MICROECONOMICS

MICROECONOMICS

HEINZ KOHLER
Amherst College

D. C. Heath and Company
Lexington, Massachusetts   Toronto

Address editorial correspondence to:

D. C. Heath
125 Spring Street
Lexington, MA 02173

Cover: Keller and Peet Associates *(photograph)*, Judith Miller *(design)*

Technical Art: Interactive Composition Corp.

For permission to use copyrighted material, grateful acknowledgment is made to the copyright holders listed on pages A-1–A-2, which are hereby considered an extension of this copyright page.

Copyright © 1992 by D. C. Heath and Company.

All rights reserved. No part of this publication may be reproduced or transmitted in any form or by any means, electronic or mechanical, including photocopy, recording, or any information storage or retrieval system, without permission in writing from the publisher.

Published simultaneously in Canada.

Printed in the United States of America.

International Standard Book Number: 0–669–21772–7

Library of Congress Catalog Number: 91-74003

10 9 8 7 6 5 4 3 2 1

ABOUT THE AUTHOR

Heinz Kohler, the Willard L. Thorp Professor of Economics at Amherst College, received his undergraduate education from the Free University of Berlin, Germany, and his M.A. and Ph.D. from the University of Michigan. Professor Kohler has taught at Amherst College for thirty years. Besides teaching principles each year, Professor Kohler has systematically rotated through the upper level courses, in order to stay "fresh" as well as up to date. Additionally, he has taught part-time at the University of Massachusetts, Amherst for nearly twenty years. He has written many successful texts: *Intermediate Microeconomics* (3d ed.), *Statistics for Business and Economics* (2d ed.), *Essentials of Statistics, Comparative Economic Systems,* and *Welfare and Planning: An Analysis of Capitalism vs. Socialism.*

PREFACE

Economics is an important subject. Those who master the theoretical knowledge of the discipline can wield a powerful set of tools capable of explaining why people act the way they do and capable of affecting—for better or worse—the lives of millions around the world. However, as practitioners of economics know all too well, the crucial theoretical core of the discipline is far from fixed. It is enlarged each year by a vast amount of newly published research. Typically this new material appears in a mathematical garb that is inaccessible to the beginner. What makes economics remarkable and what accounts for the writing of this book is the fact that the latest theoretical advances can be written up in an intuitive manner and presented in basic textbooks. This fact alone not only justifies but indeed dictates the publication of new principles of economics texts.

Economics is also an exciting subject. This fact is evidenced throughout this text by a continual link between theory and applications. Such is the case with principal-agent issues that lead to discussions of corporate raiders, takeover battles, and general problems of economic incentives. This is also the case with hundreds of other subjects, ranging from comparable worth to logrolling, from price discrimination to pollution rights, and from persuasive advertising to prisoners' dilemma games. Close to a hundred other applications, on the other hand, have been set off as self-contained boxed examples. Consider just some of the topics: Airwave Wars and Tonga Satellites; Banning Trade to Save the Elephant; The Guiding Hand of MITI; The Internationalization of the Beer Brewing Industry; Producing Cheaper Computers: The Caribbean Connection; The Lure of Venezuela's "Liquid Coal"; Broadway and the Bottom Line; Challenging Airfone's Monopoly; The Convergence of Bank Credit Cards; The Proliferation of Fragrances; The Coming Global Labor Market; Pinups at Work Are Sexual Harassment; Selling Football Teams; The Homeless; Antitrust in a Global Economy; Green Marketing; Computer Software—a Public Good; The Welfare Trap.

To the Instructor

As noted above, this text aims to introduce the beginning student to the most up-to-date theoretical knowledge that economists possess. It also illustrates the usefulness of economic theory with a wealth of applications. But there is more. Having taught economic principles continuously for over thirty years, I know that too many texts race too quickly through the important ideas in economics. As a result—year in, year out—students stumble on the same set of concepts. Most chapters of this text, therefore, contain *caution boxes* that identify the common traps into which students often fall. Additionally, special "Ideas in History" sections provide valuable perspectives on how the theoretical tools of modern-day economists were fashioned and by whom. The more than a dozen such boxes focus on such topics as The Division of Labor, The Proper Economic Role of Government, The Theory of Comparative Advantage, The Marginalist Revolution, and The Nature of the Firm; the list goes on.

Most important, perhaps, is another feature still. The trend in new (and revised) principles of economics texts is to recognize the international setting of a single economy (like the American one) and integrate various international vignettes throughout the text. This text takes the "international evolution" a step further by covering such topics as comparative advantage, the strategic trade model, and exchange rate theory early in the text (in Chapter 4) and then integrating the use of these ideas throughout.

While it has long been customary to relegate the discussion of international trade to a last chapter in the introductory text, the appearance of the topic early on in this text signals an important change: Unlike some decades ago, present-day American consumers, workers, and business managers operate in markets that are essentially international. More and more products that *consumers* buy are made abroad or are produced by foreign firms located on American soil. Given the collapse of communism in Eastern Europe, the economic unification of Western Europe, the imminent creation of a North American free trade zone, and an easing of immigration policies around the world, *workers* will find themselves increasingly in an international labor market as well. And *business managers* have long adjusted to trading products and financial capital alike in an international setting. For all these reasons and more, decision makers must operate in a global setting; it is only proper that all the chapters of this book take account of this new reality.

The book is divided into five parts. Part I, Basic Concepts, introduces scarcity, choice, and optimizing (Chapter 1); the nature of economic systems and how economists theorize about them (Chapter 2); the fundamentals of demand and supply (Chapter 3); and the important role of international trade in boosting the wealth of nations (Chapter 4).

Part II, Households and Firms, introduces consumer preferences and demand (Chapter 5); elasticity (Chapter 6); the nature of the firm, including principal-agent issues, takeover battles, and the like (Chapter 7); the technology of production (Chapter 8); and the costs of production (Chapter 9).

Part III, Markets for Goods, covers perfect competition (Chapter 10), monopoly and cartels (Chapter 11), and oligopoly and monopolistic competition (Chapter 12).

Part IV, Markets for Resources, deals with perfectly competitive labor markets (Chapter 13), imperfectly competitive labor markets (Chapter 14), markets for natural and capital resources (Chapter 15), the personal distribution of income and the problem of poverty (Chapter 16).

Part V, Government in the Microeconomy, explores the role of government in greater depth than earlier discussions of price fixing, excise taxes, and labor market laws allowed. This final section of the text addresses antitrust policy (Chapter 17), economic and social regulation (Chapter 18), externalities and environmental economics (Chapter 19), public goods and public choices (Chapter 20), and the redistribution of income (Chapter 21). For those who wish to explore the economics of health, an optional chapter is offered in the *Student Workbook* that accompanies this text.

Numerous support items have been designed to help the instructor. Some of these are built into the back of the book—a complete Glossary of key concepts and Solutions to Odd-Numbered Chapter Questions and Problems. In addition, there are a number of Appendices: the use of graphs in economics (Chapter 1a); indifference curve analysis (Chapter 5a); major concepts of business accounting (Chapter 7a); and isoquant analysis (Chapter 8a). Other support items—all written by the author of the text—include an *Instructor's Manual*, a *Test Bank*, a *Student Workbook*, and the MICEC personal computer programs. The *Instructor's Manual* contains Answers to the even-numbered end-of-chapter Questions and Problems in the text as well as various teaching suggestions. The *Test Bank* contains 75 multiple-choice questions for each text chapter (not duplicated in the *Student Workbook* described in the next section). The MICEC diskette contains numerous exercises described below.

To the Student

This text comes with a number of study aids designed to make your work easier and more successful than it would otherwise be. Some of these aids are built into the text. Consider the chapter summaries, end-of-chapter listings of Key Concepts (boldfaced in the text), end-of-chapter Questions and Problems, Solutions to odd-numbered items at the back of the book, and a complete Glossary of all the key concepts. More important, perhaps, a separate *Student Workbook* is also available. For each chapter of the text, it contains 35 multiple-choice questions, 12 true-false questions, and a number of problems—along with detailed solutions and answers to all of these. In addition, you will find a listing of Selected Readings if you want to pursue any given topic further than the text. The *Workbook* also contians an optional chapter, The Economics of Health Care. Finally, note the availability of MICEC, a personal computer diskette filled with numerous exercises on key topics throughout the text.

The MICEC Personal Computer Programs

A set of programs for IBM personal computers and compatible machines has been specially designed to accompany this text. The computer must have graphics capability and DOS version 2.1 or later. The 10 programs cover the following aspects of the text:

1. Demand and Supply
2. The Production Function
3. Costs
4. Profit-Maximization: Perfect Competition
5. Profit-Maximization: Imperfect Competition
6. Labor Markets
7. Capital Budgeting
8. Regulation
9. Externalities
10. Public Goods

The programs include about 350 graphical and tabular exercises on the subjects noted above, as well as mathematical programs to work out compounding, discounting, and net present value problems.

Initial Start-Up Procedure

Given the DOS prompt, such as **A>**, place the diskette into the computer and type:

A:MICEC

Then press the *Enter* key. Naturally, if you have placed the diskette into another drive (such as **B**), replace the **A** above by a different appropriate letter (such as **B**).

Hard Disk Installation Instructions

Instructions on how to install the programs on a computer hard disk are provided on the diskette itself. Simply follow the start-up procedure noted above, and you will find the instructions.

Acknowledgments

I would like to express my sincere gratitude to many who have helped me in the creation of this text. Many reviewers, listed below, took time to examine at least a portion of the text and gave me good advice. Often I took it; to the extent that I did not, only I am to blame.

David G. Bivin, Indiana University;

Shirley C. Browing, University of North Carolina, Asheville;

E. Miné Cinar, Loyola University of Chicago;

Raymond L. Cohn, Illinois State University;

John L. Conant, Indiana State University;

David J. Faurot, University of Kansas;

Gary M. Galles, Pepperdine University;

Peter Gomori, St. Francis College;

Simon Hakim, Temple University;

William Hogan, Southeastern Massachusetts University;

David Huffman, Bridgewater College;

E. James Jennings, Purdue University;

Bruce K. Johnson, Centre College;

Drew E. Mattson, Anoka Ramsey Community College;

Rajesh K. Mohindru, Bloomsbury University;

Daniel E. Nolle, Middlebury College;

Maurice Pfannestiel, Wichita State University;

Richard Roehl, University of Michigan, Dearborn;

Mark Rush, University of Florida, Gainesville;

Robert Thomas, Iowa State University;

Thomas S. Ulen, University of Illinois at Urbana-Champaign;

Allen L. Webster, Bradley University;

Donald A. Wells, University of Arizona, Tuscon;

James N. Wetzel, Virginia Commonwealth University;

Cathleen Whiting, Willamette University.

I am equally grateful to George Lobell, the editorial director; to Stephen Wasserstein, the developmental editor; to Judith Miller, the designer; to Cormac J. Morrissey and Mark Palmer, editors; and the rest of the D. C. Heath staff who assisted in the preparation of this text. They have guided this project through the long process of production and have created, as most will agree, a beautiful book. Last but not least, I thank Ellen Dibble, who typed the interminable first draft and, as always, did it with perfection.

Heinz Kohler
Willard L. Thorp Professor of Economics
Amherst College

CONTENTS IN BRIEF

PART I BASIC CONCEPTS 1

1 Scarcity, Choice, and Optimizing 2
1a The Use of Graphs in Economics 23
2 Economic Systems and Economic Theory 34
3 Demand and Supply: The Fundamentals 55
4 International Trade and the Wealth of Nations 85

PART II HOUSEHOLDS AND FIRMS 121

5 Consumer Preferences and Demand 122
5a Indifference Curve Analysis 139
6 Elasticity 146
7 The Firm: An Overview 174
7a Major Concepts of Business Accounting 193
8 The Technology of Production 199
8a Isoquant Analysis 219
9 The Costs of Production 226

PART III MARKETS FOR GOODS 253

10 Perfect Competition 254
11 Monopoly and Cartels 283
12 Oligopoly and Monopolistic Competition 309

PART IV MARKETS FOR RESOURCES 341

13 Perfectly Competitive Labor Markets 342

14 Imperfectly Competitive Labor Markets 368

15 Markets for Natural and Capital Resources 404

16 The Personal Distribution of Income: Riches Versus Poverty 429

PART V GOVERNMENT IN THE MICROECONOMY 457

17 Antitrust Policy 458

18 Regulation 478

19 Externalities and Environmental Economics 507

20 Public Goods and Public Choices 536

21 The Redistribution of Income 554

Solutions to Odd-Numbered Questions and Problems S-1–S-36

Glossary G-1–G-13

Index of Subjects I-1–I-4

Index of Names I-5–I-6

Acknowledgments A-1–A-2

TABLE OF CONTENTS

PART I BASIC CONCEPTS 1

1 SCARCITY, CHOICE, AND OPTIMIZING 2

The Desire for Goods 2

Resources—The Ingredients to Make Goods 3
Technology—The Knowledge to Make Goods 4
Limited Resources and Technology Produce Limited Goods 5

Scarcity—The Basic Economic Problem 5

Scarcity Requires Choice 6
Choice Brings Benefit and Cost 7

Marginalist Thinking 8

The Optimization Principle 10

A Case Study: Cancer Versus Heart Attacks 12

Conclusion 18

EXAMPLES:

1. *An Airline that Took the Marginal Route* 10
2. *The Determinants of Family Size* 11
3. *The Cherokee Decision* 16

IDEAS IN HISTORY:

The Division of Labor 19

1a The Use of Graphs in Economics 23

The System of Coordinates 23

Graphing a Demand Schedule 24
Superimposing Graphs 25

The Concept of Slope 26

Positive Slope 26
Negative Slope 27
Measuring Slope on Curves 27

Measuring Areas in Graphs 29

Other Types of Graphs 29

Time-Series Line Graphs 29
Statistical Maps 30
Bar and Column Charts 30
Pie Charts 30
Three-Dimensional Graphs 31

2 ECONOMIC SYSTEMS AND ECONOMIC THEORY 34

The Complexity of Economic Systems 34

Classifying Economic Systems 35

Who Owns the Resources? 35
What Are the Incentives for Coordination? 37

xiii

A World of Mixed Economies 42

The Nature of Economic Theory 43

Positive Economics Versus Normative Economics 45
Macroeconomics Versus Microeconomics 45

EXAMPLES:

1. Airwave Wars and Tonga Satellites 38
2. The Rise of the Welfare State 44
3. Marketization Sweeps the Communist World 46
4. Why Economists Disagree Among Themselves 48

IDEAS IN HISTORY:

On The Proper Economic Role of Government 50

3 DEMAND AND SUPPLY: THE FUNDAMENTALS 55

The Law of Demand 55

Demand Schedule and Demand Line 56
Changes in Demand 57

The Law of Supply 61

Supply Schedule and Supply Line 61
Changes in Supply 63

The Equilibrium of Demand and Supply 64

Competition Among Sellers Reduces Price in the Face of Surpluses 65
Competition Among Buyers Raises Price in the Face of Shortages 66
Graphical Summary 67

How the Equilibrium Can Change 67

Government Intervention in Markets 70

Price Floors 70
Price Ceilings 72
Excise Taxes 74

EXAMPLES:

1. Auction Markets for Art 60
2. Changing Equilibrium Prices: Fish, Moonshine, and Silver 70
3. Changing Equilibrium Prices: From Abundance to Scarcity 72
4. Of Milk and Sugar 74
5. The Story of Rent Control 77
6. Trading Human Body Parts 78

IDEAS IN HISTORY:

The Scissors Diagram 80

4 INTERNATIONAL TRADE AND THE WEALTH OF NATIONS 85

Absolute Advantage Versus Comparative Advantage 87

Comparative Advantage: A Graphical Illustration 89

Demand and Supply Revisited: The Market for Foreign Exchange 90

Free Trade: Gainers Versus Losers 93

The Concept of Consumer Surplus 93
The Concept of Producer Surplus 95
From Autarky to Free Trade 95

Government Protectionism: The Methods 97

Tariffs 97
Nontariff Barriers 99

Government Protectionism: The Arguments 103

Noneconomic Arguments 103
Economic Arguments 103
Conclusion 109

A Brief History of United States Commercial Policy 110

Conclusion 112

EXAMPLES:

1. The U.S. Sugar Import Quota 100
2. A Voluntary Export Restraint: The U.S.-Japanese Automobile Agreement 102
3. Banning Trade to Save the Elephant 104
4. The Guiding Hand of MITI 106
5. The Consumer Cost of Import Restrictions 108
6. The New North America 111

IDEAS IN HISTORY:

The Theory of Comparative Advantage 113
The Strategic Trade Model 114

PART II HOUSEHOLDS AND FIRMS 121

5 CONSUMER PREFERENCES AND DEMAND 122

Utility Maximization 122

Cardinal Utility Versus Ordinal Utility 123
Total Utility Versus Marginal Utility 123
From Marginal Utility to Individual Demand 127

The Optimization Principle Revisited 127

From Individual Demand to Market Demand 129

The Model Expanded: Two Goods and More 129

NUMERICAL EXERCISE 1: *Allocating a $9 Budget for Maximum Total Utility* 133

FOCUS 1: *Jevons' Rule* 137

EXAMPLES:

1. The Water-Diamond Paradox 125
2. Tokyo Journal: The Case of $115 Melons 131
3. Micromarketing: Hitting the Bull's-Eye 134

IDEAS IN HISTORY:

The Felicific Calculus 135
The Marginal Utility School 136

5a Indifference Curve Analysis 139

The Field of Choice 139

Indifference Curves 139

Consumers Rank Bundles of Goods 140
Consumers Always Prefer More to Less 140
Consumers Insist on a Diminishing Marginal Rate of Substitution 142
Consumer Choices Are Noncontradictory 143

The Consumer's Optimum 144

6 ELASTICITY 146

A General Definition 147

A Blind Alley 147
The Accepted Approach 149

The Own-Price Elasticity of Demand 150

A Numerical Example 150

FOCUS 1: *The Own-Price Elasticity of Demand* 151

NUMERICAL EXERCISE 1: *Calculating the Own-Price Elasticity of Demand* 151

Empirical Data 154
The Determinants of Elasticity Values 154

The Cross-Price Elasticity of Demand 155

FOCUS 2: *The Cross-Price Elasticity of Demand* 156

NUMERICAL EXERCISE 2: *Calculating the Cross-Price Elasticity of Demand* 157

Empirical Data 156

The Income Elasticity of Demand 156

Empirical Data 158

FOCUS 3: *The Income Elasticity of Demand* 159

NUMERICAL EXERCISE 3: *Calculating the Income Elasticity of Demand* 161

The Own-Price Elasticity of Supply 160

FOCUS 4: *The Own-Price Elasticity of Supply* 162

NUMERICAL EXERCISE 4: *Calculating the Own-Price Elasticity of Supply* 164

Emperical Data 160

Arc Elasticity Versus Point Elasticity 163

Measuring Point Elasticity 166

Using the PAPO Rule: A Typical Demand Line 166

Price Elasticity of Demand and Revenue 168

Applications 171

EXAMPLES:

1. *How Washington Learned About Price Elasticity* 149
2. *Agricultural Policy: Restricting Supply* 165
3. *Thinking About National Health Insurance* 167
4. *The OPEC Cartel* 169

7 THE FIRM: AN OVERVIEW 174

The Firm as a Miniature Command Economy 175

Major Types of U.S. Firms 175

Proprietorships 175
Partnerships 178
Corporations 179
Nonprofit Firms 181

Principals Versus Agents 182

Bonuses 182
Stock Options 184
Takeover Battles 185

The Goal of Firms: Profit Maximization 189

EXAMPLES:

1. *Why Entrepreneurs Often Fail as Managers* 177
2. *Fortune's Top Ten Companies* 181
3. *Businesses with Halos* 183
4. *The CEO Disease* 184
5. *Major Companies Reject Takeover Protection* 186
6. *The Globalization of Business* 188

IDEAS IN HISTORY:

The Nature of the Firm 189

7a Major Concepts of Business Accounting 193

The Balance Sheet 193

An Example 193

The Income Statement 194

An Example 194
Accounting Profit Versus Economic Profit 196

8 THE TECHNOLOGY OF PRODUCTION 199

The Production Function 200

Fixed Inputs Versus Variable Inputs 200

Total Product Versus Marginal Product 200

The Law of Diminishing Returns 202

Marginal Product Versus Average Product 202

Graphical Illustrations 203

The Total Product 203
Diminishing Returns 206
Marginal Product and Average Product 206

Economies of Scale 209

Constant Returns to Scale 210
Increasing Returns to Scale 211
Decreasing Returns to Scale 212

EXAMPLES:

1. *The Amazing Story of Two Ford Plants* 204
2. *Research and Development Labs Move Abroad* 207
3. *Luftwaffe Secret Unburied* 210
4. *The Optimum Size of Cargo Ships* 213

IDEAS IN HISTORY:

The Concept of Marginal Product 214
The Concept of X-inefficiency 215

8a   Isoquant Analysis 219

Isoquants Defined 219

Isoquants Analyzed 219

Negative Isoquant Slope Implies Positive Marginal Physical Products 221
Convex Isoquant Slope Implies Diminishing Marginal Rate of Technical Substitution 221
Horizontal and Vertical Isoquant Slopes Denote Zero Marginal Physical Products 222
Going Beyond Technology 223

The Isocost Line 223

The Producer's Optimum 224

9   THE COSTS OF PRODUCTION   226

Short-Run Costs: Tabular Illustrations 226

Fixed Cost 227
Variable Cost 228
Total Cost 228
Average and Marginal Costs 229

FOCUS 1: *Major Concepts of Cost* 230

Short-Run Costs: Graphical Illustrations 230

Fixed, Variable, and Total Costs 230
The Production Function Revisited 231
Average Fixed, Average Variable, and Average Total Costs 233
Marginal Cost 234
Key Relationships Among Cost Curves 234

NUMERICAL EXERCISE 1: *Calculating Marginal Cost* 236

NUMERICAL EXERCISE 2: *Calculating Average Total Cost* 238

Long-Run Costs 236

Constant Returns to Scale 238
Increasing Returns to Scale 239
Decreasing Returns to Scale 241
The Envelope Curve 242
Empirical Studies 242
Cost Cutting: Recent Developments 245

EXAMPLES:

1. *Increasing Returns to Scale in Beer Brewing* 240
2. *Constant Returns to Scale in Steel Making* 242
3. *Mending the Hole in Hollywood's Pocket* 245
4. *Producing Cheaper Computers: The Caribbean Connection* 246
5. *The Lure of Venezuela's "Liquid Coal"* 246

6. The Internationalization of the Beer Brewing Industry 247

IDEAS IN HISTORY:

The Envelope Curve 248

PART III MARKETS FOR GOODS 253

10 PERFECT COMPETITION 254

Varieties of Market Structure 254

The Characteristics of Perfect Competition 254

A Large Number of Independently Acting Buyers and Sellers 255
Virtual Identity of Different Units of Traded Item 256
Full Knowledge Concerning the Market 256
Unrestricted Entry into and Exit from the Market 256

The Firm's Revenue: Total, Average, and Marginal 257

FOCUS 1: Major Concepts of Revenue under Perfect Competition 257

NUMERICAL EXERCISE 1: *Calculating Average Revenue and Marginal Revenue* 259

The Maximization of Economic Profit and Short-Run Supply 260

A Profitable Business 260

NUMERICAL EXERCISE 2: *The Case of Positive Economic Profit* 263

A Zero-Profit Business 264

NUMERICAL EXERCISE 3: *The Case of Zero Economic Profit* 265

A Business Operating With an Economic Loss 265

NUMERICAL EXERCISE 4: *The Case of Negative Economic Profit, but No Shutdown* 266

A Business at the Point of Shutdown 266

NUMERICAL EXERCISE 5: *The Case of Negative Economic Profit at the Shutdown Point* 270

Summary 268

From Individual Supply to Market Supply 270

A Long-Run Perspective 271

Profit and Industry Expansion 273
Loss and Industry Contraction 274
Constant, Increasing, and Decreasing Cost Industries 275

The Efficiency of Perfect Competition 278

EXAMPLES:

1. *Shakespeare, Dickens, and Hillegass* 263
2. *Broadway and the Bottom Line* 268
3. *Struggling for Profits in Electronics* 276
4. *Eggs with Less Cholesterol?* 277
5. *Big Farms Try Organic Methods* 278

11 MONOPOLY AND CARTELS 283

The Sources of Monopoly 284

Increasing Returns to Scale 284
Concentrated Ownership of Key Resources 285

Patents and Copyrights 285
Exclusive Franchises 285

A Monopoly's Cost and Revenue 286

The Cost Curves 286
The Revenue Curves 288

NUMERICAL EXERCISE 1: Calculating Marginal Revenue 290

FOCUS 1: Major Concepts of Revenue Under Monopoly 290

The Maximization of Economic Profit 291

A Profitable Monopoly 292

NUMERICAL EXERCISE 2: The Case of Positive Economic Profit 293

A Zero-Profit Monopoly 293
A Monopoly Incurring a Loss 293
Conclusions 293

The Price Discriminating Monopoly 296

First-Degree Price Discrimination 296

NUMERICAL EXERCISE 3: First-Degree Price Discrimination 296

Second-Degree Price Discrimination 298

NUMERICAL EXERCISE 4: Second-Degree Price Discrimination 298

The Imperfections of Monopoly 298

Economic Inefficiency: $P > MC$ 298
Economic Inequity: $P > ATC$ 301

Cartels 301

Private Cartels 301
Government Cartels 305
International Cartels 305

EXAMPLES:

1. **Polaroid Versus Kodak; Hughes Aircraft Versus the U.S. Government 286**
2. **Challenging Airfone's Monopoly 287**
3. **Technological Change and the Death of the Record Industry 303**
4. **The de Beers Diamond Cartel 304**
5. **Coffee: Another Cartel Bites the Dust 305**

IDEAS IN HISTORY:

The Theory of Monopoly 306

12 OLIGOPOLY AND MONOPOLISTIC COMPETITION 309

Oligopolistic Interdependence 310

Oligopoly Decisions: Price 311

The Oligopolists' Dilemma 311
The Kinked Demand Curve 313
Gentlemen's Agreements 314
Price Leadership 315

Oligopoly Decisions: Product Quality 315

Product Differentiation 315
Hotelling's Paradox 315

Oligopoly Decisions: Advertising 317

The Theory 317
The U.S. Experience 317

Oligopoly Decisions: A Game Theory Approach 321

The Two-Person Zero-Sum Game 322
The Two-Person Nonzero-Sum Game 323

Monopolistic Competition 326

Profit Maximization 326

Empirical Studies 328

Indexes of Industrial Concentration 328
The U.S. Economy: An Overview 328

EXAMPLES:

1. The Auto Industry: Moves and Countermoves 310
2. The Convergence of Bank Credit Cards 318
3. The Proliferation of Fragrances 320
4. The Great American Health Pitch 321
5. Stalking the New Consumer 331
6. The Vending Machine Craze 334
7. Modern Day "Hamburger Wars" 335

IDEAS IN HISTORY:

The Chamberlinian Revolution 337

PART IV MARKETS FOR RESOURCES 341

13 PERFECTLY COMPETITIVE LABOR MARKETS 342

The Supply of Labor 344

The Demand for Labor 346

A Numerical Example 346
A Graphical Illustration 348

NUMERICAL EXERCISE 1: *Calculating the Average Value Product of Labor* 349

FOCUS 1: *Profit-Maximizing Rules Under Perfect Competition* 350

Market Equilibrium 349

Economic Efficiency 351

Applications and Extensions 352

Wage Differentials 352
The Iron Law of Wages 354
Cobweb Cycles 355

Government in Labor Markets 360

Minimum Wages 360
Maximum Wages 364

EXAMPLES:

1. Why Sleep? There's No Money In It 346
2. The Value of Human Life 356
3. Regional Wage Differentials and Population Change 358
4. Investing in Human Capital 359
5. When the Baby Boomers Grew Up 361

14 IMPERFECTLY COMPETITIVE LABOR MARKETS 368

Examples of Market Imperfections 368

Competition in the Labor Market, Modified by Monopoly Power in Output Markets 370

A Numerical Example 370
A Graphical Illustration 372
Monopolistic Exploitation 372

FOCUS 1: *Monopolistic Exploitation of Labor* 373

Monopsony in the Labor Market, But Competition in Output Markets 374

A Numerical Example 374
A Graphical Illustration 376
Monopsonistic Exploitation 376

FOCUS 2: *Monopsonistic Exploitation of Labor* 377

Cartels in the Labor Market: The Emergence of Labor Unions 377

Difficulties Illustrated 377
The Early Unions 380
The Labor Movement Comes to Stay 380
Helpful Laws 380
A Change in Strategy 381
Anti-Union Laws 381

Labor Union Versus Competitive Buyers of Labor 383

Possible Union Goals 384
Possible Strategies 384

Labor Union Versus Labor Monopsony 386

Discrimination in the Labor Market 387

*The Labor Market Status of Black
  Americans* 388
Two Types of Discrimination 388
*Nondiscriminatory Reasons for
  Income Differences* 392

Government and Labor Market Discrimination 392

Legislation 393
Court Decisions 396

EXAMPLES:

1. **A Case Study in Monopsony: The Baseball Player's Market** 378
2. **Keeping Unions Out** 383
3. **Comparable Worth: A Profoundly Flawed Concept?** 394
4. **Pinups At Work Are Sexual Harassment** 397
5. **The Coming Global Labor Market** 398

IDEAS IN HISTORY:

Marginal Productivity and the Exploitation of Labor 399
Bread-and-Butter Unionism 400

15 MARKETS FOR NATURAL AND CAPITAL RESOURCES 404

The Size of Tangible Wealth 404

Markets for Flows and Markets for Stocks 405

Of Time and Interest 406

*The Interest Rate: Nominal Versus
  Real* 406
*Compounding: Turning Present
  Dollars into Future Dollars* 407
*Discounting: Turning Future Dollars
  into Present Dollars* 407

Rental Markets for Natural Resources 408

Asset Markets for Natural Resources 410

Rental Markets for Capital Resources 412

Asset Markets for Capital Resources 413

*Capital Asset Prices in the Short
  Run* 413
*Capital Asset Prices in the Long
  Run* 415

Applications and Extensions 416

Pure Rent Earned by People 416
Why Interest Exists 417
*The Nature of Capital
  Budgeting* 420
The Role of Economic Profit 422

EXAMPLES:

1. **Ricardo and the High Price of Corn** 411
2. **Selling Football Teams** 416

IDEAS IN HISTORY:

The Single-Taxers 424

16 THE PERSONAL DISTRIBUTION OF INCOME: RICHES VS. POVERTY 429

Home Income Inequality is Generated 430

*The Size and Quality of Resource
  Stocks Owned* 430
*The Rate at Which Resource Stocks
  are Put to Work* 430
*The Prices of Resource
  Services* 431

The Distribution of Money Income Among U.S. Families 431

Tabular Data 432
A Graphical Exposition 432
The Gini Coefficient 434

Income and Wealth 434
The Super Rich 435
The Poor 437

The Meaning of "Needs" 437
The Meaning of "Available Income" 442
The Choice of an "Income-Receiving Unit" 442
The Choice of an "Accounting Period" 443
The Official Definition 443

Poverty Statistics 446

Overall Measures of Poverty 446

The Makeup of the Poverty Population 452

The Dynamics of Poverty 453

EXAMPLES:

1. *Is the Boss Getting Paid Too Much?* 440
2. *Income Dynamics* 444
3. *The Homeless* 448

PART V   GOVERNMENT IN THE MICROECONOMY   457

17   ANTITRUST POLICY   458

Major Types of Market Failures   458

Inefficiency Due to Market Imperfections 459
Inefficiency Due to Externalities and the Publicness of Goods 460
Inequity 462
Instability 462

The Impetus to Antitrust Legislation   462

Horizontal Mergers 462
Holding Companies 462
Trusts 463
The Robber Barons 463

The Antitrust Laws   464

The Sherman Act 464
The Clayton Act 465
The Federal Trade Commission Act 466
The Robinson-Patman Act 466
The Celler-Kefauver Act 466
Recent Amendments 467

Antitrust Policy Assessed   467

A Negligible Effect 467
A Significant Effect 468
Numerical Evidence 471

EXAMPLES:

1. *The Antitrust Division's Vietnam* 469
2. *The Breakup of Ma Bell* 470
3. *AT&T, the Unlikely Trustbuster* 472
4. *Antitrust in a Global Economy* 474

18   REGULATION   478

Economic Regulation and Social Regulation   479

The Regulation of Natural Monopolies   480

Eliminating Economic Inequity 482
Eliminating Economic Inefficiency 482
Rate-of-Return Regulation: Practical Problems 484
Rate-of-Return Regulation: An Assessment 486

The Regulation of Competitive Industries   487

The Public Interest Theory 487
Price-Fixing Schemes: Practical Problems 490
Price-Fixing Schemes: An Assessment 490
The Special Interest Theory 491
The Call for Deregulation 493

The Regulation of Health and Safety 493

Improving Market Knowledge 494
Mandating Reductions in Known Hazards 495
Of Benefits and Costs 495

Two Case Studies 497

Case 1: The Story of Airline Deregulation 499
Case 2: The Food and Drug Safety War 501

EXAMPLES:

1. *Back from the Grave: The Case of Trucking Deregulation 494*
2. *Health and Safety Regulation and the Price of Cars 496*
3. *Safeguarding the Welfare of Babies and the Disabled 498*

19 EXTERNALITIES AND ENVIRONMENTAL ECONOMICS 507

The Nature of Externalities 509

Negative Externalities 509

FOCUS 1: Negative Externalities 510

Positive Externalities 510

FOCUS 2: Positive Externalities 510

The Analysis of Pigou 510

Taxing Producers 511
Subsidizing Consumers 511

The Challenge of Coase 514

An Example 514
The Coase Theorem 516

The Tragedy of the Commons 516

The New England Commons 518

The Pollution of Nature 520

The Theory of Optimum Pollution 521
Actual Pollution in the Absence of Government Intervention 523
Types of Government Intervention 523

EXAMPLES:

1. *The Economics of Bees 517*
2. *Overfishing on the Georges Bank 519*
3. *Escaping the Commons: Lobsters and Oysters 520*
4. *Netting and Offsets, Bubbles and Banks 530*
5. *Green Marketing 532*

20 PUBLIC GOODS AND PUBLIC CHOICES 536

The Nature of Public Goods 536

Nonexcludability 536
Nonrivalness 537
Examples 537

Public Goods and Market Failure 537

The Free-Rider Problem 537
Public Finance 539

The Optimum Quantity of a Pure Public Good 539

The Elusive Marginal Social Benefit 540

The Process of Public Choice 542

Majority Voting 543
Delegating Authority 547
The Nature of Bureaucracy 547

Remedies for Government Failure 549

EXAMPLES:

1. *Computer Software: A Public Good 538*
2. *Breaking Out of the Prison Crisis 550*
3. *Privatizing Public School Functions 551*
4. *Privatizing Space Projects 551*

21 THE REDISTRIBUTION OF INCOME 554

Notions of Distributive Justice 554

Major Transfer Programs in the United States 556

Social Insurance Programs 556
Public Assistance Programs 558

The Effect of Financing Transfers by Taxes 560

The Tax Incidence Problem 560
Tax Incidence in the United States 561
Taxes and Transfers Combined 562

Behavioral Feedback Effects 562

Taxpayer Disincentives 562
Recipient Disincentives 563

An Overall Assessment 566

The Call for Welfare Reform 566

A Negative Income Tax System 566
The Cost-Incentive Dilemma 567
The Experiments 569

EXAMPLES:

1. **Headstart at Age 25** 560
2. **The Welfare Trap** 564

SOLUTIONS TO ODD-NUMBERED QUESTIONS AND PROBLEMS S-1

GLOSSARY G-1

INDEX OF SUBJECTS I-1

INDEX OF NAMES I-5

ACKNOWLEDGMENTS A-1

MICROECONOMICS

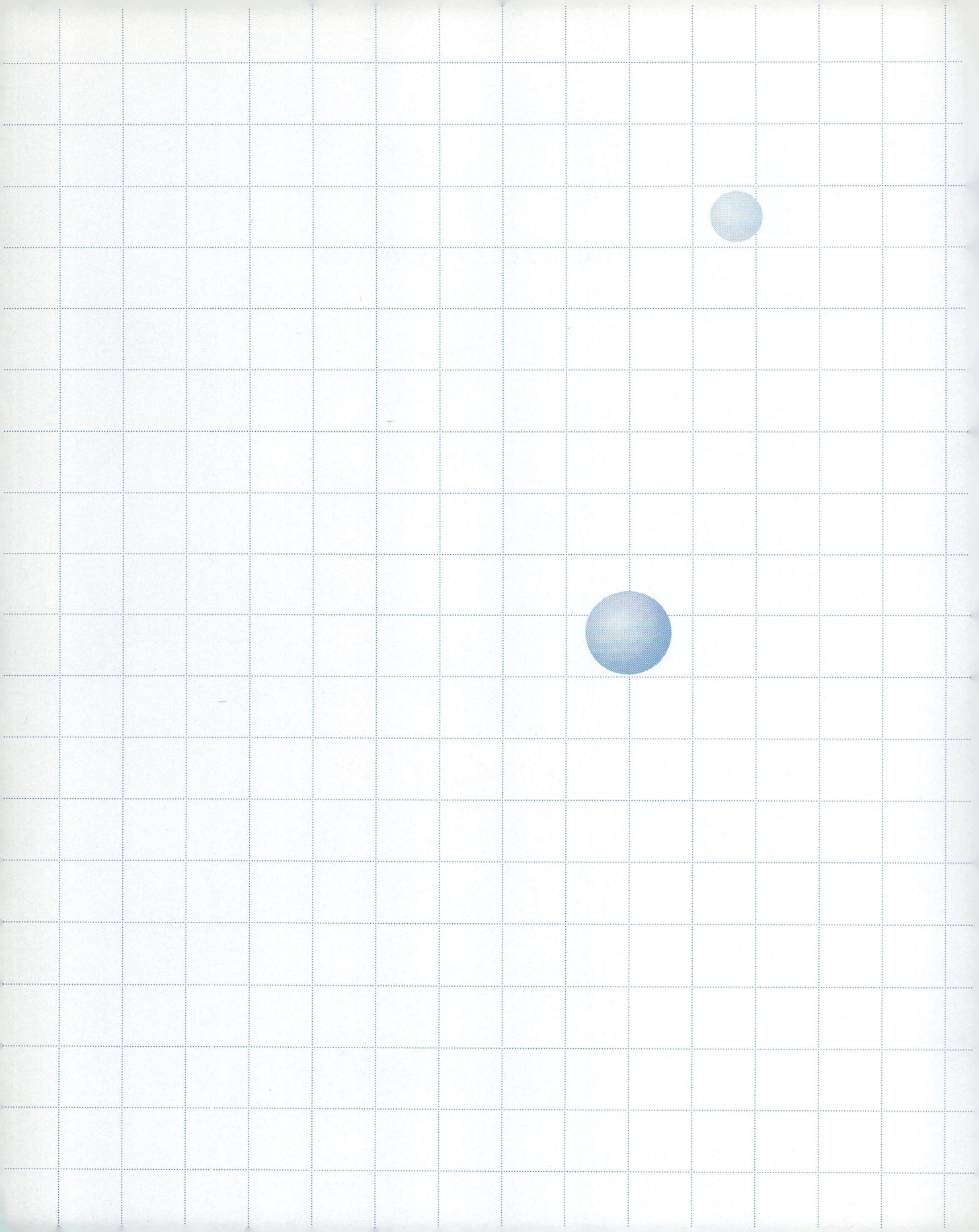

PART I

BASIC CONCEPTS

1   Scarcity, Choice, and Optimizing
1a The Use of Graphs in Economics
2   Economic Systems and Economic Theory
3   Demand and Supply: The Fundamentals
4   International Trade and the Wealth of Nations

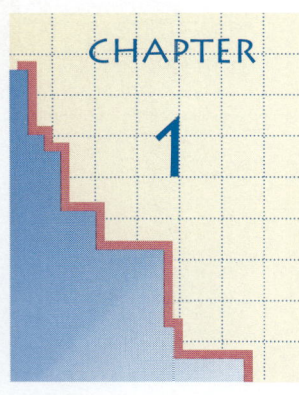

CHAPTER 1

SCARCITY, CHOICE, AND OPTIMIZING

Preview

This chapter shows that all societies must struggle with the basic economic problem of scarcity, as immense human desire for goods meets all-too-limited capacity to produce. Scarcity forces choice upon people everywhere, and choice brings both a benefit (as people receive something they want) and a cost (as people must forgo something else). While painful choices cannot be escaped in a world of scarcity, people can make the best possible (or optimal) choice by adopting "marginalist" thinking and applying the principle of optimization.

Chapter 1a immediately following this chapter introduces the use of graphs in economics.

Examples

1. An Airline That Took the Marginal Route
2. The Determinants of Family Size
3. The Cherokee Decision

Ideas in History

The Division of Labor

A worldwide problem exists. You can find it in every continent, country, and town. Wherever people live and whatever they do, the problem is with them. Small bands of Greenland Eskimos face it, so do Saharan Bedouins, Amazon Indians, farmers in Canada, and peasants in Italy, Mexico, and the Sudan. City dwellers in Moscow are not exempt, nor are those living in Washington, Nairobi, or Beijing. Everywhere and every day, people must struggle with the basic economic problem of *scarcity*. Private consumers, business executives, and government officials everywhere are eager to acquire a multitude of goods. However, it is generally impossible to produce the quantities of goods desired. Therefore, crucial choices have to made about *What* is to be produced, *How,* and *For Whom*.

The Desire for Goods

Suppose you had a magic wand that would bring you, just for the asking, any object you desired. Imagine the incredible power you would have to improve the material aspects of your life. If you were hungry, you could call for a meal. All you would have to do is ask and your wish would be fulfilled, but would you stop there?

Probably not. You might as well ask for new clothes, the fancy computer you admired last week, and that car you have dreamed about for years. All this and more could be yours: a weekend cottage by the sea, a yacht, a private plane to get you there . . . presents for family and friends . . . jet trips to Paris, the best in medical care . . . the list goes on.

Now imagine yourself as someone else, as an executive running a farm, factory, or some department of government. Surely, the magic wand would be just as welcome and would trigger more wishful thoughts: You might call for a new barn, a fancy combine, or a herd of cows; for a blast furnace, milling machine, or an entire fleet of new trucks; for police cruisers, school buildings, prison complexes; for interstate highways, national parks, nuclear submarines . . . And you might wish for all kinds of workers as well, ranging from grape pickers to truck drivers, from police officers to economics professors, from prison guards to nuclear engineers.

In short, economists believe that most of the five billion people on earth harbor desires for a staggering variety and quantity of commodities and services. For any given period of time, the extent of this desire would be revealed if people were asked—in their various capacities as private consumers, business executives, government officials, and the like—to prepare a list of commodities and services they would wish to receive if these could be had for nothing.

As we have seen, people desire various **commodities**—physical objects like food, blast furnaces, and police cruisers. People also seek **services**—the temporary use of physical objects or of other people: a seat for three hours on the New York-to-Paris supersonic jet, five minutes of a doctor's time, a truck driver's work for a day. We will refer to the tangible commodities and the intangible services that people desire simply as **goods**. And we will measure people's **desire for goods** by the quantity of goods people would take in a given period of time if goods could be had for nothing.

Resources—The Ingredients to Make Goods

In the real world, people do manage to acquire goods, but the process is more complicated and less satisfactory than in our imaginary world. Consider the **process of production** or set of activities by which people, directly or indirectly, make goods available where and when they are wanted. Regardless of which good we consider, every one is produced with the help of identifiable productive ingredients. Economists refer to them as **resources** or **factors of production;** we will use the former term throughout this book.

CAUTION

The desire for goods *refers to wishful thinking, to the quantity of goods people would want if prices were zero. This concept of desire should not be confused with people's* demand, *their ability to buy goods that are available only at positive prices. The ability to buy is all too limited. Right now, you may* desire *a new car, yet you may be quite unable to* demand *that car, to buy it at the price required. The world of magic wands is merely a device to highlight the extent of people's desire for goods.*

Customarily, economists classify resources into three major groups: human, natural, and capital. **Human resources** are people able and willing to participate in the process of production by supplying their mental or physical labor. Consider the jet trip to Paris mentioned earlier. Its production requires the labor of numerous people: ticket sellers, insurance agents, airplane mechanics, baggage handlers, security officers, flight attendants, pilots, air traffic controllers, and many more. **Natural resources** are gifts of nature in their natural state, productive ingredients not made by people and as yet untouched by them. Consider virgin land, with its plants and animals and underground minerals and fuels. Consider the world's oceans, with the predictable tides, flocks of whales and schools of fish, and deposits of oil, gas, and other minerals. Consider the atmosphere with all its life forms, wind, sunlight, and more. These things are all natural resources that might become ingredients for the production of goods. The air itself is a key ingredient for our jet trip to Paris.

Capital resources, finally, are all the productive ingredients made by people. They are "tools" in the most general sense of the word. They include all types of structures used in the process of production—assembly plants, blast furnaces, college libraries, highway bridges, and office towers. They include durable equipment used by producers, such as computers, locomotives, sewing machines, and turret lathes. They also include producer inventories: stocks of raw materials, semifinished goods, and even finished goods that have yet to reach their ultimate users. Once again, it is obvious how our jet trip to Paris requires capital resources: airport control towers, airplanes, runways, stocks of food, fuel, and much more.

CAUTION

We must anticipate a number of possible confusions with regard to the capital concept. First, many productive ingredients that one might be tempted to classify as natural resources are in fact capital resources. Consider land that has been cleared or drained, irrigated or fertilized, planted with trees or paved over; consider minerals or fuels that have been taken from the ground and shipped far from their original places of deposit; consider herds of animals that have been domesticated and specially bred. These items are no longer "gifts of nature in their natural state". They are in a sense "made by people" (iron ore in the ground is not the same as iron ore in a steel mill's yard). They are capital resources.

Second, there are occasions (for example, when discussing the sources of economic growth) when it is useful to recognize the existence of an invisible kind of capital that is embodied in people. **Human capital** *is the accumulation of past investments in people's health, general education, and training that raise the productive capacity of people. People who are in good physical condition, well educated, and highly trained tend to produce more than those without such qualities. Hence the observed productivity of human resources might be attributed to a combination of raw labor and human capital. We must be careful not to confuse human capital with the tangible items (structures, durable equipment, and producer inventories) that are classified as capital resources and are also called* **real capital.**

Third, noneconomists think of capital in still another sense, as a collection of paper claims against real capital. Such claims include money, bonds, deeds, stocks, and the like. We will refer to these paper claims as **financial capital.** *In many societies, financial capital is important, but nowhere is it directly productive. A deed or stock certificate merely indicates who owns the natural or capital resource to which this piece of paper refers. People could easily increase such paper claims a millionfold. Yet, if no corresponding increase occurred in the available quantities of human, natural, and capital resources, people would not be richer. They could not produce more goods. Just as an airline must ultimately use airplanes, fuel, pilots, runways, and the air (*not *dollars) to produce jet trips to Paris, so people in every society must mix human, natural, and* real *capital resources to produce every good they acquire.*

Technology—The Knowledge to Make Goods

Another ingredient is necessary in the process of production. The quantities of goods people produce depend not only on the physical quantities of resources they employ, but also on the state of **technology,** the knowledge that people have about how different goods can be produced. The methods of production known to people are comparable to a recipe book; at any one time, the recipes available set limits on the **productivity** of resources—the quantity of goods that can be produced *per unit* of any given type of resource. Over time, however, new recipes are discovered, productivity is raised, and therefore, identical quantities of resources yield a larger harvest of goods.

Consider during this past century how agricultural output per acre has increased as people applied new knowledge (about fertilizers, high-yield crops, hormones, pesticides) to an age-old activity. Industrial output per worker has similarly increased, often by simply introducing a new form of labor organization, such as the assembly line. Ideas in History has more to say on this subject. In the future, other advances in productivity are certain. Contemplate the promise of genetic engineering, computers and robotics, space technology, nuclear fusion, or solar energy. A mere hundred years ago, airplanes had not been invented; in 1988, an experimental aircraft circled the earth nonstop powered by nothing but solar cells. Who knows? One day, people may fly to Paris on planes powered entirely by the sun.

Limited Resources and Technology Produce Limited Goods

Every society possesses limited quantities of resources and limited technical knowledge about the processes that can turn these resources into the goods people desire. Inevitably, every society can produce only a limited quantity of goods in a given period of time. An important distinction exists, however, between stocks and flows of resources and goods. The term **stock** always refers to a quantity that is related to a given *moment* of time. Consider 50 gallons of water sitting in a tub on July 4 at 1 P.M. or 150 million people being ready for work on January 2 at 8 A.M. A particular *moment* of time has been specified in each instance. We can think of a society's resources as stocks available at a given moment of time, and these stocks are clearly finite. Thus, on January 2 at 8 A.M., a society may have 150 million people ready for work, along with acres of virgin pastureland, oceans, lakes, and cultivated fields, known cubic yards of natural gas or iron ore in the ground, blast furnaces, turret lathes, trucks and miles of road, barrels of oil in storage tanks, and so much more.

Over time, however, a society's resource stocks can be used slowly or rapidly, and, depending on the pace chosen, they yield variously sized sets of goods. The term **flow** refers to a quantity that is related to a given *period* of time. Consider 3 gallons of water per minute flowing into a tub or 950 million hours per day being worked by our 150 million people. A particular *period* of time has been specified in each of these examples. Specifying resource flows provides us with a more useful gauge of a society's production possibilities than a mere listing of resource stocks. Thus a society may have 150 million people ready for work on January 2 at 8 A.M. (a stock), but it matters whether these people will work all year long at a rate of 950 million hours per day or only at a rate of 300 million hours per day.

In summary, every society has the option of using its resource stocks at various possible rates. Whatever rates it chooses, however, the result will be finite flows of resources (263 billion labor hours per year, 4.3 trillion acre hours per year, 800 million machine hours per year, etc.). These finite flows of resources will in turn produce finite flows of newly produced goods (100 million sweaters per year, 50 million bushels of peaches per year, 20 million cars per year, etc.).

Scarcity—The Basic Economic Problem

That every society produces *finite* flows of goods in a given period creates no problem in itself. The limited flows of goods might still exceed the quantities required to fulfill everyone's desire for goods at the same time. If this were the case, all goods would be **free goods.** If all people tried to take whatever quantities they wanted at zero prices, everyone would succeed. Indeed, something would be left over still.

A few *individual* goods that are free do, in fact, exist. Air to breathe (not necessarily pure air) is available at all times and everywhere on the surface of the earth in quantities greater than desired by all people. On earth, air is a free good. Navigable air space from 2 to 3 A.M. Tuesdays over New York City (but not from 5 to 6 P.M. Fridays) is similarly available in quantities greater than desired by all people.

The typical situation is, however, quite the opposite. In any given period, the limited flows of goods that can be produced are smaller than the quantities needed to fulfill everyone's desire for goods at the same time, which makes for **scarce goods.** If all people tried to take whatever quantities they would want if goods could be had for nothing, all people would *not* succeed. And thus the basic economic problem is a **scarcity problem.** In any country and in any period of time, it is impossible to fulfill the desire for goods by all people at the same time.

CAUTION

The nature of the scarcity problem is sometimes misunderstood. The problem is not that some goods are available in small quantities only. What matters is the relationship between people's desire for goods and their production possibilities. Consider a product called frozen glass splinters. Each year, very few packages of this useless product are produced. The same is true for cans of shredded bees' wings or number one steamed cherry pits. In the entire world, their production is low indeed; yet no problems arise because nobody wants these things. There is no scarcity of them. On the other hand, every year large numbers of new automobiles come into the world—and huge quantities of bread and peaches too. Here, a problem exists because people would take even larger quantities if these goods were offered free.

Nor is the scarcity problem related to people's inability to produce whatever quantity of any one good all people want. If people wanted only a single good, all they would have to do is put to work all of their resources for this single purpose. Most likely, they could then produce more of this one good than all people wanted. Similarly, people could produce all the goods any one person wanted by concentrating all resources on satisfying this one person. Although it is possible to produce the quantity of any one good all the people want or even of all the goods one person wants, the scarcity problem lies in people's inability to produce the quantities of *all* goods that *all* people want. This scarcity of resources in relation to a virtually infinite desire for goods is the reason why we often have to go without. Figure 1 summarizes this discussion of scarcity.

Since economists are forever telling people that ours is a world of scarcity wherein people can never have all they want, economics is often called "the dismal science." Yet economists are far from content with being prophets of gloom. Their main concern is exploring the *implications* of scarcity, which allows people to minimize the impact of scarcity.

Scarcity Requires Choice

The most obvious implication of scarcity is the need to choose. Because there are not enough resources to do everything, people must decide what will be done with the resources available and what cannot be done. Decision makers every day face literally millions of choices, which are interdependent in many ways. Consider three major types of choices.

First there is the question of *What.* People in every society must decide what they are going to produce: consumption goods (such as food, clothing, and medical care) that people can enjoy immediately or capital goods (such as blast furnaces, vineyards, and warehouses) that enable people to increase their capacity to produce future goods.

Second is the question of *How.* People in every society must decide how they are going to produce the goods they have chosen. Any one good can usually be produced in innumerable ways, by using lots of labor and few capital resources or by using capital-intensive methods that require little labor. Thus, the production of rice in Vietnam involves the

FIGURE 1 The Scarcity Problem

Desire for goods

Production possibilities

Quantity of goods people desire in a year

Quantity of goods people are able to produce in a year

Unlike in a make-believe world of magic wands, in the real world, people face the unpleasant fact of scarcity. In every society the people's attempt to satisfy their desire for goods is frustrated by the lack of sufficient resources to produce the required quantity of goods. While resource flows are sufficient to produce the "pie" shown by the right-hand circle, people would like to consume the one shown by the left-hand circle. Therein lies the basic economic problem.

FIGURE 2 The Production Possibilities Frontier

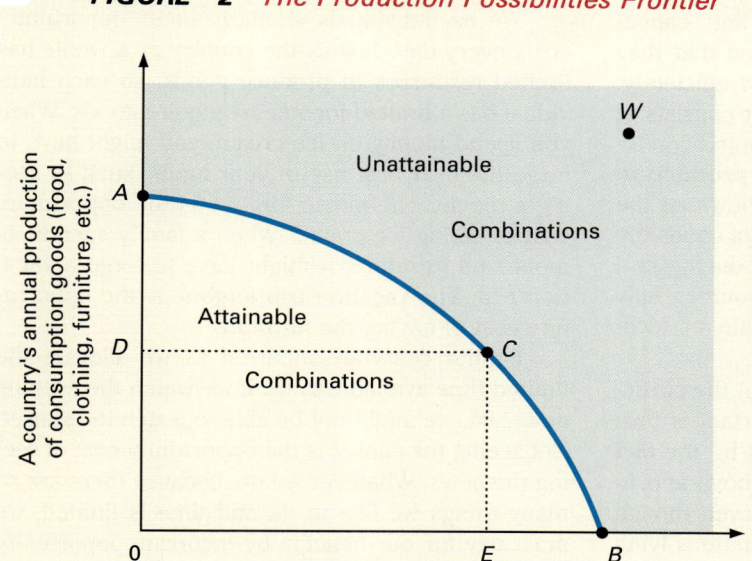

This production possibilities frontier shows all the alternative combinations of two groups of goods that the people of a country are capable of producing in a given year by using their flows of resources fully and efficiently, given their present state of technology. The frontier thus divides the set of all conceivable combinations of goods into two: attainable ones (unshaded) and unattainable ones (shaded). In a world of scarcity, there is always a frontier that restricts people's freedom to get all they want (such as combination W). People must choose within the (unshaded) world of the possible, along or inside the frontier. When they do, people receive a benefit, but they also incur an opportunity cost.

labor of many people. In California, seeds are scattered by airplane and machines do the harvesting.

Third is the question of *For Whom*. People must find a way of apportioning among themselves the goods they have produced. They must decide who is to receive the newly produced food, houses, etc., and who, by implication, is to go without. This is the issue of income distribution and it is bound to be an emotional issue everywhere.

Choice Brings Benefit and Cost

Choice, which cannot be escaped, is a mixture of pleasure and pain, of opportunity gained and opportunity lost. Resources have alternative uses, and every use of resources for one purpose means forgoing the chance to use them for another desired purpose. Every choice realizes some opportunity and thus gives people an advantage, or **benefit,** but with it also comes an opportunity forgone, a disadvantage, or **cost.** Because every desire we satisfy "costs us" the opportunity of satisfying a different desire, the opportunity lost is also referred to as the **opportunity cost.** With two alternatives, the opportunity cost of a choice is simply the forgone benefit of the discarded alternative. With many alternatives, the opportunity cost of a choice is the *most highly valued* alternative forgone.

Figure 2 illustrates these concepts.[1] Imagine the citizens of a country allocating their annual flows of resources to the production of nothing but consumption goods such as food, clothing, and furniture. By fully and efficiently using their flows of resources, they are able to produce a maximum quantity of such goods as shown by distance 0A. These same people could instead devote all their resources to making capital goods, such as blast furnaces, iron ore mines, and trucks. By using all their resources for this purpose they would produce

---

[1] Those unfamiliar with the techniques of graphing may wish to consult Appendix 1a, The Use of Graphs in Economics.

some other maximum quantity of goods, distance 0B. These people could also produce any one of the many *combinations* of consumption and capital goods lying on line AB, always assuming that they used their flows of resources fully and efficiently. Point C is one of these combinations; it consists of 0D consumption goods as well as 0E capital goods.

The entire line AB is the country's **production possibilities frontier.** This frontier shows all the alternative combinations of two groups of goods the people of a country are capable of producing in a given year by using their flows of resources fully and efficiently, given their present state of technology.

For the moment, do not worry about the particular shape of this curve. What is important is this: The existence of scarcity is illustrated by the fact that all combinations of goods lying above and to the right of line AB are unattainable, even though they may be wanted by people. Combinations lying to the left and below the line are attainable, but they would require less than the total flows of resources or less efficient production methods than are available. The production possibilities frontier restricts people's ability to have all they want. They may want combination W, but they cannot have the combinations of goods outside the frontier in the shaded region. On the other hand, people can attain any one of the combination of goods lying within the unshaded area 0AB. Presumably, people will try to use their resources fully and efficiently (rather than partly and inefficiently). If they do, they will acquire one of the combinations of goods lying precisely on curved line ACB (rather than somewhere below it).

It is now easy to see how each benefit comes with a related cost. If the people of our hypothetical country were to produce quantity 0A of consumption goods, they would have to forgo quantity 0B of capital goods. Thus the opportunity cost of 0A consumption goods would equal 0B of capital goods. Alternatively, if these people were to produce 0B of capital goods, they would have to forgo production of 0A of consumption goods. The opportunity cost of 0B of capital goods would equal 0A of consumption goods. And if they were to produce (at point C) some of both types of goods, the production of $EC = 0D$ of consumption goods would cost BE of capital goods, while producing $DC = 0E$ of capital goods would cost AD of consumption goods.

We as individuals similarly incur opportunity costs every day. Just as the country as a whole has limited resources to produce goods, so each individual has a limited income to acquire goods. When you spend money on ice cream, you might have to forgo the next best use of your funds, such as seeing a movie. The movie forgone is the opportunity cost of eating ice cream. When a family spends its money on furniture, it might have to forgo a vacation trip. The vacation trip forgone is the opportunity cost of having the furniture.

Similar costs are incurred as we allocate the limited time available to us. If we watch the evening newscast, we might not be able to watch the sunset. Not seeing the sunset is the opportunity cost of seeing the news. Whatever we do, because there are so many things we like to do and time is limited, we must pay for our benefits by incurring opportunity costs. Right now, as you read this book, there is surely something else you could do and would like to do. As long as you refrain from doing it, forgoing the next best thing is the opportunity cost of studying economics.

Marginalist Thinking

Scarcity is not popular. Most people do not like to put a rein on their desires and relinquish some of the goods they want. That necessity can be minimized, however, by not wasting resources, by *economizing* them. Let us begin with ourselves. Are we successfully economizing our own "resources"? How do we decide on the allocation of our scarce time among the many competing activities we might engage in? How do we decide on the allocation of our scarce money income among the many goods we want?

Seldom do we make all-or-nothing decisions. We rarely spend *all* our time studying economics and *none* of it doing other things. We rarely spend all our income buying food and none of it buying other goods. Usually we engage in a variety of activities in a given day, just as we buy many different goods with our income. Groups of people, like the citizens of a nation, do the same thing. They never use all their scarce resources for one purpose only.

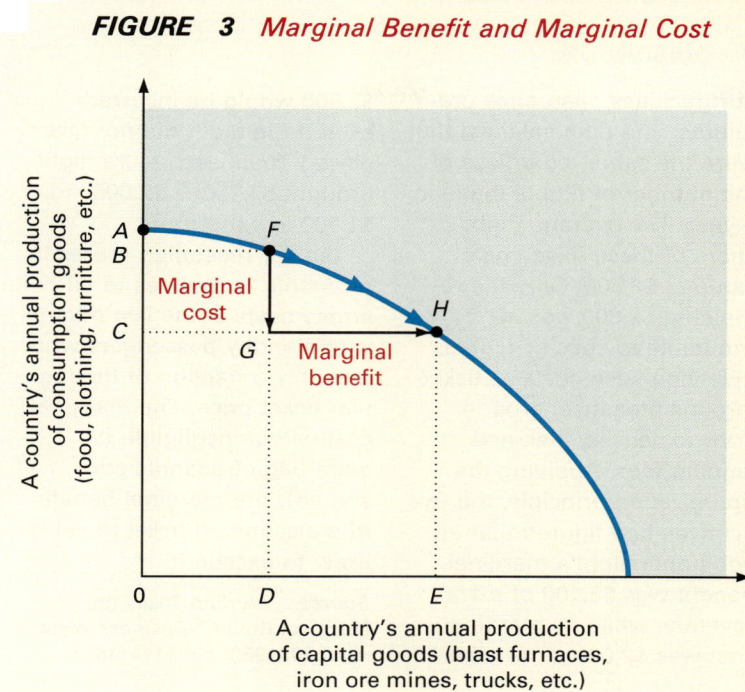

FIGURE 3 Marginal Benefit and Marginal Cost

When a country reallocates its resources from consumption goods to capital goods and moves along its production possibilities frontier from F to H, it reaps a marginal benefit GH while incurring a marginal cost FG.

They never choose a position such as A in Figure 2 (producing nothing but consumption goods) or one such as B (producing nothing but capital goods). The choices made do not involve choosing all this or all that, rather, they involve a little more of this and a little less of that.

Now consider the implications. In the context of scarcity, any act of choice brings with it not only a benefit but also a cost. Therefore, when people replace one choice with another, they will change both the benefit and the cost related to their original choice. Economists have a special name for such changes in the total benefit and cost of an activity. They call the change in an activity's total benefit that is attributable to a unit change in the level of that activity its **marginal benefit.** In addition, they call the change in an activity's total cost that is attributable to a single unit change in the level of that activity its **marginal cost** (or its marginal opportunity cost).

Figure 3 illustrates these concepts. Originally, a country is positioned at F, producing 0B of consumption goods and 0D of capital goods. (The benefit of 0D = BF of capital goods was purchased at an opportunity cost of AB of consumption goods.) Let the country move to point H (where it produces only 0C of consumption goods but 0E of capital goods). In the process, the country effectively sacrifices FG of additional consumption goods (on top of AB). These goods are the marginal cost of the resource shift. As a reward, the country can have additional capital goods (on top of BF). These goods are the marginal benefit of the resource shift.

Why would a country move from F to H, thereby producing more capital goods in the full knowledge that this action requires producing fewer consumption goods? Presumably, decision makers would do so only if they subjectively valued the marginal benefit GH of extra capital goods more highly than the marginal cost FG of extra consumption goods that must be forgone. By the same token, rational decision makers (who cared to maximize the welfare obtainable from scarce resources) could be expected to forgo a move from F to H if the marginal benefit of extra capital goods was valued less than the marginal cost of extra capital goods (mea-

EXAMPLE 1

An Airline That Took the Marginal Route

In 1962, executives at Continental Airlines, Inc., came under fire from angry stockholders who had discovered the company was *expanding* its number of flights even though it filled merely half the seats available on its Boeing 707 jets. The company took in $3,100 on each extra flight, yet the average flight's share of the company's total cost came to $4,500. This practice seemed an invitation to financial disaster.

Actually, it was not. The company's total costs included many items (such as interest on debt, rent on airport facilities, insurance premiums, and pilot salaries) that were the same regardless of the number of flights made in a year. The average flight's share of these fixed costs came to $2,500. Only the remaining $2,000 was attributable to specific flights, involving such costs as ticketing, maintenance, ground crew expenses, fuel, and landing fees. Applying the optimization principle, the executives had figured that an additional flight's marginal benefit was $3,100 of extra revenue, while its marginal cost was $2,000. (The other $2,500 would be incurred even if the flight did not take place.) Thus, each extra flight brought $3,100 − $2,000 = $1,100 in extra profit.

Similar reasoning makes it *profitable* for airlines to fill empty seats at the last minute with standby passengers who pay only a fraction of the regular ticket price. The marginal cost will be negligible (an extra bag of peanuts consumed); the marginal benefit (the discounted ticket price) is likely to exceed it.

Source: "Airline Takes the Marginal Route," *Business Week*, April 20, 1963, pp. 111–114.

---

sured in terms of forgone consumption goods). The key to the economical use of resources thus lies in **marginalist thinking,** the systematic comparison of the marginal benefit and marginal cost associated with any conceivable reallocation of fully employed resources.

The Optimization Principle

People who care to maximize the welfare they obtain from scarce resources should apply the **optimization principle:** Whenever a subjective evaluation of an activity's marginal benefit, *MB*, and marginal cost, *MC*, shows the two values to be unequal, it pays to change the level of the activity in question. If the marginal benefit is valued more than the marginal cost, an expansion of the activity will raise total welfare. If the marginal benefit is valued less than the marginal cost, a contraction of the activity will raise total welfare. Whenever marginal benefit and marginal cost are of equal value, the best possible (or optimum) level of the activity has been reached.

FOCUS 1

The Optimization Principle

a. *MB* > *MC*, expand activity.
b. *MB* < *MC*, contract activity.
c. *MB* = *MC*, activity level is optimum.

More often than not, if people follow this principle, any initial difference between the values placed on marginal benefit and marginal cost tends to disappear as people adjust the level of the activ-

EXAMPLE 2

The Determinants of Family Size

People's use of the optimization principle, even subconsciously, helps explain the number of children married couples tend to have. In the figure, the marginal cost of having a child is represented by line *MC*. Each additional child costs a constant extra amount of $10,000 per year for food, clothing, health care, education, and the like. The marginal benefit is represented by falling line *MB*. Each additional child brings smaller additional benefits to the parents. Under the circumstances, the optimum is found at *a*; the typical couple has an average of 3 children.

Let the cost of child care increase to $19,000 per year, illustrated by line *MC'*, the typical couple would only have a single child, corresponding to point *b*. Further increases in cost to $26,000 per year would reduce the number of children to zero. It has been hypothesized that increasing job opportunities for women in the United States have, in effect, during the past decades produced the trend just discussed. A woman who could earn $20,000 in an outside job would have to forgo this income to be a mother at home. Thus the true cost of child raising includes such income forgone (in addition to the child's food, clothing, and the like), just as the true cost of a college education includes the student's income forgone.

A decline in the perceived marginal benefit of having children, as from *MB* to *MB'*, would similarly reduce the chosen family size (again to zero in our example, regardless of which *MC* line prevailed). It has been hypothesized that the value of children to parents, especially as agricultural workers or providers in old age, declines in the process of economic development. As the overall importance of agriculture declines, agricultural labor is replaced by agricultural machines, and the extended family gives way to government-run social security systems. As a result, family size is smaller in the United States than in many of the poorer countries throughout the world, and it is smaller now than a hundred years ago. Within any given country and any given period of time, birth rates among the well-to-do tend to be smaller than those among the poor.

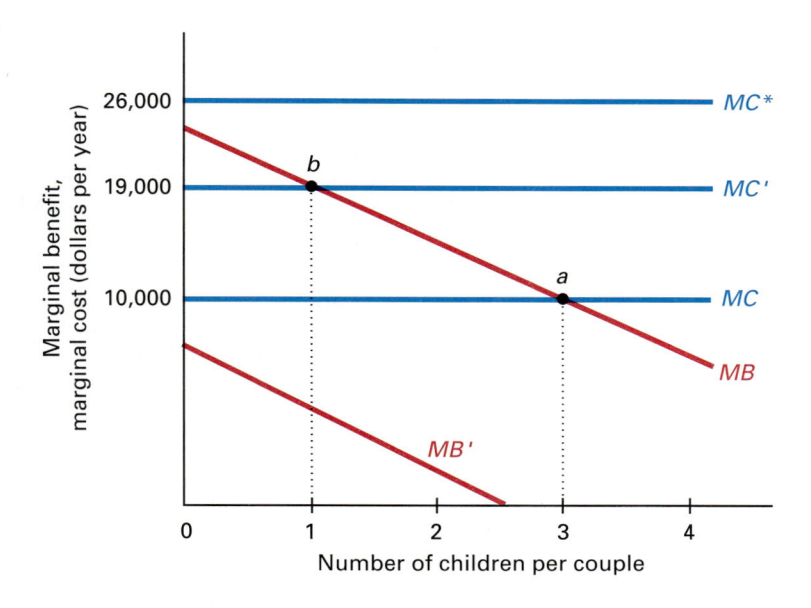

ity in question. This result occurs because the values placed on the marginal benefit tend to be smaller, and those placed on the marginal cost tend to be larger, at higher levels of an activity (and the opposite).

A Case Study: Cancer Versus Heart Attacks

Many people believe that economists focus their attention on matters of business, but nothing can be further from the truth. Economics is equally applicable to the difficult choices that scarcity forces upon private consumers and government officials. Suppose the Secretary of Health in a state government has an annual budget of $30 million. The money is to be spent on saving as many lives as possible. Two programs stand out as most promising: screening the state's population for cancer; or deploying special cardiac arrest ambulances, that are capable of saving people immediately after a heart attack. The relevant facts are summarized in Table 1. A brief look at the table tempts an immediate conclusion. By spending the entire annual budget of $30 million on cancer screening (screening everyone between the ages of 20 and 79), some 1,950 lives would be saved. By funding 60 cardiac arrest units, only 1,650 lives would be saved. The former alternative seems to be the one to pursue, yet this conclusion is entirely wrong. It focuses on all-or-nothing outcomes and ignores the optimization principle.

Let us instead take a marginalist approach. Focusing on cancer screening first, we can expand this activity gradually, one $5 million step at a time, from 0 to 6 units, which would exhaust our $30 million budget. Using the information in Part A of Table 1, we derive Figure 4. Note how the first $5 million spent (on screening only people in their 70s) would save 800 lives. This number is shown by shaded block *a* in the upper graph. Thus the total benefit of 1 unit of cancer screening equals 800 lives (point *P*). The lower graph provides the same information in a different way. The increase in cancer screening expenditure from zero to one ($5 million) unit would increase the number of lives saved from 0 to 800. It would provide an extra or marginal benefit of 800 lives. This number is shown by block *a* in the lower graph.

TABLE 1 Alternative Public Health Programs

	A. Cancer screening			B. Heart attack treatment	
Age group screened (1)	Total monetary cost (millions of dollars per year) (2)	Total benefit (number of lives saved per year) (3)	Mobile units deployed (4)	Total monetary cost (millions of dollars per year) (5)	Total benefit (number of lives saved per year) (6)
70–79	$5	800	10	$5	600
60–79	10	1,300	20	10	1,000
50–79	15	1,600	30	15	1,300
40–79	20	1,800	40	20	1,500
30–79	25	1,900	50	25	1,600
20–79	30	1,950	60	30	1,650

A superficial reading of this table leads to the conclusion that a $30 million budget will save the greatest number of lives (1,950 per year) if it is spent entirely on cancer screening. This conclusion, however, is wrong, as the optimization principle shows.

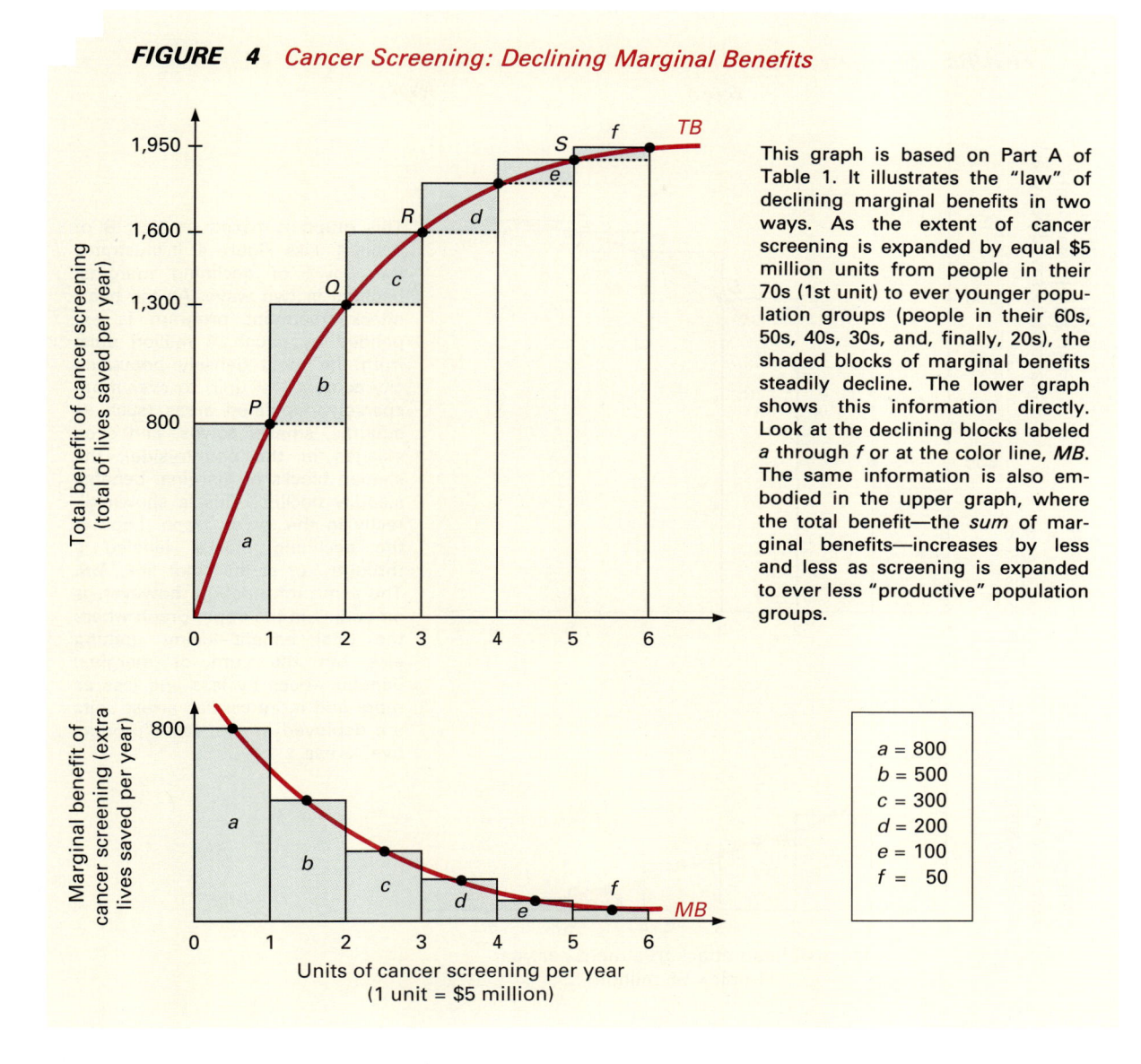

FIGURE 4 Cancer Screening: Declining Marginal Benefits

This graph is based on Part A of Table 1. It illustrates the "law" of declining marginal benefits in two ways. As the extent of cancer screening is expanded by equal $5 million units from people in their 70s (1st unit) to ever younger population groups (people in their 60s, 50s, 40s, 30s, and, finally, 20s), the shaded blocks of marginal benefits steadily decline. The lower graph shows this information directly. Look at the declining blocks labeled a through f or at the color line, MB. The same information is also embodied in the upper graph, where the total benefit—the *sum* of marginal benefits—increases by less and less as screening is expanded to ever less "productive" population groups.

a = 800
b = 500
c = 300
d = 200
e = 100
f = 50

The second $5 million spent to expand the screening process to people in their 60s would save an extra 500 lives, block b. Thus the total benefit of 2 units of cancer screening equals a + b or 800 + 500 = 1,300 lives (point Q). Once again, the marginal benefit is shown separately in the lower graph (block b). It represents the change in the total benefit (from 800 to 1,300 lives) as spending on cancer screening is raised from 1 to 2 units.

And so it would go. Eventually, by the time five $5 million units were being spent (and everyone between ages 30 and 79 was being screened), the total benefit would equal a + b + c + d + e or 800 + 500 + 300 + 200 + 100 = 1,900 lives (point S, upper graph). At this point, an additional $5 million spending on cancer screening would bring a tiny marginal benefit equal to a saving of only f = 50 lives per year. As a look at Table 1 confirms, these relatively few additional lives would be saved by including in the screening program people in their 20s (who would be less likely to have cancer than older age groups).

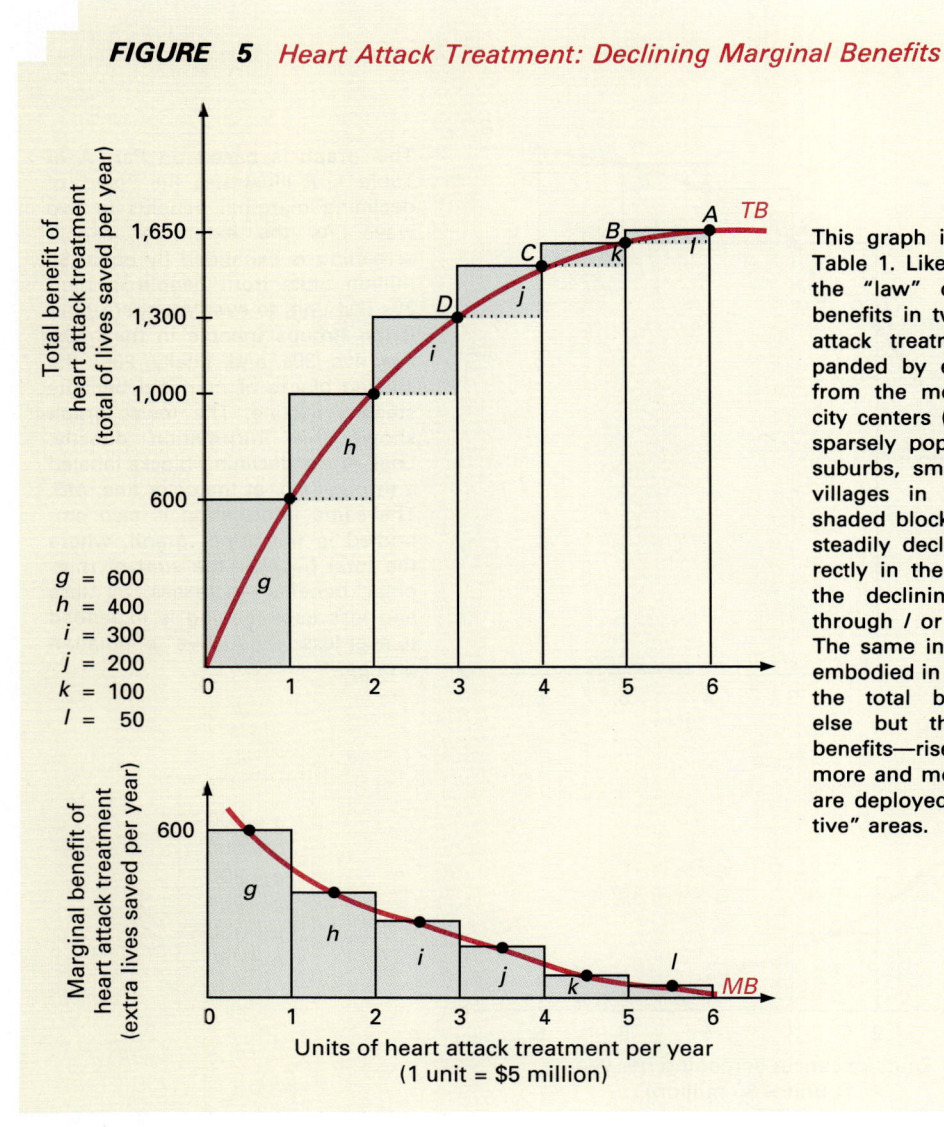

FIGURE 5 Heart Attack Treatment: Declining Marginal Benefits

g = 600
h = 400
i = 300
j = 200
k = 100
l = 50

This graph is based on Part B of Table 1. Like Figure 4, it illustrates the "law" of declining marginal benefits in two ways. As the heart attack treatment program is expanded by equal $5 million units from the most densely populated city centers (1st unit) to ever more sparsely populated areas (such as suburbs, smaller towns, and even villages in the countryside), the shaded blocks of marginal benefits steadily decline. This is shown directly in the lower graph. Look at the declining blocks, labeled g through l or at the color line, MB. The same information, however, is embodied in the upper graph where the total benefit—being nothing else but the sum of marginal benefits—rises by less and less as more and more cardiac arrest units are deployed in ever less "productive" areas.

The "Law" of Declining Marginal Benefits

Although there are exceptions to it, Figure 4 depicts the **"law" of declining marginal benefits.** All else being equal, the greater the overall level of any activity during a given period, the smaller its marginal benefit will usually be. In our example, the operation of the "law" simply reflects the fact that ever-younger age groups would be equally expensive to screen but ever less likely to have cancer and thus to provide life saving opportunities.

We can follow the same procedure with respect to Part B of Table 1. Although the numbers differ, the result is similar, as shown in Figure 5. Successive $5 million units are spent on purchasing and deploying cardiac arrest units, which each cost $500,000 per year. The first 10 units bought will be deployed where they do the most good, in the most densely populated center of a large city. Thus the marginal benefit is an impressive 600 lives saved. Successive units are deployed in ever less densely populated areas; the marginal benefits decline accordingly.

From Declining MB to Rising MC

Even in a world of scarcity, people can always have

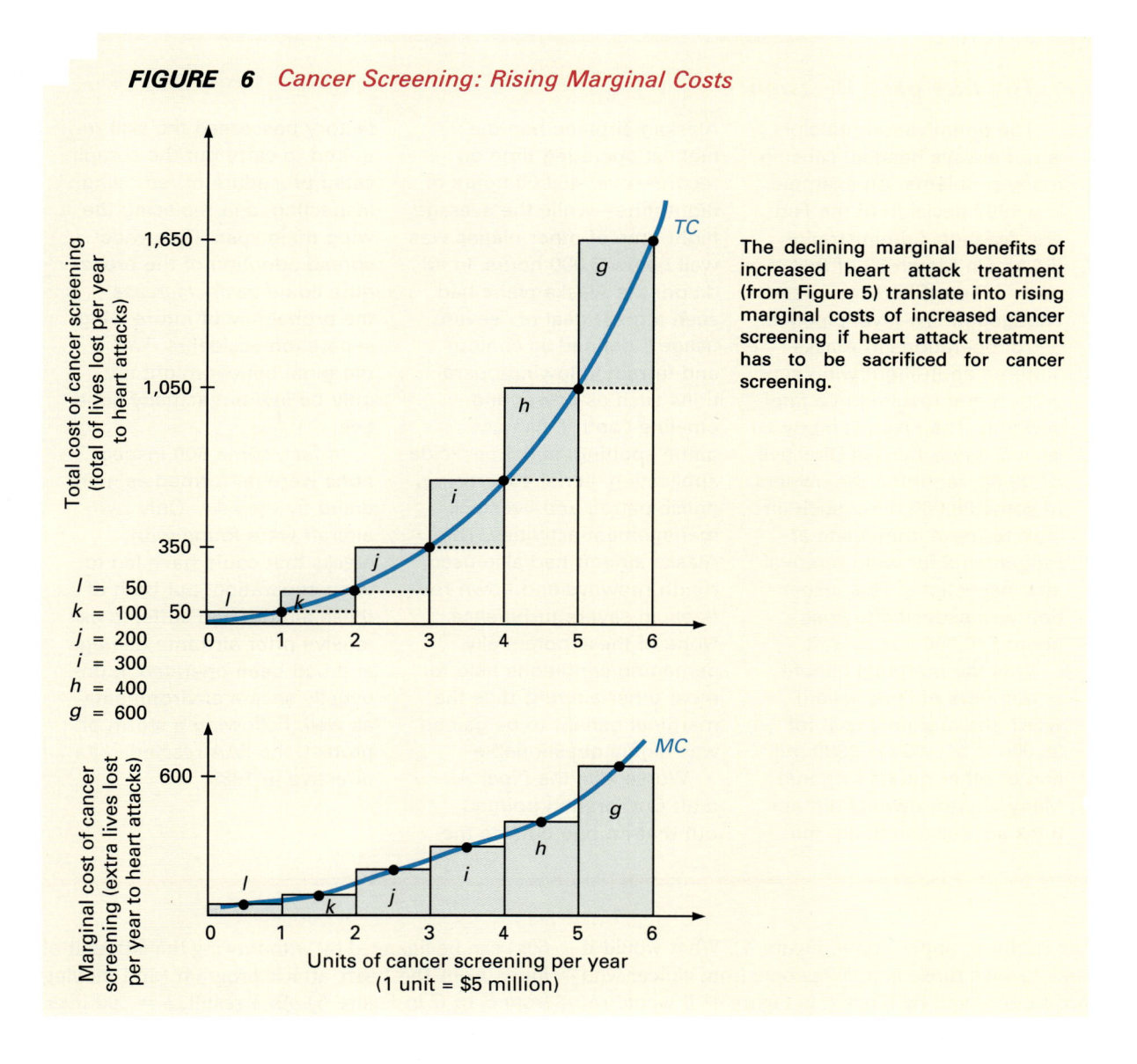

FIGURE 6 Cancer Screening: Rising Marginal Costs

The declining marginal benefits of increased heart attack treatment (from Figure 5) translate into rising marginal costs of increased cancer screening if heart attack treatment has to be sacrificed for cancer screening.

l = 50
k = 100
j = 200
i = 300
h = 400
g = 600

more of one good if they are willing to give up some amount of another good. Now we are ready to see more fully some of the implications. Scarcity is an issue in our state's public health department. The Secretary of Health could spend $500 million a year on all kinds of life saving programs but is confronted with a fixed annual budget of $30 million. As Figures 4 and 5 show, the expansion of any given program is associated with *declining* marginal benefits. If, however, the expansion of any one program comes at the cost of reducing the potential size of another program (as is inevitably the case), the *declining* marginal benefits of the expanding program are purchased at the cost of forgone and *rising* marginal benefits of the contracting program. (Review Figure 4 or 5. Note how the marginal benefits are *rising* as one contracts a given program and moves from the right-hand side to the left.) The forgone and rising marginal benefits of any contracting program can be viewed as the *rising marginal costs* of the expanding program.

An illustration is provided by Figure 6. Picture the entire public health budget spent on the heart attack program. Then 1,650 lives would be saved from heart attacks (point *A*, upper graph, Figure 5), but nobody would be saved through cancer screen-

EXAMPLE 3

The Cherokee Decision

The optimization principle is not always heeded, causing many problems. An example is a 1987 decision of the Federal Aviation Administration (FAA). On March 30 of that year, a Piper Cherokee aircraft engaged in low-level pipeline patrol operations in Alaska suffered an in-flight wing separation that resulted in a fatal accident. The FAA promptly issued Airworthiness Directive 87-08-08, requiring the owners of some 38,000 other such aircraft to make immediate arrangements for wing removal and inspections. This inspection was expected to cost about $10,000 per aircraft.

Was the marginal benefit (x numbers of lives saved) worth the marginal cost (of 38,000 × $10,000 = $380 million of other goods forgone)? Many aircraft owners did not think so. For one thing, the Alaskan airplane had the highest operating time on record—over 45,000 hours of flight time—while the average flight time of other planes was well below 5,000 hours. In addition, the Alaska plane had seen a great deal of "severe usage," defined as contour and terrain following operations such as power and pipeline control, fish and game spotting, aerial pesticide application, aerial advertising, police patrol, and livestock management activities. The Alaska aircraft had also used rough runways and flown routinely in severe turbulence. None of these potentially damaging conditions held for most other aircraft; thus the marginal benefit to be gained was highly questionable.

Worse still, the Piper Aircraft Corporation pointed out that no one outside the factory possessed the skill required to carry out the complicated procedure of removing, inspecting, and replacing the wing main spar. Thus widespread adoption of the procedure could easily *increase* the probability of future wing-separation accidents. The marginal benefit might not only be low but actually negative.

In fact, some 500 inspections were performed as mandated by the FAA. Only two aircraft were found with cracks that could have led to wing separation, but both of these aircraft had suffered extensive prior airframe damage and had been operated in unusually severe environments as well. Following a storm of protest, the FAA rescinded its directive in 1989.

---

ing (point 0, upper graph, Figure 4). What would it take to save those first 800 people from cancer who are represented by block *a* in Figure 4? It would require withdrawing a $5 million unit of funds from the heart attack program and applying it to the cancer screening program. As a result of spending 5 rather than 6 units of funds ($25 million rather than $30 million) on heart attack treatment, only 1,600 lives would be saved by that program (point *B*, upper graph, Figure 5). The 50 lives *not* saved from heart attacks (because no cardiac arrest units will be deployed in certain rural areas) are represented by block *l* in Figure 6. They are the opportunity cost of funding the first $5 million units of cancer screening (for people in their 70s).

The remaining entries in Figure 6 are similar. A second unit of cancer screening (for people in their 60s) can be financed by withdrawing the fifth unit of funds from the heart attack program (and moving from *B* to *C* in Figure 5). As a result, $k = 100$ lives are *not* saved from heart attacks. It is the marginal cost of funding the second unit of cancer screening. A third unit of cancer screening (for people in their 50s) can be similarly financed by withdrawing the fourth unit of funds from the heart attack program (and moving from *C* to *D* in Figure 5). This time, $j = 200$ lives are lost to heart attacks for lack of quick medical response and this number is the marginal cost of funding the third unit of cancer screening. The more cancer screening is expanded, the more the heart attack program must be cut and the more people are lost to heart attacks. Cutting the last unit of funds from the heart attack program (Figure 5) would result in failure to save the 600

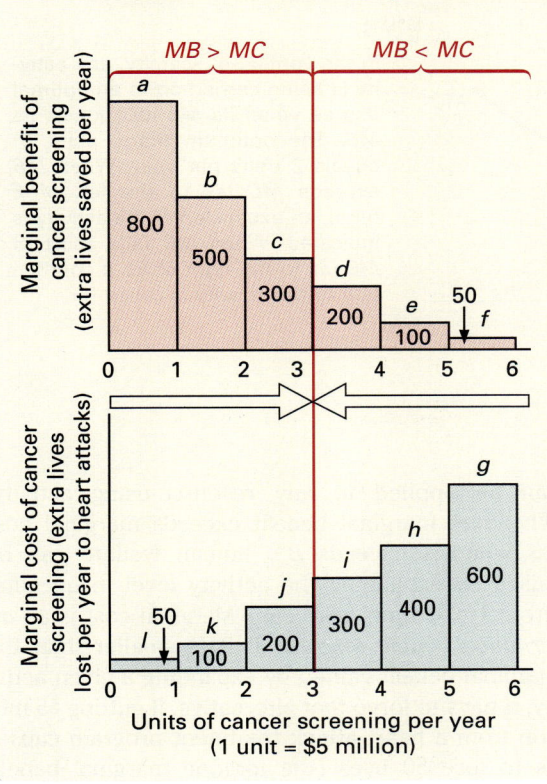

FIGURE 7 The Deadly Choice: Cancer or Heart Attacks

This graph brings together the marginal benefit and marginal cost data of Figures 4 and 6. It shows that spending three $5 million units on cancer screening is optimal. When less is spent, it pays to expand the cancer screening activity (at the expense of the heart attack program) because each expansionary step saves more lives from cancer (800, 500, 300) than are lost to heart attacks (50, 100, 200). On the other hand, when more is spent, it pays to contract the cancer screening activity (in favor of an expanded heart attack program) because each contractionary step loses fewer lives to cancer (50, 100, 200) than can be saved from heart attacks (600, 400, 300). The arrows point to the optimal level of the cancer screening activity.

lives represented by block *g*, and these 600 lives would be the marginal cost (Figure 6) of raising cancer screening from 5 to 6 units.

The Optimum Solution

We find the best possible manner in which to spend the $30 million budget by applying the optimization principle shown in Focus 1. Figure 7 brings together in a single graph the information on marginal benefits and marginal costs of cancer screening that was contained in Figures 4 and 6. The optimal level of cancer screening is revealed:

1. A first $5 million unit of the $30 million budget should clearly be spent on cancer screening because the marginal benefit (saving a = 800 lives) exceeds the associated marginal cost (failing to save l = 50 lives).

2. A second $5 million unit of the $30 million budget should also be spent on cancer screening be-

cause the (admittedly lower) marginal benefit (saving b = 500 lives) still exceeds the (admittedly higher) marginal cost (failing to save k = 100 lives).

3. A third $5 million unit of the $30 million budget should also be spent on cancer screening because the (still lower) marginal benefit (saving c = 300 lives) still exceeds the (even higher) marginal cost (failing to save j = 200 lives).

At this point, the cancer screening program would have expanded to its optimal level. Spending of additional (fourth, fifth, and sixth) units of $5 million would be associated with marginal benefits (d = 200, e = 100, and f = 50 lives) that would fall short of marginal costs (i = 300, h = 400, and g = 600 lives). Indeed, should the cancer screening program exceed the optimal level indicated by the vertical color line, one should contract the program to the 3-unit optimum level. In that case, marginal benefits of f = 50, e = 100, and d = 200 lives would

FIGURE 8 The Optimization Principle

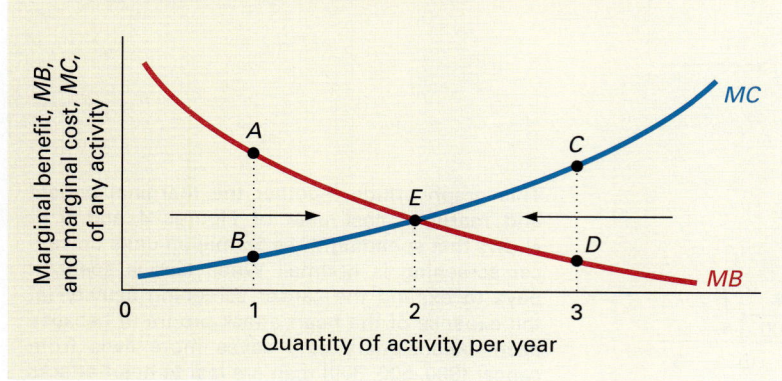

In the context of scarcity, any activity is being carried on to an optimal degree when its *MB* just equals its *MC*. The optimum (here, point *E*) equals 2 units per year. When *MB* exceeds *MC* (as to the left of *E* here), an expansion of the activity is indicated. When *MB* falls short of *MC* (as to the right of *E*), a contraction of the activity is called for.

be forgone, but larger marginal benefits of $g = 600$, $h = 400$, and $i = 300$ would be reaped elsewhere (by expanding the heart attack program to 3 units as well). The best solution, in our example, would involve spending three units of $5 million, or $15 million per year, on cancer screening and another $15 million per year on heart attack treatment. As the shaded row of Table 1 indicates, this combination would result in

1. A cancer screening program that only screened people in the 50–79 year age bracket and saved 1,600 lives a year (point *R*, Figure 4, or the sum of $a + b + c$, Figure 7)

2. A heart attack program that only deployed 30 cardiac arrest units—presumably in the most populous areas—and saved 1,300 lives per year (point *D*, Figure 5, or the sum of $g + h + i$, Figure 7)

Thus, a total of 2,900 lives per year would be saved, considerably more than the 1,950 lives that a complete 6-unit funding of the cancer screening program alone could have saved.

Conclusion

The lessons learned from the previous example can be extended to other choices. The graph in Figure 8 is a streamlined version of the two lower panels of Figures 4 and 6, superimposed upon one another. It can be applied to any resource-using activity. Whenever marginal benefit exceeds marginal cost (as when *A* exceeds *B*), human welfare can be raised by expanding the activity level in question (from 1 to 2 units per year). Marginal cost is an *alternative benefit forgone*. If it is smaller than the marginal benefit gained by expanding a given activity, it pays to forgo that alternative. If cutting $5 million from a heart attack treatment program causes us to lose 50 lives (the forgone marginal benefit from heart attack treatment being the marginal cost of cancer screening), while spending an extra $5 million on cancer screening enables us to save 800 lives (the marginal benefit), we are raising the number of lives saved.

In contrast, whenever marginal benefit falls short of marginal cost (as when *D* falls short of *C* here), human welfare can be raised by contracting the activity level (from 3 toward 2 units per year). This decision also makes sense because the alternative is more promising. Thus, cutting $5 million from a cancer screening program (and losing 50 lives to cancer) is painful yet worthwhile if the funds, when applied to heart attack treatment, could save 600 lives instead.

This optimization principle is universal for maximizing welfare under conditions of scarcity. People of all societies must apply it when deciding how to allocate their scarce resources, just as you must apply it when deciding how to allocate your scarce money income or your scarce time. Instead

IDEAS IN HISTORY — *The Division of Labor*

Adam Smith (1723–1790), a Scottish professor of logic and moral philosophy, published in 1776 *An Inquiry into the Nature and Causes of the Wealth of Nations.* The book is now considered the fountainhead of economic science; it earned Smith the title "father of economics." In his book, Smith sought to explain why some nations were rich and others poor. He focused on their *productivity,* the amount of output they produced per unit of resources. The single most important source of productivity, Smith argued, is the division of labor. "This division of labor, from which so many advantages are derived, is not originally the effect of any human wisdom, which foresees and intends that general opulence to which it gives occasion. It is the necessary, though very slow and gradual, consequence of a certain propensity in human nature which has in view no such extensive utility, the propensity to truck, barter, and exchange one thing for another."[1]

Adam Smith articulated the advantages of the division of labor with the help of a now famous example. A pinmaker, he pointed out, could not produce twenty pins in a day if he himself had to do everything required—drawing out the wire, straightening it, cutting it, pointing it, grinding it for receiving the head, making the head, and so on. Yet Smith observed that ten people, only poorly equipped with machinery but with the proper division of labor among them, were able to make 48,000 pins in one day.

This particular example refers to specialization within a firm, but Smith was well aware of the benefits from specialization on a larger scale. The wealth of nations could be increased by the kind of regional cooperation involved in all kinds of domestic markets as well as in international trade among countries (to be discussed in Chapter 4 of this book).

Smith urged that government refrain from protecting monopolies, imposing tariffs, and similar actions that would restrict free trade and ultimately the division of labor. Smith repeatedly emphasized the importance of economic liberty, the free competition among individuals pursuing their self-interest as they choose to define it. This spontaneous interaction of people in the marketplace—all persons having only their own narrow, but not necessarily selfish, ends in mind—would bring about the greatest possible prosperity that limited resources allowed.

---
[1] Adam Smith, *An Inquiry into The Nature and Causes of the Wealth of Nations* (Edinburgh: A. and C. Black 1872) Book I, p. 6.

---

of devoting all your money to ice cream or all your time to studying economics, you are better off to do a little bit of many things. Similarly for society at large, instead of devoting all the resources to expanding health care or education, building better houses or more missiles, constructing subways or cleaning up the environment, people are most likely to maximize their welfare by chosing a little bit of each. When people do too much of any one thing at the expense of other things that are also wanted, they become dissatisfied. Remember, no matter how good or desirable an activity may seem, in a world of scarcity a logical stopping point exists, beyond which an activity should be expanded no further. This is the point at which, in people's judgment, the marginal benefit and marginal cost are equal.

Examples 1 to 3 provide additional illustrations of how the optimization principle is used or ignored in everyday life.

Summary

1. Most people on earth harbor desires for a staggering variety and quantity of goods. The extent of this desire would be revealed, economists believe, if people were asked—in their various capacities as household members, business executives, government officials, and the like—to prepare a list of commodities and services they would wish to receive if these could be had in return for nothing.

2. Goods are produced with productive ingredients called resources. Resources are classified into human, natural, and capital.

3. The quantities of goods people produce depend not only on the physical quantities of resources they employ but also on the state of technology.

4. All societies have limited stocks of resources; therefore, resource flows in any period are limited, too. Given limited technical knowledge, any period's flows of goods are also limited.

5. Because people's desire for goods exceeds their ability to produce goods, every society suffers from the basic economic problem of scarcity. It is impossible, in any country and in any period we consider, simultaneously to fulfill the desire for goods by all the people.

6. The most obvious implication of scarcity is the need to choose. Consider the questions of *What, How,* and *For Whom.*

7. Choice brings a mixture of pleasure and pain because every use of resources for one purpose means forgoing the opportunity to use them for another desired purpose. Where there is scarcity, every benefit derived from a particular use of resources is accompanied by an opportunity cost. This concept is illustrated by the production possibilities frontier.

8. Successful economizing of scarce resources requires not all-or-nothing choices, but rather adopting marginalist thinking, which systematically compares the marginal benefit and marginal cost associated with a proposed reallocation of fully used resources.

9. The optimization principle tells us under what circumstances it is wise to expand one activity at the expense of another (or to curtail it in favor of another). Whenever a subjective evaluation of an activity's marginal benefit, *MB,* and marginal cost, *MC,* reveals

   a. $MB > MC$, an expansion of the activity raises welfare.
   b. $MB < MC$, a contraction of the activity raises welfare.
   c. $MB = MC$, the activity level is optimal.

10. The optimization principle is illustrated with an extended example about a government department's choice between fighting cancer or heart attacks. The lessons learned from this example can be extended to other choices as well.

Key Concepts

benefit
capital resources
commodities
cost
desire for goods
factors of production
financial capital
flow
free goods
goods
human capital
human resources
"law" of declining marginal benefits
marginal benefit
marginal cost
marginalist thinking
natural resources
opportunity cost
optimization principle
process of production
production possibilities frontier

productivity	scarce goods	stock
real capital	scarcity problem	technology
resources	services	

Questions and Problems

1. Which of the following are *natural resources* as defined in this chapter: 100 cubic feet of coal, a highway, a cow, an acre of land, sand at a beach not yet discovered by people, sunshine, a school of tuna in the ocean, a college building, a can of peas? *Hint:* Of the nine correct answers, three will be *always;* three others, *never;* and the remaining three, *maybe.* Why?

2. Which of the following are (real) *capital resources* as defined in this chapter: an automobile assembly plant, a toy truck, Ford Motor Company stock, a natural waterfall, unsold refrigerators held by an appliance dealer, an inventory of groceries held by a food store, a horse, a truck driver, a wrist watch. *Hint:* Of the nine correct answers, three will be *always;* three others, *never;* and the remaining three, *maybe.* Why?

3. "There *is* something akin to a magic wand: money. With its help we can fulfill all our material wants. If the government would just print enough and give it to us, scarcity could be eliminated in one fell swoop." Comment.

4. Refer to Figure 1. In principle, there are two approaches one might take to eliminate scarcity in the long run. What are they?

5. "Here are some examples of free goods: highways, public schools, air for purposes of communication, air for purposes of waste disposal, agricultural surpluses, and coal in the ground." What do you think?

6. Can you think of goods that were once free but are now scarce? Goods that are now free at some times or places but scarce at other times or places? Explain.

7. Once again review Figure 1. Redraw the graph for a society of abundance in which all goods are free goods. What would the graph look like if the society stood precisely at the threshold between scarcity and abundance?

8. Refer to Figure 2. How might you use the graph to depict a society (a) enjoying abundance and (b) positioned precisely at the threshold between scarcity and abundance?

9. Reconsider Figure 2. What would happen to the graph if the society in question acquired additional technical knowledge or additional quantities of resources that could only increase the output of capital goods? Could the people of this society still have more consumption goods?

10. Figure 2 is drawn convex to the origin 0 (rather than as a straight line or concave). What do you think are the implications of drawing the frontier in this way?

11. Comment on each of the following:
    a. "Leisure has an opportunity cost."
    b. "Time is money."
    c. "If I won $10 million in a lottery, scarcity would be a thing of the past—at least for me."

12. On what basis would
    a. a rational student allocate time among sleeping, eating, recreation, and studying? Among studying economics, physics, and biology? Among tennis, swimming, and going to movies?
    b. a rational nation allocate its scarce resources between private goods (like TV sets) and public goods (like roads)?

13. Comment on the following statements:
    a. "It may be wise for a household to stop the consumption of any good long before the marginal benefits have fallen to zero."
    b. "It may be wise for a government to stop

putting more resources into education (or pollution abatement or foreign aid) long before the extra benefits from such action have fallen to zero."

c. "It is unwise to maximize the total benefit of an activity, and it is just as unwise to minimize its total cost."

d. "In the absence of scarcity, the optimization principle could be violated with impunity."

14. Why do you think class attendance is always highest on exam days? Why is it so low on ordinary Friday afternoons?

15. Reconsider Table 1. Assuming the $30 million annual budget cannot be subdivided into units smaller than $5 million, prepare a table showing all possible divisions of the budget between the two programs, along with the associated numbers of lives saved. What would be the optimal division according to this table? Does it confirm the result produced by the optimization principle?

16. "I have a better way for discovering the optimal budget division in the cancer/heart attack example. Simply calculate the marginal benefits for each program (as in the lower panels of Figures 4 and 5), then spend successive $5 million units by always picking the highest potential marginal benefit not yet realized." Comment.

APPENDIX 1a

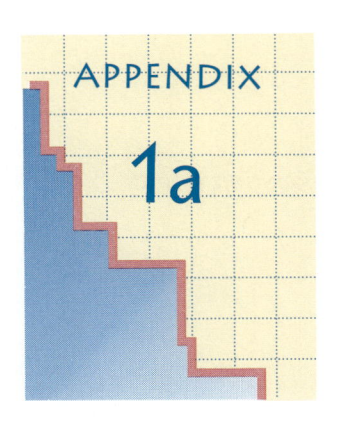

THE USE OF GRAPHS IN ECONOMICS

Graphs are useful tools for studying economics, and many are found throughout this book. This Appendix is designed for those who are unfamiliar with the nature of graphs and want to learn more about them.

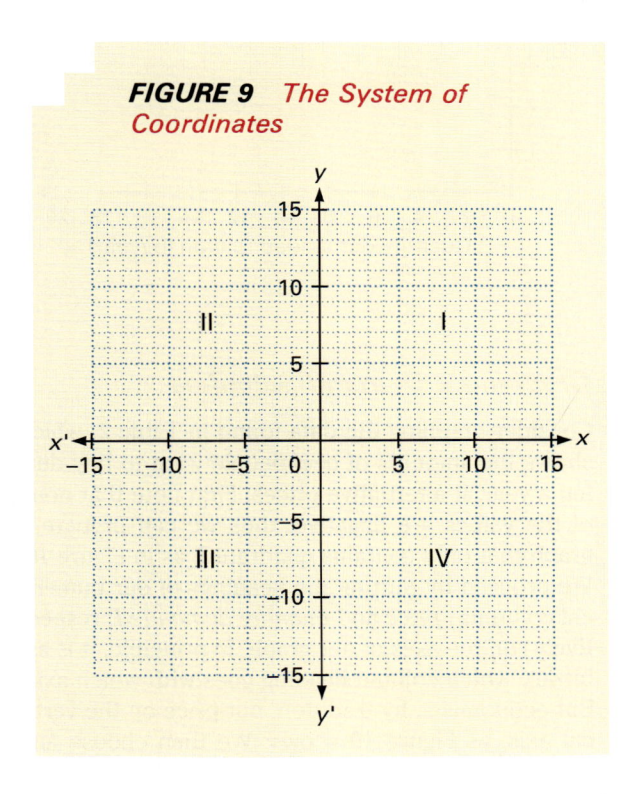

The System of Coordinates

Graphs are merely a shorthand way of presenting information that could be conveyed more laboriously in words or in tabular form. In principle, all graphs are drawn on squared paper, as in Figure 9. The paper is divided by a horizontal axis, called the **abscissa** (line $x'x$), and a vertical axis, called the **ordinate** (line yy'), into four quarters or **quadrants** (labeled I through IV). The two axes intersect at right angles at a point called the **origin** (usually labeled 0). Each axis has a scale of numerical values; the origin counts as zero. On the horizontal axis, or abscissa, all values to the left of 0 are negative, all values to the right of 0 are positive. On the vertical axis, or ordinate, all values below 0 are negative, while those above 0 are positive.

Figure 9 has been drawn so that equal distances from 0 on both axes represent equal units. Each small square equals 1 unit both horizontally and vertically. Such a procedure, however, is not a logical necessity. One often finds identical distances representing different units of measurement on the two axes, as in Figure 10. Throughout this book, once a unit of measurement has been chosen for either axis (and that choice is a matter of convenience), it will be consistently applied to that axis. We may label the fifth unit to the right of 0 on the horizontal axis not 5 but 400, but then we must label the tenth unit 800 (instead of 10), the fifteenth unit 1,200 (instead of 15), and so on. Naturally, to the *left* of 0, we must then replace -5, -10, and -15 by -400, -800, and $-1,200$ as well. (Alternative labeling procedures, such as logarithmic scales, do not concern us here.)

With the rarest of exceptions, the graphs found in this book deal with variables that only take on positive values. They are, therefore, graphed from 0 toward x or from 0 toward y. Hence the typical graph will only contain quadrant I.

FIGURE 9 The System of Coordinates

FIGURE 10 Preparing the Graph

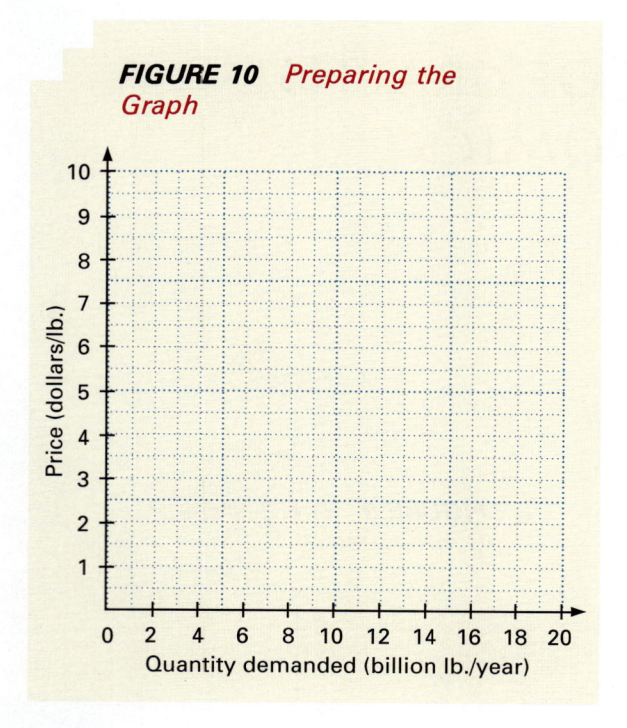

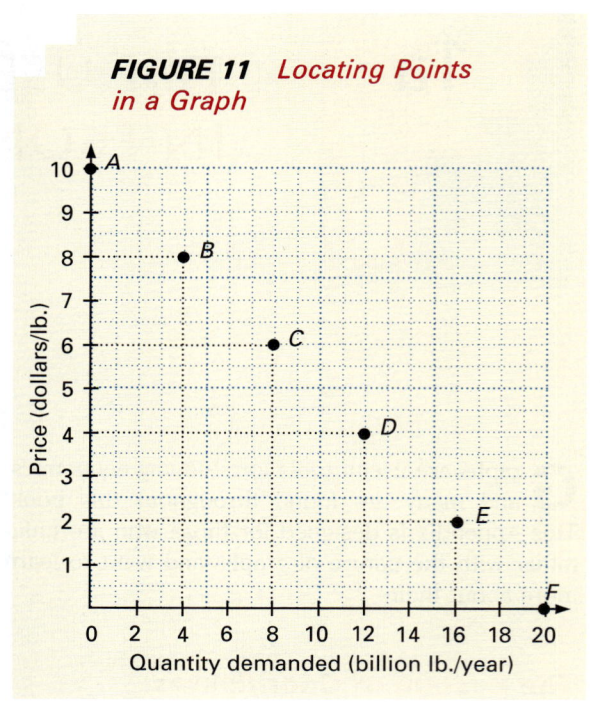

FIGURE 11 Locating Points in a Graph

Graphing a Demand Schedule

Consider graphing the data found in Table 2, which shows the amounts of beef people want to buy during a year at alternative prices. First note that none of the values are negative; thus we can prepare a graph that only contains quadrant I, as in Figure 10. We proceed by putting the headings of our numerical columns (*price* and *quantity demanded*, respectively) on the axes of our graph. In principle, it is arbitrary which column heading goes with which axis. But economists, by tradition, put price on the vertical axis, as Figure 10 shows. We then choose any convenient units of measurement for the axes. The vertical axis must have room for numbers between 0 and 10 (as the Table 2 price column indicates). The horizontal axis must have room for numbers between 0 and 20 (as the quantity-demanded column requires).

The next step involves locating the 6 price-quantity alternatives in the graph. It is akin to finding a geographic point on a map from given longitude and latitude information. Figure 11 is a copy of Figure 10 with the addition of points *A* through *F*, which represent the Table 2 alternatives. They are found by following the dotted straight lines from the relevant places on the two axes. For example, to graph alternative *B* (a price of 8 and a quantity demanded of 4), we draw a horizontal dotted line at a right angle to the vertical axis at 8 and a vertical dotted line at a right angle to the horizontal axis at 4. Where the two dotted lines meet, we locate point

TABLE 2 A Demand Schedule for Beef

Alternative	Price ($/lb.)	Quantity demanded (billions lb./yr.)
A	$10	0
B	8	4
C	6	8
D	4	12
E	2	16
F	0	20

FIGURE 12 A Finished Graph—The Demand for Beef

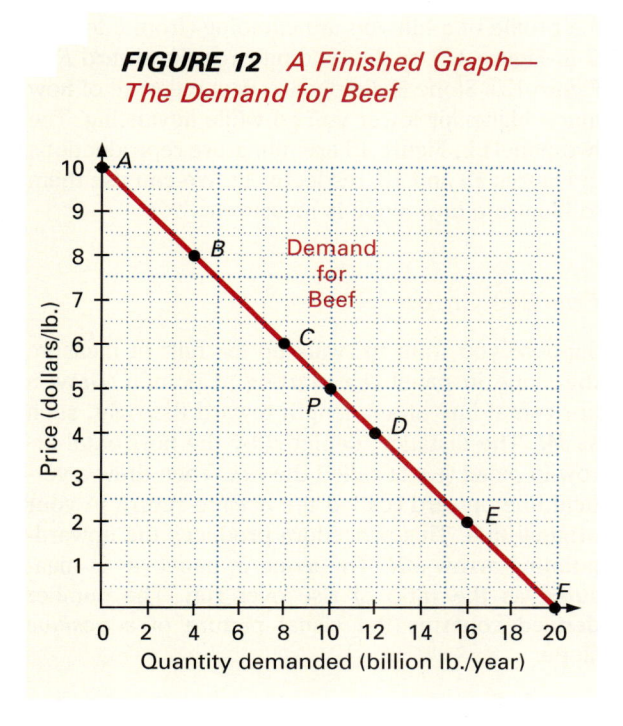

FIGURE 13 The Supply of Beef

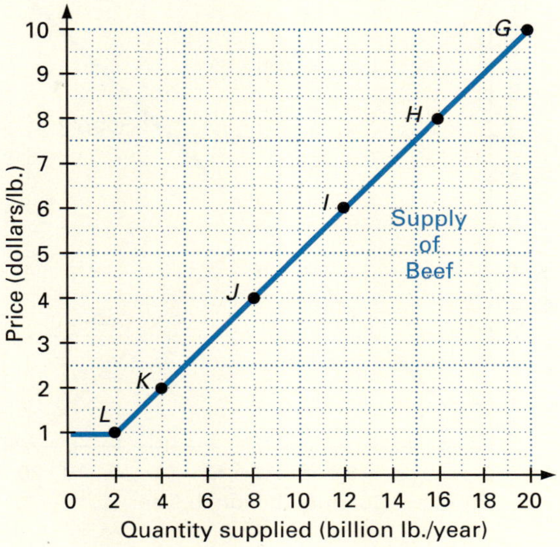

B. We proceed in the same way for all of the other Table 2 alternatives. Note that the vertical dotted line for A and the horizontal dotted line for F coincide with the respective axes of the graph and thus are not visible.

If we believe that the price-quantity relationship in Table 2 ($Q = 20 - 2P$) holds for values not shown in the table, we can connect the points by a line, such as the color line in Figure 12. On the graph, we can then read additional information not contained in Table 2. Can you see how quantity demanded equals 10 billion pounds per year at a price of $5 per pound (point P)?

Just like Figure 12, most graphs in this book are representations of numerical data, such as the data found in Table 2. When you encounter a new graph, first read the labels on the axes. You will then know immediately what the column headings of the corresponding table must have been. If *you* ever graph anything, do not forget to label the axes.

TABLE 3 A Supply Schedule for Beef

Alternative	Price ($/lb.)	Quantity supplied (billions lb./yr.)
G	$10	20
H	8	16
I	6	12
J	4	8
K	2	4
L	1	2

Note: Nothing is supplied below $1.

Superimposing Graphs

Sometimes it is useful to superimpose different graphs on the same system of coordinates. Suppose the supply of beef varies with its price as shown in Table 3. Just as Table 2 was graphed as Figure 12, the Table 3 data are graphed in Figure 13. Notice how Figures 12 and 13 both measure the price of beef (in identical units) on the vertical axis and the quantity of beef (in identical units) on the horizontal axis. Given this commonality, one can combine

26 PART I *Basic Concepts*

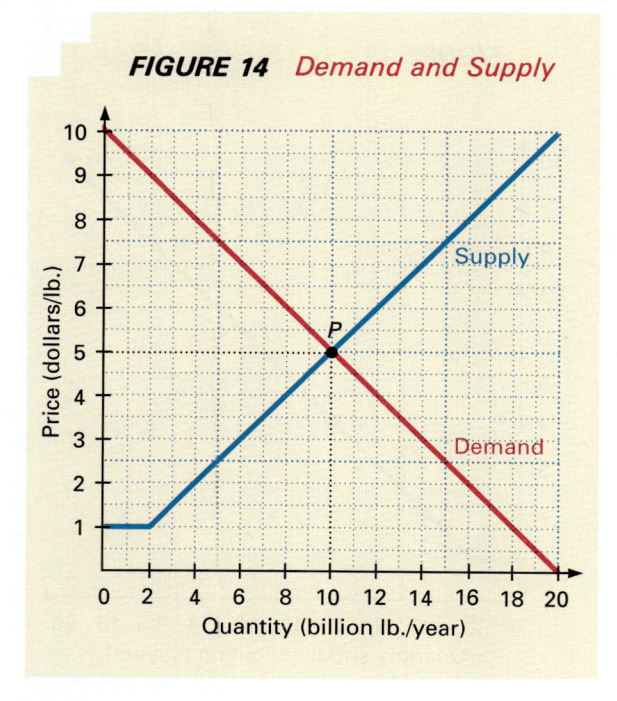

FIGURE 14 Demand and Supply

the two graphs in Figure 14. Focus on intersection P. One can tell right away that demand equals supply at a price of $5/lb and that 10 billion lb/year are then demanded as well as supplied. This information is not instantly available from Tables 2 and 3 but could be deduced by studying them at somewhat greater length.

The Concept of Slope

Economists often want to know how much one variable changes if there is a change in another, related variable. They may want to know in what direction and by how much the quantity demanded or supplied changes when the price changes by $1. Or they may be interested in the direction and extent of a change in consumer spending when income changes by $1. As long as the two variables of interest are shown on the axes of a given graph, the answers to such questions can be found by studying the *slope* of lines drawn in the graph.

Consider how often you have walked up or down a hill and how you gained or lost altitude while going forward. **Slope** is a measure of inclination of a given line (or plane) from the horizontal. Look at the line in Figure 13 or 12. Imagine it to be

the profile of a hill you are climbing (from L toward G in Figure 13) or descending (from A toward F in Figure 12). Slope is simply an exact measure of how much higher or lower you go while advancing. The two panels in Figure 15 are miniature reproductions of Figures 13 and 12, respectively. We can use them to illustrate how slope is measured.

Positive Slope

Suppose you want to "walk up the hill" or measure the slope in panel (a), starting at point J. Draw a horizontal line of any length toward the right, such as JM. The distance, depicted by the horizontal arrow in panel (a), is called the *run*. Then draw a vertical line upward (called the *rise*) to return to your original line. This procedure produces the upward-pointing arrow MH. The slope in panel (a) is measured as the ratio of rise over run. The number derived confirms the visual picture of a *positive* slope:

$$\frac{\text{Rise}}{\text{Run}} = \text{positive slope} = \frac{+4}{+8} = +\frac{1}{2}$$

For the section of the supply line we have examined, every 1-unit change toward the right is associated with a 1/2 unit change in the upward direction. Given the variables on the axes of our graph, this result indicates that a 1-unit increase in quantity supplied is associated with a 1/2 unit increase in price. Thus, a 1 billion pound increase in the quantity of beef supplied is associated with a 1/2 dollar, or 50 cent, increase in price.

CAUTION

Slope must be measured according to the units employed on the two axes, not in terms of inches. Measured by a ruler calibrated in inches, distances JM and MH are equal, but slope does not equal 1. Distance JM, as the horizontal axis tells us, represents an increase in quantity supplied from 8 to 16 billion lb./year, or of +8 billion lb./year. Distance MH, as the vertical axis tells us, represents an increase in price from $4/lb. to $8/lb., or of +$4/lb. Hence the slope is +4/+8, or +1/2.

FIGURE 15 The Concept of Slope

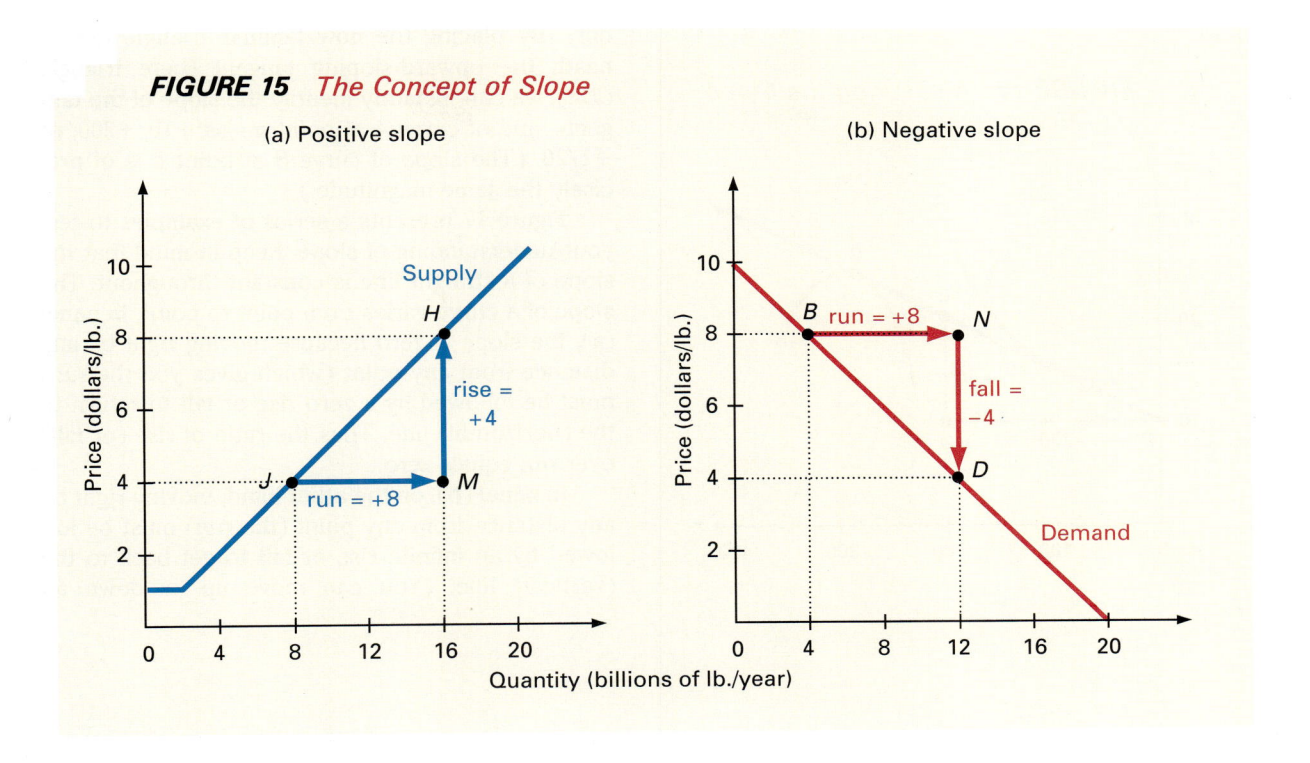

(a) Positive slope

(b) Negative slope

Negative Slope

Now imagine that you want to "walk down the hill" in panel (b) and measure the slope, starting at point B. Again you can draw a horizontal line of any length toward the right, such as BN. The distance you go forward, depicted by the horizontal arrow in panel (b), is the *run*. A vertical line down to the original line produces a *fall*, the downward-pointing arrow ND. The panel (b) slope is measured as the ratio of fall over run. The number so derived supports the visual picture of a *negative* slope:

$$\frac{\text{Fall}}{\text{Run}} = \text{negative slope} = \frac{-4}{+8} = -\frac{1}{2}$$

For the section of the demand line we have examined, every 1-unit change toward the right is associated with a 1/2 unit change in the downward direction. Given the variables on the axes of our graph, this result can be interpreted easily enough: A 1-unit increase in quantity demanded is associated with a 1/2 unit *decrease* in price. Thus a 1 billion pound increase in the quantity of beef demanded is associated with a 1/2 dollar decrease in price.

Measuring the Slope on Curves

The preceding section discussed the slope of straight lines, which is easy because the slope is the same at every point along the line. The procedure to measure the slope of a curve is slightly more complicated because the slope changes from one point to the next. The general rule illustrated in Figure 16 is simple enough:

1. Select the point on the curve at which you want to measure the slope.

2. Place a tangent on the curve at that point. (A **tangent** is a straight line that just touches a curve at a single point.)

3. Measure the slope of the tangent by the ratio of rise (or fall) over run.

4. The slope of the tangent equals the slope of the curve at the chosen point.

Suppose you wish to measure the slope of curve A at point a in Figure 16. Line CF is the tangent because it touches curve A at single point a

FIGURE 16 *Measuring the Slope on Curves*

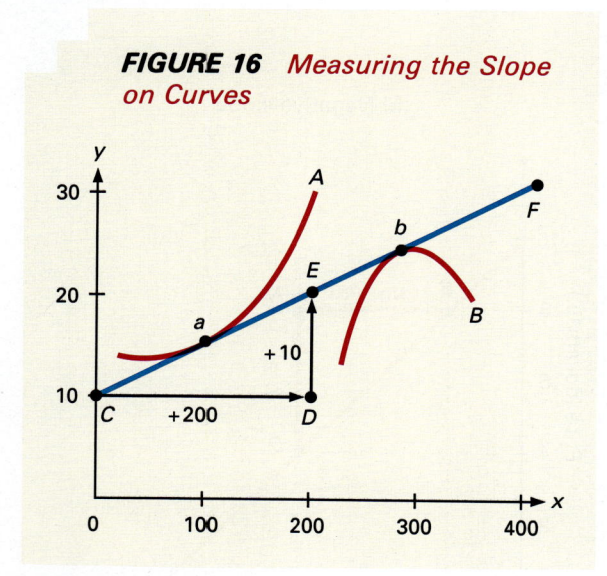

only. By placing the now familiar triangle underneath the upward-sloping tangent (here triangle CDE), we can instantly identify the slope of the tangent—and of curve A at point a—as +10/+200, or +1/20. (The slope of curve B at point b is of precisely the same magnitude.)

Figure 17 presents a series of examples to test your understanding of slope. Keep in mind that the slope of a straight line is constant throughout. The slope of a curve varies from point to point. In panel (a), the slope is zero because moving right by any distance from any point (which gives you the run) must be followed by a zero rise or fall to return to the (horizontal) line. Thus the ratio of rise (or fall) over run equals zero.

In panel (b), on the other hand, moving right by any distance from any point (the run) must be followed by an infinite rise or fall to get back to the (vertical) line. (You can move up or down an

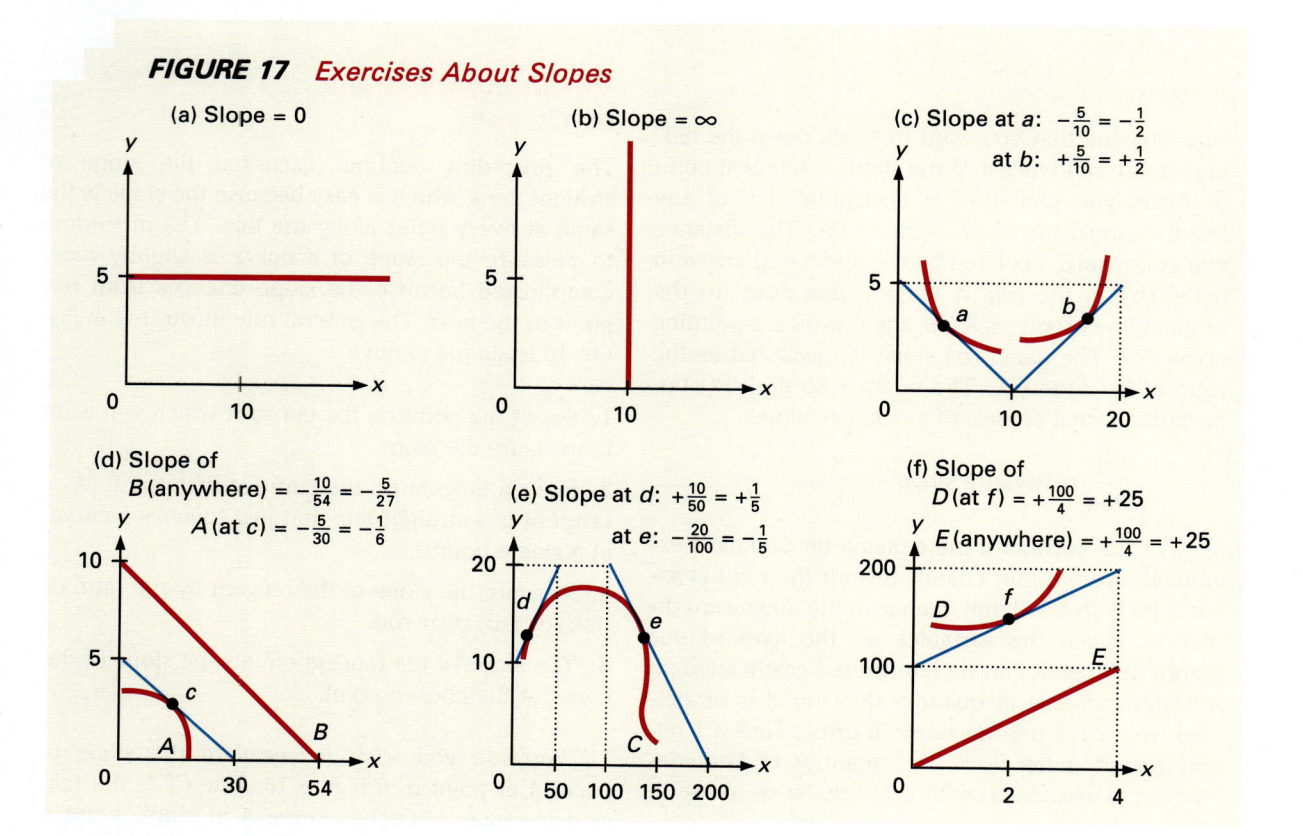

FIGURE 17 *Exercises About Slopes*

(a) Slope = 0

(b) Slope = ∞

(c) Slope at a: $-\frac{5}{10} = -\frac{1}{2}$
at b: $+\frac{5}{10} = +\frac{1}{2}$

(d) Slope of
 B (anywhere) = $-\frac{10}{54} = -\frac{5}{27}$
 A (at c) = $-\frac{5}{30} = -\frac{1}{6}$

(e) Slope at d: $+\frac{10}{50} = +\frac{1}{5}$
at e: $-\frac{20}{100} = -\frac{1}{5}$

(f) Slope of
 D (at f) = $+\frac{100}{4} = +25$
 E (anywhere) = $+\frac{100}{4} = +25$

infinite distance, but you will never reach the original line.) Thus the ratio of rise (or fall) over run equals (plus or minus) infinity. Review panels (c) through (f) on your own.

Measuring Areas in Graphs

Often it is important to find certain *areas* in graphs rather than the slope of lines. Most important in this book are rectangles and triangles, the areas of which are easily computed. Height times base gives the area of rectangles; height times base, divided by 2, the area of triangles.

Consider Figure 18. Given the demand line shown here (a copy of Figure 12), a price of $5 is associated with a quantity demanded of 10 billion lb./year (point *C*). To determine how much money consumers are spending under these circumstances, simply multiply price by quantity:

Consumer spending = $5/lb. × 10 billion lb./year
= $50 billion/year.

This answer is represented by crosshatched area 0*BCD*. The rectangle's height 0*B* represents the $5/lb. price, its base 0*D* represents the 10 billion lb./year quantity. 0*B* times 0*D* equals area 0*BCD*, the $50 billion/year total of consumer spending.

FIGURE 18 *Measuring Areas*

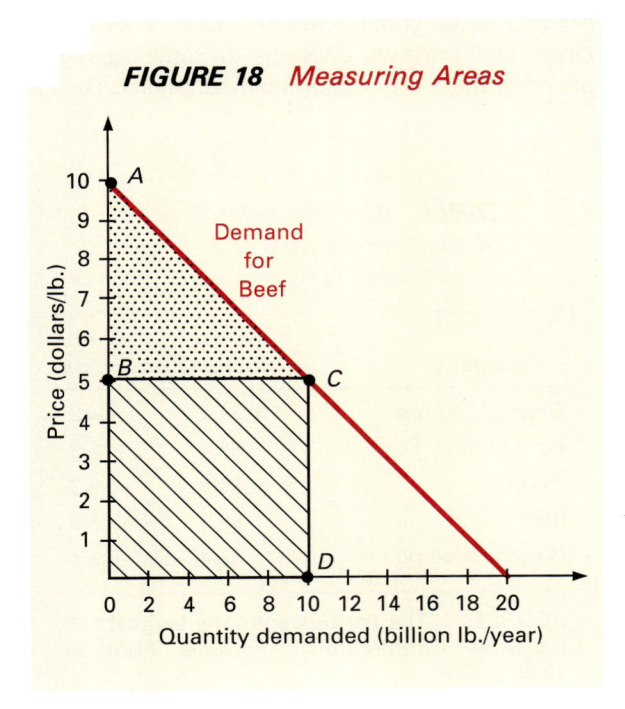

TABLE 4 *XYZ Corporation Sales of GM Cars, 1985–1994*

Year	Number (*1,000s*)
1985	12
1986	21
1987	14
1988	30
1989	24
1990	29
1991	37
1992	24
1993	18
1994	32

Similarly, we can calculate the area of dotted triangle *ABC* (the *consumer surplus* introduced in Chapter 4) by multiplying the height (distance *AB* = $5/lb.) by its base (distance *BC* = 10 billion lb./year) and dividing the result by 2.

$$\text{Consumer surplus} = \frac{\$5/\text{lb.} \times 10 \text{ billion lb./year}}{2}$$

$$= \$25 \text{ billion/year}$$

These and similar applications are used throughout this book.

Other Types of Graphs

Economics texts are filled with numerous other types of graphs, each designed to illustrate different types of information. The following sections introduce some of them.

Time-Series Line Graphs

Sometimes one is interested in the movements of a variable over time. Graph the variable's magnitude on the vertical axis and units of time (such as days, weeks, or years) on the horizontal axis. The data of Table 4 might summarize a regional car dealership's

FIGURE 19 *A Time-Series Line Graph*

[Graph: GM car sales (thousands of cars) vs. Time from 1985 to '94, labeled "Time-series line graph"]

FIGURE 20 *A Statistical Map*

[Map of U.S. states]

1972 Per Capita Personal Incomes
- $3,000 to under $4,000
- $4,000 to under $5,000
- $5,000 and above

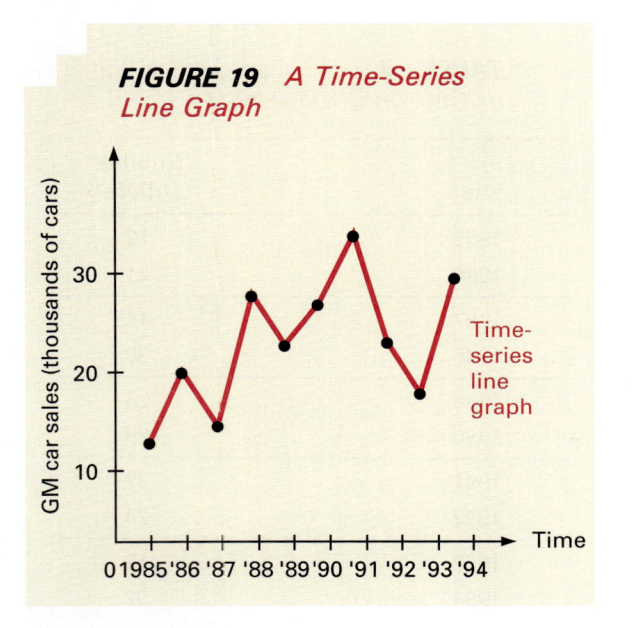

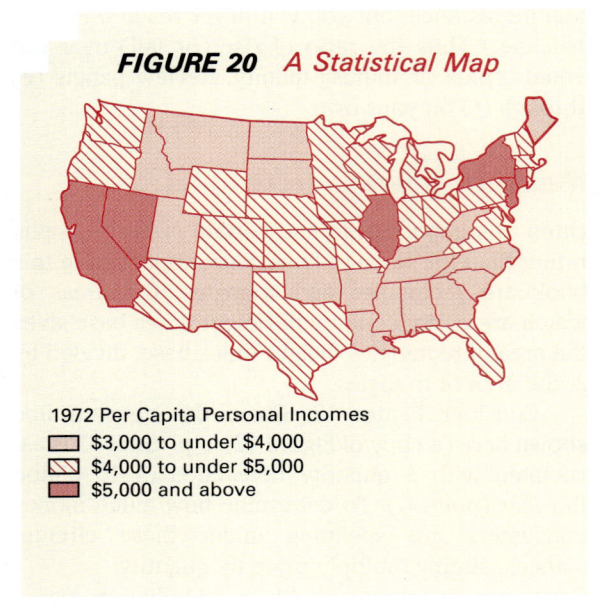

performance. The data are plotted as the ten dots in Figure 19. When successive dots plotting a variable's magnitude (measured vertically) against time (measured horizontally) are joined by a continuous line, the graph is called **a time-series line graph.**

Statistical Maps

Sometimes economists portray data about geographic areas (world regions, nations, states, or census tracts) by crosshatching, shading, or otherwise differentiating these areas on a regular geographic map. The result is a **statistical map,** such as Figure 20. Note how easy it is to decipher the graph: 1972 per capita personal income reached $5,000 or more in only 6 of the lower 48 states of the United States (California, Nevada, Illinois, New York, New Jersey, and Connecticut). On the other hand, per capita income was below $4,000 in Louisiana, Maine, and many other states.

Bar and Column Charts

Sometimes data are portrayed by a series of noncontiguous horizontal bars or vertical columns, the lengths or heights of which are proportional to the values depicted. The graphs are then referred to as **bar charts** or **column charts.** Consider the data of Table 5. They are plotted as a bar and a column chart in the two panels of Figure 21.

Pie Charts

Another useful graph is the **pie chart,** a segmented circle that portrays divisions of some aggregate, provided there are not too many divisions. The cir-

TABLE 5 *1988 Sales and Profits of the Five Largest U.S. Industrial Corporations*

Company	Sales	Profits
	(billions of dollars)	
General Motors	$121.1	$4.9
Ford Motor	92.4	5.3
Exxon	79.6	5.3
IBM	59.7	5.8
General Electric	49.4	3.4

SOURCE: "The Fortune 500: The Largest U.S. Industrial Corporations," *Fortune,* April 24, 1989, p. 354.

FIGURE 21 Bar and Column Charts

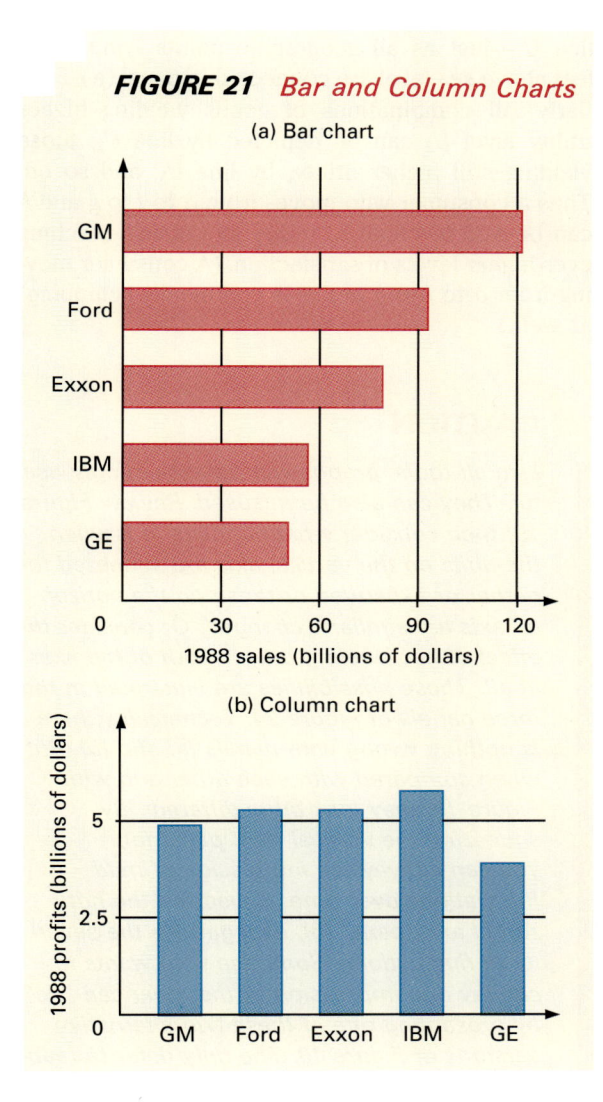

(a) Bar chart

[Bar chart showing 1988 sales (billions of dollars):
- GM: ~125
- Ford: ~92
- Exxon: ~80
- IBM: ~60
- GE: ~50]

(b) Column chart

[Column chart showing 1988 profits (billions of dollars) for GM, Ford, Exxon, IBM, GE]

FIGURE 22 A Pie Chart

(a) Figuring the central angles

[Pie chart with angles 69.8°, 36.4°, 253.8°]

(b) The finished graph

[Pie chart showing:
- Corporations 19.4%
- Partnerships 10.1%
- Proprietorships 70.5%]

United States, 1985

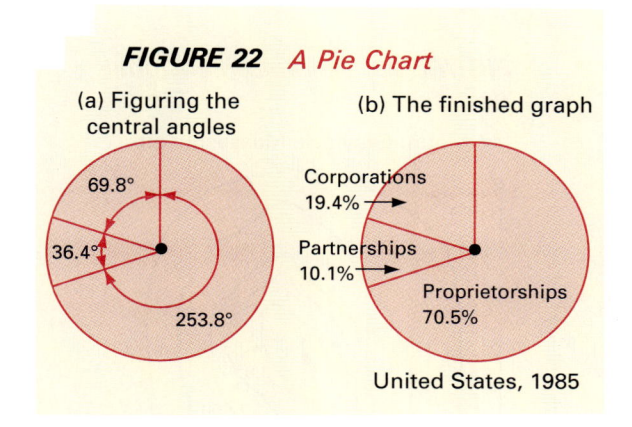

cular pie is cut into slices by radii in such a way that the central angles (and therefore, the sector areas) are proportional to the divisions being displayed. To present the data from Table 6 in a pie chart, first note that proprietorships, partnerships, and corporations made up 70.5 percent, 10.1 percent, and 19.4 percent, respectively, of the 16.92 million firm total. Divide the 360 degrees of a circle accordingly, computing central angles of .705 (360°) = 253.8°, of .101(360°) = 36.4°, and of .194 (360)° = 69.8°. The resulting graph is shown in Figure 22.

Three-Dimensional Graphs

Sometimes economists want to depict relationships not between two variables (such as price and quantity demanded) but among three variables (such as a consumer's consumption of food and of clothing and the associated satisfaction or "utility" derived from that consumption). Three-dimensional graphs, however, are hard to read. To make them usable, economists take another lesson from geographers.

Panel (a) of Figure 23 shows the typical way in which geographers depict a mountain. Starting from the origin of the graph (point 0), one axis depicts distance to the north and the other one distance to the east. Altitude (the third variable) is depicted by labeled contour lines that connect all the points of equal elevation. A picture of the 3,440 foot mountain is squeezed onto the two-dimensional paper.

Panel (b) pictures a similar type of graph used by economists. The vertical axis measures units of food consumed by a person; the horizontal axis,

TABLE 6 Major Types of Firms, United States, 1985

Type	Number (1,000s)
Proprietorships	11,929
Partnerships	1,714
Corporations	3,277
Total	16,920

FIGURE 23 Three-Dimensional Graphs

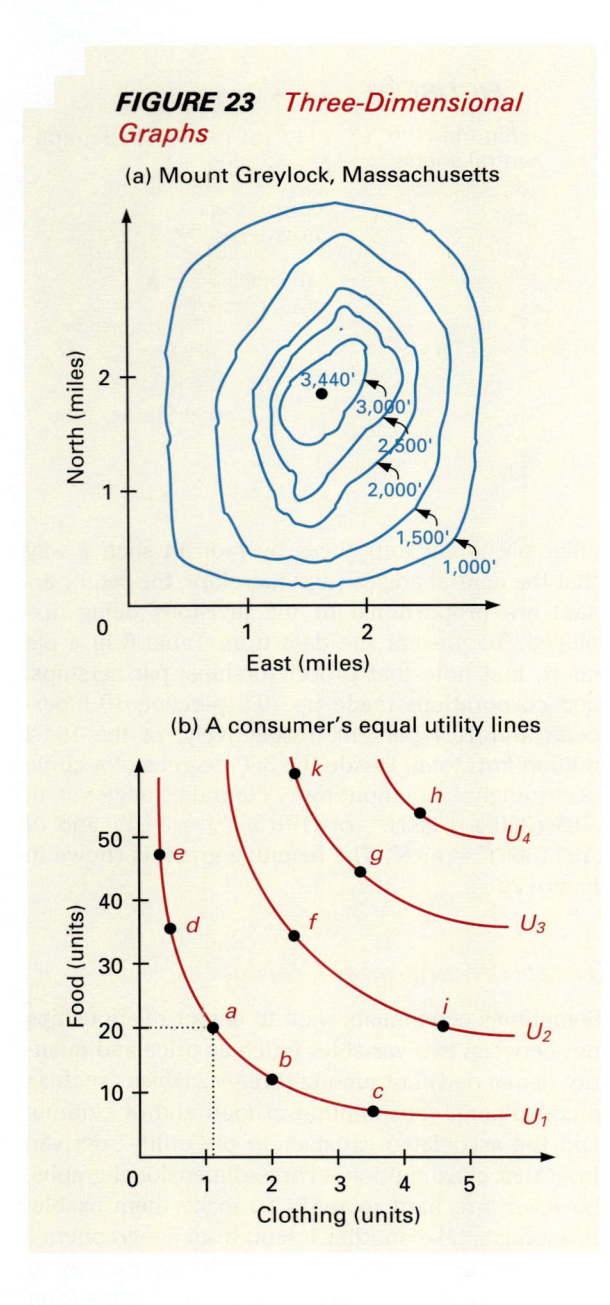

(a) Mount Greylock, Massachusetts

(b) A consumer's equal utility lines

units of clothing consumed. Thus each point in the graph (such as a) corresponds to some combination of the goods consumed (such as 20 units of food plus 1.1 units of clothing for point a). Let us designate the level of utility associated with combination a by U_1. All other combinations of the two types of goods that yield the same utility level (such as b, c, d, or e) can be connected with a by smooth line U_1—just as all geographic points lying 1,500 feet above sea level are connected in panel (a). Similarly, all combinations of goods yielding higher utility level U_2 can be depicted by line U_2; those yielding still higher utility, by line U_3, and so on. Thus a consumer who moves from a to f to g and h can be said to climb a "utility mountain," reaching ever-higher levels of satisfaction. (A consumer moving from a to i to k and h is continually "climbing" as well.)

CAUTION

Like all tools, graphs can be exceedingly useful. They can also be misused. Review Figure 19; then consider what happens to it when the units on the vertical axis are squeezed together or expanded or those on the horizontal axis are similarly changed. Or consider the effect of not labeling one or both of the axes at all. These possibilities are illustrated in the three panels of Figure 24. Technically, there is nothing wrong with panels (a) and (b). But when compared with each other and with Figure 19, they look quite different. By squeezing the vertical axis, panel (a), you can convey the impression of mild fluctuations over time. Squeezing the horizontal axis, panel (b), exaggerates the severity of fluctuations. Someone who wants to convey one impression or the other can "lie" by presenting one of these two alternative versions of Figure 19. The only defense readers have is to study graphs carefully and not to be fooled by first impressions.

Finally, consider panel (c), in which the vertical axis contains no numerical values whatsoever. Such a graph gives the impression of a rapid increase in sales over time (the kind of graph often found in advertisements), but it is totally meaningless. Did sales increase from 40 cars in 1985 to 65 cars in 1990 to 140 cars in 1995? Or did sales rise from 40 million to 65 million and 140 million cars instead? The graph tells us nothing, and its lesson is clear. Whenever you encounter a graph, carefully analyze what is measured on the axes; whenever you draw a graph, carefully label both axes so your reader knows what you mean to convey.

APPENDIX 1a The Use of Graphs in Economics 33

FIGURE 24 *How to Lie With Graphs*

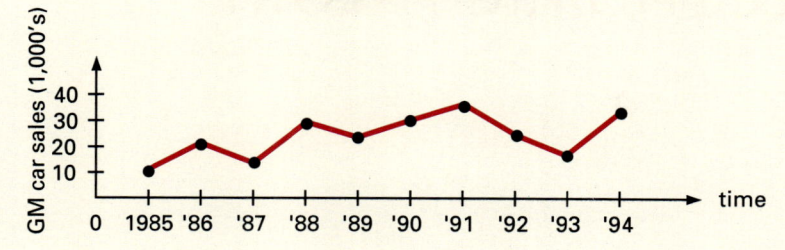

(a) Vertical axis squeezed

(b) Horizontal axis squeezed

(c) Meaningless graph

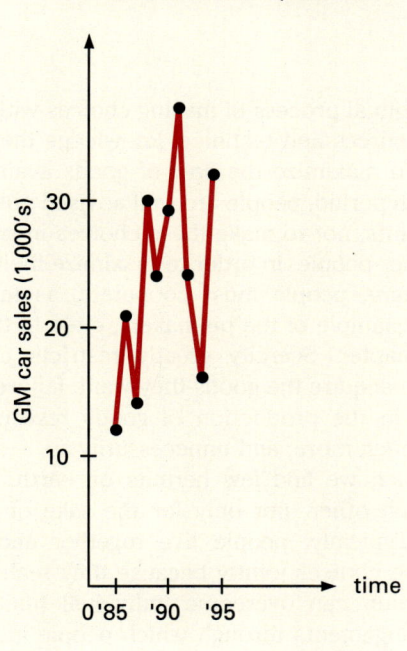

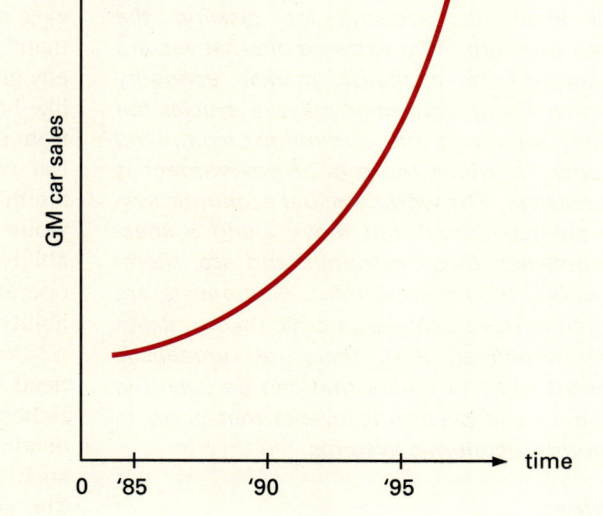

Key Concepts

abscissa	ordinate	quadrant	tangent
bar chart	origin	slope	time-series line graph
column chart	pie chart	statistical map	

CHAPTER 2

ECONOMIC SYSTEMS AND ECONOMIC THEORY

Preview

Different societies have different arrangements called economic systems *for tackling the scarcity problem. Two extreme alternatives are the laissez-faire capitalist market economy (in which the government plays a crucial but minimal role) and the communist command economy (in which the role of government is all-pervasive). The world's actual economic systems are positioned and move along a spectrum between these extremes and are, therefore, called mixed economies. Economists are engaged in developing* economic theory, *deliberately simplified and, therefore, unrealistic representations of reality that can be useful in explaining and predicting events that occur in the world's economic systems.*

Examples

1. Airwave Wars and Tonga Satellites
2. The Rise of the Welfare State
3. Marketization Sweeps the Communist World
4. Why Economists Disagree Among Themselves

Ideas in History

On the Proper Economic Role of Government

As Chapter 1 has shown, all countries wrestle with the basic economic problem of scarcity. People everywhere are engaged in a complicated and continual process of making choices with whatever resources and technical knowledge they command. To maximize the flow of goods available in any given period, people are well advised not to live like hermits, not to make these choices in isolation from other people. In order to maximize their material welfare, people must cooperate, as in Adam Smith's example of the pinmakers, cited in the previous chapter. Scarcity greatly restricts people's ability to acquire the goods they want; failure to cooperate in the production of goods restricts that ability much more, and unnecessarily so.

In fact, we find few hermits on earth. People need each other, not only for the sake of getting richer. Typically, people live together and make economic choices jointly because they realize how such action can overcome individual limitations. The arrangements through which people in a society cooperate with each other in allocating scarce resources and apportioning scarce goods among themselves is called their **economic system.** In the following sections, we explore this basic concept.

The Complexity of Economic Systems

In the early 1990s, over 150 independent nations exist on this earth. One might argue that there are just as many different economic systems because the arrangements people make for allocating their scarce resources and apportioning their scarce goods differ so widely from one nation to the next. At first sight, the only thing all these systems seem to have in common is their *complexity.*

Consider any single good you might acquire, such as a bicycle. It would take considerable effort to trace the people and other resources involved in bringing a bicycle to you. Probably the actual human, natural, and capital resources could never be identified, even after months of careful investigation. Your contact may have been only with the employees of a retail store, along with the store itself and all the equipment therein. But even at this last and most visible stage of production, there were other people at work in the background: a bookkeeper, an insurance agent in Chicago, a trucker who brought the bicycle from the factory, to name just a few. Somewhat more removed, there were the bricklayers and carpenters, the ironworkers and plumbers, the cement workers and glaziers, the electricians and telephone workers, and all who helped build that retail store, insurance agency, and bicycle factory. Hundreds more worked in the factory; thousands dug the mine to get the bauxite ore (from which aluminum is made), mined the iron ore to make the steel to make the railroad cars to ship that ore, or dug the coal or pumped the oil to make electric power that helps produce all the aluminum pipes, rubber tires, and colorful paints needed to make bicycles. Nor should we forget those who made the bulldozers and cranes, the oil tankers and trucks, the highways, warehouses, and millions of other tools all these workers required.

Now picture the millions of goods potentially available to you, day after day, in department stores, supermarkets, and many other outlets in every town across the land. Almost every one of these goods has traveled through thousands of hands, just like that bicycle. Almost every one of them has similarly traveled through time and space. Have you ever asked yourself who or what directs this complicated process on which your life literally depends? In 1845, Frédéric Bastiat, a famous French economist, pondered precisely the same issue:

On coming to Paris for a visit, I said to myself: Here are a million human beings who would all die in a few days if supplies of all sorts did not flow into this great metropolis. It staggers the imagination to try to comprehend the vast multiplicity of objects that must pass through its gates tomorrow, if its inhabitants are to be preserved from the horrors of famine, insurrection, and pillage. And yet all are sleeping peacefully at this moment without being disturbed for a single instant by the idea of so frightful a prospect. . . .

How does each succeeding day manage to bring to this gigantic market just what is necessary—neither too much nor too little? What, then, is the resourceful and secret power that governs the amazing regularity of such complicated movements, a regularity in which everyone has such implicit faith, although his prosperity and his very life depend upon it?[1]

To answer this question, we must examine the nature of economic systems.

Classifying Economic Systems

To appreciate how different societies deal with the scarcity problem, we can classify the multitude of real-world economic systems into a relatively small number of theoretical categories. Although several classification schemes are possible, we will consider two of them: who owns the resources (and thus, makes decisions about their allocation) or what type of incentive typically gets people to coordinate their specialized economic activities with those of other people. As we shall see, the alternative schemes are not unrelated.

Who Owns the Resources?

In every one of today's economic systems, government plays a crucial role. One of its functions involves the establishment of property rights in resources. A **property right** is the exclusive (but variously qualified) right to the use of something scarce. Typically, it is established by law and protected by government force. In the United States,

---

[1] Translated by the author from "Il n'y a pas de principes absolus," in *Sophismes Économiques,* in *Oeuvres Complètes de Frédéric Bastiat,* vol. 4 (Paris: Guillaume, 1907), pp. 94–97. See Bastiat, *Economic Sophisms* (Princeton, NJ: Van Nostrand, 1964) for an English edition.

you may own real estate, as evidenced by appropriate entries in a Registry of Deeds. If you own a house and a plot of land, you are free to keep all others from using them. The police and courts help you enforce that wish. At the same time, your ownership right is not absolute but variously circumscribed or "qualified." Thus, you may not have the right to burn down your house nor even to burn the brush in the back yard. You may not be allowed to dam the brook that flows across your land, and even the oil or minerals underground may not be yours. Your right to your own body is circumscribed as well: You may not sell yourself into slavery.

Clear-cut property rights in human, natural, and capital resources are an important ingredient for any peaceful society. Although the ability to satisfy their desire for goods is limited to people *as a group* (by the limited flows of resources to make these goods), any *single* person could always satisfy more of his or her individual desire for goods by seizing control of additional resources at the expense of other people. Just ask yourself why slavery has existed in many societies since time immemorial. Scarcity sets up a conflict situation. In the absence of governmental intervention to override the "law of the jungle," there develops a wild scramble to appropriate those goods-yielding resources. The strong or the cunning take for themselves as large a portion of available resource stocks as possible (while the resource ownership of the weak or not-so-clever soon amounts to little or nothing). Resources end up in the hands of a few, who literally enslave the rest of the people and take over most of the natural and capital resources as well.

To avoid this potential outcome, governments determine who owns and may exclusively use every unit of available resources. By implication, governments announce that anyone who interferes with the owner's exclusive right to use a resource breaks the law and will be punished accordingly. By assigning property rights in resources, governments distribute **economic power,** the capacity to make and enforce decisions on the allocation of scarce resources and ultimately, the apportionment of scarce goods made with the help of these resources. Example 1 provides perspectives on the birth of new property rights in recent times.

Now we can classify the world's economic systems according to the nature of property rights in resources. Nowadays, governments assign property rights in individuals solely to each individual concerned. However, the story differs with respect to nonhuman resources. Governments in some countries, such as the United States, Japan, or Germany, assign property rights in natural and capital resources *predominantly* to private individuals. Such economic systems are referred to as systems of **capitalism.** Governments in other countries, such as the Soviet Union, China, or Cuba in the 1980s, assign property rights in natural and capital resources *predominantly* to "the people as a whole" (which in effect means to the government). Such economic systems are referred to as systems of **communism.** Thus, we can classify all of the world's economic systems into two broad groups, the capitalist countries and the communist countries. The former tend to distribute economic power widely, the latter tend to concentrate it.

CAUTION

Our tentative classification of the world's economic systems into categories of capitalism *and* communism *warrants three notes of caution. First, since the late 1980s, many countries that used to be communist—ranging from Czechoslovakia, Poland, and the Soviet Union to Angola, China, and Vietnam—have either abandoned communism outright or have announced their intention to reform their systems and move them in varying degrees toward capitalism.*

Second, the group of countries here called communist never practiced communism in the strict Marxian sense. Furthermore, they called themselves socialist. *(U.S.S.R. stands for Union of Soviet* Socialist *Republics.) Western writers often refer to these economic systems as* **totalitarian socialism.** *We will use the terms communism and totalitarian socialism interchangeably.*

Third, countries here called capitalist on occasion refer to themselves as socialist as well. Social-democratic or labor parties often run the government and introduce programs to modify capitalism, such as limited nationalization of industry, environmental legislation, or tax systems that redistribute income

> *from the rich to the poor. France, Great Britain, and Sweden have been cases in point. To avoid confusion, we will refer to such societies as **democratic socialism** or **managed capitalism**.*

Two final things should be noted. First, the term *predominates* appears in our definitions of capitalism and communism in reference to the private or public ownership of resources. This word is crucial because there are always exceptions to the rule. Even in the capitalist United States, for example, some natural and capital resources clearly belong to "the people as a whole" (or the government). Public airports, national parks, post offices, and many schools fall into this category. On the other hand, even in the communist Soviet Union some natural and capital resources are owned by private individuals: Private plots of land held by peasants working on otherwise collective farms, and all the equipment used in artisan shops. Second, the very fact that property rights everywhere are variously qualified makes property always a mixture of private and public. Even in the United States, private property owners can never do absolutely anything they please. The "public interest" intervenes. Your right to a piece of land may include the right to farm it and mine the minerals below it, while excluding the right to fly over it (aviation maps are dotted with all kinds of "prohibited zones"). Similarly, you may be excluded from burning down its trees, building houses on it, or draining its pond. Your rights to a factory may include the right to produce all kinds of products in it, to rent or sell the factory to someone else, and to bequeath it at the time of your death, while excluding the right to burn the factory down (as you may wish to do in preparation for selling the land on which it stands). Nor may you be allowed to dump factory wastes into a nearby stream, to operate machinery that endangers the safety of workers, or to damage the peace of neighbors by excessive noise. In short, property rights are anything but simple. Strictly speaking, they are complex *bundles* of rights that are continually created and modified by government. However, this textbook is not on law. It is sufficient for us to say that the world's economic systems can be classified on the basis of predominantly private or public property rights. But there is an alternative approach to classifying economic systems. It takes property rights for granted and asks what makes resource owners cooperate with other people in the allocation of the resources they command.

What Are the Incentives for Coordination?

All of the world's economic systems are based on complex schemes of specialization and exchange. Particularly in the industrialized countries, most people specialize in a task that constitutes a tiny portion of the production process. They hand most if not all of what they produce to others. In turn, almost everything they consume comes from others who have similarly specialized. How do the specialized activities of millions of people fit together to form a well-coordinated whole? Who or what, for example, assures that bauxite miners dig up just the right amount of ore—not too little and not too much—so that aluminum refineries can make just the right amounts of pipes that are needed by bicycle makers?

Two extreme possibilities exist. First, the specialized activities of millions of people can be made to mesh perfectly with the help of *monetary incentives* that emerge when large numbers of people make contact with one another in markets for the purpose of trading resources or goods. Second, the specialized activities of millions of people can be made to fit together with the help of *verbal commands* that are based on a carefully worked out central plan for allocating resources and apportioning goods.

Monetary Incentives

A government that has widely distributed the property rights to resources could take limited additional steps (such as providing money as a convenient medium of exchange, establishing and enforcing laws of contract or laws against fraud) to facilitate widespread voluntary exchange of property rights to resources and goods. Beyond that, such a government might simply rely on people to follow their self-interest. It might simply say laissez-faire, let them choose as they like, let them use their economic power in any way they wish. History has shown that under such conditions there

EXAMPLE 1

Airwave Wars and Tonga Satellites

Do governments really assign and enforce property rights? Despite the fact that Registries of Deeds now record land ownership of every square inch of North American territory, it is obvious that these rights have not always existed. In 1785, the U.S. Congress was busily assigning unclaimed land to the construction of public schools in the Northwest Territory; later to the construction of railroads in the West. Today, most land is claimed, but national governments and international agencies alike are busily creating new rights in other types of scarce resources, such as the electromagnetic spectrum or the geostationary arc.

The *electromagnetic spectrum,* popularly called the airwaves, is an immense range of frequencies (radio waves, microwaves, visible light, x-rays, gamma rays, and more) that are coveted by many for voice communication, navigation, data transmission, and the like. Almost all currently available frequencies are being used by someone, and the unchecked arrival of new users would lead to serious overcrowding and bad reception for all. But new arrivals keep coming and thus create an airwaves gridlock. These would-be users include the obvious: AM and FM radio stations as well as VHF and UHF television companies. They include people engaged in airplane, boat, car, and railroad communications, and others building cellular phone companies and satellite navigation systems. They also include energy companies wanting to relay safety information from remote pipeline monitors, makers of high-definition television, and scientists with radio telescopes waiting for messages from extraterrestrials. Most of all, they include the users of millions of gadgets, such as baby monitors, cordless phones, garage door openers, pagers, TV remote controls, and ultrasonic denture cleaners.

The jammed airwaves problem came to a head in 1990 when UPS, the largest private package carrier in the United States, decided to outfit its 55,000 trucks with radio receivers and transmitters so customers could be given up-to-the-second information about deliveries. The Federal Communications Commission allocated a frequency to UPS that had been used by ham radio operators, which caused many problems. The 170,000 member American Radio Relay League picketed federal buildings in major cities across the land. It deluged the FCC, the Congress, and the White House with angry letters, and it challenged the FCC

---

emerges not utter chaos, but a well-coordinated network of human relations held together by the prospect of mutual gain through exchange. Self-interested individuals, acting in their various capacities as household members or managers of business firms, approach others with conditional offers: "If you do something for me (namely, give me so many units of money), I will do something for you (namely, give you so many labor hours or so many ingots of aluminum)." Naturally, only those who expect to gain from such an offer will accept it. Thus, numerous markets spring up—markets for resources (labor hours, acre hours, or truck hours) and markets for goods (apples, bicycles, or shoes).

Each **market** is a framework within which owners of property rights make contact with one another for the purpose of transferring ownership, usually for money.

In all of these markets, furthermore, the joint actions of would-be buyers and sellers establish the precise terms of exchange, the *prices* at which trade takes place ($6 per labor hour, $500 per acre per year, $4 per bushel of apples, or $200 per bicycle). Everyone in the economy becomes a price watcher. Would-be buyers are more likely to buy at lower prices; would-be sellers are more likely to sell at higher prices. The likely reaction of buyers and sellers to changing prices contains the key to the co-action in court. Two congressmen quickly introduced the Emerging Telecommunications Technology Act. It would take 200 megahertz of spectrum from the military (in light of the end of the Cold War) and distribute this "peace dividend" to civilian users. President Bush, in turn, chided the FCC for practically giving away scarce frequencies and included in the 1991 budget $3 billion of revenue from *selling* a portion of the airwaves to would-be owners. While the FCC had been charging favored recipients nominal annual licence fees, the average sales price of AM and FM radio stations in the 1980s came to $1.24 million, that of VHF and UHF television stations was $21.52 million. Sixty percent of these prices were attributable solely to the FCC licence.

The *geostationary arc,* a precise orbit in space about 22,300 miles above the equator, is another one of those scarce resources coveted by the telecommunications industry. When a satellite occupies this orbit, it appears stationary from earth and can be seen from half the globe, which makes it a perfect device for reducing long-distance communication costs. Unfortunately, the arc can accommodate only a finite number of satellites, fewer than people would like to use. Thus another issue of property rights has arisen. Because there is no *world* government to assign orbital slots, conflicting claims have appeared. In 1990, the South Pacific nation of Tonga (usually known for its coral reefs, volcanoes, bananas, and coconuts) made news by claiming 16 orbital slots overhead. A new company, Tongasat, offered to install a new satellite communications system.

The shareholders were King Taufa'ahau Tupou the Fourth, Princess Salote Pilolevu Tuita, and Matt C. Nilson, an American entrepreneur. The idea was quickly rejected by the Geneva-based International Frequency Registration Board and denounced by Intelsat, a 119 government satellite consortium. But the issues raised by Tonga's claim will recur.

Sources: Keith Bradsher, "The Elbowing Is Becoming Fierce for Space on the Radio Spectrum," *The New York Times,* June 24, 1990, pp. 1 and 20: Mark Lewyn and Peter Coy, "Airwave Wars," *Business Week,* July 23, 1990, pp. 48–53: "Satellites for Tonga?" *The New York Times,* September 2, 1990, p. 2; and Edmund L. Andrews, "Tonga's Plan for Satellites Set Back by Global Agency," *The New York Times,* December 1, 1990, p. 33.

---

ordinating power of this type of economy. We will discuss this topic further in Chapter 3, but for now consider two simple examples.

Imagine a situation in which factories are putting out 3 million bicycles per year, while households are buying only 2 million of them. The *surplus* of seemingly unsalable bicycles would induce producers to cut bicycle prices just to get rid of them. This cut in prices would discourage firms from producing so many bicycles in the future, while the same cut would *encourage* households to buy more of them. Can you see how annual production and sales might come to balance at 2.5 million units per year? Indeed, all kinds of further effects would, therefore, spread throughout the economy. Bicycle producers (who have cut output from 3 million to 2.5 million units per year) would, for example, buy less aluminum, rubber, and paint. The prices of these goods would fall as well and discourage their production.

Imagine, similarly, that fruit growers are offering for sale 4 million bushels of peaches per year, while households therefore are trying to buy 6 million of them. Can you see how the *shortage* of peaches would induce the growers to raise their price? This increase in price would encourage higher production or imports or even a diversion of peaches from the marmalade market to the fresh fruit market. This very price hike would also discourage households from buying so many peaches. Before long, the supply of fresh peaches would precisely match the demand for them at, say, 5.1 million units per year. The increased peach production would, in turn, raise the growers' purchases of fertilizer, labor, pesticides, and other ingredients. Similar changes in prices in these markets would induce similar increases in supply. And workers losing their jobs in bicycle factories might find new jobs in peach orchards.

These matters will be discussed at length in future chapters, but we can see already how the **price system,** the totality of interdependent prices in numerous markets for goods and resources might become an economy's invisible governor who coordinates activities by always signaling to people, inducing them to supply less and consume more of surplus things (the prices of which are falling) and to supply more and consume less of shortage things (the prices of which are rising). As self-interested, optimizing people respond to these price signals, the actions of consumers and producers cease to be inconsistent with one another (as they would be if factory owners continued to produce 3 million bicycles in a year and and households only bought 2 million or if peach growers put 4 million bushels on the market, while consumers were seeking to buy 6 million bushels of them). This type of social arrangement, in which monetary incentives established in markets spontaneously coordinate the independently taken but interdependent economic activities of self-interested people, is a **market economy.** This type of economy is also called the system of **spontaneous coordination** or of the **Invisible Hand.** Clearly, these terms indicate that the continual match-up of demand and supply in a multitude of markets occurs in this economy *spontaneously,* without the *conscious* intervention of any centralized human planner/manager. Adam Smith was the first economist to note that people in this economy seem to be guided by an "invisible hand" to employ their resources precisely in a manner that produces economic order rather than chaos. Figure 1 summarizes our discussion so far.

Verbal Commands

A government that has concentrated the ownership of most nonhuman resources in its own hands may, naturally be tempted to take a different approach. It may expand its economic role to the maximum extent, setting itself up as an economic commander-in-chief. Instead of order being created spontaneously by the interaction in markets of millions of decision-making units, the government may set out to create order consciously, deliberately, with the help of a **central economic plan,** a document specifying the future economic actions of all people in detail. Outside the government, no one makes economic decisions at all. Each adult is *told* to what degree and to whom to supply labor and is, in return, assigned specific quantities of consumption goods to be picked up at designated places. Firms are government-run, and each enterprise manager is told what types and quantities of resources to use, what types and quantities of goods to produce, and to whom to deliver them. Since everybody is told exactly what to do in physical terms, money might conceivably not enter the picture at all. Money does not speak; governmental *decrees* do the talking. The motto of the market economy is gone, replaced by another one: "Unless you do something for me (follow my commands)," the government says, "I will do something bad to you (punish you in whatever fashion I decide)."

Under such conditions, how would economic order be achieved? It would be achieved by a careful process of planning prior to the annual issuing of orders. Suppose the government had decided to give people 2.5 million new bicycles this year. Accordingly, it would make a list of all the resources needed for this purpose: so many workers in the assembly plant, so many miles of aluminum pipe, so many gallons of paint. Planners would need to think through all the consequences of each of these decisions: so many workers and trucks to be sent to mining bauxite ore, so many tons of ore to be sent to the refinery to be made into aluminum, so many barrels of oil to be pumped, to be sent to the power station to be made into electric power needed by the aluminum plant. . . .

This type of economy, in which the separate economic activities of people engaged in the division of labor are coordinated on paper by a central planning board, followed by its issuance of detailed verbal commands directed to each person, is called a **command economy.** It is also referred to as the system of **deliberate coordination** or of the **Visible Hand.** Coordination is not achieved spontaneously by people trading in markets, but deliberately by the governmental application of reason.

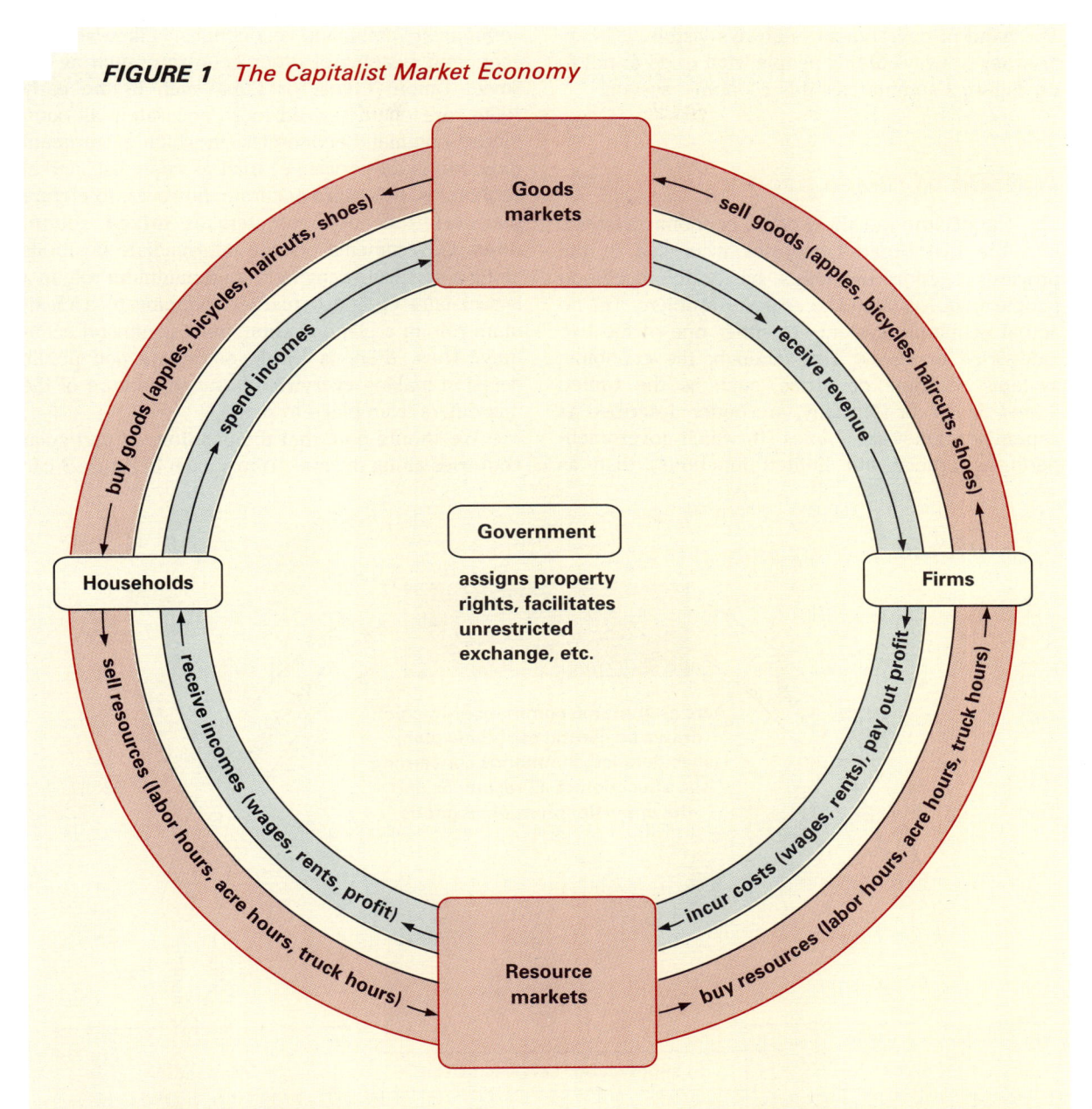

CHAPTER 2 *Economic Systems and Economic Theory* 41

FIGURE 1 The Capitalist Market Economy

[Diagram: Circular-flow diagram showing Households (left), Firms (right), Goods markets (top), Resource markets (bottom), with Government in the center. Government "assigns property rights, facilitates unrestricted exchange, etc."

Outer counter-clockwise flow (resources and goods):
- From Households to Goods markets: "buy goods (apples, bicycles, haircuts, shoes)"
- From Goods markets to Firms: "sell goods (apples, bicycles, haircuts, shoes)"
- From Firms to Resource markets: "buy resources (labor hours, acre hours, truck hours)"
- From Resource markets to Households: "sell resources (labor hours, acre hours, truck hours)"

Inner clockwise flow (money):
- From Households to Goods markets: "spend incomes"
- From Goods markets to Firms: "receive revenue"
- From Firms to Resource markets: "incur costs (wages, rents), pay out profit"
- From Resource markets to Households: "receive incomes (wages, rents, profit)"]

This circular-flow diagram provides a simplified picture of the capitalist market economy. While government is important (in that it must assign property rights and facilitate unrestricted exchange), it stands in the background. Most important are exchange relations between households (who own most resources) and firms (that produce goods). They meet each other in two types of markets. In resource markets, households sell the services of human, natural, and capital resources; firms buy them and turn them into goods. In goods markets, firms sell commodities and services; households buy them. Note the outer, counter-clockwise flow of resources and goods. Correspondingly, there is an inner, clockwise flow of money (shaded), as the costs and profits of firms become the incomes of households, while the spending of households turns into the revenue of firms.

The hand of government is always visible. It is everywhere, always telling people what to do or not to do. Figure 2 summarizes this economic system.

A World of Mixed Economies

The classification of the world's economic systems into the two broad categories discussed in the previous section highlights basic differences in people's approach to the scarcity problem. Yet no actual economic system fits either one of the two categories precisely. True enough, the economic systems of some countries, such as the United States, Japan, or Germany, are better described as capitalist market economies (in which government performs crucial but limited functions) than as communist command economies. Likewise, the economic systems of other countries, such as the Soviet Union, China, or Cuba even in the early 1990s, are characterized more accurately as communist command economies (in which government direction is all-pervasive) than as capitalist market economies. It is more accurate, however, to picture the world's economic system as **mixed economies.** Governments occupy intermediate positions along a spectrum ranging from a minimum role in a laissez-faire capitalist market economy to a maximum role in a planned communist command economy. Thus, there is a mix of private and public decision making everywhere, but the nature of the mix differs from place to place.

We should note that the positions of particular countries along the spectrum shown in Figure 3 can

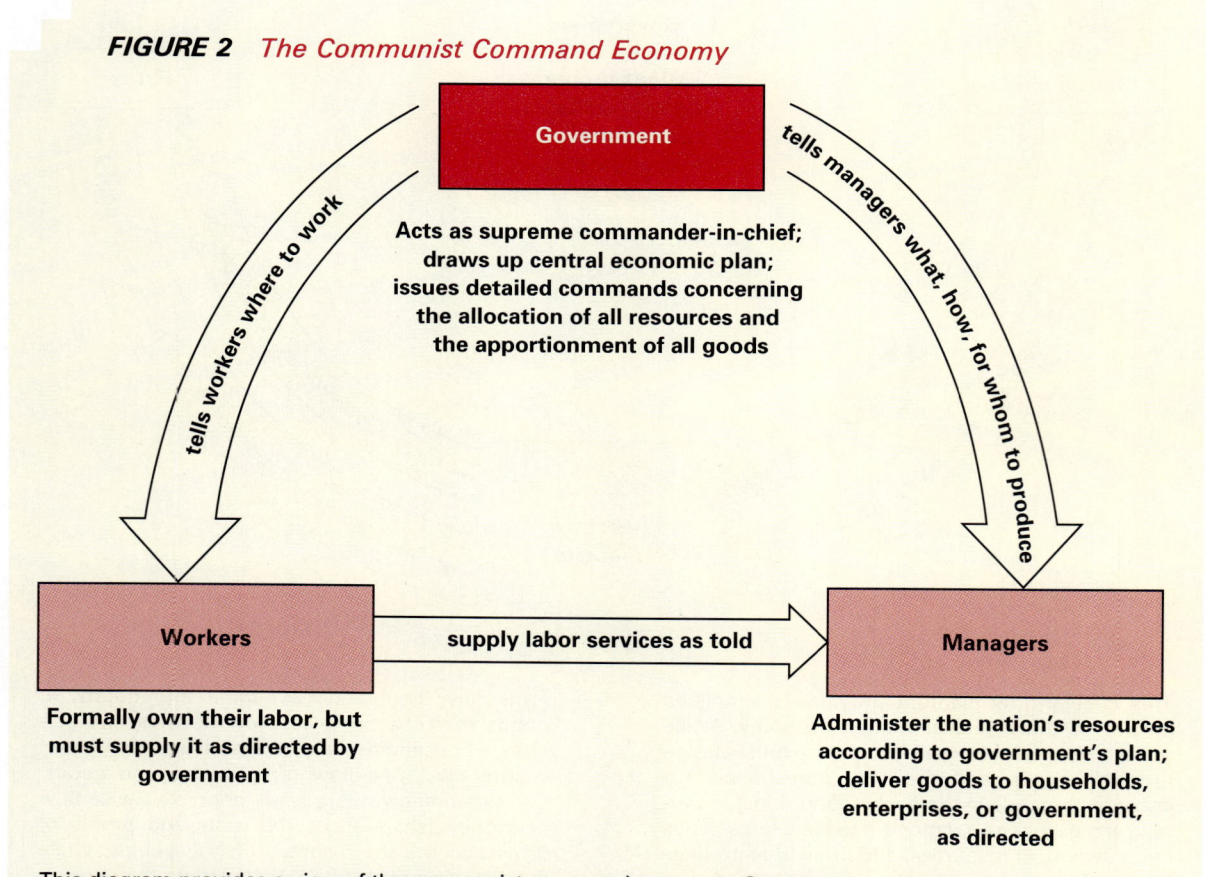

FIGURE 2 *The Communist Command Economy*

Government — Acts as supreme commander-in-chief; draws up central economic plan; issues detailed commands concerning the allocation of all resources and the apportionment of all goods

tells workers where to work → Workers — Formally own their labor, but must supply it as directed by government

tells managers what, how, for whom to produce → Managers — Administer the nation's resources according to government's plan; deliver goods to households, enterprises, or government, as directed

Workers → supply labor services as told → Managers

This diagram provides a view of the communist command economy. Government is the key decision maker, being in command of most natural and capital resources and, for all practical purposes, of human resources as well. Workers and enterprise managers are treated as subordinates. They obey the government's directives on what, how, and for whom to produce.

FIGURE 3 A World of Mixed Economies

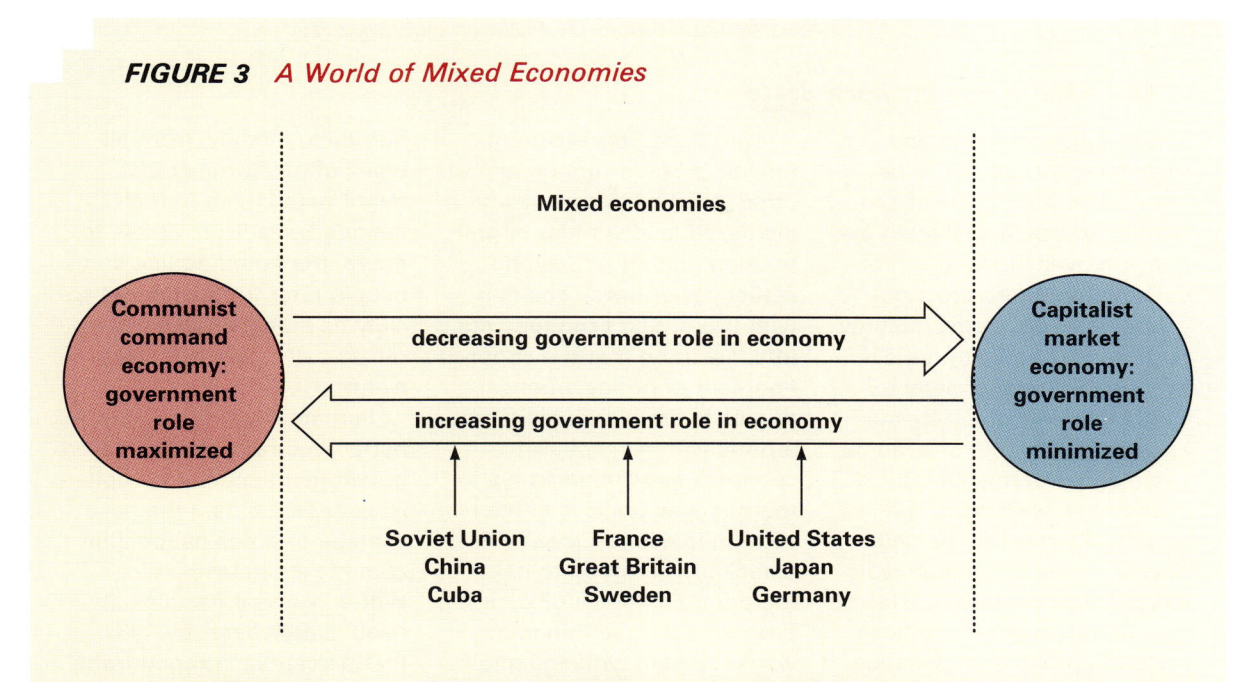

```
                            Mixed economies

  ┌──────────┐    decreasing government role in economy →    ┌──────────┐
  │Communist │                                                │Capitalist│
  │ command  │                                                │  market  │
  │ economy: │   ← increasing government role in economy      │ economy: │
  │government│                                                │government│
  │   role   │         ↑           ↑           ↑              │   role   │
  │maximized │                                                │minimized │
  └──────────┘                                                └──────────┘

              Soviet Union    France      United States
              China           Great Britain   Japan
              Cuba            Sweden      Germany
```

The two extreme forms of economic systems, described in the previous section of this chapter, are best viewed as idealized types or models rather than precise descriptions of any actual economic system. All of the world's actual systems are mixed economies, positioned at different points along a spectrum that reaches from the left-hand pole of maximum government involvement to the right-hand pole of minimum involvement.

and do change over time. Tremendous changes in capitalist market economies have occurred since the 1930s—a story told in Example 2. An equally remarkable trend in the opposite direction has also occurred in communist command economies since the 1950s—a story told in Example 3.

The Nature of Economic Theory

Having discussed the nature of the economic problem in Chapter 1 and, in this chapter, the types of economic systems people use to deal with that scarcity problem, it is fitting to ask what economists do. If we leaf through a few dozen textbooks of the discipline, we are likely to discover that "**economics** is the study of how people allocate scarce resources that have alternative uses among virtually unlimited competing ends," but that we already know. Does this mean that economists are forever engaged in *describing* the world's economic systems? Or do they choose between the good ones and the bad ones? Or do they run their institutions, be they banks, tax collection agencies, stock markets, or central planning boards?

Although economists may do all of the above, their most important task is the development of **economic theory,** of deliberately simplified and therefore, unrealistic representations of reality that can be useful in explaining and predicting events that occur in the world's economic systems. Such theorizing has nothing to do with detailed *descriptions* of reality because such descriptions can never provide us with an understanding of *why* economic events come to pass. Facts do *not* speak for themselves.

Paradoxically, true understanding is gained by an orderly *loss* of information, by ruthlessly simplifying, which is what economists do. They want to understand the economic behavior of Americans and Russians, of Chinese and Nigerians, of Australians and Japanese. They want to explain the economic choices made by family members, business managers, and government officials. Such understanding and explanation can be gained by

EXAMPLE 2

The Rise of the Welfare State

Capitalist market economies have turned out to be impressive promoters of **economic growth,** a sustained expansion over the long run of society's ability to produce goods. As a result, the quantity of goods available to the average person today greatly exceeds that consumed by our ancestors 200, 100, or even 50 years ago. Yet this long-term growth has been accompanied by short-term ups and downs in overall economic activity. These business cycle fluctuations produce reduced rates of growth and even absolute declines in output in some years. In the 1930s, however, they brought about a worldwide depression of a magnitude and length never experienced before or since. It was then that many people demanded government drop its laissez-faire attitude and take on a more active economic role. Government responded and has since been involved in policies designed to assure **economic stability,** the maintenance over time of constant or smoothly growing levels of overall output and employment, while preserving a constant general level of prices.

The Great Depression of the 1930s set in motion another trend as well: a vastly increased involvement of government, going far beyond earlier "poor laws" and such, with promoting **economic equity,** ensuring that the apportionment of goods among people is fair. As a result, governments in all capitalist countries have initiated numerous new policies of intervention in economic activities ostensibly designed to help the poor. Examples of such programs are the minimum wages to help workers, minimum prices for agricultural products to help farmers, maximum rents, fuel prices, or interest rates to help renters or home buyers. Consider the governmental support for labor unions, the governmental provision of unemployment benefits, social security systems covering child support, disability, medical care, old-age pensions, and much more. In the end, a **welfare state** has emerged, a capitalist society in which government pledges to protect people not only from the rigors of the marketplace (the unemployment or inflation associated with business cycles) but, quite literally, from all types of misfortunes that might befall them in their lifelong travel from cradle to grave. (As noted earlier, some people refer to this type of society as *managed capitalism,* others call it *democratic socialism.*)

Perhaps no single measure better illustrates the increased government activity in capitalist economies than the percentage of gross national income taken in taxes. Since World War II, it has steadily risen everywhere; by 1987, that percentage ranged from 29 in the United States and 31 in Japan to 37 in what was then West Germany, 38 in Great Britain, 46 in France, and 58 in Sweden.[1]

Critics have deplored this trend and have called it "creeping socialism"; advocates of the welfare state disagree and applaud it. Ideas in History has more to say on the subject.

---

[1] U.S. Bureau of the Census, *Statistical Abstract of the United States: 1990* (Washington, D.C.: U.S. Government Printing Office, 1990), pp. 840 and 845.

abstracting from reality, by focusing on the most essential features and forgetting about unimportant detail. Indeed, economic theorizing is akin to producing a geographic map. Note how geographers never provide us with a *detailed* picture of the world. Modern maps are drawn from satellite pictures that bring into sharp relief the broad outlines of reality. The entire North American continent can be shown on a piece of paper 8 inches square. Nothing could be more unrealistic. Entire cities are missing, as are many mountains, rivers, highways, houses, and certainly millions of trees. Yet it is precisely because such detail is omitted that geographers can create a useful image of the reality in which we live and move. Without their maps, we would literally be lost.

CAUTION

While economic theory is indispensable for those who care to understand the complex world of economic affairs, it does not follow that every theory is equally good. Consider the first maps made after Columbus came to America. They were not true to even the broad outlines of the North American continent. But surely that provided a reason for making better maps, not for giving up the map-making enterprise. The same holds for economic theory. Economists are capable of inventing theories that contribute to confusion rather than enlightenment. If that happens, one should try to make better theories, not give up theorizing altogether.

This cautionary note brings us to an important question: How can one tell whether a theory is good or bad? One school of thought to which many subscribe claims that a theory is good if it is positive economics, bad if it is normative economics.

Positive Economics Versus Normative Economics

Economists practice **positive economics** when they restrict themselves to describing the facts, explaining how they are related, and predicting the consequences of any change in circumstances. For example: "The average price of gasoline last month was $1.34 per gallon and 2 billion gallons were traded; given the way demand and supply are related to price, a 10¢ per gallon increase in the federal gasoline excise tax would raise the price to buyers by 6¢ and lower the after-tax price received by sellers by 4¢."

Economists engage in **normative economics** when they enter the realm of ethics, make value judgments about existing circumstances, and prescribe what ought to be. Examples: "The federal excise tax on gasoline *should* be raised by 10¢ per gallon in order to raise the revenue needed to help the homeless" or "The federal gasoline tax *ought* to be doubled in order to raise funds for unemployed teenagers."

In accordance with this distinction between positive and normative, a theory is good if it accurately explains what is, what causes what, and what will happen under specified conditions. Such theory is the essence of all science. Beginning in the next chapter we will see many examples of it throughout this book. A good positive theory, like a good geographic map, abstracts crucial elements from the mass of detailed circumstances and permits us to make accurate predictions on their basis alone. It is a tool that often explains much by little.

Such positive theory, however, must never be confused with normative statements, with value judgments that announce to us what is good, what is bad, and what ought to happen.

All economists, of course, have personal preferences. Being human, they have even been known to present as theory (as a map of reality) what was in fact their own value judgment. It is all too easy to ignore the aspects of reality we dislike and to overemphasize other aspects that we do like. Thus, it is tempting to reject positive conclusions when their normative implications are unpalatable to us, and it is equally tempting to accept as positive conclusions what is merely our own wishful thinking. Normative statements that masquerade as positive theory are the worst possible kind of "theory." Example 4 has more to say on the subject.

Macroeconomics vs. Microeconomics

In closing, we should finally note that economic theory is commonly subdivided into two parts, macroeconomics and microeconomics. The words

EXAMPLE 3

Marketization Sweeps the Communist World

By the 1930s Joseph Stalin had consolidated political power in his hands, and the Soviet Union was well on its way to becoming a command economy, as represented by the left-hand pole of Figure 3. Through careful economic planning, Stalin claimed, this type of economy would experience not only economic stability and equity but also unprecedented rates of economic growth. After World War II, the Stalinist model of centralized economic control was expanded to many other countries: to Poland and East Germany, to Czechoslovakia and Hungary, to Bulgaria and Rumania, to Albania and Yugoslavia, even to China, North Korea, Vietnam, and, ultimately, such far-away places as Cuba and Angola. Communism, it seemed, was sweeping the world.

This trend was contrary to the advice proffered by most economists of the past. Beginning with Adam Smith, they had consistently held that the market economy provided the best chance for increasing the wealth of nations.

The statesman, who should attempt to direct private people in what manner they ought to employ their [resources], would ... assume an authority which could safely be trusted, not only to no single person, but to no council or senate whatever, and which would nowhere be so dangerous as in the hands of a man who had folly and presumption enough to fancy himself fit to exercise it.[1]

Frédéric Bastiat answered his own question (cited earlier in this chapter) about the secret power that governs the market economy:

That power ... is the principle of free exchange. We put our faith in that inner light which Providence has placed in the hearts of all men, and to which has been entrusted the preservation and the unlimited improvement of our species, a light we term self-interest, which is so illuminating, so constant, and so penetrating, when it is left free of every hindrance. Where would you be, inhabitants of Paris, if some cabinet minister decided to substitute for that power contrivances of his own invention, however superior we might suppose them to be: If he proposed to subject this prodigious mechanism to his supreme direction, to take control of all of it into his own hands, to determine by whom, where, how, and under what conditions everything should be produced, transported, exchanged, and consumed? Although there may be much suffering within your walls, although misery, despair, and perhaps starvation, cause more tears to flow than your warmhearted charity can wipe away, it is probable, I dare say it is certain, that the arbitrary intervention of the government would infinitely multiply this suffering and spread among all of you the ills that now affect only a small number of your fellow citizens.[2]

It was only after Stalin's death in 1953 that criticism emerged in the communist world. Breaking decades of enforced silence, these modern critics pointed to an obvious and major problem endemic to all centrally planned communist economies, a flaw that is responsible for a significant degree of unnecessary scarcity. They noted that central planners, contrary to Stalin's projections (and precisely as Smith and Bastiat had predicted), were incapable of setting up and executing *well-designed* economic plans. Being less than omniscient by nature (as all humans are), the planners in Moscow, Warsaw, East Berlin, and all the other capitals inevitably failed to account for important details known only to workers and managers far removed from the planning process. As a result, there emerged widespread **economic inefficiency,** a state of affairs in which it is possible, through a judicious reallocation of resources or goods, to make some people better off without making others worse off. It is possible to reap marginal benefits without incurring marginal costs, as the following example illustrates.

Suppose central planners are about to allocate 100 tons of fertilizer between collective farms A and B. Unbeknownst to the planners, the effectiveness of the fertilizer differs between the farms. On farm A, an extra 100 tons of fertilizer would produce an extra 5 million bushels of wheat. On farm B, the marginal benefit would only equal an extra 2 million bushels of wheat. Central planners who do not know these facts may allocate half of the available fertilizer to each farm (the equal treatment makes for administrative ease and seems fair); as a result, wheat output rises by (1/2)5 + (1/2)2 = 3.5 million bushels. Yet this would be inefficient because an allocation of all 100 tons of fertilizer to farm A alone would have produced an extra 5 million bushels of wheat—1.5 million bushels more. These extra bushels could have brought bread to lots of people or even eggs and meat (if the wheat were fed to chickens instead).

An efficient allocation of fertilizer, argued Stalin's critics, rarely occurs under central planning (even then only by accident), but it would happen routinely in a market economy. In the absence of central government allocations, farmers would have to *buy* fertilizer; more productive (and revenue-richer) farmer A could easily outbid farmer B. Thus, economic inefficiency (producing 3.5 instead of 5 million bushels of wheat from a given amount of fertilizer) would be avoided.

During the decade of the 1980s, economic reforms in almost all communist countries—ranging from the Soviet Union and China to Czechoslovakia, Hungary, Poland, and even to Angola and Vietnam—have begun to dismantle the central planning apparatus and to replace it with decentralized decision making coordinated by markets. In the process, private property rights have been expanded significantly. Everywhere, the goal of reformers (such as the Soviet Union's Mikhail Gorbachev or China's Deng Xiaoping) has been the same: to reduce scarcity by increasing efficiency. Interestingly, the result has vindicated one of the most severe critics of "big government," Friedrich A. von Hayek (see Ideas in History). Yet caution is advised. A universal victory of the reforms is not assured. In the Soviet Union and China in particular, powerful opponents of change are alive and well. They complain of "creeping capitalism," and do all they can to slow down or reverse the reform movement.

---

[1] Adam Smith, *An Inquiry into the Nature and Causes of the Wealth of Nations.* (Edinburgh: A. and C. Black, 1872) Book IV, p. 200.

[2] Translated by the author from "Il n'y a pas de principes absolus," in *Sophismes Économiques,* in *Oeuvres Complètes de Frédéric Bastiat,* vol. 4 (Paris: Guillaume, 1907), pp. 94–97. See Bastiat, *Economic Sophisms* (Princeton, NJ: Van Nostrand, 1964) for an English edition.

EXAMPLE 4

Why Economists Disagree Among Themselves

Many people believe that economists can never agree on anything. As George Bernard Shaw allegedly put it, "If you took all the economists in the world and laid them end to end, they wouldn't reach a conclusion." On almost any TV show on economic affairs there is sure to be one economist saying one thing and another one saying just the opposite. Several answers come to mind to explain this disagreement.

First, the general impression just noted may be due to (possibly inadvertent) media distortion. Even if 999 out of 1,000 economists believed that raising the minimum wage would *hurt* the poor (because many of them would lose their jobs), you can be sure that the producer of a network show on the subject will find the *one* economist who holds the opposite view and pit him or her against *one* of the 999 others. Inevitably, the viewing public gets the mistaken impression of a deep split in the profession.

Second, economists (like all other people) do not always make themselves clear. Although two economists may agree, one of them (using last year for comparison without saying so) may claim that "inflation is accelerating." The other one (using the experience of the late 1980s as a benchmark) may counter that "inflation is down." Thus both may be right at the same time. Similarly, one economist may predict that "the recent tax cut will lower unemployment" (thinking of the short-run effect over the next 6 months). Another economist—interviewed by the same reporter in a different place—may claim that "the tax cut will have no effect on unemployment whatsoever" (thinking of the long-run effect over the coming decade). Once again, both could be correct.

Third, and perhaps most importantly, the perceived differences among economists may simply reflect the distinction between positive and normative economics. In fact, economists widely agree on *positive* issues (on what is). Like any other group of people, they frequently disagree on *normative* issues (on what ought to be). Table 1 contains selected results of a survey. It lists a number of propositions presented to a random sample of U.S. economists. In each case, the combined percentage of those who "generally agreed" or "agreed with provisions" is indicated, along with the percentage of those who disagreed. The closer the split comes to 100 to 0 (or 0 to 100), the more economists agree *with one another.* The closer the split is to 50/50, the more economists disagree with one another. Clearly, Table 1 shows a remarkable consensus. The disagreement is strongest on normative statements, such as propositions 7–10. Note that each of these statements contains the word *should.*

Source: J. R. Kearl et al., "A Confusion of Economists?" *The American Economic Review,* May 1979, pp. 28–37. For a more recent and international survey, see Bruno S. Frey et al., "Consensus and Dissension Among Economists: An Empirical Inquiry," *The American Economic Review,* December 1984, pp. 986–94.

---

have their origin in Greek, the term *makros* means large and *mikros* means small. Accordingly, **macroeconomics** studies issues that are economy-wide or "large"; it examines the economy as a whole and is concerned with the combined, aggregate effects of millions of individual choices on such variables as national output, the overall level of employment, the general level of prices. In contrast, **microeconomics** studies issues that do not encompass the entire economy and are in this sense "small"; it examines the economic behavior of individuals (household members, business managers,

TABLE 1 Results of a Survey of Economists

Proposition	Percentage of economists who Agreed with proposition	Percentage of economists who Disagreed with proposition
1. A ceiling on rents reduces the quantity and quality of housing available.	98	2
2. Tariffs and import quotas reduce general economic welfare.	97	3
3. Flexible exchange rates offer an effective international monetary arrangement.	95	5
4. Fiscal policy has a significant stimulative impact on a less than fully employed economy.	92	8
5. Cash payments are superior to transfers in kind.	92	8
6. A minimum wage increases unemployment among young and unskilled workers.	90	10
7. The economic power of labor unions should be significantly curtailed.	70	30
8. The government should be an employer of last resort and initiate a guaranteed job program.	53	47
9. The Federal Reserve System should be instructed to increase the money supply at a fixed rate.	39	61
10. Wage-price controls should be used to control inflation.	28	72

SOURCE: J. R. Kearl et al., "A Confusion of Economists?" *The American Economic Review,* May 1979, pp. 28–37. For a more recent and international survey, see Bruno S. Frey et al., "Consensus and Dissension Among Economists: An Empirical Inquiry," *The American Economic Review,* December 1984, pp. 986–994.

government officials) or of relatively small groups of them (the people operating in the market for peaches or bicycles or all the firms producing aluminum or medical care).

Note that the words *large* and *small* have been placed in quotation marks to warn us of their relative nature. A study of economic growth or inflation in a small country such as Jamaica would be considered macroeconomics. Yet the study of a single firm such as Exxon would be considered microeconomics, despite the fact that annual sales of Exxon exceed the entire national income of Jamaica.

IDEAS IN HISTORY

On the Proper Economic Role of Government

The 1974 Nobel Memorial Prize in Economic Science was awarded jointly to two individuals: Friedrich August von Hayek (b. 1899) and Karl Gunnar Myrdal (1898–1987). It was a strange spectacle, because these two economists agreed with one another on almost nothing. Yet, they had one thing in common, a lifelong concern with the proper economic role of government.

Hayek, born and educated in Vienna, had a distinguished career as director of the Austrian Institute for Economic Research, then as professor at the London School of Economics, the University of Chicago, and the University of Freiburg. His greatest insight, perhaps, was that markets are crucial mechanisms for utilizing knowledge. He considered the question of what institutional arrangement could best enable large numbers of people—each possessing only bits of knowledge—to cooperate with each other to achieve the best use of resources. He rejected the notion that one could put at the disposal of some center all the knowledge that ought to be used but that was initially dispersed among many. The relevant knowledge is made up of elements of such number, diversity, and variety, he argued, that its explicit, conscious combination in a single mind is impossible. Thus, Five Year Plans and even management of the entire economy by computers would necessarily yield poor results. Yet the spontaneous interaction of people in free markets can bring about that which only someone possessing the combined knowledge of all could achieve by deliberate action.

It is worth contemplating for a moment a very simple and commonplace instance of the action of the price system to see what precisely it accomplishes. Assume that somewhere in the world a new opportunity for the use of some raw material, say tin, has arisen, or that one of the sources of supply of tin has been eliminated. It does not matter for our purpose—and it is very significant that it does not matter—which of these two causes has made tin more scarce. All that the users of tin need to know is that some of the tin they used to consume is now more profitably employed elsewhere. . . . There is no need for the great majority of them even to know where the more urgent need has arisen. . . . If only some of them know directly of the new demand, and switch resources over to it, and if the people who are aware of the new gap thus created in turn fill it from still other sources, the effect will rapidly spread throughout the whole economic system and influence not only all the uses of tin, but also those of its substitutes and the substitutes of these substitutes, the supply of all the things made of tin, and their substitutes. . . .

The most significant fact about this system is the economy of knowledge with which it operates. . . . In abbreviated form, by a kind of symbol, only the most essential information is passed on, and passed on only to those concerned. . . . The marvel is that in a case like that of a scarcity of one raw material, without an order being issued, without more than perhaps a handful of people knowing the cause, tens of thousands of people whose identity could not be ascertained by months of investigation, are made to use the material or its products more sparingly. . . .

I have deliberately used the word "marvel" to shock the reader out of the complacency with which we often take the working of this mechanism for granted. I am convinced that if it were the result of deliberate human design, and if the people guided by the price changes understood that their decisions have significance far beyond their immediate aim, this mechanism would have been acclaimed as one of the greatest triumphs of the human mind. . . . But those who clamor for "conscious direction"—and who cannot believe that anything which has evolved without design (and even without our understanding it) should solve problems which we should not be able to solve consciously—should remember this: The problem is precisely how to extend the span of our utilization of resources beyond the span of the control of any one mind; and, therefore, how to dispense with the need of conscious control and how to provide inducements which will make the individuals do the desirable things without anyone having to tell them what to do.¹

Hayek concluded that markets do the best job of solving the problem of resource allocation, but only if they are free from any distortions introduced by ill-advised government. Government should only perform minimal functions, such as assigning and protecting property rights and setting up institutions to help people trade such rights among themselves.

In a best-selling book, *The Road to Serfdom* (1944), Hayek warned that the enthusiasm of governments for intervening in the market leads us down a path that ends in central planning and totalitarianism. Government intervention will, thus, cause the end of the free society, humanity's highest social achievement.

Hayek's most recent books are magnificent statements of all these themes: *The Constitution of Liberty* (1960); *Law, Legislation, and Liberty*, vol. 1, *Rules and Order* (1973); vol. 2, *The Mirage of Social Justice* (1976); and vol. 3, *The Political Order of a Free Society* (1979); and *The Fatal Conceit: The Errors of Socialism* (1989).

Myrdal was born in Gustafs, a small village in central Sweden where his father was a railroad worker. He studied law and economics at Stockholm University, so impressing his teachers that he was named to the faculty upon graduation. In addition to teaching, he became a government advisor on financial and social questions and achieved world renown through an investigation for the Carnegie Corporation on the status of blacks in the U.S., published as *An American Dilemma: The Negro Problem and Modern Democracy* (1944). Eventually, this book helped to destroy the "separate but equal" racial policy in the United States. (The book literally became a footnote to history—footnote 11 to the U.S. Supreme Court's 1954 ruling that segregation in public schools was unconstitutional. Listing sources to prove that schools could not be "separate but equal" because separation implied and enforced inferiority, the Court cited Myrdal's book.) After the Second World War, Myrdal held numerous government and United Nations positions, and he published many books on macroeconomics, international trade, and economic development, including the three-volume *Asian Drama: An Inquiry into the Poverty of Nations* (1968).

Myrdal's view on government was diametrically opposed to that of Hayek. He thought government should vigorously intervene in the economy to assure economic growth, economic stability, and economic equity. Just as he did in the United States, Myrdal left his mark on Sweden, where he drafted many economic and social programs which made him one of the leading architects of the welfare state. Myrdal faced head-on those critics (like Hayek) who warned that the welfare state was but the first step toward socialist tyranny.

In the Western countries, one of the least informed and least intelligent controversies of our time has concerned the question whether we should have a "free" or a "planned" economy. This controversy has always been unrealistic and is becoming ever more so. . . . People generally tend to keep themselves unaware of how far they have proceeded from a "free" economy; how very much regulatory intervention by organized society there actually is in their countries, and important national economic planning of a pragmatic, noncomprehensive type has in fact become. . . . Anybody who makes a plea for the ideals of a "free" economy and . . . who from these goes on to characterize what we are indulging in as "creeping socialism" and warns that we might be on the "road to serfdom," can be sure of a sympathetic audience. . . . While the actual development in our countries has continually been towards more and more planning, the antiplanning attitudes have remained respectable and popular ones. . . . My value premises are the long-inherited ones of liberty, equality, and brotherhood. . . . The trend towards economic planning has broadly implied an ever fuller realization of these ideals.[2]

Myrdal was proud of the fact that poverty and slums had disappeared from Sweden, and he was scornful of suggestions that affluence and security had made Swedes bored, depressed, frustrated, and even suicidal. "This is a fantastic lie," he said. "Why in hell should the protection of your life from economic disasters and from bad health, opening education for young people, pensions for old people, nursery care for children—why should that make you frustrated?" But he did acknowledge that the welfare state had its problems: The high rates of labor turnover and absenteeism and the large underground economy were, he said, the result of generous social services combined with high marginal tax rates. They were turning Swedes "into a nation of hustlers" and were corrupting such traditional values as honesty.

---

[1] Friedrich A. von Hayek, "The Use of Knowledge in Society," *The American Economic Review,* September 1945, pp. 519–530.

[2] Gunnar Myrdal, *Beyond the Welfare State* (New Haven, CT: Yale University Press, 1960), pp. 3, 11–13, and 15–16.

Source: Heinz Kohler, *Comparative Economic Systems* (Glenview, IL: Scott, Foresman, and Co., 1989), pp. 120–21 and 434–435. Adapted with permission.

Summary

1. The arrangements through which people in a society cooperate with each other in allocating scarce resources and apportioning scarce goods among themselves is called an *economic system*. All of the world's economic systems are based on a significant degree of specialization and thus, have in common an enormous degree of complexity.

2. The world's numerous economic systems can be classified into a smaller number of categories. One basis for such a classification is the ownership of resources; another one, the predominant incentive for people to coordinate their specialized economic activities with those of other people. Using the first criterion, one distinguishes between capitalism and communism. The second criterion distinguishes a market economy from a command economy. By combining the criteria, one defines two extreme types of economic systems: the laissez-faire, capitalist market economy (in which government plays a crucial but minimal role) and the centrally-planned, communist command economy (in which the role of government is all-pervasive).

3. The two extreme forms of economic systems

are best viewed as idealized types or models rather than precise descriptions of any actual economic system. All of the world's actual systems are mixed economies, positioned at different points along a spectrum that reaches from maximum government involvement in the economy to minimum involvement. Over time, a specific nation's economy can and does change position along this spectrum, as illustrated by the rise of the welfare state in capitalist countries as well as the recent sweep of marketization through the communist world.

4. The most important task of economists is not the description of the world's economic systems. It is, rather, the development of *economic theory*, the deliberately simplified and therefore, unrealistic representations of reality that can be useful in explaining and predicting events that occur in the world's economic systems.

5. Positive economics, which makes purely descriptive statements and predictions, must never be confused with normative economics, which makes prescriptive announcements on what is good or bad.

6. Economic theory is commonly subdivided into macroeconomics and microeconomics, depending on whether it is concerned with "large" issues that are economy-wide (the size of national output, the overall level of employment, or the general level of prices) or with "small" issues that do not encompass the entire economy (the economic behavior of individuals or relatively small groups of them).

Key Concepts

capitalism	economic stability	mixed economies
central economic plan	economic system	normative economics
command economy	economic theory	positive economics
communism	economics	price system
deliberate coordination	Invisible Hand	property right
democratic socialism	macroeconomics	spontaneous coordination
economic equity	managed capitalism	totalitarian socialism
economic growth	market	Visible Hand
economic inefficiency	market economy	welfare state
economic power	microeconomics	

Questions and Problems

1. There is no essential difference between someone using my flower garden on my land or using the air over my land as a dumping site. In the real world, the former rarely happens; the latter happens all the time. Why? Might one avoid the latter in the same way as one avoids the former?

2. Mr. A: "In the real world, governments often take away property. They force people to lend themselves to the government for limited periods (jury duty, the military draft), to sell their land to make room for a public school (eminent domain), or even to hand over some of their property without compensation (taxation). This behavior should not be allowed."

   Mr. B: "Why not? Property *is* whatever government protects. Who gives can take. The important thing is whether government

follows the due process of law or takes arbitrarily."
Discuss these points of view.

3. This chapter shows the important role of property rights in an economic system. What are some other recent instances (excluding those noted in Example 1) in which *new* property rights have been established?

4. "Although it is interesting to speculate about human relationships based *solely* on monetary incentives and exchange, in fact, even a laissez-faire capitalist market economy could not survive unless it contained islands within which command or love reigned supreme." Discuss.

5. Consider Figure 1. How do you think the government might enter the picture to increase or decrease the money supply, which is circulating in the graph's shaded segments?

6. Consider Figure 1. How might one depict in it the country's *foreign* economic relations?

7. "Although it is interesting to speculate about human relationships based on command, in fact, a pure centrally planned command system cannot survive unless it is supplemented by monetary incentives or even a strong dose of love." Discuss.

8. Classify the following propositions as positive statements or normative statements. (Hint: Positive statements can potentially be proven correct or false by appeal to factual data; normative statements involve value judgments that can never be proven correct or false.)

   a. The ceiling on interest paid on savings deposits should be removed.
   b. In the short run, unemployment can be reduced by increasing the rate of inflation.
   c. The redistribution of income is a legitimate role for the federal government.
   d. The fundamental cause of the recent rise in oil prices is the monopoly power of the large oil companies.
   e. The level of government spending should be reduced.
   f. Inflation is primarily a monetary phenomenon.
   g. National defense expenditures should be reduced to more reasonable levels.
   h. The distribution of income in the United States should be more equal.
   i. It is possible to decrease unemployment by raising the money supply.
   j. Higher unemployment benefits raise unemployment.

9. Classify the following propositions as positive statements or normative statements. (Hint: Positive statements can potentially be proven correct or false by appeal to factual data; normative statements involve value judgments that can never be proven correct or false.)

   a. There are substantial differences in IQ among the races.
   b. Extraterrestrials exist and have visited the earth.
   c. We should not worry about inflation; unemployment is the problem.
   d. We should not subsidize higher education.
   e. It is stupid to send food to Ethiopia.
   f. The earth is a mere 5,000 years old.
   g. It is time to raise the taxes on the rich to help the poor.
   h. Lower defense spending will cause a depression.
   i. Higher taxes on the rich will lower the production of capital goods and thus, the rate of economic growth.
   j. This year's drought will lower the income of farmers.

10. "Not all statements are positive or normative; there are also *analytic statements* of the if-then variety that are always necessarily correct as a matter of logic." Discuss.

CHAPTER 3

DEMAND AND SUPPLY: THE FUNDAMENTALS

Preview

This chapter focuses on a major relationship in the mixed U.S. economy, that between households as demanders of goods and firms as suppliers of goods. It considers how the forces of demand and supply interact to eliminate surpluses and shortages and to establish equilibrium. The chapter also shows how this result can be upset by government intervention that legislates price floors or ceilings or imposes taxes on market transactions.

Examples

1. Auction Markets for Art
2. Changing Equilibrium Prices: Fish, Moonshine, and Silver
3. Changing Equilibrium Prices: From Abundance to Scarcity
4. Of Milk and Sugar
5. The Story of Rent Control
6. Trading Human Body Parts

Ideas in History

The Scissors Diagram

Last chapter's Figure 3, A World of Mixed Economies, placed all of the world's economic systems between two theoretical extremes, the completely centralized, communist command economy on the one hand and the totally laissez-faire, capitalist market economy on the other. The mixed economy of the United States is positioned closer to the latter than the former pole. Thus, last chapter's Figure 1, The Capitalist Market Economy, provides a fairly good description of the major types of actors operating in the U.S. economy and of the major types of markets in which they meet. The major actors are households and firms; the major markets are those for goods and resources, respectively. In the present chapter, we learn more about the fundamental relationships in the capitalist market economy by turning to the upper loop in last chapter's diagram and focusing on the market for a single good. In such a market, households appear as consumers who demand a good, and firms appear as producers who supply it.

The Law of Demand

The quantity of any single good that the nation's consumers are able and willing to demand in a given period varies with a considerable number of factors. We will consider several of these influences later, but for now let us focus on only one of them, the good's own price. In doing so, we discover the **"law" of demand:** Other things being equal, as the price of an item falls, the quantity demanded by buyers tends to increase; the opposite is also true (as the price of an item rises, the quantity demanded tends to decrease). Three initial points must be made about this statement. First, the term *law* has been placed in quotation marks to indicate that the principle stated here is a tendency normally observed; exceptions are possible but extremely rare.

Second, the *quantity demanded* by buyers refers to amounts they are able and willing to buy; it must not be confused with the quantity buyers desire or need. A person may *desire* a Cadillac but be unable to afford one. Similarly, a person may *need* insulin, yet have no way to pay for it. In both cases, the quantity demanded is zero.

Third, the inverse relationship noted here (lower price means higher quantity, higher price means lower quantity) is believed to hold, *other things being equal*. Other factors such as the prices of other goods, the level of consumer income, or the strength of consumer tastes influence the amounts demanded as well. If changes in these other factors occur at the same time the price of an item changes, we cannot directly observe the "law" of demand, but we will see how to handle such other changes later.

Demand Schedule and Demand Line

The "law" of demand can be illustrated by a **demand schedule,** a tabular listing of the relationship between alternative prices of an item and the associated quantities demanded, other things being equal. Table 1 cannot list all possible price-quantity combinations, but it does provide a few alternatives, A through F. Read the table from top to bottom and note how a fall in price (column 2) is associated with an increase in quantity demanded (column 3), just as the "law" of demand states. Then read the table from bottom to top, noting the opposite relationship as well. A rise in price (column 2) is associated with a decrease in quantity demanded (column 3).

A **demand line** is simply a graphical representation of a demand schedule, such as Figure 1. Note how the Table 1 alternatives now appear as the six points labeled A through F.

TABLE 1   A Demand Schedule for Beef

Alternative (1)	Price, P (dollars per pound) (2)	Quantity Demanded, Q (billions of pounds per year) (3)	
A	$10	0	*Other things being equal:* prices of all other goods; consumer income; consumer tastes; consumer expectations about future prices and income; number of consumers; and more.
B	8	4	
C	6	8	
D	4	12	
E	2	16	
F	0	20	

This demand schedule shows the relationship between selected alternative prices of beef and associated quantities demanded—other things, such as those listed to the right, being equal. (You may note that this demand schedule conforms to the simple equation $Q = 20 - 2P$, with the understanding that P must lie within the $0 to $10 range. Enter any given value of P from column 2 into that equation and you can calculate the corresponding value of Q in column 3.)

FIGURE 1 A Demand Line for Beef

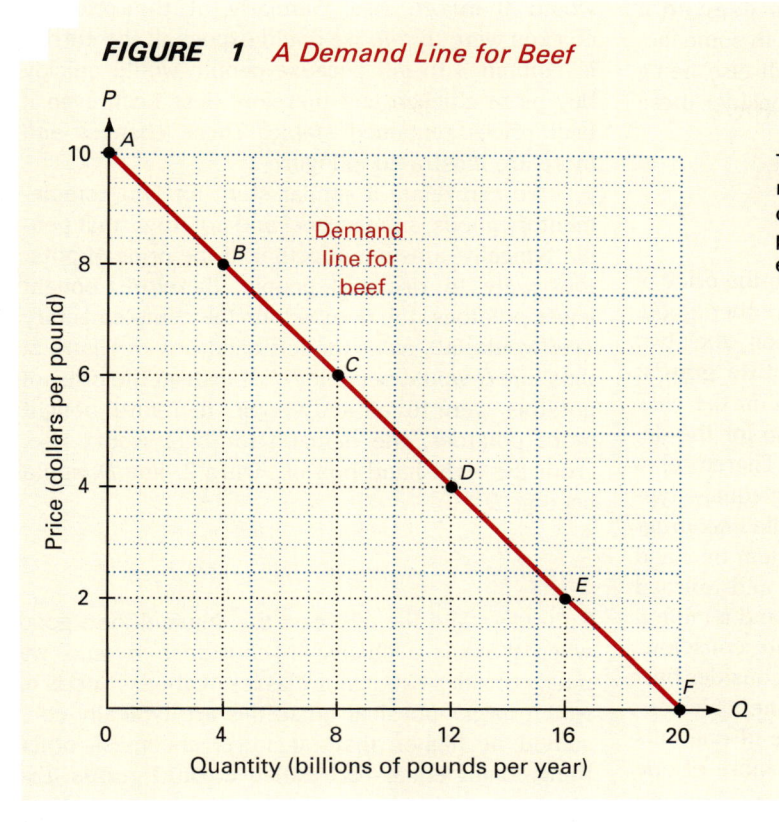

This demand line for beef, a graphical representation of Table 1, shows how quantity demanded varies with the price of beef—other things being equal.

CAUTION

Economists have a special way of talking about a movement from one row to the next in a demand schedule or from one point to another on a demand line. A change in the quantity of an item that buyers are ready to purchase is not *a change in demand but is a* **change in quantity demanded** *if this change is due to a change in the item's own price, other things being equal. Thus, a move from A to B (in either Table 1 or Figure 1) is called "an increase in the quantity of beef demanded" (from 0 to 4 billion pounds per year). It is caused by nothing but the associated price fall from $10 to $8 per pound (because all other things were held equal when our table and graph were constructed). Similarly, a move from F to E (in either Table 1 or Figure 1) is called "a decrease in the quantity of beef demanded" (from 20 to 16 billion pounds of beef per year), and it is caused by nothing but the associated price rise from $0 to $2 per pound (again, all other things were held equal).*

Given this verbal convention, whenever you hear the phrase "change in quantity demanded," you instantly know the reason for the change: a fall or rise in the item's own price. In your mind, you should picture a movement along a given demand line, such as Figure 1.

Changes in Demand

We can also illustrate the effects of changes in the other factors, such as those listed in the Table 1 box. A change in the quantity of an item that buyers are ready to purchase is a **change in demand** if this quantity change is due to a change in some factor other than the item's own price, all else being equal. To illustrate what is involved, consider these other factors one at a time.

Changes in the Prices of Other Goods

When considering the effect a change in the price of one good has on the demand for another good, three relationships can exist between the two goods. First, the goods can be **substitute goods;** the increased consumption of one can, in the view of the consumer, more or less make up for the decreased consumption of the other. Therefore, a higher price of one—other things being equal—typically discourages its consumption while *encouraging* the consumption of the other. Consider beef and chicken, apples and pears, bus travel and railroad travel, white shirts and colored shirts, and a million other such "either-or" goods. (If you are conscious of your cholesterol level, *you* may not consider beef and chicken to be substitutes, but American consumers as a group do. When the price of one falls relative to that of the other, they buy more of one and less of the other.)

Second, the goods in question can be **complementary goods;** the consumption of one is typically linked to the simultaneous consumption of the other. Therefore, a higher price of one—other things being equal—typically discourages its consumption while also discouraging the consumption of the other. Consider beef and potatoes, hamburger and ketchup, cars and gasoline, medical services and drugs, and many similar "go-together" goods. If the price of beef falls relative to that of other meats, then people buy not only more beef but also more of the potatoes they like to eat at the same time.

Third, the goods can be **independent goods.** The consumption of one is totally unrelated to the consumption of the other. Consider beef and diapers, chicken and bus travel, white shirts and potatoes, ketchup and cars.

Look again at Table 1 and imagine what would happen to all the column 3 entries if the price of chicken were to rise substantially. Given that beef is a fairly good substitute for chicken, we could expect people to buy less chicken and more beef at *any* given price of beef. All the entries in column 3 would therefore rise. Similarly, if the price of chicken were to *fall*, we could expect all the entries in column 3 to fall because people would quickly buy more chicken and therefore, less beef, even if beef prices remained stable. These changes and more are illustrated in Figure 2.

We can relate a similar story for two complementary goods, such as beef and potatoes, that people typically consume together. If the price of potatoes were to rise and people, therefore, bought fewer potatoes, the demand for the complementary beef would fall, as in the left-hand box of Figure 2; thus line D would become D^*. If instead the price of potatoes were to fall and people, therefore, bought more potatoes, the demand for beef would rise. From the right-hand box of Figure 2, line D would become D'.

Changes in Consumer Income

To understand the effect on the demand for a good when there is a change in consumer income, we must consider two major classes of goods. Goods of which *larger* physical quantities are typically consumed at higher than at lower incomes—other things being equal—are called **normal goods.** Examples include airline travel, beef, designer clothing, owner-occupied housing, or root-canal dentistry. On the other hand, goods of which *smaller* physical quantities are typically consumed at higher than at lower incomes—other things being equal— are called **inferior goods.** Think of long-distance bus travel, bologna, second-hand clothes, apartment housing, or routine tooth extractions. Now have another look at Figure 2.

An increase in income would produce the result shown in the right-hand box (and a graphical shift of D to D') for a normal good but the result shown in the left-hand box (and a graphical shift of D to D^*) for an inferior good. Similarly, a decrease in income would shift D to D' in the case of an inferior good but D to D^* in the case of a normal good.

Changes in Consumer Tastes

A change in people's general *attitude* about a good could also affect their demand for it—even if other things remained the same. Imagine what would happen if the Surgeon General announced that eating beef caused cancer. In Figure 2 people's predictably "weaker tastes" for beef would produce the results

FIGURE 2 Changes in the Demand for Beef

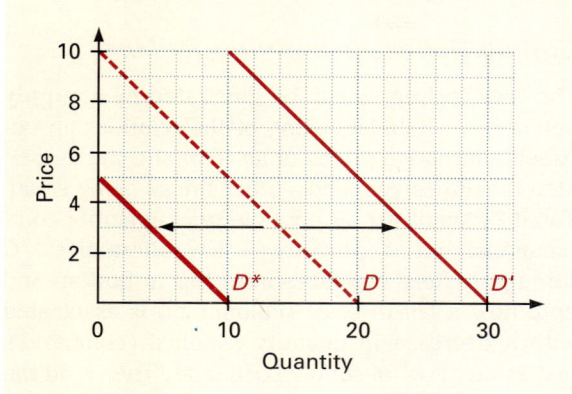

This graph illustrates how the changed price of a substitute good, such as chicken, changes the demand for beef. In the demand schedule, the entire quantity column is replaced; in the graph, the entire demand line shifts to a new position. Line D, based on the original Table 1 demand schedule, is a copy of the Figure 1 demand line. If the price of chicken rises (right-hand box), the demand for beef rises—the entire line shifts from D to D'. If the price of chicken falls (left-hand box), the demand for beef falls—the entire line shifts from D to D^*. As the legend indicates, many other factors can have similar demand-shifting effects. You will learn about these factors later in the text.

	Decrease in demand (D changes to D^*)	
	Demand for Beef (billions of lb./year)	
Price ($/lb)	D (original)	D^* (after fall in price of substitute)
10	0	0
8	4	0
6	8	0
4	12	2
2	16	6
0	20	10

Similar effects:
  rise in price of complement
  rise in income (inferior good)
  fall in income (normal good)
  weaker tastes
  expected fall in future price
  expected fall in future income (normal good)
  fall in number of consumers
  and more

	Increase in demand (D changes to D')	
	Demand for Beef (billions of lb./year)	
Price ($/lb)	D (original)	D' (after rise in price of substitute)
10	0	10
8	4	14
6	8	18
4	12	22
2	16	26
0	20	30

Similar effects:
  fall in price of complement
  rise in income (normal good)
  fall in income (inferior good)
  stronger tastes
  expected rise in future price
  expected rise in future income (normal good)
  rise in number of consumers
  and more

depicted by the left-hand box and cause a shift of D to D^*. Now imagine the Surgeon General's report told different news, that eating beef *cured* cancer. Can you see why people's "stronger tastes" for beef would initiate the change depicted by the right-hand box and the shift of D to D'?

Changes in Other Factors

In similar ways, many other factors might change the demand for a good in the current period. Consider how D might shift to D' simply because people *expect* (rightly or wrongly) future increases in price and thus, decide to stock up now. *D* might also shift to *D'* (in the case of a normal good) if people expect future increases in income and decide to anticipate the benefits by buying more on credit now. Finally *D* might shift to *D'* simply because the number of consumers is growing, perhaps from natural population growth, immigration, or even the removal of international trade barriers which suddenly allows foreigners to enter the market as buyers. Clearly, the opposites (and corresponding shifts of *D* to *D**) are possible as well.

Conclusions

From the foregoing sections, a simple conclusion should emerge. Whenever you hear the phrase "change in demand," you instantly know the reason for the change: a fall or rise in one of numerous factors *other than* the item's own price. In your mind, you should picture a *shift* of an entire demand line, as in Figure 2.

The Law of Supply

The quantity of any good that the nation's producers are able and willing to supply in a given period varies with a considerable number of factors as well. We will consider several of these influences later, but for now focus on one of them, the good's own price. We discover the **"law" of supply:** Other things being equal, as the price of an item falls, the quantity supplied by sellers tends to decrease; the opposite is also true (as the price of an item rises, the quantity supplied tends to increase).

For now, two points need to be understood about this statement. First, the term *law* has once again been placed in quotation marks to remind us that the principle just stated is a tendency normally observed for things that people can produce; exceptions are possible but rare.

Second, the direct relationship noted here (lower price means lower quantity; higher price means higher quantity) is believed to hold *other things being equal*. Such other factors as the prices of productive inputs, the producers' technical knowledge or even the prices of alternative outputs can also be expected to influence the amounts of any given good that are supplied. When changes in these other factors occur at the same time the price of an item changes, we cannot directly observe the "law" of supply. Once again, we will learn later how to deal with such complications.

Supply Schedule and Supply Line

The "law" of supply can be illustrated by a **supply schedule,** a tabular listing of the relationship between alternative prices of an item and the associated quantities supplied—other things being equal. Table 2 cannot list all possible price-quantity combinations, but it provides a few alternatives, *G* through *L*. Read the table from top to bottom and note how a fall in price (column 2) is associated with a decrease in quantity supplied (column 3), just as the "law" of supply postulates. Then read the table from bottom to top and note the opposite as well: A rise in price (column 2) is associated with an increase in quantity supplied (column 3).

CAUTION

As for demand, economists have a special name for a movement from one row to the next in a supply schedule or from one point to another on a supply line. They refer to a change in the quantity of an item that sellers are ready to provide not *as a change in supply but as a* **change in quantity supplied***, if it is due to a change in the item's own price, other things being equal. Thus, a move from G to H (in either Table 2 or Figure 3) is called "a decrease in the quantity of beef supplied" (from 20 to 16 billion pounds per year). It is caused by nothing but the associated price fall from $10 to $8 per pound (all other things were held equal when our table and graph were constructed). Similarly, a move from L to K (in Table 2 or Figure 3) is called "an increase in the quantity of beef supplied" (from 2 to 4 billion pounds of beef per year). It is caused by nothing but the associated price rise from $1 to $2 per pound (because, again, all other things were held equal). This verbal convention is analogous to the demand side. Whenever you hear the phrase "change in quantity supplied," you are in fact given the* reason *for the change: a fall or rise in the item's own price. In your mind you should then picture a* movement along *a given supply line, such as Figure 3.*

TABLE 2 A Supply Schedule for Beef

Alternative (1)	Price, P (dollars per pound) (2)	Quantity Supplied, Q (billions of pounds per year) (3)
G	$10	20
H	8	16
I	6	12
J	4	8
K	2	4
L	1	2

Note: Nothing is supplied below $1.

Other things being equal: Prices of productive inputs; technical knowledge; prices of alternative outputs; producer expectations about future prices of inputs or outputs; number of producers; and more.

This supply schedule shows the relationship between selected alternative prices of beef and associated quantities supplied—other things, such as those listed in the right-hand box, being equal. (Note that this supply schedule conforms to the simple equation $Q = 2P$, with the understanding that P cannot be less than $1 per pound. Enter any permissible value of P from column 2 into that equation and you can calculate the corresponding value of Q in column 3.)

FIGURE 3 A Supply Line for Beef

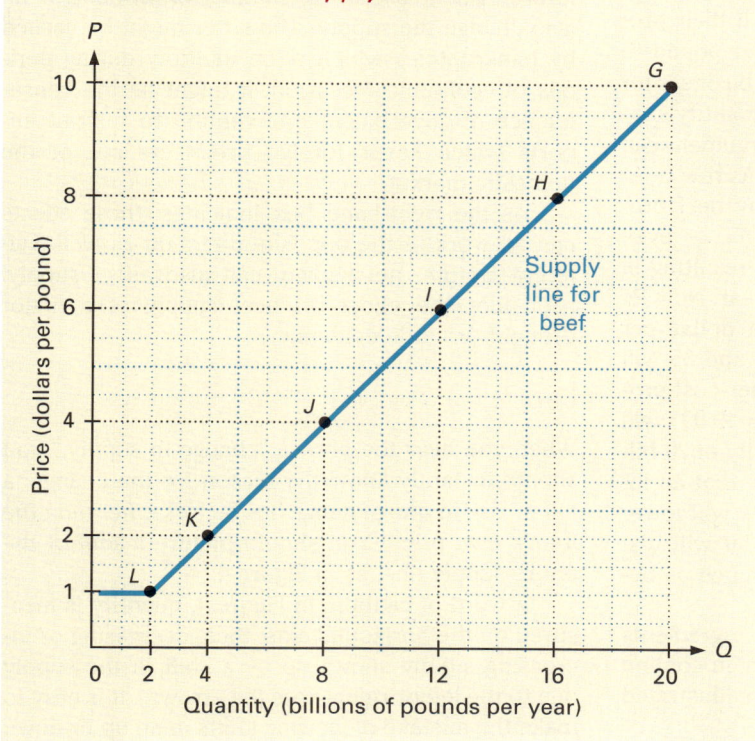

This supply line for beef, a graphical representation of Table 2, shows how the quantity supplied varies with the price of beef—other things being equal.

A **supply line** is nothing more complicated than a graphical representation of a supply schedule, as Figure 3 illustrates. The alternatives now appear graphically as the six points labeled G through L in Table 2.

Changes in Supply

Economists refer to a change in the quantity of an item that sellers are ready to provide as a **change in supply** if this quantity change is due to a change in some factor other than the item's own price, all else being equal. The other factors include those listed in the Table 2 box. Let us illustrate what is involved by considering them one at a time.

Changes in the Prices of Productive Inputs

Have another look at Table 2 and imagine what would happen to all the column 3 entries if beef producers had to pay more for animals, pastureland, human labor, and the other productive ingredients they use. As row L tells us, at a market price of $1 per pound of beef, only 2 billion pounds would be supplied per year—presumably because only a small number of producers can manage to produce beef at a cost of $1 per pound or less. If their production costs went up from, say, 84¢ per pound to $1.10 per pound, they would not stay in business for long and our 2 billion pound per year quantity supplied would fall to zero. An analogous argument can be made for any other alternative, such as row G. At a market price of $10 per pound, many beef producers—with production costs of $2, $5, or even $9.99—find it profitable to supply beef, resulting in 20 billion pounds being supplied each year. Now let everyone's production costs rise by a dollar per pound. Those with original costs of $2 and $5 will still supply at the $10 price, but the higher-cost producers (with original costs of $9.10 or $9.99) will surely drop out. Thus, the annual quantity of 20 billion pounds will drop. We can conclude that an increase in the prices of productive inputs will lower all the entries in column 3 of Table 2. It will discourage producers from producing as much as before.

Similarly, if the prices of productive ingredients were to *fall,* we could expect every entry in column 3 of Table 2 to rise. Both these effects are illustrated in Figure 4.

Changes in Technology

Consider what would happen to our Table 2 supply schedule if beef producers' technical knowledge improved. If every single combination of productive inputs (and thus, every given expenditure of costs) yielded a larger quantity of physical output, beef producers might supply a larger output quantity at any given output price. This effect is shown in the right-hand box of Figure 4 by a replacement of column S with S' and by a corresponding increase in supply in the graph. Obviously, a loss in technical knowledge (which is rare but not impossible, especially in times of war) would have the opposite effects (as shown by a shift of S to S*).

Changes in Other Factors

In the same way, all kinds of other factors might change the supply of a good in the current period. As Figure 4 indicates (left-hand box), a rise in the price of some alternative output (such as mutton or even peaches) might induce producers to use their resources to produce more of these other goods and therefore, less beef. Then S becomes S*. A similar effect can occur from the mere expectation of higher input prices or of a lower beef price in the future. A decrease in the number of producers can also change the supply. The latter might be caused by bankruptcies which often multiply during periods of economic recession. It might be the consequence of government intervention to restrict imports which keeps foreign producers out of the domestic market.

As the right-hand box indicates, these effects can all work in the opposite direction as well. Different factors, not shown, can also affect supply. (Consider the effect on beef supply of a major drought or cattle epidemic.)

Conclusion

When you hear the phrase "change in supply," you should instantly know the reason for the change: a fall or rise in one of numerous factors *other than* the item's own price. You should picture a *shift* of the entire supply line, as in Figure 4.

A word of caution: In Figure 4, quantity is measured on the horizontal axis; thus, decreasing or increasing supply shows up by a shift in the supply line to the left or right (note the arrows). It is easy to make the mistake of viewing shifts in an up or down

FIGURE 4 Changes in the Supply of Beef

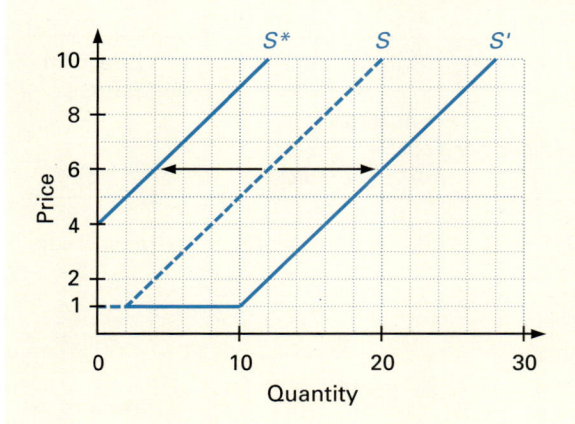

This graph illustrates how changes in the prices of productive ingredients, such as herd animals, pastureland, or human labor, affect the supply of beef. In the supply schedule, the entire quantity column is replaced; in the graph, the entire supply line shifts to a new position. Line S, based on the original Table 2 supply schedule, is a copy of the Figure 3 supply line. If the prices of inputs rise (left-hand box), the supply of beef falls—the entire line shifts from S to S*. If the prices of inputs fall (right-hand box), the supply of beef rises—the entire line shifts from S to S'. As the legend indicates, many factors can have similar supply-shifting effects.

	Decrease in supply (S changes to S*)	
	Supply of Beef (billions of lb./year)	
Price ($/lb.)	S (original)	S* (after rise in input prices)
10	20	12
8	16	8
6	12	4
4	8	0
2	4	0
1	2	0

Similar effects:
  loss of technical knowledge
  rise in price of alternative output
  expected rise in input prices
  expected fall in output price
  fall in number of producers
  and more

	Increase in supply (S changes to S')	
	Supply of Beef (billions of lb./year)	
Price ($/lb.)	S (original)	S' (after fall in input prices)
10	20	28
8	16	24
6	12	20
4	8	16
2	4	12
1	2	10

Similar effects:
  improvement in technical knowledge
  fall in price of alternative output
  expected fall in input prices
  expected rise in output price
  rise in number of producers
  and more

direction (along the vertical price axis). If this were the case, line S* would seem to lie *above* S, and you would call the shift from S to S* (incorrectly) a rise in supply. Similarly, line S' would seem to lie *below* S, and you would call the shift from S to S' (incorrectly) a fall in supply. (This potential problem does not arise in the case of demand.)

The Equilibrium of Demand and Supply

Table 3 shows what happens when numerous potential buyers and numerous potential sellers meet in a market. Columns (1) and (2) of Table 3 correspond to the demand schedule of Table 1; columns

TABLE 3 Demand and Supply Schedules Compared

Price (dollars per pound) (1)	Quantity Demanded (2)	Quantity Supplied (3)	Surplus (+) or Shortage (−) (4) = (3) − (2)	Effect on Price (5)
(billions of pounds of beef per year)				
$10	0	20	+20	pressure to fall
8	4	16	+12	
6	8	12	+4	
5	10	10	0	neutral
4	12	8	−4	pressure to rise
2	16	4	−12	
0	20	0	−20	

Comparing the Table 1 and 2 demand and supply schedules, we find only one price at which quantity demanded equals quantity supplied. This is the equilibrium price ($5); the corresponding quantity (10 billion pounds per year) is the equilibrium quantity. Competition among sellers and buyers, respectively, pushes any prevailing price down or up to this equilibrium level and thus, eliminates any innate tendency for price and quantity to change.

(1) and (3), to the supply schedule of Table 2. The same information is graphed in Figure 5, which is a combination of Figure 1 and Figure 3.

The shaded row in Table 3 and the intersection (point e) of demand and supply in Figure 5 depict the beef market's **equilibrium.** In this situation there is no innate tendency for price or quantity to change because quantity demanded and quantity supplied are just equal to one another. Let us examine the process by which equilibrium is reached.

Competition Among Sellers Reduces Price in the Face of Surpluses

Consider the first row of Table 3: Suppose sellers insisted on getting $10 per pound of beef. Even though sellers as a group would offer to sell beef at a rate of 20 billion pounds per year (column 3), we can see (column 2) that their attempts to dictate such a price would be frustrated, and they could not sell a single pound. At this price, the quantity supplied would exceed the quantity demanded. A **surplus** would exist. In cold-storage facilities throughout the country, unwanted beef would be accumulating at a rate of 20 billion pounds per year (column 4). Surely, some of the frustrated sellers would come to recognize the $10-per-pound price as inappropriate.

Some of these would-be sellers would attempt to get rid of their surplus by offering to sell beef at a lower price. This occurrence is predicted in column 5. The second row of our table tells us what would happen if the price asked fell to $8 per pound. Quantity demanded would rise to 4 billion pounds per year and quantity supplied would fall to 16 billion pounds. Both of these responses (familiar from the analysis earlier in this chapter) would still not be sufficient to solve the problem. At the $8-per-pound price, there would be a surplus of 12 billion pounds per year (row 2, column 4). Even though *some* sellers would succeed in selling beef at an annual rate of 4 billion pounds, *other* sellers would accumulate surpluses at an annual rate of 12 billion

FIGURE 5 Equilibrium of Demand and Supply

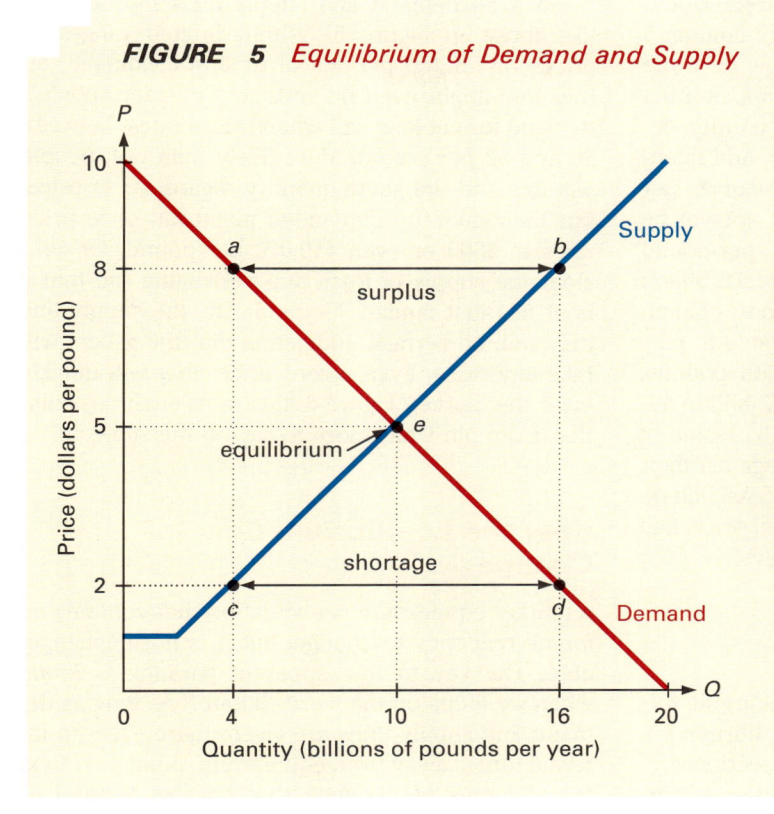

This graph illustrates the establishment, in a competitive market, of equilibrium price and equilibrium quantity (intersection *e* of the demand and supply lines). At any higher price, there would be surpluses, which tend to depress price. At any lower price, there would be shortages, which tend to raise price. At the equilibrium price, all those who want to buy can find a seller, and all those who want to sell can find a buyer.

pounds (distance *ab,* Figure 5). Some of these would-be sellers would bid against their fellows and further depress the price.

It is easy to see where this process would end. When the price had fallen to $5 per pound, there would be *equilibrium,* a situation without any built-in tendency to change. Households as a group would have adjusted their annual purchases to 10 billion pounds, and firms as a group would also have adjusted their production levels to 10 billion pounds. As economists say, the market would be "cleared." Neither a shortage nor a surplus would exist. Every seller would find a buyer, and every buyer would find a seller. Only a change in demand or supply (that is, a change in the entire quantity columns of Table 3 and a corresponding *shift* of the demand or supply line) could upset this result.

Competition Among Buyers Raises Price in the Face of Shortages

The same equilibrium would have been reached if we had originally assumed that buyers insisted on paying nothing for beef at all. Consider the last row of Table 3. Even though buyers as a group would gladly take beef at a rate of 20 billion pounds per year at a zero price (column 2), an attempt to dictate such a price would fail (column 3). Buyers would not find a single pound of beef. The quantity demanded would exceed the quantity supplied at this price; a **shortage** would come to exist. Some of these frustrated buyers would recognize that the zero price had no substance to it and was impossible.

Almost certainly, some of these buyers would offer a higher price. The lower section of column 5 predicts this occurrence. The second row from the bottom of Table 3 tells us what would happen if the price offered rose to $2 per pound. Quantity demanded would fall to 16 billion pounds, and quantity supplied would rise to 4 billion pounds per year. But again these responses would not yet be sufficient to solve the problem. At the $2-per-pound price, there still would be a shortage of 12 billion pounds per year (row 2 from the bottom, column 4). Even though *some* buyers would be able to purchase beef at an annual rate of 4 billion pounds, *other* buyers would still be looking for 12 billion additional pounds (distance *cd* in Figure 5). Some of these would-be buyers would compete against their fellows and further push up the price. As before, this pressure could only end when the price had risen to the $5-per-pound equilibrium level.

Graphical Summary

Figure 5 summarizes our story. By looking at this graph, we discover the *one* possible equilibrium position in the market: the point of intersection *e* of demand and supply. At the $5-per-pound price corresponding to *e*, and at no other price, are buyers willing and able to take exactly what sellers are willing and able to bring to the market (10 billion pounds of beef per year).

At *any* higher price we would find surpluses, measured by the horizontal distance between the two lines at a given price. At $8, for instance, the quantity supplied would be 16 (point *b*) and the quantity demanded would be only 4 (point *a*). Thus *actual* trade (were an $8 price ever to prevail) could only involve 4, whereas 12 billion other pounds would accumulate in storage facilities (distance *ab*). Hence price would tend to fall toward *e* through competition among sellers.

At any lower price we would find shortages. At $2, for instance, the quantity supplied would be only 4 (point *c*) and the quantity demanded, 10 (point *d*). Thus actual trade would only involve 4; whereas potential demanders of another 12 billion pounds (distance *cd*) would go without beef. This time, buyers would push the price up toward *e* as they competed with one another.

Ideas in History reviews the origin of the analysis presented in this chapter so far.

Not all demand and supply lines look exactly like those in Figure 5. Within limited ranges of prices or limited periods of time, for example, either line might even be vertical. Consider people's demand for cooking salt when prices range between $0 and $2 per pound. More likely than not, people will demand the same quantity regardless of price, but their quantity demanded might fall once price rises to $500 or even $10,000 per pound. Or consider the supply of fresh and perishable fish that a boat has just landed. Momentarily, the supply line may well be vertical, indicating that the fishers will take any price, even a zero price, that will quickly clear the market. Figure 6 illustrates such possibilities. Example 1 has more to say on the subject.

How the Equilibrium Can Change

A market equilibrium is a situation that contains no *innate* tendency to change, but it is not unchangeable. The key to this apparent paradox is found when we focus on the word "innate." As long as demand and supply lines are given, there exist no internal forces away from equilibrium point *e*. Yet external forces of the type that change demand or supply (see Figures 2 and 4) can easily upset a market equilibrium.

Look again at Figure 5 and imagine the consequences of a decrease or increase in demand (first shown in Figure 2), given unchanged supply. The equilibrium point *e* would move down or up along the supply line. Now picture the consequences of a decrease or increase in supply (first shown in Figure 4), given unchanged demand. Can you see how equilibrium point *e* would move up or down along the demand line?

Panels (a) through (d) of Figure 7 illustrate these changes. The figure caption summarizes the effects of the contemplated changes in demand or supply. Examples 2 and 3 provide case studies from the real world.

Two technical notes should be made about changing equilibrium. First, Figure 7 only depicts the (predictable) consequences of separate changes in demand, given supply, or in supply, given demand. Our graph does not deal with the (sometimes less predictable) consequences of *simultaneous* changes in demand and supply. End-of-chapter question 7 asks you to consider the four obvious

EXAMPLE 1

Auction Markets for Art

In 1990, a painting by Vincent van Gogh, entitled *Portrait of Dr. Gachet,* was sold for $82.5 million at Christie's (a New York auction house). At the time, no single painting had ever commanded a higher price. (The previous record, set at Sotheby's in 1987, involved a van Gogh as well: *Irises* for $53.9 million.) One can explain this outcome with the help of the Marshallian tools of demand and supply as Figure A illustrates. In the case of a unique item, the supply line will have the vertical shape shown here. Above a certain minimum price ($16 million) below which the current owner will not part with the item, a single unit is supplied—no matter what the price. The demand line has the familiar downward-sloping shape, although it may be kinked rather than smooth. Given the hypothetical demand line drawn here, in 1990 nobody would have demanded this painting above the $82.5 million price (section *ab*). There would have been a single buyer at any price between $82.5 and $40 million (section *ec*), there would have been two buyers between $40 and $16 million (section *df*), and so on. In this example, any price above $40 million and no higher than $82.5 million might have cleared the market.

The graph also shows why prices of rare art objects often rise over time. While the supply is fixed, an increase in demand can easily raise the equilibrium price from one auction to the next, as from *e* in 1990 to *e'* in 1995, if the auctioneer manages to find the highest possible equilibrium price in each case. Indeed, the price of art objects at Sotheby's rose at an average annual rate of 20.9 percent between 1984 and 1989. Considering individual categories, this percentage ranged from 9.7 for French furniture to 12.1 for English silver to 12.2 for Chinese ceramics, and 32.2 for modern (1900–1950) paintings. The most amazing event, perhaps, was the sale of an Old Master painting (*Dosso Dotti* by Giovanni de Lutero). It had just been purchased unrecognized at a country auction for $1,000; the work was resold for over $4 million when its artist was properly identified.

Sources: *The New York Times,* November 26, 1988, p. 15, May 16, 1990, p. 1; *Forbes,* March 6, 1989, p. 152; *The Wall Street Journal,* January 2, 1991, p. R22.

FIGURE A

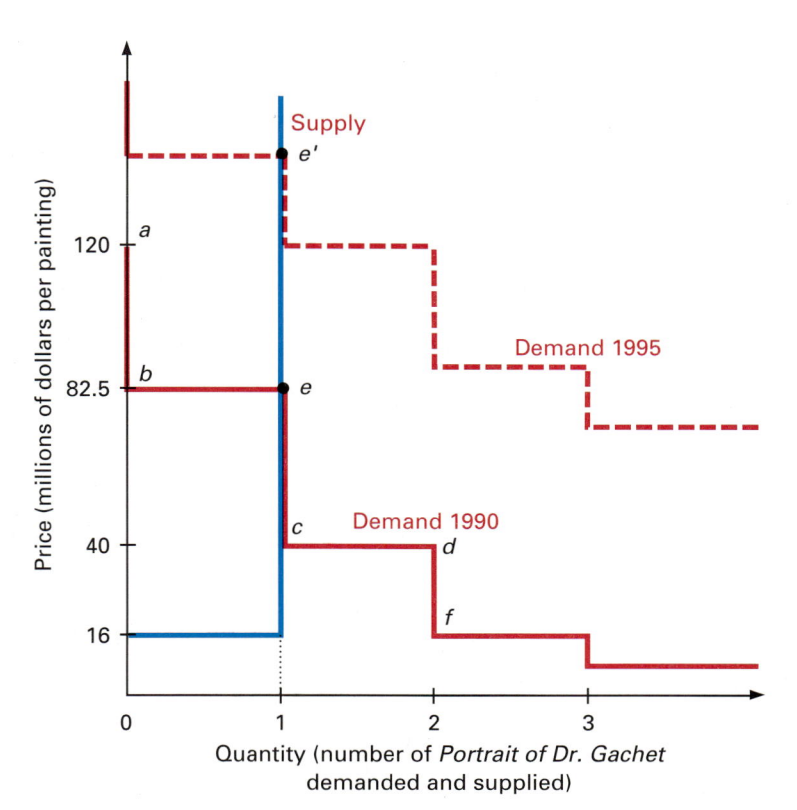

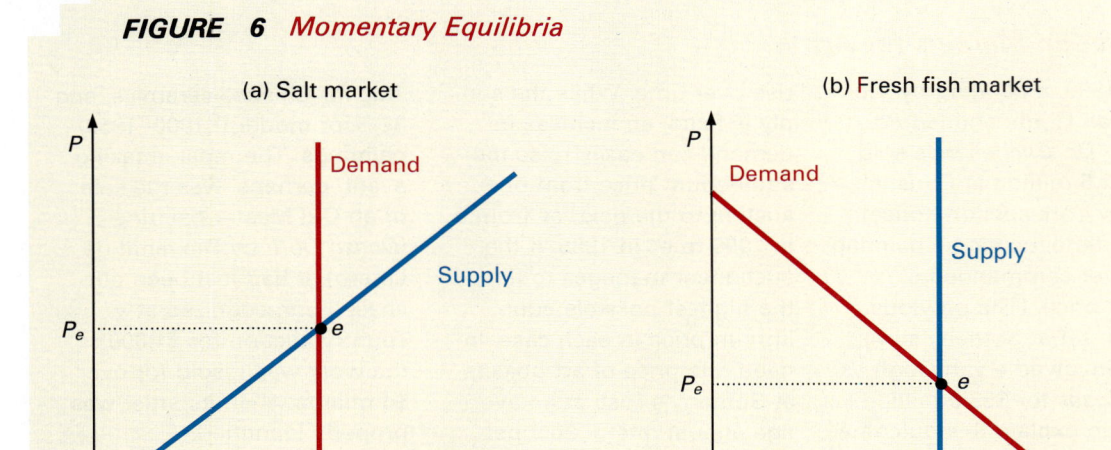

FIGURE 6 Momentary Equilibria

(a) Salt market

(b) Fresh fish market

The concept of *momentary equilibrium* refers to a limited range of prices or time such that quantity demanded or supplied is absolutely fixed, regardless of price. Thus, in panel (a), the quantity of salt demanded is unresponsive to its price. In panel (b), the quantity of fresh fish supplied is similarly unresponsive. Nevertheless, the demand-and-supply intersection at e indicates equilibrium price, P_e, and equilibrium quantity, Q_e.

cases of simultaneity not discussed here; you may wish to look now at the question and its answer at the back of the book.

Second, whenever market equilibrium changes (as from e to e' in the panels of Figure 7), one can separate the observed change in actual quantity (from Q_0 to Q_1) into four components: a change in demand, a change in supply, a change in quantity demanded, and a change in quantity supplied.

1. Any leftward shift in the demand or supply line denotes, respectively, a decrease in demand or supply (again, for any one of the reasons listed in Figures 2 and 4).

2. Any rightward shift in the demand or supply line denotes, respectively, an increase in demand or supply (again, for any one of the reasons listed in Figures 2 and 4).

3. Given the sloping lines of Figure 7, any increase in the equilibrium price signals, respectively, a decrease in quantity demanded or an increase in quantity supplied (caused by this rise in price).

4. Given the sloping lines of Figure 7, any decrease in the equilibrium price signals, respectively, an increase in quantity demanded or a decrease in quantity supplied (caused by this fall in price).

By studying Figure 8 you can train yourself to make the determinations suggested by these points.

In the final section of this chapter we consolidate our understanding of the demand-and-supply model by considering various effects of government intervention in otherwise competitive markets. Thus, we return to the issue of private versus government decision making that was introduced in Chapter 2.

FIGURE 7 *How the Equilibrium Can Change*

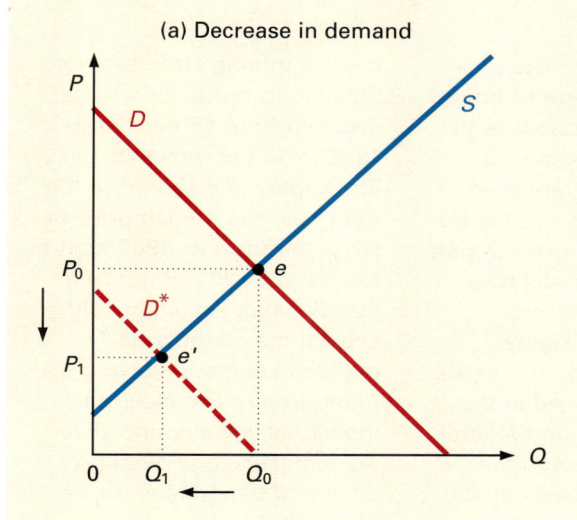

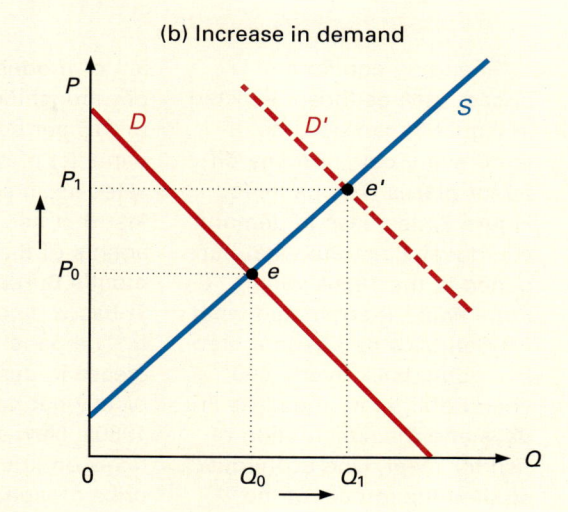

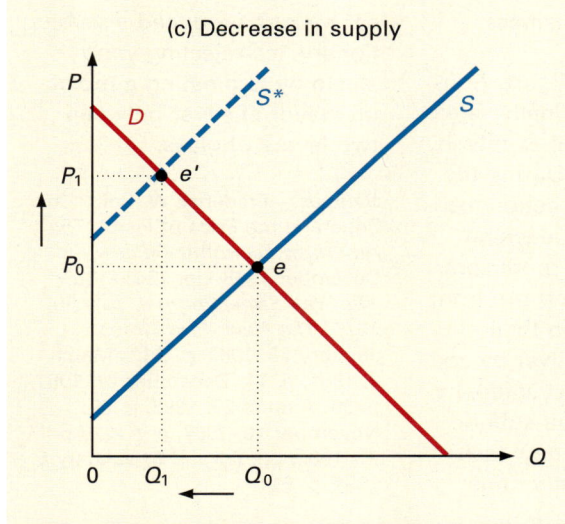

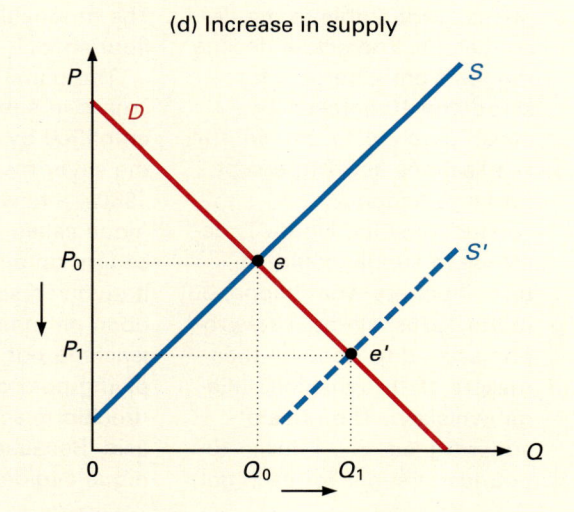

(a) Decrease in demand

(b) Increase in demand

(c) Decrease in supply

(d) Increase in supply

This graph illustrates the effects on equilibrium price and equilibrium quantity of a decrease in demand (panel a), an increase in demand (panel b), a decrease in supply (panel c), and an increase in supply (panel d)—other things being equal. In each case, an original equilibrium at e is defined by the solid lines of demand, D, and supply, S. Given the change depicted by the broken line, a new equilibrium emerges at e'. Accordingly, original price and quantity P_0 and Q_0 change to new levels denoted by P_1 and Q_1. The arrows along the axes summarize the effects.

EXAMPLE 2

Changing Equilibrium Prices: Fish, Moonshine, and Silver

Changing equilibrium prices, such as those depicted in Figure 7, can be encountered every day, in many different places. The panel (a), Figure 7, decrease in demand could well illustrate what happened in the 1960s when Pope Paul VI terminated what for Catholics had been a practice going back over 1,000 years: obligatory meatless Fridays and the substitution of fish for meat. One economist studied the impact of the Pope's decree on the fish market and discovered a 12.5 percent average decline in fish prices, attributable to the decree alone. The actual decline ranged from 2 percent for scrod and 10 percent for ocean perch to 17 percent for sea scallops and 21 percent for large haddock.

The panel (c), Figure 7, decrease in supply could, in turn, illustrate what happened in the 1970s when a catastrophe second to none hit the makers of "moonshine" (illegal whiskey). The price of sugar tripled, and it takes 10 pounds of sugar for each gallon of moonshine. The price of moonshine soared from $6 to $15 per gallon. Just as in panel (c) of our graph, its sales declined severely—a feat that had long evaded the agents of the Treasury Department's Bureau of Alcohol, Tobacco, and Firearms.

The panel (b), Figure 7, increase in demand, in turn, depicts what happened in the 1980s. New state and federal taxes on liquor raised the price of legal whiskey to $30 per gallon and, simultaneously, raised the demand for its illegal substitute. The moonshine business flourished.

The panel (d), Figure 7, increase in supply, finally, is exemplified by recent events in the silver market. During the 1980s, a new production technique called heap leaching caught on among producers. It involved scooping ore from open pit mines and then leaching out the silver by applying potassium cyanide, hydrochloric acid, and sulfuric acid. Because the new technique avoided costly underground mining and used very little labor, production costs declined from $8 per ounce in 1983 to $4 per ounce in 1990. The supply line shifted to the right, and the market price of silver fell from its 1980 high of $20.63 to $4.20 per ounce a decade later. As one would expect, the quantity demanded soared, involving the photography and electronics industries, jewelry and silverware makers, and even producers of batteries and cars. Thus, electronics makers replaced palladium with silver to connect silicon chips, and car makers produced a revolutionary, ice-rejecting windshield by laminating a molecular layer of silver between two layers of glass.

Sources: Frederick W. Bell, "The Pope and the Price of Fish," *The American Economic Review,* December 1968, pp. 1346–1350; *The Wall Street Journal,* July 30, 1975; *The New York Times,* January 23, 1980, p. A12; March 8, 1981, p. 11; December 27, 1981, p. 55; August 29, 1982, p. 37; November 16, 1987, p. A12; April 27, 1988, pp. A1 and 8; January 6, 1991, p. F11.

Government Intervention in Markets

Government intervention in markets is common, and it takes numerous forms. Three means by which government changes the equilibrium outcome that would otherwise occur are price floors, price ceilings, and excise taxes.

Price Floors

On occasion, government wants to help sellers earn more than the equilibrium price. A legislature simply enacts a law establishing a **minimum price** or **price floor** above the market equilibrium level. Transactions below that floor are henceforth illegal. The U.S. Congress has for decades set such mini-

CHAPTER 3 Demand and Supply: The Fundamentals

FIGURE 8 Analyzing a Change in Equilibrium

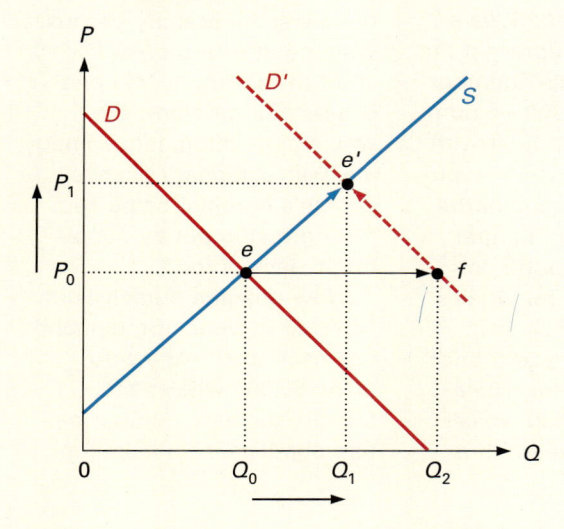

This graph is a copy of panel (b), Figure 7; it can be used to analyze the change of one equilibrium to another. The graph shows an increase in demand (of D to D'), but no change in supply (line S is unchanged). Starting at equilibrium e, the increase in demand equals ef, which produces a shortage of $ef = Q_0 Q_2$ at the old equilibrium price, P_0. The shortage makes the price rise to P_1. Because of this rise in price, quantity demanded falls along fe', but quantity supplied rises along ee'. The shortage disappears.

The establishment of above-equilibrium price floors, however, has two inevitable consequences. Given the "law" of demand, the higher price typically reduces quantity demanded. Given the "law" of supply, the higher price typically raises quantity supplied. Jointly, the two effects create a surplus, and would-be sellers are dissatisfied. Figure 9 illustrates the problem. (Students often think of a price *floor*—like the

FIGURE 9 Setting a Minimum Price for Wheat

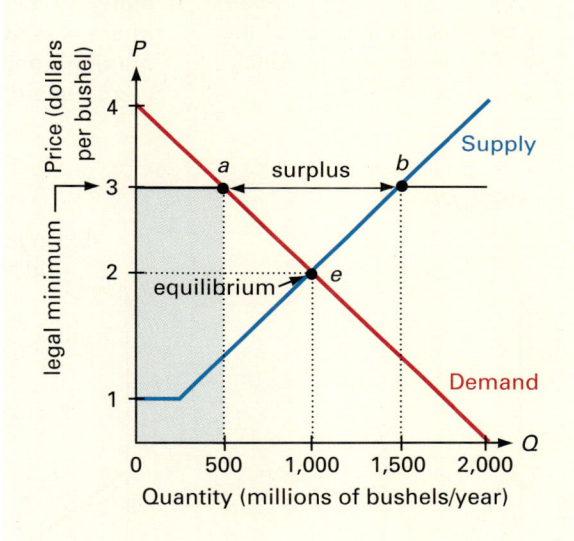

In this market for wheat, free competition among sellers or buyers would establish an equilibrium at e, corresponding to a price of $2 per bushel and a quantity traded of 1,000 million bushels per year. If government intervenes by setting a legal minimum price of $3 per bushel, a surplus of ab emerges. As price rises from the equilibrium level to the legal minimum, quantity demanded decreases along ea while quantity supplied increases along eb. Sellers are more than unhappy. In this example, their actual sales correspond to point a, not point b; thus, their revenue comes to $3 per bushel times 500 million bushels per year, or $1,500 million per year (shaded). This amount is considerably less than the hoped-for revenue from selling 1,500 million bushels. In the meantime, 1,500 − 500 = 1,000 million bushels per year (distance ab) cannot be sold and accumulate in silos.

mum prices for agricultural products ranging widely from almonds, barley, cheese, dates, flax seed, honey, milk, lemons, mohair, raisins, sorghum, and oats to peanuts, rice, soybeans, tobacco, and wool. Many state and local governments have engaged in similar actions. For almost four decades prior to 1976 (when a federal law repealed them), governments enacted **fair-trade laws,** which allowed any manufacturer to fix a minimum price for a product. If a single retailer agreed to it, all retailers were bound to it, even those who refused to sign an appropriate agreement with the manufacturer. Those selling for less could be enjoined, fined, and even jailed. Today, state and local governments fix prices for all kinds of things, ranging from electric power and liquor to insurance rates and taxi fares.

72 PART I *Basic Concepts*

EXAMPLE 3

Changing Equilibrium Prices: From Abundance to Scarcity

Sometimes the supply of something that people want is absolutely fixed, regardless of price. As a result, the supply line is vertical and stationary over time. If demand rises over time, a situation of abundance can gradually give way to one of scarcity. If demand fluctuates, times of abundance and scarcity can alternate. Look at Figure B; it can be used to explain many of the world's problems, of which we will consider two.

1. The Decline of the Whales. Let supply line S represent the annual "harvestable" number of whales, say 50,000—a number that people can hunt without depleting the whale population (because annual births exceed deaths from natural causes by this amount). In 1750, the demand for whales may have equaled D, as in panel (a). Even at a zero price (there was no fee for whale hunting), only 30,000 whales were hunted per year. Thus, there was no scarcity because demand at a zero price fell short of the supply. No one observed a problem; the whale population, let us imagine, was stationary despite people's hunting, being kept from growing not by people but by lack of food.

Now imagine ourselves in 1850. As in panel (b), demand has risen to D'. At a zero price, 50,000 whales are hunted, the very number nature supplies from a station-

FIGURE B

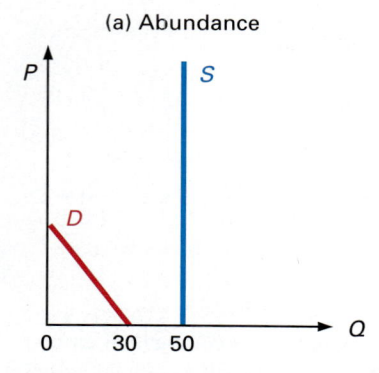

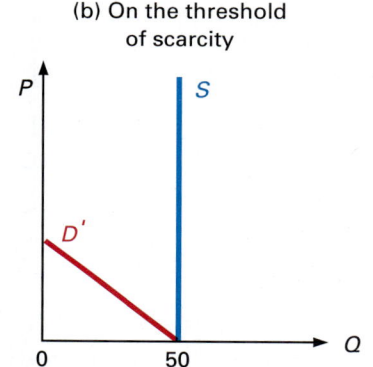

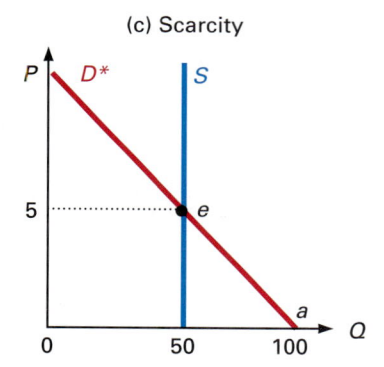

(a) Abundance (b) On the threshold of scarcity (c) Scarcity

floor of a room—as something "down below." As you can see, however, a price floor in the demand-and-supply diagram does not appear below equilibrium point e but *above* it. A price floor below e would be ineffective because higher equilibrium price would prevail.)

Government usually obliges sellers by taking additional steps beyond merely legislating the minimum price. Several possibilities exist. Figure 10 illustrates two of the more common approaches. Approach (a) saddles the government with unwanted stocks of the good in question, along with all the subsequent problems of storage and disposal; approach (b) avoids this additional expense and concern. Example 4 has more to say on the subject.

Price Ceilings

Other occasions exist when a government wants to help buyers rather than sellers. Accordingly, it legislates a **maximum price** or **price ceiling** below ary population of whales. Still, there is no scarcity; but society stands at the threshold of it. The demand, at a zero price, equals the supply.

Finally, consider ourselves in the present. As panel (c) shows, demand has risen to D^*, which exceeds supply at a zero price. Scarcity has arrived. As long as people are free to go out and hunt all the whales they want (without having to pay a fee for the privilege), people hunt 100,000 whales a year. But only 50,000 can be hunted if the whale population is to remain unchanged. As a result of the excessive hunting (point a), the population begins to decline, the supply line shifts left (not shown), and whales are in danger of extinction. A positive equilibrium price of $5,000 per whale (corresponding to point e) would cut the quantity demanded down along ae to the permissible level. Can you see how only an international agreement could enforce such limited sale of hunting rights?

2. *Airport Congestion.* Let supply line S represent the hourly number of runway operations at a major airport. Until more runways are built, only 50 airplanes can land or take off on the existing runway. Between 3 A.M. and 5 A.M. each day, demand may equal D, as in panel (a). Even at a zero price (without a fee for using the runway), only 30 planes care to use the runway. There is no scarcity because the demand, at a zero price, falls short of supply. No one complains about a problem.

Now consider the same airport between 1 P.M. and 3 P.M. on any day. As in panel (b), demand picks up and equals D'. Still, there is no problem. Even at a zero price, demand just equals supply. Finally, consider our airport between 4 P.M. and 6 P.M. on Fridays. Demand now equals D^*. Some 100 planes per hour want to use the runway; only 50 can do so. Scarcity exists. The airport manager has two choices.

First, fees can remain at zero, and a shortage of $100 - 50 = 50$ slots per hour will persist. There will be traffic congestion on the ramps and taxiways as planes wait for takeoff clearance. There will be stacks of airplanes circling 20 miles out, waiting for approach clearance and permission to land. Passengers will complain bitterly about all the delays.

Second, a fee of $500 per runway operation (corresponding to point e) could be charged on Friday afternoons only. This would cut the quantity demanded along ae from 100 to 50 slots per hour. Some planes (such as those carrying freight) would reschedule their operations to avoid the fee, others would pay it (and add the cost to each passenger's ticket price). Congestion would be gone.

---

the market equilibrium level with the understanding that transactions above that ceiling are henceforth illegal. Here, too, numerous examples exist, ranging from airport landing fees and apartment rents to tolls for bridges and highways and even prices of natural gas or sports events.

The establishment of below-equilibrium price ceilings also has two predictable consequences. Given the "law" of demand, the lower price typically increases quantity demanded. Given the "law" of supply, the lower price also typically lowers quantity supplied. Jointly, the two effects create a shortage, and government has a choice of ignoring it or dealing with it through direct rationing. In the former case, would-be buyers are likely to turn to **black markets,** in which goods are traded at illegal prices. The rationing approach, in turn, opens a Pandora's box of corruption and political favoritism as buyers attempt to influence the bureaucrats involved so as to have their rations increased or their

EXAMPLE 4

Of Milk and Sugar

Examples of what happens when government intervenes in otherwise competitive markets are provided by long-standing U.S. programs to support above-equilibrium prices of milk and sugar. (The government's dairy program dates back to 1937; the sugar program to 1933.) In a manner reminiscent of panel (a) of Figure 10, the 1990 Farm Bill committed the U.S. government to supporting a price floor of $10.10 per 100 pounds of fresh milk until 1995. This role is somewhat indirect through the purchase of butter, cheese, and dry milk by the Commodity Credit Corporation, an agency of the U.S. Department of Agriculture. Presumably, these purchases will raise the demand for fresh milk to keep the price up.

In the past, this program has cost taxpayers billions of dollars per year and has aroused the ire of many critics. Some critics were angry because this program vastly exceeded federal expenditures on other programs such as the arts and humanities, the National Park Service, the National Science Foundation, and Third World development projects. Other critics were dissatisfied because most of this money went to big farmers (who produce most of the dairy products put on the market) and not to small, poor farmers.

The 1990 Farm Bill also set a minimum price of 18¢ per pound of cane sugar and of 21.9 cents per pound of beet sugar. The Commodity Credit Corporation stands ready to make loans to producers equal to the value of their crop, calculated at these prices. The crop itself goes to the CCC as collateral. If the free market price is higher than the government price, farmers can reclaim their crops, sell them in the open market, and repay the loan. If the free market price is lower, farmers simply forfeit their crops to the government and owe nothing. Thus, the government becomes the buyer of last resort. In effect, taxpayers buy the crop and pay for storage and disposal costs as well. During fiscal years 1987–1989, U.S. taxpayers paid about $3 billion per year to sugar growers for the difference between government-set and free-market prices.

---

waiting times reduced. Figure 11 illustrates the problem. Example 5 and Example 6 have more to say on the subject of fixing prices that are too low.

Excise Taxes

In many instances, government collects revenue simply by imposing an **excise tax,** which is a tax imposed on each unit of a good traded in a market. The federal government imposes such taxes on alcohol, cigarettes, gasoline, tires, and more. State and local governments levy similar taxes on these and other goods, ranging broadly from appliances to automobiles, from clothing to hotel occupancy, and even on food. We can use our demand-and-supply model to analyze the likely effect of such taxes.

Consider Figure 12 and focus on the demand and supply lines alone. In the absence of taxation, equilibrium e would emerge. Price would equal $1 per gallon; quantity traded, 100 billion gallons per year. Now let government impose a tax of $1 per gallon. Some people think that sellers would raise the price to $2 per gallon, passing the entire tax burden on to buyers, but such analysis ignores the "law" of demand—shown in our graph by the leftward sloping demand line above point e. If the buyers' price did rise from $1 to $2 per gallon, the quantity demanded in our example would decrease to zero along ec. Sellers, on the other hand, could only count on keeping $1 of any $2 collected; the government would take the other dollar. Thus, sellers—looking at their $1 *net* price—would continue to supply a quantity corresponding to point e on the supply line, or 100 billion gallons per year.

Thus, when buyers demanded nothing (point *c*), sellers would supply *e* = *f* and a surplus of *cf* (100 billion gallons per year) would emerge. Surely, this situation is not an equilibrium.

Other people have a similarly mistaken idea. They think that sellers would simply have to absorb the entire tax burden and accept a lower net price. But such analysis ignores the "law" of supply—shown in our graph by the leftward sloping supply line below point *e*. If the sellers' net price did fall from $1 to $0 per gallon, the quantity supplied in our example would decrease to zero as well. Buyers—looking at the old $1 price—would, on the other hand, continue to demand a quantity corresponding to point *e* on the demand line, or 100 billion gallons per year. Thus, when sellers supplied nothing (point 0), buyers would demand *e* = *h* and a shortage of 0*h* (100 billion gallons per year) would emerge. This outcome could not be final either.

As you can guess from the preceeding discussion, the ultimate *equilibrium* in our example must lie between the two extremes just noted. After the

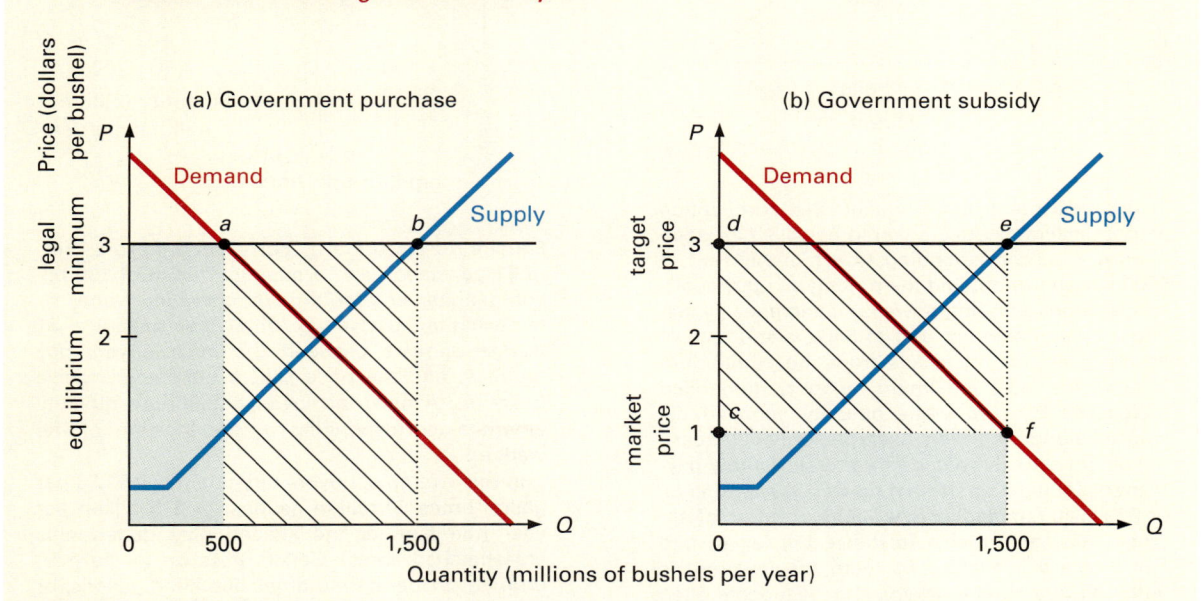

FIGURE 10 Dealing with the Surplus

This graph illustrates two of many approaches open to a government that has legislated an above-equilibrium minimum price (here of $3 per bushel) and has to deal with the ensuing surplus problem as well. First, as panel (a) demonstrates, regular consumers can buy whatever they are willing to take at the minimum price (point *a*). Subsequently, the government can use the taxpayers' money to buy up the surplus (*ab*). In this example, regular consumers end up spending $1,500 million per year (shaded area) and the government spends an additional $3,000 million per year (crosshatched area).

Second, as panel (b) demonstrates, regular consumers can be given the *entire* crop (*de*), which farmers supply when promised the "target" price of $3 per bushel. As point *f* indicates, these consumers will buy that crop, but only for $1 per bushel. Subsequently, the government can use the taxpayers' money to pay farmers a subsidy equal to the difference between the promised "target" price of $3 and the realized market price of $1. In this example, regular consumers end up spending $1,500 million per year (shaded area), and the government spends another $3,000 million per year (crosshatched area).

Note: It is only a coincidence that the shaded areas in the two panels and the crosshatched areas in the two panels are equal to each other.

FIGURE 11 Setting a Maximum Price for Apartment Rental

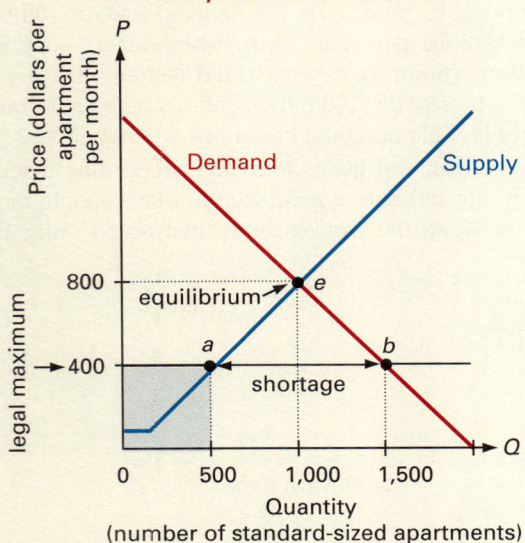

In this apartment-rental market, free competition among sellers or buyers would establish an equilibrium at *e,* corresponding to a monthly rent of $800 per apartment and the renting of 1,000 apartments. If government, however, intervenes by setting a legal maximum rent of $400, a shortage of *ab* emerges. As price falls from the equilibrium level to the legal maximum, quantity demanded increases along *eb* while quantity supplied decreases along *ea.* In this example, only 500 apartments are actually rented, for a total monthly payment of $400 per apartment times 500 apartments, or $200,000 (shaded). Yet would-be renters of another 1,000 apartments (distance *ab*) fail to find any that are available. To them the low rent is nothing but a cruel mockery. Note: Students often think of a maximum price or price *ceiling*—like the ceiling in a room—as something "high above." Yet, a price ceiling in a demand-and-supply diagram appears *below* equilibrium point *e.* (A ceiling above *e* would be ineffective because people would trade at the lower equilibrium price.)

FIGURE 12 Imposing an Excise Tax on Gasoline

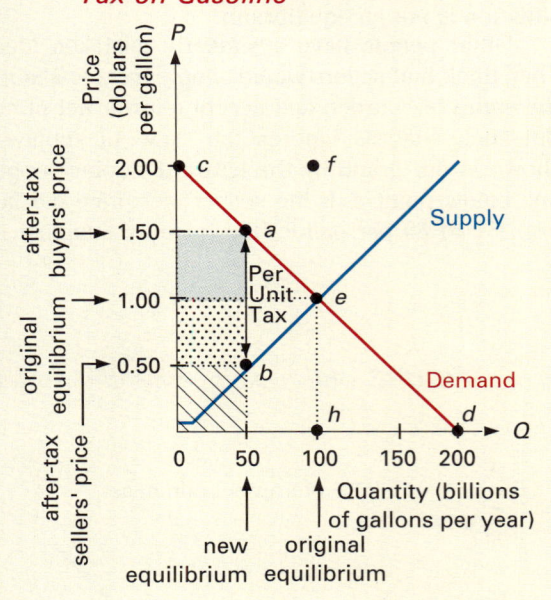

Equilibrium occurs at *e,* corresponding to a price of $1 per gallon and a quantity traded of 100 billion gallons per year. If government intervenes by imposing an excise tax of $1 per gallon, a $1 *wedge* appears between the price buyers pay (point *a*) and the price sellers ultimately receive (point *b*). A new and lower equilibrium quantity emerges (corresponding to the location of the wedge).

In this example, buyers ultimately pay $1.50 per gallon times 50 billion gallons, or $75 billion per year (the sum of the shaded plus dotted plus crosshatched areas). Sellers pass on to the government $1 per gallon times 50 billion gallons, or $50 billion per year (the sum of the shaded plus dotted areas). Thus the sellers' after-tax receipts only equal 50¢ per gallon times 50 billion gallons, or $25 billion per year (the crosshatched area). Compared to the original equilibrium price, buyers pay 50¢ more per gallon; sellers get 50¢ less. Thus, the tax burden, by coincidence, is equally shared.

excise tax has been imposed, the price paid by buyers must rise, but by less than the tax. This will cause buyers to reduce the quantity demanded. The net price received by sellers, on the other hand, must fall—again by less than the tax—and this will cause them to reduce the quantity supplied. When the fall in quantity demanded just matches the fall in quantity supplied, the new equilibrium has been reached. Fortunately for us, there is a simple, graphical way to find it.

1. Picture a vertical double arrow, such as *ab,* the length of which represents the government's tax per unit of product ($1 in our case).

2. Vertically place this double arrow between the demand and supply curves to the *left* of the old

EXAMPLE 5

The Story of Rent Control

The story depicted by Figure 11 has been confirmed by the experience of renters in many cities throughout the world. In the United States, rent control was introduced in New York in 1943 and has since spread to many other cities, ranging from Boston and Washington, D.C., to Los Angeles and San Francisco, and to well over 200 smaller towns. At the time of their enactment, rent-control laws are typically justified as a long-overdue means of putting greedy, villainous landlords in their place and of helping their innocent, overcharged victims.

Inevitably, the kind of shortage depicted by distance *ab* in Figure 11 develops and tends to grow worse over time. The short-run decrease in quantity supplied (along *ea*) as landlords quickly convert rent-controlled apartments to uncontrolled office space, private condominiums, and similar alternative uses is followed by decreases in long-run supply (not shown in Figure 11). Such a leftward shift of the entire supply line occurs when new construction comes to a halt and existing rental units disappear. At first, landlords skimp on maintenance as their profits are squeezed between fixed revenues and rising costs. A vicious circle is set up. Poor maintenance of electrical wiring turns buildings into firetraps and causes accidents, so insurance rates go up. So do city taxes for fire protection. Lack of janitorial services forces people to share water facilities. Before long, tenants end up living in vermin-infested, badly ventilated quarters. Children get lead poisoning from eating peeling paint. Everyone gets sick from breathing garbage processed by inefficient incinerators. Everyone freezes in winter when old furnaces break down and go untended. In anger, residents turn to vandalism. Insurance rates go up some more, as do city taxes for police protection.

Eventually, the rental units become so dilapidated as to be unlivable. Finally, instead of paying taxes on useless buildings, landlords abandon them, as happened to 200,000 units in New York between 1965 and 1975. In due time, most abandoned buildings fall victim to vandals who strip them of heating, plumbing, electrical installations, windows, paneling, flooring, and stairways. Before long, they are littered with garbage, blackened by arsonists, and damaged beyond repair. The charred rubble becomes inhabited by homeless people. Thus entire slums are born, and what remains are eyesores and threats to public health and safety.

In the meantime, a black market develops in which people on waiting lists attempt to acquire scarce rental units at above-ceiling prices. A million different methods are in common use. They range from outright bribes to paying "key money" to requiring any new tenant to buy worthless furniture at incredibly inflated prices.

As with so many price-fixing programs, there is no certainty that this program truly helps the poor. In New York City, for example, many tenants in rent-controlled apartments (who recently paid a median rent of $330 a month) are middle and upper income families. Many landlords are small investors of moderate income.

Source: Heinz Kohler, *Economics and Urban Problems* (Lexington, MA: D. C. Heath and Co., 1973), pp. 267–270.

EXAMPLE 6

Trading Human Body Parts

An extreme example of U.S. government price fixing is provided by the National Organ Transplant Act of 1984. By making the purchase or sale of human organs a felony, the law effectively set the legal price at zero. Yet there is a large potential market for all kinds of human body parts, ranging from kidneys, hearts, and livers to pancreas, lungs, and even skeletons. The accompanying Figure C depicts a potential market for kidneys. Thousands of Americans are waiting for kidney transplants, an operation that has been blessed with soaring success rates. At a zero price, the quantity demanded might equal 0B; as with all goods, we can expect that quantity to fall at increasingly higher positive prices. At a price of 0C, perhaps, no one would be

FIGURE C

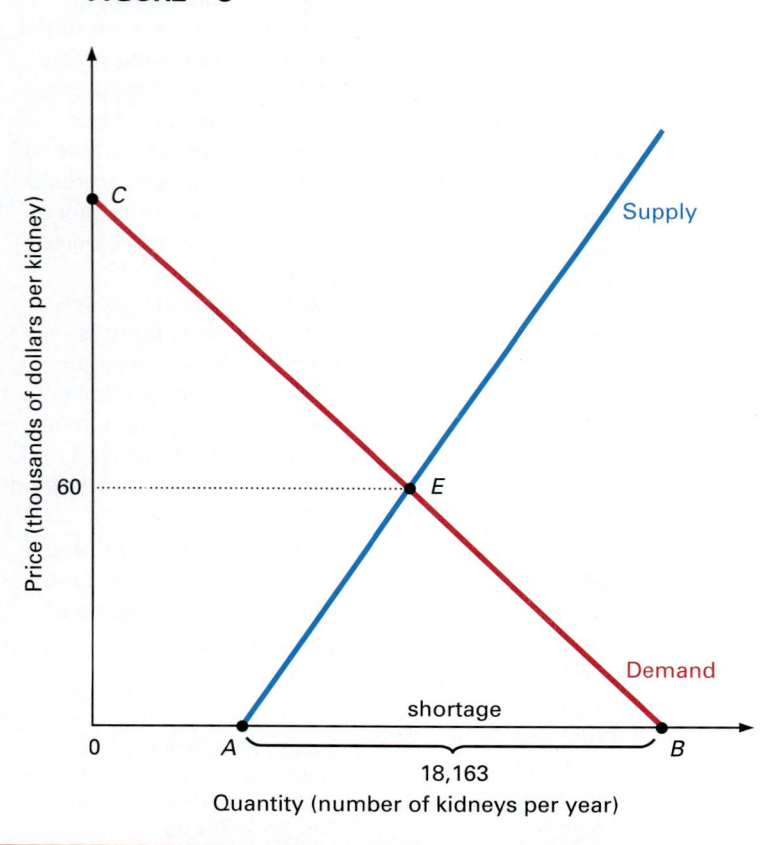

1991 Organ shortages, U.S.	
Kidneys	18,163
Hearts	1,884
Livers	1,344
Pancreas	516
Lungs	394
Heart/Lung Combinations	182

able and willing to buy kidneys. Potential recipients as well as their insurance companies would be equally unable to afford them.

The quantity supplied at a zero price, however, is not zero. It equals 0A because the government has no objections to people *donating* kidneys. Indeed, public opinion polls show that a large majority of Americans claim to be willing to give away their organs before or after death. Quite possibly, Americans like to impress questioners with their altruism; in fact, relatively few organs are donated. The result is a predictable shortage at the zero price, such as AB = 18,163 kidneys in Figure C. As the accompanying table shows, this figure equals the estimated 1991 shortage in the United States. Similar but less severe shortages existed for other organs. As a result, in 1990, some 2,206 Americans died while awaiting a transplant operation.

Why is the quantity supplied so low relative to the quantity demanded at the zero price? Medical authorities have suggested a number of reasons: The timing of a request for an organ donation tends to be disastrous; just when family members learn of a loved one's death, they are asked to hand over some of the organs—*now*. Most people cannot tolerate the thought of such a mutilation. In addition, many people believe that the potential recipients are unworthy. They may have caused their liver disease by their own drinking, for example, or may have *bought* their way to the top of the transplant list, leaving poorer persons behind.

Many economists, on the other hand, think that the shortage problem would disappear with proper monetary incentives. In our example, a $60,000 price for a kidney (the actual price recently paid in Europe) would eliminate the shortage by stimulating quantity supplied along AE and reducing quantity demanded along BE. Others have suggested indirect ways of encouraging greater supply. These might include federal tax benefits to the donor's estate or the governmental assumption of funeral expenses.

In other countries, where trade in organs and other body parts has been allowed, shortages have quickly disappeared as positive equilibrium prices have been established by demand and supply. By the same token, any interruption in supply has led to hefty price increases, just as our diagram would predict. Here is a case in point: Medical and dental schools require a continual supply of skeletons for anatomy classes. Plastic substitutes and even three-dimensional paper models simply cannot take the place of the real thing. Substitutes lack subtle detail, such as the contours showing where muscles had been attached. Accordingly, there exists a strong worldwide demand for skeletons. For decades, India supplied 15,000 a year—skeletons of all sizes and shapes, along with 50,000 skulls and other bones. Then, in 1985, the Indian government banned "this repulsive and distasteful trade." The price of skeletons soared.

Sources: Gary Putka, "Skeleton Dealers Get Jitters as They Find Nothing in the Closet," *The Wall Street Journal,* April 18, 1986, pp. 1 and 9; Glenn Ruffenach, "Trying to Cure Shortage of Organ Donors," *The Wall Street Journal,* March 13, 1991, p. B1.

IDEAS IN HISTORY

The Scissors Diagram

Economists used to be embroiled in controversy about the determinants of market prices. Some explained them by *demand* and the subjectively felt enjoyment or "utility" prospective buyers hoped to gain from consumption. Why else, argued the advocates of this view, are people ready to pay so much more for a pound of diamonds than a pound of coal? Diamonds are forever. Others held a contrary view, which seemed to make just as much sense on the surface. They explained market prices by *supply* and the objectively measured cost prospective sellers had to incur during production. Many more resources had to be expended to gather a pound of diamonds than a pound of coal.

Along came Alfred Marshall (1842–1924). He started his life in a suburb of London, England (as the son of a Bank of England cashier who once wrote a tract on *Man's Rights and Women's Duties*) and ended up as Cambridge University's most famous professor of political economy. Like Adam Smith, Marshall was a profoundly learned man, overflowing with ideas covering fields as diverse as biology, economics, history, mathematics, and philosophy. The bulk of his work is contained in *Principles of Economics* (1890). It became the leading text for decades in the English-speaking world, going through eight editions in Marshall's lifetime.

Even today, many copies of this book are sold every year, which is not surprising given that almost the entire corpus of modern microeconomics can be traced to some suggestion by Marshall. He was a master of *partial analysis*, which makes use of the "other-things-being equal" clause introduced in this chapter. (Marshall and many modern economists call it the *ceteris paribus* clause by its Latin name.) Marshall also introduced diagrammatic analysis, the impact of which any comparison of modern economics texts with pre-Marshallian ones can quickly show. Most of all, Marshall is known for solving the controversy about the market price. That price, he argued, is determined neither by demand alone nor by supply alone. Look at Figure 1 by itself and you cannot tell which price will come to prevail. Separately look at Figure 3 and you will be equally stumped. Look at the two lines together, as in Figure 5 and the answer is obvious.

Marshall referred to the kind of diagram pictured in Figure 5 as a *scissors diagram* because the demand and supply lines shown there resemble a pair of open scissors. As he put it,

We might as reasonably dispute whether it is the upper or the under blade of a pair of scissors that cuts a piece of paper, as whether value is governed by utility or cost of production. It is true that when one blade is held still, and the cutting is effected by moving the other, we may say with careless brevity that the cutting is done by the second; but the statement is not strictly accurate, and it is to be excused only so long as it claims to be merely a popular and not a strictly scientific account of what happens.[1]

Marshall's open scissors, we should note, can be held in many different ways; the many different graphs of demand and supply found in this chapter and later ones testify to this fact.

---

[1] Alfred Marshall, *Principles of Economics,* 8th ed. (London: Macmillan, 1922), p. 348.

Source: Heinz Kohler, *Intermediate Microeconomics: Theory and Applications,* 1st ed. (Glenview, IL: Scott, Foresman and Co., 1982), pp. 190–191. Adapted with permission.

equilibrium point *e* in such a way that its upper tip touches the demand line (*a*) while its lower tip touches the supply line (*b*).

3. Point *a* will indicate the new equilibrium as seen by buyers; point *b* will indicate the new equilibrium as seen by sellers.

This procedure has already been performed in Figure 12. Buyers ultimately pay $1.50 per gallon and—according to their demand line—demand 50 billion gallons of gasoline per year (point *a*). Sellers, on the other hand, collect $1.50 from buyers but must pass on $1 to the government, keeping only 50¢ per gallon for themselves. According to their supply line, sellers who receive 50¢ per gallon will supply 50 billion gallons of gasoline per year (point *b*). Demand again equals supply. As the caption to Figure 12 indicates, the government collects $50 billion in taxes.

A Final Note on Excise Taxes

This approach to figuring the effect of excise taxation is the simplest one, but it has one drawback. The three-step procedure appears to provide a solution as if by magic. Alternative approaches without that drawback exist; unfortunately, they are more complicated. One alternative assumes that sellers have to send the tax money to the government and finds the solution by shifting the entire supply line vertically upward by the amount of the excise tax, here $1. This shift signifies that under these circumstances (when sellers have to give $1 to the government for every gallon they sell), sellers would continue to supply any given quantity only if assured receipt of an extra $1 per gallon. If we drew this new supply line in Figure 12, it would be a straight line passing through points *a* and *f*. Its intersection with demand (*a*) would indicate the new price to buyers; the net price to sellers would be $1 less, just as we figured earlier.

Another alternative assumes that *buyers* have to send the tax money to the government and finds the solution by shifting the entire demand line vertically downward by the amount of the excise tax, here $1. This shift signifies that when buyers have to give $1 to the government for every gallon they buy, buyers would continue to demand any given quantity only if assured a price at the pump that was $1 per gallon lower than before. If we drew such a new demand line in Figure 12, it would be a straight line passing through points *b* and *h*. Its intersection with supply (*b*) would indicate the new price to sellers; the ultimate price to buyers would be $1 more. Again, this result is the same as our earlier ones.

In the case of an excise tax, the **economic tax incidence,** the way in which the real burden of the tax is ultimately apportioned among people, is the same regardless of the **statutory tax incidence,** the way in which the monetary burden of the tax is officially apportioned among people. The tax law may place the responsibility of sending the tax payment to the government entirely on sellers or entirely on buyers. It does not matter; the economic tax incidence is the same. In our example (but not always), half the burden falls on buyers (shaded area in Figure 12), the other half falls on sellers (dotted area).

Summary

1. This chapter elaborates upon the fundamental relationships found in the capitalist market economy by focusing on the market for a single good. In such a market, households appear as consumers who demand it, firms appear as producers who supply it.

2. According to the "law" of demand, other things being equal, as the price of an item falls, the quantity demanded by buyers tends to increase; the opposite is also true (as the price of an item rises, the quantity demanded tends to decrease).

3. The "law" of demand can be illustrated by a demand schedule, which can be graphed as a demand line. Economists have a special name for a movement from one row to the next in a de-

mand schedule or from one point to another on a demand line. They refer to a change in the quantity of an item that buyers are ready to purchase as a *change in quantity demanded* if this quantity change is due to a change in the item's own price, other things being equal. Graphically, this denotes a *movement along* a given demand line.

4. In contrast, economists refer to a change in the quantity of an item that buyers are ready to purchase as a *change in demand* if this quantity change is due to a change in some factor *other than* the item's own price, all else being equal. Graphically, a *shift* of an entire demand line from one position to another occurs. Such a shift results from a change in another good's price, a change in consumer income, in consumer tastes, and for many other reasons.

5. According to the "law" of supply, other things being equal, as the price of an item falls, the quantity supplied by sellers tends to decrease; the opposite is also true (as the price of an item rises, the quantity supplied tends to increase).

6. The "law" of supply can be illustrated by a supply schedule, which can be graphed as a supply line. Economists have a special name for a movement from one row to the next in a supply schedule or from one point to another on a supply line. They refer to a change in the quantity of an item that sellers are ready to provide as a *change in quantity supplied* if this quantity change is due to a change in the item's own price, other things being equal. Graphically, this denotes a *movement along* a given supply line.

7. In contrast, economists refer to a change in the quantity of an item that sellers are ready to provide as a *change in supply* if this quantity change is due to a change in some factor *other than* the item's own price, all else being equal. Graphically, this is denoted by a *shift* of an entire supply line from one position to another. Such a shift results from changes in the prices of productive inputs, in technology, and for other reasons.

8. When numerous potential buyers and numerous potential sellers meet in a market, an *equilibrium* emerges in which there is no innate tendency for price or quantity to change (because quantity demanded and quantity supplied are just equal to one another). Such an equilibrium is reached because competition among sellers reduces price in the face of surpluses, while competition among buyers raises price in the face of shortages.

9. While it contains no *innate* tendency to change, a market equilibrium is far from unchangeable. It will change whenever there are changes in demand, in supply, or both.

10. Government intervention in markets is common; it takes numerous forms. Discussed are three approaches to changing the equilibrium outcome that would otherwise occur: the setting of price floors, the setting of price ceilings, and the imposition of excise taxes.

Key Concepts

black markets	equilibrium	normal goods
change in demand	excise tax	price ceiling
change in quantity demanded	fair-trade laws	price floor
change in quantity supplied	independent goods	shortage
change in supply	inferior goods	statutory tax incidence
complementary goods	"law" of demand	substitute goods
demand line	"law" of supply	supply line
demand schedule	maximum price	supply schedule
economic tax incidence	minimum price	surplus

Questions and Problems

1. The following table contains a large city's demand schedule for sewage-dumping opportunities. Depending on the fee charged by those who control a nearby river, the city would like to dump raw sewage into it in the quantities indicated. Plot the schedule as a demand line.

   A Demand Schedule for Sewage-Dumping Opportunities

Alternative (1)	Price (thousands of dollars per ton) (2)	Quantity Demanded (millions of tons dumped per year) (3)
A	10	0
B	8	1.8
C	6	3.6
D	4	5.4
E	2	7.2
F	0	9.0

2. The caption of Table 1 restricts permissible prices to the $0 to $10 range. The caption of Table 2 imposes a similar restriction for prices below $1. What is the reason for these restrictions?

3. Consider the following list of paired goods. Identify them as complementary goods, independent goods, or substitute goods:
   a. shirts and neckties
   b. airline travel and rental cars
   c. home videos and drive-in movies
   d. honey and oranges
   e. wool and cotton
   f. eggs and hashbrowns
   g. cereal and footballs
   h. coal and natural gas
   i. cars and highways
   j. peanut butter and jelly
   k. TV sets and electricity
   l. coffee and cream
   m. coffee and tea
   n. right shoes and left shoes
   o. bacon and eggs
   p. rifles and ammunition
   q. red apples and yellow apples
   r. Exxon gas and Mobil gas
   s. diapers and oil filters
   t. shoes and laces
   u. new houses and old houses
   v. rail freight and truck freight
   w. turkeys and cranberry sauce
   x. tuna and salmon
   y. Federal Express and UPS
   z. strawberries and textbooks

4. What would you expect to happen to the demand for beef if, simultaneously, the price of pork fell, the price of potatoes rose, consumer income fell, and population declined? What if, in addition, people came to believe that eating beef made them live longer?

5. Reread the captions to Tables 1 and 2. Then arithmetically find the equilibrium solution, given in the shaded row of Table 3.

6. If there were a shortage or surplus in a real-world market, what signs of it could one probably observe?

7. What would be the effects, in a competitive market, on equilibrium price and quantity of the following *simultaneous* changes:
   a. demand rises, supply rises
   b. demand rises, supply falls
   c. demand falls, supply rises
   d. demand falls, supply falls

8. Figure 8 analyzed a change in equilibrium resulting from increased demand, as in panel (b) of Figure 7. Perform a similar analysis for panels (a), (c), and (d) of Figure 7.

9. Overheard in an introductory economics class: "In a competitive market, if price rises, demand falls, but falling demand lowers price, so we end up where we started." Evaluate.

10. In mid-1972, the U.S. wheat price was $1.70 per bushel. Then the Soviet Union entered the market, buying 19 million metric tons of wheat (one quarter of the U.S. crop). By the end of the summer, the price of wheat was $5 per bushel. Even the per-bushel price of rye (which the Soviets did not buy) jumped from $1.01 to $3.86, that of oats from 80¢ to $2.06, and that of soy-

beans from $3.50 to $12. Can you explain these events?

11. In the 1980s, Humpty Dumpty had a great fall. U.S. egg prices plummeted, as did the number of egg producers. Can you think of any reasons?

12. The equilibrium price depicted in Figure 5 is *stable,* that is, it would be reestablished through competition if it ever rose above or fell below this level. What would competition do, however, if market demand had the peculiar (*upward*-sloping) position given in the accompanying figure and then the price ever moved away from its equilibrium at *e*?

13. Ms. A: "I am surprised. This chapter's Figure 5, looks very much like Chapter 1's Figure 8, The Optimization Principle."
    Ms. B: "Of course. These graphs show pretty much the same thing."
    What do you think?

14. This chapter's Figure 10 illustrated two ways of dealing with surpluses that price floors might create. Can you think of a third approach?

15. Reconsider this chapter's Problem 1 and its answer at the back of the book. How could a state or federal government get this city to restrict its sewage dumping from a present 9 million tons per year to 3.6 million tons? To 1.8 million tons? To zero? In each case, what would you expect the city to do with its sewage?

16. This chapter's entire discussion has focused on markets for *goods.* Do you think graphs such as Figures 5, 9, or 11 could be equally applied to markets for *resources*? If so, can you think of examples?

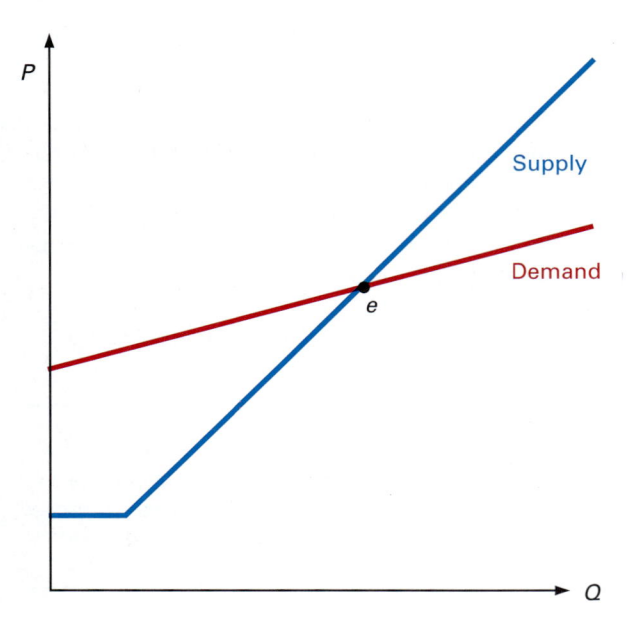

17. Figure 12 discusses the effects of an excise tax when the burden is *equally* shared by buyers (shaded area) and sellers (dotted area). What would create an *unequal* sharing of this burden?

18. Figure 12 discusses the effects of an excise tax. What do you think would be the effects of an excise *subsidy,* which provides a fixed dollar grant to buyers or sellers for each unit traded?

CHAPTER 4

INTERNATIONAL TRADE AND THE WEALTH OF NATIONS

Preview

The U.S. economy does not exist in isolation; in fact, it is becoming increasingly integrated with other economies throughout the world. As a result, everything that economists study—from the microeconomic behavior of individual firms and financial markets to the macroeconomic issues of economic growth, recession, and inflation—is connected to the global economic setting. This chapter introduces the theory of comparative advantage, which shows why countries that specialize and trade become richer in the process. And although international trade can increase the availability of goods to a country as a whole, it can harm some people, which produces a call for government protection. The types of governmental responses are discussed, and the history of U.S. trade policy is reviewed.

Examples

1. The U.S. Sugar Import Quota
2. A Voluntary Export Restraint: The U.S.-Japanese Automobile Agreement
3. Banning Trade to Save the Elephant
4. The Guiding Hand of MITI
5. The Consumer Cost of Import Restrictions
6. The New North America

Ideas in History

The Theory of Comparative Advantage
The Strategic Trade Model

Since the end of World War II, the United States economy has exhibited a remarkable trend: an ever-increasing integration—through international flows of goods, resources, and financial capital—with the economies of other countries throughout the world. The U.S. exports of commodities alone rose from $11.8 billion in 1946, then equal to 5.5 percent of the gross national product or GNP, to $389.3 billion or 7.1 percent of the GNP in 1990. (The gross national product is a comprehensive measure of the nation's annual production of new commodities and services. The concept is discussed in detail in the macroeconomics section of this book.) Similarly, the U.S. imports of commodities rose from $5.1 billion in 1946 (2.4 percent of the GNP) to $498.0 billion in 1990 (9.1 percent of the GNP). For U.S. trading partners, the volume of international trade is typically smaller, but the size of commodity exports or imports (the two tend to be roughly equal to one another) as a *percentage* of national output is often larger. In recent years, that percentage hovered around 16 in Japan, 30 in both Canada and Great Britain, and 33 in Germany.

Figure 1 summarizes the nature of U.S. merchandise trade in a recent year. Trade in services, financial capital, and the like is excluded from this illustration. What explains the emergence of international trade and its geographic and product composition?

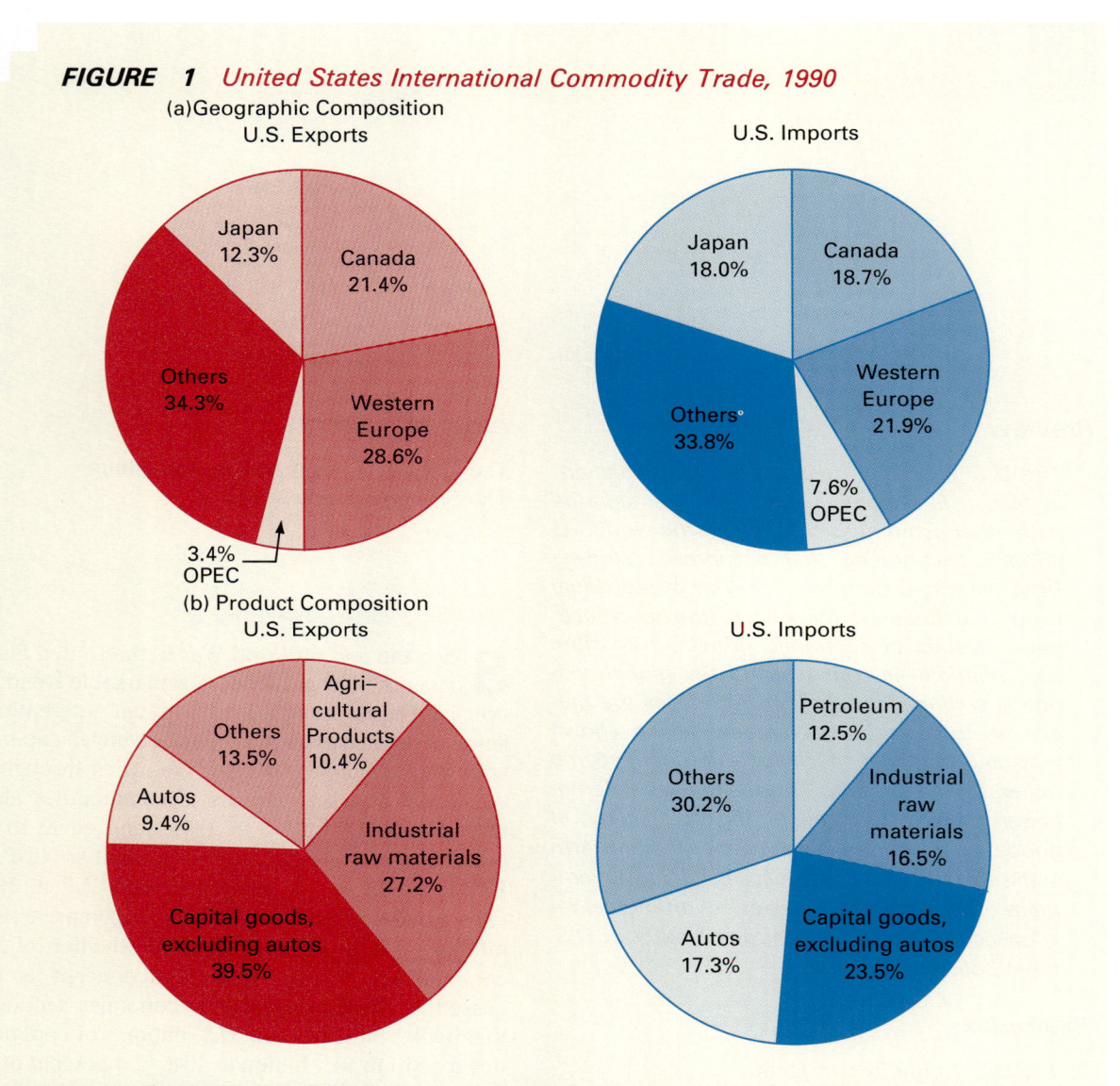

FIGURE 1 *United States International Commodity Trade, 1990*

(a) Geographic Composition

U.S. Exports:
- Canada 21.4%
- Western Europe 28.6%
- OPEC 3.4%
- Others 34.3%
- Japan 12.3%

U.S. Imports:
- Canada 18.7%
- Western Europe 21.9%
- OPEC 7.6%
- Others 33.8%
- Japan 18.0%

(b) Product Composition

U.S. Exports:
- Agricultural Products 10.4%
- Industrial raw materials 27.2%
- Capital goods, excluding autos 39.5%
- Autos 9.4%
- Others 13.5%

U.S. Imports:
- Petroleum 12.5%
- Industrial raw materials 16.5%
- Capital goods, excluding autos 23.5%
- Autos 17.3%
- Others 30.2%

As these graphs illustrate, the 1990 commodity trade between the United States and other countries ($389.3 billion in U.S. exports and $498.0 billion in U.S. imports) ranged widely with respect to geography—panel (a)—as well as product type—panel (b).

Note: The Organization of Petroleum Exporting Countries, OPEC, includes Algeria, Ecuador, Gabon, Indonesia, Iran, Iraq, Kuwait, Libya, Nigeria, Qatar, Saudi Arabia, the United Arab Emirates, and Venezuela.

Source: United States Department of Commerce, *Survey of Current Business,* March 1991, pp. 40, 51, and 52.

Absolute Advantage Versus Comparative Advantage

Economists who first considered the reasons for international trade focused on the possibility that one country might have an *absolute advantage* over another country in the production of a good, in the sense that it took fewer units of resources to produce a unit of the good. Adam Smith, for example, explained international trade in the same way he explained interpersonal trade. On one occasion, Smith pictured groups of primitive hunters, all of whom had equal access to abundant natural resources and who relied exclusively on their own labor and not on fancy capital goods ("stock" as he called it) to catch their prey. If one hunter could catch a beaver in two days, while another took four days, the former, Smith thought, would soon specialize in beaver hunting. Similarly, if one hunter could kill a deer in three days, while another could do it in one day, the latter would specialize in the hunting of deer. Before long, specialization based on absolute advantage would give rise to an exchange of goods at terms reflecting the minimum necessary labor time needed to produce each good. As Smith put it,

> *In that early and rude state of society which precedes both the accumulation of stock and the appropriation of land, the proportion between the quantities of labor necessary for acquiring different objects seems to be the only circumstance which can afford any rule for exchanging them for one another. If, among a nation of hunters, for example, it usually costs twice the labor to kill a beaver which it does to kill a deer, one beaver should naturally exchange for or be worth two deer. It is natural that what is usually the produce of two days' or two hours' labor, should be worth double of what is usually the produce of one day's or one hour's labor.*[1]

In short, if B-people were best at hunting beavers and needed 2 units of labor for each, while D-people were best at hunting deer and needed 1 unit of labor for each, then B-people would specialize in beaver production, D-people would specialize in deer production, and they would trade 1 beaver for 2 deer (because each of these quantities would contain the same quantity of labor).

The **theory of absolute advantage** explained *international* trade similarly. It claimed that citizens of every nation would specialize in the production and export of those goods they could produce with fewer units of resources than anyone else. Nations would import other goods, the production of which required fewer resources elsewhere. Thus, the nation that needed the fewest units of resources to produce clothing would specialize in producing clothing and would export it in exchange for other products. These imported products might include food that could be produced with the fewest units of resources in another place.

David Ricardo, however, had a different idea of why countries engaged in international trade. (See Ideas in History, The Theory of Comparative Advantage.) Absolute advantage, Ricardo argued, was not necessary for mutually beneficial international trade. One trading partner might be absolutely inferior in the production of every single good, thus requiring more resources per unit of each good than any other country. But, mutually beneficial trade is still possible provided the country is not equally bad at producing everything and has, therefore, a *comparative advantage* in the production of some good. According to Ricardo's **theory of comparative advantage,** mutually beneficial trade between two countries arises—regardless of the presence or absence of absolute advantage—whenever one country is *relatively* better at producing a good than the other country. This fact is indicated by the country's ability to produce a good at a lower opportunity cost (measured in terms of other goods forgone).

Given the data of Table 1, England has an absolute disadvantage in producing cloth as well as wine. Portugal has an absolute advantage in both. Ricardo, however, asks us to look at *opportunity costs*.

In England the same amount of resources (100 hours of labor) can make *either* 10 square yards of cloth *or* 100 gallons of wine. The opportunity cost of 10 square yards is 100 gallons (and that of 1 square yard is 100/10 or 10 gallons). Likewise, England's opportunity cost of 100 gallons is 10 square

---

[1] Adam Smith, *An Inquiry into the Nature and Causes of the Wealth of Nations* (Homewood, IL: Richard D. Irwin, 1776/1963), Book 1, Chap. 6, p. 38.

TABLE 1 Ricardo's Insight

(a) Labor Needed per Unit of Output

	England	Portugal
Cloth	10 hours	5 hours
Wine	1 hour	1/5 hour

(b) Output Producible by 100 Labor Hours

	England	Portugal
Cloth	10 square yards	20 square yards
Wine	100 gallons	500 gallons

Assuming that labor alone is required to produce cloth or wine, these data indicate that England is inferior (has an absolute disadvantage) and Portugal is superior (has an absolute advantage) in the production of both goods. The production of one unit of either good requires more labor in England than in Portugal (panel a), which implies that a given amount of labor (such as 100 hours) produces less of either good in England than in Portugal (panel b). Nevertheless, Ricardo noted, mutually beneficial trade is possible because England is *relatively* better at making cloth and Portugal at making wine.

---

yards (and that of 1 gallon is 10/100 or 1/10 square yard).

In Portugal the same resources (100 hours of labor) can make *either* 20 square yards of cloth *or* 500 gallons of wine. The opportunity cost of 20 square yards is 500 gallons (and that of 1 square yard is 500/20 or 25 gallons). Likewise, Portugal's opportunity cost of 500 gallons is 20 square yards (and that of 1 gallon is 20/500 or 1/25 square yard). All this information is summarized in Table 2.

Now consider Ricardo's surprising conclusion (based on either row (a) or row (b) of Table 2). If England produced another unit of cloth (marginalist thinking), it would have to give up making 10 gallons of wine.

England: +1 cloth, −10 wine

If Portugal produced one fewer unit of cloth, it could produce 25 additional gallons of wine.

Portugal: −1 cloth, +25 wine

If these changes were made simultaneously, the world would be richer by 15 gallons of wine—despite using no more resources than before. Subsequently, the two countries could trade: England might export 1 square yard of cloth for 15 gallons of wine. As a result, *both countries would be better off at the same time.*

In England, the production of cloth would be up by 1 square yard, but so would exports. The British would be left with the same amount of cloth as before. The production of wine would be down by 10 gallons, but imports would be up by 15 gallons. The British would have 5 extra gallons of wine, their reward from specialization and trade.

In Portugal, the production of cloth would be down by 1 square yard, but imports would be up by 1 square yard. The Portuguese would have the same amount of cloth as before. The production of wine would be up by 25 gallons, but exports would be up by 15 gallons. The Portuguese would have 10 extra gallons of wine, their reward from specialization and trade.

Clearly, it is no accident that the net gain of the

TABLE 2 Opportunity Costs

	England	Portugal
(a) Per 1 square yard of cloth:	10 gallons of wine	25 gallons of wine
(b) Per 1 gallon of wine:	1/10 square yard of cloth	1/25 square yard of cloth

As the shaded cells in this table indicate, in terms of other goods forgone, cloth is cheaper in England, wine is cheaper in Portugal. Thus England has a comparative advantage in making cloth, Portugal in making wine.

British (+5 gallons of wine) plus the net gain of the Portuguese (+10 gallons of wine) equals the world's output gain (+15 gallons of wine).

Comparative Advantage: A Graphical Illustration

The theory of comparative advantage can be illustrated graphically with two countries' production possibilities frontiers. Consider Figure 2. Imagine the United States initially operating on its production possibilities frontier at point *A*, while Japan is operating on its frontier at *F*. The United States has a comparative advantage in the production of rice. In the vicinity of *A* in the United States, the opportunity cost per unit of rice is roughly 1/10 or .1 unit of steel, but in the vicinity of *F* in Japan it is roughly 4/10 or .4 units of steel. By implication, Japan has a comparative advantage in the production of steel. The opportunity cost per unit of steel near *F* in Japan is roughly 10/4 or 2.5 units of rice. Near *A* in the United States it comes to roughly 10 units of rice.

Let the United States specialize in rice (produce more rice at the expense of steel) and let Japan specialize in steel (produce more steel at the expense of rice). Following the black arrows, the United States might move from *A* to *B* (producing 1 less unit of steel) and on to *C* (producing 10 more units of rice). At the same time, Japan might move from *F* to *G* (producing 10 fewer units of rice) and on to *H* (producing 4 more units of steel). Being now positioned at points *C* and *H*, the world as a whole has the same amount of rice (10 more units in the United States, 10 fewer units in Japan), but it has 3 more units of steel (1 less unit in the United States, 4 more units in Japan). Thus, there is a net gain of 3 units of steel, attributable to a reallocation of resources within each country from one industry to another.

Subsequently, international trade can enable both countries to share this net gain. Following the colored arrows, let the United States import 2 units of Japanese steel (*CD*) and export 10 units of rice (*DE*). The United States will end up at *E*, with a net gain of 1 unit of steel. As Japan receives U.S. rice (*DE* = *HI*) and pays for it by exporting steel (*IK* = *CD*), Japan ends up at *K*, with a net gain of 2 units of steel. Thus *both* countries are better off at the same time. Naturally, the U.S. net gain (+1 unit of steel) plus the Japanese net gain (+2 units of steel) equals the world's net gain (+3 units of steel).

Figure 2 also provides a strong hint concerning the determinants of comparative advantages. Because they are endowed with different quantities and qualities of human, natural, and capital resources and frequently with different technical knowledge, different countries have differently shaped production possibilities frontiers. In addition, people in different countries have different preferences and make different choices; thus, they end up at radically different points on the frontiers, as at *A* and *F*. For all of these reasons, the **marginal rate of transformation,** or the rate at which people can exchange, in the process of production, a little bit of one good for a little bit of another, differs as well. This rate is shown in Figure 2 by the exaggerated "triangles" *ABC* and *FGH*. Differences in these triangles imply differences in opportunity costs.

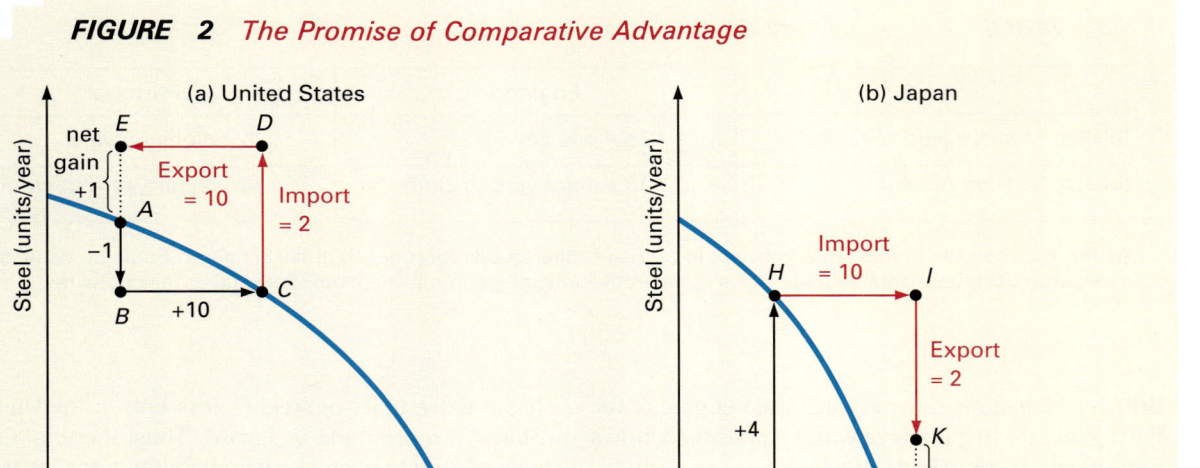

FIGURE 2 *The Promise of Comparative Advantage*

By specializing according to comparative advantage, nations can be richer than otherwise. In this example, the United States moves from A to C and Japan moves from F to H along the respective production possibilities frontiers. These internal reallocations of resources (black arrows) leave the world's output of rice unchanged, but raise the world's output of steel by 3 units. Subsequent international trade distributes this gain (colored arrows). In the end, both countries have the same amount of rice, but both have more steel. Both can consume combinations of goods (at E and K, respectively) that lie beyond their domestic production possibilities. Thus, scarcity is less intense than before.

Demand and Supply Revisited: The Market for Foreign Exchange

The importance of Figure 2 can hardly be exaggerated. Although scarcity is present in all nations, cooperation among nations can lift people beyond the confines of their domestic production possibilities frontiers and dramatically reduce scarcity. Economists everywhere are well aware of this fact, but how is the great promise of Ricardo's theory realized in everyday life? The answer depends on the type of economic system we consider.

In centrally planned command economies, such as those of Eastern Europe during Stalin's time, central planners routinely met to make the type of specialization and trade decisions that Figure 2 illustrates. In 1949, for example, the Soviet Union and her satellites formed a Council for Mutual Economic Assistance (frequently abbreviated as Comecon or CMEA) for just such a purpose. At one point, its members decided that Albania should specialize in early potatoes, Bulgaria in industrial sewing machines, Czechoslovakia in sugar beet combines, East Germany in plastics, Hungary in aluminum products, Poland in horticultural tractors, Rumania

TABLE 3 Monetary Prices

	United States	Japan
Steel	$100/unit	¥10,000/unit
Rice	$10/unit	¥4,000/unit

In market economies, the marginal rate of transformation of two goods tends to be reflected in their relative market prices. Thus, if 1 unit of steel and 10 units of rice are interchangeable in the U.S. process of production, as in panel (a) of Figure 2, they also tend to be so interchangeable in the U.S. market, as this table's U.S. prices imply. (Note how 1 unit of steel and 10 units of rice both cost $100.) Similarly, if 4 units of steel and 10 units of rice are interchangeable in the Japanese process of production, as in panel (b) of Figure 2, they also tend to be so interchangeable in the Japanese market, as this table's Japanese prices imply. (Note how 4 units of steel and 10 units of rice both cost ¥40,000.)

in reed cellulose, the Soviet Union in fishing vessels. And they formulated central output and foreign trade plans accordingly.[2]

In capitalist market economies, however, this is not how things happen. Numerous decentralized decision makers—millions of households, business managers, and government officials—make their own and separate decisions about buying from or selling to foreigners. They do not consult any central plan; they know nothing of Ricardo's theory. They simply compare the *prices* of goods here and abroad. And what do they find? With exceptions to be noted in later chapters, the relative prices in any one country often come to reflect opportunity costs. Consider once more the data of Figure 2. If the sacrifice of 1 unit of steel in the United States releases just enough resources to produce 10 additional units of rice (which is what the *ABC* "triangle" tells us), these two quantities tend to have the same monetary value. If this value were $100, then in the United States

$$\$100 = 1 \text{ unit of steel} = 10 \text{ units of rice}$$

and the respective prices are $100 per unit of steel and $10 per unit of rice.

Similarly, if 4 additional units of steel can be produced in Japan with the resources released by the sacrifice of 10 units of rice (which is what the *FGH* "triangle" tells us), these two quantities, too, tend to be of equal monetary value. If this value were ¥40,000 (the Japanese currency unit is called the *yen* and symbolized by ¥), then in Japan

$$\text{¥}40,000 = 4 \text{ units of steel} = 10 \text{ units of rice}$$

and the respective prices are ¥10,000 per unit of steel and ¥4,000 per unit of rice.

Table 3 illustrates the problem that an individual consumer of steel or rice would then face: In the absence of a dollar-to-yen rate of exchange, such a consumer could not tell where purchase would be most advantageous. Should one buy steel at $100/unit in the United States or at ¥10,000/unit in Japan? Should one buy rice at $10/unit in the United States or at ¥4,000/unit in Japan? This is the point where markets for foreign currencies, usually referred to as **foreign-exchange markets,** enter the picture. In such markets, one country's money is traded for another country's money, and these markets operate precisely as those for ordinary goods discussed in Chapter 3. The price in a foreign exchange market is called the **exchange rate** and will be expressed throughout this book as so many dollars per unit of foreign money, such as the Japanese

---

[2] For a detailed listing of those early specialization decisions, see Heinz Kohler, *Economic Integration in the Soviet Bloc* (New York: Praeger, 1965), pp. 127–140. In the last few years, as much of Eastern Europe has turned away from communism and toward capitalism, Comecon has become nearly defunct.

yen (¥), the British pound (£), or the German mark (DM). This corresponds to our accustomed way of expressing prices as so many dollars per bushel of rice, per gallon of gasoline, or per loaf of bread.

CAUTION

What is customary for Americans need not be customary for foreigners. The Japanese, naturally, think of prices in terms of yen, the British think of them in terms of pounds, the Germans in terms of marks. When it comes to exchange rates, therefore, different customs prevail. Americans may talk of a rate of 1¢ per yen; the Japanese may refer to the same reality as ¥100 per dollar. Americans may talk of a rate of $1.63 per British pound; the British may call the same thing £.61 per dollar. To make matters worse, banks, newspapers, television stations, and even textbooks differ in their handling of this matter. Nothing but extreme vigilance, therefore, can save us from confusion when talking about the foreign-exchange market.

Figure 3 illustrates how an exchange rate is determined. At some high rate, such as $.015 per yen, the quantity of yen demanded may be zero (point A). Every American may find every good cheaper in the United States, so why buy yen to purchase goods in Japan? Apply this exchange rate, for example, to Table 3 and note how a unit of Japanese steel would cost $.015 per yen times ¥10,000 = $150, while a unit of Japanese rice would cost $.015 per yen times ¥4,000 = $60. At successively lower exchange rates, however, more and more Japanese goods would become attractive to Americans and the quantity of yen demanded might rise along line AB. (Can you see, looking at Table 3, that Japanese steel would be cheaper than U.S. steel below a rate of $100 per ¥10,000, or $.01 per yen? Can you see that even Japanese rice would be cheaper than U.S. rice below a rate of $10 per ¥4,000, or $.0025 per yen?)

We can tell a similar story about supply. At some high exchange rate, such as $.015 per yen, the quantity of yen supplied would be large (point C). Every Japanese would find every good cheaper in the United States and would offer to sell yen to get the dollars needed to buy American goods. Apply

FIGURE 3 The Market for Japanese Yen

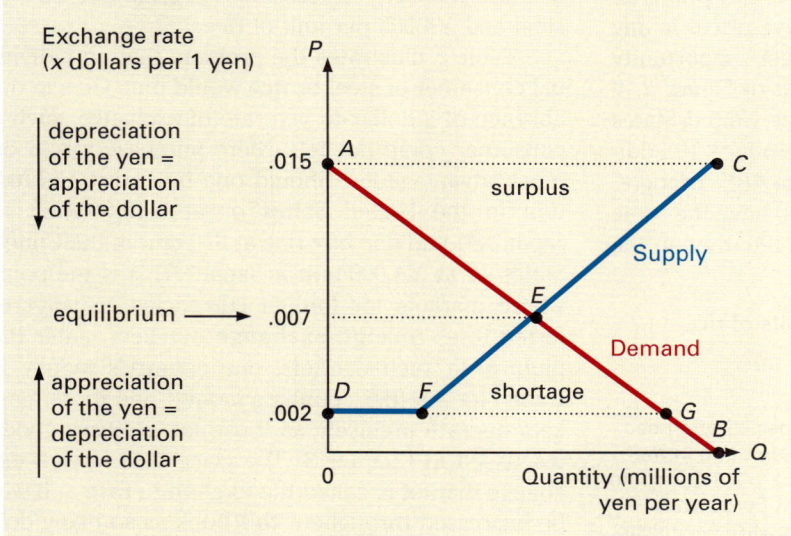

A competitive market for foreign money works just like the market for an ordinary good: The price, now called the *exchange rate,* falls in the face of surpluses and rises in the face of shortages, until equilibrium is reached.

this exchange rate to Table 3 and note how a Japanese would then picture the U.S. price of a unit of steel at $100/$.015 per yen, or ¥6,666.66, while a unit of U.S. rice would be seen to cost a mere $10/$.015 per yen, or ¥666.66. At successively lower exchange rates, however, fewer and fewer American goods would look attractive to the Japanese; at some very low rate, their appetite for American goods and their supply of yen would vanish altogether (point D).

Looking at Figure 3, we can instantly see that the only viable exchange rate is the one corresponding to point E, or $.007 per yen. At any higher rate (such as $.015 per yen) a surplus of yen (such as AC) would appear and the rate would fall. At any lower rate (such as $.002 per yen) a shortage of yen (such as FG) would exist and the rate would rise. Incidentally, as Figure 3 shows, when the exchange rate is expressed as so many dollars per yen, any fall in the rate is referred to as a **depreciation** of the yen and, by implication, as an **appreciation** of the dollar. (You can see why: A yen is then worth fewer dollars, but a dollar is worth more yen.) Analogously, any rise in the rate as defined here is an appreciation of the yen and a depreciation of the dollar.

CAUTION

If an exchange rate is expressed as x units of foreign money per dollar, all of the statements made in the text and in Figure 3 about depreciation and appreciation have to be reversed. Under those circumstances, a rise in the exchange rate, for example, denotes an appreciation of the dollar and a simultaneous depreciation of the foreign money.

Having introduced the foreign-exchange market, we are ready to see how the capitalist market economy encourages people to trade in accordance with comparative advantages. Review Table 3, given our Figure 3 equilibrium exchange rate of $.007 per yen. At this rate, the Japanese price of steel comes to $.007 per yen times ¥10,000 = $70 per unit, which is cheaper than the U.S. price. On the other hand, the American price per unit of rice comes to $10/$.007 per yen, or ¥1,428.57, which is cheaper than the Japanese price. Accordingly, Americans will buy Japanese steel and Japanese will buy American rice, just as pictured in Figure 2. Indeed, this result is not an accident. As long as relative goods prices in each country reflect the goods' opportunity costs (as in our Table 3), and as long as free markets for foreign exchange are allowed to establish equilibrium rates of exchange, the country with comparative advantage will also have the absolutely lower price, and trade in accordance with comparative advantage will occur spontaneously. Ricardo's promise will be realized; scarcity in each country will be less intense than before.

Free Trade: Gainers Versus Losers

Trade in accordance with comparative advantage increases the availability of goods to each country as a whole. Thus, the potential exists in each country to make some people better off while making no one worse off. In practice, despite the overall gain, some individuals and groups often do become worse off when nations engage in international trade. Such losers seek to undo what free trade has wrought, an issue that will occupy us for the remainder of the chapter.

To show why international trade in accordance with comparative advantage—despite the overall gain—may, nevertheless, hurt specific population groups, we examine two crucial concepts: consumer surplus and producer surplus.

The Concept of Consumer Surplus

Figure 4 may appear complicated at first sight; in fact it is quite easy to comprehend, one panel at a time. Panel (a) presents the familiar model of demand and supply. At an equilibrium price of $5 per pound, 10 billion pounds of beef per year are traded.

Panels (b) through (d) help us analyze the fate of consumers in a novel way. Panel (b) shows that there is one pound of beef for which some consumer would pay $10. This fact is shown by the height of the first vertical block next to the vertical axis, and it accounts for the vertical intercept of the demand line. Additional pounds of beef exist for which the same consumer or others would pay a

FIGURE 4 *Consumer Surplus and Producer Surplus*

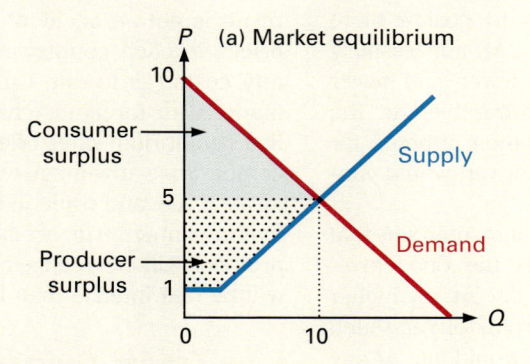

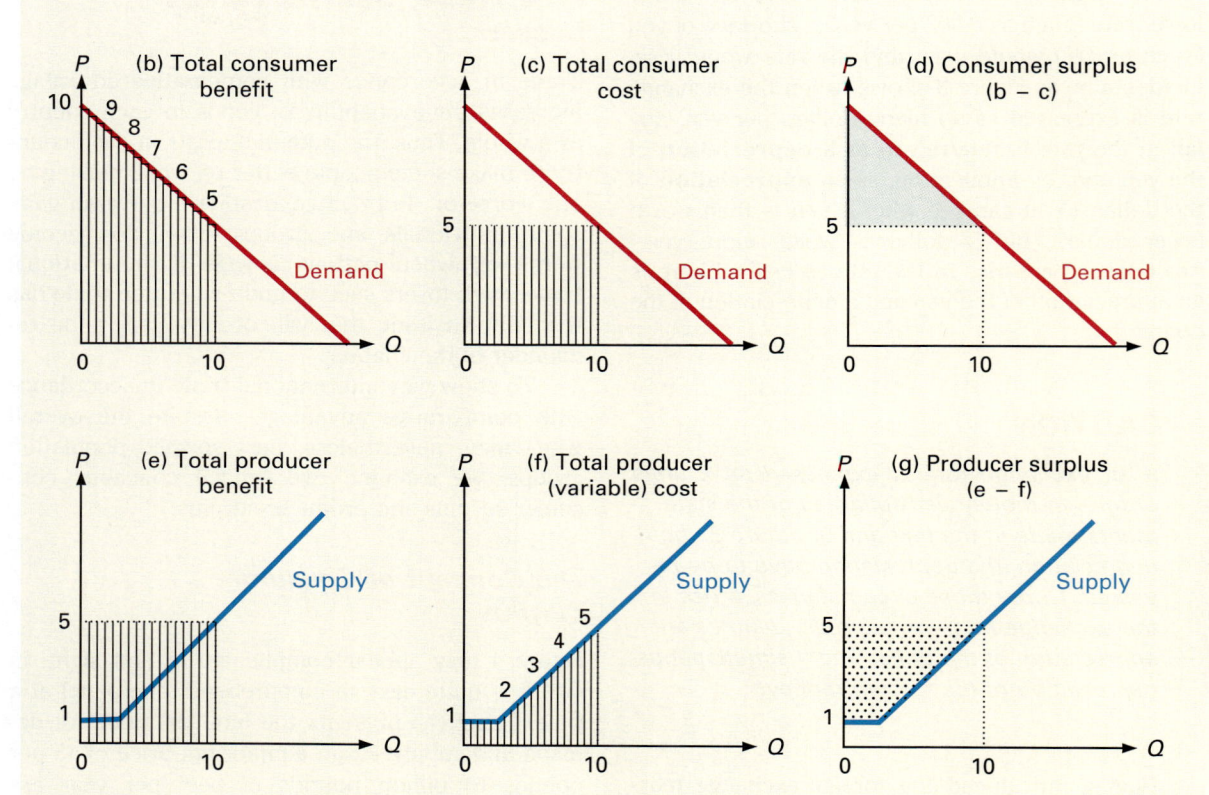

(a) Market equilibrium

(b) Total consumer benefit

(c) Total consumer cost

(d) Consumer surplus (b − c)

(e) Total producer benefit

(f) Total producer (variable) cost

(g) Producer surplus (e − f)

These graphs analyze the demand-and-supply model to highlight two crucial concepts. The difference between the maximum sum of money consumers would pay for the quantity traded (panel b) and the actual sum they do pay for it (panel c) is called the *consumer surplus* (shaded area, panel d). The difference between the actual sum of money producers receive for the quantity traded (panel e) and the minimum sum they would accept for it (panel f) is called the *producer surplus* (dotted area, panel g). The two surpluses are shown together in panel a. The sum of the shaded plus dotted areas in that panel represents the net benefit to all market participants of producing and consuming the good in question.

maximum of $9.85, $9.71, $9, $8.23, $6, and so on. Imagine all these pounds of beef lined up along the demand line, in accordance with the maximum prices consumers would pay for them. The declining blocks in panel (b), which show in descending order the maximum prices people would pay, can also be said to measure the *marginal benefits* various consumers expect to get when consuming pounds of beef. Why else would people be willing to pay a maximum of $10, $9.85, $8.23, and so on, unless they thought the enjoyment of consumption was worth that much but no more? Now consider the entire area of blocks in panel (b), right up to the last 10 billionth pound per year actually bought. It represents the *sum* of all the marginal benefits, or the *total benefit* consumers derive from the equilibrium quantity they buy.

Panel (c), in contrast, shows something else. The actual equilibrium price in this market is $5 per pound. It is paid by everyone, regardless of the willingness to pay as much as $10, $9.85, or $8.23. Thus, the vertical blocks in panel (c) measure the *marginal cost* to consumers who acquire pounds of beef. This cost is identical for all consumers. The first pound is sold for $5 and so is each additional pound, right up to the 10 billionth pound per year. The entire area of blocks in panel (c) represents the *sum* of marginal costs, or the *total cost* (or expenditure) that consumers in this market incur when buying the equilibrium quantity.

Panel (d) relates the total benefit to the total cost. The difference between the maximum sum of money consumers would pay for the quantity traded (panel b) and the actual sum they do pay for it (panel c) is called the **consumer surplus** (shaded area, panel d).

Do *you* ever receive a consumer surplus? Of course. Every time you are willing to pay up to $x for an item but find and pay a lower price, you enjoy a consumer surplus equal to the difference.

The Concept of Producer Surplus

Panels (e) through (g) similarly analyze the situation from the point of view of producers. Given the equilibrium market price of $5 per pound of beef, the (identical) vertical blocks in panel (e) represent the *marginal benefits* to producers. The first pound is sold for $5, and so is each additional pound right up to the 10 billionth pound per year. The entire area of blocks in panel (e), thus, represents the *sum* of marginal benefits, or the *total benefit* (or revenue) that producers in this market receive when selling the equilibrium quantity. Panel (f) shows some pounds of beef that low-cost producers would supply for as little as $1 per pound. These units are shown by the first set of blocks next to the vertical axis, and they account for the vertical intercept of the supply line. There are other pounds of beef, however, for which producers require a minimum of $1.25, $2, $2.73, $3, $4, and so on—presumably because they are costlier to produce. Imagine all these pounds of beef lined up along the supply line in accordance with the minimum prices at which producers would sell them. The rising blocks in panel (f), which show in ascending order the minimum prices producers must get, can also be said to measure the *marginal costs* various producers incur when producing pounds of beef. Why else would producers insist on getting a minimum of $1, $1.25, $2.73, and so on, unless these were the additional costs of bringing extra pounds of beef to market? Now consider the entire area of blocks in panel (f), right up to the 10 billionth pound per year actually sold. It represents the *sum* of marginal costs, or the *total (variable) cost* producers in this market are incurring for the equilibrium quantity they sell. (You need not worry about it here, but producers also incur a *fixed cost,* which does not show up in this graph nor vary with the quantity produced and sold.)

Panel (g) summarizes the producers' situation. The difference between the actual sum of money producers receive for the quantity traded (panel e) and the minimum sum they would accept for it (panel f) is called the **producer surplus** (dotted area, panel g). Even if you are not a producer of goods, you may have experienced something similar to the joy of reaping a producer surplus. If you have ever sold anything (a book, a car, or your labor), were willing to take as little as $x, but received more, you enjoyed a seller surplus equal to the difference.

From Autarky to Free Trade

We can now explore what happens when two countries move from **autarky,** a situation of national self-sufficiency in which no economic relations with foreigners exist at all, to a situation of international free trade. Figure 5 illustrates such a case.

Consider again the United States and Japan; the United States, we imagine, has a comparative advantage in the production of rice, while Japan enjoys a similar advantage with respect to steel. As we have already seen, in the context of free markets for goods as well as national currencies (the U.S. dollar or the Japanese yen in our example), a country with a comparative advantage in a good will also come to charge the lowest price. Accordingly, millions of individual decision makers—private consumers, business executives, government officials—will begin to buy the good in that country. In the process, the good's supply in the importing country will rise, and its high domestic price will fall toward a lower world market price. At the same time, the demand for the good in the exporting country will rise; its low domestic price will rise toward a higher world market level. Consumer and producer surpluses will be affected as a result.

Panel (a) of Figure 5 depicts this situation with respect to a good that would be imported under conditions of free trade, such as steel in the United States or rice in Japan in our example. Under autarky, domestic supply and demand would establish price P_a and quantity Q_a according to intersection e. Consumers would enjoy a consumer surplus of A (shaded); producers would reap a producer surplus of $B + C$ (dotted). With free trade, the price falls to P_f as cheaper foreign products enter the market. The solid supply line has been replaced by the dashed line to the right, which yields a new intersection at g. Given world market price P_f, the domestic quantity produced falls from Q_a to Q_p; only the lowest-cost domestic producers who can compete with the foreigners will stay in the market. At the same time, the domestic quantity consumed rises from Q_a to Q_c and the gap between Q_p and Q_c is filled with imports (fg).

Simultaneously the consumer surplus rises from A to $A + B + D$: consumers in importing

FIGURE 5 From Autarky to Free Trade

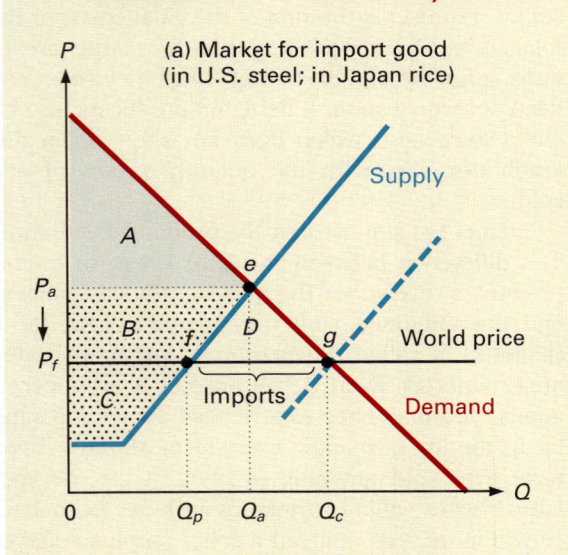

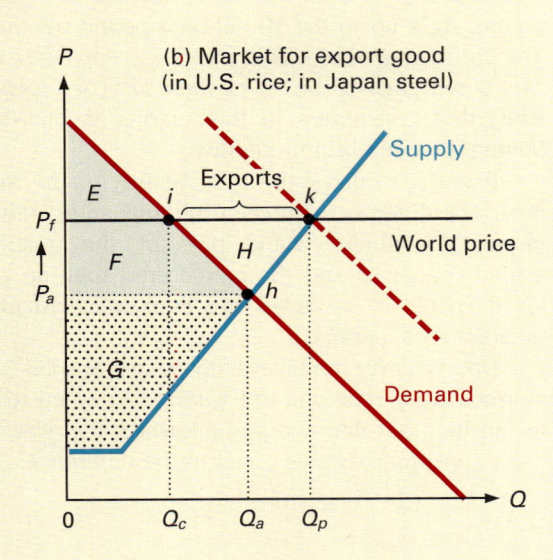

As free trade opens up between countries, a single worldwide price comes to prevail, such as P_f. The price is lower than before in the importing country, which has a comparative disadvantage in production (panel a), but higher than before in the exporting country, which enjoys a comparative advantage in production (panel b). Consumer and producer surpluses change accordingly; thus producers in importing countries and consumers in exporting countries oppose free trade, while producers in exporting countries and consumers in importing countries welcome it.

countries receive a larger quantity, Q_c, at a lower price, P_f. The producer surplus, on the other hand, falls from $B + C$ to C. Domestic producers who are suddenly competing with imports are annoyed by free trade; they sell a lower quantity, Q_p, at a lower price, P_f. The gain of consumers ($B + D$), you should note, exceeds the loss of producers (B). Hypothetically, the gainers could fully compensate the losers (by the amount B) and still enjoy a *net benefit of D*.

Panel (b) of Figure 5 helps us make a similar assessment with respect to the good that is being exported under free trade, such as steel in Japan or rice in the United States in our example. Under conditions of autarky, domestic supply and demand would establish P_a and quantity Q_a according to intersection h. Consumers would enjoy a consumer surplus of $E+F$ (shaded); producers would reap a producer surplus of G (dotted). Once free trade begins, the price rises to P_f as demand from the rest of the world augments domestic demand. The solid demand line has given way to the dashed line to the right, which yields new intersection k. Given world market price P_f, the domestic quantity consumed falls from Q_a to Q_c; only the most eager consumers (who are willing to pay P_f or more) will stay in the market. At the same time, the domestic quantity produced rises from Q_a to Q_p (even higher-cost suppliers can now enter the market), and the gap between Q_c and Q_p is sent abroad (ik).

What is the effect on consumers and producers in the exporting country? The consumer surplus falls from $E + F$ to E; consumers in exporting countries receive a smaller quantity, Q_c, at a higher price, P_f. The producer surplus, on the other hand, rises from G to $G + F + H$. Domestic producers, who are now able to sell abroad, are pleased by free trade; they sell a larger quantity, Q_p, at a higher price, P_f. Again you should note that there is a net gain to the nation. The gain of producers ($F + H$) exceeds the loss of consumers (F). Hypothetically, the gainers could fully compensate the losers (by the amount F) and still enjoy a net benefit of H.

In fact, these hypothetical compensations rarely take place. Thus producers in importing countries and consumers in exporting countries typically oppose free trade, while producers in exporting countries and consumers in importing countries support it. In the absence of compensation, producers in importing countries (U.S. steel makers and Japanese rice farmers) and consumers in exporting countries (U.S. rice consumers and Japanese steel users) are better off under conditions of autarky.

Government Protectionism: The Methods

Whenever people are worse off from free trade, they are likely to complain to their government, seeking protection from the "ruthless competition" of the world market. More often than not, government responds. Interestingly, the obvious solution of compensating the losers from the *larger* gains of the winners is rarely used. Instead, governments tend to erect barriers to international trade; the totality of measures governments take to restrict international trade is called **protectionism**.

The imposition of tariffs is the most popular trade-restricting technique. Governments are, however, equally adept at erecting nontariff barriers. Let us consider the possibilities in turn.

Tariffs

A **tariff** is simply a tax on imported goods. The tax can be a fixed dollar amount per physical unit, in which case one speaks of a **specific tariff.** Or it can be a percentage of the good's value, making it an **ad valorem tariff.** In either case, the effect in the tariff-imposing country is similar. The price of the good rises, as does the quantity supplied by domestic firms; the quantities demanded and imported fall. The country's trading partner is affected, too. Typically, the price of the good falls, as does the quantity supplied by that country's firms; the quantity demanded by domestic consumers rises.

In some cases, governments impose "scientific" or "prohibitive" tariffs, which reduce imports to zero. That approach produces a situation of autarky and could be illustrated by *reversing* all the changes shown in Figure 5. Starting with a situation of free trade and world market price P_f, we would return to a situation of autarky with domestic price P_a. Most actual tariffs are not *prohibitive;* they tend to reduce foreign trade but not eliminate it. That situation is a little more complicated, as illustrated in Figure 6.

The two panels show demand and supply lines for steel in the United States and Japan, respec-

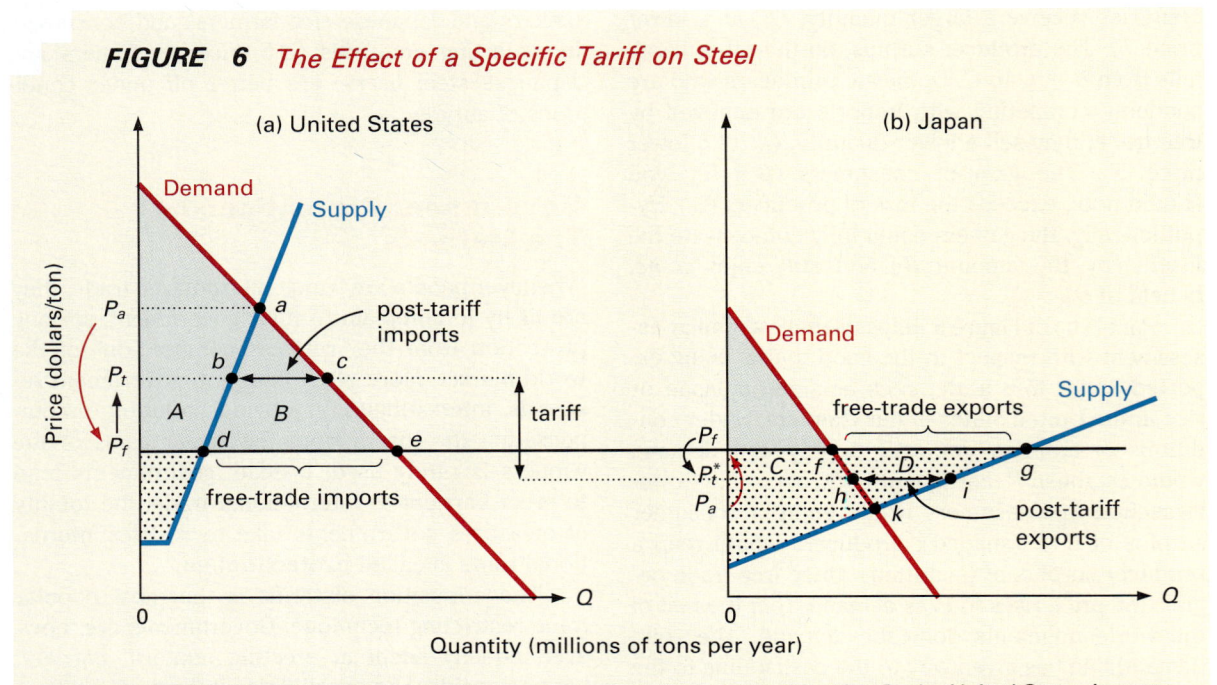

FIGURE 6 The Effect of a Specific Tariff on Steel

These graphs picture an initial situation of free trade in steel. At world market price P_f, the United States imports quantity de; Japan exports the equivalent amount fg. A U.S. tariff raises the U.S. price to P_t and lowers imports to bc. Consumer surplus $A + B$ is lost; producer surplus A is gained. The same tariff lowers the Japanese price to P_t^* and Japanese exports to $hi = bc$. Japanese producer surplus $C + D$ is lost; consumer surplus C is gained. The U.S. government collects a portion of loss $B + D$ as tariff revenue; the remainder is a deadweight loss that accrues to nobody.

tively. In the absence of foreign trade, a domestic equilibrium would be established at points a and k; the United States would have high price P_a and Japan low price P_a^*. Free trade would lower price in the importing country, while raising it in the exporting country, establishing a uniform world market price, P_f. The color arrows in Figure 6 illustrate that process, with the long horizontal line picturing free-trade world market price, P_f. Under free trade, U.S. and Japanese consumers enjoy consumer surpluses equal to the shaded triangles; producers in the two countries reap surpluses equal to the dotted areas. Quantity de is imported into the United States; the identical quantity fg is exported from Japan.

Now let the U.S. government impose a specific tariff measured by the vertical double-arrow in the center of the figure. For reasons discussed in the Chapter 3 section on excise taxes, the price faced by buyers rises from P_f to P_t (panel a), but the price received by sellers falls from P_f to P_t^* (panel b). As a consequence, a variety of changes, all visible in our graph, occur as well.

In the United States, the quantity supplied by domestic producers rises along db, and the producer surplus increases from the dotted area to include area A. Domestic producers sell more and at a higher price. The quantity demanded by consumers falls along ec, and the consumer surplus falls by $A + B$. Thus, consumers get a lower quantity at a higher price as imports fall from de to bc.

In Japan, the quantity supplied by producers falls along gi, and the original producer surplus (dotted) is reduced by $C + D$. Japanese producers sell less at a lower price. The quantity demanded by consumers rises along fh and the shaded consumer surplus rises to include C. Exports fg (equal to U.S.

FIGURE 7 The Effect of an Import Quota on Steel

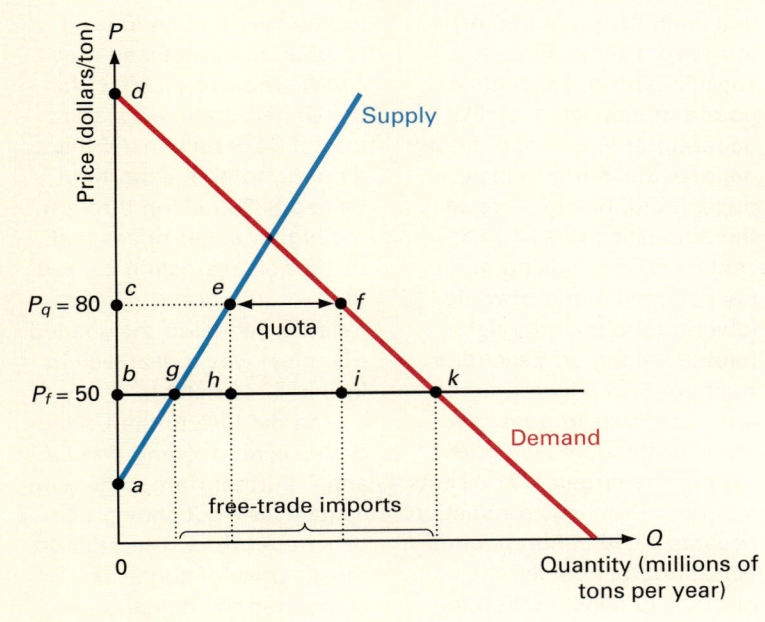

An import quota, similar in effect to a tariff but with greater certainty, reduces the volume of imports. In the quota-imposing country, the price rises, consumer surplus is lost, and producer surplus is gained. If the quota is handed out as a gift (rather than auctioned off to the highest bidder), foreign producers gain as well. Yet a deadweight loss remains (equal to triangles *geh* and *ifk*).

imports *de*) fall to *hi* (equal to lower U.S. imports *bc*). Naturally, Japanese producers are dissatisfied. Their government might seriously think of *retaliating* against the U.S. tariff by imposing tariffs on American exports to Japan. All too often, this response is precisely what happens. Then the volume of world trade shrinks and shrinks and the great promise of Ricardo's insight fails to be realized.

Note that the loss to U.S. consumers (area $A + B$) is transferred to producers only in part (area A). Similarly, the loss to Japanese producers ($C + D$) provides a smaller gain to Japanese consumers (C). What happens to lost areas $B + D$? In part, they become revenue of the tariff-imposing U.S. government; it collects an amount equal to *bc* multiplied by the size of the tariff. Another part of area $B + D$, however, vanishes. Such a welfare loss experienced by some people that is not offset by other people's gain is called a **deadweight loss**. A quick review of Figure 2 can help explain this occurrence. Just as specialization in accordance with comparative advantage produces a net gain of extra output, so anything that reverses the specialization prevents that gain. The output that might have been simply is not realized; neither are the associated monetary gains of consumers and producers involved.

Nontariff Barriers

Governments also have available an impressive array of **nontariff barriers;** nontax measures that protect domestic producers from import competition. Like tariffs, they inevitably hurt domestic consumers. The most used among nontariff barriers are import quotas.

Import Quotas

Whenever a government specifies a maximum physical quantity of a good that may be imported in a given period, it is said to establish an **import quota.** Consider Figure 7. Assume a free-trade

EXAMPLE 1

The U.S. Sugar Import Quota

In order to support a domestic price guarantee for sugar that exceeds the sugar world market price, the U.S. government since 1982 has imposed sugar import quotas (in addition to an existing tariff). The government has given limited rights to sell sugar in the United States directly to some 24 foreign governments. Figure A uses fiscal year 1983 data as an example. The domestic U.S. demand and supply are depicted by the familiar lines. The price in the world market, P_w, was 15¢ a pound, shown by the solid horizontal line. With free trade, the U.S. would have produced 6.14 billion pounds (*ab*), imported 13.04 billion pounds (*be*), and consumed 19.18 billion pounds (*ae*). Yet the U.S. government insisted on a domestic price, P_d, of 21.8 cents a pound. To achieve this goal, the government took two actions. First, a specific tariff of 2.8 cents a pound was enacted. Unlike panel (b) of Figure 6, it did *not* depress the world market price. It did, however, raise the domestic price to 17.8 cents a pound, raising quantity supplied along *bf* while lowering the quantity demanded along *ei*. Second, a quota of 5.96 billion pounds (*gh = no*) was imposed. In the end, the domestic price rose to the targeted 21.8 cents a pound. Domestic production became 12.10 billion pounds (*kn*), imports equaled the quota, and consumption fell to 18.06 billion pounds (*ko*).

The welfare effects were as follows: The consumer surplus declined by *akoe*, or $1.266 billion. The producer surplus rose by *aknb*, or $620 million. The government collected $167 million in tariff revenue (crosshatched area *cghd*). The overall effect for the United States was a net loss of $479 million. Of this amount, foreign exporters gained $238 million through the higher sugar prices that the import restriction caused (dotted area *gnoh*). The remainder (equal to the shaded triangles) was a deadweight loss of $241 million.

The net loss to the United States is an ongoing *annual* affair. Furthermore, other consequences—not shown here—occur over time. The high domestic price of sugar has stimulated the demand for and production of substitutes (such as corn sweeteners, non-caloric sweeteners, honey, and specialty sugars) and has raised *their* prices, which has, in turn, stimulated the import of sugar-containing

---

price, P_f of $50 per ton of steel prevails. Domestic production equals *bg*; the producer surplus is *abg*. Consumers buy quantity *bk* (portion *gk* of which is imported); the consumer surplus equals *bdk*. Then the government imposes a legal import limit of *hi = ef*. We can discover the consequences graphically by sliding a horizontal wedge, the length of which represents the quota, between the demand and supply lines but below their intersection. Because such a wedge represents the permissible domestic shortage (that imports are allowed to make up), the price at which the wedge just fits between the lines represents the solution.

In our case, the post-quota price, P_q, will equal $80 per ton. As price rises to that level, the quantity supplied by domestic producers rises from *bg* to *ce* and the producer surplus rises from *abg* to *ace*. Simultaneously, the quantity demanded falls from *bk* to *cf*, and the consumer surplus falls from *bdk* to *cdf*. In the process, imports fall from *gk* to *ef*, thus equaling the legal maximum.

What happens to the consumer surplus that is lost (area *bcfk*)? Part of it goes to domestic producers (*bceg*) and represents the increase in producer surplus. Part of it goes to foreign producers in the form of extra revenue (*hefi*). Another part (triangles *geh* and *ifk*) is deadweight loss. Unless quotas are auctioned off to the highest bidder (and that is rare), government collects nothing at all. Example 1 discusses a real-world situation.

FIGURE A

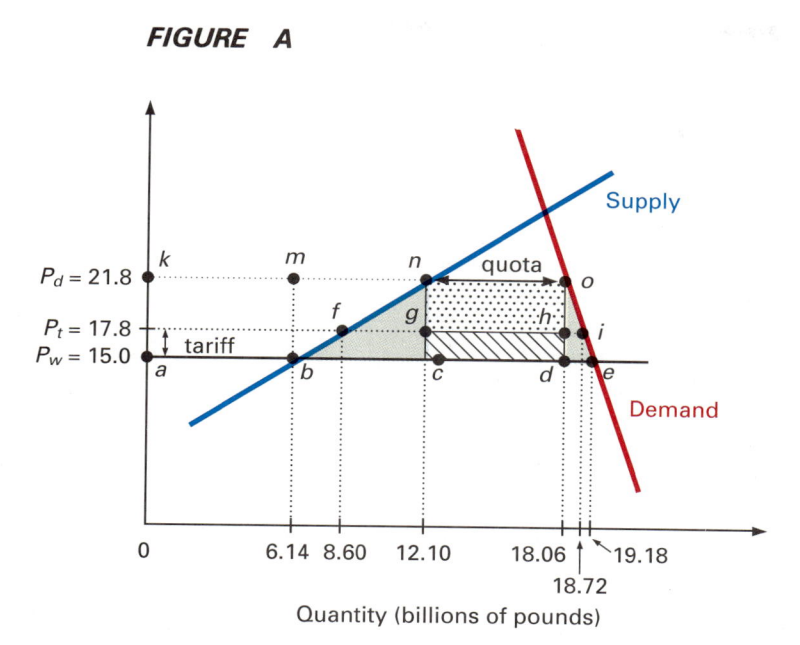

$P_d = 21.8$
$P_t = 17.8$
$P_w = 15.0$

tariff, quota

Supply, Demand

Quantity (billions of pounds): 6.14, 8.60, 12.10, 18.06, 18.72, 19.18

Labels: k, m, n, o, f, g, h, i, a, b, c, d, e

goods, especially from Canada. At one point in 1985, the world sugar price declined so much that the U.S. domestic price was 776 percent of the world price. This difference induced some firms to import Canadian pancake mix for the sole purpose of extracting sugar from it. The U.S. government responded with "emergency" trade restrictions, banning the import of syrups and putting quotas on a broad range of sugar-containing goods as well. This led to numerous political squabbles with foreign governments. Some of them claimed that the U.S. refusal to accept sugar imports spurred on the production of illegal drugs in sugar-growing areas. In 1989, when the U.S. had lowered the annual sugar quota to 2.5 billion pounds (consumption was 3.3 billion pounds), a council of 96 nations declared U.S. sugar import quotas in violation of world trade rules.

Sources: Cletus C. Coughlin and Geoffrey E. Wood, "An Introduction to Non-Tariff Barriers to Trade," *The Federal Reserve Bank of St. Louis Review,* January/February 1989, pp. 41–42; Clyde H. Farnsworth, "Sugar Quotas of U.S. Cited as Violation," *The New York Times,* June 23, 1989, p. D1.

Other Nontariff Barriers

Let us also consider a brief summary of other nontariff barriers that governments can erect. **Voluntary export restraints (VERs)** work almost exactly like import quotas, except that the party imposing them differs. VERs are agreements between importing and exporting countries in which the exporting country's government "voluntarily" limits the exports of a specified item to the importing country during a given period. Typically, the government of the importing country threatens the government of the exporting country with various unilateral sanctions (tariffs, import quotas, or even the withdrawal of military aid) until the exporter accedes to its demands. The agreement in question can be bilateral, as exemplified by the U.S.-Japanese automobile agreement (Example 2). A multilateral form of voluntary export restraints is called an **orderly marketing agreement.** An example is provided by the 1974 Multifiber Arrangement. This international agreement established special rules concerning textiles and apparel. Developed nations, in effect, put import quotas on textiles and apparel if they originated in developing nations but not if they originated in other developed nations.

Non-automatic import authorizations are import licenses that are required for specific imports and that can be granted or denied at the discretion

EXAMPLE 2

A Voluntary Export Restraint: The U.S.-Japanese Automobile Agreement

In 1981, sales of U.S.-made cars reached a 20-year low. Auto industry stockholders and workers blamed foreign imports. In order to preempt more restrictive measures that U.S. producers and labor groups were demanding (including a minimum content of American components and labor in *all* cars sold in the United States), the Japanese government acceded to a U.S. request for a 1981–1984 voluntary automobile export restraint. The following events happened during a single year (1984):

A VER of 1.68 million cars was imposed. The U.S. price of Japanese cars rose by $1,700 (22.5 percent). The subsequent reduction in competitive pressure permitted price increases on U.S.-made cars and other foreign imports as well; in the case of domestic cars by $1,185 (12 percent). The average price on all cars rose by $1,649 (17 percent). Consumers responded with an overall reduction in purchases of 1.5 million units. The shift in relative prices, however, allowed U.S. producers to increase their market share by 6.75 percentage points, enough to leave sales of U.S.-made cars unchanged. Thus, the quantity change came at the expense of foreigners. The U.S. consumer surplus fell by $6.8 billion. Of this amount, U.S. producers gained $1.25 billion, foreign producers $5.5 billion (of which $5.25 billion went to Japan). The Japanese gain provides an obvious reason why the Japanese continued the VER even after the U.S. government, in early 1985, decided not to ask for an extension.

There were two other consequences. First, the Japanese started to export larger, more luxurious cars with many more options (because it was more profitable, on the average). Second, the Japanese increased production activities on U.S. soil, as evidenced by the GM-Toyota venture in Fremont, California, the Nissan plant in Smyrna, Tennessee, and the Honda plant in Marysville, Ohio.

Sources: Cletus C. Coughlin and Geoffrey E. Wood, "An Introduction to Non-Tariff Barriers to Trade," *The Federal Reserve Bank of St. Louis Review,* January/February 1989, pp. 39–40; and Robert W. Crandall, "Detroit Rode Quotas to Prosperity," *The Wall Street Journal,* January 29, 1986, p. 30.

---

of government officials. In some cases (various steel products in the United States), government officials are supposed to grant an import license "if the particular type of product is unavailable domestically at a reasonable cost." Obviously, this leaves room for disagreement about "availability" and "reasonableness." In other cases (automotive components in the United States), the conditions under which import licenses are granted are specified in advance. For example, the imported item must be used to produce a specified export product (such as automobiles) and must constitute no more than a specified percentage of the export's value.

Variable import levies are specific tariffs that are continually adjusted to changing world market prices so as to keep the domestic price constant. The countries of the European Community often place such levies on imported agricultural products in order to maintain domestic target prices (see Chapter 3, Figure 10).

Antidumping rules are designed to prevent imports from entering a country if these imports are "unfairly traded." According to a typical complaint by domestic producers (but certainly not by consumers), goods are offered to the importing country at a price below the exporting country's domestic price or even below average cost. There may, however, exist valid reasons for both of these events. The price differential may be necessary to meet strong competition abroad, while there is none at home. Or pricing at average cost may be bad for business. (Recall Chapter 1's Example 3, "An Airline That Took the Marginal Route," which showed the importance of marginal-cost pricing.)

On occasion, however, the low import price is caused by **export subsidies,** money paid to exporters by their government to promote larger sales abroad. Instead of being delighted by this gift from abroad, governments of importing countries often retaliate by imposing **countervailing tariffs,** tariffs designed to offset the price-lowering effects of export subsidies.

Many other import barriers exist; they include deliberate delays at customs, unreasonable health and sanitary regulations, unreasonable packaging or labeling requirements, unreasonable technical standards (that require, for example, imported electrical products, which have already been adequately tested in the exporting country to be retested in the importing country), and discriminatory rules for government contracts (that give priority to domestic suppliers of satellites, supercomputers, and a whole range of other products governments buy).

Government Protectionism: The Arguments

Many reasons have been advanced in support of protectionist policies. Some of them make sense; many are quite foolish. Although the reader is free to disagree with this author's evaluations, let us briefly review some of these arguments.

Noneconomic Arguments

Noneconomic arguments for protectionism, perhaps, make the most sense of all. According to the **national-defense argument,** a sovereign nation must preserve certain key industries without which a successful national defense could not be mounted in times of war. What would a country do if war broke out and it had specialized in exporting chickens, textiles, and wheat, while importing airplanes, oil, and telephone equipment? A cutoff of these latter imports in times of war could prove fatal. (In 1973, an Arab oil embargo dealt a severe blow to the economies of western countries that were believed to favor Israel in the Yom Kippur War.)

This argument is a seductive one for creating import barriers. Unfortunately, it is being flagrantly misused by almost every industry, because *all* producers can claim that their product would be crucial for a war effort, at least indirectly. Don't soldiers have to eat? Thus, it would be disastrous to depend on foreign sources of food. For example, the U.S. watch industry has used the defense argument against the import of Swiss watches because "a decline in the U.S. watch industry would reduce the number of highly skilled workers who would be needed in the production of sophisticated weapons systems."

Most economists do not reject the national-defense argument. Rather they point out its abuses and suggest a more direct alternative: outright subsidies to preserve the industries considered crucial in times of war.

Example 3 provides another illustration of a noneconomic argument for trade restriction.

Economic Arguments

Few of the economic arguments are sound, except perhaps the first one. According to the **young-economy argument,** new industries in a developing nation must be protected against established industries in developed nations. Any developing nation is likely to have a comparative advantage in agricultural or mining products, while many of its more developed trading partners are likely to have a comparative advantage in industrial products. As a result, infant industries of the former have little chance in competing with the mature industries of the latter. For the sake of economic development, therefore, one needs *temporary* trade barriers to allow the new industries to grow and become established. Otherwise attempts to industrialize will fail repeatedly.

There is some truth to the argument (which was used by the United States against Great Britain in the 19th century). Consider how some countries never seem to escape (or escape fully) their preoccupation with agricultural and mining exports: Brazil and cotton, Bolivia and tin, Colombia and coffee, Cuba and sugar, Ghana and cocoa—the list goes on. Unless countries escape from the dominance of single industries, their entire national income varies with the world market price of a single product. Yet, once again, the argument is easily abused. Protected industries never admit to having matured, and they resist reductions in trade barriers even a century after they were first imposed.

EXAMPLE 3

Banning Trade to Save the Elephant

In 1989, journalists from around the globe were treated to an amazing spectacle. Kenyan President Daniel arap Moi ignited a towering pile of elephant tusks that had been taken from some 2,000 animals (and soaked in gasoline for the occasion). His purpose was to focus world attention on the fact that trade in ivory threatened Africa's elephants. Table A highlights the recent decline in the animal's population in countries that had more than 50,000 elephants in 1979.

Similar population declines had been occurring throughout Africa. They were partly attributable to legal "culling" in countries such as Botswana, Malawi, South Africa, and Zimbabwe, which practiced "managed" state trading. Mostly, however, they could be traced to the work of poachers who roamed the continent in heavily armed gangs as well as to rebel groups in Angola, Mozambique, Zaire, and the Sudan who wanted ivory to trade for arms. These activities were spurred on by a rise in the price of ivory from $75/kg. in 1979, to $300/kg. in 1989. The price rise, in turn, reflects rising demand for raw ivory used for jewelry, ornamental carvings, billiard balls, piano keys, and personal seals ("hankos") that the Japanese use in place of signatures.

Table B shows the major

TABLE A *Africa's Elephant Population*

Country	1979	1989
Zaire	377,700	85,000
Tanzania	316,300	80,000
Zambia	150,000	41,000
Sudan	134,000	40,000
Kenya	65,000	19,000
Central African Republic	63,000	19,000
Mozambique	54,800	18,600
Total	1,160,800	301,600

TABLE B *Cumulative Ivory Exports, 1979–1987*

Country	Tons exported
Sudan	1,452
Central African Republic	1,136
Congo	917
Tanzania	653
Zaire	640
Burundi	488
Uganda	424
Zambia	149
Kenya	131
Chad	111
Somalia	105
Zimbabwe	94
Botswana	58
Namibia	37
Cameroon	28
Total (incl. other countries)	6,828

sources of exports that killed 760,000 elephants. And where did all this ivory go? Table C has the answer for one of the years.

In 1989, it became apparent that elephants faced extinction by the turn of the century if the current rate of slaughter were to continue. In response, Tanzania proposed a worldwide ban of the ivory trade. Furthermore, the monetary returns to African countries have been minuscule, equal to .2 percent of all merchandise exports. Many governments realize that greater returns can come from tourists looking at live elephants and from the bigger and denser tusks taken from elephants that die a natural death.

Great Britain responded first to the Tanzanian request by banning imports; the rest of the European Community and the United States followed suit. Japan imposed a partial ban (on worked ivory only), stating its desire to continue raw ivory imports from sources authorized by the Convention on International Trade in Endangered Species (CITES). In 1990, CITES banned African ivory trade, but within a year Japan and Zimbabwe (which sells elephant shooting rights) requested a reversal of that policy.

What do economists have to say on the subject? They are generally no more certain that an ivory trade ban can save the elephant than a ban on cocaine can stop drug trafficking. Given continued demand, a ban on the legal ivory supply will drive up the price and make the illegal supply all the more profitable. Quite possibly, a different approach is needed, such as setting up an effective armed force to combat poachers. However, neither governments of exporting nor of importing countries are able and ready to commit the resources required, nor are conservation groups.

Indeed, history already has an example of a failed trade ban. Trade in the horn of the black rhinoceros was banned in 1975, yet its population since then has declined from 500,000 to well below 40,000. The horns are used to make dagger handles in Yemen and aphrodisiacs and fever cures in East Asia. They were selling for $90,000 apiece in 1989. At that point, Namibian wildlife authorities initiated a campaign to dehorn the remaining animals, thereby destroying their value to poachers, while possibly saving their lives. (Even that result was uncertain because the animals use their horns for browsing in the thick underbrush and for fighting among bulls, which is a crucial prelude to reproduction.)

Sources: *The New York Times,* June 2, 1989, June 17, 1989, p. 6, July 11, 1989, pp. 1 and 7, July 19, 1989, p. 5, July 21, 1989, p. 3; and *The Economist,* July 1, 1989, pp. 15–17, March 2, 1991 p. 16.

TABLE C *Ivory Imports, 1985*

Country	Tons imported
Japan	300
Hong Kong	215
Singapore	175
Macao	100
Belgium	70
Great Britain	40
United States	25
Taiwan	20
West Germany	15
Total	960

EXAMPLE 4

The Guiding Hand of MITI

Inside Japan's Ministry of International Trade and Industry (MITI), hundreds of government workers draw up blueprints designed to create and destroy comparative advantage around the world. In a methodical and sophisticated manner, they seek to "coordinate" what nations will produce and trade in the 21st century. They place special emphasis on three areas of the world: the Asian-Pacific region, North America, and Europe.

The Asian-Pacific Region. In a manner reminiscent of the Co-Prosperity Sphere that Japan's military leaders sought to establish in southern and eastern Asia in the 1930s, MITI officials of today seek to weave the economies of that region into a cohesive whole. In a recent interview, one MITI worker used the image of a flock of geese: Japan in the lead, followed by newly industrialized South Korea and Taiwan; followed by currently developing Indonesia, Malaysia, Thailand, and the Philippines; then by China; and finally by the weakest economies of all, Bangladesh, India, Vietnam. Unlike his ancestors, the worker did not count on Japan's military force to build up the grand international division of labor that MITI has in mind, but rather on annual flows of government aid and private investment funds carefully channeled in directions that fit the long-range MITI plan.

Thus, in 1990, MITI laid the groundwork for "complementary development" across the region by directing billions of dollars' worth of government aid to the construction of bridges, roads, ports, dams, and power plants—all guided by Japanese technical experts. It also directed some $8 billion of private investment funds to facilities for textiles, forest products, and plastics in Indonesia, to factories making answering machines, facsimile devices, word processors, and rubber sneakers in Malaysia, to plants building die-cast molds, furniture, and toys in Thailand. By the turn of the century, Japanese cars could be made with steering mechanisms from Malaysia, transmissions from the Philippines, and engines from Thailand.

North America. MITI has been equally concerned with helping Japanese corporations attain positions of leadership in North America. In 1990 alone, it helped channel $32.5 billion of private investments into the United States. Earlier, MITI had masterminded Sony's 1988 acquisition of CBS Records ($2 billion) as well as its 1989 purchase of Columbia Pictures ($3.4 billion). MITI stood behind the 1990 takeover by the Matsushita Electric Industrial Company of MCA/Universal Studios ($6.59

Furthermore, some industrialized countries have used a variant of the young economy argument to launch systematic attacks on foreign industries. According to the **infant-industry argument,** new industries in a developed nation must be protected against more mature foreign competitors while they become established. The "strategic trade policy" of the Japanese Ministry of International Trade and Industry (MITI) is a case in point. In the early 1960s, when Japan was already an industrialized country, MITI set out to "destroy the U.S. comparative advantage in the production of television sets."[3] It channeled financial capital to the fledgling Japanese industry, protected it from U.S. competition via high tariff and nontariff barriers, and even allowed Japanese firms to engage in domestic price

---

[3] Kozo Yamamura, "Caveat Emptor: The Industrial Policy of Japan," in Paul Krugman, ed., *Strategic Trade Policy and the New International Economics* (Cambridge, MA: MIT Press, 1986).

billion—a record at the time). In this way the Japanese maker of Panasonic, Quasar, and Technics television sets bought into the U.S. export sector and gained control of a major producer of films and television shows.

Critics wondered how the reportedly stodgy Japanese electronics maker would adjust to the world of Hollywood and fare in the booming international market for videocassettes and compact disks that feature American stars. One journalist interviewed the company's chief executive in Osaka, Japan, amid scores of docile employees, wearing uniform grayish-blue jumpsuits, chanting the company song, and reciting words of wisdom by Konosuke Matsushita. The executive pointed to buttons pinned to everyone's jacket, featuring an elephant popping out of an eggshell. "Breakthrough," he said, "is our new slogan. Just like an elephant born out of an egg, we have adopted new ways of thinking."

Europe. Even the most optimistic boosters of European unity don't expect a Super Europe, with a single currency and goods and resources moving freely from the Atlantic Ocean to the Ural Mountains, to be in place until well into the 21st century. But, beginning in the late 1980s and guided by MITI, Japanese companies have been buying up real estate, European companies, and have been setting up subsidiaries and boosting sales forces all over Europe, West and East. In 1990 alone, their investment in European Community countries came to $14 billion. The motivation has been twofold: a belief that Europe's millions will provide a superb market and a fear that a united Europe might resist imports of Japanese goods. Accordingly, MITI has urged Japanese firms to create manufacturing capacity within a potentially protectionist Europe.

Examples abound. Fujitsa bought control of International Computers, Great Britain's largest computer maker, for $1.37 billion. Hitachi built a computer disk factory in France and other factories to make television sets in Great Britain and semiconductors in Germany. Fujisama Pharmaceuticals set up drug making in Ireland, and the NEC corporation turned to computer making in Germany. Nissan got set to make cars and Matsushita telephone equipment in Great Britain. Many others have joined the low-key but relentless parade.

Sources: *The Wall Street Journal,* August 20, 1990, pp. 1 and 2; November 26, 1990, pp. 1 and 5; November 27, 1990, pp. 1, 3, 8, and 9; December 10, 1990, p. 7A; *Business Week,* January 14, 1991, p. 97; *Europe,* May 1990, pp. 15–16.

---

fixing to reap high profits. Eventually, the new firms sold TV sets at extremely low prices in the United States. In the monochrome section of the U.S. market, the Japanese share rose from less than 1 percent in 1962 to 25 percent by 1977. In the color section, it rose from 3 percent in 1967 to 37 percent by 1977. In the meantime, U.S. television industry employment plummeted by two-thirds. Example 4 has more to say on the subject.

According to the **saving-our-jobs argument** imports must be prevented from entering the country in order to save jobs in domestic import-competing industries. This argument makes little sense in the long run but is not entirely unreasonable in the short run. Its proponents argue that the import of every product that is also produced domestically inevitably reduces domestic production, employment, and income. They are correct when narrowly focusing on the import-competing domestic industry. Review panel (a) of Figure 5. The lower world-market price reduces the quantity supplied domestically along section *ef*, and output falls from

EXAMPLE 5

The Consumer Cost of Import Restrictions

Numerous studies in the 1980s have attempted to make quantitative estimates of the cost of import restrictions to U.S. consumers and the implied cost of saving jobs in domestic import-competing industries. The results, highlighted in Table D, are truly amazing. In every instance, it would have been far cheaper simply to tax consumers an amount equal to the average income of workers in the affected industries. Indeed, one study concluded that protectionist policies were equivalent in 1984 to placing an income tax surcharge on Americans ranging from 66 percent (for people in the $7,000 to $9,350 income range) to 5 percent (for people earning $58,500 and more).

TABLE D *Cost per job saved (Ratio of lost consumer surplus to number of jobs saved)*

Industry	Dollars per year
Steel	$750,000
Dairy Products	220,000
Automobiles	105,000
Book Manufacturing	100,000
Footwear	78,000
Sugar	60,000
Apparel	46,000
Textiles	42,000

Sources: Keith E. Maskus, "Rising Protectionism and U.S. International Trade Policy," *Federal Reserve Bank of Kansas City Economic Review,* July-August 1984; Susan Hickok, "The Consumer Cost of U.S. Trade Restraints," *Federal Reserve Bank of New York Quarterly Review,* Summer 1985; and Gary C. Hufbauer et al., *Trade Protectionism in the United States: 31 Case Studies* (Washington, D.C.: Institute for International Economic Studies, 1986).

Q_a to Q_p. With this fall in output goes a fall in the employment of various resources, including people. If free trade is prevented—by tariffs, quotas, or other means—this loss in employment does not occur.

As Figure 5 also shows, however, this story is incomplete. Free trade also raises exports (panel b). In export industries, the quantity supplied domestically rises (along section hk from Q_a to Q_p). With this rise in output, there is a *rise* in the use of resources, including people. Thus, the opening up of free trade does not necessarily reduce the employment opportunities of people in the nation as a whole; it simply requires a *reallocation* of resources, including people, from one industry (with a comparative disadvantage) to another industry (with a comparative advantage). Obviously, government could help with this adjustment by offering relocation and retraining assistance to workers and loans or tax preferences to firms. When it doesn't, workers who lose jobs oppose the imports, assuming that the associated rise of employment in the export industries would have occurred anyway. But, in fact, this assumption is unlikely to be true. When the United States restricts imports of steel to save jobs in that industry, the partner country is likely to retaliate and restrict its imports of U.S. products such as rice. Then the jobs saved in the steel industry are cancelled out by the jobs lost in agriculture.

A variant of the preceding argument supports restricting imports to save our high-wage standard of living from the inroads of "unfair" wages paid abroad. Once more, this idea can be fallacious. Despite high hourly wages, the U.S. has a comparative advantage in many products. Despite their low hourly wages, many other countries have a comparative disadvantage because per unit costs of production are significant and this argument ignores possible differences in productivity. If an American worker gets $15 per hour and produces 10 units of a product, while a South Korean worker gets $2 per hour and produces 1 unit of the same product, the unit cost of production favors the United States over South Korea ($1.50 versus $2).

Example 5 provides data about the cost of saving jobs through protectionism.

According to the **terms-of-trade argument,** tariffs are needed in order to assure a fair division of the gain from international specialization and trade. The argument focuses on the way the overall gain from trade is apportioned among the international trading partners. In Figure 2 the world as a whole gained 3 units of steel per year, but the gain was unevenly split. The U.S. had a net gain of 1 unit, the Japanese had a net gain of 2 units. Some people argue that such unevenness should be eliminated by appropriately adjusting the terms at which trade takes place. In our example, the United States imported 2 units of steel in exchange for 10 units of rice (note the colored arrows). If the exchange had been 2.5 units of steel for the 10 units of rice, then the net gain of each country would have been 1.5 units of steel. To achieve such an increase in the ratio of physical import quantity to physical export quantity (referred to as the **gross barter terms of trade**), some observers suggest imposing tariffs to depress the price charged by the foreign exporters. (Glance at Figure 6 and note that this can, indeed, be expected to happen.) Thus the lower price charged by foreigners will enable the tariff-imposing country to buy a larger quantity of imports and—given its export quantity—to improve the gross barter terms of trade. Once again, however, this argument collapses if foreigners retaliate, impose their own tariff, and the quantity of the initial country's exports falls as well.

The **keeping-our-money-at-home argument** for trade restriction is, perhaps, the least defensible of them all. Here it is argued that importing goods gives us the goods but the foreigners have our money; buying the same goods from domestic producers gives us both the goods *and* the money.

Hence trade restrictions are needed to prevent our money from ending up in foreign hands. Many a "Buy American" campaign has been so motivated. The argument lacks merit for a number of reasons; let us consider just two of them. First, it assumes that money is desirable for its own sake, but why should it be? Our government could produce and distribute huge quantities of money to us, so why not increase our happiness by doing just that? The answer is that goods are made with human, natural, and capital resources, not with money. Multiplying the money stock does not multiply our capacity to produce (just as printing more tickets does not increase the number of seats in a movie theater). Second, the argument ignores the fact that our money *as such* is as worthless to foreigners as it is to us. They will eventually use it to buy goods from us; thus, "our" money returns to us in any case.

Conclusion

At one time or another, each of the preceding arguments has been debated in Congress (and by foreign governments), but the arguments never seem to reach a conclusion. It is fairly easy to see why. As Ricardo's theory illustrates, *in the long run,* the citizens of a nation become richer by reallocating their resources toward what they can do relatively best and trading with other nations who similarly specialize. Taking this long run view and responding to their national constituency, almost all U.S. presidents have favored free trade.

Yet members of Congress tend to take a *short run* and more regional view. While resources are being reallocated, free trade will help some people and hurt others. Consumers who can buy cheaper import goods benefit, but the advantages are widely dispersed and of relatively minor importance to any one person. Consumers are unlikely to bombard Congress with letters of thanks if a free-trade policy is adopted. On the other hand, producers in import-competing industries and the workers they employ see their livelihood threatened by free trade. They find little solace in the other jobs that will become available in the export sector, eventually, after they retrain, relocate, and otherwise rearrange their lives. So they make their voices heard, and members of Congress will often vote for trade protection. The next section reviews the history of this tug of war.

A Brief History of United States Commercial Policy

Government measures affecting international trade are generally referred to as **commercial policy.** Such a policy is termed "easy" or "restrictive" depending on whether it encourages or discourages trade across national boundaries. In the early years of the republic, the young-economy argument held sway; U.S. policy was restrictive and focused on tariffs. By 1830, some 92 percent of imports were charged with tariffs; on the average, the tax came to 62 percent of their value. (Such a figure, however, can understate the severity of tariffs because it does not include prohibitive tariffs that shut out imports completely.)

Figure 8 summarizes the more recent history. Between 1860 and 1930, tariffs took an average 45 percent of the value of **dutiable imports** (imports subject to tariffs, also called "customs duties"). Then came the first of two occasions when the United States took the lead in setting a new course for the world's trading system. In 1930, Congress passed the Smoot-Hawley Act for higher tariffs. In a matter of two years, it helped raise the average tariff to 59 percent. Amid worldwide retaliation, trade and output plummeted everywhere.

Since 1934, however, successive administra-

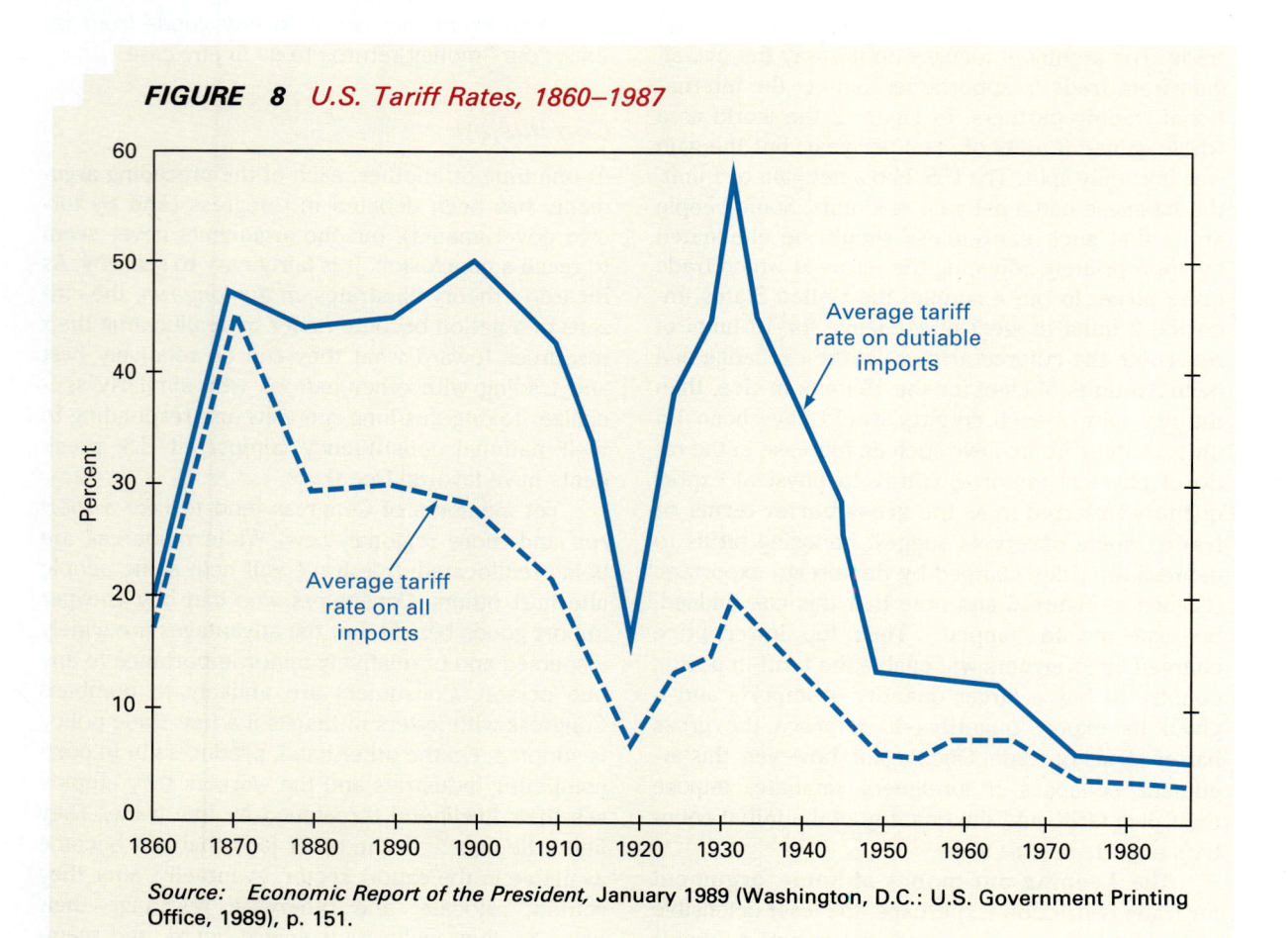

FIGURE 8 U.S. Tariff Rates, 1860–1987

Source: *Economic Report of the President,* January 1989 (Washington, D.C.: U.S. Government Printing Office, 1989), p. 151.

EXAMPLE 6

The New North America

If all goes according to plan, the entire North American continent will become a free trade zone devoid of tariffs, quotas, and other trade barriers some time during the 1990s. This plan is the result of recent agreements and discussions involving the United States and Canada on the one hand and the United States and Mexico on the other.

Canada. Canada and the United States are already each other's largest trading partners. In 1986, for example, the U.S. accounted for 71 percent of Canadian merchandise trade (exports plus imports); Canada accounted for 19 percent of U.S. trade. In 1988, an historic document was signed, the Canada-United States Free-Trade Agreement.

In many respects, this event seems a natural consequence of long-standing friendship, common economic interests, and geographic proximity. Nevertheless, it took more than a century to reach agreement. In the mid-1800s, after Great Britain repealed the Corn Laws noted in this chapter's Ideas in History, Canada proposed bilateral free trade with the United States, and a limited treaty covering natural products only was signed. However, it was abrogated during the Civil War by the United States because of close Canadian-British ties and British support for the Confederacy. After more than a century of fluctuating sentiments on the issue, the 1988 agreement finally eliminates all bilateral tariffs (in stages to be completed by 1998) and all quantitative trade restrictions (immediately). The agreement, it was thought, would particularly boost trade in agricultural products (fruits, vegetables, poultry), mining products (coal and oil), and services (banking, computer, insurance, professional and telecommunications services, plus retail and wholesale trade). Both countries expected net gains between $1 and 3 billion per year.

Mexico. Mexico is the third largest U.S. trading partner, accounting for 5 percent of U.S. exports plus imports (Canada and Japan account for 19 percent each); the U.S. accounts for two-thirds of Mexico's foreign trade.

In 1987, the United States-Mexico Framework Understanding put in place the first procedures ever for consultations regarding trade and investment relations between these two countries. The mechanism was set up to resolve disputes and to negotiate the removal of trade barriers as a supplement to GATT. In early 1991, genuine free trade discussions were set in motion and soon joined by Canada. The goal was the creation of a hemispheric free trade zone reaching from the Yukon to the Yucatan and encompassing a market of over 360 million people.

Analysts forsaw major gains associated with increased specialization and trade. They also predicted major adjustment costs in the United States where low-skill jobs would be lost to thousands of low-wage assembly plants now clustered along the U.S.-Mexican border, while high-skill jobs ranging from architecture to engineering and telecommunications would get a noticeable export boost. Another likely consequence is that the future rise in real wages south of the border would slow the flow of illegal aliens into the United States.

Sources: Economic Report of the President, February 1988 (Washington, D.C.: U.S. Government Printing Office, 1988), pp. 129–138; *Challenge,* November-December 1990, pp. 52–55; *Business Week,* November 12, 1990, pp. 102–113; *The New York Times,* November 11, 1990, p. F12; December 31, 1990, pp. 29 and 36.

tions have persuaded an always reluctant Congress to ease trade restrictions. In 1934, Congress passed the Reciprocal Trade Agreements Act. It gave the president authority to swap tariff cuts with individual countries in bilateral negotiations. Through use of this power, the tariff level in the United States by 1947 had been whittled down to 19 percent of dutiable imports (whose significance in total imports remained about the same as earlier).

After World War II, which had established a strong spirit of international cooperation among the victorious powers, the United States again took the lead during negotiations. In 1947 in Geneva, the U.S. and 22 other nations signed the General Agreement on Tariffs and Trade (GATT), an executive agreement that required no congressional action. It provided a framework for *multilateral* reductions in trade barriers. (Participants would periodically negotiate bilateral cuts; any agreements would be automatically extended to all members of GATT. Such an automatic extension of bilaterally negotiated tariff cuts to other trading partners is a practice referred to as **most-favored nation treatment.**) As Figure 8 confirms, the initial effect was not great as far as the United States was concerned. By 1965, the average tariff had been reduced to 12 percent of dutiable imports, but the percentage of all imports subject to tariffs had risen to 65 percent. Postwar renewals of the Reciprocal Trade Agreements Act had increasingly restricted the powers of the executive branch of the U.S. government; negotiations had to be conducted, after hearings, product by product. An **escape clause** made it possible to revoke tariff concessions if a domestic industry was "seriously" hurt by foreign competition. Congress set **peril points,** legal limits below which tariffs could not be lowered by the administration. The allowable reduction in tariffs was reduced again and again. In the meantime, steps were being taken elsewhere in the world to liberalize international trade.

In 1957, six European countries (Belgium, France, Italy, Luxemburg, the Netherlands, and West Germany) formed the European Economic Community (EEC), more generally known as the European Common Market. These countries decided to eliminate all trade barriers between each other over the course of a lengthy transition period. Eventually, there would be unhindered movement of goods and resources among them but a common trade barrier toward the outside world. Seven other countries set up a parallel organization in 1960, known as the European Free Trade Association (EFTA). These "outer seven" comprised Austria, Denmark, Great Britain, Norway, Portugal, Sweden, and Switzerland.

In response to these free trade blocs abroad, Congress passed the U.S. Trade Expansion Act of 1962. It provided for trade adjustment assistance to injured parties (such as workers who lost their jobs) and authorized the president to negotiate across-the-board tariff cuts up to 50 percent in exchange for comparable foreign concessions. It also gave rise to the 1964–1967 Kennedy Round of trade negotiations under the auspices of GATT. The United States, Great Britain, the EEC countries, and Japan agreed to cut tariffs (by an average 35 percent) on some 60,000 goods. By 1973, some 60 percent of U.S. imports were subject to an average tariff of a mere 8 percent.

The 1973–1979 Tokyo Round of GATT negotiations cut tariffs further (by about one third) and established agreements, called "codes," on how to deal with nontariff barriers. The U.S. average tariff rates were at an all-time low of under 4 percent. The Uruguay Round (1986–1990) attempted to continue the effort, amidst overwhelming evidence that free trade had made many a developed country rich and provided the best hope yet for developing nations. Yet four years later, in 1990, the talks broke down. Nevertheless, the United States took special steps to improve economic relations with immediate neighbors as Example 6 explains.

On the other side of the Atlantic, another giant free trade zone has been in the making. The European Common Market, renamed the European Community (EC) has expanded its membership to include Denmark, Great Britain, and Ireland (1972), Greece (1979), and Portugal and Spain (1985). The members agreed to implement their ultimate goal of completely free internal trade in 1992.

Conclusion

What, finally, has history taught us? The decades-long trend toward freer trade among GATT members has contributed significantly to their growing prosperity, just as Ricardo's theory predicts. Compare, for example, the average annual rate of

IDEAS IN HISTORY

The Theory of Comparative Advantage

Early in the 19th century, a now famous debate raged among British economists as they tried to explain the high price of corn (a term referring to many types of grain). At the time, Parliament was dominated by landowning aristocrats who benefitted as the population and demand for corn were rising, along with the price of corn. This situation, in turn, pushed up the demand for corn-growing land and the rents landowners could collect. A rising class of urban industrialists complained. They blamed the high price of corn that urban workers had to pay on the high rents charged by "greedy" landlords; they wanted to lower the price of corn so they could keep wages down and better compete in markets for industrial goods.

Among those debating the issue was David Ricardo (1772–1823) who had been born in Amsterdam but had come to England at an early age. His formal schooling ended at age 13, but he had a lucky break. Working as a broker at the London Stock Exchange, he had made a fortune on government securities purchased just before the Battle of Waterloo. Thus, he retired at age 42, bought a country estate, Gatcomb, and automatically received a seat in Parliament. Unlike his fellow landowners, Ricardo was in favor of lowering the price of corn. However, he did not think that rolling back high rents was the way to accomplish it. High rents, he argued, were the consequence, not the cause of the high price of corn. As he saw it, what was needed was a repeal of the Corn Laws that had imposed high tariffs on the importation of corn and reduced imports to nil. If the supply of corn were to rise as a result of greater imports, argued Ricardo, its price would fall, along with the demand for domestic corn-growing land and the rents its owners could earn. (In fact, Ricardo's analysis of demand and supply was correct, but he never experienced the fruits of his efforts. The Corn Laws were not repealed until 1846, long after his death.)

The Corn Law debate, in turn, led Ricardo to ponder the nature of international trade. Picking up an idea first advanced by Robert Torrens, Ricardo refined the theory of comparative advantage found in this chapter. In his 1817 masterwork, *The Principles of Political Economy and Taxation,* he presented the now famous example involving cloth and wine, England and Portugal. He showed conclusively that mutually beneficial trade was possible even under circumstances never envisioned by Adam Smith—in a situation in which one trading partner held an absolute advantage in the production of all goods at the same time. Ultimately, Ricardo's insight led to the adoption of free trade policies in many nations around the world and, whenever it did, contributed to "the wealth of nations."

We should, however, note another and equally long-lasting influence Ricardo has had, although quite unwittingly. It has come to us through Karl Marx, the father of communism. Although Marx disagreed with much of what Ricardo had to say, he studied Ricardo's writings intensively, adapted Ricardo's models of economic growth for his own purposes, and came to very different conclusions. For example, as this chapter's Table 1 illustrates, Ricardo, like Smith before him, often employed a "labor theory of value" for expository purposes, acting as if products were produced by labor alone (and capital and natural resources did not exist). Marx took the matter seriously, argued that labor alone produced all goods, should receive all goods, did in fact not receive all goods, and thus was "exploited." From that came the call to abolish capitalism by communist revolutions, which, ultimately, shaped much of the history of the 20th century.

IDEAS IN HISTORY — *The Strategic Trade Model*

Congressional critics of the U.S. free trade policy have been joined in recent years by a number of economists, such as Paul Krugman of the Massachusetts Institute of Technology and Clyde V. Prestowitz, Jr., Alan Tonelson, and Robert W. Jerome of the Economic Strategic Institute.[1] They argue that many countries cheat on free trade agreements in order to promote their favored industries and that the United States should pursue a deliberate policy of helping its important industries as well. Such a deliberate policy, they say, moved Japan from a country with a comparative advantage in "dwarf trees and cheap, breakable toys" to its present position of industrial might. (See Example 4.) Failure to pursue such a policy will, in turn, make the United States into a nation of "scrap metal collectors and lumberjacks."

Consider these examples of "cheating":

1. While U.S. free traders proudly point to the improvement in the U.S. commodity trade deficit with Japan (from $59.1 billion in 1986 to $42.7 billion in 1990) and attribute this effect to "Japan's opening of its protected market," the free trade critics focus on two other developments. First, Japanese goods simply enter the United States via Japanese-owned assembly plants in the United States or via Japanese firms located in Mexico, Thailand, and other Asian countries. Second, this Japanese "sleight of hand" is reinforced by a change in the commodity composition of trade. While the crucial U.S. manufacturing industries are being destroyed and the U.S.-Japanese deficit in their products remains the same or even rises, U.S. exports of breakfast cereals, fish, lumber, meat, and scrap metal rise. Yet, these critics say, in the long run it does matter a great deal whether a country produces computer chips or potato chips; some industries are and others aren't engines for growth.

2. Many countries subsidize chosen exporters and thereby influence who ends up with a comparative advantage in what. Thus, a European consortium of aircraft manufacturers in Britain, France, Germany, and Spain has subsidized the Airbus production. In 1990, for example, the German government paid 390 million DM (Deutsche Mark) to offset adverse exchange rate fluctuations. (The manufacturer had incurred costs in DM but made sales in dollars.) Through such policies, critics say, high-tech U.S. firms, such as Boeing and McDonnell Douglas, are squeezed out of existence. In 1980, the U.S. market share for large commercial aircraft was 87 percent, while the Airbus share was 7 percent. In 1989, the U.S. share was 64 percent, the Airbus share 27 percent. All this occurred despite "free trade" and an obvious violation of the GATT subsidies code.

3. Many countries use tax policies to promote their favored industries. Thus, in 1991, Canada repealed an old excise tax on manufacturers and introduced a broad-based goods and services tax, GST. The tax added 7 percent to the price of almost everything, except basic food, rent, health, and education. Yet exporters could get a rebate of the tax. The result of the repeal of one tax and the imposition plus rebate of another: Canadian exports to the U.S. had a 5 percent price advantage. Canadian exports to the U.S. of certain manufactured goods were expected to rise by $2 billion per year; U.S. exports to Canada of similar goods were destined to fall by $2.5 billion per year.

Examples such as these could be listed endlessly. Free trade critics suggest that the U.S. government, similar to Japan's MITI, identify industries it wishes to promote because they are engines for long-run growth. Having done so, it should put an end to competing imports and provide subsidies, tax breaks, or low-interest loans; whatever it takes to assure industry growth. *Then* it is time to pursue a strategic trade policy and invade the world market—if necessary by using the "crowbar approach" to force open markets abroad. Presumably, this refers to the use of economic, military, and political power to attain a "voluntary import expansion" abroad.

Note: In an unprecedented move, the White House in 1991 listed 22 areas of technological development that "should be nurtured as critical to the national prosperity." Said the White House Office of Science and Technology, "We most recently have been reminded, by the spectacular performance of U.S. coalition forces in the Persian Gulf, of the crucial role that technology plays in military competitiveness. It is equally clear that technology plays a similar role in the economic competitiveness of nations." Among the technologies cited for "nurturing" were intelligent vehicle/highway systems ("smart cars" and "smart highways"), microelectronics, high-definition imaging, and applied molecular biology.

---

[1] See, for example, Paul Krugman, "Is Free Trade Passé?" *Journal of Economic Perspectives,* No. 2, 1987; Paul Krugman, ed., *Strategic Trade Policy and the New International Economics* (Cambridge, MA: MIT Press, 1986); Clyde V. Prestowitz, Jr., Alan Tonelson, Robert W. Jerome, "The Last Gasp of GATTism," *Harvard Business Review,* March-April 1991, pp. 130–138.

Sources: Clive Crook, "World Trade," *The Economist,* September 22, 1990, pp. 5–40; Clyde H. Farnsworth, "New Tax to Aid Canada in Trade," *The New York Times,* January 21, 1991, pp. C1 and 2; Dominick Salvatore, "How to Solve the U.S.-Japan Trade Problem," *Challenge,* January-February, 1991, pp. 40–46; U.S. International Trade Commission, "United States Asks Dispute-Settlement Panel to Examine German Exchange Rate Guarantee Scheme for Airbus," *International Economic Review,* April 1991, p. 5; Kevin L. Kearns, "Japan's Sleight of Hand in Trade," *The New York Times,* April 7, 1991, p. F11; David E. Rosenbaum, "Trade Issues Enter Crucial Political Phase," *The New York Times,* April 9, 1991, p. D5; Martin Tolchin, "White House Lists 22 Areas for Nurturing," *The New York Times,* April 26, 1991, p. D17.

---

growth of national output from 1913–1950 with 1950–1990: In the United States, that growth rate rose from 2.8 to 3.2 percent, in Canada from 2.9 to 4.3 percent, in Japan from 1.8 to 7.4 percent, in France from 1.0 to 3.9 percent, in Great Britain from 1.3 to 2.5 percent, in Italy from 1.4 to 4.2 percent, in West Germany from 1.3 to 4.4 percent. The data are similar in the less developed world where countries with a strong, outward-looking pro-trade orientation have experienced growth rates six times as high as other countries that pursued inward-oriented policies favoring self-sufficiency.[4]

Yet it is also true that some prominent economists have recently joined protection-minded lawmakers to denounce the long-run trend toward free international trade and to demand that the U.S. government pursue a policy of *managed* trade. Ideas in History, The Strategic Trade Model, explains.

Whatever the outcome of the seemingly endless debate between free traders and protectionists, all aspects of modern economics are permeated by the fact that we live in a global economy in which the promise and problems of international trade are forever present. This is clearly true in the microeconomic world of individual consumers, workers, and firms—all of whom are affected by flows of exports and imports that, in turn, affect the prices they pay, the wages and profits they earn, the jobs they can get, and so much more. It is equally true in the macroeconomic world of government policy makers whose attempt to fight recession or inflation is continually circumscribed by international flows of commodities, services, and financial capital and by changes in exchange rates that reinforce or counteract the intended results of governmental actions.

---

[4] *Economic Report of the President* (Washington, D.C.: U.S. Government Printing Office), January 1989, p. 150, and February 1991, p. 411.

Summary

1. In recent decades, the United States economy has experienced an ever-increasing degree of integration with the economies of other countries throughout the world. Microeconomic as well as macroeconomic theorizing must take this fact into account.

2. What explains the international flows of goods? According to the theory of *absolute* advantage, the citizens of every nation specialize in the production and export of those goods they can produce with fewer units of resources than anyone else, while importing other goods the production of which requires fewer resources elsewhere. According to Ricardo's theory of *comparative* advantage, mutually beneficial trade between two countries arises—regardless of the presence or absence of absolute advantage—whenever one country is *relatively* better at producing a good than the other country, a fact that is indicated by the former country's ability to produce a good at a lower opportunity cost (measured in terms of other goods forgone). The importance of Ricardo's insight can hardly be exaggerated. It can be illustrated graphically by the fact that nations specializing acording to comparative advantage, and then trading with each other, can consume a set of goods beyond the confines of their domestic production possibilities frontiers.

3. The dramatic reduction in scarcity that Ricardo's theory promises can be realized in various ways. In command economies, conscious decisions on specialization and trade are required of central planners. In market economies, the result can be achieved through decentralized decision making with the help of special types of markets for foreign exchange. As long as relative prices of goods in each country reflect the opportunity costs of goods and as long as free markets for foreign exchange are allowed to establish equilibrium rates of exchange, a country with a comparative advantage in a good will also enjoy a lower absolute price. Thus, trade in accordance with comparative advantage will occur spontaneously.

4. While trade in accordance with comparative advantage increases the availability of goods to each country as a whole, it is possible for particular individuals or groups to lose when nations open up trade. This fact is shown with the demand-and-supply model and the concepts of consumer surplus and producer surplus. Consumers in exporting countries and producers in importing countries tend to lose from free trade, while consumers in importing countries and producers in exporting countries gain.

5. Governments often seek to mitigate the localized harm that is associated with free trade by erecting barriers to such trade. Such protectionism can take numerous forms, including the imposition of tariffs and various types of non-tariff measures, ranging from import quotas to voluntary export restraints, non-automatic import authorizations, variable import levies, antidumping rules, and more.

6. Many reasons have been advanced in favor of protectionism. Some of them make sense, many are less defensible. This chapter examines the national-defense argument, the young-economy argument, the infant-industry argument, the saving-our-jobs argument, the terms-of-trade argument, and the keeping-our-money-at-home argument.

7. The history of U.S. commercial policy began with high tariffs motivated by the young-economy argument. The 1930 Smoot-Hawley Act raised tariffs to an all-time high. In 1934, a long-range policy of tariff reductions was initiated; it was continued since 1947 under the auspices of GATT and was further stimulated by the 1957 formation of the European Economic Community. By 1990, average U.S. tariff rates reached an all-time low of under 4 percent. There is strong evidence that the decades-long trend in the U.S. and elsewhere toward freer trade has contributed significantly to the growing prosperity of the countries involved—just as Ricardo's theory predicts. Nevertheless, some recent critics suggest the substitution of a strategic policy of managed trade for a policy of free trade.

Key Concepts

ad valorem tariff
antidumping rules
appreciation
autarky
commercial policy
consumer surplus
countervailing tariffs
deadweight loss
depreciation
dutiable imports
escape clause
exchange rate
export subsidies
foreign exchange markets

gross barter terms of trade
import quota
infant-industry argument
keeping-our-money-at-home argument
marginal rate of transformation
most-favored nation treatment
national-defense argument
non-automatic import authorizations
nontariff barriers
orderly marketing agreement

peril points
producer surplus
protectionism
saving-our-jobs argument
specific tariff
tariff
terms-of-trade argument
theory of absolute advantage
theory of comparative advantage
variable import levies
voluntary export restraints (VERs)
young-economy argument

Questions and Problems

1. Consider Table 1. Make a single numerical change in part (a) of the table that would wipe out Ricardo's reason for international trade. Explain what you did.

2. Consider the following data and determine who, if anyone, has a comparative advantage and in what product.

   Resource Units Needed per Unit of Output

	France	Italy
Computers	100	150
TV sets	50	50

3. Consider the data of Problem 2 and determine whether proper specialization in production could
   a. raise the world output of computers without changing that of TV sets.
   b. raise the world output of TV sets without changing that of computers.
   c. raise the world output of both goods simultaneously.

4. Reconsider Table 2. Unlike in the text example, could the two countries increase the world's output of cloth without reducing that of wine? Explain.

5. Consider the following data and determine who, if anyone, has a comparative advantage and in what product.

   Output Producible by 100 Units of Resources

	Great Britain	Germany
Cameras	500	1,000
Trucks	5	8

6. Still using the data of Problem 5, determine a scheme of specialization and trade that would give both countries more cameras but the same number of trucks. Let the gain from trade be shared unequally.

7. "There is a basic flaw in Ricardo's theory. The output gains from specialization and trade that he pictures will be eaten up by the need to divert valuable resources from the production of other goods to the transportation industry. After all, Portuguese wine doesn't get to England by magic, nor does English cloth get to Portugal in that way." Comment.

8. Figure 2 (reproduced below) illustrates Ricardo's theory with the help of two production possibilities frontiers that are convex (bowed out) with respect to the origin of the graphs. What would it mean if the two frontiers were straight lines instead?

9. Reconsider Problem 2. If international trade in fact opened up between France and Italy, what might the "terms of trade" be, that is, how many TV sets might trade for each computer? Justify your answer.

10. Reconsider Figure 4. Can you see Chapter 1's optimization principle at work? Explain.

11. Reconsider Figure A (reproduced on the following page) and its discussion in Example 1. With the help of the graph, confirm these values mentioned in the text:

    a. the change in consumer surplus
    b. the change in producer surplus
    c. the value of tariff revenue
    d. the value of the quota
    e. the deadweight loss

12. "I am terribly confused. In Chapter 3, I learned to find the equilibrium price at the intersection of demand and supply. In this chapter's Figure 5, this ceases to be true." Comment on this remark.

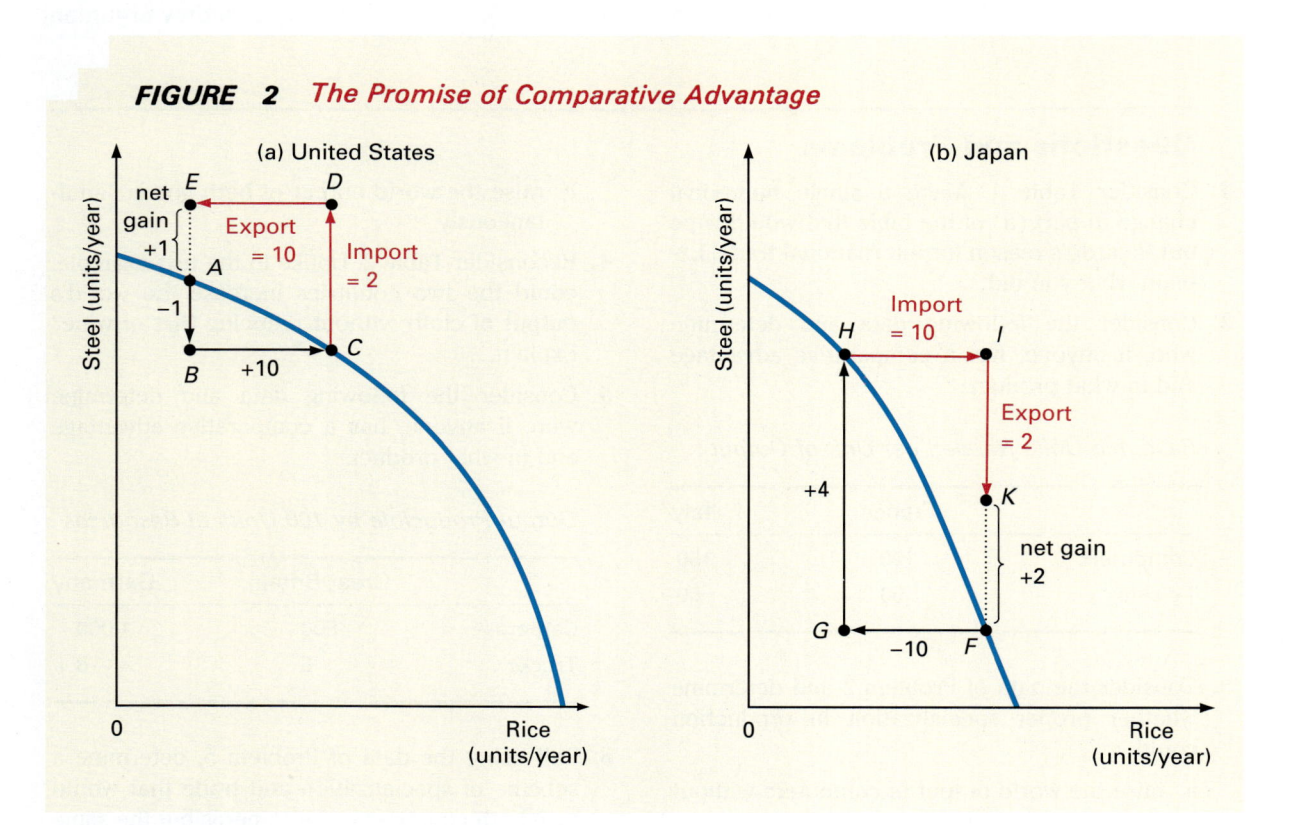

FIGURE 2 *The Promise of Comparative Advantage*

FIGURE A

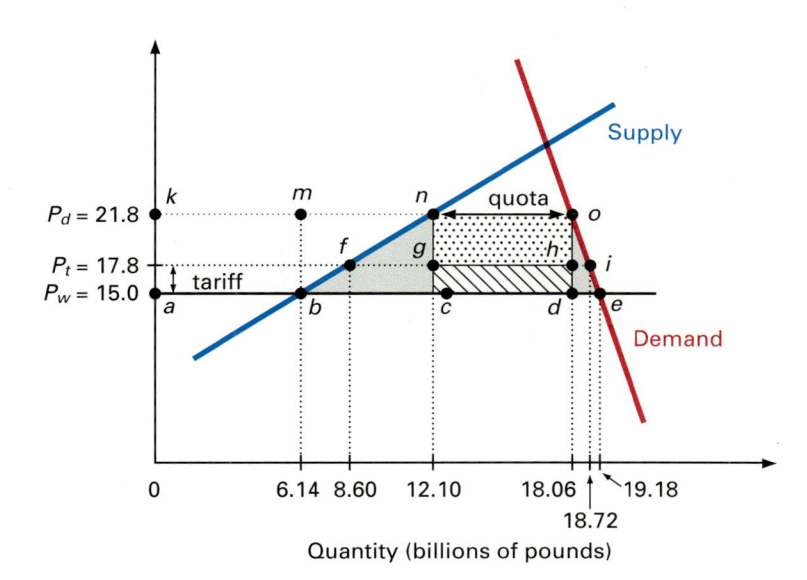

Figure shows supply and demand curves with:
- $P_d = 21.8$
- $P_t = 17.8$
- $P_w = 15.0$
- tariff between P_w and P_t
- Quantity axis (billions of pounds): 6.14, 8.60, 12.10, 18.06, 18.72, 19.18
- Labeled points: k, m, n, o, f, g, h, i, a, b, c, d, e
- quota region indicated between 12.10 and 18.06

13. Comment on these arguments for imposing tariffs:

   a. "We must impose tariffs against low-wage countries lest they undersell us in everything."
   b. "Tariffs are the best type of tax our government can impose; foreigners end up paying it."

14. Here are some actual exchange rates as of a recent date. In each case, determine whether a depreciation of the dollar would be associated with a rise or fall of the stated rate.

   a. $.1563/franc (France)
   b. .3769 dinar (Bahrain)/$
   c. $.66304/cruzado (Brazil)
   d. $.061012/rupee (India)
   e. 2,121.02 lira (Turkey)/$
   f. $1.6285/pound (Great Britain)

PART II

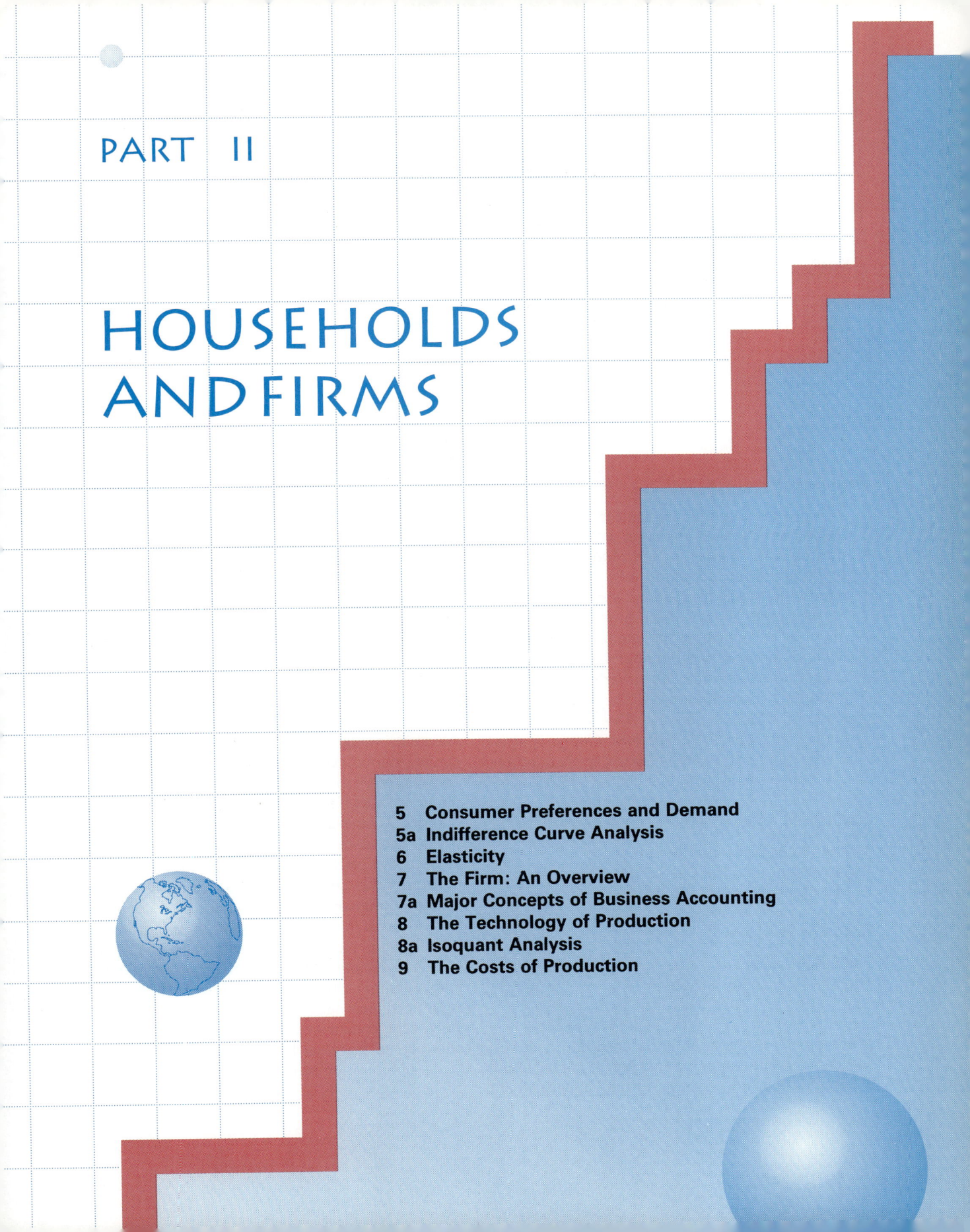

HOUSEHOLDS AND FIRMS

5 Consumer Preferences and Demand
5a Indifference Curve Analysis
6 Elasticity
7 The Firm: An Overview
7a Major Concepts of Business Accounting
8 The Technology of Production
8a Isoquant Analysis
9 The Costs of Production

CHAPTER 5

CONSUMER PREFERENCES AND DEMAND

Preview

This chapter explores the factors that lie behind the market demand line for a good that was introduced in Chapter 3. The theory of cardinal utility is introduced, along with the crucial distinction between total utility and marginal utility. Declining marginal utility is shown to explain each individual consumer's downward sloping demand, and the optimization principle is used to explain the consumer's behavior. An important criterion for utility maximization (Jevons' Rule) is derived. This chapter's appendix introduces the modern theory of consumer behavior, which is based entirely on ordinal utility measurements.

Examples

1. The Water-Diamond Paradox
2. Tokyo Journal: The Case of $115 Melons
3. Micromarketing: Hitting the Bull's-Eye

Ideas in History

The Felicific Calculus
The Marginal Utility School

Chapter 3 of this book introduced the model of demand and supply; a number of applications illustrated its power to explain what happens when consumers and producers meet one another in markets for goods. In this chapter, we take a detailed look at the demand side of the model. We begin by asking what it is that household-consumers of goods seek to accomplish.

Utility Maximization

Economists postulate that consumers, by and large, are rational beings. As such, consumers attempt to maximize welfare or **utility**, the enjoyment consumers derive from the choices they make. These choices, inevitably, are made under less than ideal circumstances. On the one hand, each consumer harbors a near-infinite desire for goods; on the other hand, each is constrained by a limited budget and positive prices, which assures that only a small portion of the desired goods can be acquired. Presumably, ordinary consumers want to squeeze the largest possible amount of satisfaction out of their limited funds just like the government official discussed in Chapter 1 (who wanted to save the maximum number of lives a limited budget would allow). Such maximum satisfaction can be achieved—provided each consumer's budget is spent with careful attention to marginal benefits and marginal costs, as the optimization principle demands (see Chapter 1, Focus 1).

CAUTION

Economists who postulate that consumers seek to maximize their utility are often misunderstood. Economists are not assuming that all consumers are completely selfish and unaccompanied by any concern for others. The utility maximization assumption is perfectly consistent with people being selfish, selfless, or a mixture of both. When citing this goal, economists merely express the belief that people will use their limited incomes to make as much progress toward their goals in life as possible, whatever these goals might be. Such progress is as important to egotists (who want goods only for themselves) as to altruists (who want goods for others).

Cardinal Utility Versus Ordinal Utility

When one thinks about the enjoyment or utility a person might derive from the consumption of any good, one thing becomes clear: Utility is a subjective quantity that cannot be measured in an obvious way. We can measure a person's blood pressure as so many pounds per square inch, height as so many inches, and weight as so many pounds. In each case, a commonly accepted unit of measurement exists, along with an instrument to do the measuring. But how are we to measure *utility* and thus, assess whether it has reached its highest possible value?

Economists of the last century, such as William S. Jevons and Alfred Marshall, seemed to have little trouble with that question. They were influenced by the British philosopher Jeremy Bentham, who argued that utility could be measured—if not in practice, at least in principle—with *cardinal numbers* (such as 1, 2, 3, and so on) that were attached to units called **utils.** If a util is viewed as a hypothetical unit of enjoyment that a consumer derives from consumption, one might say that the consumption of a loaf of bread gave a consumer 80 utils, the consumption of a pound of beef 240 utils, and the joint consumption of both provided 80 + 240 = 320 utils. Bentham and his followers even believed it possible to make meaningful comparisons of such imaginary util numbers between persons so that 240 utils for John and 60 utils for Jane came to 300 utils for both of them combined. Ideas in History, The Felicific Calculus, elaborates.

Economists of the cardinal utility school built an elaborate theory of consumer behavior upon the Benthamite foundations. Yet, there were other economists, such as Francis Y. Edgeworth (1845–1926) and Irving Fisher (1867–1947) who disagreed with the notion of cardinal utility measurement. They rejected the ideas that any individual could attach utility numbers to quantities consumed in the first place, that such numbers could then be added together, and—above all—that such numbers could be compared among individuals in any meaningful sense. These critics provided an alternative. They thought people were quite capable of attaching *ordinal numbers* (such as first, second, third, and so on) to quantities of consumption goods. Thus, a consumer could designate quantity x as first in utility, quantity y as second, quantity z as third (indicating preference of x over y and z and of y over z). But such a consumer could not ever say that x provided 300 utils, y only 180 utils, and z a mere 17.9 utils. As the appendix to this chapter shows, the ordinal utility school has now swept the field, and yet its conclusions are the same as those of the cardinal utility theorists.

Total Utility Versus Marginal Utility

The British economist William Stanley Jevons was first in the English-speaking world to offer in print a complete theory of consumer behavior that was entirely based on Bentham's cardinal utility foundation. Jevons insisted, however, that a careful distinction be made between total utility and marginal utility. Ideas in History, The Marginal Utility School, indicates how other European economists came to similar conclusions at about the same time.

Table 1 illustrates the approach Jevons took. During a given period an individual might consume various alternative quantities of a good, such as bread (column 1), given constant amounts of other goods. A total utility, measured in utils, was then associated with each of the alternative quantities (column 2). Other things being equal, this relationship between alternative quantities of a good consumed (column 1) and the associated total utility

TABLE 1 A Consumer's Utility Function

Quantity of bread consumed (lb. per week) (1)	Total utility (utils) (2)	Marginal utility (utils) (3)
0	0	
		80
1	80	
		50
2	130	
		30
3	160	
		20
4	180	
		10
5	190	
		5
6	195	

Other things being equal, the relationship between alternative quantities of bread consumed (col. 1) and the associated total utility reaped by the consumer (col. 2) is called the consumer's utility function. It can be used to calculate marginal utility (col. 3). Note how marginal utility declines (from 80 to 5 utils) as the quantity consumed rises by successive units (from 0 to 6 lb. of bread per week). The opposite is implied as well. As the quantity consumed falls (from 6 to 0 lb. of bread per week), marginal utility rises (from 5 to 80 utils).

reaped by the consumer (column 2) is called the consumer's **utility function;** Jevons viewed it as a numerical expression of the consumer's current preference or taste for the good in question. Presumably, the column (2) numbers in our table would all be larger if the consumer had a stronger taste for the good; they would all be smaller if the consumer's taste were weaker. And the numbers might change over time if the consumer's taste were to change. Similarly, different consumers with different tastes possess different utility functions at a given moment of time, and this would be expressed by differences in the column (2) util numbers.

Column (3) is derived from column (2) with the help of the marginalist thinking that Jevons pioneered. He calculated the change in total utility (column 3) that is associated with a unit change in a good's quantity consumed—other things being equal—and called it **marginal utility.** Furthermore, he argued that the consumption of any good was likely to be subject to the operation of the **"law" of declining marginal utility**: Given a consumer's tastes and the quantities of all other goods being consumed, the greater is the quantity consumed of a given good during a period, the smaller will its marginal utility usually be. This "law" is simply a special version of Chapter 1's "law" of declining marginal benefits, and the reasoning behind it is the same. Typically, consumers who want a good are eager to get a first unit of it and thus, derive a relatively high extra utility from it. In our example, as consumption rises from 0 to 1 unit, total utility rises from 0 to 80 utils; hence the extra or marginal util-

CAUTION

Table 1 does not show it, but it is conceivable that additional units consumed eventually yield zero or even negative marginal utility. Thus, a seventh unit of bread in our example may add nothing to total utility at all, and any such level of consumption at which total utility has peaked and thus is associated with a zero marginal utility is referred to as the level of **satiation.** *Consumption beyond that level subtracts from the total of utility and would not be undertaken by a rational consumer, which is why this possibility has not been shown in Table 1.*

EXAMPLE 1

The Water-Diamond Paradox

Before economists introduced the distinction between total utility and marginal utility, they were frequently confused by the low market price of "important" things and the high market price of "unimportant" things. Consider how Adam Smith was troubled by the water-diamond paradox.

Things which have the greatest value in use, frequently have little or no value in exchange; and on the contrary, those which have the greatest value in exchange have frequently little or no value in use. Nothing is more useful than water; but it will scarce purchase anything; scarce anything can be had in exchange for it. A diamond, on the contrary, has scarce any value in use; but a very great quantity of other goods may frequently be had in exchange for it.[1]

Yet the paradox disappears once one realizes that in most places on earth water is plentiful relative to demand, while diamonds are extremely scarce in relation to it. In Figure A, given identical demands for water and diamonds, the high supply of water in panel (a) produces a

FIGURE A

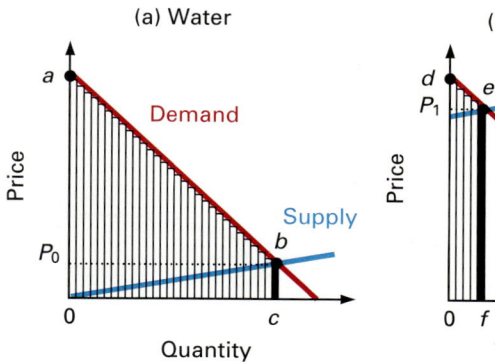

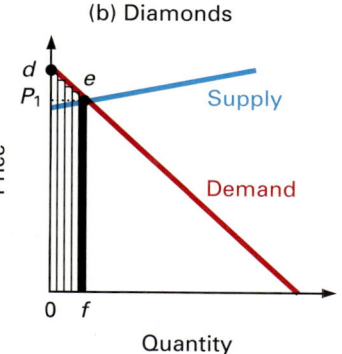

(a) Water

(b) Diamonds

low equilibrium price, P_0 (despite the fact that people would perish without water). The low supply of diamonds in panel (b) produces a high equilibrium price, P_1 (despite the fact that life could easily go on without diamonds). The total utility people derive from water quantity $0c$ (the sum of the marginal utility blocks) equals large area $0abc$. The marginal utility is small and equal to block bc. In contrast, the total utility people derive from diamond quantity $0f$ equals small area $0def$, yet the marginal utility is large and equal to block ef.

Note that Figure A depicts the typical situation; exceptions are quite possible. When water is extremely scarce, as in the American West or the Sahara Desert, the water diagram may look like panel (b). Then water's marginal utility and price is high, which explains why Western cowboys and Bedouins have killed other people to gain control of water holes. Similarly, in times of general war, people have gladly exchanged diamonds for simple food or refuge because the latter were equally scarce and precious.

---

[1] Adam Smith, *An Inquiry into the Nature and Causes of the Wealth of Nations* (1776; reprint New York: Modern Library, 1937), p. 28.

---

ity equals +80 utils. Yet as Table 1 indicates, consumers are likely to be ever less eager for additional units the higher their initial consumption level. By the time consumption rises from 5 to 6 units, total utility rises from 190 to 195 utils; hence the marginal utility equals only +5 utils.

If we read Table 1 not from top to bottom but from bottom to top, we discover an important implication of the "law" of declining marginal utility. All else being equal, the *smaller* is the quantity consumed, the *larger* is the marginal utility. People are typically less resistant to losing a unit of a good when they have much of it than when they have little of it. In our example, the consumer would lose a mere 5 utils when changing weekly bread consumption from 6 to 5 pounds, but the same consumer would lose 80 utils when sacrificing the last pound of bread and changing consumption from 1 to 0 unit.

Figure 1 is based on the Table 1 data. The top panel is a graph of column 1 and column 2; the bottom panel graphs column 1 and column 3. The

FIGURE 1 *Total Utility Versus Marginal Utility*

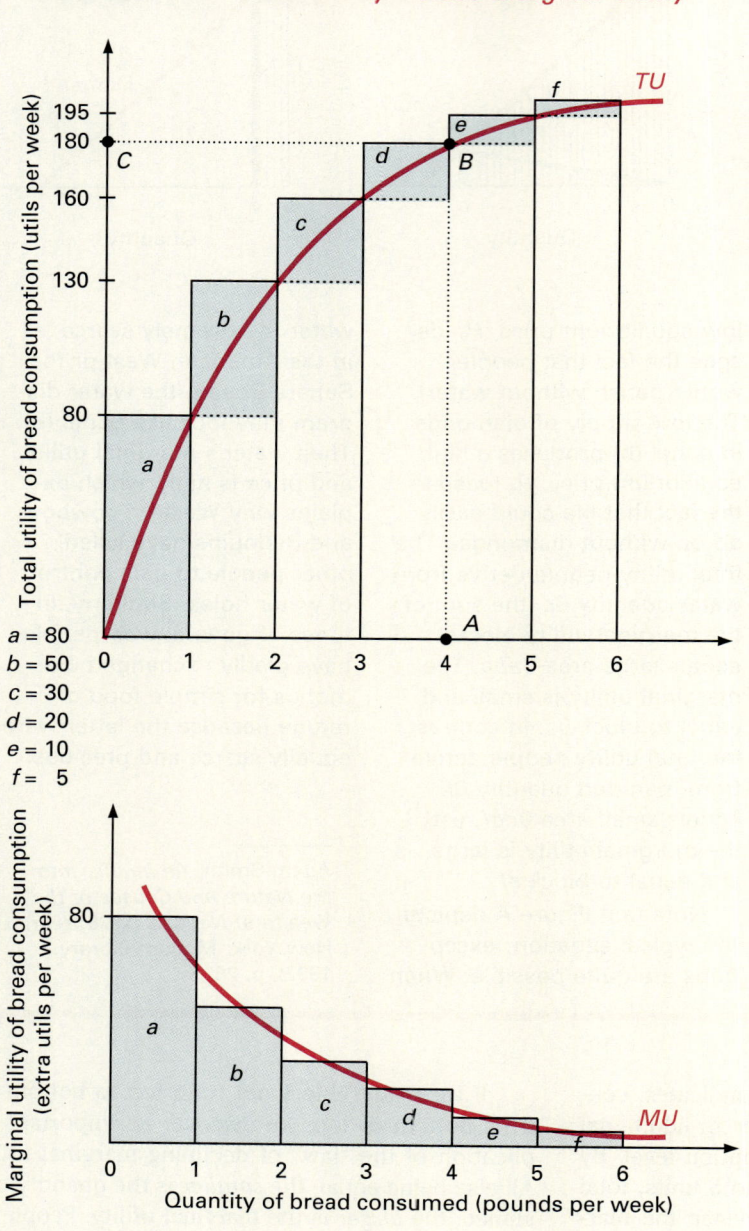

This set of graphs is based on the data in Table 1, and illustrates the "law" of declining marginal utility. It is no accident that these graphs look just like those in Chapter 1's Figure 5, "Heart Attack Treatment: Declining Marginal Benefits."

shaded blocks, measured in units of satisfaction, indicate how increased consumption is associated with ever smaller increases in total utility (top) or—what amounts to the same thing—with declining marginal utility (bottom). Note that the total utility associated with any given quantity consumed can be measured in two ways: as the *height* of the total-utility line at that quantity or as the *area* under the marginal-utility line up to that quantity. Consider the total utility associated with the consumption of 4 pounds of bread per week. In the upper graph, the *height* at point B of the total-utility line clearly equals 180 utils (follow the dotted lines from A to B to C). In the lower graph, the *area* of blocks up to 4 pounds of bread per week comes to $a + b + c + d$, or to $80 + 50 + 30 + 20 = 180$ utils as well.

Example 1 provides an interesting application of the total and marginal utility concepts.

From Marginal Utility to Individual Demand

Jevons and other economic theorists of his time noticed a close link between marginal utility and an individual consumer's demand line. They argued that declining marginal utility, as depicted in the lower panel of Figure 1, was directly responsible for the downward slope of an individual consumer's demand line. A consumer who received 80 utils from the first unit of a good might be willing to pay a maximum price of $8 for that unit. However, because of the "law" of declining marginal utility, the consumer might only receive an extra 50 utils from a second unit, an extra 30 utils from a third unit, and so on (as indicated by blocks a through f in Figure 1); the maximum price the consumer would be willing to pay for a second unit, a third unit, and so on, would accordingly decline as well, perhaps to $5, then $3, and so on. Figure 2 provides an indirect way of measuring declining marginal utility. The consumer's willingness to buy additional units only at ever lower prices can be viewed as evidence of the consumer's declining marginal utility. Thus Figure 2 shows the marginal benefit our consumer derives from bread consumption—measured in dollars rather than utils.

The Optimization Principle Revisited

It is possible to compare the marginal benefit to the marginal cost and figure the consumer's optimizing behavior. Figure 2 showed the maximum prices our consumer would pay for various units of bread; it

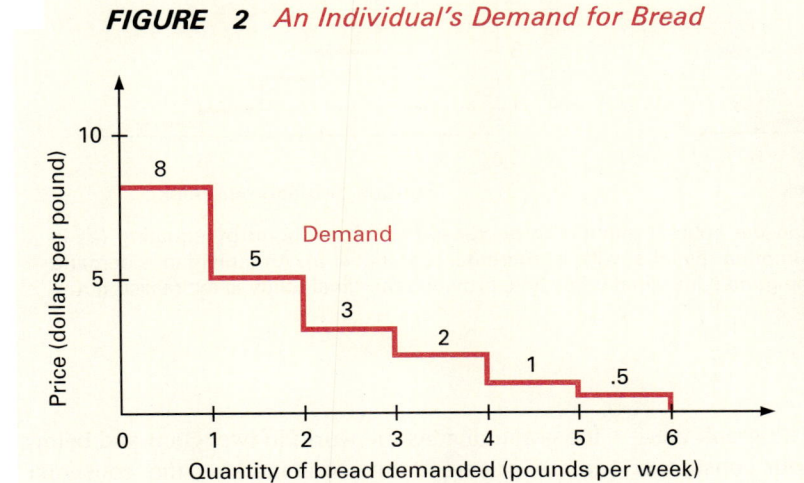

FIGURE 2 *An Individual's Demand for Bread*

This consumer's demand line for bread reflects the declining marginal utility associated with increased bread consumption (lower panel, Figure 1). Because additional units provide ever smaller marginal utility (80, 50, 30, 20, 10, and 5 utils), the maximum price the consumer is willing to pay for additional units declines as well ($8, $5, $3, $2, $1, and $.5).

FIGURE 3 *How a Consumer Can Optimize*

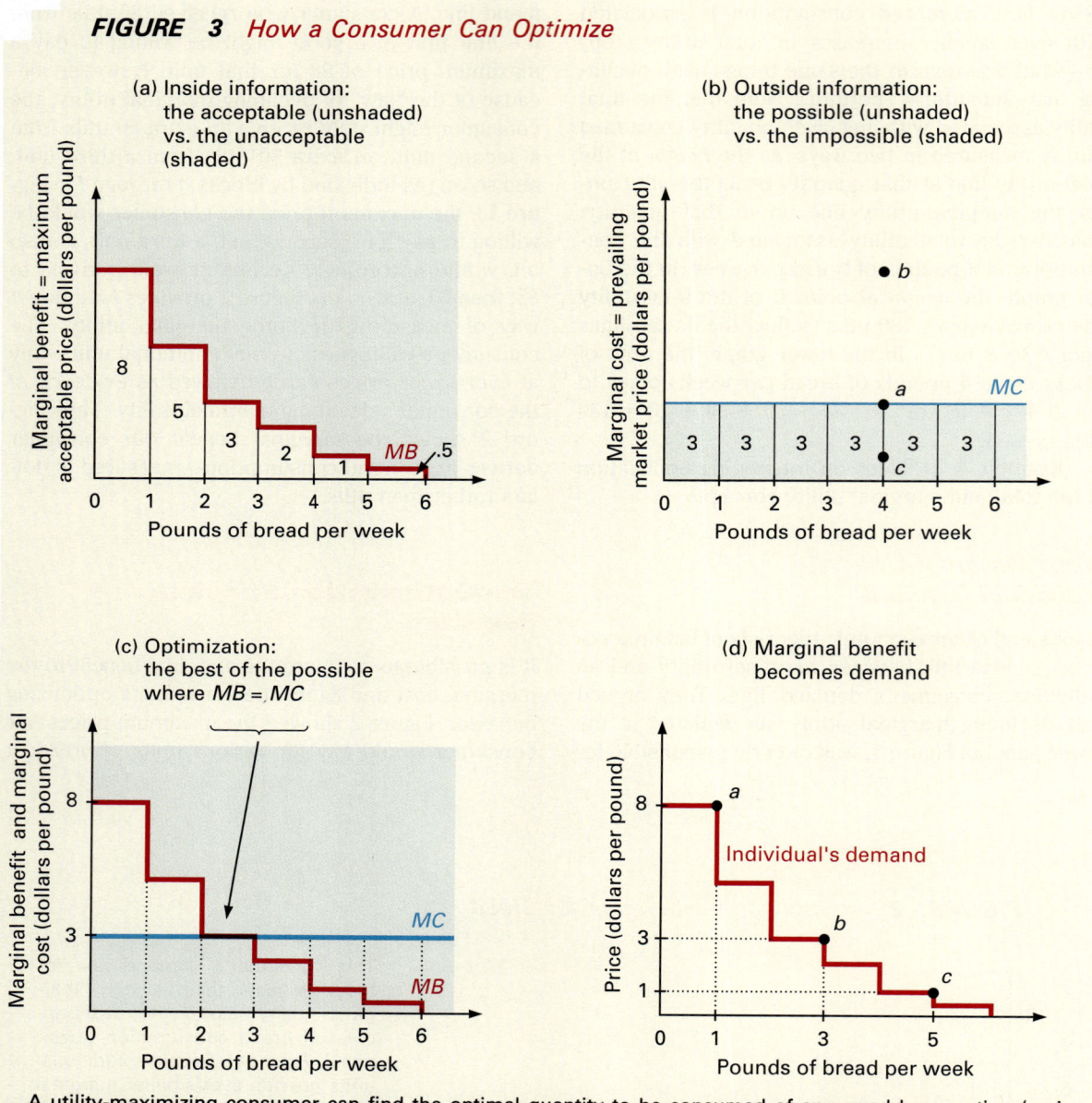

(a) Inside information: the acceptable (unshaded) vs. the unacceptable (shaded)

(b) Outside information: the possible (unshaded) vs. the impossible (shaded)

(c) Optimization: the best of the possible where MB = MC

(d) Marginal benefit becomes demand

A utility-maximizing consumer can find the optimal quantity to be consumed of any good by equating (as in panel c) the marginal benefit of consumption (panel a) with its marginal cost (panel b). An individual's demand line for a good thus comes to equal the good's marginal utility line, provided marginal utility is expressed not in utils but in dollar equivalents.

reappears as panel (a) of Figure 3. The graph contains "inside information" unique to our consumer; it reflects this particular individual's translation of subjectively felt utils into dollars. The color line in the graph divides the world in two: On it and below it are price-quantity combinations the consumer finds acceptable (unshaded); above it lie combinations that are unacceptable (shaded). This particular consumer would buy a first pound of bread for as much as $8; a sixth pound would be bought only for 50¢ or less.

Panel (b), on contrast, depicts "outside information" common to all consumers, the prevailing market price. Our consumer can buy any number of pounds for $3 each, which makes this number our consumer's marginal cost of acquiring bread. Every additional pound can be had for another $3, but none for less. Thus, the marginal cost line drawn also divides the world in two: On it and above it are price-quantity combinations the consumer could choose (unshaded); below it lie combinations that cannot be chosen (shaded). Thus, the consumer could buy 4 pounds per week at $3 each (point a) or if the consumer cared to make a gift to the seller, even at $8 each (point b), but not at $1 each (point c).

To find the optimum quantity of bread consumption, our consumer must coordinate the inside information of marginal benefits, shown in panel (a), with the outside information of marginal costs, shown in panel (b). This task is achieved in panel (c), where Chapter 1's optimization principle is applied visually by superimposing the marginal benefit and marginal cost lines. From their intersection (to which the arrow points), the optimal purchase is 3 pounds of bread per week. Only at this quantity does there exist an equality (at $3 per pound) of marginal benefit, MB, and marginal cost, MC, as Chapter 1, Focus 1, demands. At lower consumption levels, MB exceeds MC; at higher levels, MC exceeds MB. Only the 3 pound per week choice maximizes the consumer's net benefit from consuming bread; it equals the total benefit of buying 3 pounds (the sum of marginal benefits worth $8 + $5 + $3 = $16) minus the total cost of doing so (giving up 3 × $3 = $9 of other goods). This net benefit of $16 − $9 = $7 equals the unshaded area in panel (c) and is this particular buyer's *consumer surplus* (a concept introduced in Chapter 4).

Panel (d) returns us to Jevons's insight that a consumer's marginal utility line, when translated into dollar equivalents, constitutes the consumer's demand. As we have already noted in panel (c), this utility maximizing consumer would select a weekly optimum bread quantity of 3 pounds when faced with a market price of $3. This situation is now shown by point b in panel (d). Yet, if this consumer faced a higher market price of $8, the MC line in panel (c) would lie at that higher level and the $MB = MC$ optimum would occur when consuming 1 pound per week. This is shown by point a in panel (d). Finally, if this consumer faced a lower market price of $1, the MC line in panel (c) would lie at that lower level and the $MB = MC$ optimum would occur when consuming 5 pounds per week. This is shown by point c in panel (d). Thus, the dollar marginal benefit line is, in effect, the consumer's demand line for bread. The following section examines how similar demand lines for many consumers combine to create the market demand line introduced in Chapter 3.

From Individual Demand to Market Demand

Thousands, perhaps millions, of buyers may appear in any one market, but to illustrate how market demand derives from individual demands, we need not concern ourselves with such large numbers. Let us imagine just three buyers in the market for bread. Their respective demand schedules might be those shown in columns 2 through 4 of Table 2. The demand schedule of consumer A is the one graphed in panel (d) of Figure 3. The assumed demand schedules of consumers A, B, and C and the market demand schedule of column 5 are graphed in Figure 4. If we added a much larger number of individual demands, the resultant market demand line would take on the smooth shape shown in Chapter 3 and the stairstep appearance would disappear.

One more point must be made at this stage. While downward-sloping demand lines based on declining marginal utilities are typical, exceptions are possible. Example 2 explains one case.

The Model Expanded: Two Goods and More

The previous sections summarize the extent to which cardinal utility theory has been able to explain consumer choices with respect to a single good. What happens in the more realistic case when consumers choose between two goods or among a multitude of them? On this matter, too, Jevons had plenty to say. Let us follow his reasoning with the help of Table 3. Any consumer is likely to face declining marginal utilities no matter which good is

TABLE 2 Deriving the Market Demand Schedule

Price $/lb. (1)	Quantity of bread demanded (pounds per week)			
	Consumer A (2)	Consumer B (3)	Consumer C (4)	All three consumers (5) = (2) + (3) + (4)
10	0	1	0	1
9	0	2	1	3
8	1	3	1	5
7	1	4	3	8
6	1	5	3	9
5	2	6	5	13
4	2	7	5	14
3	3	8	7	18
2	4	9	7	20
1	5	10	8	23
0	6	10	8	24

A market demand schedule can be derived by adding, at each conceivable price, the quantities demanded by all potential market participants, all else being held equal.

FIGURE 4 Deriving the Market Demand Line

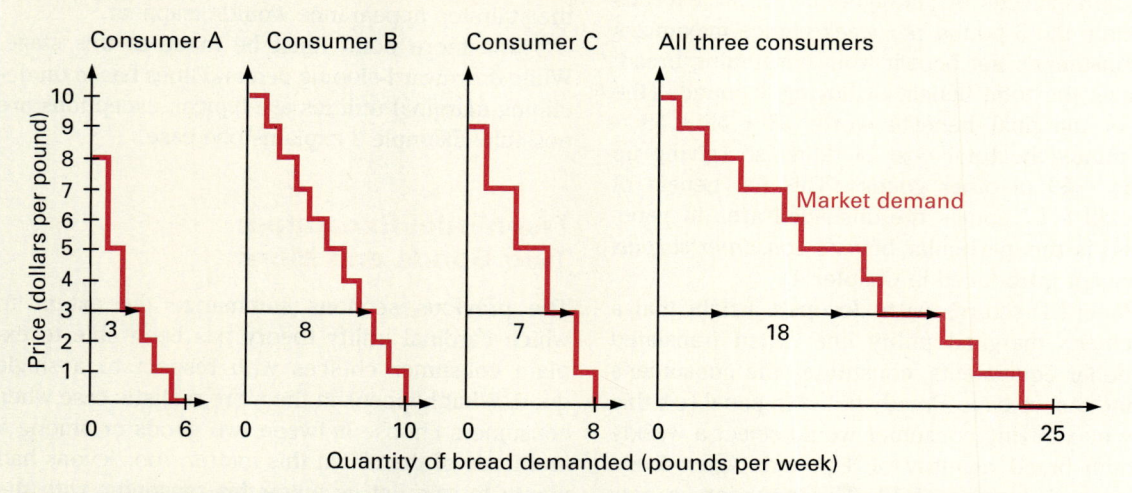

This set of graphs is based on Table 2. It shows how, all else being equal, the market demand line can be derived by adding horizontally, at each conceivable price, the quantities demanded by all potential market participants.

EXAMPLE 2

Tokyo Journal: The Case of $115 Melons

The "laws" of demand and declining marginal utility are closely linked. For most people, a larger quantity consumed is associated with a lower marginal utility; hence they buy a larger quantity only at a lower price. There are, however, rare exceptions in which a lower price makes people buy less rather than more. The matter was first noted by the American economist Thorstein Veblen (1857–1929), who wrote about people advertising their wealth through "conspicuous consumption." The more expensive a good was, the more they would buy it; when the good's price fell, they abandoned it. Recently, this *Veblen effect* was observed in Japan.

According to an age-old custom, the Japanese give one another end-of-year gifts. It is an essential part of friendships, family, and business relations. The number and value of gifts received are seen as a measure of the status of the recipient. At the end of 1990, a proper gift cost at least 10,000 yen ($75 at the time). A senior government official could look forward to much more. One of them installed four new refrigerators in anticipation of an onslaught of 3-foot whole salmons, boxes of matsutake mushrooms, New Zealand mussels, Maine lobsters, Florida stone crab claws, and California chardonnay. There were $115 melons, too, carefully wrapped in tissue from their days on the vine. But one thing was missing, the usual cases of Scotch. The importer had lowered the price below 10,000 yen and the quantity demanded had plummeted. Scotch was no longer a suitable gift. Presumably, the expensive melons would meet a similar fate: At a much lower price, people would buy fewer rather than more of them.

Source: The New York Times, December 21, 1990, p. A4.

TABLE 3 Choosing Between Two Goods

Bread			Meat		
Quantity consumed (lbs/wk)	Marginal utility (utils/lb)	Marginal-utility-to-price ratio (utils/$)	Quantity consumed (lbs/wk)	Marginal utility (utils/lb)	Marginal-utility-to-price ratio (utils/$)
Q_b	MU_b	MU_b/P_b	Q_m	MU_m	MU_m/P_m
(1)	(2)	$(3) = \frac{(2)}{\$1/lb.}$	(4)	(5)	$(6) = \frac{(5)}{\$5/lb.}$
1	80	80	1	140	28
2	50	50	2	100	20
3	30	30	3	70	14
4	20	20	4	50	10
5	10	10	5	30	6
6	5	5	6	20	4

This table contains a hypothetical consumer's marginal utility functions for bread (columns 1 and 2) and for meat (columns 4 and 5). Assuming that the price of bread, P_b, is $1 per pound, while the price of meat, P_m, is $5 per pound, the additional information in columns 3 and 6 can be derived.

being consumed; this is shown for bread in columns 1 and 2, for meat in columns 4 and 5. Furthermore, every consumer is constrained by a limited budget and positive market prices to acquiring a limited set of goods. Let our consumer's weekly budget equal $9, let the prices of bread and meat equal, respectively, $P_b = \$1$ per pound and $P_m = \$5$ per pound. How would a utility-maximizing consumer proceed?

The correct answer cannot lie in maximizing the number of pounds acquired with the $9 at hand, or in buying 9 pounds of bread rather than slightly less than 2 pounds of meat. Such an approach would be like buying the largest *number* of cereal boxes in a grocery store without ever asking how many ounces of cereal each box contains. Just as modern-day supermarkets help shoppers with unit pricing, listing the ounces of cereal gained per dollar spent on this box or that, Jevons suggested looking at the marginal utility *per dollar* rather than the marginal utility per pound. The necessary information is found by dividing the marginal utility per pound (columns 2 and 5) by the price per pound, which yields the marginal utility each dollar can bring (columns 3 and 6).

A consumer could maximize total utility by now allocating one dollar at a time—always toward the good that at the time promises the greatest increase in total utility and thus delivers the highest marginal utility for the dollar. When the marginal utility per dollar spent on bread exceeds the marginal utility per dollar spent on meat, it makes sense to spend the dollar on bread. When the marginal utility per dollar spent on bread falls short of the marginal utility per dollar spent on meat, spending the dollar on meat is preferable. Proceeding along this path, a wise consumer can allocate a given budget in the best possible way. Numerical Exercise 1 illustrates in detail the decision making process in our example.

We can draw two lessons from the preceding discussion. First, the decision making procedure suggested by Jevons (and illustrated in Numerical Exercise 1) is an application of the optimization principle. The consumer's choice here between bread and meat corresponds to the choice in Chapter 1 between fighting cancer or heart attacks. As each dollar is spent, the consumer must choose between two marginal benefits, one to be realized, the other to be sacrificed. Consider the choice between 80 utils or 28 utils when spending the first dollar. By choosing the 80-util purchase as the marginal benefit to be realized, the consumer sacrifices the 28-util purchase, hence this foregone marginal benefit is nothing but the marginal cost associated with the 80-util choice. Thus, the consumer follows the $MB > MC$ rule of Chapter 1's Focus 1.

Second, as Jevons himself realized, what our example tells us about two goods can be extended to any number of goods.

To maximize utility, a consumer should purchase such quantities of various goods that the marginal utility received per dollar of every good is the same.

This advice is now known as **Jevons' Rule.** When followed, it leads to a state of affairs, known as the **consumer optimum,** in which it is impossible to raise total utility from a given budget by buying more of one good and less of another. Jevons' Rule is formally stated in Focus 1.

FOCUS 1

Jevons' Rule

Utility is maximized when

$$\frac{MU_a}{P_a} = \frac{MU_b}{P_b} = \frac{MU_c}{P_c} = \cdots = \frac{MU_n}{P_n},$$

where the *MU*s are the marginal utilities per pound, gallon, or similar physical units of goods *a* to *n*, while the *P*s are the dollar prices of these goods per identical physical units; hence any one ratio, such as MU_a/P_a equals the marginal utility per dollar's worth of a given good.

A consumer who allocates a budget in violation of Jevons' Rule, such that MU_a/P_a exceeds MU_b/P_b, can raise total utility by buying more of good *a* and less of *b*. In the process, MU_a will fall, but MU_b will rise (remember the "law" of declining marginal utility) until the *MU/P* ratios are equal (total utility is

NUMERICAL EXERCISE 1

Allocating a $9 Budget for Maximum Total Utility

Dollar spent (1)	Available choices (P_b = $1/lb.; P_m = $5/lb.) (2)	Decision (3)	Total utility (4)	Dollars remaining (5)
1st	1st lb. of bread, yielding 80 utils or 1st 1/5 lb. of meat, yielding 28 utils	buy 1st lb. of bread	0 + 80 = 80 utils	8
2nd	2nd lb. of bread, yielding 50 utils or 1st 1/5 lb. of meat, yielding 28 utils	buy 2nd lb. of bread	80 + 50 = 130 utils	7
3rd	3rd lb. of bread, yielding 30 utils or 1st 1/5 lb. of meat, yielding 28 utils	buy 3rd lb. of bread	130 + 30 = 160 utils	6
4th	4th lb. of bread, yielding 20 utils or 1st 1/5 lb. of meat, yielding 28 utils	buy 1st 1/5 lb. of meat	160 + 28 = 188 utils	5
5th	4th lb. of bread, yielding 20 utils or 2nd 1/5 lb. of meat, yielding 28 utils	buy 2nd 1/5 lb. of meat	188 + 28 = 216 utils	4
6th	4th lb. of bread, yielding 20 utils or 3rd 1/5 lb. of meat, yielding 28 utils	buy 3rd 1/5 lb. of meat	216 + 28 = 244 utils	3
7th	4th lb. of bread, yielding 20 utils or 4th 1/5 lb. of meat, yielding 28 utils	buy 4th 1/5 lb. of meat	244 + 28 = 272 utils	2
8th	4th lb. of bread, yielding 20 utils or 5th 1/5 lb. of meat, yielding 28 utils	buy 5th 1/5 lb. of meat	272 + 28 = 300 utils	1
9th	4th lb. of bread, yielding 20 utils or 6th 1/5 lb. of meat, yielding 20 utils	a toss-up; buy, e.g., 4th lb. of bread	300 + 20 = 320 utils	0

By allocating one dollar at a time—always with a view toward reaping the highest marginal utility then available—a consumer can divide a $9 budget between two goods, while achieving maximum total utility. In this example, the purchase of 4 lb. of bread (for $4) and 1 lb. of meat (for $5) exhausts the $9 budget and raises total utility to a 320-util maximum.

maximized). Notice how our consumer in Numerical Exercise 1 has reached the ideal position by the time the 9th dollar is to be allocated. Regardless of how it is spent, total utility will be raised by 20 utils. At that point, (MU_b/P_b) = 20 utils per dollar and (MU_m/P_m) = 20 utils as well. This chapter's appendix confirms Jevons' Rule through the ordinal-utility approach.

Example 3 shows how American firms have learned to zero in on their best customers by using detailed information on the past choices that consumers have made.

EXAMPLE 3

Micromarketing: Hitting the Bull's-Eye

In the heart of the Pennsylvania Amish country, where horse-drawn carriages are still the daily mode of transportation, a new type of research company uses a mainframe computer to peek inside grocery stores thousands of miles away and collect data on the preferences of millions of consumers. Market Metrics of Lancaster regularly analyzes the information provided by 30,000 supermarket checkout scanners that record the type, quantity, and price of every product purchased. This information is collated with U.S. census data that provide detail on the economic, social, and ethnic make-up of all the people residing in the immediate neighborhood of each store. Additional information comes from consumer credit bureaus, banks, and manufacturers, all of whom learn a great deal about specific households every time one of their members applies for a credit card, takes on a mortgage, or fills out a warranty card.

This kind of research pays off because marketers love the highly targeted lists Market Metrics provides to sellers, enabling them to zero in on just the right people with laser beam precision. Consider the detail known about an Atlanta, Georgia, A&P Store and its customers. The store has 10 checkouts with scanners and 33,900 square feet of selling space. It has 20 end-of-aisle displays, 150 feet devoted to upright freezers, another 150 feet to health and beauty products, and 8 feet to powdered drinks. There is a fresh coffee grinder. Average weekly sales are $350,000, which provides a 9 percent market share. (Two Kroger stores are the main competitors.) There are 14,372 customers in the average week; given the traffic pattern and roads, most of them come from the northeast. (Access from the north and south is very difficult, average from the west.) The typical household in the area has 3 to 4 members; most of them are white. A quarter of the population is under 14; parents tend to be blue-collar workers; their average income is $42,912 per year.

This type of information on types of consumers and their choices has enabled firms to push their sales to unexpected heights. Thus, Kraft USA learned to stock one supermarket with row after row of strawberry flavored Philadelphia Cream Cheese, another with the diet version, and another with large 12 ounce cartons instead. Pepsi stocks its flavored soft drinks in stores near lots of children; Peter Pan Peanut Butter sells best among suburban households with heads aged 18–54 who have children, love theme parks, and are heavy video renters. Stouffer's Red Box Frozen Entrees do best among consumers aged 55 and up who travel frequently, give parties, and read newspapers a lot. Coors Light Beer fares best in stores surrounded by 21–34-year-olds, with middle to upper incomes and a penchant for health clubs, rock music, cookouts, and watching TV sports. Did you know West Coast metropolitan residents with incomes above $35,000 can't keep their hands off Borden's Classico pasta sauce? That Quaker Oats sales soared when it pinpointed stores whose customers were baking from scratch and couldn't resist those old-fashioned cookie tins sitting right next to oatmeal packages?

No matter how much marketers love the new approach, others are worried about Big Brother prying into American households. The privacy issue was addressed by the Computer Professionals for Social Responsibility at a Burlingame, California conference in 1991. In the preceding year, Lotus Development Corporation of Cambridge, Massachusetts had created two data bases for personal computer users. The first one, *Marketplace: Business,* provided detailed factual information about 9.2 million American firms, right down to the name and telephone number of the key purchasing executive. A second program, *Marketplace: Households,* chronicled the names, ages, addresses, lifestyles, and buying habits of 120 million consumers—without their consent. After receiving 30,000 complaints about the abuse of private information, Lotus withdrew the two products. Meanwhile, Trinet America, Inc., a Parsippany, New Jersey, firm, produced a similar product, *Lists-on-Disk.* True enough, products such as these may not give you information if you ask directly for George Bush, but, as one reporter noted, you can ask the computer for a list of executives earning more than $200,000 a year, living on the East Coast, and carrying the American Express card and, lo and behold, the printout will note a certain George Herbert Walker Bush, age 65, living at 1600 Pennsylvania Avenue, Washington, D.C. More likely than not, you will end up on such a list as well.

Sources: Michael J. McCarthy, "Marketers Zero In On Their Customers," *The Wall Street Journal,* March 18, 1991, pp. B1 and 8; and Peter H. Lewis, "Why the Privacy Issue Will Never Go Away," *The New York Times,* April 7, 1991, p. F4.

IDEAS IN HISTORY

The Felicific Calculus

Last century's cardinal utility theorists were strongly influenced by British philosopher Jeremy Bentham (1748–1832). Born in London, he was trained as a lawyer but retired early to devote his life to research and the advocacy of his utilitarian philosophy. His thoughts were expounded in *An Introduction to the Principles of Morals and Legislation* (1789) and in many other works. "Nature has placed man," said Bentham, "under the empire of *pleasure* and *pain*. . . . He who pretends to withdraw himself from this subjection knows not what he says. His only object is to seek pleasure and to shun pain."[1] Bentham suggested that human conduct be guided by a "felicific calculus," which approves of any action only if the pleasure it brings outweighs the pain it causes. He thought that the pleasure and pain of each action could be measured in units called *utils,* and he identified the social total of utility produced by all actions as the common good. He advocated that this total utility be maximized to achieve "the greatest happiness of the greatest number."

As a review of the optimization principle in Chapter 1 shows, modern economists follow in the footsteps of Bentham when they analyze human behavior based on comparisons of *benefits* and *costs* (Bentham's "pleasure" and "pain"). Yet, as this chapter's Appendix shows, the economists of today do not share Bentham's faith in the cardinal measurability of utility. Nor do they believe that a social utility maximum can be found by making interpersonal comparisons of utility.

Bentham, incidentally, received his own utility in unique ways. He let a pet pig roam freely through his mansion. He once petitioned the London City Council for permission to line his driveway with mummies, which he considered "far more aesthetic than flowers." In the end, he left his large estate to the University of London, provided his body was embalmed in a certain way, properly dressed, and allowed to attend all trustee meetings forevermore. To this day, he does, in a glass closet. The minutes record him "present but not voting."

---

[1] Jeremy Bentham, *The Theory of Legislation* (New York: Harcourt, Brace and Co., 1931), p. 2.

Source: Adapted with permission from Heinz Kohler, *Intermediate Microeconomics: Theory and Applications,* 1st ed. (Glenview, IL: Scott, Foresman and Co., 1982), p. 56.

IDEAS IN HISTORY: The Marginal Utility School

As has often been true in the history of science, the idea of *marginal utility* was "in the air" during the middle of the last century. The English-speaking world, however, learned about it from William Stanley Jevons (1835–1882), who was born in Liverpool, the son of an iron merchant. He became an assayer at the Royal Mint in Sydney, Australia. In later years, he taught political economy at Owens College, Manchester, and University College, London.

His writings covered a wide range of subjects: gold mining in Australia, Britain's dwindling coal reserves, the effect of gold discoveries on the general price level, sunspots and business cycles. Yet his immortality was achieved by his pioneering application of mathematics to economics. In a paper which he read to the British Association for the Advancement of Science in 1862, he introduced the concept of the "final degree of utility," now known as *marginal utility*.

This single decisive achievement made scientific history. His subsequent *Theory of Political Economy* (1871) contains a systematic exposition of the theory of consumer optimization based on the marginal utility concept. As he put it,

Let us imagine the whole quantity of food which a person consumes on an average during twenty-four hours to be divided into ten equal parts. If his food be reduced by the last part, he will suffer but little; if a second tenth part be deficient, he will feel the want distinctly; the subtraction of the third part will be decidedly injurious; with every subsequent subtraction of a tenth part his sufferings will be more and more serious until at length he will be upon the verge of starvation. Now, if we call each of the ten parts an increment, the meaning of these facts is, that each increment of food is less necessary, or possesses less utility, than the previous one.[1]

The achievement of Jevons was original, although he had three forerunners of whom he was unaware. W. F. Lloyd of England in 1834, J. Dupuit of France in 1844, and H. H. Gossen of Germany in 1854 had each developed the notion of marginal utility, but no one had paid attention at the time. Even after Jevons, the concept was independently derived by Carl Menger of Austria in 1871 and by Léon Walras of France in 1874. At that point, the "marginal revolution" in economics was irreversible. In Britain and the Commonwealth for a period of half a century, practically all elementary students both of logic and of political economy were brought up on Jevons.

---

[1] *The Theory of Political Economy*, 2nd. ed. (London: Macmillan, 1879), pp. 49–50.

Source: Adapted with permission from Heinz Kohler, *Intermediate Microeconomics: Theory and Applications,* 1st ed. (Glenview, IL: Scott, Foresman and Co., 1982), p. 56.

Summary

1. This chapter focuses on the demand side of Marshall's scissors diagram and tries to explain the behavior of household-consumers of goods. Economists picture consumers as trying to maximize the utility or enjoyment they derive from the choices they make.

2. Utility is a subjective quantity that cannot be measured in any obvious way. Nevertheless, economists of the last century developed an impressive theory of consumer behavior while *pretending* that utility could be measured and expressed in cardinal numbers that were attached to units, called utils. Modern theorists, as this chapter's Appendix shows, reject this idea and build their theory of consumer behavior on people's ability to make statements about utility that use ordinal numbers only.

3. The cardinal utility theory developed by Jevons introduced the crucial distinction between total utility and marginal utility and postulated the existence of a "law" of declining marginal utility.

4. Declining marginal utility, in turn, is responsible for the downward slope of an individual consumer's demand line.

5. A utility-maximizing consumer can find the best quantity to be consumed of any good by applying the optimization principle and equating the marginal benefit of consumption (which the demand line represents) with the marginal cost of consumption (the good's market price).

6. The demand lines of individual consumers can be combined to yield the familiar market demand line.

7. An expansion of cardinal utility theory from one good to two or more goods yields Jevons' Rule: To maximize utility, a consumer should purchase such quantities of various goods that the marginal utility received per dollar of every good is the same.

8. The optional Appendix to this chapter introduces the modern theory of consumer behavior that is based on ordinal utility measurements.

Key Concepts

consumer optimum
Jevons' Rule
"law" of declining marginal utility
marginal utility
satiation
util
utility
utility function

Questions and Problems

1. Review Ideas in History, The Felicific Calculus. How would you apply his felicific calculus to achieve "the greatest happiness of the greatest number" in the following cases?

    a. A hospital has just enough medicine to save the lives of three college students (economics majors) or the life of a 70-year-old man on death row, but it cannot do both.

    b. A new factory about to be built is expected to reduce neighborhood property values drastically, but it will give 250 people jobs. In addition, half the firm's profits go to build homes for the homeless.

2. Table 1 and Figure 1 show total utility approaching a maximum and therefore show marginal utility approaching zero. Do you think to-

tal utility could ever decline and marginal utility, therefore, become negative?

3. Reconsider Example 2. Can you think of other items of which people might buy more at a higher price and less at a lower one?

4. Review this chapter's Figure 3. Then consider the following variations:
   a. What would be the consumer's maximum net benefit from weekly bread consumption if the price were 50¢/lb.?
   b. What would it be if the price were $5/lb.?
   c. Given the price of $3/lb. shown in the graph, prove that the net benefit would be smaller than the $7 shown by the unshaded area in panel (c) if the consumer violated the optimization principle and consumed not 3 lb./week, but 1 or 5 lb./week.

5. What would happen to the market demand in column 5 of Table 2 if consumer B disappeared? How would it look graphically? What name would economists give to this event?

6. Let the price of good a equal P_a = $100/unit, while the price of good b equals P_b = $50/unit. Under what circumstances would a consumer of both goods have found the consumer optimum?

7. A consumer has chosen to consume quantities of various goods such that the marginal utility per pound of product is the same for all goods. Has the consumer found the consumer optimum?

8. Consider the following information about a consumer:

Good X		Good Y	
Quantity consumed	Total utility	Quantity consumed	Total utility
0	0	0	0
1	50	1	100
2	90	2	150
3	120	3	175
4	140	4	185
5	150	5	190

Compute the marginal utilities.

9. Still considering Question 8, what quantity combination of X and Y would maximize the consumer's utility?

APPENDIX 5a

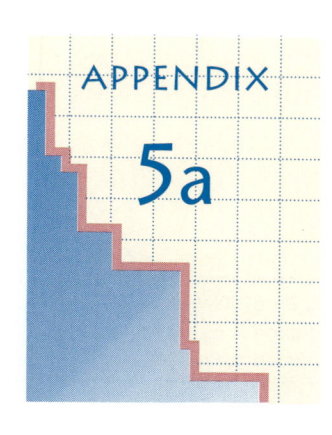

INDIFFERENCE CURVE ANALYSIS

Another British economist, Francis Ysidro Edgeworth (1845–1926), carried the theory of consumer choice beyond the realm of cardinal utility to that of ordinal utility. The theory becomes more elegant, but its conclusions remain the same as those derived by Jevons.

The Field of Choice

Consider a consumer who is about to select some combination of two goods, *a* and *b*, and who cares to maximize utility in the process. All the alternative quantity combinations, Q_a and Q_b, among which the consumer might conceivably choose are called the **field of choice,** shown in Figure 5. In fact, however, every consumer's choice is constrained by a limited budget and positive prices of goods. Let this consumer's budget $B = \$100$ per week; let the prices equal $P_a = \$10$ per unit of good *a* and $P_b = \$20$ per unit of good *b*.

The consumer could buy a weekly maximum of B/P_a or $100 per week/$10 per unit or 10 units of good *a*, as shown by point *A* in our graph. If the consumer bought this quantity, no money would be left over for the purchase of good *b*. Alternatively, the consumer could buy a weekly maximum of B/P_b or $100 per week/$20 per unit or 5 units of good *b*, point *C* in our graph. Line *AC* is called the consumer's **budget line** or **consumption possibilities frontier**; it shows all the alternative quantity combinations of two goods that the consumer is able to buy at current market prices in a given period by fully using a given budget. The budget line divides the field of choice in two: attainable combinations (unshaded) and unattainable combinations (shaded). Inevitably, the consumer must select some combination lying on the budget line (if the budget is fully spent) or lying somewhere below it (if the budget is not fully spent). We shall assume throughout that the budget is to be spent fully.

The absolute value of the budget line's slope always equals the ratio of two prices—the price of the good measured on the horizontal axis, here P_b, divided by the price of the good measured on the vertical axis, here P_a.

$$\mid \text{Budget Line Slope} \mid = \frac{P_b}{P_a}$$

As a quick look at Figure 5 confirms, the slope's absolute value equals 10/5 or 2/1. This value can also be calculated as

$$\frac{0A}{0C} = \frac{B/P_a}{B/P_b} = \frac{P_b}{P_a} = \frac{\$20}{\$10} = \frac{2}{1}$$

Having depicted the consumer's consumption possibilities, based on such *objective* factors as budget and prices, consider a second ingredient in every consumer's choice, the highly personal and *subjective* factor of preferences or tastes. Ordinal utility theorists depict these preferences with the help of a special graphical device, which we now examine.

Indifference Curves

Economists who reject the use of cardinal utility numbers by Bentham and Jevons make a number of simple assertions about consumers.

FIGURE 5 The Field of Choice

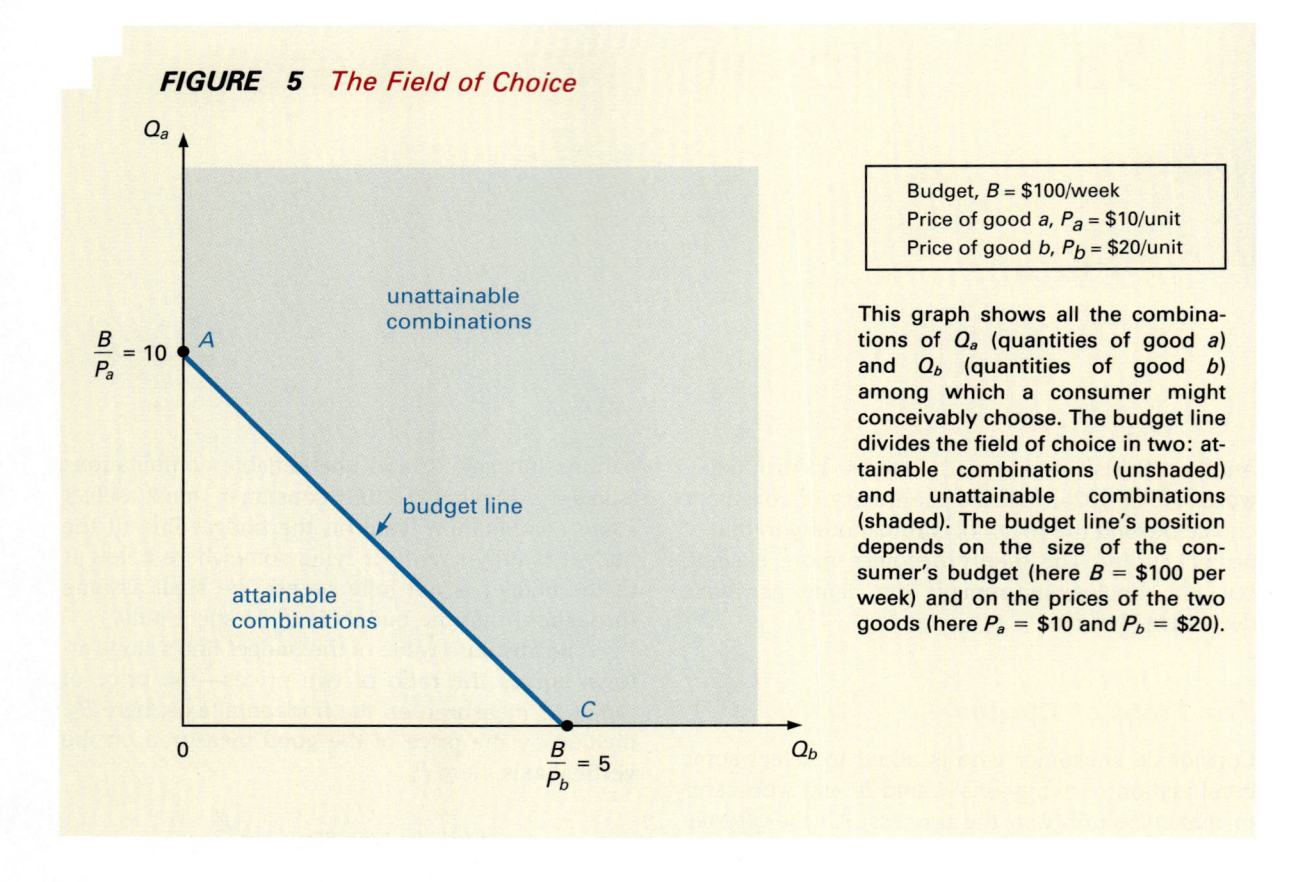

Budget, $B = \$100$/week
Price of good a, $P_a = \$10$/unit
Price of good b, $P_b = \$20$/unit

This graph shows all the combinations of Q_a (quantities of good a) and Q_b (quantities of good b) among which a consumer might conceivably choose. The budget line divides the field of choice in two: attainable combinations (unshaded) and unattainable combinations (shaded). The budget line's position depends on the size of the consumer's budget (here $B = \$100$ per week) and on the prices of the two goods (here $P_a = \$10$ and $P_b = \$20$).

Consumers Rank Bundles of Goods

It is argued, first, that consumers are unable to *evaluate* different bundles of goods (such as 5a and 3b versus 6a and 2b) by assigning cardinal utility numbers to them (such as 117 utils for the first bundle and 128 utils for the second one). Yet the same consumers can *rank* different bundles on an ordinal scale of better or worse. For any two sets of goods, A and B, that one might find in the field of choice, it is assumed, consumers can tell whether they prefer A to B or B to A or find them equally desirable (and are, therefore, indifferent between them). Ordinal utility theorists use an important device called the consumer's **indifference curve** to graph all the alternative quantity combinations of two goods that in the consumer's view yield the same (unmeasurable) total utility and among which the consumer is, therefore, indifferent. Figure 6 depicts what a typical indifference curve is believed to look like. We shall note the reasons for its shape presently.

Consumers Always Prefer More to Less

It is argued, second, that consumers always prefer more of any good to less. This implies the belief that consumers have not reached satiation with respect to any good, the situation at which they have so many units of it that total utility has peaked and marginal utility has declined to zero. The marginal utility of any good, just as in Chapter 5, Figure 1, is always believed to be positive. Figure 7 shows one implication of this belief: An indifference curve must be negatively sloped. Consider initial combination B. All combinations to the right and above B,

FIGURE 6   A Consumer's Indifference Curve

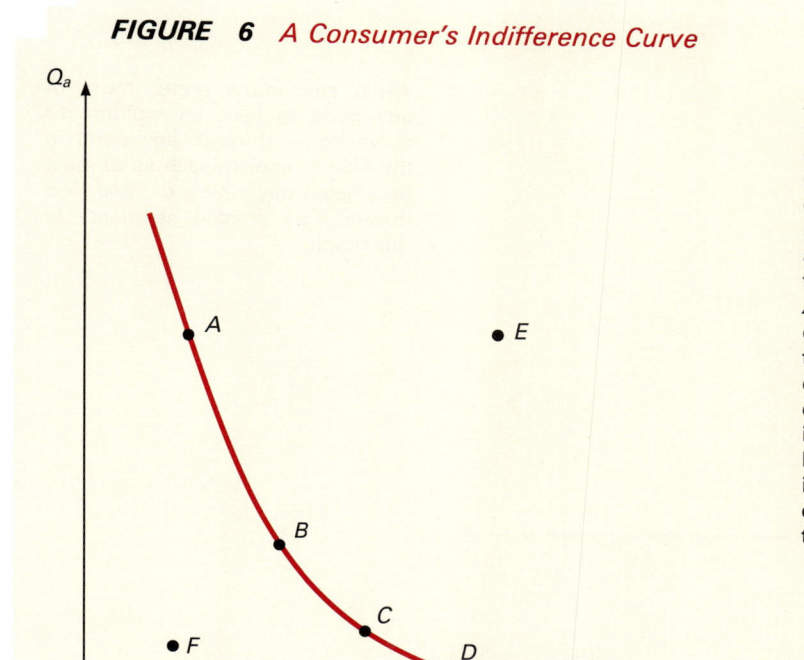

A consumer's indifference curve, such as I_1, shows all the alternative quantity combinations of two goods, such as a and b, which in the consumer's view yield the same (unmeasurable) utility total and among which the consumer is therefore indifferent. Combinations A, B, C, and D are all considered equally good. Combinations lying to the right and above a given indifference curve, such as E, are considered superior to any combination lying on the curve. Combinations lying to the left and below a given indifference curve, such as F, are considered inferior to any combination lying on the curve.

such as those in segment HBG, contain more of one or both goods and are, thus, preferred to B. They cannot lie on the same indifference curve as B. All combinations to the left and below B, such as those in segment 0KBL, contain less of one or both goods and are, therefore, considered inferior to B. Again, they cannot lie on the same indifference curve as B. Combinations considered as good as B (and, thus, lying on the same indifference curve as B) must necessarily be found in the shaded segments of the graph. This explains the negative slope of any indifference curve, such as I_1 in Figure 6.

We can look at Figure 7 in yet another way. If our consumer were to move from B toward G, the same quantity of good a would go with ever larger amounts of good b; thus total utility would rise. To keep the consumer indifferent, the quantity of a would have to be reduced so that the utility loss from less a would just cancel the utility gain from more b. Note the downward-pointing arrow in the graph. Or if our consumer were to move from B toward L, the same quantity of b would go with ever smaller amounts of a; thus total utility would fall. To keep the consumer indifferent, the quantity of b would have to be increased so that the utility gain from more b would just cancel the utility loss from less a. Note the rightward-pointing arrow in the graph. Similar reasoning would apply to a move from B toward K (less b would have to be made up by more a to remain indifferent, as the upward-pointing arrow notes) and from B toward H (more a would have to be canceled by less b to remain indifferent, as the leftward-pointing arrow notes). The conclusion, however, is the same. An indifference curve through B (or any point) must be negatively sloped.

FIGURE 7 More Is Preferred to Less

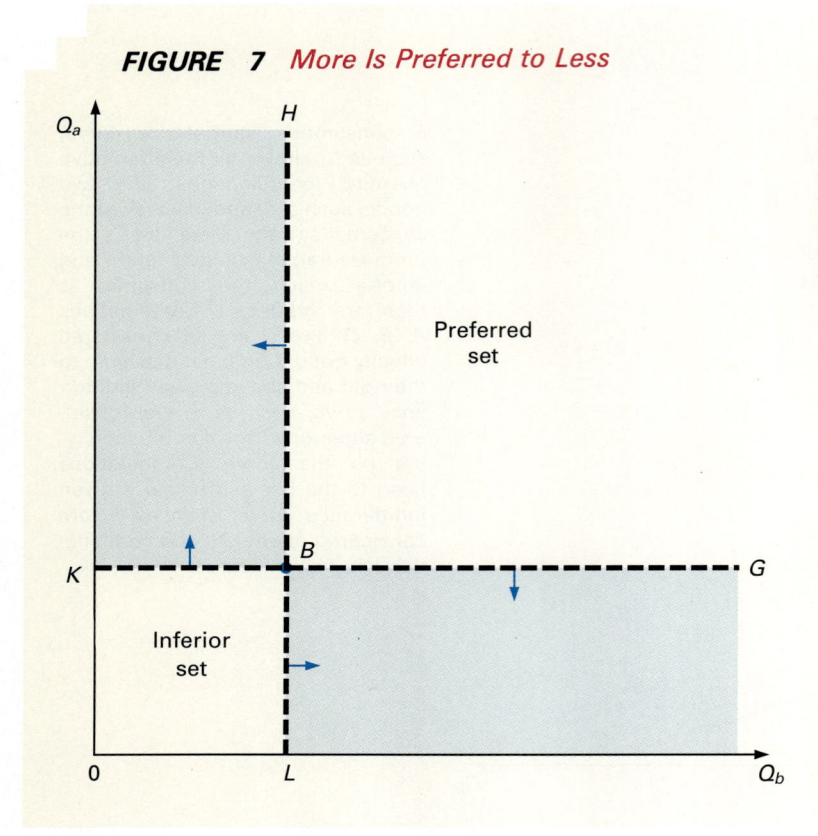

When consumers prefer more of any good to less, an indifference curve going through any point in the field of choice (such as *B*) must be negatively sloped and go through the shaded segments in this graph.

Consumers Insist on a Diminishing Marginal Rate of Substitution

It is argued, third, that consumers who substitute one good for another (moving along an indifference curve) will be indifferent about this procedure only if equal successive quantity increases of one good are paid for by ever smaller quantity decreases of the other good. The rate at which a consumer is able to sacrifice—without any feeling of utility gain or loss—a little bit of one good for a unit increase in another good is called the **marginal rate of substitution (MRS)**, as pictured in Figure 8. Consider our consumer initially consuming quantities of *a* and *b* corresponding to point *A*. According to the graph, the consumer is indifferent about gaining an additional unit of *b* if it requires sacrificing 2*a*. At new position *B*, the consumer is indifferent about gaining another *b* only if the required sacrifice is reduced to 1*a*. Then, at position *C*, the consumer's willingness to sacrifice *a* for another *b* declines even more; to remain indifferent, another *b* is accepted for a sacrifice of $\frac{1}{2} a$ only. Why should this be so and why, therefore, should the indifference curve not only be negatively sloped but also be *convex* with respect to the origin of the graph?

Ordinal utility theorists believe the reason lies in the "law" of declining marginal utility. A consumer who moves from *A* to *D* in Figure 8 gets more *b* (the marginal utility of which declines), while giving up *a* (the marginal utility of which rises). To remain indifferent, the consumer pays for (subjectively) ever-less-precious units of *b* by sacrificing ever smaller amounts of (subjectively) ever-more-precious units of *a*.

We can establish an important implication about an indifference curve's slope. Its (ever-chang-

FIGURE 8 The Diminishing Marginal Rate of Substitution

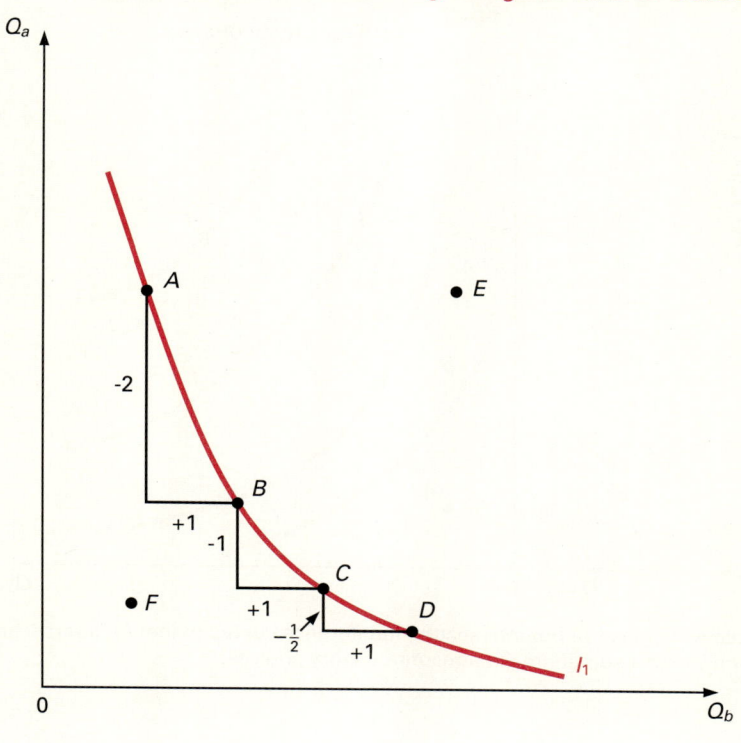

A consumer's indifference curve is not only negatively sloped but also convex with respect to the origin of the graph. This implies a diminishing marginal rate of substitution of one good for the other. In this example, between points A and D, this indifferent rate of exchange declines from 2a to 1a to ½a for an extra unit of b.

ing) absolute value is not only the marginal rate of substitution, but also equals the ratio of two marginal utilities—the marginal utility of the good measured on the horizontal axis, here MU_b, divided by the marginal utility of the good measured on the vertical axis, here MU_a.

$$|\text{Indifference Curve Slope}| = \frac{MU_b}{MU_a}$$

In Figure 8, the slope's absolute value in segment AB, for example, clearly equals 2/1. The consumer's indifference about sacrificing 2a for 1b, however, implies that the marginal utility of 2 units of a equals that of 1 unit of b.

$$MU_{2a} = MU_{1b}$$
$$MU_{1a} = .5\, MU_{1b}$$
$$\frac{MU_{1b}}{MU_{1a}} = \frac{1}{.5} = \frac{2}{1}$$

Consumer Choices Are Noncontradictory

It is argued, fourth, that consumers who rank bundles of goods do so in a noncontradictory, consistent manner; this characteristic of consumer choice is referred to as **transitivity.** For example, if a consumer prefers A to B and B to C, then A is also preferred to C. This assumption implies that different indifference curves—and we can imagine the field of choice packed with an infinite number of them—cannot touch or intersect, as illustrated in Figure 9. Panel (a) shows what would happen if transitivity were violated. According to indifference curve I_1, combination X, Y, and Z all yield the same utility total, simply referred to as level 1 (rather than some measured number, such as 739 utils). Combination W on curve I_2 contains the same amount of good b but more of good a than combination Z, hence W is preferred to Z and yields a higher utility total, sim-

FIGURE 9 A Consumer's Preferences

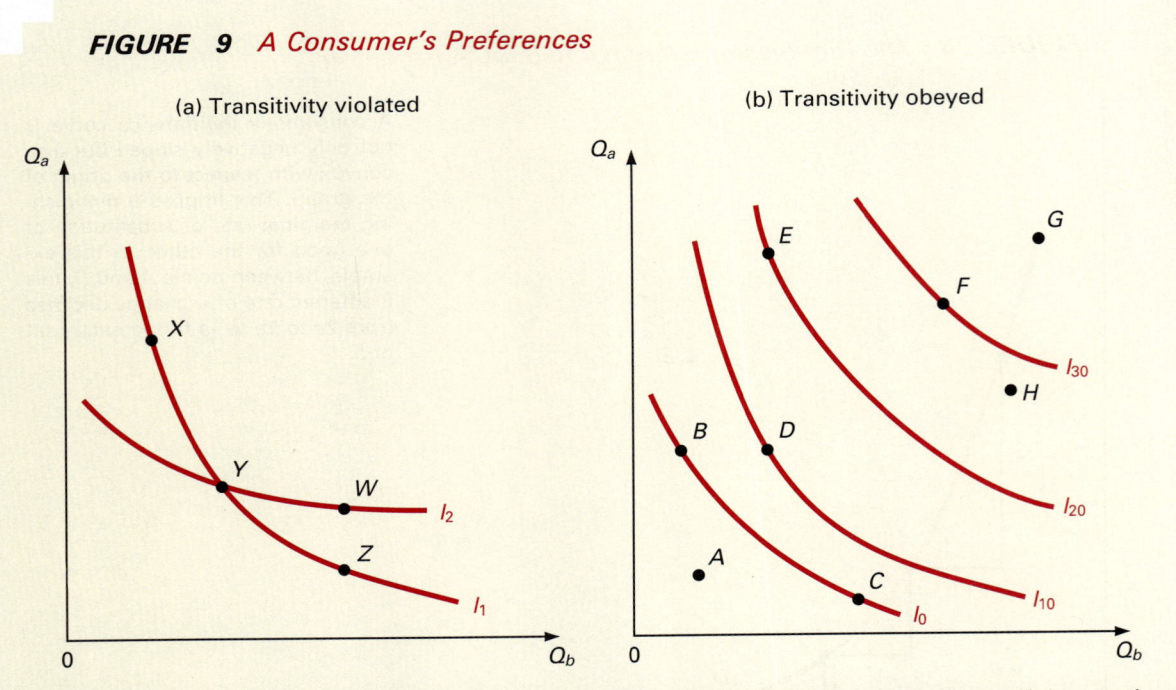

(a) Transitivity violated

(b) Transitivity obeyed

A consumer's preferences can be depicted by a set of nonintersecting indifference curves (panel *b*). Intersecting curves (panel *a*) violate the assumption that consumers make noncontradictory choices.

ply referred to as level 2. Yet, according to indifference curve I_2, W and Y yield the same level 2 utility total and are indifferently chosen. But how can Y equal Z as well as W, while W is superior to Z? Such inconsistencies are ruled out by the transitivity assumption.

Panel (b), finally, shows the way ordinal utility theorists depict a consumer's preferences. The field of choice is densely packed by a potentially infinite number of nonintersecting indifference curves. Our graph shows four of these curves; their labels are of ordinal significance only. The total utility of all the combinations of goods lying on I_0 is the same, but that of all the combinations on I_{10} is higher (we do not know by how many utils), that of all the combinations on I_{20} is higher still, and so on for I_{30}. Given this indifference curve map, we can tell how this consumer feels about any two sets of goods. If both lie on the same indifference curve, they are indifferently chosen; if one lies on a higher (or lower) curve, it is preferred (or considered inferior). Thus, G is preferred to F, F to H, H to E, E to D, D to B and C, and C to A. B and C are considered equally good; A is inferior to C.

The Consumer's Optimum

We can now combine what we have learned about the consumer's opportunities (the budget line) and the consumer's preferences (the indifference curve map). When we do, we find the optimum choice a utility maximizing consumer is expected to make. Figure 10 shows the familiar budget line and beyond it, the shaded world of unattainable combinations of goods. Indifference curves I_0 to I_3 depict the consumer's preferences. When fully spending the given

FIGURE 10 The Consumer's Optimum

A rational consumer is expected to allocate a given budget to that quantity combination of goods (here E) that yields the highest possible utility level (here I_1).

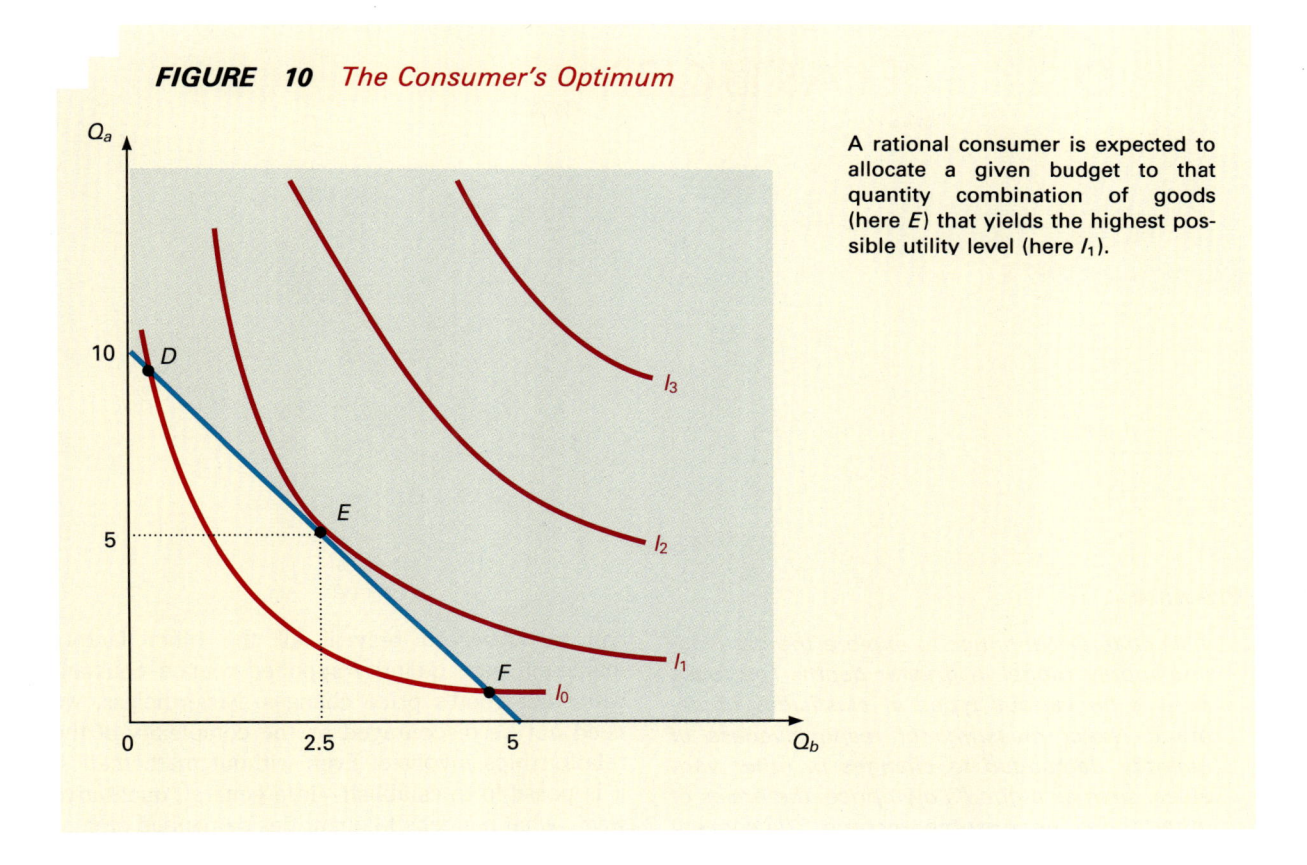

budget, the consumer will buy some combination of quantities lying on the budget line; presumably a rational consumer will buy the one combination (here E, consisting of $5a$ plus $2.5b$) that yields the highest attainable level of utility (here I_1).

Two things should be noted. First, a utility-maximizing consumer will reject combinations such as D and F that would exhaust the entire budget but yield lower utility (here I_0). Second, at optimum E, the slopes of budget line and chosen indifference curve are equal to one another.

| Budget Line Slope | = | Indifference Curve Slope |

$$\frac{P_b}{P_a} = \frac{MU_b}{MU_a}$$

This relationship implies, in turn, that at the optimum

$$\frac{MU_a}{P_a} = \frac{MU_b}{P_b}$$

The result is precisely that one suggested by Jevons' Rule and summarized in Chapter 5, Focus 1.

Key Concepts

budget line
consumption possibilities frontier
field of choice
indifference curve
marginal rate of substitution, MRS
transitivity

CHAPTER 6

ELASTICITY

Preview

This chapter continues to explore the demand-and-supply model in greater depth. The focus here is on various types of elasticities of demand—exact measures of responsiveness of quantity demanded to changes in other variables, such as a good's own price, the prices of other goods, or consumer income. The concept of elasticity of supply is introduced as well. As examples show, elasticity analysis pervades the worlds of business and government decision makers.

Examples

1. How Washington Learned About Price Elasticity
2. Agricultural Policy: Restricting Supply
3. Thinking About National Health Insurance
4. The OPEC Cartel

Demand and supply each depend on numerous factors. As we noted in Chapter 3, the "law" of demand, according to which a good's quantity demanded varies inversely with the good's price, can be observed only if all other factors influencing the quantity demanded (the prices of other goods, consumer income, and so on) remain constant while the good's own price changes. Similarly, the "law" of supply, according to which a good's quantity supplied varies directly with the good's price, can be observed only if all the other factors influencing the quantity supplied remain constant while the good's price changes. Nevertheless, we need not be discouraged by the complexity of the relationships involved. Even without mathematics, it is possible to establish—in a general, qualitative way—what happens to quantities demanded or supplied if any one of the numerous factors that influence these quantities should change. The quantity of beef demanded is likely to increase (and the quantity supplied is likely to decrease) with a lower price of beef. The lower price of a substitute is likely to decrease the demand for beef; the lower price of a complement is likely to increase it. A greater consumer income is likely to increase the demand for normal goods but decrease that for inferior goods.

Yet there are times when economic decision makers want to know more than that. They are not always content with qualitative answers ("the quantity will *rise*" or "the quantity will *fall*"); they need precise measurements of the consequences when certain key variables change. Thus, business managers who sell beef, cars, telephone services, or even theatrical performances want to know precisely what will happen to their quantitative sales and revenues when their product's price is raised or lowered, when other prices change, or when consumer incomes change. Similarly, government officials—be they concerned simply with raising tax revenue or with changing "excessive" or "insufficient" quantities consumed by people—want to know precisely what will happen when a tax or price is changed by a given amount. Will a higher excise tax on alcohol, cigarettes, or gasoline bring in extra tax revenues, or will quantity demanded fall so much as to lower tax collections? Will higher property tax rates fill the city's empty coffers or will homeowners and businesses abandon the city for suburban townships, *worsening* deficits? Will lower Amtrak fares raise ridership and revenue dramatically, or will passenger counts rise imperceptibly, raising losses? What precisely will be the response of quantities demanded and supplied if government farm programs raise the prices of agricultural goods, if national health insurance lowers the price of medical care, if poor people are given food stamps or housing vouchers, or if OPEC governments push up the price of crude oil? Questions such as these call for more than vague answers. As this chapter will show, precise answers can be provided by computing various types of **elasticity,** exact measures of responsiveness of quantity demanded or quantity supplied to changes in other variables. Because there are so many variables influencing the quantities in question, numerous elasticity measures can be calculated. This chapter will discuss four of them: the own-price elasticity of demand, the cross-price elasticity of demand, the income elasticity of demand, and briefly, the own-price elasticity of supply. All else being equal, these measures show, respectively, how a good's quantity demanded responds to a change in the good's own price, in another good's price, in consumer income, and how a good's quantity supplied responds to a change in the good's own price.

A General Definition

Let us determine how the exact measure of responsiveness that elasticity represents is calculated. First note a well-traveled blind alley.

A Blind Alley

Figure 1 helps us avoid a major error: attempting to measure the quantity response with the help of a demand or supply line's slope (or its reciprocal). Consider the demand line for beef in panel (a). Assume the supply line (not shown) shifts so as to move the market's equilibrium from A to B. Some people have been tempted to measure the responsiveness of quantity demanded to the associated price change simply via the *slope* of the demand line in the relevant section AB. Because a price change of $-\$2$/lb. leads to a quantity increase of $+4$ billion pounds per year, they have reasoned, an elasticity measure of $-2/4$ or $-1/2$ might be calculated. Others have suggested using the slope's reciprocal, or -2 in this case, which would indicate more directly that quantity is cut by 2 billion lb. for each $1 increase in price and the opposite for a price decrease.

Now consider why the preceding approach is wrong: Panels (b) and (c) of Figure 1 provide the same information as panel (a), except that the units on the axes have been changed. In panel (b), pounds are replaced by ounces on the horizontal axis; in panel (c), cents have replaced dollars on the vertical axis. Calculating elasticity now—either as the slope or its reciprocal—yields different numbers for identical circumstances ($-1/32$ or -32 and -50 or $-1/50$, respectively). At the least, this method is confusing, although a careful labeling of all ratios shows them to say the same thing:

$-\$2$/lb. yielding $+4$ billion lb./year (panel a)

is the same thing as

$-\$2$/lb. yielding $+64$ billion oz./ year (panel b),

which is the same as

-200¢/lb. yielding $+4$ billion lb./year (panel c).

This confusion is worse if one uses the slope (or its reciprocal) to calculate and compare elasticities for different goods that *have* to be measured in different physical units. Consider beef and telephone calls. If a fall in the price of beef by $2/lb. leads to a 4 billion lb./year increase in the quantity of beef demanded, while a fall in the price of telephoning by 10¢/minute leads to a 400,000 hours/year increase in the quantity of telephoning, which type of demand is more responsive to a fall in its price? There simply is no way to answer this question without using a different measure of elasticity.

FIGURE 1 Elasticity Versus Slope

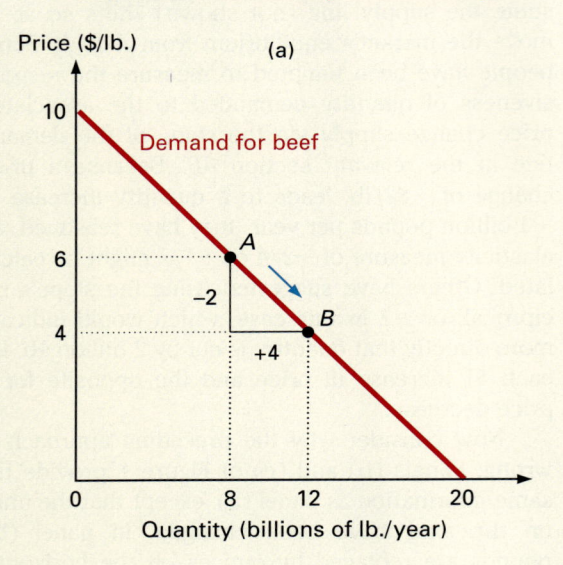

	Slope	$\frac{1}{\text{Slope}}$
a:	$\frac{-2}{4} = -\frac{1}{2}$	-2
b:	$\frac{-2}{64} = -\frac{1}{32}$	-32
c:	$\frac{-200}{4} = -50$	$-\frac{1}{50}$

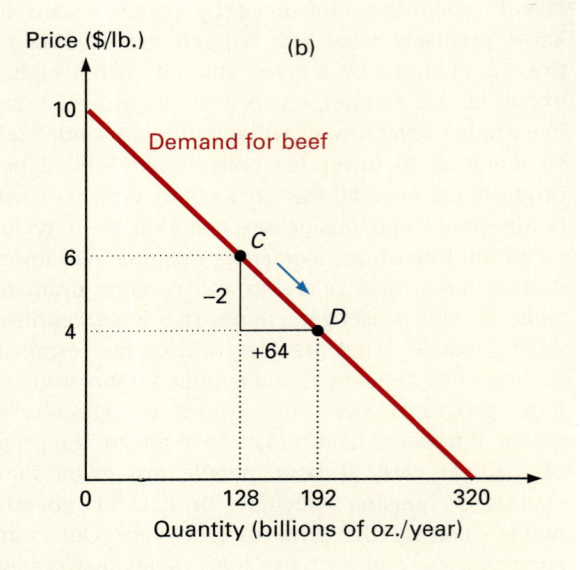

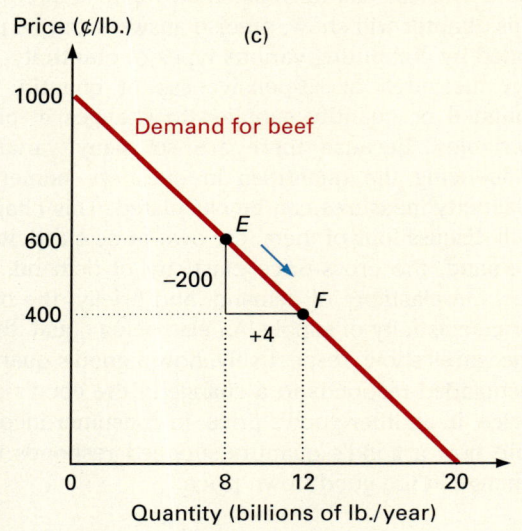

These graphs illustrate the hazard of using the demand line's slope (or its reciprocal) to calculate the responsiveness of a good's quantity demanded to a change in its price. Even under identical circumstances, different units of measurement (dollars instead of cents for price, or pounds instead of ounces for quantity) will produce different elasticity numbers. Although careful labeling of the results can clear up the confusion, the approach here suggests the difficulty in comparing elasticities of different goods whose quantities are measured in different physical units, such as beef in pounds and telephone calls in minutes.

The Accepted Approach

Economists have a way of avoiding all the problems just noted (and others still). Three major decisions are involved.

First, economists calculate elasticities by expressing changes of all variables in percentage terms rather than in such absolute units as dollars and cents for prices or pounds, ounces, and minutes for quantities. In the panels of Figure 1, whether price is expressed in dollars (panels a and b) or in cents (panel c), the price declines by the same percentage in all cases: $6 to $4 and 600¢ to 400¢ represent the same percentage decline (33.33 percent of the original price). Whether quantity is expressed in pounds/year (panels a and c) or in ounces/year (panel b), the quantity rises by the same percentage in all cases: 8 billion lb. to 12 billion lb. and 128 billion ounces to 192 billion ounces represent the same percentage increase (50 percent of the original quantity).

Second, economists calculate all percentage changes by relating the observed absolute change, such as $-\$2$, not to the original value, such as $6 (as was done in the preceding paragraph) but to the average of new and original values, such as

($4 + $6) ÷ 2, or $5. Thus, for panel (a) of Figure 1, the percentage change in price is calculated as

$$\%\Delta P = \frac{-\$2}{\frac{\$4 + \$6}{2}} \times 100 = -\frac{2}{5} \times 100 = -40\%$$

(The Greek letter delta, Δ, is used to represent "change in.") Similarly, the percentage change in quantity demanded is calculated as

$$\%\Delta Q_D = \frac{+4 \text{ billion lb.}}{\frac{12 + 8 \text{ billion lb.}}{2}} \times 100$$

$$= \frac{+4}{10} \times 100 = +40\%$$

This procedure has one major advantage over an alternative method that relates changes to original values. For any given section on a demand or supply line (such as section *AB* in panel a), it calculates the same percentage change regardless of whether the contemplated change goes from *A* to *B* (as in our example) or from *B* to *A*.

Third, economists define every type of **elasticity** as the percentage change in quantity divided by

---

EXAMPLE 1

How Washington Learned About Price Elasticity

In August of 1980, the city of Washington, D.C., tried to cure a fiscal deficit by imposing a 6 percent excise tax on gasoline. Within 4 months, the tax was repealed. Mayor Marion Barry cited "overwhelming evidence" that it had not worked.

That evidence was massive, indeed, and it had to do with price elasticity. True enough, the own-price elasticity for gasoline *in general* tends to be low (note the value of |.14| in Table 1), but that for *Washington* gasoline was high. Drivers found easily available substitutes in Maryland and Virginia (where the price was 10¢ less per gallon); the quantity demanded in Washington dropped by 33 percent within a month. Assuming that price rose by 6 percent, the forgoing quantity response implies an own-price elasticity of demand (even in the short run) of |33/6| or |5.5|. If price rose less and, as is likely, some of the tax was absorbed by dealers (see Chapter 3, Figure 12), the elasticity was even higher. Naturally, city tax revenues did not rise, and city officials were deluged by complaints from angry gas station owners.

Source: The Washington Post, November 25, 1980, p. A1.

the percentage change in whatever variable causes the quantity change—all other things being equal. The following sections of this chapter provide examples of four elasticity measures.

The Own-Price Elasticity of Demand

A good's **own-price elasticity of demand** is the percentage change in the good's quantity demanded divided by the associated percentage change in the good's own price that causes it, all else being equal.

A Numerical Example

Let us designate the quantity demanded of any good a by Q_{Da}. This quantity depends on many variables, including the good's own price P_a, the prices of other goods $P_b, P_c, \ldots, P_n$ that may be substitutes or complements, the income of consumers Y, the tastes of consumers T, and more. Mathematicians would say that Q_{Da} depends on or "is a function of" all these other variables, and they would indicate this fact by writing

$$Q_{Da} = f(P_a, P_b, P_c, \ldots, P_n, Y, T, \ldots) \quad (1)$$

Now let us focus our attention solely on Q_{Da} and P_a, holding all other factors constant (a procedure followed in Chapter 3 to graph Figure 1, A Demand Line for Beef). By changing P_a, we change Q_{Da}, all else being equal. Any observed percentage change in Q_{Da} divided by the associated percentage change in P_a is called good a's own-price elasticity of demand. In our equation let %Δ stand for "percentage change":

$$Q_{Da} = f(\underset{\downarrow}{P_a}, \underbrace{P_b, P_c, \ldots, P_n, Y, T, \ldots}_{\text{factors held constant}}) \quad (2)$$

$$E_{Da}^{o\text{-}p} = \frac{\%\Delta Q_{Da}}{\%\Delta P_a} = \text{own-price elasticity of demand for good } a.$$

Given the "law" of demand (that makes price and quantity move in opposite directions), any number so calculated is typically negative. In Figure 2, consider an original position at A with price $P_1 = \$7.50$/lb. of good a and quantity demanded $Q_1 = 5$ billion lb./year. Let price fall to $P_2 = \$5$/lb.

FIGURE 2 The Own-Price Elasticity of Demand

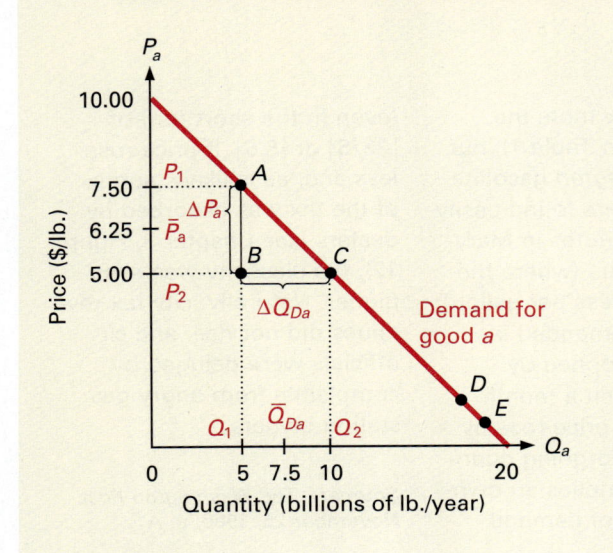

A good's own-price elasticity of demand is the percentage change in the good's quantity demanded divided by the associated percentage change in the good's own price that caused it (all else being equal). For a range such as AC, this elasticity is traditionally calculated as

$$E_{Da}^{o\text{-}p} = \frac{\%\Delta Q_{Da}}{\%\Delta P_a} = \frac{\dfrac{\Delta Q_{Da}}{\overline{Q}_{Da}} \times 100}{\dfrac{\Delta P_a}{\overline{P}_a} \times 100}$$

where ΔQ_{Da} is the absolute quantity change; $\overline{Q}_{Da}$ is the average of new and old quantities, or $(Q_2 + Q_1)/2$; while ΔP_a is the absolute price change; and $\overline{P}_a$ is the average of new and old prices, or $(P_2 + P_1)/2$. Focus 1 presents alternative versions of the same formula.

FOCUS 1

The Own-Price Elasticity of Demand

$$E_{Da}^{o\text{-}p} = \frac{\%\Delta Q_{Da}}{\%\Delta P_a} = \frac{\dfrac{\Delta Q_{Da}}{\overline{Q}_{Da}} \times 100}{\dfrac{\Delta P_a}{\overline{P}_a} \times 100} = \frac{\dfrac{Q_2 - Q_1}{\dfrac{Q_2 + Q_1}{2}} \times 100}{\dfrac{P_2 - P_1}{\dfrac{P_2 + P_1}{2}} \times 100} = \frac{\dfrac{Q_2 - Q_1}{Q_2 + Q_1}}{\dfrac{P_2 - P_1}{P_2 + P_1}}$$

where Q_1 and Q_2 are the original and new quantities of good a demanded ($Q_2 - Q_1$ equals ΔQ_{Da}), while P_1 and P_2 are the original and new prices of good a (hence $P_2 - P_1$ equals ΔP_a).

and quantity demanded rise to 10 billion lb./year (point C). The own-price elasticity of demand for good a along demand line section AC is calculated in three steps:

1. First, the percentage change in quantity demanded is computed by dividing the absolute quantity change, ΔQ_{Da} (distance BC) by the average of new and old quantities, $\overline{Q}_{Da}$, [pronounced "Q bar Da" and equaling $(Q_2 + Q_1)/2$], and multiplying the result by 100. In our case,

$$\%\Delta Q_{Da} = \frac{\Delta Q_{Da}}{\overline{Q}_{Da}} \times 100 = \frac{\Delta Q_{Da}}{\dfrac{Q_2 + Q_1}{2}} \times 100$$

$$= \frac{+5}{\dfrac{10 + 5}{2}} \times 100 = \frac{+5}{7.5} \times 100 = +66.67\%$$

2. Second, the percentage change in price is computed by dividing the absolute price change, ΔP_a (distance AB) by the average of new and old prices, $\overline{P}_a$ [which equals $(P_2 + P_1)/2$], and multiplying the result by 100. In our case,

$$\%\Delta P_a = \frac{\Delta P_a}{\overline{P}_a} \times 100 = \frac{\Delta P_a}{\dfrac{P_2 + P_1}{2}} \times 100$$

$$= \frac{-2.50}{\dfrac{5.00 + 7.50}{2}} \times 100 = \frac{-2.50}{6.25} \times 100 = -40\%$$

3. Third, the own-price elasticity of demand is computed by relating the two percentage changes as noted in equation (2):

$$E_{Da}^{o\text{-}p} = \frac{\%\Delta Q_{Da}}{\%\Delta P_a} = \frac{+66.67\%}{-40\%} = -1.67$$

NUMERICAL EXERCISE 1

Calculating the Own-Price Elasticity of Demand

We can confirm the result reached in step 3 by using our Figure 2 numbers in the last expression of Focus 1:

$$E_{Da}^{o\text{-}p} = \frac{\dfrac{Q_2 - Q_1}{Q_2 + Q_1}}{\dfrac{P_2 - P_1}{P_2 + P_1}} = \frac{\dfrac{10 - 5}{10 + 5}}{\dfrac{5 - 7.50}{5 + 7.50}} = \frac{\dfrac{5}{15}}{\dfrac{-2.50}{12.50}} = \frac{.33}{-.2} = -1.67$$

TABLE 1 Own-Price Elasticities of Demand in U.S. Markets (absolute values)

Good	|Elasticity|	Source	Good	|Elasticity|	Source
Cottonseed oil	6.92	C	Air travel (foreign)	0.70	I
Tomatoes (fresh)	4.60	I	Shoes	0.70	I
Green peas (fresh)	2.80	I	Household appliances	0.67	I
Scrod	2.20	A	Legal services	0.61	I
Legal gambling	1.91	N	Physicians' services	0.58	I
Lamb	1.90	M	Rail travel (commuter)	0.54	I
Restaurant meals	1.63	I	Jewelry, watches	0.54	I
Marijuana	1.51	K	Water	0.52	F
Peaches	1.50	G	Cigarettes	0.51	J
Butter	1.40	L	Stationery	0.47	I
Automobiles	1.35	O	Radio, TV repair	0.47	I
China, glassware	1.34	I	Sea scallops	0.46	A
Apples	1.30	G	Toilet articles	0.44	I
Giving to charity	1.29	E	Cabbage	0.40	I
Taxi service	1.24	I	Auto repair	0.36	I
Cable TV	1.20	B	Medical insurance	0.31	I

The own-price elasticities shown here are given in absolute values; their interpretation is easy. At the time of this study, a 1 percent rise in the price of cottonseed oil led to a 6.92 percent decrease in quantity demanded (and the opposite). Yet, as the last row shows, a 1 percent rise in the price of mailing letters only led to a 0.05 percent decrease in quantity demanded (and the opposite).

SOURCES: **A.** Frederick W. Bell, "The Pope and the Price of Fish," *The American Economic Review,* December 1968. **B.** Charles B. Blankart, "Towards an Economic Theory of Advice and Its Application to the Deregulation Issue," *Kyklos,* I, 1981, p. 101. **C.** G. E. Brandow, "Interrelations Among Demands for Farm Products and Implications for Control of Market Supply," *Bulletin* 680 (University Park: Pennsylvania State University Agricultural Experiment Station, 1961). **D.** Rex F. Daly, "Coffee Consumption and Prices in the United States," *Agricultural Economic Research* (Washington, D.C.: U.S. Department of Agriculture, Economic Research Service, July 1958). **E.** M. Feldstein and A. Taylor, "The Income Tax and Charitable Contributions," *Econometrica,* November 1976.

The result is a pure number (the percentage labels cancel out), which is easily interpreted. Along section *AC* of our demand line, any 1 percent change in price leads to a 1.67 percent change in quantity demanded—in the opposite direction, as the minus sign reminds us. Focus 1 presents several alternative versions of this elasticity formula.

One final point must be made. Given the law of demand (higher price → lower quantity, lower price → higher quantity), the own-price elasticity of demand is typically negative. Therefore, when people's responsiveness to a price change is high, as in our example, the calculated elasticity number may be −1.67. When people's responsiveness to a

Good	|Elasticity|	Source	Good	|Elasticity|	Source
Chicken	1.20	G	Margarine	0.30	L
Radios, TV sets	1.19	I	Potatoes	0.30	D
Beer	1.13	H	Coffee	0.25	D
Furniture	1.01	I	Eggs	0.23	C
Housing	1.00	I	Spectator sports	0.21	I
Alcohol	0.92	I	Bus travel (intercity)	0.20	I
Beef	0.92	P	Theatre, opera	0.18	I
Telephone calls	0.89	B	Natural gas (residential)	0.15	I
Sports equipment, boats, etc.	0.88	I	Gasoline and oil	0.14	I
Movies	0.87	I	Milk	0.14	C
Flowers, seeds	0.82	I	Electricity (residential)	0.13	I
Citrus fruit	0.80	G	Newspapers, magazines	0.10	I
Bus travel (local)	0.77	I	Mail (letters)	0.05	B

F. Henry S. Foster, Jr., and Bruce R. Beattie, "Urban Residential Demand for Water in the United States," *Land Economics,* February 1979. **G.** Karl A. Fox, *The Analysis of Demand for Farm Products, Technical Bulletin 1081* (Washington, D.C.: U.S. Department of Agriculture, September 1953). **H.** T. F. Hogarty and K. G. Elzinga, "The Demand for Beer," *The Review of Economics and Statistics,* May 1972. **I.** H. S. Houthakker and Lester D. Taylor, *Consumer Demand in the United States: Analyses and Projections,* 2nd ed. (Cambridge: Harvard University Press, 1970). **J.** Herbert L. Lyon and Julian L. Simon, "Price Elasticity of the Demand for Cigarettes in the United States," *American Journal of Agricultural Economics,* November 1968. **K.** Charles T. Nisbet and Firouz Vakil, "Some Estimates of Price and Expenditure Elasticities of Demand for Marijuana Among UCLA Students," *The Review of Economics and Statistics,* November 1972. **L.** A. S. Rojko, *The Demand and Price Structure for Dairy Products, Technical Bulletin 1168* (Washington, D.C.: U.S. Department of Agriculture, 1957). **M.** Henry Schultz, *The Theory and Measurement of Demand* (Chicago: Chicago University Press, 1938). **N.** Daniel B. Suits, "The Elasticity of Demand for Gambling," *The Quarterly Journal of Economics,* February 1979. **O.** U.S. Senate, Subcommittee on Antitrust and Monopoly, *Administered Prices: Automobiles* (Washington, D.C.: U.S. Government Printing Office, 1958). **P.** Elmer Working, *The Demand for Meat* (Chicago: University of Chicago Press, 1951).

price change is low, the calculated number may be $-.05$, which is a *larger* number than -1.67. Sometimes economists seek to avoid the likely confusion resulting from the fact that smaller numbers (such as -1.67) designate high responsiveness and larger numbers (such as $-.05$) designate low responsiveness. So they ignore the minus sign and simply look at the *absolute values* involved. The absolute value of $E_D = -1.67$ is then written as $|E_D| = 1.67$, which designates high elasticity; the absolute value of $E_D = -.05$ is written as $|E_D| = .05$, which designates low elasticity. (The vertical lines warn us that minus signs are being ignored.)

Empirical Data

We now review in Table 1 some of the empirical data economists have accumulated. The sources show that the studies were undertaken at many different times and places. At other times and places, different estimates reflecting the price-quantity relationships could well have been obtained. (If in Figure 2 we had calculated the elasticity for the range between D and E rather than A and C, the result would surely not have equaled -1.67.) It is important, therefore, not to view empirical elasticity data as if they indicated some inherent and permanent characteristic of the goods involved. Nevertheless, the elasticity estimates found are far from arbitrary numbers; often there are good reasons for the size of the numbers observed, as the next section will show.

The Determinants of Elasticity Values

The data in Table 1 are far from surprising. Consider some of the factors that tend to determine the size of any given own-price elasticity of demand.

The Availability of Substitutes

The extent to which substitutes for a given good are available clearly influences the responsiveness of quantity demanded to a change in the good's price. When there are many close substitutes, as for cottonseed oil, the elasticity is likely to be high (6.92 in Table 1); when there are relatively few good substitutes, as for physicians' services, the elasticity is likely to be low (0.58 in Table 1). Thus, a rise in the price of cottonseed oil—all else being equal—will cause consumers to switch to other types of cooking oil, to margarine, or even to butter; hence the quantity response in the market for cottonseed oil will be fairly high. On the other hand, a rise in the price of physicians' services—all else being equal—leaves consumers with rather undesirable alternatives: reading a medical guide book and buying over-the-counter drugs, consulting a nurse or pharmacist, or ignoring their health problem altogether. No wonder that the quantity response is relatively weak.

Look at some of the other entries in Table 1 and figure out how many can be explained by the substitute-availability factor. (For example, picture the many good substitutes for fresh tomatoes; then think of all the poor ones for telephone calls: citizens' band radio, personal visits, private messengers, the U.S. mail.)

We must note, however, that the availability of substitutes and the elasticity estimate depend in part on the narrowness with which a good is defined. Few good substitutes may exist for gasoline in general (note the elasticity estimate of .14 in Table 1), but there are many for Mobil gasoline and even more for Mobil gasoline sold at a particular location. Example 1 has more to say on that subject.

The Fraction of Consumer Budgets Involved

The extent to which a particular good takes a large or small fraction of the typical consumer's budget also influences the elasticity. Consumer responsiveness to a price change tends to be high for "important" goods that occupy a prominent place in the consumer budget, low for "unimportant" goods that occupy a negligible position in it. Consider the Table 1 own-price elasticities of demand for automobiles (1.35) or housing (1.00); compare them with those for newspapers (.10) or mailing letters (.05). A bit of introspection shows that the observed differences make sense. If your rent or mortgage payments were to rise by 20 percent (from $600 to $720 per month), you would seriously consider a quantity response, demanding considerably fewer housing services (moving to a smaller apartment or house or—what amounts to the same thing—sharing your current space with other people). Yet if your postage were to rise by 20 percent (from 29¢ to 35¢ per letter), you may hardly respond at all. People's own-price elasticities of demand for such items as matches, salt, or drinking water tend to be small; those for big-ticket items such as appliances, boats, and furniture are large.

The Passage of Time

The responsiveness to price changes tends to be greater for longer periods of time under consideration. Table 2 confirms this assertion. These observations should not be surprising; they merely corroborate the availability-of-substitutes argument made earlier. The passage of time often increases the number of substitutes available; the measured elasticity rises accordingly.

Thus, the doubling of the price of gasoline (a 100 percent increase) may reduce gasoline con-

TABLE 2 Own-Price Elasticities of Demand: Short Run Versus Long Run (absolute values)

Good	|Elasticity| Short run	Long run	Good	|Elasticity| Short run	Long run
China, glassware	1.34	8.80	Radio, TV repair	0.47	3.84
Alcohol	0.92	3.63	Toilet articles	0.44	2.42
Sports equipment,			Medical insurance	0.31	0.92
boats, etc.	0.88	2.39	Bus travel (intercity)	0.20	2.17
Movies	0.87	3.67	Theatre, opera	0.18	0.31
Flowers, seeds	0.82	2.65			
Bus travel (local)	0.77	3.54	Natural gas (residential)	0.15	10.74
Air travel (foreign)	0.70	4.00	Gasoline, oil	0.14	0.48
Shoes	0.70	1.20	Electricity (residential)	0.13	1.90
Rail travel (commuter)	0.54	1.70	Newspapers, magazines	0.10	0.52
Jewelry, watches	0.54	0.67			

The responsiveness of quantity demanded to changes in a good's own price tends to be stronger in the long run than in the short run. At the time of this study, a 1 percent rise in the price of china and glassware (first row) led to a 1.34 percent decrease in quantity demanded in the short run, but to an 8.80 percent decrease in the long run. Similar differences are observable for other goods.

SOURCE: For each item the source is the same as that listed in Table 1.

sumption by only 14 percent this year, as the short-run column of Table 2 suggests. Eventually, the cutback may equal 48 percent, as the long-run column indicates. Over a period of 5, 10, or 20 years, people make all kinds of adjustments that are not immediately available. They can change the location of their residences and jobs to reduce commuting distances. They can buy smaller, more fuel-efficient cars that use less gasoline per mile. They can use new types of energy altogether. They can even change their life-styles, taking fewer and shorter vacations and rediscovering the joys of bicycling and walking.

The Cross-Price Elasticity of Demand

A good's **cross-price elasticity of demand** is the percentage change in the good's quantity demanded divided by the associated percentage change in *another* good's price that causes it, all else being equal. Recall equation (1) but look at it in a new way:

$$Q_{Da} = f(\overbrace{P_a, P_b, P_c, \ldots, P_n, Y, T, \ldots}^{\text{factors held constant}}) \quad (3)$$

$$E_{Da}^{c\text{-}p(b)} = \frac{\%\Delta Q_{Da}}{\%\Delta P_b} = \begin{array}{l}\text{cross-price elasticity of demand}\\\text{for good } a \text{ with respect to}\\\text{the price of good } b.\end{array}$$

Given that two goods can be substitutes, complements, or independents with respect to one another, any elasticity number so calculated will be positive, negative, or zero.

Cross-price elasticity is positive in the case of substitutes because a higher price of good *b* decreases the quantity of good *b* demanded and therefore increases the quantity demanded of substitute

FOCUS 2

The Cross-Price Elasticity of Demand

$$E_{Da}^{c\text{-}p\,(b)} = \frac{\%\Delta Q_{Da}}{\%\Delta P_b} = \frac{\dfrac{\Delta Q_{Da}}{\overline{Q}_{Da}} \times 100}{\dfrac{\Delta P_b}{\overline{P}_b} \times 100} = \frac{\dfrac{Q_2 - Q_1}{\dfrac{Q_2 + Q_1}{2}} \times 100}{\dfrac{P_2 - P_1}{\dfrac{P_2 + P_1}{2}} \times 100} = \frac{\dfrac{Q_2 - Q_1}{Q_2 + Q_1}}{\dfrac{P_2 - P_1}{P_2 + P_1}}$$

where Q_1 and Q_2 are the original and new quantities of good a demanded ($Q_2 - Q_1$ equals ΔQ_{Da}), while P_1 and P_2 are the original and new prices of good b (hence $P_2 - P_1$ equals ΔP_b).

good a. In the preceding ratio, both the numerator ($\%\Delta Q_{Da}$) and the denominator ($\%\Delta P_b$) are positive. A lower price of b similarly induces greater purchases of b and lower purchases of a; both numerator and denominator are then negative, again making the elasticity ratio positive.

Cross-price elasticity is negative in the case of complements because a higher price of good b decreases the quantity of good b demanded and therefore decreases the quantity demanded of complementary good a as well. The opposite occurs when the price of good b falls. In either case, the ratio's numerator and denominator have opposite signs, so the elasticity is negative.

Cross-price elasticity, finally, is zero in the case of independent goods. Any change in the price of good b changes the quantity of good b demanded but has no effect at all on the quantity demanded of good a. Hence the value of $\%\Delta Q_{Da}$ is zero and so is the elasticity.

Focus 2 presents alternative versions of the cross-price elasticity formula; it is analogous to Focus 1, the only change being the replacement of P_a by P_b.

Empirical Data

Once again, numerous studies have collected empirical data. Table 3 presents selected estimates from U.S. and British markets.

The Income Elasticity of Demand

A good's **income elasticity of demand** is measured as the percentage change in the good's quantity demanded divided by the associated percentage change in consumer income that causes it, all else being equal. Once again we can modify equation (1) to see what is involved:

$$Q_{Da} = f(P_a, P_b, P_c, \ldots, P_n, Y, T, \ldots) \qquad (4)$$

with factors held constant.

$$E_{Da}^{Y} = \frac{\%\Delta Q_{Da}}{\%\Delta Y} = \text{income elasticity of demand for good } a.$$

Given that there are inferior goods and normal goods (smaller or larger physical quantities, respectively, are consumed as income rises), any elasticity number so calculated can be negative or positive. It is negative for inferior goods because the change in quantity demanded is opposite to the income change. It is positive for normal goods because quantity demanded and income move in the same direction. Indeed, economists distinguish two types of normal goods: those with an income elasticity of demand between 0 and 1 are called **necessities,** those with an income elasticity of demand

CHAPTER 6   *Elasticity*   **157**

NUMERICAL EXERCISE 2

Calculating the Cross-Price Elasticity of Demand

We can use Figure 3 to provide numerical examples for calculating the cross-price elasticity of demand between 2 goods.

The case of substitutes. Panel (a) pictures the case of two substitutes, coffee and tea. Originally, the demand for tea is given by the solid line and equilibrium exists at *A* (the supply line is not shown). The price of tea is $5/lb., coffee is $10/lb., and the quantity of tea demanded equals 300 lb./year. Let the price of coffee rise to $20/lb. As people substitute tea for coffee, the demand for tea rises from the solid to the broken line. All else being equal, the quantity moves from *A* to *B*. Using the Focus 2 formula (let good *a* stand for tea and good *b* for coffee), we compute

$$E_{Da}^{c-p(b)} = \frac{\%\Delta Q_{Da}}{\%\Delta P_b} = \frac{\dfrac{Q_2 - Q_1}{Q_2 + Q_1}}{\dfrac{P_2 - P_1}{P_2 + P_1}} = \frac{\dfrac{800 - 300}{800 + 300}}{\dfrac{20 - 10}{20 + 10}}$$

$$= \frac{\dfrac{500}{1{,}100}}{\dfrac{10}{30}} = \frac{.45}{.33} = +1.36$$

In this example, each 1 percent increase in the price of coffee raises the quantity of tea demanded by 1.36 percent. The cross-price elasticity for substitute goods is positive.

The case of complements. Panel (b) pictures the case of two complements, lemons and tea. Originally, the demand for tea is given by the solid line; an equilibrium exists at *C* (the supply line is not shown). The price of tea is $5/lb., a lemon is 10¢, and the quantity of tea demanded equals 300 lb./year. Let the price of a lemon rise to $1. As people buy fewer lemons, they also drink less tea; the demand for tea falls from the solid to the broken line. All else being equal, the quantity moves from *C* to *D*. Using the Focus 2 formula (now let good *a* stand for tea and good *b* for lemons), we compute

$$E_{Da}^{c-p(b)} = \frac{\%\Delta Q_{Da}}{\%\Delta P_b} = \frac{\dfrac{Q_2 - Q_1}{Q_2 + Q_1}}{\dfrac{P_2 - P_1}{P_2 + P_1}} = \frac{\dfrac{100 - 300}{100 + 300}}{\dfrac{1 - .10}{1 + .10}}$$

$$= \frac{\dfrac{-200}{400}}{\dfrac{.9}{1.10}} = \frac{-.5}{.81} = -.61$$

Here, each 1 percent increase in the price of lemons lowers the quantity of tea demanded by .61 percent. The cross-price elasticity for complementary goods is negative.

The case of independents. Panel (c) pictures the case of two independent goods, salt and tea. Originally, the demand for tea is given by the solid line; an equilibrium exists at *E* (the supply line is not shown). The price of tea is $5/lb., salt is 30¢/lb., and the quantity of tea demanded equals 300 lb./year. Let the price of salt rise to $1/lb. As people buy less salt (perhaps), their demand for tea is unaffected. The equilibrium remains at E. If one did employ the Focus 2 formula, expressions such as $\%\Delta Q_{Da}$ and $Q_2 - Q_1$ would equal zero, as would the entire elasticity number. Each 1 percent increase in the price of salt leaves the quantity of tea demanded unchanged.

FIGURE 3 The Cross-Price Elasticity of Demand

(a) Substitutes

Price of tea ($/lb.) vs. Quantity of tea (pounds per year)

Demand (given coffee price $P_1 = \$10/lb.$) — point A at (300, 5)
Demand (given coffee price $P_2 = \$20/lb.$) — point B at (800, 5)
$Q_1 = 300$, $Q_2 = 800$

(b) Complements

Price of tea ($/lb.) vs. Quantity of tea (pounds per year)

Demand (given lemon price $P_1 = 10¢$ each) — point C at (300, 5)
Demand (given lemon price $P_2 = \$1$ each) — point D at (100, 5)
$Q_2 = 100$, $Q_1 = 300$

(c) Independents

Price of tea ($/lb.) vs. Quantity of tea (pounds per year)

Demand (given salt price $P_1 = 30¢/lb.$ or $P_2 = \$1/lb.$) — point E at (300, 5)
$Q_1 = Q_2 = 300$

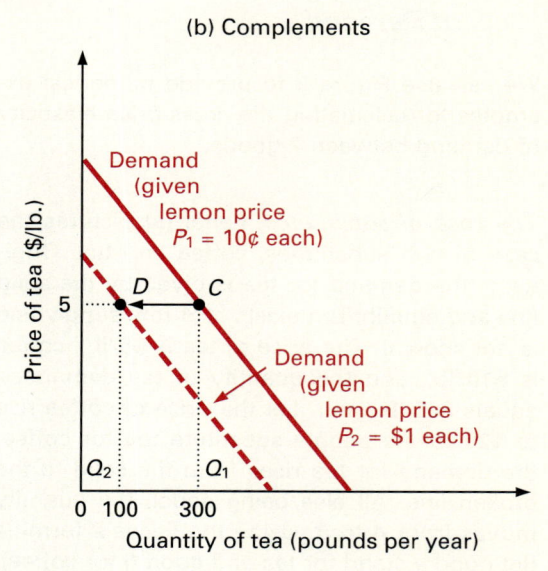

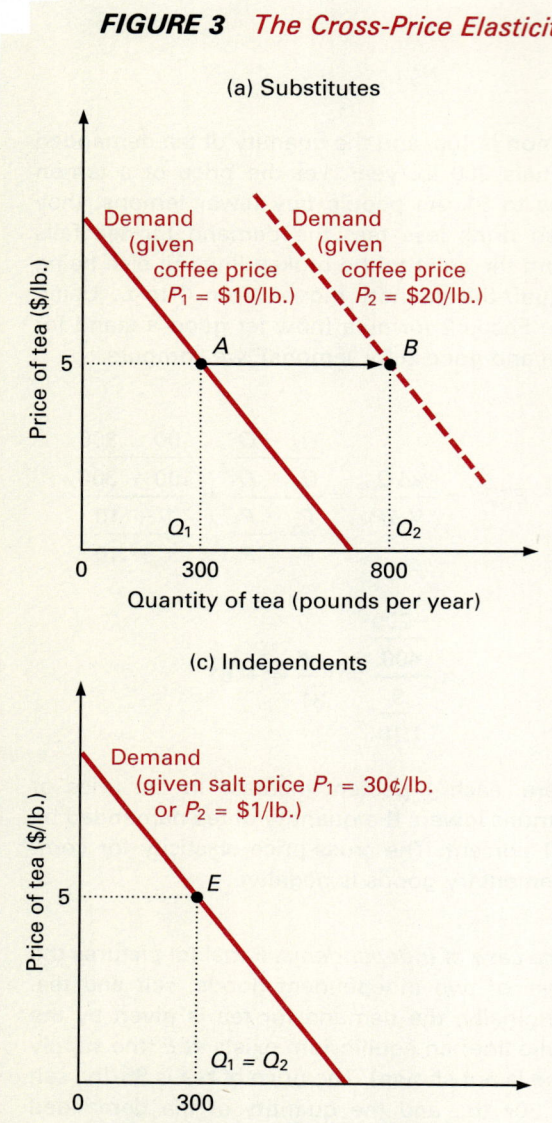

A good's cross-price elasticity of demand is the percentage change in the good's quantity demanded divided by the associated percentage change in *another* good's price that caused it (all else being equal). For any two goods, *a* and *b*, this elasticity is calculated as

$$E_{Da}^{c\text{-}p\,(b)} = \frac{\%\Delta Q_{Da}}{\%\Delta P_b} = \frac{\dfrac{\Delta Q_{Da}}{\overline{Q}_{Da}} \times 100}{\dfrac{\Delta P_b}{\overline{P}_b} \times 100}$$

where ΔQ_{Da} is good *a*'s absolute quantity change; $\overline{Q}_{Da}$ is the average of new and old good *a* quantities, or $(Q_2 + Q_1)/2$; while ΔP_b is good *b*'s absolute price change and $\overline{P}_b$ is the average of new and old good *b* prices, or $(P_2 + P_1)/2$. Focus 2 presents alternative versions of the same formula.

above 1 are called **luxuries.** No value judgment is involved; economists simply observe how people behave in a variety of markets. Given any percentage change in income, when the physical quantity consumed of a good changes by a smaller percentage than income, the good is called a necessity, when it changes by a larger percentage, a luxury. But beware: Your personal judgment about what constitutes a necessity or luxury may not coincide with the technical meaning of these terms.

Focus 3 presents alternative versions of the income elasticity formula; it is analogous to Focus 1, the only change being the replacement of the good's price, P_a, by consumer income, Y.

Empirical Data

Once again, numerous studies have collected empirical data. Table 4 presents selected estimates from U.S. markets.

TABLE 3 Cross-Price Elasticities of Demand

Good with quantity change	Good with price change	Elasticity	Source
Florida Interior oranges	Florida Indian River oranges	+1.56	Q
Margarine	Butter	+0.81	R
Butter	Margarine	+0.67	R
Natural gas	Fuel oil	+0.44	S
Beef	Pork	+0.28	R
Electricity	Natural gas	+0.20	S
Pork	Beef	+0.14	R
California oranges	Florida Interior oranges	+0.14	Q
Fruits	Sugar	−0.28	T
Cheese	Butter	−0.61	T

Empirical studies show cross-price elasticities of demand to be positive for substitutes, negative for complements.

SOURCES: **Q.** Marshall B. Godwin, W. Fred Chapman, Jr., and William T. Hanley, *Competition Between Florida and California Valencia Oranges in the Fruit Market*, Bulletin 704 (Washington, D.C.: U.S. Department of Agriculture, Economic Research Service, December 1965). **R.** H. Wold and L. Jureen, *Demand Analysis* (New York: Wiley, 1953). **S.** S. L. Taylor, and R. Halvorsen, "Energy Substitution in U.S. Manufacturing," *The Review of Economics and Statistics*, November 1977. **T.** R. Stone, *The Measurement of Consumers' Expenditure and Behavior in the United Kingdom, 1920–1938*, vol. 1 (Cambridge: Cambridge University Press, 1954).

FOCUS 3

The Income Elasticity of Demand

$$E_{Da}^{Y} = \frac{\%\Delta Q_{Da}}{\%\Delta Y} = \frac{\frac{\Delta Q_{Da}}{\overline{Q_{Da}}} \times 100}{\frac{\Delta Y}{\overline{Y}} \times 100} = \frac{\frac{Q_2 - Q_1}{Q_2 + Q_1} \times 100}{\frac{Y_2 - Y_1}{Y_2 + Y_1} \times 100} = \frac{\frac{Q_2 - Q_1}{Q_2 + Q_1}}{\frac{Y_2 - Y_1}{Y_2 + Y_1}}$$

where Q_1 and Q_2 are the original and new quantities of good *a* demanded ($Q_2 - Q_1$ equals ΔQ_{Da}), while Y_1 and Y_2 are the original and new levels of consumer income ($Y_2 - Y_1$ equals ΔY).

TABLE 4 Income Elasticities of Demand

Good	Elasticity	Source	Good	Elasticity	Source
Automobiles	2.46	A	Giving to charity	−0.70	D
Alcohol	1.54	A	Mail (letters)	0.65	C
Housing, owner-occupied	1.49	A	Tobacco	0.64	A
Furniture	1.48	A	Gasoline, oil	0.48	A
Books	1.44	A	Housing, rental	0.43	A
Dental services	1.42	A	Butter	0.42	E
Restaurant meals	1.40	A	Eggs	0.37	E
Shoes	1.10	A	Fuel oil, coal	0.27	B
Clothing	1.02	A	Electricity, residential	0.20	F
Water	1.02	A	Coffee	0	G
Beef	0.94	B	Margarine	−0.20	E
Medical insurance	0.92	A	Starchy roots	−0.20	G
Cable TV	0.83	C	Pig products	−0.20	G
Telephone calls	0.83	C	Flour	−0.36	E
Physicians' services	0.75	A	Whole milk	−0.50	G

Income elasticities of demand that are positive define normal goods, those that are negative identify inferior goods.

SOURCES: **A.** H. S. Houthakker and Lester D. Taylor, *Consumer Demand in the United States: Analyses and Projections,* 2nd ed. (Cambridge: Harvard University Press, 1970). **B.** Dale Heien, "Seasonality in U.S. Consumer Demand," *Journal of Business and Economic Statistics,* October 1983, p. 283. **C.** Charles B. Blankart, "Towards an Economic Theory of Advice and Its Application to the Deregulation Issue," *Kyklos,* 1, 1981, p. 101. **D.** M. Feldstein and A. Taylor, "The Income Tax and Charitable Contributions," *Econometrica,* November 1976. **E.** H. Wold and L. Jureen, *Demand Analysis* (New York: Wiley, 1953). **F.** L. Taylor and R. Halvorsen, "Energy Substitution in U.S. Manufacturing," *The Review of Economics and Statistics,* November 1977. **G.** Richard G. Lipsey and Peter O. Steiner, *Microeconomics,* 5th ed. (New York: Harper & Row, 1979), p. 133.

The Own-Price Elasticity of Supply

Just as there are numerous elasticities of demand, there are many elasticities of supply, each relating changes in the quantity supplied to changes in some other variable, such as the good's own price, the prices of alternative products, the prices of productive ingredients, and so on. Here we will consider only a good's **own-price elasticity of supply,** which is the percentage change in the good's quantity supplied divided by the associated percentage change in the good's own price that causes it, all else being equal. The concept is analogous to the own-price elasticity of demand, as a comparison of Focus 1 with Focus 4 shows.

Empirical Data

Economists have estimated supply elasticities in many markets. Selected results from an extended

NUMERICAL EXERCISE 3

Calculating the Income Elasticity of Demand

We can use Figure 4 to provide numerical examples for calculating different income elasticities of demand.

The case of an inferior good. Panel (a) pictures the case of an inferior good, such as intercity bus travel. Originally, the demand for this type of transportation is given by the solid line and equilibrium exists at A (the supply line is not shown). The price is 10¢/mile, aggregate consumer income is $400 million/year, and the quantity demanded by the consumers in question is 800,000 miles per year. If income rises to $500 million/year, the demand for the inferior bus travel falls from the solid to the broken line. All else being equal, the quantity moves from A to B. Using the Focus 3 formula (let good a stand for bus travel), we compute

$$E^Y_{Da} = \frac{\%\Delta Q_{Da}}{\%\Delta Y} = \frac{\dfrac{Q_2 - Q_1}{Q_2 + Q_1}}{\dfrac{Y_2 - Y_1}{Y_2 + Y_1}} = \frac{\dfrac{200 - 800}{200 + 800}}{\dfrac{500 - 400}{500 + 400}}$$

$$= \frac{\dfrac{-600}{1{,}000}}{\dfrac{100}{900}} = \frac{-.6}{.11} = -5.45$$

Each 1 percent increase in aggregate consumer income lowers the quantity of intercity bus travel demanded by 5.45 percent (or the opposites). As expected, the income elasticity of demand for an inferior good is negative.

The case of a normal good. Panel (b) pictures the case of a normal good, such as air travel. Originally, the demand is given by the solid line and equilibrium is at C (the supply line is not shown). The price is 35¢/mile, aggregate consumer income is $800 million/year, and the quantity demanded by the consumers in question is 500,000 miles per year. Let income rise to $4,000 million/year. The demand for this normal good rises from the solid to the broken line. All else being equal, the quantity moves from C to D. Using the Focus 3 formula (let good a now stand for airline travel), we compute

$$E^Y_{Da} = \frac{\%\Delta Q_{Da}}{\%\Delta Y} = \frac{\dfrac{Q_2 - Q_1}{Q_2 + Q_1}}{\dfrac{Y_2 - Y_1}{Y_2 + Y_1}} = \frac{\dfrac{3{,}500 - 500}{3{,}500 + 500}}{\dfrac{4{,}000 - 800}{4{,}000 + 800}}$$

$$= \frac{\dfrac{3{,}000}{4{,}000}}{\dfrac{3{,}200}{4{,}800}} = \frac{.75}{.66} = +1.125$$

Each 1 percent increase in aggregate consumer income raises the quantity of airline travel demanded by 1.125 percent (or the opposites). As expected, the income elasticity of demand for a normal good is positive. Moreover, the good in question is a luxury because the elasticity exceeds unity.

---

study of U.S. vegetable markets (covering 1919–1955) are given in Table 5. Short-run elasticities were calculated for one growing season, and long-run elasticities covering more extended periods were computed as well. The differences, often dramatic, are not surprising. In a given season, any 1 percent change in the price of green peas changes the quantity supplied by only .31 percent. Yet, given more time, each farm can change the quantities of formerly fixed inputs and devote more labor and land to growing peas if the price rose or less if the price fell. In addition, the number of firms in the industry can change. More firms enter the pea-growing business if the price of peas rises because that raises profit (all else being equal). By the same token, firms leave the business if price falls sufficiently to create losses. Thus, in the long run, any 1 percent change in the price of peas changes

FIGURE 4 The Income Elasticity of Demand

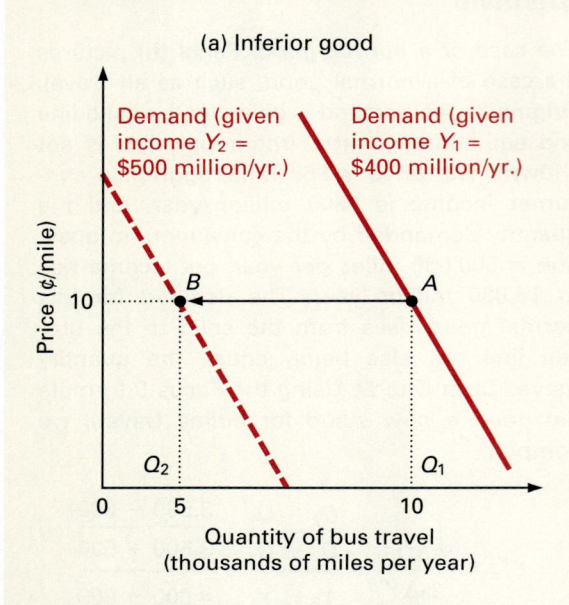

(a) Inferior good

Demand (given income Y_2 = $500 million/yr.)
Demand (given income Y_1 = $400 million/yr.)

Price (¢/mile)

B ← A at price 10

Q_2 = 5, Q_1 = 10

Quantity of bus travel (thousands of miles per year)

(b) Normal good

Demand (given income Y_1 = $800 million/yr.)
Demand (given income Y_2 = $4,000 million/yr.)

Price (¢/mile)

C → D at price 35

Q_1 = 500, Q_2 = 3500

Quantity of air travel (thousands of miles per year)

A good's income elasticity of demand is the percentage change in the good's quantity demanded divided by the associated percentage change in consumer income that causes it (all else being equal). For any good a and consumer income Y, this elasticity is calculated as

$$E_{Da}^{Y} = \frac{\%\Delta Q_{Da}}{\%\Delta Y} = \frac{\frac{\Delta Q_{Da}}{\overline{Q}_{Da}} \times 100}{\frac{\Delta Y}{\overline{Y}} \times 100}$$

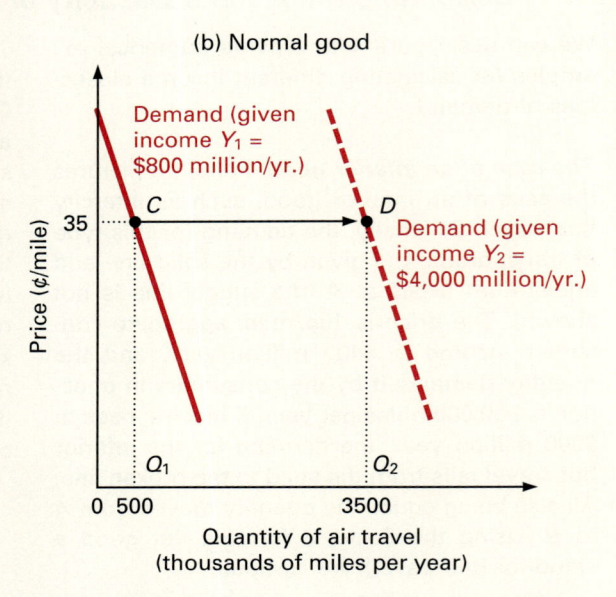

where ΔQ_{Da} is good a's absolute quantity change; $\overline{Q}_{Da}$ is the average of new and old good a quantities, or $(Q_2 + Q_1)/2$; while ΔY is the absolute change in consumer income and $\overline{Y}$ is the average of new and old income, or $(Y_2 + Y_1)/2$. Focus 3 presents alternative versions of the same formula.

FOCUS 4

The Own-Price Elasticity of Supply

$$E_{Sa}^{o-p} = \frac{\%\Delta Q_{Sa}}{\%\Delta P_a} = \frac{\frac{\Delta Q_{Sa}}{\overline{Q}_{Sa}} \times 100}{\frac{\Delta P_a}{\overline{P}_a} \times 100} = \frac{\frac{Q_2 - Q_1}{\frac{Q_2 + Q_1}{2}} \times 100}{\frac{P_2 - P_1}{\frac{P_2 + P_1}{2}} \times 100} = \frac{\frac{Q_2 - Q_1}{Q_2 + Q_1}}{\frac{P_2 - P_1}{P_2 + P_1}}$$

where Q_1 and Q_2 are the original and new quantities of good a supplied (hence $Q_2 - Q_1$ equals ΔQ_{Sa}), while P_1 and P_2 are the original and new prices of good a (hence $P_2 - P_1$ equals ΔP_a).

TABLE 5 *Own-Price Elasticities of Supply*

Good	Elasticity Short run	Elasticity Long run	Good	Elasticity Short run	Elasticity Long run
Cantaloupes	0.02	0.04	Green snap beans	0.15	∞
Lettuce	0.03	0.16	Eggplant	0.16	0.34
Green peppers	0.07	0.26	Tomatoes	0.16	0.90
Green lima beans	0.10	1.70	Kale	0.20	0.23
Shallots	0.12	0.31	Spinach	0.20	4.70
Beets	0.13	1.00	Watermelons	0.23	0.48
Carrots	0.14	1.00	Green peas	0.31	4.40
Cauliflower	0.14	1.10	Onions	0.34	1.00
Celery	0.14	0.95	Cabbage	0.36	1.20

SOURCE: Adapted from Marc Nerlove and William Addison, "Statistical Estimation of Long-Run Elasticities of Supply and Demand," *Journal of Farm Economics*, November 1958, p. 872.

quantity supplied not by .31 percent, but by 4.4 percent.

A knowledge of own-price elasticities is crucial for many decision makers. Consider the agricultural price support programs undertaken by governments in the United States and other countries. (A number of examples were provided in Chapters 3 and 4.) If the U.S. government promises sugar growers a price that lies 50 percent above the free market equilibrium level and also promises to buy whatever sugar remains unsold, it matters a great deal how sugar growers respond. Will the quantity supplied remain unchanged, will it rise by 15 percent, 50 percent, or even 275 percent? Depending on the answer, taxpayer subsidies to sugar growers may be relatively small or incredibly large.

Producers who want to manipulate prices, such as the members of the OPEC cartel, are equally interested in empirical supply elasticities. If they cut their own supply in order to drive up the price of oil, they must consider the response to the higher price by outsiders who are not part of the cartel. As long as the world market price is $5 per barrel of oil, producers in Pennsylvania who must spend $18 on drilling for each barrel of oil will shut down their wells. Let the world market price soar to $40, and Pennsylvania producers will drill day and night. For any cartel, a key question is the extent to which nonmembers will increase their quantity supplied. An empirical estimate of own-price elasticity of supply provides the answer.

Arc Elasticity Versus Point Elasticity

All types of elasticity numbers can be calculated in two different ways. First (as we have done in this chapter so far), one can concentrate on a given *section* of some demand or supply line and measure the responsiveness of quantity demanded or supplied to a fairly large change in some variable—be it the good's own price, some other price, income, or any other causal factor. Consider how we calculated the own-price elasticity of demand for section AC in Figure 2 and the own-price elasticity of supply for section AC in Figure 5. Indeed, had we graphed quantity demanded directly against the prices of other goods (Figure 3) or against income (Figure 4) we would have produced other, unconventional de-

NUMERICAL EXERCISE 4

Calculating the Own-Price Elasticity of Supply

Use Figure 5 to work out the now familiar numerical example. Imagine an original equilibrium at A (the demand line is not shown), with a price of $P_1 = \$5/\text{lb.}$ and a quantity supplied of $Q_1 = 10$ billion lb./year. Let the equilibrium move to C, raising price to $P_2 = \$7.50/\text{lb.}$ and quantity supplied to $Q_2 = 15$ billion lb./year.

We can calculate the elasticity in three steps:

1. The percentage change in quantity supplied is

$$\%\Delta Q_{Sa} = \frac{+5 \text{ billion lb.}}{\frac{15 + 10 \text{ billion lb.}}{2}} \times 100$$

$$= \frac{+5}{12.5} \times 100 = +40\%$$

2. The percentage change in price is

$$\%\Delta P_a = \frac{+\$2.50}{\frac{\$7.50 + 5.00}{2}} \times 100$$

$$= \frac{\$2.50}{\$6.25} \times 100 = +40\%$$

3. The own-price elasticity of supply is

$$E_{Sa}^{o\text{-}p} = \frac{\%\Delta Q_{Sa}}{\%\Delta P_a} = \frac{+40\%}{+40\%} = 1$$

We can instead get the same result by using the shortcut method of Focus 4:

$$E_{Sa}^{o\text{-}p} = \frac{\dfrac{Q_2 - Q_1}{Q_2 + Q_1}}{\dfrac{P_2 - P_1}{P_2 + P_1}} = \frac{\dfrac{15 - 10}{15 + 10}}{\dfrac{7.50 - 5.00}{7.50 + 5.00}} = \frac{\dfrac{5}{25}}{\dfrac{2.50}{12.50}}$$

$$= \frac{.2}{.2} = 1$$

Thus, in the relevant range of our supply line, any 1 percent change in price brings about a 1 percent change in quantity supplied as well.

FIGURE 5 *The Own-Price Elasticity of Supply*

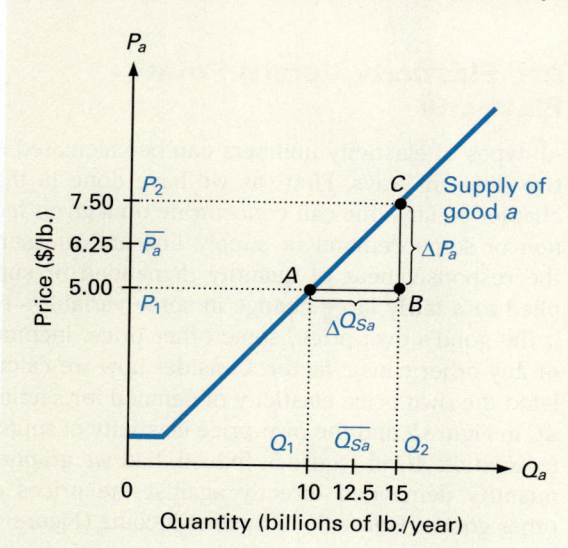

A good's own-price elasticity of supply is the percentage change in the good's quantity supplied divided by the associated percentage change in the good's own price that caused it (all else being equal). For a range such as AC, this elasticity is traditionally calculated as

$$E_{Sa}^{o\text{-}p} = \frac{\%\Delta Q_{Sa}}{\%\Delta P_a} = \frac{\dfrac{\Delta Q_{Sa}}{\overline{Q}_{Sa}} \times 100}{\dfrac{\Delta P_a}{\overline{P}_a} \times 100}$$

where ΔQ_{Sa} is the absolute quantity change; $\overline{Q}_{Sa}$ is the average of new and old quantities, or $(Q_2 + Q_1)/2$; while ΔP_a is the absolute price change; and $\overline{P}_a$ is the average of new and old prices, or $(P_2 + P_1)/2$. Focus 4 presents alternative versions of the same formula.

EXAMPLE 2

Agricultural Policy: Restricting Supply

Some 300 years ago, the British economist Gregory King (1648–1712) noted in amazement that bumper crops mean bad times for farmers, while poor crops spell good times for them. We now know the reason. In most agricultural markets, equilibrium is established in the relatively inelastic region of the demand line, as at points *b* or *e* in Figure 9 panel (b). When supply rises from a bumper crop, prices fall and gross revenues tumble. At the same time, larger crops mean higher costs for harvesting, transportation, storage, insurance, and so on, causing net revenues to tumble further. On the other hand, when supply falls in response to a poor crop and prices rise, gross revenues soar. At the same time, smaller crops mean lower costs for harvesting operations, causing net revenues to rise even more.

Figure A illustrates the typical case in which even small shifts in supply (between *S* and *S**) create huge changes in price (between *P* and *P**) because demand is relatively own-price inelastic. (Note how the section of the demand line shown lies entirely below midpoint *M.*) Figure B illustrates a hypothetical case (not usually found) in which the demand for agricultural products is relatively own-price elastic. Note how the section of the demand line shown lies entirely above midpoint *M.* Under such circumstances, identical shifts in supply (between *S* and *S'*) would cause negligible changes in price (between *P* and *P'*).

A number of government policies concerning agriculture have been based on the recognition that Figure A is typical while Figure B is not. Thus, all kinds of programs have been enacted with the aim of *deliberately* restricting agricultural production and marketing (as from *S** to *S* in Figure A). Given own-price inelastic demand, prices and farmers' revenues soar. Hence farmers are helped as if they had had a bad crop—and without a penny of taxpayer support. (For an alternative type of agricultural policy that does cost taxpayers, review Chapter 3, Figure 10.)

FIGURE A

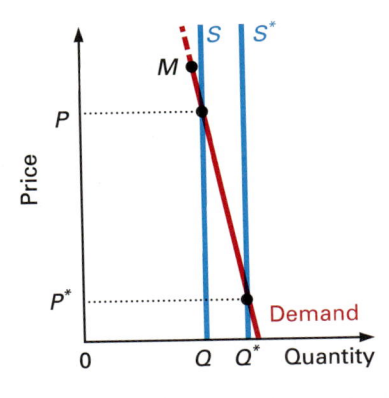

FIGURE B

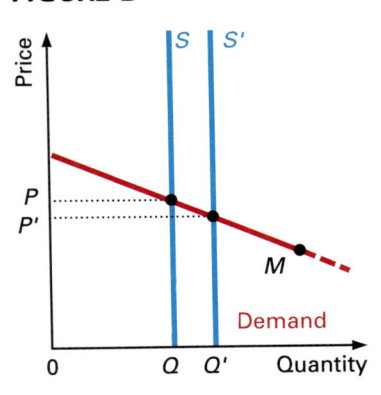

---

mand lines and could have depicted our elasticity computations with the help of demand line sections similar to *AC* in Figures 2 and 5. (End-of-chapter question 9 and its answer at the back of the book illustrate this assertion.) An elasticity measure that refers in this way to a fairly large section of a demand or supply line is called **arc elasticity,** presumably because most real-world demand and supply lines are curved rather than straight, making any given section of them look like an arc.

Economists are also interested in the effects on quantity demanded or supplied not of large but of very small changes in other variables. Take another look at Figure 2 and imagine that ΔP_a diminished until point *B* was practically next to point *A*. Naturally, ΔQ_{Da} would decrease, too, and point *C* would move very close to A. In the limit, B and C would merge with A. If we made ΔP_a and, therefore, ΔQ_{Da} infinitesimal, we would be measuring the own-price elasticity of demand at point A itself. An elasticity measure that refers in this way to a single point on a demand or supply line is called **point elasticity.** As the next section will show, point elasticity is easy to measure.

Measuring Point Elasticity

The value of point elasticity can be determined almost instantly at any point on any demand or supply line—whether it is straight or curved, sloping to the right or to the left. Three simple steps are involved.

1. Place a tangent—a straight line that *just touches* (but does not intersect) the demand or supply line—on the point P at which elasticity is to be measured.

2. Along this tangent, and using any convenient units of length, measure the distance from point P to the horizontal axis (or abscissa) as well as the distance from point P to the vertical axis (or ordinate).

3. The absolute value of the elasticity at point P equals the distance from point P to the abscissa ($P \rightarrow A$) divided by the distance from point P to the ordinate ($P \rightarrow O$). PAPO is a key word to remember.

Using the PAPO Rule: A Typical Demand Line

It is interesting to apply the PAPO rule to a typical, downward-sloping demand line and to note how the own-price elasticity of demand varies from point to point. Figure 6 shows the pattern found on every demand line of this type, regardless of its slope.

Using absolute values, elasticity equals infinity (demand is "perfectly elastic") where demand intercepts the vertical axis or ordinate (point A). Elasticity equals zero (demand is "perfectly inelastic") where demand intercepts the horizontal axis or abscissa (point B). Elasticity equals unity at midpoint M. (By definition, at the midpint, MB = MA. Hence the ratio MB/MA, which the PAPO rule makes us compute, equals 1.) Between A and M, in the demand line's upper half, the elasticity's absolute value always exceeds unity. (The PAPO rule then calls for dividing one distance, such as CB = 3, by a smaller distance, such as CA = 1). Demand in this region is said to be "relatively elastic," and elasticity falls continuously below infinity and towards unity as one moves from A toward M. Finally, between M and B, in the demand line's lower half, the elasticity's absolute value always falls short of unity. (The PAPO rule here calls for dividing one distance, such as DB = 1, by a larger distance, such as DA = 3). Demand in this region is said to be "relatively inelastic," and elasticity falls increasingly below unity and towards zero as one moves from M toward B.

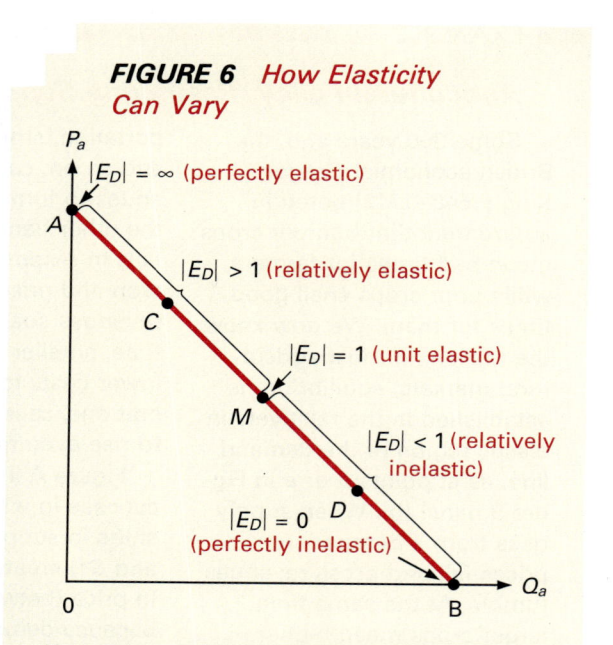

FIGURE 6 How Elasticity Can Vary

Along any straight, downward-sloping demand line, the slope (here 0A/0B) is constant throughout, but the own-price elasticity of demand varies from point to point. The PAPO rule instantly identifies any point elasticity involved. In this example, its absolute value at point A equals AB divided by zero, or what economists usually call infinity; at point C, it equals (CB/CA) = 3; at midpoint M, it equals (MB/MA) = 1; at point D, it equals (DB/DA) = $\frac{1}{3}$; and at point B, it equals zero divided by BA, or zero.

EXAMPLE 3

Thinking About National Health Insurance

Designers of national health insurance plans inevitably are concerned with elasticities. Their goal is to reduce the price people pay when receiving medical care to zero or to some tiny fraction of its cost, such as 10 percent. (Naturally, people as a group must pay for all of it in one way or another, including general taxes, government borrowing, higher interest rates, and so on.)

One study, based on U.S. 1970 data, tried to predict what Americans would do if they could have a national insurance plan covering dental care. Table A shows the ranges of elasticities revealed by the study (which computed separate values for children, adult women, and adult men). The study revealed many things, including the fact that adults considered extractions and dentures inferior goods (poor person's dentistry) and preferred preventive care and root-canal work at higher incomes. The study's overall conclusion, however, was that the use of dentists would double for adults and triple for children if direct user payments were cut to zero. Given the number of available dentists, it would be impossible to meet this demand in the short run. Long waiting periods to see doctors would be inevitable. This outcome could be avoided only by having patients pay a substantial portion of the true cost of each visit (even 25 percent would not be enough) or by phasing in a national dental insurance plan slowly (adults first, children later).

TABLE A

Service	Own-price elasticities	Income elasticities
Fillings	−0.95 to −0.58	+0.88 to +0.28
Cleanings	−1.34 to −0.14	+0.80 to +0.74
Examinations	−0.59 to −0.03	+0.73 to +0.51
Extractions	−1.51 to +0.21	−0.13 to +0.47
Crowns	−1.70 to +0.89	−0.08 to +0.93
Dentures	−0.59 to +2.20	−0.08 to +0.26
Orthodontia	−0.08	+1.24

Source: Willard G. Manning, Jr., and Charles E. Phelps, "The Demand for Dental Care," *The Bell Journal of Economics,* Autumn 1979, pp. 503–525, Table p. 512. Copyright © 1979, American Telephone and Telegraph Company.

The information summarized by Figure 6 is crucial for business executives who want to predict the consequences for their revenues when they adjust their prices. An increase in price will raise revenue if it is initiated in the relatively inelastic region of the demand line, at a point such as *D*. On the other hand, an increase in price will lower revenue if the initial position is a point such as *C*, in the relatively elastic region of demand. Thus, in the 1990–1991 season, Colorado ski resorts raised their lift ticket prices drastically (to $40 a day at Aspen), believing themselves to be operating in the *MB* section of Figure 6.

CAUTION

As Figure 6 confirms, price elasticities typically vary from one point to the next on any given demand or supply line. Therefore, it does not make sense to talk of the elasticity of a demand or supply line or curve. *Nevertheless, one often encounters statements to this effect. It is wiser to speak of the elasticity at a given* point *or along a given* arc, *the latter being the average of all the different point elasticities within the arc.*

Certain unusual demand or supply lines

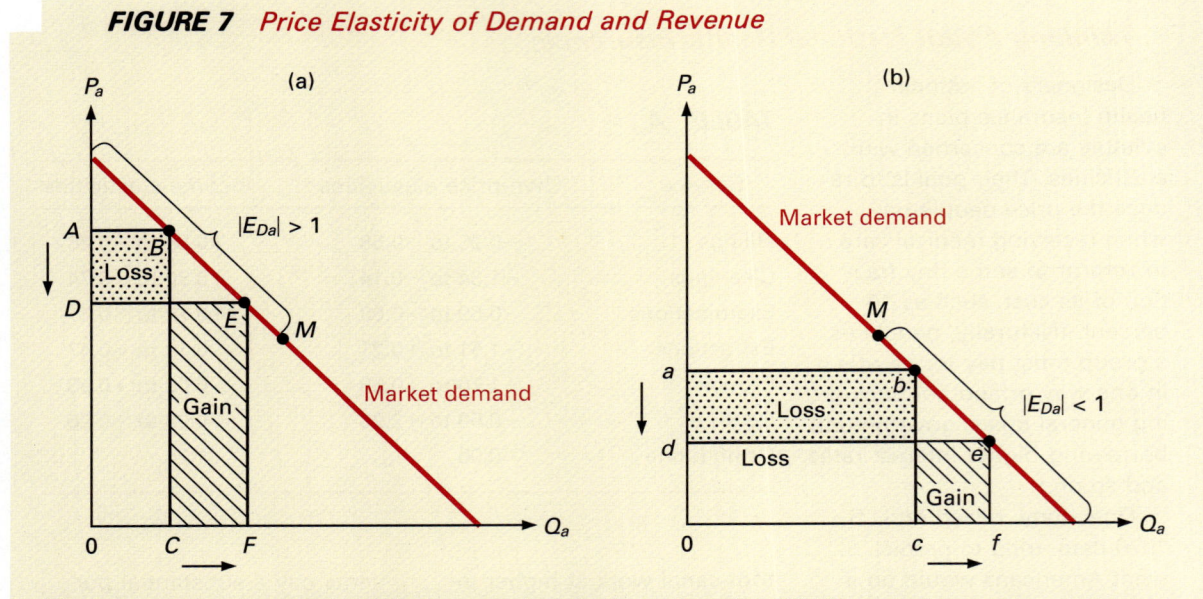

FIGURE 7 Price Elasticity of Demand and Revenue

Whenever market demand is relatively own-price elastic, as in region BE of panel (a), any price cut leads to larger dollar expenditures of consumers and thus to larger revenues of firms. When market demand is relatively own-price inelastic, on the other hand, as in region be of panel (b), any price cut leads to smaller dollar expenditures of consumers and to smaller revenues of firms. Increases in price have the opposite effects.

can have the same price elasticity at every single point, but such is the exception rather than the rule. Examples are provided by vertical demand or supply lines (price elasticity = 0), by horizontal demand or supply lines (price elasticity = ∞), and by straight supply lines that start at the origin of a graph (price elasticity = 1).

Price Elasticity of Demand and Revenue

One of the most important lessons to be learned from this chapter is the recognition of a relationship between the price elasticity of demand and the revenue of those who seek to satisfy that demand. As the remainder of the chapter will show, that relationship is simple and predictable. Whenever the absolute value of the own-price elasticity of demand exceeds unity, a decrease in price increases the total expenditures of consumers, which is the total revenues of all firms. When the elasticity falls short of unity, a decrease in price decreases the total expenditures of consumers and the total revenues of firms. An increase in price has the opposite effects in each case.

In Figure 7 both panels feature the identical market demand line. Panel (a) focuses on a price cut in the region of relatively elastic demand, above the demand line's midpoint M. When price equals OA, quantity demanded equals OC, hence the total expenditure of consumers and the total revenue of firms (price multiplied by quantity) are given by rectangle $OABC$. Let price fall to OD. Quantity demanded rises to OF; hence the consumers' expenditure and the firms' revenue equal rectangle $ODEF$. It is visually apparent that the new rectangle $ODEF$ is larger than old rectangle $OABC$; thus, the price cut has *raised* the revenue of firms. Note how the dotted area of revenue loss (from the lower price per unit sold) is more than offset by the crosshatched

EXAMPLE 4

The OPEC Cartel

At Baghdad in 1960, the governments of five countries (Iran, Iraq, Kuwait, Saudi Arabia, and Venezuela) founded OPEC, the Organization of Petroleum Exporting Countries. Eventually, other nations joined: Algeria, Ecuador, Gabon, Indonesia, Libya, Nigeria, Qatar, and the United Arab Emirates. Their goal was a simple one. The own-price elasticity of the demand for crude oil being low, joint action that reduced supply and raised price would dramatically raise the exporting countries' revenues. Figure A illustrates the cartel members' plan. Consider an original equilibrium at *a*, with price at P_0 and quantity Q_0. If the cartel members restrict supply from S to S^*, a new equilibrium emerges at *b*, with price rising to P_1 and quantity traded falling to Q_1. Given relatively price inelastic demand (the relevant demand line section shown lies entirely to the right and below midpoint *M*), seller revenues rise dramatically from $P_0 \times Q_0$ to $P_1 \times Q_1$.

Note how the gain from higher price (cross-hatched) far exceeds the loss from lower quantity (dotted).

This result did occur when the organization agreed to act at the start of 1973. Within the year, the price rose from $2.12 to $11.65 a barrel. By the end of 1980, while OPEC's average cost of production was 25¢ a barrel, the price reached $41 a barrel. OPEC's total revenue exceeded $300 billion a year, sufficient to buy up in about three years all the companies listed on the New York Stock Exchange. (The market value of their shares equaled $961.3 billion on September 30, 1979.)

In the long run, however, OPEC's initial success eroded. The long-run price elasticity of demand was much higher than the short-run elasticity. Thus, consumers conserved energy by turning to smaller cars with more miles per gallon, by turning their thermostats down in winter and up in summer, by moving to different climates, by insulating buildings, and more. And they switched to alternative fuels, such as coal, natural gas, and nuclear power. The long-run price elasticity of supply also exceeded the short-run elasticity. Thus, the high price of oil stimulated exploration activities and eventually opened vast new sources of supply outside the OPEC countries, as in Alaska, Mexico, and Europe's North Sea. The world price of oil declined accordingly, to $10 per barrel by 1986.

FIGURE A

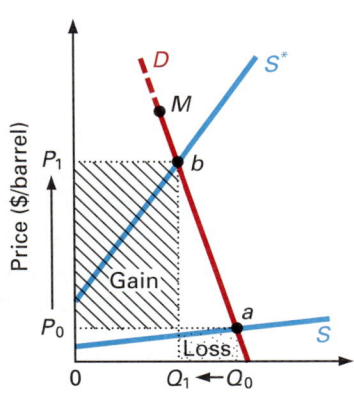

area of revenue gain (from the larger number of units sold). This result always occurs when price is cut in the region of relatively elastic demand and it should not surprise us. After all, when the own-price elasticity of demand has an absolute value above 1, any given percentage decrease in price leads to a *larger* percentage increase in quantity demanded. Thus it raises the dollar expenditure of consumers.

An example is provided to us by two publishers who made an experiment in 1989[1]. Betting on a high own-price elasticity of demand for hardcover novels, they lowered the standard price below the accepted $18.95 per book—and created best-sellers.

---

[1] Edwin McDowell, "Publishers Experiment With Lower Prices," *The New York Times,* May 8, 1989, p. D10.

TABLE 6 **Effects of Price Changes on Total Revenue (TR)**

Own-price Elasticity of demand (*absolute values*)	Price decreases	Price increases
Relatively elastic (>1)	TR rises	TR falls
Unit elastic (=1)	TR unchanged	TR unchanged
Relatively inelastic (<1)	TR falls	TR rises

The effect of a given price change on total revenue depends on the own-price elasticity of demand, which is why private business firms and governments are so interested in estimates of elasticity.

FIGURE 8 **The Total Revenue Curve**

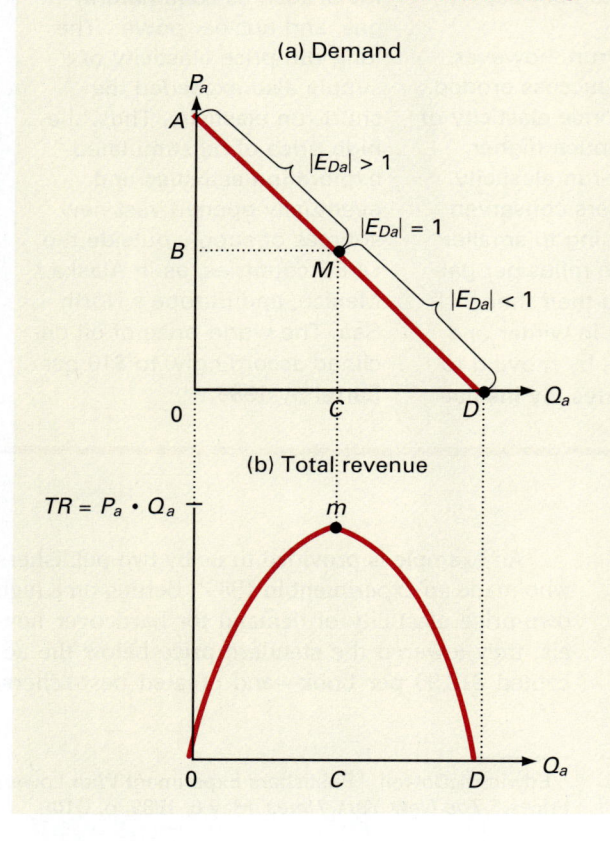

This graph illustrates the inevitable relationship between a straight, downward-sloping demand line (panel a) and the total revenue curve (panel b). At a price of A, nothing is sold, hence total revenue TR (which equals $P \times Q$) is zero. As price falls from A toward B, quantity demanded rises from 0 toward C. Because only the upper half of the demand line is involved, and thus the own-price elasticity's absolute value exceeds 1, total revenue rises. This is now shown in panel (b) by the total revenue line's rising section $0m$.

As price falls further from B toward 0, quantity demanded rises further from C toward D. Because only the lower half of the demand line is involved, and thus the own-price elasticity's absolute value now lies below 1, total revenue falls. This is shown in panel (b) by the total revenue line's declining section mD.

Total revenue reaches its maximum point m at a quantity ($0C$) that corresponds precisely to the demand line's midpoint M and, thus, to the point of unitary own-price elasticity of demand.

One case involved Bantam Books, which priced John Saul's horror novel, *Creature,* at $12.95. The second case involved Putnam's Sons and La Vyrle Spencer's *Morning Glory,* priced at $14.95.

Panel (b), on the other hand, focuses on a price cut in the region of relatively inelastic demand, below the demand line's midpoint *M*. When price equals O*a*, quantity demanded equals O*c*; the total revenue of firms equals rectangle O*abc*. Let price fall to O*d*. Quantity demanded rises to O*f*, the revenue of firms equals O*def*. It is visually obvious that new rectangle O*def* is smaller than old rectangle O*abc*; thus, the price cut has *lowered* the revenue of firms. Note how the dotted area of revenue loss (from the lower price per unit sold) fails to be offset by the crosshatched area of revenue gain (from the larger number of units sold). This result always occurs when price is cut in the region of relatively inelastic demand. When the own-price elasticity of demand has an absolute value below 1, any given percentage decrease in price leads to a *smaller* percentage increase in quantity demanded. Thus it lowers the dollar expenditure of consumers.

These points are summarized in Table 6. Figure 8 tells the same story in a different way; its caption makes it self-explanatory.

Applications

In Examples 2, 3, and 4, we consider a series of examples that show how elasticity analysis pervades the worlds of business and government decision makers.

Summary

1. Demand and supply each depend on numerous factors. Despite this complexity, the simple demand-and-supply model helps us see the general direction of change in quantities demanded or supplied when other variables change. There are times, however, when economic decision makers want a more exact measure of responsiveness; such measures are called *elasticities*.

2. Despite a temptation to do so, it is not wise to measure elasticity by a demand or supply line's slope (or its reciprocal). The problems that arise from this method can be avoided by computing changes in all variables in percentage terms. Any type of elasticity is then defined as the percentage change in quantity divided by the percentage change in whatever variable causes the quantity change—all else being equal.

3. The own-price elasticity of demand is the percentage change in a good's quantity demanded divided by the associated percentage change in the good's own price that causes it, all else being equal. Economists have measured this elasticity in many markets; some of their results are presented in this chapter. The values observed are explained by such factors as the availability of substitutes, the fraction of consumer budgets involved, and the passage of time.

4. The cross-price elasticity of demand is the percentage change in a good's quantity demanded divided by the associated percentage change in *another* good's price that causes it, all else being equal. Numerous studies have collected empirical data. They confirm theoretical expectations that cross-price elasticities are positive for substitute goods and negative for complementary goods.

5. The income elasticity of demand is the percentage change in a good's quantity demanded divided by the associated percentage change in consumer income that causes it, all else being equal. Numerous studies have collected empirical data. When positive, these income elasticities identify normal goods; when negative, inferior goods.

6. The own-price elasticity of supply is the percentage change in a good's quantity supplied divided by the associated percentage change in the good's own price that causes it, all else being equal. Economists have measured this elasticity in many markets; selected results are pre-

sented here. It is not surprising that long-run elasticities exceed short-run elasticities.

7. An elasticity measure that refers to a fairly large section of a demand or supply line is called arc elasticity; a measure that refers to a simple point on such a line is called point elasticity.

8. Point elasticity can be determined almost instantly at any point on any demand or supply line with the help of the PAPO rule. Among other things, the rule can be used to show how the price elasticity of demand varies from point to point along a typical, straight, downward-sloping demand line.

9. One of the most important lessons to be learned from elasticity analysis is the recognition of a predictable relationship between the price elasticity of demand and the revenue of those who seek to satisfy that demand.

10. A series of applications illustrate how elasticity analysis pervades the worlds of business and government decision makers.

Key Concepts

arc elasticity

cross-price elasticity of demand

elasticity

income elasticity of demand

luxuries

necessities

own-price elasticity of demand

own-price elasticity of supply

point elasticity

Questions and Problems

1. Consider Chapter 3, Table 1. Calculate price elasticities of demand for each successive pair of rows.

2. Consider these numbers relating to Henry Ford's Model T:

Year	Price	Quantity Sold	Total revenue
1909	$900	58,022	$ 52.2 million
1914	440	472,350	207.8 million
1916	360	730,041	262.8 million

Calculate the own-price elasticity of demand for Ford cars

a. for the period 1909–1914.
b. for the period 1914–1916.

3. Consider Figure 2. Compute the arc elasticity in the DE range, given that P and Q equal 2 and 16 for D, 1 and 18 for E.

4. Which of the following are likely to have positive cross-price elasticities of demand: automobiles and oil, gin and tonic, a Harvard education and a Yale education, ham and cheese, men's shoes and women's shoes, gasoline and diapers. Give reasons for your answers.

5. A study of rats (John H. Kagel, Raymond C. Battalio, Howard Rachlin, and Leonard Green, "Demand Curves for Animal Consumers," *The Quarterly Journal of Economics,* February 1981, pp. 1–15) revealed these elasticities:

a. Own-price elasticity of demand
   Food   − .18
   Root beer   −2.22
b. Cross-price elasticity of demand
   Water/food   .13
   Saccharin solution/food   .18
   Collins mix/root beer   4.12
   Cherry cola/root beer   .72

Interpret the numbers.

6. Comment on the truth or falsity of each of the following statements:
   a. The U.S. own-price elasticity of demand for oranges equals $|.8|$. Therefore, California growers can increase their revenues by raising price.
   b. The own-price elasticity for steak in general is likely to be lower than that for steak sold by Stop and Shop.
   c. The own-price elasticity for iceberg lettuce is likely to be higher than that for all types of lettuce.
   d. On two parallel, downward-sloping demand lines, the own-price elasticity of demand is the same at any given price.
   e. On two parallel, downward-sloping demand lines, the own-price elasticity of demand is the same at any given quantity.
   f. Luxuries, unlike necessities, have an income elasticity of less than unity.

7. One researcher (James H. Gapinski, "The Economics of Performing Shakespeare," *The American Economic Review,* June 1984, pp. 458–466) studied Britain's Royal Shakespeare Company and found an own-price elasticity of demand of $-.657$ and an income elasticity of demand of 1.327. Interpret these results.

8. A study by George W. Hilton, *Amtrak: The National Railroad Passenger Corporation* (Washington, D.C.: American Enterprise Institute, 1980) noted an own-price elasticity of demand for rail travel in general of -2.2, but of $-.67$ in the Boston-Washington corridor, and an income elasticity of $-.6$. Interpret these results.

9. When discussing Figures 3 and 4, the text mentions the possibility of drawing unconventional types of demand lines that relate a good's quantity not to its own price but to
   a. the price of a substitute good.
   b. the price of a complementary good.
   c. the price of an independent good.
   d. income (assuming the good is an inferior good).
   e. income (assuming the good is a normal good).

   Using the examples of Figures 3 and 4, draw a series of such unconventional demand lines.

10. Consider Chapter 3, Table 2, A Supply Schedule for Beef. Calculate price elasticities of supply for each successive pair of rows.

11. Do you think supply elasticities, like demand elasticities, can also be defined for variables other than a good's own price?

12. Who is likely to bear the burden of an excise tax if
    a. supply is upward sloping while demand is vertical?
    b. supply is upward sloping while demand is horizontal?

CHAPTER 7

THE FIRM: AN OVERVIEW

Preview

This chapter explores the nature of the firm in a market economy where it is an island of central economic planning and management in contrast to the world around it. No matter how accomplished, the coordination of people's specialized activities is never costless, and some such activities can be coordinated with less cost by managers than by markets. The major types of firms in the U.S. economy are profit-seeking proprietorships, partnerships, and corporations, and nonprofit firms. Principal-agent problems are discussed (in particular those arising from the separation of ownership and management in large corporations), so are possible solutions. Profit maximization is identified as the primary goal of most firms.

An appendix introduces two major concepts of business accounting: the balance sheet and the income statement.

Examples

1. Why Entrepreneurs Often Fail as Managers
2. *Fortune's* Top Ten Companies
3. Businesses with Halos
4. The CEO Disease
5. Major Companies Reject Takeover Protection
6. The Globalization of Business

Ideas in History

The Nature of the Firm

As noted earlier in this book, people who care to maximize the flow of goods available to them in any given period are well advised not to employ their scarce resources in isolation from other people. This lesson has been widely accepted throughout the world. By specializing in the production of particular goods and then trading with others who similarly specialize, people everywhere routinely manage to squeeze a larger flow of goods from the available resources than they could otherwise procure. Within as well as among countries, this complex division of labor, we must now recall, can be coordinated in one of two ways: It can be coordinated *spontaneously,* through a system of markets in which people make voluntary contracts with one another (usually about trading commodities and services for money); or *deliberately,* through a system of central planning in which monetary incentives are replaced by verbal commands that managers issue to subordinates who are expected to obey. (For a quick review, see Chapter 2, Figure 1, The Capitalist Market Economy, and Figure 2, The Communist Command Economy.)

Now consider a market economy in somewhat greater detail and focus on the **firm,** the institution that buys productive ingredients in resource markets, uses them to produce goods, and sells these products in goods markets. In stark contrast to the world of markets that surround it, the firm itself is an island of central economic planning and management.

The Firm as a Miniature Command Economy

In the U.S. economy, the specialized activities *among* households and firms generally mesh through market relationships. Monetary contracts specify who shall do what. Worker A works a total of 35 hours a week for Firm X and receives $300 in return. Firm X delivers 50 cars to Firm Y and receives $250,000. Firm Z delivers 5 sacks of groceries to Consumer A who pays $91.32 for them. And so on. Millions of monetary contracts ultimately decide what is produced, how, and for whom.

Yet the specialized activities of people *within* households or firms (the latter alone are of concern in this chapter) are generally *not* coordinated with the help of market relationships. Within the typical firm all the buying and selling that pervades the rest of the economy comes to an abrupt halt. Take Adam Smith's pin factory (noted in Chapter 1), in which numerous individuals divided among themselves the tasks required for producing a single product, pins. It would not be inconceivable to organize the pinmakers' activities on the basis of market relationships. Worker A could *buy* metal and use owned or rented tools to draw out the wire and *sell* the wire to Worker B. Worker B could use owned or rented tools to cut the wire into appropriate lengths and *sell* the pieces to Worker C. Worker C could create sharp points on the pieces just bought and *sell* the resultant products to Worker D. Worker D could use additional tools to grind the pieces for receiving the head and *sell* these products to Worker E. Worker E could buy heads from Worker F, attach them to the pieces received from Worker D, and *sell* the finished pins to Worker G. Worker G, in turn, could market the pins to their ultimate consumers.

Yet such a series of contracts is unlikely to be made, either in Adam Smith's pin factory or in any modern-day firm. In the typical firm, workers enter into a single monetary contract: an agreement to work x hours per week in return for y dollars per week and to accept—during the specified working time and within reasonable limits—the verbal orders of a boss. Workers are then provided with raw materials and tools and are *told* what to do: draw out the wire, point it, grind it, make the head, attach the head, package the pins, and send them to the warehouse. Workers do what they are told, each just handing over their work to the next person without payment. Thus, each individual firm is a miniature of the command economy discussed in Chapter 2. Why is it that in so many countries the price system dominates the relationships among households and firms but ceases to work within the confines of those firms? The answer was provided by Ronald Coase in 1937, as Ideas in History, The Nature of the Firm, explains.

Coase's insight—that the division of labor will ultimately be coordinated either by markets or by central managers, depending on which is less costly—has been confirmed by numerous events. Chapter 2, Example 3, Marketization Sweeps the Communist World, provided an example of what happens when managerial coordination of specialized activities is carried too far and the entire economy becomes a single firm. Yugoslavia's experience in recent decades illustrates an opposite case, in which market coordination was expanded to such an excessive degree that its costs far exceeded those of managerial coordination.

Having discussed the nature of the firm in general, we now turn to the major types of firms in the U.S. economy (and other market economies throughout the world).

Major Types of U.S. Firms

Table 1 provides data concerning proprietorships, partnerships, and corporations in the United States. We will discuss each of these categories and then note other, minor types of firms.

Proprietorships

As Table 1 shows, the most common type of firm in the United States is the **proprietorship,** a firm owned and operated by a single person. (It is also referred to as a *sole* proprietorship or a *single* proprietorship.) Nonfarm proprietorships accounted for almost 71 percent of 17.5 million profit-seeking U.S. businesses in 1986, yet they produced only 6.1 percent of the $9.2 trillion of business sales. Proprietorships tend to be small firms. Of the 12.4 million nonfarm proprietorships in 1986, some 46 percent operated in the service sector (architects, doctors,

TABLE 1 Major Types of U.S. Firms, 1986

Type	Number		Sales	
	In thousands	%	Billion dollars	%
Proprietorships (nonfarm)	12,394	70.7	559	6.1
Partnerships	1,703	9.7	379	4.1
Corporations	3,429	19.6	8,282	89.8
Total	17,526	100.0	9,220	100.0

SOURCE: U.S. Bureau of the Census, *Statistical Abstract of the United States: 1990* (Washington, D.C.: U.S. Government Printing Office, 1990), p. 521.

lawyers, writers); 18 percent in wholesale and retail trade; 13 percent in construction; 9 percent in finance, insurance, real estate; and only 3 percent in manufacturing. The remaining 11 percent were scattered throughout the rest of the economy.

Table 2 summarizes the advantages and disadvantages of this type of business organization.

Advantages

1. *Ease of formation and liquidation.* It is exceedingly easy to create a proprietorship or bring it to an end. No complicated forms have to be filled out or filed, no fees paid, no lawyers involved. A person simply announces that he or she is in business (or has ceased to operate). So far as the law is concerned, the single proprietor *is* the firm; the firm has no separate existence from its owner. Naturally, the owner must comply with existing laws. Someone setting out to run a restaurant must comply with zoning ordinances, satisfy health department requirements, and perhaps get a liquor license, but there are no special rules that single out the proprietorship as opposed to everyone else.

2. *Owner in complete control.* The proprietor is also the manager, solely responsible for everything that happens in the firm. People who value independence, like to work for themselves, and want to be their own boss are attracted by this feature. They have complete control over all of the firm's assets and profits, but are also responsible for all the firm's debts and losses.

TABLE 2 The Proprietorship: Major Characteristics

Advantages	Disadvantages
1. Ease of formation and liquidation.	1. Unlimited liability of owner.
2. Owner in complete control.	2. Limited ability to acquire funds.
3. Profits taxed as regular personal income.	3. Limited managerial skill.
	4. Firm's life tied to owner's.

■ EXAMPLE 1

Why Entrepreneurs Often Fail as Managers

In the mid-1980s, when Marc Hyman started his own business in New York, he was obsessed with being "on top of everything." He was in charge of production, selling, maintenance, dealing with employees and suppliers, keeping records, arranging financial matters, and so forth. "I wasn't willing to listen to other people," he recalls. "I thought, 'I am the daddy of this. I put in thousands of hours. I know better than anyone else.'" At first the business flourished, yet its very growth brought financial and personal grief. The story is typical.

The very traits that lead people to start successful businesses—ambition, self-confidence, creativity, hands-on-involvement in perfecting every detail—are also the traits that can impede the business as it grows. A growing proprietorship requires a radical change in management style: the ability to delegate authority. Those founders who insist on never taking a day off, keeping tabs on everything, studying every sales order, reading every invoice, inspecting every packing list, eventually invite disaster. Once sales top $1 million a year, then $13 million, then $75 million, founders must let others share responsibility, let others babysit their "child." If they don't, more and more things go wrong and their offspring dies because an individual person cannot take care of it no matter how hard they try.

Source: Carrie Dolan, "Entrepreneurs Often Fail as Managers," *The Wall Street Journal,* May 15, 1989, p. B1.

---

3. *Profits taxed as regular personal income.* Naturally, the tax collector requires the single proprietor to keep careful records of sales revenues and costs (see the appendix to this chapter) and to report the difference—a profit if it is positive, a loss if it is negative. The U.S. Internal Revenue Service, for example, requires the filing of a special form, Schedule C, for this purpose. The resultant business profit (or loss) is simply added to (or subtracted from) the owner's other income, if any. Any profit is taxed at the regular personal income tax rate.

Disadvantages

1. *Unlimited liability of owner.* A major disadvantage of the proprietorship is the legal principle of **unlimited liability,** according to which the firm's owner is responsible for all business debts without limit—up to the full extent of the owner's personal wealth and regardless of the amount of money the owner has invested in the business. Thus, a proprietor who originally put $50,000 into a business but eventually finds the firm owning nothing and owing $2 million can be called upon to hand over to creditors everything that is owned, no matter how unrelated to the business: houses and cars, personal bank accounts and stock certificates, furniture and stamp collections, life insurance policies and the children's bicycles. This risk affects the behavior of proprietorships; they are unlikely to engage in high risk ventures, even if the expected payoff is high. Business bankruptcy means family bankruptcy.

2. *Limited ability to acquire funds.* The amount of financial capital that a proprietorship can acquire tends to be limited by the owner's initial wealth, money that can be borrowed from relatives and friends, and the owner's credit at a local bank. If the business is profitable, additional funds become available over time. But typically it is next to impossible to acquire significant outside funds, which severely limits the firm's chances for growth. This fact also explains why successful firms move from proprietorships to partnerships and corporations during their history.

3. *Limited managerial skill.* While being one's own boss can be an advantage, it also limits the managerial resources of the firm to whatever skills the single owner possesses. As firms grow, the owner's skills are not always sufficient. Example 1 casts light on this issue.

4. *Firm's life tied to owner's.* The firm's life is inextricably tied to that of the owner. If the owner dies, the firm ceases to exist.

Partnerships

As Table 1 shows, the **partnership,** an unincorporated firm owned and operated by a fixed number of two or more persons, is the least common type of business in the United States. Partnerships accounted for fewer than 10 percent of the 17.5 million profit-seeking U.S. businesses in 1986 and produced only 4.1 percent of all business sales. Of the 1.7 million partnerships in 1986, some 50 percent operated in finance, insurance, and real estate; 19 percent in services; 10 percent in wholesale and retail trade; and only 2 percent in manufacturing.

Table 3 summarizes the advantages and disadvantages of this type of business organization.

Advantages

1. *Ease of formation and liquidation.* Like a proprietorship, a partnership can be established and brought to an end fairly easily, by simple agreement among the partners. Although no lawyers are required, it is good business practice to draw up a written document that specifies who the partners are, who is to contribute how much of the original capital, who is to carry out which duties, how profits and losses are to be apportioned, how the firm can be liquidated, and so on.

2. *Greater access to funds.* Compared to the proprietorship, the partnership has greater access to funds. The sources are the same as for the single proprietor, but there are more owners whose access to funds can be pooled.

3. *Greater access to managerial skill.* The different management skills of partners can be pooled just as their capitals can; the partnership has more managerial resources on which to draw. In addition, different partners can specialize in different managing tasks according to their talents.

4. *Profits taxed as regular personal income.* As in the case of proprietorships, partnership profits or losses are treated by tax collectors as regular personal income. Each partner must report his or her share on personal income tax returns.

Disadvantages

1. *Unlimited liability of owners.* The principle of unlimited liability, discussed earlier with respect to single proprietors, applies fully to each owner in a partnership. Thus, a given partner among three equal partners may have invested a mere $100,000 in the business. Yet if the day comes that the other partners skip town and the business goes bankrupt—holding no assets, but debts of $5 million—that partner could become personally responsible for *all* of the $5 million debt. This risk is inherent in a partnership. Some have argued it is

TABLE 3 *The Partnership: Major Characteristics*

Advantages	Disadvantages
1. Ease of formation and liquidation.	1. Unlimited liability of owners.
2. Greater access to funds (compared to proprietorship).	2. Complicated decision making (compared to proprietorship).
3. Greater access to managerial skill (compared to proprietorship).	3. Firm's life tied to original owners.
4. Profits taxed as regular personal income.	

precisely this fact that enhances public confidence in the partnership. People who take such an enormous risk must surely be honest and reliable; hence it is safe to deal with partnership firms. Allegedly, this reasoning explains the prevalence of partnerships in such fields as accounting, investment banking, law, and medicine.

Although rare, there also exists a **limited partnership,** a partnership jointly owned by one or more general partners (who carry unlimited liability) and one or more limited partners (whose liability for the firm's debts is limited to their original investment in the firm). This type of business, presumably, enhances a partnership's ability to raise funds because people may be willing to invest money as limited partners (they cannot lose more than the amount so invested), but unwilling to take on the risks and managerial responsibilities of general partners.

2. *Complicated decision making.* Compared to the single proprietorship where one person decides everything, decision making in a partnership is more complex. Every general partner has the legal right to make binding decisions for the entire partnership; presumably, it takes a considerable amount of trust and goodwill to run a partnership smoothly under such circumstances. Imagine, for example, that you are a general partner in a firm, having invested $10,000 of your own money and sharing 5 percent of the firm's profits and losses. You know that *anything* any one of the other partners does can potentially burden you with millions of dollars of debt. Wouldn't you want to keep a close eye on as much of the business activity as possible? So would all your partners, in turn, who wouldn't want to rely on blind faith either. As a result, any decision is likely to be more complicated than it would be in a single proprietorship.

3. *Firm's life tied to original owners.* The death or withdrawal of any one owner ends the life of the partnership. Even where there are procedures for the orderly replacement of a partner who wants to withdraw, the original partnership is considered dissolved and a new one formed.

Corporations

As Table 1 shows, corporations made up just over 19 percent of U.S. profit-seeking firms in 1986 but accounted for almost 90 percent of all business sales. In that sense, they are by far the most important type of business. A **corporation** is a legal entity, chartered by government, and separate and distinct from the persons who own it. In the United States, a corporation can be chartered by a state or by the federal government. Like a human being, this "legal person" can own property, incur debt, earn income, enter into contracts, sue and be sued, and pay taxes. The owners are called **stockholders,** as evidenced by their holding marketable certificates of ownership, called **stock certificates.**

CAUTION

Since the invention of the corporation, there are two types of persons so far as the law is concerned. Human beings are real *persons; corporations are looked upon as fictitious,* legal *persons. Thus, the term "person" in the definitions given here has to be interpreted with care. It includes both possibilities; a corporation can be owned by human beings or by other corporations.*

Table 4 summarizes the advantages and disadvantages of this form of business.

Advantages

1. *Limited liability of owners.* The limited liability of stockholders is the most important advantage of the corporate form of business. **Limited liability** is the legal principle that makes each stockholder separately liable for a corporation's debts, but only up to the amount of money already spent when acquiring the stock certificates held. Thus, if you spend $100 on a stock certificate, you can never be called upon to pay another cent. The worst that can happen to you is that the corporation goes bankrupt and the value of your stock falls to zero.

2. *Easy access to funds.* Related to the limited liability feature is the fact that corporations find it much easier to acquire large sums of financial capital than proprietorships and partnerships do. Given limited liability, many small investors can be persuaded to buy stock certificates because their personal wealth is not at risk beyond the stock purchase itself. Selling $100 stock certificates to a hundred million people brings in $10 billion, a sum that no proprietorship or partnerships could hope to amass. Example 2 provides an illustration of the incredible size of some of America's corporations.

3. *Easy access to managerial skills.* Unlike single proprietors or business partners, stockholders need not become involved in running the firm they own. Indeed, many of them have no desire to do so. Those who wish may attend the annual stockholders' meeting and vote for a board of directors. The board then sets broad company policy but appoints and supervises a group of managers to run the firm on a day-to-day basis. Owners need not have management skills; still, they can in this way recruit high-quality managers for the firm. And owners can replace these managers if they are dissatisfied with management performance.

4. *Permanent life of firm.* Potentially, a corporation has an eternal life. Being a separate entity in the eyes of the law, its existence is not affected by what happens to its human owners. Individual stockholders can die and bequeath their certificates to others; they can sell their shares or buy new ones. The corporation continues unchanged. Indeed, the stock of large corporations is listed and continually traded in organized markets, such as the New York Stock Exchange. That of smaller corporations is similarly traded by stockbrokers on so-called over-the-counter markets. (This ability of individual owners to give up their ownership share at a moment's notice, simply by selling it to someone else, is another reason for the ease with which corporations can raise financial capital.)

Disadvantages

1. *Complexity of formation.* Compared to the other two forms of business, the formation of a corporation is complex, which is why it is rarely created for temporary business ventures. A charter must be obtained from a government, numerous forms must be filed, and fees must be paid. A lawyer is required.

2. *Double taxation.* A major disadvantage of the corporate form of business is that a corporation—a fictitious legal person—is also treated as such for tax purposes. The federal government and most state governments impose a corporate income tax on corporate profit (ranging from 15 to 34 percent in recent years). The remaining profit after taxes is then used for one of two purposes. It is either divided among stockholders and paid out to them as **dividends** or it is retained by the business as **undistributed corporate profit.** Dividends are then taxed again as personal income received, a practice referred to as **double taxation.** Thus it is possible that a dollar of corporate profit turns into 34¢ of corporate income taxes and, if 66¢ are paid in dividends, into another 22¢ of personal income taxes, yielding only 44¢ of net income to stockholders.

There is one exception, however, that exists. Certain small-business corporations, called **S-corporations,** are able to escape the double taxation, provided that the number of their stockholders does not exceed 35. In 1986, there were 826,000 such firms.

TABLE 4 *The Corporation: Major Characteristics*

Advantages	Disadvantages
1. Limited liability of owners.	1. Complexity of formation.
2. Easy access to funds.	2. Double taxation.
3. Easy access to managerial skills.	3. Separation of ownership and control.
4. Permanent life of firm.	

EXAMPLE 2

Fortune's *Top Ten Companies*

Business publications, such as *Business Week, Forbes,* or *Fortune,* regularly carry feature articles about America's corporations. Table A provides pertinent data on the ten largest U.S. Industrial Corporations in 1990, ranked by sales. The sales of each of these giants exceeded the revenues of most of the fifty states as well as the national incomes of many of the world's nations.

TABLE A

Company	Sales	Profits	Assets	Employees
	(billions of dollars)			(thousands)
1. General Motors	$126.0	$−2.0	$180.2	761.4
2. Exxon	105.9	5.0	87.7	104.0
3. Ford Motor	98.3	.9	173.7	370.4
4. IBM	69.0	6.0	87.6	373.8
5. Mobil	58.8	1.9	41.7	67.3
6. General Electric	58.4	4.3	153.9	298.0
7. Philip Morris	44.3	3.5	46.6	168.0
8. Texaco	41.2	1.5	26.0	39.2
9. DuPont	39.8	2.3	38.1	144.0
10. Chevron	39.3	2.2	35.1	54.2

SOURCE: "The Fortune 500: The Largest U.S. Industrial Corporations," *Fortune,* April 22,1991, pp. 286, 312, 314, 316, 322, and 324.

---

3. *Separation of ownership and control.* The separation of corporate ownership from corporate management has its advantages. It improves the availability of funds from people who want to be investors but abhor the hassle of running a firm. It improves the chances of finding high-quality managers because managers need not be selected from among a narrow group of owners. Yet, at the same time, there emerges a possible conflict of interest. Owners typically want to see their firm earn high profits. Such profits translate into high dividends (if owners hold on to their stock) or into rising stock prices and the realization of capital gains (if owners sell their stock). Managers, on the other hand, may have alternative goals that conflict with those of stockholders. This issue is discussed in a later section of this chapter.

Nonprofit Firms

The previous sections have discussed the major types of profit-seeking businesses found in the United States, but **nonprofit firms** that are typically exempt from taxation exist as well. They include nonprofit corporations that have no stockholders and are run by self-perpetuating boards of trustees, various types of cooperatives, and public enterprises.

Consider nonprofit corporations, such as charities, churches, and country clubs; colleges, educational TV stations, and hospitals; labor unions, research firms, and theater companies. All of them rely on membership fees, donations, and market sales to generate revenue; all of them return the excess of revenue over cost to future operations.

Consider cooperative enterprises, such as consumer coops, credit unions, electric power coops, farmers' marketing coops, rural telephone coops, and worker coops. In one way or another, all of these are run for the benefit of members; any excess of revenue over cost is returned to members—for example, on the basis of purchases made in the case of many consumer coops, or on an equal basis in the case of many labor-owned worker coops.

Consider, finally, a multitude of government enterprises that often sell products in competition with private firms, ranging from railroad transportation and mail service to garbage collection and drinking water. Often such firms incur losses that are subsidized by general tax revenues; any "profits" accrue to the governments involved. Example 3 examines the nonprofit sector in the U.S. economy.

Principals Versus Agents

Corporations, although not the most numerous type of firm in the U.S. economy, are the most important type when considering factors such as sales, assets, or number of employees. Given the corporation's dominance, it is important to ask how efficiently it approaches the scarcity problem, how well it manages the task of turning scarce resources into the largest possible set of goods. Corporate owners certainly are eager to have any given set of resources turned into the largest possible quantity of product, or to have any given output produced at the lowest possible resource cost, because such actions yield high profits, and, thus, the dividends or rising stock prices that owners seek. Yet some critics fear that corporate managers may pursue other goals. The separation of ownership and control, they think, may allow managers to seek the quiet life, the minimization of risk, uncertainty, and unpleasant surprises, along with personal comforts—plush offices, corporate jets, and extravagant expense accounts. Such actions are unlikely to maximize profits for the owners. Example 4 recalls recent instances in which corporate managers thwarted the stockholders' profit maximization goal.

We are discussing here the **agency problem** that arises whenever people employ others to perform a task on their behalf. How can the superior party (the **principal** who exercises authority over subordinates) make sure that the subordinate party (the **agent** who is charged with acting on behalf of the superior party) truly acts in the latter's interest? How can one prevent the agent from pursuing goals that conflict with either the letter or spirit of the principal's instructions?

In some situations, the problem is minor. A single proprietor (principal) may hire two workers (agents) but still work along with them. Here no conflict of interests will arise because the agents can be perfectly monitored by the principal. They cannot do A when told to do B; they cannot do an inferior job; they cannot work at a pace unreasonably slow. All these and other violations of the principal's interests can be quickly identified and punished; by loss of the offending agent's job if necessary.

In other situations, however, problems arise. In a large corporation, such as General Motors, there is no way the millions of stockholders (the principals) can personally monitor the management (the agents) to make sure that it provides what stockholders want: the largest possible profits. It becomes important, therefore, for principals to devise indirect ways of motivating their agents to act on the principals' behalf.

Bonuses

One common approach to the agency problem involves paying bonuses. This method is used by managers when *they* are the principals and seek to motivate their workforce to give their best. General Motors' top managers cannot monitor in person the behavior of the company's employees (who numbered 761,400 in 1990). Thus, they motivate them not only by wages based on time but also by piecework rules and profit-sharing plans that focus on the quantity and quality of output produced. As a

EXAMPLE 3

Businesses with Halos

A 1989 survey revealed the existence of nearly a million and a half nonprofit firms in the United States. Jointly, they had nearly $800 billion in revenues, as Table A indicates.

What were the names of the firms involved? Almost all of them will be familiar to you. In the health care field, there was Kaiser; the health and welfare funds included the Aid Association for Lutherans. The largest pension fund was TIAA-CREF, the Teachers Insurance and Annuity Association/College Retirement Equities Fund, with $16.6 billion of revenues. Among educational institutions, Harvard had the top revenue ($1.6 billion). Public benefit organizations included charities such as the American Red Cross and the American Cancer Society; as well as scientific and cultural groups such as the National Geographic Society, the Public Broadcasting Service, and the Smithsonian Institution. Others engaged in research and testing, ranging from the Rand Corporation to the Educational Testing Service, and Underwriters Laboratories. Agricultural cooperatives included many household names as well: Agway, Ocean Spray, Sunkist. The federal corporations involved the providers of deposit insurance and the Federal Reserve Banks; membership organizations included the Teamsters Union with $1.5 billion of revenues and the American Association of Retired Persons with $286 million.

Many for-profit firms were opposed to the competition that the nonprofits provided. College stores sold everything from books, computers, and software to T-shirts, toiletries, and travel tours. The American Association of Retired Persons offered prescription drugs, homeowner's insurance, and mutual funds; the YMCA (Young Men's Christian Association) had health clubs in competition with commercial clubs. Critics argued that this competition was unfair and that the benefits available to tax-exempt nonprofits were not deserved. Why should a college's bookstore be tax exempt and even get a 1/3 discount at the U.S. Postal Service, they asked, when no such privileges are granted to the bookstore on Main Street? Many nonprofits were making profits all along but routinely dispersed them to their employees in the form of travel allowances, low interest loans, and fancy offices, critics said. They pointed to the Ford Foundation's crystal palace in New York, to the American Red Cross's Beaux-arts headquarters in Washington, D.C., and they urged Congress to repeal the tax-exempt status of these firms.

Source: James Cook, "Businessmen with Halos," *Forbes,* November 26, 1990, pp. 100–114.

TABLE A *1989 Revenue of U.S. Nonprofit Firms (billions)*

Health care	$170
Health and welfare funds	130
Pension funds	100
Education	85
Public benefit organizations	85
Agricultural cooperatives	70
Religious organizations	53
Federal corporations	45
Electric cooperatives	23
Credit unions	20
Membership organizations	15
	$796

EXAMPLE 4

The CEO Disease

In a recent exposé, *Business Week* provided examples of what the magazine considered unacceptable behavior on the part of America's corporate chief executive officers. Instead of doing their best to serve the profit interests of stockholders, argued the magazine, some executives succumb to the CEO disease, an unhealthy narcissism that leads them to follow an egotistic agenda of their own. Some examples:

Walter J. Connolly, Jr., CEO of the Bank of New England, was cited for destroying employee morale by condescending, contemptuous attitudes, surrounding himself with yes-men (they *were* all men), and making $1.2 billion in bad loans that produced bankruptcy.

F. Ross Johnson, CEO of RJR Nabisco, was cited for excessive greed that produced a palatial hangar in Atlanta complete with 26 pilots and 10 planes, along with a 3-story structure filled with marble floors, inlaid mahogany walls, and a roomy atrium that featured a Japanese garden.

Armand Hammer, CEO of Occidental Petroleum, was cited for spending $50 million of corporate funds to build an art museum bearing his name.

James E. Stewart, CEO of Lone Star Industries, took the nation's largest cement company into bankruptcy, while running up a $2.9 million expense account for commuting between Florida and his Connecticut home in the company jet.

Other CEOs have been accused of running companies not for their owner-stockholders, but for groups of variously defined "stakeholders": employees, suppliers, customers, neighbors. The idea that corporations should be "nice" to people in and around them is often cited as a prime example of violating the principal-agent contract.

Source: "CEO Disease," *Business Week,* April 1, 1991, pp. 52–59; "Stakes, Shares, and Digestible Poison Pills," *The Economist,* February 2, 1991, p. 61.

---

result, top managers figure, lower levels of management and production workers alike will pursue with vigor the goals set at the top of the firm's hierarchy.

And stockholders, through their elected boards of directors, pursue a similar strategy with respect to top managers. To make them seek maximum profit (and to abandon alternative goals that may please managers but not stockholders), they provide managers with more than fancy salaries. Many of them receive bonuses based on performance.

A famous recent example involved the late J. Hugh Liedtke, chief executive officer of Pennzoil Co. For "exceptional and extraordinary services" stockholders supplemented his salary with a $10 million bonus. (During the company's legal battle with Texaco, Inc., Pennzoil won a $7.5 billion jury award; then, to avoid extended court appeals, the parties settled for $3 billion in 1988. This move doubled Pennzoil's net worth.)

Stock Options

Many corporate managers are given a **stock option,** the right to buy a specified number of company shares at a specified price before a specified date. Suppose a manager is given the right of buying 10,000 shares of company stock at the present price of $30/share at any time before July 1, 1998. If the company has large profits, the price of its stock may rise to $50/share. The manager can then exercise the option, buy 10,000 shares at $30, and resell them for $50 each. The gain is $200,000, a nice reward for a job well done. If, on the other hand, the company has no profits or incurs losses, the market price of its stock may stagnate or even fall to $25/

share. In that case, the manager's option is worthless.

Takeover Battles

There exists yet another way to motivate corporate managers to work hard on behalf of the stockholders. Failure to earn high profits will cause many stockholders to sell their shares. The increased supply in the stock market will lower the stock price and induce corporate raiders to make a takeover bid. The 1980s were marked by an unprecedented wave of corporate takeovers.

A **takeover** is an action in which one corporation or a group of financiers (known as the acquirers) buy a sufficiently large percentage of the outstanding stock of another corporation (known as the target company) to dominate the stockholders' meeting and either shake up the firm's management or take control of the firm. Persons who specialize in seeking out corporations for takeover are generally referred to as **corporate raiders;** they are usually motivated by the belief that the target company's stock market evaluation is low relative to the value of its assets and debts or that the firm's actual profits are far below their potential. Table 5 lists major transactions that occurred in the 1980s. Note that takeovers have become a worldwide phenomenon. Thus, in 1989, an investor group including James Goldsmith, Jacob Rothschild, and Kerry Packer made a $21 billion offer to buy up BAT Industries, a London-based conglomerate that owned the Benson & Hedges, Kool, and Lucky Strike cigarette companies, the Hardee's hamburger chain, the Farmers Group insurance firms, the Marshall Field's and Saks Fifth Avenue department stores, as well as paper mills in India and Portugal, tobacco processors in Zaire and Zimbabwe, and more.)

The Attack

Counting on the fact that the target company will have higher profits (and, therefore, higher stock prices) once a better management is in charge, corporate raiders can do one of two things: They can make a **tender offer,** a proposal to buy a controlling interest in the corporation by purchasing stock from current stockholders at a fixed price that

TABLE 5 Recent Corporate Takeovers

Target company	Principal acquirer	Value (billions)
RJR Nabisco	Kohlberg, Kravis, Roberts	$24.5
BAT Industries	Hoylake Investments	21.0
Warner	Time	14.0
Gulf	Standard Oil	13.4
Kraft	Philip Morris	12.9
Time	Paramount	12.2
Getty Oil	Texaco	10.1
Dome Petroleum	Amoco Canada	9.0
SmithKline Beckman	Beecham Group	7.8
Conoco	DuPont	7.4
Federated	Campeau	6.6
Marathon	USX	6.5

Corporate takeovers mushroomed during the 1980s. This partial listing indicates the enormous values involved.
SOURCE: Keith Brasher, "A Far-Flung Corporate Empire," *The New York Times,* July 12, 1989, pp. D1 and 6.

exceeds the current market price. They can also ask stockholders for their **proxies,** permissions to vote on behalf of current stockholders at the next stockholders' meeting.

A successful tender offer or proxy fight puts the raiders in a position to control the stockholders' meeting, install a new management, and, it is hoped, raise company profits—a result clearly in the interest of stockholders. Indeed, the new management might even liquidate the company if selling off the pieces is worth more than the company's stock. (According to recent studies, past takeovers have in fact raised long-run stockholder wealth, as described above. Stockholders who have sold their shares in response to a tender offer have instantly gained from the higher price per share; others who held on to their shares or acquired new ones have benefitted from higher dividends or capital gains later on.)

The Defense

Usually, a takeover is initiated by a group that is unfriendly toward the current management; such a **hostile takeover** tends to be fiercely resisted by that management. Current managers argue that attemped takeovers divert their attention "from product to paper," it forces them to deal with the takeover threat and to neglect normal activities, such as efficiently producing and marketing high-quality products. In addition, managers say, takeovers destroy a company—either because it is deliberately liquidated or because the takeover process upsets established ways of doing things. The process, say the managers, causes valuable employees and customers to sever their relationships and, ultimately, dumps problems of rising unemployment and plummeting tax revenues on local governments. Furthermore, managers do not want to lose their own jobs. Accordingly, they take measures to defend against hostile takeovers. Sometimes they use **poison pills,** techniques such as selling off the best company assets or taking on dangerously risky ventures that are deliberately designed to make the target company less attractive to corporate raiders. At other times, managers pay **greenmail,** an arrangement that uses company

---

EXAMPLE 5

Major Companies Reject Takeover Protection

In 1990, the state of Pennsylvania passed the toughest antitakeover law in the United States. A "control share provision" disenfranchised holders of large blocks of stock if the stock was acquired within 12 months of a takeover bid. A "stakeholder provision" empowered corporate directors to put the interests of certain nonowners, such as customers and employees, ahead of their fiduciary duty to stockholders while a takeover bid existed. A "disgorgement provision" forced corporate raiders who had failed in their takeover to turn over any profits made to the target company.

Yet the law included an option that allowed companies to exclude themselves from all this protection. Major firms such as H. J. Heinz, the Mellon Bank, the Sun Company, and Westinghouse did just that. They argued that the "protection" offered merely protected the jobs of inefficient managers and that the best way to prevent takeovers was to run a company well. In addition, many large investors threatened to sell their shares in protected companies. These investors included the $60 billion Public Employees Pension Fund and numerous smaller funds ranging from the pension fund of the City of Flint, Michigan, to the firefighters in Houston, Texas.

Some companies, however, did not reject the government's help. They included Alcoa (Aluminum Company of America) and PPG Industries, both major Pennsylvania firms.

Source: Leslie Wayne, "Many Companies in Pennsylvania Reject State's Takeover Protection," *The New York Times,* July 20, 1990, pp. A1 and D4.

funds for buying up, at extremely high prices, the raiders' block of company stock. On other occasions managers engineer a **friendly takeover** by someone, called a **white knight,** who would maintain the current management.

The preceding actions, however, confirm to outsiders that the current management is unsure of itself and is vulnerable to criticism. Accordingly, these defensive techniques inadvertently draw attention to a possible takeover target. As a result, many managers have taken another route to fend off raiders: They have lobbied the government to enact **antitakeover laws** designed to delay or discourage corporate takeovers. Such laws have been passed at the federal level (the Williams Act) and in over three dozen states. Typical provisions include the following. A **delay period** mandates a lengthy waiting period between the time a corporate raider makes a tender offer and the date of its expiration. **Disclosure statements** require the publication of details about the personal background and finances of corporate raiders. **Fair price provisions** force successful corporate raiders to pay the same price per share to all former stockholders, even to those who refused to surrender their shares before the expiration of a tender offer. **Supermajority requirements** link the acquisition of corporate control by a raider to unusually difficult conditions, such as the ownership of 85 percent of all shares, an approving two-thirds vote of current stockholders, and the like. Yet, not all corporations seek such government help as described in Example 5.

Encouraging Takeovers

Numerous studies have shown that takeovers, whether successful or not, increase the efficiency of target firms, raise their profitability, and provide stockholders with a significant increase in wealth. Thus, from the stockholders' point of view, corporate raiders are welcome allies and should not be discouraged. Accordingly, stockholders have provided many corporate managers with incentives *not* to resist takeovers that are likely to raise the price of company stock. One incentive is the **golden parachute,** an exceedingly generous promise of

TABLE 6 *Recent Golden Parachutes*

Executives	Company	Total Package (millions of dollars)
1. F. Ross Johnson, CEO	RJR Nabisco	$53.8
2. E. A. Horrigan, Vice-Chmn.	RJR Nabisco	45.7
3. Gerald Tsai, Jr., Chmn.	Primerica	46.8
4. Edward P. Evans, Chmn.	Macmillan	31.9
5. Kenneth A. Yarnell, Pres.	Primerica	18.4
6. John D. Martin, Exec. v-p	RJR Nabisco	18.2
7. Sanford C. Sigoloff, Chmn.	Wickes	15.9
8. Whitney Stevens, Chmn.	J. P. Stevens	15.7
9. Philip L. Smith, Chmn.	Pillsbury	11.0
10. Wilhelm A. Mallory, Sr. v-p	Wickes	7.5

In recent years, corporate executives whose companies were taken over by corporate raiders have collected large golden parachute benefits.

SOURCE: Business Week, May 1, 1989, p. 47.

EXAMPLE 6

The Globalization of Business

Increasingly, business executives find that the pursuit of maximum profit requires the globalization of their firms. The term is a catchall that describes the need for companies, if they are to prosper, to treat the world as their stage. The trend has been spurred by at least three processes.

First, the world financial system became more open and unified during the 1980s, which makes it now possible for many firms to get financial capital not only locally, but from numerous sources around the world. Naturally, to remain competitive, the cheapest capital source must be sought out.

Second, improvements in computer and communications technology have effectively reduced the distance between markets. Many a firm finds it just as easy to use labor located in the United States as in Mexico, Poland, or Vietnam. Oftentimes, their output can easily be sold worldwide as well.

Third, foreign competition in all the big economies has raised the ratios of imports to national output. To stay alive, domestic firms are well advised to get resources wherever they are cheapest and to sell wherever they can. If they don't, others will.

As a result, the nature of firms operating in the international market is changing. In the past, such firms tended to be highly centralized, with headquarters in one place, such as New York, where all strategic decisions were made concerning operations abroad and from whence orders flowed to company divisions around the world. There were also multinational companies, essentially holding companies that combined autonomous subsidiaries in a variety of countries under a common name. Nowadays, we see the emergence of *transnationals,* firms that "think globally and act locally." They have no geographic center, no national ax to grind. They combine production on a global scale (to maximize the cost savings associated with mass production) with an eager search for world-class technology (by facilitating the sharing of ideas among experts in many countries). And yet, they have deep local roots in numerous places, carefully adjust their products to the preferences, customs, and laws of different markets.

One example is ABB (Asea Brown Boveri), a company formed in 1987 by the merger of a Swedish and Swiss firm. The firm has a tiny headquarters in Zurich, but doesn't consider itself a Swiss concern, nor a Swedish one. The firm's 240,000 employees are spread around the world; their official language is English. They produce electrical systems and equipment—such things as locomotives, subway cars, trolleys, and signaling devices. The firm's 1990 sales topped $25 billion; 57 percent of this revenue was earned in Europe, 28 percent in North America, 15 percent in Asia. Production occurred in 60 countries; it involved the frequent rotation of technologists to share expertise. (If the Japanese can bring out a new model five times faster than the Germans, the German employees must learn the trick as well.) And marketing relied on the maximum use of local talent—selling in France cannot be directed by someone in New York; it must be kept in the hands of those who are keenly aware of the French concern with environmentally friendly goods or ethical business behavior.

Sources: "Management Education: Passport to Prosperity," *The Economist,* March 2, 1991, pp. 3–26; and William Taylor, "The Logic of Global Business," *Harvard Business Review,* March–April 1991, pp. 91–105.

pay and other benefits to a corporate manager that is due in the event of a corporate takeover that eliminates the manager's job. Thus, managers are enticed to raise company profits. If they succeed, they will personally gain through stock options. If they fail, they still gain through golden parachutes. In one famous case, Michel Bergerec, the chief executive officer of Revlon, received $54 million of golden parachute benefits when Revlon was taken over by Pantry Pride (*Business Week,* May 5, 1986, p. 56.) Table 6 has more to say on the subject.

The Goal of Firms: Profit Maximization

There exists considerable literature on maintaining that corporate managers have effectively expropriated corporate owners and are, therefore, pursuing whatever goals fit managers best. Some say managers seek to maximize sales, others see them maximizing the growth of their firms (as measured by sales, assets, or number of employees). Others still argue that corporate managers seek the quiet life and personal comforts.

Yet most economists hold that the techniques discussed in the previous section—techniques designed to bring managerial actions in line with stockholder interests—work reasonably well. It is wiser to assume that proprietorships, partnerships, and corporations seek to maximize profits for their owners because a) this is more often true than not and b) there is a process of natural selection that in the long run eliminates firms that neglect the profit-maximization goal, while causing firms that embrace it to prosper. Experience shows that the assumption of profit maximization is remarkably accurate in predicting the behavior of firms. Example 6 reports on a new trend that serves the purpose of profit maximization.

IDEAS IN HISTORY

The Nature of the Firm

In the 1930s, the world was fascinated by a grand social experiment. In the Soviet Union, Joseph Stalin abolished the last vestiges of the market economy and replaced it with a command economy on a scale hitherto unknown. There were obvious and enormous costs. Millions of people who might otherwise have been tilling the soil, building roads, or sewing clothes were engrossed in the task of setting up a central plan and verifying its execution. Was the market economy superior because it avoided such costs? Hardly, argued Ronald Coase (b. 1910), then a professor at the London School of Economics.

Coase noted that a market coordination of people's specialized activities is also costly, but the costs are less obvious. Whenever there is buying and selling of anything, it is necessary for the seller to have a recognized property right in the item concerned. Thus, the existence of markets assumes the existence of government defining and enforcing property rights, perhaps by a system of laws, courts, and police. Usually, government also provides a medium of exchange, perhaps through some kind of banking system. Surely, argued Coase, these institutions require considerable resources: lawmakers, judges, police officers, and bankers, to name a few. More resources still must be expended as would-be traders gather information. Thus, buyers must find out who is willing to sell the commodity or service they care to acquire and at what price. (Conceivably, there exist thousands of alternative sources of supply, along with a wide range of prices.) Sellers face a similar task of identifying potential buyers and the prices they are willing to pay. And the potential trading partners must confirm that the product involved is of the desired quantity and quality. Then buyers and sellers must devote further time and energy to choosing their actual trading partners, negotiating and writing up appropriate contracts (who delivers what, when, where, and at what price), and physically carrying out the agreed-upon exchange. Additional resources may be needed to straighten out misunderstandings and to deal with possible failures to carry out contracts (which could involve a full-fledged case in court).

Coase referred to the resources used to bring buyers and sellers together and to facilitate the coordination of people's specialized activities through voluntary market exchanges as **transactions costs** or **market coordination costs**. (Alternatively, these costs can also be thought of as the forgone output these resources might have produced.) In turn, Coase referred to analogous costs that must be incurred whenever spontaneous market transactions are replaced by centralized planning and management as **managerial coordination costs**. (Again such costs could be measured instead by the forgone output these resources might have produced.)

Over time, Coase argued, experience will show whether the division of labor involved in the production of any product is more cheaply coordinated through market exchanges among independent contractors or through the central direction of some manager. To the extent that market coordination costs for any given task are smaller than managerial coordination costs, the division of labor will come to be coordinated through monetary arrangements made in markets. To the extent that market coordination costs are larger, the division of labor will come to be coordinated through verbal directives issued by managers (the "autocratic" firm, as we know it, will be created to carry out the task in question). Yet, Coase noted, such a firm will not grow without limit to perform ever-more additional tasks. As it takes on more and more tasks, and long before it comes to encompass the entire economy, the marginal cost of managerial coordination will grow to exceed the marginal cost of market coordination. Then the miniature command economy that the firm represents will have reached its natural limits.

Source: Ronald H. Coase, "The Nature of the Firm," *Economica,* New Series 4 (November 1937), 386–405.

Summary

1. This chapter explores the nature of the firm, one of the market economy's major institutions, and notes that the firm—in stark contrast to the world around it—is itself an island of central economic planning and management.

2. Ronald Coase was the first to ask why it is that the price system in so many countries dominates the relationships among households and firms but ceases to work within the confines of market economy firms. His answer focused on a comparison of transactions costs (market coordination costs) with managerial coordination costs. To the extent that market coordination costs for any given task are smaller than managerial coordination costs, the division of labor will be coordinated through monetary arrangements made in markets. To the extent that market coordination costs are larger, the division of labor will be coordinated through verbal directives issued by managers. Then the autocratic firms will spring up to carry out the task in question.

3. In the U.S. economy, three major types of profit-seeking firms exist: the proprietorship, the partnership, and the corporation. The advantages and disadvantages of each of these are discussed in detail (and are summarized in Tables 2–4). Certain nonprofit firms play a relatively minor role.

4. Because of the separation of ownership and management in the corporation and because of its frequently large size, principal-agent problems arise. How can stockholders make sure that professional managers truly act on their behalf? Principals who cannot personally monitor their agents must devise indirect ways of motivating them to act in the principals' interest. Bonuses, stock options, and the threat of corporate takeovers provide examples.

5. Despite considerable literature to the contrary, most economists assume that firms seek to maximize profits. This assumption has proven remarkably accurate in predicting the behavior of firms.

6. The optional Appendix to this chapter introduces two major concepts of business accounting: the balance sheet and the income statement. It also introduces a crucial distinction between accounting profit and economic profit.

Key Concepts

agency problem
agent
antitakeover laws
corporate raiders
corporation
delay period
disclosure statement
dividends
double taxation
fair price provision
firm
friendly takeover
greenmail
golden parachute
hostile takeover
limited liability
limited partnership
managerial coordination costs
market coordination costs
nonprofit firms
partnership
poison pills
principal
proprietorship
proxies
S-corporations
stock certificates
stockholders
stock option
supermajority requirement
takeover
tender offer
transactions costs
undistributed corporate profit
unlimited liability
white knight

Questions and Problems

1. Some large firms generate their own electricity, build their own internal telephone network, make their own parts, do their own bookkeeping, and ship their products on their own fleet of trucks. Other firms buy electricity, phone service, parts, and bookkeeping and transportation services from other firms. Can you explain it?

2. Mr. A: "This chapter gives me an idea. If all firms were owned and run by their workers, everyone could be richer because workers would earn the equivalent of wages *and* profits."

   Mr. B: "Of course, and if all supermarkets and other retail stores were replaced by consumer cooperatives, workers could get the food and other goods they buy for less, which would make them richer still."

   What do you think?

3. Consider the centrally planned communist command economy that Joseph Stalin tried to run. Neither Stalin nor his close associates (the principals) could possibly monitor the behavior of millions of peasants and workers (the agents who were supposed to work long and hard to carry out the instructions laid down for them in the central economic plan). There were endless possibilities for infractions of the rules. Peasants might tend their personal gardens (or simply rest under a tree) instead of weeding the collective fields. Workers might use factory materials and tools to make clothes for themselves rather than produce clothes for export as stated in the plan. How might one tackle the principal-agent problem in the context of a command economy (in which stock markets, stock options, and corporate takeovers do not exist)? (Hint: The answer requires some reading; a good textbook on comparative economic systems will help.)

APPENDIX 7a

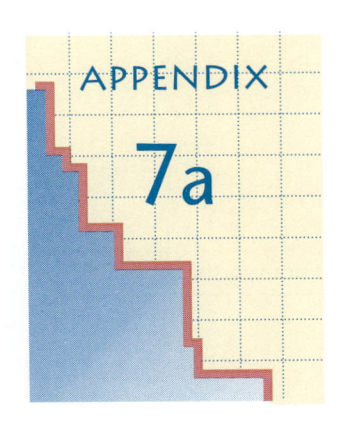

MAJOR CONCEPTS OF BUSINESS ACCOUNTING

Much of what we know about business organizations comes to us through studying records kept by accountants. This appendix introduces two major accounting reports, the balance sheet and the income statement.

The Balance Sheet

The **balance sheet** is a systematic listing, referenced to a particular moment of time, of a specified party's assets, liabilities, and net worth. Usually the party in question is a single firm, but a balance sheet can be drawn up for anyone, including individuals, various groupings of persons, firms, or governments, and so on.

The things of value owned by the party in question are called **assets;** debts are called **liabilities.** The difference between assets A and liabilities L can be positive or negative and is called **net worth** NW. Thus, by definition,

$$NW \equiv A - L \qquad (1)$$

It follows from equation (1) that assets always and necessarily equal the sum of liabilities plus net worth.

$$A \equiv L + NW \qquad (2)$$

Equation (2) is the basic **balance sheet identity.** It says that assets always equal or "balance" liabilities plus net worth (a fact that follows logically from the definition of net worth).

An Example

Table 1 presents the balance sheet of a hypothetical firm. All the entries are stocks rather than flows; they all refer to a particular *moment* of time (here the end of 1992).

On the asset side, the firm owned cash (coins, paper bills, and checking accounts) of $21 million at the moment the balance sheet was drawn up. It also had short-term claims on others, probably customers, of $317 million; and held government securities (such as Treasury bills, notes, and bonds) of $52 million. There were inventories (of raw materials, semi-finished goods, and finished goods) worth $785 million, and the firm's buildings and equipment came to $1,308 million. Finally, the firm owned land and miscellaneous other items valued, respectively, at $123 million and $29 million. Thus total assets equaled $2,635 million, representing the accountants' best estimate of the amount of money the owners could get if they liquidated the firm and literally sold everything the firm owned. That hypothetical amount of money, however, is not what the owners could keep. There were debts, as the liability side shows, of $1,064 million. Some were immediately payable, perhaps to workers and various types of suppliers; note the $58 million accounts payable. Other liabilities, such as the $900 million of corporate bonds issued, were longer term. Finally, there was additional debt of $106 million, perhaps a tax payment due in a few months.

By definition, assets of $2,635 million minus li-

TABLE 1 Balance Sheet, ABC Corporation, December 31, 1992 (millions of dollars)

Assets		Liabilities and net worth	
Cash	$ 21	Liabilities	
Accounts receivable	317	Accounts payable	$ 58
Government securities	52	Bonds	900
Inventories	785	Other	106
Plant and equipment	1,308		$1,064
Land	123	Net worth	
Other	29	Stock	$1,000
		Surplus	571
			$1,571
Total	$2,635	Total	$2,635

abilities of $1,064 million equals net worth of $1,571 million. This amount is the hypothetical amount of money the firm's owners could keep if they sold all the assets and paid off all their debts. A corporation's net worth always equals the original value of stock certificates issued (here $1,000 million) plus "surplus," which is the sum of all the profits ever retained minus all the losses ever made.

A final note: Accountants value assets at their actual historical cost at time of purchase minus an estimate, where applicable, of value loss through wear and tear since that time (depreciation). Accountants try to deal with objectively verifiable figures; they ignore the effects of price fluctuations over time. Thus, a depreciable asset such as a blast furnace bought for $50 million ten years ago and half used up is considered a piece of equipment worth $25 million, even if its current market value, driven up by inflation, equals $62 million.

The Income Statement

The **income statement** is a systematic listing, for a specified period of time, of a specified party's revenue, cost, and profit. (Once again, the party in question is usually a single firm, but income statements for other parties or even groups of them can be drawn up as well.)

Revenue and cost are figured on an accrual basis. Thus, revenue is assigned to the period in which it is earned through the sale of something; it does not necessarily represent a cash receipt. Similarly, any cost is assigned to the period in which it is incurred; it does not necessarily represent payments of cash. The difference between revenue R and cost C can be positive or negative and is called **profit, Π**. (A negative profit is called a loss.) Thus, by definition

$$R - C \equiv \Pi \qquad (3)$$

An Example

Table 2 presents the income statement for our hypothetical firm. All the entries here are flows rather than stocks; they all refer to a specified *period* of time (the entire year of 1992). This income statement lists revenue from sales (after discounts and returns) of $29.2 million for the year; other such statements might include other forms of revenue, such as receipts of interest, rents, or royalties.

TABLE 2 *Income Statement, ABC Corporation for the Year Ended December 31, 1992 (millions of dollars)*

Revenue		
	Sales	$30.9
−	Discounts and returns	1.7
		$29.2
− **Cost**		
	Wages	$ 7.3
	Raw materials	4.8
	Depreciation	3.6
	Interest	2.4
	Rent	1.7
	Property and sales taxes	1.5
		$21.3
= **Profit**		$ 7.9
	Corporate income taxes	$ 3.1
	Dividends	3.0
	Undistributed profit	1.8

The various categories of cost are fairly self-explanatory; however, the way accountants derive the numbers is not equally obvious. Consider two examples of the discretionary power wielded by accountants in determining values.

The Valuation of Inventories

The valuation of inventories, as of raw materials used to produce goods, can take one of two routes. According to the FIFO method (first in, first out), any given piece of inventory used now is assumed to have been the oldest one in stock and is, therefore, evaluated at the oldest prices paid for it. In a period of rapidly rising prices, this method has the effect of measuring raw material costs at older, lower prices. Thus, it raises the reported profit figure. FIFO may be helpful if the firm is about to borrow money or issue new stock and wishes to impress would-be investors. It is also useful at times when tax rates are low but are expected to rise in the near future. Then it is better to report high profit now and pay a lower tax rate than to report high profit in future years and pay a higher rate.

According to the alternative LIFO method (last in, first out), any given piece of inventory used now is assumed to have been the latest one bought and is, therefore, evaluated at the most recent prices. In a period of rapidly rising prices, this method has the effect of measuring the raw material cost at current, higher prices. Thus it lowers the reported profit figure. This may be a useful strategy if high current tax rates are expected to give way to lower rates in future years.

The Figuring of Depreciation

Accountants allocate the cost of long-lasting assets (such as buildings, blast furnaces, and trucks) not to the year in which the assets are bought but to a series of years over which the assets are used and, presumably, used up. The monetary estimate of this gradual wear and tear of such long-lasting assets is called **depreciation.** Tax law, however, allows several alternative methods of figuring depreciation. The choice made affects the reported cost and, therefore, profit. Under the *straight-line method* of computing depreciation allowances, the original cost of the asset is reduced by any expected salvage value and the amount so derived is divided by the number of years the asset is expected to be in use. Consider a $100,000 truck that is to be used for 5 years and then to be sold for $5,000 at the end. The $95,000 difference would be divided by 5, yielding an annual depreciation allowance of $19,000. (The $3.6 million figure for depreciation found in Table 2 comes from totalling similar numbers for all the firm's depreciable assets.) Under an *accelerated method* of computing depreciation allowances, deductions are larger in the early years of an asset's use, smaller later on. The result is higher cost (lower reported profit) in early years, followed by lower cost (higher reported profit) in later years. Consider our $100,000 truck and the depreciation of its assumed $95,000 value loss by the "double declining balance method." Instead of figuring depreciation of 1/5 ($95,000) or $19,000 in each year, accountants double the fraction to 2/5 in the first year and then figure future allowances at 2/5 of each year's remaining balance. This method would yield depreciation figures for the first 5 years as shown below:

1st year: 2/5($95,000) = $38,000; balance = $57,000

2nd year: 2/5($57,000) = $22,800; balance = $34,200

3rd year: 2/5($34,200) = $13,680; balance = $20,520

4th year: 2/5($20,520) = $ 8,208; balance = $12,312

5th year: 2/5($12,312) = $ 4,925; balance = $ 7,387

The remainder is then depreciated similarly in future years or in a lump sum when the asset is actually sold.

Accounting Profit Versus Economic Profit

The "bottom line" of our hypothetical income statement shows profit of $7.9 million for the year. Note that this profit is called **accounting profit.** It always is the difference between a firm's sales on the one hand and its explicit cost plus depreciation on the other hand. Sooner or later, any **explicit cost** involves a payment made to outside parties (workers, raw material suppliers, money lenders, landlords, and goverments in our case). Depreciation, in contrast, is an **implicit cost** that does not involve a payment by the firm to anyone but recognizes the use of some resource; in this case, it is the extent to which long-lived assets owned by the firm have been used up in the process of production.

Our hypothetical income statement also shows the disposition of the firm's accounting profit: $3.1 million of it was paid out in corporate income taxes, $3 million of it was paid to stockholders as dividends, the remaining $1.8 million was retained in the business. (This amount equals the difference between the surplus figure shown in the Table 1 balance sheet for 1992 and a similar surplus figure in the balance sheet for 1991.)

As later chapters will show, economists make use of still another type of profit figure, called **economic profit.** This concept equals accounting profit minus all types of implicit costs not considered in its computation, notably the value of resource services supplied to the firm without pay by its owners. Consider a single proprietor who works 60 hours a week in the business and has invested $50,000 in it. In the next best alternative, this person might have earned wages of $300 a week or $15,600 a year by working all that time for someone else and might have earned interest of $5,000 a year by lending the funds to someone else. When this labor and money is used in the proprietor's own business, the opportunity of earning $15,600 + $5,000 = $20,600 a year elsewhere is forgone. This opportunity cost, economists argue, should be added to the cost the proprietor's accountant measures even if no explicit payment of wages and interest is made. (Such a payment would have been made if the labor and funds had been supplied by an outsider.) If this adjustment is made, the computed figure of accounting profit is reduced by the amount of these additional implicit costs. The result is economic profit.

For example, let the proprietor's accounting profit equal $30,000 (or $10,000) a year. In our case (with implicit cost of $20,600 a year), the economic profit would be figured, at

$$\$30{,}000 - \$20{,}600 = \$9{,}400 \text{ a year}$$

(or $10,000 − $20,600 = −$10,600 a year).

Data on economic profit are more useful than data on accounting profit in predicting the likely behavior of firms.

When economic profit, as in the case above, equals $9,400 a year, the firm's owner (who made an accounting profit of $30,000 a year and could have earned $20,600 a year outside the business) has earned $9,400 a year *more* by being in business than would have been earned by doing the next best thing (working for someone else and lending the money to others). Economists predict that such an owner is likely to stay in business.

On the other hand, when economic profit, as in the second case above, equals −$10,600 a year, the firm's owner (who made an accounting profit of $10,000 a year and could have earned $20,600 a year outside the business) has earned $10,600 a year *less* by being in business than by doing the next best thing (working for someone else and lending the money to others). Economists predict that such an owner is likely to go out of business. By focusing on accounting profit alone (and noting numbers of +$30,000 and +$10,000) this distinction would be missed entirely.

In the case of corporations, similar adjustments can be made. Stockholders typically do not work in the firms they own, but they do invest funds that could earn a return elsewhere. The Table 1 balance sheet shows a net worth of $1,571 million. If this amount were invested in the best available outside opportunity, an annual return of 10 percent or $15.71 million might be earned. This sum could, therefore, be viewed as implicit interest and might be deducted from the ABC Corporation's accounting profit to derive the economic profit. An accounting profit of $7.9 million minus implicit interest of $15.71 million yields an economic profit of −$7.81 million.

The stockholders of ABC Corporation, having invested $1,571 million in the firm, in fact earned $7.9 million in 1992 (accounting profit). Yet, they could have earned (we assumed) $15.71 million by investing their money elsewhere. Thus, they were worse off by $7.81 million (as the *negative* economic profit indicates). Economists would predict difficulties for any ABC Corporation attempt to get more money from stockholders—despite the firm's $7.9 million accounting profit. Economists would also predict that stockholders might try to withdraw their money from this firm (which any *individual* can do by selling ABC stock, thereby depressing its price).

Key Concepts

accounting profit
assets
balance sheet
balance sheet identity
depreciation
economic profit
explicit cost
implicit cost
income statement
liabilities
net worth
profit

Questions and Problems

1. Because equation (2) in this Appendix holds separately for every single firm, it also holds for any group of firms. One can add together the assets of all U.S. corporations and the resultant sum necessarily equals the sum of all corporations' liabilities and net worth. Given the December 31, 1985, data below (stated in billions of dollars) construct a *Consolidated Balance Sheet* of all U.S. corporations.

Accounts payable	892
Land	141
Other assets	3,825
Other liabilities	5,877
Accounts receivable	3,318
Government securities held	917
Corporate bonds issued	
Short term	1,001
Long term	1,699
Inventories	715
Cash	683
Plant and equipment	3,174

SOURCE: U.S. Bureau of the Census, *Statistical Abstract of the United States, 1989* (Washington, D.C.: U.S. Government Printing Office, 1989), p. 520.

2. Because equation (3) in this Appendix holds separately for every single firm, it also holds jointly for any group of firms. Thus one can produce a *Consolidated Income Statement* for all U.S. corporations as a group. Do so for 1985 when revenue from all sources equaled $8,398 billion and all explicit costs plus depreciation equaled $8,158 billion.

3. Consider the following data about a student; then compute the student's net worth (in dollars).

IOU issued to roommate	$20
Cash	$100
Tuition due	$5,000
Car	$1,100
Books	$400
Clothing	$500
Annual income	$4,500

CHAPTER 8

THE TECHNOLOGY OF PRODUCTION

Preview

This chapter focuses on the fundamental task of every firm: the physical combining of inputs to create output. The technical possibilities are summarized by a production function *that relates alternative input combinations used during a period to maximum possible output quantities associated with each, given the state of technical knowledge. This input-output relationship is explored in detail, both for the short run (when some inputs are fixed) and the long run (when all inputs can be varied). Appendix 8A introduces isoquant analysis, a more sophisticated approach to production functions.*

Examples

1. The Amazing Story of Two Ford Plants
2. Research and Development Labs Move Abroad
3. Luftwaffe Secret Unburied
4. The Optimum Size of Cargo Ships

Ideas in History

The Concept of Marginal Product
The Concept of X-inefficiency

The previous chapter discussed the general nature of the firm as an island of central economic planning and management within a market economy. We now begin a more detailed analysis of such a firm's behavior by focusing on the fundamental aspect of every firm's life: the combining of all kinds of productive ingredients to create some kind of product that people want. Far removed from the concerns of the accountant (who counts dollars and cents of revenue, cost, and profit), this chapter involves the nonmonetary world of the production engineer who turns physical quantities of *inputs* (hours of labor, land, or machine time) into physical quantities of *output* (bushels of apples, yards of cloth, or gallons of gasoline).

To learn about this basic component of a firm's life, let us perform a thought experiment that involves you. Imagine yourself, initially, as a school teacher; your spouse works as a part-time editor. Between the two, you barely make ends meet. Then a letter arrives: You have inherited a mountain in Vermont from your grandfather, complete with 1,000 apple trees, cold-storage barns, and other equipment used in apple-growing. Suddenly, you have many kinds of choices. You could sell the orchard, put the money in a bank, and supplement your current incomes with interest earned. You could lease the orchard to a neighbor in Vermont and enjoy the rental income it brings. Or you could be daring, quit your current jobs, and start a new life running the Crisp Apple Company. Assume you choose the latter; in the process, you will learn much about the technology of a firm.

The Production Function

Arriving in Vermont and searching through grandfather's belongings, you might discover careful records of what economists call the **production function.** It is the technical relationship, stated in physical (not in value) terms, between alternative combinations of inputs used during a period and the maximum possible output quantities associated with each of these input combinations, given the state of technical knowledge. A production function in an equation is stated as

$$Q^* = f(L, T, K, t)$$

Any firm's maximum possible output (Q^*) is a function of, depends on, or varies with the employed quantities of human resources or labor (L), natural resources (T), and capital resources (K), and also with the state of technical knowledge (t).

Sooner or later, producers learn from experience the value of Q^* for any specified combinations of L, T, K, and t. In grandfather's case, the information was probably not expressed this formally; assume it was jotted down in numerous pages of a thick book. One of those pages might look like Table 1. Summarizing grandfather's many years of experience as an orchardist, the table predicts what you could expect to happen if you followed in his footsteps and managed the orchard well. Thus, the data in Table 1 can be invaluable to your decision making.

Fixed Inputs Versus Variable Inputs

First of all, Table 1 helps you distinguish between **fixed inputs** and **variable inputs** or productive ingredients, the quantities of which, respectively, cannot be varied or can easily be varied in the period under consideration. The Table 1 records refer to a given year, a period too short to add to the stock of mature apple trees (they require a minimum of five years to be grown) and too short as well to construct new cold-storage barns or arrange for new spraying machines. (We shall assume that no one committed to running this orchard would want to *decrease* the existing quantities of these inputs, as by putting a chain saw to the apple trees and going into the firewood business, or by burning down the cold-storage barns and putting up condos in their place.) Thus, for purposes of making decisions for the next year, consider these inputs as fixed and unalterable in quantity. The entire set of these inputs is referred to as 1 unit in column (1). On the other hand, we assume, you can hire or fire workers at any time during the next year. This type of input, therefore, is considered a variable one (column 2). Table 1 lists 10 possible combinations (A through J) of fixed and variable inputs that your orchard might utilize during the next year.

CAUTION

*Fixed inputs are often associated with "the short run" and variable inputs with "the long run," but this association must be treated with caution. A time period so short that a firm cannot vary the quantity of at least one of its inputs is called the **short run** by economists. A time period so long that a firm can vary the quantities of all of its inputs is called the **long run**. The length of the time involved, however, can differ for firms in different industries. An apple producer may need five years to increase the number of fruit-bearing trees; a vendor selling apples in the street may be able to increase all relevant inputs in a single day. Thus, the short run may equal 5 years for one, but 1 day for the other. In addition, no type of input—even for a given firm and a given period—is intrinsically fixed or variable. Take labor employed by an orchard. From the point of view of 1-year decision making, a day laborer (who can be hired or fired at will) is a variable input, but a worker with a 3-year contract is a fixed input.*

Total Product Versus Marginal Product

Consider what else grandfather's records show. As alternative (A) indicates, if you assigned your orchard and all its equipment to the apple-growing business for a year (and, thus, used one unit of fixed inputs as defined in Table 1), but neglected to employ any workers (applied zero units of the variable input), you would not harvest a single apple. A combination of spring frost, summer drought, and various pests would ruin your crop (row A, col. 3). Even if apples grew on your trees, no one would pick or market them.

The picture changes drastically in alternative B with a single full-time worker. Sprinkling blossoms

TABLE 1 The Production Function

	Inputs per year		Output per year		
	Fixed[a]	Variable[b]	Maximum total product,[c] Q^*	Marginal physical product of labor,[d] MPP_L	Average physical product of labor,[e] APP_L
	(1)	(2)	(3)	(4) = $\Delta 3/\Delta 2$	(5) = (3)/(2)
A.	1	0	0		0
B.	1	1	2,000	+2,000	2,000
C.	1	2	9,000	+7,000	4,500
D.	1	3	14,000	+5,000	4,667
E.	1	4	16,500	+2,500	4,125
F.	1	5	18,000	+1,500	3,600
G.	1	6	18,750	+750	3,125
H.	1	7	18,750	0	2,679
I.	1	8	18,000	−750	2,250
J.	1	9	14,000	−4,000	1,556

Each row of this table shows a conceivable input combination used in a year (columns 1 and 2) and the associated maximum total product (column 3). Given the state of technical knowledge and an orchard with fixed quantities of natural and capital resources, equal successive additions of workers eventually yield declining additions to the crops (columns 3 or 4), which exemplifies the *law of diminishing returns*. Caution: The variable input's eventually declining marginal physical product (to which the law refers) should not be confused with that input's average physical product (column 5).

[a] Fixed (1,000 apple trees, 2 cold-storage barns, 4 spraying machines, etc.)
[b] Variable (number of full-time workers)
[c] Bushels of apples
[d] Extra bushels/extra worker
[e] Bushels per worker

against frost and watering roots during the drought, perhaps, is rewarded by a total product of 2,000 bushels (row B, column 3). Moving from row A to row B, an *extra* worker employed for a year yields an *extra* 2,000 bushels of apples per year, and this marginal benefit is typically given a special name. Other things being equal, such a physical change in the total product that is attributable to a unit change in one input in the productive process is called that input's **marginal physical product, MPP.** The marginal physical product of labor in Table 1 can be calculated by noting the change in the total product evidenced by the difference between any two adjacent numbers in column (3). This difference is associated in our example with a unit change in the labor input in column (2). The results are shown directly in column (4).

Now imagine yourself abandoning alternative B in favor of C. If you hire a second worker for the year, the maximum total product jumps from 2,000 bushels to 9,000 bushels (which implies a marginal physical product of +7,000 bushels). The two workers may be able to do what one alone cannot accomplish: prune some of the trees or fertilize them, wrap the trunks to keep rodents away, place beehives in the orchard to help pollinate the blossoms, and more. Each tree may thus bear more and larger apples.

Hiring a third, fourth, fifth, and sixth worker can be similarly productive—though on a less marked scale. Thus, additional workers may fix and run the pesticide spraying machines, harvest more of the apples, and give more attention to the cold-storage barns. As a result, fewer apples are eaten by worms, remain unpicked, or spoil before reaching the market. Yet, as column (4) reveals, there is a limit to these returns.

The Law of Diminishing Returns

Proceeding on the path of hiring ever more workers, you would soon come to face a technological fact: Given the fixed number of apple trees and quantity of equipment that you have, equal successive additions of workers eventually yield ever smaller additions to the crop, which illustrates a famous law. The **law of diminishing returns** states that given technical knowledge and fixed quantities of all other inputs, equal successive increases of any one input to any given production process will, after some point (the point of diminishing returns) yield ever smaller increases in output. These declining marginal physical products can even fall to zero and become negative.

This law is illustrated in column (4) of Table 1. After 2 workers are employed in the orchard (the maximum *total* product then is 9,000 bushels/year), the marginal physical product per extra worker declines from its maximum of +7,000 bushels to +5,000 bushels, then +2,500 bushels, and so forth, reaching, ultimately, −4,000 bushels. Accordingly, as more and more workers are hired, other things being equal, the maximum product that can be attained from the orchard (column 3) rises by less and less, fails to rise, and even declines.

Eventually, there would be too many workers relative to the fixed number of trees and quantity of equipment. Once trees were saturated with fertilizer, water, and tender loving care, additional workers would have nothing to do except eat apples and get in each other's way. Inevitably, the law of diminishing returns (a special version of Chapter 1's law of declining marginal benefits) would take effect.

An important point is that each of the persons employed can be assumed to be an *equally good* worker. The fourth person hired need not be any weaker, lazier, or less intelligent than the second or third, even though he or she would add less to the total crop. Nor need the ninth person be any different from the fourth. Their different performances would result from the different *circumstances* existing when these workers arrived on the scene. If worker number 9 were hired first, he or she would produce a marginal physical product of +2,000 rather than one of −4,000 bushels. If worker number 1 were hired last, he or she would produce a marginal physical product of −4,000 rather than of +2,000 bushels.

By the same token, were you to *fire* any one of seven workers in the orchard, no matter whether he or she was hired first, fourth, or seventh, the total produced would not change at all because the product associated with six rather than seven workers is the same (see the entries in column 3). This fact may seem surprising but merely reflects the truth that people by themselves produce nothing. Their productivity depends on the world in which they are placed: It depends on the quantity and quality of the natural, capital, and other human resources that already exist in this world when they enter it. Just ask yourself this: What would *your* marginal physical product be if you were to join the productive process—just as you now are—in Central Africa or in 4th-century Tibet rather than in the present-day United States? There can be little doubt that it would be much lower than it is here and now. Ideas in History, The Concept of Marginal Product, provides a wider perspective on this issue.

Marginal Product Versus Average Product

Table 1 also makes a distinction between marginal product (column 4) and average product (column 5). The marginal physical product is the change in total product associated with a unit change in the variable input quantity. In contrast, the **average physical product** is the ratio of total product to the total quantity of an input used. This quantity of goods produced *per unit* of any given type of resource is also referred to as the **productivity** of the input in question. Table 1, column 5, shows the average physical product of the variable labor input used and could be labeled "the productivity of labor."

CHAPTER 8   *The Technology of Production*   **203**

FIGURE 1   A Production Function

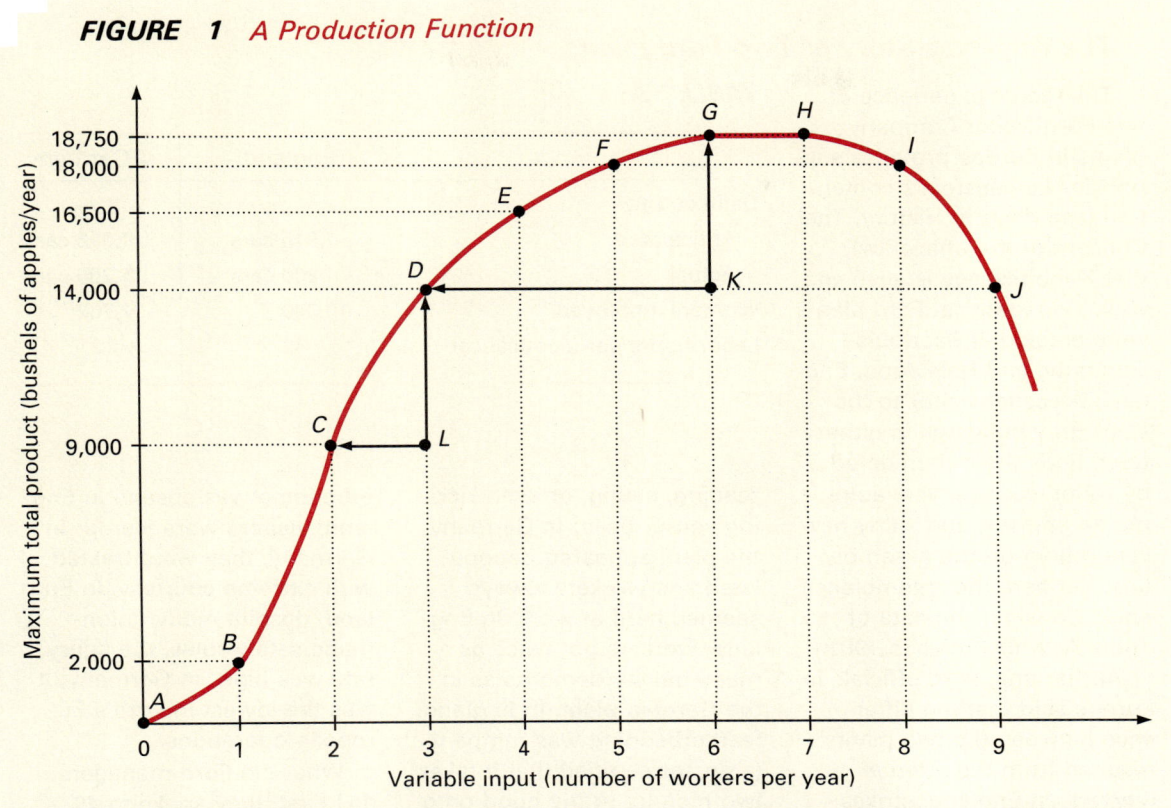

This graph of columns (2) and (3) of Table 1 depicts a typical firm's production function. It assumes a given state of technical knowledge and fixed amounts of all other inputs, such as natural and capital resources.

CAUTION

While one can calculate labor productivity numbers such as those in column 5, one should not conclude (as some theorists have) that labor alone is responsible for the output produced (and, perhaps, should get all of it). In our example, if 4 workers are employed, their average physical product is 16,500/4 or 4,125 bushels per worker per year, but this output was produced jointly *by the workers and all the nonlabor inputs listed in column 1. One could just as well divide the total product (column 3) by the total quantity of nonlabor input used (column 1) and would then derive a series of numbers (like those in column 3) that could be called "the productivity of nonlabor inputs."*

Graphical Illustrations

It is helpful to study the Table 1 data in still another way. Consider the graphical illustrations presented in the following sections.

The Total Product

Figure 1 is based on the first three columns of Table 1. It shows the ten alternative input combinations along with the associated maximum possible output quantities (A through J). All the output/input combinations lying on the positively sloped section of the red line are said to denote situations of **technical efficiency,** wherein it is impossible, with current technical knowledge, to raise output from given inputs or, alternatively, to produce a given output by using less of one input without using

EXAMPLE 1

The Amazing Story of Two Ford Plants

The recent experience of two Ford Motor Company plants in Europe provides support for Leibenstein's contention (see Ideas in History, The Concept of X-inefficiency), that X-inefficiency is alive and well. Two identical Ford plants were erected at Saarlouis, Germany, and Halewood, England. A casual visitor to the sleek gray buildings in either town finds them dominated by robot welders, vast automated presses, and shiny new cars rolling off the assembly line. Yet here the resemblance ends. Consider the data of Table A, which refer to 1981.

At the time, Ford officials in Europe said that the difference between the two plants resulted from the *attitude of workers.* In England, strikes were frequent; in Germany, unknown. In England, workers were visible everywhere, often reading, eating, or even kicking soccer balls; in Germany, the plant appeared depopulated and workers always seemed hard at work. In England, workers got twice as many quality demerits as in the German plant. In England, featherbedding was rampant (a doctor certified that it takes two men to lift the hood onto the car body, but in fact one man did it while the other one watched); in Germany, featherbedding was absent. In England, visitors were jeered; in Germany, they were treated with extreme courtesy. In England, despite many union-made safety rules, the injury rate was high; in Germany, it was the lowest in Ford's European operations.

What did Ford managers do? First, they spoke to 40 workers at a time, then to groups of 200, until all 10,000 had been reached. The mes-

TABLE A

	England	Germany
Daily output		
Anticipated	1,015 cars	1,015 cars
Actual	800 cars	1,200 cars
Workers employed	10,040	7,762
Labor hours per identical car	40	21

---

more of another input. By implication, **technical inefficiency** describes a situation wherein the just-mentioned feats *are* possible.

Consider, for example, the technical inefficiency of output/input combinations K and L. If the orchard used 6 workers and produced 14,000 bushels of apples per year (point K), it would be technically inefficient since (grandfather's records show) better management could raise output to 18,750 bushels/year (point G) or could produce 14,000 bushels/year with as few as 3 workers (point D). Note the arrows originating at K. Point L is also inefficient because a better manager could raise the output of 3 workers from 9,000 to 14,000 bushels/year (note the arrow from L to D) or could produce the same 9,000 bushels/year with only 2 workers (note the arrow from L to C). Thus, any output/input combinations underneath the positively sloped section AG of our production function is similarly inefficient from a technical point of view.

Consider any point on the horizontal or negatively sloped section of the production function, such as H, I, or J. The output associated with H could be produced with 1 fewer worker at G. The output associated with I could be produced with 3 fewer workers at F. That of J could be produced with 5 fewer workers at D.

Does such technical inefficiency ever occur? Ideas in History, The Concept of X-inefficiency, and Example 1 explore this issue.

TABLE B

	England		Germany	
	1980	1988	1980	1988
Daily output	716 cars	1,027 cars	1,130 cars	1,332 cars
Workers employed	11,315	7,789	8,458	7,240
Output per worker	15 cars	31 cars	31 cars	42 cars

sage was clear: Europe 1992 was on the horizon. On the economically unified continent, Ford would face competition from highly productive German and Japanese firms. As things were going, the strife-ridden British plant would not survive.

Second, to counteract the widespread notion that this discrepancy was merely company propaganda, some 2,000 British workers were flown to Germany to see the other plant. Third, the visits to Germany were followed by face-to-face discussions over beer. Gradually, the daily walkouts in Britain gave way to conflict resolution by committee. Peace at the Halewood plant became news; as a *Liverpool Echo* headline put it, "Smooth Night Shift at Ford."

Fourth, new equipment was installed to raise productivity, but the 160 jobs eliminated were cut by attrition rather than dismissals.

Table B indicates the results of the management campaign to improve worker attitudes. British labor productivity doubled during the 1980s, yet was still trailing that in Germany, as the Germans had increased productivity as well.

Sources: Steven Rattner, "A Tale of Two Ford Plants: German Unit Far Outpaces One in Britain," *The New York Times,* October 13, 1981, pp. D1 and D4; Heinz Kohler, *Comparative Economic Systems* (Glenview, IL: Scott, Foresman and Co., 1990), pp. 26–27; and Steve Lohr, "How a British Ford Plant Became Productive Again," *The New York Times,* November 28, 1989, pp. A1 and D6.

A final note: In the long run, when formerly fixed inputs can be varied and technical knowledge can be gained or lost, an entirely new production function can emerge. This fact is illustrated in Figure 2. An upward shift (P_1 to P_2) illustrates some kind of improvement; for example, note how 4 workers become capable of producing a maximum not of 10,000 bushels/year (point b) but of 17,200 bushels/year (point c). This may be the result of their having access to larger quantities or better qualities of nonlabor resources (more trees, more productive trees, an improving climate, more or better fertilizers, and the like); it can also denote improvements in technical knowledge (such as the application of scientific discoveries to the precise timing of fertilization).

In contrast, a downward shift (P_1 to P_0) illustrates some kind of deterioration; note, for example, how 4 workers lose their ability to produce 10,000 bushels/year (point b) and become capable of only producing a maximum of 3,700 bushels/year (point a). This may be the result of their having access to smaller quantities or lower qualities of nonlabor resources (trees having died or been destroyed by earthquakes or pests, a deteriorating climate, and the like); it can also denote losses in technical knowledge (due, for example, to the killing of people in war). Examples 2 and 3 show how technical knowledge and scientific research and development change over time.

FIGURE 2 Long Run Changes in a Production Function

Over time, a firm's production function can change, as from P_1 to P_2 or from P_1 to P_0 in this graph.

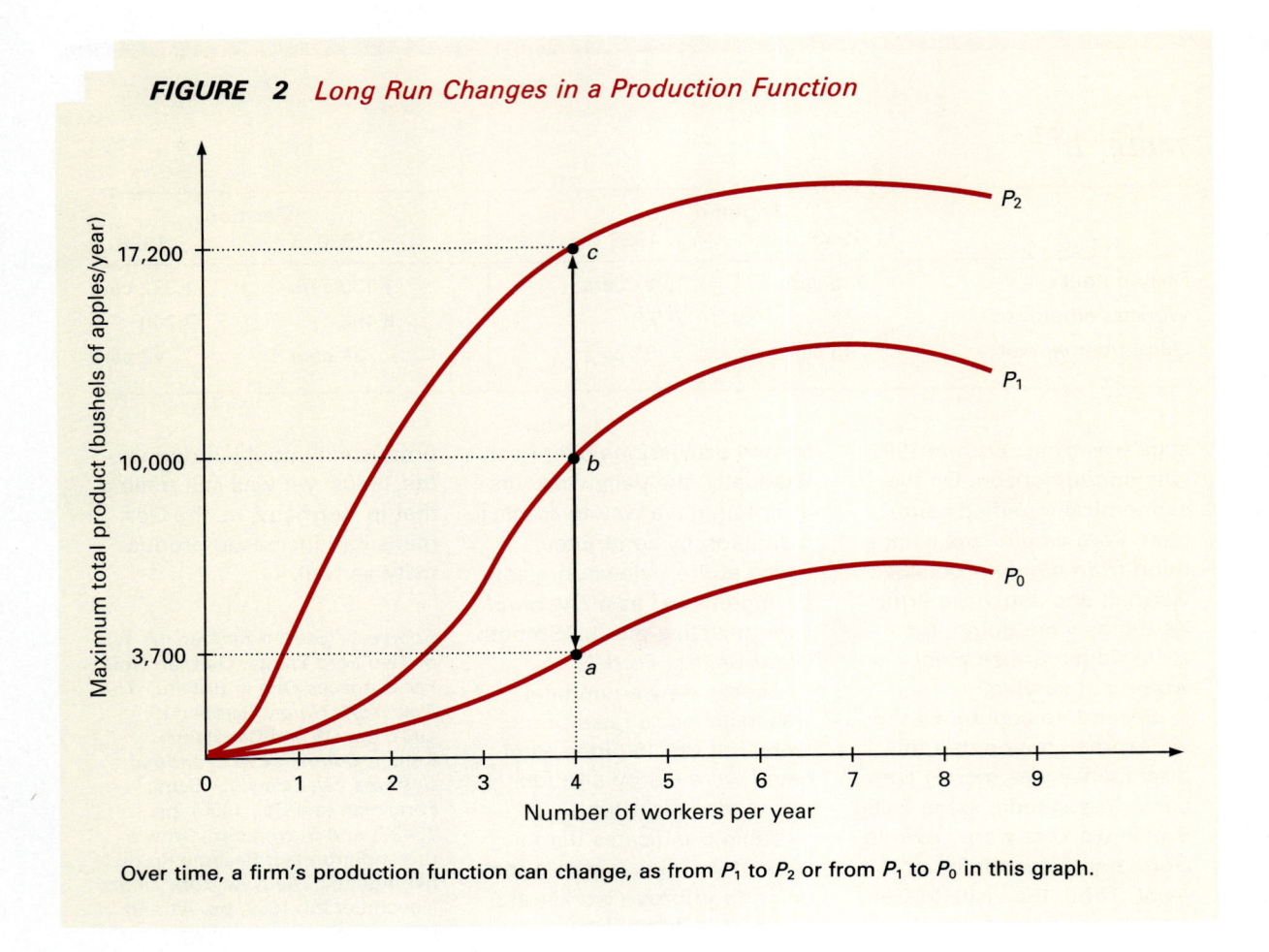

Diminishing Returns

Figure 3 looks at the total product curve in yet another way. It highlights the marginal physical products that are associated with unit increases in the variable labor input, other things being equal. Just as in column 4 of Table 1, the marginal physical product is rising as labor input is increased from 0 to 2 workers. Then the **point of diminishing returns** is reached (point C). It is the inflection point on the total product curve where increasing positive slope (from A to C) gives way to decreasing positive slope (from C to J), and beyond which the variable input's marginal physical products decline.

Marginal Product and Average Product

Figure 4 finally, relates the total product curve to the curves of marginal product and average product that are derived from it. As in earlier graphs, the total product curve rises at an increasing rate up to the point of diminishing returns; the shaded boxes of marginal physical product rise accordingly. Thereafter, the total product rises at a decreasing rate up to a maximum and then declines; accordingly, the boxes of marginal physical product get smaller (shaded) and even become negative (crosshatched).

EXAMPLE 2

Research and Development Labs Move Abroad

Last chapter's Example 6 noted the emergence of the *transnational firm* that views no single country as its home. Traditional domestic firms find it perfectly natural to produce component A in Michigan and component B in Oregon, assemble product C in New York, and sell it in all 50 states. So it is just as natural for the transnational firm to manufacture components in many countries, assemble them in other countries, and market the resultant product worldwide. Research and development activities (R&D) that used to be undertaken by firms only at their domestic headquarters are now becoming internationalized as well.

Japanese firms, for example, consider it important that their R&D teams have frequent contact with the firm's customers. As a result, Japanese automotive design facilities have moved to North America and Europe, along with growing exports of Honda and Toyota cars. Sony, Hitachi, and Fujitsu have similarly established electronics research facilities near foreign export markets. The same process is at work in reverse. Many American firms that are eager to compete with the Japanese in markets around the world have established industrial laboratories in Japan. IBM, in 1991, moved most of its small systems R&D to Japan, from where many components of IBM products had been coming for some time. Before long, IBM's new 5.5 lb. notebook computer was brought out and subjected to market tests not in the United States, but on the other side of the Pacific. Dow Chemicals, Eastman Kodak, Texas Instruments, and many more have made major breakthroughs in laboratories set up in Japan. Among them was a Kodak video camera that converts images into electronic data via a light-sensitive chip, known as a charged-couple device, CCD. The idea involves capturing a picture on film, digitizing it with a scanner, and storing it on a compact disk. Then Kodak's Rochester lab took over, making it possible for users to display the film on a TV screen, print it on a color printer, or even merge it with documents in a computer. The future of high-definition television is closely related to this new technology as well.

Other firms with labs around the world have joined forces to develop a *lingua franca* for the electronics age, a universal digital code that could be used by computers to represent letters and characters in all the world's languages. If the Unicode becomes a worldwide standard, people in different countries could communicate by electronic mail, and software companies could develop programs that can work in different languages. Right now, an American computer cannot understand the codes used by a French computer. With the new code, any computer could understand and display everything from French accents to Chinese ideographs, along with letters in Bengali, Hebrew, Arabic, and Russian.

The proposed Unicode standard would represent letters and symbols by a sequence of 16 zeroes and ones (instead of 8, as in the U.S. ASCII code), which allows for 65,536 different combinations. That is enough to give each character used in all the living languages of the world its own unique sequence, with enough combinations left over to include eventually such obsolete scripts as cuneiform and hieroglyphs as well. With such a code in place, worldwide production technologies, driven by computer-guided robots, are likely to emerge.

Sources: Andrew Pollack, "Universal Computer Code Due," *The New York Times,* February 20, 1991, pp. D1 and D5; and David E. Sanger, "When the Corporate Lab Goes to Japan," *The New York Times,* April 28, 1991, pp. F1 and 6.

FIGURE 3 *The Law of Diminishing Returns*

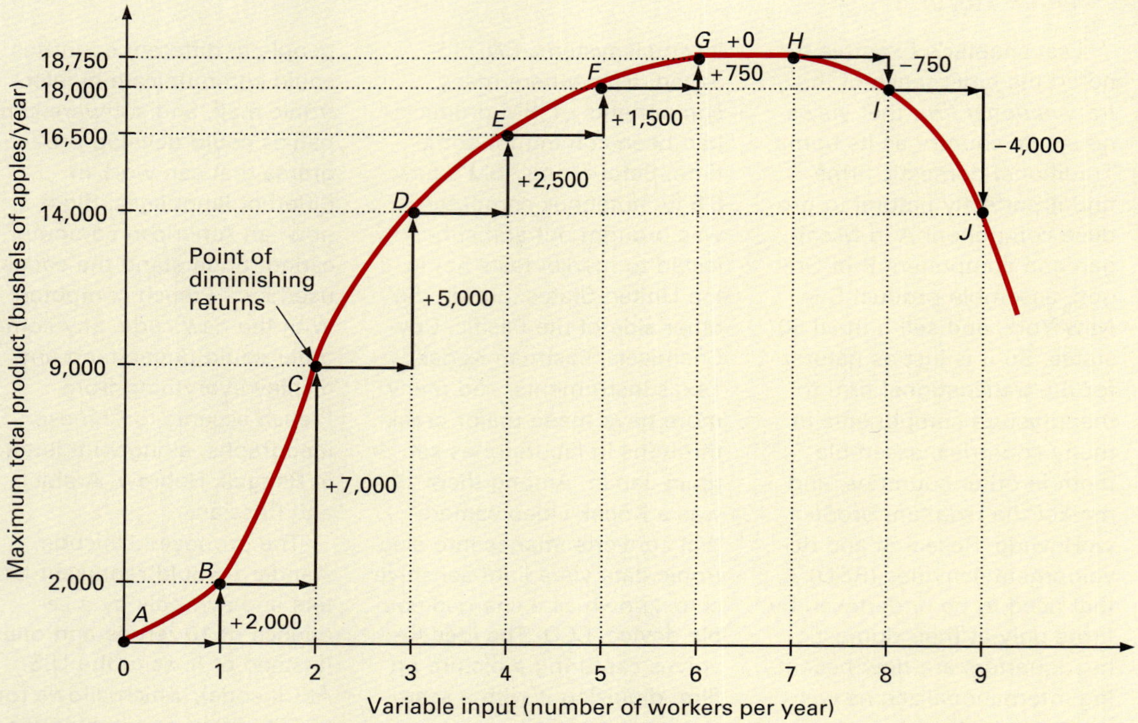

This graph, based on Table 1, illustrates the law of diminishing returns for an apple orchard. Given technical knowledge and fixed quantities of some inputs (1,000 apple trees, 2 cold-storage barns, 4 spraying machines, etc.), equal successive increases of the variable labor input after some point—the point of diminishing returns (here C)—yield ever smaller increases in output. After point G, these declining marginal physical products even fall to zero and below.

The average physical product line, based on columns (2) and (5) of Table 1, similarly rises and then falls. Of particular interest here is the relationship between the average physical product APP and the marginal physical product MPP. As long as MPP exceeds APP (to the left of point M) and regardless of whether MPP itself is rising or falling, APP rises. Once MPP falls short of APP (to the right of point M), APP falls. Indeed, this is a general rule. The behavior of average "anything" (be it product, cost, or even a student's grades) is always related in the following way to the behavior of marginal "anything":

As long as marginal is above average, it pulls up the average. When marginal is equal to average, average does not change. When marginal is below average, it pulls down the average.

Students are apt to be quite familiar with this phenomenon without realizing it. Anyone receiving a new grade (a *marginal* grade) knows how it can pull up or pull down one's grade *average*. A marginal grade above average will pull up the average; a marginal grade below the average will pull the average down. This effect is true, furthermore, regardless of what the marginal grade itself is doing. Each

FIGURE 4 Total, Marginal, and Average Product

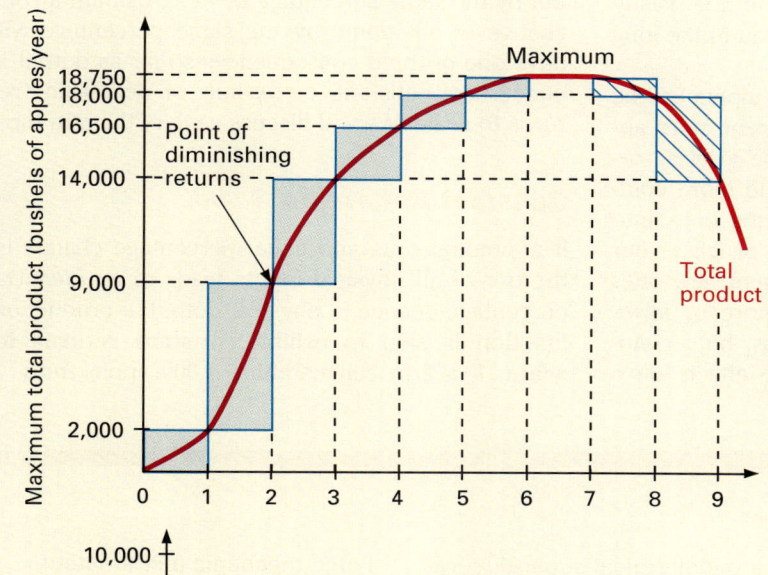

This graph is based on Table 1. Given the state of technology and the fixity of some inputs, increases in the variable input are associated with at first rising and then falling levels of total, marginal, and average products. Note in particular how the average physical product (*APP*) rises as long as the marginal physical product (*MPP*) lies above it (left of *M*), and how *APP* falls once *MPP* lies below it (right of *M*). Also note how the marginal physical product becomes negative once the total product begins to decline, as the crosshatched boxes illustrate.

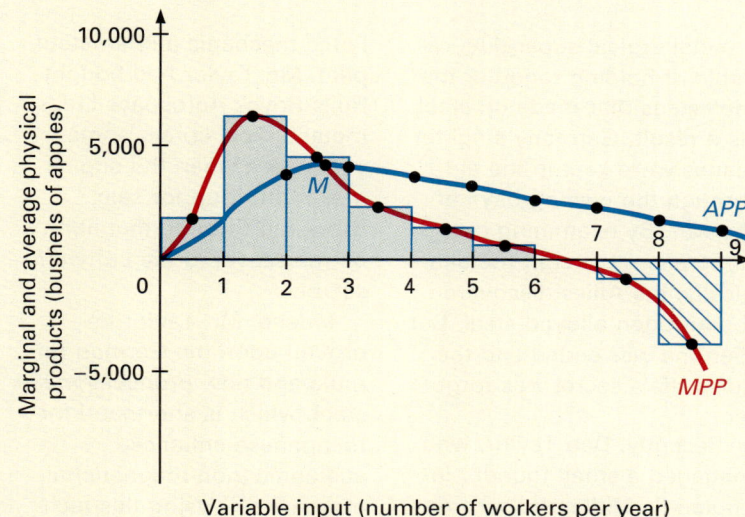

new grade can be better than the last one (marginal grades are rising); yet if these new (and improving) grades are below the average, the average will still go down. Each new grade, on the other hand, can be worse than the last one (marginal grades are falling); yet if these new (but deteriorating) grades are above the average, the average will still go up.

Economies of Scale

If you were to run the Crisp Apple Company, the kinds of choices available to you in the short run are summarized by Table 1 and the graphs derived from it. Presumably, you would reject the technically inefficient alternatives (*H* through *J*) and would hire a maximum of six full-time workers. As the next chapters show, the precise number will depend on which of the technically efficient alternatives yields the greatest profit. Before proceeding to that topic, however, we should note the vastly greater array of choices available to you in the long run.

Given enough time, none of your inputs will be fixed. You can clear more land and plant more apple trees; you can convert part of the existing orchard into housing lots. You can build more cold-storage barns; you can change existing ones into condos or even a motel. You can sell or lease your spraying machines; you can buy or rent new ones instead. And you can always hire more or fewer workers. The possibilities are endless, but economists have particular interest in the effects on a firm's maximum possible output of variations in the *scale* of the productive process. Scale varies when all inputs are not only changed at the same time, but by the same percentage as well. A simultaneous change of all inputs by the same percentage will have one of three consequences so far as output is concerned: constant, increasing, or decreasing returns to scale. We will discuss each of them in turn.

Constant Returns to Scale

If a simultaneous and equal percentage change in the use of all physical inputs leads to an *identical* percentage change in physical output, a production function is said to exhibit **constant returns to scale.** If a firm can combine 1,000 apple trees, 2

■ EXAMPLE 3

Luftwaffe Secret Unburied

People often find it hard to believe that technical knowledge can be lost, but it does happen. The most famous and long-lasting example, perhaps, is the recipe for producing a Stradivarius violin; a mundane example of much more recent origin involves steel making.

During World War II, German scientists faced a problem. To keep their air force flying, they needed exhaust valves made of high strength, corrosion resistant steel that could withstand extremes of temperature, both high and low. Traditionally, such characteristics were found in a nickel-steel alloy, but Germany's supplies of nickel were dwindling fast. A technological breakthrough came when it was discovered that nitrogen could be substituted for nickel. Nitrogen acted like a metallurgical superglue, capable of holding together the molecules that made up steel. As a result, Germany's fighter planes were kept in the air through the waning days of the war. By examining captured enemy aircraft metallurgically, the Allies discovered the nitrogen alloyed steel. But then the war ended and the Luftwaffe's secret was forgotten.

Recently, Dan Taylor, who managed a small foundry in England's Midlands, became alarmed at the tripling of nickel prices (from under $2/lb. in 1979 to over $6/lb. in 1989). One of the foundry's major tasks was the production of turbocharger casings for the auto industry; they had to be made of steel heavily laced with nickel to increase the tolerance to heat changes. A former Royal Air Force mechanic and amateur pilot, Mr. Taylor had bought Rolls-Royce Aerospace Ltd.'s metallurgical library some years back when the engine maker put it up for sale. Browsing through that library, he rediscovered the Luftwaffe secret.

Indeed, Mr. Taylor improved upon the German formula and now produces *mean* steel, which is shorthand for manganese-enhanced austenitic (non-magnetic) nitrogen steel. Using this technology, the foundry can produce a turbocharger housing for $24 with mean steel; it costs $46 when made with nickel-alloy steel.

Source: Steve Lohr, "Luftwaffe Secret Spurs New Steel," *The New York Times,* August 30, 1989, pp. D1 and D4.

TABLE 2 Constant Returns to Scale

	Scale 1			Scale 2		
	Inputs (respective units/year)		Output (bushels/year)	Inputs (respective units/year)		Output (bushels/year)
	Land and capital (1)	Labor (2)	Apples (3)	Land and capital (4)	Labor (5)	Apples (6)
A.	1	0	0	2	0	0
B.	1	1	2,000	2	2	4,000
C.	1	2	9,000	2	4	18,000
D.	1	3	14,000	2	6	28,000
E.	1	4	16,500	2	8	33,000
F.	1	5	18,000	2	10	36,000
G.	1	6	18,750	2	12	37,500

If a simultaneous and equal percentage change in the use of all its physical inputs leads to an identical percentage change in its physical output, a firm's production function is said to exhibit *constant returns to scale*. Note how, in this example, the doubling of all inputs also doubles total output. When columns (1) and (2) become columns (4) and (5), column (3) becomes column (6). The same process works in reverse as well. If constant returns to scale exist, halving of all inputs halves the associated outputs. Be careful, a *doubling* of all inputs (an increase of 100 percent) is not a requirement. Under constant returns to scale, all inputs can be changed by *any* percentage (+10.7 percent or −3.9 percent), and output will change by the same percentage (up or down).

cold-storage barns, 4 spraying machines, etc., with 5 workers to produce 18,000 bushels of apples per year (alternative *F* in Table 1 or Figure 1), it seems natural that it should be able to combine twice the inputs (2,000 apple trees, 4 cold-storage barns, 8 spraying machines, 2 etc., with 10 workers) to produce twice the output (36,000 bushels of apples per year). This reasonable possibility is illustrated by Table 2.

Increasing Returns to Scale

If a simultaneous and equal percentage change in the use of all physical inputs leads to a *larger* percentage change in physical output, a production function is said to exhibit **increasing returns to scale.** If you increase all the column (6) entries in Table 2 (and only those), you have a numerical example. The reasons for such an occurrence are not so obvious. They often include the advantages derived from specialization, as well as the operation of certain physical laws.

Advantages of Specialization

As the scale of production becomes larger, the production process can be divided into a multitude of ever-narrower tasks, and various inputs can be assigned exclusively to performing each of these tasks. Imagine expanding the apple orchard from 1,000 to 10,000 to 100,000 and even to 1 million trees, while other inputs expand proportionately. It then becomes possible to let workers concentrate on what they can do best, to assign them full time to tasks for which they have inherent talents. A worker with a knack for mechanics can work all day and every day maintaining the orchard's trucks when there are 400 of them, which would hardly be possible if there was only one. Other people can, similarly, specialize in driving trucks, pruning trees, bookkeeping, or marketing; others still in apple picking, bee keeping, research, or even caring for the workers' children.

Even when talents are not inherent in people, "practice makes perfect." The random assignment of people to narrow tasks is likely to make them more proficient at performing those tasks and thus, to raise productivity compared to a small-scale operation. When productions occur on a small scale, any given person frequently moves from one job to another and thus loses valuable time while moving between different locations, changing tools, and warming up for a new task.

Finally, the simplicity and repetitiveness of narrowly specialized, large-scale operations often allows for the use of machines, which can also raise productivity. Consider how a large orchard may use airplanes to spray pesticides and fancy robots to sort, wash, and pack the fruit. No firm that produces only 2,000 bushels a year could seriously consider those options.

The Operation of Certain Physical Laws

The operation of certain physical laws can also explain the existence of increasing returns to scale. Consider a box that is 1 foot long, 1 foot wide, and 1 foot high. It has six sides with a surface area of 1 square foot each. Hence the box as a whole has a surface area of 6 square feet; its volume equals 1 cubic foot. Now increase length, width, and height by a factor of 5. The surface area of each side becomes 25 square feet, that of the entire box, $6 \times 25 = 150$ square feet; the volume grows to $5 \times 5 \times 5 = 125$ cubic feet. Thus a 25-fold increase in surface area produces a 125-fold increase in volume. Frequently, the input quantities needed to construct "containers," such as cargo ships, office buildings, pipelines, or warehouses, depend on their surface area, but their output (cargo transported, office space rented, crude oil shipped, or commodities stored) depends on their volume. Larger scale, therefore, yields more output per unit of input.

Decreasing Returns to Scale

If a simultaneous and equal percentage change in the use of all physical inputs leads to a *smaller* percentage change in physical output, a production function is said to exhibit **decreasing returns to scale.** If you decrease all the column (6) entries in Table 2 (and only those), you have a numerical example. Why should such a phenomenon occur? More often than not, economists think, it has to do with the fact that managerial coordination becomes more difficult on a larger scale.

If you ran your apple orchard with six workers, you could easily keep an eye on things. You would probably work right along with everyone else and make sure that everyone worked reasonably hard, did a good job, and always did the type of work that was most important at the time. But imagine that your business grew from 1,000 apple trees in Vermont to a million trees in 15 states. Your 6 workers would turn into 60, then 6,000, then 600,000. Things would happen every day of which you could not possibly be aware. Some workers on your payroll may just sleep under trees instead of pruning them, watering them, or picking apples. Others may do a careless job, pruning trees incorrectly, applying the wrong kind of fertilizer (or the right kind at the wrong time), taking a shortcut and harvesting apples *en masse* by shaking the trees rather than climbing a ladder and carefully picking one apple at a time. As a result, fewer apples will grow on each tree, or those reaching the storage barn will be bruised and rot in a week. Can you see how output per worker may fall with larger scale?

This problem, the principal-agent problem noted in the last chapter and in this chapter's Ideas in History, The Concept of X-inefficiency, is not always easily solved. Even if you hired supervisors to make sure ordinary workers did their work properly, the greater quantity of apples produced would be accompanied by a greater quantity of labor (including more supervisory personnel), and output per worker may still decline compared to the days when your firm was small.

Nor should all the problems be blamed on workers. Management itself may be responsible for decreasing returns to scale. The larger a firm becomes, the longer and more complex the communications channels within it become. There are so many workers and supervisors, division heads, and vice presidents in charge of an increasing number of departments. All of them must pass crucial information up the corporate hierarchy so that top management can make proper decisions, which must in turn be passed down the hierarchy.

Now imagine what happens when messages going up or down that hierarchy become garbled or simply fail to reach their destination. If wrong decisions are made, or if correct decisions are made too late, crucial output-raising opportunities are missed. Example 4 provides a real-world illustration about returns to scale.

EXAMPLE 4

The Optimum Size of Cargo Ships

In recent years, the average size of cargo ships has increased rapidly, but a limit to this trend is in sight. The output of a ship can be viewed as the *quantity of cargo it hauls per mile.* Because the quantity of labor and materials required to build a container is a function of its surface area, while holding and hauling capacity is a function of the volume enclosed, the hauling operations of a ship tend to be subject to increasing returns to scale. As a result, the hauling cost per ton tends to *decrease* with larger ship size.

A ship in port, however, is a different matter from a ship at sea. The output of a ship in port is better viewed as the *quantity of cargo it loads or unloads per day.* The capacity to handle cargo in port tends to be a function of the length of the ship, because length determines the number of possible hatches and cranes. Because length cannot grow in proportion to volume, the handling operations of a ship tend to be subject to decreasing returns to scale. The handling cost per ton tends to *increase* with larger ship size.

Increasing returns to scale in *hauling* cargo must, therefore, be traded off against decreasing returns to scale in *handling* it. This relationship yields an optimum ship size where the marginal benefit of large size (lower hauling cost per ton) equals the associated marginal cost (higher handling cost per ton).

In 1980, the Chevron Shipping Company subjected four of its supertankers to "downsizing," a process akin to removing the center leaf of a dining room table and shoving the table back together again. Four 200,000-ton ships were sliced apart, a 100-foot section was removed from the middle of each, and the remainder was rewelded together. The result was a set of four 150,000-ton tankers capable of operating in ports that were previously inaccessible.

Sources: Jan Owen Jansson and Dan Shneerson, "Economies of Scale of General Cargo Ships," *The Review of Economics and Statistics,* May 1978, pp. 287–293; "Shrinking the Oversized Supertanker," *The New York Times,* July 18, 1980, pp. D1 and 6; and Heinz Kohler, *Intermediate Microeconomics: Theory and Applications,* 3rd ed. (Glenview, IL: Scott, Foresman and Co., 1990), p. 133.

IDEAS IN HISTORY: The Concept of Marginal Product

The law of diminishing returns and the concept of marginal physical product on which it is based have an interesting history. It starts with Johann Heinrich von Thünen (1783-1850), who was born into an old feudal family in Oldenburg, Germany. On his father's estate, he developed an early interest in agriculture and mathematics. Although he attended an agricultural college near Hamburg and later the University of Göttingen, he never graduated, preferring the career of a practical farmer.

On his estate in Mecklenburg, he kept meticulous farm accounts from 1810 to 1820, costing every plot of land, every bushel of rye, every cow and goose. Von Thünen therefore became the first investigator who put his occupational life into the service of scientific economic research. He was thus the first practitioner of *econometrics* (the application of statistical methods to the study of economics). The data he collected served as the empirical basis for his discovery of the law of diminishing returns.

Von Thünen also developed a theory of income distribution based on the concept of marginal productivity. He stated that the (real) wage of all workers, in a large firm employing many workers, would tend to equal the marginal product of the last worker employed. Consider Table 1, row G. If a 6th worker raises annual output by 750 bushels of apples per year, no employer would pay more than 750 bushels as a wage. If all workers are alike and 6 are hired, all get this wage regardless of the chronological order in which they are hired. Von Thünen applied this thinking to capital as well, suggesting that the profit of capital would equal the marginal product of the last portion of capital employed.

Von Thünen was, however, baffled by certain results. If his theory of actual wage (or profit) determination was correct, all units, except for the labor (or capital) unit hired last, would be receiving less than the marginal products associated with the chronological order of their hiring. (See Table 1, column 4.) This result seemed unfair. Such thoughts led von Thünen into normative economics. Living in the days when social revolution incited by the misery of workers seemed imminent, he looked for an *ethical principle* that would reconcile the claims of workers (demanding "the whole product of labor") with those of the owners of capital and land (offering "bare subsistence" to the workers). Von Thünen suggested a compromise, a "natural wage," w, equal to the geometric mean between a worker's subsistence requirements, a, and total product, p. In his own eyes, the formula $w = \sqrt{ap}$ was his highest achievement. He had it engraved on his tombstone to indicate not how wages actually were determined but how they ought to be determined in a just society.

Von Thünen exhibited great concern for his own workers. At a time when most employers treated farm hands like cattle, he supported a doctor, nurse, and cottage-hospital for the free treatment of all workers and their families on his estate. He provided sick pay and retirement pensions. In return, however, he required punctilious performance of duty, paying workers by piece rates whenever possible.

His thoughts are preserved in his single major book, *The Isolated State in Relation to Agriculture and Political Economy*, which appeared in four installments between 1826 and 1863. In his book, von Thünen also introduced the concept of *human capital*:

The reluctance to view a man as capital is especially ruinous of mankind in wartime; here capital is protected, but not man, and in time of war we have no hesitation in sacrificing one hundred men in the bloom of their years to save one cannon. In a hundred men at least twenty times as much capital is lost as is lost in one cannon. But the production of the cannon is the cause of an expenditure of the state treasury, while human beings are again available for nothing by means of a simple conscription order. . . . When the statement was made to Napoleon, the founder of the conscription system, that a planned operation would cost too many men, he replied: "That is nothing. The women produce more of them than I can use."¹

Unfortunately for economic science, von Thünen's many original ideas never had the influence they deserved. He received little honor in any country, especially in Germany where economic theorists and political liberals were equally despised. von Thünen was both, and his lack of academic status did not help. In Britain, Ricardo's brilliant advocacy of policies (see Chapter 4, Ideas in History) eclipsed the German thinker's theoretical advances. It took nearly a century after Ricardo before an economist of world renown, Alfred Marshall (see Chapter 3, Ideas in History), would say: "I loved von Thünen above all my other masters."²

---

[1] Translated by the author from Johann Heinrich von Thünen, *Der Isolierte Staat in Beziehung auf Landwirtschaft und National-ökonomie*, 3rd. ed. (Berlin: Von Wiegandt, Hempel, and Parey; 1875), vol 2, pp. 146 and 148.
[2] A. C. Pigou, ed., *Memorials of Alfred Marshall* (London: Macmillan, 1925), p. 360.

Source: Heinz Kohler, *Intermediate Microeconomics: Theory and Applications,* 1st. ed. (Glenview, IL.: Scott, Foresman and Co., 1982), pp. 134–135. Adapted with permission.

IDEAS IN HISTORY *The Concept of X-inefficiency*

Some 25 years ago, a now classic article, "Allocative Efficiency vs. 'X-Efficiency'" challenged economists. Its author was Harvey Leibenstein (b. 1922), a professor of economics at the University of California, Berkeley; now he teaches at Harvard. Leibenstein urged economists to reach beyond their traditional study of how to achieve an efficient allocation of resources *among* firms (asking whether given inputs are best used by firm A or firm B) and to focus their attention on the possibility that inputs were inefficiently allocated *within* firms. Take another look at the definition of the production function; it is about the relationship of inputs to the *maximum* output obtainable therefrom. Leibenstein argued that many firms were, in fact, not achieving the maximum possible output from the inputs they employed. They were actually operating at a point such as K in Figure 1, a situation he called **X-inefficiency** and that he attributed mainly to insufficient worker supervision or motivation.

In the Preface to his *Beyond Economic Man: A New Foundation for Microeconomics* (1976), Leibenstein introduces his thoughts on X-inefficiency with a quotation from Tolstoy's *War and Peace*:

. . .Military science assumes the strength of an army to be identical with its numbers. Military science says that the more troops the greater the strength. Les gros battaillons sont toujours raison *(Large battalions are always victorious)*. . . .

In military affairs the strength of an army is the product of its mass and some unknown x. . . .

That unknown quantity is the spirit of the army, . . .

The spirit of an army is the factor which multiplied by the

mass gives the resulting force. To define and express the significance of this unknown factor—the spirit of an army—is a problem for science.

This problem is only solvable if we cease arbitrarily to substitute for the unknown x itself the conditions under which that force becomes apparent—such as the commands of the general, the equipment employed, and so on—mistaking these for the real significance of the factor, and if we recognize this unknown quantity in its entirety as being the greater or lesser desire to fight and to face danger.[1]

Leibenstein expands:

Without straining his meaning too much, Tolstoy's argument is similar to one of the central theses of this volume, despite the fact that his concern is the art of war, and mine economics, one of the arts of peace. To shift to the common language of economics, what Tolstoy is saying is that merely knowing the observable inputs (the number of guns, men, the commands of the generals, and so on) does not tell you the outcome, contrary to the claims of the "military scientists." Something else is involved, an X-factor that Tolstoy equates with "spirit." Similarly, in . . . this volume I argue that knowing the allocation of inputs and the state of the arts of production is not enough, there is also something else involved—what I have called the X-efficiency element.[2]

Leibenstein suggested that slack he called X-inefficiency was likely to occur as firms grew beyond the stage at which a single owner could keep a watchful eye on everything. He focused on the distinction (noted previously in this text) between *principals* (owners) and *agents* (people working for others). He argued that in firms exceeding perhaps 10 persons, agents are free to make many decisions. This is so because employment contracts clearly specify rates of pay in advance but cannot possibly specify every task workers must perform in return. These contracts are necessarily vague and incomplete on all matters relating to worker effort. As a result, workers have discretion as to the type of activities they perform, the pace of these activities, and their quality (Leibenstein called this area of worker discretion the *APQ bundle*—in reference to *activity type*, *pace*, and *quality*).

The larger a firm, the farther removed from actual operations owners must necessarily be, but agents have discretion even in a relatively small firm. Consider our orchard with just 15 employees. A supervisor may send out workers to root-feed the trees; to prune, spray, or water them; to pick apples; to fix the truck; or to put a new roof on the storage barn. Or workers may be sent out to select their own activities. In either case, the activity types selected may not be the best ones for maximizing output; workers may do their work at a pace unreasonably slow; they may do a sloppy job. The effect on output can be disastrous. Yet, Leibenstein contends, X-inefficiency can be reduced—not by putting a supervisor next to every worker but by motivating workers better, by raising their spirit, the X-factor.

---

[1] Harvey Leibenstein, *Beyond Economic Man: A New Foundation for Microeconomics* (Cambridge, MA: Harvard University Press, 1976), p. vii.

[2] *Ibid.*, pp. vii and viii.

Source: Adapted, with permission, from Heinz Kohler, *Intermediate Microeconomics: Theory and Applications,* 1st. ed. (Glenview, IL: Scott, Foresman and Co., 1982), p. 138.

Summary

1. This chapter focuses on the most fundamental aspect of every firm's life: the physical task of combining inputs to create output. The technical possibilities can be summarized by a *production function* that relates alternative input combinations used during a period to maximum possible output quantities associated with each, given the state of technical knowledge.

2. A typical production function is analyzed in a variety of ways: by distinguishing fixed and variable inputs; the total product, marginal product, and average product; and by noting the operation of the law of diminishing returns.

3. A series of graphs of the production function are used to illustrate all of the aforementioned concepts. In addition, such concepts as technical efficiency or inefficiency are depicted, situations in which it is, respectively, impossible or possible to raise output from given inputs. Various reasons for long run changes in the production function are also explored.

4. In the long run, when all inputs can be varied, an expanded array of choices is available to any producer. Of particular interest are changes in a firm's scale when all inputs are not only changed at the same time but also by the same percentage. The consequences can be constant, increasing, or decreasing returns to scale (percentage changes in output that equal, exceed, or fall short of those in inputs).

5. The Appendix to this chapter introduces a more sophisticated approach to the analysis of production functions.

Key Concepts

average physical product
constant returns to scale
decreasing returns to scale
fixed inputs
increasing returns to scale
law of diminishing returns

long run
marginal physical product
point of diminishing returns
production function
productivity

short run
technical efficiency
technical inefficiency
variable inputs
X-inefficiency

Questions and Problems

1. Consider the data to the right. Assume other inputs and technical knowledge to be fixed. Calculate the marginal and average physical products of labor.

2. Take another look at Figure 4. What do you think is happening to the average physical product of the fixed *nonlabor* inputs as labor input is raised?

3. This chapter introduces the law of diminishing returns in connection with the operations of a

Alternative	Labor (hrs/day)	Total product (tons/day)
A	0	0
B	100	1,000
C	200	1,800
D	300	2,400
E	400	2,800
F	500	3,000

firm. Leaf through earlier chapters of this text and determine whether such a law might apply to other situations as well.

4. "If the law of diminishing returns did not hold, one could grow the world's entire annual crop of wheat in a single flowerpot." Evaluate.

5. Are the following statements true or false? Explain.
   a. In the presence of diminishing returns, a firm can do nothing to increase the marginal physical product of its variable input.
   b. When marginal physical product rises, average physical product rises.
   c. When marginal physical product falls, average physical product falls.
   d. When total physical product rises, average physical product rises as well.
   e. When total physical product rises, marginal physical product rises as well.

6. There are many critics of Leibenstein's X-inefficiency theory. Can you think of an argument against it? (Hint: Apply the optimization principle.)

7. Make a table indicating what must happen to the *average* physical product of all inputs when a firm's scale of operations is expanded or contracted and its production function is subject to
   a. constant returns to scale.
   b. increasing returns to scale.
   c. decreasing returns to scale.

8. How do you think one could discover whether a real-world industry was subject to constant, increasing, or decreasing returns to scale?

9. One economist (James H. Gapinski, "The Production of Culture," *The Review of Economics and Statistics,* November 1980, p. 584) recently estimated production functions for five of the fine arts: theater, opera, symphony, ballet, and modern dance. He measured output by the number of cultural experiences enjoyed by patrons and then related it to three types of inputs: labor services of artists, labor services of "adjuvants" (administrators, box office and maintenance help, parking lot attendants, promotional personnel, stage hands, ushers, and the like), and capital services (of structures, musical instruments, stage sets, costumes, scores, scripts, and the like).

The accompanying table shows some of his results: the factor by which output changed when all inputs were simultaneously multiplied by some coefficent, such as 0.25 or 4.00.

Scale co-efficient	Theater	Opera	Symphony	Ballet
0.25	0.2823	0.2802	0.3079	0.1315
0.75	0.7610	0.7640	0.7741	0.7309
1.25	1.2398	1.2359	1.2263	1.2036
2.00	1.9438	1.9517	1.9129	1.4531
3.00	2.7445	2.9391	2.8260	1.3347
4.00	3.2361	3.9701	3.6750	1.1139

Interpret the results.

10. Are the following statements true or false? Explain.
    a. The existence of increasing returns to scale refutes the law of diminishing returns.
    b. In the presence of decreasing returns to scale, a firm can do nothing to increase the average physical product of its inputs.
    c. In the presence of increasing returns to scale, a decrease in scale reduces the average physical products of all inputs.
    d. In the presence of decreasing returns to scale, an increase in scale reduces the average physical products of all inputs.
    e. X-inefficiency is a form of technical inefficiency.

APPENDIX 8a

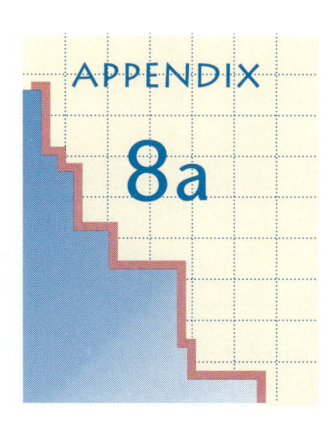

ISOQUANT ANALYSIS

The body of Chapter 8 presented the theory of production from two points of view: the short run (only a single input could be varied) and the long run (all inputs were variable). This appendix discusses an intermediate case in which two inputs are variable while other inputs and technical knowledge are fixed. It also anticipates some of next chapter's material by linking the theory of production (which tells a firm what is technically possible) and the theory of profit maximization (which helps it find what is most desirable).

Consider a producer of apples who, during a given period, can freely vary the quantities of labor L and capital K, while being constrained by a fixed quantity of land T and a given state of technical knowledge t. The production function can be written as

$$Q^* = f(L, K), \text{ given } T \text{ and } t,$$

where Q^* represents the maximum possible output quantity.

Figure 5 is a short-hand way of endowing our equation with numerical content. The table is read like a mileage chart: All else being equal, using 3 units of capital plus 1 unit of labor per year yields a maximum total product of 870 bushels of apples per year; using 5 units of capital plus 6 units of labor yields 2,740 bushels of apples per year, and so on for all other combinations.

Note that the production function shown here is subject to diminishing returns with respect to either one of the variable inputs. Hold capital constant at any level while increasing labor by equal units (moving along any row from left to right), and you will find maximum output rising by ever-decreasing amounts. Hold labor constant at any level while increasing capital by equal units (moving along any column from bottom to top), and you will also find maximum output rising by less and less.

Isoquants Defined

The information in Figure 5 can also be pictured graphically by replacing each of the bushel numbers in the grid by a dot and connecting the dots representing identical bushel numbers by a smooth line. Figure 6 graphs the selected bushel numbers highlighted in color in Figure 5. Each of the lines found by this procedure is called a **production indifference curve, equal-product curve,** or **isoquant.** Each is a graph of all the alternative combinations of two input quantities that yield the same maximum total product and among which a producer would be indifferent from a purely technical point of view. As we shall see later, this definition does not mean indifference from a profit-maximizing point of view. Different input combinations, such as *a* and *b*, that produce the same output (and, thus, bring the same revenue) may cost different amounts of money and thus simply different profits. To avoid misunderstanding, it is probably wiser to call the production indifference curve by one of its two other names.

Isoquants Analyzed

It is important to understand some of the things isoquants can tell us about production functions.

FIGURE 5 A Complex Production Function

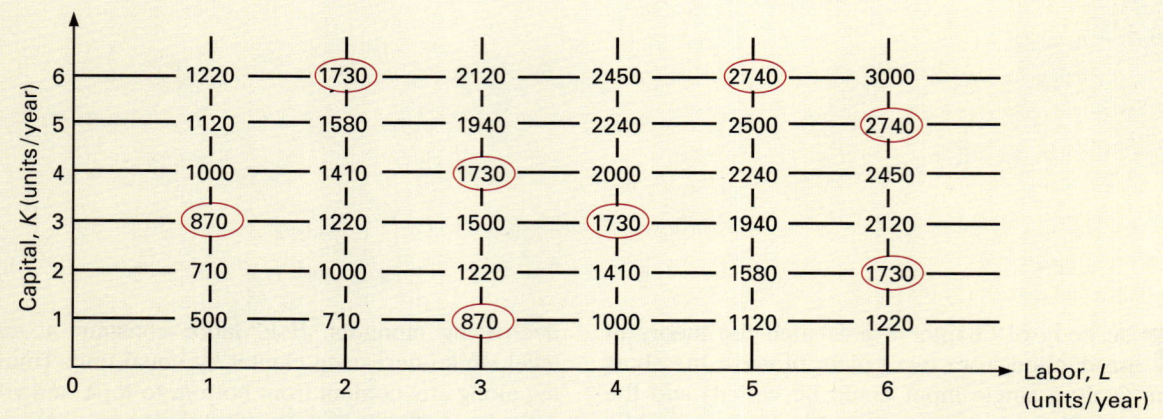

Capital, K (units/year)	L=1	L=2	L=3	L=4	L=5	L=6
6	1220	(1730)	2120	2450	(2740)	3000
5	1120	1580	1940	2240	2500	(2740)
4	1000	1410	(1730)	2000	2240	2450
3	(870)	1220	1500	(1730)	1940	2120
2	710	1000	1220	1410	1580	(1730)
1	500	710	(870)	1000	1120	1220

Given a fixed quantity of land (not shown) and the current state of technical knowledge, different combinations of capital and labor yield the alternative maximum quantities of total product shown in this grid. The equation of this particular production function is $500\sqrt{K \cdot L}$. Thus 6K and 6L yield an output of $500\sqrt{6 \cdot 6} = 500\sqrt{36} = 500(6) = 3000$, as shown.

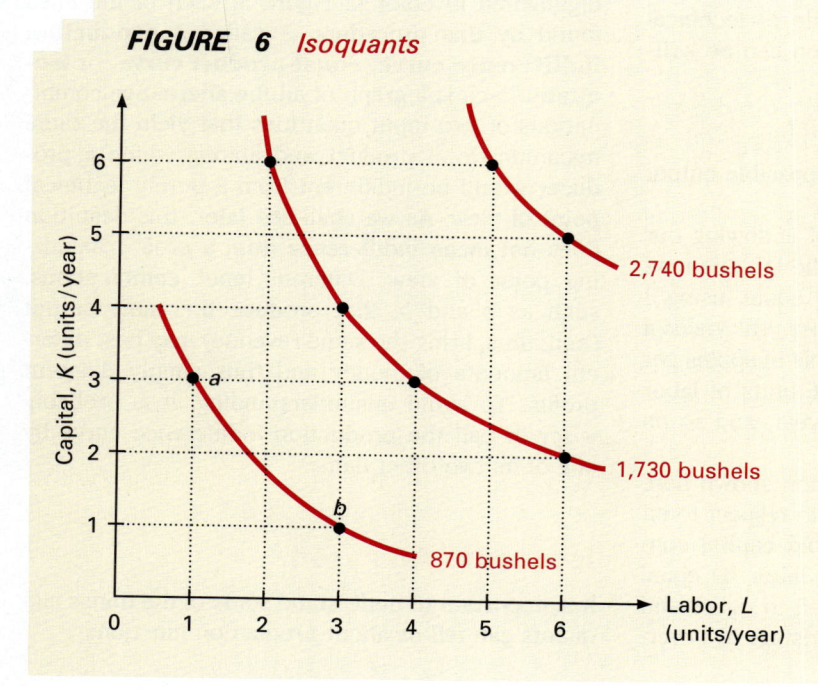

FIGURE 6 Isoquants

A complex production function, such as Figure 5, can be graphed with a set of isoquants such as those shown here. Given fixed quantities of other inputs and technical knowledge, each isoquant (meaning "equal-quantity line") shows all the alternative combinations of two inputs (here capital and labor) that yield the same maximum total product (here bushels of apples per year).

Negative Isoquant Slope Implies Positive Marginal Physical Products

No producer will use any input to the extent that it *reduces* total product (thus yielding *negative* marginal physical products). The negative slope of our isoquants supports this decision. Figure 7 reproduces the 1,730-bushel isoquant of Figure 6. Let the producer initially operate at point *c*, producing 1,730 bushels per year with a combination of 6*K* plus 2*L* (plus unspecified quantities of other inputs). If 2*K* are withdrawn from the process of production, output can be maintained only by adding 1*L*, which moves our producer to point *d* (4*K* plus 3*L* are used). This move implies that capital's marginal physical product was *positive* and the withdrawal of capital must by itself have reduced output; otherwise, it would not have been necessary to add labor to keep output unchanged. The success of this substitution of labor for capital further implies that labor's marginal physical product was positive as well; otherwise, the addition of labor at point *g* could not have succeeded in bringing output back to its original level.

Convex Isoquant Slope Implies Diminishing Marginal Rate of Technical Substitution

Economists have a special name for the rate at which a producer is technically able to exchange— without affecting the quantity of output produced— a little of one input (such as capital) for a little of another input (such as labor). It is called the **marginal rate of technical substitution (MRTS).**

Our Figure 7 isoquant is not only negatively sloped but also convex with respect to the origin of the graph. This shape implies that the *MRTS* is not a constant (as it would be along a straight-line isoquant), but it diminishes as substitution of one input for another proceeds. If our producer (having moved from *c* to *d*) wanted to substitute ever more labor for capital (moving on to *e* and *f*), output could be kept unchanged only if equal increases in labor went hand in hand with *ever smaller* sacrifices of capital (or equal sacrifices of capital were compensated by *ever larger* increases of labor). This characteristic of the production function ultimately reflects changes in the inputs' marginal physical products.

FIGURE 7 The Marginal Rate of Technical Substitution

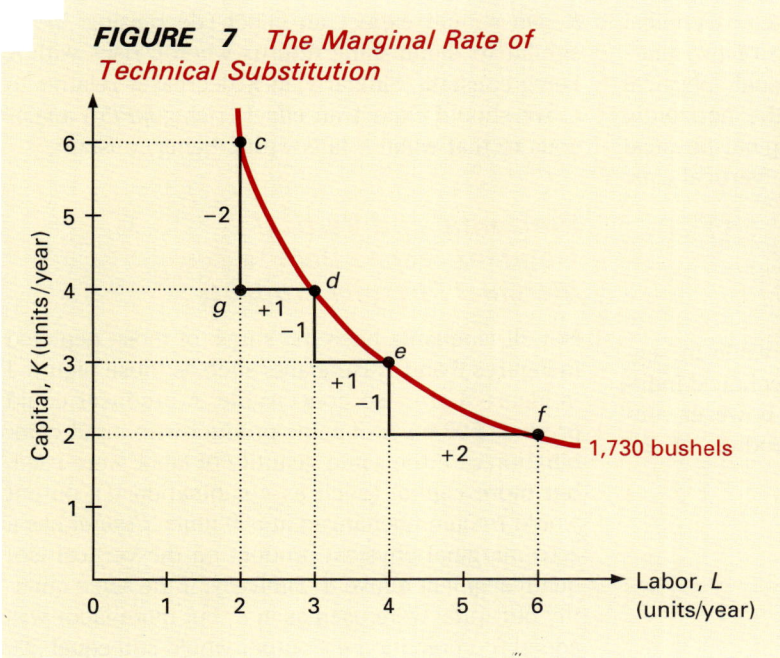

A typical isoquant is not only negatively sloped, but also convex with respect to the origin of this graph. This implies a diminishing marginal rate of technical substitution of one input for the other. In this example, between points *c* and *f*, this technical rate of exchange declines from 2*K* to 1*K* and again to $\frac{1}{2}K$ for an extra unit of *L*.

FIGURE 8 Right-Angled Isoquants

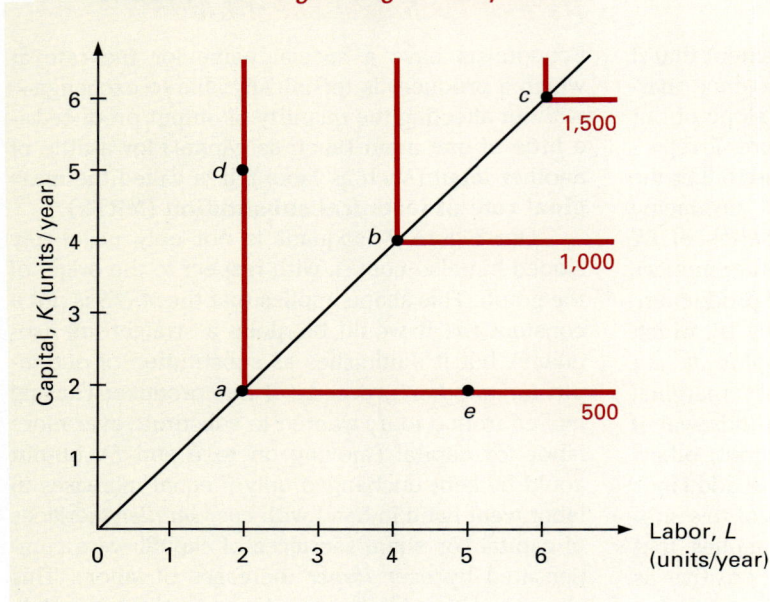

Horizontal and vertical segments of isoquants are not impossible but imply zero marginal physical products and, thus, denote technical inefficiency.

The diminishing *MRTS* can be measured by the absolute value of the isoquant's slope, which in our case changes from |2| in segment *cd* to |1| in segment *de* and then to |1/2| in segment *ef*. This absolute value is not only the marginal rate of technical substitution but also equals the ratio of two marginal physical products—the marginal physical product of the input measured on the horizontal axis, here MPP_L, divided by the marginal physical product of the input measured on the vertical axis, here MPP_K.

$$|\text{Isoquant Slope}| = \frac{MPP_L}{MPP_K}$$

In Figure 7, the slope's absolute value in segment *cd*, equals 2/1. The producer's technical indifference about sacrificing 2*K* for 1*L*, however, implies that the marginal physical product of 2*K* equals that of 1*L*, or

$$MPP_{2K} = MPP_{1L}$$
$$MPP_{1K} = .5\ MPP_{1L}$$
$$\frac{MPP_{1L}}{MPP_{1K}} = \frac{1}{.5} = \frac{2}{1}$$

In our example, the diminishing absolute value of the *MRTS* implies a diminishing ratio of MPP_L / MPP_K, which makes sense given that *L* increases and *K* decreases. As *L* increases relative to *K*, we should expect an effect (decreasing MPP_L) similar to diminishing returns when *L* rises with *K* being constant. Similarly, as *K* decreases relative to *L*, we should expect an effect (rising MPP_K) analogous to that when *K* falls with *L* being constant.

Horizontal and Vertical Isoquant Slopes Denote Zero Marginal Physical Products

Not all isoquants have the shape of those depicted in Figures 6 and 7. Isoquants such as those pictured in Figure 8 are also conceivable. A producer could produce 500 units of some product with input combination *a*. If the same quantity of labor were used, but more capital (such as combination *d*), output would remain unchanged at 500 units. *Capital has a zero marginal physical product on the vertical isoquant segment above a.* Similarly, if the same quantity of capital were used as in *a*, but more labor was added (combination *e*), output would still equal 500

FIGURE 9 The Isocost Line

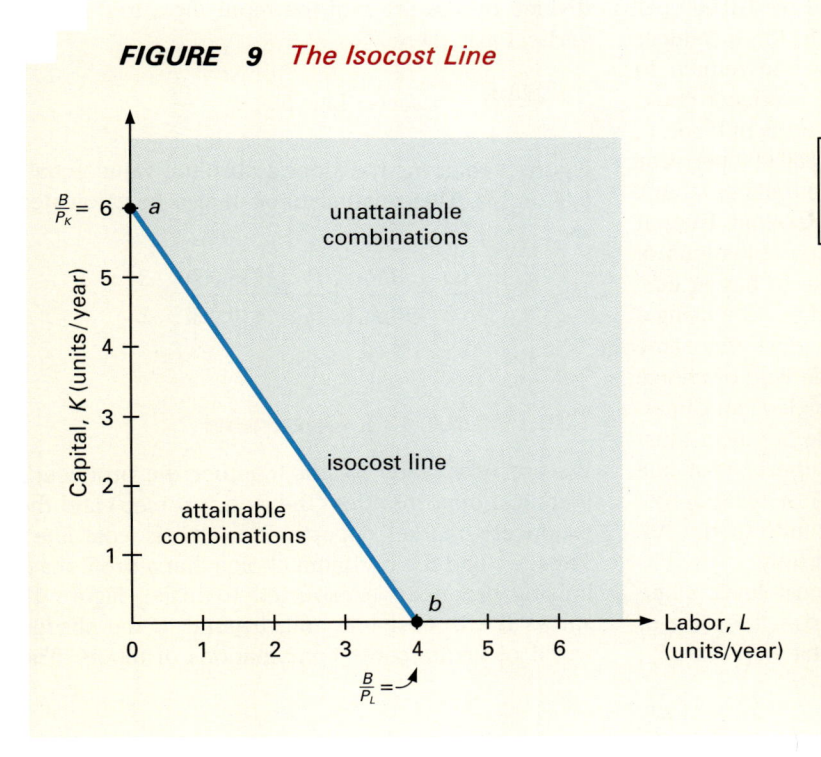

Budget, $B = \$60{,}000$/year
Price of capital, $P_K = \$10{,}000$/unit
Price of labor, $P_L = \$15{,}000$/unit

This graph depicts a *field of choice,* all the alternative input combinations among which a producer might conceivably choose. The isocost line divides the field of choice in two: attainable combinations (*unshaded*) and unattainable combinations (*shaded*). The isocost line's position depends on the size of the firm's budget (here $B = \$60{,}000$/year) and on the prices of the two inputs (here $P_K = \$10{,}000$ and $P_L = \$15{,}000$).

units. This result implies a zero marginal physical product of *labor* on the horizontal isoquant segment to the right of a.

No producer would use additional capital or labor that added nothing to output. To avoid such technical inefficiency, a producer facing the isoquants depicted in Figure 8 would produce 500 units of output *only* with input combination a. Output quantities of 1,000 or 1,500 units would, similarly, be produced only with combinations b or c. In a case such as this, input substitution makes no sense. All levels of output would be produced (at points such as a, b, or c) with the same capital-to-labor ratio, the one given by the slope of a line from 0 to c and beyond.

Going Beyond Technology

We can take our analysis a step further and ask which input combination (therefore, which output quantity) would be chosen by a producer facing the technical possibilities summarized by the isoquants given in Figure 6. Various answers are possible, all of which anticipate material introduced in later chapters. We shall, therefore, provide only one possible answer. This answer makes three assumptions: the producer 1) wants to maximize profits, 2) faces prices of inputs and of output that will not vary with the choices the producer makes, and 3) operates with a fixed budget for purchasing the variable input quantities used. Under the circumstances, a producer would spend the fixed budget on that input combination which maximizes physical output and—given output prices—maximizes revenue. Maximum revenue from a given cost implies maximum profit.

The Isocost Line

First determine which input combinations can, in fact, be purchased. Figure 9 imagines a producer who is constrained by a budget of $60,000/year and prices equal to $P_K = \$10{,}000$ per unit of capital and $P_L = \$15{,}000$ per unit of labor.

The producer could buy a yearly maximum of B/P_K or 6 units of capital, K, as shown by point a in our graph ($60,000 per year divided by $10,000 per unit equals 6 units of capital). If the producer bought this quantity, no money would remain to purchase labor L. Alternatively, the producer could buy a yearly maximum of B/P_L or 4 units of labor, L, as shown by point b in our graph ($60,000 per year divided by $15,000 per unit equals 4 units of labor). Line ab is called the producer's **isocost line**; it shows all the alternative quantity combinations of two inputs that the producer is able to buy at current market prices in a given period by fully using a given budget and that, therefore, cost the same amount. The isocost line divides the field of choice into attainable combinations (unshaded) and unattainable combinations (shaded). The producer must select some combination lying on the isocost line (if the budget is to be spent fully) or lying somewhere below it (if the budget is not fully spent). Assume that the budget is to be spent fully.

The absolute value of the isocost line's slope always equals the ratio of two prices—the price of the input measured on the horizontal axis, here P_L, divided by the price of the input measured on the vertical axis, here P_K.

$$|\text{Isocost Line Slope}| = \frac{P_L}{P_K}$$

Figure 9 confirms the slope's absolute value equals 6/4 or 3/2. This relationship can also be calculated as

$$\frac{0a}{0b} = \frac{B/P_K}{B/P_L} = \frac{P_L}{P_K} = \frac{\$15,000}{\$10,000} = \frac{3}{2}$$

The Producer's Optimum

We are now ready to put together the producer's technical opportunities (the isoquant map) and the producer's market opportunities (the isocost line). Thus, we find the optimum choice that a profit maximizing producer is expected to make. Figure 10 shows the isocost line and, beyond it, the shaded world of unattainable combinations of inputs. The

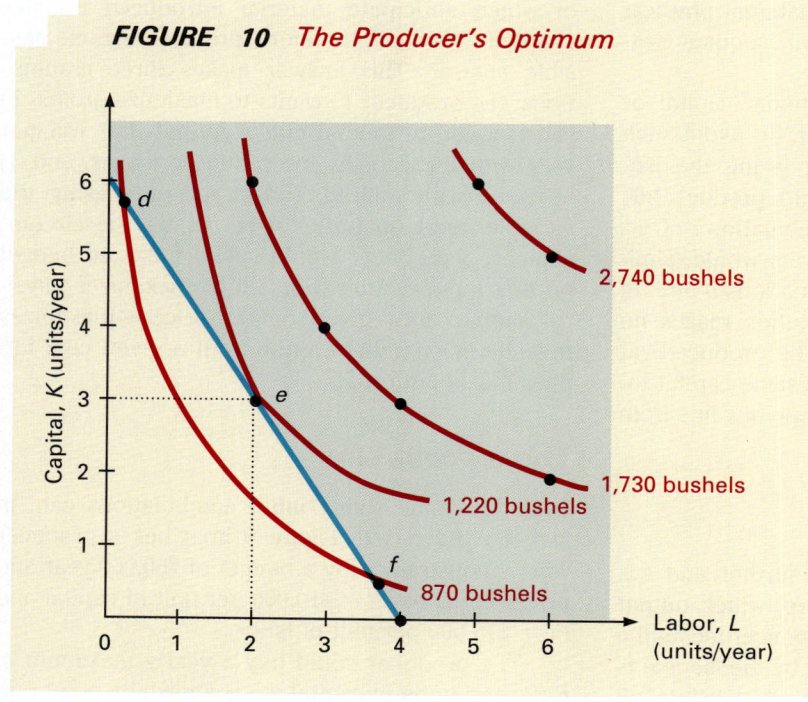

FIGURE 10 *The Producer's Optimum*

A profit-maximizing producer is expected to allocate a given budget to that quantity combination of inputs (here e) that yields the highest possible output (here 1,220 bushels/year).

color isoquants depict the technical possibilities. When fully spending a given budget, the producer will buy some quantity combination of inputs lying on the isocost line; presumably a profit maximizing producer will buy the one combination (here e, consisting of $3K$ plus $2L$) that yields the highest attainable level of output (here 1,220 bushels per year). Given output price, this output yields the highest attainable revenue and thus the highest attainable profit for the assumed budget.

Two additional conclusions should be noted. First, a profit-maximizing producer will reject combinations such as d and f that would exhaust the entire budget but yield lower output (870 bushels/year). Second, at optimum e, the slopes of isocost line and chosen isoquant are equal to one another. From what we learned earlier:

$$|\text{Isocost Line Slope}| = |\text{Isoquant Slope}|$$

$$\frac{P_L}{P_K} = \frac{MPP_L}{MPP_K}$$

Thus, at the optimum:

$$\frac{MPP_L}{P_L} = \frac{MPP_K}{P_K}$$

Profit maximization requires that the marginal physical product *per dollar* of any input be equal to that of any other input. If an extra dollar spent on labor yielded a larger increase in output than an extra dollar spent on capital, it would be wise to spend the dollar on labor rather than capital. Given the law of diminishing returns, this choice would eventually reduce the MPP_L until the above equality was reached.

Key Concepts

equal-product curve
isocost line
isoquant
marginal rate of technical substitution, *MRTS*
production indifference curve

CHAPTER 9

THE COSTS OF PRODUCTION

Preview

This chapter further explains the behavior of firms by connecting physical quantities of inputs and monetary costs. Various categories of costs are introduced, both for the short run (when firms have at least one input that is fixed) and the long run (when firms can freely vary the quantities of all inputs). The study of theoretical cost curves is supplemented by empirical evidence and numerous case studies of cost cutting in the global markets of our time.

Examples

1. Increasing Returns to Scale in Beer Brewing
2. Constant Returns to Scale in Steel Making
3. Mending the Hole in Hollywood's Pocket
4. Producing Cheaper Computers: The Caribbean Connection
5. The Lure of Venezuela's "Liquid Coal"
6. The Internationalization of the Beer Brewing Industry

Ideas in History

The Envelope Curve

Most firms produce goods for the purpose of reaping the largest possible profit for themselves. Managers must identify, from among all the input-output combinations that are technically possible (as summarized by the production function), the one combination that maximizes the difference between revenue and cost. Revenue is brought in by the sale of output; costs are incurred when inputs are purchased.

Recall the important distinction between the *short run* and the *long run*. A time period so short that a firm cannot vary at least one (and, perhaps, even several) of its inputs is the short run. A time period so long that a firm can vary the quantities of *all* of its inputs is the long run. In accordance with these definitions, we can also distinguish short-run and long-run costs.

Short-Run Costs: Tabular Illustrations

Let us pursue the story begun in the last chapter. Having inherited the apple orchard, you and your spouse have quit your former jobs and spent long hours studying the business' data. You now know about the technology of apple growing (the kind of data found in last chapter's Table 1). Beyond that, you are now on your own. You may well decide not to initiate any long-run changes, such as planting more apple trees or inviting bids for the construction of new cold-storage barns. For the time being, let us assume, you decide to stick with grandfather's nonlabor inputs and to choose one of the technically efficient alternatives (A–G) found in the previous chapter. These alternatives are reproduced here as columns (1)–(3) of Table 1. These data lend themselves to calculating three types of costs—fixed, variable, and total.

Fixed Cost

The cost associated with the presence of fixed inputs is called **fixed cost, FC.** It is the monetary value of the fixed inputs used in a period. As long as a firm operates in the short run (when certain inputs cannot be varied and are, therefore, called fixed), fixed cost cannot be escaped. Furthermore, it does not vary with the level of production, even when operations are shut down and production is cut to zero. (In the long run, when all inputs can be varied, fixed cost does not exist.)

Table 2 provides a possible list of costs you have taken on by deciding to run the Crisp Apple Company. There is one **explicit cost,** which is a highly visible cost, that sooner or later involves a payment by a firm to an outside party. In this example, it is a payment to the local government of $5,000 in property taxes. There are three items of **implicit cost,** which is a hidden cost that does not involve a payment and that the owners of a firm incur when using their own resources in their firm "free of charge" rather than hiring them out to collect the maximum possible income available elsewhere.

The magnitude of implicit cost is figured by asking what the firm's owners could have earned from these resources in the *best available* outside alternative. Assume that the orchard (land, trees, equipment, and all) could have been sold for a sum of money that would have yielded $20,000 of interest per year. If it could also have been leased to a

TABLE 1 Short-Run Cost Alternatives

	Inputs per year		Output per year	Costs		
	Fixed[a]	Variable[b]	Maximum total product[c]	Fixed cost[d], FC	Variable cost[d], VC	Total cost[d], TC = FC + VC
	(1)	(2)	(3)	(4) = (1) · $50,000	(5) = (2) · $15,000	(6) = (4) + (5)
A.	1	0	0	50,000	0	50,000
B.	1	1	2,000	50,000	15,000	65,000
C.	1	2	9,000	50,000	30,000	80,000
D.	1	3	14,000	50,000	45,000	95,000
E.	1	4	16,500	50,000	60,000	110,000
F.	1	5	18,000	50,000	75,000	125,000
G.	1	6	18,750	50,000	90,000	140,000

As long as it has some inputs it cannot vary, such as the column (1) unit of orchard, equipment, and management team, a firm operates in the short run. It has a fixed cost for these fixed inputs (column 4). Yet the firm might be able to vary other inputs, such as the column (2) number of workers. Thus it can vary other costs (column 5). By doing so, it can vary its total cost (column 6) as well as its level of production (column 3).
[a]Fixed (in this example) = 1000 apple trees, 2 coldstorage barns, 4 spraying machines, etc.
[b]Variable (number of full-time workers)
[c]bushels of apples
[d]dollars per year

TABLE 2 Calculating Fixed Cost

(a) Explicit costs:	
Property taxes	$ 5,000
(b) Implicit costs:	
Forgone potential interest	20,000
Forgone potential salary (spouse 1)	18,000
Forgone potential salary (spouse 2)	7,000
Total	$50,000

The costs of running a firm include explicit costs and implicit costs, as shown here for the fixed cost of an orchard.

neighbor for $14,000 of rental income per year, the relevant figure, as Table 2 shows, is the $20,000 of forgone interest per year. By running the orchard, you and your spouse are forgoing a potential interest income of $20,000 per year (a sum you would have earned if your decision had been *not* to run the orchard and to do the next best thing, selling rather than leasing the orchard).

By running the orchard, you and your spouse are also forgoing potential salaries of, say, $18,000 per year as a full-time school teacher and $7,000 per year as a part-time editor. Assuming these to be the best possible jobs available to you, these forgone salaries are implicit costs as well. Total fixed cost is $50,000.

Given our decision to run the company for a year, and regardless of how many apples you produce, you are burdened with a $50,000 disadvantage—money that you must pay out (explicit cost) or that you will fail to take in (implicit cost). An entry in every row of Table 1, column (4) indicates the monetary value of the fixed inputs listed in column (1).

Variable Cost

The cost associated with the use of variable inputs is called **variable cost, VC.** It is the monetary value of the variable inputs used in a period. The magnitude of this cost can be varied at the discretion of a firm by changing the quantity of the variable inputs used, and thus the level of output.

In our example, hired workers are the only variable input used; thus, the variable cost depends entirely on the number of workers hired and the prevailing annual wage. Assuming the annual wage to equal $15,000 per worker, we can fill in the data of Table 1, column (5) by multiplying each of the column (2) entries by $15,000.

Total Cost

The cost associated with the use of all inputs—fixed and variable—is **total cost, TC.** It is the sum of fixed and variable costs, as Table 1, column (6) indicates. Looking at Table 1, you can easily see what your total cost of producing any of the column (3) output levels would be. If you select alternative E, you could combine 1 unit of fixed input (consisting of 1,000 apple trees, 2 cold-storage barns, 4 spraying machines, and your husband-wife management team) with 4 hired workers to produce 16,500 bushels of apples this year. Your total cost would be $110,000. Of this amount, $65,000 would be explicit—paid out to other parties: $5,000 in property taxes and $60,000 in wages to workers. Another $45,000 would be your own potential incomes forgone—the implicit costs listed in Table 2.

If your total revenue were equal to the $110,000 total cost, the Crisp Apple Company's *economic profit* would be zero. This would mean that you, the owners, after paying $65,000 to others, would end up with the remaining $45,000—precisely the *same* income—section (b), Table 2—that you could have earned by *not* running the company. Thus, running the business would have given you no advantage over the next best alternative, which is what *zero economic profit* indicates. On the other hand, if total revenue were to equal $150,000 (exceeding total cost by $40,000) or were to equal $90,000 (falling short of total cost by $20,000), the economic profit would be $40,000 or −$20,000, respectively. These results would indicate that the owners' income exceeded the next best alternative (by $40,000) or fell short of it (by $20,000). Accordingly, economists would predict the firm in question to stay in business (when owners take home $85,000 by running the firm rather than Table 2's $45,000 by not running it) or to go out of business (when owners take home $25,000 by running the firm rather than $45,000 by not running it).

Average and Marginal Costs

From the cost data discussed so far, other types of cost can be derived, as shown in Table 3. Columns (1) to (4) of Table 3 reproduce relevant data from Table 1. **Average fixed cost, AFC,** shown in column (5), equals fixed cost, FC, divided by total product, Q. In row B, as long as the orchard produces 2,000 bushels per year (which requires the use of 1 unit of our fixed inputs, imposing a fixed cost of $50,000 per year), the average fixed cost equals $50,000/year divided by 2,000 bushels/year, or $25/bushel. Similar calculations can be made for alternatives C through G by dividing the fixed-cost entry (column 2) by the corresponding total-product entry (column 1). The results are given in column (5) and show a steadily declining average fixed cost as output expands. If a fixed dollar amount (representing the cost of the orchard's fixed inputs) is spread over ever more units of output, a single bushel's share of the fixed total is bound to decline.

Average variable cost, AVC, shown in column (6), equals variable cost, VC, divided by total

TABLE 3 *Short-Run Cost Concepts—An Expanded View*

	Total product, Q (bushels of apples/yr) (1)	Fixed cost, FC (2)	Variable cost, VC (dollars per year) (3)	Total cost, TC (4)	Average fixed cost, $AFC = FC/Q$ (5) = (2)/(1)	Average variable cost, $AVC = VC/Q$ (dollars per bushel) (6) = (3)/(1)	Average total cost, $ATC = TC/Q$ (7) = (4)/(1)	Marginal cost $MC = \dfrac{\Delta TC}{\Delta Q}$ (extra $/extra bushel) (8) = $\dfrac{\Delta(4)}{\Delta(1)}$
A.	0	50,000	0	50,000	?	?	?	
B.	2,000	50,000	15,000	65,000	25.00	7.50	32.50	$\dfrac{+15,000}{+2,000} = 7.50$
C.	9,000	50,000	30,000	80,000	5.56	3.33	8.89	$\dfrac{+15,000}{+7,000} = 2.14$
D.	14,000	50,000	45,000	95,000	3.57	3.21	6.78	$\dfrac{+15,000}{+5,000} = 3.00$
E.	16,500	50,000	60,000	110,000	3.03	3.64	6.67	$\dfrac{+15,000}{+2,500} = 6.00$
F.	18,000	50,000	75,000	125,000	2.78	4.17	6.95	$\dfrac{+15,000}{+1,500} = 10.00$
G.	18,750	50,000	90,000	140,000	2.67	4.80	7.47	$\dfrac{+15,000}{+750} = 20.00$

This table is based on Table 1 and introduces four additional concepts of cost (columns 5 to 8). Note that any type of average cost always equals the *level* of some cost total (FC, VC, or TC, as the case may be) divided by the associated *level* of total product (Q). Marginal cost, as the pointers indicate, always equals the *change* in total cost (ΔTC) between any two input/output alternatives divided by the corresponding *change* in total product (ΔQ).

product, Q. Consider row B. As long as the orchard produces 2,000 bushels per year (which requires the use of one worker, imposing a variable cost of $15,000 per year), the average variable cost equals $15,000/year divided by 2,000 bushels/year, or $7.50/bushel. Similar calculations can be made for alternatives C through G by dividing the variable-cost entry (column 3) by the corresponding total-product entry (column 1). The results are given in column (6) and reveal average variable cost first declining and then rising as total production expands. Given our particular production function (Table 1, columns 1–3), which shows unit increases in worker input yielding at first rising and then falling additions to output, equal $15,000/year additions to wage costs (each of which buys an extra worker) are bound to yield at first falling and then rising average variable cost.

Average total cost, ATC, shown in column (7), equals total cost, TC, divided by total product, Q. In row B, as long as the orchard produces 2,000 bushels per year (which requires the combined use of 1 unit of our fixed inputs plus 1 worker, imposing a total cost of $50,000 + $15,000 = $65,000/year), the average total cost equals $65,000/year divided by 2,000 bushels/year, or $32.50/bushel. Inevitably, this figure also equals the sum of average fixed cost ($25/bushel) plus average variable cost ($7.50/bushel). Similar calculations can be made for alternatives C through G by dividing the total-cost entry (column 4) by the corresponding total-product entry (column 1)—or, more simply, by adding the average fixed cost and average variable cost. The results are given in column (7) and reveal average total cost first declining and then rising as total production expands. This trend reflects the combined influences of steadily declining average fixed cost and of first declining and later rising average variable cost.

Marginal cost, MC, finally, is the *change* in total cost divided by the associated *change* in total product. A change from alternative A to B involves a change in total cost (column 4) from $50,000/year to $65,000/year and a change in total product (column 1) from 0 to 2,000 bushels/year. Marginal cost comes to $+$15,000/year divided by $+$2,000 bushels/year, or $+$7.50/extra bushel. Similar calculations can be made for all the other alternatives, C through G, by always dividing the change in total cost, ΔTC, by the corresponding change in total

FOCUS 1

Major Concepts of Cost

1. Average Fixed Cost
$$AFC = \frac{FC}{Q}$$

2. Average Variable Cost
$$AVC = \frac{VC}{Q}$$

3. Average Total Cost
$$ATC = \frac{TC}{Q} = \frac{FC}{Q} + \frac{VC}{Q} = AFC + AVC$$

4. Marginal Cost
$$MC = \frac{\Delta TC}{\Delta Q} = \frac{\Delta VC}{\Delta Q}$$

product, ΔQ. The results are given in column (8) and reveal marginal cost first declining and then rising as total production expands. Once again, as in the case of average variable cost, this behavior reflects the nature of our particular production function in which marginal physical products are at first rising and later falling as equal units of variable input are added.

Focus 1 summarizes our discussion so far.

Short-Run Costs: Graphical Illustrations

We can learn even more about a firm's costs of production by depicting the output-cost relationships graphically.

Fixed, Variable, and Total Costs

Figure 1 graphs the Table 3, column (2) to (4) cost data against the column (1) total-product data. Panel (a) graphs fixed cost only. The seven dots represent alternatives A through G; the horizontal line connecting them is the orchard's fixed cost; regardless of output produced, it equals $50,000/year.

FIGURE 1 Fixed, Variable, and Total Costs

(a) Fixed cost

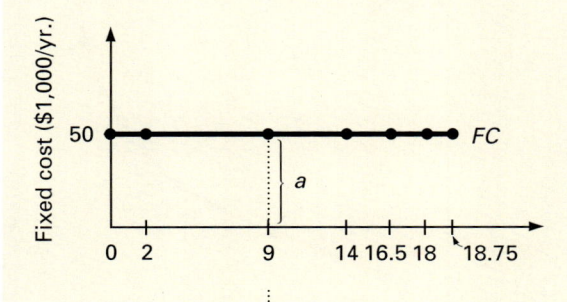

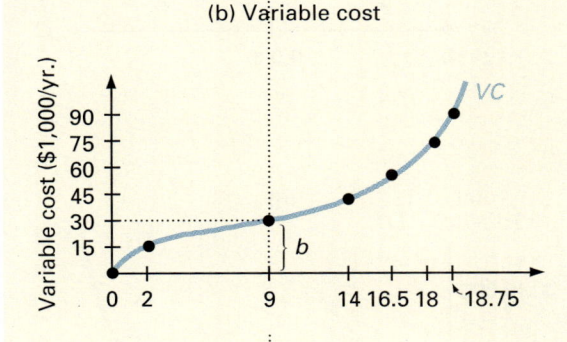

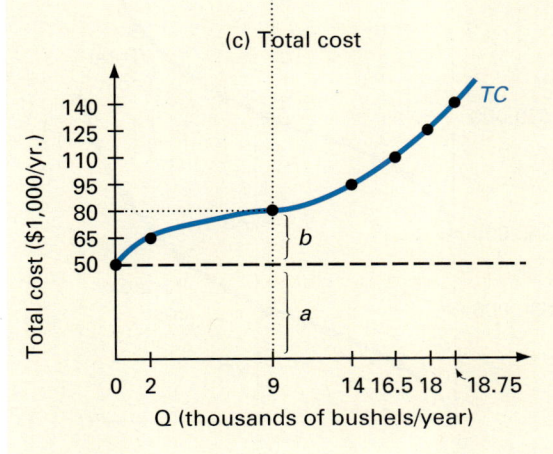

(b) Variable cost

(c) Total cost

Q (thousands of bushels/year)

These graphs provide an illustration of the types of costs in Table 1. Note that total cost equals $50,000 at an output level of zero, revealing fixed costs and indicating that the firm is operating in the short run. (In contrast, a total cost curve starting at origin 0 would indicate the absence of fixed cost and, thus, depict the firm's long-run cost alternatives).

Panel (b) graphs variable cost only. Once again, the seven dots represent alternatives A through G; the smooth line drawn through the dots depicts the rising variable cost as output expands.

Panel (c) graphs the total cost. Each of the seven dots represents the sum of the given output level's fixed plus variable costs. Thus, if output equals 9,000 bushels/year, the total cost equals $80,000/year, which is the sum of the $50,000 fixed cost (a) plus the $30,000 variable cost (b). Note that the panel (a) line of fixed cost reappears as the dashed line in panel (c); the variable cost curve of panel (b) has been placed on top of it to yield total cost.

The Production Function Revisited

The Figure 1 cost curves can also be derived directly from our firm's production function. Examine Figure 2. Panel (a) depicts the orchard's production function, embodied in columns (1) to (3) of Table 1 and first graphed as last chapter's Figure 1. Alternative C has been highlighted by point a: Using 2 units of labor, L yields an output Q of 9,000 bushels of apples/year, given fixed amounts of other inputs and technical knowledge. Panel (b) depicts the identical relationship as panel (a) with the axes reversed.

In panel (c), each variable input quantity has been multiplied by its price, in our case by the assumed price of labor, $P_L = \$15,000$/year. On the vertical axis, the use of 2 workers now shows up as the incurring of 2 ($15,000) = $30,000 of variable cost. As a result, the panel (b) production function turns into the panel (c) variable cost curve. Instead of saying that 2 workers yield 9,000 bushels of output (point a, panel b), we now say that $30,000 of wage cost yields 9,000 bushels of output (point a, panel c).

Panel (d) adds our assumed fixed cost of $50,000/year to the variable cost curve. The resulting total cost curve is precisely the one depicted in panel (c) of Figure 1. You should note, however, that in Figure 1 panel (c), total cost was derived by adding variable cost on top of fixed cost; in Figure 2 panel (d), the same goal is achieved by adding fixed cost on top of variable cost. The $30,000 variable cost of producing 9,000 bushels/year (point a) plus $50,000 of fixed cost, yields $80,000 of total cost (point b).

FIGURE 2 *Production Function and Cost Curves*

(a)

Output, Q (bushels/year)

9,000 — a

Production function

0   2   → Q
Variable input, L (workers/year)

(b)

L

Production function

2 — a

0   9,000   → Q

(c)

Variable cost, VC = L · P_L

2($15,000) = $30,000

Variable cost

0   9,000   → Q

(d)

Total cost, TC = VC + FC

$140,000

$80,000 — b

$50,000   FC

$30,000 — a

VC

Total cost

Variable cost

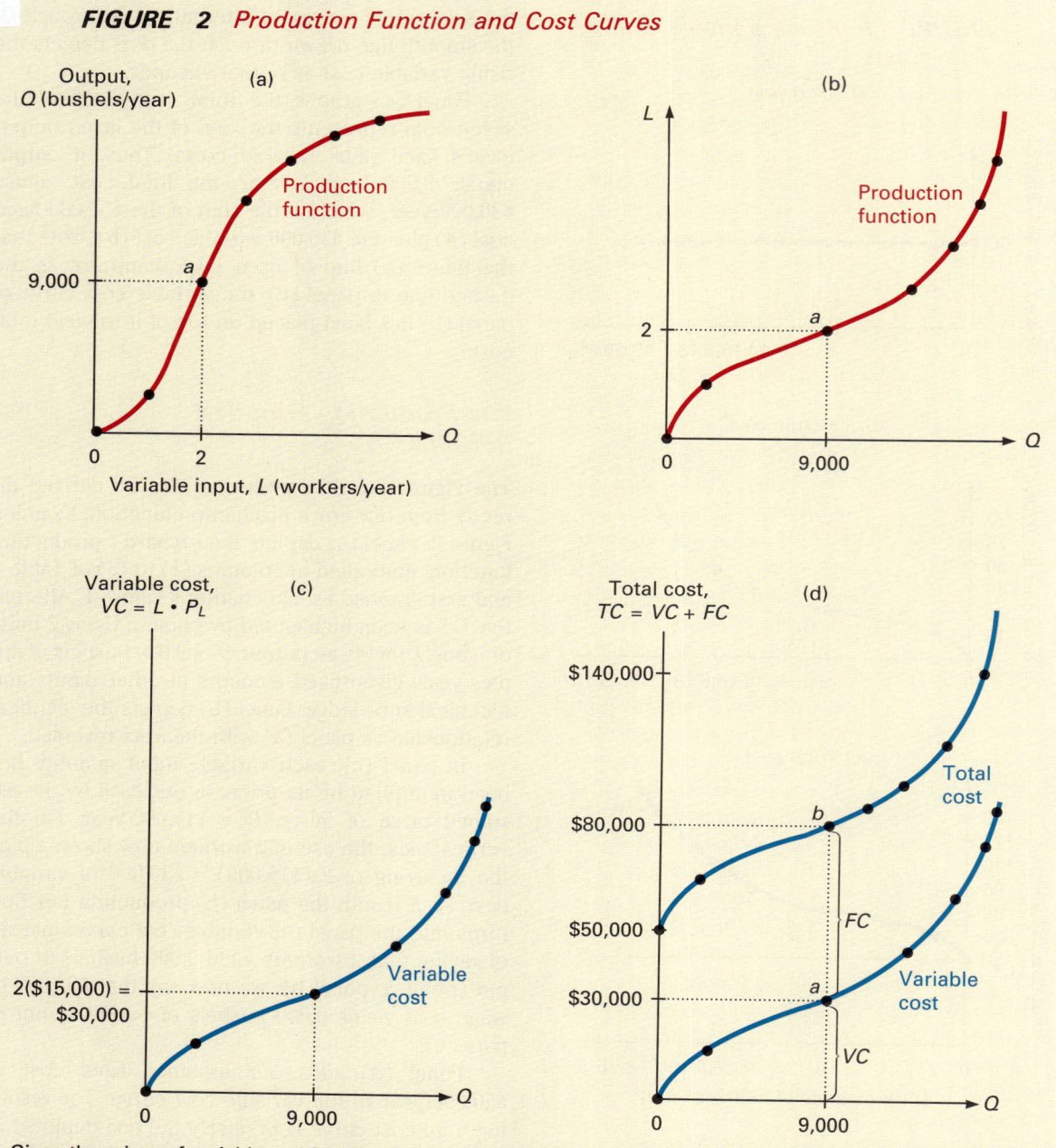

0   9,000   → Q

Given the prices of variable and fixed inputs (here of $15,000 per unit and $50,000, respectively), one can derive the total cost curve by a series of manipulations of the underlying production function.

Average Fixed, Average Variable, and Average Total Costs

Figure 3 graphs our Table 3, columns (5) to (7) average cost data against the column (1) total product data. Note how the curve of average fixed cost declines as output rises (for the reasons noted earlier), while the curves of average variable cost and average total cost are U-shaped. Given that $ATC = AFC + AVC$ (Focus 1), it follows that $ATC - AVC = AFC$; hence, the ever-declining average fixed cost can also be seen by the ever-narrowing gap between the curves of average total cost and average variable cost. At an output of 18,000 bushels/year, average fixed cost equals $2.78/bushel, as shown by distance cd in Figure 3. It is also shown indirectly, however, by distance ab, which is ATC (of $ad =$ $6.95) minus AVC (of $bd = $4.17). In future applications throughout this book, the average fixed cost curve will not be shown because the value of AFC can always be derived by looking at the vertical gap between ATC and AVC.

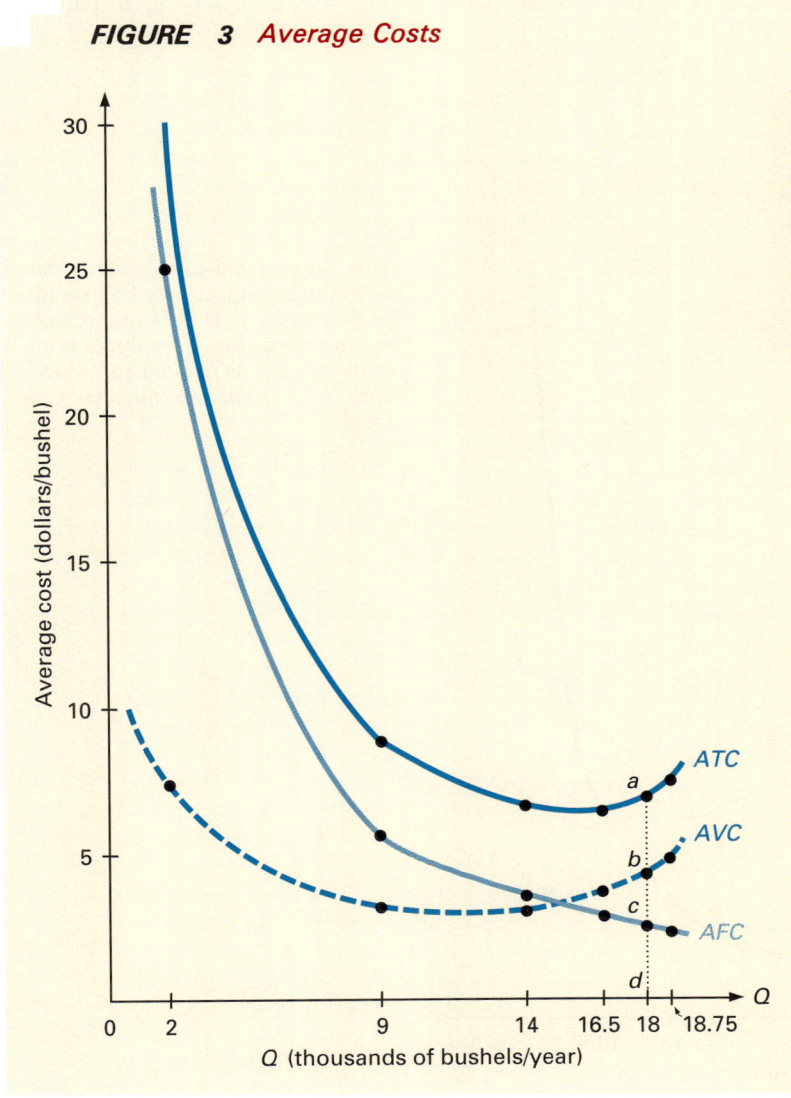

FIGURE 3 *Average Costs*

This graph provides an illustration of the three types of average costs computed in Table 3. Note how average fixed cost can be read directly on the *AFC* line (for example, as distance *cd* when 18,000 bushels/year are produced) or indirectly as the vertical gap between average total cost and average variable cost (for example, as distance *ab*).

Marginal Cost

Figure 4 graphs the Table 3, column (8) data of marginal cost against the column (1) total product data. For comparison, the associated curves of average variable cost and average total cost have been added to the graph. The relationship confirms last chapter's general rule about marginal "anything" and average "anything." As long as marginal cost lies below either average variable cost (to the left of *b*) or average total cost (to the left of *c*), and regardless of whether marginal cost itself is falling or rising as output rises, the average cost in question declines. The moment marginal cost lies above either type of average cost (to the right of *b* or *c*), the average cost in question rises. By implication, the marginal cost curve passes through the minimum points of *AVC* as well as *ATC*.

Key Relationships Among Cost Curves

It is interesting to relate the total and variable cost curves, shown in Figure 1, to the average and marginal cost curves depicted in Figure 4.

Total Cost Versus Marginal Cost

Consider Figure 5. Note that the total cost curve's *slope*, measured by the ratio $\Delta TC/\Delta Q$ in panel (a),

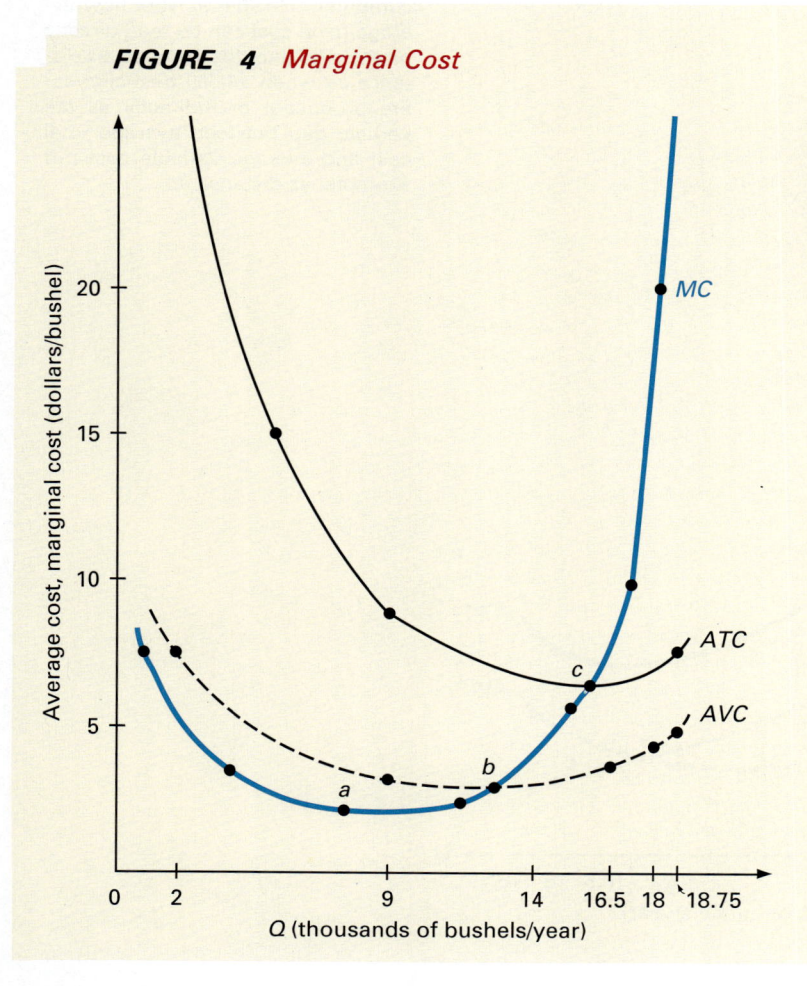

FIGURE 4 *Marginal Cost*

This graph pictures a typical relationship among curves of average and marginal cost. It is no accident that marginal cost goes through the minimum points of average variable cost (at *b*) and average total cost (at *c*).

CHAPTER 9　The Costs of Production　235

FIGURE 5　Total Cost Versus Marginal Cost

(a)

Total cost ($1,000/year) vs Q (1,000 of bushels/yr)

Points on TC curve: a (0, 50), b (2, 65), c (7.6), d (16.5, 110), e (18, 125)

$$MC = \frac{\Delta TC}{\Delta Q} = \frac{+15}{+1.5} = +10$$

$$MC = \frac{\Delta TC}{\Delta Q} = \frac{+15}{+2} = +7.50$$

Point of inflection

(b)

Marginal cost (dollars/extra bushel) vs Q (1,000 of bushels/yr)

Points on MC curve: f (1, 7.5), g (7.6, minimum point), h (17.25, 10)

Marginal cost is nothing but the total cost curve's slope, measured by the ratio $\Delta TC/\Delta Q$.

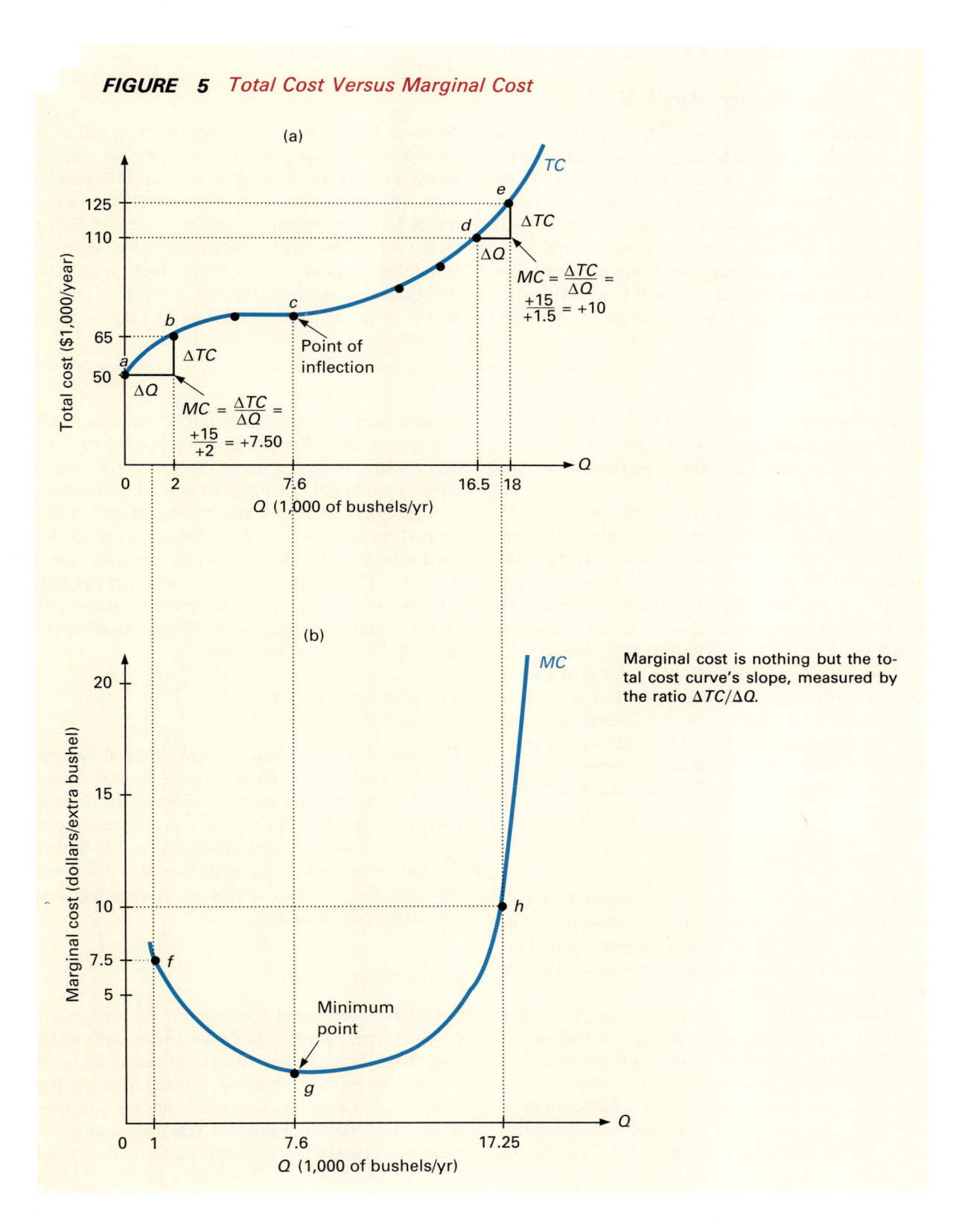

NUMERICAL EXERCISE 1

Calculating Marginal Cost

Example 1: As output in Figure 5 is raised from 0 to 2,000 bushels/year, our firm's total cost rises along section *ab* from $50,000 to $65,000/year. The change in total cost (+$15,000/year) divided by the change in total product (+2,000 bushels/year) comes to +$7.50/bushel and represents the marginal cost in the chosen output range. It is plotted separately (in the middle of that range) in panel (b), which gives us point *f* on the *MC* curve.

Example 2: As output is raised from 16,500 to 18,000 bushels/year, our firm's total cost rises along section *de* from $110,000 to $125,000/year. The change in total cost (+$15,000/year) divided by the change in total product (+1,500 bushels/year) comes to +$10/bushel and represents the marginal cost in that output range. It is plotted separately (in the middle of the range) in panel (b), which gives us point *h* on the *MC* curve.

---

is the marginal cost, measured by the *height* of the *MC* curve in panel (b). (For a review of the concept of slope, see Appendix 1, The Use of Graphs in Economics.)

Figure 5 tells us one more thing. As long as total cost rises at a decreasing rate with higher output, as between *a* and *c*, the point of inflection, the slope of *TC* is falling and so is the level of *MC*, as from *f* to *g* in panel (b). When total cost rises at an increasing rate as output expands, as between *c* and *e*, the slope of *TC* is rising and so is the level of *MC*, as from *g* to *h* in panel (b). The total cost curve's point of inflection (where positive but decreasing slope gives way to positive and increasing slope) therefore corresponds to the marginal cost curve's minimum point. Points *c* and *g* correspond to the identical output quantity (7,600 bushels/year).

Total Cost Versus Average Total Cost

Consider Figure 6. Note that the average total cost of any chosen output level, *TC/Q*, can easily be calculated as the slope of a ray emanating from origin 0 and aiming at the total cost curve right above the output level in question.

Picture a whole series of rays, always originating at 0 in panel (a) and aiming, successively, at points along the total cost curve farther and farther to the right, such as *a*, *b*, and *c*. The ever-changing slope of these rays, traces out the behavior of average total cost as output expands. Note how that slope (*ATC*) continually declines until one ray (0*b* in our example) just touches the *TC* line at a single point, such as *b*. The *ATC* line in panel (b) declines accordingly, as from *g* toward *h*. Yet rays aiming at points to the right of tangency point *b* begin to have ever greater slopes—compare the slope of the dashed ray 0*c* with that of the tangency ray 0*b*. Accordingly, the *ATC* line in panel (b) rises, as from *h* toward *i*. The point of tangency in panel (a) thus corresponds to the minimum point in panel (b). Points *b* and *h* correspond to the identical output quantity (15,800 bushels/year).

Variable Cost Versus Average Variable Cost

The relationship between variable cost and average variable cost can be depicted in a fashion analogous to the previous section's discussion for total cost. The ever-changing slopes of rays emanating at origin 0 and aiming, successively, at points farther and farther to the right along the *variable cost* curve measure the changing levels of average variable cost as output expands.

Long-Run Costs

In this final section of the chapter, we turn to the *long run*. Remember, it is a time period sufficiently long that a firm can vary the quantities of *all* of its inputs. Once again, imagine yourself running the Crisp Apple Company. However cautious you may be in your first year, eventually you may want to expand or contract not only the number of orchard

CHAPTER 9 The Costs of Production

FIGURE 6 *Total Cost Versus Average Total Cost*

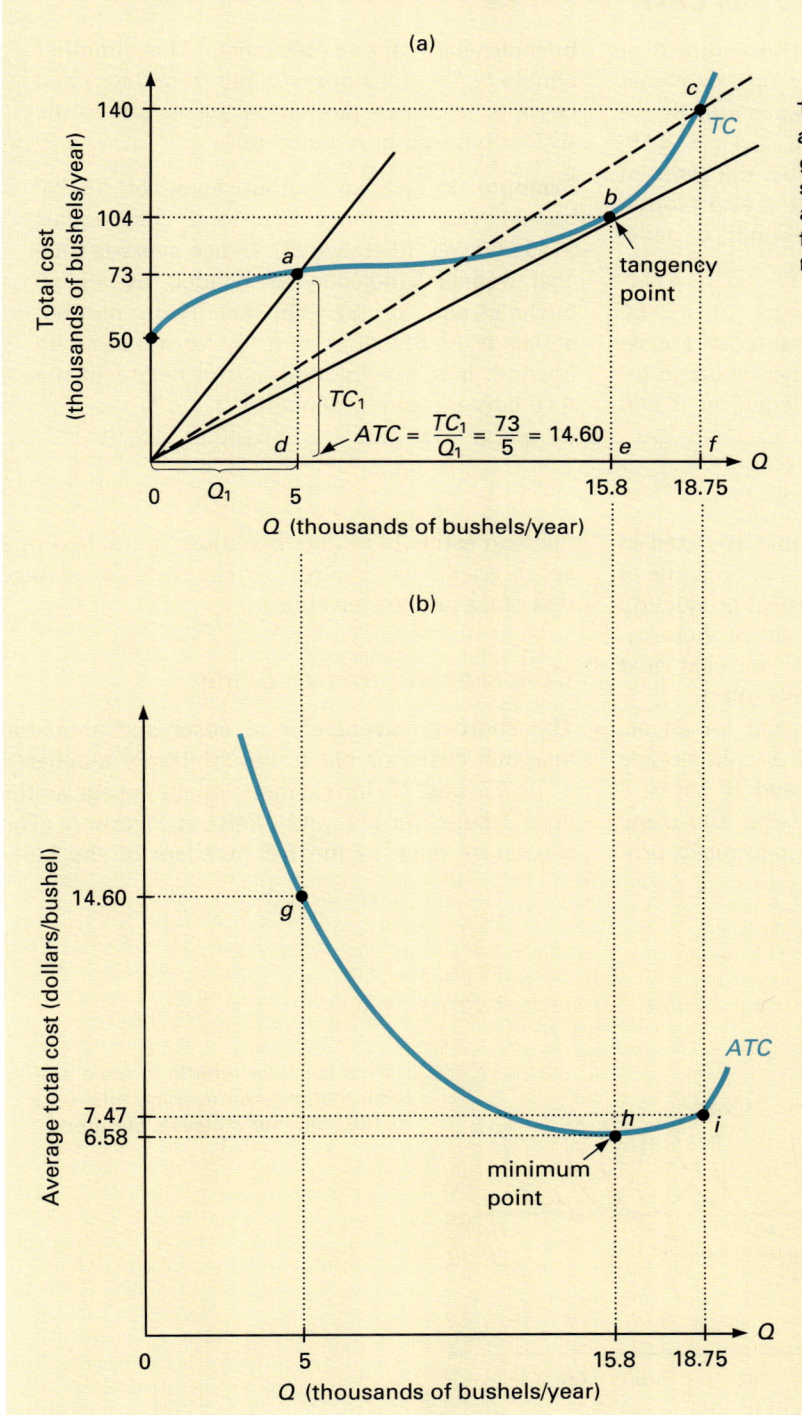

(a)

(b)

The behavior of average total cost as output expands (panel b), can be gauged from the ever-changing slopes of rays emanating at origin 0 and aiming, successively, at points farther and farther to the right along the total cost curve (panel a).

$ATC = \dfrac{TC_1}{Q_1} = \dfrac{73}{5} = 14.60$

NUMERICAL EXERCISE 2

Calculating Average Total Cost

Example 1: At an output level in Figure 6 of $Q = 5,000$ bushels/year (distance $0d$), total cost equals $TC_1 = \$73,000$/year (distance ad). Hence average total cost equals $(TC_1/Q_1) = \$14.60$/bushel. This number equals $ad/0d$, the *slope* of a ray from 0 to a and beyond. It is also plotted as the *height* of the ATC curve—point g, panel (b).

Example 2: At an output level of 15,800 bushels/year (distance $0e$), total cost equals $\$104,000$/year (distance be). Hence average total cost equals $\$104,000$/year divided by 15,800 bushels/year, or $\$6.58$/bushel. This number equals $be/0e$, the slope of a ray from 0 to b and beyond. It is also plotted as the height of the ATC curve—point h, panel (b).

Example 3: At an output level of 18,750 bushels/year (distance $0f$), total cost equals $\$140,000$/year (distance cf). Hence average total cost equals $\$140,000$/year divided by 18,750 bushels/year, or $\$7.47$/bushel. This number equals $cf/0f$, the slope of a ray from 0 to c and beyond. It is also plotted as the height of the ATC curve—point i, panel (b).

---

workers but also the other inputs that are fixed in the short run. Imagine a whole series of orchards of different size, each one being a physical production facility defined by a different-sized set of those inputs that are fixed in the short run and that economists often refer to as the firm's **plant**.

You might, draw up one blueprint for an orchard with 1,000 apple trees and 2 cold-storage barns, another one for 5,000 trees and 10 barns, a third one for 25,000 trees and 50 barns, and many more. For each of these blueprints, you might produce an estimate of data like those in Table 3 or a set of graphs like Figure 1 or Figure 4. Three basic outcomes are conceivable.

Constant Returns to Scale

The short-run average total costs and short-run marginal costs for blueprints arbitrarily numbered 4, 13, 27, and 35, for example, might appear as the lines labeled SRATC and SRMC in Figure 7. (The subscripts refer to the file numbers of the blue-

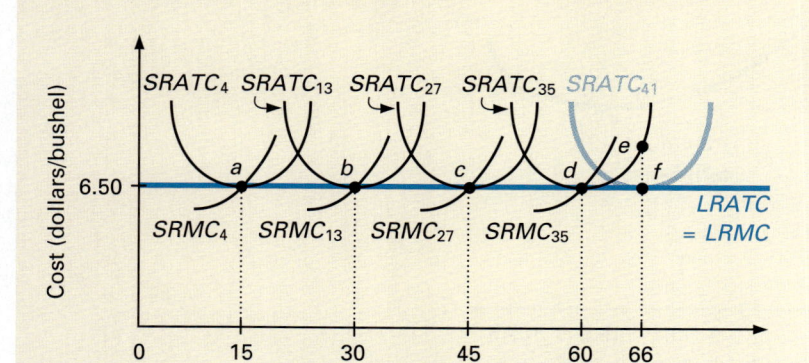

FIGURE 7 Long-Run Costs Under Constant Returns to Scale

When constant returns to scale prevail, the long-run average total cost is the same for all levels of output.

prints: They have only ordinal significance, so larger numbers refer to larger plants.) Figure 7 implies constant returns to scale. Look at each prospective orchard's **capacity output** or (what engineers call) its **optimal rate of plant operation,** which refers to the output level at which a given plant achieves minimum average total cost (points a, b, c, or d, respectively).

By using 1,000 apple trees, 2 cold-storage barns, etc., and by running that plant at capacity, you might be able to produce 15,000 bushels of apples per year at an average total cost of $6.50/bushel (point a). By doubling, tripling, or quadrupling all inputs, you might double, triple, or quadruple physical output as well as total cost. As a result, your *average* total cost would remain unchanged and you would simply move from a to b to c or to d. You might discover that, given enough time to adjust all inputs, *any* output can be produced at the same low $6.50/bushel ATC. Thus, your *long-run* average total cost LRATC is described by a horizontal line. The long-run marginal cost coincides with it. (Marginal above average would pull the average up; marginal below average would pull the average down.)

The line of long-run average total cost is tangent to all the curves of short-run average total cost and indicates the lowest possible average total costs for all conceivable output levels that a firm might produce. It is called the **planning curve.** It was given this name because it helps owners of firms make long-range plans.

CAUTION

Figure 7 must be interpreted with care. Once fixed inputs corresponding to any given blueprint are in place, the average total cost encountered in the short run is shown by the line labeled SRATC. For example, given the existence of plant 35 (which produces 60,000 bushels/year when run at capacity), an output of 66,000 bushels/year can be produced, but only at an average total cost of $7.50/bushel (point e). The orchard would then be said to operate "above capacity." Yet, as the horizontal line of LRATC indicates, one could produce even 66,000 bushels/year at $6.50/bushel (point f), provided a larger plant (blueprint 41) was put in place and run at its capacity.

Increasing Returns to Scale

Figure 8 depicts another possible outcome. As you contemplate larger and larger orchards, you might

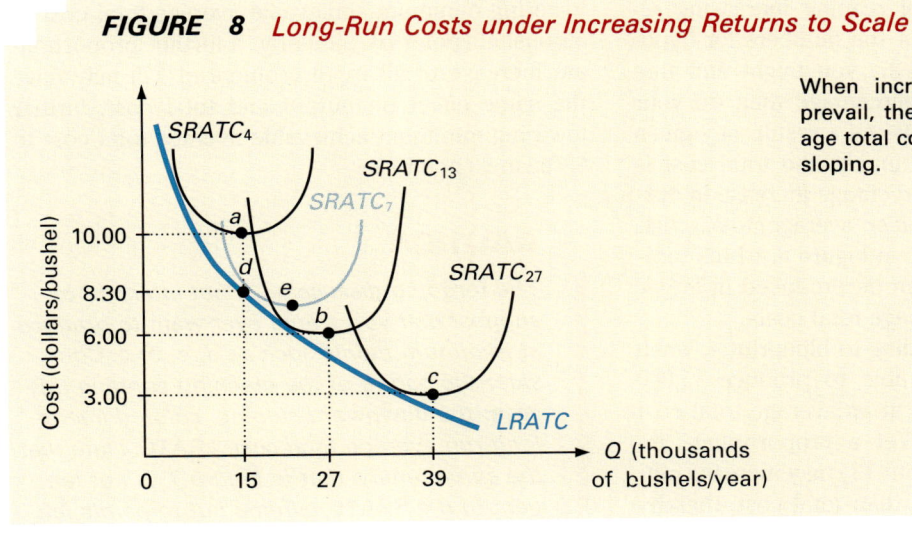

FIGURE 8 Long-Run Costs under Increasing Returns to Scale

When increasing returns to scale prevail, the curve of long-run average total cost (*LRATC*) is downward sloping.

EXAMPLE 1

Increasing Returns to Scale in Beer Brewing

Between 1950 and 1983, the average size of U.S. breweries rose rapidly and their number declined form 369 to 33. One economist, Victor Tremblay, studied the experience of 3 national breweries (Anheuser-Busch, Pabst, and Schlitz) as well as that of 19 regional companies. He estimated and then compared short-run average total costs for 6 different periods and made inferences about long-run costs. He found not only significant economies of scale but also an increase in their prevalence over time. Listed below are some of his findings.

At the level of a single plant:

1. Plant construction costs per barrel of capacity were 35 percent less for a 5 million barrel plant than for a 1 million barrel plant.

2. Increased automation of brew houses reduced labor costs markedly. In 1953, some 64,800 workers helped produce 88.2 million barrels. By 1983, some 29,500 workers produced 195.1 million barrels.

3. Faster packaging equipment lowered average cost. In 1952, a "high speed line" filled 300 12-oz. cans per minute; by 1986, its successor filled 2,000 such cans per minute.

At the level of the firm:

1. Significant cost savings were achieved by multiplant firms that could mount national (rather than regional or local) advertising campaigns.

2. Further savings were reaped after innovations in water treatment made it possible to hold water and beer quality constant across the country. This technology allowed production to be decentralized, while still achieving a homogeneous product. It also served to reduce transportation costs.

Source: Victor Tremblay, "Scale Economies, Technological Change and Firm Cost Asymmetries in the U.S. Brewing Industry," *Quarterly Review of Economics and Business,* Summer 1987, pp. 71–86.

---

discover the possibility of reaping increasing returns to scale. Working out the numbers for hypothetical plants 4, 13, and 27, you might find that output rises by a larger percentage than do your simultaneously rising inputs. As a result, any given percentage increase in all inputs and total cost is associated with a larger percentage increase in output and therefore with *lower* average total cost. Consider points *a*, *b*, and *c* in Figure 8, which indicate how larger outputs can be produced in larger plants with ever lower average total costs.

An orchard corresponding to blueprint 4, when run at capacity, may be able to produce 15,000 bushels of apples per year at an average total cost of $10/bushel (point *a*). Yet a proportionate increase of *all* inputs (blueprint 13) may increase output by a larger percentage than total cost, thereby lowering minimum achievable average total cost to $6/bushel (point *b*). Similarly, a further proportionate increase of all inputs (blueprint 27) may have the same effect on output and total cost, further lowering minimum achievable average total cost to $3/bushel (point *c*).

CAUTION

The forgoing discussion is not intended to suggest that you would ever want *to produce at minimum points such as* a, b, *or* c. *Consider the nature of the planning curve in this case: the downward-sloping, colored line of long-run average total cost,* LRATC. *Note that the curve, unlike that in Figure 7, is not tangent to the* SRATC *minima but to points left* of them. *When increasing returns to scale exist, it is cheaper to produce any given output, such as that corresponding to a, b, or c, by setting up a larger plant and running it* below *capacity than by putting together an appropriately designed smaller plant capable of producing the chosen output level when run at its capacity. For example, if you wanted to produce 15,000 bushels of apples per year, you could set up plant 4 and run it at its capacity, point* a. *Your average total cost would be $10/bushel. But you could also set up plant 7 and run it at* d *(below its capacity at* e*); your average total cost would then be only $8.30/bushel.*

Decreasing Returns to Scale

Figure 9 depicts yet a third outcome. With ever larger orchards, you might discover decreasing returns to scale. Working out the numbers for plants 35, 41, and 59, you might find that output rises by a smaller percentage than your simultaneously rising inputs do. As a result, any given percentage increase in all inputs and total cost is associated with a smaller percentage increase in output and therefore with *higher* average total cost. Consider points *d*, *e*, and *f* in Figure 9, which indicate how larger outputs can be produced in larger plants only with higher average total costs.

An orchard corresponding to blueprint 35, when run at capacity, may be able to produce 48,000 bushels of apples per year at an average total cost of $2/bushel (point *d*). Yet a proportionate increase of all inputs (blueprint 41) may increase output by a smaller percentage than total cost, thereby raising minimum achievable average total cost to $4/bushel (point *e*). Similarly, a further proportionate increase of all inputs (blueprint 59) may have the same type of effect on output and total cost, further raising minimum achievable average total cost to $7/bushel (point *f*).

Once again, this does not mean that you would want to produce at minimum points *d*, *e*, or *f*. Consider the nature of the planning curve in this case: the upward-sloping, colored line of long-run average total cost, *LRATC*. Note that the curve, unlike that in Figure 7, is not tangent to the *SRATC* minima but to points to the right of them. When decreasing returns to scale exist, it is cheaper to produce any given output, such as that corresponding to *d*, *e*, or *f*, by setting up a smaller plant and running it *above* capacity than by putting together an appropriately designed larger plant capable of producing the chosen output level when run at its capacity. For example, if you wanted to produce 77,400 bushels of ap-

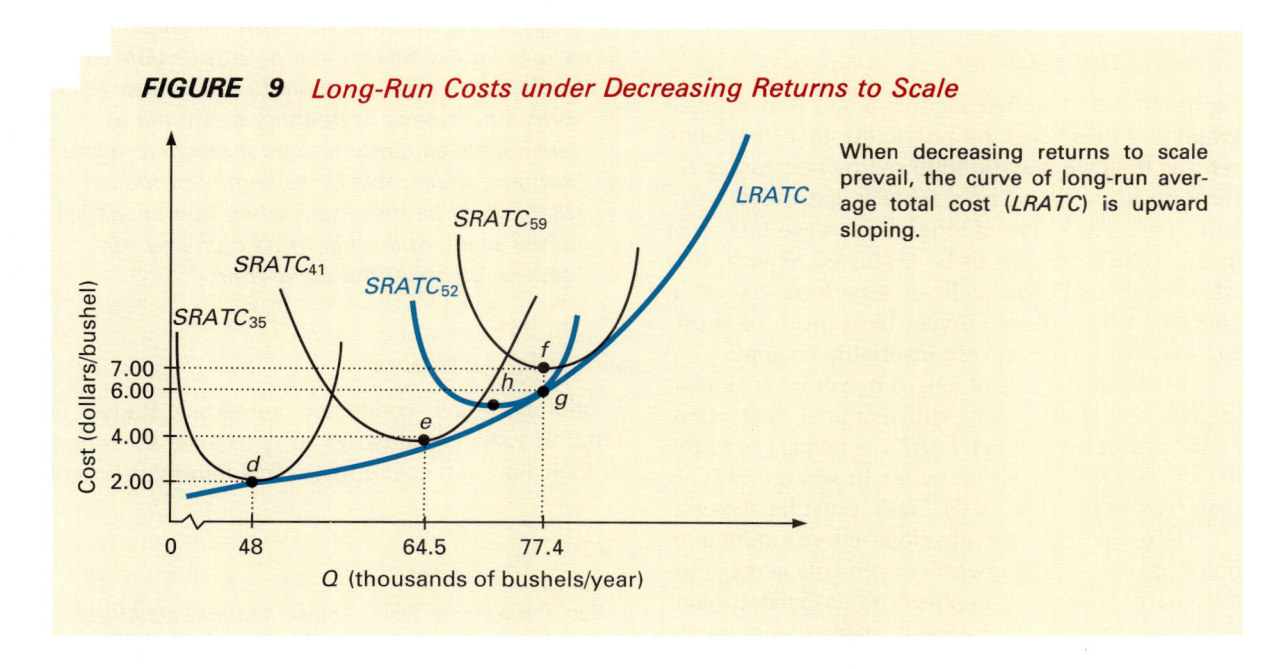

FIGURE 9 *Long-Run Costs under Decreasing Returns to Scale*

When decreasing returns to scale prevail, the curve of long-run average total cost (*LRATC*) is upward sloping.

EXAMPLE 2

Constant Returns to Scale in Steel Making

While increasing returns to scale have contributed to fewer breweries (Example 1), constant returns to scale in steel making have been cited as the reason for a recent explosion in the number of certain types of steel makers.

The production of steel sheets used to be the exclusive province of a few large, integrated steel companies, such as USX Corporation, Bethlehem Steel, LTV Corporation, Inland Steel Industries, Armco, and National Steel.

Since 1979, however, tiny steel firms have seized 25 percent of domestic shipments in the 40 million ton/year market for flat-rolled steel. By remelting scrap and employing nonunion labor, and similar devices, it was discovered that these "minimills" could match the lowest costs achieved by giant firms, at least in the low-quality section of the market that supplies the construction and oil industries. By 1989, when the Nucor Corporation opened its new Crawfordsville, Indiana, plant and Birmingham Steel readied its new Houston plant, the high-quality section of the market (involving appliance manufacturers and the auto industry) was being invaded as well. Analysts predicted that beginning in 1992 one new minimill will be opened in the United States each year.

Source: Rick Wartzman, "Minimills Take Aim at Big-Steel Markets," *The Wall Street Journal,* April 19, 1989, p. B8.

---

ples per year, you could set up plant 59 and run it at its capacity point *f*. Your average total cost would be $7/bushel. Or you could set up smaller plant 52 and run it at *g* above its capacity at *h*; your average total cost would then be $6/bushel only.

The Envelope Curve

Figure 10 puts together Figures 8 and 9 in a single graph and illustrates the possibility that increasing returns to scale may be followed by decreasing returns to scale as a firm's scale is expanded again and again. The curve of long-run average total cost in this case turns out to be U-shaped as well. It is what mathematicians call an **envelope curve,** a curve to which other curves (here those of short-run average total cost) are invariably tangent.

A U-shaped curve of long-run average total cost implies the kind of long-run marginal cost curve *LRMC* drawn here. When *LRATC* is falling (as to the left of *d*), *LRMC* must lie below it; when *LRATC* is rising (as to the right of d), *LRMC* must lie above it.

Note also that the envelope curve's minimum point (*d*) reveals the lowest conceivable average total cost of producing apples. The associated plant (35) that can yield the lowest possible minimum average total cost is called the **optimum plant.**

CAUTION

The downward-sloping section of our LRATC *curve to the left of* d *has been explained by increasing returns to scale and the upward-sloping section to the right of* d *by decreasing returns to scale. As more advanced texts show,[1] other factors can be responsible as well. Some firms manage to lower their input prices by means of quantity discounts as their scale expands; others manage to offset some of their costs by selling by-products that would be discarded when operations are small scale. Still other firms own and run several plants at the same time.*

Empirical Studies

Economists have conducted numerous studies of firms in various industries to determine the shape of their long-run cost curves. This information is of

---

[1] See, for example, Heinz Kohler, *Intermediate Microeconomics: Theory and Applications,* 3rd. ed. (Glenview, IL: Scott, Foresman and Co., 1990), p. 156.

FIGURE 10 The Envelope Curve

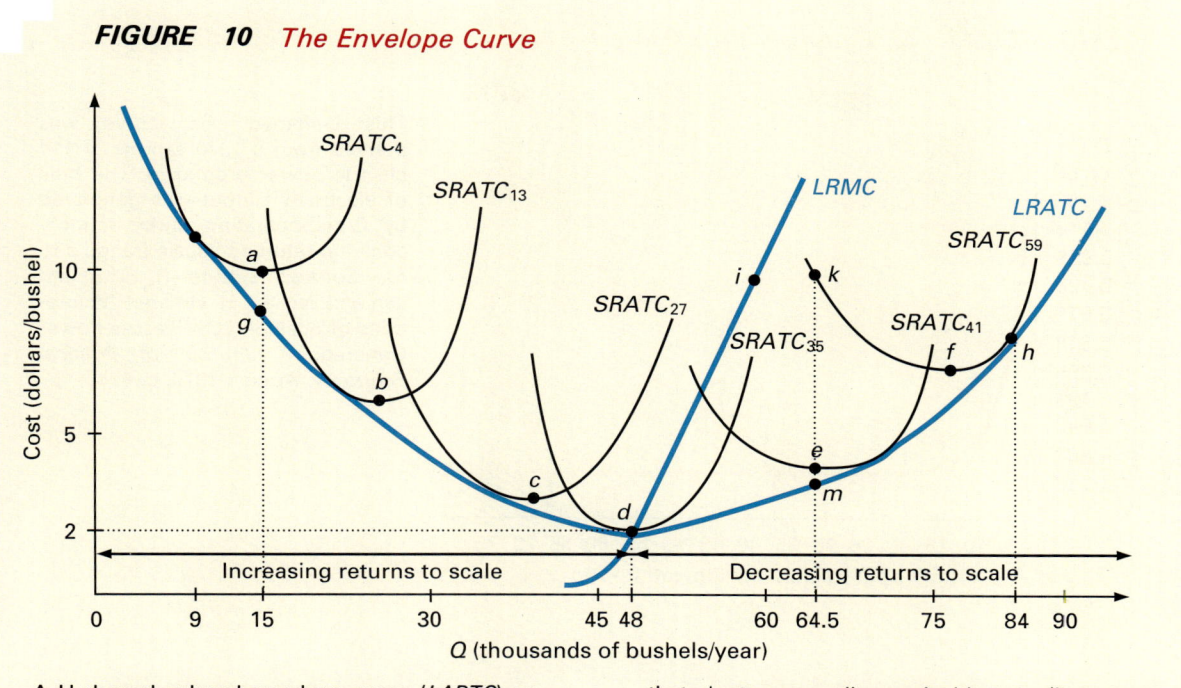

A U-shaped colored envelope curve (LARTC) appears when increases in a firm's scale produce at first increasing and then decreasing returns. The curve envelops all the short-run curves, touching each one only at a single point. The curve's minimum point (here d) reveals the *optimum plant*, or that plant among all conceivable ones (here number 35) with the lowest possible minimum average total cost (here $2/bushel). For more on the subject, see Ideas in History, The Envelope Curve.

interest for a variety of reasons. Such knowledge can help explain the typical size of firms in an industry, which, given demand, explains their number.

If the *LRATC* curve looks like that in Figure 7, one would expect firms of many different sizes to intermingle in an industry. Small firms can easily compete with large firms because all firms achieve the same lowest possible *ATC*. If, on the other hand, the *LRATC* curve looks like that in Figure 10, firms will tend toward a single size, that of the optimum plant. Only a firm of that size (plant 35 in our example) can achieve the lowest possible *ATC*. Even if run at capacity, firms with smaller plants (4, 13, or 27) or larger plants (41 or 59) could never match the low *ATC* of plant 35. Note how points *a*, *b*, and *c* are much higher than *d*, as are points *e* and *f*.

Empirical evidence is overwhelming that long-run average total cost curves are a mixture of our Figures 8 and 7, that is L-shaped, with the horizontal portion of the letter L covering a rather wide range of output. Figure 11 provides an example. Note how increasing returns to scale exist until a certain critical output level is reached at point *a*. That output level, called **minimum efficient scale, MES,** is the lowest output level associated with the long-run average total cost curve at which minimum long-run *ATC* can be achieved. In Figure 11, output above *MES* point *a* is essentially associated with constant returns to scale.

Table 4 provides some interesting data from the mid-1960s. It also highlights the fact that firms can often capture additional cost savings (for example, in administrative, marketing, or transportation expenses) by operating more than one *MES* plant. For more on the subject see Examples 1 and 2.

FIGURE 11 An Empirical Cost Curve

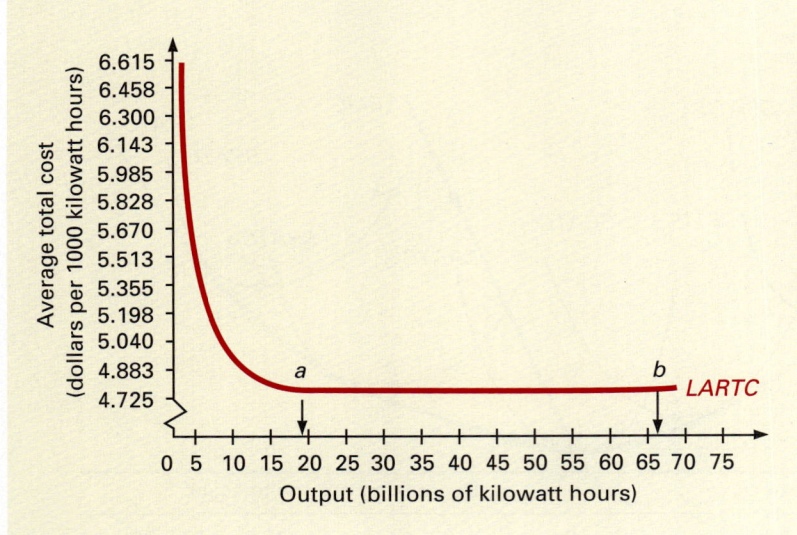

This L-shaped cost curve was derived from a 1970 sample of 114 electric power producers. The bulk of electricity output was generated by firms operating under roughly constant returns to scale (range *a* to *b*). *Source:* Laurits R. Christensen and William H. Greene, "Economies of Scale in U.S. Electric Power Generation," *Journal of Political Economy,* August 1976, p. 674.

TABLE 4 Results of U.S. Cost Studies

Product	Annual output of MES plant	Number of plants owned by MES firm	Annual output of MES firm as percent of U.S. output
Auto batteries	1 million	1	2%
Beer	4.5 million barrels	3–4	10–14%
Broad-woven fabrics	37.5 million square yards	3–6	1%
Cigarettes	36 billion	1–2	6–12%
Paints	10 million gallons	1	1.4%
Refined petroleum	73 million barrels	2–3	4–6%
Refrigerators	800,000	4–8	14–20%
Shoes	1 million pairs	3–6	1%
Steel	4 million short tons	1	3%

The results of the U.S. cost studies given here are easily interpreted. Take beer. At the minimum efficient scale, MES (a point corresponding to *d* in Figure 10 or *a* in Figure 11), a brewery produces 4.5 million barrels/year. A firm can achieve further cuts in costs by combining 3 to 4 such plants under its administration. Such an MES firm will supply 10–14 percent of the U.S. market. Hence there is room for only 7 to 10 such firms in the national market.

SOURCE: F. M. Scherer, A. Beckenstein, E. Kaufer, R. D. Murphy, and F. Bougeon-Maassen, *The Economics of Multi-Plant Operation* (Cambridge, MA: Harvard University Press, 1975), pp. 80 and 336.

Cost Cutting: Recent Developments

In the chapter "The Firm: An Overview," we noted that business managers have strong incentives to keep their costs down. If they allow their cost curves to drift upwards over time, they are reducing their chances to make profit and to keep their jobs. Examples 3–6 in the remainder of this chapter, provide illustrations from recent years that indicate how cost cutting is on every manager's mind.

EXAMPLE 3

Mending the Hole in Hollywood's Pocket

In recent years, Hollywood production costs—for films as well as television shows—have been skyrocketing. Measured in dollars of constant 1980 purchasing power, the *average* cost of making a film rose from $13 million in 1980 to $31 million in 1989. All elements of cost were involved, ranging from camera operators and directors to scripts, stars, and advertising. Consider some of the prices paid: one cameraman's wage rose from $6,000 to $12,000 per week; director Irwin Winkler was paid $1 million for *Basic Instinct,* a film he never even finished. Screenwriter Shane Black got $750,000 for *Lethal Weapon,* then $1.7 million for *The Last Boy Scout.* Arnold Schwarzenegger received $10 million for *Total Recall* and $12 million for *The Terminator II*. The Walt Disney Company spent $46 million to make *Dick Tracy,* then $54 million to advertise it. Makers of television shows have fared no better, regardless of the type of cost involved.

Then major studios fell into Japanese hands. Having acquired CBS Records in 1988, Sony took possession of Columbia Pictures in 1989. In 1990, the Matsushita Electric Industrial Company took over MCA/Universal Studios (see Chapter 4, Example 4, The Guiding Hand of MITI). Before long, Hollywood producers were motivated to control their rising costs.

Television producers are now sending their animation work to Japan, Korea, the Philippines, Taiwan, even mainland China. Plans involve sending more work to Indonesia, Thailand, even Vietnam. The making of a top quality cartoon of the type American children watch on Saturday mornings, for instance, requires hundreds of artists to draw 18,000 separate frames for a half-hour show; a full-length feature, such as Disney's 1989 movie *The Little Mermaid,* requires over 100,000 frames. An Asian worker does such tedious and time-consuming work for a quarter of an American's cost. (Depending on experience, in 1990 a Hollywood animator earned between $750 and $2,000 a week.)

Picture this: In a gray concrete building on a dusty side street in the South China town of Shenzhen, a young woman sits at a metal desk, carefully painting a sketch of Disney's character Baloo the Bear. She speaks no English; she has never traveled anywhere. Yet just weeks later, her work will be seen around the globe. She is among many workers who help produce reasonably priced TV shows, ranging from *The Wizard of Oz* and *Garfield* to *Peter Pan and the Pirates* and even *Teen-Age Mutant Ninja Turtles*.

True enough, sometimes there are slipups. Picture our Chinese worker painting background scenery and characters in a football game. She has never heard of football before. So she paints all the players' uniforms in different colors, and when the quarterback passes the ball to his receiver, the two are wearing different colored uniforms. To the American viewer, this looks like an interception. But all in all, here is a way of cutting costs.

Sources: Barbara Basler, "Peter Pan, Garfield and Bart—All Have Asian Roots," *The New York Times,* December 2, 1990, pp. H35 and H36; and Geraldine Fabrikant, "The Hole in Hollywood's Pocket," *The New York Times,* December 10, 1990, pp. D1 and D4.

EXAMPLE 4

Producing Cheaper Computers: The Caribbean Connection

St. Kitts, the pastoral Caribbean island of mountainous rain forests and sugar-cane covered hillsides, also houses half a dozen factories that do not fit into the scenery at all. They help the U.S. electronics industry control its costs. Inside those factories, workers twist tiny copper wires into transformers and mount fingernail-sized parts onto computer circuit boards. Eventually, these products end up back in the U.S. Thus, in 1989, U.S. electronics imports from Caribbean countries ranged from $83.6 million (Dominican Republic) to $11.3 million (St. Kitts) to $2.1 million (Netherland Antilles).

Each year companies like Allen Bradley, General Electric, Intel, and Westinghouse import well over $250 million of electronics components from the Caribbean, often paying minimum wages such as those in Table A. This trade has been encouraged by governments on both sides. In the Caribbean, there are 10- to 15-year corporate tax holidays for foreign investors, along with low-priced leases on government plants, and government-financed training for employees. On the U.S. side, there is the Caribbean Basin Initiative, which allows duty free entry of many products assembled abroad by U.S. firms.

TABLE A Minimum Wages in 1990

Jamaica	$0.27/hour
Dominican Republic	0.50/hour
St. Kitts	1.08/hour
Netherland Antilles	1.18/hour

Sources: Jim McNair, "Caribbean Still Holds Low-Cost Lure for U.S. Manufacturers," *Chicago Tribune,* November 4, 1990, p. 12D; United States International Trade Commission, *International Economic Review,* August 1991, p. 5.

EXAMPLE 5

The Lure of Venezuela's "Liquid Coal"

With oil prices soaring, electric power companies have been seeking relief in alternative fuels. Venezuela's *Orimulsion* seems to fit the bill. The product has been marketed since 1990 and consists of a bitumen and water emulsion that is liquid and easy to handle like oil but is priced closer to coal. (The 1990 average price of Orimulsion was $1.20 a barrel compared to heavy fuel oil #6 that cost $19 a barrel and did precisely the same thing.)

The new product comes from the dry, flat plains of northeastern Venezuela, where extra heavy crude oil and bitumen lie in abundance some 500 to 4,000 feet below the surface. When heated salt water is forced into the deposits and pumped up, a material close to Orimulsion is at hand. By 1996, Venezuela expects to produce 700,000 barrels a day; already it has identified 1.2 trillion barrels of deposits.

Power plants in Canada, Britain, and Japan have successfully tested the "liquid coal." It can be burned like oil, but requires smokestack scrubbers to catch sulfur emissions that can cause acid rain. Still, despite the new investments, the Florida Power and Light Company estimates saving $3–5 billion over the next 15 years. Power companies in Maine, Massachusetts, and Virginia were looking to cut costs in the same way.

Source: James Brooke, "Venezuela Pushing 'Liquid Coal,'" *The New York Times,* October 16, 1990, pp. D1 and D2.

EXAMPLE 6

The Internationalization of the Beer Brewing Industry

In recent years, increasing returns to scale (noted in Example 1) and trade barriers have both contributed to an internationalization of beer brewing. Three developments illustrate the point.

First, where the quantity demanded abroad has been relatively small compared to that demanded domestically, breweries have increased their domestic production, taken advantage of the lower average costs shown in Figure 8, and have exported the product. As a result, world trade in beer has risen rapidly from $149 million in 1965 to $2.08 billion in 1987. Table A shows the five largest exporters and importers in 1987.

Second, where the quantity demanded abroad has been relatively large compared to that demanded domestically, lowest costs have often been achieved by licensing foreign brewers to produce and market the product of a domestic brewer. Thus, knowledge was traded for royalties, and direct exports were avoided. This process also made it easy to circumvent trade barriers, to cut transportation costs (beer is 90 percent water), and to solve the problem of limited shelf life by saving time lost during transportation. Thus, Anheuser-Busch licensed Guinness to brew Budweiser in Ireland; similar licenses were granted to Labatt in Canada, National in Israel, Oriental in Korea, and Suntory in Japan. In 1990, some 30 such agreements were in effect throughout the world.

Third, where trade barriers were high, direct investment abroad was preferred. This approach was often reinforced by lower labor costs, lower energy costs, and fewer government regulations. Thus, Australia's Elders IXL owns Courage Lt. in Britain and Carling O'Keefe in Canada; Australia's Bond owns Pittsburgh Brewing and G. Heileman. Tatsuuma-Honke and Asahi of Japan set up plants in Colorado. Most of the trade barriers so overcome have been nontariff barriers. One example, Canada has employed discriminatory markups against foreign beer at its provincial liquor outlets and discriminatory marketing techniques as well, including smaller packages and no refrigeration for foreign beer, a 1988 GATT study pointed out.

Source: Jeffrey D. Karrenbrock, "The Internationalization of the Beer Brewing Industry," The Federal Reserve Bank of St. Louis, *Review,* November/December 1990, pp. 3–19.

TABLE A *World Beer Trade in 1987 (in 1,000 HL)*

Exporters		Importers	
1. Netherlands	5,725	1. United States	10,991
2. Germany	5,706	2. Great Britain	4,093
3. Czechoslovakia	2,698	3. France	2,446
4. Belgium	2,537	4. Italy	2,163
5. Canada	2,416	5. Germany	1,302

1HL = 100 liters = 26.4 gallons

IDEAS IN HISTORY

The Envelope Curve

Here is a story that will warm your heart. It concerns a now famous Canadian economist who introduced economists to the envelope curve. Jacob Viner (1892–1970) was born in Montreal and studied at McGill and Harvard. For many decades, he taught economics, first at the University of Chicago, later at Princeton. His presidency of the American Economic Association in 1939 was only one of a large number of honors bestowed upon him (among them honorary degrees from thirteen institutions of higher learning).

Viner's major interest was international trade, but among microeconomists, Viner is best known for his brilliant article on "Cost Curves and Supply Curves," which appeared in the *Zeitschrift für Nationalökonomie* (September 1931, pp. 23–46). In this article, Viner introduced much of the material contained in this chapter, but he also made a single famous mistake (which should not detract from his achievement). Attempting to produce a graph such as this chapter's Figure 10, he instructed his draftsman to draw a smooth curve of long-run average total cost in such a way that it passed through all the minimum points of short-run average total cost (such as *a* through *f*) without ever rising above any short-run curve. His draftsman objected that this could not be done. Viner insisted; the result was a rather impossible graph.

Viner had confused the minimum short-run average total cost achievable in a given plant (such as *a* for plant 4 or *f* for plant 59) with the minimum long-run average total cost achievable for a given rate of production (such as *g* for 15,000 bushels/year or *h* for 84,000 bushels/year). The latter may well require the underutilization or overutilization of some plant. Two decades later, when his justly famous article was readied for reprinting, Viner declined the opportunity to revise it.

I do not take advantage of the opportunity [to revise] . . . . The error in Chart IV is left uncorrected so that future teachers and students may share the pleasure of many of their predecessors of pointing out that if I had known what an "envelope" was I would not have given my excellent draftsman the technically impossible and economically inappropriate assignment.[1]

---

[1] "Supplementary Note (1950)" in American Economic Association, *Readings in Price Theory* (Chicago: Irwin, 1952), p. 227.

Source: Adapted, with permission, from Heinz Kohler, *Intermediate Microeconomics: Theory and Applications,* 1st. ed. (Glenview, IL.: Scott, Foresman and Co., 1982), p. 164.

Summary

1. This chapter brings us closer to understanding the behavior of firms by making connections between physical quantities of inputs and monetary costs. Thus, the monetary value of fixed inputs used in a period is that period's fixed cost; the monetary value of variable inputs used is variable cost; their sum is the firm's total cost. From these short-run concepts of cost other categories can be derived, including average fixed cost, average variable cost, average total cost, and marginal cost.

2. The various relationships between output and each category of short-run cost are also pictured graphically.

3. Long-run costs are the costs encountered by a firm when there is sufficient time to vary the quantities of *all* inputs, thus, none of them are fixed. Long-run cost curves are derived for situations of constant, increasing, and decreasing returns to scale. The theoretical cost curves are supplemented by empirical evidence. Empirical studies have shown many real-world cost curves to be L-shaped, revealing a sequence of first increasing and then constant returns as scale is expanded.

4. A variety of examples illustrate how cost cutting works in the global markets of our day.

Key Concepts

averaged fixed cost, *AFC*
average total cost, *ATC*
average variable cost, *AVC*
capacity output
envelope curve
explicit cost
fixed cost, *FC*
implicit cost
marginal cost, *MC*
minimum efficient scale, MES
optimal rate of plant operation
optimum plant
planning curve
plant
total cost, *TC*
variable cost, *VC*

Questions and Problems

1. Look again at Table 1. Determine what would happen to fixed cost, variable cost, and total cost if
    a. the price of fixed inputs rose (or fell).
    b. the price of variable inputs rose (or fell).
    c. the quantity of fixed inputs were smaller (or larger)—given technical knowledge.
    d. technical knowledge advanced (or regressed).

   In each case, what would happen to the entries in columns (4) to (6) and how would these changes affect Figure 1?

2. Consider the following production function. Then assume the price of fixed inputs to be $10,000, while that of variable inputs is $20,000/unit. Calculate fixed, variable, and total costs.

	Fixed inputs	Variable inputs	Output
A.	1	0	500
B.	1	1	900
C.	1	2	1,200
D.	1	3	1,400
E.	1	4	1,500

3. Reconsider Problem 1 and your answer to it. Now determine, in each case, what would happen to the curves of average fixed cost, average variable cost, and average total cost in Figure 3.

4. Reconsider Problem 2 and your answer to it. Then calculate average fixed cost, average variable cost, average total cost, and marginal cost.

5. Consider Table 2.
   a. How would you adjust the entries if you learned that the husband-wife team worked twice as many hours in their own business as they did earlier in their outside jobs?
   b. What if they would gladly *pay* $2,000 per year just for the privilege of being their own bosses?

6. Mr. A: "Marginal cost is alleged to equal the change in total cost divided by the associated change in total product. It is so calculated in column (8) of Table 3. Yet, when I calculate the change in *variable* cost divided by the associated change in total product, I get the same results. I am confused."
   Ms. B: "You are right. I am stumped, too."
   Comment on this exchange.

7. Invent a numerical example that shows how the law of diminishing returns is related to rising marginal costs.

8. Consider the accompanying figure. Then identify:
   a. the marginal cost curve.
   b. the average total cost curve.
   c. the average variable cost curve.
   d. the average fixed cost curve.
   e. the capacity output level.
   f. the planning curve.

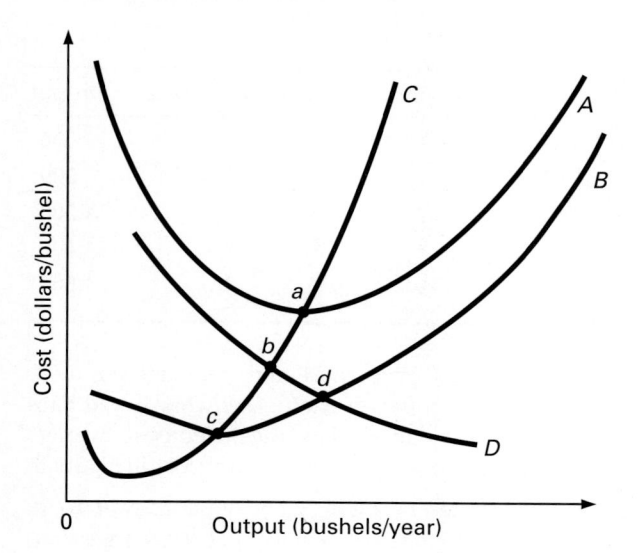

9. Reconsider Figure 6. Then use the data contained in this chapter
   a. to draw a similar graph, entitled Variable Cost Versus Average Variable Cost.
   b. to explain your graph verbally.

10. Are each of the following true or false?
    a. If marginal cost were to fall with higher output, average total cost would have to fall.
    b. The total variable cost at any output level equals the sum of marginal costs up to that output level.
    c. If the apple orchard discussed in this chapter were run by a surgeon, its fixed cost would be higher.
    d. The minimum point on a curve of short-run average total cost shows the lowest average total cost of production for a given fixed cost.
    e. The long-run average total cost curve shows the lowest possible average total cost for producing any given output when the firm has time to make all the adjustments in input combinations it wants to make.
    f. The slope of a straight short-run total cost line equals marginal cost.
    g. The slope of a straight short-run total cost line equals average variable cost.
    h. The slope of a straight short-run total cost line equals average total cost.

11. Have another look at Figure 8. When plant 4 is replaced by plant 13, and assuming physical input quantities change by the same percentage as does total cost, what is the percentage change in inputs between *a* and *b*? The percentage change in output?

12. Have another look at Figure 9. When plant 35 is replaced by plant 41, and assuming physical input quantities change by the same percentage as does total cost, what is the percentage change in inputs between *d* and *e*? The percentage change in output?

13. Have another look at Figure 10. Using any Figure 9 data, calculate the precise value of *LRMC* in the 48,000 to 64,500 bushel range.

14. "Depending on the size of its plant, a firm's average total cost of producing any given output

level can take on many different values." Evaluate. (Hint: Look at Figure 10.)

15. The accompanying table contains data for several short-run average total cost curves. Graph these curves; then draw in a long-run average total cost curve.

16. If you have read the appendix to the previous chapter, draw an isoquant map and isocost lines to show why the total cost of producing a given output in the long run may be lower than in the short run.

	Plant #1			Plant #2			Plant #3			Plant #4	
Point	Q	SRATC	Point	Q	SRATC	Point	Q	SRATC	Point	Q	SRATC
A	200	12.0	F	500	8.7	M	1,000	6.0	T	1,530	11.0
B	230	9	G	590	5.7	N	1,210	3.5	U	1,640	9
C	650	6.8	H	770	3	P	1,530	2.3	V	1,800	7.3
D	1,120	10	I	1,110	3	Q	1,760	4	W	2,330	9.2
E	1,200	12	K	1,480	5.8	R	1,880	6	X	2,400	12
			L	1,700	10.8	S	1,970	8			
			N	1,210	3.5						
			U	1,640	9						

PART III

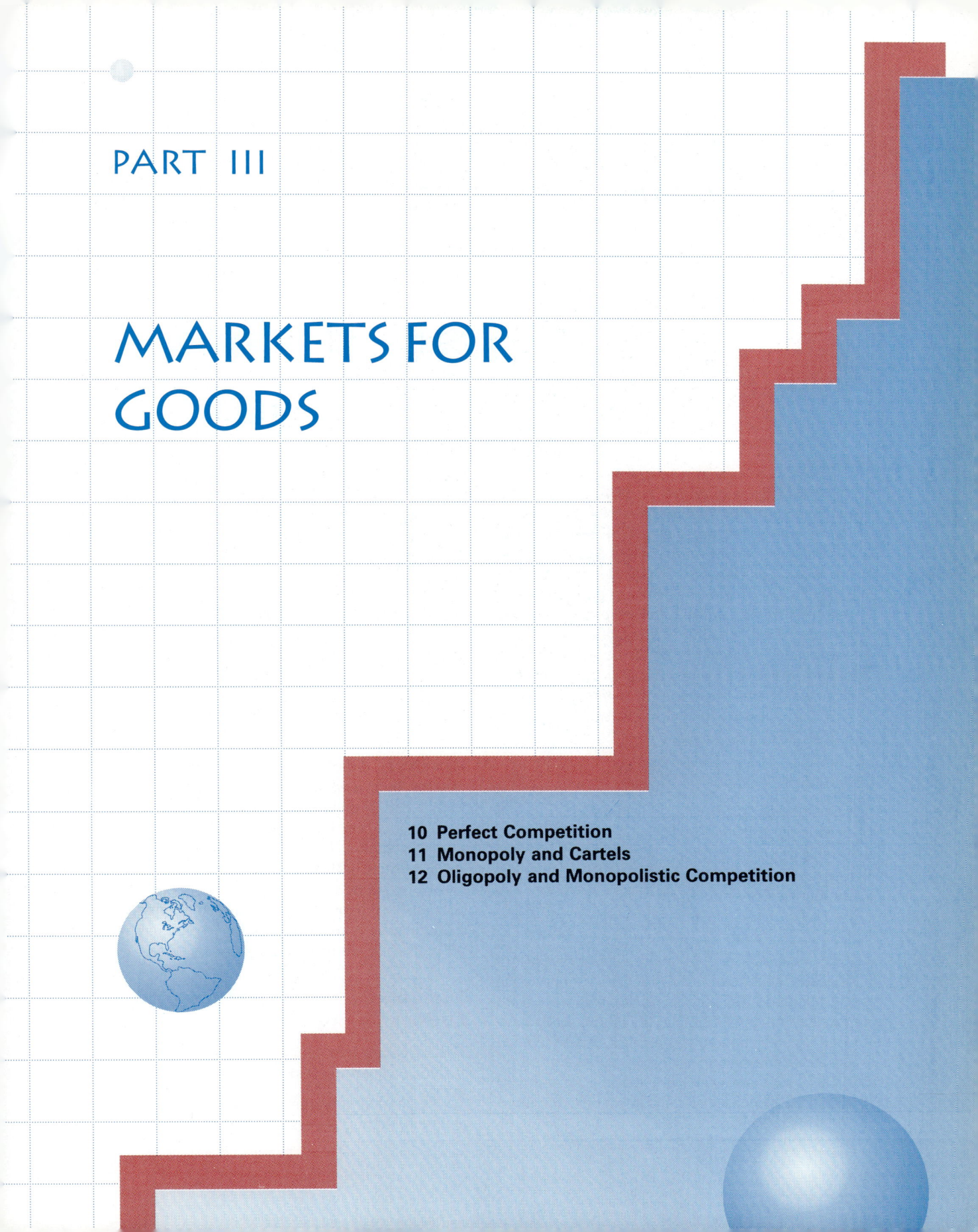

MARKETS FOR GOODS

10 Perfect Competition
11 Monopoly and Cartels
12 Oligopoly and Monopolistic Competition

CHAPTER 10

PERFECT COMPETITION

Preview

A market is said to be perfectly competitive when it contains a large number of independently acting buyers as well as sellers, when buyers view all the units of the traded item as identical regardless of its source, when traders possess full knowledge relevant to trading, and when entry into and exit from the market is free to all. This chapter discusses the profit-maximizing behavior of firms in such an environment. It explores the long-run fate of industries in the presence of profits and losses and the question of what makes this type of market structure "perfect."

Examples:

1. Shakespeare, Dickens, and Hillegass
2. Broadway and the Bottom Line
3. Struggling for Profits in Electronics
4. Eggs with Less Cholesterol?
5. Big Farms Try Organic Methods

In the long run, the minimum efficient scale of firms and the size of market demand at prevailing prices influence the number of firms in any given market. Economists often classify all the firms operating in a given market and producing an identical or similar product as members of the same **industry.** They then describe the market or industry structure on the basis of various criteria, the number of firms being one.

Varieties of Market Structure

The major characteristics of a market or industry that determine how it is organized are said to define the **market structure** or **industry structure.** They include the following:

1. The number of firms operating in the market
2. The nature of the product traded
3. The degree to which market knowledge is available to traders
4. The conditions of entry into or exit from the market

Markets can differ with respect to any one of these criteria; thus, a wide variety of market types potentially exist. (If each criterion had only two different values, such as "few firms versus many firms" for criterion number 1, there could be 16 different market structures.) This chapter and the next two discuss four major types of market structure: perfect competition, monopoly and cartels, oligopoly, and monopolistic competition. Table 1 provides a preview of what will be discussed.

The Characteristics of Perfect Competition

The following four characteristics define a market structure called **perfect competition:**

1. The market contains a large number of independently acting buyers as well as sellers.

TABLE 1 Varieties of Market Structure

Major type	Distinguishing characteristics				Example
	Number of firms	Nature of product	Extent of market knowledge	Conditions of entry and exit	
A. Perfect competition	many	homogeneous	perfect	free	wheat farmers
B. Monopoly/cartel	one	homogeneous	limited	restricted	electric power companies
C. Oligopoly	few	homogeneous or differentiated	limited	restricted	auto producers
D. Monopolistic competition	many	differentiated	limited	free	restaurants

This table summarizes characteristics of major types of market structure.

2. Buyers view all units of the traded item as identical regardless of the source of its supply.

3. Buyers as well as sellers possess full knowledge relevant to trading in the market.

4. Nothing impedes entry into or exit from the market for either buyers or sellers.

These characteristics are listed in row A of Table 1; they will now be discussed in greater detail.

A Large Number of Independently Acting Buyers and Sellers

Perfect competition requires that the number of buyers as well as sellers in a given market be large and that each of these traders act independently of all the others. This condition raises the question of the meaning of largeness: Do we need 10,000 buyers and 10,000 sellers? Would 5,000 buyers and 300 sellers do as well? Where does "smallness" end and "largeness" begin?

Economists consider the number of buyers or sellers to be large when the ordinary transactions of any one trader do not affect the price at which exchanges take place. Think of yourself as buying apples. Given the amounts you are likely to buy in a week, month, or year, your actions will not affect the prevailing price. If the supermarket price is $5/bushel, you can buy 1 bushel, 7 bushels, or none at all; the price will remain the same. Think of the typical orchardist anywhere; even the largest of them sells an insignificant percentage of the nation's crop. Whether that orchardist sells 10,000 bushels/year, 70,000 bushels/year or none at all, the going price will be virtually unchanged.

Many markets exist in which the number of buyers as well as of sellers is large in the sense just noted. Therefore, many markets conform to the first criterion of perfect competition. In such markets, all participants are **price takers** who must take or leave the price that the forces of demand and supply have established and who cannot influence that price by any individual actions of their own. Consider the organized commodity exchanges. In places like the Chicago Board of Trade, the Minneapolis Grain Exchange, or New York's Coffee, Sugar, and Cocoa Exchange all kinds of products are traded—ranging from wheat, soybeans, and pork bellies to coffee, plywood, and gold—and no single buyer or seller can do a thing about the prevailing price. The same is usually true in many other markets that do not involve goods, such as markets for stocks, bonds, and foreign exchange. Any single buyer or seller of IBM stock, U.S. bonds, and French francs is a price taker as well.

Yet, as the next two chapters will show, and rows B to D of Table 1 anticipate, there are other markets for goods or resources in which the number of buyers or sellers is small (possibly because large numbers of them act in collusion) and in which individual traders often do have the power to push prices down or up. For example, on the selling side, think of electric power companies, auto producers, the OPEC cartel, or labor unions.

Virtual Identity of Different Units of Traded Item

Perfect competition also requires that all the different units of a given traded item are considered identical by buyers and are, thus, interchangeable. Because each unit is seen as a perfect duplicate of every other unit, buyers do not care from which particular seller they acquire the units they buy.

The markets for many agricultural and mining products (such as cotton, potatoes, or wheat; bauxite, iron ore, or petroleum) fit this description fairly well. So do many financial markets, such as those for stocks, bonds, or foreign exchange. Typically, buyers do not care whether the wheat about to be purchased was grown by farmer Jones or farmer Smith. Nor do buyers of IBM stock care whether the shares they acquire come from the broker downtown or the neighbor next door.

Under such circumstances, advertising by any one seller, designed to take customers away from other sellers in the same market, makes no sense. Picture farmer Jones taking out ads—in magazines and newspapers, renting billboards along highways, buying radio and television time, sending letters to thousands through the mail, or even employing an army of traveling salespeople—just to tell everyone that "Farmer Jones's wheat is the best." People would ridicule Jones for wasting all that money in a futile campaign.

Yet again, as later chapters will show, and rows C and D of Table 1 anticipate, other markets exist in which the traded goods or resources are far from homogeneous. Think of automobiles or restaurants, of doctors, lawyers, and other types of labor. In many such markets advertising is common, and it does make sense because buyers care very much about the exact source of their supply.

Full Knowledge Concerning the Market

Perfect competition requires that all buyers and sellers are fully aware of the existence of potential trading partners and of the qualities and prices of goods and resources traded. Once again, the commodity exchanges or the organized stock, bond, and foreign exchange markets are examples of institutions that spread the relevant knowledge to all. The Chicago Board of Trade standardizes quality by carefully defining the unit of any traded item. Thus, a unit of plywood, every trader in that market knows, equals "a boxcar of 36 banded units of 66 pieces each (2,376 pieces), sized 48″ by 96″ (76,032 square feet total), four- or five-ply, half-inch thick, exterior glue 32/16, free on board, Portland, Oregon." Specialists continually compare prices and quantities offered and asked and then equate demand and supply in the market. All potential traders can watch the ticker tape announcing the current equilibrium price—all these data being transmitted within seconds to numerous places around the country and often around the world.

Yet, there are other markets to be discussed and exemplified by rows B to D of Table 1, in which market knowledge is limited because contact between potential buyers and sellers is less organized and communication among them is sporadic rather than continuous. Thus, traders have to find each other through a lengthy process of *search,* and even then uncertainty remains. Might there be other sellers willing to sell for less? Might there be other buyers willing to pay more? Is the quality of traded items really what sellers claim?

Unrestricted Entry into and Exit from the Market

Perfect competition requires that anyone, at any time, is free to become a buyer or seller in a given market and can do so on the same terms as existing traders. Similarly, anyone is able to stop being a buyer or seller in the market at any time. Such a condition, once again, holds in the market for wheat, iron ore, IBM stock, and many more, but it is by no means a characteristic found everywhere.

New and smaller firms may have a cost disadvantage relative to established larger firms when there are increasing returns to scale (a situation depicted in last chapter's Figure 8, "Long-Run Costs Under Increasing Returns to Scale," and typical in the electric power industry). Market entry might also be restricted by government licensing (taxicabs in many cities) or by quotas (foreign sellers of sugar or of labor). Similar restrictions can exist with respect to market exit. Union contracts sometimes contain provisions against plant closings. Many state and local laws require 90-day notices concerning plant closings and impose various exit penalties, such as worker severance pay. Rows B and C of Table 1 cover these possibilities.

The Firm's Revenue: Total, Average, and Marginal

The perfectly competitive firm, like any firm, seeks to maximize the difference between total revenue and total cost and thus to earn the largest possible profit. In order to understand a perfectly competitive firm's behavior, we must focus on the alternatives it faces with respect to revenue and cost. Half of that task was completed in the last chapter; we now turn to the other half.

The physical quantities of inputs used, when multiplied by input prices, translate into a firm's costs. The cost curves derived apply fully to any firm, including the perfectly competitive firm. The next step is to note that the physical quantity of output produced, when multiplied by the output price, translates into a firm's revenue. To illustrate what is involved, we turn again to our apple orchard example and consider Table 2. Column (1) reproduces the output quantities associated with technically efficient input/output combinations A through G, which we encountered with the production function. Assume that a perfectly competitive apple market establishes an equilibrium price of $10/bushel. Being a price taker, your ultimate input/output choice will not affect this price; hence you can multiply the given market price of $10 by each of the alternative output quantities of column (1) to find associated alternative values of total revenue (column 2). **Total revenue, TR,** is the market price, P, multiplied by total product, Q.

Average revenue, AR, shown in column (3), equals total revenue, TR, divided by total product, Q. In row B, as long as the orchard produces 2,000 bushels/year (which sell at $20,000/year), average revenue equals $20,000/year divided by 2,000 bushels/year, or $10/bushel. Note $AR = P$ because $TR = P \cdot Q$ and $AR = (TR/Q)$.

Marginal revenue, MR, finally, is the *change* in total revenue divided by the associated *change* in total product. A change from alternative A to B involves a change in total revenue from $0/year in row A to $20,000/year in row B of column (2) and a change in total product from 0 in row A to 2,000 bushels/year in row B of column (1). Marginal revenue is +$20,000/year divided by +2,000 bushels/year, or +$10/extra bushel. Similar calculations can be made for alternatives C through G by dividing the change in total revenue, ΔTR, by the corresponding change in total product, ΔQ. The results are given in column (4) and reveal an important fact. *A perfectly competitive firm's marginal revenue, like its average revenue, is always equal to the market price.*

Figure 1 tells this story graphically. Panel (a) depicts demand and supply lines in the apple market (of the type discussed in Chapter 4). The market's equilibrium price equals $10/bushel (point E). From the point of view of an individual firm (which

---

FOCUS 1

Major Concepts of Revenue Under Perfect Competition

1. Total Revenue

$$TR = P \cdot Q$$

2. Average Revenue

$$AR = \frac{TR}{Q} = \frac{P \cdot Q}{Q} = P$$

3. Marginal Revenue

$$MR = \frac{\Delta TR}{\Delta Q} = P$$

where P is the market-determined output price, which an individual firm cannot influence.

TABLE 2 *Concepts of Revenue*

	Total product, Q (bushels of apples/yr) (1)	Total revenue, $TR = P \cdot Q$ ($/yr) (2) = $10 \cdot$ (1)	Average revenue, $AR = \frac{TR}{Q} = \frac{P \cdot Q}{Q} = P$ ($/bushel) (3) = $\frac{(2)}{(1)}$	Marginal revenue, $MR = \frac{\Delta TR}{\Delta Q} = P$ (extra $/extra bushel) (4) = $\frac{\Delta(2)}{\Delta(1)}$
A.	0	0	?	
				$\frac{+20,000}{+2,000} = 10$
B.	2,000	20,000	10	
				$\frac{+70,000}{+7,000} = 10$
C.	9,000	90,000	10	
				$\frac{+50,000}{+5,000} = 10$
D.	14,000	140,000	10	
				$\frac{+25,000}{+2,500} = 10$
E.	16,500	165,000	10	
				$\frac{+15,000}{+1,500} = 10$
F.	18,000	180,000	10	
				$\frac{+7,500}{+750} = 10$
G.	18,750	187,500	10	

This table is based on the production function of our apple orchard example from the chapter, "The Technology of Production." It introduces three revenue concepts. Total revenue, *TR*, is simply market price *P* multiplied by total product *Q*. Average revenue, *AR*, always equals the *level* of total revenue (*TR*) divided by the associated *level* of total product (*Q*). Inevitably, average revenue equals the market price *P*. (If $TR = P \cdot Q$ and $AR = (TR/Q)$, then $AR = P$.) Marginal revenue, on the other hand, as the pointers indicate, always equals the *change* in total revenue (ΔTR) between any two output alternatives divided by the corresponding *change* in total product (ΔQ). For a perfectly competitive, price-taking firm, this value always equals *P* as well.

cannot influence price), the price is a given, as shown by the horizontal line in panel (b). The firm can sell all it wants at the $10 price. It need not (and presumably will not) sell for less. It cannot sell a single bushel for a penny more (because buyers can find all the bushels they want from other sellers for $10). In short, our firm can sell 1 bushel or 2,000, it can sell 9,000 bushels or 14,000; the price will always be the same. As the horizontal line in panel (b) indicates, each bushel will sell for pre-

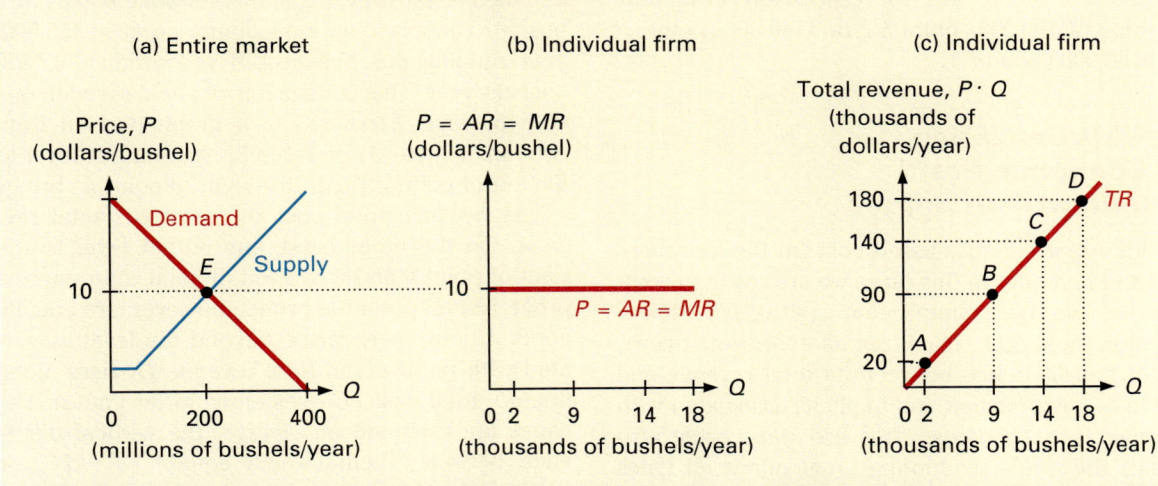

FIGURE 1 The Perfectly Competitive Firm and Its Revenue

(a) Entire market — Price, P (dollars/bushel) vs Q (millions of bushels/year); Demand and Supply intersect at point E at price 10, quantity 200 (with 400 shown on axis).

(b) Individual firm — $P = AR = MR$ (dollars/bushel); horizontal line at 10 across Q (thousands of bushels/year) with marks at 0, 2, 9, 14, 18.

(c) Individual firm — Total revenue, $P \cdot Q$ (thousands of dollars/year); TR is a straight line through origin with points A (2, 20), B (9, 90), C (14, 140), D (18, 180).

The forces of demand and supply in a perfectly competitive market establish an equilibrium price, such as $10/bushel at point E (panel a). This price becomes a given for any individual firm. Each and every unit can be sold at that price; thus the height of the horizontal line in panel (b) measures not only the market's equilibrium price, but also the firm's average revenue and marginal revenue. By implication, the perfectly competitive firm's line of total revenue is a straight line, such as TR in panel (c). Its slope measures price, average revenue, and marginal revenue at the same time.

cisely $10. Therefore, the average revenue will be $10; so will marginal revenue (each *extra* bushel will bring an extra $10).

As panel (c) indicates, a perfectly competitive firm's total revenue line must be a straight line starting at the origin of the graph. Because each and every unit sells for precisely the same amount ($10 in our example), total revenue rises in perfect proportion to quantity sold. If 1 bushel is sold, total revenue is $10; if 2 bushels are sold, it equals $20;

NUMERICAL EXERCISE 1

Calculating Average Revenue and Marginal Revenue

The total revenue line's slope simultaneously measures what is shown separately in panel (b): price, average revenue, and marginal revenue. Consider the average revenue associated with any one of the four quantities listed on the horizontal axis of panel (c). Whether we figure $AR = (TR/Q)$ as the ratio (in thousands) of 20/2 (point A), 90/9 (point B), 140/14 (point C), or 180/18 (point D), the answer is the same (and equal to the price): $10/bushel.

Similarly, consider the marginal revenue between any two output quantities. The value of $MR = (\Delta TR/\Delta Q)$ always equals $10/bushel as well. If output rises from 9,000 to 14,000 bushels/year, total revenue rises from $90,000 at B to $140,000 at C. Thus, $MR = (+\$50,000/+5,000)$, or $10/bushel. If output falls from 9,000 to 2,000 bushels/year, total revenue falls from $90,000 at B to $20,000 at A. Thus, $MR = (-\$70,000/-7,000)$, or again $10/bushel.

and if 2,000 bushels are sold, it equals $10 times 2,000, or $20,000 (point *A*). By the same token, 9,000 or 14,000 or 18,000 bushels, respectively, bring total revenue of $90,000 (point *B*), or $140,000 (point *C*) or $180,000 (point *D*).

The Maximization of Economic Profit and Short-Run Supply

Having separately discussed cost (in the last chapter) and revenue (in this one), we are ready to combine the two. We examine what a perfectly competitive firm must do to maximize its **economic profit, Π,** or the difference between its total revenue and the total cost (explicit and implicit) associated with producing that revenue. This economic profit also equals the firm's accounting profit minus all types of implicit cost not considered in its computation, notably the value of resource services supplied to the firm without pay by its owners. Profit maximization can be achieved by applying the optimization principle that was introduced in Chapter 1.

> *To maximize economic profit in the short run (when some of its inputs are fixed), a perfectly competitive firm must adjust its rate of production until the rising marginal cost of production equals the given marginal benefit of production (which is nothing else but the market-determined price of its output). There is, however, one exception to the rule: If its total revenue is insufficient to cover variable cost, the firm does better by shutting down and producing nothing at all.*

Following is a series of examples that utilize the data of our orchard business.

A Profitable Business

Table 3 summarizes earlier data concerning the orchard business. By comparing total revenue and total cost, we determine the total profit associated with each output alternative. From column (4), it is apparent that an output level between alternatives *E* and *F* is ideal from a profit-maximizing point of view. The same conclusion is reached from applying the optimization principle and comparing the marginal benefit of production directly with the marginal cost (columns 5 to 7).

Figure 2 illustrates what happens in the orchard business if the production function and cost data assumed so far prevail and market price equals $10/bushel. You can reap a maximum profit of $55,500/year running this business, if you produce 17,250 bushels/year. This conclusion can be derived in one of two ways. Panel (a) is a graph derived from columns (1) to (3) of Table 3.[1] Any output level to the left of point *a* (or to the right of point *d*) brings a loss because total cost then exceeds total revenue. On the other hand, any output level to the right of point *a* and to the left of point *d* produces a profit. Not all potential profits, however, are equally good. As output is raised beyond the level associated with point *a* and total revenue *TR* rises along line *ab*, total cost *TC* rises along lower line *ac*. Because lines *ab* and *ac* diverge, the vertical difference between them (which equals *TR* − *TC*, or profit, Π) gets larger, reaching a maximum of *bc* = $55,500/year at an output of 17,250 bushels/year. If output is raised beyond that level, profit does not immediately disappear, but it does decline. Note how lines *bd* and *cd* then *converge;* so the vertical difference between them (profit, Π) declines with larger output.

The optimum output volume thus involves total revenue of $172,500/year (distance *bf*), total cost of $117,000/year (distance *cf*), and an economic profit of $55,500/year (distance *bc*). It is important to remember what these numbers represent. If you were to prepare an income statement (and if last chapter's data still held), it would look like this:

Income Statement, Crisp Apple Company, 1992

Sales revenue		$172,500
Costs		
Property taxes	$ 5,000	
Wages	67,000	72,000
Taxable accounting profit		$100,500

---

[1] The total revenue line is a graph of Table 3, column (2) versus (1): the total cost line, a graph of column (3) versus (1). The table's row A, column (3) entry—total cost at a zero output—reveals fixed cost equal to $50,000/year. Hence variable cost equals the column (3) entries minus $50,000.

TABLE 3 Maximizing Profit

Total product, Q (bushels of apples/yr)	Total revenue, TR	Total cost, TC	Profit, Π	Marginal revenue, $MR = \frac{\Delta TR}{\Delta Q} = P$	Marginal cost, $MC = \frac{\Delta TC}{\Delta Q}$	Advice given by optimization principle
	(dollars per year)			(dollars per extra bushel)		
(1)	(2) = $10(1)	(3)	(4) = (2)−(3)	(5) = $\frac{\Delta(2)}{\Delta(1)}$	(6) = $\frac{\Delta(3)}{\Delta(1)}$	(7)
A. 0	0	50,000	−50,000			
				10	7.50	
B. 2,000	20,000	65,000	−45,000			
				10	2.14	P > MC, expand output
C. 9,000	90,000	80,000	+10,000			
				10	3.00	
D. 14,000	140,000	95,000	+45,000			
				10	6.00	
E. 16,500	165,000	110,000	+55,000			
				10	10.00	P = MC, output optimal, profit maximized
F. 18,000	180,000	125,000	+55,000			
				10	20.00	P < MC, contract output
G. 18,750	187,500	140,000	+47,000			

This table combines revenue and cost data concerning our orchard business. The data are based on the production function introduced in the chapter, "The Technology of Production," as well as on assumed market prices of inputs and output ($50,000 per unit of fixed input, $15,000 per unit of variable input, and $10 per bushel of apples). As columns (4) and (1) suggest, the profit-maximizing level of output lies somewhere between alternative E and F. This outcome is shown more clearly by comparing marginal benefit and marginal cost in columns (5) and (6). Note that any firm's marginal benefit from production equals its marginal revenue, but in the case of a perfectly competitive firm this, in turn, equals the market price. In this case, MB = MR = P; and profit is maximized when P = MC.

Yet the $100,500 figure would not contradict the $55,500 figure calculated in the preceding paragraph. As last chapter's Table 2, "Calculating Fixed Cost," indicates, we assumed that you could have earned interest and wage income of $45,000 outside the orchard business. Thus we included this amount as a fixed, implicit cost of running the business. In this example, you are earning $100,500/year (and must pay taxes on it), but you are only earning $55,500/year more than you would have earned elsewhere. This *extra* income from running the business is what economic profit indicates. When it is positive, as in this case, you are doing well. Your gamble on forgoing the best alternative to run the orchard has paid off. Example 1 provides a real-world example of this kind of situation.

262 PART III *Markets for Goods*

FIGURE 2 A Profitable Business

(a)

Revenue, cost, profit ($1,000/yr)

- 200 — *d*
- 172.5 — *b* — Total cost
- 150 — Π — Maximum profit
- Total revenue
- 117.0 — *c* — Variable cost
- 100 — FC
- 67.0 — *e*
- 50 — *a*
- VC
- *f*
- 0 2 9 14 16.5 ↑18 20 — Total product (thousands of bushels/year)

Profit-maximizing output: 17.25

TR:	$172,500	= *bf*
− FC:	50,000	= *ce*
− VC:	67,000	= *ef*
= Π :	55,500	= *bc*

(b)

Price, cost (dollars/bushel)

- 20
- 15
- 10.00 — A ——————— B — Marginal revenue = price
- Marginal cost
- ≈ 6.78 — C ——— D — Average total cost
- 5 — E — FC — Average variable cost
- ≈ 3.88 — F
- VC — G
- 0 2 9 14 16.5 ↑18 20 — Total product (thousands of bushels/year)

Profit-maximizing output: 17.25

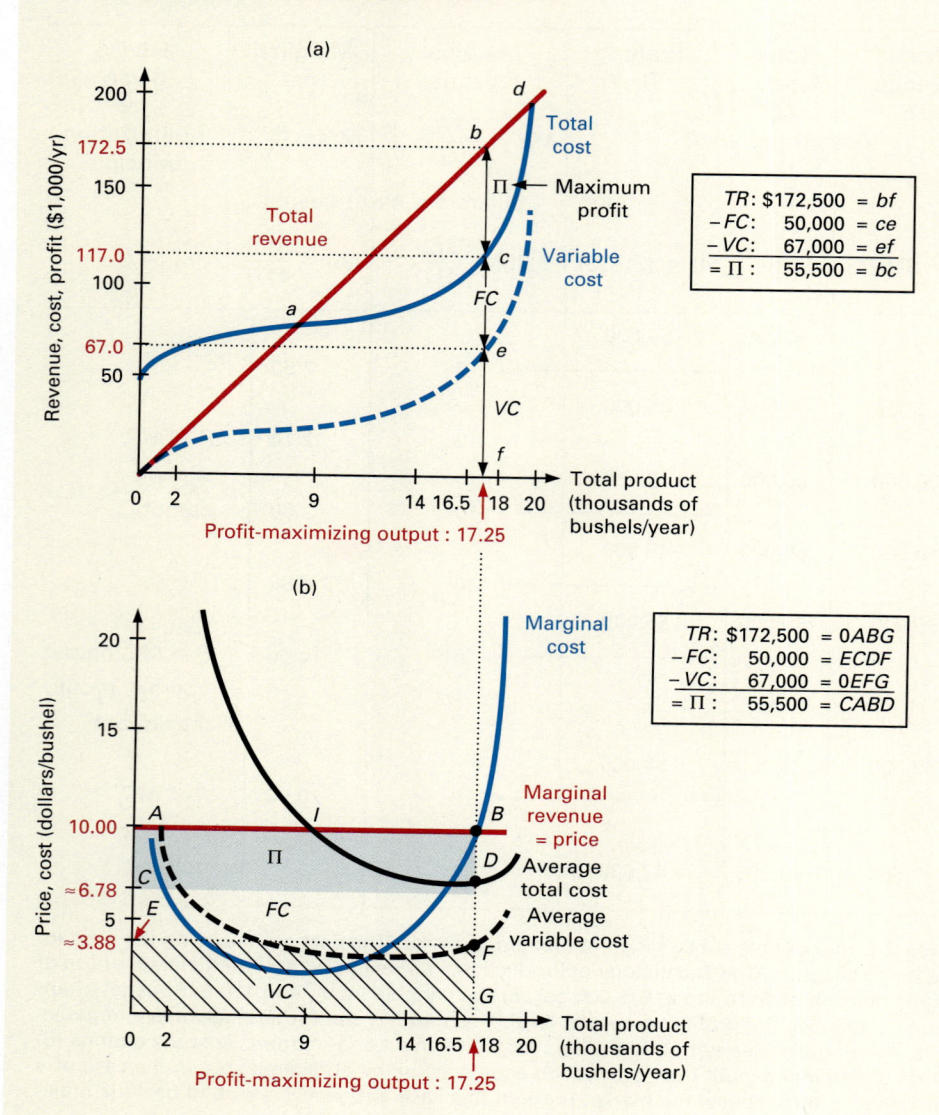

TR:	$172,500	= 0*ABG*
− FC:	50,000	= *ECDF*
− VC:	67,000	= 0*EFG*
= Π :	55,500	= *CABD*

If product price were $10/bushel (clearly above minimum average total cost), this perfectly competitive firm would find its optimal rate of production at 17,250 bushels/year, where rising marginal cost just equals marginal benefit (point *B*). Note that no exception to the *P* = *MC* rule is required; total revenue easily covers variable cost.

EXAMPLE 1

Shakespeare, Dickens, and Hillegass

"In 1775," begins the Cliffs Notes summary of Charles Dickens's *A Tale of Two Cities,* "people viewed their era as exceptionally good or exceptionally wicked." That passage lacks the poetry of Dickens's original—"It was the best of times, it was the worst of times"—but that did not stop students from snapping up 100,000 copies of this study aid in 1988, at $3.50 each.

Cliffs Notes, Inc. of Lincoln, Nebraska, was founded by Clifton Hillegass over three decades ago to produce summaries of literary works in "comfortable terms." The business started in his basement, then moved to a former supermarket, a tombstone factory, and finally into a windowless, corrugated steel structure wedged between a billiard equipment company and a Goodwill Industries warehouse. The major customers are high school students. By now Cliffs Notes has over 200 titles, and over 90 million copies have been sold to date.

The business is quite a money machine. It pays no royalties; authors of the notes receive a flat fee, of perhaps $2,000; and overhead is low. In 1988 *The Scarlet Letter* and *Macbeth* each sold 150,000 copies; *A Tale of Two Cities* sold 100,000; altogether, 5 million copies were sold. They cost 35 cents each to print; despite a $1 million tab for advertising (in magazines like *Scholastic* and *Seventeen*), the income statement looked like this:

Sales revenue	$11 million
Costs	9 million
Accounting profit	$ 2 million

Mr. Hillegass received 20 buy-out offers for about $70 million.

Source: Fleming Meeks, "Shakespeare, Dickens, and Hillegass," *Forbes,* October 30, 1989, pp. 206–209.

NUMERICAL EXERCISE 2

The Case of Positive Economic Profit

Panel (b) of Figure 2 provides an important alternative approach. Follow the optimization principle and search for an equality of marginal benefit/marginal revenue/market price (they all mean the same thing to a perfectly competitive firm) with rising marginal cost. Inevitably, you find point *B* and the associated profit-maximizing output level of 17,250 bushels/year.

In panel (b), however, yearly dollar amounts (such as total revenue, total cost, fixed cost, variable cost, and profit) are represented by *areas* (rather than distances). At the optimum output level, total revenue is shown as price (*BG*) times quantity (0*G*), or by rectangle 0*ABG*. Obviously, it equals $10/bushel times 17,250 bushels/year, or $172,500/year, just as did *distance bc* in panel (a).

Total cost, similarly, equals average total cost *DG* (slightly over $6.78/bushel) times quantity 0*G* (17,250 bushels/year), or rectangle 0*CDG* ($117,000/year), just as did distance *cf* in panel (a). We can also figure fixed cost and variable cost. Fixed cost equals average fixed cost *DF* (slightly under $2.90/bushel) times quantity 0*G* (17,250 bushels/year), or white rectangle *ECDF* ($50,000/year), just as did distance *ce* in panel (a). Variable cost equals average variable cost *FG* (slightly over $3.88/bushel) times quantity 0*G* (17,250 bushels/year), or crosshatched rectangle 0*EFG* ($67,000/year), just as distance *ef* in panel (a).

By implication, profit equals average profit *BD* (slightly under $3.22/bushel) times quantity 0*G* (17,250 bushels/year), or shaded rectangle *CABD* ($55,500/year), just as distance *bc* in panel (a).

A Zero-Profit Business

We can also use these tools of analysis to illustrate the case of your business making no economic profit. Imagine a fall in the market price of apples from our assumed $10/bushel to $6.58/bushel (your minimum average total cost). In Figure 3, the cost curves are the same as in Figure 2, but the total and marginal revenue lines reflect the assumed lower market price of apples. The slope of the total revenue line in panel (a) and the height of the marginal revenue line in panel *b* now equal 6.58.

In panel (a), there now exists no output level at which total revenue exceeds total cost. Only an out-

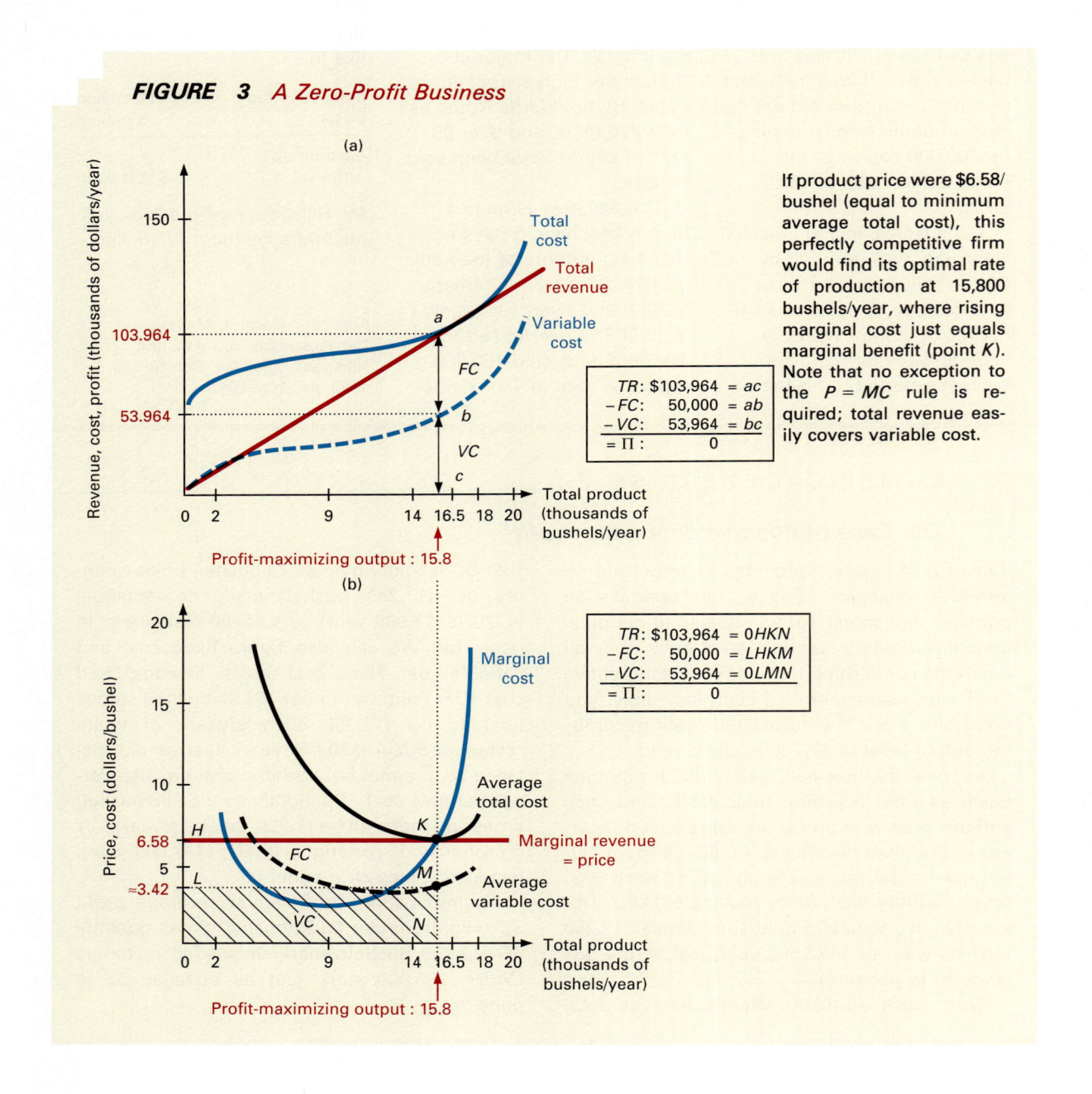

FIGURE 3 A Zero-Profit Business

If product price were $6.58/bushel (equal to minimum average total cost), this perfectly competitive firm would find its optimal rate of production at 15,800 bushels/year, where rising marginal cost just equals marginal benefit (point *K*). Note that no exception to the $P = MC$ rule is required; total revenue easily covers variable cost.

put of 15,800 bushels/year (corresponding to point *a*) can avoid losses. Even then, the economic profit and loss is precisely zero. At that optimum output level, total revenue equals $103,964/year (distance *ac*); total cost (fixed plus variable) is the same. If you were to prepare an income statement now, it would look like this:

Income Statement, Crisp Apple Company

Sales revenue		$103,964
Costs		
Property taxes	$ 5,000	
Wages	53,964	58,964
Taxable accounting profit		$ 45,000

Thus, your personal income would not be zero, but $45,000/year. You would be earning precisely the same amount you could have earned in your best outside alternative. Your *extra* income from running the business (your *economic* profit) would be zero. You would have no reason to rejoice; neither would you have reason for regret.

Any output level at which total revenue equals total cost (as at point *a*), and at which average revenue or price, therefore, equals average total cost (as at point *K*), is called a **break-even point.** When the market price of output also equals *minimum* average total cost (as in Figure 3), a firm cannot escape choosing the break-even level of production.

A Business Operating with an Economic Loss

Now imagine a further fall in the market price of apples from $6.58/bushel to $5/bushel (which lies under the orchard's minimum average total cost, but above its minimum average variable cost). In Figure 4, as before, the cost curves are unchanged; the total and marginal revenue lines reflect the assumed lower market price of apples. The slope of the total revenue line in panel (a) and the height of the marginal revenue line in panel (b) now equal 5.

In panel (a), total cost now exceeds total revenue at every conceivable output level. The firm is destined to make losses, at least in the short run, until market conditions improve or it can rid itself of fixed inputs and cease to operate. Nevertheless, losses are minimized at an output level of 14,000 bushels/year, which equates output price and marginal cost. (Economists still talk of profit *maximization* here because choosing a profit of say, $-\$25,000$ over a profit of $-\$50,000$ means choosing the *larger* number of the two.) At the optimum output level, total revenue equals $70,000/year (distance *bd*), total cost (fixed plus variable) equals $95,000/year (distance *ad*); thus profit equals $-\$25,000$/year

---

NUMERICAL EXERCISE 3

The Case of Zero Economic Profit

Panel (b) of Figure 3 provides the now familiar alternative to finding maximum profit. By equating price with marginal cost at *K*, you can find the optimum output level: At that output level, total revenue equals price *KN* ($6.58/bushel) times quantity 0*N* (15,800 bushels/year), or rectangle 0*HKN* ($103,964/year), which corresponds to distance *ac* in panel (a). Total cost equals average total cost *KN* ($6.58/bushel) times quantity 0*N* (15,800 bushels/year), or rectangle 0*HKN* ($103,964/year), which corresponds to distance *ac* in panel (a) as well. Of this total, fixed cost equals average fixed cost *KM* (slightly over $3.16/bushel) times quantity 0*N* (15,800 bushels/year), or white rectangle *LHKM* ($50,000/year), which corresponds to distance *ab* in panel (a). Variable cost equals average variable cost *MN* (slightly under $3.42/bushel) times quantity 0*N* (15,800 bushels/year), or crosshatched rectangle 0*LMN* ($53,964/year), which corresponds to distance *bc* in panel (a). There is no economic profit.

(distance *ab*). If you were to prepare an income statement now, it would look like this:

Income Statement,
Crisp Apple Company, 1992

Sales revenue		$70,000
Costs		
Property taxes	$ 5,000	
Wages	45,000	50,000
Taxable accounting profit		$20,000

Thus, your personal income would not be zero, but $20,000/year. Given your forgone opportunity to earn $45,000/year elsewhere, you would be earning $25,000/year *less* by running the orchard business, as the $25,000 negative economic profit in Figure 4 indicates. It is likely that the business would be closed down eventually. Still, given the fact that total revenue more than covers variable cost, closing down at once is ill advised. That decision would reduce your variable costs to zero, along with your output and total revenue. But you would still have $50,000 of fixed cost. The economic loss would equal $50,000, which is worse than $25,000. As panel (a) of Figure 4 shows, producing 14,000 bushels/year brings revenue of $70,000 (*bd*), which more than covers the $45,000 variable cost (*cd*). It leaves $25,000 of funds (*bc*) to cover at least *some* of the fixed cost. Taking home the $20,000 shown in the income statement is not as good as earning $45,000 elsewhere, but it is better than earning nothing at all. Example 2 provides a real-world example of the kind of situation just described.

A Business at the Point of Shutdown

Finally, consider the case in which a business might shut down even in the short run. Let the market price of apples fall even further from $5/bushel to $3.10/bushel (which equals the orchard's minimum average variable cost). In Figure 5, the cost curves, once again, are unchanged; the total and marginal revenue lines reflect the assumed lower market price of apples. The slope of the total revenue line in panel (a) and the height of the marginal revenue line in panel (b) now equal 3.10.

In panel (a), total cost now exceeds total revenue at every conceivable output level. Even variable cost exceeds total revenue at every output quantity except one (point *b*). The firm is destined to make losses, at least in the short run, until market conditions improve or it can rid itself of fixed inputs and cease to operate. As always, losses are minimized at an output level at which price equals

---

NUMERICAL EXERCISE 4

The Case of Negative Economic Profit, but No Shutdown

Panel (b) of Figure 4 can lead you to the same conclusion just derived. By equating price with marginal cost at *S,* you can find the optimum output level of 14,000 bushels/year. At that output level, total revenue equals price *SV* ($5/bushel) times quantity 0*V* (14,000 bushels/year), or rectangle 0*RSV* ($70,000/year), which corresponds to distance *bd* in panel (a). Total cost equals average total cost *QV* (slightly over $6.78/bushel) times quantity 0*V* (14,000 bushels/year), or rectangle 0*PQV* ($95,000/year), which corresponds to distance *ad* in panel (a). Of this total, fixed cost equals average fixed cost *QU* (slightly over $3.57/bushel) times quantity 0*V* (14,000 bushels/year), or white-plus-dotted rectangle *TPQU* $50,000/year), which corresponds to distance *ac* in panel (a). Variable cost equals average variable cost *UV* (slightly over $3.21/bushel) times quantity 0*V* (14,000 bushels/year), or crosshatched rectangle 0*TUV* ($45,000/year), which corresponds to distance *cd* in panel (a). Thus, economic profit equals the average loss *QS* (slightly over $1.78/bushel) times quantity 0*V* (14,000 bushels/year), or dotted rectangle *RPQS* (−$25,000/year).

FIGURE 4 Operating with a Loss

(a)

If product price were $5/bushel (below minimum average total cost but above minimum average variable cost), this perfectly competitive firm would find its optimal rate of production at 14,000 bushels/year, where rising marginal cost just equals marginal benefit (point S). Note that no exception to the $P = MC$ rule is required; total revenue easily covers variable cost.

TR:	$70,000	= bd
−FC:	50,000	= ac
−VC:	45,000	= cd
= Π:	−25,000	= ab

(b)

TR:	$70,000	= 0RSV
−FC:	50,000	= TPQU
−VC:	45,000	= 0TUV
= Π:	−25,000	= RPQS

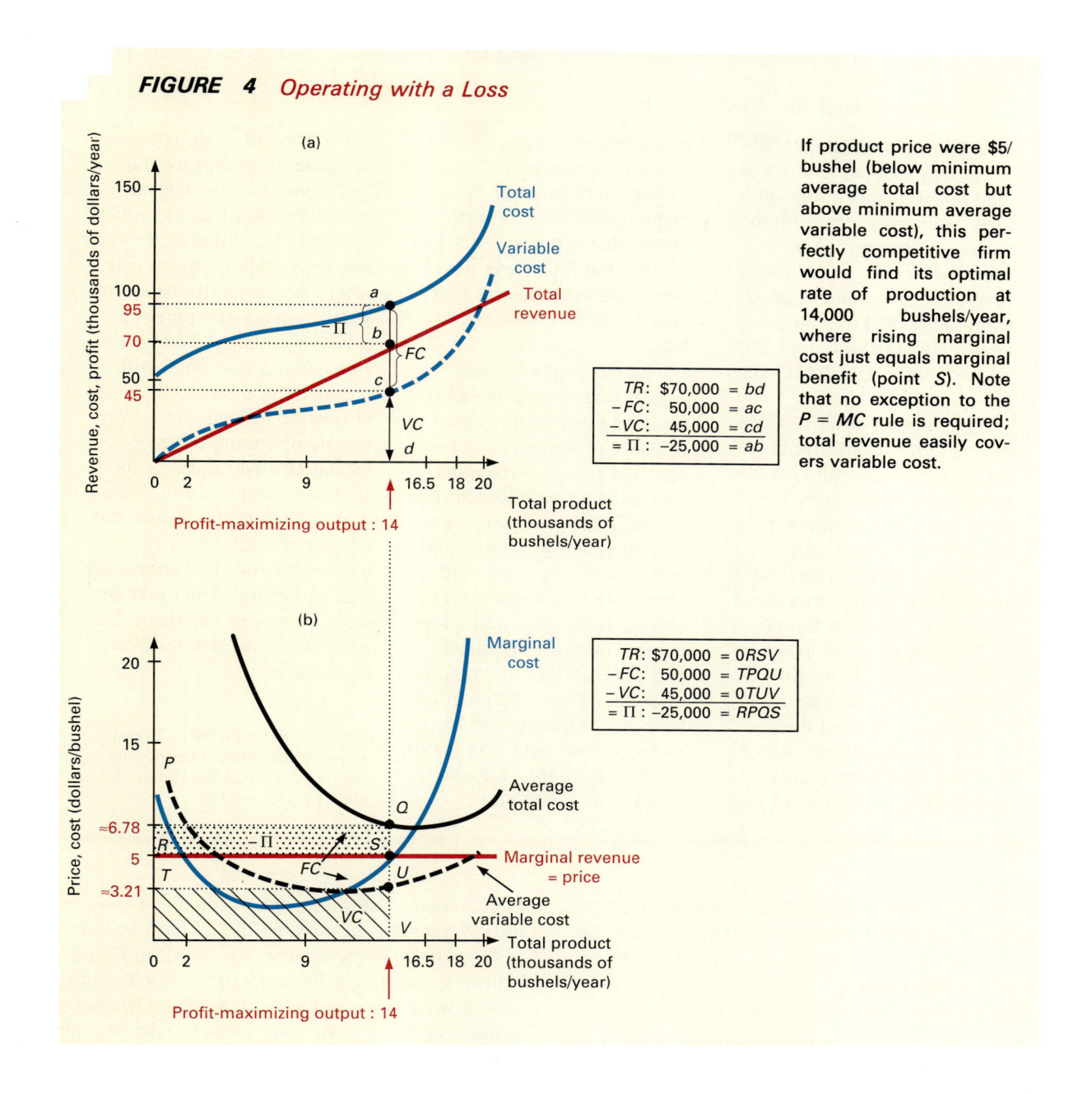

rising marginal cost—provided total revenue covers variable cost. Such an output level exists: 12,300 bushels/year. This optimum output is associated with total revenue of $38,130/year (distance *bc*) and total cost (fixed plus variable) of $88,130/year (distance *ac*); thus profit equals −$50,000/year (distance *ab*). It is equal to fixed cost and would be the same if the firm shut down at once. An output level at which total revenue equals variable cost [as at point *b*, panel (a)] and at which average revenue or price, therefore, equals average variable cost [as at point Z, panel (b)], is called a **shutdown point**. When the market price of output also equals *minimum* average variable cost (Figure 5), a firm that chooses to operate at all will do so at the shutdown level of production.

EXAMPLE 2

Broadway and the Bottom Line

With rare exceptions, Broadway theaters are not doing well. Typically, they survive, but barely, covering their variable costs and *some* of their fixed costs. While total revenues have been soaring from below $50 million per year in 1973 to well over $250 million in the late 1980s, costs have also been rising.

The largest portion of total cost is labor. Unlike other businesses, opportunities for substituting machinery for labor are strictly limited or fiercely resisted by labor unions. It takes just as long to design a stage barge for Cleopatra or bewail the death of Anthony as it did in Shakespeare's days. Union work rules are today at least as complex as those of the medieval guilds; the number of workers from each craft is specified for each theater and every circumstance. Featherbedding is rampant. Thus, a minimum number of musicians is specified for each show. Nor is it permissible to replace the musicians with electronic synthesizers that could replace entire orchestras.

Hourly wages for scenery assemblers, box office workers, and stage hands equal a multiple of the national average; the fees and royalties that must be paid to actors, choreographers, composers, directors, set designers, and writers are very high. Add New York City taxes on real estate, utility bills, and advertising. Elaborate stage sets can also run into the millions of dollars. (The 1,000 feet of fluorescent tubing and 22 miles of fiber optic conductor used in *Starlight Express* came to $2.5 million.)

Yet none of these costs can be escaped, except by shutting down entirely. Unlike movie theaters that can follow people to the suburbs, Broadway must stay on Broadway, where parking and restaurants are expensive and personal safety is an issue. The typical show, being burdened with pre-opening production costs of over $8 million and facing weekly operating costs of $400,000, never recoups its costs in revenue. Even if every seat is filled in the house, the break-even point may require a two-year run; few shows are that successful. The most notable exception has been *Cats*, which returned $10 for every $1 invested.

Source: Peter Passell, "Broadway and the Bottom Line," *The New York Times,* December 10, 1989, pp. H1 and H8.

If you were to make that choice and then prepared an income statement, it would look like this:

Income Statement,
Crisp Apple Company, 1992

Sales revenue		$38,130
Costs		
Property taxes	$ 5,000	
Wages	38,130	43,130
Accounting profit		−$ 5,000

In this case, your personal income would equal −$5,000. Given your forgone opportunity to earn $45,000/year elsewhere you would be earning $50,000/year *less* by running the orchard business, as the $50,000 negative economic profit in Figure 5 indicates. You might be tempted to shut the business down at once and save yourself the trouble of running it. If you did, your variable cost, output, and revenue would all drop to zero; in the short run, your fixed cost would remain the same and would equal your economic loss.

Summary

We can summarize our discussion so far with five simple points:

1. A firm will operate with positive economic

CHAPTER 10 *Perfect Competition* **269**

profit (at an output level that equates *P* and *MC*) because it indicates earnings in excess of the owners' best alternative (Figure 2).

2. A firm will operate with zero economic profit (at an output level that equates *P* and *MC*) because implicit cost (counted as part of fixed cost) is then fully covered by total revenue; hence owners earn in their firm precisely what they could have earned elsewhere, and shutting down would deprive them of these earnings (Figure 3).

3. A firm will operate with a loss falling short of fixed cost (at an output level that equates *P* and

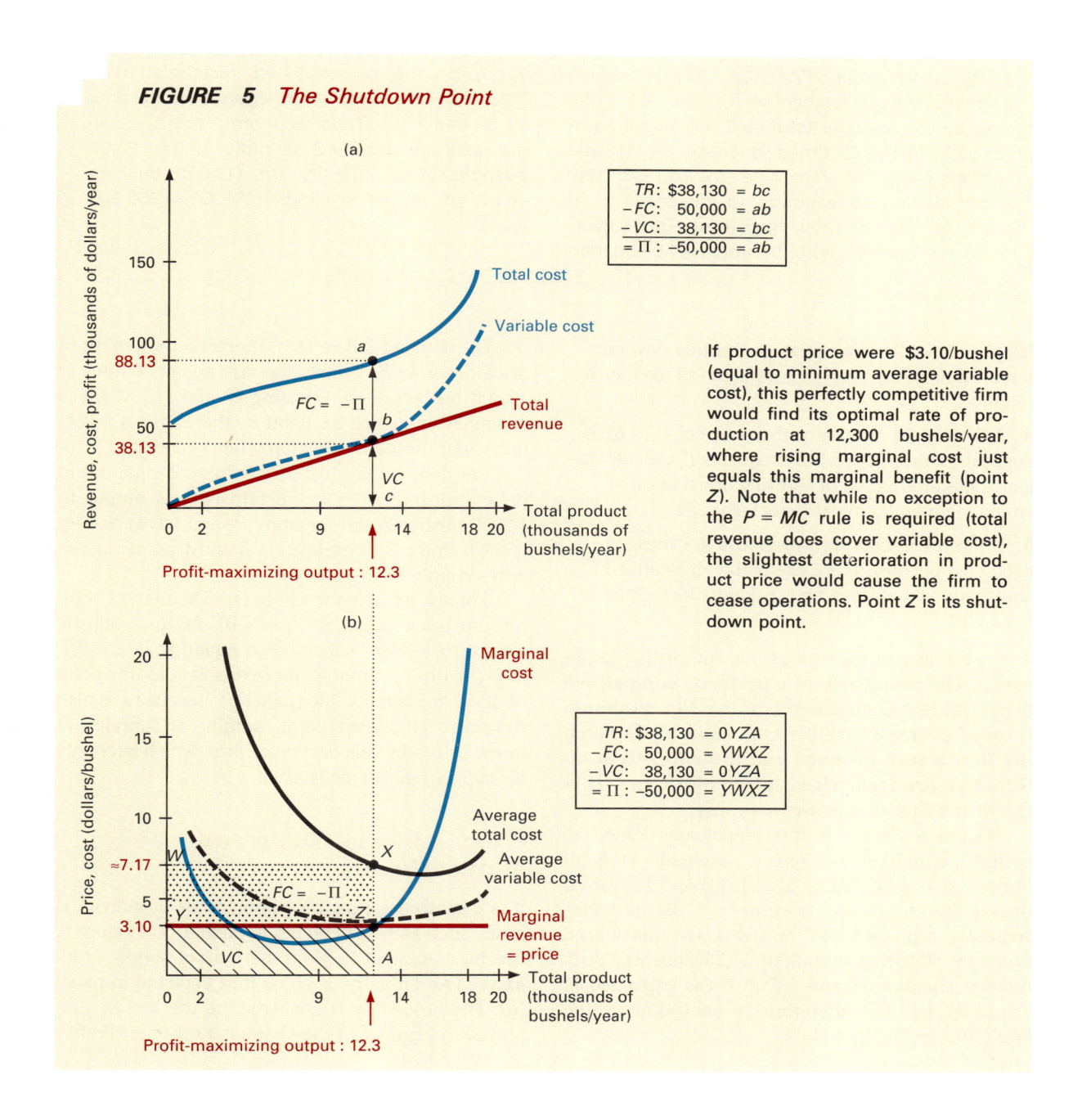

FIGURE 5 *The Shutdown Point*

(a)

TR:	$38,130	= bc
−FC:	50,000	= ab
−VC:	38,130	= bc
= Π :	−50,000	= ab

If product price were $3.10/bushel (equal to minimum average variable cost), this perfectly competitive firm would find its optimal rate of production at 12,300 bushels/year, where rising marginal cost just equals this marginal benefit (point Z). Note that while no exception to the *P* = *MC* rule is required (total revenue does cover variable cost), the slightest deterioration in product price would cause the firm to cease operations. Point *Z* is its shutdown point.

(b)

TR:	$38,130	= 0YZA
−FC:	50,000	= YWXZ
−VC:	38,130	= 0YZA
= Π :	−50,000	= YWXZ

NUMERICAL EXERCISE 5

The Case of Negative Economic Profit at the Shutdown Point

In panel (b) of Figure 5, by equating price with marginal cost at Z, you can find the optimum output level of 12,300 bushels/year. At that output level, total revenue equals price ZA ($3.10/bushel) times quantity 0A (12,300 bushels/year), or rectangle 0YZA ($38,130/year), which corresponds to distance bc in panel (a). Total cost equals average total cost XA (slightly under $7.17/bushel) times quantity 0A (12,300 bushels/year), or rectangle 0WXA ($88,130/year), which corresponds to distance ac in panel (a). Of this total, fixed cost equals average fixed cost XZ (slightly under $4.07/bushel) times quantity 0A (12,300 bushels/year), or dotted rectangle YWXZ ($50,000/year), which corresponds to distance ab in panel (a). Variable cost equals average variable cost ZA ($3.10/bushel) times quantity 0A (12,300 bushels/year), or the crosshatched rectangle 0YZA ($38,130/year), which corresponds to distance bc in panel (a). Thus, economic profit equals the average loss XZ (slightly under $4.07/bushel) times quantity 0A (12,300 bushels/year), or dotted rectangle YWXZ (−$50,000/year).

MC) because the alternative of shutting down at once would yield a bigger loss equal to fixed cost (Figure 4).

4. A firm might operate with a loss equal to fixed cost (at an output level that equates P and MC) because the alternative of shutting down at once would yield an identical loss (Figure 5).

5. No firm will operate with a loss in excess of fixed cost because there exists the alternative of shutting down at once and making a loss equal to fixed cost.

The preceding discussion has an interesting implication: **The rising arm of a perfectly competitive firm's marginal cost curve above the minimum level of average variable cost shows how much the firm would produce and offer to sell at alternative product prices in the short run. It is the firm's line of short-run supply.**

Figure 6 illustrates this graphically. Panel (a) pictures a market for apples, originally in equilibrium at a with supply S and demand D_1. Given the equilibrium market price of $P_1 = 10$, the representative firm pictured in panel (b) maximized profit by adjusting output to 17,250 bushels/year, thereby equating P_1 and MC at B (as explained in Figure 2). Point B, therefore, is one point on the firm's supply line (panel c).

Let demand fall to D_2. The market equilibrium price drops to $P_2 = 6.58$; the firm adjusts output to 15,800 bushels/year, equating P_2 and MC at K (as explained in Figure 3). Point K, therefore, is a second point on the firm's supply line (panel c).

Let demand fall to D_3. The market equilibrium price drops to $P_3 = 5$; the firm adjusts output to 14,000 bushels/year, equating P_3 and MC at S (Figure 4). Point S, therefore, is a third point on the firm's supply line (panel c).

Finally, let demand fall to D_4. The market equilibrium price drops to $P_4 = 3.10$; the firm adjusts output to 12,300 bushels/year, equating P_4 and MC at Z (Figure 5). Point Z, therefore, is a fourth point on the firm's supply line (panel c). Because Z is also the firm's shutdown point, nothing is supplied at lower prices by this particular firm, which accounts for supply line segment AZ.

From Individual Supply to Market Supply

It is easy to see how the supply lines of individual firms, such as that depicted in panel (c) of Figure 6, can be combined to yield the market supply of all firms in an industry, such as that depicted in panel (a). The procedure is analogous to the one we employed in Figure 4 of the chapter "Consumer Prefer-

FIGURE 6 From Marginal Cost to Supply

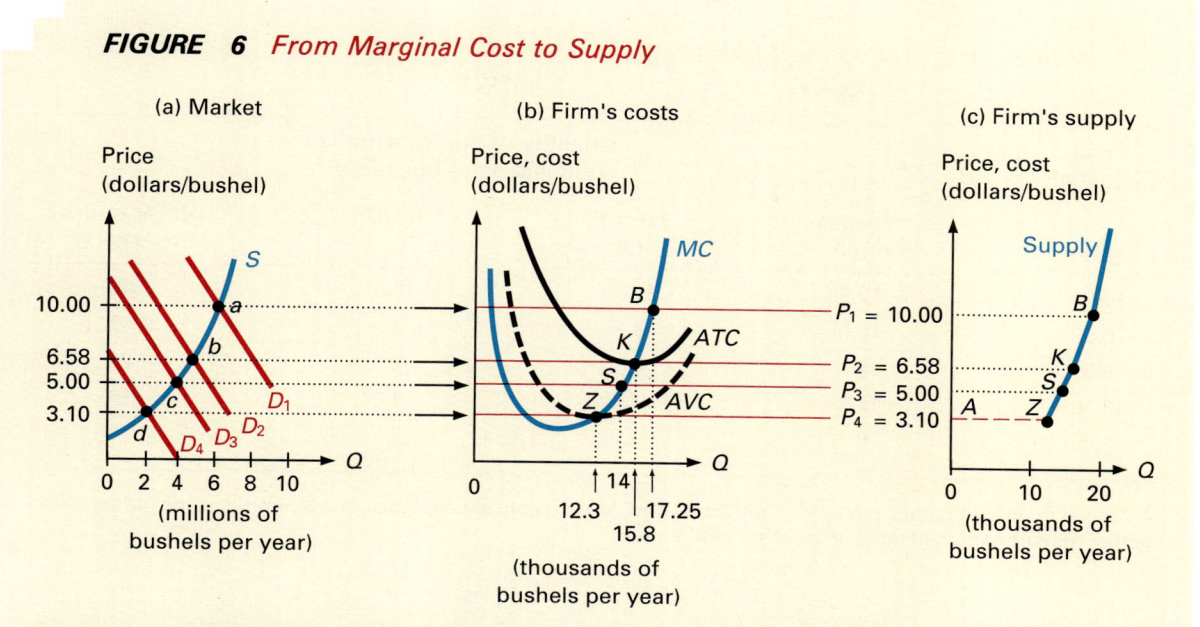

(a) Market

Price (dollars/bushel)

(b) Firm's costs

Price, cost (dollars/bushel)

(c) Firm's supply

Price, cost (dollars/bushel)

$P_1 = 10.00$
$P_2 = 6.58$
$P_3 = 5.00$
$P_4 = 3.10$

For a perfectly competitive firm, the rising arm of the marginal cost curve, above the minimum level of average variable cost (here at Z) is, in fact, the firm's short-run supply. It indicates how much the firm would produce and offer to sell at alternative product prices.

ences and Demand," when aggregating individual demands into market demand. Although we know that hundreds, thousands, and perhaps even millions of sellers might appear in a perfectly competitive market, we can illustrate the procedure with a much simpler example. Imagine that just three sellers exist in the apple market. Their respective supply schedules might be those shown in columns 2 through 4 of Table 4. Note how the supply schedule of firm A is the one graphed in panel (c) of Figure 6. The assumed supply schedule of firms B and C can be similarly graphed and so can the market supply schedule of column 5. The result is Figure 7.

A Long-Run Perspective

Our discussion so far has focused on the short run, in which firms have fixed inputs that cannot be changed. Yet the kind of short-run equilibria depicted by Figures 2–5 may not represent states of rest when seen in a longer perspective. Consider Figure 2. If you were the owner of that orchard, earning from it an additional $55,500 on top of your next best alternative, you might be tempted to use some of that profit to expand your business. Other people, noting your good fortune, might take advantage of the unrestricted entry of perfectly competitive markets and go into the orchard business as well. Indeed, both of these reactions are likely. In the presence of positive economic profit, firms in a perfectly competitive market tend to become larger and more numerous in the long run.

This process works in the opposite direction as well. If you were the owner of the firm in Figure 5, earning from it each year $50,000 *less* than in your next best alternative, you might be tempted to contract the size of your operations or to shut down altogether. Your competitors would have similar plans, and the unrestricted exit that perfectly competitive markets allow would make it easy to do. In

TABLE 4 Deriving the Market Supply Schedule

Price ($/bushel) (1)	Quantity of apples supplied (thousands of bushels/yr)			
	Firm A (2)	Firm B (3)	Firm C (4)	All three firms (5) = (2)+(3)+(4)
10.00	17.25	12.75	10	40
6.58	15.8	8.2	8	32
5.0	14	6	6	26
3.10	12.3	1.7	4	18
2.00	0	1	2	3

A market supply schedule can be derived by adding, at each conceivable price, the quantities supplied by all potential market participants, all else being held equal.

FIGURE 7 Deriving the Market Supply Line

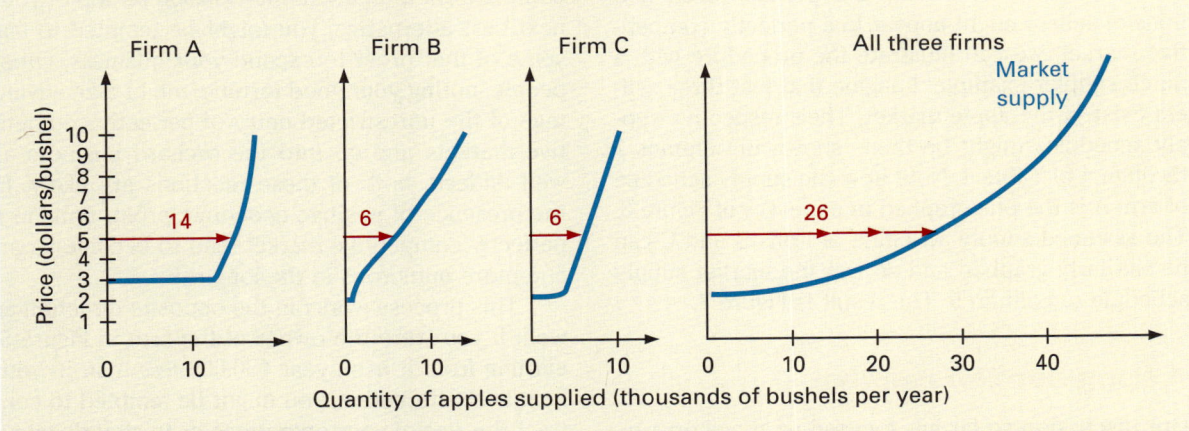

This set of graphs, based on Table 4, shows how, all else being equal, the market supply line can be derived by adding horizontally, at each conceivable price, the quantities supplied by all potential market participants. Thus market supply is a summation of the marginal cost curves (above minimum AVC) of all firms operating in the market.

the presence of negative economic profit, firms in a perfectly competitive market tend to become smaller and less numerous in the long run. There are, however, further implications.

Profit and Industry Expansion

Consider Figure 8. Panel (a) depicts an original market equilibrium, with a price of $10/bushel and quantity traded of 400 million bushels/year (point *a*). The typical firm (in Figure 2) produces 17,250 bushels/year and thereby equates its marginal cost *MC* with market price *P* at *c*. It also reaps a profit equal to the shaded rectangle. This profit attracts new firms into the industry. Supply rises from *S* toward *S**; market equilibrium moves from *a* to *b*, where a new equilibrium price of $7.80/bushel is reached. Our typical firm adjusts its output volume to 15,250 bushels/year, thereby equating its *MC* with new and lower market price *P** at *e* (in a manner reminiscent of Figure 3). Indeed, this outcome is inevitable in the long run. The typical firm's eco-

FIGURE 8 *A Profitable Industry Expands*

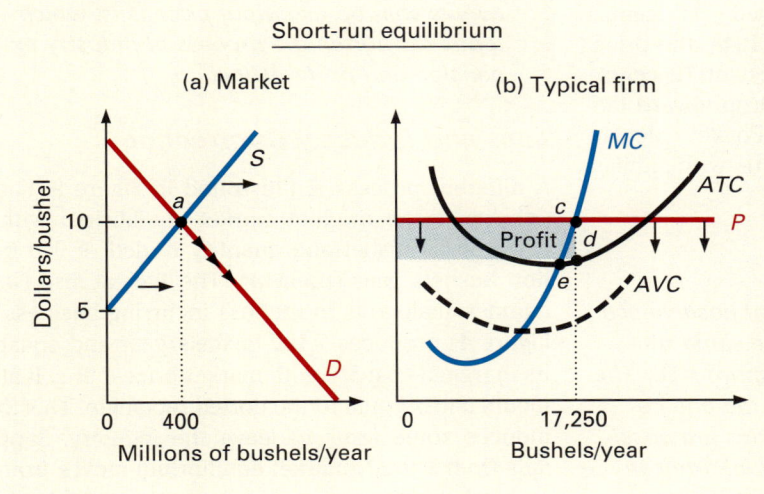

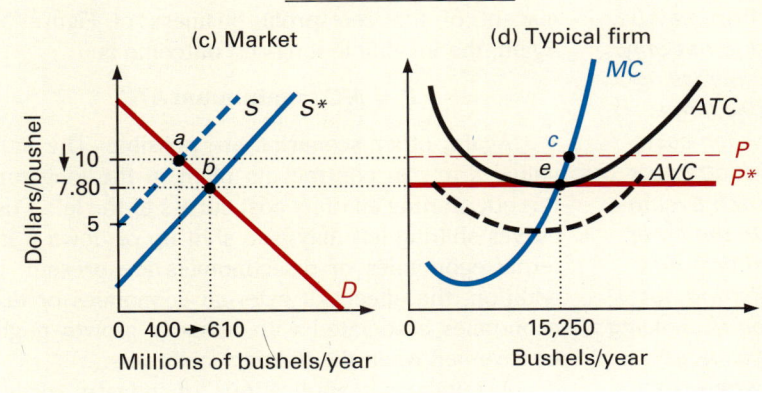

When markets are perfectly competitive, a short-run equilibrium in which the typical firm reaps a positive economic profit (panel b) contains within it the seeds for long-run change. The number or size of firms will grow, attracted by the prospect of profit. As supply rises (from *S* to *S**), the market price will fall (from $10 to $7.80/bushel). The process will come to an end only when the typical firm makes zero economic profit and *P = MC =* minimum *ATC*, as at *e* in panel (d).

Caution: This succinct example assumes that the entire adjustment occurred through the entry of new firms and that no changes occurred in the cost curves of existing firms. Other scenarios are possible, but the end result is always the same: *P = MC =* minimum *ATC*, as at *e* in panel (d).

nomic profit is zero; price equals not only marginal cost but also minimum average total cost.

In the long run, **P = MC = minimum ATC.**

An example of this process (even though it does not involve perfect competition) is provided by the history of the ball point pen. When introduced in 1945, the Reynolds International Pen Company produced it at an average total cost of 80 cents, but sold it for $19.98. Within a year, there were others (Eversharp and Sheaffer) who offered the pen at $15. Next came the Ball Point Pen Company and a $9.95 price; so Reynolds dropped its price to $3.85. (Enormous sales exceeding tens of thousands of pens per day helped lower its average total cost to 30 cents.) By late 1946, a hundred firms offered the new type of pen for $2.98. In 1947, the Continental Pen Company charged 98 cents, Reynolds 88 cents. A year later, in 1948, the price stood at 39 cents, average total cost at 10 cents. Since then, price has continued to drop toward the lowest possible average total cost. Pocket calculators and laptop computers provide us with similar scenarios in more recent times.

CAUTION

Industry expansion in the face of positive economic profit always leads to the same ultimate outcome: P = MC = minimum ATC. *The process, however, need not be the one depicted in Figure 8. Other scenarios are possible. Unlike Figure 8, the individual firm can expand its plant in the long run, thereby shifting all of its cost curves to the right. As the last chapter has shown, however, cost curves shifting right may also shift down or up. The growth of an* individual firm *may be associated with cost curves shifting not only to the right but also down when increasing returns to scale are encountered as larger plants are put into operation or when costs rise as a single administrative unit attempts to run ever more plants. Under such circumstances, a firm is subject to* **internal economies.** *On the other hand, the growth of an individual firm may be associated with cost curves shifting not only to the right but also up when decreasing returns to scale are encountered as larger plants are put into operation or when costs rise as a single administrative unit attempts to run ever more plants. Under such circumstances, a firm is subject to* **internal diseconomies.**

In addition to the preceding effects, production functions may change and input prices may rise or fall in the process of industry *expansion. When industry growth causes favorable changes in the production functions of all firms (raising output per unit of input) or causes decreases in input prices,* **external economies** *occur. Cost curves will shift down as output price falls, which tends to prolong the process of industry expansion and profit extinction. When industry growth causes unfavorable changes in production functions of all firms (lowering output per unit of input) or causes increases in input prices,* **external diseconomies** *occur. Cost curves shift up as output price falls, which tends to shorten the process of industry expansion and profit extinction.*

Loss and Industry Contraction

A different process is illustrated in Figure 9. Panel (a) depicts an original market equilibrium with a price of $5/bushel and quantity traded of 900 million bushels/year (point *a*). The typical firm (in a manner analogous to the loss-incurring business of Figure 4) produces 7,100 bushels/year and equates its marginal cost *MC* with market price *P* at *c*. It also incurs a loss equal to the dotted rectangle. This loss induces some firms to leave the industry. Supply falls from *S* to *S**; market equilibrium moves from *a* to *b*, where the new equilibrium price is $7/bushel. Our typical firm adjusts its output volume to 8,000 bushels/year and thereby equates its *MC* with new and higher market price *P** at *e* (in a manner reminiscent of the zero-profit business of Figure 3). Again, the inevitable long-run outcome is

P = MC = minimum ATC.

Again, other scenarios are possible. The individual firm can contract its plant in the long run, thereby shifting all of its cost curves to the left. Cost curves shifting left may also shift up or down if internal economies or diseconomies are present. In addition, the effects of external economies or diseconomies associated with industry growth might be reversed when the industry contracts.

A number of applications of industry expansion and contraction are provided by Examples 3, 4, and 5.

FIGURE 9 An Unprofitable Industry Contracts

Short-run equilibrium

(a) Market

(b) Typical firm

Long-run equilibrium

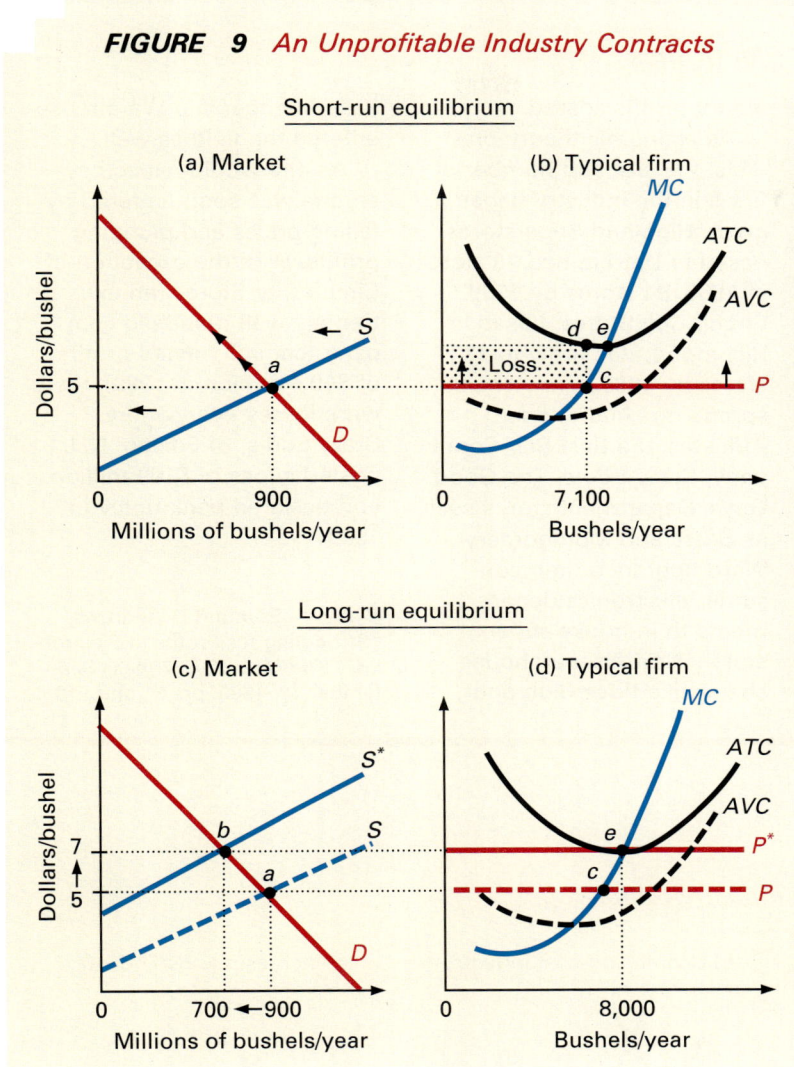

(c) Market

(d) Typical firm

When markets are perfectly competitive, a short-run equilibrium in which the typical firm makes an economic loss (panel b) contains within it the seeds for long-run change. The number or size of firms will contract, repelled by the losses being incurred. As supply falls (from S to S^*), the market price will rise (from \$5 to \$7/bushel). The process will come to an end only when the typical firm makes zero economic profit and $P = MC =$ minimum ATC, as at e in panel (d).

Caution: This succinct example assumes that the entire adjustment occurred through the exit of firms and that no changes occurred in the cost curves of surviving firms. Other scenarios are possible, but the end result is always the same: $P = MC =$ minimum ATC, as at e in panel (d).

Constant, Increasing, and Decreasing Cost Industries[2]

In the long run, a perfectly competitive industry will be populated with firms making zero economic profit because any profit or loss invites changes that produce a situation in which $P = MC =$ minimum ATC. As the preceding note of caution implies, however, the level of minimum ATC that prevails after an industry has expanded or contracted may not be the same as the one prevailing before the expansion or contraction. Consider a long-run equilibrium as that depicted by panels (c) and (d) in Figure 9. Product price is $P^* = \$7$/bushel, which is also the minimum average total cost of the typical firm (point e). Let this equilibrium be upset by an increase in demand. Price would rise above P^*; the typical firm would produce more, and positive profit would appear. As a result, the process of industry expansion would begin. New firms would enter the industry, existing firms would grow, supply would

---

[2] Optional section.

EXAMPLE 3

Struggling for Profits in Electronics

The processes of industry expansion and contraction apply in many circumstances, even when industries are not perfectly competitive. An example of how profits induce industry expansion, which *destroys* profits, is provided by the U.S. consumer electronics industry. In the late 1970s, consumers first became aware of videocassette recorders, VCRs; in 1979, industry sales were a mere $389 million nationwide. Then the VCR craze set in, spreading like wildfire. By 1986, annual sales reached $5.2 billion; a year later more than half of American households had acquired a VCR. Industry profits soared.

As economic theory predicts, the size and number of firms in the industry began to grow. Highland Superstores, based in Detroit, had 18 stores in 1980, 84 stores by 1989. Circuit City Stores, based in Richmond, Va., grew to 133 stores by 1989. Many chains sprang up: Audio Video Affiliates, the Best Buy Company, Crazy Eddie, The Good Guys. Department stores such as Sears and Montgomery Ward upgraded their consumer electronics departments to in-house superstores. No-frills warehouse chains like Price Club and Pace Membership Warehouse entered the field as well.

As one would expect, everyone was soon battered by falling prices and plunging profits. With the exception of Circuit City Stores (an extremely well managed company that still posted profits of $69.5 million in 1989), there were losses everywhere. Crazy Eddie, of Edison, N.J., posted a loss of $109 million and declared bankruptcy in 1989.

Source: Edmund L. Andrews, "Struggling for Profits in Electronics," *The New York Times,* September 10, 1989, pp. F1 and F10.

FIGURE 10 Long-Run Industry Supply Curves

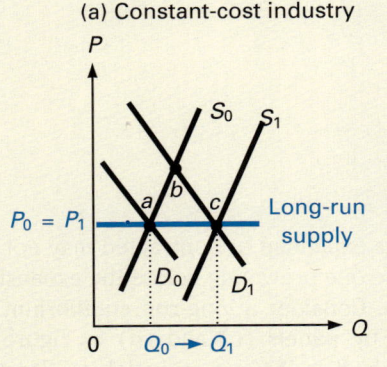

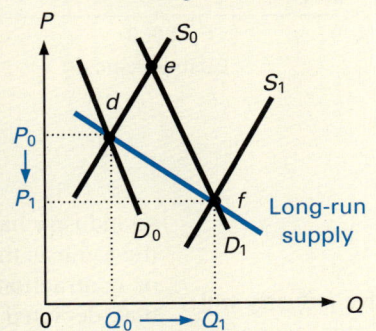

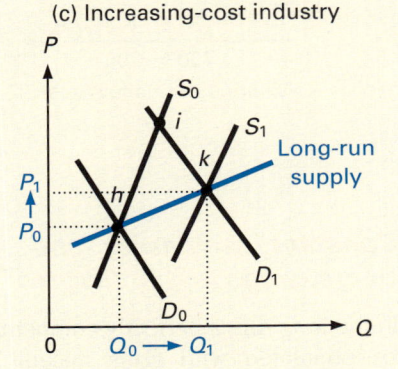

Long-run industry supply curves can be horizontal, downward sloping, or upward sloping. When internal and external economies (associated, respectively, with the growth of individual firms or of the entire industry) are absent or are precisely offset by internal and external diseconomies, the panel (a) picture emerges. In the long run, any output can be supplied at the same price. If economies overwhelm diseconomies, panel (b) applies; more of the product can be supplied in the long run at a lower price. Finally, when diseconomies overwhelm economies, panel (c) applies; more of the product can be supplied in the long run but only at a higher price.

rise, and price would fall. But would price fall back to P^*? Not necessarily. Three outcomes are possible. First, when external economies or diseconomies are absent (or mutually offsetting) the ultimate product price (after the industry has ceased to expand) will equal the initial price; such an industry is a **constant-cost industry.** Its long-run supply is a horizontal line. Second, when external economies are present, the ultimate product price (after the industry has ceased to expand) will be lower than the initial price; such an industry is a **decreasing-cost industry.** Its long-run supply is a downward-sloping line. Third, when external diseconomies are present, the ultimate product price (after the industry has ceased to expand) will be higher than the initial price; such an industry is an **increasing-cost industry.** Its long-run supply is an upward-sloping line.

Figure 10 illustrates this discussion. In panel (a), an initial short-run equilibrium is established by demand D_O and supply S_O at a. Firms earn zero economic profit; a is a long-run equilibrium as well. Demand rises to D_1; at the new equilibrium b positive profit is widespread. The industry expands and supply rises to S_1. At the final zero-profit equilibrium at c, price is the same as before ($P_1 = P_O$).

In panel (b), an initial short-run equilibrium is established by D_O and S_O at d. Firms earn zero economic profit; hence d is a long-run equilibrium as well. Demand rises to D_1; at the new equilibrium e positive profit is widespread. The industry expands and supply rises to S_1 because external economies

■ EXAMPLE 4

Eggs with Less Cholesterol?

Here is another example of the link between industry size and profits. The American Heart Association recommends that adults consume no more than 300 milligrams (mg) of cholesterol per day. The substance is found in animal fats and eggs; it blocks blood vessels, causing serious heart disease. A single egg contains 220 mg of cholesterol, twice as much as two 4-oz. pork chops. Small wonder the U.S. egg industry has faced a continuous slide in sales. From 1984 to 1989 alone, sales dropped from $4.1 billion to $3.1 billion, profits tumbled, and *the number of producers has been cut in half.*

The egg industry decided to fight back. Said one industry spokesperson: "Our intent is to sell more eggs and get the American people to feel better about eggs. We're sick and tired of the American Heart Association telling people they're going to die if they eat an egg." To reverse the industry's decline, some major egg producers have introduced new husbandry techniques that are "more sensitive to the needs of chickens." Innovations include the following:

1. More nutritious diets, including a secret mixture of grain and minerals that is said to enhance the chickens' ability to metabolize cholesterol

2. A reduction in stress, allegedly accomplished by providing chickens with more space, better lighting (blue light, simulating sunlight), better ventilation (including machines that filter dust from the air), automated feeding and watering equipment (neutralizing radio-wave emissions from electric motors and removing metals and bacteria from the water itself)

Advertisements claim that the result is a "light and natural" egg with only 185–210 mg. of cholesterol, which is safer to eat. The Washington, D.C., Egg Nutrition Center tested the "low cholesterol" eggs and found no difference between them and ordinary eggs. The government described the ads as a marketing gimmick, fined some companies (Pennsylvania's Full Spectrum Farms and California's Rosemary Farms) for "false and misleading" advertising, and barred the low-cholesterol labels.

Source: Keith Schneider, "Eggs With Less Cholesterol: Industry's Salvation or Sham?" *The New York Times,* May 15, 1989, pp. A1 and B6.

EXAMPLE 5

Big Farms Try Organic Methods

What has happened to the egg industry (see Example 4) might happen to other food producers as well. The consuming public has become increasingly aware of the dangers of food tainted by synthetic chemicals such as inorganic fertilizers, herbicides, pesticides, or growth regulators. Anticipating what might happen to them if demand drops, some of California's largest farms have begun experimenting with growing fruits and vegetables organically.

Farm operators, such as Marko Zaninovich, the Nunes Company, and the Superior Fruit Company grow iceberg lettuce, persimmons, strawberries, and table grapes with manure, naturally derived insect killers, and other organic substances. Strips of cowpeas and vetch supply nitrogen to the soil; weeds are battled with hands, hoes, and mechanical cultivators (rather than herbicides); vacuum cleaners are used to suck insects off vines; and French prune trees are planted to provide a home for the wasps that feed on grape leaf hoppers.

Results so far show that these methods work well in California's hot and dry climate. However, they fail in warm and moist places (such as Florida) where pests and plant diseases are more prevalent. Consumers have been willing to pay 10 to 50 percent more for organically grown food. As one would expect, this premium has provided a strong incentive to cheat. Pacific Organics, a California company, went bankrupt after a government investigation proved that its "organically grown" carrots had been grown with chemicals in Mexico.

Source: Keith Schneider, "Big Farm Companies Try Hand at Organic Methods," *The New York Times,* May 28, 1989, pp. A1 and A24.

---

are present. At the final zero-profit equilibrium at *f*, price is lower than before ($P_1 < P_0$).

In panel (c), an initial short-run equilibrium is established by D_0 and S_0 at *h*. Firms earn zero economic profit; hence *h* is a long-run equilibrium as well. Demand rises to D_1; at the new equilibrium *i* positive profit is widespread. The industry expands and supply rises to S_1 because diseconomies come into play. At the final zero-profit equilibrium at *k*, price is higher than before ($P_1 > P_0$).

The Efficiency of Perfect Competition

In this section, we ask a final question. What is so "perfect" about perfect competition? Two answers come to mind.

First, a perfectly competitive market contains within it a strong tendency for **technical efficiency,** a situation in which it is impossible, with current technical knowledge, to raise output from given inputs or, alternatively, to produce a given output by using less of one input without using more of another input. This efficiency is achieved by perfect competition in the long run when P = minimum ATC. In that situation, any given physical output is produced with a minimum expenditure of physical inputs. As Figures 8 and 9 show, any situation in which output is *not* produced at minimum ATC [as at points *d* in panels (b)] gives rise to profits or losses and sets into motion changes that ultimately bring about the result P = minimum ATC. [See points *e* in panels (d).]

Second, a perfectly competitive market is perfect in the sense that it produces **economic efficiency,** a situation in which it is impossible to make a person better off without making another person worse off because all *mutually beneficial* transactions have already been carried out. It is achieved when $P = MC$. To understand what is involved, we can make use of the concepts of consumer surplus and producer surplus, first introduced in Chapter 4 and now reviewed in Figure 11.

Figure 11 shows a perfectly competitive market for apples. Given the demand and supply lines

FIGURE 11 Economic Efficiency

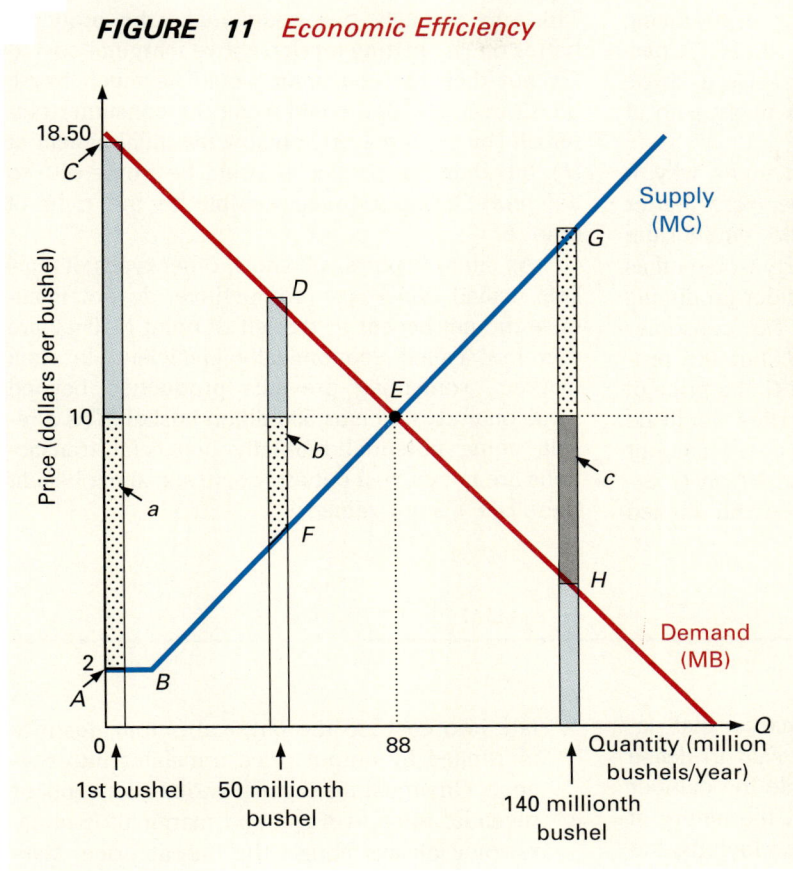

A perfectly competitive market establishes an equilibrium price and quantity, here at demand and supply intersection E. Because demand reflects the marginal benefits of consumers, while supply reflects the marginal costs of producers, MB and MC are equated at the equilibrium point as well. As a result, the social net benefit of the activity in question (here of producing and consuming apples) is maximized (here as area ACEB).

shown, an equilibrium price of $10/bushel is established and 88 million bushels are traded (point *E*). We must now consider that the whole purpose of any market is to bring buyers and sellers together in order to carry out exchanges that both parties consider beneficial. Thus, the first bushel bought and sold (right next to the vertical axis) provides a net benefit to *both* buyer and seller. Some buyer is willing to pay as much as $18.50 for that bushel (the height of column *a*) yet can buy the bushel for $10 (the equilibrium price). From the point of view of that buyer, the marginal benefit *MB* is $18.50. The marginal cost *MC* is only $10; thus a marginal net benefit of $8.50 is reaped. The shaded section of column *a* represents this *consumer surplus*.

At the same time, some seller is willing to supply that first bushel for as little as $2 (as the height of the supply line indicates) yet can sell the bushel for $10 (the equilibrium price). For that seller, the marginal benefit *MB* is $10; the marginal cost *MC* is only $2; thus the marginal net benefit is $8. The dotted section of column *a* shows this *producer surplus*.

Together, the shaded and dotted segments represent the joint net benefit from producing, selling, buying, and consuming that first bushel. A similar story, of course, can be told about the second and third bushel, the 1 millionth bushel, and the 50 millionth bushel (column *b*). As more and more bushels are sold and bought, the *sizes* of (shaded) consumer surpluses and (dotted) producer surpluses will change. Their decline reflects, respectively, the diminishing marginal utility of consumption and the rising marginal cost of production. Yet, right up to the 88 millionth bushel, there will be net benefits or *mutually beneficial* transactions. By the time the equilibrium quantity of 88 million bushels is sold, the total net benefit from apple producing and consuming is maximized (area *ACEB*). A perfectly competitive market does not miss a single transaction from which both parties might gain at the same time.

Another look at Figure 11 can show why it would *not* be possible to make either party better off by trading bushels beyond the equilibrium amount without making the other party worse off as a result. Focus on column *c* and consider producing and selling a 140 millionth bushel. The consumer would reap a marginal benefit of *H,* but the producer would incur a marginal cost of *G.* If a price of $10 were charged and paid, both parties would be worse off. The producer would lose an amount equal to the dotted segment because *MC* at *G* exceeds $10. The consumer would lose the shaded segment of column *c* because *MB* at *H* falls short of $10. Sure enough, one could make the producer better off (by setting a price above marginal cost at *G*), but then the consumer would be much worse off. Conversely, one could make the consumer better off (by setting a price below marginal benefit at *H*), but then the producer would be worse off. No *voluntary* transaction is possible to the right of point *E.*

As later chapters will show, other types of markets, called *imperfectly* competitive, do not maximize the net benefit to the left of point *E.* They are therefore called economically inefficient. In such markets, something prevents production beyond some quantity (such as 50 million bushels). As a result, some potential mutually beneficial transactions are not carried out and some social net benefit (here *DEF*) is not gained.

Summary

1. The major characteristics of a market that determine how it is organized are said to define the *market structure.* They include the number of firms operating in the market, the nature of the product traded, the degree to which market knowledge is available to traders, and the conditions of entry into or exit from the market. This chapter defines four major types of market structure—perfect competition, monopoly and cartels, oligopoly, and monopolistic competition—and focuses on perfect competition.

2. Perfect competition is a market structure characterized by a large number of independently acting buyers and also by a large number of independently acting sellers, by buyers viewing all units of the traded items as identical, regardless of the source of its supply, by buyers as well as sellers possessing full knowledge relevant to trading in the market, and by the absence of impediments to entry into or exit from this market for either buyers or sellers.

3. To understand the behavior of the profit-maximizing, perfectly competitive firm, we study its revenue as well as its cost. Just as physical input quantities multiplied by input prices translate into cost, so the physical output quantity multiplied by output price translates into revenue. One must distinguish various concepts of revenue: total, average, and marginal. Average revenue always equals the output price. Marginal revenue equals output price under perfect competition only.

4. Economic profit is the difference between total revenue and the total cost (explicit and implicit) associated with producing that revenue. To maximize economic profit in the short run (when some of its inputs are fixed), a perfectly competitive firm must adjust its rate of production until the rising marginal cost of production equals the given marginal benefit of production (which is the market-determined price of its output). There is, however, one exception to this rule. If its total revenue is insufficient to cover variable cost, the firm does better by shutting down at once and producing nothing at all. A series of examples show that the rising arm of a perfectly competitive firm's marginal cost curve, above the minimum level of average variable cost, constitutes the firm's short-run supply.

5. All else being equal, market supply can be derived by adding horizontally, at each conceivable price, the quantities supplied by all potential market participants. Thus, market supply is a summation of the marginal cost curves (above minimum AVC) of all firms operating in the market.

6. In the long run, firms in a perfectly competitive industry tend to become larger and more numerous in the presence of positive economic profit. They tend to become smaller and less numerous in the presence of negative economic profit. This process of industry expansion or contraction eventually produces a state of zero economic profit and an equality of product price with marginal cost and minimum average total cost. Long-run industry supply curves can be horizontal, downward sloping, or upward sloping.

7. Perfect competition is called perfect because it contains within it a strong tendency toward both technical efficiency and economic efficiency. Technical efficiency is a situation (P = minimum ATC) in which it is impossible, with current technical knowldege, to raise output from given inputs or alternatively, to produce a given output by using less of one input without using more of another input. Economic efficiency is a situation ($P = MC$) in which it is impossible to make a person better off without making another person worse off because all mutually beneficial transactions have already been carried out.

Key Concepts

average revenue, AR	economic profit, Π	industry structure	perfect competition
break-even point	external diseconomies	internal diseconomies	price takers
constant-cost industry	external economies	internal economies	shutdown point
decreasing-cost industry	increasing-cost industry	marginal revenue, MR	technical efficiency
economic efficiency	industry	market structure	total revenue, TR

Questions and Problems

1. Consider Figure 2. In panel (b), the optimization principle is applied to find the profit-maximizing output level where marginal benefit (in the form of marginal revenue = price) equals marginal cost (point B). What principle is applied in panel (a)?

2. In Figure 2, what would happen to the firm's profit-maximizing output level if the government imposed
   a. a $3 tax per bushel of apples?
   b. a $10,000 license fee?
   c. a 30 percent tax on profit?

3. The text discusses break-even points with respect to Figure 3 and identifies them as a in panel (a) and K in panel (b). Do such points exist in Figure 2?

4. The text section, A Business Operating with an Economic Loss, ends with the claim that the firm's loss would be $50,000 if it shut down at once. Interpret the meaning of that claim.

5. Suppose you were running the orchard depicted in Figure 5, the market price fell to $2.57/bushel, and you violated the profit-maximization rule ("shut down at once if product price falls below minimum average variable cost"). If you then equated marginal cost with price by producing 9,000 bushels/year, what would happen to you? Compute your fixed cost, variable cost, total cost, and economic profit.

6. Consider Figure 6. Make a list of factors that would *shift* the supply line derived in panel (c).

7. A perfectly competitive firm faces a price and

marginal revenue of $10 per bushel. Its average total cost is given in the accompanying table. Graph these data; then figure out the profit-maximizing output. Show the firm's short-run supply curve in the graph, if you can.

Q (bushels/year)	ATC (dollars/bushel)
20	14.00
40	11.60
60	9.50
80	8.10
100	7.30
120	7.00
140	6.80 (minimum)
160	6.90
180	7.00
200	7.40
220	8.00
240	9.10
260	10.20
280	12.00
300	14.00

8. Consider the accompanying figure and identify
   a. line *A*.
   b. line *B*.
   c. line *C*.
   d. line *D*.
   e. the short-run supply line.
   f. the average revenue line.
   g. the break-even point on the short-run supply line.
   h. the shutdown point on the short-run supply line.
   i. the average fixed cost curve.

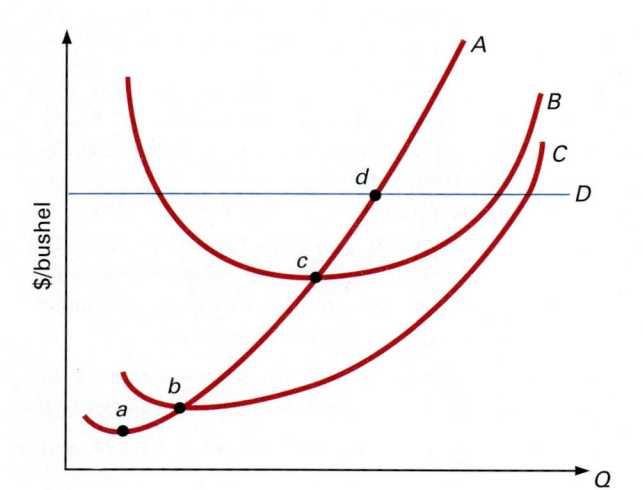

9. Look at the chapter "Consumer Preferences and Demand" and reread Figure 3. Draw an analogous four-panel graph for the perfectly competitive firm. Then interpret the meaning of the unshaded (net benefit) area in panel (c).

10. Are the following statements true or false?
    a. "The most profitable level of production for any firm is obviously the one at which average total cost is minimized."
    b. "Total variable cost at any output level equals the sum of marginal costs up to that output level."
    c. "The slope of a total revenue line equals marginal revenue, but only if the *TR* line is straight."
    d. "The slope of a total cost line equals marginal cost."
    e. "The short-run supply of a perfectly competitive firm equals the rising arm of marginal cost."
    f. "In perfect competition, profits ultimately serve as an inducement to bring price down to minimum average total cost."
    g. "In perfect competition, losses ultimately serve as an inducement to bring price up to minimum average total cost."

11. Given the market demand for its product, what do you think would happen to an industry under perfect competition if its inputs were gradually becoming exhausted? Explain.

12. The text notes that external economies or diseconomies might take the form of changes in the production function of all firms. Can you think of some examples?

13. "There is a subtle mistake in this chapter's Figures 8 and 9. In Figure 8, industry output rises—compare panels (a) and (c)—while that of the typical firm *declines*—compare panels (b) and (d). In Figure 9, industry output falls—compare panels (a) and (c)—while that of the typical firm *rises*—compare panels (b) and (d). Surely, this is contradictory." Comment.

CHAPTER 11

MONOPOLY AND CARTELS

Preview

This chapter introduces monopolies and cartels, extreme departures from the conditions of perfect competition. The reasons for the appearance of monopoly are explored, the rules of monopoly profit maximization are developed, and the major flaws of monopoly are examined. The incentive of competitive sellers to form cartels is considered, along with typical difficulties encountered by such would-be conspirators.

Examples

1. Polaroid Versus Kodak; Hughes Aircraft Versus the U.S. Government
2. Challenging Airfone's Monopoly
3. Technological Change and the Death of the Record Industry
4. The de Beers Diamond Cartel
5. Coffee: Another Cartel Bites the Dust

Ideas in History

The Theory of Monopoly

When markets are perfectly competitive, no single buyer, when acting alone, has the power to influence the prevailing equilibrium price. If any one buyer insisted on paying a lower price, no seller would be willing to accommodate that wish. Plenty of other competing buyers would be willing to pay the equilibrium price, and every seller would be aware of this fact. Similarly, if any one seller charged an above-equilibrium price, all potential buyers would vanish. Plenty of other competing sellers would be willing to accept the equilibrium price, and every buyer would be aware of these alternatives. In this chapter and the next, however, we turn to other, so-called **imperfectly competitive markets** in which one or more of the characteristics of perfect competition are absent and individuals often do have the power to dictate prices.

Consider the case of a market in which a single seller offers an item for which no good substitutes are available and into which the entry of other sellers is severely restricted or even impossible. Such a situation defines a **monopoly.** By threatening to withhold the product from would-be buyers, such a single seller also has the power to influence the price at which exchanges take place. Examples are provided by the de Beers Consolidated Mining Company (selling diamonds), by Polaroid (selling instant-photography cameras and films), by local sellers of cable TV and telephone services, and by electric power companies.

Consider, instead, a market in which all existing sellers conspire to put up a joint front toward buyers, acting as if they were one and making joint price and output decisions. Such a **cartel** has the same power that a monopoly does. Examples are provided by the Organization of Petroleum Exporting

Countries (OPEC), by government-sponsored price-fixing schemes for agricultural products, and by labor unions.

As later chapters show, lack of competition can also exist on the buyers' side of a market. In some markets, there is only a single buyer and the entry of other buyers is blocked or highly unlikely. Such a buyer, called a **monopsony,** by threatening would-be sellers not to buy from them, can influence the price at which transactions occur. Examples are provided by the markets for aircraft carriers, nuclear submarines, or space shuttles (which, presumably, are bought by the federal government only); by markets for raw tobacco that might be supplied by numerous farmers facing a single processing company; or by markets for labor supplied in isolated towns containing a single dominant employer. (Think of such "company towns" as Butte, Montana, and the Anaconda Copper Company; Corning, New York, and the Corning Glass Company; Hershey, Pennsylvania, and the Hershey Chocolate Company; and Barstow, California, and the Santa Fe Railway.)

Unlike last chapter's price takers, imperfectly competitive sellers and buyers who have the power to influence the prices at which transactions take place are called **price setters.** This chapter will focus on two types of price setters, monopolies and cartels.

The Sources of Monopoly

A number of reasons for the appearance of a monopoly exist. They include increasing returns to scale, the concentrated ownership of key resources, patents and copyrights, and exclusive franchises. We will discuss each of these factors in turn.

Increasing Returns to Scale

A firm may be subject to increasing returns to scale, such as the electric power company depicted in Figure 1. The downward-sloping straight line represents the market demand for electric power; the curved heavy line measures the firm's long-run average total cost, *LRATC*. It envelops a multitude of short-run curves, each representing the average total costs associated with a given plant, such as plants number 5, 21, 28, or 32 shown in the graph.

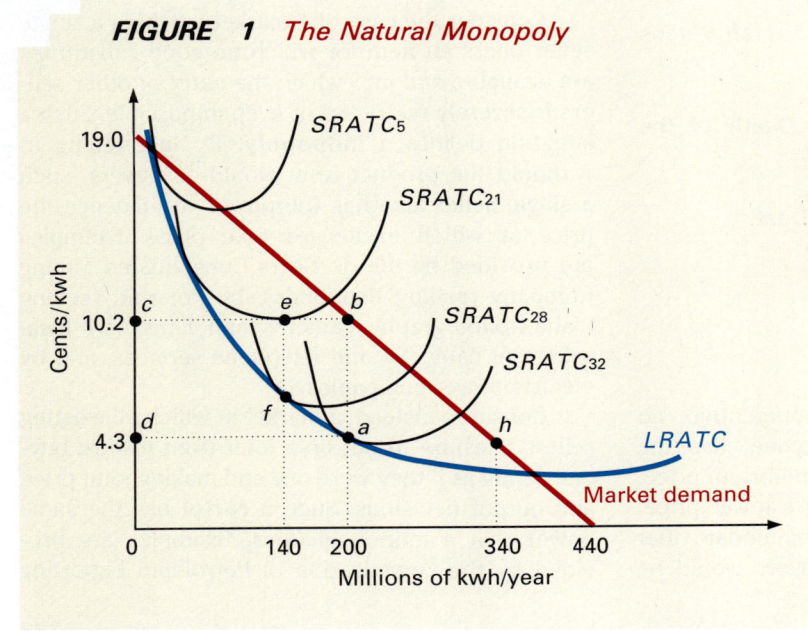

FIGURE 1 **The Natural Monopoly**

Increasing returns to scale may be responsible for the "natural" appearance of monopoly because the first firm to take advantage of them can supply the entire market demand at a lower average total cost than any larger number of firms could achieve.

Whenever a firm's *LRATC* is declining throughout the range of quantities that might be demanded in the market, the situation produces a **natural monopoly.** A monopoly "naturally" develops because increasing returns to scale make it possible for one firm to produce all that the market demands at any given price and to do so at a lower average total cost than would be encountered by several firms each producing smaller quantities.

The first firm to recognize this fact might build plant #32 and operate it at point *a*, producing 200 million kilowatt hours (kwh) per year at an average total cost of 4.3¢ each. This quantity can be sold, as point *b* indicates, for 10.2 cents/kwh, yielding a profit of 5.9¢/kwh (*ab*) or $11.8 million/year (*abcd*). Any potential rival who wanted to match the 10.2¢/kwh price would have to build a plant of size #21 at least and run that plant at its capacity at *e*. (An even larger plant, such as #28, could in the long run produce the same 140 million kwh/year output for less if run below *its* capacity at *f*.) Yet if such a newcomer appeared on the scene, market supply would rise from the original 200 million kwh/year to 200 + 140 = 340 million kwh/year and that quantity could only be sold at the 4¢/kwh price corresponding to *h*. Such a price would create a loss for the newcomer since *h* is lower than either *e* or *f*. The prospect of such a loss would keep the newcomer from ever entering the market. Such a natural monopoly, resulting from technical factors, is common for producers of electric power, gas, water, and local telephone service. It is not, however, the only source of monopoly, as the following sections will show.

Concentrated Ownership of Key Resources

Firms can also become monopolies if they own all of the known quantities of some key resource without which the industry's product cannot be produced. Alcoa (the Aluminum Company of America) once controlled most of the bauxite deposits from which aluminum is made; American Metal Climax, in a single Colorado mountain, once owned most of the world's molybdenum; and the International Nickel Company once possessed most of the world's nickel.

Not all such "artificial" monopolies, however, are based on the concentrated ownership of natural resources. New York's Metropolitan Opera Company once held a virtual monopoly in American opera, simply because all the experienced singers had signed long-term contracts with the Met.

Patents and Copyrights

Another type of artificial monopoly arises when the government grants patents and copyrights. A **patent** is an exclusive right to the use of an invention. A patent is limited to a period of 17 years and permits the holder to prevent all others from producing a specified product (such as Polaroid's instant-picture camera) or using a specified process (such as Alcoa's process for turning alumina into aluminum ingots). A **copyright** is an exclusive right to the publishing, sale, or reproduction of a literary, musical, or artistic work. It is also granted for a limited period.

These protections are designed to encourage the production, disclosure, and dissemination of items that can be copied by others easily and cheaply but that can be created in the first place only by engaging in a risky and expensive venture. Presumably, the creators will try to recoup their development expenses during the period of artificial monopoly by setting an appropriately high price. Although the period in question is limited, the sellers in question often gain an impregnable market position by the time this protection expires. Instances of past monopolies that were based on patents include aluminum, cash registers, cellophane, instant-picture cameras, rayon, scotch tape, shoe machinery, and xerography. Example 1 reports on recent court battles concerning copyrights.

Exclusive Franchises

The oldest source of monopoly, perhaps, is the **exclusive franchise,** a government grant to a single seller of the exclusive right to produce and sell a good. Ancient kings and queens used to grant this privilege to their favored subjects. By setting them free to gouge the general public, they could enrich them without depleting the royal coffers. The British East India Company (involved in the Boston Tea Party) is a famous case in point, but modern governments often do the same thing. Consider the monopolies bestowed upon the U.S. Postal Service

EXAMPLE 1

Polaroid Versus Kodak; Hughes Aircraft Versus the U.S. Government

An example of a monopoly based on patents is provided by the instant-picture camera, invented and patented by Polaroid in the late 1950s. In 1976, when the original patent expired, Kodak entered the market with an instant picture camera of its own. Polaroid sued for patent infringement.

By 1985, when Kodak had sold 16.5 million such cameras and held a 25 percent market share, a court ruled in favor of Polaroid. Seven Polaroid patents that had not yet expired had indeed been infringed. Kodak was ordered to cease production of its cameras and their associated films, which made the existing cameras worthless to their users. Kodak exchanged each of them for other products or one share of company stock. Thus, Polaroid's monopoly was restored, and it instantly sued for $5.7 billion in damages.

A similar case involves the Hughes Aircraft Company, which developed the crucial technology for positioning satellites. Patented in 1973, the system employs sensors that use the sun to record a satellite's position in space, relay the information to a ground station, which relays a new position to the satellite's antenna. The satellite then fires a small propulsion jet in precise bursts to change the satellite's position. The positioning ability is essential for the geostationary satellites used extensively in communications, both civilian and military. The U.S. government used the Hughes system in over 100 satellites. When a 1983 court convicted the United States of patent infringement, Hughes Aircraft sued for $3.3 billion in damages.

Source: Edmund L. Andrews, "Patent Case May Cost U.S. Billions," *The New York Times,* April 22, 1989, pp. 35 and 36.

---

and on radio and television stations by the federal government. Monopolies are also granted by state governments to airport car rental companies, auto insurance companies, or restaurant chains operating along state turnpikes; and by local governments to dozens of firms, ranging from cable TV companies and garbage collectors to liquor stores, taxi companies, and food sellers at sports events. Example 2 tells of a recent monopoly based on an exclusive franchise.

A Monopoly's Cost and Revenue

To understand the profit-maximizing behavior of a monopoly, we must study its cost and revenue. Having detailed the perfectly competitive firm's cost and revenue in the last two chapters, we can quickly note the differences one might expect if the market contains only a single seller who is protected from the entry of other sellers.

The Cost Curves

The cost curves of a monopoly have the same general shape as those of a perfect competitor. Like any firm, a monopoly faces a production function that determines which physical inputs can be converted into how much output, and it also faces the need to buy the physical inputs at the prevailing market prices. While the cost curves have the same *general* shape as those depicted in Figures 1 through 6 of the chapter "The Cost of Production," a subtle difference (although not a logical necessity) is conceivable. All the cost curves may well be higher than they would be if the firm operated in a competitive environment. At least three reasons for such a possibility are usually advanced.

Technical Inefficiency

Because a monopoly does not face the threat of competition, it is often argued, its management can relax and afford to get less than the maximum pos-

EXAMPLE 2

Challenging Airfone's Monopoly

Since he left the army where he first learned about micro-wave radio transmissions, John D. Goeken has proven to be a brilliant pioneer in tele-communications technology. In the 1960s, he founded Microwave Communications, Inc., a company then providing 2-way radio service to truck drivers and now known as MCI, the second largest long-distance telephone company (after AT&T). He also set up the FTD Mercury Network, which processes millions of orders for florists each year. Then, in 1976, he founded Airfone, a company that was soon granted an exclusive franchise by the Federal Communications Commission (FCC) to provide public telephone service on commercial airliners while in flight. Eventually, Mr. Goeken sold Airfone to the GTE Corporation.

The availability of airfone service, however, rose slowly, being found on 37 planes in 1984, on 1,108 planes by 1989 (then 27 percent of the U.S. fleet). The price was $7.50 for the first three minutes and $1.25 for each additional minute. The quality of the service was far from perfect; users complained about being cut off in the middle of conversations. Then Mr. Goeken founded the Goeken Group and challenged the FCC to let him share the 4 megahertz assigned to the Airfone monopoly. He would provide higher quality air phone service, he said, and would do so at lower rates, while adding numerous additional services: the inflight ability to transmit and receive data and facsimiles (on lap top computers), to make airline, rental car, and hotel reservations on 800-numbers, and even to call up quotes on corporate stocks.

In late 1989, the FCC decided to end the Airfone monopoly. It granted licenses to four additional firms: Goeken's In-Flight Phone Corporation, the American Skycell Corporation, the Clairtel Communications Group, and the Mobile Telecommunications Technologies Corporation. Meanwhile, the GTE Corporation settled a Goeken suit challenging its monopolistic behavior by paying Goeken and other original Airfone founders $15.5 million in damages.

Sources: Calvin Sims, "Challenging Airfone's Monopoly," *The New York Times,* September 5, 1989, pp. D1 and D3, January 2, 1990, p. D2; Mark Lewyn, "Ground to Airfone: Prepare for Hostile Fire," *Business Week,* February 12, 1990, p. 88; Keith Bradsher, "Founder of Airfone Wins Big Settlement With GTE," *The New York Times,* March 21, 1991, pp. D1 and D5.

---

sible quantity of output from any given set of inputs. As a result of such bad management, any given set of output is produced with more inputs and thus at a higher cost than necessary. The fixed, variable, and total cost curves—and the average and marginal cost curves derived from them—simply lie higher in a monopoly graph than they would if a perfectly competitive firm were involved. As a result, it is alleged, a monopoly's output is never produced at the lowest possible average total cost achievable for that output level.

Yet caution is advised. Recall the chapter, "The Firm: An Overview," and the discussion of principal-agent problems. Might not the stockholders of a monopoly firm be able to motivate managers to do their best by the same techniques (stock options, golden parachutes, and the like) that allegedly work so well in other firms? Might not the managers of a monopoly firm be just as concerned about losing their jobs through takeovers as any other managers are?

Lack of Innovation

Because a monopoly does not face the threat of competition, it is further argued, its management—even if it achieves technical efficiency at any given point in time—may not be interested in *advancing* technical knowledge so that even more output can be gained from given inputs than was previously thought possible. Such advances would, over time, shift up the production function (that relates physical input quantities to maximum possible output) and, therefore, shift down all the cost curves derived from it. In the monopoly case, it is alleged, cost curves would simply fail to shift down over time.

Such a result, once again, is possible but certainly not assured. Outsiders who think that technical improvements can be made (and that costs, therefore, can be reduced and profit raised) are always waiting to take over a lethargic firm. Managers know this threat and can best protect their jobs by innovating at a rapid rate. Indeed, monopolies that achieve positive economic profit, unlike perfect competitors, need not fear having their profit competed away through industry expansion, as described in the last chapter. Therefore, such *permanent* monopoly profit can be used to finance research and development (R & D) programs that improve production functions over time much more rapidly than could be achieved under perfect competition's ever-present tendency toward zero economic profit.[1]

Rent Seeking

The most important possibility, perhaps, for monopoly cost curves being excessively high is associated with **rent seeking,** a set of activities through which monopolies expend valuable resources not to produce goods but to obtain, strengthen, and defend their monopoly positions (and to gain long-lasting profit). Some 10,000 registered lobbyists are in Washington (all of whom could be engaged in producing scarce goods) with the main purpose of manipulating government agencies into granting exclusive franchises and similar privileges to the firms that employ them. Their employment implies that the costs for producing the affected firms' output are higher than necessary. Or consider all the lawyers employed in the kind of court battles described in Examples 1 and 2.

The Revenue Curves

For revenue, a major difference emerges between a monopoly and a perfectly competitive firm. While a monopoly satisfies the entire market demand at a price it is free to set, a perfectly competitive firm satisfies a negligible fraction of market demand and does so at a price it cannot influence.

Table 1 can help us see what is involved. Columns 1 and 2 represent the market demand for electric power. It is produced, we assume, by a monopoly firm. People often think that such a monopoly can do "anything it wants" because buyers are trapped. After all, there is no good substitute for electric power, they say. Yet, the power generating firm can trap buyers only in the sense that they cannot get electric power from anyone else; in another sense, buyers are free. Once a price has been announced, buyers can decide on the quantity they will take; the monopoly firm must reckon with this fact. In our example, people would gladly take 250 million kwh/year if electricity could be had for nothing (row F), but at 4¢/kwh, they will only buy 200 million kwh/year (row E). Some air conditioners will then be turned off in the summer. Some houses will be heated with oil or wood in the winter, while other people will save electric power by wearing warmer clothes. Now picture the firm raising the kilowatt-hour price even more—from 4¢ (row E) to 8¢, 12¢, 16¢, and even 20¢ (row A). The quantity demanded falls more and more, vanishing altogether in the end. It is doubtful that the monopoly firm will raise its price to 20¢; selling nothing at a high price per unit is unlikely to maximize its profit.

The *total revenue TR* associated with price-quantity combinations A to F is given in column 3. As for the perfectly competitive firm, it equals output price times quantity. The firm's *average rev-*

---

[1] What is the empirical evidence? It seems that a blend of small and large firms (which are neither perfect competitors nor monopolies and which are operating in an environment with moderate barriers to market entry) is most conducive to technical advance. Where the entry of new firms is very easy, the fear of rapid imitation of R & D successes seems to discourage such inevitably expensive programs. Where entry of rivals is impossible, the lack of any competitive threat seems to discourage such an effort as well. For more on the subject, see Heinz Kohler, *Intermediate Microeconomics: Theory and Applications*, 2nd ed. (Glenview, IL: Scott, Foresman and Co., 1986), pp. 388–389.

TABLE 1 A Monopoly's Revenue

	Market Demand		Revenue		
	Price, P ($/kwh)	Quantity, Q (millions of kwh/yr)	Total revenue, $TR = P \cdot Q$ (millions of $/yr)	Average revenue, $AR = \dfrac{TR}{Q} = \dfrac{P \cdot Q}{Q} = P$ ($/kwh)	Marginal revenue, $MR = \dfrac{\Delta TR}{\Delta Q}$ (extra $/extra kwh)
	(1)	(2)	(3) = (1)·(2)	(4) = $\dfrac{(3)}{(2)}$	(5) = $\dfrac{\Delta(3)}{\Delta(2)}$
A.	.20	0	0	20	
					$\dfrac{+8}{+50} = .16$
B.	.16	50	8	16	
					$\dfrac{+4}{+50} = .08$
C.	.12	100	12	12	
					$\dfrac{0}{+50} = 0$
D.	.08	150	12	8	
					$\dfrac{-4}{+50} = -.08$
E.	.04	200	8	4	
					$\dfrac{-8}{+50} = -.16$
F.	0	250	0	0	

A monopoly faces the entire market demand, given in columns (1) and (2). It can set its output price at any level it wishes, column (1), but must then live with the consequences, columns (2)–(5). A crucial different emerges between perfect competition and monopoly. If the monopoly charges a uniform price of all its customers (as assumed here), the monopoly's marginal revenue [column (5)] lies below its price [column (1)]; under perfect competition, $P = MR$ always.

enue AR is again the ratio of total revenue over output quantity; therefore, it is the same as the firm's chosen output price (column 4). Column 5, finally, contains a surprise. As we calculate the monopoly's *marginal revenue MR* (or the change in total revenue divided by the associated change in output quantity), we note an important fact. *As long as a monopoly charges a uniform price of all its customers (as we have assumed), a monopoly's marginal revenue, unlike its average revenue, is always smaller than its chosen price.* We can explain this phenomenon with the help of a simple numerical exercise based on Table 1.

Figure 2 tells the story graphically. Panel (a) graphs columns (3) and (2) of Table 1 and thus pictures total revenue. Panel (b) graphs the associated lines of average revenue (always equal to market demand) and of marginal revenue, using the data of

NUMERICAL EXERCISE 1

Calculating Marginal Revenue

Case 1: Imagine the monopoly charging an initial price of 16¢/kwh and selling 50 million kwh/year (alternative B). If it drops its price to 12¢/kwh, sales rise to 100 million kwh/year (alternative C). Two consequences are involved. The 50 million kwh/year previously sold are now sold for 12¢ instead of 16¢ each. This change will delight old customers but means a *loss* of revenue to the firm of 4¢/kwh on 50 million kwh/year, or $2 million/year. On the other hand, an additional 50 million kwh/year are sold to new customers, also at 12¢ each, a *gain* of revenue to the firm of $6 million/year. The $6 million revenue gain outweighs the $2 million revenue loss, making for a +$4 million total-revenue change. Accordingly, the change in total revenue per extra kilowatt-hour sold equals +$4 million/year divided by +50 million kwh/year, or +8¢/kwh; note the second entry in Table 1, column 5.

Case 2: Imagine the monopoly charging an initial price of 8¢/kwh and selling 150 million kwh/year (alternative D). If it drops its price to 4¢/kwh, sales rise to 200 million kwh/year (alternative E). Again, two consequences are involved. Old customers get 150 million kwh/year for 4¢/kwh less than before; the firm's revenue *loss* is $6 million/year. New customers buy an extra 50 million kwh/year at the new 4¢/kwh price, bringing in a revenue *gain* of $2 million/year. The $6 million revenue loss outweighs the $2 million revenue gain, making for a −$4 million total-revenue change. Accordingly, the change in total revenue per kilowatt hour sold equals −$4 million/year divided by +50 million kwh/year, or −8¢/kwh; note the fourth entry in Table 1, column 5.

FOCUS 1

Major Concepts of Revenue Under Monopoly

1. Total Revenue
   $TR = P \cdot Q$

2. Average Revenue
   $AR = \dfrac{TR}{Q} = \dfrac{P \cdot Q}{Q} = P$

3. Marginal Revenue
   $MR = \dfrac{\Delta TR}{\Delta Q} < P$

where P is the output price chosen by the monopoly firm and uniformly charged of all its customers.

---

columns 4, 5, and 2 of Table 1. The relationships involved are identical to those in Table 6 and Figure 10 of the chapter "Elasticity."

As long as the absolute value of the own-price elasticity of demand exceeds 1 (as between A and M), lower price goes with higher total revenue (between 0 and m). Accordingly, marginal revenue is positive (between A and G). Yet, total revenue rises at a decreasing rate toward maximum m, hence the positive marginal revenue between A and G also falls.

Once the absolute value of the own-price elasticity of demand falls below 1 (between M and F), lower price goes with lower total revenue (between m and n). Accordingly marginal revenue is negative (between G and H). Because total revenue falls at an increasing rate to the right of m, the marginal revenue between G and H is not only negative but also falls.

FIGURE 2 The Monopoly and Its Revenue

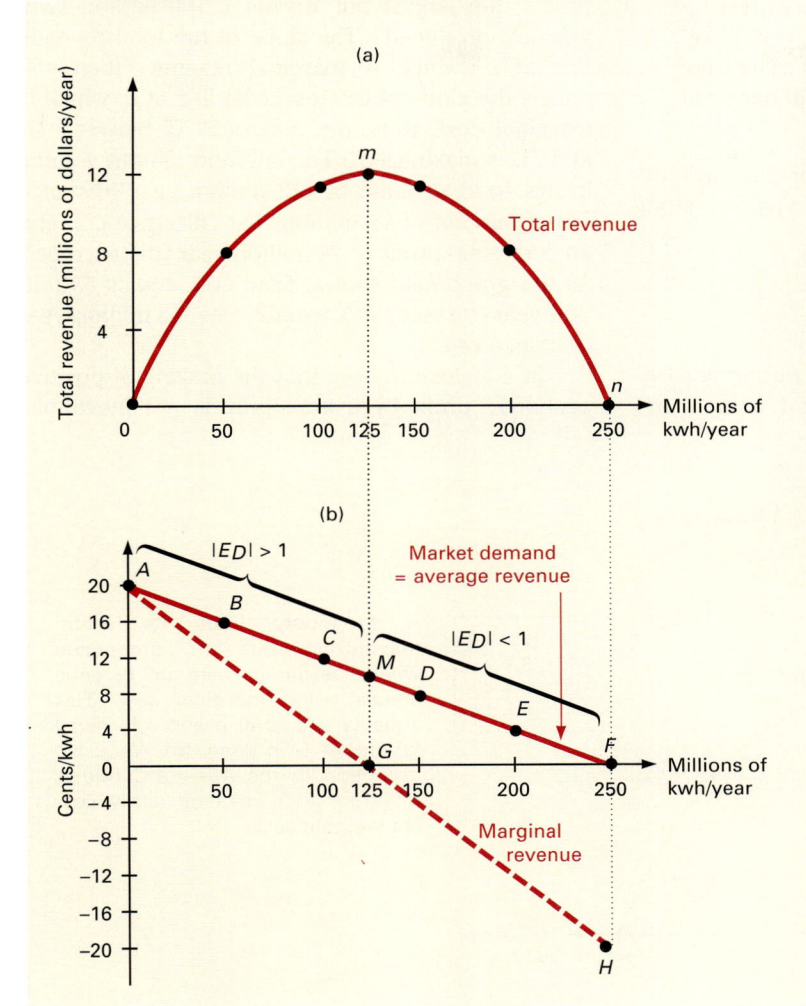

A monopoly is confronted with the entire market demand, such as line AF. It can set the price of its output at any level it wishes; the quantity demanded adjusts accordingly. Starting at A in panel (b), successive price reductions always raise quantity demanded. As price is lowered, total revenue rises (from 0 toward m) and marginal revenue is positive (along AG) as long as the own-price elasticity of demand E_D has an absolute value greater than 1 (between A and M). On the other hand, as price is lowered, total revenue falls (from m toward n) and marginal revenue is negative (between G and H) once the own-price elasticity of demand has an absolute value of less than 1 (between M and F).

Thus, it is no accident that total revenue is maximized (at m) and marginal revenue is zero (at G) precisely at that quantity (125 million kwh/year) at which the own-price elasticity of demand equals |1|, as at point M. A marginal revenue line associated with a straight demand line always begins at the demand line's vertical intercept (point A) and then bisects the distance between origin 0 and the horizontal intercept (point F), as at G. Thus, 0G = GF.

The Maximization of Economic Profit

Given a monopoly's cost and revenue, we now ask how a monopoly maximizes its economic profit. The answer, once again, involves the optimization principle.

To maximize economic profit, a monopoly must adjust its rate of production until the rising marginal cost of production equals the

292 PART III *Markets for Goods*

declining marginal benefit of production (its marginal revenue). There is, however, one exception to the rule. If its total revenue is insufficient to cover variable cost (and price, therefore, is below average variable cost), the firm does better by shutting down at once and producing nothing at all.

We illustrate this rule with a series of examples, using the revenue lines introduced in Figure 2 along with varying sets of cost data.

A Profitable Monopoly

Consider Figure 3. In panel (a), any output level to the left of point a (and to the right of point d) brings a loss because total cost then exceeds total revenue. Output levels between a and d produce profits; the largest one occurs if 100 million kwh/year are produced. (The slope of the total revenue line at b, which is marginal revenue, then just equals the slope of the total cost line at c, which is marginal cost; thus, the difference Π between TR and TC is maximized.) The optimum output volume brings total revenue of $12 million/year (distance bf), total cost of $8 million/year (distance cf), and an economic profit of $4 million/year (distance bc). As the graph also shows, fixed cost equals $3 million/year (distance ef), variable cost $5 million/year (distance ce).

In conclusion, note that the making of positive economic profit by a monopoly is not inevitable.

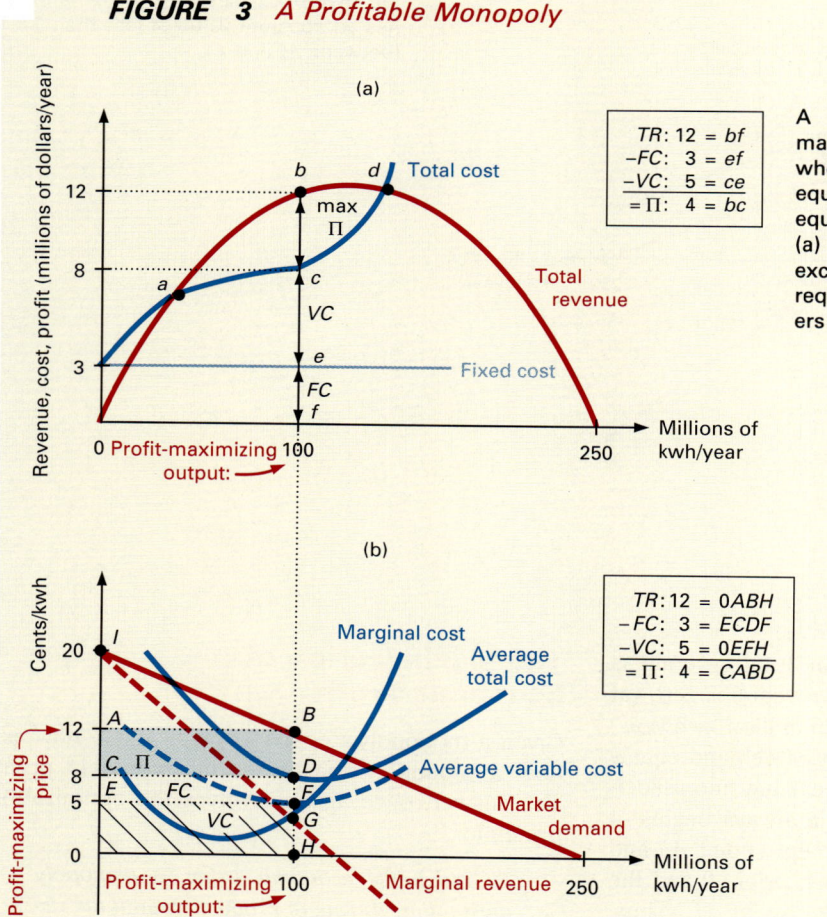

FIGURE 3 A Profitable Monopoly

TR: 12 = bf	
$-FC$: 3 = ef	
$-VC$: 5 = ce	
= Π: 4 = bc	

A monopoly finds its profit-maximizing rate of production where declining marginal revenue equals rising marginal cost. This equality occurs at b and c in panel (a) and at G in panel (b). *Note:* No exception to the $MR = MC$ rule is required; total revenue easily covers variable cost.

TR: 12 = 0ABH	
$-FC$: 3 = $ECDF$	
$-VC$: 5 = 0EFH	
= Π: 4 = $CABD$	

NUMERICAL EXERCISE 2

The Case of Positive Economic Profit

Panel (b) of Figure 3 allows us to find maximum profit in a different way. Up to an output volume of $H = 100$ million kwh/year, every kilowatt hour produced adds more to total revenue (note the marginal revenue along segment *IG*) than it adds to total cost (note the lower marginal cost line left of *G*). Thus, profit rises. To the right of *G*, the opposite is true. (Marginal cost then exceeds marginal revenue, and raising output lowers profit.) Having decided on the profit-maximizing output level (the level 0*H* corresponding to point *G*), the monopoly sets a price designed to sell that quantity, or *BH* = 12¢/kwh. Accordingly, total revenue is measured by price *BH* times quantity 0*H*, or rectangle 0*ABH* ($12 million/year), which corresponds to *bf* in panel (a). Fixed cost equals average fixed cost *DF* (3¢/kwh) times quantity 0*H* (100 million kwh/year), or white rectangle *ECDF* ($3 million/year), which corresponds to *ef* in panel (a). Variable cost equals average variable cost *FH* (5¢/kwh) times quantity 0*H* (100 million kwh/year), or crosshatched rectangle 0*EFH* ($5 million/year), which corresponds to *ce* in panel (a). By implication, maximum possible profit equals average profit *BD* (4¢/kwh) times quantity 0*H* (100 million kwh/year), or shaded rectangle *CABD* ($4 million/year), which corresponds to *bc* in panel (a).

If demand were to fall or costs were to rise, the monopoly could make zero profit or even incur a loss. The sections that follow illustrate two such possibilities.

A Zero-Profit Monopoly

Figure 4 depicts demand conditions identical to those in Figure 3 but with higher costs. In panel (a) only one output level exists at which losses can be avoided (point *a*). At this 100 million kwh/year level of production, total revenue just equals total cost, and profit is zero. As before, panel (b) provides the same information in a different way. The equality at *F* of marginal revenue and marginal cost points to the best output level; the demand line shows the price at which it can be sold (point *B*). At any higher price, less would be demanded; at any lower price, more. But the firm is not interested in selling less or more; it wants to sell the profit-maximizing output level and therefore sets the corresponding 12¢/kwh price.

A Monopoly Incurring a Loss

Figure 5 depicts a scenario in which costs are higher still. The firm cannot avoid making a loss. In the long run it will shut down, but in the short run it pays to operate because total revenue more than covers variable cost. As a look at panel (a) shows, the inevitable short-run loss is minimized (by distance *ab*) if 100 million kwh/year are produced. Panel (b) tells the same story. Marginal revenue equals marginal cost at *G*. Output 0*H* can be sold at a price of *DH*, and total revenue then equals rectangle 0*CDH*. This revenue more than covers the crosshatched rectangle of variable cost. As a result, a part of fixed cost (white rectangle *ECDF*) can be covered as well, leaving another part (dotted rectangle *CABD*), which is the firm's economic loss. Yet, in the short run, while fixed cost cannot be escaped, the $3 million/year loss is preferable to shutting down at once and incurring a $10 million/year loss equal to fixed cost. Ideas in History, Antoine Cournot and the Theory of Monopoly, tells about the economist who developed this theory.

Conclusions

From the forgoing discussion a number of pertinent conclusions emerge. We will consider four of them.

First, a monopoly finds its profit-maximizing position by adjusting its output (and therefore the level of its marginal cost) until rising marginal cost

FIGURE 4 A Zero-Profit Monopoly

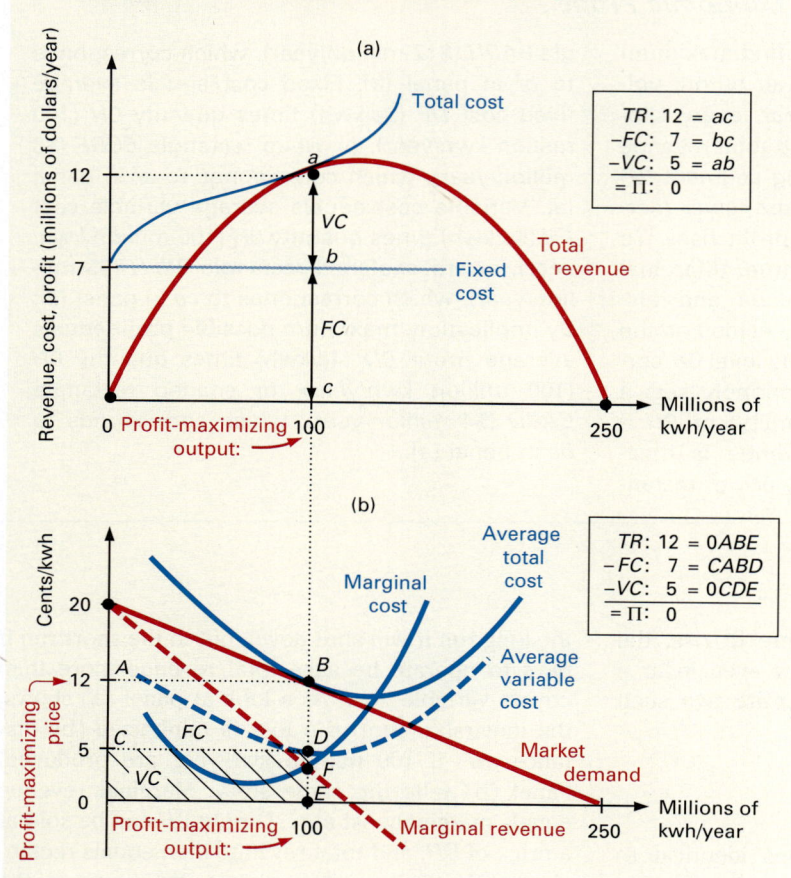

A monopoly finds its profit-maximizing rate of production where declining marginal revenue equals rising marginal cost. This equality occurs at *a* in panel (a) and at *F* in panel (b). *Note:* Although the firm makes zero profit, no exception to the *MR* = *MC* rule is required; total revenue easily covers variable cost (as well as all fixed cost).

Panel (a):
TR: 12 = ac
−FC: 7 = bc
−VC: 5 = ab
= Π: 0

Panel (b):
TR: 12 = 0ABE
−FC: 7 = CABD
−VC: 5 = 0CDE
= Π: 0

equals falling marginal revenue. But marginal cost is always positive and never zero or negative. Therefore, at the chosen output level, marginal revenue is positive as well. *A monopoly will never choose an output level at which marginal revenue is zero or negative.* (This conclusion makes a lot of sense: Why would any firm produce another unit of output—which inevitably *increases* its total cost—if the sale of that unit adds nothing to total revenue or even reduces it? Such an action would reduce profit and would, therefore, not be taken.)

Second, if the profit-maximizing output level is always associated with positive marginal revenue [along segment *AG* in panel (b), Figure 2], then the following is also true. *The price chosen by a monopoly will always lie in the elastic section of the de-* mand line facing it [as in section *AM* in panel (b)]. A monopoly that charges a price corresponding to inelastic demand (as section *MF*) cannot be maximizing profit. It could increase profit by cutting production and raising price.

Third, unlike a perfectly competitive firm, *a monopoly does not have a supply curve.* If anything, a monopoly only has a supply *point;* it confronts its customers with a single price-quantity combination that it has chosen and says "take it or leave it." Consider point *B* in Figure 3, point *B* in Figure 4, or point *D* in Figure 5. A supply line, after all, shows all the alternative quantities a firm or group of firms would supply at all conceivable prices that the forces of demand and supply might establish. In the case of monopoly, however, market forces do not

FIGURE 5 A Monopoly Incurring a Loss

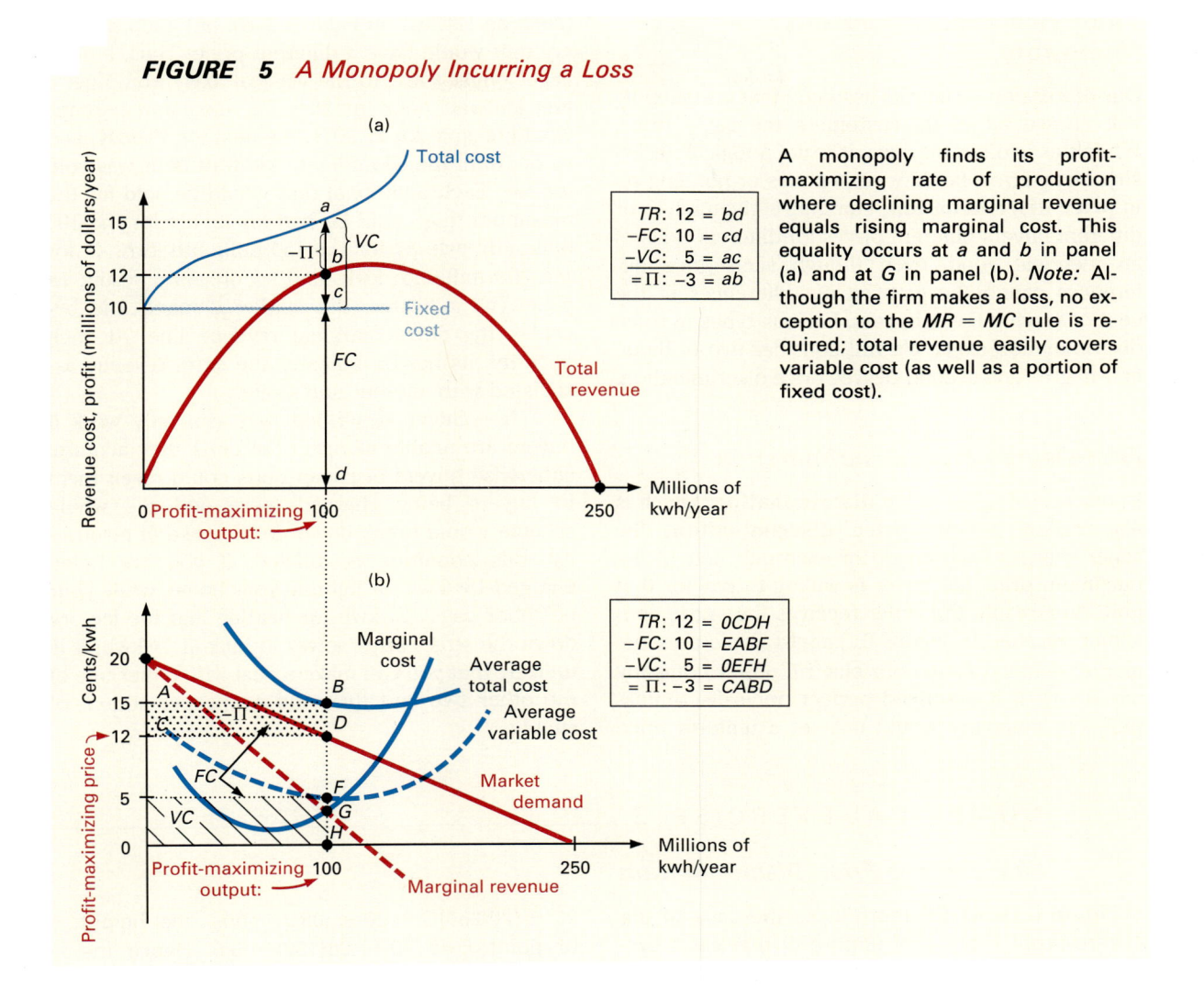

(a)

TR: 12 = bd
−FC: 10 = cd
−VC: 5 = ac
=Π: −3 = ab

(b)

TR: 12 = 0CDH
−FC: 10 = EABF
−VC: 5 = 0EFH
=Π: −3 = CABD

A monopoly finds its profit-maximizing rate of production where declining marginal revenue equals rising marginal cost. This equality occurs at *a* and *b* in panel (a) and at *G* in panel (b). *Note:* Although the firm makes a loss, no exception to the $MR = MC$ rule is required; total revenue easily covers variable cost (as well as a portion of fixed cost).

---

establish a price that the firm must simply accept. The firm makes its own conscious choice on the matter, asking itself which price among the many that it might set would make customers willingly buy the quantity that would maximize its profit (because at that quantity $MR = MC$).

Fourth, we should note that *any profit made by a monopoly may well be permanent profit*. Consider the profitable firm depicted in Figure 3. If the firm were a perfect competitor, the existence of profit would quickly raise the size and number of firms in the industry. This expansion would raise market supply and lower output price. Over time—regardless of whether the industry was one of constant, decreasing, or increasing cost—the profit would tend to disappear. No such thing happens in the case of monopoly because market entry to other firms is blocked. Thus, the profit pictured in Figure 3 can be reaped year after year.

However, as Figures 4 and 5 indicate, positive monopoly profit is not a certainty; like any firm, a monopoly can also incur zero profit or even a loss. On that account, however, a monopoly has another advantage over the perfectly competitive firm. It can improve its profit position by engaging in *price discrimination*.

The Price Discriminating Monopoly

Our discussion so far has assumed that a monopoly will charge all of its customers the same price. While this is often the case, it is not a logical necessity. Many firms, be they monopolies or not, engage in **price discrimination,** charging a given buyer or different buyers different prices for different units of an identical good, even though such price differences cannot be justified by differences in the cost of serving these buyers. Various types of price discrimination exist. We will consider two of them, first-degree and second-degree price discrimination.

First-Degree Price Discrimination

Under **first-degree price discrimination,** which is also called **perfect price discrimination,** the seller charges each buyer for each unit bought the maximum price the buyer is willing to pay for that unit. As a result, the seller receives the entire consumer surplus. In Figure 6, panel (a) pictures the market demand facing our electric power company monopoly. If it practiced perfect price discrimination, the company would not set a uniform price (such as 12¢/kwh in Figures 3–5), but each and every unit would have a different price. Thus, a most eager buyer (next to the vertical axis) would get a first kilowatt hour for 20¢. The next unit perhaps would be sold for 19.997¢, the next for 19.984¢, and so on, until the 50 millionth kilowatt hour was sold for 16¢. Each additional unit would be sold for the maximum that could be had for it: 12¢ for the 100 millionth kwh, 8¢ for the 150 millionth kwh, 4¢ for the 200 millionth kwh, and so on. As a result, as panel (b) indicates, the market demand line becomes the firm's marginal revenue line. At each quantity, its height indicates the extra revenue associated with another unit's sale.

The scheme described here can only work if buyers are unable to resell the units they acquire. Otherwise buyers of cheap units could resell them to buyers being charged more and the whole scheme would break down. In the case of electricity, this condition is fulfilled. If you are being charged 18¢/kwh for lighting your home, while your neighbor pays 12¢/kwh for heating and the factory down the street buys power in bulk at 7¢/kwh, it is unlikely that you can make a deal with either one of the other two and thus find a cheaper source of supply.

NUMERICAL EXERCISE 3

First-Degree Price Discrimination

Figure 6 panel (b) reproduces the case of the zero-profit monopoly (Figure 4) that set a uniform price of 12¢/kwh and produced 100 million kwh/year (point *B*). By practicing first-degree price discrimination, this monopoly can equate marginal revenue with marginal cost at *F* and produce 130 million kwh/year. Its total revenue then equals area 0*AFG*, or $19.24 million/year. Its total cost (rectangle 0*CEG*) equals average total cost *EG* (10.6¢/kwh) times output 0*G* (130 million kwh/year), or $13.78 million/year. Hence its profit, once zero, rises to $19.24 − 13.78 = $5.46 million/year (triangle *ACD* minus triangle *DEF*).

Using algebra, you can also calculate this result. The equation of the demand and marginal revenue line, as the intercepts reveal, is $P = 20 - (20/250)Q = 20 - .08Q$. Thus, the height of point *F* is $20 - .08(130) = 9.6$. Hence the rectangle 0*HFG* (which is part of total revenue) equals 9.6¢/kwh times 130 million kwh/year, or $12.48 million/year. Triangle *AFH*, which is the remaining part of total revenue, equals height *AH* (or $20 - 9.6 = 10.4$¢/kwh) times base *HF* (or 130 million kwh/year), divided by 2, or $6.76 million/year. Hence total revenue equals $12.48 + 6.76 = $19.24 million/year.

Alternatively, one could figure the area of triangle 0*AI* (at 20¢/kwh times 250 million kwh/year, divided by 2, or $25 million/year) and deduct from it triangle *FGI* (9.6¢/kwh times 120 million kwh/year, divided by 2, or $5.76 million/year). The result is $19.24 million/year as well.

FIGURE 6 *Monopoly with First-Degree Price Discrimination*

(a)

(b)

TR: 19.24 = 0AFG
−TC: 13.78 = 0CEG
= Π: 5.46 = ADC − DEF

Profit-maximizing output

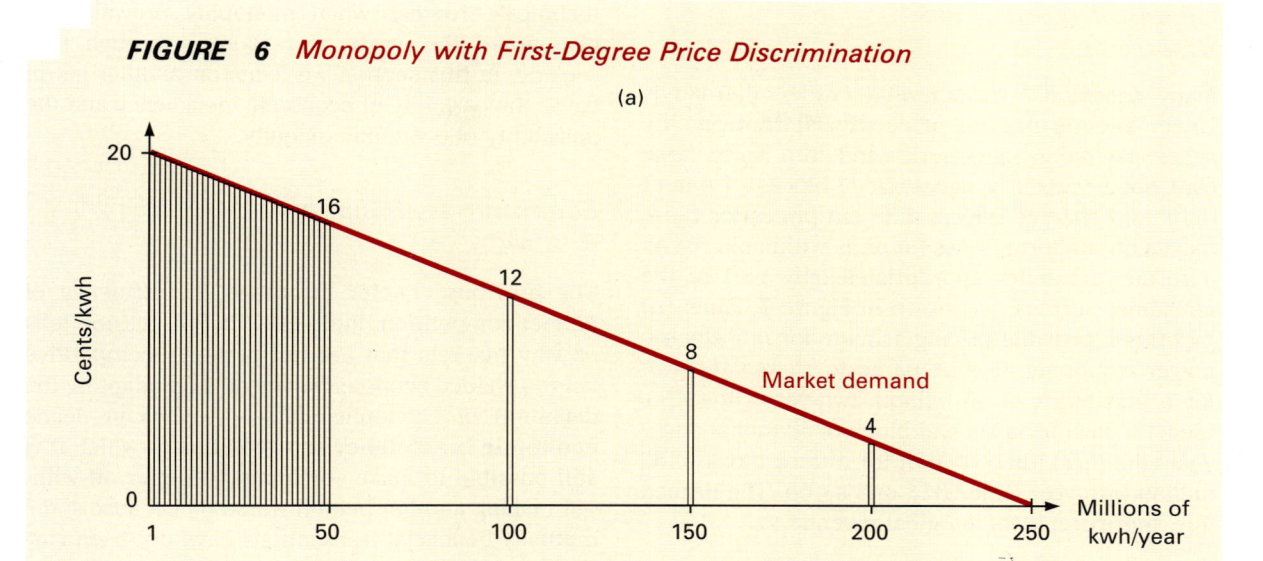

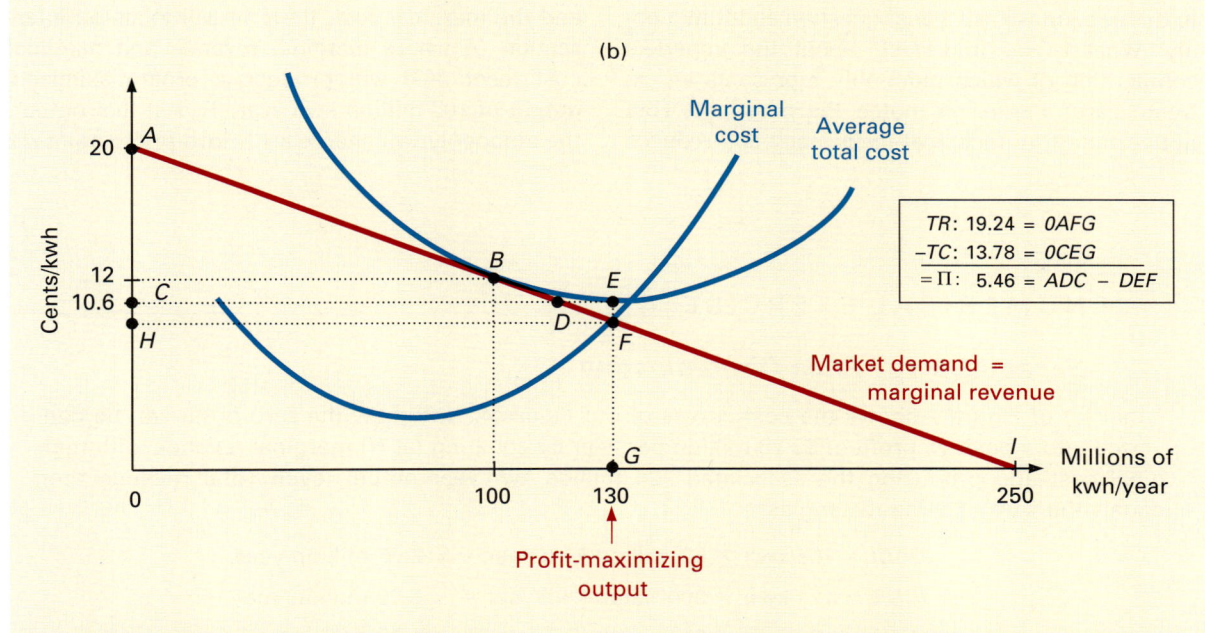

A monopoly that practices first-degree price discrimination charges a different price for every unit sold (always the maximum the unit's consumer is willing to pay) and thus effectively converts the market demand line confronting it into its line of marginal revenue. By then following the profit-maximizing rule of equating marginal revenue with marginal cost (here at *F*), the firm can reap a larger profit than uniform pricing can bring. In this example, a zero profit when charging uniform price *B* = 12 cents/kwh and selling 100 million kwh/year (depicted in Figure 4) is converted into a hefty positive profit of $5.46 million/year (triangle *ADC* minus triangle *DEF*) by charging numerous alternative prices along line *AF* and selling 130 million kwh/year (*0G*).

Second-Degree Price Discrimination

Many sellers use a somewhat cruder alternative. Under **second-degree price discrimination,** the seller partitions market demand into fairly large (but not necessarily equal-sized) blocks of output units and charges buyers different prices for these blocks but uniform prices for units within blocks. As a result, the seller appropriates only part of the consumer surplus, as shown in Figure 7. Panel (a) pictures a possible pricing scheme for our electric power monopoly. It is prepared to charge 16¢/kwh for a first block of 50 million kwh/year (line *AB*), then 12¢/kwh for a second block of 50 million kwh/year (line *CD*), then 8¢/kwh for a third block of 50 million kwh/year (line *GM*), and so on. The dashed line, therefore, is its marginal revenue.

The Imperfections of Monopoly

In this section we ask a final question about monopoly: What is so "imperfect" about the imperfect competition of which monopoly represents an extreme case? Earlier we noted the possibility (but not certainty) of technical inefficiency and reduced technical progress when monopoly prevails. We also noted the waste of resources through rent seeking. In this section we focus on another set of flaws: the certainty of economic inefficiency and the possibility of economic inequity.

Economic Inefficiency: $P > MC$

The previous chapter discussed the efficiency of perfect competition. Indirectly, that discussion tells us why markets that are not perfectly competitive fail to produce economic efficiency. By adapting the definition of economic efficiency, we can define **economic inefficiency** as a situation in which it is still possible to make some person better off without making another person worse off because some mutually beneficial transactions have not been carried out. Monopoly produces such a situation *and contains no tendency to eliminate it.*

Consider Figure 8. Given the market demand line, the dashed marginal revenue line it implies, and the marginal cost, the firm will focus on intersection *b*, where marginal revenue and marginal cost meet, and will produce a profit-maximizing output of 100 million kwh/year. To sell that output, the monopoly will charge a 12¢/kwh price (point *a*).

NUMERICAL EXERCISE 4

Second-Degree Price Discrimination

Panel (b) of Figure 7 shows the cost curves of our Figure 4. Note how the zero profit can be converted into a positive profit of $2.28 million per year by equating (at *H*) marginal revenue with marginal cost and producing the associated 124 million kwh/year output level. Total revenue then equals the sum of three rectangles:

$$
\begin{aligned}
0ABI &= 16¢/\text{kwh} \times 50 \text{ million kwh/year} = \$\ 8.00 \text{ million/year} \\
+ ICDK &= 12¢/\text{kwh} \times 50 \text{ million kwh/year} =\ \ \ \ 6.00 \text{ million/year} \\
+ KGHL &= \ \ 8¢/\text{kwh} \times 24 \text{ million kwh/year} =\ \ \ \ 1.92 \text{ million/year} \\
&\text{Total Revenue} = \$15.92 \text{ million/year}
\end{aligned}
$$

Total cost equals rectangle 0*EFL*, which is average total cost *FL* (11¢/kwh) times output 0*L* (124 million kwh/year), or $13.64 million/year. Hence total profit equals $15.92 − 13.64 = $2.28 million/year. This profit, too, is an improvement over the zero profit of Figure 4, although less dramatic than under perfect price discrimination.

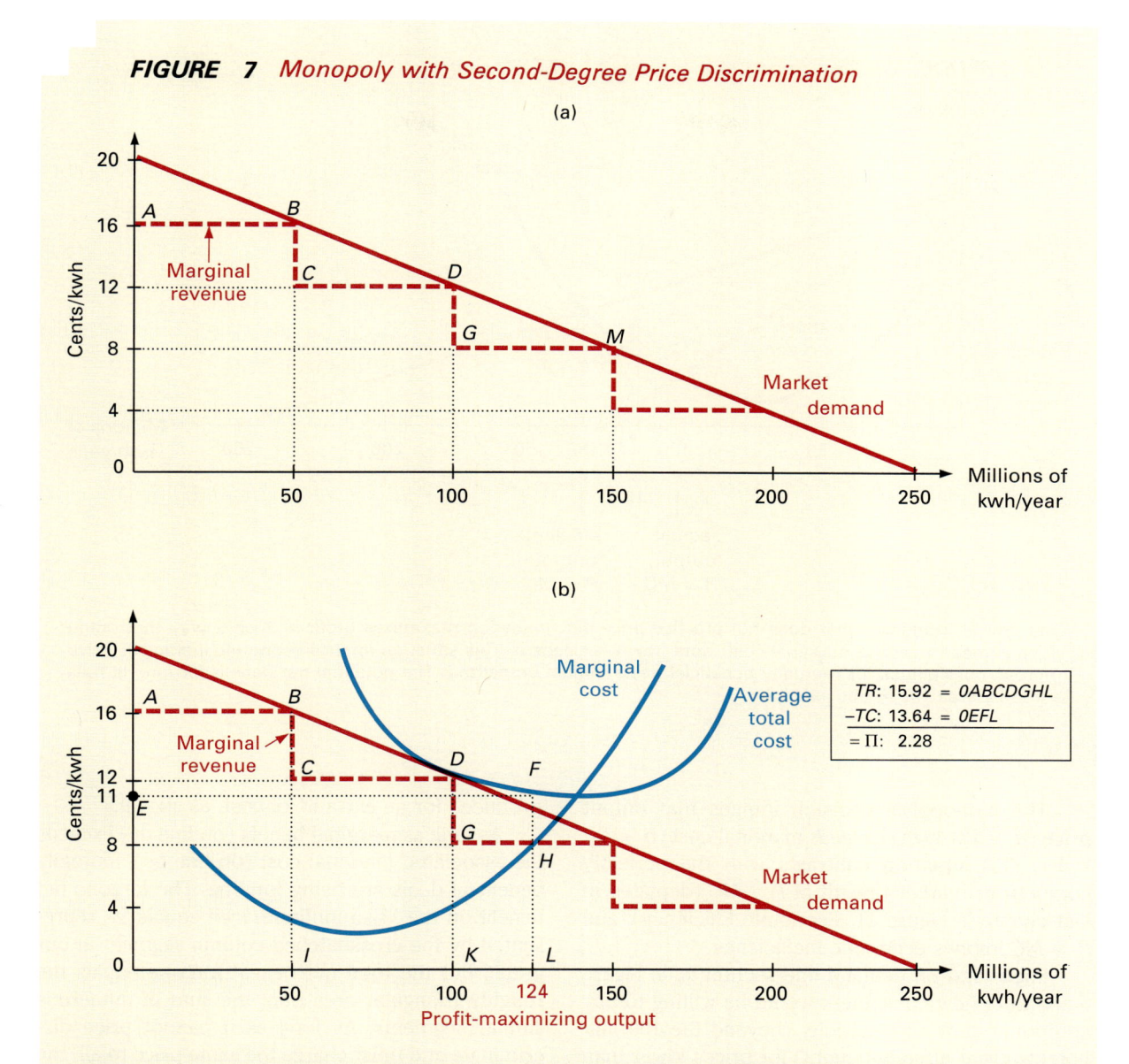

FIGURE 7 Monopoly with Second-Degree Price Discrimination

(a)

(b)

TR: 15.92 = 0ABCDGHL
−TC: 13.64 = 0EFL
= Π: 2.28

A monopoly that practices second-degree price discrimination charges different prices for various blocks of units sold, such as *AB, CD,* and *GM* in panel (a). As a result, the dashed, stair-step line measures its marginal revenue. By then following the profit-maximizing rule of equating marginal revenue with marginal cost (here at *H*), the firm can reap a larger profit than uniform pricing can bring. In this example, a zero profit when charging uniform price *D* = 12 cents/kwh and selling 100 million kwh/year (depicted in Figure 4) is converted into a respectable profit of $2.28 million/year by charging alternative prices along lines *AB, CD,* and *GH* and selling 124 million kwh/year (*OL*).

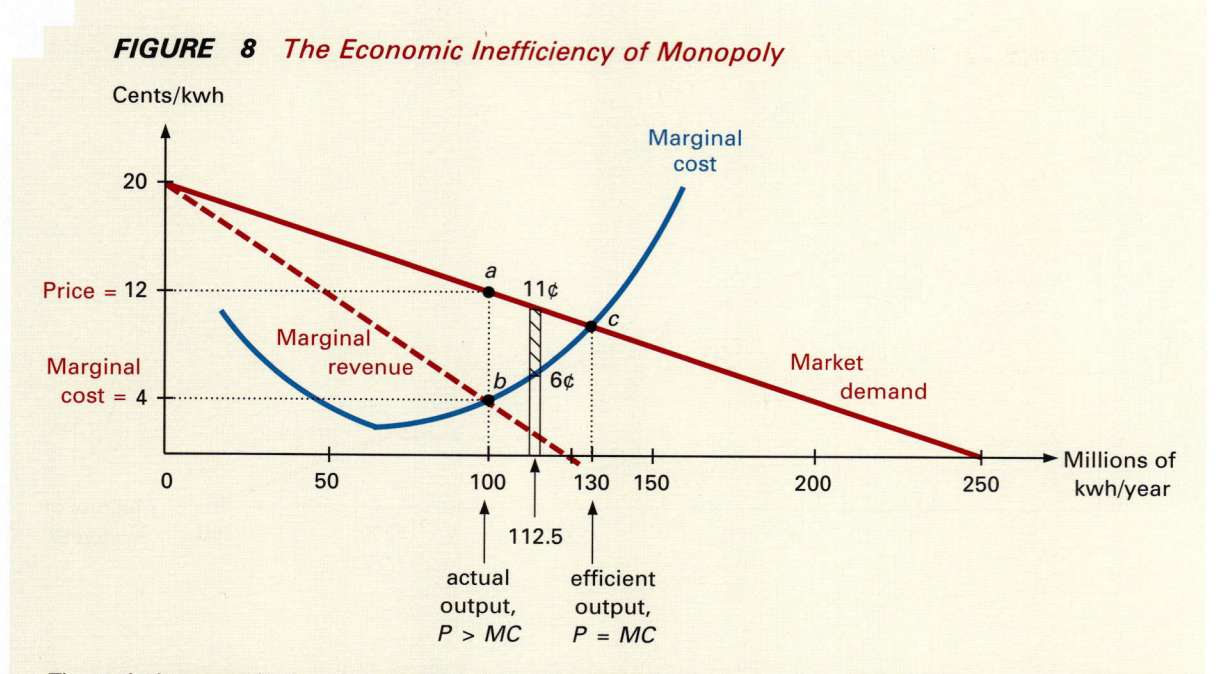

FIGURE 8 The Economic Inefficiency of Monopoly

(Cents/kwh vs. Millions of kwh/year)

- Price = 12
- Marginal cost = 4
- Point a at 11¢, point b at 6¢, point c on market demand
- Actual output: 100 (P > MC); 112.5; Efficient output: 130 (P = MC)

The typical monopoly that does not practice price discrimination maximizes profit in such a way that output price comes to exceed marginal cost; note how *a* exceeds *b*. This situation implies economic inefficiency: Numerous possibilities for mutually beneficial deals remain unrealized. The potential net benefit forgone is measured by area *abc* in this example.

The monopoly's decision implies that output price (*a* = 12¢/kwh) *exceeds* marginal cost (*b* = 4¢/kwh). This situation contrasts with the perfectly competitive market's result of *P* = *MC* (depicted in last chapter's Figure 11, Economic Efficiency); and *P* > *MC* implies economic inefficiency.

Focus first on demand line section *ac* in Figure 8 and note how consumers would be willing to buy additional units of electricity (beyond the 100 million kwh/year already bought) for prices lower than 12¢/kwh (point *a*). Some consumer would gladly buy a 112.5 millionth kilowatt hour for 11¢, as the graph indicates. The potential prices paid by additional consumers for additional units (prices measured along line *ac*) are in effect the marginal benefits consumers expect from extra electric power consumption.

Second, focus on marginal cost line section *bc*. The producer would be able to produce additional units of electricity (beyond the 100 million kwh/year already produced) at extra costs above 4¢/kwh (point *b*). A 112.5 millionth kilowatt hour could be produced for an extra 6¢ of cost, as shown.

As long as marginal benefit (on line *ac*) exceeds the associated marginal cost (on line *bc*), mutually beneficial deals are being forgone. The forgone net benefit on the 112.5 millionth kwh equals 5¢, represented by the crosshatched column segment in our graph, but the total net benefit forgone equals the roughly triangular area *abc*, the sum of numerous similar segments. As long as it cannot price discriminate and must charge the same price to all, the monopoly has no interest in producing the extra 30 million kwh/year that would eliminate the economic inefficiency just noted. Its profit is maximized by producing 100 million kwh/year.

Were it to produce more and lower its price to all in order to sell the extra output, its profit would fall. Thus, economic inefficiency persists; the potential net benefit of *abc* remains unrealized. This forgone net benefit, which is the cumulative excess of marginal benefits over marginal costs between the actual monopoly output and the higher efficient output, is also called the **social cost of monopoly.**

FIGURE 9 Forming a Cartel

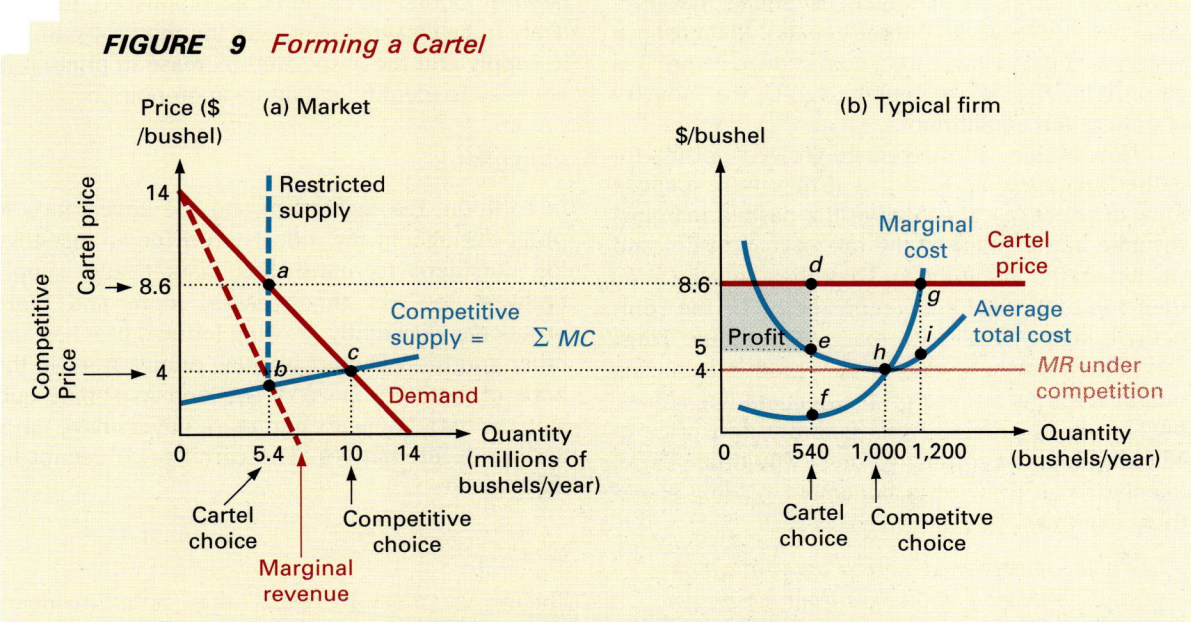

(a) Market

Price ($/bushel) — Cartel price 8.6, Competitive Price 4
- Restricted supply (vertical dashed line)
- Competitive supply = ΣMC
- Demand
- Marginal revenue (dashed)
- Points: a (at 8.6), b, c (at 4)
- Quantities: 5.4 (Cartel choice), 10 (Competitive choice), 14

(b) Typical firm

$/bushel — 8.6 Cartel price, 5, 4 MR under competition
- Marginal cost
- Average total cost
- Profit area
- Points: d, e, f, g, h, i
- Quantities: 540 (Cartel choice), 1,000, 1,200 (Competitive choice)

By forming a cartel and then restricting supply and raising price, formerly competitive sellers can transform zero profit into positive profit.

Economic Inequity: P > ATC

Others fault monopoly for yet another reason. When economic profit is being made (see Figure 3) output price exceeds average total cost. Given that market entry is blocked to other firms, the profit can be permanent. This transfer of purchasing power from the monopoly's customers to the monopoly's owners is often considered "unfair" or inequitable.

But caution is advised. As Figures 4 and 5 show, the reaping of economic profit by a monopoly is not a logical necessity; it is a lucky circumstance. A monopoly can also incur zero profit or negative profit. Furthermore, even if profit is positive, the issue in question remains a normative one about which reasonable people can disagree. One may ask: Who are the monopoly's customers? Who are its owners? The answers are not self-evident. The customers might be retired people, living on social security checks; they could also be successful business firms, earning billions of dollars per year. The owners might be a handful of multimillionaires; they could also be ordinary working people whose labor union invested their pension funds in corporate stocks. There is no certainty that the customers are "poor" and the owners are "rich."

Example 3 provides an illustration of how fragile "monopoly profits" can be—be they fair or not.

Cartels

It is easy to see why sellers in a competitive market might be tempted to form a cartel, to put up a joint front toward buyers, to act as if they were a monopoly. If their joint venture succeeds, they can replace the tendency toward zero profit by the permanence of positive profit. In principle, the formation of a cartel is easy, as Figure 9 shows.

Private Cartels

Panel (a) pictures a competitive market for, say, oranges. Demand and supply have established an equilibrium at c. The price equals $4/bushel; the quantity traded is 10 million bushels/year. Panel (b) pictures the fate of the typical firm. It faces a marginal revenue equal to the market price, it adjusts output so that rising marginal cost equals that marginal revenue at h. Its output equals 1,000 bushels/year; given the average total cost shown, its profit is zero. At h, $P = MC$ = minimum ATC; the industry is in long-run equilibrium.

Now picture all the orange growers getting together and agreeing to act as if they were a single firm. In panel (a), they derive the dashed marginal revenue line implied by the line of market demand (as illustrated in Figure 2). Then they equate (at b) their joint marginal cost (represented by the competitive supply line) with marginal revenue. Thus, 5.4 million bushels/year is the profit-maximizing output level. As point a on the demand line shows, buyers would purchase this quantity at a price of $8.60/bushel. Accordingly, the would-be cartel members can draw up a document reading something like this:

> *We, the undersigned, hereby agree to cut our joint production of oranges from the present level of 10 million bushels/year to 5.4 million bushels/year and each and every one of us will, therefore, reduce the present quantity offered for sale by 46 percent. We also agree to charge a price of $8.60 per bushel, not a penny less or more.*

For the typical firm in panel (b), cutting its output by 46 percent from 1,000 bushels/year to 540 bushels/year, and selling this amount for $8.60/bushel (point d), brings total revenue of $8.60/bushel times 540 bushels/year, or $4,644/year. Given average total cost of $5/bushel (point e), total cost equals $5/bushel times 540 bushels/year, or $2,700/year. Hence economic profit of $4,644 − 2,700 = $1,944/year is reaped (the shaded rectangle). It equals the average profit (de = $3.60/bushel) times the quantity sold and represents a visible improvement over the zero profit once earned at point h.

In spite of the potential profits to be earned, such private cartels are difficult to form and maintain. Three major problems arise.

Organizational Difficulties

The actions described above are often illegal, and it is next to impossible to get large numbers of sellers together in secret (which helps explain why orange cartels do not exist in the real world). Even if the next to impossible could be accomplished, there is likely to be disagreement over the required cutback in supply and the associated increase in price. It is not easy to identify and agree upon point a.

Outsiders

In addition, the high price and the appearance of profit throughout the industry provide an incentive for outsiders to enter the market and supply oranges, too. As time passes, more and more producers—currently growing lettuce, peaches and other goods—will start planting orange trees in the hope of getting a piece of the loot. As supply outside the cartel appears and rises, buyers have more and more alternatives. The cartel price cannot be maintained.

Cheating by Insiders

Finally, we must recognize that cartel members themselves have a strong incentive to cheat. Picture yourself as the manager of the typical firm. You can be grateful, indeed, that your long-time zero economic profit at h—thanks to the cartel—has become the shaded rectangle of positive economic profit. But you also see that price along segment dg exceeds your marginal cost along segment fg. Your profit could be larger still if you produced a quantity corresponding to g (where cartel price equals marginal cost). That potential profit equals an average $3.80/bushel ($gi$) times 1,200 bushels/year, or $4,560/year, more than twice what the cartel agreement has wrought. For many cartel members, the temptation to cheat is overwhelming, but the consequence is clear: As panel (a) supply rises from a toward c, the market price drops until all the profit is gone.

Privately arranged cartels, therefore, rarely succeed. In 1968, when the National Farmers' Organization tried to organize a cattle cartel, only 10 percent of the farmers joined initially. Among them, many cheated. Before long, angry would-be cartel members blew up cattle scales and sat on the roads obstructing cattle shipments by the chiselers. Yet the incentive to cheat was too strong; some farmers even used house trailers to conceal their "illegal" shipments.

Example 4 reports on a famous exception to the rule, a private cartel that has had success.

EXAMPLE 3

Technological Change and the Death of the Record Industry

Records, such as the 45 rpm vinyl single, have been around for a long time. The phonograph was invented in 1877 by Thomas Edison; since then, the playing of records has become a staple of American culture, associated with everything from sock hops to jukeboxes and rock-and-roll. At one time, the Columbia Record Company enjoyed a "near monopoly" in the recording industry and, as some put it, reaped billions of "unfair profits" year after year. But no more.

A whole generation has grown up that does not even own a turntable. Sales of records in the United States peaked at 344 million albums in 1977 and have been declining ever since. In 1989, only 37 million albums were sold, which came to less than 4 percent of the recording industry's dollar sales. The reason is technological change.

In 1989, some 400 million cassette tapes were sold, along with more than 200 million compact disks. These two products highlight technological changes in recording and reproducing sound. Old-style record companies relied on cutting grooves into vinyl. Newcomers use a different technique. Compact disks (CDs) store music in a computer-like code. A sound wave is sampled so many times a second and a number is stored on the disk. In the CD player, a laser beam reads the numbers and reconstructs the sound waves. The result, furthermore, is less subject to distortion, hisses, and pops; nor do the new products degrade in quality over time as records do. No wonder that the record makers' "monopoly profits" have vanished.

Among audiophiles, to be sure, the matter is far from closed. To some, the new recording technique does not sample the sound wave enough. The digital numbers stored are similar to a dotted line, not a continuous curve. To them, music recorded on the new devices sounds cold and antiseptic. Says the senior editor of *The Absolute Sound:* "Digital preserves music like formaldehyde preserves frogs. You kill it and it lasts forever." "Nonsense," rejoins the senior editor of *Audio Magazine*. "The missing frequencies are so high that only dogs can hear them." Meanwhile, the trend has been the same around the world. In 1991, Tower Records, which runs Britain's biggest music stores, decided to clear vinyl from its shelves for good. The price of records had crept up toward the CD level and made their continued sale unprofitable.

Sources: Andrew Pollack, "Recording Enters a New Era, and You Can't Find It on LP," *The New York Times,* April 1, 1990, pp. 1 and 24; and "Vinyl Records: End of Track," The Economist, May 11, 1991, p. 88.

EXAMPLE 4

The de Beers Diamond Cartel

If you were to visit Southern Namibia where the Orange River flows into the Atlantic Ocean, you would see a strange sight indeed. A fleet of 336 earth moving vehicles is digging up an area 200 miles long (along the shore), 60 miles wide (into the Namib Desert) and 60 feet deep. In this *prohibited zone* only de Beers Consolidated Mines, Ltd. is allowed for the next twenty years. While the giant machines move entire dunes from one place to another, mechanized vacuum cleaners probe the sand like giant anteaters; whirring ferris-wheel-like excavators, with buckets instead of seats, chew through layers of compacted sand; and conveyor belts criss-cross the beach, shuttling sand to screening plants. Even the ocean has been pushed back 300 yards behind a movable sea wall some 60 feet thick. Everyone is looking for that glint in the sand first spotted in 1908 when Zacharias Lewala, a railroad worker, was cleaning sand off the tracks.

Mr. Lewala obediently turned the diamond over to August Stauch, his supervisor, who promptly took out a prospecting license from the German colonial authorities and left Mr. Lewala with nothing at all. Before long de Beers, the South African company founded in 1888 by Cecil Rhodes, was in charge. It has run a worldwide diamond cartel ever since. Nowadays, de Beers handles nearly 90 percent of the world's uncut diamonds; it is not unusual for its stockholders to earn over 40 percent on their investment in a single year.

In a recent year, the company bought diamonds for about $10 a carat; the retail price of a D-flawless grade diamond was $18,000 a carat. (A *carat* equals 200 milligrams or 1/142 of an ounce. It was named for the carob seed, known for its consistency in weight.) Key to de Beers' market control are its secret "sights" at places such as London, Kimberley, and Lucerne, where wholesalers and cutters meet every five weeks. Attendance is by invitation only and is limited to about 300 persons—provided they have faithfully followed de Beers' policies on pricing and sales in the past.

In 1982, Zaire pulled out of the cartel, deciding to sell its *boart* (industrial-grade diamonds) independently to producers of abrasive wheels, cutting tools, and phonograph needles. Within days, de Beers flooded the market from its $1.7 billion inventory of boart. The price dropped by 66 percent, and a humbled Zaire returned to the cartel. At the same time, a major new mine in Australia (potentially capable of raising world diamond output by 40 percent and "spoiling" the market) obediently joined the Central Selling Organization, as the de Beers Syndicate is called. Even countries like Angola and the Soviet Union have always used de Beers as their marketing agent.

Sources: Paul Gibson, "De Beers: Can a Cartel Be Forever?" *Forbes,* May 28, 1979, pp. 45–46; "How de Beers Dominates the Diamonds," *The Economist,* February 23, 1980, pp. 101–102; *The Wall Street Journal,* February 22, 1982; July 7, 1983; August 7, 1983; and October 25, 1989, p. A14; *The New York Times,* July 26, 1990, pp. A1 and D5.

Government Cartels

Given all the difficulties just noted, it is easy to see why would-be cartel-makers often turn to government. If government can be persuaded to *force* everyone to join, to keep outsiders from "spoiling" the market, and to put "chiselers" in jail, all would be fine. On many occasions, government does lend a hand. The reasons are not difficult to comprehend.

For one thing, legislators have to be elected. Therefore, would-be cartel-members make favored legislators the beneficiaries not only of their votes but of monetary contributions. Once elected, these officials are expected to show their proper gratitude and to make laws establishing and maintaining cartels. This relationship engenders other rewards: job offers for spouses and children, for legislators losing an election, all-expenses paid vacations, and gifts of jewelry and cars. Before long, laws *legislate* a hike in the industry's price, a mandatory cutback in supply, and perhaps even an increase in demand, often in the form of governmental purchases. (The Chapter 3 section on government intervention describes these and other actions.)

International Cartels

On occasion, governments even join with other governments to form international cartels. The practice goes back hundreds of years, the most notable example in recent years is provided by OPEC, the Organization of Petroleum Exporting Countries. More often than not, however, international cartels flounder for the very reasons noted with respect to private cartels (organizational difficulties, the appearance of outside suppliers, and cheating by members).

Recent examples of potential international cartels that have *failed* to come off the ground or to work include cartels among producers of bananas (Central America, Ecuador), bauxite (Australia, the Dominican Republic, Ghana, Guinea, Guyana, Haiti, Indonesia, Jamaica, Sierra Leone, Surinam, Yugoslavia), coffee (Brazil, Colombia), copper (Chile, Peru, Zaire, Zambia), grain (Australia, Canada, the United States), natural rubber (Indonesia, Malaysia, Sri Lanka, Thailand), phosphate (Morocco, Tunisia), and tea (India, Sri Lanka). Example 5 provides a recent case in point.

EXAMPLE 5

Coffee: Another Cartel Bites the Dust

In 1962, as part of his Alliance for Progress designed to help the poorer countries of Latin America, President John F. Kennedy made a suggestion. He urged the creation of an International Coffee Organization, essentially a 72 nation cartel that would set export quotas for producing nations low enough to drive up the price of coffee and, thus, engineer an income transfer from coffee drinkers in rich countries to coffee growers in poor countries.

For some 27 years, the scheme worked, mainly because the governments of *consuming* nations cooperated with those of the major producing countries—Brazil, Colombia, Mexico, the Ivory Coast. In the 1980s, the first signs of trouble appeared. Unable to agree among themselves, producers increased their joint output by 21 percent to an annual total of 12.5 billion pounds. At the same time, demand in the developed countries fell. The remaining demand also changed away from the Robusta beans of South America and Africa toward the milder Arabica strains of Central America and Mexico. As a result, the world coffee price during the 1980s tumbled from a high of $1.27/lb. to a low of 70¢/lb., the lowest level since the Great Depression of the 1930s. On July 3, 1989, strangled by market forces, the organization came to an end.

Source: Peter Fuhrman, "Another Cartel Bites the Dust," *Forbes,* October 30, 1989, pp. 41–42.

IDEAS IN HISTORY

The Theory of Monopoly

The theory of monopoly and much of the material found in this chapter goes back to one man and the now famous book he published in 1838. The man was Antoine Augustin Cournot (1801–1877); the book *Researches into the Mathematical Principles of the Theory of Wealth* made him the founder of mathematical economics. Unfortunately, the book had little impact at the time; it was rediscovered many years later when William Jevons (see Ideas in History, The Marginal Utility School, in the chapter "Consumer Preferences and Demand") paid glowing tribute to Cournot.

Cournot was born at Gray, France. He studied mathematics at the École Normale Supérieure in Paris. While a student, he worked as a secretary for one of Napoleon's generals. Later, he became a professor of mathematics at the University of Lyons and Rector, first at the Academy of Grenoble and then at the Academy of Dijon. His book had few equals in economics for sheer originality and boldness of conception. It contained the nucleus of Alfred Marshall's economics (see Ideas in History, The Scissors Diagram, in Chapter 3). Unlike any previous economics book, it developed a theory of the monopoly firm, introducing for the first time demand, marginal revenue, and total revenue functions (such as those in Figure 2), contrasting these with total and marginal costs (as in Figures 3–5), and deriving clearly the profit-maximizing principle of marginal revenue equal to marginal cost.

In one famous example, Cournot described the profit-maximizing choice of the owner of a natural spring (whose marginal cost was zero) as equivalent to maximizing total revenue. If marginal cost is zero and the marginal cost line, thus, coincides with the Figure 2, panel (b) horizontal axis, the $MR = MC$ point (G) coincides with maximum total revenue m, Figure 2, panel (a). A hundred years after his death, the members of OPEC whose marginal cost was *near* zero (and who held an asset much like a natural spring) came to the same conclusion.

Cournot produced his work in defiance of dispiriting conditions. During many years, he was troubled by an infirmity of the eyes that made continuous work impossible and eventually led to blindness.

Source: Adapted, with permission, from Heinz Kohler, *Intermediate Microeconomics: Theory and Applications,* 1st ed. (Glenview, IL: Scott, Foresman and Co., 1982), p. 329.

Summary

1. This chapter and the next turn to markets in which one or more of the characteristics of perfect competition are absent and that are, therefore, imperfectly competitive. Monopolies and cartels are the focus here. The former are single sellers of items for which no good substitutes are available and who operate in markets into which the entry of others sellers is severely restricted or even impossible. The latter are conspiracies by all existing sellers in a market to put up a joint front toward buyers, acting as if they were one.

2. A number of reasons for the appearance of monopoly exist. They include increasing returns to scale (leading to "natural" monopoly), the concentrated ownership of key resources, patents and copyrights, and exclusive franchises (all of which can produce "artificial" monopolies).

3. To understand the profit-maximizing behavior of a monopoly, we study its cost and revenue. The cost curves of a monopoly can be expected to have the same *general* shape as those of a perfect competitor. They might, however, be higher than if the firm operated in a competitive environment. This position might be the consequence of technical inefficiency, of reduced innovative activity, and of rent seeking, an activity that expends valuable resources not to produce goods but to obtain, strengthen, and defend the monopoly position itself.

    On the revenue side, a major difference emerges between a monopoly and a perfectly competitive firm. For a monopoly charging a uniform price of all its customers, marginal revenue always lies below price.

4. To maximize its profit, a monopoly must follow the optimization principle. It must adjust its rate of production until the rising marginal cost of production equals its declining marginal revenue—provided the output price equals or exceeds average variable cost. A series of examples illustrate the rule and highlight a number of implications. A monopoly never chooses an output level at which marginal revenue is zero or negative; the price chosen by a monopoly will always lie in the elastic section of its demand line; a monopoly does not have a supply curve; and any profit made by a monopoly may be permanent profit.

5. The theory of monopoly is extended by considering the possibility of price discrimination, the practice of charging a given buyer or different buyers different prices for different units of an identical good. First-degree and second-degree price discrimination are considered.

6. Besides the possibility of technical inefficiency, reduced technical progress, and resource waste through rent seeking, the imperfections of monopoly include economic inefficiency and, possibly, economic inequity.

7. Sellers in competitive markets are tempted to form cartels because such a venture, if successful, can replace an ever-present tendency toward zero profit by the permanence of positive profit. Private cartels rarely succeed—because of organizational difficulties, the appearance of outside suppliers, and cheating by members. Government-sponsored and international cartels are possible alternatives.

Key Concepts

cartel
copyright
economic inefficiency
exclusive franchise
first-degree price discrimination
imperfectly competitive markets
monopoly
monopsony
natural monopoly
patent
perfect price discrimination
price discrimination
price setters
rent seeking
second-degree price discrimination
social cost of monopoly

Questions and Problems

1. "Examples of pure monopoly are hard to find; almost all goods have fairly good substitutes. Consider aluminum, cellophane, local newspapers, railroad transportation, in fact, any domestically made good." Can you think of substitutes in the cases cited?

2. Consider Case 1 in this chapter's Numerical Exercise 1. Illustrate the move from B to C graphically; then explain your graph.

3. Consider Case 2 in this chapter's Numerical Exercise 1. Illustrate the move from D to E graphically; then explain your graph.

4. Adam Smith: "The price of monopoly is upon every occasion the highest which can be got." Comment.

5. Consider Figure 3.

    a. At which point, to the left and right of B, must average total cost intersect market demand?

    b. To which point on the marginal cost curve does the total cost curve's point of inflection (between a and c) correspond?

    Explain your answers.

6. Consider the following data for a monopoly that does not price discriminate. Determine its profit-maximizing price and quantity.

Price	Quantity	Total cost
10	5	20
9	6	22
8	7	24
7	8	26
6	9	28
5	10	30

7. "The author of a book who receives a fixed percentage of sales revenue will disagree with the profit-maximizing publisher on the ideal price." Comment.

8. The mere right to have a monopoly often sells for impressive sums of money. Thus, New York taxicab licenses have sold for $68,000, American Baseball League franchises for $25 million, TV station licenses for $50 million, and truck operating rights for $2.5 million. Can you explain it?

9. As the previous question indicates, the issue of an exclusive franchise (such as a TV station license or an air route) amounts to a gift of millions of dollars because the recipients of the license can get a huge annual income, just as they could from a multimillion-dollar bank account. How could the government restrict the number of TV stations, air routes, etc. (to avoid signal interference, traffic congestion, etc.) without giving a favored recipient a personal fortune?

10. Make a list of real-world examples of first- or second-degree price discrimination.

11. Consider Figure 9. Draw up an income statement for the typical firm
    a. before the cartel.
    b. after the cartel.

12. Make a list of government-sponsored cartels—past or present.

CHAPTER 12

OLIGOPOLY AND MONOPOLISTIC COMPETITION

Preview

This chapter explores the middle ground between such extreme market structures as perfect competition and monopoly/cartel. Oligopolistic markets that are dominated by the competition of two or more large firms (as in the auto industry) give rise to various forms of interdependent behavior explored here. Also studied are monopolistically competitive markets that, in contrast, contain large numbers of firms (such as restaurants) offering differentiated products for which consumers can find numerous substitutes. Empirical studies, finally, reveal the relative importance in the United States of the different market structures studied in this chapter and the preceding two.

Examples

1. The Auto Industry: Moves and Countermoves
2. The Convergence of Bank Credit Cards
3. The Proliferation of Fragrances
4. The Great American Health Pitch
5. Stalking the New Consumer
6. The Vending Machine Craze
7. Modern Day "Hamburger Wars"

Ideas in History

The Chamberlinian Revolution

The previous two chapters focused on two extreme forms of market structure. One of these was *perfect competition*, a situation in which innumerable firms offer a homogeneous product to innumerable buyers and in which all market participants are price takers who possess perfect knowledge about the market and are equally free to enter or leave it. The other extreme was the case of *monopoly* (or *cartel*), a situation in which a single price-setting seller confronts buyers (or in which several sellers conspire to act as one) and in which market entry to other sellers is blocked. In this chapter, we consider markets in which features of competition and monopoly are interwoven. The *oligopolists* and *monopolistic competitors* about to be discussed here have been seriously analyzed by economists only since the 1930s, as Ideas in History, The Chamberlinian Revolution explains.

Many markets contain neither innumerable sellers nor a single seller but are dominated by a handful of firms that may be offering a homogeneous product (like cement, steel bars, or tin cans) or a differentiated product (like automobiles, computers, or turret lathes). More often than not, entry into such markets is restricted (by any one of the factors that are potentially able to create monopoly and that were noted in the previous chapter) and market knowledge is less than perfect. Such a market structure, in which a large percentage of sales is made by a very small number of firms that compete with one another in the sale of homogeneous or differentiated products, in which the entry of new firms is difficult, and in which market knowledge is imperfect, is called an **oligopoly.**

Another type of market structure in which innumerable firms compete because restrictions to market entry or exit are absent, in which the products traded are differentiated from one seller to the next, and in which traders possess less than perfect market knowledge, is just as common. Such **monopolistic competition** is exemplified by barber shops, drug stores, restaurants, and the like. We will consider these two market structures in turn.

Oligopolistic Interdependence

The most important feature of oligopoly is the high degree of interdependence that inevitably emerges among the relatively small number of firms operating in the market. Because only a few sellers really matter, every seller is intensely aware that the actions of any one can significantly affect the well-being of the others. Unlike the perfectly competitive wheat farmer who is only vaguely aware of hundreds of thousands of fellow farmers who also supply wheat, the oligopolistic seller of cars is facing a handful of *identifiable* rivals. When competition is thus restricted to a few, any one firm is bound to monitor the decisions made by other firms concerning output quantity, pricing, product quality, advertising, and the like. These decisions are often attempts to gain market share at the expense of others; therefore, they elicit a reaction. In situations of oligopoly, one encounters **strategic behavior,** a type of behavior that always arises among a small number of actors who have conflicting interests and are mutually conscious of the interdependence of their actions and that tries to anticipate the reactions of others to one's own decisions. The type and extent of those reactions, however, will vary with

EXAMPLE 1

The Auto Industry: Moves and Countermoves

A perfect example of oligopolistic moves and countermoves is provided by the recent behavior of the three U.S. auto companies, General Motors, Ford, and Chrysler. GM first decided to forgo all-out competitive warfare with foreign auto makers in the small-car market and to acquire a small car by entering a joint venture with one of its foreign competitors. The result was the Geo. Before long, Ford followed suit and acquired the Festiva; Chrysler traveled the same route to produce the Dodge Colt.

Each move engendered a countermove, and joint ventures with foreign companies proliferated throughout the industry. By the end of the 1980s, GM had *stock ownership* in two Japanese companies, Isuzu (40%) and Suzuki (5%), in one Korean company, Daewoo Motors (50%), and in one British firm, Lotus (100%). Ford followed suit with Korea's Kia Motors (10%), Japan's Mazda (25%), and Britain's Aston Martin Lagonda (100%). So did Chrysler with Japan's Mitsubishi (22%) and Italy's Lamborghini (100%) and Maserati (16%).

GM, in turn, set up *joint ventures* with Volvo (making trucks in North Carolina), Toyota (making cars in Melbourne, Australia, and Fremont, California), and Suzuki (making utility vehicles in Canada). Not to be outdone, Ford arranged a joint venture with Nissan (building minivans in Cleveland, Ohio) and Volkswagen (for producing cars in Brazil). Chrysler was close behind, producing cars with Mitsubishi in Illinois, with Hyundai in Canada, and jeeps with Renault.

At the time of this writing, rumors were that Ford would buy into Sweden's Saab and Chrysler into Italy's Fiat. General Motors, meanwhile, was challenging Japan's dominance by setting up car making facilities in Southeast Asia from India to China. The Japanese themselves were players in the game as well, moving from exporting cars *to* the United States to producing cars *in* the United States. Accordingly, they set up assembly plants, engine factories, engineering centers, design studios, and research circumstances. Indeed, when any one move calls forth a countermove, when that one causes another one, and so on, the final result is hard to predict. Example 1 provides a recent case in point.

No single theory of oligopoly can be expected to capture the array of outcomes for all conceivable circumstances in which oligopolists face one another. The following sections introduce a few of many competing theories for explaining oligopolistic decision making. Each one of them may well be applicable to a particular time and place; none can be considered of universal validity.

Oligopoly Decisions: Price

Many theories attempt to explain the pricing behavior of oligopolistic firms. All stress that oligopolists have to keep a sharp eye on pricing decisions.

The Oligopolists' Dilemma

Let market demand, in Figure 1, be represented by the downward-sloping solid line; the implied marginal revenue, by dashed line MR. Let each firm's marginal and average total cost equal the horizontal line. Each oligopolist is aware of two extreme possibilities. First, cooperation among the small number of firms in the industry could restrict their joint output to the quantity Q_m that a monopoly would choose (and that corresponds to the equality at b of marginal revenue with marginal cost). That output could be sold at the monopoly price P_m according to point a, and would provide maximum industry profit equal to the shaded rectangle. Unfortunately for oligopolists, such a cartel arrangement is illegal—a matter to be discussed in detail in a later chapter, "Antitrust Policy."

TABLE A *Auto Factories Shut Down and Opened on U.S. Soil Since 1982*

	Factories Shut Down			Factories Opened	
1987	General Motors	Norwood, OH	1982	Honda	Marysville, OH
1988	General Motors	Leeds, MO	1983	Nissan	Smyrna, TN
	Chrysler	Kenosha, WI			
	General Motors	Pontiac, MI	1984	Toyota-GM	Fremont, CA
1989	General Motors	Framingham, MA	1987	Mazda	Flat Rock, MI
1990	General Motors	Lakewood, GA	1988	Mitsubishi-Chrysler	Normal, IL
	Chrysler	Detroit, MI		Toyota	Georgetown, KY
	Chrysler	St. Louis, MO	1989	Subaru- Isuzu	Lafayette, IN
				Honda	E. Liberty, OH
			1990	General Motors	Spring Hill, TN

facilities throughout the land. In 1989, they sold over a million cars and trucks in the United States for the first time ever, capturing 26 percent of the market. By 1995, they hope to surpass General Motors' share of the U.S. market (roughly 33 percent). Given the story told by Table A, this seems possible.

Sources: James B. Treece and Joan Hoerr, "Shaking Up Detroit," *Business Week,* August 14, 1989, pp. 74–80; Jerry Flint, "Make Love, Not War," *Forbes,* October 2, 1989, pp. 46 and 48; "Losing Control," *The Wall Street Journal,* February 16, 1990, pp. 1 and 5; and Jerry Flint, "Somewhere East of Suez," *Forbes,* December 24, 1990, pp. 68–69.

FIGURE 1 The Oligopolists' Dilemma

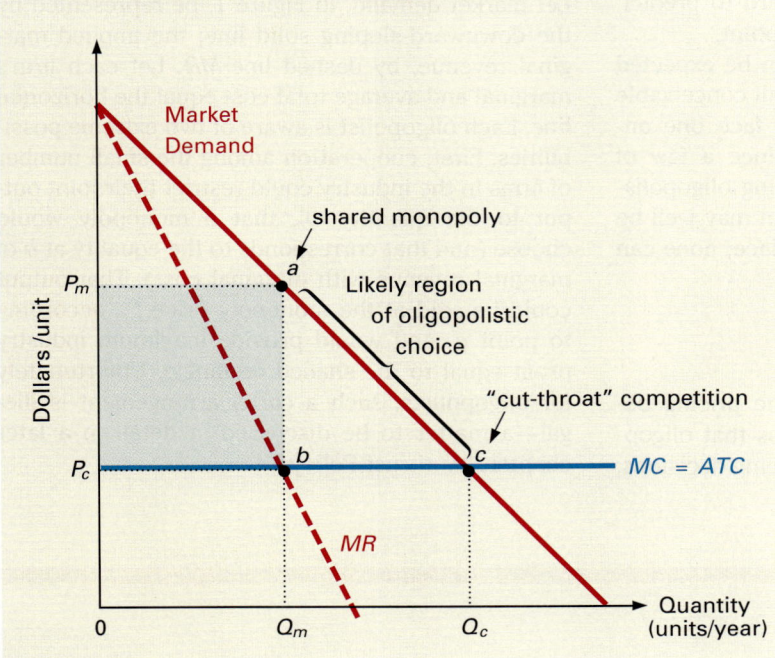

By illegally cooperating with one another, firms in an oligopolistic industry could reap monopoly profit (here by consciously choosing the price/output combination given by point *a*). By engaging one another in competition instead and attempting to lure away each other's customers with lower prices, oligopolists might end up with no profit at all (here by inadvertently choosing the price/output combination given by point *c*).

Second, even if the competing oligopolists managed to make separate output and pricing decisions that yielded Q_m and P_m for the industry as a whole, that result would be highly unstable in the absence of an enforceable cartel agreement. Each firm would know that additional units could be sold at prices (along demand line section *ac*) that would exceed marginal cost (along segment *bc*); hence each firm, by producing more and charging less, could gain additional profit—at the expense of other firms. If all firms acted independently and followed this line of reasoning, the industry would end up producing the quantity Q_c that a competitive industry would provide. It would sell, according to point *c*, at a competitive price P_c that equaled marginal cost. In our example (where marginal cost also equals average total cost), industry profit would be zero under these circumstances.

Barring a secret conspiracy to monopolize the market, how is each individual firm to act? It may be tempting for any one firm to raise price toward P_m, but then the other firms may not raise their price and may supply the first firm's customers at the old price. Before long, the first firm's market share would shrink, profits giving way to losses or even bankruptcy. Should the firm then *cut* its price? Whether done openly or via secret discounts and rebates, such an action has the potential of luring away the customers of the firm's rivals. No rival firm welcomes this scenario. Before you know it, the industry can be involved in a chain of "predatory price cutting," a **price war** in which rival firms successively cut their prices below those of competitors and, perhaps, even below their own costs. Thus, the attempt to move to point *a* in Figure 1 may lead to point *c* instead. Such mutually ruinous price cutting occurred, for instance, 100 years ago among railroads hauling freight between New York and Chicago, in the 1880s among oil companies, in the 1930s among cigarette producers, in the 1950s among producers of electrical equipment, and in the 1960s among steel companies. More recently, the practice was revived among New England banks, among airlines, and among many rent-a-car companies. And, as is true of all wars, price wars are apt to be bitter experiences for all participants. Profits disappear and the existence of firms is threatened. Sooner or later, survivors may look for other ways to compete and will leave prices alone.

The Kinked Demand Curve

In 1939, Paul M. Sweezy developed a theory that predicted a pronounced rigidity of prices in oligopolistic markets. Figure 2 pictures an oligopolist, such as a producer of steel, selling 200,000 tons/year at $30/ton (point *a*). The producer perceives two subjectively estimated demand lines. One of these is a line from *b* to *c* and beyond, which indicates the firm's estimated sales at alternative prices on the assumption that its rivals exactly match any price change it initiates. The other demand line, from *d* to *e* and beyond, indicates the firm's estimated sales at alternative prices if rivals do not react to the price changes our firm makes.

A hypothetical price increase from $30 to $40/ton of steel is expected to reduce quantity demanded from *a* to *c* if rivals match the price hike but from *a* to *d* if rivals keep their prices unchanged to lure customers away from our firm. Similarly, a hypothetical price decrease from $30 to $20/ton of steel is expected to raise quantity demanded from *a* to *e* if rivals do nothing and customers, therefore, are lured away from them; but only from *a* to *f* if rivals match the price cut.

Sweezy reasoned that an oligopolist assumes ri-

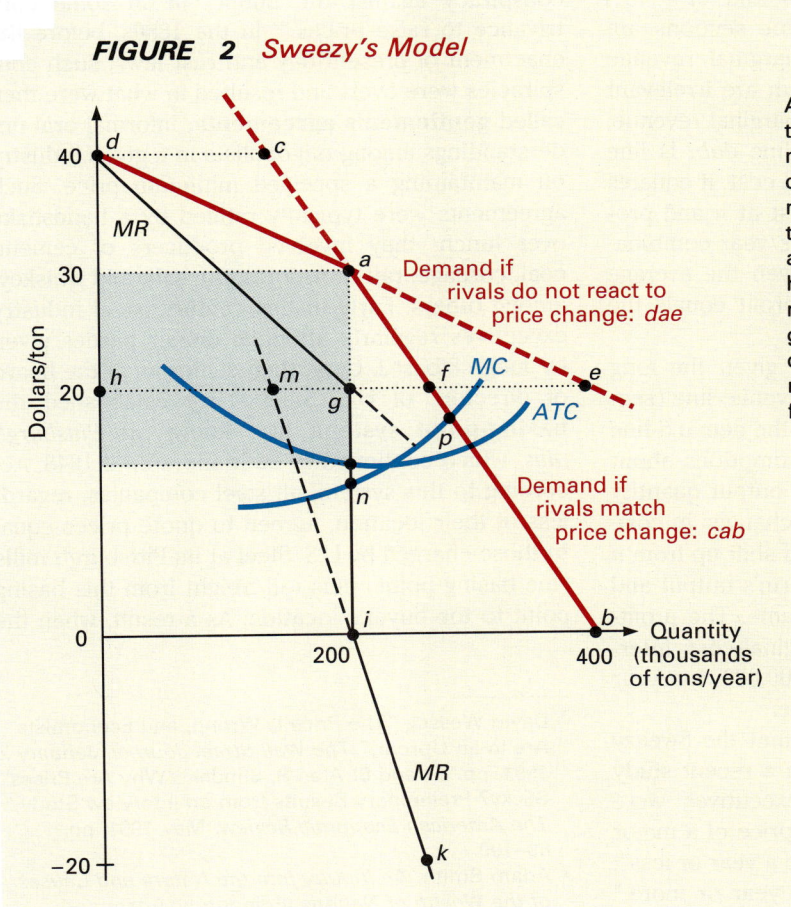

FIGURE 2 *Sweezy's Model*

An oligopolistic firm that assumes the worst of its rivals (they will match price decreases but not increases) ends up with a kinked demand line, such as *dab*. A discontinuous marginal revenue line, such as *dgik*, is associated with it, which helps explain why the profit-maximizing firm might stick with a given price/quantity choice, such as combination *a*, even in the face of major shifts in marginal cost (up from *n* to *g*, down from *n* to *i*).

vals will *not* match price increases but *will* match price decreases. Hence a firm's effective demand line will have a kink at the level of the current price, such as point *a* in our graph. An oligopolist's **kinked demand line,** such as line *dab*, thus is relatively flat above the current price and relatively steep below it, reflecting that price increases are not expected to be matched by competitors (which will greatly reduce quantity demanded), while price decreases are expected to be matched promptly (which will raise quantity demanded only a bit).

Corresponding to hypothetical demand line *de* and beyond, we can derive marginal revenue line *dg* and beyond. (Recall that marginal revenue always lies halfway between a straight demand line and the vertical axis; thus, distance *hg* = *ge*). Corresponding to hypothetical demand line *bc* and beyond, a marginal revenue line can, similarly, be derived; only a portion of it (segment *kim*) is shown in Figure 2. (Again, distances *hm* = *mf* and 0*i* = *ib*.) Given that the dashed demand line sections are deemed irrelevant, the dashed marginal revenue line sections corresponding to them are irrelevant as well. Thus, our firm's relevant marginal revenue, corresponding to kinked demand line *dab*, is line *dgik* and beyond. Given its marginal cost, it equates marginal revenue and marginal cost at *n* and produces the $30/ton and 200,000 tons/year combination corresponding to point *a*. Given the average total cost line shown, the firm's profit equals the shaded rectangle.

Sweezy's conclusion was that given the long vertical segment of the marginal revenue line (segment *gi*)—a direct consequence of the demand line kink and the firm's pessimistic assumptions about its rivals—the firm will not change output quantity or price even in the face of major changes in cost. In our example, marginal cost could shift up from *n* to *g* or down from *n* to *i*, yet the firm's output and price decision would remain the same. The profit-maximizing marginal-revenue/marginal-cost intersection would still dictate the 200,000 ton/year output volume and the $30/ton price.

There is substantial evidence that the Sweezy model captures a part of reality. In a recent study by Alan Blinder, 200 business executives were asked how often they changed the price of a major product. Over 55 percent said "once a year or less"; only 14 percent said "four times a year or more." Fear of competitors' reactions was given as one reason for infrequent price changes.[1] Nevertheless, the model presented here is far from universally applicable. Numerous empirical studies have discovered a considerable degree of price *flexibility* in some oligopolistic markets, which is why alternative theories abound.

Gentlemen's Agreements

While the Sweezy model has oligopolists making pricing decisions independently of one another (as the law requires of them), other economists have postulated that oligopolistic firms communicate among themselves and thus reach some understanding on pricing policies that brings them closer to the maximization of monopoly profit (point *a* of Figure 1). As Adam Smith observed, "people of the same trade seldom meet together, even for merriment and diversion, but the conversation ends in a conspiracy against the public, or in some contrivance to raise prices."[2] In the 1880s, before the enactment of present-day antitrust laws, such conspiracies were overt and resulted in what were then called **gentlemen's agreements,** informal oral understandings among oligopolists in a given industry on maintaining a specified minimum price. Such agreements were typically ratified by a handshake over lunch; they involved producers of cement, coal, cordage, rail transportation, salt, and whiskey, among others. Early in this century, steel industry executives regularly attended dinner parties given by Judge Elbert J. Gary, then chairman of the board of directors of U.S. Steel. They established the **basing-point system,** also known as *Pittsburgh plus,* which continued to be in force until 1948. According to this system, all steel companies, regardless of their location, agreed to quote prices equal to those charged by U.S. Steel at its Pittsburgh mills (the basing point) plus rail freight from this basing point to the buyer's location. As a result, when the

---

[1] David Wessel, "The Price Is Wrong, and Economists Are in an Uproar," *The Wall Street Journal,* January 2, 1991, pp. B1 and 6; Alan S. Blinder, "Why Are Prices Sticky? Preliminary Results from an Interview Study," *The American Economic Review,* May 1991, pp. 89–100.

[2] Adam Smith, *An Inquiry Into the Nature and Causes of the Wealth of Nations* (Edinburgh: Adam and Charles Black, 1872/1776), p. 59.

U.S. Navy Department on May 26, 1936 opened 31 sealed bids for a certain quantity of rolled steel, it found 31 identical prices of $20,727.26 each.

Noting how well the steel companies' system worked, other industries adopted similar practices. Thus, the U.S. Engineer's Office at Tucumcari, New Mexico, also in 1936, received 11 secret bids for the delivery of 6,000 barrels of cement. Each of them was identical, right up to the sixth decimal point: $3.286854/barrel.[3]

Despite the fact that such price fixing agreements are now illegal, they do continue. At one point in the 1970s, the U.S. Justice Department estimated that one third of all U.S. firms were involved in such schemes, ranging from the producers of beef, beer, and bread to those of eggs, milk, and soft drinks. Similar arrangements existed among the members of professional societies, ranging from accountants, architects, and doctors to engineers and real estate brokers.

Price Leadership

Given the illegality of gentleman's agreements, a more subtle form of price fixing seems to have developed in their place. In many oligopolistic industries, one observes a practice called **price leadership** according to which one firm, the price leader, announces and occasionally changes the price of the industry's product, while other firms immediately follow suit. Such price leadership has been exercised by Alcoa (aluminum), General Motors (automobiles), Chase Manhattan (banking), Reynolds (cigarettes), Kellogg (cereals), General Electric (turbogenerators), and many more.

Oligopoly Decisions: Product Quality

Analyzing the decision making of interdependent oligopolists with respect to price is difficult, even though this variable is easy to measure and can only move in two directions—up or down. Analysis becomes more complicated when one studies issues of product quality.

---

[3] These examples are from Max E. Fletcher, *Economics and Social Problems* (Boston: Houghton Mifflin, 1979), pp. 172–173.

Product Differentiation

Some oligopolists do compete with one another in marketing seemingly homogeneous products, such as aluminum, cement, gasoline, or steel, while others are selling clearly heterogeneous goods, such as automobiles, ready-to-eat cereals, or turbogenerators. Yet in all cases, opportunities for **product differentiation** exist. These involve deliberate actions by producers to make their product, in the eyes of consumers, distinct from the close substitutes that rival firms supply. There are literally hundreds of ways in which such differentiation can be achieved. The most obvious approach involves changing the physical aspects of goods: their color, durability, flavor, octane rating, size, speed of operation, style, and the like. Another approach focuses on legal aspects, such as the introduction of a brand name or trademark that may imply physical differences that do not exist. Consider such physically identical products as generic aspirin, Bayer, Cope, or Excedrin. Finally, products can be differentiated in infinite ways by varying the conditions of sale. Buyers may admit to products being identical but their purchasing decisions are linked to other attributes: a store that is clean, easily accessible, and closer to home; free convenient parking; more business hours per day; more and friendlier clerks; music while you shop; carpeted floors; trading stamps; attractive reusable containers; the provision of easier credit terms, prompter delivery, better warranties; faster repair and maintenance. But competition through product differentiation has its limits, as discussed in an analysis by Harold Hotelling.

Hotelling's Paradox

Hotelling set out to analyze product differentiation based on a single variable—seller location—and arrived at an unexpected and startling conclusion. His reasoning is illustrated by Figure 3. Line (a) represents a line of geographic distance from west (W) to east (E), such as the Chicago to New York railroad, an interstate highway, Main Street, or a strip of beach. Stretched out along the line, and uniformly distributed along it, are 9 buyers, but you can think of them as 9 million buyers. Hotelling envisioned two sellers, A and B, appearing on the scene. In the eyes of buyers, their products are identical, as are their prices. The only possible reason for preferring

FIGURE 3 Hotelling's Paradox

(a) W ├──•──•──•──•──**A**──•──•──**B**──•──•──┤ E
        1   2   3   4   5   6   7   8   9

(b) W ├──•──•──•──•──•──•──**A B**──•──•──┤ E
        1   2   3   4   5   6   7   8   9

(c) W ├──•──•──•──•──•──•──**B A**──•──•──┤ E
        1   2   3   4   5   6   7   8   9

(d) W ├──•──•──•──•──**A B**──•──•──•──•──┤ E
        1   2   3   4   5   6   7   8   9

Line of indifference

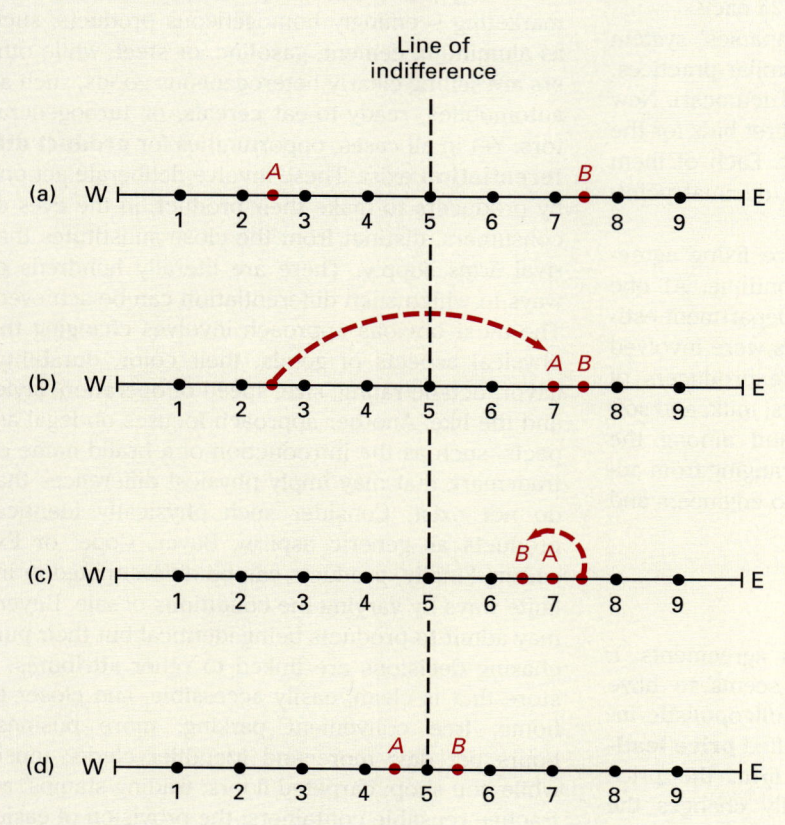

Under certain conditions, oligopolistic competition by means of product differentiation can lead to a situation in which products are hardly differentiated at all.

one seller to the other would be differences in transportation costs, that is, product differentiation based on seller location. Assume that each buyer wants to contact a seller only once; each seeks to buy a single unit, and transporting that unit costs $1 for each of the distances between the black dots. Which locational distribution of A and B would be ideal in the sense of minimizing society's transportation cost?

Hotelling's answer is given in panel (a). The ideal locations would be at the points labeled *A* and *B* on the top line. Under the circumstances, buyers 1 to 4 would buy from *A*, buyers 6 to 9 would buy from *B*, and buyer 5 would be indifferent about the source of supply. Given this ideal degree of locational product differentiation, buyers 2, 3, 7, and 8 would spend 50¢ each on freight, buyers 1, 4, 6, and 9 would spend $1.50 each, leaving buyer 5 to spend $2.50 (regardless of whether A or B was the source of supply). Thus, total transportation cost would be minimized at $10.50.

Yet, that result would not occur, Hotelling argued. The panel (a) solution, if it ever existed, would give each seller a 50 percent market share in the long run, but either seller could improve upon that outcome by relocating right next to the other seller, as is shown in panel (b) for seller *A*. Given *A*'s relocation, *A* would capture buyers 1 to 7, leaving only 8 and 9 to buy from *B*. Thus *A* would have a market share of nearly 78 percent.

Presumably, *B* would respond, as panel (c) shows. *B* could "jump over" *A* and relocate between buyers 6 and 7, thereby inducing buyers 1 to 6 to buy from it and leaving only buyers 7 to 9 for *A*. As a result, *A*'s market share would fall to 33 percent and *B*'s rise accordingly.

The only stable outcome would be the one depicted in panel (d). As in panel (a), each firm would then have a 50 percent market share, their products would scarcely be differentiated, and society's transportation cost would be well above the panel (a) minimum. (Can you show why it would now equal $16.50 instead of the minimum possible $10.50?) **Hotelling's paradox,** thus, states that oligopolistic competition by means of product differentiation can lead to a situation in which products are hardly differentiated at all. Furthermore, Hotelling's insight has far wider applications than shown here. The horizontal lines in Figure 3, for example, might represent not geographic distances between west and east, but all kinds of other quality "distances" among products. Thus, *W* might represent not the western edge of a market, but the blandest possible beer, the sweetest type of cider, or the softest possible cheese. Point *E*, similarly, might then stand for the most bitter beer, the most sour cider, the hardest possible cheese. The dots, in turn, could represent numerous intermediate qualities of the products just named, and the numbers along the line of "characteristics space" might represent the buyers who prefer the given product quality "located" there. The interpretation, however, would be similar. Given the production of only two types of beer, buyers would be served best if brands *A* and *B* were produced as in panel (a). In that case, no buyer would be forced to buy a brand that was more than 2.5 steps away from the buyer's ideal type, and many buyers would find a brand that was closer to their ideal. Yet, the panel (a) divergence would not persist. Producers would attempt to gain market share by changing the character of their products until the panel (d) outcome emerged. Then there would be two types of beer, hardly distinguishable from each other, and many buyers, such as 1 and 9, would have to live with a product, such as A or B, that was far removed from their ideal choice.

Examples 2 and 3 have more to say on the paradox that Hotelling introduced.

Oligopoly Decisions: Advertising

As we saw in an earlier chapter, for firms operating in perfectly competitive markets, advertising makes no sense. Each firm can sell all it wants at the market equilibrium price. For oligopolists facing downward-sloping demand curves, advertising may well be worthwhile.

The Theory

Figure 4 illustrates what is involved. In both panels of the graph, a firm's initial demand and marginal revenue are represented by lines *D* and *MR*, respectively; its initial cost conditions—constant marginal and average total costs—are pictured by the horizontal line, $MC = ATC$. Accordingly, the firm maximizes profit by equating *MR* with *MC* at point *a*, producing an output volume of Q_0 and charging a price P_0 suggested by point *b*. The firm's initial profit equals the crosshatched rectangle. We then assume that the firm incurs **selling costs,** such as advertising expenditures, designed to increase the demand for its product. Its cost curve shifts up to the dashed line $MC' = ATC'$. Two consequences are possible; they are shown in panels (a) and (b), respectively.

In panel (a), demand rises from *D* to *D'*. The firm's marginal revenue rises from the dashed line *MR* to the dotted line *MR'*. Maximum profit is achieved by equating *MR'* with *MC'* at point *c*, producing higher output volume Q_1, and charging higher price P_1 (point *d*). The firm's new profit is higher than before and equals the shaded rectangle. Advertising was a success.

In panel (b), demand fails to rise. Given its higher costs, the firm achieves maximum profit by equating unchanged *MR* with new *MC'* at point *e*, producing lower output volume Q_1, and charging higher price P_1 (point *f*). The firm's new profit is lower than before and equals the shaded rectangle. Advertising was a failure.

The U.S. Experience

In the United States, advertising is big business. In 1990, firms spent $130.1 billion on advertising, which came to over $500 for every man, woman,

EXAMPLE 2

The Convergence of Bank Credit Cards

The world is full of examples that corroborate the story told by Figure 3. One of these cases involves recent developments in the market for bank credit cards. The market might be represented by a line connecting two poles. At one extreme stands the American Express card, introduced in 1958 and long aimed at upper-income spenders buying big-ticket items at top-line establishments throughout the world. (In 1989, there were 33 million such cards, accepted at 2.7 million places in 130 nations.) At the other extreme stand Visa, Mastercard, and the Discover Card, typically used by lower-income spenders for all kinds of mundane purposes. Table A shows selected 1988 data on the charges made by the owners of such cards.

In the late 1980s, the issuers of both types of cards decided to challenge the traditional division of the bank credit card market by lower and upper income sectors. Both reached toward the center of the market. On the one hand, American Express tried to shed its "snob card" image and attempted to convey the idea that its card was useful at places other than Tiffany's. While its "gold card" continued to carry a $75 annual fee (plus $35 for each additional card), its "basic green card" was promoted to middle-income groups at a mere $55 per year. And the company that collected 3.5 percent of the purchase price from ritzy stores actively sought to persuade non-traditional sellers to accept its card. The American Express card was test marketed at McDonald's, doctors' offices and hospitals, movie houses, and even self-service gas pumps.

At the same time, Visa and Mastercard (with annual fees between $15 and $20 and merchant charges of 2.25 percent) moved to attract the middle of the market with "premium cards." Sears, Roebuck issued the Discover card and introduced special incentives: a zero annual fee to users, an unusually low 2 percent merchant charge, and a 1 percent cash-back feature for those charging in excess of $3,000 per year. AT&T in 1990 introduced the Universal credit card aimed at the middle of the market as well. Before year's end, the company had 4.5 million new accounts.

Sources: Jon Friedman and John Meehan, "Can Amex Win the Masses—And Keep Its Class?" *Business Week,* October 9, 1989, pp. 134–138; and *The New York Times,* January 22, 1991, p. B8.

TABLE A

Issuer	Billions of dollars charged, 1988
American Express	$88.9
Citibank	27.0
First Chicago Bank	9.2
Bank of America	8.7
Chase Manhattan Bank	7.7
Sears Discover	7.2
Maryland Bank	6.8

FIGURE 4 The Effects of Advertising

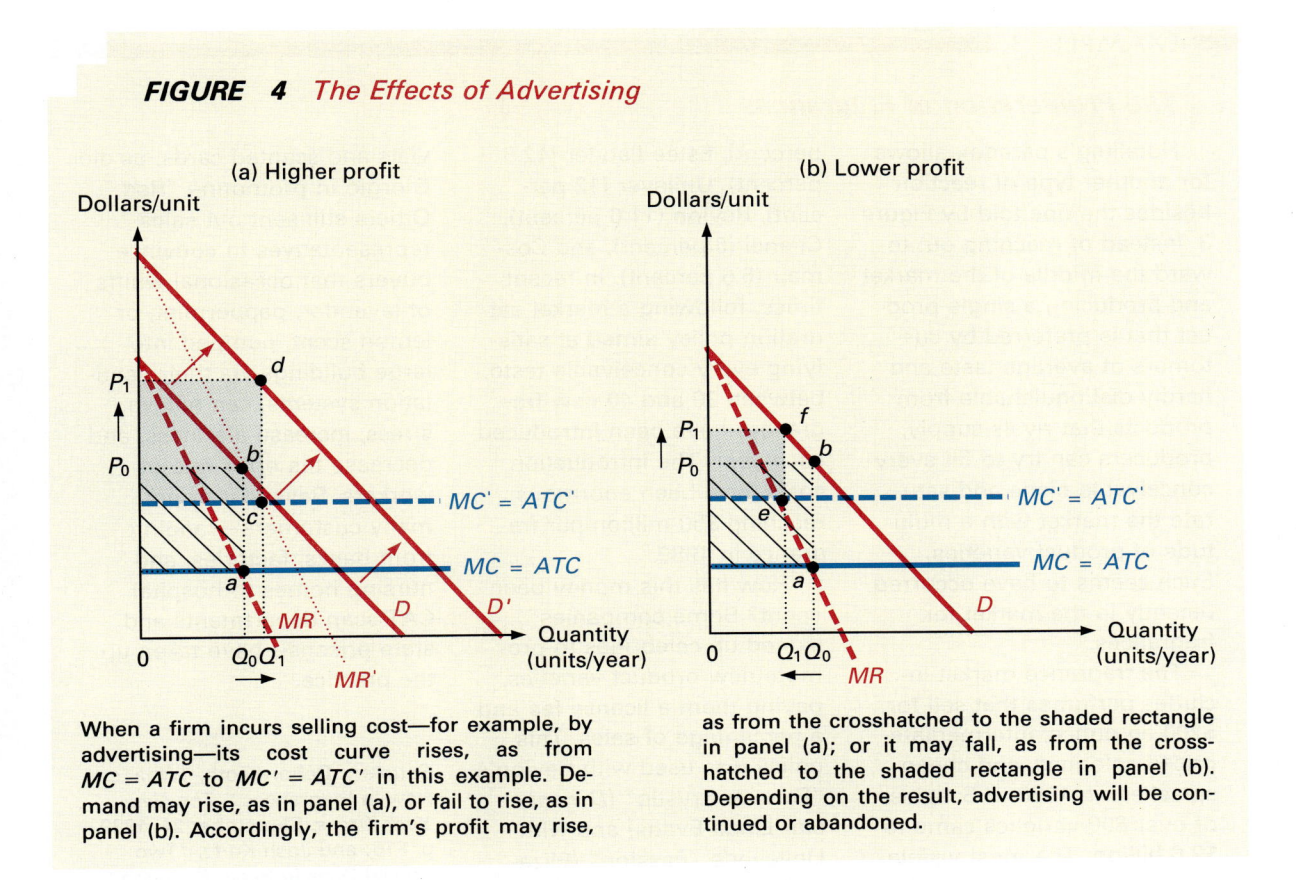

(a) Higher profit

(b) Lower profit

When a firm incurs selling cost—for example, by advertising—its cost curve rises, as from $MC = ATC$ to $MC' = ATC'$ in this example. Demand may rise, as in panel (a), or fail to rise, as in panel (b). Accordingly, the firm's profit may rise, as from the crosshatched to the shaded rectangle in panel (a); or it may fall, as from the crosshatched to the shaded rectangle in panel (b). Depending on the result, advertising will be continued or abandoned.

and child. As the term is used here, advertising includes every type of selling cost, from newspaper and magazine ads to advertisements on radio and television; from telephone book yellow pages, store window displays, and billboards along roads to free samples, trading stamps, contests and games; from direct solicitations by mail or phone to the activities of salespeople, banner-towing airplanes, and blimps.

Advertising, furthermore, comes in two varieties, although it is often difficult to distinguish the two. Some advertising is **informative advertising,** which provides much needed truthful information to prospective buyers concerning available sellers, products, prices, and the like. On the other hand, **persuasive advertising** is designed to divert people's attention from facts to images and to make them buy more as a result of imagined advantages. More often than not, the messages broadcast by the persuaders are totally meaningless. Not so long ago, we used to be told: "Blondes have more fun." "Ours is the most expensive perfume in the world." "This cigarette has the honest taste." "Put a tiger in your tank." and "Coke is it!" Nowadays, we hear about "The choice of a new generation" and "We build excitement." But do these statements mean that the products in question are superior to competing ones? Certainly, that is the impression the advertisers hope to leave, but it is not what the advertisements are saying.

Persuasive advertising attempts to condition people to become loyal to a particular seller and a particular product. Without being linked to any objectively important advantages in the product, such persuasion serves to build prestige for a particular firm by linking its product in people's minds with favorable circumstances until people shout, as Tareyton smokers did on television screens some two

EXAMPLE 3

The Proliferation of Fragrances

Hotelling's paradox allows for another type of reaction besides the one told by Figure 3. Instead of reaching out toward the middle of the market and producing a single product that is preferred by customers of average taste and hardly distinguishable from products that rivals supply, producers can try to fill every conceivable niche and saturate the market with a multitude of product varieties. Such seems to have occurred recently in the market for fragrances.

The fragrance market includes perfumes that sell for $200 an ounce, intermediate priced colognes, and cheap splashes; in 1988, U.S. sales of over 800 varieties came to $2.6 billion. The most visible competitors and their market shares included Avon (19.5 percent), Estée Lauder (12.5 percent), Unilever (12 percent), Revlon (11.6 percent), Chanel (6 percent), and Cosmair (5.6 percent). In recent times, following a market saturation policy aimed at satisfying every conceivable taste, between 30 and 40 new fragrances have been introduced each year. The introduction costs have been enormous, reaching $50 million per fragrance in 1989.

How has this money been spent? Some companies signed up celebrities to promote new product varieties, paying them a license fee and a percentage of sales. This policy was used with Revlon's "Forever Krystle" (*Dynasty* star Linda Evans) and with Unilever's "Passion" (Elizabeth Taylor). Other companies mailed out millions of sample vials and scented cards, as did Giorgio in promoting "Red." Others still sent out sales representatives to convince buyers that occasional whiffs of lavender, peppermint, or lemon scent, pumped into large buildings via their ventilation systems, can relieve stress, increase alertness, and decrease the error rate of workers. Believe it or not, many customers—ranging from banks, factories, and nursing homes to hospital CAT scan departments and state prisons—have taken up the practice.

Source: Debora Toth, "What's New In Fragrances," *The New York Times,* September 24, 1989, p. F15; and Josh Kurtz, "Two Crucial Days in Scent Peddling," *The New York Times,* December 23, 1990, p. F5.

---

decades ago, "We'd rather fight than switch!" A case study of persuasive advertising is provided by Example 4.

One issue has interested economists greatly: Does advertising prevent new firms from entering an industry or does it help them do so? Theoretically, either proposition might make sense. Heavy advertising by existing firms can create **brand loyalty,** an attitude that causes consumers of a highly advertised product to make automatic repeat purchases of the same brand and to cease sampling other brands. The presence of brand loyalty might discourage new firms from entering a market because they can only gain customers by incurring prohibitively high advertising expenses or charging considerably lower prices than existing firms. On the other hand, heavy advertising by new firms can also provide new information to consumers who are not particularly tied to existing products, thus helping new firms gain a foothold in a market that could not be gained any other way. Empirical studies indicate that both cases occur. In some situations, advertising has created brand loyalty and has erected entry barriers against new firms. In other cases, ad-

EXAMPLE 4

The Great American Health Pitch

Persuasive advertising (with minimal informational content) occurred recently in food industry ad campaigns. They have converted America's supermarket aisles into a medicine show reminiscent of the snake oil era. In 1989, the food industry spent $3.6 billion on advertising, almost a third of which provided messages about people's health.

To avoid heart attacks, these messages said, one should lower one's cholesterol intake, which can be achieved by consuming olive oil and foods containing oats and psyllium, ranging from oat bran to new types of bagels, blueberry muffins, cereals, pasta, and (the name notwithstanding) even potato chips. The advertisers failed to mention, however, that most of the "oats" products contained only trace amounts of oats, while containing large quantities of fat, salt, and sugar that have been linked to high blood pressure, obesity, and—ultimately—heart attacks.

To fight off colon cancer, additional messages said, one should consume high-fiber cereal (such as Kellogg's All-Bran, General Mills' Fiber One, or Ralston-Purina's Bran News). The advertisers failed to mention, however, that their claims were based on a poorly executed cross-national study that compared relatively high colon-cancer rates among Americans with relatively low rates abroad without controlling for other differences (besides fiber consumption) that could easily explain the observed differences in cancer rates.

To improve one's general health, still other messages said, one should consume fewer calories. Highly recommended were Healthy Choice and Right Course frozen dinners, along with the regular use of such products as diet drinks, light ice milk, and extra light oil. The advertisers failed to mention, however, that the low calorie counts were often achieved by redefining the serving size (from 12 to 6 ounces in the case of diet drinks) and that many of the low calorie foods contained ingredients (such as saturated coconut oil) that were anything but healthy. Contrary to what the name seems to suggest, the "extra light oil" label referred only to the oil's airy texture, color, and taste; it had nothing to do with its calorie count.

Sources: Claudia H. Deutsch, "Has Kellogg Lost Its Snap?" *The New York Times,* September 24, 1989, pp. F1 and F14; and Zachary Schiller et al., "The Great American Health Pitch," *Business Week,* October 9, 1989, pp. 114–122.

---

vertising has been a means of overcoming brand loyalty and of tearing down barriers to market entry.

Oligopoly Decisions: A Game Theory Approach

As has been noted, none of the preceding theories claim to be a universally valid model of oligopolistic behavior. Each has its uses but is restricted to a particular set of circumstances observed at a narrowly defined time. We now turn to another way of modeling the behavior of interdependent oligopolists. This approach seems to be more fruitful than most; it comes to us from theorists such as John von Neumann (1903–1957) and Oskar Morgenstern (1902–1977), who studied games that people play. In this connection, a **game** is any decision-making situation in which people interact with other people and in which these other people actively seek to thwart the attainment of the first people's goals. Thus, **game theory** is a method for studying decision making in situations of conflict in which the

TABLE 1 *A Zero-Sum Game: Fighting Over Market Shares*

		Firm A's gain (+) or loss (−) of market share (in percent)			
		Firm B			Row minimum (B's choice, given A's = worst outcome for A)
		Product 4	Product 5	Product 6	
Firm A	Product 1	+6	0	+8	0 Maximin
	Product 2	−8	−4	+16	−8
	Product 3	+8	−2	−6	−6
Column maximum (A's choice, given B's = worst outcome for B)		+8	0 Minimax	+16	

A game with a saddle point—the colored number—is the most simple game of all.

fates of people seeking different goals are interlocked so that the payoff to people's choices depends not only on them and objective circumstances but also on other people's choices. As a result, oligopolistic firms, like chess or poker players, must base their decisions on what they expect others to do and therefore, on what they think others expect them to do and even on what they think the others think they expect them to do.

The Two-Person Zero-Sum Game

The simplest of games involves two persons only and is characterized by the winnings of one being exactly matched by the losses of the other. The game is called a **zero-sum game** because the sum of winnings and losses equals zero. Table 1 illustrates this situation and introduces the terminology game theorists employ: players, control variables, and payoffs. In this example, the *players* are two firms, A and B, which compete with each other by introducing newly differentiated products. Each firm has three *control variables,* each can introduce one of three products: products 1, 2, or 3 in the case of Firm A, products 4, 5, or 6 in the case of Firm B. The resultant *payoffs,* measured in terms of market share percentages gained or lost by Firm A (which in a zero-sum game implies a corresponding loss or gain by Firm B), are given in the main body of the table.

In the first row Firm A can introduce Product 1. It will gain 6, 0, or 8 percent of the market, respectively, depending on whether Firm B introduces Product 4, 5, or 6. The next two rows are similarly interpreted. How then should each firm act, given that any one action can lead to widely varying results?

Von Neumann and Morgenstern suggested that each firm might imagine itself in the place of its rival and thus anticipate the rival's reaction to any action it was about to take. Wouldn't it be likely, they asked, that the rival would always adopt the most damaging counterstrategy?

Thus, if Firm A introduces Product 1, Firm B introduces Product 5 and neither party gains or loses market share. If Firm A chooses Product 2, Firm B introduces Product 4, reducing A's market share by 8 percent and raising its own accordingly. Finally, if Firm A chooses Product 3, Firm B chooses Product 6, reducing A's market share and raising its own by 6 percent. All these outcomes (negative for Firm A) are shown in the last column of Table 1, labeled "row minimum."

If we repeat this reasoning from the point of view of Firm B, we find that B's introduction of Products 4, 5, or 6 will be greeted by A's introduction of Products 3, 1, or 2, respectively. Each of these countermoves is best for A and worst for B under the circumstances. All these choices by A, given prior choices by B, are listed in the last row of Table 1, labeled "column maximum."

If all firms always expect the worst of their rivals (as von Neumann and Morgenstern assumed), each firm will try to choose the best among a list of worst possible outcomes. Thus, A will focus on the last column of our table and "maximin," i.e., select the maximum among all the possible minima shown there (the *maximum minimorum*). In our example, this **maximin strategy** will cause A to introduce Product 1. The worst that can then happen to A (if B introduces Product 5) is a 0 percent change in A's market share. This is better than an 8 or 6 percent market-share *loss* that might be associated with A's Products 2 or 3 (provided B makes the smartest countermove).

Reasoning similarly, Firm B will focus on the last row of our table, which shows A's maxima and B's minima. Accordingly, B will "minimax," i.e., select the minimum among all of its opponent's possible maxima (the *minimum maximorum*). This **minimax strategy** will cause B to introduce Product 5. The worst that can then happen to B (if A introduces Product 1) is a 0 percent change in B's market share, which is better than an 8 or even a 16 percent market-share *loss* that might be associated with B's Products 4 or 6 (provided A makes the smartest countermove).

The result is shown by the colored number in Table 1. Firm A will introduce Product 1; Firm B, Product 5; neither firm will gain or lose market share. The combination of strategies that equates maximin and minimax in a game is called a **saddle point.** In our example, it produces a zero payoff for both parties. Neither player can do better than choosing the saddle point strategy again and again.

The Two-Person Nonzero-Sum Game

People can, however, play a **nonzero-sum game** in which the winnings and losses of all players add to a positive or negative number. The most famous game of this type, called the **prisoners' dilemma game,** is one in which the best common choice of strategies is unstable, offers great incentives to cheat, and leads to the worst possible choice, as shown in Table 2. The police, it is imagined, have arrested two suspects in an armed burglary case. They are locked in separate rooms and each is told:

> If you confess, but your buddy keeps quiet, we will allow you—in return for your cooperation—to plead guilty to a lesser charge. You will get off with 2 years in jail, but your buddy will get a 9 year sentence. You have one hour to decide.

The offers made by the police are clearly illustrated by the cells labeled B and C in Table 2, but what will our suspects do? Imagine yourself in the position of Suspect 1. If you confess, you can end up in jail for 6 years or 2 years, depending on whether your buddy confesses or keeps quiet; the worst of the two outcomes is given in the last column's upper cell. If you keep quiet, you can end up in jail for 9 years or 1 year, again depending on your buddy's action; the worst of these two outcomes is given in the last column's lower cell. Repelled by the prospect of 9 years in jail, you will "maximin" and confess.

An analogous argument can be made for your buddy, of course. The worst possible outcomes for Suspect 2 are given in the table's last row; once again, confession is preferable to not confessing (and the associated risk of 9 years in jail). Thus, *both* prisoners will confess, and both will go to jail for 6 years (cell A). But if they had both been quiet—the police having less than perfect evidence—both would have gotten away with only 1 year in jail (cell D).

The preceding analysis is easily applied to oligopolistic firms competing against one another by changing prices or advertising expenditures. Table 3 imagines two oligopolists who would neither gain nor lose profit (cell D) if both maintained current prices. Yet each firm knows that a 15 percent cut in its price—given the other firm's price—would yield a $5 million profit increase, along with a $9 million profit decrease to the other firm (cells B

TABLE 2 The Prisoners' Dilemma

Each suspect's loss of free time via jail sentence

		Suspect 2		Row minimum (the worst for Suspect 1)
		Confess	Keep quiet	
Suspect 1	Confess	A −6 years / −6 years	B −9 years / −2 years	−6 years Maximin
	Keep quiet	C −2 years / −9 years	D −1 year / −1 year	−9 years
Column minimum (the worst for Suspect 2)		−6 years Maximin	−9 years	

The prisoners' dilemma illustrates game situations in which the best common choice of strategies (block D in this example) is unstable, offers great incentives to cheat, and leads to the worst possible choice (block A).

TABLE 3 A Price War

Each firm's annual profit increase (+) or decrease (−) compared to original position (in million dollars)

		Firm B		Row minimum (the worst for Firm A)
		Cut price 15 percent	Maintain price	
Firm A	Cut price 15 percent	A −7 / −7	B −9 / +5	−7 Maximin
	Maintain price	C +5 / −9	D 0 / 0	−9
Column minimum (the worst for Firm B)		−7 Maximin	−9	

The game pictured here is also a prisoners' dilemma game. The best common strategy is found in cell D; the worst one (cell A) is chosen.

and C). And a simultaneous price cut by both would reduce the profit of each by $7 million (cell A). Repelled by the prospect of a $9 million profit decrease, both firms will decide *not* to maintain their price. They will "maximin" by cutting price and end up in cell A (the worst possible outcome) rather than in D (the best possible one).

Table 4 tells a similar story in which two oligopolists fight each other through advertising campaigns. Originally, both firms spend $500,000/year on advertising, both gain some customers and revenue, but the effects cancel each other, hence there is no net effect on profit (cell A). If either firm cut its advertising budget to $100,000/year (while the other firm made no change), many customers would abandon the former firm for the latter; the former would lose, the latter would gain profit (cells B and C). On the other hand, if both firms cut their ad budgets at the same time, neither firm would lose customers and revenue, but both would gain profit (cell D). For the now familiar reasons, both firms could do best by cutting their ad budgets at the same time, but will, in fact, "maximin" and choose the worst possible case (cell A).

It is fairly easy to see what it would take to escape the prisoners' dilemma game. The dilemma feeds on uncertainty and distrust, which would evaporate if the two opposing parties (the prisoners locked in separate rooms) could cooperate with each other. Thus, a cartel agreement could put both parties into cell D instead of A. (Can you see why U.S. tobacco companies were delighted, not grieved, when the U.S. government banned cigarette ads on TV? The ban effectively produced a cartel agreement forcing the warring factions simultaneously to "disarm.") At the same time, Tables 3 and 4 also indicate why cartel agreements provide each participant with a strong incentive to cheat. In Table 3, once Firm B has agreed to maintain price, Firm A can do even better than in cell D by cutting its price and moving to cell B. (And once A has promised to maintain price, Firm B can do better by moving from cell D to cell C). In Table 4, similarly, once either firm has promised to eliminate its ads, the other firm can do better by *not* abandoning *its* ads. As cheating Firm A tries to abandon cell D for B, and cheating Firm B tries to abandon cell D for C, both end up back in cell A.

TABLE 4 An Advertising War

Each firm's annual profit increase (+) or decrease (−) compared to original position (in million dollars)

Firm A		Firm B Spend $500,000	Firm B Spend $100,000	Row minimum (the worst for Firm A)
	Spend $500,000	A: 0 / 0	B: −0.5 / +1.5	0 ← Maximin
	Spend $100,000	C: +1.5 / −0.5	D: +0.3 / +0.3	−0.5
Column minimum (the worst for Firm B)		0 ↗ Maximin	−0.5	

The game pictured here is also a prisoners' dilemma game. The best common strategy is found in cell D; the worst one (cell A) is chosen.

Monopolistic Competition

As noted at the beginning of this chapter, monopolistic competitors, like many (but not all) oligopolists, offer products that are differentiated from one seller to the next. In other respects, however, this type of market structure differs significantly from an oligopoly. Most importantly, restrictions to market entry or exit do not exist and the number of firms is large, which accounts for the absence of strategic behavior.

Profit Maximization

Figure 5 can help us understand the behavior of the typical firm in this kind of environment. In panel (a), a restaurant on Main Street faces a downward-sloping demand along with the implied line of marginal revenue. Unlike the perfectly competitive wheat farmer (who is a price taker), the owner of the restaurant has some control over price. The restaurant has its own identifiable product that is not precisely duplicated anywhere else. It also has a

FIGURE 5 *The Monopolistic Competitor*

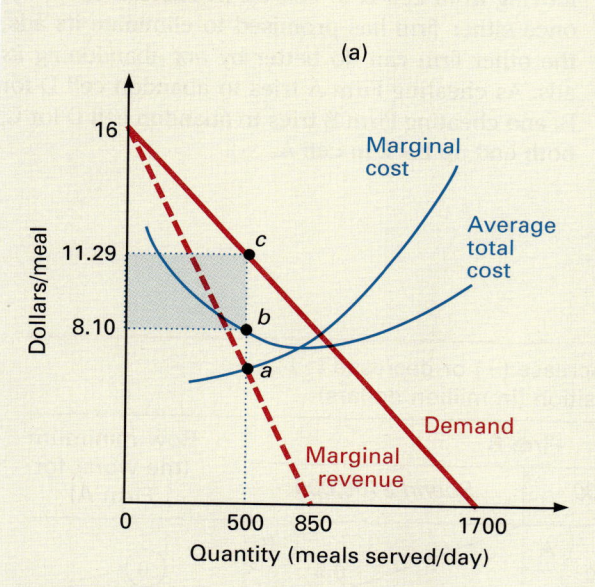

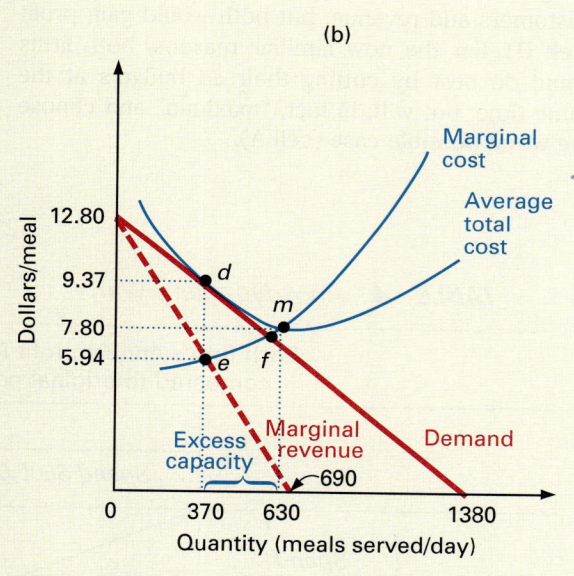

The earning of positive economic profit by monopolistically competitive firms, as in panel (a), invites the entry into the market of new competitors who supply slightly differentiated but similar products. As a result, some customers are lost and the demand facing the typical firm declines over time. The process comes to a halt when price equals average total cost and economic profit has completely disappeared, as in panel (b). Initial losses are similarly eliminated by the exit of firms from the market and an increase in demand experienced by the surviving firms (not shown).

Although the zero-profit ($P = ATC$) long-run result is reminiscent of the fate of perfectly competitive firms, there are major differences: Unlike the long-run result of perfect competition ($P = MC =$ minimum ATC), the long-run result of monopolistic competition implies $P > MC$ (compare d and e) and, thus, economic inefficiency. It also implies $P >$ minimum ATC (compare d and m) and, thus, excess *capacity*.

group of more or less steady customers. Yet, if it raises its price too much (to $16/meal in our case), all of its customers will vanish because there are many close substitutes for this restaurant's meals, including similar meals offered by other restaurants and food cooked at home. Given the cost curves shown in panel (a), our restaurant maximizes profit by selecting that output quantity (500 meals/day) at which declining marginal revenue and rising marginal cost are equal to one another (point a). To sell that ideal quantity, the manager sets the price at $11.29/meal (point c). Because the associated average total cost equals $8.10/meal (point b), a profit of $bc = \$3.19$/meal is made. This situation implies a total profit equal to the shaded rectangle of $3.19/meal times 500 meals/day, or $1,595/day.

If our restaurant were a genuine monopoly, the economic profit just calculated ($1,595/day or $582,175/year over and above the owner's next best job opportunity) might be reaped again and again, year after year. But not so in the case of monopolistic competition. Other people would observe the restaurant's good fortune and would seriously consider abandoning their low-paying jobs and going into the restaurant business as well. "If Joe (who was always so *dumb* in school) can do it," they might say, "we can do it." Soon another restaurant opens up across the street, another one around the corner on Pleasant Street, and then another one right next door. Slowly, Joe's customers will drift away; some may just want variety and to try something new, others may prefer a place for lunch 200 feet closer to where they work. In the process, the demand line facing Joe begins to shrink. Profit shrinks accordingly, and the whole process comes to an end when profit has completely disappeared. Eventually, as Figure 5, panel (b), indicates, our restaurant will be serving 370 meals/day, corresponding to intersection e of the new marginal revenue line and the old marginal cost line. The associated profit-maximizing price ($9.37) just equals the restaurant's average total cost (point d), and all of the economic profit is gone. In this respect ($P = ATC$ and economic profit = zero), the long-run outcome is the same as under perfect competition. In other respects, however, significant differences exist.

First, while price equals marginal cost under perfect competition, *price exceeds marginal cost,* $P > MC$, under monopolistic competition. In panel (b) of Figure 5, price ($d = \$9.37$) exceeds marginal cost ($e = \$5.94$) at the profit-maximizing output volume (370 meals/day). This situation implies failure to produce additional units of output that could be produced at marginal costs measured along ef but would be valued by potential customers along higher demand line section df. The potential mutually beneficial deals that this divergence implies are not being carried out; the extent of the implied economic inefficiency is measured by area def.

Second, while price equals *minimum* average total cost under perfect competition, *price exceeds minimum average total cost,* $P > $ minimum ATC, under monopolistic competition. In panel (b) of Figure 5, price ($d = \$9.37$) exceeds minimum average total cost ($m = \$7.80$). Our firm is producing 370 meals/day at an average total cost of $9.37/day, while its average total cost could be as low as $7.80 if it produced its capacity output of 630 meals/day corresponding to minimum ATC point m. This difference between a monopolistically competitive firm's capacity output (corresponding to minimum ATC) and its lower but profit-maximizing level of actual output is called **excess capacity.**

Such excess capacity can be observed in many places. Barber shops, cinemas, motels, and restaurants are rarely filled, and clerks in many retail stores usually have spare time that could be used to serve extra customers. Yet, the higher-than-minimum average total cost that such excess capacity implies need not be a total waste. The fact that many firms permanently operate at a fraction of their capacity provides customers with *diversity,* which is certainly worth something to them. What if 4 out of 10 restaurants were closed so that the remaining restaurants could always operate at capacity and produce at minimum average total cost? As panel (b) of Figure 5 indicates, you may then be able to get a meal at $7.80 rather than $9.37, but you would have fewer restaurants from which to choose. The surviving ones may be less conveniently located, may not produce the type of meal you prefer, and may make you wait longer to be served. Soon you would long for the good old days when restaurants were abundant, less crowded, and always ready to serve you.

Examples 5, 6, and 7 provide illustrations of monopolistic competition in action.

Empirical Studies

A number of empirical studies have attempted to determine the relative importance of various types of market structures in the United States. We will consider two of them.

Indexes of Industrial Concentration

One type of study focuses on the extent to which particular markets are dominated by large firms. It computes **concentration ratios,** numbers that show the percentage of domestic sales that is attributable to a stated number of largest domestic firms in an industry, usually the 4, 8, 20, or 50 largest companies. Thus a 4-firm concentration ratio of 91 would indicate that the 4 largest domestic firms in the industry accounted for 91 percent of domestic sales in the year for which the data were gathered.

A 1972 government study of 450 U.S. industries showed this 4-firm concentration ratio to lie between 0 and 19 for 87 industries, between 20 and 39 for 168 industries, between 40 and 59 for 118 industries, and at 60 or above for the remaining 77 industries.[4] Tables 5 and 6 provide further detail. The numbers shown in these tables must, however, be interpreted with care.

Understatements of Market Power

For one thing, the ratios refer to the nation as a whole, but some markets are effectively limited to a much smaller area. Some products, such as bricks or cement, may have prohibitively high transportation costs: other products, such as cut flowers or fresh strawberries, may be extremely perishable. In such a situation, a national concentration ratio may be extremely small. There may be 3,000 firms of equal size, each supplying a given county; hence the 4 "largest" firms would ship 4/3,000 of output and the 4-firm concentration ratio would equal a mere .13 percent. Yet this would *understate* the market power of the firms; in any given county, buyers would find only a single supplier!

[4] U.S. Bureau of the Census, Census of Manufactures, 1972 *Special Report Series: Concentration Ratios in Manufacturing,* MC72–(SR)–2 (Washington, D.C.: U.S. Government Printing Office, 1975).

The same effect occurs when the industry classification is extremely *broad.* Consider "farm machinery" in Table 6. Although the 4 largest domestic firms supply only 46 percent of domestic sales (and even the 50-firm ratio only equals 78), it is still possible for buyers to face pure monopolies—if each of the 1,868 firms supplies a *particular* machine that has no substitutes and that no one else supplies.

Overstatements of Market Power

On the other hand, high concentration ratios could also *overstate* the market power of firms. Consider industries producing products, such as automobiles or aluminum ingots, for which many good substitutes (such as *imported* cars or *recycled* aluminum) are available. In cases such as these, the 4 largest domestic firms may supply 100 percent of domestic sales, yet buyers may have numerous near-perfect alternatives.

Once again, the industry classification must be watched. If it is extremely *narrow,* a high concentration ratio may be meaningless. Consider "cereal breakfast foods" in Table 5, an industry in which the 4 largest firms "control" 90 percent of the market. There are innumerable breakfast-food substitutes; the market power of these 4 firms is undoubtedly much less than the 90-percent ratio seems to imply.

The U.S. Economy: An Overview

A recent study by William G. Shepherd classified the nation's economic activities by major sectors (agriculture, mining, construction, manufacturing, and the like) and then estimated the degree of competition prevailing in each. His results are summarized in Table 7. Part I of the table introduces the government's 89 "standard-industrial-classification" or SIC categories. It also shows Shephard's classification scheme with respect to the degree of competition prevailing. An activity was classified as *pure monopoly* (category 1) when a single, price-setting producer held a market share near 100 percent and entry into the market was blocked. An activity was classified as involving a *dominant firm* (category 2) when one price-setting producer held a market share between 50 and over 90 percent and when entry barriers were high. An activity was classified as

TABLE 5 Concentration Ratios in the United States—Part I

Industry	4-firm ratio	8-firm ratio	Number of firms
Electron receiving tubes	95	99	21
Motor vehicles, car bodies*	93	99	254
Primary lead	93	99	2
Cereal breakfast foods	90	98	34
Electric lamps	90	94	103
Turbines, generators	90	96	59
Household refrigerators/freezers	85	98	30
Cigarettes	84	n.a.	13
Cathode-ray (TV) tubes	83	97	69
Household laundry equipment	83	98	20
Carbon/graphite products	80	91	58
Primary aluminum	79	92	12
Organic fibers (noncellulosic)*	78	90	37
Household vacuum cleaners	75	91	34
Chocolate, cocoa products	74	88	39
Calculating/accounting machines	73	89	74
Photographic equipment, supplies*	72	86	702
Tires, inner tubes*	70	88	121
Metal cans	66	79	134
Roasted coffee	65	79	162
Guided missiles, space vehicles*	64	94	20
Sanitary paper products	63	82	72
Motor vehicle parts, accessories*	62	70	2,194
Aircraft*	59	81	151
Soap, detergents*	59	71	554
Storage batteries	57	85	138
Glass containers	55	76	27
Wine, brandy	53	68	183
Malt beverages	52	70	108
Pet food	51	71	147

The data in this table refer to 1972 or 1977 (asterisk). They indicate that in many U.S. industries, concentration ratios are high and the number of firms is small.

SOURCES: U.S. Bureau of the Census, *Statistical Abstract of the United States 1985* (Washington, D.C.: U.S. Government Printing Office, 1986), p. 764, and the source cited in footnote 4.

TABLE 6 Concentration Ratios in the United States—Part II

Industry	4-firm ratio	8-firm ratio	20-firm ratio	50-firm ratio	Number of firms
Construction machinery	47	59	75	86	807
Farm machinery	46	61	70	78	1,868
Blast furnaces, steel mills	45	65	84	95	395
Electronic computing equipment	44	55	71	85	808
Refrigeration/heating equipment	41	51	67	82	731
Toilet preparations	40	56	74	90	644
Gray iron foundries	34	44	60	73	865
Bread, cake, and related products	33	40	54	68	2,549
Petroleum refining	30	53	81	94	192
Pharmaceuticals	24	43	73	91	655
Paper mills	23	42	70	92	171
Periodicals	22	35	52	67	2,860
Plastics, resins	22	37	60	87	221
Radio/TV equipment	20	33	57	73	1,873
Meat packing	19	37	49	62	2,404
Newspapers	19	31	45	62	7,821
Fluid milk	18	28	43	60	1,516
Sawmills, planing mills	17	23	36	49	6,966
Bottled, canned soft drinks	15	22	36	50	1,758
Commercial printing					
Letterpress	14	19	25	31	14,375
Lithographic	6	10	17	26	10,964

The data in this table refer to 1977. They provide examples of relatively low ratios, typically associated with large numbers of firms.

SOURCE: U.S. Bureau of the Census, *Statistical Abstract of the United States 1985* (Washington, D.C.: U.S. Government Printing Office, 1986), p. 764.

tight oligopoly (category 3) when the 4-firm concentration ratio exceeded 60 percent, there were medium to high entry barriers, and rigid prices were cooperatively set (either privately or through governmental price-fixing schemes). All remaining activities—loosely oligopolistic, monopolistically competitive, and perfectly competitive—were classified as *effectively competitive* (category 4). All of these industries had a 4-firm concentration ratio below 40 percent, low entry barriers, unstable market shares, little collusion, flexible prices, and low profits.

EXAMPLE 5

Stalking the New Consumer

New York's Madison Avenue—the heart of America's advertising industry—originally flourished selling mass produced goods to mass audiences via the mass media: newspaper, magazines, radio, and network television. It used to be that the industry could simply saturate daytime or evening soap operas and be fairly confident that most of America's households knew about the Jolly Green Giant, the Hefty, Hefty Cinch Sak, or whatever else the advertisers cared to sell. But no more, for which three reasons are often cited.

First, the network TV audience has been steadily shrinking. Between 1979 and 1989, it fell from 78 percent of all households to 57 percent during the daytime and from 92 percent to 67 percent during evening prime time. And those who do watch, surveys show, pay less attention than ever to a 30 second commercial, (which cost $185,000 in 1989).

Second, many producers have turned to "micromarketing," flooding any given market with innumerable variations of a basic product in an attempt to reach every conceivable market niche in which small audiences want products customized to their special tastes. Before long, Oreos were joined by Fudge Covered Oreos, Oreo Double Stufs, and Oreo Big Stufs; Tide by Liquid Tide, Tide with Bleach; and so on. Advertisers have found it impossible to tell network TV audiences about literally hundreds of variations of a product a given firm is offering. (Counting merely the brands that yielded total revenues in excess of $1 million, the number of cereals, for example, rose from 84 in 1979 to 150 in 1989; that of toothpastes from 10 in 1979 to 31 in 1989.)

Third, a technological innovation—the supermarket barcode scanner—can provide an avalanche of data and makes it possible to find out which specialized audience is buying which specialized products at what prices. If Oreo Big Stufs sell well in supermarkets situated in big-city Italian neighborhoods but nowhere else, producers know which population group to target in their advertising. The outreach to specialized groups can occur in hundreds of ways other than the once favored network television. Involved are direct mail solicitations; local cable TV; displays, posters, and loudspeakers *inside* stores; magazines aimed at special audiences (teenagers, the elderly, African-Americans, Hispanics, and so on). In addition, ads are being placed in a multitude of unexpected locations: in high-school cafeterias and classrooms, in beauty parlors, and doctors' offices, in the middle of books or board games, on video cassettes, shopping carts, and blood-pressure monitors, and at innumerable special events, rainging from beauty contests, chili-cooking contests, and sing-in-the shower contests to neighborhood block parties, hydroplane races, and the Carnaval Miami. For all these reasons, modern-day advertisers of consumer goods are aiming at a mosaic of minorities rather than a homogeneous mass market reflecting America, the melting pot.

Indeed, some advertisers have begun to target individual consumers. If you get lots of collect phone calls, MCI may offer you a personal 800 number; if you call area code 413 a lot, AT&T may offer a special deal for that area. If you buy certain types of books or redeem certain types of coupons, a personal letter offering similar products may soon be in your mailbox. Believe it or not, work is underway to create individualized TV ads as well.

Sources: Zachary Schiller, "Stalking the New Consumer," *Business Week,* August 28, 1989, pp. 54–62; Randall Rothenberg, "Change in Consumer Markets Hurting Advertising Industry," *The New York Times,* October 3, 1989, pp. 1 and D23; and Kathleen Deveny, "Segments of One," *The Wall Street Journal,* March 22, 1991, p. B4.

TABLE 7 The Trend of Competition by Sectors, United States, 1939–1980

Part I

SIC category	Sector	Competition category[a]	Amount of national income in each category ($ million)		
			1939	1958	1980
0–9	Agriculture, forestry, and fisheries	1	0	0	0
		2	0	0	0
		3	507	2,681	7,462
		4	5,519	15,229	47,261
10–14	Mining	1	0	0	0
		2	0	0	0
		3	211	443	1,116
		4	1,422	5,254	25,354
15–17	Construction	1	0	0	0
		2	0	0	0
		3	1,688	8,367	17,346
		4	654	10,624	70,247
20–39	Manufacturing	1	135	372	0
		2	2,053	6,777	18,032
		3	6,588	40,358	124,428
		4	9,318	60,234	317,042
40–49	Transportation and public utilities	1	3,827	9,557	38,171
		2	120	7,974	24,133
		3	3,856	9,917	35,828
		4	743	9,683	64,186

Part II

Sectors of the economy	National income in each sector, 1978[b] ($ billion)	The share of each sector that was effectively competitive		
		1939 (%)	1958 (%)	1980[b] (%)
Agriculture, forestry and fisheries	54.7	91.6	85.0	86.4
Mining	24.5	87.1	92.2	95.8
Construction	87.6	27.9	55.9	80.2
Manufacturing	459.5	51.5	55.9	69.0
Transportation and public utilities	162.3	8.7	26.1	39.1
Wholesale and retail trade	261.8	57.8	60.5	93.4
Finance, insurance and real estate	210.7	61.5	63.8	94.1
Services	245.3	53.9	54.3	77.9
Totals	**1,512.4**	**52.4**	**56.4**	**76.7**

[a]1 is "pure monopoly," 2 is "dominant firm," 3 is "tight oligopoly," and 4 is "effectively competitive" (loose oligopoly, monopolistic competition, and perfect competition).

Part I (continued)			Amount of national income in each category ($ million)		
SIC category	Sector	Competition category[a]	1939	1958	1980
50–59	Trade	1	0	0	0
		2	0	0	0
		3	5,313	23,019	17,238
		4	7,291	35,227	244,542
60–69	Finance, insurance, and real estate	1	0	0	0
		2	880	203	0
		3	2,194	14,582	12,384
		4	4,917	26,090	198,351
70–89	Services	1	36	0	0
		2	213	1,185	0
		3	3,231	16,364	54,296
		4	4,074	20,831	190,950
Totals		1	3,998	9,929	38,171
		2	3,266	16,139	42,165
		3	23,588	115,731	272,098
		4	33,938	183,172	1,157,933
Percent of total national income		1	6.17	3.06	2.53
		2	5.04	4.97	2.79
		3	36.41	35.61	18.02
		4	52.38	56.37	76.66

Part III		The share of each category in national income		
Competition categories		1939	1958	1980
	($ billion)	(%)	(%)	(%)
1. Pure monopoly	38.2	6.2	3.1	2.5
2. Dominant firm	42.2	5.0	5.0	2.8
3. Tight oligopoly	272.1	36.4	35.6	18.0
4. Others: effectively competitive	1,157.9	52.4	56.3	76.7
Total	**1,512.4**	**100.0**	**100.0**	**100.0**

[b]1980 figures reflect competitive conditions as of 1980. The industry weights are based on 1978 data for national income, the latest year available.

SOURCE: William G. Shepherd, "Causes of Increased Competition in the U.S. Economy, 1939–1980," *The Review of Economics and Statistics,* November 1982, pp. 613–626.

EXAMPLE 6

The Vending Machine Craze

In recent years, the vending machine industry, symbol of America's perpetual quest for convenience, has been on a roll. Sales have more than doubled from $11 billion in 1978 to nearly $23 billion in 1988. At the same time, the composition of sales has changed drastically from 27 percent cigarettes and 65 percent food and beverages in 1978 to a mere 8 percent cigarettes and 91 percent food and beverages in 1988. This reflects, in part, people's fear of lung cancer and growing agitation and legislation against smoking in public. It also reflects the attempt by some 8,000 vending machine companies (that contract with owners of buildings to place machines on their property) to differentiate their products. Indeed, technological innovations have opened up tantalizing new opportunities. These include:

1. A new "retort" process that vacuum seals food and makes refrigeration unnecessary. This has enabled operators to offer almost any type of food, from french fries to fruit juices and microwave dinners.

2. More sophisticated refrigerator dispensing units. This has made it possible to supplement basic sandwiches with all kinds of cold platters.

3. Paper money and credit card acceptors. This has enabled operators to expand their market to customers without change.

But the battle has just begun. At the time of this writing, the industry was fiercely lobbying Congress for a new $1 coin because inflation has made nickels, dimes, and quarters ever less useful for vending machine sales. Plans were underway to sell blue jeans, computer programs, toothpaste, and videotapes through vending machines as well. And many coffee-dispensing machines were being equipped with coffee grinders to let customers create a higher-quality brew.

Source: Jack Steinberg, "What's New in Vending Machines," *The New York Times,* October 8, 1989, p. F17.

The Table 7 entries are easily interpreted. Consider agriculture, forestry, and fisheries in 1939. In that year, this sector contributed $6,026 million to national income. Of this amount, nothing was produced by pure monopoly or dominant firms; $507 million was produced by tight oligopolies, the remaining $5,519 million (or 91.6 percent of the total) by effectively competitive firms.

Part II of Table 7 summarizes the degree to which each sector's output was produced under conditions of effective competition in each of the three years studied. Note how the 91.6 percent figure just calculated reappears in that table's first row. Part III of Table 7 summarizes the data in yet another way by showing the importance in the economy as a whole (and for each of the three years studied) of each of the four competition categories. Two major conclusions stand out.

First, as the boldfaced totals of Part II indicate, there has been a major advance in competitiveness since 1958. Shepherd attributed the jump from 56.4 to 76.7 percent to vigorous antitrust action, increased import competition, and deregulation. Second, by 1980, as the last column of Part III indicates, roughly three quarters of U.S. output was produced under conditions of effective competition.

EXAMPLE 7

Modern Day "Hamburger Wars"

An example of monopolistic competition in action is provided by the fast food industry (1989 U.S. sales of $56 billion). Typically, outlets are run by independent owner-operators; many are affiliated with one or another of the franchising companies listed in Table A. On average, firms operating under McDonald's golden arches produced the greatest revenue in 1989. The organization made sales of $18 billion and operated 10,577 outlets in 50 countries, some 8,014 of them in the United States. The total sales of the nearest competitor, Burger King, came to less than a third of McDonald's.

McDonald's success has been attributed to a variety of factors, including the following:

1. A careful selection of franchisees. Each year, there are 20,000 applicants, a mere 2,000 of which are seriously considered. After lengthy interviews, credit checks, and the like, only 150 are admitted to a 2-year training program that includes working 20 hours a week at a franchise without pay (cleaning toilets, sweeping floors, working the counter, keeping the books) and attending "Hamburger University" at $700 a week, where a 4-volume training guide must be digested. Graduates must invest a minimum of $66,000 of their own money in the franchise they receive.

2. Careful site selection. Before the golden arches go up, the parent company assures itself of a sufficiently large number of potential customers at the chosen site. In recent years, the company has even used NASA photographs to analyze traffic patterns and has pinpointed sites near hospitals, military bases, and even in tiny hamlets near busy road intersections for future outlets.

3. Strict standards set by headquarters. To assure customers a predictable product across the land, the parent company provides franchisees with extensive direction. It prescribes the architecture, the items on the menu, the recipes, the prices, the operating procedures, and much more.

4. Generous parent company support of franchisees, involving heavy advertising ($1 billion in 1989) and financial help in bad times.

5. Continuous innovation. As

TABLE A

Franchising parent company	1989 average sales per franchise (1,000s of dollars)
McDonald's	1,600
Burger King	984
Hardee's	920
Jack in the Box	900
Wendy's	759
Arby's	610
Kentucky Fried Chicken	597
Taco Bell	589
Pizza Hut	520
Domino's	485

EXAMPLE 7

Modern Day "Hamburger Wars" (continued)

needed, new and improved architecture is introduced: an extra lane, a larger window, multiple windows—all designed to let people pass through the place in 45 seconds or less. In addition, new and varied products are provided at carefully chosen intervals. The basic hamburger is almost a memory now, long replaced by more sophisticated versions and joined by breakfast food in 1973 (Egg McMuffin), by packaged salads in 1987, by pizzas in 1989 (ridiculed in a Pizza Hut ad as the "McFrozen"). Health-conscious consumers are being accommodated with oat-bran muffins, low-calorie salad dressing, low-fat milk, french fries cooked in vegetable oil, and the McLean Deluxe, a low-fat hamburger. Finally, hundreds of small changes are designed to cater to every customer's taste: larger tabletops, movable chairs, dimmed lights at supper time, and diaper-changing stations.

Other fast food vendors have countered McDonald's innovations with ones of their own, and they have tried to lure away customers by offering deep discounts, contests, premiums, and more. Thus, the Kentucky Fried Chicken Company has marketed a fried chicken without skin to counter the McLean Deluxe. Burger King put up a 29 cent "mini-hamburger" when McDonald's priced its basic hamburger at 49 cents in response to 49 cent tacos sold by Taco Bell. Major companies usually considered "outside" the industry, such as Campbell Soup and Kraft General Foods, are competitors as well. Given that three quarters of American households have microwaves, one major campaign has attempted to provide working parents with microwavable foods as a home alternative to fast food outlets. Campbell's Great Starts and Super Combos or Kraft's Zappetites are directly aimed at the fast food breakfast business.

All this competition has spilled over national boundaries as well. In 1986, 20.3 percent of McDonald's profit was earned abroad; the figure rose steadily to 38.2 percent in 1990. By then, McDonald's had 11,800 outlets, of which 3,300 were abroad. While U.S. sales were flat, foreign sales grew by leaps and bounds. Asian markets, ranging from Japan, Hong Kong, and Taiwan to Singapore, the Philippines, and Malaysia, grew at rates exceeding 50 percent a year. In South Korea, there were only four restaurants and "hanging out at McDonald's" was the trendy thing to do. The company quickly moved to put 30 restaurants in place by 1993; almost instantly, Wendy's opened 13 outlets and Burger King 12.

Sources: Barbara March, "Going for the Golden Arches," *The Wall Street Journal,* May 1, 1989, p. B1; Eben Shapiro, "For McDonald's, Pizza May Be the Next McHit," *The New York Times,* September 20, 1989, p. D1; Brian Brenner and Gail DeGeorge, "The Burger Wars Were Just a Warmup for McDonald's," *Business Week,* May 8, 1989, pp. 67 and 70; Damon Darling, "South Koreans Crave American Fast Food," *The Wall Street Journal,* February 22, 1991, pp. B1 and 3; Ronald Henkoff, "Big Mac Attacks With Pizza," *Fortune,* February 26, 1990, pp. 87–89; Anthony Ramirez, "Low-Fat McDonald's Burger Is Planned to Answer Critics," *The New York Times,* March 13, 1991, pp. A1 and D9; and Eric N. Berg, "An American Icon Wrestles With a Troubled Future," *The New York Times,* May 12, 1991, pp. F1 and F6.

IDEAS IN HISTORY

The Chamberlinian Revolution

Back in 1838, Antoine Cournot, the French economist featured in the last chapter, pointed out the importance of intermediate market structures that are properly described neither by the theory of perfect competition nor the theory of monopoly. At that time, his teachings failed to take hold. Almost a century passed before economists paid attention to the fact that many sellers hold a monopoly in some product but are, nevertheless, subject to the competition of numerous, admittedly imperfect substitutes. The point was reexplored by a 1927 Ph.D. thesis written by Edward Hastings Chamberlin (1899–1967) and his subsequent book, *The Theory of Monopolistic Competition: A Reorientation of the Theory of Value* (1933). His brilliant exposition and original contributions swept the profession. Despite the fact that Joan V. Robinson of Cambridge, England, advanced similar ideas at the same time, economists soon spoke of the "Chamberlinian revolution" in microeconomics.

Chamberlin spent the rest of his life at Cambridge, Massachusetts, teaching economics at Harvard and editing the prestigious *Quarterly Journal of Economics.* His term "monopolistic competition" included what is now generally termed (differentiated) oligopoly as well as monopolistic competition. As he wrote in the 8th edition of his book,

Monopolistic competition is a challenge to the traditional viewpoint of economics that competition and monopoly are alternatives and that individual prices are to be explained in terms of either the one or the other. By contrast, it is held that most economic situations are composites of both competition and monopoly and that, wherever this is the case, a false view is given by neglecting either one of the two forces . . . . This seems to be a very simple idea . . . . Its inherent reasonableness was never better expressed than by a student who observed to me . . . "Chapter IV is easy—you don't say anything in it."

My own observation of Chapter IV, however, would be quite different . . . . It contains not a technique, but a [new] way of looking at the economic system; and changing one's economic Weltanschauung is something very different from . . . adding new tools to one's kit . . . . This concept of a blending of competition and monopoly is . . . in fact the key to . . . understanding. (pp. 204–207)

Source: Adapted, with permission, from Heinz Kohler, *Intermediate Microeconomics: Theory and Applications,* 1st ed. (Glenview, IL: Scott, Foresman and Co., 1982), p. 353.

Summary

1. This chapter considers the middle ground between the poles of perfect competition and monopoly/cartel, a world of oligopolists and monopolistic competitors in which features of competition and monopoly are found side by side. An *oligopoly* is a market structure in which a large percentage of sales is made by a mere handful of firms that compete with one another in the sale of homogeneous or differentiated products, in which the entry of new firms is difficult, and in which market knowledge is imperfect. On the other hand, *monopolistic competition* is a market structure in which innumerable firms compete because restrictions to market entry or exit are absent, in which the products traded are differentiated from one seller to the next, and in which traders possess less than perfect market knowledge.

2. The most important feature of oligopoly is the high degree of interdependence that inevitably emerges among the relatively small number of firms operating in the market. It gives rise to strategic behavior; as a result, no single theory of oligopoly captures the rich array of possible outcomes for all conceivable circumstances.

3. Numerous theories have tried to explain the pricing behavior of oligopolistic firms that, on the one hand, have a strong incentive to collude in establishing a shared monopoly, but on the other hand, have a strong individual incentive to cheat on any such agreement. A number of alternative price-setting theories are discussed: Sweezy's kinked demand line, gentlemen's agreements, and price leadership.

4. Another key aspect of oligopolistic competition involves product differentiation—deliberate actions taken by producers to make their product, in the eyes of consumers, distinct from the close substitutes that rival firms supply. Such actions are widespread but may, under certain circumstances, lead to Hotelling's paradox.

5. Another major feature of oligopolistic competition still is advertising. By incurring selling costs, firms attempt to increase the demand for their products and their profit. Advertising in the United States is massive in scope and comes in two varieties: informative and persuasive. Depending on the circumstances, advertising by existing firms can create brand loyalty and prevent new firms from gaining a foothold in a market. But advertising can also be a means of overcoming brand loyalty and of tearing down barriers to market entry.

6. The most successful approach to modeling the behavior of interdependent oligopolists involves game theory. It is a method for studying decision making in situations of conflict in which the fates of people seeking different goals are interlocked. The payoff to people's choices depends not only on themselves and objective circumstances but also on other people's choices. A number of examples illustrate zero-sum and nonzero-sum games that oligopolists play.

7. Strategic behavior is absent among monopolistic competitors, but they do have some control over price. Like all firms, they maximize profit by choosing an output volume that equates marginal revenue with marginal cost. Because of the absence of entry barriers, profit is zero in the long run, but—unlike in perfect competition—price (then equal to average total cost) remains above marginal cost and also above the *minimum* average total cost.

8. A number of empirical studies have attempted to determine the relative importance of various types of market structures. Reviewed in detail are government studies of U.S. concentration ratios and a study by Shephard on the 1939–1980 trend of competition in the United States. The latter study reveals a major advance in competitiveness since 1958.

Key Concepts

- basing-point system
- brand loyalty
- concentration ratios
- excess capacity
- game
- game theory
- gentlemen's agreements
- Hotelling's paradox
- informative advertising
- kinked demand line
- maximin strategy
- minimax strategy
- monopolistic competition
- nonzero-sum game
- oligopoly
- persuasive advertising
- price leadership
- price war
- prisoners' dilemma game
- product differentiation
- saddle point
- selling costs
- strategic behavior
- zero-sum game

Questions and Problems

1. Can you think of any *criticism* of Sweezy's model (Figure 2)?
2. Construct a new theory, akin to Figure 2, that assumes that the typical oligopolist expects rivals to match price increases but not to match price decreases.
3. Reconsider Figure 3 and its associated text. Calculate the total transportation cost for the locational solutions given in panels (b) and (c).
4. Can you think of other examples besides the ones mentioned in the text where Hotelling's paradox is at work?
5. Consider Table 1. Interpret the meaning of
   a. the Product 3 row.
   b. the Product 6 column.
6. Consider Figure 5. Draw up the firm's daily income statement
   a. for the situation in panel (a).
   b. for the situation in panel (b).
7. Still considering Figure 5, what would have happened if the panel (a) situation involved a *loss*? Show such a situation graphically; then explain it.
8. As this chapter indicates, buyers and sellers in imperfectly competitive markets often have less than perfect knowledge concerning the market. What can they do about it?
9. Can you think of any *reasons* for the high concentration ratios found in many industries?

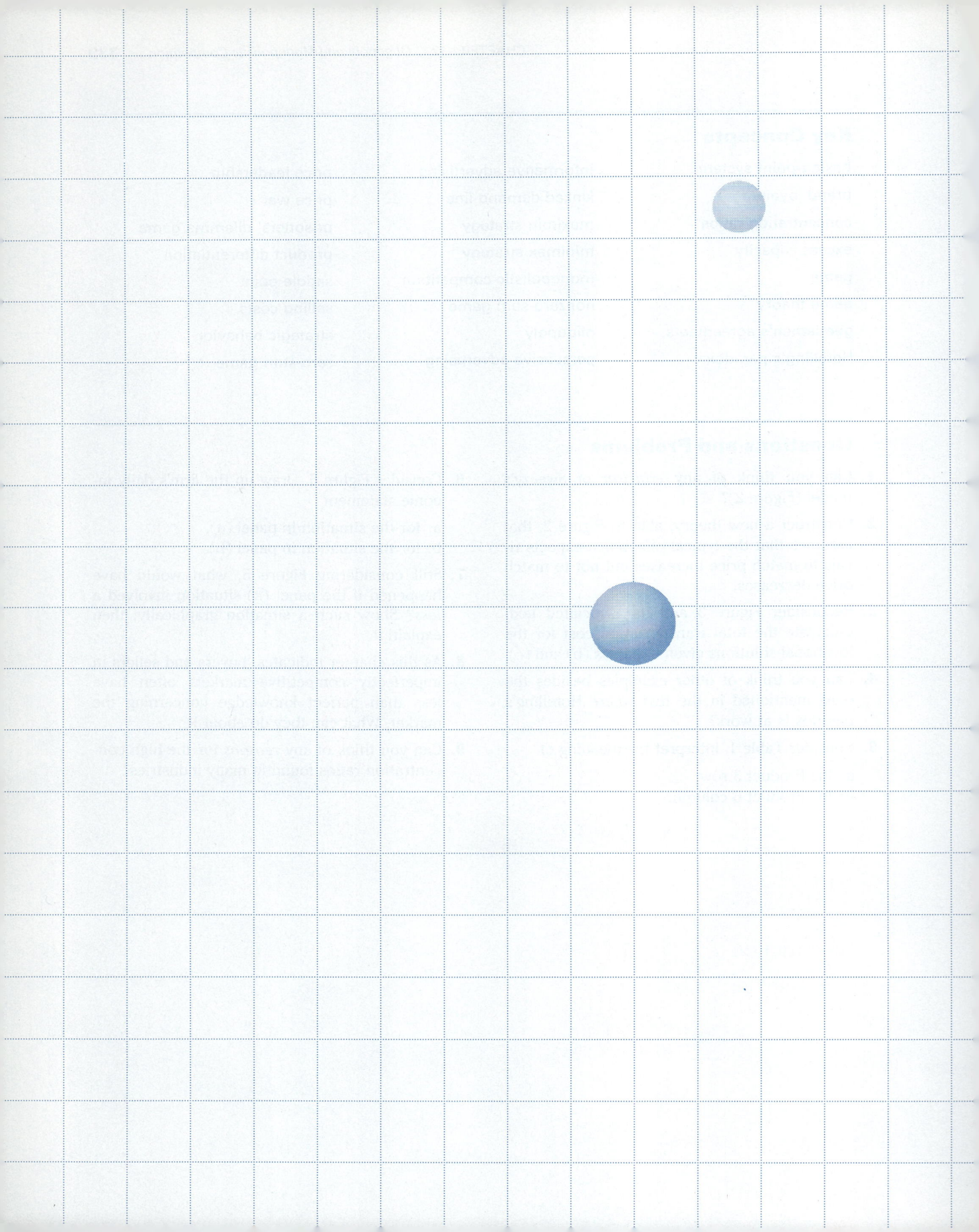

PART IV

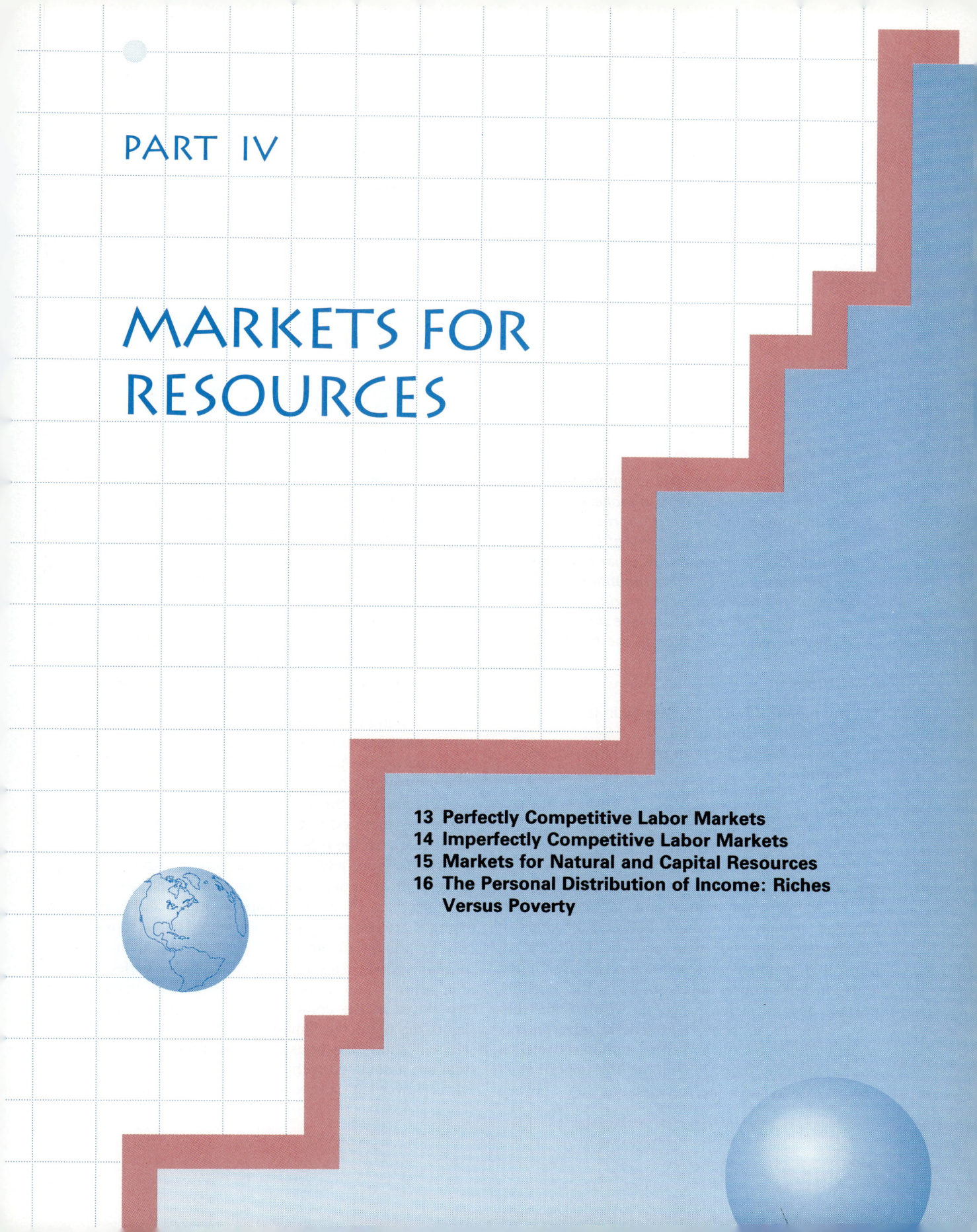

MARKETS FOR RESOURCES

13 **Perfectly Competitive Labor Markets**
14 **Imperfectly Competitive Labor Markets**
15 **Markets for Natural and Capital Resources**
16 **The Personal Distribution of Income: Riches Versus Poverty**

CHAPTER 13

PERFECTLY COMPETITIVE LABOR MARKETS

Preview

This is the first of several chapters that study the roles of households as suppliers and firms as demanders in markets for resources. This chapter focuses on the supply of labor and the demand for it and examines what happens under conditions of perfect competition. This theory explains numerous real-world phenomena, ranging from occupational wage differentials to "cobweb cycles" and even to the military draft.

Examples

1. Why Sleep? There's No Money In It
2. The Value of Human Life
3. Regional Wage Differentials and Population Change
4. Investing in Human Capital
5. When the Baby Boomers Grew Up

Part III of this book focused on markets for goods in which commodities and services are exchanged, usually for money, between all kinds of buyers who demand them and the multitude of firms that produce and sell them. In the United States in 1990, households were by far the most important buyers, acquiring goods worth $3,658 billion, while local, state, and federal governments bought $1,098 billion and firms purchased capital goods worth another $745 billion. The upper half of Figure 1 highlights the key relationship between households and firms in a world of perfectly competitive goods markets. In each of many such markets, the households' marginal benefits *MB* that are associated with the consumption of a good (upper left) sum to market demand *D*. The firms' marginal costs *MC* that are associated with the production of goods (upper right) sum to market supply *S*. The equilibrium price, established at intersection *a*, becomes each firm's marginal cost of acquiring the good and each firm's marginal benefit of selling it. (Follow the arrows to the left and right of point *a*.) Each trader optimizes by selecting a quantity that equates marginal benefit with marginal cost. The particular household pictured here optimizes by demanding q_0; the particular firm pictured here optimizes by supplying q_1.

In Part IV of this book, we focus on markets for resources pictured in the lower half of Figure 1. In these markets, the roles of households and firms are reversed. Households appear as sellers rather than buyers; firms appear as buyers rather than sellers. The services of human, capital, and natural resources are offered by their household owners, usually for money, to firms that want to use them to produce goods. Although we will consider perfectly competitive and imperfectly competitive market structures in the coming chapters, Figure 1 highlights the perfectly competitive case. As this chapter will show, the households' marginal costs *MC* that are associated with the supply of resource services (lower left) sum to market supply *S*. The firms' marginal benefits *MB* that are associated with the use of resource services (lower right) sum to market demand *D*. In analogy to the goods market, market forces in any resource market determine an equilibrium price at intersection *b* that becomes, respectively, the marginal benefit to any given household of selling the resource service (note the arrow to the left of point *b*) and the marginal cost to

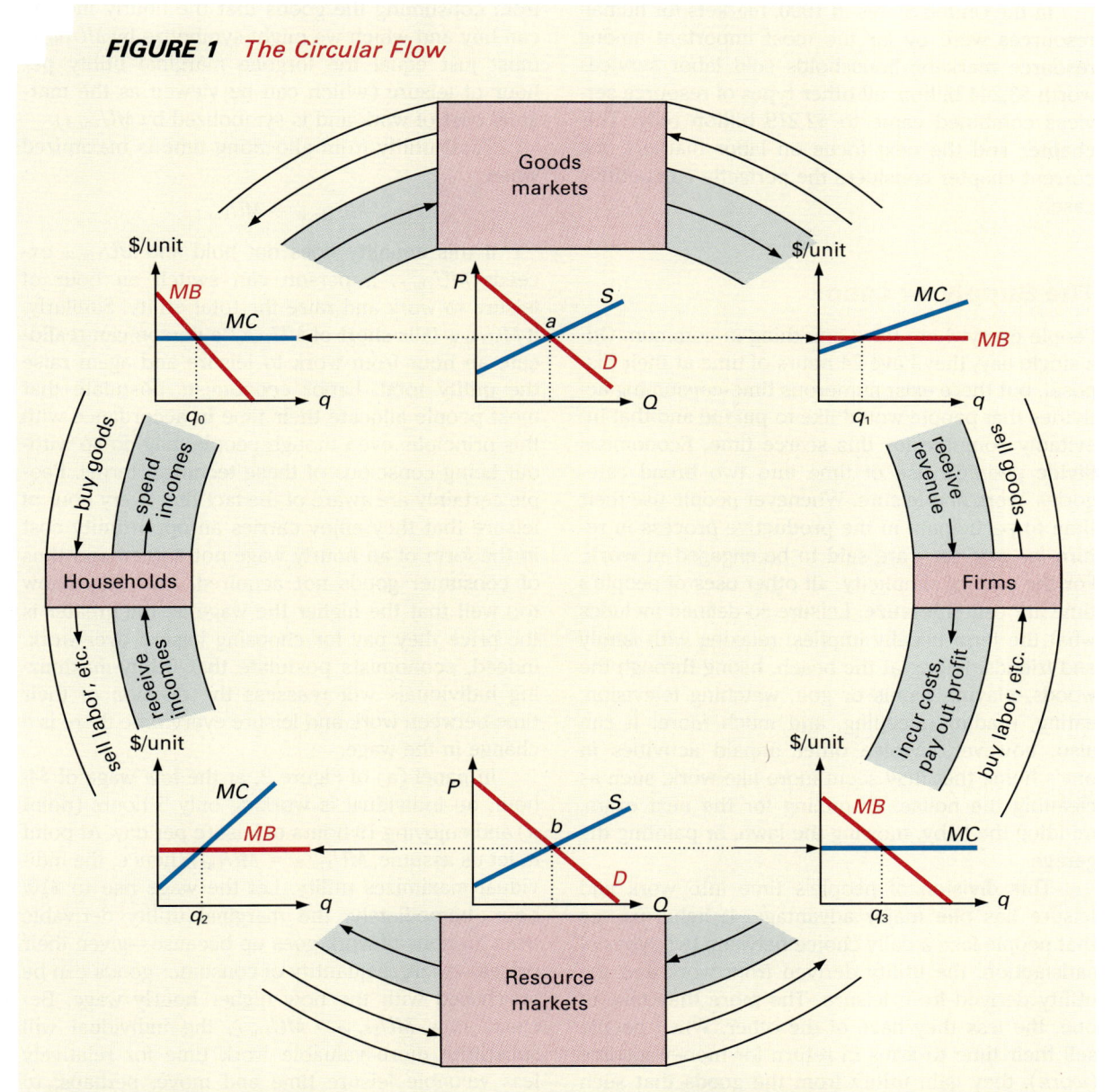

FIGURE 1 *The Circular Flow*

This diagram pictures the circular flow of goods and resource services first encountered in Chapter 2, Figure 1, The Capitalist Market Economy, but does so in the context of perfectly competitive markets.

any given firm of buying the resource service (note the arrow to the right of point *b*). Once again, each trader optimizes by selecting a quantity, such as q_2 or q_3, that equates marginal benefit with marginal cost.

In the United States in 1990, markets for human resources were by far the most important among resource markets; households sold labor services worth $3,244 billion; all other types of resource services combined came to $2,219 billion only. This chapter and the next focus on labor markets; the current chapter considers the perfectly competitive case.

The Supply of Labor

People everywhere have one thing in common. On a single day, they have 24 hours of time at their disposal, but there exist numerous time-consuming activities that people would like to pursue and that inevitably compete for this scarce time. Economists divide people's use of time into two broad categories: work and leisure. Whenever people use their time to participate in the productive process in return for pay, they are said to be engaged in **work**. For the sake of simplicity, all other uses of people's time are called **leisure**. Leisure so defined includes what the term usually implies: relaxing with family and friends, lolling at the beach, hiking through the woods, playing tennis or golf, watching television, eating, reading, sleeping, and much more. It can also, however, involve other unpaid activities in one's home that may seem more like work, such as cleaning the house, cramming for the next exam, minding the baby, mowing the lawn, or painting the garage.

This division of people's time into work and leisure has one major advantage. It helps us see that people face a daily choice between two types of satisfaction, the utility derived from work and the utility derived from leisure. The more they take of one, the less they have of the other. When people sell their time to firms in return for money income (*work*), they gain utility from the goods that such income can buy (maybe even from the process of working itself), but they also forgo the utility from alternative uses of time in leisure activities. A person who wants to maximize the total utility derived from the available time must split that time between work and leisure in such a way that the marginal benefit from either activity just equals the associated marginal cost (the optimization principle). If an individual divides time optimally, the marginal utility per hour of work (which, typically, is derived from consuming the goods that the hourly income can buy and which we might symbolize by $MU_{1\,hr.W}$) must just equal the forgone marginal utility per hour of leisure (which can be viewed as the marginal cost of work and is symbolized by $MU_{1\,hr.L}$).

Total utility from allocating time is maximized when

$$MU_{1\,hr.W} = MU_{1\,hr.L}$$

If this equality does not hold and $MU_{1\,hr.W}$ exceeds $MU_{1\,hr.L}$, a person can switch an hour of leisure to work and raise the total utility. Similarly, if $MU_{1\,hr.W}$ falls short of $MU_{1\,hr.L}$, a person can reallocate an hour from work to leisure and again raise the utility total. Labor economists postulate that most people allocate their time in accordance with this principle, even though people may do so without being conscious of these technical terms. People certainly are aware of the fact that every hour of leisure that they enjoy carries an opportunity cost in the form of an hourly wage not earned and thus of consumer goods not acquired. And they know too well that the higher the wage is, the greater is the price they pay for choosing leisure over work. Indeed, economists postulate that utility-maximizing individuals will reassess the division of their time between work and leisure every time there is a change in the wage.

In panel (a) of Figure 2, at the low wage of $4/hour, an individual is working only 5 hours (point *a*) and enjoying 19 hours of leisure per day. At point *a*, let us assume, $MU_{1\,hr.W} = MU_{1\,hr.L}$; hence, the individual maximizes utility. Let the wage rise to $10/hour. Immediately, the marginal utility derivable from an hour of work goes up because—given their prices—a larger quantity of consumer goods can be purchased with the now higher hourly wage. Because now $MU_{1\,hr.W} > MU_{1\,hr.L}$, the individual will substitute more valuable work time for relatively less valuable leisure time and move, perhaps, to point *b*, supplying 10 hours of labor and consuming only 14 hours of leisure per day. This **substitution effect** makes the individual supply more labor at a higher wage, thus, substituting work and consumption goods for leisure because more utility is gained

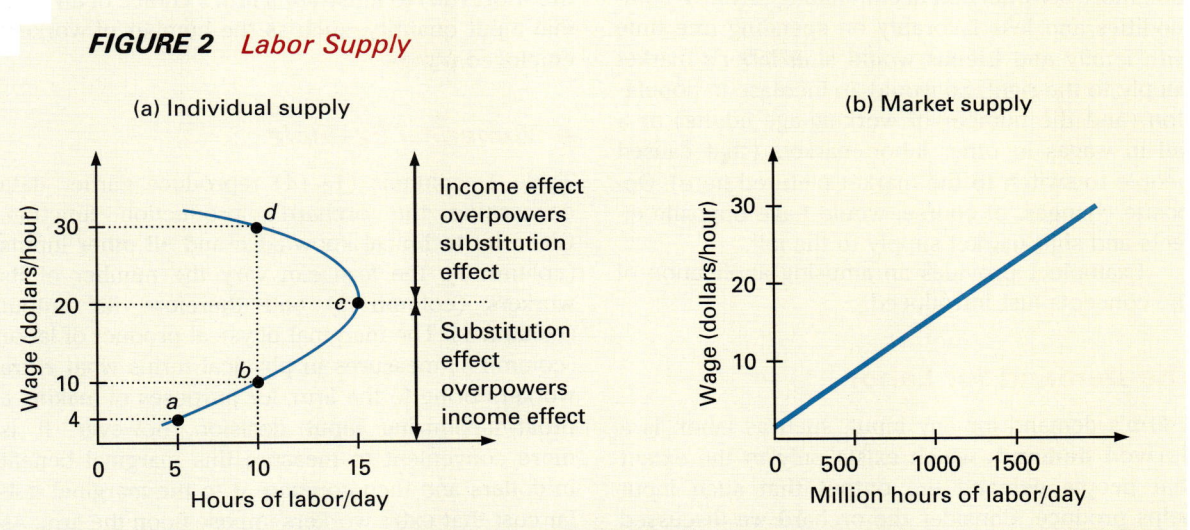

FIGURE 2 Labor Supply

(a) Individual supply

A backward-bending individual labor supply curve is plotted with Wage (dollars/hour) on the vertical axis and Hours of labor/day on the horizontal axis. Points shown: a (5, $4), b (10, $10), c (15, $20), d (10, $30). Above point c: "Income effect overpowers substitution effect." Below point c: "Substitution effect overpowers income effect."

(b) Market supply

An upward-sloping straight line with Wage (dollars/hour) on the vertical axis (from 0 to 30) and Million hours of labor/day on the horizontal axis (0, 500, 1000, 1500).

Although an individual's labor supply line may be backward-bending (panel a), the entire market's supply line is likely to be positively sloped throughout (panel b). All other things being equal, a higher wage calls forth a larger quantity of labor supplied. Changes in other relevant factors will shift the supply line to the right or left.

---

from the addition of consumption goods than is lost from the sacrifice of leisure. (The opposites happen at a lower wage.)

But, economists speculate, another force is at work as well. Note how the individual's income at *b* (10($10) = $100/day) is much larger than at *a* (5($4) = $20/day). It is likely that a richer individual will want to consume more not only of all kinds of ordinary consumption goods (such as airplane rides, cars, and television sets) but also of the leisure time that their use often requires.

As noted in the chapter "Elasticity," as people's incomes rise, they tend to consume more of so-called *normal goods;* in a sense, leisure is a normal good. More of it can be "bought" by working less and sacrificing some income and ordinary consumption goods. Thus, there is an **income effect** that is likely to work counter to the substitution effect and that makes an individual supply less labor at a higher wage because being richer incites the desire to consume more leisure as well. (Once again, the opposites are likely to happen at a lower wage.)

In our example, the substitution effect out-weighs the income effect until the wage has risen to $20/hour. At higher wages still, the income effect overpowers the substitution effect and the quantity of labor supplied declines. Thus, the individual's labor supply is a backward-bending line.

As panel (b) indicates, the supply line for any given labor market as a whole may well be positively sloped at all conceivable wages. For one thing, the bending point *c* will not come at the same wage for all individuals; hence a horizontal summation of individual supply lines may eliminate the bend. More importantly, even if existing workers insist on working fewer hours per week and fewer weeks per year at higher wages, such higher wages may draw new workers into the market, including people who are unwilling to work at all at lower wages and others who were working in other geographic areas or occupations.

As always, the market supply line, which relates the quantity of labor supplied to the wage, is drawn on the assumption of other things being equal. Changes in other relevant factors will shift the supply line to the right or left. For example, a widespread change in people's tastes that made them look more favorably on accumulating physical commodities and less favorably on spending free time with family and friends would shift labor's market supply to the right. So would an increase in population (and the number of working-age adults) or a fall in wages in other labor markets (that caused people to switch to the market pictured here). Opposite changes, of course, would have opposite effects and shift market supply to the left.

Example 1 provides an amusing application of the concepts just introduced.

The Demand for Labor

A firm's demand for any input, such as labor, is a **derived demand,** which exists only to the extent that people demand the output that such input helps produce. Consider the orchard we discussed in earlier chapters. Without a steady demand for apples, this firm would have no reason to demand the services of workers, cold-storage barns, spraying machines, or acres of land. We can now expand that example (a perfectly competitive orchard in the short run) to illustrate a firm's choice of an optimal input quantity, such as the number of workers employed.

A Numerical Example

Table 1, columns (1)–(4) reproduce earlier data concerning the orchard's production function. Given its technical knowledge and all other inputs (column 1), the firm can vary the number of its workers (column 2) and therefore its output (column 3). The marginal physical product of labor (column 4) measures in physical terms what extra workers bring to the firm; for purposes of making a profit-maximizing input decision, however, it is more convenient to measure this marginal benefit in dollars and then compare it to the marginal dollar cost that extra workers impose upon the firm. As long as our firm operates in perfectly competitive markets (assumed throughout this chapter), the volumes of its output and inputs will not affect the price of its output, P_0, nor the price of any input it buys, here W, the wage of labor.

EXAMPLE 1

Why Sleep? There's No Money In It

Most people spend a third of their life asleep. One is tempted to think that the need to sleep is dictated by biology and beyond the realm of personal choice, but this is not so, a recent study asserts. Apparently, a certain *minimum* of sleep is fixed by biology—beyond that, it's a matter of discretion that is strongly influenced by the available alternatives.

According to research performed by Jeff Biddle and Daniel Hamermesh, who had 706 people aged 23 to 65 keep diaries of their allocation of time, a clear *substitution effect* is at work; a 20 percent increase in the wage causes people to sleep 1 percent less; a doubling of the wage makes them spend 20 fewer minutes in bed each day. Given differences in wages they face, the average woman sleeps more than the average man, the unemployed sleep more than the employed, and the lesser educated sleep more than the more educated. Yet men and woman doing identical work sleep the same amount of time.

Because many of their subjects had similar incomes, only a weak *income effect* was noted. A stronger income effect was found by comparing people over time and space. Apparently, being richer, we sleep more now than a century ago, and people in richer nations sleep more than people in poorer lands.

Sources: Jeff E. Biddle and Daniel S. Hamermesh, *Working Paper* #2988, National Bureau of Economic Research; "Sleep and the Allocation of Time," *Journal of Political Economy,* October 1990, pp. 922–943; *The Economist,* July 29, 1989; and *The New York Times,* August 2, 1989, pp. D1 and 2.

TABLE 1 The Input Decision

Inputs per year		Output per year		Marginal benefit and marginal cost of labor use	
Fixed[a]	Variable[b]	Maximum total product,[c] Q^*	Marginal physical product of labor,[d] MPP_L	Marginal benefit = marginal value product of labor,[e] $MVP_L = MPP_L \cdot P_0$	Marginal cost = market-given wage,[e] W
(1)	(2)	(3)	(4) = $\frac{\Delta(3)}{\Delta(2)}$	(5) = (4) · $10	(6)
1	0	0			
1	1	2,000	+2,000	20,000	15,000 ⎫
1	2	9,000	+7,000	70,000	15,000 ⎪
1	3	14,000	+5,000	50,000	15,000 ⎬ MB > MC
1	4	16,500	+2,500	25,000	15,000 ⎭
1	5	18,000	+1,500	15,000	15,000 optimum
1	6	18,750	+750	7,500	15,000 ⎫ MB < MC
1	7	18,750	+0	0	15,000 ⎭

A perfectly competitive firm will employ that quantity of any input that maximizes the firm's profit because it equates the marginal benefit with the marginal cost of input use. In this example (labor is the only variable input), the optimum requires equating labor's marginal value product with its wage.

[a] Fixed inputs (1,000 apple trees, 2 cold-storage barns, 4 spraying machines, etc.)
[b] Variable inputs (number of full-time workers)
[c] Maximum total product (bushels of apples)
[d] Marginal physical product of labor (extra bushels/extra worker)
[e] Extra dollars per extra worker

Now assume that any amount of apples can be sold at $P_0 = \$10$/bushel and that any number of workers can be hired at $W = \$15,000$/year. If you were the manager of this orchard, you could combine the internal technical information of columns (1)–(4) with the outside price information that relevant markets supply (which we have just assumed) to fill in the last two columns of Table 1. In column (5), each marginal physical product has been multiplied by the $10/bushel output price to yield labor's **marginal value product, MVP**. Thus $MPP_L \cdot P_0 = MVP_L$.

All else being equal, a first worker (who adds 2,000 bushels to physical output) adds $20,000 to the firm's revenue (each extra bushel can be sold for $10). A second worker (who adds 7,000 bushels to physical output) adds $70,000 to the firm's revenue (these extra bushels can be sold for $10 as well). And so it goes, until, in the end, a seventh worker adds nothing to output and nothing to revenue. The data of column (5), thus, represent the dollar marginal benefits of using additional workers.

Column (6) shows the associated marginal cost. Because any number of workers can be hired at $15,000 per worker per year, each extra worker hired raises the firm's cost by $15,000/year.

Focusing exclusively on columns (5) and (6), one can figure the profit-maximizing number of workers to employ. As long as the marginal benefit of hiring workers exceeds their marginal cost, the firm's profit can be raised by hiring more workers. Once this marginal benefit falls short of marginal cost, the firm's profit can be raised by hiring fewer workers. Naturally, the equality of marginal benefit and marginal cost denotes maximum profit. At the assumed $15,000 annual wage, the desire to maximize profit dictates hiring more than 4 and a maximum of 5 full-time workers.

A Graphical Illustration

Figure 3 helps us see that all else being equal, the lower the wage, the larger the quantity of labor demanded by a firm (and by all firms as a group). In panel (a), the column (2) and (5) data of Table 1 have been plotted and connected by the smooth line labeled marginal value product of labor, MVP_L. In addition, a line of labor's **average value produce, AVP**, has been plotted; it equals labor's average physical product multiplied by our assumed $10/bushel output price. Thus $AVP_L = APP_L \cdot P_0$, as shown in Numerical Exercise 1.

The average value product of labor has been plotted as the dashed line in panel (a) of Figure 3; it shows how the firm's total revenue per worker varies with the number of workers it employs. No firm will hire labor at a wage that exceeds the average value product of labor (see the AVP_L curve on our graph). Labor's average value product reaches a maximum at $m = \$47,500/\text{year}$. If the firm hired *any* amount of labor above this wage, labor's average value product would be less, and the firm's total wage cost (which is its total variable cost in our example) would exceed its total revenue. Then the firm could do better by shutting down at once and incurring a loss equal to its fixed cost. Our firm will hire no workers (and produce nothing) once the market wage exceeds the $47,500/year indicated by

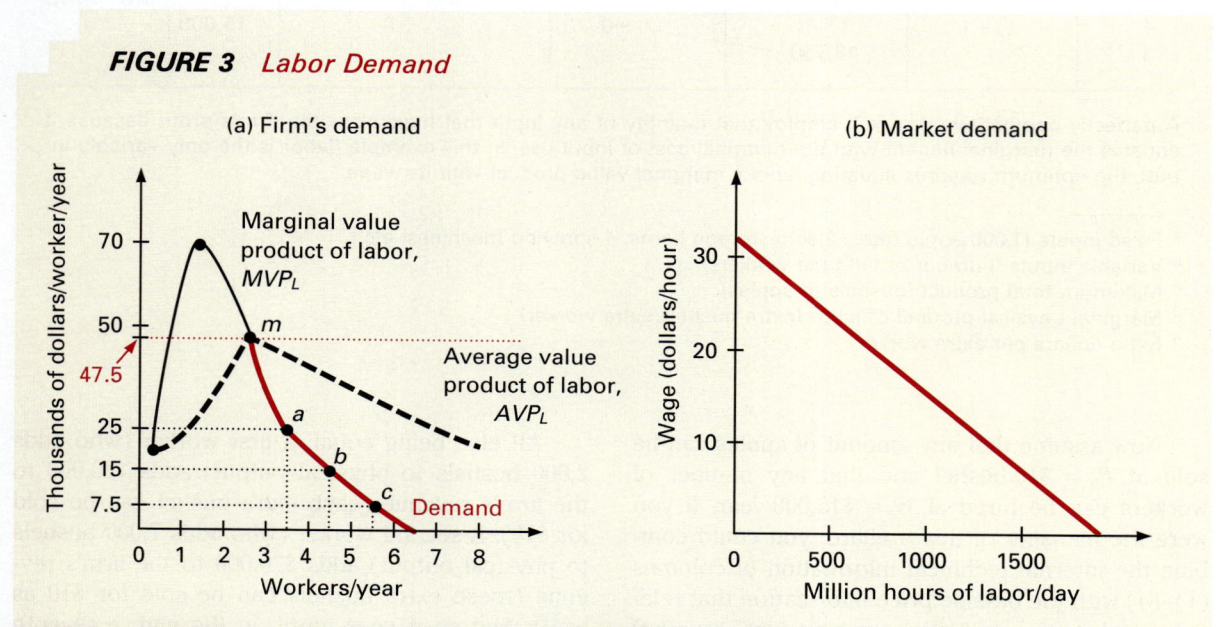

FIGURE 3 Labor Demand

(a) Firm's demand

(b) Market demand

When operating in perfectly competitive markets exclusively, a firm's demand for labor equals a section of its downward-sloping marginal-value-product-of-labor line (here shown in color in panel a). The section in question lies below the maximum at *m* of labor's average value product, which assures that the firm's total revenue will equal or exceed its variable labor cost. The horizontal summation of the demand lines of individual firms yields market demand (panel b).

NUMERICAL EXERCISE 1

Calculating the Average Value Product of Labor

The average physical product of labor is not directly shown in Table 1, nor is the average value product. Both can be calculated easily. The average physical product of labor is found by dividing any column (3) entry by the corresponding entry in column (2). Thus, it equals the maximum total product Q^* that can be produced with any given quantity of the variable labor input (and that we assume is in fact produced by our well-managed firm) divided by the associated labor quantity L. Hence $APP_L = (Q^*/L)$. When 3 full-time workers produce 14,000 bushels of apples per year, the average physical product of labor equals 14,000/3 or 4666.67 bushels per worker per year.

$$APP_L = \frac{Q^*}{L} = \frac{14{,}000 \text{ bushels/year}}{3 \text{ workers}}$$

= 4,666.67 bushels per worker per year.

When we multiply this expression by the $10 per bushel output price, we get the average value product of labor of $46,666.67 per worker per year.

$$AVP_L = APP_L \cdot P_o = 4{,}666.67 \text{ bushels per worker per year } (\$10/\text{bushel})$$

= $46,666.67 per worker per year.

---

the dotted horizontal line. If the wage lies at or below the maximum at m of labor's average value product, total revenue will equal or exceed the variable labor cost and labor will be demanded. How much labor will be demanded is shown in the color section of the MVP_L line. As we noted in the previous section, at a $15,000/year wage, the firm's profit is maximized when hiring 4–5 workers (point b). The same principle (equating labor's marginal value product with its wage) would lead our firm to demand only 3–4 workers at a $25,000/year wage (point a), but 5–6 workers at a $7,500/year wage (point c). Thus, the downward-sloping MVP_L line below maximum AVP_L represents a competitive firm's demand for labor.

As always, the market demand line, which relates the quantity of labor demanded to the wage, is drawn on the assumption of other things being equal. Changes in other relevant factors will shift the demand line to the right or left. As always, the market demand line shown here is drawn on the assumption of all other things being equal. Changes in other relevant factors can shift it to the right or left. For example, market demand would shift to the right if the number of firms rose (and there were more individual demand lines to be added together). It would shift right as well if the demand lines of individual firms shifted right as a result of factors that raised labor's marginal value product to each firm. Consider such factors as improvements in technical knowledge or increases in the quantities of complementary inputs that raise labor's marginal physical product. Consider the effect of increases in output price. Opposite changes, of course, would have opposite effects and shift market demand to the left. Focus 1 summarizes our discussion here and in earlier chapters.

Market Equilibrium

As in perfectly competitive markets for goods, equilibrium is established in markets for resources through the interaction of market demand and market supply, as Figure 4 illustrates. The equilibrium at e is associated with a wage of $16/hour at which 1,000 million labor hours per day are bought and sold. At any higher wage, there would be surpluses (such as ab). Unemployed workers would compete with one another for nonexistent jobs. In the process, the wage would fall, lowering the quantity supplied along be and raising the quantity demanded along ae. At any lower wage, there would be shortages (such as cd), and frustrated managers

FOCUS 1

Profit-Maximizing Rules Under Perfect Competition

Input Decision: Equate marginal benefit with marginal cost of input use. Assuming maximum $AVP_i \geq P_i$ (which assures total revenue ≥ total variable cost and any loss < fixed cost), profit is maximized when

$$MVP_i = P_i$$

which implies

$$MPP_i \cdot P_o = P_i$$

$$MPP_i = \frac{P_i}{P_o}$$

$$P_o = \frac{P_i}{MPP_i}.$$

AVP_i is the input's average value product; MVP_i is the input's marginal value product; MPP_i is the input's marginal physical product; P_i is the market-given input price; and P_o is the market-given output price.

Output Decision: Equate marginal benefit with marginal cost of production. Assuming $P_o \geq$ minimum AVC (which assures total revenue ≥ total variable cost and any loss < fixed cost), profit is maximized when

$$P_o = MC_o.$$

P_o is the market-given output price, and MC_o is the marginal cost per unit of output.

Note: The two rules are, in fact, equivalent because

$$\frac{P_i}{MPP_i} = MC_o$$

FIGURE 4 Labor Market Equilibrium

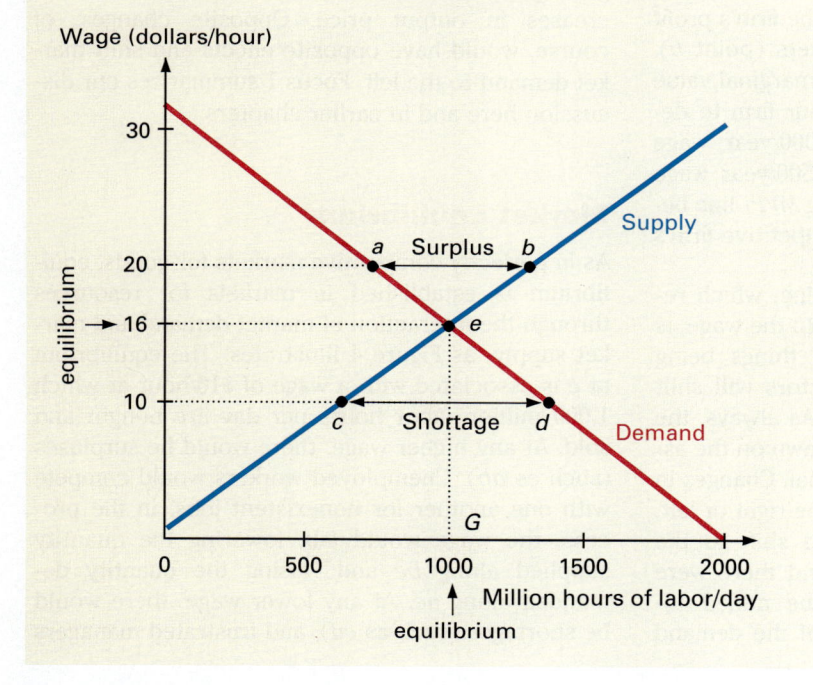

This graph illustrates the establishment, in a perfectly competitive labor market, of equilibrium price and equilibrium quantity (corresponding to intersection e of the demand and supply lines). At any higher wage, there would be surpluses (such as ab), tending to depress the wage. At any lower wage, there would be shortages (such as cd), tending to raise the wage. At the equilibrium wage (here $16/hour), all those who want to buy can find a seller, and all those who want to sell can find a buyer.

of firms would compete with one another for workers who do not seem to exist. In the process, the wage would rise, raising the quantity supplied along *ce* and lowering the quantity demanded along *de*. In either case, the equilibrium at *e* would result. And, as in goods markets (see Chapter 3), any change in supply or demand would establish a new equilibrium price that similarly equated the quantities sellers and buyers wanted to trade.

Economic Efficiency

Like perfectly competitive goods markets, perfectly competitive labor markets in equilibrium maximize the sum of consumer and producer surplus and create **economic efficiency,** a situation in which it is impossible to make a person better off without making another person worse off because all *mutually beneficial* transactions have already been carried out.

Figure 5 pictures a perfectly competitive market for labor. Given the demand and supply lines shown, an equilibrium wage of $16/hour is established and 1,000 million hours are traded (point *E*).

Since the purpose of any market is to bring buyers and sellers together to carry out exchanges that both parties consider beneficial, it is easy to see why the first hour bought and sold (next to the vertical axis) provides a net benefit to *both* buyer and seller.

Some eager buyer is willing to pay as much as $32 for that first labor hour (the height of column *a*), yet can buy the hour for $16 (the equilibrium wage). From the point of view of that buyer, the marginal benefit *MB* is $32, the marginal cost *MC* is $16; thus a marginal net benefit of $16 is reaped. This difference (the shaded section of column *a*) is called a *consumer surplus* (the consumer being the firm "consuming" labor).

At the same time, some seller is willing to supply that first hour for as little as $2.25 (as the height of the supply line indicates), yet can sell the hour for $16 (the equilibrium wage). From the point of view of that seller, the marginal benefit *MB* is $16, the marginal cost *MC* is $2.25 (the minimum acceptable compensation for the leisure hour sacrificed). The marginal net benefit is $13.75, as represented by the dotted section of column *a*. It is called a *pro-*

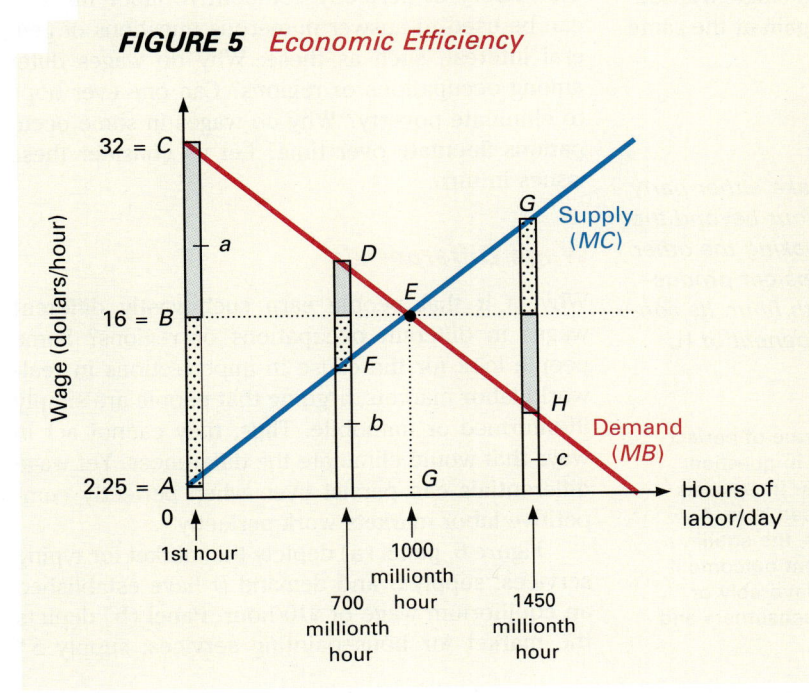

FIGURE 5 *Economic Efficiency*

A perfectly competitive labor market establishes an equilibrium wage and quantity, here at demand and supply intersection *E*. Because demand reflects the marginal benefits of labor-consuming firms, while supply reflects the (psychological) marginal costs of labor-producing workers, *MB* and *MC* are equated at the equilibrium point as well. As a result, the social net benefit of the activity in question (here of producing and consuming labor) is maximized (here as area *ACE*). It is the sum of consumer surplus *BCE* and producer surplus *ABE*. In this case, the consumers, of course, are labor using firms; the producers are labor supplying households.

ducer surplus (the producer being the worker "producing" labor services).

Together, the shaded and dotted segments represent the joint net benefit from producing, selling, buying, and consuming that first labor hour. A similar story can be told about the second hour and the third, about the 1 millionth and the 700 millionth (column b). As more and more hours are sold and bought, the *sizes* of (shaded) consumer surpluses and (dotted) producer surpluses will change. Their decline reflects, respectively, the diminishing marginal value product of labor consumed and the rising marginal psychic cost of labor produced. Yet, right up to the 1,000 millionth hour, there will be net benefits or *mutually beneficial* transactions. By the time the equilibrium quantity of 1,000 million hours is sold, economic efficiency is reached—the total net benefit from labor producing and consuming is maximized (and equal to area *ACE*). The difference between the maximum sum of money consumers would pay for the quantity traded (*OCEG*) and the actual sum they do pay for it (*OBEG*) is the total consumer surplus (*BCE*); the difference between the actual sum of money producers receive for the quantity traded (*OBEG*) and the minimum sum they would accept for it (*OAEG*) is the total producer surplus (*ABE*). The perfectly competitive market is perfect because it maximizes the sum of the two surpluses; it does not miss a single transaction from which both parties might gain at the same time.[1]

CAUTION

It would not be possible to make either party better off by trading a single hour beyond the equilibrium amount without making the other party worse off as a result. Consider producing and selling a 1,450 millionth hour. Its consumer would reap a marginal benefit of H, but its producer incur a marginal cost of G. If a wage of $16 were charged and paid, both parties would be worse off (by the shaded and dotted segments, respectively), because MC at G exceeds $16, while MB at H falls short of it. One could make the worker better off (by setting a wage above marginal cost at G), but then the firm would be worse off by far. Conversely, one could make the firm better off (by setting a wage below marginal benefit at H), but then the worker would be worse off. No voluntary transaction is possible to the right of point E.

As the next chapter will show, there are other types of labor markets (*imperfectly* competitive) that do not maximize the net benefit to the left of point *E* and that are, therefore, called economically inefficient. In such markets, something prevents trades beyond some quantity, such as 700 million hours in our example. As a result, some potential mutually beneficial transactions are not carried out and some social net benefit (such as *EFD*) is not realized.

Applications and Extensions

The theory of perfectly competitive labor markets can be used to answer numerous questions of general interest, such as these: Why do wages differ among occupations or regions? Can one ever hope to eliminate poverty? Why do wages in some occupations fluctuate over time? Let us consider these issues in turn.

Wage Differentials

Why is it that people earn such vastly different wages in different occupations or regions? Some people look for the cause in imperfections in real-world labor markets, arguing that people are simply ill-informed or immobile. Thus, they cannot act in ways that would eliminate the differences. Yet wage differentials can persist even when perfectly competitive labor markets work perfectly.

Figure 6, panel (a) depicts the market for typing services; supply *S* and demand *D* have established an equilibrium wage of $10/hour. Panel (b) depicts the market for housepainting services; supply *S**

---

[1] The forgoing conclusion about the virtue of perfect competition assumes that the traders in question are the only ones who reap benefits or incur costs in connection with the activity described here. As a later chapter, "Externalities," shows, the equilibrium outcome may not be the efficient outcome if outside parties are affected as well—favorably or unfavorably—by the activities of the consumers and producers discussed here.

FIGURE 6 Wage Differentials

(a) Wage of typists (dollars/hour); curves D and S intersect at 10, 50 million hours.

(b) Wage of housepainters (dollars/hour); curves S* and D* intersect at 20, 70 million hours. The differential between 10 and 20 is labeled.

Million hours of labor per year

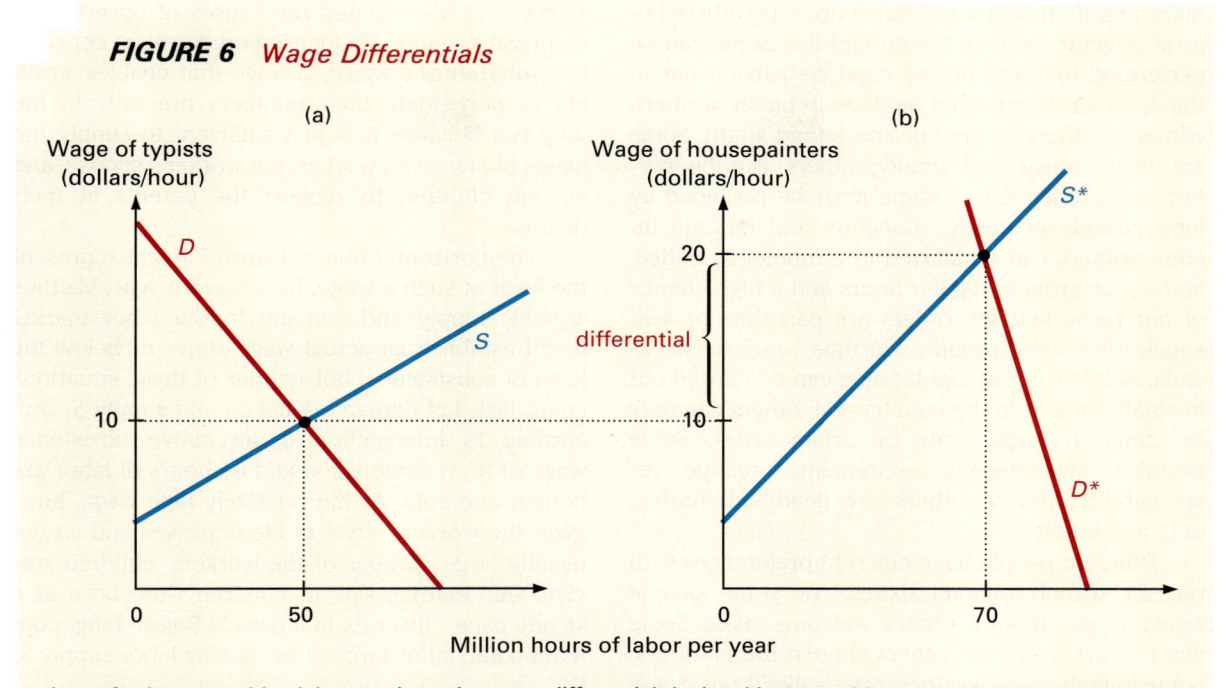

In perfectly competitive labor markets, the wage differential depicted here would not persist if all people and all jobs were alike. As people left low-paying jobs (panel a), supply would decrease and the wage would rise. As people entered high-paying jobs (panel b), supply would increase and the wage would fall. The process would end once the wages were equalized. Biological differences in people or nonmonetary differences in jobs, on the other hand, might prevent such a migration of workers and make the differential permanent.

and demand D^* have established an equilibrium wage of $20/hour. If all people were alike and all jobs were alike, the $10/hour wage *differential* would not persist under perfectly competitive conditions. Given the perfect knowledge and the free mobility found in perfectly competitive labor markets, typists would leave their occupations to become housepainters. As a result, supply S in panel (a) would fall and supply S^* in panel (b) would rise. As some typists became housepainters, the wages of the remaining typists would rise, but those of all housepainters would fall. The process would continue until the wages in the two occupations had equalized. But all people are not alike, nor are jobs, which is why differences in wages could persist even in perfectly competitive labor markets.

Differences in People

Certain biological differences exist among people. Consider how people differ in height, intelligence, strength, weight, and more. Some seem to have a natural talent for athletics, mathematics, or music; others are inept in these fields. Some are 7 feet tall, weigh 300 pounds, and are strong as an ox; others barely reach 5 feet, weigh 90 pounds, and have trouble lifting a 50 pound bag. To the extent that such personal qualities cannot be changed, wage differentials may well persist. Consider a typist who weighs 90 pounds and has trouble lifting a 50-pound bag; how could such a person ever handle the 40-foot ladders that housepainters move around and that weigh 200 pounds each?

Differences in Jobs

Probably even more important are differences in jobs and people's diverging preferences with respect to such differences. Unlike sellers of apples or of steel, sellers of labor must personally accompany what is being sold. As a result, the nonmonetary aspects of jobs have an added importance, and jobs differ in a thousand ways. Some are safe; others impose grave risks as to health and life. Some can be performed indoors; others must be carried out in the open air. Some must be done in harsh northern climates; others in the hot and humid south. Some are dirty, noisy and smelly; others can be performed in fancy dress. Some must be preceded by long periods of costly education and forgone income; others can be started at a moment's notice. Some jobs provide regular hours and a high chance of not being laid off; others are part-time or seasonal; others still require overtime, work on weekends, holidays, or at night. Some can be carried out in small firms or in the countryside; others can only be done in large firms or urban areas. Some promise advancement, excitement, prestige, responsibility, power; others are dead-end, boring, dull, and lonely.

Different people have different preferences with respect to job characteristics. To some people safety is paramount, others welcome risks. Some like to work at a desk; others cherish the outdoors. Some love the cold weather; others like it hot. Some love city life, others abhor it. Some seek out responsibility, others run from it. The list goes on....

Returning to Figure 6, even if all the typists and all the housepainters were equal physically, imagine what would happen if typists *preferred* their clean, safe, and regular work in air-conditioned offices to the alternative of climbing ladders to dizzying heights, being attacked by a merciless sun, and ending each day bathed in sweat and coated with paint. In that case, the panel (a) supply would not decline, the panel (b) supply would not rise, and the $10/hour wage differential would persist despite the absence of artificial restraints to market exit or entry.

To the extent that existing wage differentials merely offset nonmonetary differences in the perceived attractiveness of jobs, they will persist even under perfect competition. Such wage differentials are called **equalizing wage differentials** or **compensating wage differentials.**

Examples 2, 3, and 4 provide applications of the theory of wage differentials.

The Iron Law of Wages

Another application of labor market theory comes form the Reverend Robert Thomas Malthus (1766–1834), who investigated the causes of poverty and its possible cures. He focused on a crucial concept, the **subsistence wage,** a wage that enables workers to perpetuate their numbers precisely in the long run because it is just sufficient to supply the needs of any given worker, the worker's spouse, and enough children to replace the parents at their deaths.

The horizontal line in Figure 7 might represent the level of such a wage. In any given year, Malthus argued, supply and demand in the labor market might establish an actual wage above or below the level of subsistence, but neither of these situations could last. Let demand equal D_1 and supply S_1. According to intersection a, an above-subsistence wage of W_2 is established and Q_0 hours of labor are bought and sold. At the relatively high wage, however, the workers' style of life improves and an unusually large number of the workers' children survive. (As Malthus saw it, children were born at a steady pace, "like rats in a barn.") Before long, population and labor force grow, raising labor supply to S_2.

As Figure 7 indicates, a new equilibrium emerges at b; the equilibrium wage drops to W_1, the subsistence wage, and Q_1 hours of labor are bought and sold. Many more children die from lack of food, housing, and medical care; population growth comes to an end.

Alternatively, let demand equal D_1 and supply S_3. According to intersection c, a below-subsistence wage of W_0 is established and Q_2 hours of labor are bought and sold. At the relatively low wage, the workers sink into utter misery; many die, along with spouses and children. As famine and disease sweep the land, population and labor force decline, lowering labor supply to S_2. Once again, an equilibrium is established at b; the subsistence wage is reestablished, and the population decline ends.

As if in obedience to an **iron law of wages,** population changes assure that wages, ultimately, end up at the level of subsistence. Even long-run increases in the demand for labor, as from D_0 to D_1 and D_2, Malthus thought, would not raise wages permanently. Given an original equilibrium of D_0 and S_1 at d, a rise of demand to D_1 would *temporarily* raise the wage to W_2 (according to intersection a), but population would grow and labor supply rise to S_2. Thus, the wage would drop back to W_1 (according to intersection b). A further rise of demand

FIGURE 7 The Iron Law of Wages

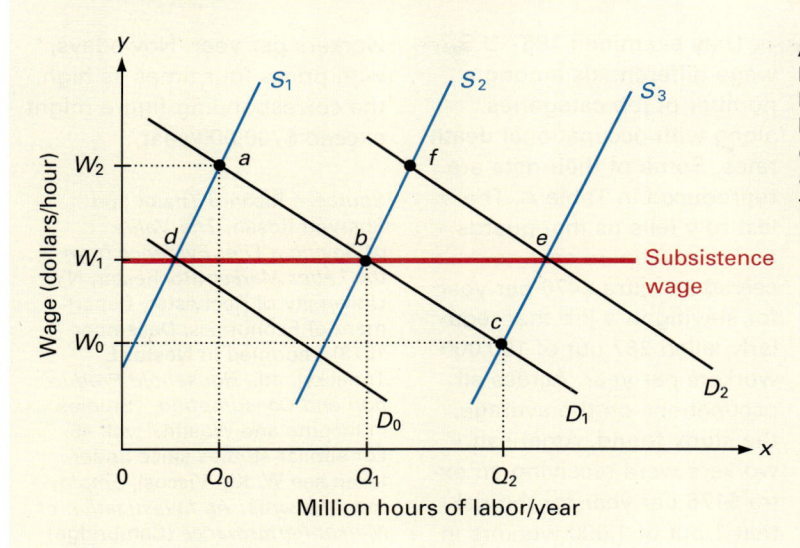

As Malthus saw it, the supply of labor was infinitely elastic at the level of the subsistence wage. Any higher wage would quickly be reduced through population growth, and any lower wage would be raised through population decline.

to D_2 would fare the same. Given S_2, the wage would temporarily rise to the level shown by point *f*, but population would grow and labor supply rise to S_3. In the end, more people would be as miserable at point *e* as fewer people once were at points *b* or *d*.

The Reverend Malthus could only think of one thing for people to do to escape the poverty trap: Forgoing sex and putting an end to the ceaseless increase in labor supply when times were good. Since the days of Malthus, many things have changed, of course, not the least of which are changes in sexual mores and the appearance of numerous means of artificial birth control. Nevertheless, the Malthusian predictions seem eerily accurate in many of the world's poorer countries where population growth repeatedly negates all efforts at economic improvement. So far as the world's richer countries are concerned, modern economists do not subscribe to the Malthusian description of population dynamics. Consider Example 2 in Chapter 1 that considers the determinants of the family size and indicates that people may well *choose* to stop the expansion of their families long before they have sunk into poverty. Nevertheless, even in richer countries, real wages are adversely affected when population growth soars. See *this* chapter's Example 5.

Cobweb Cycles

Economists have long observed a strange phenomenon in certain markets, a phenomenon called a **cobweb cycle**. The term describes the tendency of the prices and quantities of some goods or resources to rise above and then fall below some intermediate level in successive periods. In markets for certain types of skilled labor, real wages over time follow a cyclical pattern, being high for some years, then low for another set of years, and so on.[2] The simple tools of supply and demand developed in this chapter explain what is happening.

The supply of certain skilled types of labor, such as the services of astronomy professors, dentists, lawyers, medical doctors, or nuclear engineers, tends to be fairly inelastic in the short run. From one year to the next, even a large increase in

---

[2] See Richard B. Freeman, "A Cobweb Model of the Supply and Starting Salary of New Engineers," *Industrial and Labor Relations Review,* January 1976, pp. 236–246; and Robert J. Flanagan, Robert S. Smith, and Ronald Ehrenberg, *Labor Economics and Labor Relations* (Glenview, IL: Scott Foresman and Co., 1984), pp. 212–215.

EXAMPLE 2

The Value of Human Life

Newspapers are filled with stories about workers dying on the job because of cave-ins in mines, drownings at sea, explosions on oil rigs, falls from skyscrapers, motor vehicle accidents, and more. Other workers die more slowly and in less spectacular ways, being exposed to arsenic, asbestos, benzene, cotton dust, lead, vinyl chloride . . . Yet, as Adam Smith put it in 1776, if the knowledge of work hazards were widespread and workers were mobile, workers would leave dangerous jobs for safer ones and this shift in supply would raise wages in dangerous occupations above those in safer ones until the differential was deemed large enough to compensate the remaining workers for the added risk.

In order to test the hypothesis advanced by Smith, two economists, Richard Thaler and Sherwin Rosen, set out to see whether wage differentials based on job hazards exist.

They examined 1967 U.S. wage differentials among a number of job categories, along with occupational death rates. Some of their data are reproduced in Table A. The last row tells us that guards and doorkeepers each received an extra $470 per year for staying in a job that regularly killed 267 out of 100,000 workers per year. Across all occupations on the average, the study found, American workers were receiving an extra $176 per year for the risk that 1 out of 1,000 workers in their occupation would die on the job during any given year.

This finding implies that workers on the average put an implicit value of $176,000 on their own lives. (The average worker would die once in 1,000 years on the job.) The finding also implies that in the late 1960s the average firm with 1,000 workers could have saved itself $176,000/year in wage costs by eliminating the risk that killed 1 out of 1,000 workers per year. Nowadays, with prices four times as high, the corresponding figure might exceed $700,000/year.

Source: Richard Thaler and Sherwin Rosen, *The Value of Saving a Life: Evidence from the Labor Market* (Rochester, NY: University of Rochester, Department of Economics, December 1973), reprinted in Nestor E. Terleckyj, ed., *Household Production and Consumption,* "Studies in Income and Wealth," vol. 40. For similar studies since undertaken see W. Kip Viscusi, *Employment Hazards: An Investigation of Market Performance* (Cambridge: Harvard University Press, 1979); Robert S. Smith, "Compensating Wage Differentials and Public Policy: A Review," *Industrial and Labor Relations Review,* April 1979, pp. 339–352; Alan Marin and George Psacharopoulos, "The Reward for Risk in the Labor Market: Evidence from the U.K. and a Reconciliation with Other Studies," *Journal of Political Economy,* August 1982, pp. 827–853; and J. Paul Leigh, "Compensating Wages for Job-Related Death: The Opposing Arguments," *Journal of Economic Issues,* September 1989, pp. 823–842.

---

the wage will not greatly increase the number of workers in these fields. A large decrease in the wage, likewise, will not much reduce the quantity of services supplied. Astronomy professors and nuclear engineers may well prefer remaining in their professions at lower wages than retraining for higher-paying jobs bolting steel beams together 50 stories off the ground or putting out oil rig fires in the Gulf of Mexico.

The long run, however, is another matter. Just as profits made by firms in a competitive industry tend to draw in new firms, currently high incomes of professional people encourage younger people to enter the occupations in question. Thus, with a lag of several years (reflecting the period of schooling required), the supply of such labor services goes up. The reverse also holds. Just as losses made by firms in a competitive industry tend to encourage the exit of firms, currently low incomes of professionals discourage younger people from entering

TABLE A Differential Wages and Death Rates, United States, 1967

Occupation	Extra wage (dollars/year)	Occupational deaths (number/100,000 workers/year)
Fishers	$ 33	190
Fire fighters	77	44
Police officers, detectives	137	78
Electricians	164	93
Teamsters	201	114
Sawyers	234	133
Crane or derrick operators	259	147
Sailors	287	163
Bartenders	310	176
Mine operatives	310	176
Taxicab drivers	320	182
Locomotive stokers	327	186
Structural ironworkers	359	204
Boilermakers	405	230
Lumberjacks	451	256
Guards, doorkeepers	470	267

SOURCE: Adapted from Richard Thaler and Sherwin Rosen, *The Value of Saving a Life: Evidence from the Labor Market* (Rochester, NY: University of Rochester, Department of Economics, December 1973). Reprinted in Nestor E. Terleckyj, ed., *Household Production and Consumption*, "Studies in Income and Wealth," vol. 40, p. 288. Copyright © 1976 National Bureau of Economic Research, Inc. Reprinted by permission.

the affected fields. Gradually, the supply of workers in the market falls because new entrants fail to replace those who retire. The effect on wages is predictable; the entry or exit of workers in labor markets eventually lowers or raises the wages prevailing in such markets.

Figure 8 illustrates the process with respect to the market for nuclear engineers. Originally, assume demand D_0 and short-run supply S_0 establish the equilibrium given by point a. Measured in dollars of constant purchasing power, the wage equals W_0 and Q_0 engineers are employed. Let demand rise to D_1. Given long-run supply S^*, the wage-quantity combination at E may eventually emerge, but getting there may take many years. In the short run, supply S_0 is fixed; the given number of engineers find themselves in a "sellers' market"; their wage rises rapidly to W_4 (note the arrow pointing to intersection b). The high wage may persist for a number of years, while college students prepare themselves

EXAMPLE 3

Regional Wage Differentials and Population Change

Figure 6 illustrates how wages can differ between occupations. Similar differences can often be observed between geographic regions. All else being equal (notably the characteristics of workers, jobs, and the attractiveness of the geography involved), such differences should give rise to worker migrations from low-wage regions to high-wage regions.

It is important, however, not to be fooled by differences in money wages that are possibly offset by similar differences in living costs. If Alaska money wages are twice as high as those in Mississippi, but food, clothing, housing, and the like cost twice as much too, there is no advantage in moving. Economists who study labor migrations, therefore, compare *real* wages, the ratio of money wages to consumer prices.

In the United States between 1940 and 1970, real wages in the North were higher than in the South; accordingly, millions of people migrated north. By the end of that period, real wages were equalized. (In 1970, on average, nominal wages in the North were 12 percent higher than in the South, but so were living costs.) After 1970, on the other hand, real wages in the West, the North Central States, and the South were often higher than in the Northeast; as Table A indicates, people moved accordingly.

Sources: P. Coelho and M. Ghali, "The End of the North-South Wage Differential," *The American Economic Review,* December 1971, pp. 932–937; D. Bellante, "The North-South Differential and the Migration of Heterogeneous Labor," *The American Economic Review,* March 1979, pp. 166–175; and William E. Cullison, "Equalizing Regional Differences in Wages: A Study of Wages and Migration in the South and Other Regions," *Federal Reserve Bank of Richmond Economic Review,* May/June 1984, pp. 20–33.

TABLE A

| Region | Real wages as percent of south | | | | Population change 1970–1980 (percent) |
| | 1978 | | 1981 | | |
	Men	Women	Men	Women	
New York	80	88	77	90	−6.0
Rest of Northeast	88	93	93	98	−1.3
North Central	92	94	96	102	+2.2
West	99	105	95	103	+15.4
South	100	100	100	100	+27.4

EXAMPLE 4

Investing in Human Capital

One explanation of persistent differences in wages among occupations is that some people incur high educational costs (in terms of income forgone and actual out-of-pocket expenditures). During one period in their lives, they acquire *human capital* (an engineering degree, an economics Ph.D., a law degree, an M.D.) and later get a lifelong return from this capital. The extra income later received from the learned abilities is equivalent to the income one might receive from owning a truck, a factory, or a piece of land (that might, similarly, be acquired after years of saving and sacrifice). The figure illustrates what is involved.

The individual pictured might be able to earn a steady $20,000/year having a high-school degree, as indicated by the horizontal color line. The individual might instead make an investment in higher education beginning at age 18, forgoing the $20,000 annual income for 8 years and paying out $16,000/year for tuition and the like on top of that. The reward after age 26 is a steady lifetime income of $40,000/year, or a $20,000/year *excess* over the income of high-school friends who have chosen not to make this 8-year sacrifice.

Assuming that the extra $20,000/year return of this investment comes to an abrupt end at age 65, the investment yields an annual return of 10.5 percent. (If you put $36,000 in a bank for 8 years in a row and received 10.5 percent interest per year, you could also withdraw $20,000/year for the remaining 39 years before your account was exhausted.) Studies of actual educational investments made in the U.S. revealed the 1979 data given in Table A. They also showed annual returns between 10 and 15 percent in the 1950s and 1960s, and returns of only about 7.5 percent in the 1970s and 1980s (reflecting relatively higher college fees and lower starting salaries).

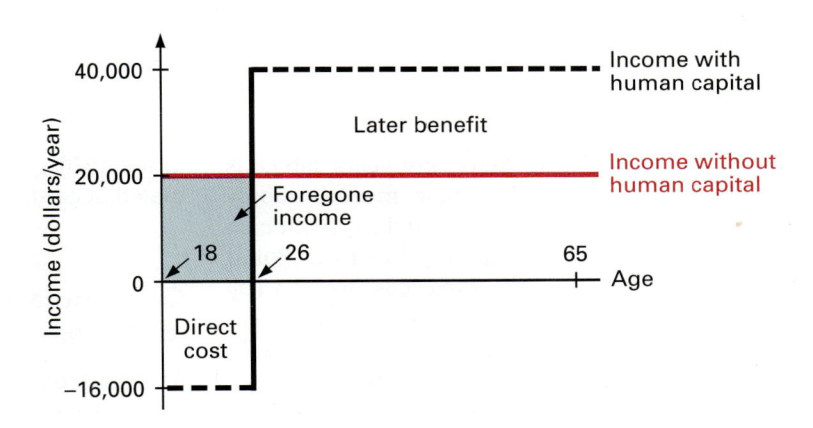

TABLE A

Yrs. of school completed	Lifetime income of men from age 18 to death (1981 dollars)	Extra lifetime income over previous category
Fewer than 12 years	$ 601,000	—
High school, 4 years	861,000	$260,000
College, 1–3 years	957,000	96,000
College, 4 years	1,190,000	233,000
College, 5 or more years	1,301,000	111,000

Source: U.S. Bureau of the Census, *Statistical Abstract of the United States: 1985* (Washington, D.C.: U.S. Government Printing Office, 1985), p. 453.

FIGURE 8 A Cobweb Cycle for Labor

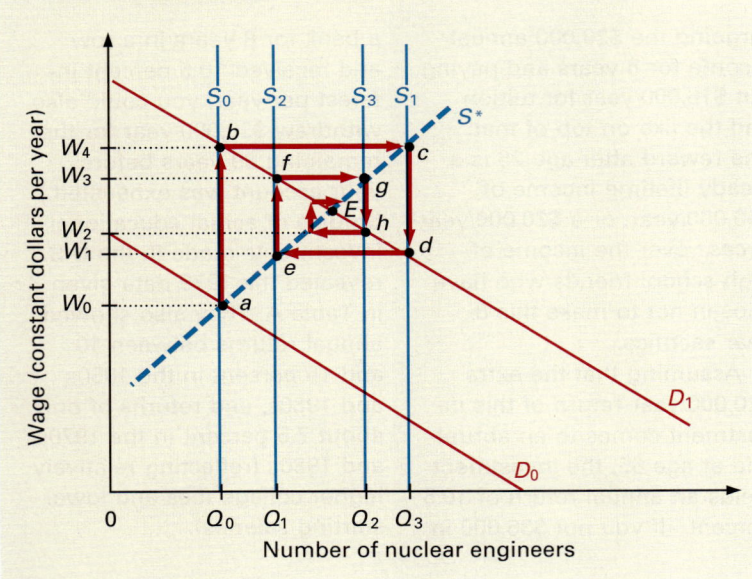

In some labor markets, supply may respond to wages with a considerable lag of time, as illustrated here by dashed supply line S^* in the market for nuclear engineers (that relates the wage now to the quantity supplied a number of years hence). Any change in demand (as from D_0 to D_1) may set off a long procession of short-run equilibria (as here from a to b to d, f, h, ...), which conjures up the image of a cobweb among strands of grass.

for this promising field. Some six years later, as those graduates enter the labor market, supply finally responds to the high wage and (as point c on the long-run supply line suggests) rises to S_1. But at the wage of W_4, supply then exceeds demand (by bc), and firms have an easy time hiring nuclear engineers for lower wages. The going wage falls to W_1 (corresponding to arrow cd). Yet, as the line of long-run supply S^* indicates, supply at W_1 will eventually correspond to point e. Over the years, fewer and fewer students enroll in the field and supply reaches S_2, which raises the wage to W_3 (point f). And so it goes. Given W_3, supply rises to S_3 (point g), but given S_3, the wage drops to W_2 (point h). For years on end, wages and quantities dance around point E, following the pattern drawn by the colored arrows (and resembling a cobweb). Long before E is reached, demand may change again and another cobweb may begin.

In the early 1950s, the U.S. market for (all types of) engineers was said to be in surplus. That was followed by a shortage near the end of the decade and lasting into the early 1960s. By the late 1960s, there was another surplus, followed by a shortage in the 1970s. Salaries and college enrollments fluctuated accordingly.

Government in Labor Markets

As discussed in the last section of Chapter 3, government can modify the way goods markets work by setting price floors or price ceilings and by imposing excise taxes. We now note that the results achieved by perfectly competitive labor markets can be similarly modified. In particular, we consider minimum wages and maximum wages.

Minimum Wages

An example of wishful thinking overwhelming hard analysis is provided by the history of minimum wage legislation in the United States. A government might well want to enact a law that establishes a *wage floor* above a currently prevailing equilibrium level. It seems an easy way to alleviate and perhaps

EXAMPLE 5

When the Baby Boomers Grew Up

Recent developments in U.S. labor markets have confirmed the Malthusian prediction that— all else being equal— wages will be depressed by a larger population and labor supply. After World War II, U.S. birth rates soared. Two decades later, the earlier baby boom had its predictable effect on the labor market. The population of 20-year-olds looking for jobs was 44 percent larger. True enough, *money* wages did not fall, but what happened to real wages as a result of the earlier baby boom?

The issue is somewhat complicated because real wages tend to rise over time with technical advances and other factors of economic growth. One economist decided to test the matter by comparing the *ratio* of real wages received by younger workers to those received by older workers during two relevant periods, assuming that inexperienced 20-year-olds were not competing in the same markets as experienced older workers and that, therefore, the influx of the baby boomers into labor markets should reduce the growth of their real wages *relative to* that of everyone else. Table A shows some of the results, which confirm the hypothesis for workers at all levels of education. Note how increases between columns (1) and (2) led to decreases between columns (3) and (4). Another baby boom in the early 1970s can be expected to have a similar effect in the early 1990s.

Source: Finis Welch, "Effects of Cohort Size on Earnings: The Baby Boom Babies' Financial Bust," *The Journal of Political Economy,* October 1979, pp. 565–598.

TABLE A

Yrs. of school completed	% of labor force with fewer than 5 yrs. work experience		Real wages of new entrants relative to peak earners	
	1967–1969 (1)	1973–1975 (2)	1967–1969 (3)	1973–1975 (4)
Fewer than 12 years	8.9	15.4	.53	.46
High school, 4 years	15.0	20.8	.63	.55
College, 1–3 years	19.0	25.2	.59	.52
College, 4 or more years	18.7	22.9	.63	.54

---

even abolish the poverty of low-wage workers. In addition, such a law does not directly cost the government a cent. The U.S. government first set a minimum wage of 25¢/hour in 1938 with the Fair Labor Standards Act. As the first row of Table 2 indicates, that wage equaled 40.3 percent of average manufacturing wages prevailing at the time; thus the law did not affect many labor markets because workers were already earning more. In addition, the law only covered 43.4 percent of all nonsupervisory employees; it excluded farm workers, household workers, employees of state and local governments, and many more. As Table 2 also indicates, Congress has raised the minimum wage over the years with regularity (to account for the erosion of its purchasing power by inflation). It has also extended the coverage of the law. By 1991, when the minimum stood at $4.25/hour, about 80 percent of all workers were

TABLE 2 The Federal Minimum Wage

Year	Nominal minimum wage	Minimum wage as a percentage of average manufacturing wage	Percentage of nonsupervisory employees covered by law
1938	$0.25	40.3	43.4
1939	0.30	47.6	47.1
1945	0.40	39.2	55.4
1950	0.75	52.1	53.4
1956	1.00	51.3	53.1
1961	1.15	49.6	62.1
1963	1.25	50.8	62.1
1967	1.40	49.6	75.3
1968	1.60	53.2	72.6
1974	2.00	45.2	83.7
1975	2.10	43.5	83.3
1976	2.30	44.1	
1978	2.65	43.0	
1979	2.90	43.3	
1980	3.10	42.6	
1981	3.35	41.9	
1990	3.80	35.1	
1991	4.25		80.0

Over the years, Congress has raised the U.S. minimum wage with regularity; it has also extended its coverage.

covered. But again, many workers who already earned more were unaffected and many others were illegally paid less than the minimum.[3]

What does economic theory tell us about the likely effects of minimum wages? Consider Figure 9 and imagine it to describe a typical competitive market for unskilled labor, such as that found in the fast-food industry. Originally, an equilibrium wage of $4/hour exists and 100 million hours of labor/day are being bought and sold (point *e*). Let the government enact a $6/hour minimum wage. Immediately, quantity demanded falls (along demand line

---

[3] Enforcement of the law was extremely lax, fines for violating it were low, and one (somewhat earlier) study estimated that between 30 and 50 percent of those who might have benefited from the law were paid too little. See Orley Ashenfelter and Robert S. Smith, "Compliance with the Minimum Wage Law," *Journal of Political Economy*, April 1979, pp. 335–350.

A 1990 law, however, provided for a sub-minimum, training wage for 16 to 19 year olds. In 1991, it equaled $3.61 per hour but could be paid only at a person's first job and for a maximum of 6 months. Few employers paid this wage, being unable to get workers or considering the effect "demoralizing."

FIGURE 9 Setting a Minimum Wage

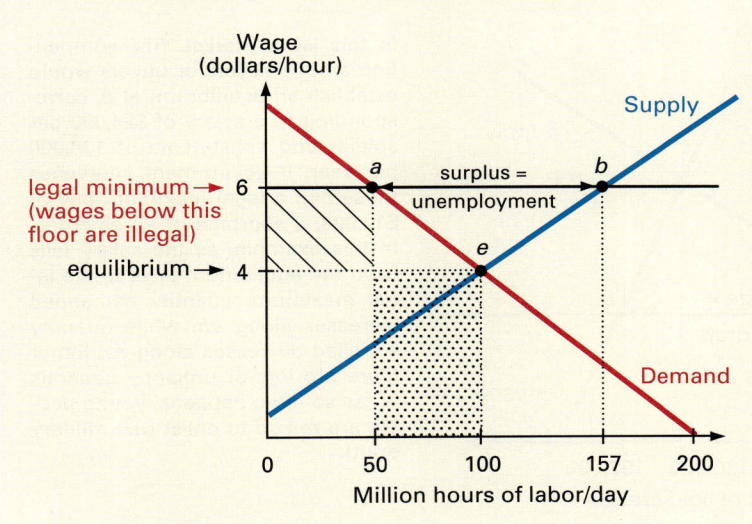

The enactment of an above-equilibrium minimum wage in a perfectly competitive labor market, here of $6 per hour, creates unemployment (*ab*). If the income of workers who lose their jobs (dotted area) exceeds the extra income of workers still employed (cross-hatched area), workers' total income declines.

segment *ea*), while quantity supplied rises (along supply line segment *eb*). A surplus of labor (unemployment) emerges; it equals *ab* = 107 million labor hours/day.

If the demand for labor is relatively elastic (as to the left of point *e*), workers as a group are hardly helped. In this example, their actual labor sales correspond to point *a*, not point *b*; thus, their income comes to $6 per hour times 50 million hours per day, or $300 million per day. This is a lot less than the hoped-for income from selling 157 million hours. In the meantime, 157 − 50 = 107 million hours per day (distance *ab*) cannot be sold in this market and remain unemployed or earn lower wages elsewhere. Many real-world examples corroborate our theory.

In the 1970s, the minimum hourly wage went from $2.30 to $2.65. The reaction of the fast-food chains was swift. They lowered their employees' weekly hours (by opening later and closing earlier). They hired fewer teenagers and more adults (who were more skilled and experienced, had lower turnover rates, and reduced company training costs). They substituted capital for labor (by installing computerized cash registers and overnight cookers).[4] In the end, those who were still employed were clearly better off (as measured by the cross-hatched rectangle in Figure 9). Those who lost their jobs (and the dotted-rectangle income) were worse off. Those additional workers who were entering the market in response to the higher wage (note segment *eb*) but were unable to find work were not helped. Indeed, workers in *other* markets (not shown here) may have been hurt as well. Picture some of the unemployed (*ab*) looking for jobs in other fields not covered by the minimum wage. Their entry would raise the supply and lower the wage in these other markets—to the dismay of those workers.

Numerous empirical studies of minimum wage effects have found the following. Many workers are unaffected because they already earn more than the minimum. Others are unaffected because employers ignore the law, others still because employers who pay higher nominal wages can make up for it by re-

---

[4] See Paul Ingrassia, "Quick Adjustment: Fast-Food Chains Act to Offset the Effects of Minimum-Pay Rise," *The Wall Street Journal,* December 22, 1977, p. 1.

FIGURE 10 Setting a Maximum Wage

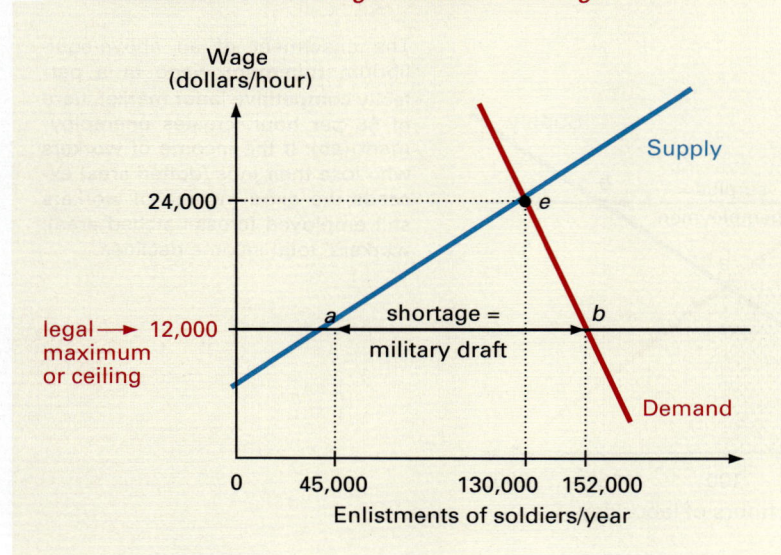

In this labor market, free competition among sellers or buyers would establish an equilibrium at e, corresponding to a salary of $24,000 per soldier and enlistments of 130,000 per year. If government intervenes by setting a legal maximum pay of $12,000, a shortage of ab emerges. In this example, as the salary falls from the equilibrium level to the legal maximum, quantity demanded increases along eb, while quantity supplied decreases along ea. Either there are lots of unhappy generals or, as so often happens, young people are *forced* to enlist (the military draft).

ducing fringe benefits, such as low-cost meals; subsidized housing; holiday, vacation, or sick pay; health insurance and pension benefits. Most importantly, the employment level of teenagers (and even more so of African-American teenagers) has been reduced with every increase of the minimum wage. As a result, there has been a long-term upward trend in the ratio of teenage to overall unemployment. Before the $1.15/hour minimum went into effect, this ratio was 2.5, in the year following the increase it became 2.7. When the minimum rose to $1.25/hour, the ratio rose to 3.1; when the minimum rose to $1.60, the ratio rose to 3.6.[5] The attempt to help the working poor, it seems, has proven to be the most effective method yet of keeping the nation's teenagers idle.

Maximum Wages

On other occasions government enters labor markets not to set minimum wages (to help sellers of labor) but to set maximum wages (to help buyers of labor). A now ancient example dates from medieval Europe and the time of the Black Death. Around 1350, up to a third of many countries' populations was wiped out by the plague, which caused a severe decline in the supply of labor. The survivors, however, inherited the unchanged physical wealth, which made them richer and more eager to consume. The demand for labor failed to fall much and a severe labor shortage emerged. Governments tried to prevent the pressure on wages to rise by

---

[5] Yale Brozen, "The Effect of Statutory Minimum Wage Increases on Teen-Age Employmnent," *The Journal of Law and Economics,* April 1969, pp. 109–122. A partial listing of other studies includes Thomas G. Moore, "The Effect of Minimum Wages on Teenage Unemployment Rates," *Journal of Political Economy,* July/August 1971, pp. 897–902; Douglas K. Adie, "Teen-Age Unemployment and Real Federal Minimum Wages," *Journal of Political Economy,* March/April 1973, pp. 435–441; Finis Welch, "Minimum Wage Legislation in the United States," *Economic Inquiry,* September 1974, pp. 285–318; Jacob Mincer, "Unemployment Effects of Minimum Wages," *Journal of Political Economy,* August 1976, pp. S87–S104; James F. Ragan, "Minimum Wages and the Youth Labor Market,"

The Review of Economics and Statistics, May 1977, pp. 129–136; Robert Swidinsky, "Minimum Wages and Teenage Unemployment," *Canadian Journal of Economics,* February 1980, pp. 158–171; and Robert H. Meyer and David A. Wise, "The Effects of the Minimum Wage on the Employment and Earnings of Youth," *Journal of Labor Economics,* no. 1, 1983, pp. 66–100.

setting maximum wages. Apparently their efforts failed; in many places, wages rose from 50 to 100 percent within three years.

A more recent example concerns the U.S. Pentagon and the Vietnam War. It also involves death. Given the demand and supply shown in Figure 10, an equilibrium might be reached at point *e*. At a $24,000 annual wage per soldier, 130,000 soldiers would enlist each year and the same number would be demanded by the government. The budgetary cost would come to $3.12 billion/year. Now let Congress legislate a lower maximum wage of $12,000 per soldier per year. The quantity supplied would fall from *e* to *a*, the quantity demanded would rise from *e* to *b*. A shortage of *ab* would emerge. As Congress did during the Vietnam War, it could *force* an appropriate increase in supply by instituting a military draft, calling up $ab = 107,000$ soldiers/year. The government's budgetary cost would be down, to $1.824 billion in this example.

In reality, in the 1960s, military wages were set way below comparable civilian wages. After 1973, when an all-volunteer army was substituted, these wages rose to a level 14 percent above similar civilian jobs, reflecting nonmonetary differences between these types of employment. In the 1980s, the compensating wage differential equaled about 20 percent.

Summary

1. In markets for resources, the roles of households and firms (whose actions in goods markets were studied in previous chapters) are reversed. Households appear as sellers rather than buyers; firms appear as buyers rather than sellers. This chapter focuses on their interaction in labor markets under conditions of perfect competition.

2. People's use of time can be divided into two broad categories: work and leisure. When people sell their time to firms in return for money income (*work*), they gain utility from the goods that such income can buy (and possibly even from the process of working itself). But they also forgo the utility that could have been reaped from alternative uses of time in *leisure* activities. Their total utility from the use of their time is maximized when time is split between work and leisure in such a way that the marginal utility per hour of work just equals the marginal utility per hour of leisure. From this principle one can derive an individual's supply curve of labor (relating labor quantity supplied to the prevailing wage). Individual labor supplies can be summed to yield market supply.

3. The demand for any input, such as labor, is a derived demand that exists only to the extent that people demand the output such input helps produce. A perfectly competitive firm will employ the quantity of any input that maximizes the firm's profit because it equates the marginal benefit of input use (such as labor's marginal value product) with the marginal cost of input use (such as labor's wage). From this principle one can derive a firm's demand curve for labor (relating labor quantity demanded to the prevailing wage). Individual labor demands can be summed to yield market demand.

4. As in perfectly competitive markets for goods, equilibrium is established in markets for resources, such as labor, through the interaction of market demand and market supply.

5. A perfectly competitive labor market in equilibrium, just like a perfectly competitive goods market, produces economic efficiency, a situation in which it is impossible to make a person better off without making another person worse off because all mutually beneficial transactions have already been carried out.

6. The theory of perfectly competitive labor markets can be applied to answer numerous ques-

tions of general interest. Those that are discussed here include possible reasons for occupational wage differentials, for the persistence of poverty, and for persistently fluctuating wages over time.

7. The results achieved by perfectly competitive labor markets can be modified by the intervention of government. Considered here are the setting of minimum wages or maximum wages.

Key Concepts

average value product, AVP
cobweb cycle
compensating wage differentials
derived demand
economic efficiency
equalizing wage differentials
income effect
iron law of wages
leisure
marginal value product, MVP
subsistence wage
substitution effect
work

Questions and Problems

1. The manager of a shopping mall was concerned about shoplifting and experimented with employing different numbers of detectives on otherwise identical days.[6] The results are given in the accompanying table:

Number of detectives on duty	Total value of thefts prevented/day
0	$ 0
1	200
2	300
3	380
4	440
5	480
6	500

a. Assuming the manager wants to maximize profit, derive the manager's demand schedule for store detectives.
b. How many detectives would be hired at a wage of $60/day? Explain.

2. A firm has collected the following selected data on the average and marginal value products of its workers. Derive the firm's labor demand curve graphically.

	Number of workers employed	Marginal value product of labor	Average value product of labor
a.	200	$110	—
b.	400	140	—
c.	760	155 (max.)	—
d.	1,000	147	—
e.	1,150	127	$127
f.	1,240	100	—
g.	1,400	52	—
h.	1,500	20	—
i.	100	—	40
j.	500	—	98
k.	1,500	—	115
m.	1,800	—	70
n.	1,900	—	40

---

[6] Adapted from Robert J. Flanagan, Robert S. Smith, and Ronald G. Ehrenberg, *Labor Economics and Labor Relations* (Glenview, IL: Scott, Foresman and Co., 1984), pp. 56–58.

	Theater	Opera	Symphony	Ballet
Marginal physical product (MPP)	0.5943	0.2909	0.0870	0.5899
Ratio of input price to output price (P_i/P_o)	1.057	0.735	1.431	0.855

3. A firm operates in perfectly competitive labor markets and is maximizing profit. It faces an output price of $50/unit and input price of $200/unit. Determine

   a. the input's marginal physical product.
   b. the input's marginal value product.

4. A recent study[7] of 164 performing arts companies discovered the above data with respect to the labor of artists:

   a. Assuming perfect competition, were the companies studied maximizing profits? Explain.
   b. Would you change your opinion if these were nonprofit organizations heavily subsidized by gifts? Explain.

5. In earlier chapters, a "marginal versus average rule" was applied, for example, to the relationship between marginal cost and average variable cost (or average total cost). What examples in this chapter confirm this rule?

6. What would be the effect on a competitive labor market if the government, as it often does, instituted a massive training program for the type of labor in question? Would employment rise by the number of newly trained workers? Explain.

7. In the 1970s, New York City established wage levels for fire fighters and police officers that were 40 percent above the wages of comparable workers, such as skilled mechanics and truck drivers. Similarly, the wages of sanitation workers were set at a level 60 percent higher than for laborers.[8] What effects would you predict?

8. Let government enter a labor market and set a minimum wage far above the equilibrium level, creating massive unemployment. How could government deal with this unemployment? (Hint: Review Chapter 3, Figure 10, Dealing with the Surplus.)

9. The chapter discusses the case of maximum wages with respect to military labor markets. Can you think of any other examples?

---

[7] James H. Gapinski, "The Production of Culture," *The Review of Economics and Statistics,* November 1980, pp. 578–586.

[8] Robert J. Flanagan, et al., *Economics of the Employment Relationship* (Glenview, IL: Scott, Foresman and Co., 1985), p. 46.

CHAPTER 14

IMPERFECTLY COMPETITIVE LABOR MARKETS

Preview

This chapter explores what happens in labor markets when some of the conditions that characterize perfect competition fail to be fulfilled. Competitive workers may confront a single buyer of labor (as in a "company town"). On the other hand, competitive firms might have to deal with a group of associated workers acting like a single seller (a labor union). Or a single buyer might have to deal with a single (labor union) seller. Other types of labor market imperfections, such as discrimination by sex or race, are discussed as well, as are recent government efforts to end such behavior.

Examples

1. A Case Study in Monopsony: The Baseball Players' Market
2. Keeping Unions Out
3. Comparable Worth: A Profoundly Flawed Concept?
4. Pinups at Work Are Sexual Harassment
5. The Coming Global Labor Market

Ideas in History

Marginal Productivity and the Exploitation of Labor
Bread-and-Butter Unionism

The previous chapter focused on labor markets operating in a world in which markets for goods as well as resources were perfectly competitive. Now we are ready to explore how the results then obtained must be modified when the products of labor or labor services themselves are traded in markets that fail to be perfectly competitive. The task before us is fairly complex because the conditions of perfect competition are numerous and thus can be violated in many different ways.

Examples of Market Imperfections

Table 1 helps us identify possible forms of market imperfections that would modify the results obtained in the previous chapter. The row headings of Table 1 indicate two alternative ways in which labor services might be supplied; the column headings define four alternative situations on the buying side. The cells of the table, accordingly, represent eight different market configurations. Case A is the situation analyzed in the last chapter. Every labor market was then assumed to contain large numbers of independently acting sellers and buyers. As a result, no market participant, acting alone, could influence the market price; everyone was a price taker. All the workers that sold labor and all the firms that bought labor had to accept the market's equilibrium wage as a given; labor-buying firms were equally impotent with respect to market prices of outputs they produced.

Now consider the ways in which even this first condition of perfect competition—traders so numerous that everyone is a price taker—can be violated. Case B points to the possibility that price-taking sellers of labor might meet price-taking buyers of labor who exercise monopolistic price-setting power in their output markets. This fact alone changes the nature of the labor market equilibrium obtained. Cases C and D introduce a less subtle change in circumstances. Perfectly competitive sellers of labor confront a single buyer for whom they have no good substitute because the entry of other such buyers into the market is blocked or highly unlikely—a **monopsony**. The monopsonistic buyer may sell output either competitively (Case C) or monopolistically (Case D). Cases E–H illustrate situations in which workers exercise monopoly power by forming a **labor union**—a cartel for the joint sale of their labor—and then confront any of the aforementioned situations on the buying side.

The labor market imperfections highlighted by Cases B through H in Table 1 are by no means the only possible ones. Perfect competition also requires that buyers view all units of the traded item as identical, regardless of the source of supply; that buyers as well as sellers possess full knowledge relevant to trading in the market; and that there be no impediments to entry into or exit from the market for either buyers or sellers. In many real-world labor markets, these conditions are violated as well. Consider employers who indulge their personal preferences by systematically *discriminating* among different types of workers whom they know to be equally qualified; clearly, they are not treating all labor units as homogeneous. Consider how market knowledge is often far from perfect, which gives rise

TABLE 1 *Selected Labor Market Configurations*

		Labor demand is exercised by			
		Perfectly competitive buyers who are		A single buyer (monopsony) who is	
		perfectly competitive sellers of output	monopolistic sellers of output	a perfectly competitive seller of output	a monopolistic seller of output
Labor supply is provided by	Perfectly competitive sellers	A	B	C	D
	a labor union (i.e., a cartel of workers acting like a single seller)	E	F	G	H

The previous chapter analyzed the combination of circumstances represented by Case A, in which everyone is a price taker in every market. In this situation, competitive sellers of labor face competitive buyers of labor who are also competitive sellers of output. Cases B through H, in contrast, illustrate a variety of alternative market configurations in which buyers or sellers do exercise a measure of control over price. All of these cases are discussed in this chapter.

to such costly activities as search, signaling, and screening. (As we will also see, in the face of imperfect market knowledge some employers who harbor no malevolent feelings may discriminate against members of particular groups because they can cut screening costs by ruling out individuals who are costly to assess but who belong to groups whose *average* characteristics are known to be undesirable.) Consider, finally, how labor market entry is often restricted to particular individuals or groups by a variety of factors, ranging from social custom to formal legislation to labor union rules. We study these and other examples of imperfect competition in the following sections.

Competition in the Labor Market, Modified by Monopoly Power in Output Markets

Case B of Table 1 involves perfectly competitive sellers of labor confronting perfectly competitive buyers of labor, but the latter exercise price-setting power in their respective *output* markets. The firms involved might be pure monopolies (electric power companies); they might be oligopolies (automobile producers); they might even be monopolistic competitors (auto repair shops). All such firms have one thing in common: Unlike perfect competitors, they each face a downward-sloping demand curve for their product. Hence they can sell more output only by lowering output price. If we assume that these firms are not engaging in price discrimination and are charging a uniform price of all customers, their marginal revenue is always lower than output price:

$$MR < P_o$$

Such firms entering a labor market find themselves among innumerable independently acting other buyers, while facing many (noncolluding) sellers. (All the firms mentioned, along with thousands of other firms, might compete for the same type of labor. Will the quantity of labor demanded by any one firm be the one that equates labor's marginal value product with labor's price, that is, the market-determined equilibrium wage? That was the outcome in the last chapter, as a review of Focus 1 shows. Given the changed circumstances analyzed here, the answer is "no," as can be deduced from Table 2.

A Numerical Example

First consider Part A of Table 2. Column (1) lists alternative labor quantities a firm might use (along with fixed amounts of other inputs not specified). Column (2) shows the maximum possible output quantities that are associated with the labor inputs shown. As the numbers indicate, by using more labor, the firm can produce more output. But if it does produce more output in this way *and cares to sell it,* its downward-sloping demand line forces it to lower the output price, column (3). Given data on output quantity Q_o and output price P_o we can calculate the total revenue TR that is associated with alternative amounts of labor used.

Note how column (4) equals column (2) multiplied by column (3). The extra revenue brought in by an extra worker (column 5) is the marginal benefit derived by employing that worker. This change in the firm's total revenue that is associated with a unit change in labor used is called the **marginal revenue product of labor, MRP_L**. In our example, it is measured by the change in the column (4) values (directly shown in column 5) as we hire one additional worker at a time.

Naturally, a profit-maximizing firm compares this marginal benefit with the marginal cost of hiring additional workers, which in a competitive labor market is simply the equilibrium wage. We assume that wage is $2,640 per worker per month (column 6). Our firm does best by hiring 5 workers, the number that equates the marginal benefit and marginal cost just discussed. Up to that point, additional workers add more to the firm's revenue than to its cost; hence profit rises. (The second worker hired, for example, adds $8,085 to revenue but only $2,640 to cost.) Beyond that optimum point, additional workers add less to the firm's revenue than to its cost; hence profit declines. (The seventh worker, for example, adds $960 to revenue but $2,640 to cost.) Thus we conclude:

> A firm that is a perfect competitor in the labor market but wields monopoly power in the output market, maximizes profit by employing a quantity of labor that equates the marginal revenue product of labor with the market-given wage:

$$MRP_L = W$$

TABLE 2 The Input Decision Revisited: Monopoly Power in the Output Market

Part A

Quantity of labor, L	Quantity of output, Q_o	Price of output, P_o	Total revenue, $Q_o \cdot P_o = TR$	marginal benefit and marginal cost of labor use	
				marginal benefit = marginal revenue product of labor, $MRP_L = \Delta TR/\Delta L$	marginal cost = market-given wage, W
(no. of full-time workers)	(units/ month)	($/unit)	($/month)	(extra $/month/extra worker)	
(1)	(2)	(3)	(4) = (2)·(3)	(5) = Δ(4)/Δ(1)	(6)
0	0	15.00	0	—	—
1	800	13.80	11,040	11,040	2,640 ⎫
2	1,500	12.75	19,125	8,085	2,640 ⎪
3	2,100	11.85	24,885	5,760	2,640 ⎬ MB > MC
4	2,600	11.10	28,860	3,975	2,640 ⎭
5	3,000	10.50	31,500	2,640	2,640 optimum
6	3,300	10.05	33,165	1,665	2,640 ⎫
7	3,500	9.75	34,125	960	2,640 ⎬ MB < MC
8	3,600	9.60	34,560	435	2,640 ⎭

Part B

Quantity of labor, L	Marginal physical product of labor, $MPP_L = \Delta Q_o/\Delta L$	Marginal revenue, $MR = \Delta TR/\Delta Q_o$	Marginal revenue product of labor, $MRP_L = MPP_L \cdot MR$	Marginal value product of labor, $MVP_L = MPP_L \cdot P_o$	Wage, W
(no. of full-time workers)	(extra units/ extra worker)	(extra $/ extra output unit)	(extra $/month/extra worker)		
(7)	(8) = Δ(2)/Δ(1)	(9) = Δ(4)/Δ(2)	(10) = (8)·(9) = (5)	(11) = (8)·(3)	(12)
0	—	—	—	—	—
1	800	13.80	11,040	11,040	2,640
2	700	11.55	8,085	8,925	2,640
3	600	9.60	5,760	7,110	2,640
4	500	7.95	3,975	5,550	2,640
5	400	6.60	2,640	4,200	2,640
6	300	5.55	1,665	3,015	2,640
				2,640	2,640
7	200	4.80	960	1,950	2,640
8	100	4.35	435	960	2,640

A firm that is a perfect competitor in the labor market but has monopoly power in the output market maximizes profit by employing that quantity of labor (here 5 full-time workers) that equates the marginal revenue product of labor with the market-given wage (columns 5 and 6). That chosen labor quantity falls short of the one (here between 6 and 7 workers) that equates the marginal value product of labor with the wage (columns 11 and 12).

Part B of Table 2 teaches two additional lessons. First, as columns (7) to (10) indicate, the marginal revenue product of labor (previously calculated in column 5) always equals the marginal physical product of labor (as in column 8) multiplied by the firm's marginal revenue (as in column 9). Recall that the *marginal physical product of labor* is the change in labor's total product (the change from one row to the next in column 2) divided by the associated change in labor input (the change from one row to the next in column 1 or 7). *Marginal revenue*, on the other hand, is the change in total revenue (from one row to the next in column 4) divided by the associated change in output (from one row to the next in column 2). Thus the marginal revenue product of labor can be calculated in an alternative way:

$$MRP_L = MPP_L \cdot MR$$

Second, as columns (10) to (12) indicate, as more and more labor is used by a firm that possesses monopoly power in the output market (marginal revenue, therefore, lies below output price), labor's marginal revenue product ($MPP_L \cdot MR$) declines much faster than its marginal value product ($MPP_L \cdot P_o$). As a consequence, this section's profit-maximizing rule (hire additional workers until the MRP_L has fallen to W) leads to the employment of fewer workers than last chapter's rule (hire additional workers until the MVP_L has fallen to W). This difference is evident in columns (11) and (12) of our table. If our firm were to follow the $MVP_L = W$ rule, it would employ between 6 and 7 workers, but then it would find itself in a position at which labor's marginal revenue product (somewhere between $1,665 and $960 in column 10) fell short of the market wage ($2,640 in column 12). Thus the firm's profit would not be maximized.

A Graphical Illustration

The new profit-maximizing rule can be illustrated graphically. Figure 1 is based on Table 2. The downward-sloping line of labor's marginal revenue product MRP_L is a graph of column (1) versus column (5) or of column (7) versus column (10). It represents the firm's demand for labor. The horizontal line, labeled W, is the assumed equilibrium wage (from columns 6 and 12) that has been established by the interaction (not shown) of competitive market supply with market demand (the summation of innumerable MRP_L lines such as the one shown here). Following the profit-maximizing rule noted in the previous section, the firm optimizes at d and hires 5 workers. Its total wage bill comes to $2,640/worker/month times 5 workers, or $13,200/month (area $0ade$).

Figure 1 also contains a dashed line of labor's marginal value product, MVP_L, derived from columns (7) and (11) of Table 2. It enables us to address a further issue. Firms that have monopoly power in their output markets tend to hire fewer workers than they would hire in the absence of such power and they pay them less than their marginal value product. Economists have a special name for this situation.

Monopolistic Exploitation

As a quick review of last chapter's Figure 3, Labor Demand, shows, in the *absence* of output market monopoly power (when firms are price takers with respect to the goods they sell), a firm operating in a competitive labor market hires the quantity of labor that equates labor's falling marginal value product with the equilibrium wage established in that market. In our present example, this quantity would correspond to hiring (intersection f) 6 to 7 workers rather than the 5 workers actually chosen. The lower quantity demanded here shows how labor market behavior is modified by the presence of monopoly power in the selling of output. Monopolistic sellers of goods restrict output below the competitive level at which output price equals the marginal cost of production and choose the lower level that equates marginal revenue with marginal cost. Here we see the mirror image of that behavior. The quantity of *input* used is similarly restricted (from f to d in our graph).

In addition, labor's marginal value product now exceeds the wage it receives; note the gap cd in our graph. This discrepancy disturbs some economists, as Ideas in History, Marginal Productivity and the Exploitation of Labor, explains. Some economists consider the *equality* of labor's marginal value product and labor's wage as morally just; they argue that each worker should be paid a wage precisely equal to the value of output gained when the

FIGURE 1 The Demand for Labor Reconsidered

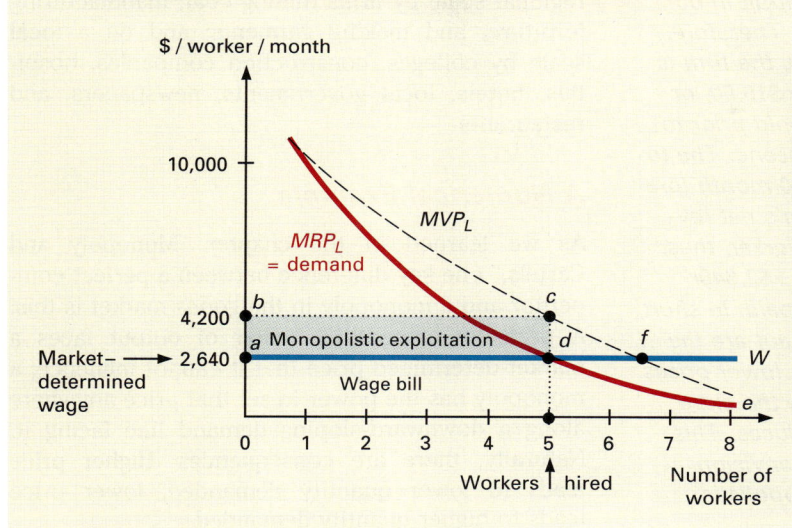

A firm operating in a perfectly competitive labor market, but possessing monopoly power in the output market, demands labor according to a line of labor's marginal revenue product, MRP_L, rather than labor's marginal value product, MVP_L. At the given, market-determined wage of $W = \$2{,}640$ per month, it demands a labor quantity corresponding to d, not f. Accordingly, labor's wage falls short of its marginal value product (by cd). Whenever such a divergence is caused by the employer's monopoly power in the output market (which makes labor's marginal revenue product fall short of its marginal value product), labor faces *monopolistic exploitation*.

---

last worker was hired, a value that would be lost if that worker *or any identical worker* were to be removed from the productive process. As a look at Table 2 can confirm, the last (5th) worker hired raises output from 2,600 to 3,000 units, or by 400 units/month. These units sell for $10.50 each; thus the worker's marginal value product equals 400 times $10.50, or $4,200/month (point c, Figure 1). Yet the worker's wage equals only $2,640/month, which these economists argue is *unjust*. Indeed, when labor's wage falls short of its marginal value product (gap cd in Figure 1) and when this divergence is caused by the employer possessing monopoly power in the output market (which makes marginal revenue fall short of output price and, therefore, the marginal revenue product of labor fall short of its marginal value product), these economists talk of **monopolistic exploitation** of labor. The extent of labor's monopolistic exploitation in our example is shown by the shaded area in Figure 1 and equals $1,560/month ($cd$) times 5 workers, or $7,800/month.

FOCUS 1

Monopolistic Exploitation of Labor

A situation in which $W < MVP_L$ because

1. $MR < P_o$, and therefore $MRP_L < MVP_L$ and
2. a perfectly competitive buyer in the labor market who has monopoly power in the output market maximizes profit by hiring a labor quantity such that

$$MRP_L = W$$

CAUTION

Many economists are more than unhappy with this use of the emotionally laden term exploitation, *which suggests that the firm is pocketing something that rightfully belongs to its workers. As these critics see it, the above numerical reasoning is faulty. The 5th worker hired does, indeed, add 400 units to output and these 400 units do sell for $10.50 each. Thus, the firm does gain $4,200 in revenue. Yet this is not the whole story. When the 5th worker raises output from 2,600 to*

> *3,000 units/month, the firm realizes that it can sell the extra output only by lowering its output price, from $11.10 to $10.50/unit in our example (as Table 2 can show). Therefore, while gaining revenue of $4,200, the firm is also losing revenue of $11.10 − $10.50, or 60¢ on each of the 2,600 units sold prior to the 5th worker's arrival on the scene. The total revenue loss comes to $1,560/month (precisely equal to gap cd). The firm's net revenue gain from hiring the 5th worker, thus, comes to +$4,200 − $1,560, or +$2,640/month, which equals the wage paid. In short, the* consumers *of the firm's output are the ones who pocket the gap* cd *via lower prices without which they will not take the extra output that the last worker produces. This situation is hardly what people envision when they hear the term "monopolistic exploitation."*

Monopsony in the Labor Market, but Competition in Output Markets

In Case C of Table 2, perfectly competitive sellers of labor confront a *monopsony*—a single buyer only for whom good substitutes are not available. Such a situation is fairly common. A typical example is the "company town," dominated by a single employer. Think of many small towns where a college or university dominates the scene. Think of Barstow, California, and the Santa Fe Railway; Corning, New York, and the Corning Glass Company; Hershey, Pennsylvania, and the Hershey Chocolate Company; Butte, Montana, and the Anaconda Copper Mining Company. Such dominant employers have "captured" work forces to the extent that workers cannot or will not leave the area or switch occupations (being ignorant of alternatives, afraid of the unknown, too poor to afford a move or retraining, reluctant to leave pretty scenery, family, or friends, or, perhaps, even reasonably happy with their monopsonistic employer).

Even when there are several major employers in a given area, labor market monopsony may result when such employers (whether it is legal or not) agree to act jointly in the hiring of labor and not to compete with each other for workers. Such **antipirating agreements** have been reached on a national scale by major league sports clubs and various departments of the federal government; on a regional scale by firms mining coal, manufacturing furniture, and making garments; and on a local scale by colleges, construction companies, hospitals, hotels, local governments, newspapers, and restaurants.

A Numerical Example

As we learned in the chapter "Monopoly and Cartels," one key difference between a perfect competitor and a monopoly in the *goods* market is this: A perfectly competitive seller of output faces a market-determined price that it cannot influence; a monopoly has the power to set that price anywhere along a downward-sloping demand line facing it. Naturally, there are consequences. Higher price leads to lower quantity demanded; lower price leads to higher quantity demanded.

In the labor market, a similar difference emerges between perfectly competitive buyers of labor and a monopsony. Any given perfectly competitive buyer of labor faces a market-determined wage that it cannot influence (such as W in Figure 1). A monopsony has the power to set the wage anywhere along an upward-sloping supply line facing it. A lower wage leads to a lower quantity of labor supplied; a higher wage leads to a higher quantity supplied. This relationship is indicated in columns (1) and (2) of Table 3. The monopsony is free to set the wage at any level it pleases, but the quantity of labor supplied to it varies accordingly. Thus, if it wants more workers, it must offer a higher wage. As long as all workers are alike and all of them are always paid the same wage (and this we assume), the labor supply schedule of columns (1) and (2) contains an important implication. When more workers are hired, the **marginal labor cost, MLC** (column 4), which is the change in the firm's total labor cost (the change from one row to the next in column 3) divided by the associated change in labor input used (the change from one row to the next in column 2) comes to *exceed* the wage that each new worker receives (column 1).

By setting a wage of $200/week, the monopsony is able to attract 1,000 workers; its total wage bill is $200,000/week. In order to get 2,000 workers to work for it, the firm has to raise the wage it offers to $300/week. But it will not, we assume, pay $300/

TABLE 3 The Input Decision: Monopsony

Monopsony's wage W ($/worker/wk) (1)	Quantity of labor supplied L (no. of full-time workers) (2)	Total labor cost TLC = W·L ($/week) (3) = (1)·(2)	Marginal cost and marginal benefit of labor use	
			Marginal cost = marginal labor cost MLC = Δ TLC/Δ L (4) = Δ(3)/Δ(2)	Marginal benefit = marginal value product of labor MVP$_L$ (extra $/wk/extra worker) (5)
200	1,000	200,000	200	1,100
300	2,000	600,000	400	1,000
400	3,000	1,200,000	600	900
500	4,000	2,000,000	800	800 — optimum
600	5,000	3,000,000	1,000	700
700	6,000	4,200,000	1,200	600
800	7,000	5,600,000	1,400	500

For rows 1–3: MC < MB and MB > MC.
For rows 5–7: MC > MB and MB < MC.

A firm that is a perfect competitor in the output market but a monopsony in the labor market maximizes profit by employing that quantity of labor (4,000 full-time workers in this example) that equates the marginal labor cost with the marginal value product of labor (columns 4 and 5). Note how the firm's marginal labor cost exceeds the wage it sets as long as it does not price-discriminate and any higher wage it pays to attract new workers is also paid to all the other workers previously employed.

week to the 1,000 workers newly hired, while continuing to pay only $200/week to the 1,000 (equally skilled) workers hired originally. In the absence of price-discrimination, the firm must not only pay an extra $300/week × 1,000 = $300,000/week to the new employees. It must also give *raises* of $100/week to its 1,000 old-time employees. These raises add another $100/week × 1,000 = $100,000/week to the firm's wage bill; they bring the total increase in labor cost to $400,000/week (note the difference between the first two entries in column 3 of Table 3). So far as the firm is concerned, each of the extra 1,000 workers hired effectively cost it an extra $400/week—although the firm's wage is pegged at $300/week. Accordingly, the firm will figure its profit-maximizing input quantity by comparing not the wage (column 1) but the marginal labor cost (column 4) with the value of the marginal product that workers produce (column 5).

As long as the marginal cost of labor use falls short of the associated marginal benefit, the firm can raise its profit by hiring more labor. Workers in the second group of 1,000 workers hired add on the average $400/week to the firm's cost (as shown in column 4), but they add $1,000/week to the firm's revenue (column 5). It pays to hire them.

On the other hand, hiring more than 4,000 workers would be counterproductive. A fifth batch of 1,000 workers would, on average, add $1,000 to the firm's cost and only $700 to its revenue. If 5,000 or 6,000 or 7,000 workers ever *were* employed by our firm, it could do better by reducing its work force (to the 4,000 worker optimum). Such a move would reduce its cost (column 4) by more than its revenue (column 5). Again, it would raise profit. We conclude:

A firm that is a perfect competitor in the output market but wields monopsony power in the labor market maximizes profit by employing a quantity of labor that equates the marginal value product of labor with the marginal labor cost.

$$MVP_L = MLC$$

A Graphical Illustration

The profit-maximizing rule just highlighted can be illustrated graphically as well. Figure 2 is based on Table 3. The dashed black line represents the market supply and thus the wage-quantity choices available to the monopsony. For reasons noted previously, the firm's marginal labor cost exceeds any wage it cares to select; accordingly, the line of marginal labor cost shown here diverges from the line of labor supply. The firm optimizes at point c by equating the marginal value product of labor with the marginal labor cost. Having chosen the profit-maximizing number of workers (4,000 workers), the firm announces a wage that will attract precisely this number of workers: $500 per worker per week (point d). As in the previous section, we note a gap (cd) between labor's marginal value product and its wage. This gap, too, has a special name.

Monopsonistic Exploitation

When labor's wage falls short of its marginal value product (gap cd in Figure 2) and when this divergence is caused by the employer possessing monopsony power in the labor market (which makes the marginal labor cost exceed any wage the firm

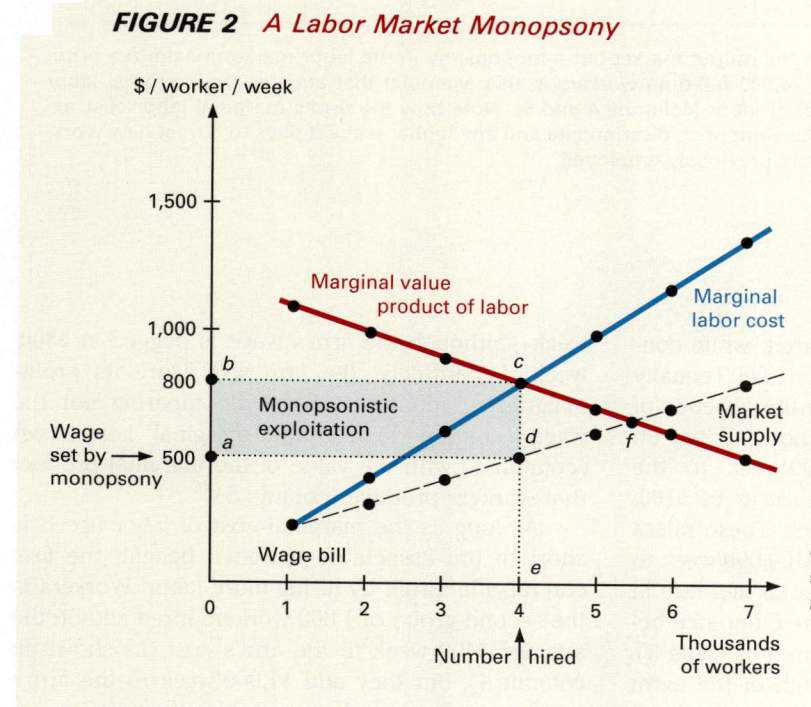

FIGURE 2 A Labor Market Monopsony

Just as the line of marginal revenue lies below the demand line for a monopoly in the goods market, so the line of marginal labor cost lies above the supply line for a monopsony in the labor market. In this example, the firm maximizes profit by equating at point c labor's marginal value product with the marginal labor cost. In order to get the 4,000 workers this choice implies, the firm sets a wage of $500/week (point d). Accordingly, labor's wage falls short of its marginal value product (by cd). Whenever such a divergence is caused by the employer's monopsony power in the labor market (which causes the marginal labor cost to exceed the wage), labor is said to face *monopsonistic exploitation*.

sets), economists talk of **monopsonistic exploitation** of labor.

The extent of labor's monopsonistic exploitation is shown by the shaded area in our graph and equals $300/week (*cd*) times 4,000 workers, or $1,200,000/week.

FOCUS 2

Monopsonistic Exploitation of Labor

A situation in which $W < MVP_L$ because

1. $MLC > W$ and
2. a monopsony in the labor market that is a perfect competitor in the output market maximizes profit by hiring a labor quantity such that

$$MVP_L = MLC$$

CAUTION

In the examples discussed so far, all workers receive the same wage. Although it is true that the last workers hired do not receive wages equal to the value of their marginal product, the difference is paid as raises to fellow workers who were previously employed. So who is "exploiting" whom? Some monopsonies, however, discriminate among different workers with respect to the wages they pay; in that case, the story is an entirely different one. (See Example 1.)

Cartels in the Labor Market: The Emergence of Labor Unions

As we have seen in the chapter "Monopoly and Cartels," the sellers of goods can possibly improve their lot by forming a cartel, restricting supply, and raising the price of whatever they are trying to sell. As we also saw, any attempt to do so is likely to encounter a variety of obstacles, ranging from organizational difficulties to the influx of outside suppliers and cheating by insiders. In the absence of government help, cartels among sellers of goods (in particular, among *numerous* sellers of goods) are unlikely to succeed in the long run. Almost the same thing holds with respect to sellers of resource services.

Consider the associations of wage earners known as *labor unions*. Although such unions serve a variety of functions, one of them is the control of labor supply and the establishment of a jointly negotiated minimum wage. Nowadays in the United States, we take the existence of labor unions for granted, but their relative success (16 percent of the labor force are union members) is in large part due to governmental protection. It wasn't always so, as the next section illustrates.

Difficulties Illustrated

Picture yourself in a different world, a hundred years ago. Imagine that all the electricians in a city got together (which in itself is a difficult task) and agreed to demand double the hourly wages for half the hours worked. Without government help, how could they enforce such a demand? The electricians could threaten employers with work slowdowns or even **strikes,** concerted refusals to work. They could set up a **picket line,** a line of striking workers parading around the work site, encouraging other workers (such as bricklayers, carpenters, or teamsters) not to cross the line. They could even institute a **labor boycott,** an organized attempt to persuade their employers' customers not to buy products of the firms until the labor dispute has been settled. But what if employers turned the tables on the workers with a **lockout,** a refusal to let workers work until the labor dispute has been settled? If employers called the workers' bluff and locked them out of their plants until a lack of income brought them back to work, the entire unionization effort could come to a halt.

Even if employers met union demands and paid the same amount of money for half the hours worked, how could the union keep any one electrician from trying to work, at the new wage of, say, $16 per hour, *twice* the allowable time? And if one tried it, how could it keep all the workers from trying it at the same time? Such an attempt would give employers the power to nudge the wage down to $14 and $13 and finally to $8 per hour where it was before.

EXAMPLE 1

A Case Study in Monopsony: The Baseball Players' Market

Baseball was the first sport to be organized professionally in the United States. From the very beginning, team owners recognized that competition for talented players would drive up their salaries; from the owners' point of view, such competition was to be avoided.

The Reserve Clause Before long, a scheme developed. A player who wanted to play professional baseball with a major league team could get a first contract only by signing a **reserve clause,** giving all rights to his future services to the original team's owners. No other team would touch the player thus "reserved" by the team that had first signed him on.

In future years, the owners of the team could dispose of the player's services in any way they saw fit. They could keep the player on (and either raise his salary, keep it unchanged, or even cut it by a prearranged maximum percentage each season). They could sell the contract to another team (and then the player had to report to the new owners within three days or never play again). They could terminate the contract (in which case, each team in the league, in inverse order of season standings, could purchase the contract; and the player was then bound to that team in the same way as to the original team). Naturally, this arrangement gave power to team owners to keep player salaries down. The typical player faced a pure monopsony. He could play for the current owners of his contract at whatever salary they offered or he could play not at all.

The Age of Free Agency The reserve clause was challenged repeatedly, but without success. Before World War I, the Federal League tried to become a third major league but could not get players. It went to court and lost. So did the Mexican League in the 1940s. Individual players did not fare any better. Curt Flood, star outfielder for the St. Louis Cardinals, didn't like being traded to Philadelphia. His case challenging the reserve clause went all the way to the U.S. Supreme Court, but he lost and gave up baseball. Then, in 1975, pitchers Andy Messersmith, Dave McNally, and Jim "Catfish" Hunter all managed to have their contracts invalidated and became free agents. Before long, more than 100 players changed uniforms and salaries (which had averaged $28,000 in 1970) rose at a dizzying rate. Jim Hunter landed a 5-year $3.5 million contract with the New York Yankees. Pete Rose left the Cincinnati Reds to get $800,000 a year with the Philadelphia Phillies. By 1982, some 13 players got over $1 million a year each; Montreal's Gary Carter and the New York Mets' George Foster earned what was then the most ($2 million a year). The average player's salary rose from $44,700 in 1975 to $146,500 in 1980 and to $580,000 in 1990. By then, 220 players earned over $1 million; 10 of them over $3.5 million. Darryl Strawberry's contract with the Los Angeles Dodgers called for $3.8 million in each of 5 years.

A single player may well be worth this much to a team. If a player could draw even 10 percent more fans for home games (and many could), some 250,000 extra tickets might be sold in a season. At $4 per ticket, this increase would bring in an extra $1 million. In addition, a team would get 40 percent of extra gate receipts from games on the road and above all, high broadcast fees. In 1989, CBS signed a 4-year contract with Major League Baseball to broadcast 16 regular-season games, the All-Star Game, and all post-season games. The price tag was $1.06 billion. In addition, teams get other fees from local contracts. The Yankees have a 12-year, $500 million deal with the Madison Square Garden cable network.

Measuring Monopsonistic Exploitation One economist recently measured the extent of monopsonistic exploitation of baseball players in 1968–1969, while the reserve clause was in effect. Selected results of this study are reproduced in Table A. For different types of players (columns 1 and 2), each player's contribution to the team's gross revenue was estimated (column 3) from added gate receipts, broadcast fees, etc. Subtracting added costs, such as training, transportation, nonplayer salaries, equipment and sales expenses, and the like, net marginal revenue product was figured (column 4). As a comparison of columns (4) and (5) indicates, average and star players received as salaries considerably less than their contributions to their teams' net revenue.

Recent Developments Team owners seem to have struck back recently. A 1987 arbitrator's ruling held that team owners had once again colluded. The evidence: In 1985, some 62 free agents received a total of 5 bids. In 1987, there were no bids at all. Because of this fact, some key players (Doyle Alexander, Bob Boone, Andre Dawson, Rich Gedman, Ron Guidry, Bob Horner, Lance Parrish, and Tim Raines) were dubbed the "untouchable eight."

Sources: Simon Rottenberg, "The Baseball Players' Labor Market," *Journal of Political Economy,* June 1956, pp. 242–258; Gerald W. Scully, "Pay and Performance in Major League Baseball," *The American Economic Review,* December 1974, pp. 915–930; Jeremy Gerard, "NBC to Pay N.B.A. $600 million for TV Rights," *The New York Times,* November 10, 1989, pp. D17 and D20; Timothy Tregarthen, "Are Professional Athletes Worth the Price?" *The Margin,* November 1988, pp. 6–8; and Norm Alster, "Major League Socialism," *Forbes,* May 27, 1991, pp. 138–146.

TABLE A

Type of player (1)	Career performance (2)	Marginal revenue product		Salary (5)
		Gross (3)	Net (4)	
	Lifetime Slugging Average			
Mediocre hitters	255	$121,200	$−39,100	$ 9,700
	283	135,000	−25,300	20,000
Average hitters	338	256,600	128,300	29,100
	375	285,100	156,800	39,000
Star hitters	427	405,800	290,500	42,200
	525	499,000	383,700	68,000
	Lifetime Strikeout-to-Walk Ratio			
Mediocre pitchers	1.50	139,500	−20,800	9,000
	1.66	154,300	−6,000	18,100
Average pitchers	2.07	269,600	141,300	23,300
	2.46	316,000	187,700	43,700
Star pitchers	2.79	464,900	349,600	47,200
	3.54	595,000	479,700	86,300

SOURCE: Adapted from Gerald W. Scully, "Pay and Performance in Major League Baseball," *American Economic Review,* December 1974, pp. 915–930.

Even if members were loyal to each other and did not cheat, how could the union prevent the electricians of other cities from appearing on the scene and offering to work for $8? How could it keep employers from then firing union workers and hiring those others? Or how could it prevent the employers from moving to other cities?

Workers could form a national union involving hundreds of thousands of workers. But other regional unions might already exist and have no desire to join the national group. The presence of other unions might lead to a series of **jurisdictional strikes** wherein workers belonging to one union, in an attempt to force the recognition of a single union, walk off the job to interrupt the work being done by fellow workers belonging to another union.

Even if all workers joined a single union, and even if cheaters were still absent among the larger number of workers in this national union (a highly improbable case), what would prevent foreign electricians from immigrating and working for $8? Or what would prevent employers from shifting electrical work to foreign subsidiaries? An international union? Even that would not assure success. New technical-school graduates may appear on the scene, and *they* may offer to work for $8. Or employers may come up with a labor-replacing device that can do the work of people and can do it for $8. Or firms may decide to produce different products that involve no electricians at all.

For all these reasons, the success of unions is always elusive. They must constantly worry about their "security," which is where government enters. In the early days, government did not help, as a look at the history of U.S. unionism shows.

The Early Unions

Labor unions have existed in the United States almost since the days of independence. In Boston, New York, and Philadelphia, carpenters, shoemakers, and printers banded together as early as 1791. These organizations of workers, however, were weak and short-lived. Not only did they face the militant opposition of employers, but there were also legal impediments. The first U.S. labor unions (as in England, France, and Germany), faced the **conspiracy doctrine,** according to which courts looked upon unionized workers who "conspired" to raise wages and were, thus, "interfering with freedom of contract" as common criminals. It was only in 1842 that the Massachusetts Supreme Court established the legality of unions as such. Still, many of their actions continued to be held illegal, and unions had no general impact for many decades thereafter.

The Labor Movement Comes to Stay

The Knights of Labor, founded in 1869, was the first national union of importance, but it vanished after reaching its peak of influence in 1886. In that same year, the American Federation of Labor (AFL) was founded. As the unions of a century earlier, those belonging to this federation were **craft unions,** or unions of workers, such as carpenters, electricians, or plumbers, who shared a common set of skills but did not necessarily work for the same employer.

Under the leadership of Samuel Gompers, craft unions developed a practical-minded philosophy. Unlike the Knights of Labor, who had called for the establishment of a "cooperative, noncapitalist order," the AFL had no aspirations to revolutionize society. It was concerned with bread and butter for its members as long as it was *more* and *now* (See Ideas in History, Bread-and-Butter Unionism.)

Membership in the AFL and other unions grew to almost a million by 1900 (3.3 percent of the labor force) and to 5 million by 1920 (11.7 percent of the labor force). It then declined until, in the 1930s, government intervened. Public opinion blamed big business for the Great Depression and began to favor the self-protection of workers via unions and the creation of "countervailing power" in labor unions. This sentiment was reflected in legislation helpful to union organization.

Helpful Laws

The Norris-La Guardia Act of 1932 (which was validated by the U.S. Supreme Court in 1938) took a first and giant step toward protecting labor unions. It exempted unions from the antitrust laws, one of which stated that "every contract . . . or conspiracy in restraint of trade . . . is hereby declared illegal" (Sherman Act, 1890). The 1932 act also outlawed one of the most powerful weapons of employers: the use against unions of the **injunction,** a court decree, enforceable by arrest and jail, forbidding certain actions. Although unions as such had been legalized in 1842, many of their actions could still be blocked. Employers found it easy to obtain injunctions against strikes, peaceful picketing, and even membership drives. Such injunctions, once obtained, automatically made a union a wrongdoer in the eyes of the law if it persisted in actions that were vital to its functioning.

President Roosevelt's New Deal quickly broadened the freedoms granted to labor. The National Labor Relations Act (Wagner Act) of 1935 affirmed the right of unions to organize and to bargain collectively. It made collective bargaining contracts legally enforceable. (Such **collective bargaining contracts** between labor unions and employers specify compensation, hours worked, and numerous other conditions of employment for a specified term.) The Wagner Act went even further. First, it guaranteed unions recognition by employers by *ordering* employers to bargain with the duly elected representatives of their workers if a majority of them wanted to bargain collectively. Second, the law outlawed a number of **antiunion practices,** such as firing workers for joining a labor union, refusing to hire them if sympathetic to unions, threatening to close the firm if workers join a union, interfering with or dominating the administration of a union, and refusing to bargain with a union.

A Change in Strategy

As government threw its support to labor, the labor movement itself underwent a significant change. Some labor leaders abandoned the principle that union membership be limited to specific skills. Instead, workers were to be organized in **industrial unions** that collected all workers of a given industry in a single organization without regard to particular skills. As a result, millions in the mass production industries (autos, electrical products, steel) qualified for membership in the new Congress of Industrial Organizations (CIO). Under the leadership of John L. Lewis in the 1930s, the CIO engaged in massive organization drives. Often there was violence. In famous sitdown strikes, the new unions seized the auto plants. These were the days when Walter Reuther, the auto union leader, was beaten by the hired strongmen of the Ford Motor Company. One by one, the industrial giants—Ford, General Motors, U.S. Steel—succumbed, recognizing a CIO union as their workers' bargaining agent. Union membership soared from below 4 million in 1930 (7.5 percent of the labor force) to over 14 million in 1948 (23.5 percent of the labor force).

Anti-Union Laws

By the end of World War II, the now giant unions learned to use their strength. Some tried to keep out competing workers by restricting union membership to a few (charging high initiation fees, administering impossible entrance tests, or simply denying access to women, blacks, Jews, or any other easily identifiable group). Others forced employers to establish a **closed shop** (in which only union members are hired) or to set up a **union shop** (in which all employees, within a short time after hiring, have to become union members or at least pay union dues as a condition of continued employment). Others still discouraged labor-saving technical changes by forcing employers to continue paying workers even when their work was being done or could have been done by machines. (Thus musicians forced broadcasters to employ "standby orchestras" while records were being played; painters restricted the width of paint brushes so jobs took longer to complete; and firemen who used to stoke steam boilers forced railroads to keep them on, riding diesel locomotives that did not have steam boilers. Such workers who did not work or did unnecessary work might as well have taken along a featherbed and slept on the job, which is why this practice is called **featherbedding**.) Unions also organized paralyzing strikes in steel, coal, and shipping, along with jurisdictional strikes resulting from two unions fighting each over the same group of workers. (Should an electrician working for U.S. Steel be a member of the AFL Electrical Workers' Union or of the CIO Steelworkers' Union?)

The public became alarmed and Congress responded. Labor, it was argued, had been given an overdose of power. To counter it, Congress passed the Taft-Hartley Act of 1947. The new act outlawed the closed shop (but not the union shop). In so doing, Congress favored the view of employers that a fundamental principle of freedom was violated if people were forced to join an organization; that employers, found it difficult to hire the best workers

FIGURE 3 Union Membership in the United States

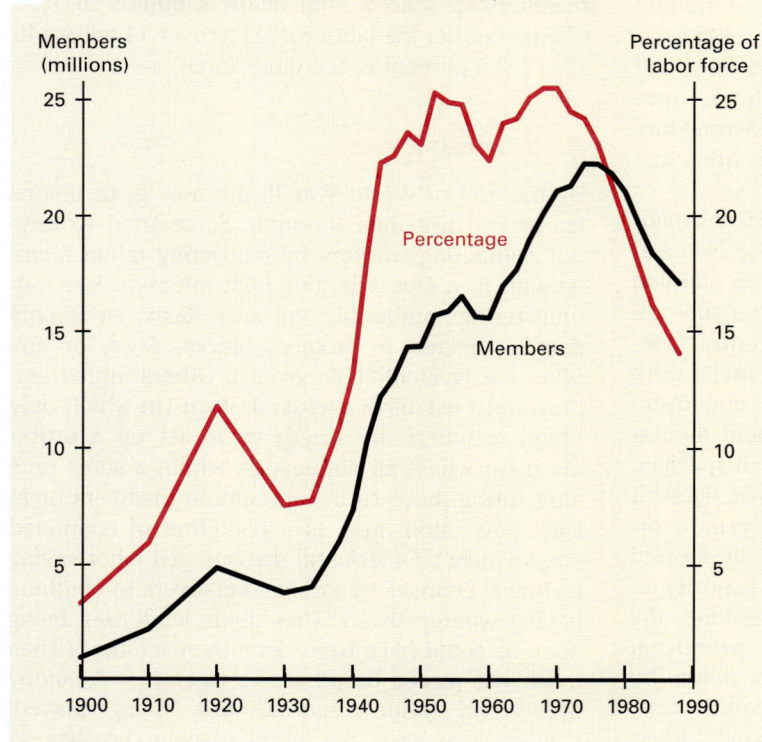

Measured as a percentage of the labor force, the explosive growth of U.S. labor union membership between 1930 and 1950 has been followed by two decades of stagnation, then decline. Thus, in 1990, the percentage of the labor force that was unionized was the same as 50 years ago. In other countries where labor unions tend to be closely allied with certain political parties, union membership is considerably more significant: recently, it equaled 53 percent of the labor force in Great Britain and 95 percent of the labor force in Sweden.

SOURCE: Data from Leo Troy and Neil Sheflin, *Union Sourcebook* (West Orange, NJ: Industrial Relations Data and Information Services, 1985), Table 3.41; and *Statistical Abstract of the United States: 1990*, pp. 378 and 419.

for a job (because they were restricted to taking those whom the union admitted to its membership); and that union leaders, having an assured membership, were likely to become irresponsible and dishonest. Many states have since passed so-called **right-to-work laws,** outlawing the union shop also.

The new act also banned **unfair union practices,** including refusal of a union to bargain with an employer, featherbedding, striking without 60 days' notice, and striking to force the recognition of one union where another has already been certified. In addition, unions were required not to charge excessive initiation fees, to make financial reports to their members, disclose their officers' salaries, and refrain from using dues for political contributions. The act also empowered employers to sue unions for breach of contract and to engage (without coercion) in anti-union activities. Finally, it allowed the president to ask for eighty–day court suspensions of strikes or lockouts that "imperil the national health and safety."

In 1959, the Landrum-Griffin Act was passed against a background of hearings by the McClellan committee into labor racketeering. It had exposed "gangsterism, bribery, and hoodlumism" in the affairs of some unions. Some union leaders had taken union funds for personal use, had taken payoffs from employers for union protection, and were involved in blackmail, arson, and murder. In answer to such labor racketeers who fattened themselves by extortion from both workers and employers, the act put still more curbs on union power. It was particularly concerned with the misuse of union funds. Members of unions were also guaranteed the right to vote in secret. The list of unfair union practices was lengthened.

For two decades since the Taft-Hartley Act, and despite a friendly merger of the AFL and CIO unions in 1955, union membership as a percentage of the labor force failed to grow; thereafter, it declined as indicated in Figure 3. The decline has been attributed to numerous factors, including the following:

EXAMPLE 2

Keeping Unions Out

In 1990, Mike Johnson, a skilled worker at the nonunion Borg-Warner automotive plant in Frankfort, Illinois, had a problem with his boss. He had been bypassed for an overtime repair job that he had done before and that he wanted badly. Rather than stew about it, as nonunion workers might, he took his supervisor to court—company court. This option is now open to ever more workers in nonunion firms and operates like a union grievance procedure. In Mike Johnson's case, three fellow workers, another supervisor, and the plant manager listened to both sides of the story, then awarded him $210 in extra pay—the amount he would have gotten from the extra work.

At least a third of nonunion firms have adopted similar procedures, including well-known corporations such as Bank of America, Federal Express, IBM, John Hancock, NBC, Polaroid, and TWA. They have introduced generous fringe benefits as well, ranging from health and life insurance plans to stock options and profit-sharing. These steps are designed to persuade workers that unions are not needed to defend their interests and that the only sure way of raising the welfare of workers is raising productivity and company profits along with worker benefits.

Many firms point to the experience of the U.S. auto industry. In the 1980s, the labor productivity of nonunionized Japanese plants in the United States was consistently higher than that of the unionized "Big Three"—General Motors, Ford, and Chrysler. In 1989, it took an average 5 workdays to make a GM car; it took 4.4 at Chrysler, 3.4 at Ford, and fewer than 3 in Japanese plants. During the 1980s, employment in the Big Three auto plants dropped (from 618,000 to 405,000 workers at GM alone) and the United Auto Workers Union lost a third of its membership (some 500,000 workers). At the same time, employment at Japanese-owned U.S. auto plants soared as lower production costs got translated into lower prices and higher sales for comparable cars. By the year 2000, some industry analysts predict, the names of the "Big Three" will be Toyota, Nissan, and Honda.

Sources: "Losing Control," *The Wall Street Journal,* February 16, 1990, pp. 1 and 5; and Ted Rohrlich, "Settling the Score In-House," *Los Angeles Times,* November 28, 1990, pp. 1 and 15.

---

1. A relative decline of employment in industries (manufacturing, mining) and regions (East, Midwest) traditionally unionized in favor of industries (trade, services) and regions (South, Southwest) traditionally not unionized

2. Stronger competition in goods markets from foreign firms and new domestic firms in deregulated industries, which has forced employers to go bankrupt or resist union demands (e.g., by substituting capital for labor, relocating geographically, or challenging union certifications)

3. A decline in worker "taste" for unions because they believe that desired benefits can be reached through voluntary employer action (fringe benefits, promotion and dismissal rules, etc.) or social legislation (on pension plans, health and safety, etc.)

Example 2 has more to say on the matter. Having reviewed labor union history, we now turn to an analysis of their behavior in labor markets.

Labor Union Versus Competitive Buyers of Labor

Let us first consider what would happen if a labor union were formed in a situation (Case E of Table 1) in which perfect competition had previously existed in all goods and resource markets. The demand and supply lines of Figure 4 might depict the original circumstances with an equilibrium at intersection *i*. The wage rate equals $10/hour and 133.33 million labor hours are bought and sold each day. Although unions pursue many goals (better working conditions, clear-cut grievance procedures, health and life insurance, pension plans, paid vacations, and more), let us focus on the money wage. Presumably, a union facing the demand line shown in our graph (which under the assumed competitive conditions reflects labor's marginal value product, MVP_L) would want to raise the wage above the $10/hour competitive level corresponding to point *i*. Along section *ia* of that demand line, the union faces a variety of possible choices; all of them involve a trade-off between higher wages and reduced employment opportunities of workers (a reflection of the law of downward-sloping demand).

Possible Union Goals

Among the more interesting choices that a union might make are those depicted by points *f* and *c*.

Maximizing Total Wage Income

The wage/employment combination corresponding to *f* (which lies at the midpoint of the labor demand line and, therefore, corresponds to a price elasticity of demand equal to absolute 1) would maximize the total income of the workers (at a level of $1,500 million/day, equal to rectangle 0*efo*). This choice would raise the workers' wage to $15/hour but reduce their employment to 100 million hours/day. At the same time, a surplus of *fg* would appear in the market, with which the union would somehow have to deal.

Maximizing Economic Rent

The wage/employment combination corresponding to *c* would maximize the workers' **economic rent,** the excess of workers' actual income (area 0*bcn*) over the minimum income necessary to bring forth the quantity being supplied (area 0*kmn*), which, presumably, is equal to the maximum value of alternative uses of the workers' time.

In the absence of a union, someone would have supplied a first labor hour for as little as 0*k* (because no better alternative existed), while additional hours would have been supplied for ever-increasing wages measured along supply-line segment *km*. A 76.67 millionth hour would have been supplied by someone for as little as *mn*. Thus, the area 0*kmn* measures the workers' next best alternatives and thus the absolute minimum amount for which 76.67 million hours of labor would have been supplied. The shaded excess of actual income over this minimum income necessary to bring forth the quantity being supplied is equivalent to the concept of *producers' surplus*—the producers in this case being the workers who supply labor rather than firms that supply goods. The maximum economic rent is found by the associated workers by viewing their market like a monopoly that faces the labor demand line and seeks to maximize profit. The monopoly labor union equates the implied marginal revenue from selling labor with the marginal opportunity cost of supplying labor at point *m*, which suggests an ideal labor "output" level of *n* and a price of *c*.

Possible Strategies

Given its wage/employment goal, a union can pursue various strategies. Let us consider the two most obvious ones.

Fixing the Wage

A union of workers can simply announce its chosen wage ($15 or $18.50 per hour) and threaten to strike unless precisely that wage is paid. Employers who do not want a strike can accept the union wage as a given and profit-maximize by hiring *ef* = 100 or *bc* = 76.67 million labor hours per day, respectively. In this scenario, the union lets employers ration jobs among would-be workers and determine who is or is not employed.

The unemployed (*fg* or *cd*, respectively) might be left to fend for themselves, possibly entering other labor markets and depressing wages there. As an alternative, the union could support government programs of unemployment benefits or welfare assistance for the unemployed, which would shift the burden not to workers in other markets but to taxpayers in general. Such an approach is equivalent to subsidizing farmers for *not* producing crops "supported" by above-equilibrium minimum prices set by the government.

FIGURE 4 Labor Union Versus Competitive Buyers of Labor

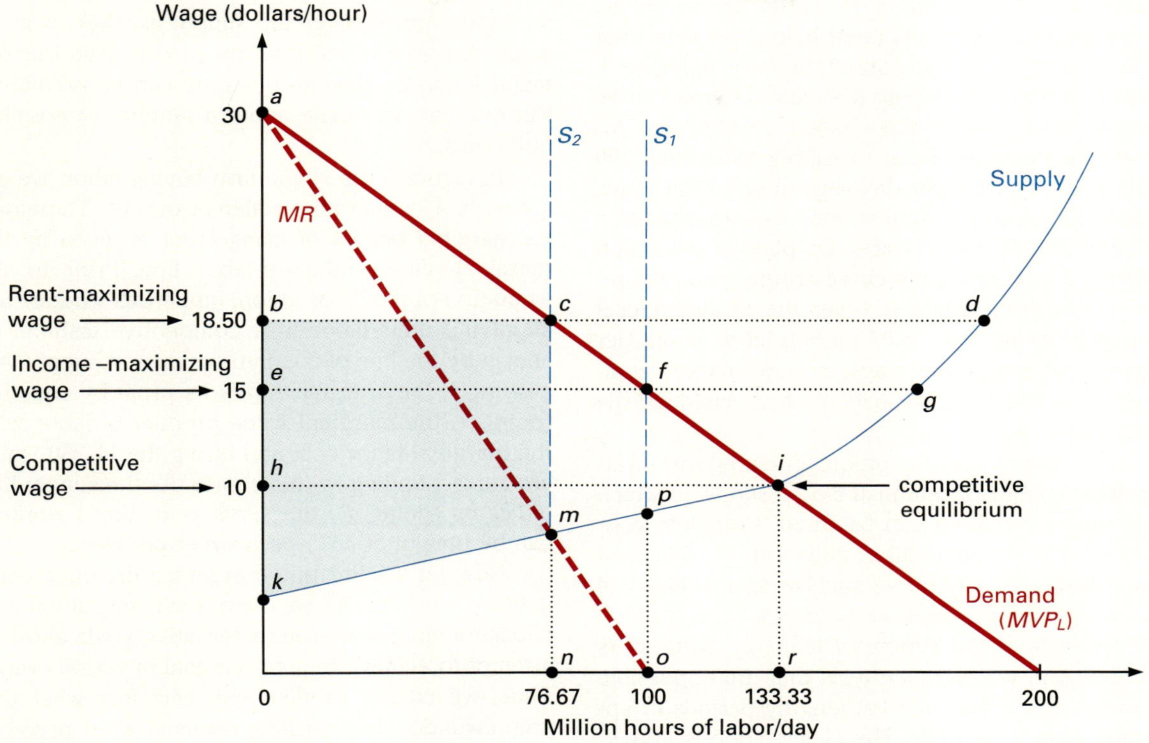

A labor union formed in a previously competitive market is likely to push the wage above the competitive equilibrium level (here $10/hour, corresponding to point i). Many wage/employment combinations are available to the union along demand line segment ai. Combination f would maximize the worker's total income (as area Oefo). Combination c would maximize their economic rent (as in shaded area kbcm).

Another possibility yet involves policies designed to increase the demand for labor until the demand line in our example passes through point g or d, respectively. Thus, some unions have introduced featherbedding practices, forcing employers to use more workers than are necessary. For example, printers have insisted on setting "dummy type" for advertising copy, which newspapers do not need when advertisers submit ready-to-print copy. Electricians have insisted on tearing apart and rewiring prewired equipment. Airline pilots have insisted on a third licensed pilot in the cockpit where a flight engineer would suffice. In addition, unions have supported programs of public-service jobs through which the government buys surplus labor in the same way that it buys surplus agricultural crops. Unions have, similarly, supported policies that raise the private demand for labor by raising the demand for certain goods. Laws can *mandate* private consumer purchases regardless of whether consumers wish to buy the goods (aircraft emergency locator transmitters, automobile safety belts, household fire alarms). Consider the governmental tariffs and quotas that restrict imports or the union-instigated "Buy American" or "Watch for the Union Label" campaigns.

Fixing the Quantity of Labor Supplied

As an alternative to fixing a chosen wage above the competitive equilibrium level, unions can simply fix the quantity of labor supplied below the level that competition would bring about. In terms of Figure 4, picture a union twisting the labor supply curve around point p into the dashed vertical line S_1. Given the implied refusal to supply more than 100 million labor hours per day regardless of the wage, a new market equilibrium would be established at f, yielding the \$15/hour wage. Or picture the union twisting the labor supply curve around point m into the dashed vertical line S_2. Given the implied refusal to supply more than 76.67 million labor hours per day regardless of the wage, a new market equilibrium would be established at c, yielding the \$18.50/hour wage.

It is easy to see why unions pursuing this strategy have sought to establish *closed shops,* in which only union members can be hired. Complete control over the supply of labor goes to the union (and lets it turn a supply curve such as *kpd* in Figure 4 into a vertical line such as S_1 or S_2). Such a union can easily limit the supply of labor by limiting its membership, via entrance tests that are impossible to pass, high initiation fees, lengthy periods of apprenticeship, and more. The closed shop is now illegal, but numerous other devices can restrict the supply of labor. Ask yourself why unions have been supporters of laws setting maximum hours, limiting immigration, "protecting" women. The latter type of laws, voided by the U.S. Supreme Court in 1971, barred women from jobs requiring the lifting of weights in excess of 25 pounds (but they were free to lift heavier children at home); they also barred them from "dangerous" occupations, including bartending, bellhopping, border patrol, coal mining, criminal investigating, meter reading, pinsetting, shoe shining, and truck driving.

Labor Union Versus Labor Monopsony

A labor union can also be in a situation (Case G of Table 1) in which a monopsony dominates the labor market. Whenever a monopoly seller thus confronts a monopsony buyer, the market configuration is called a **bilateral monopoly**. (This use of the term is regrettable because *monopoly* means "single seller," but the situation does *not* involve the confrontation of two single sellers but of a single seller with a single buyer.) When a labor union thus has monopoly power over the supply of labor, while a single buyer has monopsony power over the demand for it, no definite outcome can be predicted. But one can speculate about a number of possible outcomes.

In Figure 5 the single firm buying labor, we assume, is a competitive seller of output. Therefore, its marginal benefit of using labor is given by the marginal-value-product-of-labor line. Prior to the formation of the labor union, numerous workers are supplying their labor in a competitive fashion, as shown by the line of competitive market supply. Accordingly, the firm maximizes its profit by equating (point b) the marginal value product of labor with the marginal labor cost and hiring the 11,250 workers corresponding to this choice. As the supply line indicates (point d), the services of these workers can be bought at \$325 per worker per week.

Now let a labor union organize the once competitive workers. As we have seen, the union can choose among numerous alternative goals and can attempt to achieve the chosen goal in various ways. Thus, we cannot predict with certainty what this union will do. Nevertheless, consider a few possibilities.

If the union acted like a true monopoly to maximize the workers' economic rent, it would treat the firm's marginal-value-product-of-labor line like a demand line for labor, derive the implied line of marginal revenue, and equate (point e) this marginal revenue from selling labor with the marginal opportunity cost of supplying it. Accordingly, it would supply 9,000 workers at a price of \$640 per worker per week (point a). Compared to the monopsony's choice, the union would want to supply fewer workers and do so at a higher wage. The actual outcome would be left to the bargaining process.

Other possibilities, however, exist. If the unionized workers simply insisted on a minimum weekly wage of \$400 per worker (and the monopsony agreed), the outcome corresponding to point c would emerge. Compared to the monopsonistic choice at d, there would be a higher wage and higher employment as well. If the unionized workers instead insisted on a minimum weekly wage of

FIGURE 5 Labor Union Versus Labor Monopsony

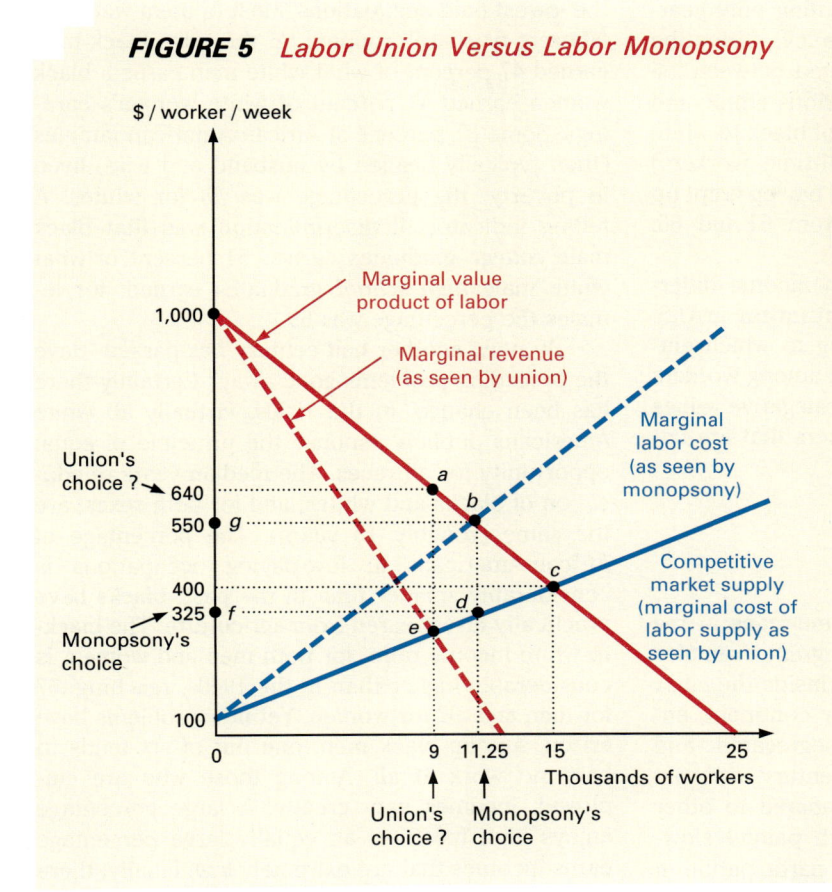

If a labor union is formed to face a monopsony, the precise outcome is impossible to predict. Depending on the parties' bargaining skills and the union's goals, the monopsonistic choice (point d) might be maintained or replaced by various other wage/employment combinations, including a, b, or c.

$550 per worker (and the monopsony agreed), the outcome corresponding to point b would emerge. Compared to the monopsonistic choice at d, there would be a higher wage and the same employment level. Other outcomes such as choice a are possible as well.

Discrimination in the Labor Market

Earlier in this chapter, we noted that labor markets can be imperfect for many reasons, not merely because the number of independently acting buyers or sellers fails to be large. We now consider what happens when buyers of labor fail to view identical workers as identical, when full knowledge relevant to trading is absent, or when impediments to entry into or exit from the labor market exist.

Consider the following Biblical passage:

And the Lord spake unto Moses, saying, Speak unto the children of Israel and say unto them, When a man shall make a singular vow, the persons shall be for the Lord by thy estimation. And thy estimation shall be of the male from twenty years old even unto sixty years old, even thy estimation shall be fifty shekels of silver, after the shekel of the sanctuary. And if it be a female then thy estimation shall be thirty shekels. (Leviticus 27:1–4)

The statement puts the worth of a woman at 60 percent of that of a man, and it is positively prophetic. In the United States, for instance, the 1986 ratio of female to male wage income (counting only year-round, full-time white workers) was .64; during the preceding three decades, it fluctuated between .56 and .65. The story is similar for various ethnic and racial minorities. In 1986, the ratio of black to white income (again for year-round, full-time workers) equaled .70 for men, .89 for women, having crept up over the preceding three decades from .61 and .66, respectively.

Many observers attribute such income differences to a long history of **discrimination** in U.S. labor markets, a practice according to which employers make irrelevant distinctions among workers and systematically place positive or negative values on personal characteristics of workers that are unrelated to their productivity.

The Labor Market Status of Black Americans

The economic history of African-Americans in the United States provides the most flagrant examples of discrimination, both outside and inside the labor market.[1] Brought by force to a new continent, enslaved, freed, denied education, segregated, and suppressed, they entered the 20th century with vast deficits of resource ownership compared to other races. True enough, gradually, with painful slowness, they have legally attained full participation in American life: schooling, skilled jobs, political and civil rights.

Although slavery ended in the 1860s, for close to another century the majority of whites openly advocated discrimination against blacks with respect to schooling, employment, and more. "Whites first" was a common slogan. Even in 1945, the median education level of black males and females was 5.4 and 6.2 years, respectively (half had more, half had less), while the corresponding numbers for white males and females were 8.7 and 8.8 years. Also in the 1940s, blacks were invariably found in the lowest paid occupations. Most of them were day laborers or share croppers. At the time, black men earned 47 percent of what white men earned; black women earned 41 percent of white women's earnings. Some 81 percent of African-American families (then typically headed by husband and wife) lived in poverty; the percentage was 48 for whites. A telling indicator of discrimination was that black male *college* graduates earned 51 percent of what white male *high school* graduates earned; for females the percentage was 59.

By now, another half century has passed. Have the preceding problems gone away? Certainly there has been change. In the 1990s, virtually all white Americans publicly espouse the principle of equal opportunity for all races. The median years of education of blacks and whites, and for both sexes, are the same (roughly 13 years). The percentage of African-Americans in low-paying occupations is considerably smaller than in the past; blacks have practically disappeared from agriculture. The black-to-white income ratio, for both men and women, is considerably higher than in the 1940s, reaching .67 for men and .97 for women. Yet new problems have arisen. Among black men, one out of six tends to have no work at all. Among those who are employed, incomes vary greatly. A large percentage enjoys high incomes; an equally large percentage earns incomes that are extremely low. Finally, there has been a notable change in the black family. More often than not, it is headed by a woman only, and about a third of such families live in poverty.

To understand these trends and to help shape policies that can alleviate the long-run consequences of slavery, economists study the nature of labor market discrimination in detail.

Two Types of Discrimination

Labor market discrimination with respect to race, sex, or any other criterion comes in two forms. It can involve the indulgence of "malevolent tastes" or the exercise of "statistical prejudgment."

Malevolent Tastes

Employers may simply indulge their own "malevolent tastes" or they may accommodate those of customers and other employees who do not want to interact with women, blacks, Jewish people, or an-

---

[1] The following discussion is based in part on the most recent review of that history: Henry J. Aaron, "Symposium on the Economic Status of African-Americans," *Journal of Economic Perspectives,* Fall 1990, pp. 3–7; and Gerald D. Jaynes, "The Labor Market Status of Black Americans: 1939–1985," *ibid.,* pp. 9–24.

other specific group. As a result, employers may put men on the high-paid assembly line and women in the lower-paid typing pool. They may let male pilots fly the passengers, while letting female pilots fly the freight. They may let women sell the residential real estate and men the more lucrative commercial pieces. They may turn pretty white women into TV announcers, but let pretty black women handle the telephone switchboard. As a result of such inexplicable "tastes," workers who differ from one another in no relevant fashion may find themselves segregated into separate labor markets and earning different wages for identical work. Figure 6 illustrates what is involved. Panel (a) depicts a nondiscriminatory labor market for jet pilots of whom, we assume, half are men and half women. According to the equilibrium shown, 14,000 pilots are hired and each paid $60,000 a year. Let the market be split artificially in two. Major airlines (that specialize in carrying passengers and demand 75 percent of the pilots) will hire male pilots only. Other operators (that specialize in carrying freight and demand 25 percent of the pilots) will hire female pilots only. Mobility between the two market fragments is completely restricted. Half the pilots supply their services in the female market, S_F; the other half in the male market, S_M. As panels (b) and (c) indicate, women end up with a $42,000 salary per year, men with $72,000 per year. The female to male income ratio is .58.

In a perfectly competitive labor market, this result could not persist because all units traded would be seen as identical by their buyers. In our example, well-informed and mobile woman pilots would quickly bid for the (here) male-only jobs, lowering the supply in market (b) and raising it in market (c). Or profit-maximizing firms would leave market (c), lowering its demand, and enter market (b), raising its demand. (By substituting expensive men for equally qualified and cheaper women, profits would be raised.) Either way, the wage in market (b) would rise, that in market (c) would fall until workers with equal skill got equal pay.

In real-world labor markets, malevolent tastes of employers that split labor markets have often been camouflaged with "good" reasons. Some employers have blamed their customers. Retail store owners have argued that they would lose all their white customers were they to employ black salespeople. Airline companies have argued that no one would fly with them were they to use *female* captains and *male* stewards. Television stations have argued that only *youthful* announcers attract a large audience. Owners of snack bars have claimed their business would collapse unless *teenage girls* tended to it.

Employers have also blamed their workers or the unions to which they belong. Contractors have argued that their white employees would walk off the job were they asked to word side by side with blacks or that men would rather quit than take orders from a woman. Others have cited collective bargaining contracts to hire union members only, but (alas) certain groups of people may not be members of this union. Unions, in turn, have kept certain groups of people out of their ranks by charging high initiation fees that members of such groups cannot pay or by administering entrance tests they are likely to fail. In 1971, the steamfitters union required applicants for its apprenticeship program to relate (among other things) Shakespeare with *Othello,* Dante with *Inferno,* Dali with painting, and Walt Whitman with poetry, and also to explain *modiste, debutante, myth,* and *verity.* Since the test was based on white middle-class education and experience, fewer than 20 percent of whites but 67 percent of nonwhites failed it.

Employers have also cited placement tests of their own as reasons for not hiring or promoting. Yet some of these tests are hardly objective or indeed relevant for the job. A test used in 1971 to promote common laborers to coal miners required an explanation of B.C., *adept,* and *adopt.*

Statistical Prejudgment

Another reason besides pure malevolence may prompt employers to discriminate against some people in favor of others. Inevitably employers are not omniscient, and the acquisition of crucial information about potential employees can be time-consuming and costly. Consider an employer who is looking for moderately healthy and well educated workers who are also honest, reliable, strongly motivated to perform high-quality work, and likely to stay with the firm for many years (making a prospective investment in their firm-specific training worthwhile). A personnel manager might proceed with an expensive **search,** which is any activity designed to discover information relevant to proper

FIGURE 6 *A Dual Labor Market*

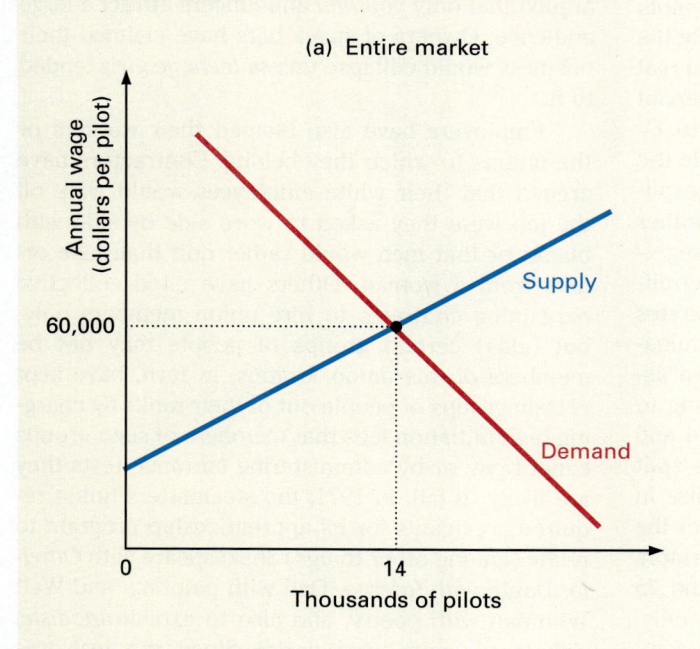

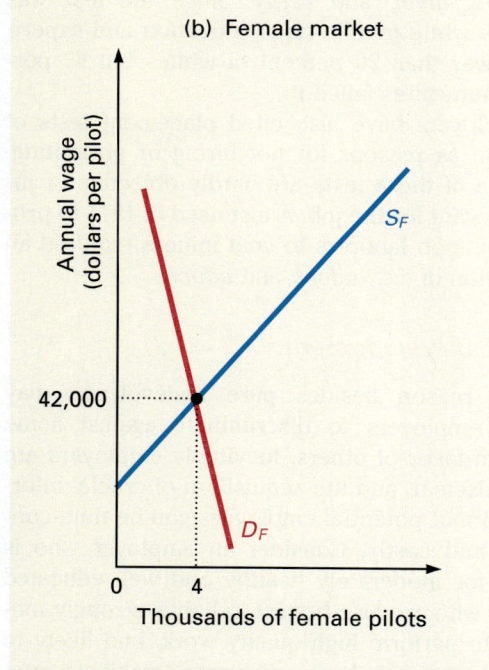

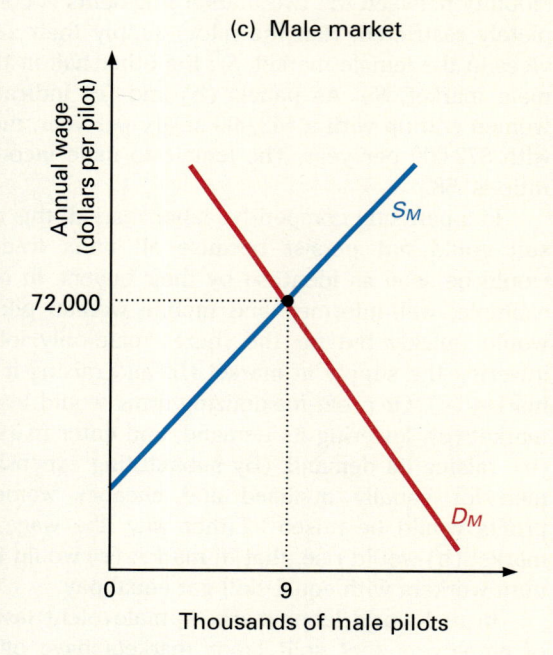

(a) Entire market

Annual wage (dollars per pilot)

60,000

Supply

Demand

0   14
Thousands of pilots

(b) Female market

Annual wage (dollars per pilot)

42,000

S_F

D_F

0   4
Thousands of female pilots

(c) Male market

Annual wage (dollars per pilot)

72,000

S_M

D_M

0   9
Thousands of male pilots

When workers of a given skill are divided into noncompeting groups and confined to different segments of the labor market, differences in pay among them can arise and persist.

decision making that is currently possessed by other people. After a job-opening ad brings applications, a background check could be made of all applicants. Did they graduate from high school, hold other jobs? What kind of high school was it and what were the applicant's grades? Were there disciplinary problems or athlete-of-the-year awards? What do landlords, neighbors, doctors, and previous employers have to say? Was the rent paid on time? Was there much drunkenness, sickness, and switching from job to job? Has there been trouble with the police? The list goes on.

Having collected the information just described, the personnel manager could proceed with an equally expensive process of **screening,** an activity by which buyers (here buyers of labor) select high-quality sellers and reject low-quality ones. Some applicants may accommodate such screening by **signaling,** which is any activity designed by sellers to convince buyers of the high quality of what is being offered for sale. Thus would-be sellers of labor may attach to their applications impressive documents, ranging from college diplomas and all-A transcripts to credit-bureau reports and letters of recommendation by former employers.

Yet few employers are willing to incur the costs associated with an exhaustive background check of prospective employees. (A thorough FBI background check on a recent vice presidential candidate is said to have cost over $100,000.) Many employers will be tempted to take a cost-saving shortcut. They may know (or think they know) that members of certain *groups,* such as women, possess certain characteristics *on the average.* Women, perhaps, spend fewer years in the labor force than do men. (In 1980, the expected working life of a 20-year-old woman was 27.2 years, that of a 20-year-old man 36.8 years, mainly because many women have two careers during their lifetimes—one in the market and one in the home.)[2] Women may be less eager than men to stay in jobs that require long hours and extensive overtime, again because of home responsibilities that have traditionally been considered theirs. (In fact, fully employed women who work year round work about 10 percent fewer hours in market jobs than do men.) Women may be less likely than men to stick with any given job; they may quit jobs to have and rear children; they may follow their husbands to other geographic locations (the reverse, so far at least, is less often true); they may switch to a job closer to home (because shorter commuting time means more time for the home).

An employer who knows these things about women in general (and let us assume for the moment that they are true) may simply decide that women are less desirable workers than are men. From the employer's point of view, spending $5,000 on training each new employee will be more effective when hiring men who stay with the firm for an average of 12 years than on hiring women who stay with the firm for an average of 8 years. Such an employer, therefore, may *prejudge* every applicant simply on the basis of sex, rejecting women and accepting men. As normally understood, the term **prejudice** denotes a preconceived irrational opinion that leads to bias against some people and unfair partiality toward others. It is seen as an attitude of mind that interferes with fair judgment. But from the point of view of the profit-maximizing firm, prejudice may be seen as a perfectly rational attitude that facilitates cost saving in the face of imperfect information.

This type of "statistical discrimination" has numerous implications. Even if the above information about women and men "in general" is true, many *individual* women and men will be incorrectly stereotyped. A particular woman who is rejected may be a much better prospect than a particular man who is hired. Yet the cost-saving employer will prejudge each as if the individual possessed the known average features of the entire group. Indeed, as far as the employer is concerned, it does not matter by which irrelevant feature people are identified as members of an "undesirable" group—whether the feature is sex, color of skin, physical stature, unkempt appearance, foreign accent, vulgar speech, cross-eyes, or red hair. As long as relevant and costly-to-observe characteristics of people are highly correlated with superficial but easily observable ones, employers who use the latter as a predictor of the former will, on average, come out ahead. Thus, judging before all the returns are in and projecting onto individuals certain known group characteristics (assuming they are truly known and not

---

[2] See Shirley Smith, "Revised Work-Life Tables Reflect 1979–1980 Experience," *Monthly Labor Review,* August 1985, pp. 23–30.

just imaginary) can pay for itself—even if many individuals suffer by being judged incorrectly.

So far as the *victims* of discrimination are concerned, it makes little difference whether the denial of labor market opportunities resulted from an employer's malevolent tastes or statistical prejudgment. In either case, a job denied is a job denied. One can suspect that in today's environment, which makes the exercise of malevolent tastes illegal, employers may try to hide malevolent tastes under the seemingly more "acceptable" mantle of statistical prejudgment. These thoughts notwithstanding, not all income differences between races and sexes are automatically the result of discrimination.

Nondiscriminatory Reasons for Income Differences

A 1977 study by Ronald Oaxaca attributed at least a quarter of the observed income gap between U.S. women and men to factors other than discrimination. He explained by other factors as much as 40 percent of the black/white income gap.[3] Other researchers of the subject have found larger or smaller numbers, but all agree that income differentials as such prove nothing about labor market discrimination. The observed income gaps can reflect numerous factors, including differences in worker preferences, in worker productivities (possibly the result of discrimination *outside* the labor market), as well as genuine discrimination in the labor market. Let us consider some of these factors.

Worker Job Preferences

As noted in last chapter's section on wage differentials, jobs differ in numerous ways and are never equally attractive to everybody. Different people may end up with different monetary incomes simply because they themselves discriminate among jobs, which gives rise to equalizing wage differentials. If all jobs are equally open to all, but men are more apt to take risks than women, it may just happen that men crowd into risky, high-paying jobs, while women prefer less risky, lower-paying jobs. Under the postulated conditions, the resultant income gap between the sexes cannot be attributed to discriminating employers.

Worker Productivities

As we also noted in the last chapter, genuine differences exist not only among jobs but also among workers. Some of these differences are clearly *relevant* to their performance on the job. To the extent that a job requires physical strength, high intelligence, formal education, or on-the-job experience, employers who prefer workers with these characteristics to others without them are not making irrelevant, discriminatory distinctions. Some of these relevant characteristics, such as physical strength or intelligence, may be primarily genetic and impossible to change. Others, such as the human capital embodied in people through education and training, may be quite amenable to change during people's lifetimes. As a result, one may ask why it is that certain people (such as women) often do not possess certain acquirable characteristics (such as engineering degrees or pilot's licenses) that would land them certain jobs that go mainly to other types of people (such as men). The cause may lie in what economists call *premarket* discrimination (such as the instilling of beliefs about occupations that are "women's work" or "men's work," respectively). As a result, girls grow up to be nurses or typists, while boys become engineers or jet pilots.[4]

Government and Labor Market Discrimination

In the past 30 years, government has stepped into the labor market in a determined effort to end discrimination by sex, race, ethnic origin, age, religion,

---

[3] Ronald Oaxaca, "Theory and Measurement in the Economics of Discrimination," *Equal Rights and Industrial Relations* (Madison, WI: Industrial Relations Research Association, 1977).

[4] In 1981, women made up 43 percent of all workers, but their representation was much lower in high-paying jobs and much higher in low-paying jobs. Thus women made up 11 percent of wholesale sales representatives, 17 percent of stock and bond sales agents, 20 percent of managers and administrators. Yet 97 percent of practical nurses were women, 97 percent of sewers and stitchers, 85 percent of hairdressers, 51 percent of professional cooks. For more on the subject, see Robert J. Flanagan, et al., *Economics of the Employment Relationship* (Glenview, IL: Scott, Foresman and Co., 1985), p. 203.

and any other criterion that is usually irrelevant for performing a job. The governmental effort has involved legislation as well as court actions.

Legislation

Most important originally were the Equal Pay Act of 1963 and certain sections of the Civil Rights Act of 1964, which severely curbed the powers of employers and labor unions to discriminate in matters of pay and hiring or membership on the basis of irrelevant criteria.

The Equal Pay Act outlawed separate pay scales for men and women using similar skills and performing work under identical conditions. But such a law by itself leaves the door open for discriminatory practices in hiring. Accordingly, Title VII of the Civil Rights Act made it also unlawful for any employer who had at least 2 employees and was engaged in interstate commerce "to refuse to hire or to discharge any individual, or otherwise to discriminate against any individual with respect to . . . compensation, terms, conditions, or privileges of employment, because of such individual's race, color, religion, sex, or national origin." It is also unlawful for any labor organization to exclude individuals from membership, to segregate membership, to refuse to refer members for employment, or to discriminate in admission to apprenticeship programs on the basis of race, color, religion, sex, or national origin.

The Civil Rights Act also set up an Equal Employment Opportunities Commission. Originally, it could receive complaints concerning employer and union discrimination, attempt a reconciliation of the parties involved, and help them go to court. Since the passage of the Equal Employment Opportunities Act of 1972, the commission has also been empowered to issue cease-and-desist orders and initiate suits of its own.

In addition, the federal government has pressured employers and unions actively to seek out women and minorities and to set up and implement **affirmative action plans,** labor market programs designed not only to end discriminatory practices but also to make deliberate efforts at overcoming the present effects of past discrimination. Under the Federal Contract Compliance Program, set up in 1965, federal agencies, federal contractors (firms that supply goods to the federal government), and labor unions of their workers were asked to submit affirmative action plans concerning discrimination in hiring, on-the-job training, compensation, promotion, layoffs, recall, discharge, and in the case of unions, concerning admission to membership or apprenticeship programs. Those who did not comply lost federal contracts.

The new requirements led to a host of problems. Consider an insurance company employing 1,000 office workers, only 10 of whom are African-American. An affirmative action plan may specify that the percentage of blacks employed by the company (now 1%) shall be changed to reflect the percentage of blacks available for the type of job in question. But, employers have asked, how is "availability" to be determined? If one considers the percentage of blacks in the *actual applicant pool,* the company may already be in compliance if only 1 out of 100 applicants is black. This may be so because the firm is located in a white neighborhood and blacks live far away and do not care to commute. It may be so because hiring is done by word of mouth and, given the current predominance of white employees living in all-white communities, few blacks hear about jobs. It may be so because blacks are aware of the company's past discrimination in hiring and therefore, do not even bother to apply. It may be so because the company is offering a package of wages and fringe benefits that is particularly discouraging to blacks. (If the company offers no day care allowances, its current staff of white men may not care; potential black woman employees may care a great deal.)

Alternative definitions of "availability" can be equally tricky. Should one consider the percentage of African-Americans in a *potential* applicant pool, such as among all the present office workers in the region? Once again, the company may find itself in compliance if only 1 percent of all office workers in the relevant 3-county area are black; but, this also can be the result of past discrimination. Some have urged the government to define "availability" by the percentage of blacks—regardless of skill—in the regional or even national population. By such a criterion, our company would surely be out of compliance. If the relevant percentage was 15, the firm would have to set up a goal of 150 black office workers and thus increase its present employment of such workers by 140.

Problems could remain. What if an additional

EXAMPLE 3

Comparable Worth: A Profoundly Flawed Concept?

Philosophers since Aristotle have argued about "morally just" prices of goods. The Roman emperor Diocletian published a list of such prices and stood ready to execute sellers who overcharged. A thousand years later, Thomas Aquinas drew up a list of his own and warned violators of eternal damnation. Economists, on the other hand, have always had trouble with the idea that a good's value was *intrinsic* to it and independent of market conditions. As they see it (note Chapter 3), no good ever has a fixed, unchangeable worth. Rather, its value varies with demand and supply. Increase demand, given supply (or decrease supply, given demand), and a good's value goes up because it is scarcer than before. Decrease demand, given supply (or increase supply, given demand) and a good's value goes down because it is less scarce. At any one time, a good's value is simply an indicator of the degree of scarcity then prevailing. And scarcity is never fixed but can become more or less intense.

Yet among those concerned about labor market discrimination the idea of a "just price" has recently been revived. As they see it, one *can* establish the intrinsic worth of different jobs. Subsequently, one can insist on **comparable worth,** a standard designed to assure equal pay for equal-quality workers holding jobs of equal intrinsic value. The idea is simple enough. Instead of letting the labor market establish wages, wages are to be set by a political process. Committees of "consultants," made up of employers, employees, representatives of labor unions, women's groups, and the like, evaluate each job by assigning, up to, say, 800 "worth-points" to it. [In Minnesota recently, 188 government jobs were evaluated in this way, considering 1) knowledge and skills, 2) mental demands, 3) accountability, and 4) associated working conditions.] Figure A helps us see what is supposed to happen next. Market forces have established an initial equilibrium wage, W_1, for librarians (according to intersection a), but a higher equilibrium wage, W_2, for fire fighters (according to intersection b). A "worth-point" study establishes that the job of a librarian is intrinsically worth the same as that of a fire fighter. Accordingly, an identical wage, W_0, is set for both, which is where trouble begins.

In response to the higher wage, the quantity of librarians supplied rises along S_L from a to d; the quantity demanded falls along D_L from a to c. A surplus cd of librarians ensues. On the other hand, in response to the lower wage, the quantity of fire fighters demanded rises along D_F from b to f, but the quantity supplied falls along S_F from b to e. Shortage ef of fire fighters is the consequence. Given the surplus in the librarian market, it is not inconceivable that hiring standards will be tightened to reduce the excess

FIGURE A

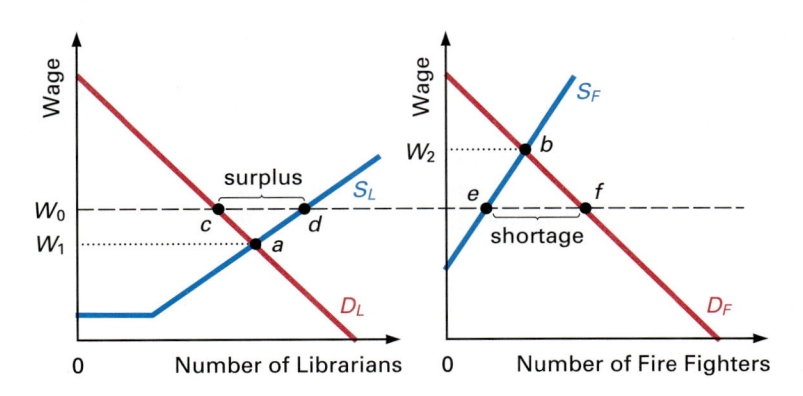

[Left graph: Wage vs Number of Librarians, showing D_L demand curve, S_L supply curve, with W_0 above equilibrium creating a surplus between points c and d, and equilibrium wage W_1 at point a.]

[Right graph: Wage vs Number of Fire Fighters, showing D_F demand curve, S_F supply curve, with W_2 at point b above the intersection, and a shortage between points e and f.]

supply. Before long, only librarians with an M.A. degree rather than a B.A. will be hired. Given the shortage in the fire fighters market, on the other hand, hiring standards may be relaxed to increase the insufficient supply. Before long, even high-school dropouts will be accepted for the job. But consider what this implies. Workers of different quality (as measured by the human capital embodied in them) will then get equal pay. Before long, no doubt, a librarian with an M.A. will sue the city for paying librarians the same amount as high-school drop-out fire fighters get.

As the Commission on Civil Rights put it, comparable worth is a "profoundly and irretrievably flawed concept." Nevertheless, at the time of this writing, the approach was being applied by 12 U.S. state governments and by numerous employers in Canada, both in the public and private sector. Based on a comparative worth study, a court in 1983 ruled that the State of Washington had discriminated on the basis of sex when it paid practical nurses (mostly women) $739/month, while paying campus police (mostly men) $1,070/month. The court ordered retroactive payments of $800 million to the nurses. And in 1991, some local governments in California enacted "prevailing wage laws," forcing nonunion employers engaged in private construction projects to raise hourly wages from $12.39 to the union level of $27.97.

Sources: Robert J. Flanagan et al., *Economics of the Employment Relationship* (Glenview, IL: Scott, Foresman and Co., 1985, pp. 219–223; June O'Neill, Michael Brien, and James Cunningham, "Effects of Comparable Worth Policy: Evidence from Washington State," *The American Economic Review,* May 1989, pp. 305–309; and Andrew Pollack, "Business Groups Fight Laws in California on Wage Scales," *The New York Times,* February 5, 1991, pp. D1 and D6.

140 black office workers simply cannot be found because no blacks are trained in the requisite skills? Should the company be required to hire unqualified black workers and train them? Should it hire unqualified black workers and offer them a higher wage than white workers to enable the former to get training on their own? (And wouldn't such a procedure violate the Equal Pay Act?) In addition, should the firm fire 140 white workers to make room for 140 black ones? Or should it simply hire black workers only as people retire or quit until the firm's labor force was 15 percent black? And wouldn't either one of these procedures constitute **reverse discrimination,** deliberate discrimination against some people on the grounds of righting past wrongs against other people, and thus conflict with Title VII of the Civil Rights Act? It is easy to see why all these matters have ended up in the courts.

Court Decisions

When the antidiscrimination laws were first tested in the courts, many individuals attacked employers and unions with **class-action suits,** legal suits charging that a given individual has been victimized and that the individual's treatment was typical of an entire class of "similarly situated" individuals (such as all women or all blacks or all applicants). The courts obliged, often by awarding monetary settlements of enormous size. Frequently, the courts also ordered other types of remedial action on the part of convicted offenders, such as the establishment of goals or quotas for hiring women and minorities. These examples led to spontaneous changes in personnel administration throughout the land. In order to avoid such lawsuits, many firms and unions set up sexblind and colorblind personnel policies. Others went further than that and established "voluntary" affirmative action plans that gave *preference* to women and minority groups.

A recent example involved a suit by black employees and job applicants against Northwest Airlines. Although the company operates in cities with large black populations (Detroit, Memphis, Minneapolis-St. Paul), only 5 percent of employees were black in 1991. Compared to whites, fewer blacks were promoted and more were discharged. The airline settled the class-action suit by agreeing to accelerate the hiring and promotion of blacks and the training of black mechanics and pilots.[5] Yet arrangements such as this often give rise to court battles. Men and whites in general charge reverse discrimination, citing section 703(j) of Title VII of the Civil Rights Act: "This statute shall not require any employer, employment agency, labor organization, or joint labor-management committee . . . to grant preferential treatment to any individual or to any group because of employment imbalances." Is affirmative action illegal? The U.S. public and the U.S. Supreme Court are sharply divided. Consider these examples:

1. *University of California Regents* v. *Bakke,* 438 U.S. 265 (1978). In the early 1970s, Allan Bakke, a white male engineer, twice sought admission to the medical school at the University of California at Davis. Twice he was rejected, but under the university's affirmative action program (that reserved 16 of 100 places of the entering class to minority students) minority applicants with substantially inferior grades and test scores were admitted. Bakke sued for having been denied admittance solely because of his race. In 1978, the U.S. Supreme Court agreed with Bakke. It ordered him admitted and ruled the university's rigid quota system illegal. But the Court also noted that race may be used as one of many criteria of admission.

2. *United Steel Workers* v. *Weber,* 443 U.S. 193 (1979). Brian Weber, a white employee of the Kaiser Aluminum and Chemical Company, also brought a charge of reverse discrimination for having been denied admittance to an apprenticeship

---

[5] "Airline Creates Affirmative Action Program to Settle Job Bias Suit," *The New York Times,* May 12, 1991, p. A20.

EXAMPLE 4

Pinups at Work are Sexual Harassment

A boss can't say to a woman worker "Have sex with me or else," but the posting of nude female pictures at America's workplaces is prevalent. It may explain in part why women earn less than men. Thus argued Lois Robinson, a Florida welder, when she took her employer, Jacksonville Shipyards, Inc., to court.

At the time, there were only six women among the shipyard's 852 well-paid craft workers. Not a single woman held any supervisory job. The reason, argued the plaintiff, was simple enough. Women were being evaluated not on their merits as craft workers but in terms of their sexual worth. They were being constantly bombarded with sexual comments by male co-workers and had to perform their work surrounded by pinup calendars. Many displayed close-ups of women's genitals; one gave a frontal view of a nude female with the words "U.S.D.A. Choice" written on it. Complaining to managers did not help. As Ms. Robinson's superior put it, men have a "constitutional right" to post such pictures.

The judge disagreed. The shipyard's boys' club atmosphere, the verdict read, with its unrelenting visual assault on the sensibilities of female workers, violated Title VII of the 1964 Civil Rights Act. The shipyard's work atmosphere deterred women from entering and continuing professional jobs no less than a sign declaring "For Men Only."

Apparently, the message has been getting out. Companies ranging from Corning and CBS to DEC and Honeywell have instituted programs of visually inspecting offices and plants to eliminate not only pinups but lewd graffiti, obscene messages on answering machines, and sexually provocative electronic mail. Educational programs, including films and role playing, tell employees to change their ways or lose their jobs.

Sources: Amy Dockser Marcus and Ellen Joan Pollock, "Pinups at Work Violate Harassment Law, Judge Rules," *The Wall Street Journal,* January 23, 1991, p. B2; Tamar Lewin, "Nude Pictures Are Ruled Sexual Harassment," *The New York Times,* January 23, 1991, p. A14; and Michele Galen et al., "Ending Sexual Harassment: Business Is Getting the Message," *Business Week,* March 18, 1991, pp. 98–100.

---

program that favored blacks. His suit was rejected. Although Title VII does not *require* preferential treatment of anyone, the Court held, it *permits* such treatment. Employers may volunteer to give preference to women or blacks, as long as they use a flexible, nonquota plan that considers race and sex along with other criteria, as long as this scheme is viewed as temporary, and as long as it does not require other employees to be laid off. If the procedure hurts innocent newcomers, so be it.

But note: In a landmark 1989 decision involving white fire fighters and the city of Birmingham, Alabama, the U.S. Supreme Court ruled that victims of reverse discrimination are free to challenge even court-approved affirmative action programs in court. Many observers threw up their hands and accused the Supreme Court of "double talk." Examples 3 and 4 provide further evidence of recent court battles. Example 5 reports on a remarkable trend that is bound to affect all these developments.

EXAMPLE 5

The Coming Global Labor Market

In recent times, we have witnessed the emergence of global markets for cars, computers, television sets, and even corporate bonds. More likely than not, by the year 2000, a worldwide labor market will have emerged as well. For some time, firms have been moving operations abroad to take advantage of cheap labor; this trend will be augmented by increasing labor flows across national frontiers.

Forecasters predict that in the coming decades most of the world's new jobs will be generated in the industrialized world, but 95 percent of all new workers will emerge in the less developed countries. In the developed world, low birth rates and longer life spans guarantee an aging population and an extremely low growth of the labor force. The average annual labor force growth between 1985 and 2000 is projected at 1 percent for the United States, .5 percent for Japan, −.3 percent for Germany, and .5 percent for all the industrialized nations as a group. In addition, female labor force participation rates are already high (58.6 percent on the average) and a greater use of women is unlikely to reverse the trend. In the less developed world, on the other hand, birth rates are high, relatively fewer woman are now in the labor force, and the population is young. Accordingly, the average annual labor force growth between 1985 and 2000 is projected at 3 percent for Mexico, 2.8 percent for Pakistan, 2.4 percent for the Philippines, and 2.1 percent for all the less developed nations as a group.

One can also foresee that an increasing share of the world's *educated* workers will come from the poorer nations. Thus, in 1970, the United States, Canada, Europe, and Japan produced 31.3 percent of the world's high school graduates; the poor countries produced 55.6 percent. By 1986, the percentages had changed to 22.7 and 69.9. Also in 1970, the United States, Canada, Europe, and Japan produced 59.6 percent of the world's college graduates; the poor countries 22.9 percent. By 1986, these percentages had changed to 42 and 49.1, respectively. In addition, high school students around the world consistently outperform Americans in science and other fields and high percentages of U.S. graduate school degrees are awarded to foreigners.

Those who study these trends predict that massive international labor movements will occur to bring together the jobs of the industrialized world with the increasingly educated labor force in the rest of the world. This will be facilitated by the ever lower cost of air travel and the general breakdown of immigration barriers in North America, Western Europe, Eastern Europe, and Japan. Already, New York hospitals hire nurses from Dublin and Manila; engineering firms find staff in China and England; and Indians and Turks write software programs in Silicon Valley. Likewise, hundreds of thousands of Yugoslavs work in Germany, Algerians in France, Egyptians throughout the Middle East. More likely than not, the trend will accelerate and generate explosive social and political tensions in many places. One case in point: American workers increasingly complain that their Japanese bosses favor Asians and discriminate against non-Asians in pay and promotions. In 1991, employees of Matsushita Electric's Quasar Company and of the Sumitomo Corporation of America won discrimination suits and millions of dollars in damages. Undoubtedly, the internationalization of the labor market will equalize not only wages and vacation times but also safety standards and other working conditions around the world.

Sources: William B. Johnston, "Global Work Force 2000: The New World Labor Market," *Harvard Business Review,* March/April 1991, pp. 115–127; and Deborah L. Jacobs, "Costly Lessons in Discrimination," *Forbes,* May 27, 1991, pp. 186–188.

IDEAS IN HISTORY

Marginal Productivity and the Exploitation of Labor

About 100 years ago, the American economist John Bates Clark (1847–1938), cofounder of the American Economic Association and professor at Columbia University, turned his attention to an ancient riddle. How does one allocate, among two or more cooperating inputs, the total product which they jointly produce? This problem had long been viewed as unsolvable, akin to deciding whether the father or the mother was responsible for the baby. (Sir William Petty, who lived from 1623 to 1687 and was called the true founder of economics by Karl Marx, called labor the father of production and land the mother.) Clark "solved" the problem by noting that the value of output in a world of perfect competition will, in the long run, precisely equal the sum of incomes earned by the suppliers of labor, land, and capital—each unit of which would earn the marginal value product of the input in question. Thus, an output of $10 million might be associated with a labor income of $7 million, land income of $1 million, and capital income of $2 million, suggesting that labor had produced 70 percent, land 10 percent, and capital 20 percent of the output.

Clark did not confine himself to explaining what portion of output might be attributable to which input under conditions of perfect competition (positive economics). He argued that the kind of income distribution among workers, landowners, and capitalists that perfect competition would produce was also the only one that was fair and just and desirable under any and all circumstances (normative economics). A famous book, *The Distribution of Wealth: A Theory of Wages, Interest, and Profits* (1899) testifies to these thoughts.

Similar ideas appeared some three decades later in the work of a British economist, Joan Violet Robinson (1903–1983). Teaching at Cambridge University, she was a pioneer in the study of the firm operating in imperfectly competitive markets. "It is customary," she wrote in *The Economics of Imperfect Competition* (1933), "in setting out the principles of economic theory, to open with the analysis of a perfectly competitive world, and to treat monopoly as a special case. . . . This process can with advantage be reversed . . . . It is more proper to set out the analysis of monopoly, treating perfect competition as a special case." The book covered much of the same ground as Chamberlin's (see Ideas in History, The Chamberlinian Revolution, in the chapter "Oligopoly and Monopolistic Competition"), but it also dealt with other matters, notably the *exploitation* of labor. As she saw it, this condition existed whenever workers were earning a wage below the marginal value product of their labor.

The Economics of Imperfect Competition established for its author a worldwide reputation at a young age. This renown was maintained through a lifelong penchant for travel, debate, and social criticism. Joan Robinson became a vehement Marxian critic of the market economy, denouncing the system of private property on which it rests and the great evils of unemployment and exploitation that she attributed to it.

Source: Adapted, with permission, from Heinz Kohler, *Intermediate Microeconomics: Theory and Applications,* 1st ed. (Glenview, IL: Scott, Foresman and Co., 1982), pp. 239 and 392–393.

IDEAS IN HISTORY

Bread-and-Butter Unionism

No single person, perhaps, has been more influential in the American labor movement than Samuel Gompers (1850–1924). He was born in London, England, into a Jewish family that had emigrated from Amsterdam. His father was a cigar maker and extremely poor; Sam had to abandon his formal education at age 10 to follow his father into the cigar trade. At age 13, having moved with his family to New York, Gompers became active in the workers' self-education movement. He overcame a stammer and learned to speak and write effectively, although in a somewhat ponderous prose. Reading to his fellow cigar makers while they worked (and rolled his cigars for him), Gompers became acquainted with the works of Marx, Engels, and other European socialists but rejected their conclusions. Unlike the Knights of Labor, he did not believe that workers could improve their lot by radical political action, such as substituting a collective ownership of the means of production for private property.

Gompers spurned the replacement of capitalism by socialism and instead focused on what became known as "bread and butter" trade unionism. Skilled craftsmen would pay high dues to a central account controlled by national officers. They would build up a fund for strikes and other benefits, such as unemployment, sickness, and death payments. The workers' most potent weapon, the strike, would be strictly controlled by national, not local, officers and thereby used strategically for maximum effect to increase wages everywhere. "Unions, pure and simple," said Gompers, "are the natural organization of wage workers to secure their present material and practical improvement. . . . The way out of the wage system is through higher wages."

In 1886, Gompers was instrumental in bringing America's craft unions together in the American Federation of Labor, AFL. Except for one year in which a socialist faction within the AFL deposed him, he was the organization's president until his death. Throughout, he emphasized *voluntarism,* the idea that working *men* could improve their lot only through voluntary membership in trade unions that would, in turn, bargain with individual employers. (Gompers considered children and women as "unorganizable.") He mistrusted government. Like the Marxists, he viewed it as a tool of "ruling classes" that would hardly have the interest of workers in mind. As a result, the AFL under his leadership even *opposed* government legislation concerning maximum hours, minimum wages, unemployment compensation, and health insurance. The AFL's attitude on the matter changed only after Gompers' death, when President Roosevelt in the 1930s initiated the social legislation now known as the New Deal.

Source: Irwin Yellowitz, "Samuel Gompers: A Half Century in Labor's Front Rank," *Monthly Labor Review,* July 1989, pp. 27–33.

Summary

1. This chapter explores what happens when the products of labor or labor services themselves are traded in markets that fail to meet some of the conditions characterizing perfect competition.

2. Even if all sellers and buyers of labor are price takers in the labor market, the nature of the market's equilibrium is modified when the buyers of labor exercise monopoly power in their respective output markets. Such buyers then determine the profit-maximizing labor input quantity by equating not labor's marginal *value* product, but labor's marginal *revenue* product with a market-determined wage. As a result, they pay a wage below labor's marginal value product and employ less labor than otherwise. Labor is said to be *monopolistically exploited*.

3. Another type of labor market imperfection involves a perfectly competitive seller of output who is the only buyer of labor in a given labor market—a monopsony. Such a buyer determines the profit-maximizing labor input quantity by equating labor's marginal value product not with a market-determined wage (which does not exist) but with the marginal labor cost (implied by the upward-sloping labor supply line that the firm faces). The firm itself then sets the wage, paying whatever wage makes workers supply the optimal input quantity the firm has chosen. As a result, such a firm also pays a wage below labor's marginal value product and employs less labor than otherwise. Labor is said to be *monopsonistically exploited*.

4. Sellers of labor can form cartels, which can take the form of labor unions. Labor unions are difficult to establish and maintain. As a brief review of their history shows, however, U.S. unions have enjoyed government support since the 1930s.

5. The effects of union-imposed increases in wages differ with the conditions unions encounter on the demand side of the labor market. If the demand side is competitive, wage increases cause employment to fall. The union can choose among a number of outcomes, including a maximization of the workers' total wage income or of their economic rent. The chosen outcome can be achieved in a variety of ways, as by fixing the higher wage and letting employers ration jobs or by fixing the lower labor quantity supplied and letting the market raise the wage. Such union policies can be supplemented by policies to help the unemployed.

6. If a union imposes wage increases on a monopsony, the effect on the level of employment is less certain. Depending on the extent of the wage increase, employment can rise, remain unchanged, or fall.

7. In the United States, the ratio of female/male or black/white wage incomes lies considerably below 1. Studies show that perhaps three quarters of this income gap can be attributed to discrimination, yet another labor market imperfection. About one quarter of the gap can be explained by differences in worker job preferences and productivities, although differences in present productivities can themselves be the result of discrimination *outside* the labor market. A review of the economic history of black Americans dramatically illustrates the effects of discrimination.

8. In the past 30 years, government has stepped into the labor market in a determined effort to end discrimination. Recent actions by legislatures and the courts range broadly from civil rights laws and affirmative action plans to court decisions about comparable worth and the sexual harassment of women at work.

Key Concepts

affirmative action plans
antipirating agreements
antiunion practices
bilateral monopoly
class-action suits
closed shop
collective bargaining contracts
comparable worth
conspiracy doctrine
craft unions
discrimination
economic rent
featherbedding
industrial unions
injunction
jurisdictional strikes
labor boycott
labor union
lockout
marginal labor cost, MLC
marginal revenue product of labor, MRP_L
monopolistic exploitation of labor
monopsonistic exploitation of labor
monopsony
picket line
prejudice
reserve clause
reverse discrimination
right-to-work laws
screening
search
signaling
strikes
unfair union practices
union shop

Questions and Problems

1. Part A of the following table shows the total number of pizzas produced by a perfectly competitive firm when employing the numbers of workers indicated. (For the time being, ignore Parts B and C.)

Part A		Part B	Part C
No. of workers	No. of pizzas/week	Price/ pizza	Wage per worker/week
1	50	$8.00	$200
2	95	7.50	220
3	135	7.00	240
4	170	6.50	260
5	200	6.00	280
6	225	5.50	300
7	245	5.00	320
8	260	4.50	340
9	270	4.00	360

   a. Assuming each pizza sells for $8, determine the schedule of labor's marginal value product.
   b. If workers are paid a competitive wage of $120 per week, how many are employed by the profit-maximizing firm? How many at $160 per week?
   c. Rework your answers to (b), assuming each pizza sells for $4.

2. Again consider the table, but now look at Parts A and B only. Part B clearly indicates that the firm is a monopolistic competitor in the pizza market.

   a. Determine the schedule of labor's marginal revenue product.
   b. If workers are paid a competitive wage of $160 per week, how many are now employed by the profit-maximizing firm? How many at $312.50 per week?

3. Again consider the table, Parts A and C only. Assume the pizza firm is a labor monopsony.

a. Determine the firm's schedule of marginal labor cost.
   b. If pizzas sell at a competitive price of $8 each, how many workers will the profit-maximizing firm employ?
   c. Rework your answer to (b) on the assumption that a labor union enforces a uniform weekly wage of $360 per worker. Of $240 per worker.

4. Reconsider Figure 5. Determine whether there is any labor unemployment if
   a. the monopsony's choice prevails.
   b. the union's rent-maximizing choice prevails.
   c. the union's income-maximizing choice prevails.
   d. the union insists on a weekly wage of $400/worker.

5. Reconsider Figure 2. What do you think would happen in this market if the monopsony practiced perfect price discrimination in the labor market?

6. The abolition of the reserve clause, some have argued, will prove to be a disaster for baseball. The rich teams will sign all the star players. The poor teams will end up with the mediocre players. All the games will be unbalanced and a bore. What do you think of this argument?

7. Reconsider Table 1. Graph Case D and indicate the extent of monopolistic or monopsonistic exploitation, if any.

8. Reconsider Table 1, Selected Labor Market Configurations.
   a. Graph Cases F and H, assuming the union is rent-maximizing.
   b. In each case, indicate the extent of monopolistic or monopsonistic exploitation, if any.

9. Carefully review last chapter's section on Economic Efficiency. Then study this chapter's labor market graphs (Figures 1, 2, 4, and 5) and determine whether the outcomes depicted there are economically efficient.

10. Joan Robinson (discussed in the first of this chapter's Ideas in History) claimed that labor unions can remove monopsonistic exploitation but *cannot* remove monopolistic exploitation. Assess this claim, using appropriate graphs.

11. Mr. A: "It is extremely difficult to determine whether and how much real-world labor unions have raised the wages of their members relative to unorganized workers."
    Ms. B: "Don't be silly. All you have to do is compare the wages of workers in the economy's unionized sectors with those of workers in nonunionized sectors."
    What do you think?

12. Do you think it could ever pay labor unions to *decrease* wages?

13. Do you think labor unions can affect labor productivity (output per worker)?

14. In 1991, Continental Airlines dismissed a Boston ticket agent, Teresa Fischette, for not wearing makeup. At the time, the company was in bankruptcy; its officials were trying to create a "new company image" with respect to aircraft, facilities, and personnel. A personal appearance code was part of the plan to rescue the firm. Do you think the action was justified? Or was it sex discrimination?

15. In 1991, a full-page advertisement for Sears showed a young woman seated at a computer terminal with the caption "The difference between me and my mother? She still thinks software is a nightgown." What do you think are the consequences of such unflattering stereotyping of older women?

16. In 1991, Bruce McNall and Wayne Gretzky—respectively owner and star of the Los Angeles Kings hockey team—bought the Toronto Argonauts, a football team. Then they signed on Raghib "Rocket" Ismail, Notre Dame's game-breaking receiver and kick returner, for a guaranteed 4-year salary of $18.2 million, plus a possible $8 million for drawing fans, and a 10 percent share of any increase in the team's value. What could possibly justify such payments?

CHAPTER 15

MARKETS FOR NATURAL AND CAPITAL RESOURCES

Preview

This chapter highlights a crucial difference between markets for human resources on the one hand and those for natural and capital resources on the other. While human resources can only be rented for limited periods of time, firms that want to use natural and capital resources have two options. They can enter rental markets and acquire limited flows of resource services, or they can enter asset markets, buy stocks of these resources outright and thus acquire exclusive ownership rights to all future flows of resource services. This chapter explores the nature of these markets and explains the relationship between rental prices and purchase prices of natural and capital resources. In the process, you will learn about the difference between pure rent and quasi rent, about the reasons for the existence of interest, about compounding and discounting, the nature of investment decisions, the role of economic profit, and more.

Examples

1. Ricardo and the High Price of Corn
2. Selling Football Teams

Ideas in History

The Single-Taxers

In 1990, almost three quarters of the U.S. national income consisted of payments to labor; all nonlabor incomes combined—rent, interest, and profit—made up the remaining quarter. Given these relative magnitudes, the labor markets discussed in the previous two chapters are far more important than the markets for nonlabor resources. In another sense, of course, markets for natural and capital resources are just as crucial. Labor by itself produces nothing; the gifts of nature and the capital produced by people in the past are badly needed inputs that now make people as productive as they are.

The Size of Tangible Wealth

In 1985, the tangible wealth owned by Americans came to $12.5 trillion or about three times their annual output of commodities and services (officially referred to as the gross national product). This wealth amounted to $52,000 per person, but not all of it was used in the productive process outside people's homes. Table 1 shows the make-up of tangible wealth as defined in recent government surveys. That composition has been remarkably stable over the past few decades. In 1985, business plant and equipment constituted about 30 percent of the total; the 27 percent share of residential structures (including apartment dwellings as well as owner-occupied single-family homes) was next in importance. Natural resources, simply called "land," came to almost 25 percent of the total; this figure included anything from agricultural acreage to coal mines and household land holdings. Consumer durables (with an 11 percent share) included fixed assets held by households other than houses and land, such as automobiles, refrigerators, and television sets. Finally, business inventories (with a 7 percent share) consisted of all the raw materials, semi-finished goods, and finished goods in the hands of businesses.

If we exclude owner-occupied houses (part of row 2), household land holdings (part of row 3), and consumer durables (row 4), we have an estimate of the natural and capital resources used by the business sector. In 1985, the quantity of such nonlabor resources came to $35,500 per worker. In physical terms, or evaluated at constant prices, that amount came to twice as much as in 1950. This chapter deals with the markets in which businesses acquire natural and capital resources.

Markets for Flows and Markets for Stocks

In the modern world, firms that want to use human resources can do so in only one way. In return for the payment of wages, they can buy the services of people for limited periods of time. That is, they can "rent" people, but they cannot buy people outright. All the labor markets discussed in the two preceding chapters, thus, are markets for the *flows* of human services. In such markets, invariably, specified numbers of labor hours are traded for specified periods of time: 7 hours per day, 35 hours per week, 1,700 hours per year, and the like.

Similar markets exist for the flows of natural and capital resources. If they wish, firms can rent from their respective owners 600 acres of pastureland for a year, a coal mine for a decade, a truck for a month, a pipeline for 49 years. Yet, in the case of nonhuman resources, firms have still another option. Instead of renting the flows of nonhuman resource services for limited periods of time, firms can buy directly the *stocks* of resources that produce these flows. Pastureland and coal mines, trucks and pipelines, warehouses and blast furnaces can all be purchased outright. The purchasers of natural and capital resource stocks acquire the exclusive right to *all* the future services that the resource stocks might produce. In the following sections, therefore, we will consider four types of markets: markets for natural resource services and for capital resource services (in which *rental prices* similar to wages are established for the flows of these resource services) and markets for natural re-

TABLE 1 *The Composition of U.S. Tangible Wealth (in percent of total)*

	12/31/1950	12/31/1985
1. Plant and equipment	26.5	30.3
2. Residential structures	29.0	27.4
3. Land	20.7	24.4
4. Consumer durables	12.6	11.1
5. Business inventories	11.2	6.8
	100.0	100.0

SOURCES: Federal Reserve System, *Balance Sheets for the U.S. Economy, 1946–85* (Washington, D.C., April 1986); and U.S. Bureau of Economic Analysis, *Fixed Reproducible Tangible Wealth in the United States, 1925–85* (Washington, D.C., 1987). For further detail, see *Survey of Current Business, October 1990,* pp. 31 and 32.

source stocks and for capital resource stocks (in which *purchase prices* or *asset prices* for these resource stocks are determined). The two types of markets and the two types of prices established therein are closely linked, which is not surprising. After all, someone who *rents* an acre or a truck buys the flow of its services for a brief period of time; someone who *purchases* an acre or a truck outright and thus becomes its owner, buys the right to enjoy the flows of its services for all future periods of time. Depending on the expected lifetime of the asset involved, the purchase price is bound to be some kind of multiple of the rental price.

Of Time and Interest

The passage of time plays an inevitable role in the relationship between the rental price and the purchase price of a natural or capital resource because the stocks in question tend to be more or less *durable*. If properly maintained, an acre of pastureland may provide productive services forever, a new truck may last a decade, a pipeline a century. As a result, any would-be purchaser of such assets can look forward to a series of expenditures and receipts that stretches from the present possibly far into the future. A truck may cost $50,000 now and an additional $5,000 in each of the next 10 years (for maintenance and repairs, fuel, insurance, taxes, and the like). In each of these years, it may also bring $12,000 in added income (in the form of rental receipts or revenue from hauling freight). Yet firms do not add together and compare the projected expenditures and receipts as if the passage of time did not matter. Such an approach would compare the expenditure of $50,000 + 10($5,000) = $100,000 with the projected receipt of 10($12,000) = $120,000 and rejoice in the prospect of a $20,000 profit. The problem with such an approach goes beyond the fact that the future is *uncertain* and that one or more of the projected receipts may fail to materialize or may be devalued by inflation. Even if all the projected dollar expenditures and receipts were to occur with absolute certainty and even if there were no changes in the general price level over time, and thus, future dollars had the same purchasing power as present dollars (and that let us assume throughout this chapter), the above direct comparison of dollars to be paid or received in different periods of time would still be flawed. Because present dollars can be lent or must be borrowed at *interest*, a dollar now is not the same thing as a dollar in a year, in two years, in ten years, or at any other point in time.

The Interest Rate: Nominal Versus Real

The interest rate to which people refer in everyday conversation is the **nominal rate of interest**. It indicates the percentage by which the dollar amount returned to a lender exceeds the dollar amount lent. Thus, if someone lends $1,000 at a nominal rate of 18 percent per year, that person would receive $1,180 of money a year later. If the general price level had not changed in the meantime, the lender could buy 18 percent more goods, which would be the lender's reward for having postponed spending for a year.

Yet changes in the general price level (called *inflation* when prices rise and *deflation* when prices fall) would change the result. If in the above example prices rose during the year, the lender's ability to acquire goods with the interest dollars received would be correspondingly reduced; if prices fell, the opposite would occur. To illustrate what is involved, economists define a **real rate of interest** as the percentage by which the *purchasing power* (or actual quantity of goods) returned to a lender exceeds the purchasing power lent.

The real rate of interest always equals the nominal rate minus the inflation rate (deflation being indicated by a negative inflation rate).

Real interest rate =
  nominal interest rate − inflation rate

If the nominal interest rate is 18 percent per year, but prices rise at an annual rate of 6, 12, or 18 percent, then the real interest rate equals 18 − 6 = 12 percent, 18 − 12 = 6 percent, and 18 − 18 = 0 percent, respectively. If prices were to fall by 10 percent, the real interest rate would equal 18 − (−10) = 28 percent.

Because changes in the general price level are part of macroeconomics, we will assume no such changes for the remainder of this chapter. Thus, the nominal and real interest rate will be considered the same. We will simply talk of *the* interest rate.

Compounding: Turning Present Dollars into Future Dollars

Consider a world in which an interest rate of 10 percent per year prevails. In such a situation, a single dollar lent now (in year 0) can be turned into $1.10 in 1 year, into $1.21 in 2 years, into $1.331 in 3 years, into $1.4641 in 4 years, into $1.6105 in 5 years, and so on to $2.5937 in 10 years. All this is illustrated in the first column of Table 2. Similar data are given in the other columns for other interest rates.

The process of making dollars of different dates comparable is called **compounding** when the interest rate is used to compute the future value of present dollars.

If we denote the future value at time t by FV_t, the present value at time 0 by PV_0, and the interest rate by i, we can write:

The Compound-Interest Formula
$$FV_t = PV_0 (1 + i)^t$$

Note in Table 2 how $1 at time 0 is said to turn into $1.6105 in 5 years, given an annual interest rate of 10 percent (which literally means 10 per 100). The compound-interest formula confirms this result:

$$FV_5 = \$1\left(1 + \frac{10}{100}\right)^5 = \$1(1.1)^5 = \$1(1.6105)$$
$$= \$1.6105$$

Discounting: Turning Future Dollars into Present Dollars

The compounding process can be reversed as well. Anyone living in a world with 10 percent interest per year and expecting with certainty to receive $1.6105 in 5 years (we also assume certainty throughout this chapter) might just as well accept $1 now as an exact equivalent. When lent at 10 percent interest per year, this present $1 would turn into $1.6105 in 5 years. In the same way, as Table 2 indicates, when the interest rate equals 25 percent per year, $9.3132 to be received in 10 years are as good as $1 now or $1.5625 in 2 years from now.

The process of making dollars of different dates

TABLE 2 *Compound Interest and Discount Factors*

Year	10 percent	15 percent	20 percent	25 percent
0	1	1	1	1
1	1.1000	1.1500	1.2000	1.2500
2	1.2100	1.3225	1.4400	1.5625
3	1.3310	1.5209	1.7280	1.9531
4	1.4641	1.7490	2.0736	2.4414
5	1.6105	2.0114	2.4883	3.0518
6	1.7716	2.3131	2.9860	3.8147
7	1.9487	2.6600	3.5832	4.7684
8	2.1436	3.0590	4.2998	5.9605
9	2.3579	3.5179	5.1598	7.4506
10	2.5937	4.0456	6.1917	9.3132

A single dollar will turn into various larger amounts when compounded at interest. (Note how $1 turns into $1.6105 in 5 years at 10-percent interest per year.) Conversely, any given future amount can be discounted to find its earlier-period equivalent. (At 15-percent interest per year, $2.66 equals $1 seven years earlier or $1.15 six years earlier.)

comparable is called **discounting** when the interest rate is used to compute the present value of future dollars. The interest rate itself is then called the **discount rate**.

If we denote the future value at time t by FV_t, the present value at time 0 by PV_0, and the interest rate by i, we can write:

The Discounting Formula

$$PV_0 = \frac{FV_t}{(1+i)^t}$$

This formula is simply a different version of the compound interest formula. Note in Table 2 how $9.3132 at year 10 is shown to be equivalent, at an interest rate of 25 percent per year, to $1 at time 0. The discounting formula confirms this result:

$$PV_0 = \frac{\$9.3132}{\left(1 + \frac{25}{100}\right)^{10}} = \frac{\$9.3132}{(1.25)^{10}} = \frac{\$9.3132}{9.3132} = \$1$$

Thus, Table 2 shows not only future equivalences of $1 for various years and interest rates but also the discount factors by which future amounts must be divided to arrive at present-value equivalents. What, for example, is the present value of $1 to be received in 10 years? Depending on whether the interest rate is 10, 15, 20, or 25 percent, the present day equivalent is $1 divided by 2.5937, 4.0456, 6.1917, or 9.3132, respectively. These values come to 38.55¢, 24.72¢, 16.15¢, or 10.174¢.

Figure 1 shows the two processes in still another way. Having discussed them, we are ready to turn to the main subject of this chapter: the markets for natural and capital resources.

Rental Markets for Natural Resources

Markets in which firms rent the services of natural resources (acres of pastureland, mineral deposits, and the like) can be analyzed like labor markets so far as the demand side is concerned. Consider a market for the services of agricultural land. Picture any firm adding successive acres of land to its production process, while being constrained to using given amounts of all other inputs and currently available technology.

The law of diminishing returns will come into play. Under the postulated conditions, as succes-

FIGURE 1 *Compounding and Discounting*

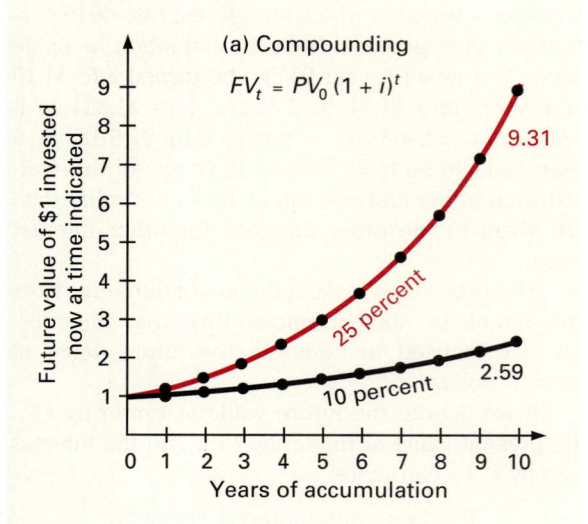

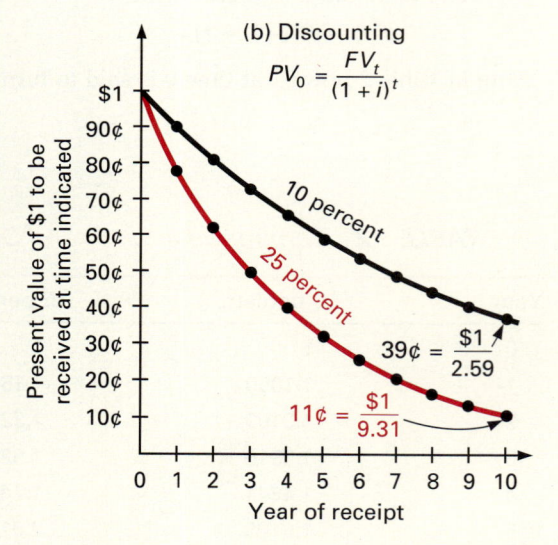

(a) Compounding
$FV_t = PV_0 (1+i)^t$

(b) Discounting
$PV_0 = \frac{FV_t}{(1+i)^t}$

In a world in which money can be lent and must be borrowed at interest, any present dollar can be compounded into a larger amount of future dollars. Any future dollar can be discounted into a smaller present-dollar equivalent. As panel (a) indicates, the longer the time span, the greater is the future value of a present dollar, but for any given time span, a higher interest rate produces a larger future value. As panel (b) shows, the farther away the receipt of a dollar, the less is its present value, but for any given time span, a higher interest rate produces a smaller present value.

sive acres are added to the firm's production process, its total output may grow, but sooner or later it will grow by less and less. The marginal physical product of land, MPP_T, will decline. If the firm is a perfect competitor in the output market and its output price P_o remains unaffected, the firm's marginal benefit from using land (the marginal value product of land, $MVP_T = MPP_T \cdot P_o$) will decline as more and more acres are employed. Accordingly, the firm will demand more land only if the rental price of land declines. If, on the other hand, the firm wields monopoly power in the output market and its output price declines as more acres help produce more output (and its marginal revenue, MR, therefore, lies below the output price), the firm's marginal benefit from using land (now the marginal *revenue* product of land, $MRP_T = MPP_T \cdot MR$) will also decline as more acres are put to work. Again, the firm will employ more land only if the rental price of land declines. In either case, the firm's rental demand for land will be downward-sloping and so will the demand by all firms combined, which is shown in Figure 2.

On the other hand, if, as is true of many natural resources, land can be neither produced nor destroyed by people but is simply made available to them as a fixed "gift of nature," its supply can be viewed as totally price inelastic. Note the vertical supply line in our graph. Regardless of whether the right to use an acre for a year (an "acre-year") sells

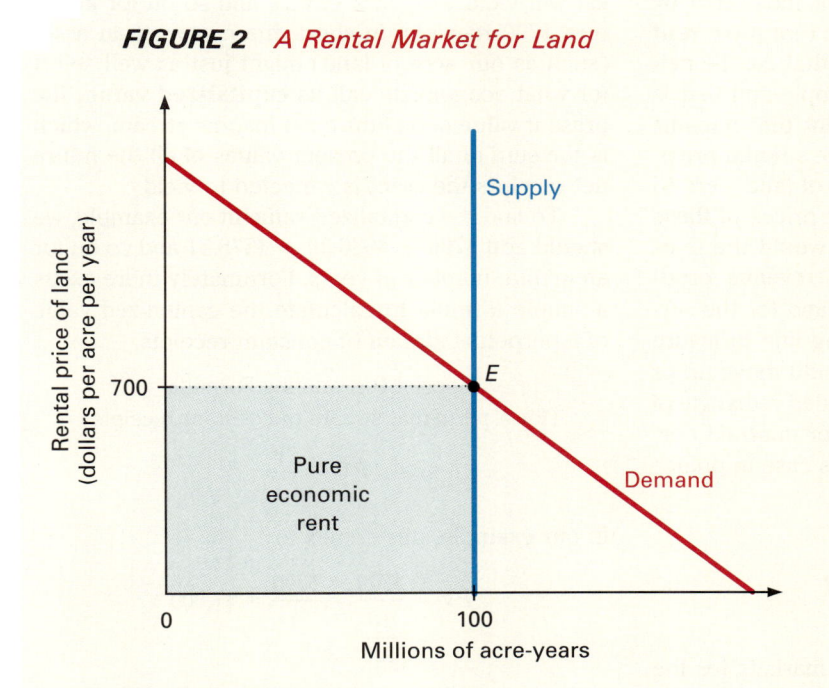

FIGURE 2 A Rental Market for Land

This graph illustrates a market in which the services of acres of land are being traded. These services are measured in acre-years, each acre-year representing the right to use one acre for one year. The demand line represents the sum of the declining marginal value product or marginal revenue product lines of numerous firms. Given nature's fixed supply (the vertical line), a rental price of $700 per acre per year emerges, corresponding to point E. (Shortages at lower prices would drive the price up; surpluses at higher prices would push the price down.) The owners of land come to enjoy a *pure rent* equal to the shaded rectangle.

for nothing, for $100, for $700, or for $20,000, the quantity of acre-years supplied is exactly the same. Given nature's supply, demand alone determines the rental price, here at $700 per acre per year, corresponding to intersection E. The owners of the land receive a rental income equal to the shaded area in our graph, or $70 billion per year.

When discussing the labor markets, we referred to the excess of workers' actual income over the minimum income necessary to bring forth the quantity being supplied as *economic rent*. We apply the same concept to the rental income received by the owners of land, but there is one difference. The land owners' *entire* income (shaded in our graph) represents economic rent because (as the vertical supply line indicates), there is no minimum payment to bring forth supply. The same amount of land would be supplied even at a zero price. Economists have a special name for the economic rent illustrated by our example. They call an economic rent **pure rent** when it is generated by a resource that can be neither produced nor destroyed by people and that is supplied by nature in a fixed amount that remains forever unresponsive to the resource's rental price.

If the demand for the products of land were to rise or fall, all else being equal, the prices of these products would rise or fall and so would the marginal value products (or marginal revenue products) of land. Accordingly, the demand for the services of land (the downward-sloping line in Figure 2) would rise or fall and point E would move up or down along the supply line. The shaded rectangle of pure economic rent would expand or contract correspondingly. Example 1 is a famous case in point.

Asset Markets for Natural Resources

It is not difficult to see how rental markets for the services of natural resources are closely related to the asset markets in which stocks of natural resources are traded outright. Consider again the agricultural land now renting for $700 per acre per year. Someone who sold such an acre outright would give up (and someone who bought such an acre outright would acquire) the right to *all* of its future services and, thus, let us assume, the right to receive $700 in all future years. (We will assume this to be known with certainty; advanced courses might describe the $700 figure as an expected annual average to be received, with actual receipts varying above and below that average.) A potential seller, however, could not insist on getting the infinite sum of $700 + $700 + $700 + . . . , nor would a potential buyer pay such an amount.

Dollars located at different points in time are not of equal value in a world in which interest exists. If the interest rate were 10 percent per year, someone expecting to receive $700 in 1 year (from the ownership of an acre of land) might just as well accept $700/1.10, or $636.36 now as an equivalent ($636.36 invested now at 10 percent interest will yield $636.36 times 1.10, or $700 in a year). By the same token, someone expecting $700 in 2 years could trade that right for $700/1.21, or $578.51 now (again because $578.51 invested at 10 percent interest will yield $700 in 2 years), and so on for all future $700 receipts. In short, the owner of an asset (such as our acre of land) might just as well sell it for what economists call its **capitalized value,** the present value of its future net income stream, which is the sum of all the present values of all the future net receipts the asset is expected to yield.

To find the capitalized value in our example, we should add $700 + $636.36 + $578.51 and so on for an infinite number of years. Fortunately there exists a simple formula to calculate the capitalized value of a perpetual stream of constant receipts.

Special Discounting Formula
(for a perpetual stream of constant receipts)

$$PV = \frac{FV}{i}$$

In our example, this comes to

$$PV = \frac{\$700}{\frac{10}{100}} = \frac{\$700}{.1} = \$7{,}000$$

A price of $7,000 per acre would fully compensate a current owner for giving up all the rights to our acre's assumed future rental receipts (of $700 per year, forever). A sum of $7,000 invested at 10 percent interest yields an internal return of $700 per year as well. We can conclude:

The purchase price of a natural resource will come to equal its capitalized value which, in turn, reflects the resource's rental price (or the net income

EXAMPLE 1

Ricardo and the High Price of Corn

The British economist David Ricardo (Chapter 4, Ideas in History) was a famous participant in early 19th century parliamentary debates on the high price of grain, referred to as "corn." We can illustrate his arguments with the tools developed in this chapter.

Consider panel (a) of Figure A. As Ricardo's opponents saw it, given supply S but rising demand, the price of wheat had continually risen from P_0 in 1800 to P_1 in 1810 and to P_2 in 1820. At the same time, as in panel (b), there had occurred "an unconscionable increase" in rents collected by landlords. The way to bring down the high price of wheat was obvious; let government enforce a decrease in rents.

Not so, argued Ricardo. As he saw it, the high rents were the consequence, not the cause, of the high price of wheat. As pictured in panel (a), population and the demand for wheat were rising rapidly, but the supply of wheat was fixed at S because the government had discouraged the import of wheat by high tariffs, and additional wheat had to be squeezed from a fixed supply of British soil. Accordingly, the equilibrium in the wheat market moved from a to b and to c, raising the price of wheat as previously indicated.

The ever-increasing price of wheat, in turn, raised the demand for the fixed domestic supply of wheat-growing land, as shown in panel (b). It displaced the equilibrium from f to g and to h and increased the landlords' rental income as shown.

The solution, argued Ricardo, was to permit the free import of wheat. This policy might raise the supply in the wheat market to dashed line S^* by 1810, moving the equilibrium from a not to b but to d. It might raise the supply to S^{**} by 1820, moving the equilibrium not to c but to e. The price of wheat would stay down (at P_0), the demand for British wheat-growing land would remain at its low 1800 level, and the landlords' rental income would remain at that low level as well.

FIGURE A

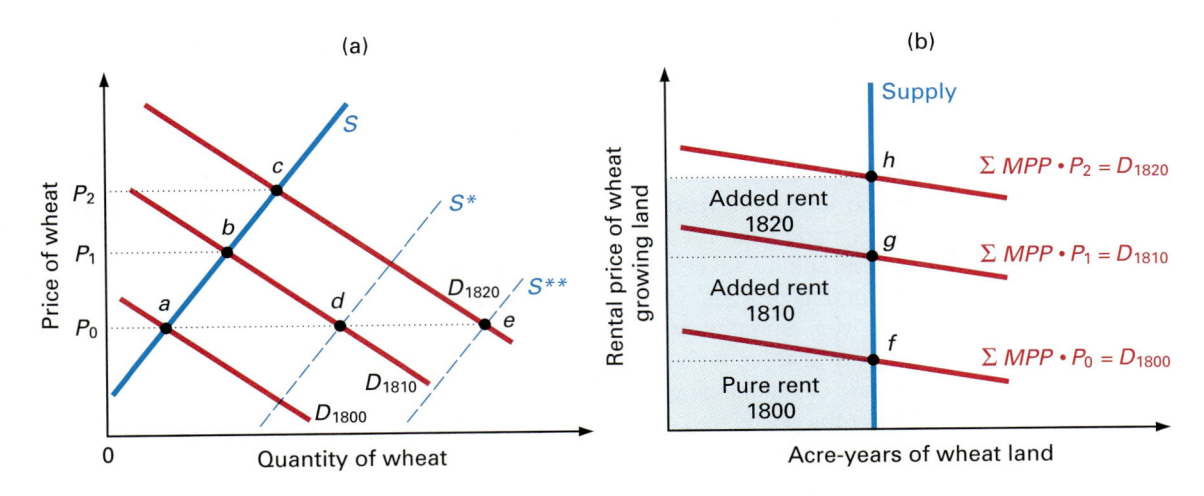

that can otherwise be generated from it) and the current rate of interest.

If the purchase price exceeded the capitalized value, all owners would want to sell the asset, nobody would want to buy it, and the price would fall until it equaled the capitalized value. (If our acre were priced at $10,000, every owner would gladly give it up along with its rental income of $700 per year, because a one-time $10,000 receipt, invested at the assumed 10 percent interest per year, would bring $1,000 of interest income per year. On the other hand, no one would want to give up $10,000, along with the interest income of $1,000 per year which that sum could generate, if the asset then purchased only yielded $700 a year.) Similarly, if the purchase price fell short of the capitalized value, no owner would want to sell the asset, lots of people would want to buy it, and the price would rise until it equaled the capitalized value. (If our acre were priced at $5,000, every owner would be reluctant to give it up, along with its rental income of $700 per year because a one-time $5,000 receipt, invested at the assumed 10 percent interest per year, would only bring $500 of interest income per year. On the other hand, everyone else would be ready to give up $5,000, along with the interest income of $500 per year which that sum could generate, because the asset then purchased would yield $700 per year.)

Rental Markets for Capital Resources

Markets in which firms rent the services of capital resources (assembly plants, trucks, warehouses, and the like) can be analyzed just like markets for human or natural resources so far as the demand side is concerned. Consider a market for the services of trucks. Picture any firm adding successive numbers of trucks to its production process, while being constrained to using given amounts of all other inputs and currently available technical knowledge. Once again, the law of diminishing returns will come into play. Under the postulated conditions, as successive trucks are added to the production process, total output may grow, but sooner or later it will grow by less and less. The marginal physical product of capital MPP_K will decline. If the firm is a perfect competitor in the output market and its output price P_o remains unaffected, the firm's marginal benefit from using capital (the marginal value product of capital, $MVP_K = MPP_K \cdot P_o$) will decline as more and more trucks are employed. Accordingly, the firm will demand more trucks only if the rental price of trucks declines. If, on the other hand, the firm wields monopoly power in the output market and its output price declines as more trucks help produce more output (marginal revenue therefore, lies below the output price), the firm's marginal benefit from using capital (the marginal *revenue* product of capital, $MRP_K = MPP_K \cdot MR$) will decline as well as more trucks are put to work. Again, the firm will employ more capital only if the rental price of trucks declines. In either case, the firm's rental demand for trucks will be downward sloping and so will the combined demand by all firms, which is shown in Figure 3.

On the supply side of the market, we can expect a significant difference to the situation found in natural resource markets. Capital resources, unlike natural resources, are made by people rather than supplied by nature. While nature's supply may be unresponsive to price, things supplied by people are not. We should not be surprised if a higher rental price of trucks will encourage people to increase the stock of trucks (by raising the rate of production above that of depreciation) and then to increase the quantity of trucks offered in the rental market. Likewise people can reduce the stock of capital in existence. A lower rental price of trucks will cause people to decrease the stock of trucks (by reducing the rate of production below that of depreciation) and then to decrease the quantity of trucks offered in the rental market. These factors explain the sloping supply line in our graph.

In our example, demand and supply together establish a rental price of $8,000 per truck per year (intersection *E*). Truck owners require a minimum payment equal to the crosshatched area in Figure 3 in order to supply the 90,000 truck-years that are being supplied. Their actual receipts (of $8,000 times 90,000 or $720 million per year) exceed this minimum by an amount equal to the shaded triangle, which, therefore, represents economic rent. Unlike earlier, this economic rent is not a *pure* rent. Economists call an economic rent **quasi rent** when it is generated by a resource that can be produced and destroyed by people and that is, therefore, in the long run, supplied in amounts that vary with the

FIGURE 3 *A Rental Market for Trucks*

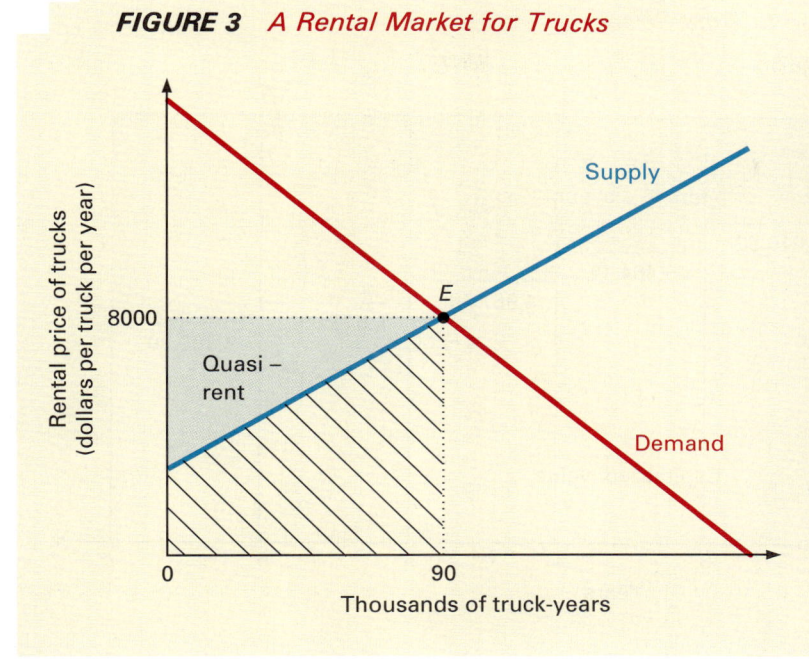

This graph illustrates a market in which the services of trucks are being traded. These services are measured in truck-years, each truck-year representing the right to use one truck for one year. The demand line represents the sum of the declining marginal-value-product or marginal-revenue-product lines of numerous firms. Given the upward-sloping supply, a rental price of $8,000 per truck per year emerges, corresponding to point E. (Shortages at lower prices would drive the price up; surpluses at higher prices would push the price down.) The owners of trucks come to enjoy a *quasi rent* equal to the shaded triangle.

resource's rental price. Ideas in History, The Single-Taxers, has more to say on the distinction between pure rent and quasi rent.

Asset Markets for Capital Resources

It is not difficult to see how rental markets for the services of capital resources are related to the asset markets in which stocks of capital resources are traded outright.

Capital Asset Prices in the Short Run

Consider our previous example in which trucks were renting at $8,000 per year. Unlike indestructible types of natural resources and like all capital goods, trucks have a finite life. Assume that an owner can rent out a truck for 7 years, whereupon it is used up and must be scrapped. Assume also that the first rental receipt comes in 1 year; that the $8,000 per year rental price represents the owner's net income (because the renter is responsible for repairs, insurance, taxes, and the like); and that the current interest rate equals 10 percent per year. The resultant stream of net rental income is represented by the height of the seven blocks in Figure 4. If the first $8,000 rental payment is received 1 year from now, we can figure its present value with our discounting formula as

$$PV_0 = \frac{FV_1}{(1+i)^2} = \frac{\$8,000}{\left(1+\frac{10}{100}\right)^1} = \frac{\$8,000}{(1.1)} = \$7,272.72$$

Or we can simply apply to our $8,000 receipt the relevant discount factor (1.1) from Table 2.

We can, similarly, figure the present value of the second rental receipt as

$$PV_0 = \frac{FV_2}{(1+i)^2} = \frac{\$8,000}{\left(1+\frac{10}{100}\right)^2} = \frac{\$8,000}{(1.21)} = \$6,611.57$$

Or we can divide $8,000 by the relevant discount factor (now 1.21) that applies to a 10 percent interest rate and a 2-year time span.

Proceeding along this route, we can calculate all the other present-value components of our 7-

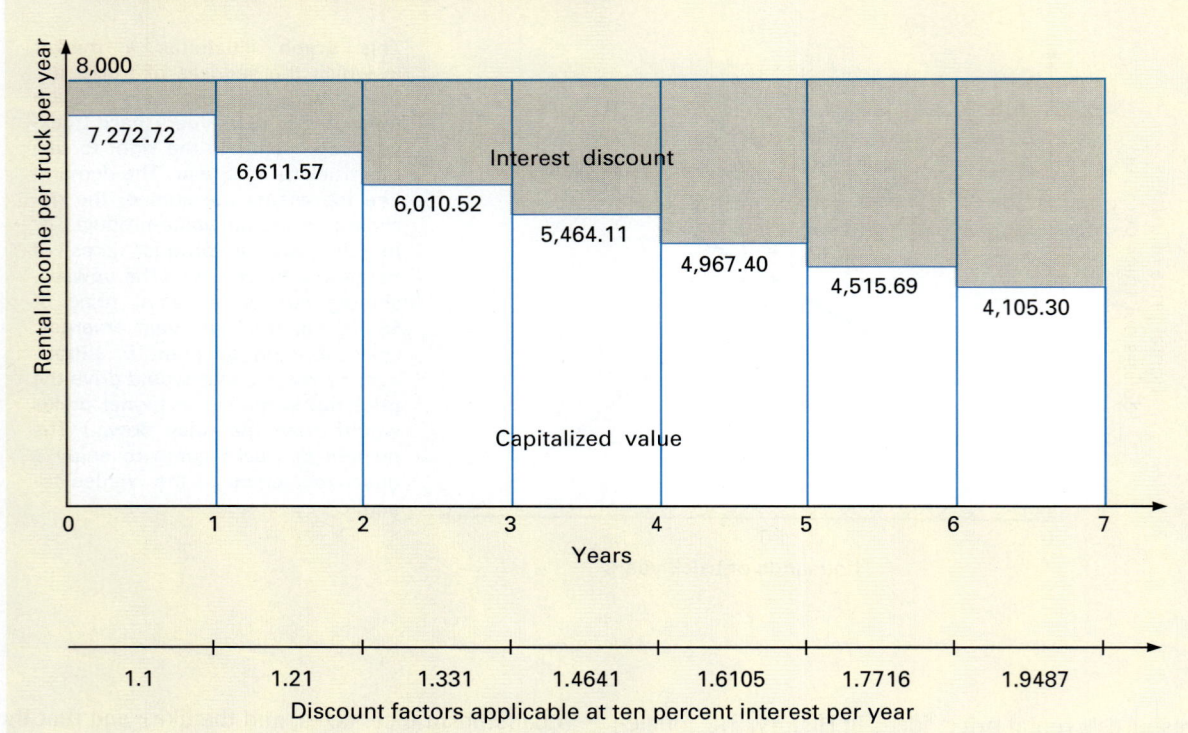

FIGURE 4 Capitalizing an Income Stream

Rental income per truck per year

Year	Value
0	8,000 / 7,272.72
1	6,611.57
2	6,010.52
3	5,464.11
4	4,967.40
5	4,515.69
6	4,105.30

Interest discount

Capitalized value

Discount factors applicable at ten percent interest per year: 1.1, 1.21, 1.331, 1.4641, 1.6105, 1.7716, 1.9487

An income stream (here represented by 7 blocks of $8,000) has a present or capitalized value that can be found by discounting separately each component part at the applicable interest rate and then summing the results. In this example, the stream's present value equals

$$PV_0 = \frac{FV_1}{(1+i)^1} + \frac{FV_2}{(1+i)^2} + \frac{FV_3}{(1+i)^3} + \frac{FV_4}{(1+i)^4}$$
$$+ \frac{FV_5}{(1+i)^5} + \frac{FV_6}{(1+i)^6} + \frac{FV_7}{(1+i)^7}$$

and the seven right-hand parts of the equation correspond to the white portions of the seven blocks in the graph. Given that each future value, FV, equals $8,000 and the interest rate i, equals 10 percent per year, the seven parts sum to $38,947.31, which is shown by the white area in the graph. The upper shaded area of $17,052.69 has been discounted away. Note how later dollars shrink more than earlier dollars as the time perspective of interest is applied—just as farther objects shrink more than nearer ones in spatial perspective.

year income stream. Note, for example, how the last and seventh rental receipt is equivalent to a present dollar value of

$$PV_0 = \frac{FV_7}{(1+i)^7} = \frac{\$8,000}{\left(1+\frac{10}{100}\right)^7} = \frac{\$8,000}{1.9487} = \$4,105.30$$

The capitalized value of the entire income stream thus equals

$$PV_0 = \frac{FV_1}{(1+i)^1} + \frac{FV_2}{(1+i)^2} + \frac{FV_3}{(1+i)^3} + \frac{FV_4}{(1+i)^4}$$
$$+ \frac{FV_5}{(1+i)^5} + \frac{FV_6}{(1+i)^6} + \frac{FV_7}{(1+i)^7}$$

$$PV_0 = \$7,272.72 + \$6,611.57 + \$6,010.52 + \$5,464.11$$
$$+ \$4,967.40 + \$4,515.69 + \$4,105.30$$
$$= \$38,947.31$$

This amount represents the price at which an owner might just as well sell the truck outright. (If an owner deposited this sum in a bank at 10 percent interest per year, the owner could make seven annual withdrawals of $8,000 from the account starting one year from now. After the seventh withdrawal, the deposit would be gone. Thus, the owner would get precisely the same income stream as the one produced by owning and renting the truck.) While the owner of the truck would be willing to part with it for $38,947.31 (or more), no buyer would pay more than this amount. Anyone possessing this sum could put it in a bank and get a 7-year income stream of $8,000 per year at the prevailing interest rate of 10 percent. Why would such a person pay more than this amount to buy a truck that yields the same income stream? As with natural resources, we conclude:

The purchase price of a capital resource will come to equal its capitalized value which, in turn, reflects the resource's rental price (or the net income that can otherwise be generated from it) and the current rate of interest.

If the purchase price exceeded the capitalized value, all owners would want to sell the asset, nobody would want to buy it, and the price would fall until it equaled the capitalized value. Consider our truck priced at $50,000. At this price, every owner would gladly give it up (along with the 7-year rental income of $8,000 per year) because a one-time $50,000 receipt invested at the assumed 10 percent interest per year would bring an $8,000 per year income for *more than* 7 years. (In the first year, the interest of $5,000 could be supplemented by drawing down $3,000 of principal; the remaining $47,000 could be reinvested for another year, and so on.) On the other hand, no one would want to give up $50,000 and thus the more than 7-year stream of $8,000 per year, if the asset thus purchased only yielded $8,000 per year for 7 years.

Similarly, if the purchase price fell below the capitalized value, no owner would want to sell the asset, many people would want to buy it, and the price would rise until it equaled the capitalized value. Consider our truck priced at $25,000. At this price, every owner would be reluctant to give it up (along with the 7-year rental income of $8,000 per year) because a one-time $25,000 receipt invested at the assumed 10 percent interest per year would enable the investor to draw out $8,000 per year for fewer than 7 years. Others, however, would be ready to give up $25,000 and thus a fewer than 7-year stream of $8,000 per year because the asset thus purchased would yield $8,000 per year for 7 years.

Capital Asset Prices in the Long Run

As we have now seen, the price at which a natural resource or a capital resource can be bought outright will ultimately come to equal the capitalized value of the net income stream that an owner can expect to get from the asset. In the case of destructible and reproducible capital assets, however, another condition will pertain as well.

In the long run, the asset price of a capital good will not only equal the capitalized value of its future income stream but will also equal the average total cost of producing the good.

Consider once again our hypothetical truck, capable of generating a net income of $8,000 per year for 7 years and priced at its capitalized value of $38,947.31. If such trucks could only be produced at an average total cost of $50,000, nobody would produce them while their price was so much lower. Over time, the number of trucks would decline; so would the supply of truck rental services, as depicted in Figure 3. Accordingly, the equilibrium rental price would rise above $8,000 per truck per year. As Figure 4 confirms, all the blocks in the graph would grow to reflect the new and higher rental price and so would the white present-value portions in each block. The capitalized value would be larger than before, but as long as it was less than $50,000, the supply of truck rental services would still shift left. The process would continue until the asset price of a truck equaled the $50,000 average production cost.

A similar process would occur whenever the average total cost of producing a truck fell short of the capitalized value and equaled, say, $25,000 per truck. Given the $38,947.31 asset price, more trucks would be produced, which would increase the number of trucks as well as the supply of truck rental services (in Figure 3). Accordingly, the equilibrium rental price would fall below $8,000 per truck per year. All of the Figure 4 blocks would shrink; so would the white area of capitalized value in the graph. The process would continue until the asset

EXAMPLE 2

Selling Football Teams

In recent years, many professional football teams have changed hands. Have you ever asked yourself how the old and new owners come up with a price? The answer has to do with the capitalization of income streams.

The owner of a football franchise earns revenue from many sources: gate receipts, advertising, TV broadcasting rights, and so on. Broadcasting rights alone can be massive revenue producers. Thus, in 1989, ABC, CBS, NBC, and ESPN signed 3-year broadcasting contracts with football team owners totaling $1.428 billion. (At the same time, CBS paid 1.06 billion for a 4-year baseball contract; NBC and the Turner Network paid $670 million for a 4-year basketball contract; NBC paid $401 million for the exclusive right to broadcast the 1992 Summer Olympics; and CBS paid $243 million and $300 million, respectively, for similar rights to the 1992 and 1994 Winter Olympics.) Naturally, the team owners also incur many types of costs, ranging from stadium rentals and player salaries to transportation and administration. The difference between projected revenues and costs yields projected net revenues (analogous to the $8,000 net income blocks in Figure 4). These net revenues can be capitalized, which provides a basis for setting the team's price. Table A summarizes data on recent sales.

Sources: Hal Lancaster, "Football Team's Sale is Strictly Business," *The Wall Street Journal,* April 18, 1989, p. B1; *The New York Times,* November 10, 1989, p. D17; and *Business Week,* May 6, 1991, p. 60.

TABLE Sales of Football Franchises

Year	Team	Price
1984	Denver Broncos	$ 72 million
	Dallas Cowboys	85 million
1985	New Orleans Saints	70 million
	Philadelphia Eagles	65 million
1988	New England Patriots	82 million
	Seattle Seahawks	99 million
1989	Dallas Cowboys	> 150 million
1990	Toronto Argonauts	5 million

---

price of a truck equaled the $25,000 average production cost. Example 2 has more to say on the subject of capitalizing income streams. The next section introduces additional applications and extensions of this material.

Applications and Extensions

Pure Rent Earned by People

Earlier in this chapter, *pure rent* was described as a return to a resource that can neither be produced nor destroyed by people and that is supplied by nature in a fixed amount that remains forever unresponsive to the resource's rental price. It is tempting to expand this concept beyond the realm of natural resources. Certain people have unique aspects that are just as impossible to reproduce as Manhattan Island, an oil field in Texas, or an iron ore range in Minnesota. Consider famous athletes, corporate executives, models, movie actors, scientists, singers, or TV personalities. Many of them supply a special talent that no one else can supply, and they probably would supply it regardless of the price they receive. Most of their income is like pure rent. A huge increase in income, even in the long run, will not increase the quantity supplied because nature does the supplying; people have no control over it. By the same token, even a huge cut in income is unlikely to reduce the quantity supplied.

Consider Figure 5, which might depict the sup-

FIGURE 5 A Boxer's Market

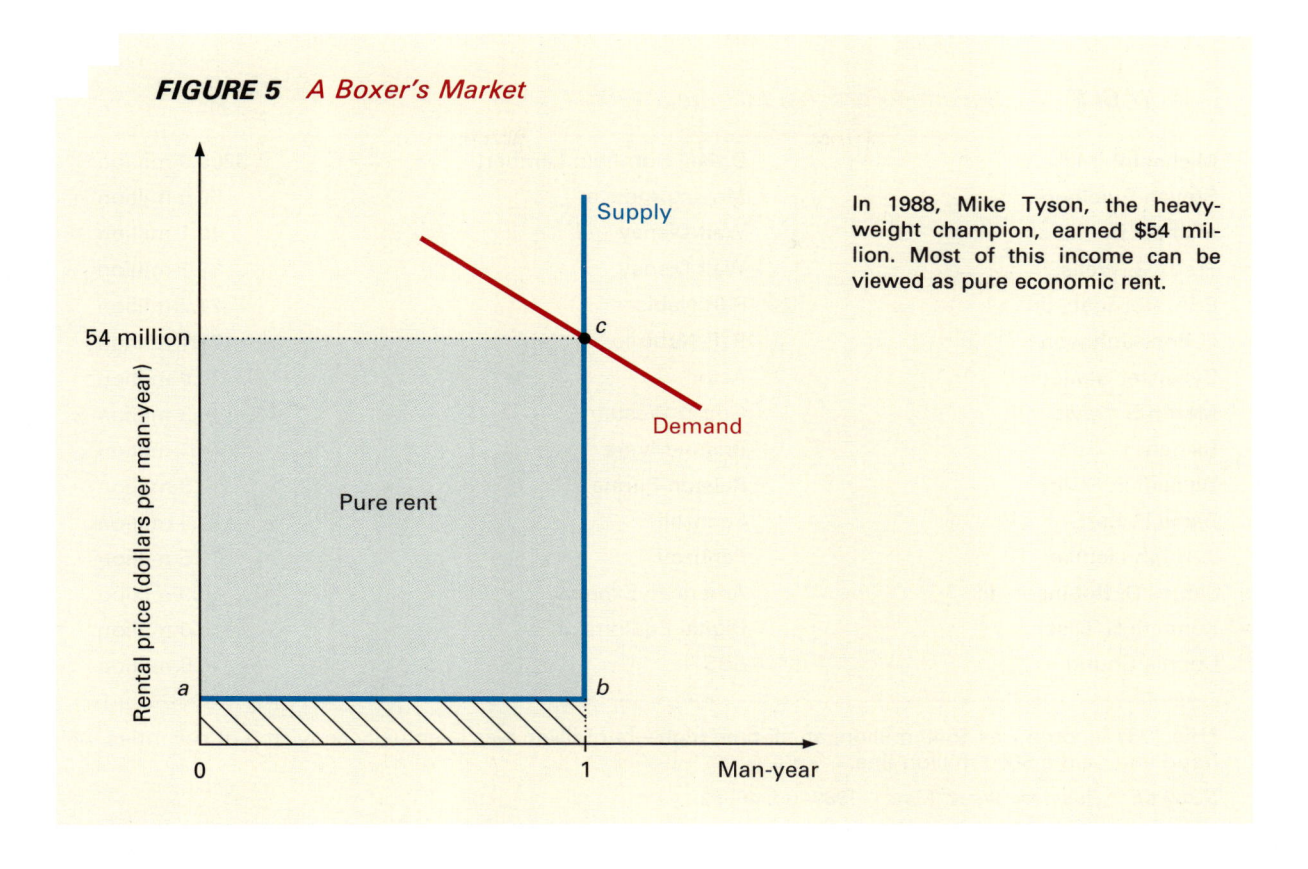

In 1988, Mike Tyson, the heavyweight champion, earned $54 million. Most of this income can be viewed as pure economic rent.

ply of services to the boxing market by Mike Tyson, the heavyweight champion, in 1988. True enough, he might not have worked for an income of less than the crosshatched area; but, given that tiny minimum, he supplied his full-time services, making his supply line *abc* and beyond. Given the demand, his salary came to $54 million that year, most of which was pure rent. An increase in the rental price would not have coaxed out a greater quantity of Mike Tysons supplied; even a massive cut in price would not have decreased the quantity. Similar rents, undoubtedly, were earned by all of the people listed in Table 3.

Why Interest Exists

Throughout this chapter, we have taken the existence of interest for granted, but why does it exist? The question has been debated throughout history and, unlike modern-day economists, many have concluded that interest is immoral. Such certainly was the view of Moses and Aristotle, of Mohammed and Thomas Aquinas and, more recently, of Karl Marx, Joseph Stalin, and the Ayatollah Khomeini. Karl Marx explained the existence of interest in modern capitalist societies by property relationships. Under capitalism, he argued, a small number of capitalists own all the country's natural and capital resources, while most people—the workers—own nothing but their bodies. To produce anything and thus get the food, clothing, and shelter needed for life, the workers must have access to the precious nonhuman resources the capitalists hold. But the capitalists allow workers to use land and capital only in return for a portion of the output the workers produce with the help of these resources. Accordingly, the capitalists deduct their "interest" from the value of output and pay wages to workers that do not equal that value. Thus interest, Marx argued, is like a forced payment of blackmail, a form of exploitation; it is a phenomenon of the "class struggle" between the haves and the have-nots. He also thought that interest would vanish in a socialist society in which there are no capitalists and in

TABLE 3	Selected Personal Incomes, 1988	
Michael R. Milken	Drexel Burnham Lambert	$200.0 million*
Steven Spielberg	Movie producer	50.0 million
Michael D. Eisner	Walt Disney	40.1 million
Frank G. Wells	Walt Disney	32.1 million
E. A. Horrigan, Jr.	RJR Nabisco	21.7 million
F. Ross Johnson	RJR Nabisco	21.1 million
Sylvester Stallone	Actor	20.0 million
Martin S. Davis	Gulf & Western	16.3 million
Richard L. Gelb	Bristol-Myers	14.1 million
William P. Stiritz	Ralston-Purina	12.9 million
Baine P. Kerr	Pennzoil	11.5 million
J. Hugh Liedtke	Pennzoil	11.5 million
James D. Robinson, III	American Express	10.9 million
Kenneth H. Olsen	Digital Equipment	10.0 million
Connie Chung	CBS	6.0 million

*His 1987 income was $550 million, an all-time high—but Milken was eventually convicted of securities fraud and paid a $600 million fine.

SOURCE: *Business Week,* May 1, 1989, pp. 46–93.

which the workers own all of the natural and capital resources.

Yet Marx's explanation (as well as many a similar one) is suspect because interest has arisen in most societies throughout history regardless of property relations. The best answer to the puzzle of its existence, perhaps, has been given by the Austrian economist and statesman Eugen von Böhm-Bawerk (1851– 1914). He viewed interest as a phenomenon connected with the passage of time and traced it to two specific sources, consumer time preference and producer time productivity.

The concept of **time preference** describes an attitude typical of consumers everywhere that makes them value current goods more highly than future goods of like kind and number. Living in a world of scarcity and being mortal, consumers are impatient to consume and to do it *now*. They do not want the unpleasant task of abstinence and waiting. Therefore, consumers can be persuaded to save income and lend it to someone else (thus giving up current consumption goods) only by the promise of a future return that *exceeds* the current sacrifice. Thus, impatient consumers who lend part of their income now insist on getting their money back in the future along with an interest premium (which enables them to acquire an amount of future consumption goods in excess of the amount currently sacrificed). As a result of this attitude, consumers lend funds only at positive rates of interest. And they are likely to lend larger amounts at higher interest rates, which produces an upward-sloping supply of loanable funds, such as line S in Figure 6.

The concept of **time productivity,** on the other hand, denotes the ability of producers to cut the production of consumption goods now, use the resources so released to make capital goods, and then employ these capital goods to produce a permanently larger flow of consumption goods in the future. This technological fact enables producers to pay the interest premium that impatient consumers demand before they are willing to give up their claim on current consumption goods.

Böhm-Bawerk's own example illustrates dramatically that the technological interest premium that producers *can* pay (like the impatience premium that consumers insist on being paid) is totally unrelated to the nature of the economic system. Böhm-Bawerk asked us to think of Robinson Crusoe, all alone on his apparently deserted island, surrounded by nothing but natural resources and possessing no tools of any kind. With his bare hands and perhaps a stick, Crusoe might catch 8 small fish a day. Over time, his daily food production might equal 8 . . . 8 . . . 8 . . . and so on, forever. Now suppose, Böhm-Bawerk argued, that Crusoe went hungry for a day and sacrificed the 8 fish he might have caught. He could then use his time to make a net and build a canoe. Starting the next day, being the new and proud owner of *capital,* Crusoe's production possibilities would be greatly expanded. Using the net and canoe, he could paddle to the middle of a lake or venture onto the ocean and catch 16 fish a day in half the time. And he could spend the other half of his time repairing his net and canoe, thereby making them last forever. As a result, Crusoe's food production would equal the series 8 . . . 0 . . . 16 . . . 16 . . . and so on, *forever*. The 8-fish sacrifice on a single day would have yielded an 8-fish *increase* in output on all future days—a return of 100 percent interest per day. Naturally, had Crusoe lived in a society and simply borrowed money from other people to *buy* a net and canoe, he would have been able to pay a maximum of 100 percent interest per day for the privilege. In our society this time productivity of producers stands behind their demand

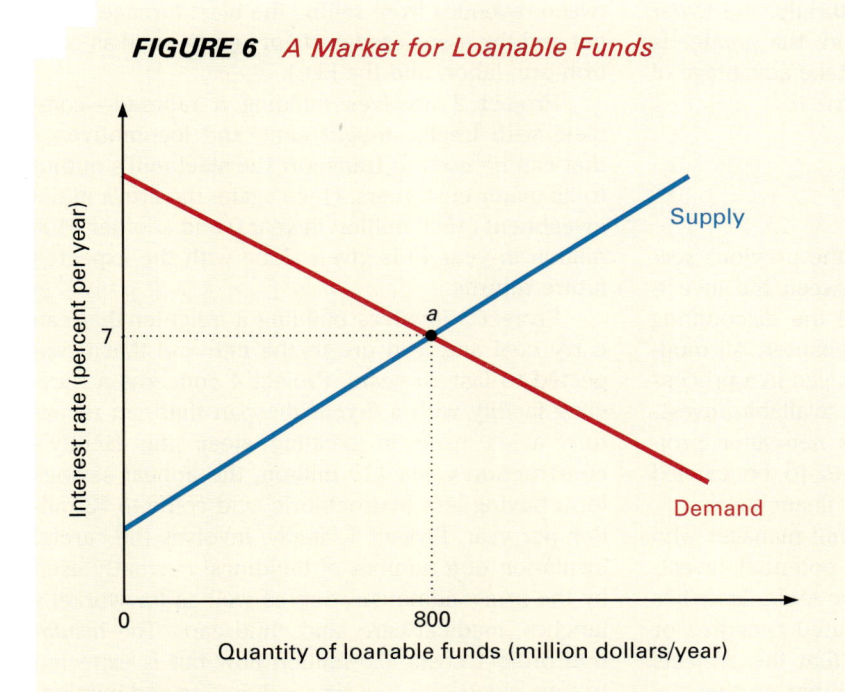

FIGURE 6 *A Market for Loanable Funds*

Supply and demand in the loanable-funds market determine an equilibrium interest rate (here 7 percent per year). Behind the upward-sloping line of supply stands the *time preference* of impatient consumers who would rather consume now than later (but who can be persuaded into postponing consumption by an interest reward). Behind the downward-sloping line of demand stands the *time productivity* of producers who may be able to convert a current sacrifice of consumption goods into a larger quantity of future consumption goods from which the interest reward can be paid.

TABLE 4 A Steel Mill's Investment Opportunities

	Net cash flows, excluding financing cost at end of indicated year (millions of $)						
Project	0	1	2	3	4	5	later years
1. Blast furnace	−100	+4	+4	+4	+4	+4	+4 through year 30
2. Railroad	−500	−100	0	+20	+30	+30	+30 through year 40
3. Freighter	−50	+5	+5	+5	+5	+5	+5 through year 20
4. Recycling	−10	+3	+3	+3	+3	+3	0
5. Insulation	−20	+8	+8	+8	+8	0	0

The investment opportunities of any firm can be described by sequences of dated cash flows, as is shown here.

for loanable funds (Figure 6). Naturally, the lower the interest rate that must be paid, the greater is the likelihood that producers will take advantage of opportunities to build capital goods.

The Nature of Capital Budgeting

We now pursue the story told in the previous section and note the connection between the investment decisions of businesses and the discounting process discussed earlier in this chapter. All modern businesses are continually engaged in a process of **capital budgeting,** identifying available investment opportunities (like Crusoe's net-canoe project), selecting investment projects to be carried out, and finally, arranging for their financing.

Consider the case of a steel mill manager who might be contemplating the five potential investment projects listed in Table 4. The table describes each project by a sequence of dated (positive or negative) cash flows. We assume that the projects are totally independent of one another so that the cash flows connected with any one project are not affected by the acceptance or rejection of any other project.

Project 1 involves constructing a new blast furnace at an expenditure of $100 million at the end of year 0. The blast furnace is expected to last for 30 years and to yield, at the end of each of these future years, a net return of $4 million (the difference between revenues from selling the blast furnace's output and the associated costs of inputs, such as coal, iron ore, labor, and the like).

Project 2 involves building a railroad—complete with tracks, freight cars, and locomotives—that can be used to transport the steel mill's output to its major customers. Once again, the firm's initial investment ($500 million in year 0 and another $100 million in year 1) is given along with the expected future returns.

Project 3 involves building a freighter that can carry coal and iron ore to the mill and that is expected to last 20 years. Project 4 concerns a recycling facility with a 5-year lifespan that can recapture acids used in pickling steel; the facility's construction costs $10 million, the annual savings form buying less hydrochloric acid come to $3 million per year. Project 5, finally, involves the careful insulation of a number of buildings, currently used by the firm's administration as well as for worker's lunches, medical care, and child care. The insulation project costs $20 million now but is expected to save electricity (for air conditioning and heating) of $8 million for 4 years (after which time the buildings are to be converted to other uses).

The listing of possible projects is, however, only a first step in capital budgeting. The presumably profit-maximizing manager must now decide which projects, if any, are worthwhile to carry out. Given what we have learned about interest and time, one approach, surely, would be *wrong*: The

TABLE 5 Net Present Values of a Steel Mill's Investment Projects (in millions of dollars)

Project	0 percent	Annual Interest Rate 5 percent	10 percent	15 percent	20 percent
1. Blast furnace	20	−38.51	−62.29	−73.74	−80.08
2. Railroad	530	−144.89	−357.12	−443.05	−485.06
3. Freighter	50	12.31	−7.43	−18.70	−25.65
4. Recycling	5	2.99	1.37	.06	−1.03
5. Insulation	12	8.37	5.36	2.84	.71

For alternative annual interest rates, this table shows the year 0 net present values of the investment projects listed in Table 4. If an annual interest rate of 10 percent prevails, projects 1 to 3 are not worthwhile; undertaking them would amount to making instant losses equal to the negative net present values shown in the 10-percent column. Projects 4 and 5, however, are worthwhile; if they are carried out, the firm is making profits, in terms of current dollars, of $1.37 million and $5.36 million, respectively.

Consider the $5.36 million net present value of project 5 at the 10 percent interest rate. The number indicates that a firm could spend the $20 million shown in row 5 of Table 4 and thus assure itself a 4-year stream of receipts of $8 million per year. In million dollars, those receipts are now worth

$$PV_0 = \frac{8}{\left(1 + \frac{10}{100}\right)^1} + \frac{8}{\left(1 + \frac{10}{100}\right)^2} + \frac{8}{\left(1 + \frac{10}{100}\right)^3} + \frac{8}{\left(1 + \frac{10}{100}\right)^4}$$

$$= \frac{8}{1.1} + \frac{8}{1.21} + \frac{8}{1.331} + \frac{8}{1.4641}$$

$$= 7.28 + 6.61 + 6.01 + 5.46 = 25.36$$

Thus project 5 amounts to exchanging $20 million for $25.36 million, providing a $5.36 million gain.

manager cannot simply add the negative and positive numbers in any given row and rejoice when the sum turns out to be positive. Unless the interest rate is zero, dollars spent or received at different points in time are not comparable. But the manager can make them comparable by applying proper discount factors to each of the entries in a given row and totalling the separate present-value results. Such an addition of the present values of all the negative and positive components of an investment project is said to yield the project's **net present value**. As Table 5 shows, these values depend on the market rate of interest with the help of which the discounting process must be carried out. The higher is that rate, the lower is a project's net present value.

Given the information in Table 5, a profit-maximizing manager's actions are clear. If the market rate of interest (which the firm could earn by lending its own funds or would have to pay to borrow other people's funds) is zero (an unlikely case), all of the projects are worthwhile (because all of the net present values in that column are positive); thus the firm demands the $680 million of loanable funds (indicated in Table 4) that are needed to carry out all of the projects. More realistically, if the market rate of interest is 5 percent per year, only projects 3 to 5 are worthwhile, and the quantity of loanable funds demanded by the firm drops to $80 million. If the market rate of interest is 10 or 15 percent per year, only projects 4 and 5 are worthwhile, and the quantity of loanable funds demanded drops to $30 million. Finally, at an interest rate of 20 percent per year, only project 5 remains worthwhile; the quan-

The Role of Economic Profit

Why is the total value of output, some economists have asked, not simply divided among the suppliers of the three types of resources—human, natural, and capital—that produce the output? Why don't wages, rent, and interest constitute the total of income? Why is there a fourth type of income called *economic profit*? A number of explanations have been advanced; none of them seems to tell the whole story. Let us consider three possible answers.

A Return to Monopoly Power

Some of the economic profit that arises in any economy is nothing else but a return to the successful exercise of monopoly power. Many firms try to create conditions that permit them to set and maintain prices in excess of average total cost (and thus in excess of payments for the services of human, natural, and capital resources). Not all manage to succeed, but those who do earn monopoly profit.

A Return to Risk-Bearing

Throughout this chapter and indeed, throughout this book, we have ignored uncertainty. In the real world, it is all too common. Consider the kinds of investment projects discussed in the previous section. To decide on their worthwhileness, one must estimate cash flows far into the future. But when the future becomes the present, those cash flows may fail to materialize or they may take on entirely different magnitudes. As a result, an investment project judged to be profitable now may turn out to be more or less profitable once time has run its course.

tity of loanable funds demanded drops to $20 million. (As these numbers indicate, the firm's demand for loanable funds, like the demand line in Figure 6, is downward sloping.)

Many people are risk-averse and avoid what they consider risky gambles of this type. Others, who are willing to act in the face of uncertainty and are ready to bear the inevitable risk, may be rewarded for this service to society by profit; but they may also take a loss.

A Phenomenon of Disequilibrium

Yet a third interpretation of economic profit has to do with the fact that markets are not always in equilibrium; as a result, economic profit can be earned during an interim period during which a new equilibrium is being approached. Economic profit might occur as a consequence of increases in demand and may later disappear as supply adjusts. Or economic profit may be earned as a consequence of a firm's cost-reducing innovations but then disappear as others imitate the innovations, market supply rises, and product price falls as a result.

Figure 7 illustrates these points. Section A depicts a competitive industry's long-run equilibrium. Market demand D and supply S have established an equilibrium price of P_0 and an equilibrium quantity of Q_0 according to intersection a. The typical firm maximizes profit by equating market price P_0 with marginal cost MC at b. Market price also equals average total cost ATC. There is no economic profit.

Section B shows how economic profit might emerge temporarily as a result of higher demand. As demand rises from D (now dashed) to D', a new price of P_1 is established. The typical firm equates the new price with marginal cost at d and produces higher output q_1. Its price now exceeds average total cost by de; economic profit equal to the shaded area is earned. Nevertheless, the profit is temporary. As was explained in the chapter "Perfect Competition," such a profit will induce the growth of existing firms or the entry of new firms in the industry. Eventually, market supply will rise, lowering market price. The process will continue until price and average total cost have again been equated and economic profit is gone.

FIGURE 7 Economic Profit and Disequilibrium

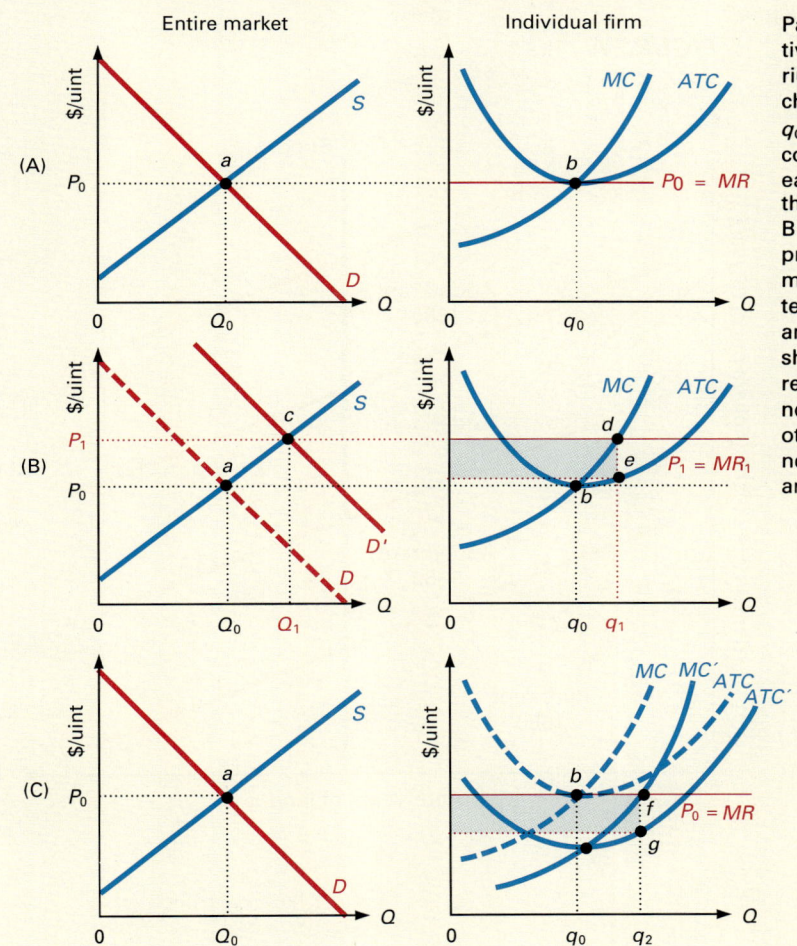

Part A pictures a perfectly competitive industry in long-run equilibrium. All firms maximize profit by choosing an output level (such as q_0) that equates price and marginal cost. Market price P_0 also equals each firm's average total cost ATC; there are no economic profits. Parts B and C illustrate how economic profit might arise. In part B, a rise in market demand raises price to P_1; temporarily, the typical firm earns an economic profit equal to the shaded area. In part C, a cost-reducing innovation reduces the innovating firm's cost curves; until others imitate the innovation, economic profit equal to the shaded area is earned.

Section C, finally, shows how economic profit might emerge temporarily when an innovating firm manages to find a way of producing any given output with fewer resources. As a result, the firm's cost curves will decline, as from MC and ATC (now dashed) to MC' and ATC' in our graph. Given market price P_0, our firm maximizes profit by equating price and marginal cost at f and producing output q_2. Its price exceeds average total cost by fg, and it earns economic profit equal to the shaded area. Eventually, however, other firms will imitate the innovator's success. Their joint action will raise market supply, lower market price, and destroy the economic profit pictured here.

IDEAS IN HISTORY — The Single-Taxers

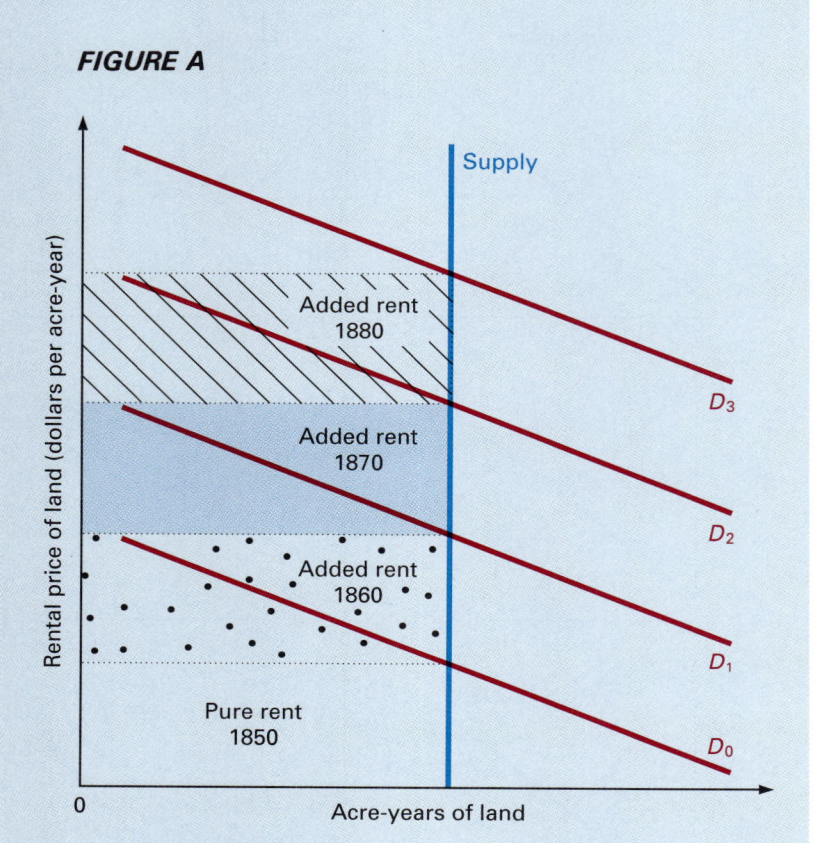

Late last century, an interesting proposal swept the country: Let the government abolish all taxes except one, a tax on the pure rent collected by the owners of land. Figure A illustrates what was involved. Given a fixed supply of both the stock of land and of the services derived from it, went the argument, the rental income earned by landowners is a *pure rent* and its size is entirely determined by demand. Given demand D_0 in 1850, the landowners' income equals the bottom white rectangle in the graph. In the following decades, let population grow, along with the demand for nature's fixed supply of land, as from D_1 to D_2 to D_3. The landowners' rental income grows accordingly: adding an amount equal to the dotted rectangle by 1860, the dotted plus shaded rectangles by 1870, and the dotted plus shaded plus cross-hatched rectangles by 1880.

This scenario was popularized by Henry George, a self-educated man whose fervently religious upbringing bestowed upon him a missionary zeal for "Social Justice." George pointed to high U.S. birth rates and the millions of immigrants pouring into the country, moving ever westward. As he saw it, the rising demand for land gave an entirely unjustified windfall to the owners of land, as pictured in Figure A. Such windfall gains could and should be taxed away without any adverse effects on the quantity of land supplied. (George was careful to suggest that the "unearned" pure-rent income from the site value of land be taxed, not income from improvements made on the land.) Moreover, he thought, such a tax could defray the entire expenses of government.

Henry George (1837–1897) was born in Philadelphia, where his father held a job as a clerk in the customshouse. Henry quit school at age 14 and took a job running errands. Restless and quick-tempered, he never held a job for very long. During the course of his life, he was a clerk in a marine store, a seaman, a printer, a gold prospector, a weigher in a rice mill, a publisher (*The San*

FIGURE A

Francisco Post), a soldier of fortune, a reporter, a managing editor, a State Inspector of Gas Meters, a foreign correspondent, a lecturer, and a politician. Once he was a candidate for the newly established chair of economics at the University of California at Berkeley. During an invited lecture, characteristically, he killed his prospects by attacking orthodox economics and criticizing university education as impractical and useless.

George's ideas about the single tax, in turn, were ignored by the leading economists of his day, such as Jevons, Marshall, and Menger. (These economists had abandoned the classical notion that economic rent was an income peculiar to land and argued that it could be earned by any type of resource.) But George's ideas proved incredibly popular among the poor. He wrote many books, his 1879 work *Progress and Poverty* becoming the all-time best-seller in economics, selling millions of copies worldwide. Accordingly, it brought international fame to George. (Among his admirers was John Dewey, the philosopher, and Leo Tolstoy, the novelist.) Before long, George found himself in politics. In 1886, running as the candidate of the Labor and Socialist Parties, he was almost elected mayor of New York, easily outpolling another would-be politician, Theodore Roosevelt. (Indeed, historians believe that George's narrow defeat was the result of widespread election fraud.) George died during a second campaign for the same post, still promoting his **single tax**.

In the end, George's idea proved unworkable. At least four reasons can be given. First it is impossible in practice to separate pure rent from other types of income that are also called "rent." Consider the "rent" provided by the parcel of land at the corner of New York's Fifth Avenue and 50th Street (site of Rockefeller Center and Saks Fifth Avenue). Only some of it is a pure rent return to the unique site. A large part of it is a return to the capital invested in the buildings. Another part merely reimburses the landlord for such things as air conditioning, heating, and general maintenance expenses. There is simply no way to disentangle these returns. Second, if one agreed on a single tax on pure rent, one should also tax the pure rent component, discussed earlier in this chapter, that is contained in the "wages" many people earn. Third, a single-tax on pure rent (even broadly defined) would not supply sufficient revenues to defray the expenses of modern governments. George's optimism on this account was quite unwarranted. Fourth, a 100 percent tax on pure rents would destroy an important role that such rents play: guiding the resources in question to those users who value them most highly. If the owner of a pure-rent-earning resource received zero income no matter how that resource was used, there would be no incentive to guide that resource to the most productive employment. For all these reasons and more, most economists nowadays reject George's proposals for tax reform.

Still, while his single-tax proposals proved unacceptable, his ideas linger. New York City's Henry George School and a few supporters at the University of Missouri still promote them. Some cities in Pennsylvania (such as Harrisburg, Pittsburgh, and Scranton) have taken advantage of a state law allowing a tax on the assessed value of land to substitute for the conventional property tax (which puts great weight on the value of buildings standing on the land). Cities in Australia and New Zealand do the same; and many cities all over the world, confusing real-world "rent" with pure rent, impose rent controls with disastrous consequences. (Recall the discussion in Chapter 3.)

Sources: James A. Gherity, *Economic Thought: A Historical Anthology* (New York: Random House, 1965), pp. 491–492; and Eugene Carlson, "It's the Land Tax, by George, That Sets Pennsylvania Apart," *The Wall Street Journal,* March 12, 1985, p. 33.

Summary

1. Only about a quarter of the U.S. national income goes to pay for the services of nonlabor resources, yet natural and capital resources are crucial ingredients without which people would produce nothing. In a recent year, the stocks of these inputs came to $35,000 per worker.

2. A crucial difference exists between markets for human resources and those for natural and capital resources. While human resources can only be rented for limited periods of time, firms that want to use natural and capital resources have two options. They can enter rental markets and acquire limited flows of resource services, or they can enter asset markets, buy the stocks of these resources outright, and thus acquire exclusive ownership rights to *all* future flows of resource services.

3. The passage of time plays a crucial role in the relationship between the rental price and the purchase price of a natural or capital resource. It makes it impossible to compare directly expenditures and receipts associated with the use of resources at different points in time. In a world in which present dollars can be lent or must be borrowed at interest, a dollar now is not the same as a dollar at any other time. Dollars of different dates can, however, be made comparable by compounding or discounting.

4. The rental price of a natural resource is established in a market in which the resource's marginal value product (or marginal revenue product) determines demand. But nature supplies a fixed amount of services that is permanently unresponsive to the rental price. Accordingly, all of the income earned by the resource's owner is *pure rent*.

5. Rental markets for the services of natural resources are closely related to the asset markets in which stocks of natural resources are traded outright: The purchase price of a natural resource ultimately comes to equal the present value of the asset's future net income stream, which is also called its *capitalized value*.

6. Markets in which firms rent the services of capital resources can be analyzed just like markets for natural resources so far as the demand side is concerned. On the supply side, a major difference emerges. While nature's supply of natural resources may be unresponsive to price, people's supply of capital resources will respond to the price for their services. Accordingly, resource owners in this market cannot earn pure rent but may earn a *quasi rent*.

7. Rental markets for the services of capital resources, too, are closely related to the asset markets in which stocks of capital resources are traded outright: The purchase price of a capital resource ultimately comes to equal the present value of the asset's future net income stream. In addition, it comes to equal the asset's average cost of production.

8. A number of applications and extensions of the preceding analysis are considered. These include the earning of pure rent by people (rather than land), the question of why interest exists, the nature of capital budgeting, and the role of economic profit.

Key Concepts

capital budgeting
capitalized value
compounding
discounting
discount rate
net present value
nominal rate of interest
pure rent
quasi rent
real rate of interest
single tax
time preference
time productivity

Questions and Problems

1. Using the compound-interest formula, calculate the value of $1 in 4, 7, and 19 years at an annual interest rate of
   a. 3 percent.
   b. 7 percent.
   c. 11 percent.

2. In 1623, Dutch settlers purchased Manhattan Island from American Indians (who, according to legend, did not even own it) for $24. If the Indians had invested these $24 at, say, 7 percent a year for the 369 years between 1623 and 1992, what would their bank account have been in 1992?

3. Instead of accepting it on faith, try to *derive* the compound-interest formula found in the text.

4. Using the discounting formula, calculate the present value of $1 to be received in 2, 5, and 8 years at an annual interest rate of
   a. 5 percent.
   b. 10 percent.

5. Suppose you were a $7 million winner at a state lottery drawing. You get the amount won in 20 equal annual installments (the first one now), each time paying 40 percent in combined federal and state taxes. Are you really a $7 million multimillionaire, as your local newspaper and TV station will claim? Exactly what are your winnings worth *now*? Explain.

6. Review Figure 2. As the text indicates, the annual rental price of $700 per acre that is shown there translates into an asset price of $7,000 per acre under the conditions of an eternal income stream. What would happen to the acre's price if the demand for its services fell or rose and the annual rental price became $100 or $1,000?

7. Imagine a campaign to recycle paper was initiated "in order to save trees." If many people responded, would this save trees?

8. "The idea that nature supplies natural resources in fixed amounts that are unresponsive to their prices (because people can't destroy or augment these resources) is positively absurd." Comment.

9. In the section Asset Markets for Capital Resources it is alleged that in a world of 10 percent interest per year the owner of a truck that yields seven $8,000 annual net receipts (starting 1 year from now) might just as well take $38,947.31 now as an exact equivalent. Prove it.

10. "A household thinking about buying a durable consumer good, such as a washing machine, is in fact engaged in an investment decision just like a firm that is contemplating the acquisition of a blast furnace." Comment and explain by numerical example.

11. When OPEC engineered a rapid increase in crude oil prices, a number of things happened. The prices of coal mines soared, so did the prices of nearby mining supply stores, car dealerships, and residential houses, so did the market price of medallions (government licenses) needed to run new York City taxicabs and the prices of used-car rental firms. Can you explain it?

12. "The text explains why capital asset prices in the long run come to equal the average total cost of their production. The process at work here is precisely the same as that underlying the Iron Law of Wages." What do you think?

13. In 1978, California's Proposition 13 eased the tax burden on property owners. By the mid-1980s, an unexpected consequence had emerged. For every $1 decrease in property taxes, property values had risen by $7. (*See* Kenneth T. Rosen, "The Impact of Proposition 13 on House Prices in Northern California: A Test of the Interjurisdictional Capitalization Hypothesis," *Journal of Political Economy,* February 1982, pp. 191–200.) Can you explain it?

14. Mr. A: "I notice that all the gas stations near the interstate charge higher prices than stations located elsewhere."
    Ms. B: "Of course. They have to because land near the interstate costs so much more."
    Comment on this exchange.

15. In a recent year, certain female models, working only 15 to 30 days a year, were earning up to $300,000 a year. (*See* Gwen Kinkead, "The

Price of Beauty is Getting Beyond Compare," *Fortune,* December 3, 1979, pp. 60–66.) Can you explain it?

16. Suppose a life insurance company approached you with the following offer: "You pay us $200 now and every year for another 24 years or until you die, if you die first. We pay you $7,000 in 24 years or at death, if you die first. Because $200 times 25 only equals $5,000, you (or your beneficiaries) are certain to get back every cent you pay and then some." Is this a good deal for you or the insurance company? How did you go about finding an answer?

17. Suppose you could spend $3,000 now moving to another state. As a result, starting 1 year from now, your income would be higher than otherwise by $800 a year for 5 years. How would you go about finding out whether such an "investment" was worthwhile?

18. A bank recently advertised: "Surprise! Only the Heritage Bank will pay your savings interest in advance. Deposit $5,000 in a 5-year certificate. Today. The Heritage Bank will pay you $1,221.01 in interest. Today." How would you go about finding out whether such a savings plan was a good deal?

19. Suppose a person were crippled in an auto accident and lost the ability to earn income, forever. How might a jury determine an appropriate lump-sum compensation payment?

20. Here is a statement often heard: "This man, positively, is worth his weight in gold." How would you go about judging the validity of this statement?

CHAPTER 16

THE PERSONAL DISTRIBUTION OF INCOME: RICHES VERSUS POVERTY

Preview

This chapter analyzes the factors that determine the apportionment of the national income among individuals. These factors include the size and quality of human, natural, and capital resource stocks owned, the rate at which these stocks are put to work, and the rental prices established in various markets for flows of resource services. Data on the personal distribution of money income and wealth in the United States are reveiwed in detail. We meet the richest people in America and study the problem of poverty.

Examples

1. Is the Boss Getting Paid Too Much?
2. Income Dynamics
3. The Homeless

Even casual observation tells us that the annual incomes of different people differ markedly. Consider the recent fortunes of two American families. First, among the richest in 1989, was the Mars family, consisting of Forrest E. Mars, Sr., 85, of Las Vegas, Nevada; Forrest E. Mars, Jr., 58, of McLean, Virginia; John F. Mars, 53, of Arlington, Virginia; and Jacqueline Mars Vogel, 49, of Bedminster, New Jersey. They were the owners of Mars Inc. with a net worth of $12.5 billion. In 1988, the family income came to $780 million, derived from selling $8 billion of Milky Way and Snickers bars, along with M & M's, Uncle Ben's Rice, Kal Kan pet food, and more.[1]

Second was the Jackson family, consisting of James Jackson, 63, and his wife Beth, as well as a daughter, 31, and a son, 29. In late 1989, you could find them at Chicago's O'Hare Airport, surrounded by small canvas tote bags, seemingly four more faces among tens of thousands headed home for Thanksgiving. But the Jacksons were not going anywhere. They had no home. They lived in the airport's cavernous terminals, slept on its banks of rigid plastic seats, bathed in its public restrooms, roamed its long, polished concourses, killing time, keeping warm, and hustling for change. If they were lucky, they could earn $15 a day, returning baggage carts for the refund, carrying luggage to the parking lot, and flagging down taxicabs.[2]

In the language of economists, the last three chapters dealt with the *functional* distribution of income: the present chapter turns to the *personal* distribution of income. The **functional distribution of income** is concerned with the apportionment of the national income among large and possi-

---

[1] See Julianne Slovak, "The Billionaires," *Fortune,* September 11, 1989, p. 73.
[2] See William E. Schmidt, "O'Hare Airport Now Host to Many Homeless," *The New York Times,* November 23, 1989, pp. A1 and 22.

bly overlapping groups of people who supply, respectively, the services of human, natural, or capital resources. Such services are demanded by firms that produce the goods we all seek. In the present-day United States, roughly 75 percent of the national income goes to people who supply human resources and receive wages; the remaining 25 percent goes to suppliers of natural and capital resources and takes the form of rent, interest, and profit. It is tempting to think of the recipients of wages as one group of people and of the recipients of rent, interest, and profit as a different group of people, but that view would be a mistake. Many individuals receive more than one type of income. But whatever its type, people receive vastly different amounts of income. The current chapter takes account of this fact. Recognizing that suppliers of human, natural, and capital resources are not distinct groupings of people but that many individuals are simultaneously members of more than one of these groupings, those who study the **personal distribution of income** focus on the apportionment of income among individuals without regard to the type of income being received and, thus, without regard to the type of resource services that are being supplied by the individuals involved.

How Income Inequality Is Generated

It is fairly easy to figure out how inequalities in personal incomes are generated. Except for governmental *redistributions* of income (discussed later in this book), individuals in the U.S. economy receive money income in return for supplying resource services to the process of production. Thus, the income earned by any one person depends on three things: 1) on the size and quality of the stocks of human, natural, and capital resources owned, 2) on the rate at which these resource stocks are put to work, and 3) on the rental prices that are established in various markets for the flows of resource services in question.

The Size and Quality of Resource Stocks Owned

Different individuals own different amounts and qualities of resource stocks. As a result, people possess markedly different *abilities* to earn income. Take human resources. Despite the fact that every individual owns a single human body, it would be foolish to argue that human resource stocks are equally distributed among people. Genetic differences endow people with different physical stature, strength, and intelligence. In addition, as people grow up, accidents occur and some people end up handicapped relative to other people. Above all, due to differences in effort or luck, people acquire vastly different amounts and types of human capital. Some individuals are offered the best in health care throughout their lives, extensive education, vocational training, and on-the-job experience; others have no such luck. Even among those who are given the opportunities just noted, some will reject them, while others eagerly grasp them, working hard for a reward that lies far in the future. As a result, some adults come to possess a vast array of marketable skills, others none at all. Some speak seven languages, know how to construct or program computers, how to engineer a new gene, how to pilot a jet. Some know how to build furniture or a house, repair a TV set or a blocked artery in someone's heart; others know how to grow alfalfa, oranges, or wheat, put satellites into orbit, and write beautiful books. Others still know little more than they did when they were five years old.

Similar differences exist with respect to tangible stocks of natural and capital resources. Some people inherit vast acres of agricultural land, coal mines, and oil deposits; some are the recipients of apartment houses, factories, hotels, and office buildings. Others inherit none of these but acquire them during their lifetimes as a result of hard work or sheer luck; others still own no natural or capital resources at all.

The Rate at Which Resource Stocks Are Put to Work

The second reason money incomes of different people come to differ is that people may differ in their *willingness* to contribute flows of resources to the process of production. Consider two people with identical bodies and with identical amounts of human capital. One person may choose to stay out of the labor force entirely and supply zero labor hours in the market. The other one may work 65 hours per week. As a result, the person not in the labor market will earn no wages at all; the one holding down two jobs earns a large amount. The same holds with respect to nonhuman resources. The owners of such resource stocks are free to make different choices with respect to the hours of resource services they supply. The owner of one truck may run it 24 hours a day; the owner of another one, only 7 hours a day. The income of the former will exceed that of the latter.

The Prices of Resource Services

A third reason for income differences among people is, of course, the inevitable divergence in prices of resource services. People who have different things to sell—even if they sell the same number of hours per week—will, most likely, get different incomes given different prices per unit of what they have to sell. Given the demand and supply conditions in their respective markets, an economics Ph.D. may command one hourly wage, a jet pilot quite a different one, and a plumber a different one still. If each works 35 hours a week for 50 weeks a year, the respective annual incomes will nevertheless differ. Similarly, given the demand and supply conditions in the respective markets, an acre of wheat-growing land is unlikely to earn the same annual rent as an acre of forest land. The consequences will be different annual incomes for their respective owners, even if identical numbers of acres are being supplied.

In addition, numerous other factors come into play when rental prices for resources are established, ranging from the monopsonistic behavior of resource-buying firms to the monopolistic behavior of labor unions to equalizing wage differentials, discrimination in the labor market, and more. Consider the section on Wage Differentials in the chapter "Perfectly Competitive Labor Markets" or recall the discussion of Discrimination in the Labor Market in the chapter "Imperfectly Competitive Labor Markets." For reasons given there—good or bad—even people supplying the same type of labor and the same quantity of labor can earn different rates of pay. (A good reason: You do job X for 35 hours a week working during the daytime and earn $8 per hour; a fellow worker does the same job working just as many hours but does so during the night time, earning $12 per hour. A bad reason: You do job X for 35 hours a week during the daytime and, being female, earn $8 per hour; a male fellow worker does the same job working just as many daytime hours but earns $12 per hour.) Similar differentials can arise in markets for nonhuman resources. The owner of capital who is willing to employ it in a risky, innovative venture may earn much more (or much less) than the owner of identical capital who avoids risk.

Finally, resource markets are not always in equilibrium. A sudden increase in the demand for one product will raise the demand for all the inputs producing that product and raise their prices, at least temporarily. The resource suppliers involved will earn more than before. At the same time, a fall in the demand for another product may lower the prices of inputs employed in the making of that product (and set up a strong incentive for their owners to switch these resources from where they are wanted less to where they are wanted more). In the meantime, though, those who supply labor hours or acre-hours or truck-hours to the contracting industry will suddenly find themselves with lower incomes, while others who supply identical resources to the expanding industry earn much more.

In summary, individuals in the U.S. economy earn different incomes because they own different quantities and qualities of resource stocks in the first place, because they choose to supply different amounts of resource services from the stocks they own, or because markets establish different prices per unit of resource services. In the next section, we consider some recent statistics on the subject.

The Distribution of Money Income Among U.S. Families

The U.S. government collects systematic data on the personal distribution of money income in a variety of ways. One set of data tells us about the incomes of *households,* each of which consists of all the persons occupying a given housing unit. (A *housing unit* is defined as a house, an apartment, a group of rooms, or a single room the occupants of which do not live and eat with any other person in the structure and have direct access to their separate living quarters from the outside or through a common hall.) Another set of data focuses on the income of *families,* each of which is a group of two or more persons who are related by birth, marriage,

TABLE 1 The Distribution of Money Income Before Taxes Among U.S. Families in 1989

Income class (1)	% of families in class (2)	% of total income received by families in class (3)	% of families in class and lower ones (4)	% of total income received by families in class and lower ones (5)
Under $16,003	20	4.6	20	4.6
$16,003–$28,000	20	10.6	40	15.2
$28,001–$40,800	20	16.5	60	31.7
$40,801–$59,550	20	23.7	80	55.4
$59,551–$98,962	15	26.7	95	82.1
$98,963 and over	5	17.9	100	100.0

In 1989, some $2,743 billion of aggregate family income was distributed in the highly uneven fashion shown here among 66 million U.S. families. (An additional $682 billion of income went to some 35 million individuals not living in families.)

SOURCE: U.S. Bureau of the Census, Current Population Reports, Series P-60, No. 168, *Money Income and Poverty Status in the United States: 1989* (Washington, D.C.: U.S. Government Printing Office, 1990), p. 29.

or adoption and are residing together; unrelated individuals residing in the same place are counted separately. A third set of data simply counts the incomes of individuals, regardless of their possible membership in households or families.[3]

Tabular Data

Table 1 contains the most recent data available on the subject. Note how the poorest 20 percent of all families (with 1989 incomes under $16,003) received only 4.6 percent of that year's aggregate family income, while the richest 20 percent of families (with 1989 incomes above $59,550) received 44.6 percent of the total. Quite often the extent of this income inequality is pictured graphically.

---

[3] For a recent set of such definitions, see U.S. Bureau of the Census, Current Population Reports, Series P-60, No. 162, *Money Income of Households, Families, and Persons in the United States: 1987* (Washington, D.C.: U.S. Government Printing Office, 1989), Appendix A.

A Graphical Exposition

A graphical device called the **Lorenz curve** provides a summary picture of the way in which income (in this case) or wealth (in other cases) is apportioned among the members of any group and highlights the extent of equality or inequality among them. To graph the data of Table 1, we simply draw a square, as in Figure 1, measuring the percentage of total money income received on the vertical axis and the percentage of families on the horizontal axis. Families are arranged from left to right from the one with the lowest to the one with the highest income.

The Line of Perfect Equality

Now consider a straight line from the bottom left corner at 0 to the right corner at e. It is the **line of perfect equality,** or the hypothetical position of the Lorenz curve if the same amount of money income went to each family. If all families in the country shared total income equally, it would be true that 20 percent of all families shared 20 percent of

FIGURE 1 The Lorenz Curve

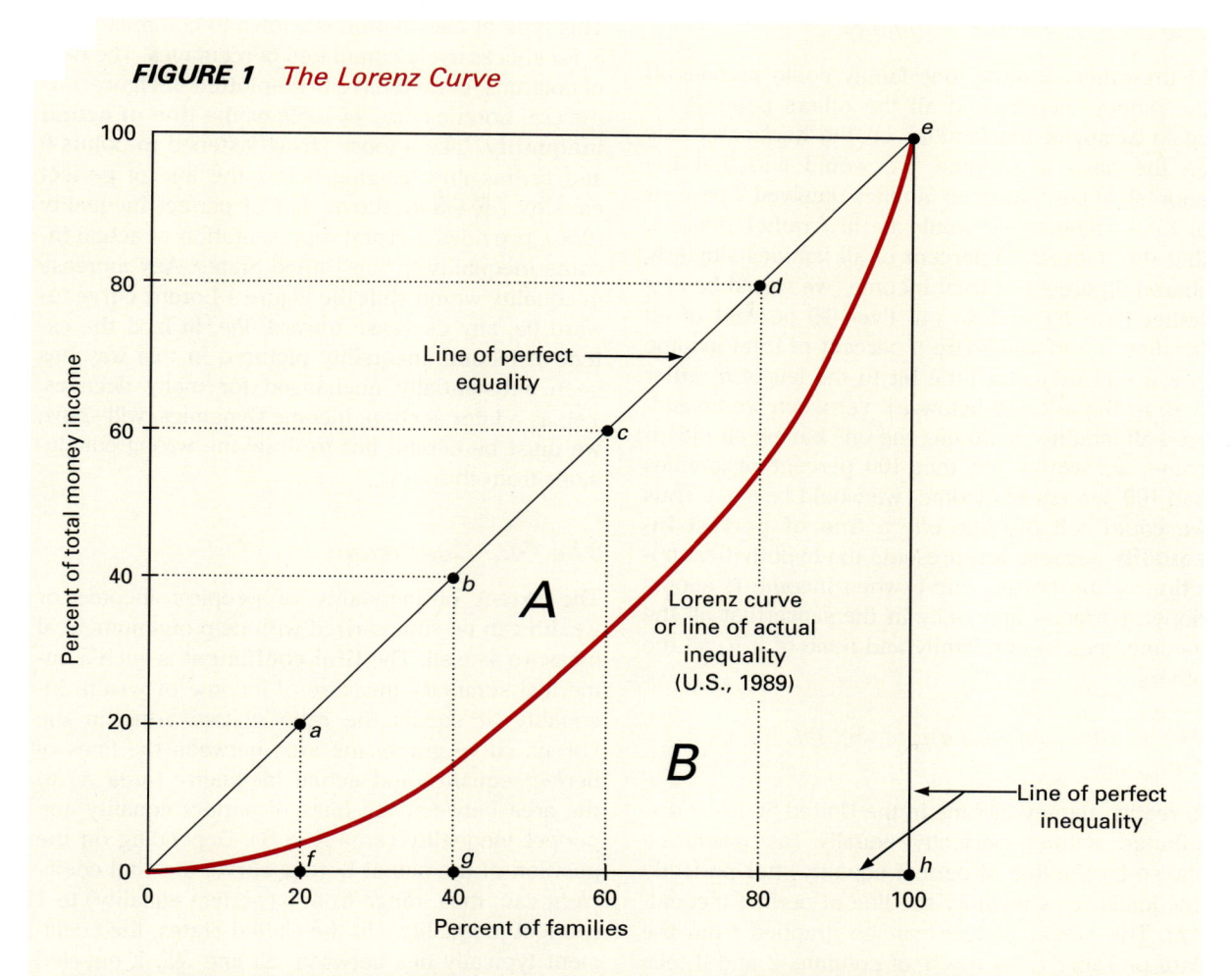

This Lorenz curve pictures the apportionment of money income among U.S. families in 1989 by plotting the data found in columns (4) and (5) of Table 1. The ratio of area A to $A + B$ is the Gini coefficient, a summary measure of income inequality as the text explains; its 1989 value was .401.

total income (at a), that 40 percent of all families shared 40 percent of total income (at b), and so on, until 100 percent of all families shared 100 percent of total income (at e).

CAUTION

The line of perfect equality should not be called one of perfect equity, or justice, for there is no objective way of defining what apportionment of income is perfectly just. But one can determine objectively whether income is apportioned perfectly equally, whether that is considered just or not. The line of perfect equality does not tell what is just, it only tells us what the Lorenz curve would look like if money income among U.S. families were distributed in a perfectly equal way.

The Line of Perfect Inequality

At the other extreme, one family could receive all the money income and all the others none. If we again arranged the families on the horizontal axis on the basis of income, we would find that the poorest 20 percent of all families received 0 percent of total income (we would be at *f* rather than *a*), that the poorest 40 percent of all families similarly shared 0 percent of total income (we would be at *g* rather than *b*), and so on. Even 99 percent of all families would still share 0 percent of total income (we would be just a little bit to the left of *h* rather than to the left and below *e*). Yet when we considered all families, including the one having all the income, we would find that 100 percent of families had 100 percent of income (we would be at *e*). Thus we could call the line 0*he* a **line of perfect inequality** because it represents the hypothetical position of the Lorenz curve when income is apportioned perfectly unequally in the sense that all the income goes to one family and none of it to all the others.

The Lorenz Curve, Line of Actual Inequality

In reality, money income in the United States is distributed neither perfectly equally (as would be shown by the line of perfect equality) nor perfectly unequally (as shown by the line of perfect inequality). The actual picture can be graphed from the data of Table 1. As row 1 of columns 2 and 3 tells us, the 20 percent of the poorest families (each of whom received less than $16,003 in 1989) received only 4.6 percent of total income. Under perfect equality, they would have received 20 percent of the total. Next are families who received between $16,003 and $28,000 in 1989. They comprised another 20 percent of the total number of families, but received only 10.6 percent of total income. And so it goes.

In order to draw the actual Lorenz curve for the United States in 1989, the data of columns 2 and 3 have been added cumulatively in columns 4 and 5, respectively. If the 20 percent poorest families received 4.6 percent of total income—row 1, columns 2 and 3—and if the 20 percent next poorest received 10.6 percent—row 2, columns 2 and 3—then 20 + 20 = 40 percent of poorest families must have received 4.6 + 10.6 = 15.2 percent of total income.

This type of information is shown in columns 4 and 5, for successively cumulated percentages. The data of columns 4 and 5 have been plotted in Figure 1 as the U.S. Lorenz curve of 1989, or the **line of actual inequality**. Like a loose string fastened to points 0 and *e*, this line hanging below the line of perfect equality (0*e*), and above that of perfect inequality (0*he*), provides a visual representation of actual income inequality in the United States. Any increase in equality would shift the Figure 1 Lorenz curve toward 0*e*, any decrease toward 0*he*. In fact, the extent of income inequality pictured in this way has been substantially unchanged for many decades. Yet, as a later section, Income Dynamics, will show, we must be careful not to draw the wrong conclusions from this fact.

The Gini Coefficient

The extent of inequality of people's income or wealth can be summarized with help of a numerical measure as well. The **Gini coefficient** is such a numerical summary measure of income or wealth inequality; it equals the ratio of two areas in the Lorenz curve graph: the area between the lines of perfect equality and actual inequality (area *A*) to the area between the lines of perfect equality and perfect inequality (area *A* + *B*). Depending on the position of the actual Lorenz curve, the Gini coefficient can, thus, range from 0 (perfect equality) to 1 (perfect inequality). In the United States, the coefficient typically lies between .35 and .45; it equaled .401 for the 1989 family income distribution depicted in Figure 1.

Income and Wealth

As noted earlier, the unequal ownership of human capital and of natural and real capital resource stocks is one of the reasons for the observed inequality in personal incomes just pictured with the Lorenz curve. It would be interesting, therefore, to contrast our personal-income-distribution data with data on the personal distribution of wealth, with wealth being defined as the dollar value, at a specified moment of time, of the stocks of human capital, natural resources, and real capital held by people. Such data, unfortunately, are impossible to come by, but fairly good substitutes are given in Table 2.

TABLE 2 The Distribution of Wealth Among U.S. Households—December 31, 1983

Size of wealth (1)	% of households in class (2)	% of total wealth held by households in class (3)	% of households in class or lower ones (4)	% of total wealth held by households in class or lower ones (5)
Under $206,340	90.0	32.6	90.0	32.6
$206,340–$1.4 million	9.0	33.6	99.0	66.2
Over $1.4 million–$2.5 million	.5	7.4	99.5	73.6
Over $2.5 million	.5	26.4	100.0	100.0

At the end of 1983, wealth in the United States was distributed even more unequally than income, as a comparison of these data with those of Table 1 can show.

SOURCE: *The Wall Street Journal,* August 22, 1986, p. 6.

The wealth data given in the table refer to households' net worth, the difference between their assets and liabilities.[4] According to U.S. accounting conventions, assets do *not* include dollar estimates of human capital owned (such as the values of plumbing skills, economics Ph.D.'s, or medical degrees), and they do include all sorts of other things (such as holdings of money, bonds, and cars) besides the natural and capital resource stocks that we really want to count. There can be little doubt, however, that the ownership of natural and capital resource stocks is highly correlated with wealth as defined here. As Table 2 shows, at the end of 1983, the 90 percent least wealthy households (each with a net worth of under $206,340) owned only 32.6 percent of total wealth. The wealthiest 10 percent of all households owned the remaining 67.4 percent of total wealth, with the top *one-half* percent of households (each with a net worth in excess of $2.5 million) holding over a quarter of total wealth. These things do not change rapidly and, most likely, still hold today.

Figure 2 provides a visual picture of the two distributions just discussed. It is striking how income is distributed so much less unequally than wealth, but it is not difficult to explain. Although most American families own negligible stocks of natural and real capital resources and have only their labor to sell, many earn respectable incomes on their *human* capital, which is not measured in our wealth data but helps labor capture, as we have seen, the lion's share of the national income.

In the following sections we take a more detailed look at the two groups on the extreme ends of the U.S. income distribution, the super rich and the super poor.

The Super Rich

Not surprisingly, the top income recipients in the United States are also the wealthiest as measured by net worth. Once a year, *Forbes* magazine publishes a list of the country's 400 wealthiest individuals, complete with detailed stories of how they got

---
[4] For a quick review of these basic accounting concepts, see the Appendix "Major Concepts of Business Accounting" that follows the chapter "The Firm—An Overview."

FIGURE 2 *Lorenz Curves of Income and Wealth*

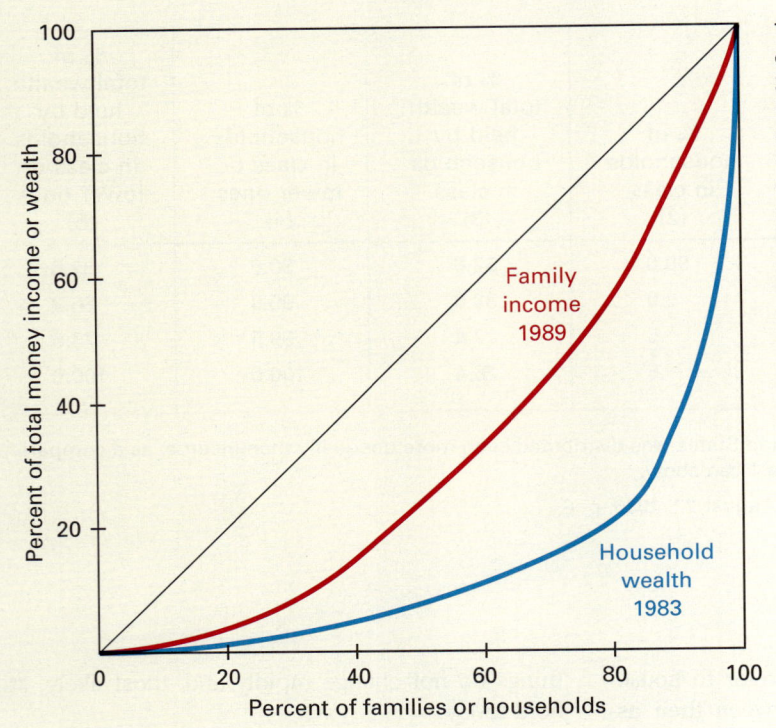

This graph pictures the data from columns (4) and (5) of Tables 1 and 2. Their message is clear: In the United States, income is much less unequally distributed than wealth (which, as it is defined here, includes not only the ownership of natural and real capital resources, but also that of other assets, such as money, bonds, and private cars). More likely than not, the less unequal distribution of income reflects many people's ownership of human capital (which is not measured by available data on wealth).

there.[5] In 1989, the 400 wealthiest as a group had a net worth of $134 billion; that of individuals ranged from $5.2 billion at the very top to a "mere" $275 million at the 400th position; there were 66 billionaires. It is interesting to look at the paths to riches that the 346 men and 54 women on the list have taken. Fully 40 percent got there through inheritance, as one might expect, but 54 percent did it by themselves, starting out poor and becoming rich after decades of hard work (18-hour days, 365 days of the year, are common), combined with shrewd decision making and, undoubtedly, a measure of luck. The remaining 6 percent on the list received a modest fortune through inheritance or marriage and expanded it over time.

Consider these examples of "self-made" individuals: 1) Josephine Esther Mentzer, now known as Estée Lauder, 83. Born to Hungarian immigrant parents in Queens, New York, she peddled skin creams for her uncle, then struck out on her own selling creams and fragrances to New York department stores. Her cosmetics company is now worth $5.2 billion. 2) William Henry Gates III, 35, created his first computer program at age 13, and scored a perfect 800 on the math SAT. At 19, he dropped out of Harvard to found Microsoft, producing software now thought to be indispensable to the computer

---

[5] See, for example, "The Richest People in America: The Eighth Annual Forbes 400," *Forbes,* October 23, 1989, entire issue. For an alternative look at the richest people in the entire world, see Jennifer Reese, "The Billionaires," *Fortune,* September 9, 1991, pp. 42–114.

industry. A voracious worker and masterful marketer, his net worth is $3.9 billion.

In what fields do the 400 wealthiest individuals operate? In order of importance, some 20 percent are connected with manufacturing of one kind or another, 19 percent with real estate, 18 percent with the media, and 16 percent with finance. The remaining 27 percent are found in numerous other fields. (The $415 million net worth of John Rangos, Sr., for example, was derived from landfill operations, a new boom industry created by environmental concerns about waste cleanup and disposal. The $325 million net worth of Joe Jamail was derived from a law practice, in particular the defeat of Texaco by Pennzoil.)

Table 3 provides a variety of detail. Example 1 provides another perspective.

The Poor

In his 1964 State of the Union Message, President Johnson committed the nation to a War on Poverty. In the same year, Congress passed the Economic Opportunity Act and made it "the policy of the United States to eliminate the paradox of poverty in the midst of plenty." Many of the government policies that proceeded from this initiative are discussed in a later chapter, "The Redistribution of Income," but we can note here how governmental concern with poverty has led to the collection of vast amounts of information on the subject. People who are worried about the poor must first ask themselves what they mean by "poverty." Such a definition is crucial for measuring the extent of poverty and ultimately for determining the degree of success from policies to abolish it. The definition of poverty, however, involves a number of difficult conceptual problems. Inevitably, they have sparked extensive discussion during the past three decades; we consider them in turn.[6]

The Meaning of "Needs"

The first and most obvious issue involves the determination of people's needs. Two possibilities exist. One can define a person's needs by an absolute standard or by a relative standard.

An Absolute Standard

An **absolute standard of poverty measurement** defines a person's "needs" as a fixed market basket of bare necessities without which the person cannot survive and declares the person "poor" if the set of goods available to the person is less than that basket of goods. Naturally, such market baskets will vary among families because families differ in size, composition, and location. A family of nine needs more food than a family of two; babies need less food than hard-working adults; the elderly often need more medical care than teenagers. And, given the climate, any family in Maine needs more clothing and fuel than any family in Florida.

Consider what a minimum diet might be. In 1945, the National Research Council established a physiological minimum for different types of individuals. Its diets contained what were then considered optimum amounts of calories, protein, minerals, and vitamins, but left out such "luxuries" as variety and palatability. For a moderately active man, such a diet involved the annual consumption of the following:[7]

- 370 pounds of wheat flour
- 57 cans of evaporated milk
- 111 pounds of cabbage
- 23 pounds of spinach
- 285 pounds of dried navy beans

To establish "need," one might proceed to evaluate such a minimum diet. At Amherst, Massachusetts, in December 1989, it cost $418.86 to purchase the above quantities. An average family (3.17 persons at the time) might, therefore, have needed $1,327.79 for food annually. Because families typically have to devote twice as much money to nonfood items, such as clothing and shelter, one might triple the minimum food figure and designate $3,983.37 per year as the rock-bottom minimum income required by an average family. That number could then be considered the average "poverty line" dividing the poor from the nonpoor. Once every

---

[6] This section and those that follow rely heavily on the excellent article by Isabel V. Sawhill, "Poverty in the U.S.: Why Is It So Persistent?" *Journal of Economic Literature,* September 1988, pp. 1073–1119.

[7] See George J. Stigler, "The Cost of Subsistence," *Journal of Farm Economics,* May 1945, pp. 303–314.

TABLE 3 **The Wealthiest Americans in 1991**

Name	Net worth	Comments
1. Sam Moore Walton, 73	$21.1 billion	Founder of Wal-Mart stores, which had 1990 sales of $32.6 billion, outselling retail giant Sears. Still works out of drab two-story office building in Bentonville, Arkansas and attends potluck suppers at the local church.
2. Forrest Mars Sr., 87 Forrest Mars Jr., 60 John Mars, 55 Jacqueline Mars Vogel, 50	$12.5 billion	Owners of M&M/Mars, Uncle Ben's Rice, Pedigree pet food, Mars Electronics. Helps supply every American with 21 lbs. of candy per year. Snickers reigns supreme, M&Ms comes next.
3. Samuel I. Newhouse Jr., 63 Donald E. Newhouse, 61	$12.1 billion	Owners of Advance Publications and Newhouse Broadcasting. Holdings include Condé Nast magazines (*Vanity Fair*) and Random House and Alfred A. Knopf book publishing. Also 31 newspapers, including Newark *Star-Ledger* and Portland *Oregonian*.
4. John Werner Kluge, 76	$7.1 billion	Owner of Metromedia, a major television broadcaster, and of real estate, including New York City's Empire Hotel.
5. Estée Lauder, 83	$5.2 billion	Owner of cosmetics empire. Started with nothing. Born of Hungarian immigrant parents in Queens, New York City. Her uncle whipped up face creams over a gas stove; she peddled them to New York's department stores, including Saks Fifth Avenue.
6. Anne Cox Chambers, 71 Barbara Cox Anthony, 68	$4.8 billion	Owners of Cox Enterprises, a broadcasting and newspaper empire. Includes the Atlanta *Constitution*.
7. Charles Koch, 55 David Koch, 51	$4.7 billion	Owners of oil refineries, cattle ranches, and chemical factories.
8. Warren Edward Buffet, 61	$4.4 billion	Part-owner of Berkshire Hathaway textile mills.
9. Jay Pritzker, 69 Robert Pritzker, 65	$4.2 billion	Owners of Hyatt hotels, the Marmon Group, Ticketmaster, and Conwood chewable tobacco. Recently diversified into aluminum tubing, leather tanning, gypsum mining, environmental consulting, freight car leasing, and medical supplies.
10. Perry Bass, 77 Sid Richardson Bass, 48 Edward Perry Bass, 46 Robert Muse Bass, 43 Lee Marshall Bass, 34	$4.0 billion	Investments in Disney, securities, and real estate. Gave $25 million to Stanford; $80 million to Yale for the study of Western civilization.
11. William Gates III, 35	$3.9 billion	Part owner of software giant Microsoft. Expanding into new fields, including electronic dictionary and thesaurus.
12. Leslie Wexner, 54	$3.6 billion	Starting with a small Columbus, Ohio, sportswear shop, built chain of 4,000 stores, including Limited and Victoria's Secret. Part owner of Sotheby's auction house. Recently gave $250 million to the Ohio Higher Education Trust.

13. A. Alfred Taubman, 67	$3.4 billion	Part owner of Sotheby's, Woodward & Lothrop, John Wanamaker, A&W Restaurants. Began putting up commercial buildings in suburban Detroit, moved on to gas stations, shopping malls, real estate, art.
14. John T. Dorrance III, 47 Bennett Dorrance, 45 Mary Alice Dorrance Malone, 41	$3.1 billion	Descendants of Campbell Soup Company founder.
15. Ronald Owen Perelman, 48	$3.1 billion	Owner of conglomerate, including MacAndrews & Forbes, Revlon, Coleman Co., National Health Laboratories, Marvel Comics, S&Ls.
16. Richard M. DeVos, 65	$3.0 billion	Started Amway in 1959; sells household cleaners, detergents, cosmetics, vitamins.
17. H. Ross Perot, 61	$3.0 billion	Owner of Perot Systems Corp; recently sold Electronics Data Systems to General Motors. Investor in real estate, oil and gas production.
18. Jay Van Andel, 67	$3.0 billion	Part-owner of Amway; also sells biodegradable products. Recently commended by the United Nations for work protecting the environment.
19. Sumner Redstone, 68	$2.9 billion	Owner of National Amusements, Inc., one of the largest motion picture circuits in U.S. Also controls Viacom, producer of *Roseanne*.
20. Edward Gaylord, 72	$2.7 billion	Owner of Oklahoma Publishing and Gaylord Broadcasting as well as Opryland USA, a sprawling country music theme park in Nashville.
21. Laurence Alan Tisch, 68 Preston Robert Tisch, 65	$2.2 billion	Part-owners of Loews Corp., including CBS, banks, N.Y. Giants.
22. William Bernard Ziff, 61	$2.2 billion	Owner of Ziff Communications, real estate, computer magazines (*PC Magazine*).
23. Walter H. Annenberg, 83	$2.1 billion	Son of East Prussian immigrant, made fortune publishing the *Daily Racing Form*, *Seventeen*, *TV Guide*.
24. Paul Allen, 38	$1.9 billion	Part-owner of Microsoft, Portland Trail Blazers pro-basketball team, Asymetrix. Plays guitar in a rock band called Threads.

SOURCE: Jennifer Reese, "The Billionaires," *Fortune*, September 9, 1991, pp. 42–114.

family had reached the minimum income level so designated, poverty could be declared dead.

A Relative Standard

A **relative standard of poverty measurement** defines a person's "needs" as a market basket of goods that varies over time and space and always equals a designated *percentage* of the goods that are available to the average person in the society. Unlike the absolute standard, which ignores the quantities of goods available to other people, the relative standard demands such a comparison. If, as in 1989, the median family income equals $34,213 per year (half of all families had less, half had more), the relative approach might designate 45 percent of the median,

EXAMPLE 1

Is the Boss Getting Paid Too Much?

Last chapter's section Pure Rent Earned by People indicated that many individuals who receive exceedingly high income do so not by selling services of natural and capital resources but by selling their own labor. More often than not, individuals in this category are top business executives. In the United States in 1988, their average total pay was $2,025,485, which was 93 times an average factory worker's $21,725; 72 times an average school teacher's $28,008; and 44 times an average engineer's $45,680. Comparing the millions of dollars of executive pay with the mere thousands of dollars earned by ordinary factory workers, school teachers, or engineers, people often ask: Are these people getting paid too much?

As noted in the last chapter, in one sense, the answer may be "yes." To the extent that the high incomes in question represent pure economic rent (and a reduction in this rent would, therefore, not reduce the labor quantity supplied), part of the payment is unnecessary and thus excessive. In another sense, however, the high payments may well be justified. Consider a chief executive officer whose superb management has raised the value of the company by $1 billion over the course of 3 years. Is it really unreasonable for the company's stockholders to pay 10 percent of this gain to the man or woman who made them this much richer? Such a payment would come to $100 million over the period in question, or $33.3 million per year.

Business Week magazine recently investigated executive pay in 354 companies from this point of view. Some

TABLE A Executive Pay Versus Stockholders' Return, 1986–1988

Executives Who Gave Stockholders the Most for Their Pay . . .

Executive	Firm	Executive total pay (*thousands*)	Stockholder return (*percent*)	Performance index
1. R. Lee Taylor II	Holly Farms	$816	108	254
2. Dwight H. Hibbard	Cincinnati Bell	1,930	238	175
3. Wm. T. McCormick Jr.	CMS Energy	1,863	225	174
4. Robert E. Price	Price	686	7	156
5. Bert Ballengee	Southwestern Pub. Serv.	821	27	154

. . . And Those Who Gave Shareholders the Least

1. Lee A. Iacocca	Chrysler	$41,930	38	3.3
2. Michael D. Eisner	Walt Disney	50,201	136	4.7
3. John H. Gutfreund	Salomon	9,452	−40	6.3
4. James D. Robinson III	American Express	16,648	9	6.5
5. Paul Fireman	Reebok Intl.	39,916	173	6.8

of its conclusions are embodied in Tables A and B. Table A compares the total pay of executives (salary, bonus, etc.) over the 1986–88 period with their stockholders' return over this three-year period (including both share-price appreciation and dividends). The performance index given in the last column is based on the stockholder-return to executive-total-pay ratio in comparison with similar ratios for other executives in the same industry group. The precise method of index construction is not important here, but note that a stockholder-return to executive-total-pay ratio above the industry average produces a high index (stockholders get relatively much for the money they pay their managers), while the opposite yields a low index. As is indicated, the index was highest for R. Lee Taylor II of Holly Farms; it was lowest for Lee A. Iacocca of Chrysler.

Table B looks at the same issue in a different way, comparing the total pay of executives over the 1986–1988 period with their companies' average return on common equity over this same period. Once again, the performance index is based on a comparison of each executive's performance with that of his or her peers in the same industry. According to Table B, Allen Born of Amax did the best; Robert D. Hunsucker of Panhandle Eastern, the worst.

Clearly then, by the respective criteria employed here, some executives are not being paid too much, but others are.

Source: *Business Week,* May 1, 1989; the tables are based on p. 49.

TABLE B *Executive Pay Versus Company Profitability, 1986–1988*

Executives Whose Companies Did the Best Relative to Their Pay . . .

Executive	Firm	Executive total pay (*thousands*)	Average return on equity (*percent*)	Performance index
1. Allen Born	Amax	$2,904	18.6	1,827
2. David S. Tappan, Jr.	Fluor	1,939	−2.0	379
3. John D. Ong	B. F. Goodrich	3,224	9.8	203
4. Walter F. Williams	Bethlehem Steel	2,035	1.8	184
5. Morton L. Mandel	Premier Industrial	1,052	24.7	184

. . . And Those Whose Companies Did the Worst

1. Robert D. Hunsucker	Panhandle Eastern	2,204	−17.2	−100
2. Walter J. McCarthy, Jr.	Detroit Edison	1,392	5.3	−59
3. Richard A. Clarke	Pacific Gas & Elec.	1,523	6.4	−22
4. James L. Ketelsen	Tenneco	3,068	−1.3	−13
5. Joseph J. Pinola	First Interstate	4,254	−3.7	−12.5

or $15,396 per year, as the "poverty line" and declare all families who have a lower income to be poor. Naturally, if such a relative standard is adopted, poverty can *never* be eliminated, unless the incomes of all persons are identical.

The relative standard has been popular since at least the time of Adam Smith. As he put it, "By necessaries, I understand not only the commodities which are indispensably necessary for the support of life, but whatever the custom of the country renders it indecent for creditable people, even of the lowest order, to be without."[8]

Presumably, if Smith lived today, he would argue that the rock-bottom income figure calculated in the previous section should be increased substantially to include funds for items, such as used cars, black-and-white television sets, or rotary-dial telephones, that are generally considered necessities by current social standards even though they are clearly not a physiological requirement for life.

The Meaning of "Available Income"

A second conceptual issue involves the measurement of the income actually available to people. It must be compared to the (absolute or relative) poverty line in order to classify people as poor or nonpoor as well as to determine the size of the **poverty gap,** the difference between poor people's needed income and their actual income. Presumably, one should determine actual income by counting people's money income from all sources, including currently earned wages, rent, interest, and profit. But questions arise. Should one count income before taxes or after taxes? Should one count or ignore the cash transfers (such as unemployment benefits, welfare payments, or pensions) that poor people receive from the government or their former employers? Should one include in "income" a monetary estimate of in-kind benefits, such as the receipt from government or employers of free food (food stamps, lunches at school or work), free housing (subsidized public or employer-provided housing), free medical care (Medicaid or employer-paid health insurance)? How should one treat people's access to credit? How about the assets people own, ranging from savings accounts to homes, land, and animals and to consumer durables, such as cars? And, given the fact that hours worked are a choice variable (people can often *choose* to work 10 or 60 hours a week), how should one treat the fact that different people consume vastly different amounts of leisure time? Answers to all these questions must be given before the extent of poverty can be gauged.

Consider two families of identical size, both "need" $12,000 a year. Family A has earned cash income of $10,000 a year (and pays $1,000 in taxes). Family B has earned cash income of $3,000 a year (and pays no taxes). Are both families poor? And is B poorer than A? What if family B, unlike family A, received $4,000 in unemployment and pension benefits, $2,000 worth of food stamps, $1,000 worth of Medicaid, had $15,000 in the bank (and could easily borrow more), and also lived in its own home free and clear? What if members of family B, unlike those of family A, were working—by choice—only 8 hours a week outside the home, but were growing fresh fruits and vegetables on their own land and getting eggs, milk, and meat from their animals in the barn? Would you still want to count family B as poor? These issues must be resolved before poverty can be measured and attacked.

The Choice of an "Income-Receiving Unit"

A third conceptual issue concerns the question of which income-receiving unit is appropriately considered when carrying out the comparison between "needs" and "income available." One could consider all individuals as separate units, but this view would cause virtually all of the nation's children to be counted as poor. All of them have needs, few of them have income of their own. One could instead focus on *households* as the relevant unit, looking at the combined needs of all the persons occupying a given housing unit and comparing that need with their combined available income. One could, finally, gather analogous data for *families,* groups of two or more persons who are related by birth, marriage, or adoption and are also residing together.

The choice made here will have a major impact on the extent of poverty measured and also on the way it is perceived to change over time. Consider a choice that selects the family as the basic unit of measurement. Such a choice seems most reasonable. Given the large extent of income-sharing that

---

[8] Adam Smith, *An Inquiry into the Nature and Causes of the Wealth of Nations* (Edinburgh: Adam and Charles Black, 1776/1872), p. 393.

traditionally occurs within families, it seems odd to count as poor family members who have no personal income but have easy access to the income of others within the family. But now consider the growing trend of middle-aged women, teenage children, and the elderly establishing smaller, fragmented households, splitting off from the middle-aged men with whom, in the past, they might have continued to live. Such a fragmentation of the traditional family reduces the access of many family members to the income of richer relatives. It causes the measured incidence of poverty to rise. Should one worry about it or should one ignore it as the inevitable price that people must pay for their own behavior, for the greater independence that they seek? Would your answer differ if those who split off from the family were forced to do so?

The Choice of an "Accounting Period"

A fourth conceptual issue concerns the proper accounting period over which "needs" and "income available" are to be compared. Is one to consider a month, a year, a lifetime? Estimates of poverty are likely to be extremely sensitive to the choice made because flows of consumption and income for most people are highly uneven over time. Many whose *lifetime* income is extremely high can, nevertheless, have unusually high needs or low incomes in some years and even more so in selected months. Consider the effects of a newborn child, a major illness, sudden unemployment, a temporary return to school, a divorce. Example 2 has more to say on this subject.

The Official Definition

The U.S. government has made choices on all of the issues in the preceding sections. Inevitably, these choices leave some people unhappy, but other choices would merely shift this unhappiness to others. The best we can do is understand what the official definition of poverty is and what, therefore official data on poverty do and do not tell us.

First, the U.S. government has rejected a relative definition of poverty and adopted an absolute standard. In the early 1960s, it established a family **poverty line,** an income level that separates the poor below it from the nonpoor above it, at a money income of $3,000 per year. The $3,000 figure was calculated to assure a family's minimum need in the way of food, clothing, medical care, and shelter, the latter including such "luxuries" as heat, a refrigerator, cold and hot water, an indoor flush toilet, a bed for every person, electric lighting, and enough furnishings to have a common meal. The government's argument was similar to ours earlier in this chapter. In 1959, argued the Department of Agriculture, a minimum nutritional meal cost 22.8 cents per person. With the average family size known to be 3.65 persons per family, a bare daily minimum of food was considered to cost about $2.50, or somewhat below $1,000 per year per average family. This figure was then tripled.

By the mid 1960s, extensive criticism of the government's standard had emerged. The standard failed to account for deviations from the average in the circumstances of actual families. Inflation over the years had also eroded the purchasing power of the $3,000 annual figure. Following a congressional mandate, the Social Security Administration in 1964 developed a more sophisticated standard that set different poverty lines for 100 different family types and then tied them to the consumer price index. (If the index rises by 7.1 percent in a year due to inflation, so do all of the poverty lines; if it falls by 1.3 percent, the poverty lines fall accordingly.) Federal Interagency Committees further revised the standards in 1969 and 1980.

The present poverty lines are fewer in number. They are still based on the cost of a nutritionally adequate diet (the Department of Agriculture's 1961 "economy food plan") for families of different size and composition, generally multiplied by 3. (A 1955 government survey showed that families spent an average 35 percent of after-tax income on food.) Table 4 shows some of the recent standards used by the U.S. Bureau of the Census.

Second, when the U.S. government classifies people as poor or nonpoor with the help of its poverty lines, it defines people's actual income as money income before taxes and *excluding* noncash benefits such as food stamps, Medicaid, public housing, and more. Included in the money income figure are wages, rents, interest, unincorporated business profits, dividends (but not capital gains), as well as all types of cash transfers, such as unemployment and social security benefits, public assistance payments, and pensions. (Using independent sources for comparison, the government estimates that respondents to its surveys underreport their money income by about 10 percent.)

EXAMPLE 2

Income Dynamics

Data on the personal distribution of money income, such as those found in Table 1 and embodied in Figure 1, can be highly misleading and not only because money income data ignore the receipt by many people of significant amounts of income in kind. More importantly, such single-year data ignore the fact that most people go through a predictable cycle of earning relatively low incomes in their youths, ever-growing incomes until retirement, and usually lower incomes thereafter. As a result, it would be possible for all the inhabitants of a country to have identical *lifetime* incomes, yet the Lorenz curve would look precisely like our Figure 1, recording great inequality year in and year out. In every year, the young and retired would show up at the bottom of that year's income distribution; prime-age earners would show up at the top. Yet, over time, any given individual would move forward and backward through all the rows of Table 1. Thus, any one-year Lorenz curve would merely reflect the age distribution of the population. There would always be low-income people and there would always be high-income people, but they would always be *different* people.

A group of researchers at the University of Michigan's Survey Research Center has been working for years to find out whether the hypothetical scenario outlined in the preceding paragraph applies to the United States. Under the direction of James N. Morgan and Greg J. Duncan, researchers in 1968 selected a 5,000-family sample of Americans that was indistinguishable from the American population as a whole. Ever since, yearly interviews have been conducted with the *same* families, including members that split off, such as children moving out on their own, adults moving on to new lives after becoming widowed or divorced, and so forth. By 1983, the group included 16,000 individuals, living in 6,500 families.

This Panel Study on Income Dynamics (PSID) has yielded fascinating results and has confirmed the suspicion that the "snapshot" character of annual income-distribution data significantly distorts our thinking and causes us to

TABLE A *Changes in Family Income, 1979–1978*

Family income quintile, 1971	Family income quintile, 1978					
	Highest	Second	Third	Fourth	Lowest	Total
Highest	48.5	29.5	14.0	4.5	3.5	100%
Second	22.0	31.5	25.5	15.0	6.0	100%
Third	14.0	18.5	30.5	23.5	13.5	100%
Fourth	9.0	13.5	21.5	34.5	21.5	100%
Lowest	6.0	7.0	9.5	22.0	55.5	100%

miss much of the "movie" of real life.

Selected results from the ongoing PSID study are given in Tables A and B; they show an amazing degree of movement within the American income distribution. The left-hand column of Table A ranks families by 1971 income from the highest fifth (or *quintile*) to the lowest and then notes along each row where each of these groups ended up in 1978. Note that only 48.5 percent of those who were among the top fifth of income recipients in 1971 still were there in 1978. Some 29.5, 14, 4.5, and 3.5 percent, respectively, had dropped to successively lower fifths. Similarly, of those who were in the second income quintile in 1971, only 31.5 percent found themselves in the same position in 1978. Some 22 percent were better off, some 25.5, 15, and 6 percent were in lower income quintiles. If there had been no such mobility in the income distribution, all the circled numbers in the table's diagonal would have equaled 100 percent.

Table B draws on other data from the PSID study and notes how young people fared relative to their parents. The left-hand column classified parents by their average 1969–81 income quintiles. Along each row we see what happened to their offspring. Consider the top row. Only 36 percent of children whose parents were in the top income quintile ended up in that top quintile as well; 23, 19, 13, and 9 percent, respectively, ended up in successively *lower* quintiles. Or consider the bottom row: Only 44 percent of children whose parents were in the bottom income quintile ended up in that quintile as well; 27, 18, 9, and 2 percent, respectively, ended up in successively *higher* quintiles. Again, if there had been no such mobility, all the circled numbers would equal 100 percent.

Source: Mark Lilla, "Why the 'Income Distribution' Is So Misleading," *The Public Interest,* Fall 1984, pp. 62–76. For a first report on the study itself, see Greg J. Duncan, et al., *Years of Poverty, Years of Plenty: The Changing Fortunes of American Workers and Families* (Ann Arbor, MI: University of Michigan Institute for Social Research, 1984).

TABLE B *Intergenerational Economic Mobility, 1969–1981*

Parent's average family income quintile	Young adult's average family income quintile					
	Highest	Second	Third	Fourth	Lowest	Total
Highest	36	23	19	13	9	100%
Second	25	26	22	17	10	100%
Third	17	26	23	23	11	100%
Fourth	15	19	19	24	23	100%
Lowest	2	9	18	27	44	100%

TABLE 4 Selected U.S. Poverty Lines, 1989

Individuals	
1 person	$6,311
15–64 years	6,452
65 years and over	5,947
Families	
2 persons	$8,076
householder 15–64 years	8,343
householder 65 years and over	7,501
3 persons	9,885
4 persons	12,675
5 persons	14,990
6 persons	16,921
7 persons	19,162
8 persons	21,328
9 persons or more	25,480

Different poverty lines are defined in the United States for unrelated individuals and for families of different size and composition.

SOURCE: U.S. Bureau of the Census, Current Population Reports, Series P-60, No. 168, *Money Income and Poverty Status in the United States: 1989* (Washington, D.C.: U.S. Government Printing Office, 1990, p. 86.

CAUTION

In response to recent criticism and following a congressional directive, the Census Bureau has begun to calculate people's "available income" in nine alternative ways, in addition to the official calculation. These alternative calculations include the value of selected noncash benefits and use different methods of valuing such benefits.[9] *The most comprehensive measure includes money income as defined earlier in this section plus the* market value *of food, housing, and medical benefits received in kind. (If three free visits to the doctor were provided and used and such visits ordinarily cost $40 each, $120 is added to the available-income figure.) Another alternative measures the value of these noncash benefits at their* worth to the recipient, *which is usually lower than market value. (For example, if three free visits to the doctor were provided and therefore used, and if such visits ordinarily cost $40 each but similarly situated families who pay for them are known to make only two visits to the doctor, only $80 is added to the available-income figure.)*

---

[9] See U.S. Bureau of the Census, Technical Paper 58, *Estimates of Poverty Including the Value of Noncash Benefits, 1987.*

Finally, we should note that the U.S. government makes comparisons between "available income" and appropriate poverty lines in three different ways: for persons, households, and families. In all cases, the comparisons are made for annual rather than shorter or longer accounting periods. The Census Bureau knows that certain population groups, such as the homeless, are missed in its surveys. To that extent, its data underrepresent the problem of poverty. For more on that subject see Example 3.

Poverty Statistics

Having discussed how poverty is defined, we now turn to the data collected by the U.S. government to understand the overall extent of poverty and also the makeup of the poverty population.

Overall Measures of Poverty

Figure 3 summarizes what happened to poverty in America during the past three decades. The black line on top measures the total number of poor persons (rather than families or households) counted by the Census Bureau in each of the indicated years. Note how the number of poor persons fell dramatically during the 1960s, from 39.5 million in 1959 (the first year for which the data were tabulated) to 24.1 million in 1969. The downward movement ceased during the 1970s, when poverty fluctuated within the 23 to 26 million range. Subsequently, the number of poor persons rose markedly

FIGURE 3 The History of U.S. Poverty, 1959–1989

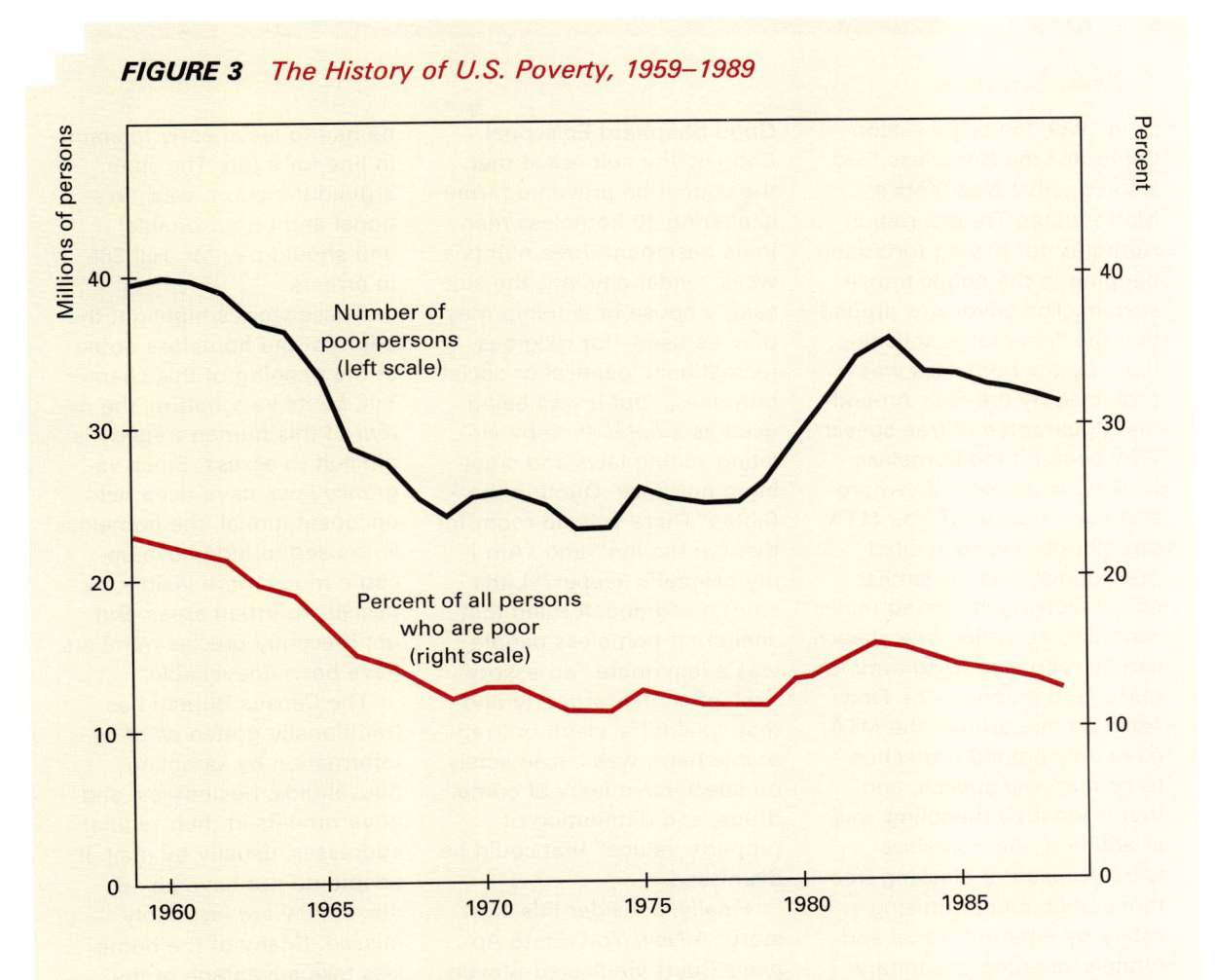

[Graph showing: Number of poor persons (left scale, millions) and Percent of all persons who are poor (right scale), from 1960 to 1985.]

This graph summarizes the recent history of U.S. poverty, based on the official government definition of the poverty concept. The black line measures the absolute number of poor persons; the color line, the poverty rate. *Source:* U.S. Bureau of the Census, Current Population Reports, Series P-60, No. 168, *Money Income and Poverty Status in the United States: 1989* (Washington, D.C.: U.S. Government Printing Office, 1990), p. 57.

to 35.3 million by 1983, then fell to 31.5 million in 1989.

The color line at the bottom of Figure 3 measures the extent of poverty in an alternative way, as the **poverty rate,** or the percentage of all the people in a given group (here the entire population) who are poor. That line more or less mirrors the changes in absolute numbers. The poverty rate fell from 22.4 percent of all persons in 1959 to 12.1 percent by 1969. It fluctuated between 11.1 percent and 12.6 percent during the 1970s, then rose to 15.2 percent in 1983. By 1989, some 12.8 percent of all persons were poor.[10]

---

[10] It is interesting to compare this figure with alternatives calculated in the source cited in footnote 9. If "available income" is redefined to include in-kind receipts of food, housing, and medical care, the 13.5 percent 1987 poverty rate falls to 8.5 percent if the market value of these items is used; it falls to 11 percent if the items' "worth to recipients" is used.

EXAMPLE 3

The Homeless

In 1989, the Legal Action Center for the Homeless filed a suit against New York's Metropolitan Transportation Authority for having forbidden begging in the public transit system. The advocates argued that the "charitable solicitation" by the homeless was protected by the First Amendment guarantee of free speech. Why couldn't the homeless walk up to anyone anywhere and ask a question? The MTA thought otherwise. It cited precedents (such as similar suits involving shopping malls) according to which free speech can be regulated as to time, place, and manner. The First Amendment, argued the MTA, gave only limited protection to *commercial* speech, and that is what panhandling was. In addition, the homeless were accused of blocking free movement, compromising safety by entering tracks and tunnels, creating unsanitary conditions, and playing radios loudly.

At the same time, the State Supreme Court returned a verdict in another suit filed by a New York City condominium against the Partnership for the Homeless, which was coordinating the nation's largest private shelter system and had set up 147 shelters in houses of worship, such as the condominium's neighbor, the Good Shepherd Episcopal Church. The suit asked that the church be prevented from sheltering 10 homeless men in its basement three nights a week. Under city law, the suit said, a house of worship may only be used "for religious, recreational, political or social purposes," but it was being used as a *hotel,* thereby violating zoning laws and creating a nuisance. Quoting the Bible ("There was no room for them in the inn" and "Am I my brother's keeper?"), the court disagreed. It ruled that sheltering homeless people was a legitimate "accessory use" of church property and that "plaintiffs' claim of irreparable harm was based solely on speculative fears of crime, drugs, and diminution of property values" that could be dismissed.

Finally, consider this 1991 story: A New York State Appeals Court vindicated Steven Hill, a homeless longshoreman, who had fought welfare officials over a 57 cents per day breakfast allowance. While the state was giving a $2.14 daily food allowance to homeless people, this man's allowance had been reduced by 57 cents because he was eligible for a *free* breakfast at a shelter. Mr. Hill always missed the breakfast because it was being served late and he had to leave early to stand in line for a job. The state, argued the court, was "irrational and unreasonable" and should pay Mr. Hill $85 in arrears.

These stories highlight the plight of the homeless noted at the opening of this chapter. Yet, by its very nature, the *extent* of this human tragedy is difficult to assess. Since vagrancy laws have been held unconstitutional, the homeless who used to hide have become much more visible, especially in urban areas. But until recently precise numbers have been unavailable.

The Census Bureau has traditionally gotten *all* of its information by sampling households, businesses, and governments at their regular addresses, usually by mail. If people do not have an address, they are inevitably missed. (Many of the homeless take advantage of the *general delivery* service provided at post offices and originally designed for sailors, tourists, and city newcomers. That service, however, is usually available only for 30 days, and the alternative of renting a post office box is not only costly but unavailable to people who do not have a permanent address.) Given the lack of solid information, various people have estimated the number of America's homeless anywhere from 250,000 to 3 million in the past. Recently a figure close to the lower end of this range was found to be accurate. Between 2 and 4 a.m. on March 21, 1990, the U.S. Census Bureau conducted its first count of the homeless. All across the land, its agents swept through abandoned buildings, all-night movie houses, bus stations, and doorways; canvassed church basements, city shelters, drug detox centers, hospital emergency rooms, and subsidized hotels; peeked into the shadows of parks and underpasses, of parked cars and even California's foothill caves. The total count: 228,621.

Although the number is disputed, we know this about the homeless: They consist of three groups, roughly of equal size. The first group is severely disabled, usually mentally ill, and ended up in the streets in the 1970s when the confinement of people in state mental hospitals was vilified as "brutal, costly, and unconstitutional." As a result, the chronically ill were deinstitutionalized, but they were not welcomed in the homes or neighborhoods of all those who had fought with such zeal for their "humane treatment." A second group consists of women—often battered and teenage, often with young children. Some 60 percent of them have been physically or sexually abused and became "runaways" (leaving home with or without permission but not returning) or "throwaways" (having been told to leave by parents who provided no alternative care and no possibility of return). A third group of homeless is made up of men, often violent and addicted to alcohol and drugs. Clearly, all these data suggest that the problem of homelessness is *not* primarily a housing problem.

A final note: counting the homeless, like counting the poor in general, is fraught with conceptual problems. The following persons, for example, were encountered by census takers. All of them considered *themselves* homeless. Would you be willing to classify them as such?

a. A man living in a cardboard box leaning against the back of a railroad station

b. A man doubled up illegally in a friend's apartment without knowledge of the landlord

c. A teenager sleeping in a shelter for the homeless because of a fight with her (affluent) parents

d. A woman with a home, hiding in a shelter to escape bill collectors

e. A family living in an overcrowded house and wishing for a bigger house

Sources: David Wessel, "Street Sweep," *The Wall Street Journal,* November 14, 1989, pp. 1 and 16; Ann Hagedorn and Milo Geyelin, "Homeless Advocates Sue for Right to Beg," *The Wall Street Journal,* November 29, 1989, p. B8; Robert D. McFadden, "Homeless Shelter in Church Is Upheld," *The New York Times,* December 12, 1989, p. B3; Michael Freitag, "Subway Security Plan Fails to Purge the Unruly Homeless," *The New York Times,* January 24, 1990, pp. A1 and B2; J. C. Barden, "Toll of Troubled Families: Flood of Homeless Youths," *The New York Times,* February 5, 1990, pp. A1 and B8; Jason De Parle, "General Delivery: Mail Call for the Homeless," *The New York Times,* February 24, 1990, pp. A1 and 30; Mireya Navarro, "Census Peers Into Corners to Count Homeless," *The New York Times,* March 21, 1990, pp. A1 and B3; Robert C. Ellickson, "The Homelessness Muddle," *The Public Interest,* Spring 1990, pp. 45–60; Ronald Sullivan, "Court Victory for Homeless: 57¢ for Breakfast," *The New York Times,* February 3, 1991, p. 32; Peter H. Rossi, *Down and Out in America: The Origins of Homelessness* (Chicago: University of Chicago Press, 1989); and Dennis Hevesi, "Census Count of Homeless Is Disputed," *The New York Times,* April 3, 1991, p. A26.

TABLE 5 *The Composition of the U.S. Poverty Population in 1989*

Characteristic (1)	Number below poverty line and composition of total (2)		Poverty rate (*Percentage in given row category who were poor*) (3)
	Millions	*Percent*	
1. Race, origin			
All Persons	**31.5**	**100.0**	**12.8**
White	20.8	65.9	10.0
African-American	9.3	29.5	30.7
Asian, Native American	1.4	4.6	16.4
Hispanic[a]	5.4	17.2	26.2
2. Age			
All persons	**31.5**	**100.0**	**12.8**
Under 18 years	12.4	39.4	19.4
18–64 years	15.7	49.9	10.3
65 years and over	3.4	10.7	11.4
3. Living arrangements			
All persons	**31.5**	**100.0**	**12.8**
Living in families	24.1	76.3	11.5
Living alone	6.7	21.5	19.2
Living in subfamilies	.7	2.2	54.4
All persons in families	**24.1**	**100.0**	**11.5**
Living in families with female head, no husband present	11.7	48.5	35.9
Living in all other families	12.4	51.5	7.0
4. Farm and nonfarm residence			
All persons	**31.5**	**100.0**	**12.8**
Farm residence	.5	1.6	11.1
Nonfarm residence	31.0	98.4	12.9
Metropolitan areas	**22.9**	**100.0**	**12.0**
in central cities	13.6	59.3	18.1
suburbs	9.3	40.7	8.0

[a] Hispanics may be of any race and are included in the respective racial categories; in fact, over 90 percent are white.

Characteristic (1)	Number below poverty line and composition of total (2)		Poverty rate (*Percentage in given row category who were poor*) (3)
5. Geographic region			
All persons	**31.5**	**100.0**	**12.8**
Northeast	5.1	16.0	10.0
Midwest	7.0	22.3	11.9
West	6.5	20.6	12.5
South	12.9	41.1	15.4
6. Educational attainment households heads			
25 years and over	**5.9**	**100.0**	**9.4**
Zero school years	.1	2.1	45.6
Elementary school			
1–7 years	1.0	16.2	25.5
8 years	.5	8.0	15.9
High school			
1–3 years	1.4	23.1	19.2
4 years	2.1	35.0	8.9
College			
1 or more years	.9	15.6	3.6
7. Work experience			
All persons, 15 years and over	**20.5**	**100.0**	**10.7**
Worked full time	2.9	14.0	3.1
Worked part time	5.5	27.1	13.5
Did not work	12.1	58.9	20.7
All persons, 15 years and over, who did not work	**12.1**	**100.0**	**20.7**
Ill or disabled	2.7	22.0	32.5
Keeping house	3.8	31.7	21.6
Going to school	2.0	16.5	22.9
Retired	2.3	19.1	10.9
Unable to find work	.7	6.1	53.3
Other	.6	4.6	44.5

SOURCE: U.S. Bureau of the Census, *Current Population Reports*, Series P-60, No. 168, *Money Income and Poverty Status in the United States: 1989* (Washington, D.C.: U.S. Government Printing Office, 1990), pp. 56–58, 65, and 67.

The data that allow us to measure the number of poor persons and the poverty rate also let us compute the overall poverty gap, or the amount of additional income that would be needed to bring the means available to every poor person up to the poverty line. In 1989, the average poor family fell short by $4,969; the average poor unrelated individual by $2,836. Overall, the poverty gap equaled $138.8 billion, 2.7 percent of that year's gross national income.

The Makeup of the Poverty Population

Census data provide us with detailed information about the makeup of the poverty population. Table 5 brings together selected data on the subject. As in the table, consider the seven characteristics in turn.

Race and Ethnic Origin

Of the 31.5 million persons who were poor in 1989, Section 1 tells us, almost two thirds were white; most of the remainder were black. The poverty rate, however, was highest for blacks and a particular subcategory of mostly white persons, Hispanics. Among all black persons, 30.7 percent were poor; among all Hispanics, 26.2 percent were poor.

Age

Of the 31.5 million persons who were poor in 1989, Section 2 tells us, 39.4 percent were under 18 years of age, almost 11 percent were elderly. It used to be that the elderly were extremely poor, but not any more. The poverty rate was highest for the very young (19.4 percent); that of the elderly (11.4 percent) was below the 12.8 percent national average.

Living Arrangements

Of the 31.5 million persons who were poor in 1989, Section 3 tells us, 76.3 percent lived in traditional families (groups of two or more persons who were related by birth, marriage, or adoption and were residing together). Some 21.5 percent lived alone; the rest, in "subfamilies," defined as a married couple with or without children, or one parent with one or more children, living in a household headed by another (related or unrelated) person. Note how the poverty rate among persons living in families (11.5 percent) was below the 12.8 percent national average, while that for persons living alone (19.2 percent) or living in subfamilies (54.4 percent) were above that average.

Note also the additional detail provided for persons living in families. Poverty in this category was concentrated in female-headed families (with no husband present), whose poverty rate reached 35.9 percent.

Farm and Nonfarm Residence

Of the 31.5 million persons who were poor in 1989, Section 4 tells us, 98.4 percent lived in nonfarm areas; not surprisingly, given the large percentage of all poor people considered, their poverty rate (12.9 percent) equaled the national average. Interesting additional detail is provided by focusing on the 22.9 million poor persons living in metropolitan areas. Of these, 59.3 percent were found in central cities, where the poverty rate was 18.1 percent (compared to a suburban rate of 8 percent).

Geographic Region

Section 5 shows the distribution of the poor among four major geographic regions. Poverty rates in the Northeast, Midwest, and West were lower than the 12.8 percent national average; that in the South (15.4 percent) lay above it.

Educational Attainment

The Section 6 data focus on the educational attainment of poor household heads aged 25 and above. The poverty rate of this group was 9.4 percent on the average but varied dramatically with years of schooling completed. Some 45.6 percent of those without any schooling were poor; the rate declined steadily to 3.6 percent for those with at least 1 year of college. Nothing can more forcefully illustrate the importance of owning human capital.

Work Experience

The Section 7 data, finally, focus on the 1989 work experience of persons aged 15 and above. The poverty rate for this group as a whole was 10.7 percent but varied substantially with the amount of work people performed. Among those who worked full time, only 3.1 percent were poor; 13.5 percent of part-time workers were, as were 20.7 percent of those who did not work at all.

Why did people not work? Of the 12.1 million poor persons, aged 15 and above, who did not work at all, 22 percent were ill or disabled (and the poverty rate in that group was 32.5 percent). Another 31.7 percent were keeping house, 16.5 percent were going to school, 19.1 percent were retired; only 6.1 percent were unable to find work. In that group, the poverty rate was the highest (reaching 53.3 percent).

Conclusion

Our table goes a long way toward explaining the reasons for poverty. First and foremost is people's inability to get any income from work—either because they are not expected to work (consider children, students, mothers with young children, and the retired) or because they are unable to work (consider the ill and disabled or the involuntarily unemployed). Second in importance is people's inability to earn a sufficiently high income when they do work, which is strongly related to their educational attainment and possibly to discrimination in the labor market. (For a review of that subject, see the section Discrimination in the Labor Market in the chapter "Imperfectly Competitive Labor Markets.")

To corroborate what has just been said, consider this: Of the 31.5 million poor persons in 1989, some 12.4 million were under 18, some 3.4 million were 65 years and over, and some 3.5 million were mothers, aged 18–64, who lived with children and no husband. Those groups alone accounted for 61 percent of the poor.

The Dynamics of Poverty

Example 2 earlier in this chapter warned us not to be overly impressed by the inequality of income revealed by the statistics of any given year and commonly depicted in the Lorenz curve graph. The same kind of warning must be issued with respect to a given year's poverty statistics. The poor may be always with us, but, as time passes, they are not necessarily the same people. The PSID study noted earlier in this chapter confirmed a remarkable rate of turnover in the poverty population. A significant portion of those who are poor in any one year were not poor in the prior year and will not be poor in the next year. Consider Table 6 which is based on the PSID study. Nearly a quarter of the people studied were poor for at least one year during the 1969–78 decade, yet only 5.4 percent were poor for five or more years, only 2.6 percent were poor for eight or more years, and fewer than 1 percent were poor during the entire decade.

Thus, the study reached two surprising results. First, a large proportion of American families falls below the poverty line at *some* time (and this is usually caused by short-term occurrences, such as birth, death, divorce, layoffs, or returning to school). Second, only a tiny percentage of American families is persistently poor. Recent U.S. government studies, such as the Census Bureau's Survey of Income and Program Participation (SIPP), have reached identical conclusions. A 1984 study that measured poverty not on an annual basis, but on a monthly basis, found 26.2 percent of all persons poor in *some* month of that year, but only 5.9 percent were poor in every month. (The official *annual* statistic measured a poverty rate of 14.4 percent, as Figure 3 shows.) Lifetime data, similarly, measure only a tiny fraction of the U.S. population as poor.

TABLE 6 The Dynamics of Poverty, 1969–1978

Poor in 1978	6.8%
Poor one or more years	24.4%
Poor five or more years	5.4%
"Persistently poor" (eight or more years)	2.6%
Poor all ten years	0.7%

This table shows the percentage of persons covered by the Michigan Panel Study on Income Dynamics who were poor in 1978, as measured by the U.S. government's poverty lines. The table compares this result with the same people's poverty status during the 1969–1978 decade.

SOURCE: Greg J. Duncan et al., *Years of Poverty, Years of Plenty: The Changing Fortunes of American Workers and Families* (Ann Arbor, MI: University of Michigan Institute for Social Research, 1984).

Summary

1. Even casual observation tells us that the annual incomes of different people differ markedly. This chapter analyzes the factors that determine the apportionment of the national income among individuals—the personal distribution of income.

2. Except for governmental redistributions of income, the income earned by any one person in the U.S. economy comes to depend on three things: the size and quality of human, natural, and capital resource stocks owned; the rate at which these stocks are put to work; and the rental prices that are established in various markets for the flows of resource services in question.

3. The U.S. government collects systematic data on the personal distribution of money income among households, families, and individuals. Data on the 1989 income distribution among families are reviewed, depicted graphically by a Lorenz curve, and described numerically by the Gini coefficient.

4. The unequal ownership of wealth (one reason for the observed inequality in personal incomes) can be pictured by a Lorenz curve as well. In the United States, wealth is distributed even more unequally than income. More likely than not, the less unequal distribution of income reflects many people's ownership of human capital (which is not measured by available data on wealth).

5. A detailed look at the higher income recipients in the United States reveals them to be also super rich in terms of wealth. Among the 400 richest people in America, 40 percent got there through inheritance, as one might expect, but a surprising 54 percent started out poor.

6. Since the passing of the 1964 Economic Opportunity Act, the U.S. government has collected information on the subject of poverty. A clear definition of "poverty" is a crucial prerequisite for measuring its extent, but it involves a number of difficult conceptual problems. These concern the meaning of "needs," the meaning of "available income," the choice of an "income receiving unit," and the choice of an "accounting period." The official U.S. government definition is reviewed.

7. Recent U.S. poverty statistics are examined, including total numbers, poverty rates, and the makeup of the poverty population. The data point strongly to major reasons for poverty: people's inability to get income from work (consider children, students, the retired; the ill, disabled, or involuntarily unemployed) or people's inability to earn a sufficiently high income when they do work (which is strongly related to their educational attainment and possibly to discrimination in the labor market).

8. Over time, a remarkable turnover in the poverty population occurs. Few people are persistently poor, but a large proportion of the population is poor at some time.

Key Concepts

absolute standard of poverty measurement
functional distribution of income
Gini coefficient
line of actual inequality
line of perfect equality
line of perfect inequality
Lorenz curve
personal distribution of income
poverty gap
poverty line
poverty rate
relative standard of poverty measurement

Questions and Problems

1. Take the income distribution data found in the following table and draw a Lorenz curve. Was the distribution more or less unequal in 1935–1936 than in 1989? (Hint: Redraw the 1989 line on the same graph, using the data of Table 1.)

   The Distribution of Money Income Among U.S. Families in 1935/1936

Income class	% of families in class	% of total income received by families in class
Under $2,000	77.7	45.4
$2,000–$2,999	13.1	19.5
$3,000–$3,999	4.4	9.2
$4,000–$4,999	1.7	4.5
$5,000–$7,499	1.6	5.8
$7,500–$9,999	0.6	3.2
$10,000 and over	0.9	12.4

2. "If we were to draw a Lorenz curve for different occupations, we should find the curve for lawyers out further from the line of perfect equality than that for doctors. That for doctors, in turn, would be out further than that for college teachers, and that for college teachers out further than that for army officers." Try to explain.

3. Consider Table A in Example 2. Interpret the meaning of the row and column labeled "lowest."

4. Consider Table B in Example 2. Interpret the meaning of the row and column labeled "third."

5. Take a look at Table 4. Using the definitions shown there, consider your family and all your acquaintances. Are any of them poor? On the basis of your determinations, do you consider the definitions reasonable? Why or why not?

6. "As Table 5 shows, in 1989, some 65.9 percent of all poor persons where white. Thus, it is absurd to argue that poverty hits black people the most."
   Evaluate this statement.

7. "There is one sure way to eliminate poverty: giving jobs to all the poor."
   Evaluate this statement.

8. There has been much talk about the "feminization" of poverty in the United States in recent times. Using sources such as those listed in this chapter, collect data for a number of years. Then prove or disprove the assertion. Also ask yourself if it is possible for the *number* of poor people in a given category to decline over time, while the group's poverty *rate* continues to rise.

9. What, do you think, would life be like in the United States if we had a per capita income of $330 per year, as people in China did in 1988? How do the Chinese manage? How do Indians manage with just about the same? Why did Marco Polo wonder at the wealth of China, and why did Vasco da Gama marvel at that of India? Were they richer in the past?

10. Mr. A: "Poverty invariably comes from exploitation."
    Ms. B: "You are crazy. Look at the facts. Poor people everywhere are poor not because they produce so much and someone takes it away from them, but precisely because they produce so little."
    Evaluate.

PART V

GOVERNMENT IN THE MICROECONOMY

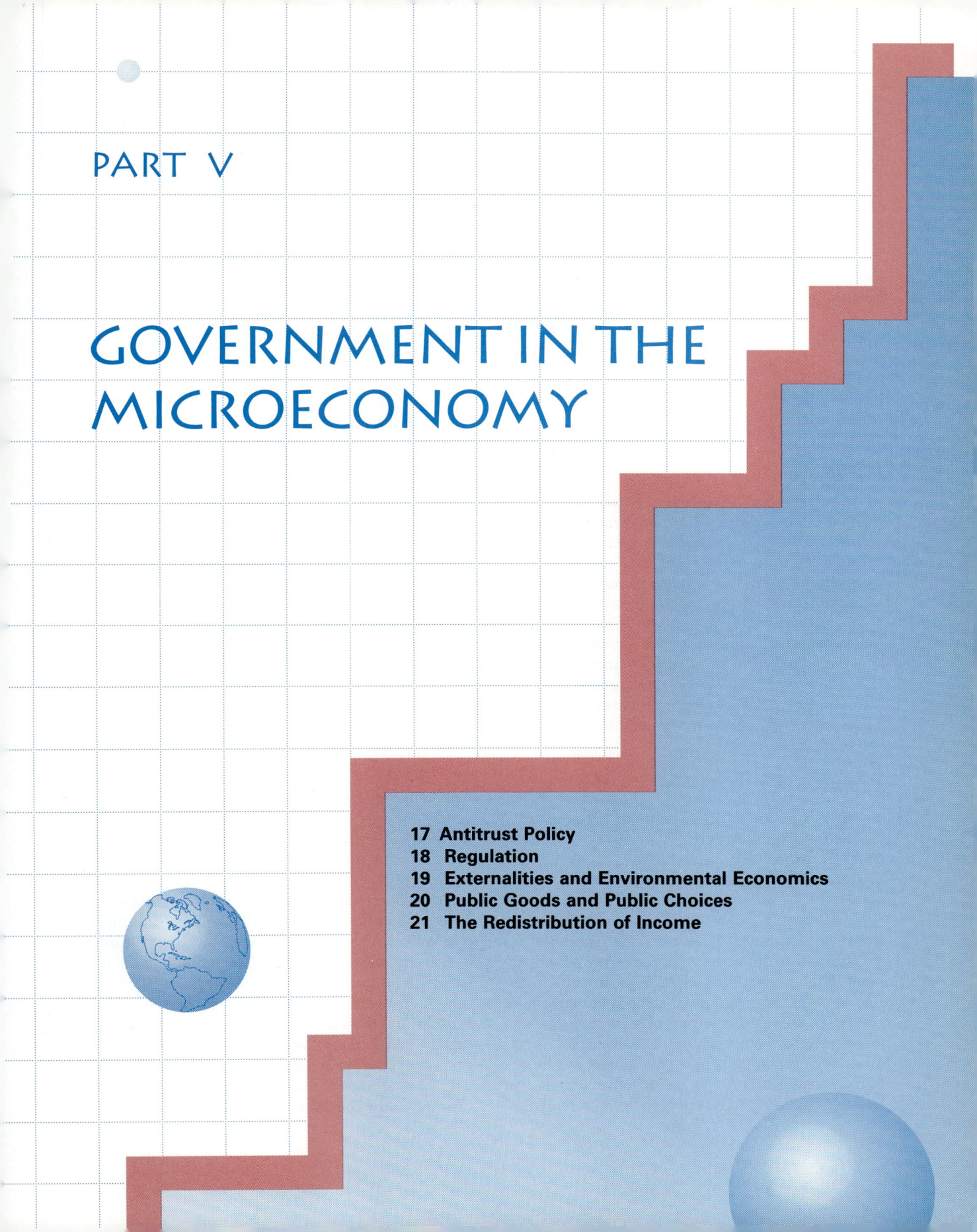

17 Antitrust Policy
18 Regulation
19 Externalities and Environmental Economics
20 Public Goods and Public Choices
21 The Redistribution of Income

CHAPTER 17

ANTITRUST POLICY

Preview

This is the first of several chapters that explore how governments deal with certain shortcomings of the market economy called market failures. *In this chapter we deal with antitrust policy, systematic governmental efforts designed to limit the market power of monopolies, oligopolies, and other imperfectly competitive firms and to create conditions under which free competition can flourish. The ultimate aim of such policy, now pursued for over a century, is to eliminate inefficiencies and inequities attributable to imperfectly competitive conditions.*

Examples

1. The Antitrust Division's Vietnam
2. The Breakup of Ma Bell
3. AT&T, the Unlikely Trustbuster
4. Antitrust in a Global Economy

Previous chapters have provided numerous occasions to note the important role of government in the market economy. We discussed the setting of price floors and price ceilings in markets for goods, as well as the setting of minimum wages in labor markets. We analyzed the effects of excise taxes. We even studied how government has helped farmers and workers set up effective cartels and how all kinds of laws—concerning import quotas, tariffs, labor market discrimination, and more—shape the behavior of people in all kinds of markets in which they buy and sell. Yet all these examples served the function merely of helping us understand how markets work; the discussion of government was incidental, not central. In the remainder of the book, we will take a *systematic* look at the economic role that government plays. In particular, we will discuss the government's attempt to deal with a variety of market failures.

Major Types of Market Failures

As recent political events in Eastern Europe have so vividly shown, centrally planned economies are unlikely to satisfy large masses of people in the long run. Any attempt to run national economies by the method of the Visible Hand (the central allocation of all resources by a government for purposes defined by that government) is likely to lead to massive inefficiencies and a considerably larger degree of scarcity than is necessary. The method of the Invisible Hand has proven vastly superior in the long run. It involves a decentralized allocation of resources by millions of separate individuals who merely follow their own interests, but whose actions are coordinated and thus made compatible with one another through a system of prices that provide continuous and unmistakable signals to all concerned. Nevertheless, market economies exhibit a number of typical shortcomings, called **market failures,** that can possibly be corrected by governmental action. Any list of such shortcomings is bound to include inefficiency, inequity, and instability. Each of these problems will be addressed in this or other chapters; we provide a brief preview here.

Inefficiency Due to Market Imperfections

Inefficiency can take many different forms, but some of them are already familiar to us from earlier discussions of alternative types of market structures. A perfectly competitive market, for example, contains within it a strong tendency for *technical efficiency,* a situation in which it is impossible, with current technical knowledge, to raise output from given inputs or, alternatively, to produce a given output by using less of one input without using more of another input. Under perfect competition in the long run, any product price comes to equal the minimum average total cost of producing the product (and any physical output is therefore produced with a minimum expenditure of physical inputs): $P = \text{minimum } ATC$.

Perfectly competitive markets also produce *economic efficiency,* a situation in which it is impossible to make any person better off without making another person worse off because all mutually beneficial transactions have already been carried out. This is achieved, as we have seen, because profit-maximizing firms see to it that output price equals the marginal cost of production: $P = MC$. Figure 1 illustrates the results just noted. The forces of demand and supply might establish an equilibrium price of $7 per unit, as in panel (a). This price becomes the marginal revenue faced by the typical firm, as in panel (b). In order to maximize profit, the firm chooses an output volume of 8,000 units, which equates marginal cost with marginal revenue and

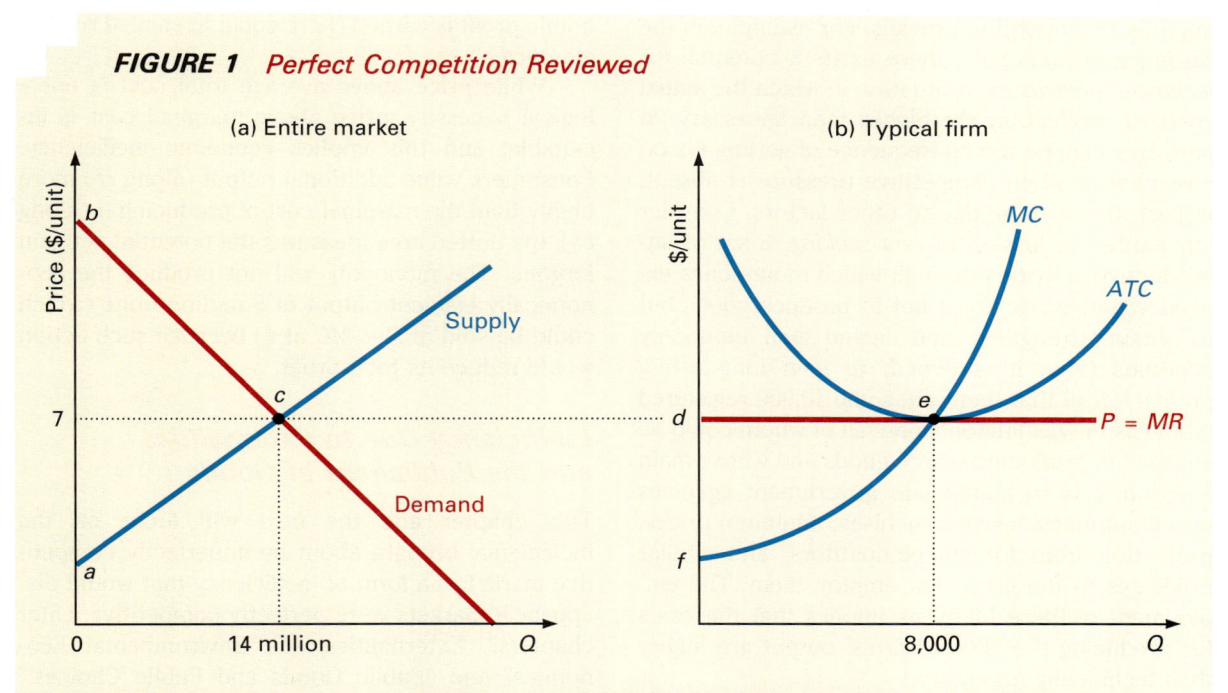

FIGURE 1 *Perfect Competition Reviewed*

A perfectly competitive firm always chooses an output volume (here 8,000 units) that equates (here at *e*) the market price of its product with marginal cost. In the long run, as shown here, price equals minimum average total cost as well. Thus, the typical firm's long-run economic profit is zero.

price (at e): $P = MC$. In the long run (depicted here), price equals not only marginal cost but minimum average total cost as well. If the ATC curve were lower, the typical firm would earn economic profit, the size and number of firms in the industry would expand, market supply would rise, and the equilibrium price would fall until it equaled the lower minimum ATC. If the ATC curve were higher, the typical firm would incur losses, the size and number of firms in the industry would contract, market supply would fall, and the equilibrium price would rise until it equaled the higher minimum ATC. Thus, in the long run, $P = $ minimum ATC, which implies technical efficiency as well as zero economic profit.

While each firm expands output as long as price (along de) exceeds marginal cost (along fe), this profit-maximizing behavior leads to economic efficiency. As panel (a) shows, every unit that consumers value more highly (along bc) than the associated marginal cost that producers must incur (along ac) is in fact being produced.

As we have also seen, things are different when imperfect competition prevails. For example, in the presence of monopoly, there exists a potential for *technical inefficiency,* a situation in which the actual costs of production are higher than necessary. In part, this may be the consequence of getting lax on cost control when competitive pressure is absent. In part, this may be due to other factors. Consider our earlier discussion of *rent seeking,* a set of unproductive activities through which monopolies expend valuable resources not to produce goods but to obtain, strengthen, and defend their monopoly positions (and, it is hoped, to gain long-lasting profit). Recall that there are some 10,000 registered lobbyists in Washington alone, all of whom could be engaged in producing scarce goods and whose main function it is to manipulate government agencies into granting exclusive franchises, minimum prices, protection from foreign competitors, and similar privileges to the firms that employ them. The employment of these lobbyists implies that the costs for producing the affected firms' output are higher than technically necessary.[1]

In addition, a monopoly may well produce at a price that exceeds average total cost, even in the long run, and thus yields permanent economic profit for its owners. Finally, by producing an output level at which output price exceeds the marginal cost of production, any monopoly is certain to create *economic inefficiency.* In such a situation it is still possible to make some person better off without making another person worse off because some mutually beneficial transactions have not been carried out. Yet a profit-maximizing monopoly has no desire to eliminate this bad result.

Figure 2 illustrates the effects just noted. In order to maximize profit, the monopoly chooses an output volume of 5 million units which equates marginal revenue and marginal cost (at e). This output can be sold at a price of \$10 per unit; thus price exceeds marginal cost (by ce): $P > MC$. The firm's average total cost may well be inflated due to rent-seeking activities (not shown); nevertheless, because market entry is blocked to other firms, price may exceed average total cost even in the long run (here by cd). Whenever $P > ATC$, a positive economic profit is earned (here equal to shaded rectangle $abcd$).

While price above average total cost is not a logical necessity, price above marginal cost is inevitable, and this implies economic inefficiency. Consumers value additional output (along cf) more highly than the marginal cost of producing it (along ef); the dotted area measures the potential net gain forgone. The monopoly will not produce the economically efficient output of 8 million units (which could be sold at $P = MC$ at f) because such action would reduce its total profit.

Inefficiency Due to Externalities and the Publicness of Goods

This chapter and the next will focus on the inefficiency brought about by imperfectly competitive markets—a form of inefficiency that would disappear if markets were perfectly competitive. Later chapters, "Externalities and Environmental Economics" and "Public Goods and Public Choices,"

---

[1] The term "lobbyists" was coined during the administration of President Ulysses Grant. He frequented the Willard, a hotel near the White House, and was mobbed by hordes of petitioners whenever he entered the lobby. "Get these Goddamn lobbyists away from me," he is said to have yelled.

FIGURE 2 Monopoly Reviewed

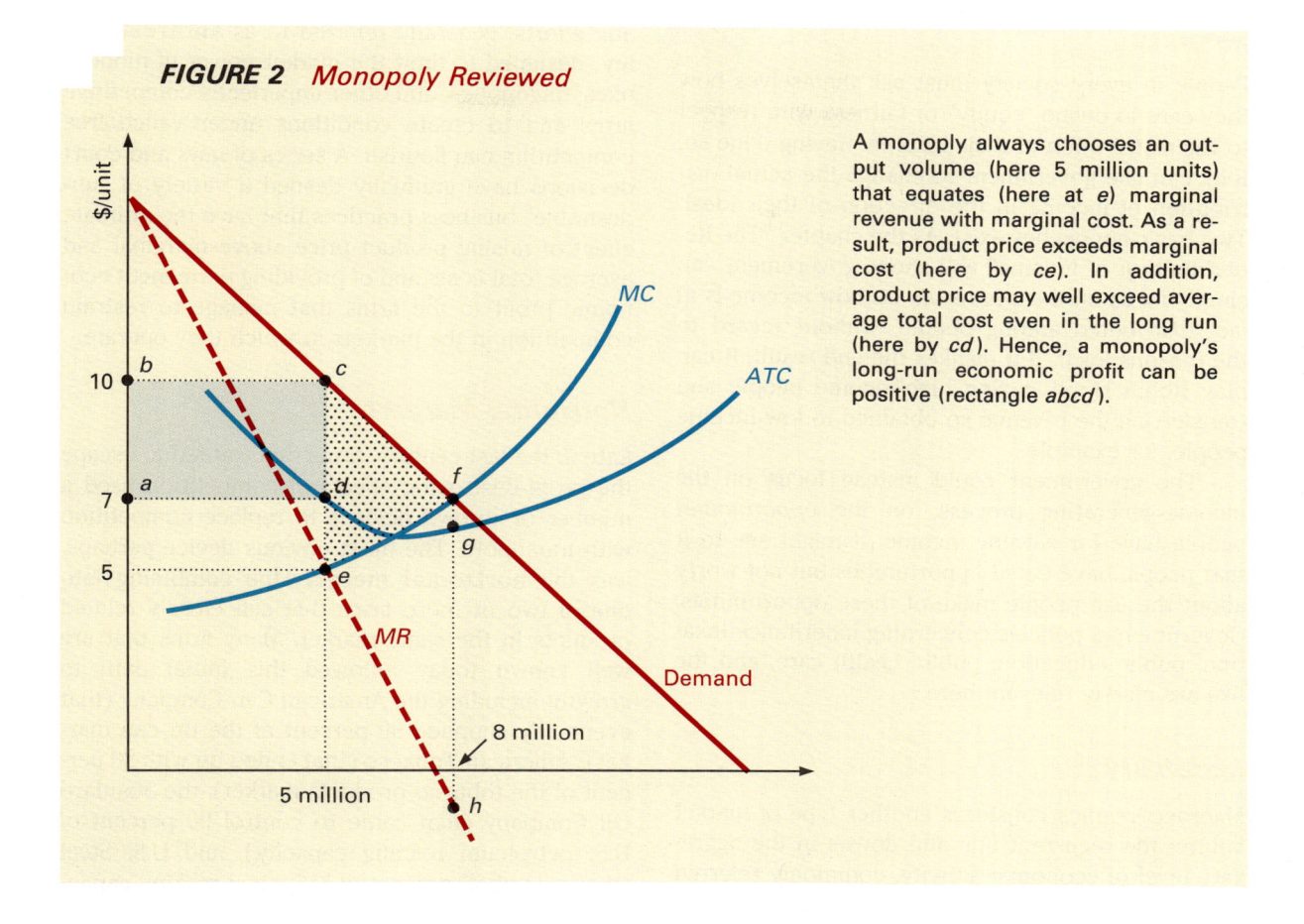

A monopoly always chooses an output volume (here 5 million units) that equates (here at *e*) marginal revenue with marginal cost. As a result, product price exceeds marginal cost (here by *ce*). In addition, product price may well exceed average total cost even in the long run (here by *cd*). Hence, a monopoly's long-run economic profit can be positive (rectangle *abcd*).

will instead be concerned with inefficiencies that even perfect competition cannot cure. As we will see, the behavior of consumers or producers who make mutually beneficial deals with one another in markets sometimes has effects on outside parties. These effects can be of two kinds. They can be detrimental, unfavorable, or "negative," imposing costs in the form of decreased utility or output on neighbors who are not being compensated for this injury—to their dismay. (Examples of such *negative externalities,* as they are called, are the noise dumped on innocent bystanders by snowmobilers or the wastes dumped into the natural environment by factories that spoil, say, the catch of nearby fishing companies). The effects in question can also be beneficial, or "positive," providing benefits in the form of increased utility or output for neighbors who are not being charged for this favor—to their delight. (Examples of such *positive externalities* are the advantage given to others by those who buy and install telephones—others can now call them—or by those who plant flowering orchards and thereby increase the output of nearby beekeepers.)

An extreme case of positive externalities is, in fact, provided by so-called *public goods.* Examples are the provision of national defense or a system of criminal justice, or even the snow-plowing of city streets, from which all members of a society can benefit at the same time and units of which cannot be sold to people individually. As a result, competitive markets fail to produce such goods entirely, even if such goods are desired by everyone and their marginal benefit clearly exceeds their marginal cost.

Inequity

People in every society must ask themselves how they care to define "equity" or fairness with respect to the distribution of their income. Having done so, they can use government to change the actual distribution of income in the direction of their ideal. Two basic appoaches exist. As the chapter "The Redistribution of Income" will show, government can simply focus on the *end result,* on how income is in fact distributed among people, without regard to the reasons for it. If it dislikes the end result, it can play Robin Hood, taxing high-income people and transferring the revenue so obtained to low-income people, for example.

The government could instead focus on the income-generating process, on the *opportunities* people have for earning income. It might see to it that people have equal opportunities but not worry about the use people make of these opportunities. Governmental policies concerning inheritance taxation, public education, public health care, and the like are clearly relevant here.[2]

Instability

Macroeconomics considers another type of market failure; the recurrent ups and downs in the aggregate level of economic activity, commonly referred to as *business cycles*. That discussion concerns varying levels of unemployment of resources, changes in the overall level of prices (inflation and deflation), and, in the long run, "inadequate" or "excessive" rates of economic growth.

The Impetus to Antitrust Legislation

The remainder of this chapter focuses on governmental efforts to remove inefficiencies and inequities that are attributable to the lack of perfect competition in markets. During the past 100 years, the U.S. government has been engaged in systematic efforts, generally referred to as **antitrust policy,** designed to limit the market power of monopolies, oligopolies, and other imperfectly competitive firms and to create conditions under which free competition can flourish. A series of laws and court decisions have gradually defined a variety of "undesirable" business practices that have the ultimate effect of raising product price above marginal and average total costs and of providing permanent economic profit to the firms that manage to restrain competition in the markets in which they operate.

Horizontal Mergers

Late in the last century, firms that wanted to escape the profit-destroying effects of competition used a number of shrewd devices to replace competition with monopoly. The most obvious device perhaps, was the **horizontal merger,** the combining into one of two or more firms that sell closely related products in the same market. Many firms that are well known today followed this initial path to growth, including the American Can Company (that eventually supplied 90 percent of the tin can market), American Tobacco (that ended up with 90 percent of the tobacco products market), the Standard Oil Company (that came to control 90 percent of U.S. petroleum refining capacity), and U.S. Steel (that gained 65 percent of U.S. steel-making capacity). Similar results were achieved by the Corn Products Refining Company (now CPC International), Dupont, Eastman Kodak, International Harvester, International Paper, International Salt, National Lead (now NL Industries), Pittsburgh Plate Glass (now PPG industries), Standard Sanitary (now American Standard), United Fruit (now United Brands), U.S. Gypsum, and U.S. Rubber (now Uniroyal).

Holding Companies

Another favorite method of eliminating competition was the formation of a **holding company,** a corporation established for the sole purpose of acquiring a controlling stock interest in two or more competing corporations and then running their affairs jointly, as if they were a single company. This device was made possible by an 1888 New Jersey law permitting one corporation to buy stock in another and by later legislation permitting a New

---

[2] The *Student Workbook* that accompanies this text contains an optional chapter, "The Economics of Health Care," which considers one of these possibilities in detail.

Jersey corporation to do business anywhere. A holding company did not have to own any productive assets directly, yet its owners could often control a vast industrial empire. Indeed, with some luck, the owners could do so with a minimal financial investment of their own, as a simple example can show.

Consider a railroad company with real estate and equipment worth $1 billion. Suppose these assets were acquired with cash raised from selling $500 million of *bonds* (that is, interest-bearing IOU's) and $500 million of *stock certificates* (that is, ownership shares). Suppose further that two types of stock certificates were issued, $300 million of *nonvoting preferred stock* (that promises preferential treatment to holders—for example, with respect to the frequency and size of dividend payments—in return for not voting on corporate affairs) and $200 million of *common stock* (that, under the circumstances, alone carries the right to vote). Then someone can control the $1 billion corporation with absolute certainty by owning just over half of the common stock, or just over $100 million of it. More than that! If the stock ownership is widely dispersed, one can count on the fact that most stockholders do not bother to go to the annual stockholders' meeting and vote. As a result, someone owning a smaller block of common stock can easily dominate the election of directors who run company affairs. Suppose, for example, that a person owning not a fraction above 50 percent but a mere 10 percent of common stock ($20 million in our case) can control the $1 billion firm. Such a person could, similarly, control 10 railroad companies, with $10 billion of assets, by owning a mere $200 million of common stock. But this is not the end of the story.

Let holding company A own these $200 million of common stock (that control $10 billion of railroad company assets). A clever person can endow holding company A with the 200 million *dollars* needed to buy that stock by selling, say $100 million of bonds, $60 million of nonvoting preferred stock, and $40 million of common stock (that alone carries the right to vote in this example). Making the same assumptions as before (wide dispersal of common-stock ownership and general stockholder apathy), our clever manipulator might control holding company A (and, indirectly, $10 billion of railroad company assets) by owning a mere 10 percent, or $4 million of holding company A's common stock.

Yet one can go further and pyramid holding company upon holding company. For example, let holding company B own the controlling interest of $4 million of holding company A stock. Using the same procedure as before, our clever financier can control company B with as little as $80,000 of B's common stock. And that person could form holding company C and control it (and, thus company B, company A, and the $10 billion of railroad companies) with a mere $1,600 of personal funds! Indeed, many actual holding companies (including American Can, American Tobacco, the Associated Gas and Electric Company, U.S. Rubber, and U.S. Steel) greatly exceeded our example in complexity.

Trusts

A third device yet for creating monopoly was the **trust,** an arrangement placing two or more competing corporations under the "trusteeship" of a single board of directors who were to run the companies' affairs jointly, as it they were a single firm. Under the plan, the original stockholders would surrender their stock certificates (and, thus, the right to run enterprise affairs) to the "trustees" in return for nonvoting *trust certificates*. Like the original stockholders, the holders of trust certificates would be entitled to all the profits made. Because most stockholders were interested in earning dividends and not in running company affairs, and because the formation of trusts and the associated elimination of competition was expected to produce monopoly profits, many stockholders went along. The number of trusts aspiring to monopoly grew rapidly, which explains why the emerging antimonopoly policy of the government came to be called *antitrust* policy.

The Robber Barons

During the last third of the 19th century, many famous trusts emerged in such diverse fields as cordage, lead, linseed oil, petroleum, sugar, and whiskey. Equally famous were the men who ran them and whose names became household words: Philip Armour (meat processing), Andrew Carnegie (steel), Jay Gould (railroads), J. P. Morgan (banks), John D. Rockefeller, Sr. (oil), Cornelius Vanderbilt (steamships). The wheelings and dealings of these men created fortunes for them at the expense of the masses of overcharged customers, and they soon came to be known as "the robber barons." In turn, they showed the greatest contempt for the public. "I owe the public nothing," said J. P. Morgan; "The public be damned," echoed Cornelius Vanderbilt.

Consider the story of John D. Rockefeller, Sr. In 1870, he formed the Standard Oil Company with an investment of $4,000. Soon, he joined with other refining companies to force the railroads into providing special discounts to the group (and to refuse such discounts to competitors). He even managed to get the railroads to pay *his* group a fee for every shipment of oil they made for rival refineries. He freely resorted to blackmail and employed an army of toughs who fought pitched battles to enforce his demands. By 1879, he controlled 90 percent of the oil refining business and all of the country's pipelines. Three years later, he formed the Standard Oil Trust and ran 40 associated firms as a single unit. By judiciously closing down refining capacity, he reduced output and raised prices until he had achieved monopoly profit. Eventually, the public was fed up and government responded with a series of laws to which we now turn.

The Antitrust Laws

The first antitrust law, passed in 1890, is probably one of the shortest pieces of legislation on record.

The Sherman Act

> Section 1. Every contract, combination in the form of trust or otherwise, or conspiracy, in restraint of trade or commerce among the several States, or with foreign nations, is hereby declared to be illegal. Every person who shall make any such contract or engage in any such combination or conspiracy, shall be deemed guilty of a misdemeanor, and, on conviction thereof, shall be punished by fine not exceeding five thousand dollars, or by imprisonment not exceeding one year, or by both said punishments, in the discretion of the court.
>
> Section 2. Every person who shall monopolize, or attempt to monopolize, or combine or conspire with any other person or persons, to monopolize any part of the trade or commerce among the several States, or with foreign nations, shall be deemed guilty of a misdemeanor, and, on conviction thereof, shall be punished by fine not exceeding five thousand dollars, or by imprisonment not exceeding one year, or by both said punishments, in the discretion of the court.

Without setting up any agency to enforce its provisions, and without defining its terms, the Sherman Act simply forbade individual or joint efforts to "restrain trade" and to "monopolize." An enforcement agency, the Antitrust Division fo the U.S. Department of Justice, was not set up until 1903. Even then, its efforts were hampered by the fact that the act's language was vague enough to give wide latitude of interpretation to the courts. Thus lawyers asked: Did the act outlaw already *existing* monopolies (that is, certain *market structures*) or only the attempt or even only the *successful* attempt to establish monopoly (that is, certain types of *business conduct*)?

Before long, the courts ruled that certain types of business conduct, such as price fixing among alleged competitors, were illegal as such (per se); the matter of market structure, however, remained unresolved for two decades.

The Rule of Reason

It took until 1911 for the U.S. Supreme Court to enunciate its famous **Rule of Reason,** according to which only deliberate and unreasonable restraint of trade was illegal under the Sherman Act, while market dominance as such was not. To be guilty of monopolization, argued the Court, a firm must have the *intent* to exercise monopoly power and on that basis engage in actions that restrain trade *unreasonably*. Both the Rockefeller family's Standard Oil Company and the Duke family's American Tobacco Company were found guilty under the new rule and were dissolved into several independent firms. They were guilty, however, by virtue of the vicious tactics used to dispose of smaller competitors. This interpretation by the Court narrowed the scope of the Sherman Act considerably. Subsequently, International Harvester, United Shoe Machinery Corporation, Eastman Kodak, and U.S. Steel were found *not* guilty, precisely because they held near-monopolies which they had "thrust upon them," that were achieved, that is, without their having made predatory attacks on competitors. Mere size as such (per se) or the existence of unexerted power, the Court held in 1920, was no offense.

Bigness Illegal Per Se

Yet in 1945, in a case involving Alcoa, the Court reversed tradition by shifting its attention from business conduct to market structure (the number and size of competing firms found in a market). Alcoa was found guilty because of bigness alone (it supplied, the government figured, 90 percent of newly produced aluminum), even though its conduct had not been offensive. Under this new interpretation, duPont was found innocent in 1956, but the United Shoe Machinery Corporation was forced, in 1969, to set up two rival companies.

Ever since the 1945 decision, in one court case after another, one perennial problem has emerged. It concerns the definition of the relevant market in which the accused firm allegedly exercises monopoly power. Alcoa, for example, believed it had a 33 percent share of the aluminum ingot market because it thought the market included production *for sale* from new ore and from scrap as well as imports. The government, on the other hand, ignored recycled aluminum and imports, while including production of ingots from new ore regardless of whether it was for sale. (A large amount was for Alcoa's internal use.) Thus, the government derived a 90 percent market share. Similar controversies have arisen repeatedly. Did duPont hold a 1956 monopoly in cellophane (which, given its patent, was strictly speaking true) or did it merely supply 20 percent of all flexible wrapping materials (which was true as well)? Was the 1963 market relevant to the Philadelphia National Bank banking in the city itself (36 percent share) or national banking (4 percent share)? Was the 1975 market relevant to Xerox that for plain-paper copiers (90 percent share) or that for all copying equipment (65 percent share)?

Explicit Collusion Illegal Per Se

The courts have been less uncertain about the Sherman Act's intent on matters of collusion concerning prices, output, market shares, or territorial allocations. Consistently, they have held explicit collusive agreements among supposedly competing firms to be illegal per se, that is, regardless of intent or consequences. They have been less consistent on pricing behavior that is consciously parallel but involves no direct communication (as when a large firm occasionally publishes a list of its prices and all other firms follow its lead).

The Clayton Act

In the years following the enactment of the Sherman Act, powerful new business combinations came into being in many industries (steel, farm machinery, tin cans, etc.). Again and again, the practices used to achieve them were held not to violate the act. So Congress enacted another law, the Clayton Act of 1914, that clearly focused on conduct rather than market structure and spelled out illegal acts in detail.

The new act forbade **price discrimination,** a practice according to which sellers charge a given buyer (or different buyers) different prices for different units of an identical good. However, the act permitted such discrimination if different prices were due to "differences in the grade, quality, or quantity of the commodity sold"; if lower prices made "only due allowance for differences in the cost of selling or transportation"; or if lower prices were offered "in good faith to meet competition." The prohibition was designed to protect small firms from larger rivals who frequently slashed prices on particular goods in specific markets only in order to eliminate small competitors.

The act also outlawed **exclusive contracts,** by which sellers "lease or make a sale or contract for sale of . . . commodities . . . on the condition that the lessee or purchaser thereof shall not use or deal in the . . . commodity . . . of a competitor." Such contracts were common in automobile retailing and soft-drink bottling. A car dealer who wanted to sell Fords, for example, would get such cars only by promising not to sell GM cars.

The act further outlawed **requirements contracts,** according which buyers agree to purchase all of their requirements of a commodity from a given seller only. For example, electric power companies often had had to sign such contracts with suppliers of coal or oil; gas stations had been forced into such deals by suppliers of batteries, gasoline, and tires.

Similarly outlawed were **tying contracts,** according to which buyers of one good are forced to purchase another good from the same seller as well. For example, buyers of land had often been made to buy the services of a particular railroad for shipping the products of that land, buyers of IBM card-sorting machines had been made to purchase IBM tabulating cards, and buyers of canning machines had been made to buy particular types of tin cans.

The Clayton Act also forbade **interlocking stockholdings,** an arrangement by which one corporation acquires the stock of a competing corporation or purchases (as a holding company does) the stock certificates of two or more corporations that are competitors. In addition, the act enjoined large direct competitors from **interlocking directorates,** arrangements under which two or more competing corporations have at least some members on their boards of directors in common.

None of these and other prohibitions, however, was absolute. They applied only where the stated conduct would "substantially lessen competition or tend to create a monopoly."

The Federal Trade Commission Act

Also in 1914, Congress passed the Federal Trade Commission Act, which sweepingly forbade "all unfair methods of competition." The commission created by the act was empowered to issue "cease and desist" orders against violators and has ever since shared antitrust law enforcement with the Justice Department's Antitrust Division. In 1990, for example, the FTC challenged one manufacturer (a maker of swimming pool cleaner) who was trying to force retailers into maintaining a certain minimum price; it attacked price fixing by the makers of infant formula and video games; and it filed consumer protection suits on such matters as 900 telephone numbers and alcohol advertising addressed to minors.

A 1938 amendment, the Wheeler-Lea Act, additionly outlawed "unfair or deceptive acts or practices" in and of themselves, regardless of whether or not they can be shown to hurt competitors. This has enabled the Federal Trade Commission to control deceptive advertising practices. For example, a 1981 ad showed a picture of a slim actress and the words, "California Avocados. Only 17 calories a slice. Would this body lie to you?" Apparently it did. The ad also promised consumers specific quantities of vitamins and potassium, but the size portion that would justify that claim contained 132 calories. The ad was challenged and withdrawn. In the 1990s, the FTC has challenged ads on Kellogg's Special K ("Keep the muscle, lose the fat"; there was no evidence), 40+ Bran Flakes ("the maximum amount of fiber plus iron for people over 40"; the product was not formulated for people over 40), Mobil's Hefty Degradable Trash Bags (they degrade in sunlight only, but most such bags are buried in landfills), Heinz's Recyclable Tomato Ketchup Bottles (they are in fact rarely recycled because collection systems and processing plants do not exist), and numerous types of gas additives ("approved by the federal government, adds 4 miles to the gallon"; an outright lie with respect to over 100 brands tested).

The Robinson-Patman Act

The Robinson-Patman Act of 1936 amended the Clayton Act to protect small independent wholesalers and retailers from mass distributors (such as chain stores or mail-order houses). The bargaining strength of mass distributors, argued the smaller independent distributors, enabled them to pay "unjustified" lower prices for their purchases and then to undercut competitors. In fact, as subsequent developments showed, much of their superior competitive strength came from streamlining internal operations. The act forbade differential quantity discounts among those buying the same quantity. It forbade *any* quantity discounts *if* they helped to create monopoly; and, given the same effect, it forbade the charging in one locality of lower prices than elsewhere.

Unfortunately, this law created great uncertainty for firms ready to engage their competitors in price competition. Court decisions since the 1930s, however, have cleared the matter up somewhat. According to the United Shoe Machinery case of 1953, price discrimination is illegal when practiced by dominant firms, but it is allowed when practiced sporadically by smaller firms.

The Celler-Kefauver Act

The Celler-Kefauver Act of 1950 is yet another Clayton Act amendment, designed to discourage mergers by closing a loophole in the Clayton Act. It prohibits not only the acquisition, for purposes of monopolization, of competitors' shares of stock, but also the use of such stock by proxy and the direct acquisition of the assets of a competitive firm.

The act has been used to challenge not only traditional types of *horizontal* mergers among competing firms selling identical goods in identical markets (as in the Bethlehem-Youngstown Steel case of 1956), but also *vertical* mergers (as in the Brown and Kinney Shoe case of 1962) and *conglomerate* mergers (as in the Procter and Gamble/Clorox case of 1967). A **vertical merger** involves the combining into one of two or more firms that are related as suppliers and users of each other's products—as when an electric power company merges, on the one hand, with the coal mines and railroads that supply it with fuel and, on the other hand, with the aluminum refiners that use massive amounts of electric power. A **conglomerate merger,** on the other hand, involves the combining into one of two or more firms that have neither competitive nor supplier-customer relations and that operate in different industries or geographic markets. As an example, consider a telephone company, such as ITT, that branches into renting cars (Avis), building homes (Levitt and Sons), baking bread (Continental), running hotels (Sheraton), and publishing books (Putnam's), which is precisely what the International Telephone and Telegraph Company did.

Recent Amendments

The government's antimerger weapons were further refined by the 1970 Antitrust Improvement Act, also known as the Hart-Scott-Rodino Act. That act replaced the word "corporations" by "persons" in the Celler-Kefauver Act and, thereby, made the antimerger rules applicable not only to legal persons (corporations), but also to real persons (human beings) who might own large unincorporated businesses. The act also established a 30–50 day premerger notification system according to which firms contemplating a merger must notify the Antitrust Division (ATD) or Federal Trade Commission (FTC) prior to consummating the merger.

The 1974 Consumer Product Warranty and Federal Trade Commission Improvement Act empowered the FTC to impose fines of $10,000 per day unless firms pay refunds and damages in fraud cases. And the same year's Antitrust Procedures and Penalties Act changed antitrust violations from misdemeanors to felonies and raised the maximum fines to $1 million for corporations and $100,000 and three years in jail for individuals.

Antitrust Policy Assessed

What have been the long term effects of the antitrust laws? Have they restrained monopoly and fostered competition? These questions, naturally, are very difficult to answer because we can only speculate as to what would have happened in the absence of such laws. Let us consider some of the arguments often heard.

A Negligible Effect

There are those who argue that antitrust policy has had only a negligible effect on the degree of monopoly power exercised in the U.S. economy. They point, first of all, to a lack of funds given to the enforcement agencies (the Justice Department's Antitrust Division and the Federal Trade Commission), which results in low annual numbers of indictments. They point to the extraordinary complexity of trials and, should conviction occur, to extremely lenient punishments. They point to continued large-scale violations of the laws.

The facts are these: From the days of trust-busting Theodore Roosevelt to the 1930s, when another President Roosevelt initiated a trust-busting campaign of his own, the funding of antitrust agencies has been only sufficient to bring a dozen court cases per year. From then until 1970, an average fifty cases per year have been given intensive investigation and brought to court. During the 1970–1985 period, the annual number of all antitrust cases filed by the government has fluctuated between 51 and 115 (and that of price fixing cases between 3 and 22)—still a negligible number so far as critics are concerned. In 1988, the Antitrust Division's budget was $48 million; the division's legal staff was 300, down from 400 in 1981. (At the time, the ATD paid an annual salary of $29,000 to a new law school graduate; major law firms in Washington and New York were offering an average entry-level salary of $74,000.)

Furthermore, many of the big cases against monopoly do take a long time (5.5 years on the average) and create an impossible volume of evidence (hundreds of thousands of pages). Conviction, therefore, follows indictment only after a considerable lag and is far from certain. Example 1, which tells the story of the *U.S.* v. *IBM*, illustrates both of these points dramatically. Private suits do not fare any better. After 5 years, the jury in the *Memorex* v. *IBM* case couldn't reach a verdict. Given the complexities, said the judge, no jury could have made a rational decision.

Even when cases are carried to the point of conviction, penalties are usually low and rarely take the form of imprisonment. (In a 1961 electrical equipment industry case, in which 29 firms were convicted of a conspiracy to fix prices and rig bids, seven executives, coming from such renowned firms as General Electric, Westinghouse, and Allen-Bradley, were sentenced to 30 days in jail, but 9 of those days were remitted for good behavior.) Traditionally, penalties have taken the form of fines and have been small in relation to, say, the convicted firms' assets, net worth, or even profits.

Is it any wonder, critics ask, that antitrust laws, like speed laws, are continually and obviously violated on a large scale?

A Significant Effect

There are others who are unwilling to accept any of the arguments presented in the preceding section. They believe that the antitrust laws have had a significant positive impact regarding the economy's competitiveness.

For one thing, they argue, the degree of enforcement should not be judged by counting the number of indictments filed by the government. Many more suits are brought by private parties, as shown by Table 1.

Nor should too much attention be paid to lengthy court cases actually carried through to the point of *conviction*. Frequently, the government prosecutor and the accused party reach a **consent agreement,** a deal according to which the law suit is dropped in exchange for voluntary ameliorative action by the accused party, such as spinning off a subdivision, creating a competitive firm with appropriate assets and personnel; making patents or even trade secrets available to competitors at reasonable cost; or withdrawing a deceptive advertisement. This short-circuits a long court proceeding and spares the accused of not only substantial legal fees, but also open court embarrassment and certain other consequences should conviction occur: treble damage action by injured parties, consumer brand switching due to injury to the firm's "image," refusal of the government to do business with such firms, and sanctions by administrative agencies (such as failure to renew licenses for broadcasting). Example 2 provides a dramatic illustration of what a consent agreement can do.

We should note, however, that consent agreements also open up vast possibilities for corruption. An accused party that has potentially hundreds of millions of dollars to lose by conviction might engineer a favorable outcome out of court for a much smaller sum, possibly including campaign contributions or other favors. Three government suits against ITT, including one seeking the divestiture of the Hartford Fire Insurance Company, for instance, were dropped in 1971 on President Nixon's orders after ITT had promised, in repeated secret meetings with top administration officials, to underwrite a

TABLE 1 Antitrust Cases Filed in the United States, 1941–1984 (average annual numbers)

Period	Cases filed by Government	Private parties	Total
1941–45	36	59	95
1946–50	51	106	157
1951–55	39	209	248
1956–60	63	233	296
1961–65	69	720	789
1966–70	55	654	709
1971–75	78	1,295	1,373
1976–80	75	1,448	1,523
1981–84	112	1,155	1,267

Private parties file considerably more antitrust suits in the United States than does government.

SOURCE: S. C. Salop and L. J. White, "An Economic Analysis of Private Antitrust Litigation," *Georgetown Law Journal,* April 1986, Table 1.

EXAMPLE 1

The Antitrust Division's Vietnam

Not all antitrust suits brought by the U.S. government are successful; the most spectacular failure, perhaps, was *United States* v. *The International Business Machines Corporation* (IBM).

In 1969, the U.S. government indicted IBM, then the largest company in the world, for attempting to monopolize the market for "general-purpose electronic digital computer systems." The government charged that IBM held an unacceptable 72 percent market share. IBM itself calculated a 32 percent share by including in the relevant market military computers, computer leasing and servicing, and even programmable hand-held computers.

Apart from the issue of market structure, the government, however, also pointed to matters of business conduct; in particular, IBM's deliberate erection of obstacles to the entry and growth of rival firms. Those obstacles, argued the government, included the following: First, "bundling" computer hardware with maintenance and programming services and selling the combination at a single price, which kept independent maintenance and programming firms at bay. (IBM argued that "bundling" was desired by customers who highly valued IBM's reliability and expertise.)

Second, leasing rather than selling its mainframe computers, which imposed heavier capital requirements on potential imitators. (IBM argued that leasing was preferred by customers who were risk-averse and unwilling to own machines that might be outdated overnight in a time of rapid technical advance.)

Third, introducing ever new families of computers, such as the System 370 "fighting machines," which outdated the machines of rival companies or made the accessories of rival companies incompatible with IBM hardware; then this strategy was reinforced with sharply reduced prices. (Was it now, IBM asked, a crime to introduce ever better-working products and to sell them at ever lower prices?)

Even before the trial began in 1975, the government had collected more than 50 million documents for it. Then it spent three years presenting its case (and filling 72,000 pages of trial transcripts). It took three more years for IBM to present its defense. By 1981, the government had spent $10 million on the case; IBM had spent $100 million in its defense. However, from the government's point of view the outlook was bad. The Sherman Act had declared restraint of trade and monopolizing to be illegal, yet—unlike monopolies that restrict output and raise price—IBM's output had grown rapidly and its prices had fallen steadily. (A calculation costing $1.50 when the trial began cost a fraction of a penny then.) One law professor (Robert H. Bork) dubbed the case "the antitrust division's Vietnam," and in 1982, the government gave up, calling the evidence "flimsy" and the suit "without merit."

Source: The New York Times, numerous issues.

---

planned Republican national convention to the tune of $400,000; as well as to divest itself of Avis, the Canteen Corporation, and two smaller insurance companies. Before all this was over, ITT and the White House attempted to prevent a Securities and Exchange Commission subpoena of ITT memos and letters on the above deal. When this failed, the Commission joined the former two in foiling the investigations of the House Commerce Committee and the Senate Judiciary Committee. In the end, top ITT and administration officials perjured themselves before the Senate committee.

This example gave rise to the 1974 Antitrust Procedures and Penalties Act that established new

EXAMPLE 2

The Breakup of Ma Bell

In 1876, Alexander Graham Bell invented the telephone; over the next 100 years, his Bell System put a phone in practically every American home. Then, in 1974, the U.S. Department of Justice charged Ma Bell, officially known as the American Telephone and Telegraph Company (AT&T), with the illegal monopolization of the telephone business. No conviction ever occurred, but some 10 years later, on January 1, 1984, AT&T voluntarily consented to have its $153.5 billion of assets split up. Two thirds of the assets went to seven new regional phone companies (Ameritech, Bell Atlantic, Bell South, Nynex, Pacific Telesis, Southwestern Bell, and U.S. West) and one third to a new AT&T. The name Bell and the old company symbol (a bell in a circle) was reserved for the seven new companies. The new AT&T agreed never to use it again. Before long, it introduced a new corporate logo.

What has happened since? First, there has been a noticeable increase in competition in the long-distance telephone market, along with a sharp decline in rates. Consider the appearance of numerous new firms, such as MCI and GTE-Sprint. Second, there has appeared vigorous competition in the market for telephone equipment, involving both domestic and foreign firms. As a result, prices of telephones, answering machines, and the like have plummeted (and product variety has multiplied manifold) compared to the days when the old AT&T's Western Electric (now AT&T Technologies) held an equipment monopoly.

Third, local telephone rates and fees for installing and servicing equipment have risen sharply. This is not surprising because, in its zeal to have everyone sign up, Ma Bell used to price long-distance service above and local service below marginal cost. (Just prior to the breakup, this cross-subsidy came to over $10 billion per year.) Since the breakup, there exists no legal connection between the local companies and the long distance carriers; thus each type of firm has to cover its own costs.

What does the public think of it all? Americans have been delighted by the drop in long-distance rates but annoyed by the predictable rise in local rates (and the difficulty of having the phone fixed when it breaks—it doesn't belong to Ma Bell any more). As a result, a *Business Week*/Harris poll showed some 64 percent thought the Bell system breakup was a dreadful mistake.

Sources: Andrew Pollack, "AT&T, U.S. Agree on Final Aspects of Bell Breakup," *The New York Times,* August 4, 1983, pp. 1 and D4; idem, "Jostling in the Over-crowded Phone Market," *The New York Times,* October 21, 1984, pp. F1 and 8; and "Did It Make Sense to Break Up AT&T?" *Business Week,* December 3, 1984, pp. 86–124.

---

rules for reaching consent agreements: The accused firm must file with the case judge a list of all contacts with government officials; the government prosecutor must give the judge (and publish in major newspapers) a sixty-day advance notice of any proposed out-of-court settlement, spelling out how the settlement will cure the problems giving rise to the suit in the first place; and the judge can accept or reject the settlement proposal after noting public response.

Finally one should note the effects that the 1974 Antitrust Procedures and Penalties Act has had on the severity of punishment. Consider Table 2, which shows an increase in both fines and jail sentences. As a result, the argument concludes, the ghost of Senator Sherman has become an *ex-officio* member

TABLE 2 Antitrust Convictions in the United States, 1955–1980

	1955–1974 (*Misdemeanors*)	1975–1980 (*Felonies*)
Individuals		
Number of offenders	664	216
Conviction rate[a]	83%	76.6%
Average fine (1967 dollars)	$3,468	$7,996
Probability of jail	.07	.42
Average days in jail (if sent to jail)	48	107
Corporations		
Number of offenders	1,371	274
Conviction rate[a]	85%	86.7%
Average fine (1967 dollars)	$15,009	$76,622

[a] Ratio of number of guilty pleas, nolo contendere pleas, and trial convictions to number of defendants.

Since the enactment of the 1974 Antitrust Procedures and Penalties Act (that changed antitrust offenses from misdemeanors to felonies), the severity of punishment has increased.

SOURCE: Mark A. Cohen, "The Role of Criminal Sanctions in Antitrust Enforcement," *Contemporary Policy Issues,* October 1989, pp. 40–41.

of every corporate board of directors. Business executives will do their best not to come into conflict with the law. Therefore, antitrust laws have primarily preventive effects.

Numerical Evidence

A number of alternative numerical measures have been utilized by those seeking to judge the success of antitrust efforts; we consider some of them here.

Lerner Indexes

One measure focuses on the fact that profit-maximizing firms will choose output volumes where price *equals* marginal cost under perfect competition, but where price *exceeds* marginal cost under conditions of monopoly (and other types of imperfect competition.). As a result, suggested Abba P. Lerner in 1934, the gap between output price P and marginal cost MC can be used to measure the degree of monopoly power exercised by a firm. This **Lerner index** is calculated as the difference between output price and marginal cost, divided by output price, as follows:

$$\text{Lerner index} = \frac{P - MC}{P}$$

For a perfectly competitive firm, $P = MC$; hence the index comes to equal 0. The more price is raised above marginal cost, the closer the index gets to 1. There are those who have tried to measure the impact of antitrust policy by computing Lerner indexes for different firms in an industry and comparing them over time. Such comparisons, however, must be treated with the greatest of care, as Example 3 explains.

Concentration Ratios

One can also compute *concentration ratios* of the type first introduced in the chapter "Oligopoly and

EXAMPLE 3

AT&T, the Unlikely Trustbuster

When Lerner indexes decline over time and, thus, the affected firms' ability to keep price above marginal cost is reduced, we would be rash to attribute this effect to the successful pursuit of antitrust policies. This is so because other causes may be at work as well; the exposure of national monopolies to the fresh wind of *foreign* competition would be one such possibility.

Since its 1984 breakup, AT&T has, for example, been rapidly expanding its operations in Europe where high-priced national telephone monopolies used to rule supreme. Thus, AT&T spent $400 million on a new seabed fiber cable that can handle 80,000 calls at the same time, which doubled its U.S.-to-Europe capacity by 1991. The company also enlisted the help of the Federal Communications Commission to pressure the European state monopolies into reducing their access charges. Most of all, AT&T provided Americans with the ability to escape Europe's monopoly prices when calling from Europe, either by calling international 800 numbers or taking advantage of USA Direct service via the AT&T card. In 1991, for example, a Venice to Chicago 5-minute peak time call cost $14 so far as Italy's state monopoly was concerned; AT&T charged less than half the amount. Table A provides a number of further examples which have hardly escaped the attention of European customers. Fed up with dilapidated equipment, interminable delays, and extortionate rates, Europe's phone users have been assailing the entrenched bureaucrats who run their phone systems, and prices have begun to come down. As Nobel Prize–winning economist Milton Friedman has put it, "The most effective anti-monopoly policy is a policy of free international trade."

So far as AT&T is concerned, the price war has only begun. In 1990, it received 17 percent of its revenue from abroad; by the end of the decade, it will be 50 percent.

Source: Peter Fuhrman, "An Unlikely Trustbuster," *Forbes*, February 18, 1991, pp. 100–104.

TABLE A *1991 Telephone Rates (5-minute call, peak time)*

AT&T		National monopoly	
U.S. to France	$6.18	France to U.S.	$ 7.86
U.S. to Germany	6.18	Germany to U.S.	10.55
U.S. to Great Britain	5.20	Great Britain to U.S.	6.50
U.S. to Spain	6.14	Spain to U.S.	19.50

TABLE 3 *Selected Herfindahl Indexes*

Market structure	Herfindahl index	
Single firm: $S_1 = 100$	$S_1^2 = 100^2 =$	10,000
Two firms of unequal size: $S_1 = 80, S_2 = 20$	$S_1^2 + S_2^2 = 80^2 + 20^2 =$	6,800
Three firms of equal size: $S_1 = S_2 = S_3 = 33.3$	$S_1^2 + S_2^2 + S_3^2 = 33.3^2 + 33.3^2 + 33.3^2 =$	3,327
Ten firms of equal size: $S_1 = S_2 = \ldots = S_{10} = 10$	$S_1^2 + S_2^2 + \ldots + S_{10}^2 = 10^2 + 10^2 + \ldots + 10^2 =$	1,000

The Herfindahl index is a new government measure of the market power of firms. The fewer are the firms in a market or the more dominant a firm is in it, the greater is the index.

Monopolistic Competition." Recall that each of these ratios shows the percentage of domestic sales that is attributable to a stated number of largest domestic firms in an industry, usually the 4, 8, 20, or 50 largest companies. Presumably, one can compare changes in concentration ratios over time, or differences in such ratios between the United States and other industrialized economies, and draw conclusions about the effects of antitrust policies. In fact, such intertemporal comparisons have shown little change over the long run.[3]

Herfindahl Indexes

Others have opted to compute more sophisticated indexes of concentration, based on new guidelines the Antitrust Division developed in 1984 to direct its own merger policy. The guidelines were formulated to enable firms to figure out ahead of time whether a contemplated merger is going to be challenged by the government. First, the government defines a firm's **market share** S as the ratio, in a given year, of the firm's dollar sales in a market to the total dollar sales of all firms in that market, multiplied by 100. Thus, if the firm has sales of $100 million in a market in which total sales equal $400 million, its market share equals ($100 million ÷ $400 million) · 100, or 25 percent. Second, the government computes a measure of industrial concentration for the market in question which is more sophisticated than the traditional *concentration ratio* that we have met in an earlier chapter. This measure is called the **Herfindahl index, H,** and equals the sum of the squared market shares of all firms operating in the market. Thus, for n firms in a market, the Herfindahl index is $H = S_1^2 + S_2^2 + S_3^2 + \ldots + S_n^2$. Clearly, this index can range up to a maximum of 10,000 for the pure monopoly case, because the market share of a single firm is 100 percent and $100^2 = 10,000$. Table 3 provides a number of alternative examples.

Third, the government's general merger policy is defined with the help of the Herfindahl index, as indicated in Table 4. However, the general policy outlined in the table is modified by other considerations, such as the existence of foreign competition, the likelihood of a firm's bankruptcy unless the merger occurs, the heterogeneity of products (that assures continued competition on the quality plane) and the likelihood of new firms springing up if price is raised.

Clearly, the movement of Herfindahl indexes for

---

[3] One aggregative U.S. time series lists the percentage of national output (value added) produced in industries with 4-firm concentration ratios above 50 percent (in which, that is, the 4 largest firms produce more than half of the output). That percentage was 32.9 in 1901, 29.0 in 1972, and never strayed much from the 30 percent mark in the intervening years. See P. W. McCracken and T. G. Moore, "Competition and Market Concentration in the American Economy," Subcommittee on Antitrust and Monopoly, U.S. Senate, March 29, 1973.

EXAMPLE 4

Antitrust in a Global Economy

We are living in a world in which many firms not only transcend the boundaries of their traditional industries by building conglomerate empires but in which national boundaries become blurred as well by firms operating in many countries at the same time. These facts have interesting applications for antitrust policy.

It is still possible to speak of telephone companies, computer makers, television networks, movie studios, publishers, and providers of financial services as separate businesses, but barely so. As the examples of AT&T and the seven "Baby Bells" created in 1984 indicates, and as the recent history of Japan's Matsushita and Sony shows, the kinds of firms just noted are converging into a single huge industry, operating worldwide. In part, the reason is technological: Once signals from phones, television, and other information sources are translated into digital form, they are, technically speaking, identical. Bursts of 0s and 1s can bring us a phone call from home, an episode of "Cheers," a Haydn symphony, or the latest set of interest rates. Indeed, the digital code involved can be sent via the same line and decoded by the same machine. It is only natural for firms in this emerging mega-industry to seek to encompass everything from the creation of programs (cop shows, movies, databases) to the construction and operation of distribution systems (cables, satellites, wires) to the making of appliances (faxes, personal computers, telephones, television sets) that can receive and manipulate the programs involved in the world's homes and offices.

But firms in different countries play by different rules. In Japan, for example, companies prefer to conspire rather than compete with one another, and when Japanese firms begin to do business in the United States, they are apt to continue that practice. Families of firms with interlocking directorates and interlocking stockholdings, known as *keiretsu*, dominate the Japanese economy. The most prominent groups are centered on Mitsui, Mitsubishi, Sumitomo, Fuji, Sanwa, and Dai-Ichi Kangyo. These groups

TABLE 4 Merger Policy Guidelines

Premerger value of Herfindahl index	Policy
< 1,000	The market is considered unconcentrated: a merger is likely to go unchallenged.
1,000 to 1,800	The market is considered moderately concentrated; a merger is challenged if it raises the index by 100 points or more.
> 1,800	The market is considered highly concentrated; a merger is challenged if it raises the index by 50 points or more.

Since the 1980s, the Antitrust Division has followed a merger policy as outlined in this table. Note how easy it is to predict how much the Herfindahl index will rise as a result of a merger of two firms:

1. Before the merger, two independent firms with market shares a and b contribute $a^2 + b^2$ points to the index.
2. After the merger, the combined larger firm contributes $(a + b)^2$ points.
3. Thus, the index rises by $(a + b)^2 - a^2 - b^2$, which equals $(a^2 + 2ab + b^2) - a^2 - b^2 = 2ab$. One only need multiply the two firms' premerger market shares and double the result.

alone combine some 12,000 companies that coordinate everything from investment plans and employment practices to political contributions. Most of all, every member of such a group is expected to provide economic favors to the keiretsu partners. (In 1990, for example, Japanese car makers in the U.S. got 90 percent of all components from keiretsu partners.)

The problem for antitrust enforcement is obvious. American consumers as well as American exporters are clearly affected by the anticompetitive behavior of American subsidiaries of foreign firms, even if the price fixing and the carving up of markets is arranged abroad. Do U.S. antitrust laws still apply? Foreign governments are sensitive to the issue, fearing an infringement of their sovereignty. Yet there is a precedent. In a famous 1945 case, Judge Learned Hand ruled that as long as a conspiring company does business in the United States, the fact that the conspiracy took place abroad does not prevent the U.S. from exercising jurisdiction in the case.

More likely than not, this precedent will be tested a great deal in the years to come. Thus, in 1991, a major antitrust suit was being fought by Go-Video, Inc., a small Scottsdale, Arizona, company. Its owner, R. Terren Dunlap, had invented and patented a dual-deck VCR that could copy tapes without the need for two machines. The suit charged Japan's electronics giants (Hitachi, Matsushita, NEC, Sony, and more) with conspiracy to monopolize the U.S. market for home entertainment gear.

Sources: Julie A. Lopez, Mary L. Carnevale, "Phone Firms Are Becoming Poles Apart," *The Wall Street Journal,* February 9, 1990, p. B5; Clyde H. Farnsworth, "Antitrust Extension Is Weighed," *The New York Times,* April 16, 1990, pp. D1 and D7; "Inside the Charmed Circle," *The Economist,* January 5, 1991, p. 54; "Everything That Communicates Must Converge," *Fortune,* January 14, 1991, pp. 35–36; and Eduardo Lachica, "U.S.-Japan VCR Antitrust Suit to Start," *The Wall Street Journal,* April 1, 1991, pp. B1 and B6.

---

different markets over time can be used to gauge the extent to which competition or monopoly has increased in relative importance.

Aggregative Studies

Finally, all kinds of aggregative studies can be consulted to judge the effects of antitrust policies. One study, "The U.S. Economy: An Overview" (by William G. Shepherd) was noted in the chapter "Oligopoly and Monopolistic Competition." It concluded that competition in the U.S. economy has increased remarkably between 1939 and 1980—a development that was, among other things, attributed to vigorous antitrust action. But still, the conclusion remains speculative.

Other studies, however, have similarly concluded that antitrust efforts have had perhaps not a dramatic but at least a positive influence on the degree of competition prevailing. At the very least, antitrust policy can be credited with having made monopolization much more difficult. By prohibiting the most efficient forms of collusion (such as open cartel agreements, interlocking stockholdings, interlocking directorships, and many mergers) and by outlawing many entry barriers (such as price discrimination, exclusive contracts, requirements contracts, and tying contracts), antitrust policy has made monopolization much costlier and less beneficial for would-be monopolists. They must do it secretly and are liable to prosecution; their secret deals are legally unenforceable and are, thus, more likely to be subject to cheating. However, as Example 4 explains, antitrust enforcement may become increasingly difficult in the years ahead.

Summary

1. This is the first of several chapters that explore how government deals with certain shortcomings that are typical of the market economy and are called *market failures*. They include various forms of inefficiency (attributable to market imperfections, externalities, and the publicness of goods), as well as inequity and instability.

2. Antitrust policy involves systematic governmental efforts designed to limit the market power of monopolies, oligopolies, and other imperfectly competitive firms and to create conditions under which free competition can flourish. The policy first evolved late in the 19th century in response to the activities of the "robber barons" who engaged in various anticompetitive practices, including horizontal mergers and the formation of holding companies and trusts.

3. The history of antitrust legislation and major court decisions based on these laws are discussed in detail. Court cases reveal that the Sherman Act has been used to correct *business conduct* (making price fixing and other types of collusion illegal per se) as well as *market structure* (making market dominance illegal, first, if it results from "unreasonable" behavior and, later, per se). Other antitrust laws have clearly focused on specific types of business conduct.

4. It is difficult to assess the overall effects that antitrust efforts have had because one can only speculate about the state of the economy in their absence. Some argue that antitrust policy has had a negligible effect; others claim that it has had a significant and pro-competitive impact on the economy. Numerical measures of antitrust policy effects make use of Lerner indexes, concentration ratios, Herfindahl indexes, and more, but do little to clarify the issue. Even if antitrust laws have not had a dramatic impact, they have at least had a positive influence on the degree of competition prevailing. They certainly have increased the costs and lowered the benefits of attempts to monopolize.

Key Concepts

antitrust policy
conglomerate merger
consent agreement
exclusive contracts
Herfindahl index
holding company
horizontal merger
interlocking directorates
interlocking stockholdings
Lerner index
market failures
market share
price discrimination
requirements contracts
Rule of Reason
trust
tying contracts
vertical merger

Questions and Problems

1. Have another look at Figure 2. The text claims that the monopoly's profit (shaded) would be smaller if the monopoly produced the economically efficient output of 8 million units and charged the associated price equal to marginal cost (at f). Prove that the profit would, indeed, be smaller (and, thus, explain why the monopoly wouldn't volunteer to produce the efficient output level).

2. Why do would-be monopolists waste society's resources on unproductive rent-seeking?

3. As the text indicates, U.S. courts must struggle with the definition of "the relevant market" be-

fore they can decide whether firms are monopolizing it. Consider the following issues and ask yourself how you would decide:

a. Is cellophane sold in the same market as wax paper, Saran wrap, and other flexible wrapping materials?
b. Are glass jars sold in the same market as tin cans?
c. Is insulated aluminum cable sold in the same market as copper cable?
d. Do New York banks operate in the same market as Philadelphia banks?
e. Are different grades of Illinois coal sold in the same market?

4. In 1967, the U.S. Department of Justice admitted that it had prepared a draft of a legal complaint aimed at breaking up General Motors. Newspapers called it an "antitrust bomb," and the "biggest antitrust news since President Theodore Roosevelt's crusade early in the century." Would you favor such a move? Justify your answer.

5. "The Clayton Act provisions against exclusive contracts, requirements contracts, and tying contracts are a serious mistake." Evaluate this position.

6. Certain groups of individuals are exempted from the antitrust laws. They can do all the colluding they want. These groups include nonprofit agricultural cooperatives, labor unions (since the 1930s), sports organizations (the NBA, NFL, etc.), export associations (Webb-Pomerene Act of 1918), and government-regulated industries. Do you think such exemptions are ever justified?

7. Have another look at Figures 1 and 2. At their profit-maximizing output levels, compute Lerner indexes for the two firms depicted there.

8. The following table gives market shares of firms in five industries. Calculate the associated Herfindahl indexes.

Industry	Market share of firms				
	1	2	3	4	5
A	50	50	–	–	–
B	80	20	–	–	–
C	25	25	25	25	–
D	60	10	10	10	10
E	20	20	20	20	20

9. Compute the Herfindahl index for each of the following:
a. an industry with 200 equal-sized firms.
b. an industry with 100 equal-sized firms.
c. an industry with 10 equal-sized firms.
d. an industry consisting of a dominant firm with a 70 percent market share plus a competitive fringe of 100 equal-sized firms.

10. The following percentages were the actual U.S. beer market shares in 1984: Anheuser-Busch 35%, Miller 20%, Stroh 13%, Heileman 9%, Coors 7%, Pabst 6%, and five others 2% each.
a. Compute the Herfindahl index.
b. Determine whether the Antitrust Division would approve a merger of two of the 2 percent firms.
c. Determine whether it would approve a merger of Anheuser-Busch and Miller. Of Coors and Pabst. Of Heileman and Pabst.

11. The following percentages were the actual U.S. soft-drink market shares in 1981: Coca-Cola 35.9%, Pepsi 24.6%, Dr. Pepper 6.5%, Seven-Up 5.9%, Royal-Crown 4.3%, and twelve others 1.9% each.
a. Compute the Herfindahl index.
b. Determine whether the Antitrust Division would approve a merger of two of the 1.9 percent firms.
c. Determine whether it would approve a merger of Coca-Cola and Dr. Pepper. Of Pepsi and Seven-Up.

CHAPTER 18

REGULATION

Preview:

Governments at all levels set thousands of detailed rules that govern business behavior; this activity is referred to as regulation. *This chapter explores* economic *regulation (that is concerned with market entry, pricing, and output in particular industries) as well as* social *regulation (that deals with economy-wide issues, such as the health and safety of consumers or workers). Finally, two case studies explore the world of regulation in detail: One deals with the life and death of the CAB (the Civil Aeronautics Board, an agency once concerned with the economic regulation of the airlines industry). The other helps us appreciate the impossible task placed before the FDA (the Food and Drug Administration, an agency concerned with social regulation).*

Examples

1. Back from the Grave: The Case of Trucking Regulation
2. Health and Safety Regulation and the Price of Cars
3. Safeguarding the Welfare of Babies and the Disabled

The previous chapter focused on the federal government's *general* efforts, collectively known as antitrust policy, to limit the market power of imperfectly competitive firms and to create conditions under which free competition can flourish. But governments at all levels—local, state, and federal— are also engaged in setting hundreds of thousands of *detailed* rules of business behavior that specify who may produce what types and quantities of products, the manner in which production takes place, how goods are marketed, what prices may be charged and more. This activity is referred to as **regulation** and constitutes the subject matter of this chapter.

One of America's favorite foods, the cheeseburger, for example, is subject to literally thousands of government regulations. There are rules about permissible grazing practices of cattle, the use of growth hormones, conditions in slaughterhouses. There are rules about meat processing and others about the nature of the end product: A hamburger patty must be made from fresh or frozen chopped beef, containing no more than 30 percent fat and no binders, extenders, or additional water. There are more rules about pesticides used in the growing of wheat that turns into hamburger buns. These buns must each be enriched with a minimum of 1.8 mg of thiamine, 1.1 mg of riboflavin, and between 8 and 12.5 mg of iron. The lettuce used must be fresh; not soft, overgrown, burst, or "ribby"; a tomato must be mature, not overripe or soft. The pickles must come in slices 1/8 to 3/8 inches thick; the ketchup, believe it or not, must flow a maximum 9 cm in 30 seconds at a temperature of 69°F. If mayonnaise is used, it

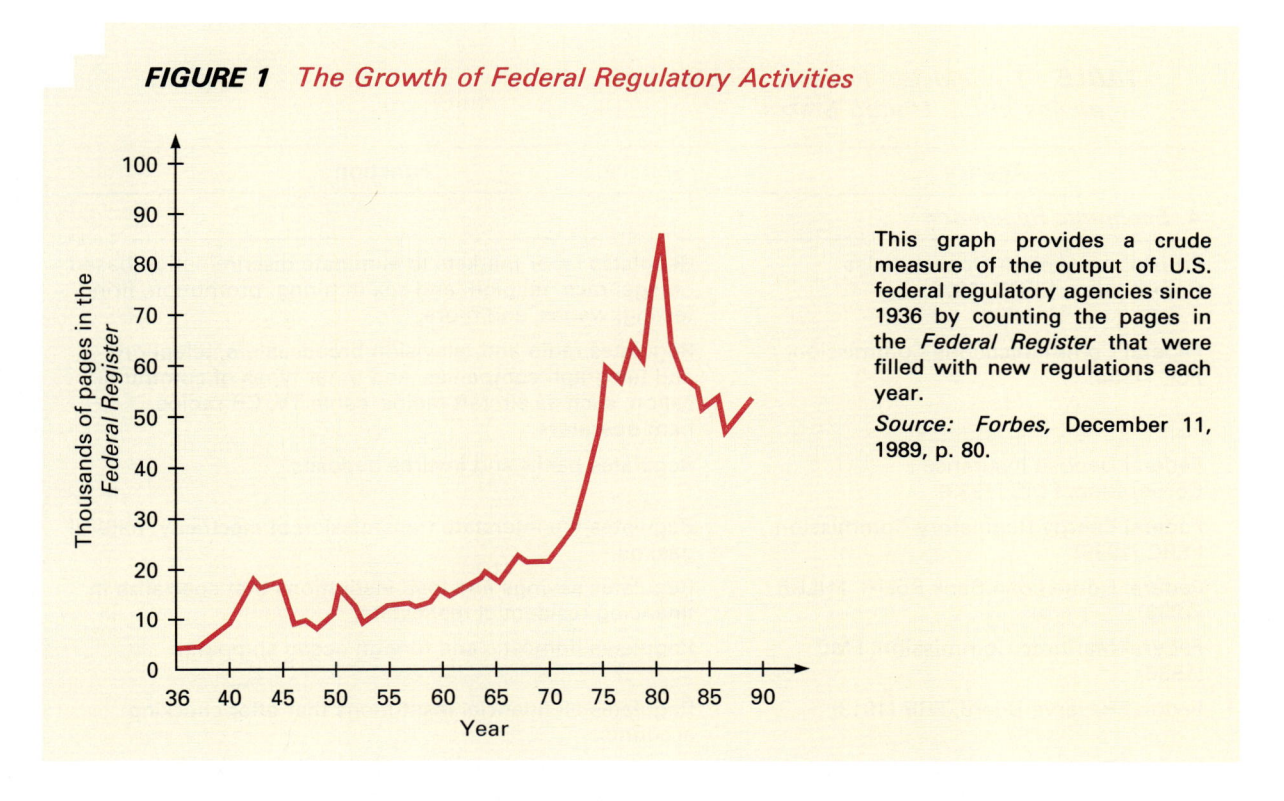

FIGURE 1 The Growth of Federal Regulatory Activities

This graph provides a crude measure of the output of U.S. federal regulatory agencies since 1936 by counting the pages in the *Federal Register* that were filled with new regulations each year.
Source: *Forbes,* December 11, 1989, p. 80.

must not be colored yellow to look like egg yolk, and yellow cheese must contain no less than 50 percent of milk fat, having been made from milk that was pasteurized or has been cured for a minimum of 60 days at a temperature of 35°F or more.[1]

Economic Regulation and Social Regulation

As the preceding examples imply, government regulation comes in two forms. First, there is **economic regulation,** a type of regulation aimed at particular industries that specifies rules concerning market entry, pricing, output, and the like. Second, there is **social regulation,** a type of regulation not targeted at specific industries and concerned with economy-wide issues, such as the health and safety of consumers or workers.

In 1991, there were over 100 regulatory agencies at the federal level alone, responsible for a staggering array of regulations. The oldest of these agencies, the Interstate Commerce Commission (ICC) had been created in 1887 in response to a public outcry against the abuses of market power that the railroad companies exercised in support of John D. Rockefeller's oil trust. Fully a quarter of all federal regulatory agencies were born as recently as the 1960s and 1970s. Table 1 provides information on major agencies and their respective areas of concern.

Figure 1 provides an admittedly crude measure of the output of U.S. federal regulatory agencies since the 1930s. The graph presents an annual count of the new pages filled in the *Federal Register,* a government publication that records all rules and notices issued by federal regulatory agencies. By this measure, regulatory activity peaked in 1980, declined during the Reagan years, and then resumed its upward trend.

Figure 2 provides an alternative and equally indirect output measure for the years since 1970.

---

[1] As reported by *U.S. News and World Report,* February 11, 1980.

TABLE 1 **Selected Federal Regulatory Agencies in the United States**

Agency	Function
A. Economic Regulation	
Equal Employment Opportunities Commission, EEOC (1972)	Regulates labor markets to eliminate discrimination based on age, race, religion, and sex in hiring, promotion, firing, testing, wages, and more.
Federal Communications Commission, FCC (1934)	Regulates radio and television broadcasters, telephone and telegraph companies, and other types of communication, such as aircraft radios, cable TV, CB radios, ham operators.
Federal Deposit Insurance Corporation, FDIC (1933)	Regulates banks and insures deposits.
Federal Energy Regulatory Commission, FERC (1935)	Regulates the interstate transmission of electricity, natural gas, oil.
Federal Home Loan Bank Board, FHLBB (1933)	Regulates savings and loan institutions that specialize in financing residential real estate.
Federal Maritime Commission, FMC (1936)	Regulates domestic and foreign ocean shipping.
Federal Reserve Board, FRB (1913)	Regulates all financial institutions that offer checking accounts.
Federal Trade Commission, FTC (1914)	Regulates trade practices to protect consumers from "unfairness," false advertising.
Interstate Commerce Commission, ICC (1887)	Regulates interstate surface transportation, including inland water and coastal shipping, pipelines, railroads, trucking.
National Labor Relations Board, NLRB (1935)	Regulates labor markets by certifying union elections and enforcing collective bargaining agreements.
Securities and Exchange Commission, SEC (1934)	Regulates all new issues of securities and all securities markets.

Measured in 1982 purchasing power, the spending by federal regulatory agencies rose steadily during the 1970s, followed by stagnation in the 1980s. Note that by this measure economic regulation in all years was of considerably lesser importance than social regulation. The following sections of this chapter will consider the nature of the two types of regulation in detail.

The Regulation of Natural Monopolies

The oldest form of regulation concerns *natural monopolies*, situations in which the long-run average total cost of every potential firm is declining throughout the range of quantities that might conceivably be demanded in the entire market; hence industry output—whatever its size—can be produced most cheaply only if no more than one firm exists. Monopoly is "natural" and desirable for technical reasons. (Such a situation was discussed in the section The Sources of Monopoly in the chapter "Monopoly and Cartels.") Figure 3 might depict such a firm. If left to its own devices, the electric power company depicted here will maximize economic profit by producing 208.42 million kilowatt hours (kwh) per year because that quantity equates at point *e* marginal cost *MC* with marginal revenue *MR*. This quantity can be sold by setting a price of

Agency	Function
B. Social Regulation	
Animal and Plant Health Inspection Service, APHIS (1907)	Regulates packing plants.
Consumer Product Safety Commission, CPSC (1972)	Regulates consumer product industries, requires reporting of defects, redesign, and labeling to reduce risk of injury.
Environmental Protection Agency, EPA (1970)	Regulates activities producing air, water, and noise pollution and toxic substances, enforces environmental standards.
Federal Aviation Administration, FAA (1934)	Regulates aviation industry.
Food and Drug Administration, FDA (1906)	Regulates food, drug, and cosmetics industries to assure purity, safety, and efficacy (of drugs); requires proper labeling.
National Highway Traffic Safety Administration, NHTSA (1970)	Regulates motor vehicle safety through safety standards, protects consumers from reset odometers, and promotes fuel economy via uniform national speed limit.
Mine Safety and Health Administration, MSHA (1973)	Regulates mine safety and miners' health.
Nuclear Regulatory Commission, NRC (1947)	Regulates civilian nuclear power facilities to protect public health and safety, as well as the environment.
Occupational Safety and Health Administration, OSHA (1971)	Regulates workplace health and safety.

These are just some of over 100 federal regulatory agencies that affect almost every aspect of economic life in the United States. The dates indicate the year of agency establishment. Agencies are often concerned with both economic and social regulation; they have been sorted according to the main direction of their activities.

10 cents/kwh (point c). Given the associated long-run average total cost ATC of 4.2 cents/kwh (point d), a profit of cd = 5.8 cents/kwh is made. This translates into an economic profit of $8.75364 million/year (equal to shaded rectangle $abcd$), year after year.

Critics often point to this *permanent* economic profit as the undeserved consequence of the firm's monopoly power and, thus, designate the shaded rectangle as a sign of *economic inequity*. They also note the presence of *economic inefficiency* because the price at c exceeds the marginal cost at e, which means that additional kilowatt hours, beyond the chosen quantity, would be valued by consumers at prices measured along demand-line segment cf, but could be produced at lower marginal costs measured along ef. The dotted triangle cef depicts the extent of this inefficiency, or the potential net benefit that is being forgone because the firm's profit would be lower if it produced output beyond the chosen quantity and charged an appropriate lower price to sell it.

This situation gives rise to demands for government intervention, but given the firm's economies of scale (depicted by the declining curve of long-run average total cost), it would be undesirable to employ the antitrust laws and break the firm up into numerous smaller competitors. For any given level of industry output, the lowest average total cost can only be achieved by a monopoly. Such situations

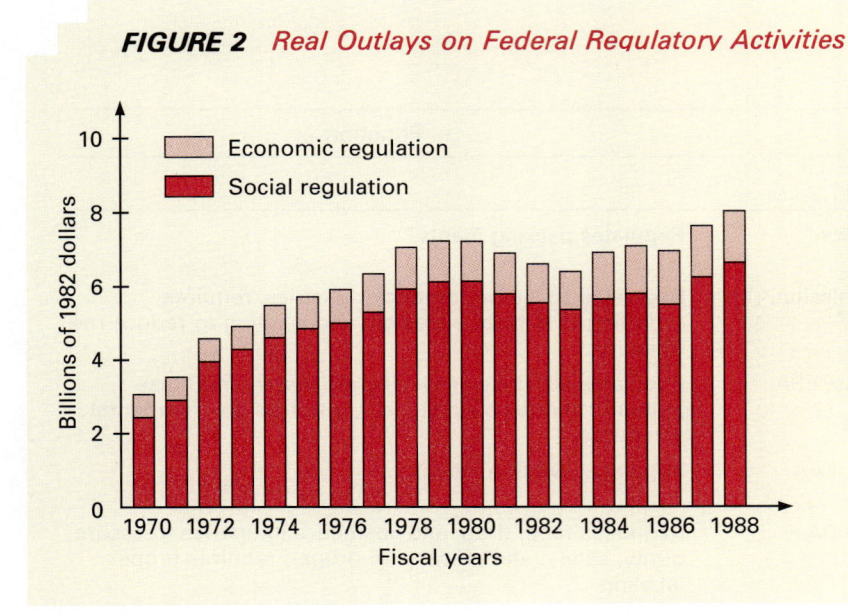

FIGURE 2 Real Outlays on Federal Regulatory Activities

Measured in constant 1982 purchasing power, real outlays on U.S. federal regulatory agencies have climbed from $3 billion in 1970 to $8 billion in 1988.

Source: *Economic Report of the President,* January 1989 (Washington, D.C.: U.S. Government Printing Office, 1989), p. 195.

are frequently associated with production of electric power, gas distribution, pipeline or railroad transport, and local telephone service. Accordingly, government sanctions the existence of natural monopolies in such industries, but, at the same time, it insists on regulating the behavior of the monopoly firm, in particular with respect to its pricing and output decisions. Figure 4 depicts two of the more obvious choices a government regulator might be tempted to make.

Eliminating Economic Inequity

A regulator might force the firm to produce an output quantity (here 379.79 million kwh/year) that can be sold at a price (here 2.6¢/kwh) precisely equal to long-run average total cost. By focusing on the price-quantity combination represented by point *b* in our graph, such a regulator would completely eliminate the monopoly's economic profit and, thus, the perceived economic inequity noted earlier.

Under this solution, price would still exceed marginal cost (here by distance *ba*) and a small amount of economic inefficiency (dotted triangle *abd*) would persist.

Eliminating Economic Inefficiency

A regulator might instead force the firm to produce an output volume (here 416.84 million kwh/year) that can be sold at a price (here 1¢/kwh) precisely equal to long-run marginal cost. By focusing on the price-quantity combination represented by point *d* in our graph, such a regulator would completely eliminate the economic inefficiency noted earlier.

But, as our graph also indicates, under this second solution, average total cost (at *c*) would exceed the chosen price (at *d*). A loss of *cd* = 1.5¢/kwh would be made, or a total loss of $6.2526 million/year (the shaded rectangle). This loss would occur year after year and inevitably drive our firm into bankruptcy, unless it was subsidized.

Another possibility, however, exists: A government regulator could mandate the efficiency-producing output quantity corresponding to the intersection of demand and marginal cost at point *d*

FIGURE 3 The Natural Monopoly Reviewed

Cents/kwh

- 19.0
- Profit maximizing price → 10.0 ● b .... ● c
- 4.2 ● a .... ● d
- ● e
- 440   Millions of kwh/year
- 208.42 Profit-maximizing quantity

Market demand
Marginal revenue
Long-run marginal cost
Long-run average total cost

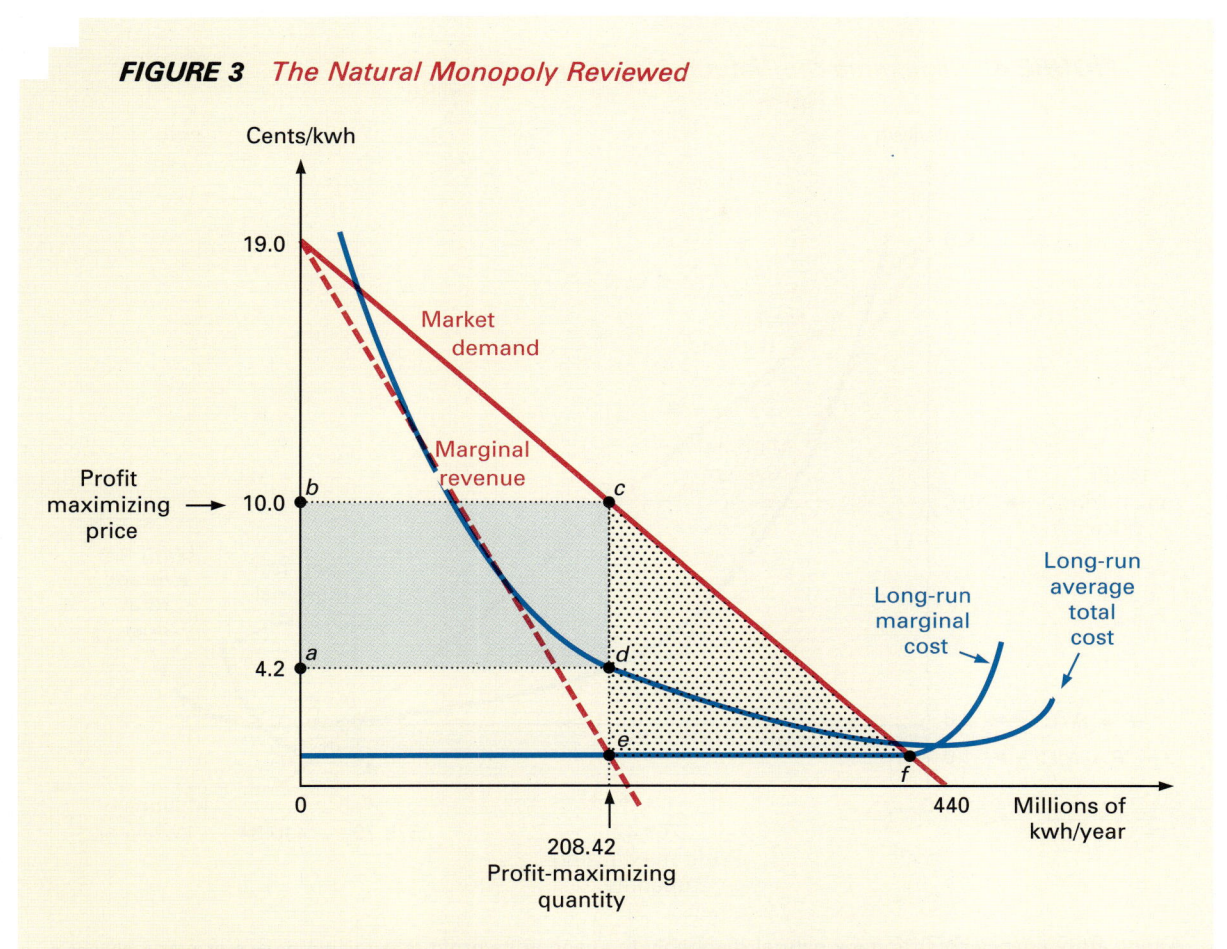

The natural monopoly poses a dilemma. On the one hand, monopoly is desirable because the declining curve of long-run average total cost allows a single firm to produce any given industry output at a lower *ATC* than a number of smaller competitive firms could achieve. On the other hand, monopoly is objectionable because a monopoly firm always prices its ouput above marginal cost; quite possibly, price exceeds average total cost as well. Critics view $P > ATC$ (distance *cd*) as a sign of *economic inequity* and measure its overall extent by the shaded profit rectangle *abcd*. In addition, they view $P > MC$ (distance *ce*) as a sign of *economic inefficiency* and measure its extent by the dotted triangle *cef*.

and then eliminate the loss by allowing the monopoly to price-discriminate. Consider Figure 5. If that monopoly produced the government-mandated output quantity corresponding to point *d*, or $416.84 million kwh/year, its average cost would equal 2.5¢/kwh (point *c*), and its total cost $10.421 million/year (rectangle 0*bce*). At a uniform $P = MC = 1$¢/kwh, the firm would make a loss equal to the shaded rectangle, as we have seen. But if it charged a price of $P_1 = 17.26$¢/kwh for the first $Q_1 = 38.46$ million kwh sold and *then* charged $P_2 = MC = 1$¢/kwh for the remaining $Q_2 = 378.38$ million kwh, its total revenue would cover its total cost:

$$P_1 \cdot Q_1 = \$6.638 \text{ million/year}$$
$$P_2 \cdot Q_2 = \$3.783 \text{ million/year}$$
$$\text{Total Revenue} = \$10.421 \text{ million/year}$$

FIGURE 4 *Regulating the Natural Monopoly*

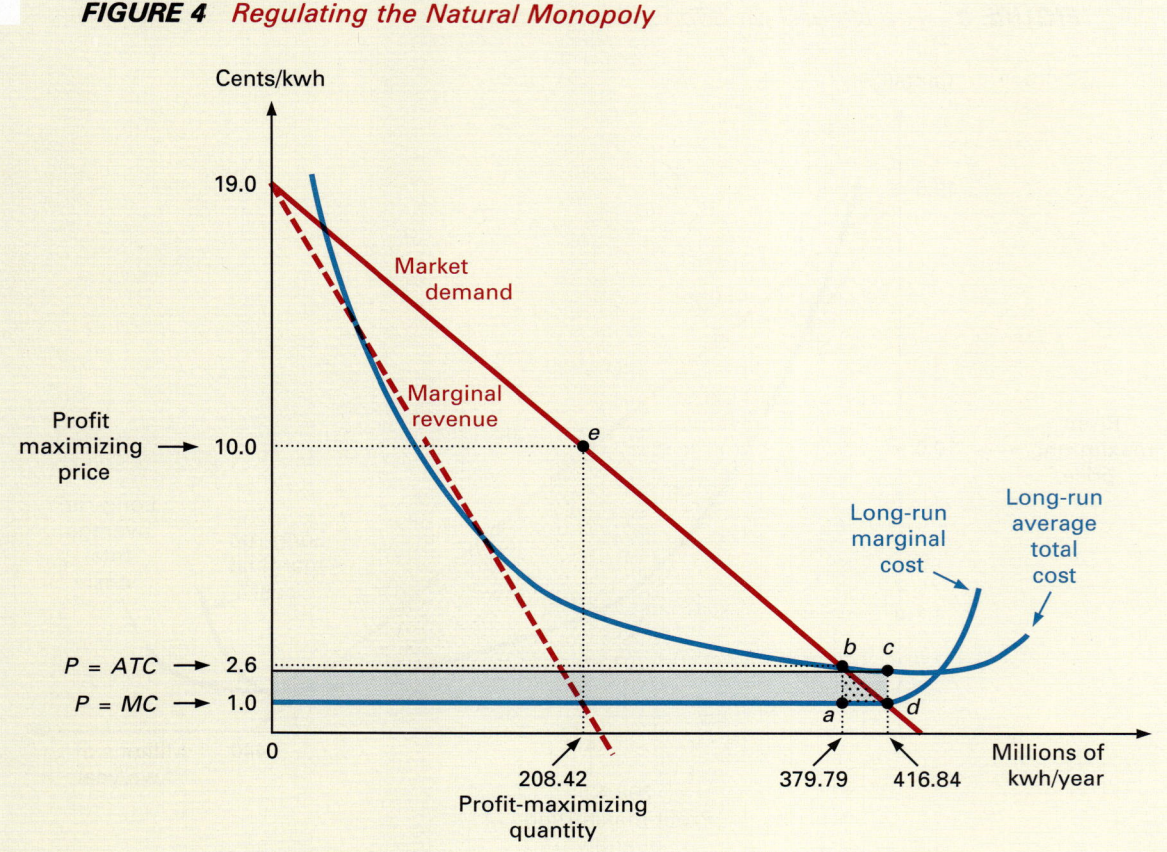

A regulatory agency could force a natural monopoly to abandon its profit-maximizing choice at *e* and accept a less palatable price-quantity combination such as *b* or even *d*. At combination *b*, P = ATC and economic profit is zero; a small remnant of economic inefficiency (triangle *abd*), however, remains. At combination *d*, P = MC and economic inefficiency is gone, yet the firm is condemned to making an eternal loss (and going bankrupt unless it is subsidized) because ATC > P.

Thus, its seems, economic inequity and economic inefficiency could be eliminated at the same time.[2]

---

[2] We need not pursue the rather complicated mathematics that lets us find the values of P_1 and P_2 here, but if you have ever looked at an actual electric bill, you know that regulators allow utilities in fact to price-discriminate in this way. For small amounts of power bought, the price is high; for additional units, it is lower.

Rate-of-Return Regulation: Practical Problems

Unfortunately, government regulators are not omniscient. They do not have access to the detailed data on demand and cost that are contained in our textbook graphs. As a result, real-world regulators of natural monopolies typically seek to bring about a situation (depicted by point *b* in Figure 4) in which the monopoly makes a zero economic profit and they do not worry excessively about their inability

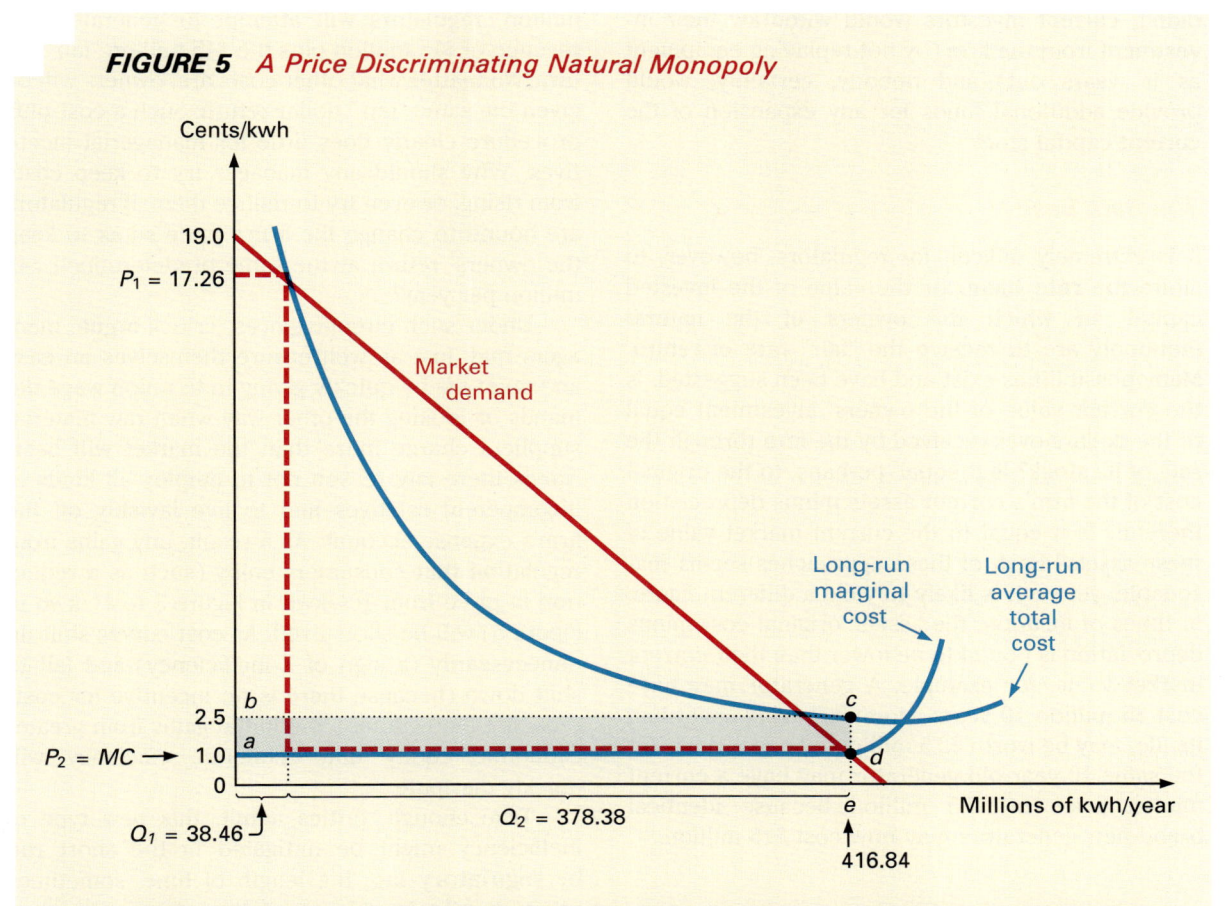

FIGURE 5 A Price Discriminating Natural Monopoly

A government regulator who forced a natural monopoly to produce an output volume (here at *e*) that eliminated every trace of economic inefficiency (because $P = MC$ at *d*) could eliminate the resulting loss (shaded rectangle *abcd*) by permitting price discrimination. In this example, selling Q_1 units at P_1 and the remaining Q_2 units at P_2 produces total revenue precisely equal to total cost. As a result, economic inequity and economic inefficiency are eliminated at the same time.

to eliminate every last trace of economic inefficiency (triangle *abd*).

To achieve the zero-economic-profit goal, regulators seek to set a price (or a pricing structure) such that total revenue covers all explicit and implicit costs: wages, raw materials, depreciation, taxes, and a "fair" return on the investment made by the firm's owners. All this, of course, makes a lot of sense. An inability to cover all costs would put the firm out of business. It would be unable to attract workers, buy raw materials, and keep or expand its capital. Yet the determination of a "fair" dollar return on the invested capital tends to be anything but easy.

The "Fair" Rate of Return

It is not too difficult to come up with a "fair" *rate* of return that owners should be allowed to earn. If investors can get a return of 9 percent in other industries that pose a comparable risk, regulators could select 9 percent as a "fair" rate as well. If they didn't, current investors would withdraw their investment from the firm (by not replacing equipment as it wears out) and nobody, certainly, would provide additional funds for any expansion of the current capital stock.

The Rate Base

It is extremely difficult for regulators, however, to figure the **rate base,** or the value of the invested capital on which the owners of the natural monopoly are to receive the "fair" rate of return. Many possibilities exist and have been suggested. Is the current value of the owners' investment equal to the dollars ever received by the firm through the sale of its stock? Is it equal, perhaps, to the original cost of the firm's current assets minus depreciation thereon? Is it equal to the current market value of these assets? Each of these approaches seems reasonable, yet each is likely to yield a different figure. In times of inflation, the assets' original cost minus depreciation is bound to be lower than their current market value, for example. A generator may have cost $5 million 10 years ago and, having spent half its life, may be worth $2.5 million on paper now. Yet the same 10-year-old generator may have a current market price of $7.5 million because identical brand-new generators may now cost $15 million.

Rate-of-Return Regulation: An Assessment

Critics are worried that the approach to regulation just described, which is typical so far as natural monopolies are concerned, is bound to fail. As they see it, even if regulators finally make a decision and promise owners a "fair" return of, say, 9 percent on, say, $500 million of current assets (valued at original cost minus depreciation thereon), further problems will quickly arise.

Owners then know how prices are set: If general operating costs equal $30 million a year, regulators will attempt to generate total revenue of $30 million (to cover wages, raw materials, taxes, and the like) plus $45 million (9 percent of $500 million, the "fair" dollar return).

If general operating costs double to equal $60 million, regulators will attempt to generate total revenue of $60 million plus the $45 million "fair" return. If general operating costs halve to equal $15 million, regulators will attempt to generate total revenue of $15 million plus the $45 million "fair" return. No matter what other costs are, owners will be given the same "fair" dollar return. Such a cost-plus procedure clearly does little for managerial incentives. Why should any manager try to keep costs from rising, or even try to reduce them, if regulators are bound to change the firm's price so as to keep the owners' return at the same predetermined $45 million per year?

Under such circumstances, critics argue, managers may just as well ensure themselves an easy and quiet life by quickly giving in to union wage demands or looking the other way when raw material suppliers charge more than the market will bear. Nor is there any reason not to employ all kinds of incompetent relatives and to live lavishly off the firm's expense account. As a result, any gains from regulation that consumers enjoy (such as a reduction in price from 10¢/kwh in Figure 3 to 1¢/kwh in Figure 5) will be short-lived. As cost curves shift up unnecessarily (a sign of X-inefficiency) and fail to shift down (because there is no incentive for cost-reducing innovations), the initial gains from greater economic equity and economic efficiency will quickly dissipate.

True enough, critics admit, this new type of inefficiency might be mitigated in the short run by **regulatory lag,** the length of time, sometimes years, that it takes government regulators of natural monopolies to review a firm's performance and possibly adjust its price. If the lag is long, the owners of well-managed regulated firms can reap a positive economic profit (and, thus, a more-than-"fair" return) by cutting costs, but the incentive is slight. For one thing, managers always know that regulators will catch up with them and slash prices if they are found with their profits up. In addition, regulators often force firms to make up for "excessive" profits by giving retroactive rebates to their "fleeced" customers. Thus the restoration of managerial incentives through regulatory lag is far from certain; in any case, it implies the failure of regulators to achieve what they set out to do.

On the other hand, regulatory lag can also cause firms to earn a less-than-fair return on the owners' investment. This can happen if costs are rising—for example, as a result of inflation—and regulators are too slow in adjusting prices upwards. Such firms will be sorely tempted to cut costs by reducing the *quality* of the goods they supply, and they will certainly be unable to attract any new funds for expansion.

Finally, critics note that technical inefficiency is likely to occur even in the absence of regulatory lag in the form of the **Averch-Johnson effect**: Whenever the "fair" rate of return that regulators guarantee a natural monopoly exceeds the current rate of interest, its owners will make unnecessary investments in the firm and, thus, fail to produce its output at the lowest possible average total cost.[3] Consider the selection of a "fair" rate of return of 9 percent per year, as in our earlier example. If the general interest rate is only 7 percent, any $10 million added to the firm's capital stock—even if it produces no output whatsoever—will yield an annual gain of $200,000 to investors: They could have earned $700,000 elsewhere; they will get a $900,000 return by virtue of the regulators' pricing formula (that promises the stated "fair" rate of return on the rate base of the firm).

The Regulation of Competitive Industries

A second form of economic regulation targets firms in competitive industries. Look again at the regulatory agencies listed in Table 1 and you will see that most of the regulated industries can by no stretch of the imagination be labeled natural monopolies. Why then are they regulated? Two opposing theories, the public-interest theory and the special-interest theory, compete for an explanation.

The Public-Interest Theory

According to the **public-interest theory of regulation,** government regulates firms in otherwise competitive industries because it wants to achieve certain goals that it considers to be in the public interest and that would otherwise not be achieved.

---

[3] See Harvey Averch and Leland L. Johnson, "Behavior of the Firm under Regulatory Constraint," *The American Economic Review,* December 1962, pp. 1052–1069. Note also Robert M. Spann, "Rate of Return Regulation and Efficiency in Production: An Empirical Test of the Averch-Johnson Thesis," *The Bell Journal of Economics and Management Science,* Spring 1974, pp. 38–52.

Unfortunately, the term *public interest* tends to remain undefined, but, more often than not, one gains the impression that the advocates of this type of regulation want to correct the distribution of income in a fashion that suits their personal values. In some cases, this involves the setting of below-equilibrium *maximum* prices because the traded items, such as fuel or housing, are considered "vital necessities" and "too important to be priced by the market." Clearly such price ceilings are meant to help "poor" buyers. In other cases (agricultural and labor markets, in particular, come to mind), this type of regulation involves the setting of above-equilibrium minimum prices; the intent of such price floors is to help "poor" sellers.

Figure 6 illustrates what is involved (and reviews material discussed in Chapter 3). Panel (a) pictures a competitive market for, say, natural gas or rental housing. In the absence of government intervention, price equals 0C and quantity traded equals 0J according to demand and supply intersection D. The sum of consumer surplus (CAD) and producer surplus (CDH) is maximized; economic efficiency prevails. Let government set a below-equilibrium maximum price of 0E. (This happened not so long ago when the federal government regulated the price of natural gas; local governments often institute rent controls.) The consequences are predictable. Quantity demanded rises along DG; quantity supplied falls along DF. Before long, a shortage of FG occurs and the actual quantity traded falls from 0J to 0I. The consumer surplus then equals ABFE; those consumers who buy quantity 0I at the lower price are better off. The producer surplus equals EFH; even those who still sell the item in question are worse off. In addition, serious economic inefficiency occurs: The shaded triangle BDF represents a deadweight loss of previous consumer and producer surplus; in other words, additional output IJ that consumers value along BD, and that producers could produce at lower marginal cost along FD, is not being produced.

Panel (b) tells the analogous story for a competitive market for, say, sugar or labor services. In the absence of government intervention, price equals 0R and quantity traded equals 0W, according to demand and supply intersection S. The sum of consumer surplus (RLS) and producer surplus (RSU) is maximized; economic efficiency prevails. Let government set an above-equilibrium minimum

FIGURE 6 Price Ceilings and Price Floors

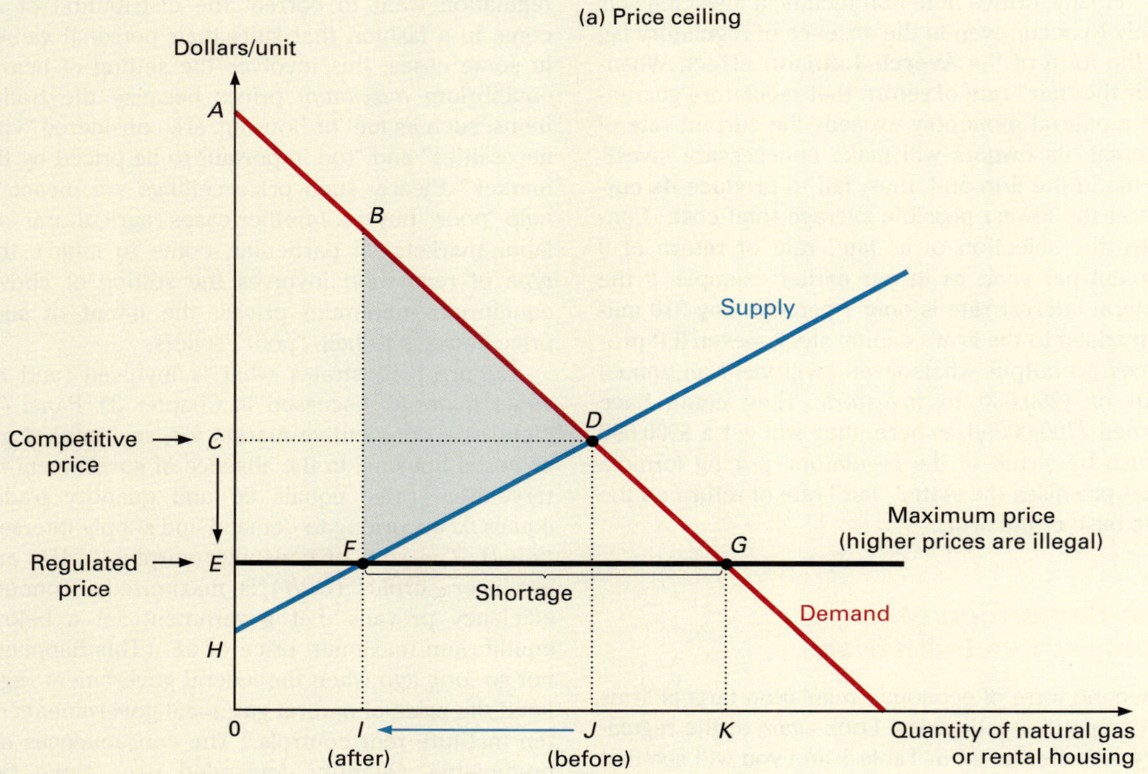

(a) Price ceiling

When government regulates firms in a competitive market, it may seek to help buyers by setting a below-equilibrium *maximum price*, or *price ceiling*, thereby outlawing higher prices (panel a). Or it may seek to help sellers with an above-equilibrium *minimum price*, or *price floor*, thereby outlawing lower prices (panel b). In either case, only *some* members of the favored group are helped. In the first case, a shortage occurs and not all buyers

price of 0M. (This happens routinely when the federal government fixes minimum prices for agricultural products or sets minimum wages.) The consequences are predictable. Quantity demanded falls along SN; quantity supplied rises along SP. Before long, a surplus of NP occurs and the actual quantity traded falls from 0W to 0V. The consumer surplus then equals MLN; those consumers who buy quantity 0V at the higher price are worse off. The producer surplus then equals UMNT; those who still sell the item in question are better off. In addition, economic inefficiency occurs: The shaded triangle NST represents a deadweight loss of previous consumer and producer surplus; put differently, additional output VW that consumers value along NS, and that producers could produce at lower marginal cost along TS, is not being produced.

Throughout this century, such price fixing has been carried on not only by the multitude of federal "alphabet agencies," such as those noted in Table 1 (the FCC, the FMC, the FTC, the ICC, and the like), but also by state and local governments. Thus state liquor commissions set liquor prices, and state insurance commissions set insurance rates. City

(b) Price floor

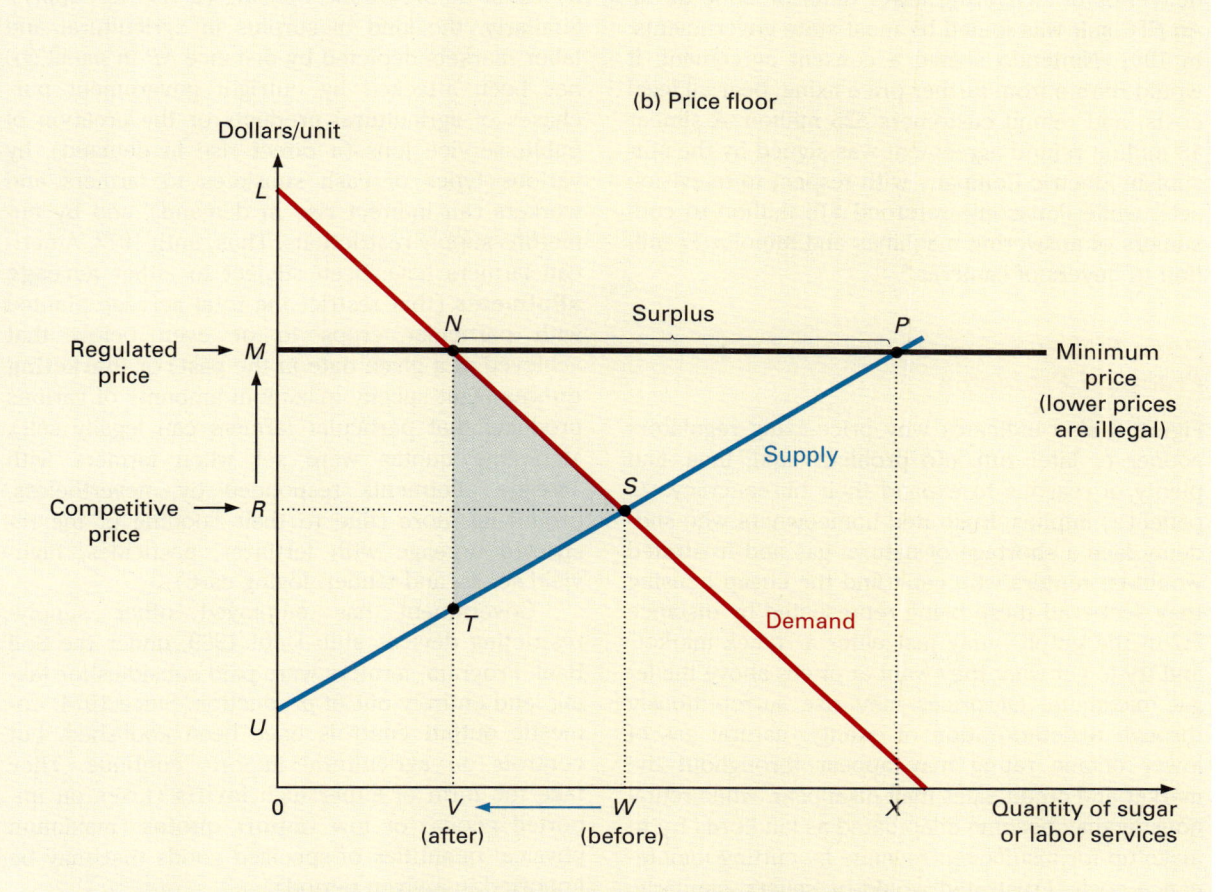

[Figure: Price floor diagram with Dollars/unit on vertical axis and Quantity of sugar or labor services on horizontal axis. Supply curve rises from U through S; Demand curve falls from L through S to the right. Regulated price (Minimum price) line MP is horizontal above competitive price R. Points N and P on the minimum price line define the surplus region. Shaded triangle NST shows inefficiency. V (after) and W (before) on horizontal axis; X marks quantity at minimum price. Label: "Minimum price (lower prices are illegal)".]

can buy what they wish; in the second, a surplus occurs and not all sellers can sell what they wish. In both cases, economic inefficiency appears where the price that a marginal consumer is willing to pay (at B or N) comes to exceed the price that a marginal producer is willing to accept (at F or T). The extent of economic inefficiency is measured by the shaded triangles.

councils set maximum rents that landlords may charge, and city transport commissions set rates on buses, subways, and taxis. And for some 38 years prior to 1976 (when a federal law repealed them), states as well as cities promoted minimum retail prices for almost everything. Their so-called **fair trade laws** allowed any manufacturer to fix a minimum price for a product and, if even a single retailer agreed to it, to bind all retailers to it, even those who refused to sign an appropriate agreement with the manufacturer. Those selling for less could be enjoined, fined, and even jailed. As recently as 1974, 36 states, including California and New York, still had such laws. All were justified by "the public interest."

Although legally dead, the matter is by no means closed. All kinds of manufacturers continue to attempt to get retailers to respect "manufacturer-suggested" minimum prices; since 1990, the Federal Trade Commission has focused its attention precisely on cases such as these. Thus, Nintendo of America, Inc., while holding an 80 percent share of the U.S. video-game market, fixed retail prices and punished noncompliant retailers by slowing down deliveries or delivering fewer units or none at all. An FTC suit was joined by most state governments; in 1991, Nintendo signed a consent agreement: It would refrain from further price fixing, bear all legal costs, and refund customers $25 million. A similar $8 million refund agreement was signed by the Mitsubishi Electric Company with respect to television sets, while Panasonic returned $16 million to consumers of answering machines and Minolta $7 million to buyers of cameras.[4]

Price-Fixing Schemes: Practical Problems

Figure 6 also indicates why price-fixing regulators sooner or later run into problems and, thus, find plenty of reasons to expand their bureaucracy. As panel (a) implies, frustrated homeowners who suddenly face a shortage of natural gas and frustrated would-be renters who can't find the cheap housing they seek—all these being represented by distance *FG* in the graph—may just enter a "black market" and try to get what they want at prices above the legal maximum. Or prices may rise surreptitiously through a deterioration of quality: natural gas of lower octane rating may appear throughout the market and credit sales may disappear, while rental housing may become dilapidated as landlords try to make up for insufficient revenue by cutting maintenance costs. Frustrated would-be sellers, similarly, will try their best to get rid of surpluses below the minimum price. Before long, our regulators will get embroiled in combatting black market transactions involving "price gouging," "chiseling," and other types of "unconscionable" behavior. And they will do their very best to shore up their price fixing by cutting demand and raising supply in the face of shortages (panel a), while raising demand and cutting supply in the face of surpluses (panel b).

For example, a few years ago in the natural gas market, the kind of shortage depicted by distance *FG* in panel (a) has been attacked by rationing natural-gas hookups for newly constructed houses (a cut in demand) and, in the rental housing market, by constructing public housing (a rise in supply). Similarly, the kind of surplus in agricultural and labor markets depicted by distance *NP* in panel (b) has been attacked by outright government purchases of agricultural products or the creation of public-service jobs (a direct rise in demand), by various types of cash subsidies to farmers and workers (an indirect rise in demand), and by numerous supply restrictions. Thus, until 1973, American farmers have been subject to either **acreage allotments** (that restrict the total acreage planted with particular crops to or even below that achieved at a given date in the past) or **marketing quotas** (that specify maximum amounts of various products that particular farmers can legally sell). Marketing quotas were set when farmers with acreage allotments responded by, nevertheless, producing more (due to their flooding of the restricted acreage with fertilizer, pesticides, high-yield seeds, and tender, loving care).

Government has employed other supply-restricting devices still. Until 1969, under the Soil Bank Program, farmers were paid subsidies for taking land entirely out of production. Since 1974, domestic output controls have been abolished, but controls on agricultural imports continue. They take the form of either high **tariffs** (taxes on imported goods) or low **import quotas** (maximum physical quantities of specified goods that may be imported in a given period).

Similar supply restrictions abound in labor markets. Consider federal laws restricting immigration. Consider how every state in the union requires the licensing of a multitude of "professions," broadly defined to include not just architects, dentists, doctors, lawyers, and psychologists (as one would expect) but also barbers, contractors, dance instructors, dog groomers, egg graders, morticians, travel agents, and sellers of yachts! Under the guise of certifying training and competency and enforcing "ethical" behavior, these licensing procedures restrict the number of practitioners with a view to upholding the prices they can charge.

Price-Fixing Schemes: An Assessment

Price-fixing schemes are not only cumbersome; in the view of many critics, they are also a particularly

---

[4] Paul M. Barrett, "Nintendo's Latest Novelty is a Price-Fixing Settlement," *The Wall Street Journal,* April 11, 1991, pp. B1 and B6.

poor way of redistributing income. Consider a single example, a study of trucking regulation in the 1970s.[5] According to the study, regulation raised freight rates from 10 to 20 percent above the competitive level and cost shippers an extra $4 billion a year. Yet of this amount, owners of trucking firms and members of the teamsters' union gained only $1.4 billion and $1.2 billion a year, respectively. The remainder was dissipated in pure waste ($1.4 billion), a consequence of driving circuitous routes, making empty return trips, and obeying all kinds of other silly rules prescribed by the regulators. Thus, whatever one's view of the desirability of redistributing income, trucking regulation was an inefficient way of carrying it out. Those doing the trucking (owners and drivers) only gained 65 cents for every extra dollar that shippers were made to pay. And this brings us to an alternative view of what the regulation of competitive markets is all about.

The Special-Interest Theory

A number of economists under the leadership of Nobel laureate George J. Stigler (b.1911), reject the public-interest theory of government regulation as an explanation of why government regulates.[6] Theirs is a more cynical view. According to their **special-interest theory of regulation,** government regulates firms in otherwise competitive industries because self-interested politicians and bureaucrats (who have a lot to gain from this) respond to requests for regulation by those who want to escape the rigors of competition and seek to set up viable cartels. As these economists see it, regulation is not thrust upon market participants against their will and for the sake of the "public interest"; it is actually *demanded* by them. Thus firms or labor unions want help in keeping other suppliers out. They want to cut supply and raise prices and assure that no one cheats in the process. They want to support their price-raising schemes by engineering higher demand for whatever they happen to sell; hence they welcome government contracts or subsidies, the suppression of substitutes, and the promotion of complements. (Thus, airlines seek contracts or subsidies to carry U.S. mail; commercial TV stations try to keep cable TV out of their market; truckers want greater highway capacity.) And all these firms willingly pay a reward for the government's help in campaign contributions, job offers, votes, and more. Before long, according to this view, the demand for regulation coaxes out an appropriate supply on the part of politicians and bureaucrats. We will consider the process involved presently.

The "Capture" of Legislators

Legislators at all levels of government, the argument goes, can be induced to rig markets directly, or to set up appropriate agencies to do the rigging, by channeling a number of rewards to them. Because all legislators must be elected, campaign contributions play a pivotal role. Such contributions, no doubt, go to incumbent legislators or to their challengers depending on who shows the "proper" attitude with respect to matters that contributors care about. Some will seek minimum prices—for airplane trips, auto insurance, labor, liquor, milk, sugar, taxi rides, or whatever else they have to sell. Others will look for legislators willing to restrict supply—whether by sanctioning cartels, exclusive franchises, and limits on immigration or via import quotas, marketing quotas, and professional licensing rules. Others still will lobby for higher demand—the awarding of government contracts, subsidies for peanuts and wheat, and public-service jobs for the unemployed.

In recent years, the size of campaign contributions made by businesses, labor unions, and political action committees (PACs) has been impressive, reflecting the fact that modern-day radio and TV campaigns are very expensive. (During 1988, victorious congressional candidates spent an average $389,950 to get elected.) Strictly speaking, only contributions made from people's personal incomes are legal; those made with corporate funds are not. Still, as recently as the 1970s, major corporations

---

[5] Thomas Gale Moore, "The Beneficiaries of Trucking Regulation," *The Journal of Law and Economics,* October 1978, pp. 327–344.

[6] See George J. Stigler, "The Theory of Economic Regulation," *The Bell Journal of Economics and Management Science,* Spring 1971, pp. 3–21; Richard A. Posner, "Theories of Economic Regulation," *The Bell Journal,* Autumn 1974, pp. 335–358; and Sam Peltzman, "Toward a More General Theory of Regulation," *The Journal of Law and Economics,* August 1976, pp. 211–240.

spent over $100 million on federal election campaigns. Following rather aggressive solicitation of funds by top Nixon administration officials, the list of corporations that eventually admitted illegal contributions includes American Airlines, Ashland Oil, Braniff Airlines, Goodyear Tire and Rubber, Gulf Oil, Minnesota Mining and Manufacturing (3M), and Phillips Petroleum. Nowadays, contributors tend to be more careful. In 1988, PACs made up of corporate officers, dairy farmers, dentists, and doctors to others put together by seafarers, teachers, and truckers managed to spend $159 million on federal election campaigns alone—quite legally.

Once elected, these officials are, of course, expected to show proper gratitude toward their beneficiaries, which is why President Bush proposed outlawing business and labor union PACs. Having been generously financed, elected officials are naturally expected to vote in the "right" way and to lend a sympathetic ear to professional lobbyists who will point out the public interest involved in all types of legislation under consideration. This boils down, of course, to pointing out the special interest of those who lobby and whose incomes are being advanced by the legislation. In the meanwhile, the voices of those whose incomes are being eroded by the very same legislation go unheard. This is so because the interests of the organized special pleaders is visible and concentrated: It may involve $100 million of extra revenues coming to a single firm, or a small group of them, as a result of higher legal prices, a subsidy, or a government contract. On the contrary, the interest of their unorganized victims is invisible and diffuse: It may involve 50 cents being lost by each of 200 million consumers or taxpayers. The former can afford to hire full-time professional lobbyists (together with large staffs of lawyers, public relations people, and so on). They can easily inundate the overworked staffs of every single legislator with good advice on the meaning of "sound public policy." They can orchestrate, if necessary, a letter campaign by thousands who have a lot to gain. The millions who lose are silent. Thus legislators get a biased view of things. And by thus accommodating the demand for regulation, the compliant legislators can gather further rewards: more campaign funds in the future, more votes from those with new jobs in new plants built in their home districts by beneficiaries grateful for their help, job offers in case of a lost election, all-expenses-paid vacations, and, perhaps, even jobs for their children.

The "Capture" of Regulators

Now consider the regulatory bodies set up by the legislative branch of government. They, too, are systematically influenced by those they are supposed to "regulate." They, too, get rewards for being compliant when approached by the special interests.

Many regulators have strong bonds with the regulated anyway. Nothing is more natural (and, indeed, frequently required when complex issues are involved) than putting doctors on a professional licensing board for practitioners of medicine, airline industry officials on the Civil Aeronautics Board (the CAB used to regulate the airlines), electric power company executives on the Federal Energy Regulatory Commission. The proper lobbying effort will see to it that this is exactly what happens. (No wonder that regulators are sometimes found to have a personal financial interest in companies they regulate.) In 1974, for example, 19 officials of the FERC, which had raised natural gas prices, held natural gas company stock.

Even when the regulators and the regulated are strangers initially, chummy relations quickly develop. Regulators cannot help but have frequent contact with the regulated: There are formal public hearings before the commissions involved, as well as over 100,000 nonpublic meetings a year in which specific issues are "informally adjudicated."

The federal regulatory agencies, for instance, employ so-called administrative law judges. They gather evidence, conduct hearings, and make decisions on the government-sponsored cartels involving rates charged, the number of firms allowed, and so on. This procedure is typically lengthy and even then any decision can be appealed to the full regulatory commission as well as challenged in court. A recent railroad merger case took 3 years and 275 days of hearings before the ICC to decide. It produced a veritable paper nightmare of 50,000 pages of transcripts and 100,000 pages of exhibits. A recent satellite communications pricing case before the FCC took 11 years to decide. Thus there is plenty of occasion for regulators and the regulated to get to know each other—not only during endless hearings, but also during informal contacts over lunch, at business conventions, and at social gatherings. Before long, government officials and industry executives are personal friends. This means, in turn, that friendly regulators (like friendly legislators whose reelection bids fail) can expect future jobs from those they now regulate. So can members of their families. And that is how self-interest explains regulatory policy. It is nothing else, the argument concludes, but public pocket picking cloaked in public-interest rhetoric.

The Call for Deregulation

The 1980s may well be remembered as roundup time for runaway regulators. It was a time when at least some of the excesses of government regulation were brought to a halt. In response to widespread criticism, Congress enacted a number of laws reducing or even eliminating the regulation of competitive industries.

The Natural Gas Policy Act of 1978 provided for the deregulation of crude oil prices by 1981 and of natural gas prices by 1985. The Airline Deregulation Act of 1978 mandated the abolition of an entire regulatory agency, the Civil Aeronautics Board, by 1985. Thus, the government removed controls on market entry and exit, routing, and fares to which the industry had been subject for nearly half a century. A later section in this chapter, Case 1: The Story of Airline Deregulation, examines the effects in detail.

Laws enacted in the early 1980s severely restricted the powers of the Interstate Commerce Commission with respect to trucks, railroads, and intercity buses. The Motor Carrier Reform Act of 1980, for example, put an end to the antitrust exemption long enjoyed by the trucking industry's rate-setting bureaus; it promoted free market entry and exit and returned to truckers the rights to set their own prices, determine their own routes, and choose the type of cargo they carry. The Staggers Rail Act of 1980 freed many railroad fares from government control and the Bus Regulatory Reform Act of 1982 ended entry and fare regulation for intercity buses. And the Federal Communications Commission moved on its own to end most regulation of radio and television broadcasters as well as of cable TV and telecommunications companies.

In 1989, when the President's Council of Economic Advisors made an interim tally, it figured that deregulation was saving airline passengers $15 billion per year, users of trucking services between $39 and $63 billion per year, and railroad customers between $9 and $15 billion per year. Nevertheless, to the extent that deregulation is partial, troubles remain, as Example 1 explains.

The Regulation of Health and Safety

As we have noted in earlier chapters, it is one of the conditions of perfect competition that buyers and sellers possess perfect knowledge concerning all matters relevant to their trading in a market. In many markets such knowledge, however, is lacking. Buyers of foods may have no idea about the ingredients contained therein and nothing short of a costly chemical analysis could reveal possible impurities or health hazards. Buyers of cars, electronic equipment, toys, and a million other products, similarly, have no easy method for ascertaining the quality of these products, including such features as their life expectancy or safety. Buyers certainly would be foolish to rely on self-serving statements of sellers who have a lot to gain from exaggerating the quality of goods they want to sell. As we saw in an earlier chapter ("Imperfectly Competitive Labor Markets"), buyers of labor have an equally hard time identifying high-quality workers and in this market, too, sellers have natural incentives to hide flaws (such as lack of experience, ill health, low motivation, insufficient training, and the like). Sellers in many markets face similar problems. Just consider how difficult it is for workers who wish to sell their labor to become informed with respect to possible hazards on the job—in particular, if such threats to health and safety are hidden, not only because employers have an incentive to hide them but also because they are by nature difficult to detect. Just as pesticides used in apple orchards may, some three decades later, cause cancer in regular consumers of cider, so may invisible vapors of benzene kill an unsuspecting worker after decades of fixing cars in a garage.

True enough, people could make private efforts to gain the crucial information they need to make well-informed choices. Consider the systematic

EXAMPLE 1

Back from the Grave: The Case of Trucking Regulation

Imagine how you would feel if you took a supersaver flight to Florida and four years later got a bill from the airline asking you to pay the difference to the full fare. That is precisely what happened to many shippers who negotiated lower prices with trucking companies following the enactment of the Motor Carrier Reform Act of 1980. Thus, in 1990, General Mills received a $457,000 bill from the trustees of the Overland Express, a bankrupt Indianapolis hauler. Similar bills totaling $200 million went to Bordens, Chrysler, General Tire, International Paper, Kellogg, and Sears.

The 1980 deregulation act had in fact not abolished the ICC bureaucracy; it had merely given truckers the right to set their own prices, *subject to their filing of appropriate price schedules with the ICC.* As the number of interstate carriers increased from 14,000 to 44,000 during the 1980s, prices plummeted, but many of the 1 million price changes per year were never filed with the ICC, which made them illegal. As some trucking firms went under, their trustees saw the obvious loophole and initiated retroactive billing at original prices. They were supported by the Teamsters' Union, concerned with back wages and health and pension benefits. Customers called it an "unconscionable disavowal of contract," but the U.S. Supreme Court upheld the letter of the law and ruled in favor of back billing.

Source: William Tucker, "Back from the Grave," *Forbes,* May 13, 1991, pp. 49 and 53.

---

evaluation of products by the Consumers' Union, which issues its findings in the monthly *Consumer Reports* (and which attempts to preserve objectivity by refusing to accept advertising money from manufacturers). It seems much easier and is considerably cheaper, however, to have government find and provide relevant information to us all or to see to it that hazards are eliminated; and that idea has spawned the type of regulation discussed in this section. The regulation of health and safety takes two forms: a) it seeks to improve market knowledge, thereby enabling people to make informed choices on matters affecting their health and safety; and b) it mandates that firms reduce or eliminate known hazards to health and safety.

Improving Market Knowledge

As we saw in the previous chapter, antitrust laws have long outlawed false advertising; more recent laws require would-be sellers not only to refrain from spreading misinformation but also to take the positive step of filling the void and providing correct information. Numerous laws see to it that sellers identify the quality of their products in detail and then disclose that information to prospective buyers through appropriate labels concerning product content, performance, grade, and the like. The Textile Fiber Products Identification Act of 1958, for example, requires that all textiles be identified by generic names (such as polyester) rather than trademarks (such as Dacron), and that the precise percentages of different types of fibers contained in a product be revealed. Thus, a blanket might be labeled as containing 50 percent polyester, 30 percent cotton, and 20 percent wool, while the mattress on which it lies is described as made from 50 percent blended cotton felt, 38 percent cortex pad, and 12 percent urethane foam.

Similar laws require analogous information on the precise content of processed foods, the performance characteristics of durable goods, the grade of agricultural products, and even the nature of consumer credit. Thus, a can of V8 vegetable juice is labeled to contain "tomato juice from concentrate, reconstituted juices of carrots, celery, beets, parsley, lettuce, watercress, and spinach, as well as salt, vitamin C (ascorbic acid), natural flavoring, and citric acid." A car may be labeled to contain a 4-cylinder, 97-cubic inch displacement engine with a 2-barrel carburetor that gives 39 miles per gallon on the open highway and involves a fuel cost of $423 per year if driven 15,000 miles. Similar "energy efficiency ratings" must be displayed on major home appliances, such as dishwashers, freezers, refrigerators, and water heaters. Basic agricultural products, such as butter, eggs, fruit, grain, meat, and vegetables, must be graded A, B, or C by U.S. Department of Agriculture standards. And consumer loans must reveal how interest is calculated (by add-on or discount; annually, monthly, weekly, or daily), and what the total dollar finance charge is.

Mandating Reductions in Known Hazards

The first government agency directly concerned with issues of health and safety, the Food and Drug Administration, was created in 1906; but most of the present-day regulatory agencies in this field were created since 1970. Changes in the attitudes of U.S. courts have created ever-stronger incentives for manufacturers to identify and reduce hazards associated with their products. Early in this century, courts followed the **doctrine of caveat emptor** (let the buyer beware), according to which buyers alone were responsible for the consequences of their purchases. It was up to buyers to ascertain the quality of products at the time of purchase and to use these products properly thereafter. If they ran into trouble later (and fell off a ladder, for example), buyers couldn't blame sellers for deception, fraud, or negligence (with respect to the ladder's construction, design, or labeling, for instance). All this began to change with a 1916 landmark case, *MacPherson* v. *Buick Motor Company*. When the wooden wheel of McPherson's car collapsed and he suffered injuries, Buick was held liable because it had used defective materials. Thus, the **doctrine of caveat venditor** (let the seller beware) was born; it made sellers responsible for the effectiveness and safety of their products and made them liable for consequences if these products had been "negligently produced." With that decision, the long-held implicit assumption that buyers and sellers shared similar market knowledge, or could acquire it with equal ease, was discarded.

Since 1970, many new agencies, such as the Consumer Product Safety Commission, the Environmental Protection Agency, the National Highway Traffic Safety Administration, and the Occupational Safety and Health Administration, have been set up to identify hazards to health and safety and to issue regulations that reduce or even eliminate them. Yet despite their good intentions, the government regulators of health and safety have been embroiled in bitter controversy. The reason goes back to a matter discussed in the first chapter of this book: In a world of scarcity, for every benefit, there is a cost. It is all too easy to focus on benefits, while forgetting the inevitable costs.

Of Benefits and Costs

To reap the benefits of health and safety regulation (or, for that matter, any type of regulation), three types of cost must be incurred. Figure 2 earlier in this chapter indicated the most obvious type of cost: the *direct administrative cost* of running the regulatory agencies themselves. These costs, however, are by no means the only ones; nor are they the major ones. There are, second, *direct compliance costs* that must be incurred by the affected parties and, third, a host of *indirect costs* that are much more difficult to quantify.

In fiscal 1979, for example, the budgets of federal regulatory agencies came to $4.8 billion, but the private sector compliance costs (that included, incidentally, $25 billion for filling out more than 4,400 federal forms) came to a whopping $97.9 billion. This compliance cost added 7 cents to the price of every pound of hamburger, $22 to the average hospital bill, $666 to the price of every new car, and $2,000 to that of every new home.[7] Thus, the total direct costs ($4.8 billion + $97.9 billion, or $102.7 billion) came to roughly $500 for every American citizen. Today, this number is considerably higher. Example 2 provides a breakdown of the $666 added to new cars.

The indirect costs of health and safety regulation

---

[7] See Murray L. Weidenbaum, "The Costs of Government Regulation of Business," in *The Cost of Government Regulation,* Hearings before the Subcommittee on Economic Growth and Stabilization of the Joint Economic Committee, Congress of the United States (Washington, D.C.: U.S. Government Printing Office, 1978), pp. 31–59.

EXAMPLE 2

Health and Safety Regulation and the Price of Cars

Government regulations concerning health and safety inevitably raise the prices of many goods. One study computed the cumulative effect of a mere decade of federal regulations on the price of a domestically made car. As the accompanying table shows, measured in 1977 dollars, the regulations raised the price by $666.

Adding the effects of substantially tightened emission standards introduced in 1980–1981 and taking account of inflation changes the total to $2,741 per car in 1990 dollars. Given the improvements listed in the accompanying table, you may or may not consider the added health and safety worth the price.

Yr. of regulation	Government-mandated equipment	Estimated increase in retail price (in 1977 $)
1968	Seat and shoulder belts, standards for exhaust emissions	$47.84
1968–69	Windshield defrosting systems, door latches, lamps, etc.	14.53
1969	Head restraints	27.48
1970	Reflective devices and further emission standards	14.77
1968–70	Ignition locking and buzzing systems, interior impact protection	12.75
1971	Fuel evaporative systems	28.33
1972	Improved exhaust emission and warranty changes; seat-belt warning system	42.37
1972–73	Exterior protection	95.29
1973	Reduced flammability materials, etc.	8.72
1969–73	Improved side-door strength	20.85
1974	Interlock system and improved exhaust emissions	133.50
1975	Additional safety features and catalytic converter	146.66
1976	Hydraulic brakes, improved bumpers, removal of interlock system, etc.	41.54
1977	Leak-resistant fuel system, etc.	21.25
1978	Redesign of emissions controls	9.99
	Total	$665.87

Sources: Murray L. Weidenbaum, "The Costs of Government Regulation of Business," in *The Cost of Government Regulation,* Hearings before the Subcommittee on Economic Growth and Stabilization of the Joint Economic Committee, Congress of the United States (Washington, D.C.: U.S. Government Printing Office, 1978), pp. 31–59; and Robert W. Crandall, "What Have Auto-Import Quotas Wrought?" *Challenge,* January–February, 1985, pp. 40–47.

(similar to those noted with respect to regulating natural monopolies) include a slower pace of technical advance. The issue was recently addressed in a study by Edward Denison.[8] He noted that pollution and job safety standards alone cut the annual rise in productivity (output per unit of input) by a quarter in the mid-1970s. This was traced to the fact that firms had to devote an increasing share of their research and development expenditures, as well as of their plant and equipment investment funds, toward satisfying government regulations.

Unfortunately, as critics have noted, government officials often tend to compare the perceived benefits of their regulations merely with the direct administrative cost, ignoring direct compliance costs as well as indirect costs. As a result, they implement all kinds of regulations the net benefit of which is in fact quite questionable. Consider Table 2 which illustrates the Consumer Product Safety Commission's zeal to protect Americans from the thousands of gadgets they buy. In the majority of cases, the ratio of total benefits to total costs of commission projects was below unity, indicating that costs exceeded benefits. In addition, the commission's own priority rankings had little in common with the ranking of the benefit-cost ratios, which suggests a serious misallocation of resources. Thus, the CPSC made power mower safety its top priority in 1977, yet the associated benefit-cost ratio was only .40 (the project's total benefits were estimated by the commission's own staff at about $112 million; total costs, at about $285 million). At the same time, another project with a benefit-cost ratio of 2.70 (bathtubs and showers) was relegated to priority level 12.

Example 3 provides vivid illustrations of how the difficulty of weighing benefits and costs continues to haunt government regulators today.

Two Case Studies

This final section presents two case studies from the world of regulation. One deals with the life and death of the CAB; the other helps us appreciate the impossible task placed before the FDA.

TABLE 2 *An Assessment of Consumer Product Safety Regulation*

Consumer Product Safety Commission projects ranked by priority	Benefit-cost ratio
1. Power mowers	0.40
2. Gas space heaters	1.85
3. Public playground equipment	2.02
4. Glazing materials	0.91
5. Upholstered furniture	0.48
6. Television sets	0.09
7. Ranges and ovens	0.87
8. Extension cords	0.10
9. Trouble lights	0.75
10. Matches	0.37
11. Ladders	0.94
12. Bathtubs and showers	2.70
13. Power saws (portable)	0.40
14. Chain saws	0.67
15. Over-the-counter antihistamines	2.52
16. Petroleum distillates	0.25
17. Drain cleaners	1.08
18. Power saws (nonportable)	0.16
19. Wearing apparel	0.02
20. Rust remover	0.34
21. Ammonia	0.11

These data on the Consumer Product Safety Commission's 1977 projects illustrate a serious misallocation of resources.

SOURCE: Henry G. Grabowski and John M. Vernon, "Consumer Product Safety Regulation," *The American Economic Review,* May 1978, p. 286.

---

[8] Edward F. Denison, "Effects of Selected Changes in the Institutional and Human Environment upon Output per Unit of Input," *Survey of Current Business,* January 1978, pp. 21–44.

EXAMPLE 3

Safeguarding the Welfare of Babies and the Disabled

In July, 1989, when a United Airlines DC-10 crashed in Sioux City, Iowa, a 23-month-old toddler was ripped from his mother's arms and died. Six months later, another baby was fatally injured when an Avianca 707 ran out of fuel over Long Island, New York, and crashed. Safety advocates urged the Federal Aviation Administration to *require* all airlines to restrain children under 2 in specially designated seats and to give up the long-standing practice of allowing small children to have free rides on parents' laps.

Yet, a Harvard Medical School study raised serious doubts about the worthwhileness of such a regulation, however well intentioned. According to the study, a maximum of 3 babies' lives would be saved over a 5-year span, but many more lives would be lost as cost-conscious parents abandoned airline travel for much more dangerous highway travel. (20 percent of families interviewed said they would switch to car travel rather than pay for an extra seat, and the highway accident death rate was 20 times that of airline travel.) The study also estimated that the airlines would sell an extra 3.3 million seats per year at an estimated $205 million, making the cost of saving a baby from an airline fatality just about $341 million per life.

Regulators in 1991 ran into a similar quandary when trying to enforce the 1990 Americans With Disabilities Act. The Act prohibits discrimination against people with physical or mental impairments in employment, telecommunications services, transportation, public accommodations, and more. It provides a $50,000 fine for a first offense and a $100,000 fine for each subsequent offense. While the benefits to the affected population were fairly obvious, the costs to some 5 million establishments were often mind-boggling.

Here are some of the rules that regulators were contemplating (for large businesses as of early 1992, for small businesses as of early 1993): Banks, concert halls, daycare centers, doctors' and lawyers' offices, gymnasiums, hotels, museums, retail stores, theaters, and even funeral homes have to place ramps over stairs and, where applicable, widen aisles to provide access to people in wheelchairs. Restaurants must provide menus in Braille, pencils and pads for the deaf and speech-impaired, hire sign-language interpreters, or provide home-delivery service. Banks must construct handicapped accessible automatic teller machines; gas stations must provide special self-service pumps. Hotels must install special telephones for the deaf and speech-impaired so they can make outside calls, call the front desk, and order room service. Movie theaters must provide *integrated* seating so that the disabled can sit with their non-handicapped friends. And no one may ask for a driver's license to cash a check; the blind and retarded clearly wouldn't be able to comply.

As you can well imagine, the costs of some of these regulations will be trivial; those of others, enormous. At the time of this writing, the debate raged on.

Sources: Peter Passell, "See Who's Dying for Regulation," *The New York Times,* September 12, 1990, p. D2; Steven A. Holmes, "U.S. Rules Would Force Businesses to Make Alterations for the Disabled," *The New York Times,* February 22, 1991, p. A14.

Case 1: The Story of Airline Deregulation[9]

In 1938, the U.S. Congress created the Civil Aeronautics Board and charged it with regulating interstate airline service. Before long, the CAB had created a cartel among the ten airlines then existing. The commission put an end to what it called "excessive, destructive, and cut-throat competition" by enforcing market-sharing and output restrictions and providing each airline with "route security." This quickly translated into high fares and assured the survival of even the highest-cost producers. As later studies showed, on identical routes served by CAB-regulated interstate airlines and by nonregulated *intrastate* airlines (such as California's *Pacific Southwest* and Texas's *Southwest*), the fares of the latter airlines were about 50 percent below the rates of CAB carriers. Yet for 40 years, and despite notoriously high fares, the CAB refused to allow the creation of even a single new interstate airline. In its own words, such a move was "not required by the public interest, convenience, and necessity." The advocates of the special-interest theory of regulation had found a perfect case in point.[10]

The idea of deregulation that the special-interest theorists advanced was eventually supported by three presidents (Ford, Carter, and Reagan), by the CAB itself (under economist Alfred E. Kahn), and by influential members of Congress (such as Senator Edward Kennedy). And in 1978, the Airline Deregulation Act was passed. It called for the abolition of the CAB by the end of 1984 and predicted that the destruction of the airline cartel and the introduction of competition would produce decreased costs and fares, higher traffic volume, and reasonable industry profits. Not surprisingly, deregulation was opposed by the major airlines and the associated labor unions. They predicted higher fares, less traffic (in particular, a loss of service to small communities), plummeting profits, unemployment of airline labor, less safety, and, ultimately, greater industry concentration. Consider what did happen.

Costs

As was to be expected, dozens of new airlines entered the industry. Despite soaring interest rates, fuel prices, and landing fees, the new entrants achieved remarkably lower costs. By the time the CAB was gone (on January 1, 1985), the average cost per seat mile was 8¢ for the older carriers; it was 6¢ for Continental and 5.3¢ for People's Express. The newcomers gained this advantage in part because they were not locked into high-wage union contracts, but also because of innovative management. People's Express, for example, had no labor union but instituted a generous employee stock ownership plan. It provided "no-frills" service to customers, making passengers pay $3 for each bag checked and 50¢ for a cup of coffee. It cross-utilized labor: while not flying, pilots might do the accounting and flight attendants might take care of the ticket counter; the airline boasted of not having a single secretary. In addition, it arranged for aircraft maintenance and baggage handling on the basis of the lowest bids received from outside contractors.

This competition quickly had an effect on the older carriers. Even by 1984, American and United (then jointly accounting for a third of domestic air travel) had negotiated new contracts with their unions that set up more flexible work rules as well as **two-tier wage structures** that allowed the companies to pay lower wages to newly hired employees than to previously hired ones, even if both types of workers did identical work. Eastern and TWA announced that they needed similar union

---

[9] *Sources:* Kenneth Labich, "Fare Wars: Have the Big Airlines Learned to Win?" *Fortune,* October 29, 1984, pp. 24–28; "Airline Deregulation: Maintaining the Momentum," *Economic Report of the President,* February 1988 (Washington, D.C.: U.S. Government Printing Office, 1988), Ch 6; *Business Week,* January 9, 1989, p. 88; *The Economist,* February 4, 1989, pp. 68 and 71; Kenneth Labich, "Should Airlines Be Reregulated?" *Fortune,* June 19, 1989, pp. 82–90; Peter Passell, "A Plan to Ration Airport Runways," *The New York Times,* June 28, 1989, p. D2; and numerous issues of *The New York Times* and *The Wall Street Journal.*

[10] Consider that in 1971, half of 24 former CAB members were employed by firms they used to regulate. In 1974, the chairman of the CAB was taken on an all-expenses-paid golfing trip to Bermuda by Boeing and United Aircraft Company officials, and he journeyed through Europe with a TWA vice-president—all while issues vital to these firms were being decided by the CAB.

concessions in order to survive in the new competitive environment. By the late 1980s, 70 airline contracts sanctioned two-tier wage structures and many companies, in addition, were speeding up the decline in their wage bills by offering cash bonuses and travel benefits to long-time employees in return for early retirement.

Fares

The lower costs achieved by new entrants soon translated into lower fares. On the San Francisco–Los Angeles route, for example, a PSA ticket had long cost $69. When newly created Pacific Express charged $49, PSA lowered its price to $44. Similar price-slashing scenarios unfolded all over the United States. In 1982–1983, Pan Am offered a $99 ticket to anywhere within its domestic system; in 1984 one could fly from New York to Chicago for $59 and coast-to-coast for $119. By 1986, over 90 percent of all passengers were taking advantage of such bargain fares despite the fact that they were often associated with advance-purchase, length-of-stay, limited refund, and off-peak-hour restrictions. As a recent study noted, during the first decade of deregulation, air travelers gained over $100 billion via lower prices.

Traffic Volume

As the law of demand would predict, falling fares went together with a surging volume of traffic. People's Express, for example, carried 2.2 million passengers on its New York–Boston route in 1981; the number had grown to 4.3 million by 1984. Overall, from 1978 to 1988, passenger-miles flown rose by 85 percent, and the annual number of airline passengers jumped from 275 million to 455 million. One single set of statistics vividly illustrates the great democratization of air travel that deregulation and lower fares have brought about: In 1971, 50 percent of all Americans had never flown in an airplane; by 1988, it was only 25 percent.

Not surprisingly, the increased traffic volume overtaxed many airport facilities. In 1986, for example, there were 62 scheduled departures at Newark between 8 and 9 A.M., which led to predictable delays in bad weather. Still, despite the ubiquity of this problem, there were only two new airports on the drawing board (Austin and Denver), the first since the 1974 construction of Dallas/Fort Worth.

Profits

Economic theory predicts that a swarm of new entrants into a competitive market will lower prices and ultimately eliminate economic profit. (Recall the section on profit and industry expansion in the chapter "Perfect Competition.") In the early 1980s, industry expansion stimulated by deregulation went hand-in-hand with soaring fuel prices. To nobody's surprise, the profit picture was mixed. Some major carriers (American, Delta, United) did well; others (Eastern, Pan Am, TWA) saw red ink. Together with the growth of newcomers, there was a rash of bankruptcies (Braniff, Continental, Pacific Express, Air 1), but some of these firms reemerged later—*without* a union contract (Continental). And there was a rash of cost-cutting mergers as well. By the late 1980s, American had swallowed Air Cal, Delta had acquired Western, Northwestern had taken in Republic, TWA had merged with Ozark, United had bought Pan Am's Pacific routes, USAir had merged with Piedmont. And Texas Air had bought Continental and Eastern, then merged with Frontier, New York Air, and People's Express. Overall, the first decade of deregulation produced net profits of less than 1 percent.

Service to Small Communities

Contrary to dire predictions made by early critics of deregulation, service to small towns has, in fact, risen when measured in available seat-miles. However, the presence of major airlines (making infrequent flights) has dwindled in favor of a larger number of commuter air lines (making more frequent flights). All this has been part of a major route realignment that has produced the new *hub-and-spokes* system. Each major airline now has selected for itself a large central airport (the hub), where it typically enters into decades-long leases of airport gates and terminal buildings (along with veto power over the construction of new airport facilities). Numerous flights (the spokes) feed passengers from all directions into the hub; other flights take them away from it. If passengers can be persuaded (by conveniently timed connections, automatic baggage transfer, and price advantages) to stay with the same airline throughout, possible losses made on short flights *to* the hub can be made up by high *load factors* (high percentages of filled seats) in flights *from* the hub.

Consider how American created a hub at Dallas/Fort Worth, Continental at Houston, Delta at Atlanta and Salt Lake City, Eastern at Miami, Northwest at Detroit and Minneapolis/St. Paul, People's Express at Newark, TWA at St. Louis, United at Chicago and Denver, and USAir at Pittsburgh.

Unemployment

Contrary to dire predictions made by early critics of deregulation, industry employment has risen. Employment at new airlines has increased more than employment at old airlines has declined, raising over-all employment by 4.8 percent between 1978 and 1989.

Safety

Contrary to dire predictions made by early critics of deregulation, there has been no decline in the industry's safety record. In the nine years preceding deregulation, U.S. airlines had 300 accidents; in the nine following years, 180 accidents. Figure 7 provides a more systematic illustration. In addition, one may wish to consider an indirect effect. Since 1978, as airline travel has surged, fewer people have been on the roads; auto accidents have declined by 600,000 per year, auto deaths by 1,700 per year. (Admittedly, some of the reduction in highway deaths can also be attributed to the lower 55 m.p.h. national speed limit introduced then.)

Industry Concentration

By the early 1990s, the airline industry shakeout (who will survive, who will disappear) had not been completed; thus one can only speculate about the future. One likely scenario, however, is the emergence of a tight oligopoly of, perhaps, six major carriers (American, Delta, Northwest, Texas Air, United, and USAir) with a combined market share of over 90 percent.

This outcome is all the more likely given the government's failure to challenge the merger of some 20 airlines since the mid-1980s, which has created near-monopolies at some hubs. For example, after the acquisition of Ozark gave TWA 82 percent of St. Louis airport gates, it raised fares 18 percent. Table 3 illustrates the near-monopolies that some U.S. carriers have recently achieved at their chosen hubs. One notable exception exists: Miami leases its 100 gates by the month only. As a result, it was served by 87 airlines in 1989 and its 12 million passengers enjoyed fares 23 percent below those found at similar hubs.

One should note, however, that long-distance travelers, such as those flying coast-to-coast, have numerous options despite the hub "monopolies." They can fly on many different airlines, via different hubs—and this competition keeps prices down.

Case 2: The Food and Drug Safety War[11]

In 1906, the U.S. Congress created the Food and Drug Administration to clean up unsanitary practices in the food industry, eliminate poisonous adulterants and preservatives from the things we eat and drink, and assure the purity of drugs. By 1990, the FDA's regulatory task, unlike its budget, had mushroomed out of control. With a mere 7,500 employees, the agency was mandated to inspect all of our milk, fruits, and vegetables, millions of different types of processed foods, cosmetics, and drugs, and even a long list of medical devices, including hearing aids and pacemakers, eyeglasses and tongue depressors. Some 24 laws passed since 1980 instructed the FDA to take up additional concerns, ranging from drugs for curing AIDS to "fake fat" and other products of the emerging biotechnology industry. But the FDA was quite unable to meet its obligations under the law, as its own officials put it.

---

[11] *Sources:* Tom Alexander, "Time for a Cease-Fire in the Food-Safety Wars," *Fortune,* February 26, 1979, pp. 94–99; Bruce Ingersoll, "Tide of Imported Food Outruns FDA Ability to Spot Contamination," *The Wall Street Journal,* September 27, 1989, pp. 1 and 14; Scott Kilman, "Aflatoxin Resurfaces in Some Midwest Corn, Hinting Problem Is Bigger Than Once Thought," *The Wall Street Journal,* September 27, 1989, p. C16; Philip J. Hilts, "A Guardian of U.S. Health Is Failing Under Pressures," *The New York Times,* December 4, 1989, pp. 1 and B10; David E. Henderson, "Peanut Butter Risk Analysis," *NLA* (New Liberal Arts Program) *News,* December, 1989, pp. 4–7; Bruce Ingersoll, "FDA Finds Bunk in Bottled-Water Claims," *The Wall Street Journal,* April 10, 1991, pp. B1 and 4; Bruce Ingersoll, "FDA Takes on 'No Cholesterol' Claims," *The Wall Street Journal,* May 15, 1991, pp. B1 and 5; and John Carey and Zachary Schiller, "The FDA Is Swinging A Sufficiently Large Two-By-Four," *Business Week,* May 27, 1991, p. 44.

FIGURE 7 U.S. Airline Accident Rates

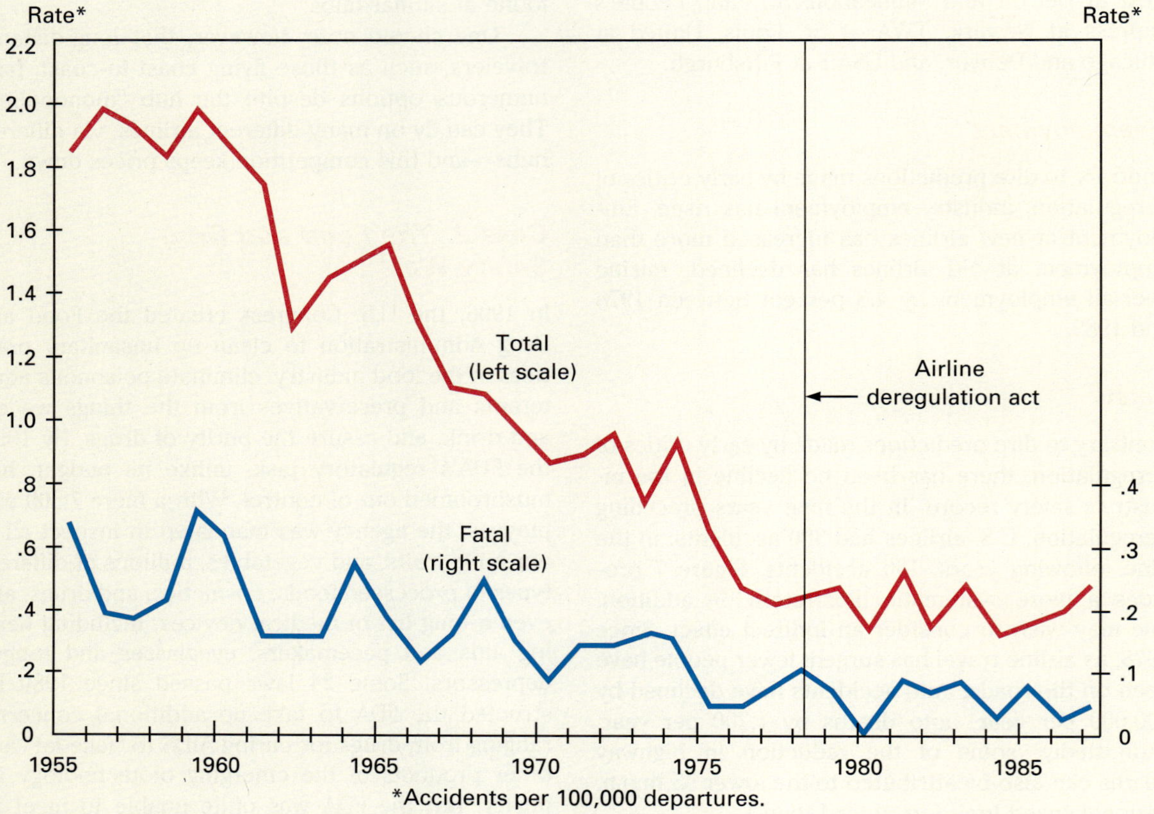

[Graph showing Total accident rate (left scale, 0–2.2) and Fatal accident rate (right scale, 0–.4) from 1955 to 1987, with a vertical line marking the Airline deregulation act around 1978. *Accidents per 100,000 departures.]

As these 1954–1987 data indicate, neither total nor fatal accident rates experienced by U.S. carriers have risen significantly since the industry was deregulated.

Source: *Economic Report of the President,* February 1988 (Washington, DC: Government Printing Office, 1988), p. 209.

Food Imports

In 1989, hundreds of Americans fell ill because they ate imported foods that sailed through customs uninspected. Involved were Canadian lobsters, Chinese prune candy, Danish soft cheese, Guatemalan chewing gum, Hong Kong frozen rabbits, Hungarian jam, Indian frog legs, Japanese horseradish, and Samoan tuna among others. The tide of imported food simply outran the FDA's ability to check: A single inspector was stationed at Nogales, Arizona, where 700 trucks of Mexican fruits and vegetables entered the United States on an average day. A total of six inspectors covered 1,200 miles of Gulf Coast and Mexican border. A handful of others inspected foreign plants; usually the plants failed. In a Philippine tuna cannery, "baskets of decomposing fish were sitting on maggot-covered floors, beneath roosting birds; polluted water was used, cooking was inadequate." Altogether, 9 percent of a million foreign food shipments were checked visually, 1 percent were tested in a lab, and 40 percent of those tested failed. But, the FDA figured, shipments rejected at one entry point were simply sent in through a different one. The odds of being caught twice were nearly nil.

TABLE 3 *How Carriers Dominate Hubs*

Hub	Airline	Percentage of hub passengers carried by airline in 1988
Pittsburgh	US Air	85
St. Louis	TWA*	82
Salt Lake City	Delta	80
Minneapolis/St. Paul	Northwest	78
Houston	Continental*	77
Dallas/Fort Worth	American	64
Detroit	Northwest	60
Atlanta	Delta	58
Chicago O'Hare	United	50
Miami	Eastern*	45

* in bankruptcy in 1991

SOURCE: Carl H. Lavin, "Battling It Out for Airport Control," *The New York Times,* August 20, 1989, p. F4.

New Drugs

The FDA is mandated to review the safety and effectiveness of new drugs within 6 months; the actual process takes 10 years on the average, which is not surprising. In order to meet all the rules, one drug company's application for approval of a muscle relaxant came to 456 volumes, weighed more than a ton, and stood taller than 8 stories. Worst of all, this was not an unusual case.

Food Additives

The 1968 Delaney amendment to the Food and Drug Act prohibited the use of any food additives shown to cause cancer in people or animals, whether added deliberately or inadvertently during growing, processing, or packaging. That simple amendment by itself could easily absorb the FDA's budget a hundred times over. Consider the case of aflatoxin B, the product of a fungus growing on peanuts and suspected of causing liver cancer. How could the FDA determine the reality and extent of the risk?

1. It clearly could not perform deliberately arranged, controlled studies on people, feeding, say, lots of suspect peanut butter to one group of people and none of it to an otherwise similar group. (In any case, the effect might not show up for 30 years.)

2. It could compare the health statistics of two groups of people (West African peanut lovers and West European peanut haters, say), provided one of the groups had been accidentally exposed to the suspected toxin while the other had not. (Still, doubts would remain: Could possible differences in health be attributed to other factors instead?)

3. It could perform animal tests, assuming (perhaps wrongly) that hamsters, rabbits, rats, or monkeys respond to the suspected toxin the way people would. Thus, a million rats might be put on a regular diet, another million like rats on an identical diet plus a dose of aflatoxin B. If, after a certain time, there were 50 deaths in group 1 but 60 deaths in group 2, the 10 excess deaths per million might be attributed to aflatoxin B. (Again, doubts would appear: What dose should be used? What period of time should be allowed to elapse? In any case, all this would be costly and time-consuming. One actual study used 24,000 mice, took 90 tons of food, 150 workers, and 4 years; it cost $12 million.)

In fact, the FDA has identified aflatoxin B as a potent carcinogen (cancer-causing substance) and has ruled that no food may contain more than 20 parts per billion. And other tests have shown that all kinds of natural and manufactured substances—ranging from eggs, ice water, sodium nitrite, and vitamin D to estrogen, food coloring agents, and saccharin—also cause cancer if fed to test animals in large enough quantities in a short enough time. Accordingly, the FDA has moved to ban coloring agents (such as carbokn black and red dye #2), spoilage, retarding nitrites, saccharin sweeteners, and more.

The nitrite ban, for example, affected bacon, ham, sausages, and canned luncheon meats; the saccharin ban affected diet drinks, lipsticks, and prescription drugs. Yet contrary to the advice given by the Chapter 1 case study "Cancer Versus Heart

Attacks," the FDA has been ignoring the costs of its actions: The use of nitrites (now banned) inhibits the growth of botulism toxins that used to kill thousands of people each year; the use of of saccharin (now banned) used to reduce blook sugar problems, obesity, and tooth decay in thousands more. Thus, critics say, the FDA is avoiding some cancer deaths at the cost of many more deaths from other causes.

Food and Drug Labeling

The FDA is also supposed to standardize and vouch for the accuracy of product labels. According to the Nutrition and Labeling Act of 1990, the task is to be completed by 1993; success is unlikely, given billions of products. Recently, the FDA examined the bottled-water industry. Some 52 brands were tested, 31 percent were tainted with bacteria, kerosene, and mold. Almost all of them were falsely labeled. Words such as "artesian," "glacial," and "naturally pure," along with pictures of moon-lit lakes, mountain streams, and waterfalls, suggested far-off natural sources. In fact, tap water was a common source. Similarly deceptive are many "no cholesterol" labels, often accompanied by pictures of hearts and electrocardiographs. In fact, products such as Crisco and Mazola vegetable oils are 100 percent fat and bad for the heart.

Summary

1. This chapter deals with *regulation,* the setting by government of detailed rules of business behavior that specify who may produce what types and quantities of products, the manner in which production takes place, how goods are marketed, what prices may be charged, and more. While *economic* regulation is concerned with market entry, pricing, and output in particular industries, *social* regulation deals with economy-wide issues, such as the health and safety of consumers or workers. In 1990, there existed over 100 regulatory agencies at the federal level of government alone.

2. Economic regulation includes the regulation of natural monopolies. On the one hand, a natural monopoly is desirable because it can produce any given industry output at a lower average total cost than a number of smaller competitive firms could achieve. On the other hand, a natural monopoly is likely to produce undesirable consequences: economic inequity and economic inefficiency. As a result, government sanctions the existence of natural monopolies, but insists on regulating their pricing and output decisions. More often than not, this takes the form of rate-of-return regulation which is difficult to carry out and likely to produce a number of negative effects so far as managerial incentives are concerned.

3. Another form of economic regulation targets firms in competitive industries. Two competing explanations are offered for this fact. According to the *public-interest theory* of regulation, competitive firms are regulated because government wants to achieve certain goals that it considers to be "in the public interest" and that would otherwise not be achieved. (One such goal might be a "proper" distribution of income; governmental price-fixing schemes are often undertaken in its pursuit. Such price fixing, however, is a most inefficient way of redistributing income.) According to the *special-interest theory* of regulation, government regulates firms in otherwise competitive industries because self-interested politicians and bureaucrats (who have a lot to gain from this) respond to requests for regulation by those who want to escape the rigors of competition and seek to set up viable cartels. (These obvious abuses have been partially reversed since the 1980s when a series of deregulation laws took effect.)

4. Following the explosive growth of new regulatory agencies since 1970, the most important type of social regulation nowadays is the regulation of the health and safety of consumers and workers. The relevant agencies take two approaches: a) they seek to improve market knowledge, thereby enabling people to make

informed choices on matters affecting their health and safety, b) they mandate that firms reduce or even eliminate known hazards to health and safety.

5. Two case studies explore the world of regulation in depth. One deals with the life and death of the CAB; the other helps us appreciate the impossible task placed before the FDA.

Key Concepts

acreage allotments
Averch-Johnson effect
doctrine of caveat emptor
doctrine of caveat venditor
economic regulation
fair trade laws
import quotas
marketing quotas
public-interest theory of regulation
rate base
regulation
regulatory lag
social regulation
special-interest theory of regulation
tariffs
two-tier wage structure

Questions and Problems

1. "I simply don't see what is so difficult about establishing a natural monopoly's *rate base*. Let the regulators simply read the section Asset Markets for Capital Resources in this book (in the chapter "Markets for Natural and Capital Resources"). Then they will learn how easy it is to capitalize an income stream, such as a natural monopoly's stream of profits. In no time at all, they will be able to figure what the owners' investment is worth."
Evaluate this position.

2. "The theory of natural-monopoly regulation contains a serious flaw: Even though increasing returns to scale imply that the industry's output can be produced most cheaply by a single firm, it does not follow that such a firm will inevitably charge a monopoly price unless it is regulated. Government can auction off the right to be this single producer to the firm that agrees to sell the good in question at the lowest price. As long as the inputs required for production are available to many potential firms and firms do not collude, there can be vigorous competition among many firms at the bidding stage. More likely than not, such franchising will produce the competitive price or something close to it, and subsequently no regulation will be needed." Evaluate this position.

3. In 1988, the Federal Communications Commission proposed a new method of natural-monopoly regulation: the setting of a long-term *price cap,* a maximum price the firm may charge during a specified period, such as 10 years, while letting the firm choose the actual price and make all other decisions on its own.
What, do you think, would be the consequences?

4. "If there is a reason for airlines and buses to be franchised and regulated, then this reason must hold also for firms delivering milk and collecting garbage at people's homes." Discuss.

5. A 1974 government study showed that Louisiana, which licenses TV repairers, had about the same incidence of fraud and 20 percent higher prices on TV repairs than the District of Columbia, where the repairers were not licensed. Try to explain.

6. In the early 1970s, 40 percent of trucks on U.S. roads were empty because ICC regulations (limiting them either to agricultural produce only or to specific types of nonagricultural cargo only), in effect, forbade them to carry cargo on return trips after making deliveries. Can you explain this?

7. "The deregulation of potentially competitive in-

dustries, such as the airlines or trucking industries, hurts many innocent people because the elimination of monopoly power destroys valuable assets. The people who are hurt ought to be compensated."
Evaluate this position.

8. "Deregulation of the airline industry clearly isn't working. Consider how major airlines are building monopoly positions at their 'fortress hubs' with long-term leases of all available ground facilities, veto power on new construction (and, thus, on new competitors), 'marketing arrangements' with commuter airlines (that travel the spokes), frequent-flyer programs (that tie customers to a given airline), and tricky computer-reservation systems (that list the sponsoring airline first and provide bonuses that tie travel agents to a given airline as well). Consider, finally, the growing financial links between U.S. and foreign airlines that pave the way toward a single worldwide mega-carrier. It is time to reregulate the industry."
Evaluate this position.

9. "Health and safety regulation ought to be restricted to developing and disseminating crucial information. Subsequently, consumers and workers ought to be allowed to make up their own minds on the extent to which they care to take risks. After all, people make such evaluations every day in a million ways; once they are appropriately informed, they do not need a paternalistic government to tell them which risks to avoid."
Evaluate this position.

10. In the 1980s, the Food and Drug Administration allowed General Mills (producer of a cereal called Benefit) and Kellogg (producer of a cereal called Heartwise) to claim that the psyllium contained in the cereal reduced cholesterol and, thus, heart disease. (Psyllium is a grain grown in India that contains a high percentage of soluble fiber.) At the same time, the FDA denied Procter and Gamble the right to make the identical claim for its laxative Metamucil that also contained psyllium. Can you explain it?

11. "Some 20 million American workers are exposed to *benzene,* a substance found in gas and oil. In concentrations of over 20 parts per million (ppm), it causes leukemia in adults. Most affected are workers in gasoline marketing, oil refining, and tire manufacture as well as others making adhesives, insecticides, paints, pharmaceuticals, pesticides, plastics, polyurethane foam, and solvents. The government ought to put a quick stop to the exposure of workers to benzene."
Evaluate this position.

12. In 1989, the Long Island Lighting Company gave up its battle with the Nuclear Regulatory Commission over the licensing of a brand-new 800-megawatt nuclear power plant at Shoreham. It decided never to operate the $5.5 billion plant despite impending electric power shortages throughout the Northeast. The company did not think it could ever allay people's fears of a Chernobyl-type accident.

    Think about the benefits and costs of the decision not to operate the plant.

13. Mr. A: "Ralph Nader and all the governmental regulators of health and safety whom he has spawned are best described as fanatics. Fanatics always know what is good for us better than we do, and they always know their duty: make us do what is good for us (with our money, of course)."

    Mr. B: "You are so right and that's why the government should adopt *sunset laws* that terminate the life of regulatory agencies after a specified number of years, unless the agency can justify its continued existence by proving that it has produced benefits in excess of costs in the past. Sunset laws would quickly put an end to nit-picking regulations that impose huge costs for tiny benefits."

    Evaluate this exchange.

14. Table 3 seems to suggest that airline passengers are at the mercy of near-monopolies. Yet the low industry profits, also noted in the text, contradict this impression. Can you explain the discrepancy?

CHAPTER 19

EXTERNALITIES AND ENVIRONMENTAL ECONOMICS

Preview

This chapter deals with situations termed externalities, *in which the consumption or production activities of some people favorably or unfavorably affect the utility or output of other people. Think of a family that plants beautiful gardens that also bring joy to its neighbors—a favorable externality from the realm of consumption. Then think of the sulfur dioxide emitted from the smokestack of a power plant that creates acid rain and destroys the crops of farmers—an unfavorable externality from the realm of production.*

Economists have developed an elaborate set of theories that explain why externalities exist and what can be done about them. These theories are discussed here; so are recent governmental attempts to put them to practical use.

Examples

1. The Economics of Bees
2. Overfishing at the Georges Bank
3. Escaping the Commons: Lobsters and Oysters
4. Netting and Offsets, Bubbles and Banks
5. Green Marketing

A perfectly competitive market, we noted in an earlier chapter, leads to a remarkable result: Provided the traders in question are the only ones who reap benefits or incur costs in connection with the activity in question, such a market establishes an equilibrium quantity of production and consumption that maximizes the activity's social net benefit and is, thus, *economically efficient*. Figure 1 reviews what is involved. The graph depicts a perfectly competitive market for apples. As always, the market demand line reflects the horizontal summation of marginal benefits gained by potential apple buyers. We will henceforth refer to the marginal benefit that the purchaser of a good derives from its consumption as the **marginal private benefit, MPB.** Thus, the purchaser of the first bushel in our example expects to derive a marginal private benefit of $20 and is, therefore, willing to pay a maximum of $20 for it. Purchasers of the 10 millionth, 20 millionth, and 33 millionth bushel, on the other hand, evaluate the associated marginal private benefits at $15, $10, and $4, respectively, and are prepared to pay only correspondingly lower maximum prices. If, as we have assumed so far, outside parties are not affected by the apple consumption of apple buyers, the **marginal social benefit, MSB**— or the change in the total benefit, from the point of view of all members of society, that is associated with a unit change in the consumption of a good—is the same as the marginal private benefit *(MPB = MSB)*.

The market supply line, in turn, reflects the horizontal summation of marginal costs incurred by potential apple sellers. We will henceforth refer to the marginal cost that the producer of a good incurs

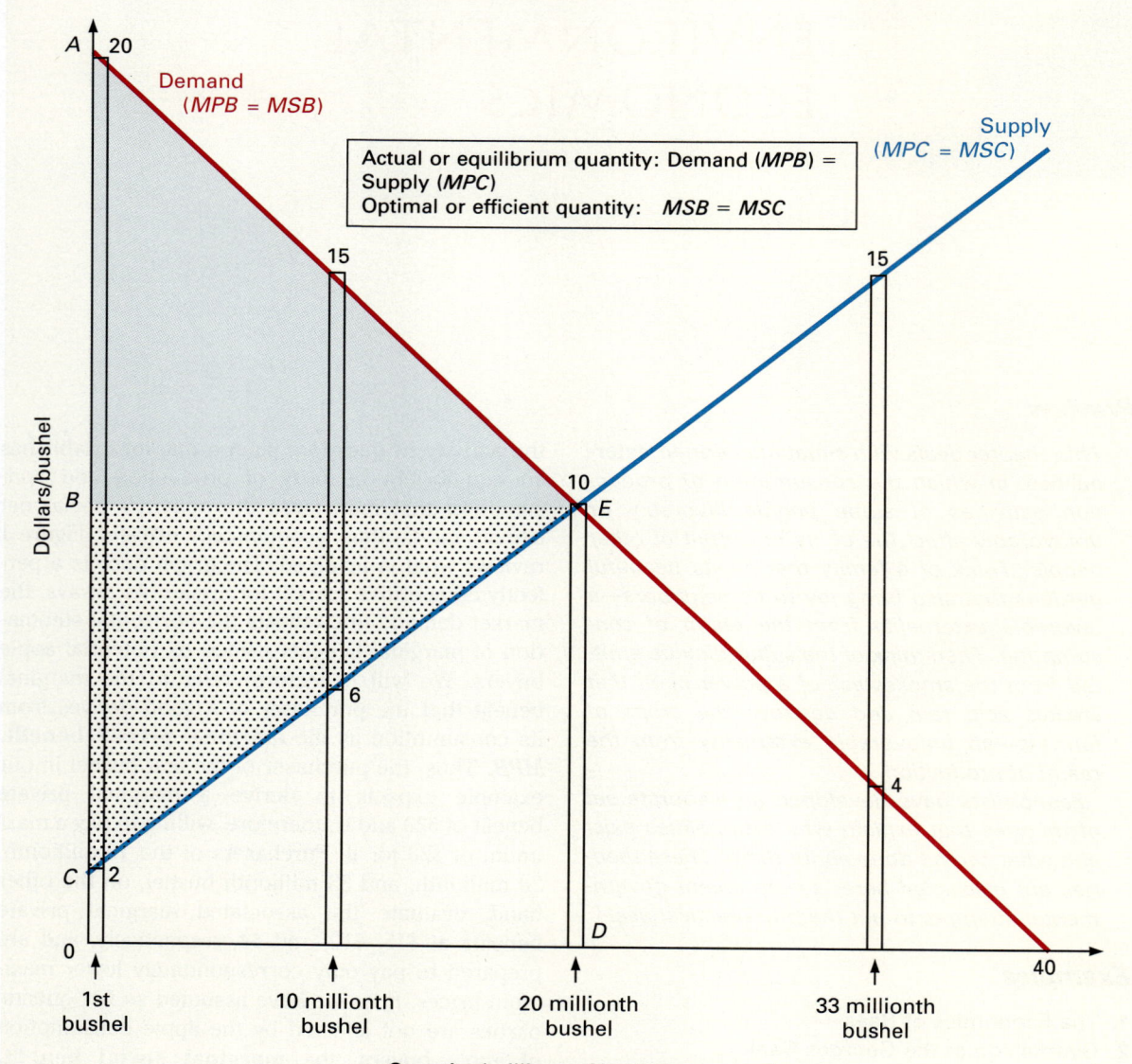

FIGURE 1 Perfect Competition and Economic Efficiency

Actual or equilibrium quantity: Demand (*MPB*) = Supply (*MPC*)
Optimal or efficient quantity: *MSB* = *MSC*

This graph illustrates the situation in which a perfectly competitive equilibrium and economic efficiency coincide. A perfectly competitive market always establishes an actual or equilibrium quantity of production and consumption (here 0D = 20 million bushels/year) that equates (here at *E*) demand (marginal private benefit *MPB*) with supply (marginal private cost *MPC*). If the activities of consumers and producers do not affect third parties (which we here assume), marginal private benefit also equals marginal social benefit, while marginal private cost also equals marginal social cost. In this case, the equilibrium quantity corresponding to demand/supply intersection *E* is also the optimal, or economically efficient, quantity that equates the marginal social benefit with the marginal social cost and thus maximizes the social net benefit (here *AEC*).

in its production as the **marginal private cost, MPC.** Thus, the seller of the 1st bushel in our example incurs a marginal private cost of $2 and is, therefore, willing to accept a minimum price of $2 for it. Sellers of the 10 millionth, 20 millionth, and 33 millionth bushel, on the other hand, incur marginal private costs of $6, $10, and $15, respectively, and are prepared to accept only correspondingly higher minimum prices. If, as we have assumed so far, outside parties are not affected by the apple production of apple sellers, the **marginal social cost, MSC**—or the change in total cost, from the point of view of all members of society, that is associated with a unit change in the production of a good—is the same as the marginal private cost ($MPC = MSC$).

We are now ready to note two important facts. First, a perfectly competitive market *always* establishes an actual (or equilibrium) quantity of production and consumption (here $0D = 20$ million bushels per year) that equates (here at E) demand (or marginal private benefit, MPB) with supply (or marginal private cost, MPC). Second, if the activities of consumers and producers do not affect third parties (therefore, $MPB = MSB$ and $MPC = MSC$), the perfectly competitive market's equilibrium quantity also equals the optimal or economically efficient quantity, explained below.

Note how, in this example, the marginal social benefit (along AE) exceeds the marginal social cost (along CE) until ouput $0D$ is reached. Until $0D$ is reached, each additional unit produced and consumed produces a positive social net benefit: $20 - 2 = $18 for the first bushel, $15 - 6 = $9 for the 10 millionth bushel, and so on. By the time the 20 millionth bushel per year has been produced, the total social benefit (or the sum of all the marginal social benefits of $20 + \cdots + $15 + \cdots + $10) equals $0AED$. The total social cost (or the sum of all the marginal social costs of $2 + \cdots + $6 + \cdots + $10) equals $0CED$. The social net benefit then equals $0AED - 0CED = AEC$ (the sum of the shaded consumer surplus and the dotted producer surplus in this example). The social net benefit associated with the equilibrium quantity of 20 million bushels is also the maximum possible one. This is so because additional units, such as the 33 millionth bushel, that are associated with a marginal social cost (such as $15) in excess of marginal social benefit (such as $4) are, quite properly, not being produced.

All of this prepares us to appreciate the subject matter of this chapter. It deals with situations in which the happy coincidence in Figure 1 between the actual and the optimal is upset because the marginal social benefit does not equal the marginal private benefit, or because the marginal social cost does not equal the marginal private cost.

The Nature of Externalities

This chapter focuses on so-called nonpecuniary or real **externalities,** which are direct effects that the actions of some consumers or producers have on the utility of other consumers or on the output of other producers, none of whom have invited these effects. Because such externalities occur when the actions of some people quite thoughtlessly are allowed to spill over onto the lives of their neighbors, these externalities are also called **spillover effects** or **neighborhood effects.**

As we noted when discussing *market failures* in an earlier chapter, externalities can be either negative or positive.

Negative Externalities

So-called **negative externalities** occur when the consumption or production activities of some people impose costs in the form of decreased utility or decreased output on other people who, to their dismay, are not being compensated for this injury. Consider the noise inflicted on bystanders by users of lawnmowers, motorcycles, radios, or snowmobiles. Consider the sewage dumped by proud owners of new houses who spoil the use of artesian wells, brooks, lakes, or even ocean fronts enjoyed by their neighbors. Consider the reduced catch that fishing companies experience when mining companies or paper mills dump wastes into bodies of water. Consider the fall in everybody else's output when extra boats are crowded onto ocean fisheries, extra cattle onto grazing lands, extra drilling platforms onto oil-bearing lands. In cases such as these, the extra consumption or production of some people is said to impose a **marginal external cost, MEC,** in the form of lowered utility or output, on other people.

In the presence of marginal external cost, the marginal social benefit (MSB) associated with the consumption activities in question lies below the marginal private benefit because the increased utility reaped by the direct consumers (*MPB*) is partly offset by the decreased utility (*MEC*) suffered by neighbors. Similarly, the marginal social cost (*MSC*) associated with the production activities in question lies above the marginal private cost because an additional cost (*MEC*) is imposed on others who must either accept a reduction in output or incur higher costs to keep their output from falling. Focus 1 summarizes our discussion so far.

Positive Externalities

So-called **positive externalities** occur when the consumption or production activities of some people provide benefits in the form of increased utility or increased output for other people who, to their delight, are not being charged for this favor. Consider the joy homeowners may bring their neighbors by planting beautiful flower gardens, installing telephones, or even getting vaccinated against the flu. Consider how firms that drain mines may raise the output of neighboring mines, how lumber companies that plant trees may change the local weather and increase the crops of nearby farms, how beekeepers may raise the productivity of cranberry bogs and orchards in the vicinity of their hives.

In cases such as these, the extra consumption or production of some people is said to provide a **marginal external benefit,** *MEB* in the form of increased utility or output for other people.

In the presence of marginal external benefit, the marginal social benefit (*MSB*) associated with the consumption activities in question lies above the marginal private benefit because the increased utility reaped by the direct consumer (*MPB*) is augmented by the increased utility (*MEB*) snatched by neighbors. Similarly, the marginal social cost (*MSC*) associated with the production activities in question lies below the marginal private cost (*MPC*) because an additional benefit (*MEB*) is provided to others who can simply enjoy a costless increase in output or reduce their own costs, while producing the same output as before. Focus 2 summarizes our discussion.

CAUTION

> *It is important not to confuse pecuniary and nonpecuniary externalities, a mistake that is fairly common. The externalities discussed in this chapter are* nonpecuniary, *which means they have nothing to do with monetary matters, such as higher or lower prices that consumers or producers might confront as a result of neighbors' activities. Thus, if your neighbor mows the lawn and the noise drives you crazy, you are not incurring any monetary expense; you are paying a marginal external cost in terms of decreased well-being. Similarly, if your neighbor installs a new telephone, your own phone doesn't suddenly become cheaper, but you can reap a marginal external benefit (if you are so inclined) by chatting away the hours of the day. Similar statements can be made with respect to producers who are affected by the production activities of others.*

The Analysis of Pigou

The British economist Arthur C. Pigou (1877–1959) was first to recognize that externalities would upset the link between perfectly competitive markets and economic efficiency; but he also suggested a cure.

FOCUS 1

Negative Externalities

MSB < *MPB*	if neighboring consumers suffer utility loss (*MEC*)
MSC > *MPC*	if neighboring producers suffer output loss (*MEC*)

FOCUS 2

Positive Externalities

MSB > *MPB*	if neighboring consumers receive utility gain (*MEB*)
MSC < *MPC*	if neighboring producers receive output gain (*MEB*)

As Pigou saw it, in the presence of externalities, one of two policies should be pursued:

1. Whenever the actual free market level of production and consumption achieved by equating demand and supply (where $MPB = MPC$) is larger than the optimal level (where $MSB = MSC$), the government should reduce the actual level to the optimal level by imposing an appropriately sized excise tax.

2. Whenever the actual free market level of production and consumption achieved by equating demand and supply (where $MPB = MPC$) is smaller than the optimal level (where $MSB = MSC$), the government should increase the actual level to the optimal level by granting an appropriately sized excise subsidy.

A couple of examples can illustrate what Pigou had in mind.

Taxing Producers

Figure 2 depicts a perfectly competitive market for iron ore, which assumes a negative externality among firms: Mining companies dump wastes into lakes and ultimately reduce the output of fisheries.[1]

Market demand, as always, reflects the marginal private benefits *MPB* of the direct consumers (in this case, the users of iron ore). Market supply, as always, is determined by the marginal private costs *MPC* of direct producers (here the mining companies). The process of consumption, we now assume, has no effects on outside parties; thus, marginal social benefit *MSB* equals marginal private benefit *MPB* in this example. Given the waste dumping of the mining companies, however, the marginal social cost *MSC* of this activity lies *above* the marginal private cost *MPC* to the extent of the marginal external cost *MEC* (which measures the fishing companies' output loss).

It is easy to see what will in fact happen under the circumstances. As long as government does not intervene, demand and supply will determine a price of P_1 and a quantity of Q_1 according to intersection *e*. Yet this free market outcome is not the efficient one from the social point of view: Marginal social benefit and marginal social cost equate at *c*; the optimal quantity is Q_2.

Pigou's solution: Let government impose an excise tax on the offending producers equal to the $MSC - MPC$ gap at the optimal output level (here equal to *ci* per ton of iron ore). As a result, the price to buyers will rise (here to P_3) and quantity demanded will fall (from *e* to *c*). At the same time, the price to sellers will fall (here to P_2) and quantity supplied will fall (from *e* to *i*). The new level of production and consumption Q_2 will equal the optimal one. (If it wants, government can use its tax revenue to compensate the fishing companies for the remaining but lower level of output loss.)

Subsidizing Consumers

Figure 3 depicts a perfectly competitive market for flower bulbs, which, we assume, involves a positive externality among households. The buyers of flower bulbs create beautiful gardens and increase the welfare of neighbors who enjoy them as well.

Market demand, as always, reflects the marginal private benefits *MPB* of the direct consumers (in this case, the bulb-planting gardeners). Market supply, as always, is determined by the marginal private costs *MPC* of direct producers (here the producers of flower bulbs). The process of production, we assume, has no effect on outside parties; thus, marginal social cost *MSC* equals marginal private cost *MPC*. Given the neighborly joys created by the flowering gardens, however, the marginal social benefit of this activity *MSB* lies *above* the marginal private benefit *MPB* to the extent of the marginal external benefit *MEB* (that measures the neighbors' utility gain).

It is easy to see what will in fact happen under the circumstances. As long as government does not intervene, demand and supply will determine a price of P_1 and a quantity of Q_1 according to intersection *g*. Yet this free market outcome is not the efficient one from the social point of view: Marginal

---

[1] In the late 1970s, at its Silver Bay, Minnesota, plant on the North Shore of Lake Superior, the Reserve Mining Company processed taconite ore into pellets that contained up to 75 percent iron and were used by the steel industry. In the process, the plant discharged 500 million gallons of water and 60,000 tons of rock tailings into the lake daily. The tailings caused a rapid decrease of dissolved oxygen in the lake and this *eutrophication* killed aquatic life. See Jerrold M. Peterson, "Estimating an Effluent Charge: The Reserve Mining Case," *Land Economics,* August 1977.

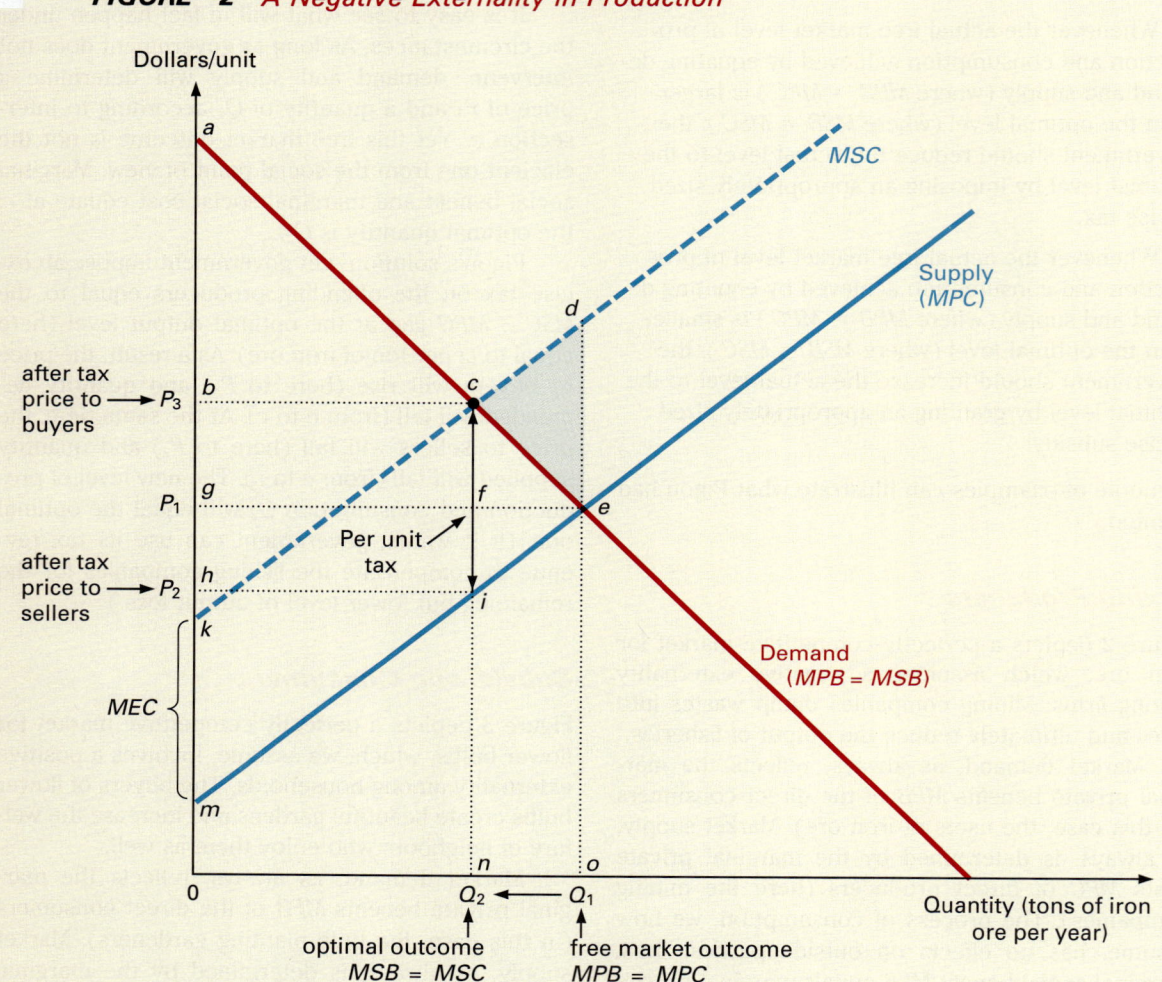

FIGURE 2 A Negative Externality in Production

In the presence of a negative externality in production (here fish killed by a waste-dumping mining company), the marginal social cost MSC lies above the marginal private cost MPC. Accordingly, the optimal level of production and consumption Q_2 lies below the level Q_1 that the free market achieves. According to Pigou, a per-unit tax on the offending producers (equal to the $MSC - MPC$ gap ci at the optimal output level) is the cure. By eliminating output units with marginal social costs (along dc) that exceed marginal social benefits (along ec), Pigou argued, the taxing scheme provides a net social benefit of shaded triangle cde.

social benefit and marginal social cost equate at e; the optimal quantity is Q_2.

Pigou's solution: Let government grant an excise subsidy to the consumers who so please their neighbors—a subsidy equal to the $MSB - MPB$ gap at the optimal output level (here equal to ek per unit of bulbs). As a result, the price to buyers will fall (here to P_2) and quantity demanded will rise (from g to k). At the same time, the price to sellers will rise (here to P_3) and quantity supplied will rise (from g to e). The new level of production and consumption Q_2 will equal the optimal one.

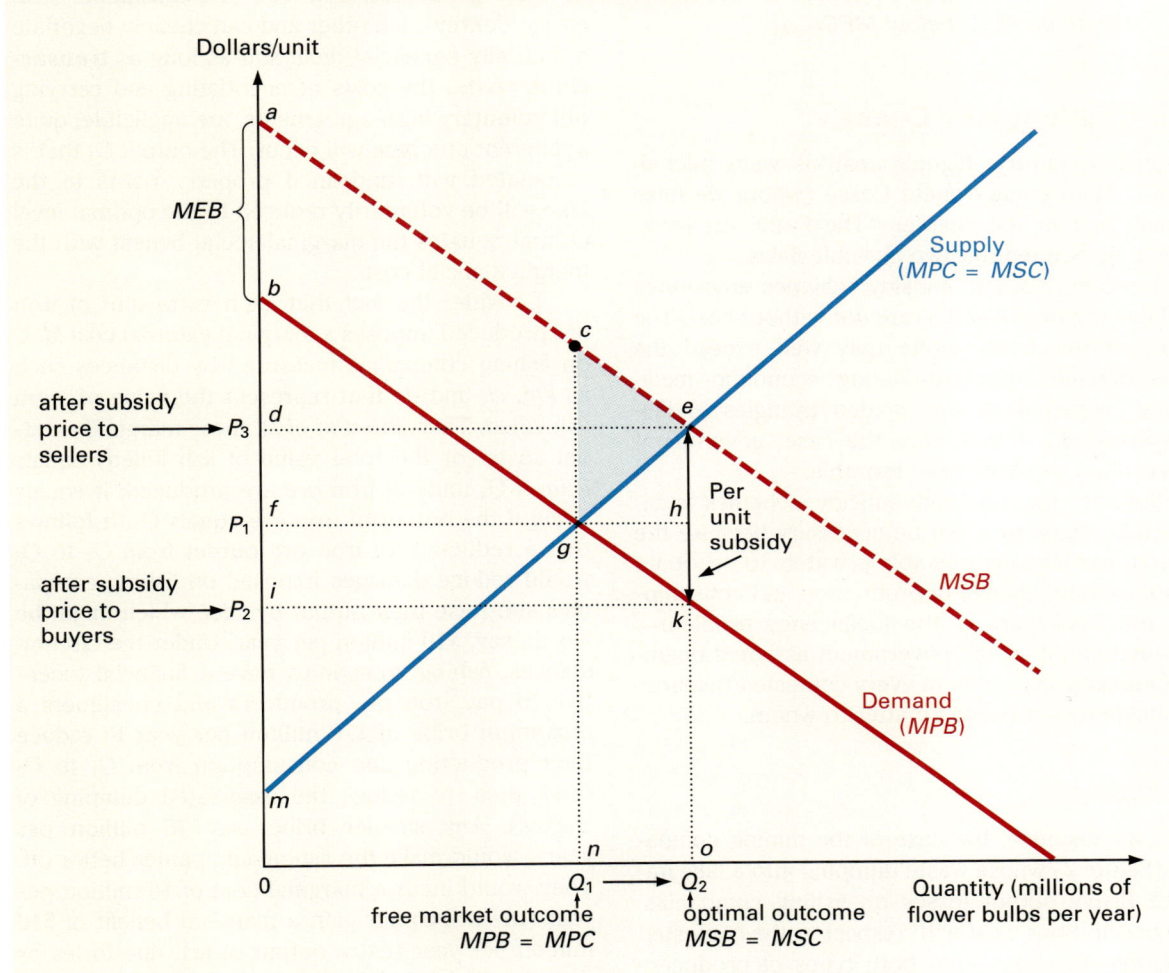

FIGURE 3 A Positive Externality in Consumption

In the presence of a positive externality in consumption (flower gardens enjoyed by neighbors), the marginal social benefit *MSB* lies above the marginal private benefit *MPB*. Accordingly, the optimal level of production and consumption Q_2 lies above the level Q_1 that the free market achieves. According to Pigou, a per-unit subsidy to the consumers who so please their neighbors (equal to the *MSB* − *MPB* gap *ek* at the optimal output level) is the cure. By encouraging the production of extra output units with marginal social benefits (along *ce*) that exceed marginal social costs (along *ge*), Pigou argued, the subsidy scheme provides a net social benefit of shaded triangle *ceg*.

CAUTION

You should not conclude from the preceding two examples that Pigou always recommended taxing *producers* and subsidizing *consumers*. His argument, rather, was that those responsible for negative externalities should be taxed, while those responsible for positive externalities should be subsidized.

For example, offending motorcyclists whose noise depressed *MSB* below *MPB* would be taxed. Similarly, producers of honey who enhanced the pollination of nearby orchards and raised their output would be encouraged by subsidies—a reward for pushing MSC below MPC.

The Challenge of Coase

For half a century, Pigou's analysis went unchallenged. Then came Ronald Coase (whom we have already met in the chapter "The Firm—An Overview"); he pointed out two possible flaws.

First, the tax and subsidy schemes envisioned by Pigou (Figures 2 and 3) are not without cost. The administrative costs alone may well exceed the gains derived from eliminating economic inefficiency (depicted by the shaded triangles in Figures 2 and 3). If that were the case, government intervention would not be desirable.

Second, the tax and subsidy schemes envisioned by Pigou may not be necessary because the affected parties might be able privately to negotiate an appropriate change in production and consumption that took care of the inefficiency problem—provided only that the government assigned unambiguous property rights in every contested resource to somebody—it doesn't matter to whom.

An Example

Take, for instance, the case of the mining companies (Figure 2) whose waste dumping into a lake imposed heavy output losses on fishing companies. Two possibilities exist with respect to the contested resource—the lake—that both types of producers would like to use: Legal rights to the lake could be given either to the mining companies or to the fishing companies.

Property Rights Given to Mining Companies

If the government assigns property rights in the lake to mining companies, they have the right to do with it as they please, which includes using it as a dumping site. Fishing companies would then have no legal grounds for complaint if fish are killed because of waste dumping. Thus, it seems that the free market outcome first depicted in Figure 2 and now reviewed in Figure 4 will occur. According to demand and supply intersection e, it seems, the price of iron ore will be P_1 and the quantity traded Q_1. Not so, argues Coase. As long as the parties involved (fishers, iron ore producers, and iron ore consumers) can easily identify each other and can cheaply negotiate a mutually beneficial deal, and as long as **transactions costs,** the costs of negotiating and carrying out voluntary legal agreements, are negligible, quite a different outcome will occur. The output Q_1 that is associated with undefined property rights in the lake will be voluntarily reduced to the optimal level Q_2 that equates the marginal social benefit with the marginal social cost.

Consider the fact that each extra unit of iron ore produced imposes a marginal external cost *MEC* on fishing companies measured by distances such as *km*, *ci*, and *de* that represent the value of extra fish killed. Thus, the *sum* of all these marginal external costs (or the total value of fish killed) equals *kcim* if Q_2 units of iron ore are produced; it equals *kdem* if the output of iron ore equals Q_1. It follows that a reduction of iron ore output from Q_1 to Q_2 would reduce damages imposed on fishing companies and raise their output by *cdei*, which might be worth, say, $10 million per year. Under the circumstances, fishing companies have a financial incentive to pay iron ore producers and consumers a *maximum* bribe of $10 million per year to reduce their production and consumption from Q_1 to Q_2 (and, thus, to reduce the associated dumping of wastes). Any smaller bribe—say $6 million per year—would make the fishing companies better off. They would incur a marginal cost of $6 million per year (the bribe) but gain a marginal benefit of $10 million per year (extra output of fish due to lesser dumping of wastes).

Would iron ore producers and consumers be interested in such a deal? Of course they would. If the production of iron ore equaled Q_1, the producers would gain sales revenue of $P_1 \cdot Q_1 = 0geo$, while incurring a variable cost of $0meo$. The producer surplus (equal to the fixed cost plus profit) would equal *mge*. If the production of iron ore were cut to Q_2 while the price stayed at P_1, the producers would gain sales revenue of $P_1 \cdot Q_2 = 0gfn$, their variable cost would equal $0min$, and the producer surplus would shrink to *mgfi*, or by *fei*. This dotted triangle would represent a loss in profit and would, thus, equal a *minimum* bribe the producers would require to make the output cut.

By the same token, any output cut from Q_1 to

FIGURE 4 The Coase Theorem

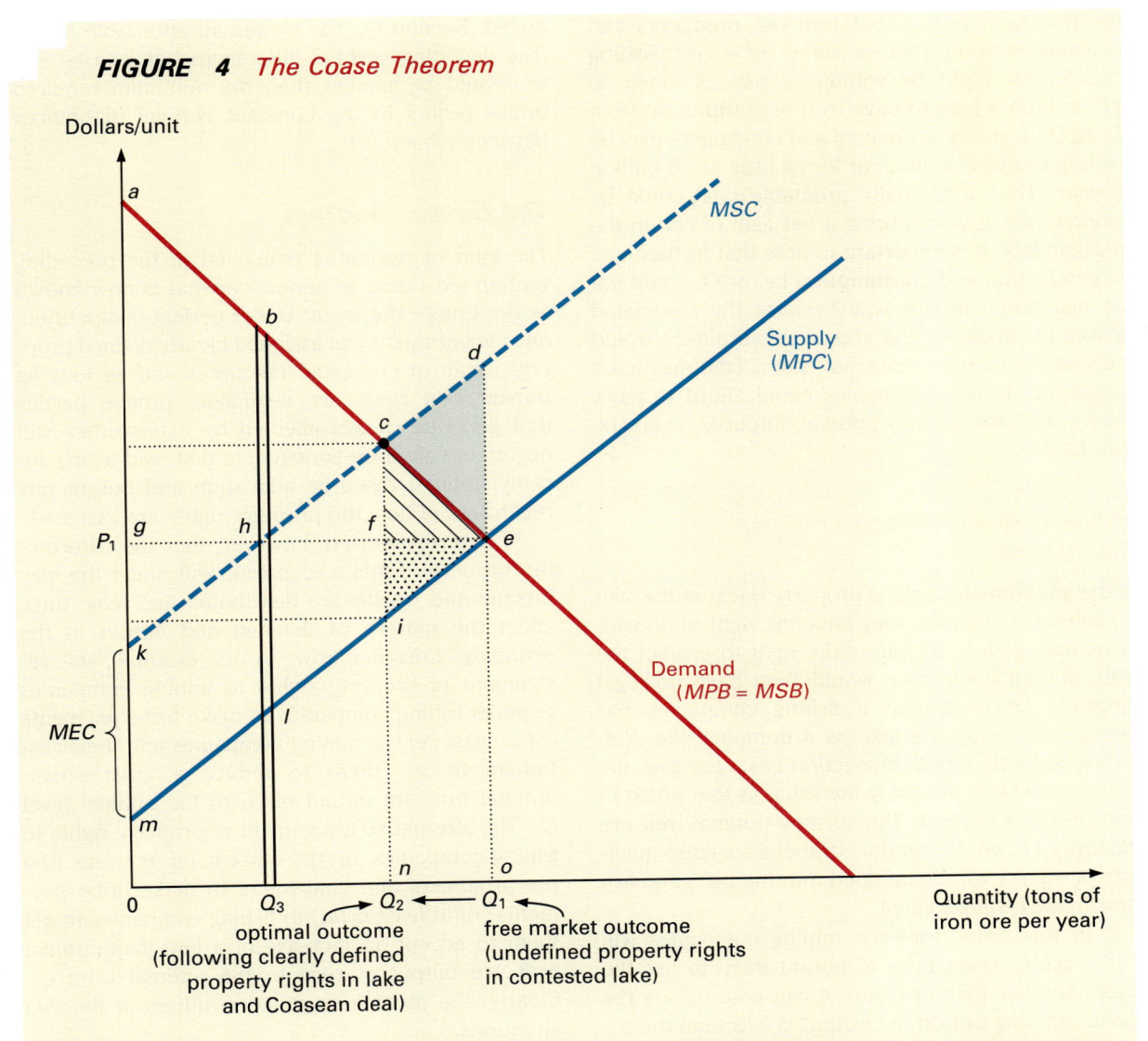

Iron ore producers generate wastes that are dumped into a lake and kill fish. Given perfect competition and low transactions costs, if property rights in the lake are given to the miners, iron ore output will be reduced from Q_1 to Q_2 (and fish output will be increased by *cdei*) because fishers can afford to pay a maximum of *cdei* to bring this about, while makers and users of iron ore require a minimum payment of only *cei*. If property rights in the lake are given to the fishers, iron ore output will be increased from 0 to Q_2 (and fish output will be reduced by *kcim*) because makers and users of iron ore can afford to pay a maximum of *acim*, while fishers require a minimum payment of only *kcim*.

Q_2 would necessitate a corresponding cut in consumption. If the price stayed at P_1, this would reduce the consumer surplus from *aeg* to *acfg*, or by *cef*. This crosshatched triangle would represent the minimum bribe consumers would require to make the consumption cut.

As our graph shows, the maximum bribe that fishing companies might pay (*cdei*) clearly exceeds the minimum bribes that iron ore producers and consumers would require ($fei + cef = cei$). Fishing companies might be willing to pay as much as $10 million a year to have iron ore output cut from Q_1 to Q_2. Iron ore producers and consumers may be willing to make such a cut for as little as $6 million a year. Thus a mutually profitable deal could be worked out. It would bring a net gain of cde to the participants. It is important to note that further cuts in production and consumption below Q_2 could *not* be negotiated in this way because the associated losses in producer and consumer surpluses would exceed the marginal external cost ci (the maximum bribe that fishing companies could afford to pay). As a result, the socially optimal output Q_2 would be produced.

Property Rights Given to Fishing Companies

If the government assigns property rights in the lake to fishing companies, they have the right to do with it as they please, including the right to protect the fish. Mining companies would then have no legal grounds for complaint if fishing companies bar them from using the lake as a dumping site. Yet, Coase showed, when transaction costs are low, the outcome will be precisely the same as that noted in the previous section. The socially optimal iron ore quantity Q_2 will be produced, the associated quantity of wastes will be dumped into the lake, and fish worth $mkci$ will be killed.

In this case, however, mining companies will bribe fishing companies to permit them to use the lake. Another look at Figure 4 can help us see the point: As long as iron ore output is less than the socially optimal Q_2, the maximum bribe that iron ore producers and consumers can afford exceeds the minimum bribe that fishing companies require. As a result, a Coasean deal will be struck to produce the iron ore, dump the wastes, and kill the fish.

For example, a first unit of iron ore sold at price P_1 yields an extra consumer surplus of ag and an extra producer surplus of gm. The sum of am (say, $18) greatly exceeds the associated fish kill of km ($5). An intermediate bribe of $10 would make both parties better off. Similarly, unit number Q_3 would bring extra producer and consumer surplus equal to bl, but smaller extra fish kill equal to hl. Once again a bribe would be made. Note that similar negotiations would break down once Q_2 units are produced. Beyond Q_2, the maximum affordable bribes (the declining vertical differences between ce and ie) would be smaller than the minimum required bribes (equal to the constant vertical differences between cd and ie).

The Coase Theorem

The kind of reasoning employed in the preceding section led Coase to announce what is now known as the **Coase theorem:** Under perfect competition, once government has assigned clearly defined property rights in contested resources and as long as transactions costs are negligible, private parties that generate or are affected by externalities will negotiate voluntary agreements that lead to the socially optimal resource allocation and output mix regardless of how the property rights are assigned.

Coase recognized, however, that the nature of the property rights assignment will affect the way income and wealth are distributed and may, thus, affect the pattern of demand and output in the economy. Consider how, in our example, the assignment of property rights to mining companies requires fishing companies to make bribe payments (of at least cei) to mining companies and their customers to get them to reduce a greater-than-optimal iron ore output of Q_1 to the optimal level Q_2. The alternative assignment of property rights to fishing companies, on the other hand, requires iron ore producers and consumers to make bribe payments (of at least $kcim$) to fishing companies to get them to accept an increase of a less-than-optimal iron ore output of zero to the optimal level Q_2. Clearly, the income distribution differs in the two situations.

Example 1 tells the story of Coasean deals in U.S. agriculture. The remainder of the chapter investigates what happens when the conditions for Coasean deals—clearly defined property rights and negligible transactions costs—are not fulfilled.

The Tragedy of the Commons

Consider a natural resource, such as a body of land, water, or air, that is freely accessible to all—"common property." In such circumstances, a tragic situation often develops: As more and more people use the resource in question, its quality progressively declines and it is eventually destroyed. An example from history can illustrate what is involved.

EXAMPLE 1

The Economics of Bees

An interesting example of Coasean deals in the face of externalities is provided by agreements routinely made between beekeepers and farmers. On the one hand, farmers receive advantages from bees that aid pollination and thereby increase the size of crops. Involved are almonds and apples, blueberries and cherries, cabbage and cranberries. Accordingly, farmers are willing to pay "pollination fees" for the privilege of having bees on their land. On the other hand, beekeepers receive advantages from farmers who grow plants whose nectar increases the production of honey, including alfalfa, fireweed, mint, and red clover. Accordingly, beekeepers are willing to pay "apiary rent" for the right to place their hives on the farmers' land.

The accompanying table presents data collected in the state of Washington during the 1970–1971 growing season, indicating the kinds of deals struck. In some cases, payments were made by farmers to beekeepers, as in the case of almonds that require pollination services but do not increase honey production. In other cases, payments went from beekeepers to farmers, as in the case of fireweed that improves honey output but does not require pollination services. In other cases still, payments go both ways, as in the case of alfalfa and red clover.

Beekeeping can be quite a business, too. In 1989, Pennsylvania beekeeper David Hackenburg received $60,000 just for delivering his 1,500 hives to pollinate blueberries in Maine and apples in Pennsylvania. Nationwide, beekeepers received $40 million for providing farmers with a million hives. And it is well worth it. According to a Cornell University study, every dollar paid for pollination returns $60 in additional production.

Sources: Steven N. S. Cheung, "The Fable of the Bees: An Economic Investigation," *The Journal of Law and Economics,* April 1973, pp. 11–33; and Sanford L. Jacobs, "Farmers are Abuzz About the Benefits of Trucked-in Bees," *The Wall Street Journal,* July 6, 1989, pp. 1 and 6.

Seasons	Plants	Pollination fees	Apiary rent/hive
Early spring	Almond (California)	$5–8	0
	Cherry	$6–8	
Late spring (major pollination season)	Apple and soft fruits	$9–10	0
	Blueberry (with maple)	$5	0
	Cabbage	$8	0
	Cherry	$9–10	0
	Cranberry	$9	0
Summer and early fall (major honey season)	Alfalfa	0	13–60¢
	Alfalfa (with pollination)	$3–5	0
	Fireweed	0	25–63¢
	Mint	0	15–65¢
	Pasture	0	15–65¢
	Red clover	0	65¢
	Red clover (with pollination)	$3–6	0
	Sweet clover	0	20–25¢

The New England Commons

Many New England towns of the past had a tract of grazing land, called the *commons,* that was considered community property and was open for all to use. Residents were free to place as many cows on the commons as they liked. Yet the carrying capacity of any pasture is clearly limited; hence more cows meant less grass per cow and a lower average selling weight, as Table 1 illustrates.

How many cows would people place on the commons? Each individual would compare the marginal private benefit (weight of mature cow times price per pound) with the marginal private cost (the price of a calf plus *zero* maintenance cost) and decide accordingly. Let a cow's sales price be $1 per pound; let a calf cost $100. Then people in our example would put up to 11 cows on the commons; they could expect them to weigh 100 lb. on the average, to bring $100 in revenue, and just make up for the cost of the calf. As long as there were fewer cows, any individual could make a profit by spending $100 on a calf, placing, say, an eighth cow on the commons, and selling the 220 lb. cow for $220. Such an individual would be quite unperturbed by the fact that the 220 lb. personal gain (and the associated profit of $120) was accompanied by seven other cows becoming slimmer by 40 lb. each, making for a negative marginal *social* benefit of + 220 lb. − 7 (40 lb.) = − 60 lb., as column (4) indicates.

Indeed, things could get worse over time, as they often did. The excessive number of cows on the commons may well reduce its productivity over time. Because the pasture can never recover from the constant overgrazing, all the entries in columns (2) to (4) of our table decline over time. Eventually, the common pasture might become totally useless for grazing.

It is instructive to ask what a sole private owner of our grazing land would do. Such an owner would care very much about the weight of other

TABLE 1 Cows on the Commons

Number of cows (1)	Average weight (lbs. per cow) (2)	Total weight (lbs., all cows combined) (3) = (1) · (2)	Marginal social benefit (change in total pounds when adding one cow) (4) = $\frac{\Delta (3)}{\Delta (1)}$
1	500	500	500
2	460	920	420
3	420	1,260	340
4	380	1,520	260
5	340	1,700	180
6	300	1,800	100
7	260	(1,820)	20
8	220	1,760	−60
9	180	1,620	−140
10	140	1,400	−220
11	100	1,100	−300

As more and more cows (1) are placed on a common pasture, their average weight (2) declines. The total weight (3) of all cows combined rises to a maximum (encircled) and then declines; the marginal social benefit (4) falls throughout.

cows as an additional cow is placed on the pasture—the other cows wouldn't be other people's cows. As a result, such an owner would focus on the data in column (4) and place no more than 6 cows on the land—the sixth cow would weigh 300 lb. But the owner's five other cows would weigh 300 lb. rather than 340 lb. and a gain of 300 lb. minus a loss of 200 lb. (5 cows times 40 lb.) comes to 100 lb., as column (4) indicates. This translates into a dollar marginal benefit of $100, just equal to the price of a calf. Private ownership, thus, would avoid the overgrazing and the destruction of the land.

Examples 2 and 3 provide other illustrations of the issues we have just discussed.

EXAMPLE 2

Overfishing at the Georges Bank

The shallow waters of Georges Bank, lying from 50 to 200 miles off the New England Coast, have been a major fishing ground since colonial times. Some 200 species of fish and shellfish spawn and feed there, including cod, haddock, flounder, lobster, and scallops. In 1978, the U.S. catch was valued at $82 million, that of foreigners at $85 million. Similar annual catches were expected for the remainder of the century.

Then, in 1979, the U.S. Department of the Interior announced its intention to auction off oil and gas drilling rights for Georges Bank. Over the next 20 years, it argued, some 6.3 million acres of offshore tracts could yield 123 million barrels of oil and 870 billion cubic feet of gas, worth a total of $7 billion. Even if a major oil spill occurred and the expected $3.34 billion of fish and shellfish had to be given up (a highly unlikely event), the marginal benefit would be far greater than the marginal cost.

Others disagreed. The Commonwealth of Massachusetts, along with environmental groups and fishing companies, sued the U.S. and successfully delayed the auctioning of drilling rights. In the meantime, Congress enacted a 200-mile territorial limit that prohibited foreign vessels from fishing within that boundary. And New England's fishing companies responded to the new opportunities.

They replaced their weathered, wooden boats with bigger, more sophisticated steel vessels. And just as the number of cows once placed on the New England commons grew rapidly, so too did the number of boats fishing at Georges Bank. For a time, total output grew. But then, in 1989, disaster struck: Catches of cod, flounder, and haddock fell to levels half as large as a decade earlier. In port towns like New Bedford, fish processors were operating at 45 percent capacity and employment was cut in half compared to 1982. Overfishing had done precisely what oil spills might have done. "There's no haddock," said Dennis Hogan, Jr., captain of the *Integrity*. "It's gone, it's wiped out." As to other types of fish, "I've caught more fish in one morning than we now catch in 10 days," he said.

In 1991, the U.S. government moved to reverse the trend. It announced that it would privatize fishing rights within the 200 mile coastal zone. The first (transferable) rights issued concerned cod, flounder, haddock, lobster, scallops, and yellowtail in the North Atlantic and various types of clams in the Mid-Atlantic Region. Then, rights to menhaden and shrimp were handed out in the Gulf of Mexico and to halibut, King crabs, salmon, and pollock in the North Pacific.

Sources: The New York Times, October 12, 1979, p. A30, April 3, 1989, pp. A1 and 12, June 19, 1989, p. A13; *The Daily Hampshire Gazette,* September 6, 1984; and Peter Passell, "U.S. Starts to Allot Fishing Rights in Coastal Waters to Boat Owners," *The New York Times,* April 22, 1991, pp. A1 and B8.

EXAMPLE 3

Escaping the Commons: Lobsters and Oysters

In colonial times, almost anyone could catch lobsters weighing 25 pounds, but those days are gone. Not so long ago, lobsters in Maine were at the point of extinction—the result of overfishing. Then groups of fishers banded together to reverse the clock. Claiming "accustomed rights" of their families, they banned outsiders from their lobstering area and effectively appropriated some of the sea's acreage. In addition, they imposed strict limits on their own catch with respect to numbers, age, and size of lobsters. The accompanying table compares their subsequent experience with that of fishers in adjacent, uncontrolled areas. As the data indicate, the private property arrangement raised productivity as well as income compared to the uncontrolled-access area in which lobster traps, like cows on the commons, were crowded together.

Similarly encouraging results have been achieved in privately owned oyster beds in Louisiana and Virginia (compared to common-property beds in adjacent states, such as Mississippi and Maryland). From 1950 to 1969, for example, the average annual income of oyster fishers in Louisiana and Virginia was $3,207 and $2,453, respectively; in Mississippi and Maryland it was $870 and $1,606, respectively.

Sources: James A. Wilson, "A Test of the Tragedy of the Commons," In Garrett Hardin and John Baden, *Managing the Commons* (San Francisco: W. H. Freeman and Company, 1977), pp. 96–111; and Richard J. Agnello and Lawrence P. Donnelley, "Prices and Property Rights in the Fisheries," *Southern Economic Journal,* October 1979, pp. 253–262.

	Access to catch area	
Features compared	Controlled	Uncontrolled
1. Number of trap hauls	5,896	4,837
2. Number of lobsters	5,762	2,951
3. Weight of lobsters (kg.)	3,106	1,568
4. Lobsters per trap haul	.98	.61
5. Weight per trap haul	.53	.32
6. Average income of fishers	$22,929	$16,449

The Pollution of Nature

In 1989 the Environmental Protection Agency (EPA) released a long-awaited report based on a survey of 19,000 manufacturing plants. The report, mandated by the Emergency Planning and Community Right-to-Know Act of 1986, measured the manufacturers' 1987 dumping of 328 types of chemicals into the natural environment. The result of this toxics release inventory exceeded any previous estimate by far. The reporting firms (which were only the larger ones) had released 22.5 billion pounds of potentially hazardous substances—2.7 billion pounds into the air, 12.9 billion pounds into surface waters and underground wells, 4.3 billion pounds into the soil, and the remaining 2.6 billion pounds to treatment facilities. These numbers shocked many across the land.

Yet the EPA study by no means defines the full extent of the waste dumping problem. Additional huge quantities are being dumped by nonreporting, smaller firms (including pesticide-using agriculture), by households (mainly in the form of automobile exhaust and garbage), and by governmental units (mainly in the form of sewage).

Even after two decades of operation (the EPA was created in 1970), the federal agency has only limited knowledge about the concentrations of wastes found in particular places, the exact timing of releases, and the extent of exposure suffered by people, animals, plants, and more. There are millions of sources of wastes; waste dumping claims millions of victims. Clearly, the transactions costs required to make private Coasean deals among those who generate wastes and others who are adversely affected by them are prohibitive. Realizing this fact, Congress has passed four key laws (plus later amendments) that empower the EPA to deal with the mess: the Clean Air Act of 1970, the Water Pollution Control Act of 1972, the Resource Conservation and Recovery Act of 1976, and the Superfund Act of 1980. Just like the FDA, discussed in the previous chapter, the EPA has long been overwhelmed by its impossible task. In theory, however, the way to proceed is fairly easy to grasp.

The Theory of Optimum Pollution

Economists suggest that a government agency—like the EPA—that wants to tackle the environmental pollution problem must first of all recognize that in a world of scarcity all human activities have costs as well as benefits. Just like the public health officials discussed in Chapter 1 (who had to *restrict* their cancer-screening program when the resources could save more lives in other pursuits), EPA administrators must make unpalatable choices. They must restrict waste abatement and permit some waste dumping (and, possibly, permit some cancer deaths following people's exposure to hazardous wastes) if a further reduction of that dumping carries an unacceptable cost (for example, an even larger number of deaths from other causes). An EPA administrator, in short, must compare the marginal social cost and the marginal social benefit of waste dumping in order to identify the level of waste dumping that equates the two, maximizes the social net benefit, and thus brings about a level of **optimum pollution.**

To see what is involved consider Figure 5, which pretends to measure the effects of a city's sewage dumping into a river.

The line labeled *MSC* represents the eventually rising marginal social cost of sewage dumping. The first 40 million tons dumped in a year have no harmful effect on anything; nature absorbs these wastes easily and without a trace (hence the *MSC* line coincides with the horizontal axis between 0 and point *f*). Further dumping, however, begins to cause damages—first to riverfront property, then to boats and fish, then to birds feeding on fish, and, finally, to human health. Follow the rising *MSC* line to the right of *f* and note how the 120 millionth ton of sewage dumped adds $40 to the damage already sustained (point *g*) and brings the total cost to *fgh*. The 200 millionth ton of sewage, in turn, adds $80 to the damages done (point *c*) and raises the total to *ckf*. The 280 millionth ton of sewage dumped adds another $120 to the total (point *i*) and makes it reach *fim*.

Now consider the line labeled *MSB* between points *a* and *e;* it represents the declining marginal social benefit of sewage dumping. The first ton of sewage dumped in a year saves society $180 of other goods that would have to be forgone if resources were diverted to treating or recycling that unit (point *a*). Dumping the 120 millionth, 200 millionth, or 280 millionth ton saves society, similarly, $120, $80, or $40 of other goods (points *b, c,* and *d*). The decline in the dollar figures just noted reflects a common experience: Given a large initial volume of waste emissions (such as 0*e* = 360 million tons per year), it is often very cheap to reduce emissions a bit (and move, say, from *e* to *m*), but it gets increasingly costly to increase the level of abatement (and move from *m* to *k, h, f,* or even 0). Thus cutting 1 ton of sewage out of 360 million tons may cost a mere 10¢ and involve only such *first-stage sewage treatment* as filtering out the coarser solids prior to dumping. For this reason, the 360 millionth ton, *when dumped,* benefits society to the extent of 10¢ (point *e*). By dumping that 360 millionth ton, people can have 10¢ worth of other goods rather than 10¢ worth of first stage sewage treatment. Yet cutting out another ton of sewage when dumping has already been cut to 200 million tons per year may cost $80 and involve such *second-stage sewage*

FIGURE 5 Optimum Pollution

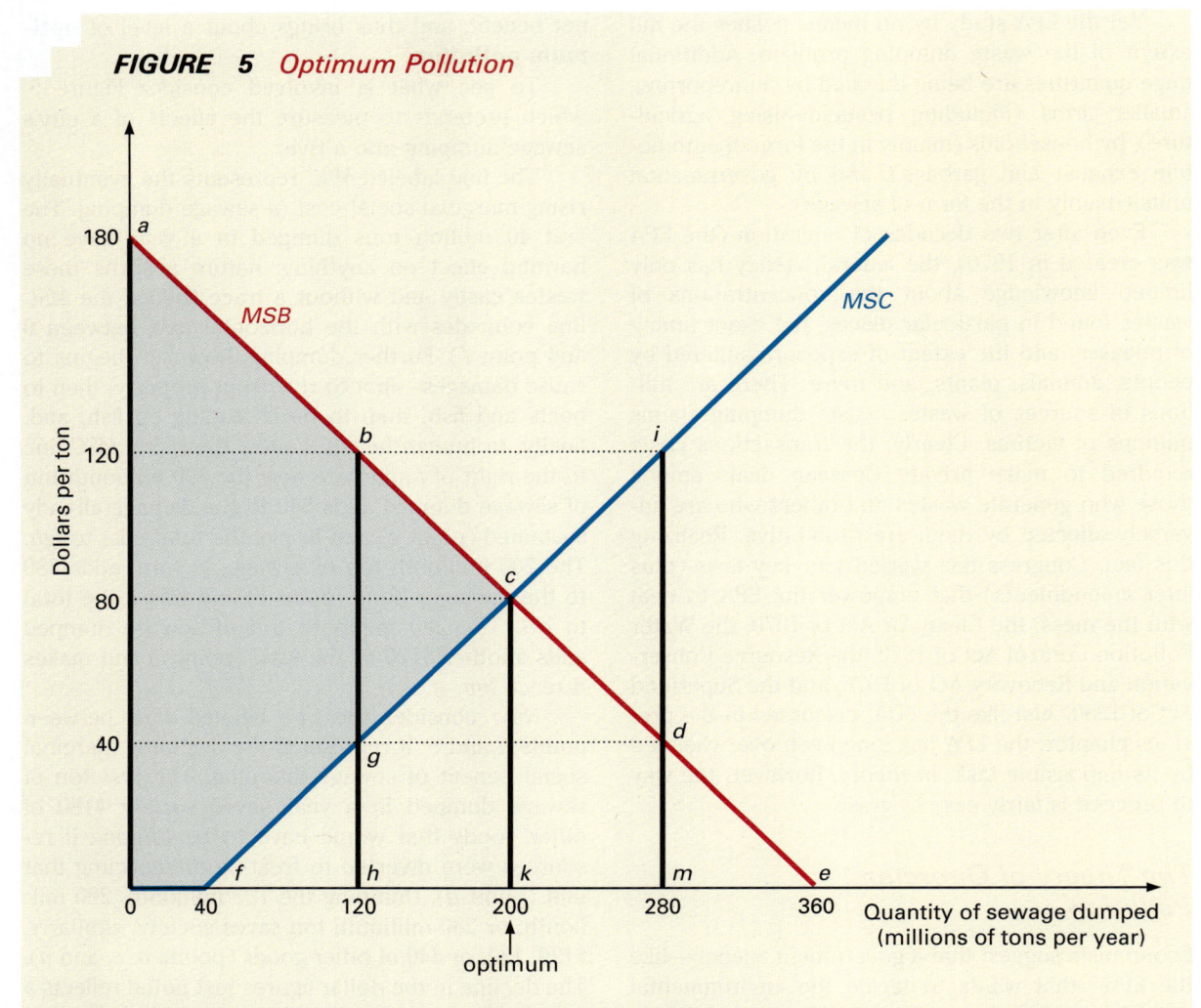

Optimum pollution occurs when waste dumping is carried to the point (here 200 million tons per year) that equates (at c) the marginal social benefit MSB of dumping with the associated marginal social cost MSC. This level maximizes the social net benefit of dumping (shaded area). Those who insist on zero pollution are asking society to sacrifice this net benefit. They are asking to save goods destroyed by waste dumping and worth ckf while ignoring the fact that other goods worth the larger amount 0ack have to be sacrificed to achieve the zero-pollution goal.

treatment as building holding ponds and using benign bacteria to break down organic materials from human wastes and garbage disposals into "innocuous" compounds. For this reason, the 200 millionth ton, *when dumped,* benefits society to the extent of $80 (point c). By dumping that ton of sewage, people can have $80 of other goods rather than $80 of second-stage sewage treatment. Finally, cutting out even the first ton of sewage dumped (and, thus, not dumping any sewage at all) may involve a fairly large marginal abatement cost of $180 and may have to involve such *third-stage sewage treatment* as mixing the effluent with lime (to remove phosphates), spraying it from a 50-foot tower (to remove ammonia gas), filtering it through coarse coal, then fine sand, then granulated carbon, and chlorinating it. The result, believe it or not, is drinking water; its production, clearly, is a costly proposition. For this reason, the 1st ton of sewage, *when dumped,* benefits society to the extent of $180 (point *a*). By dumping it, people can have $180 of other goods rather than $180 of third-stage sewage treatment.

Now note this: The *area* under the *MSB* line up to any chosen quantity equals the *sum* of the marginal social benefits derived from waste dumping, that is, the sum of $180 + $179 + $178 + . . . + $120 and so on. This sum is the total social benefit of dumping the quantity in question—the value of other goods *not* sacrificed for the sake of waste treatment. Dumping 120 million tons of sewage per year, for example, saves society 0*abh* of other goods; dumping 200 million tons saves 0*ack* of other goods; dumping 280 million tons saves 0*adm* of other goods.

It is easy to see why optimum pollution in our example is produced by the dumping of 200 million tons of sewage per year. Up to this quantity, every ton dumped saves society goods that are valued more highly (along *ac*) than those destroyed by pollution damage (along *fc*). The optimum level of pollution equates (at *c*) the marginal social benefit of dumping with its marginal social cost. At that level of dumping, the total social benefit equals 0*ack*; the total social cost, *ckf*. And the social *net* benefit is maximized as shaded area 0*acf*.

Note that dumping more than 200 million tons per year would reduce the social net benefit below this maximum because additional dumping would destroy goods valued more highly (along line *ci* and beyond) than those saved by dumping rather than abating wastes (valued along line *ce*). Likewise, dumping fewer than 200 million tons per year would reduce the social net benefit below the shaded maximum because additional abatement would destroy goods valued more highly (along line *ca*) than those saved by dumping less (valued along line *cf*0).

Actual Pollution in the Absence of Government Intervention

In the absence of government intervention, the optimum level of pollution identified in the preceding section would, however, not be achieved. We can see why by looking at Figure 6, which presents Figure 5 in a new way. The line that showed the marginal social benefit of dumping is now viewed as the *demand for pollution opportunities* by would-be dumpers of wastes. This change of view makes sense because the amount of money that waste dumpers would have to spend on abating any given ton of waste ($180 for the 1st ton, $80 for the 200 millionth ton, and so on) is also the maximum amount they would pay for the right simply to dump that ton.

Now assume, as is so often the case, that property rights in our river are ill-defined. The river is a commons—anybody's property or nobody's property. Anyone can use the river and for any purpose. In that case, our city government faces a *supply of pollution opportunities* that coincides with the horizontal axis: it can do all the dumping it wants and at a zero price.

Because demand and supply meet at point *d*, 360 million tons of sewage will in fact be dumped each year. Each one of these tons costs nothing to dump, but saves the city some money that it would otherwise have to spend on treating or recycling its wastes. The incentive to dump *all* of the sewage is strong.

Our graph also indicates how the maximum possible social net benefit from dumping (the shaded area) is reduced (by an amount equal to the dotted area) when actual dumping exceeds the optimum. As sewage beyond the 200 million ton optimum is dumped, marginal social costs are incurred (along *ab*) that clearly exceed the marginal social benefits (along *ad*). Yet the sewage-dumping city does not care. It is better off by *acd; other* people (who sustain the pollution damage) are worse off by *abdc*.

Types of Government Intervention

The preceding section indicated why waste dumping into the natural environment is likely to be excessive in the absence of government intervention. In the past two decades, however, governments at all levels, although hampered by fragmentary data, have attempted to reduce levels of actual dumping toward lower and often ill-defined optimal levels. Let us consider the major types of approaches they have taken.

FIGURE 6 Actual Pollution

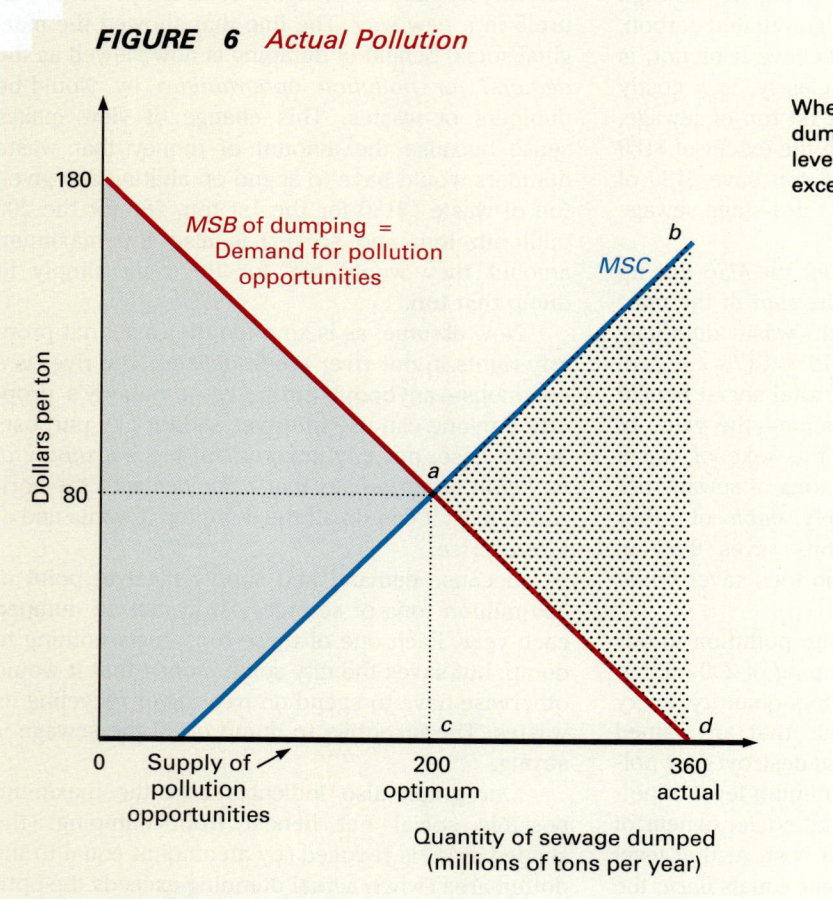

When property rights in potential dumping sites are ill-defined, the level of actual pollution may well exceed that of optimum pollution.

Axes: Dollars per ton (vertical, showing 80 and 180); Quantity of sewage dumped (millions of tons per year) horizontal, showing 200 optimum and 360 actual.

Curves: MSB of dumping = Demand for pollution opportunities; MSC. Points labeled a, b, c, d. Supply of pollution opportunities indicated on horizontal axis at 0.

Moral Suasion

Some governments have tried voluntarism. They have appealed to people's consciences and *exhorted* them not to litter in the national parks, not to incinerate their trash, not to dump raw sewage, not to use leaded gas, and not to use detergents loaded with phosphates. On occasion, governmental suasion has been reinforced by private campaigns. In 1969, for example, Vahlsing, Inc., a potato processor, was the target of a nationwide boycott because of its pollution of the Prestile Stream in Maine.

Unfortunately, altruism is a notoriously weak force for social change. Typically, any one household, firm, or even local government produces a tiny amount of the total environmental damage that we jointly manage to inflict. As a result, any one person can be certain that any sacrifices made for the sake of the environment, although costly to that person, will have no noticeable impact overall. In addition, even if that person could be convinced that all other people *were* doing their share to reduce the damage done, that single person would still have no incentive to act: If only one person were to cheat, the overall result would be indistinguishable from one in which everyone was heeding the call for "responsible citizenship." Thus, the moral-suasion approach is likely to perpetuate actual pollution in excess of optimal pollution.

The Outright Ban

Governments have also gone to the other extreme and instituted outright bans on polluting activities supported, of course, with variously severe penalties for noncompliance. If successful, such bans create zero actual pollution, which may well be less than the optimum, as the caption to Figure 5 reminds us.

In the early 1970s, for example, Oregon and New York banned disposable beverage containers; Connecticut and New York banned phosphates in laundry detergents. And the U.S. federal government banned the use of DDT, a chlorinated hydrocarbon that not so long ago had brought to its developer the Nobel Prize in medicine. (By killing the malaria mosquito, the substance single-handedly wiped out malaria in India, preventing 750,000 deaths per year.) Nevertheless, the DDT ban may have been a wise one because there was widespread evidence that the marginal social cost of DDT contamination exceeded the benefit even at very low levels, making zero dumping optimal. Used as a pesticide, DDT had quickly spread around the world, killing off whole species of animals, causing cancer in humans, and slowing the photosynthesis in plants that produce most of the oxygen on which all life on earth depends.

In the 1990s, the ban is still a popular policy. Thus Vermont banned the use of disposable diapers (they accounted for 20 percent of its trash), and the U.S. banned all asbestos products (that, after a century of use, were producing 10,000 cancer deaths per year).

Setting Standards

The most common approach to pollution abatement has involved the setting of standards. **Input standards** are rules that specify the type of inputs polluters may use. (For example, electric power plants may be told to use coal with a specified maximum sulfur content in order to reduce ultimately the level of sulfur dioxide in the air.) **Emission standards** are rules that specify maximum quantities of stated pollutants that may be released by any one polluter. (For example, an electric power plant may be told not to release more than 150 tons of sulfur dioxide per year from a particular smokestack.) Finally, **ambient standards** are rules that specify the quantity of stated pollutants that a given environment may contain. (For example, the air over New York City may be slated to contain no more than 3 parts per million of sulfur dioxide.)

The standard-setting approach has one serious drawback. It is likely to be extremely and unnecessarily costly. There is, first of all, the administrative cost. The quality of the environment has to be monitored. Standards have to be agreed upon on the basis of scientific evidence concerning emission toxicity and persistence. Pollution has to be traced to its sources, and polluters have to be made aware of the standards applying to them. Then there is the enforcement cost. Unlike traffic violations, which can bring harm to the violator (an accident), the violation of input or emission standards brings a clear benefit to the violator (lower costs); people are therefore much more inclined to break such rules.

Third, and most important, there is the compliance cost. Take the case of emission standards. Because marginal waste abatement costs differ among polluters, the total abatement cost can only be minimized if standards are carefully tailored to the special circumstances of each polluter. That is, emission standards must be toughest for those who can avoid waste dumping at the lowest marginal cost and most lenient for those who are saddled with the highest marginal abatement cost. More often than not, this is also desirable for reasons of equity, because those polluters who have already avoided some pollution voluntarily are likely to have the highest marginal cost for further reductions in emission. Yet the equitable and least-cost achievement of a given ambient standard by setting *differentiated* emission standards would spell an administrative nightmare. Thus government can almost certainly be relied upon to set *uniform* emission standards for all polluters. This may be both inequitable and unnecessarily expensive.

Taxing the Dumping of Wastes

The government can also impose taxes to curb the dumping of wastes, as Pigou taught us. Consider Figure 7 which is based on our earlier example. As before, optimum pollution equals 200 million tons per year, corresponding to the equality at point c of the marginal social benefit and the marginal social cost of dumping. In the absence of government intervention, 360 million tons per year would be dumped (point f). Let the government now announce that unlimited dumping is allowed, provided a tax of $80 is paid for each ton of sewage dumped—the tax being equal to the marginal social cost of dumping (ce) at the optimum level of pollution ($0e$). This action raises the supply of pollution opportunities from the horizontal axis (where we found it in Figure 6) to the parallel line going through point c.

FIGURE 7 Taxing the Dumping of Wastes

Dollars per ton

- a at 180
- MSB of dumping = Demand for pollution opportunities
- MSC of dumping
- b, c, d along 80 — Supply of pollution opportunities
- Tax per unit dumped: from 0 to 80
- e at 200 (optimum = actual after tax)
- f at 360 (actual before tax)

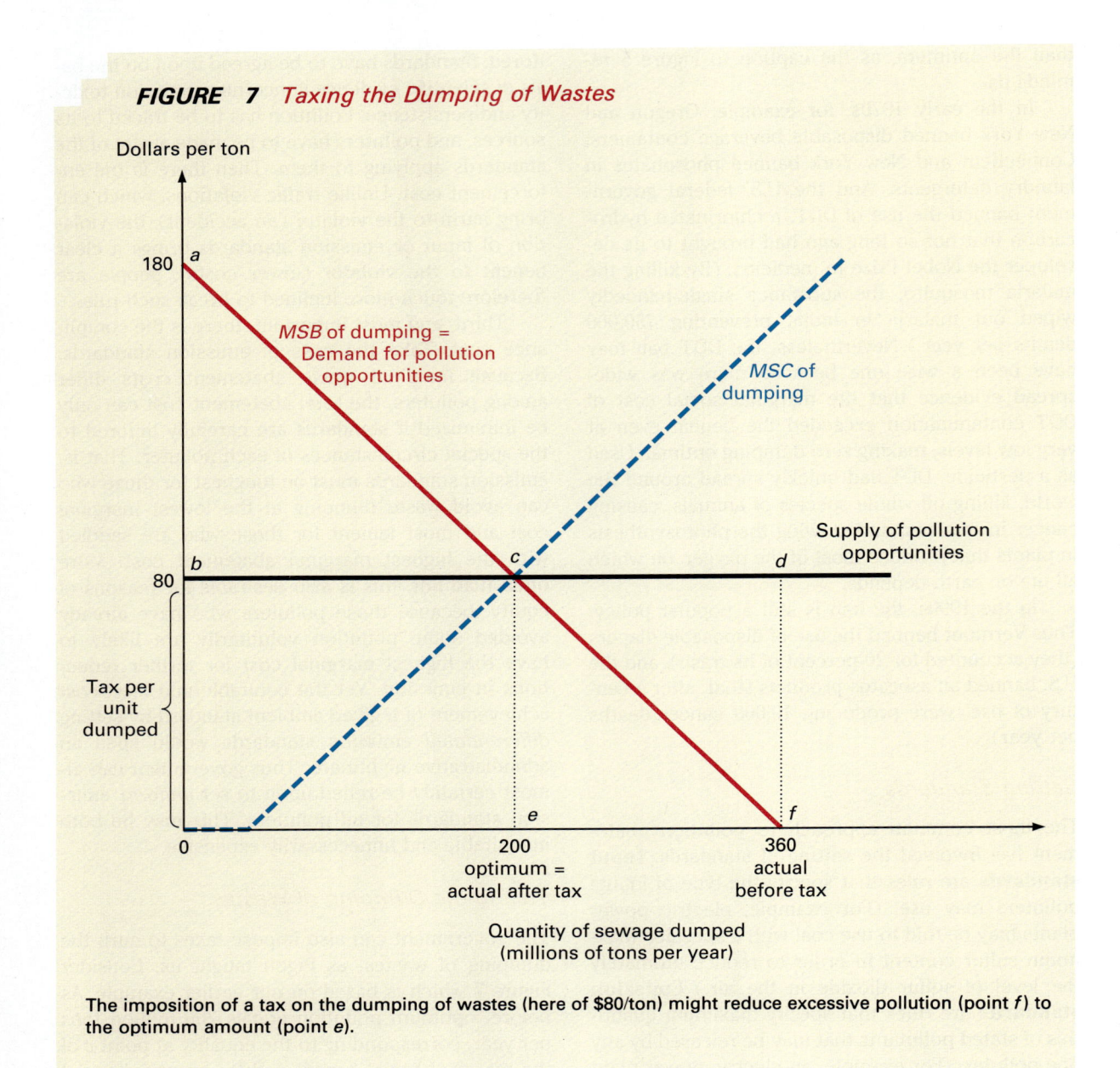

Quantity of sewage dumped (millions of tons per year)

The imposition of a tax on the dumping of wastes (here of $80/ton) might reduce excessive pollution (point f) to the optimum amount (point e).

Would-be polluters, as a result, will reduce dumping to the optimal amount. As they will see it, it is worthwhile to dump the first 200 million tons because the required dumping tax (0bce) is less than the alternative abatement expenditure (0ace). On the other hand, dumping the remaining 160 million tons (ef) is no longer worthwhile. The dumping tax would come to cdfe; the wastes could be abated for half that amount (cfe).

Examples of this approach include fees for waste disposal in waterways charged by Maryland, Michigan, and Vermont (as well as a number of Western European countries); taxes on nondegradable packaging imposed by Iowa, Maine, Massachusetts, Minnesota, and New York; and federal government taxes on sulfur found in coal, natural gas, and oil, and on lead found in gasoline.

Subsidizing the Abatement of Wastes

Pigou's alternative approach, the subsidizing of beneficial activities, has been tried as well. Consider Figure 8. Once again, actual pollution, in the absence of government intervention, equals 360 million tons per year (point *e*); optimum pollution equals 200 million tons per year (point *d*). At the optimum, the marginal social cost of dumping (which is the marginal social benefit of abating) equals the marginal social benefit of dumping (which is also the marginal social cost of abating). Now let the government continue to permit unlimited dumping at a zero price (the supply of pollution opportunities lies on the horizontal axis), but let it also grant a subsidy of $80 for each ton of sewage abated—a subsidy equal to the marginal social benefit of abating (*bd*) for the optimal amount of abatement (*ed*). This action effectively lowers the demand for pollution opportunities from the *MSB* line (now dashed) to the solid line reaching from *c* to *f*.

Would-be polluters, as a result, will reduce dumping to the optimal amount and, thus, abate quantity *ed*. From their perspective, it is worthwhile to dump the first 200 million tons because the dumping is costless (along 0*d*), and the abatement cost (equal to 0*abd* before the subsidy) is still positive (0*cd*) after the subsidy (of *cabd*) is received. On the other hand, dumping the remaining 160 million tons (*de*) is no longer worthwhile. If this amount is abated (at a total cost of *dbe*), a subsidy of *dbef* is received, creating a net gain of shaded triangle *def*.

Examples of such subsidies—all imperfect substitutes for the per-unit subsidy—have included income tax credits for purchases of pollution abatement equipment, as well as accelerated depreciation privileges, low-interest loans, and exemptions from property and sales taxes.

Marketing Pollution Rights

A final approach to achieving optimum pollution is illustrated in Figure 9. Once again, we make use of our earlier example. In the absence of government intervention, actual pollution equals 360 million tons per year (point *e*), but—as the *MSB/MSC* intersection indicates—optimum pollution equals 200 million tons per year (point *d*). Now let the government ban all dumping *unless* the polluter holds an appropriate number of **pollution licenses** or **pollution rights**, each of these being a transferable certificate allowing its owner to dump one unit of specified wastes into a specified environment. In our example, having identified the dumping of 200 million tons of sewage into the river as optimal, the government might issue a strictly limited supply of 200 million pollution rights per year, each of these allowing the holder to dump 1 ton of sewage per year into the specified river.

As before, the marginal social benefit of dumping (which is also the marginal social cost of abatement that dumping can avoid) will determine the maximum prices that various would-be dumpers are prepared to pay for the right to pollute. Hence the *MSB* line turns into the demand for pollution rights. Given the governmental supply, an equilibrium price of $80 per right emerges in our example (point *c*). As a result, the first 200 million tons of sewage per year are dumped. These polluters prefer paying $80 per right (along *bc*) to treating these tons at a higher cost (along *ac*). The remaining 160 million tons per year are abated instead. It is cheaper to treat them (at marginal abatement costs measured along *ce*) than to pay the $80 per ton price for the right to pollute. As a result, the market mechanism here described achieves any given pollution avoidance in the cheapest possible way.

In addition, we should note, any party that seeks rights to nature's waste-receiving capacity and wants them badly enough to pay the equilibrium price can acquire such rights. In most cases, this would be polluters. But the purchasers could also be special-interest groups, such as conservationists. Disagreeing with the government's decision to allow *some* pollution, they might buy up pollution rights for the express purpose of *not* using them, of keeping them out of the hands of potential waste dumpers.

Note, finally, that all firms operating under such a scheme will have higher production costs—either because they must pay the dumping fee for whatever wastes they create or because they must incur abatement costs. This will, ultimately, lower the profits of the firms' owners or raise the prices paid

FIGURE 8 Subsidizing the Abatement of Wastes

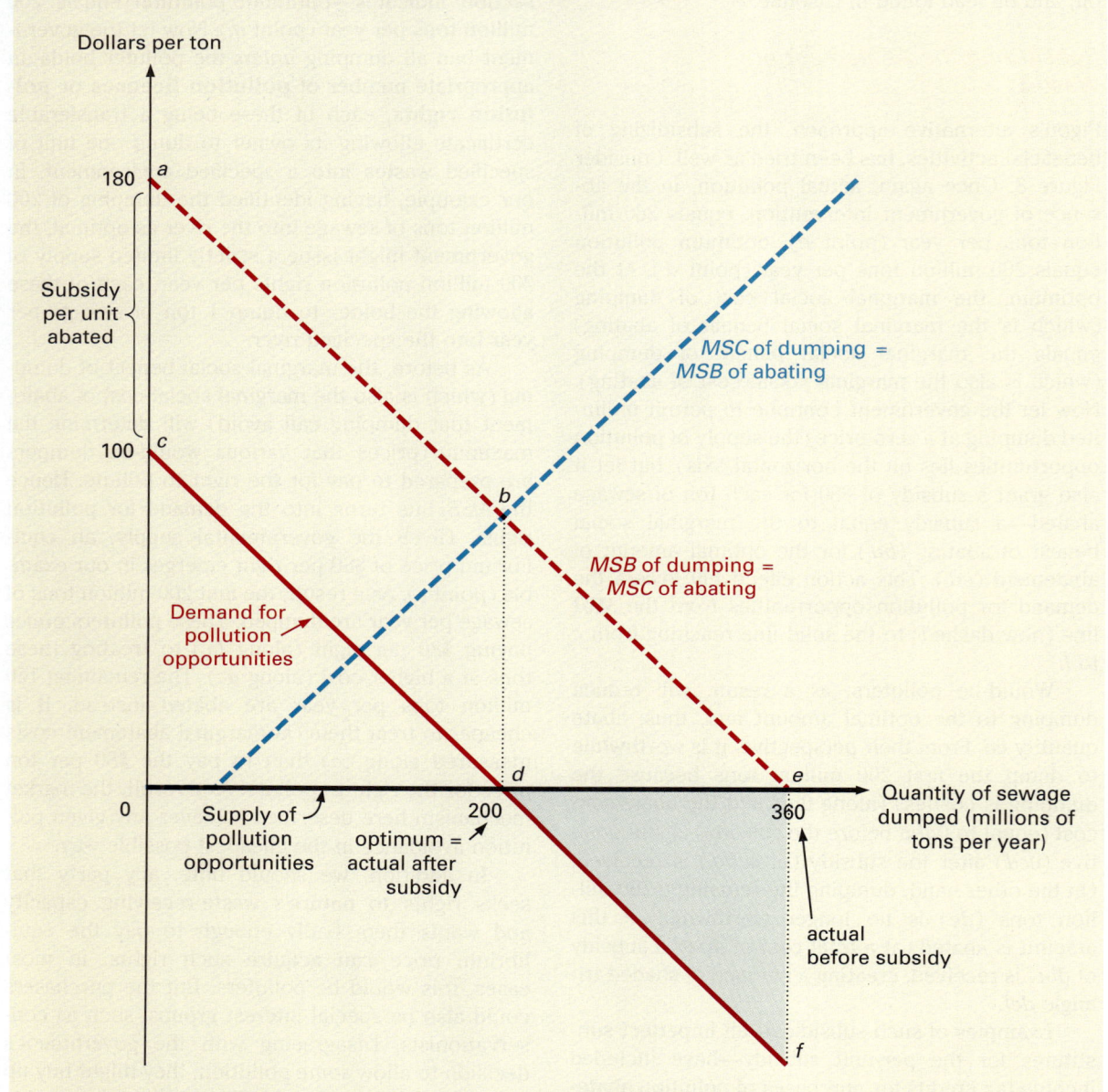

The granting of a subsidy for waste abatement (here of $80/ton) might reduce excessive pollution (point *e*) to the optimum amount (point *d*).

FIGURE 9 Marketing Pollution Rights

The creation of a market for strictly limited pollution rights might reduce excessive pollution (point e) to the optimum amount (point d).

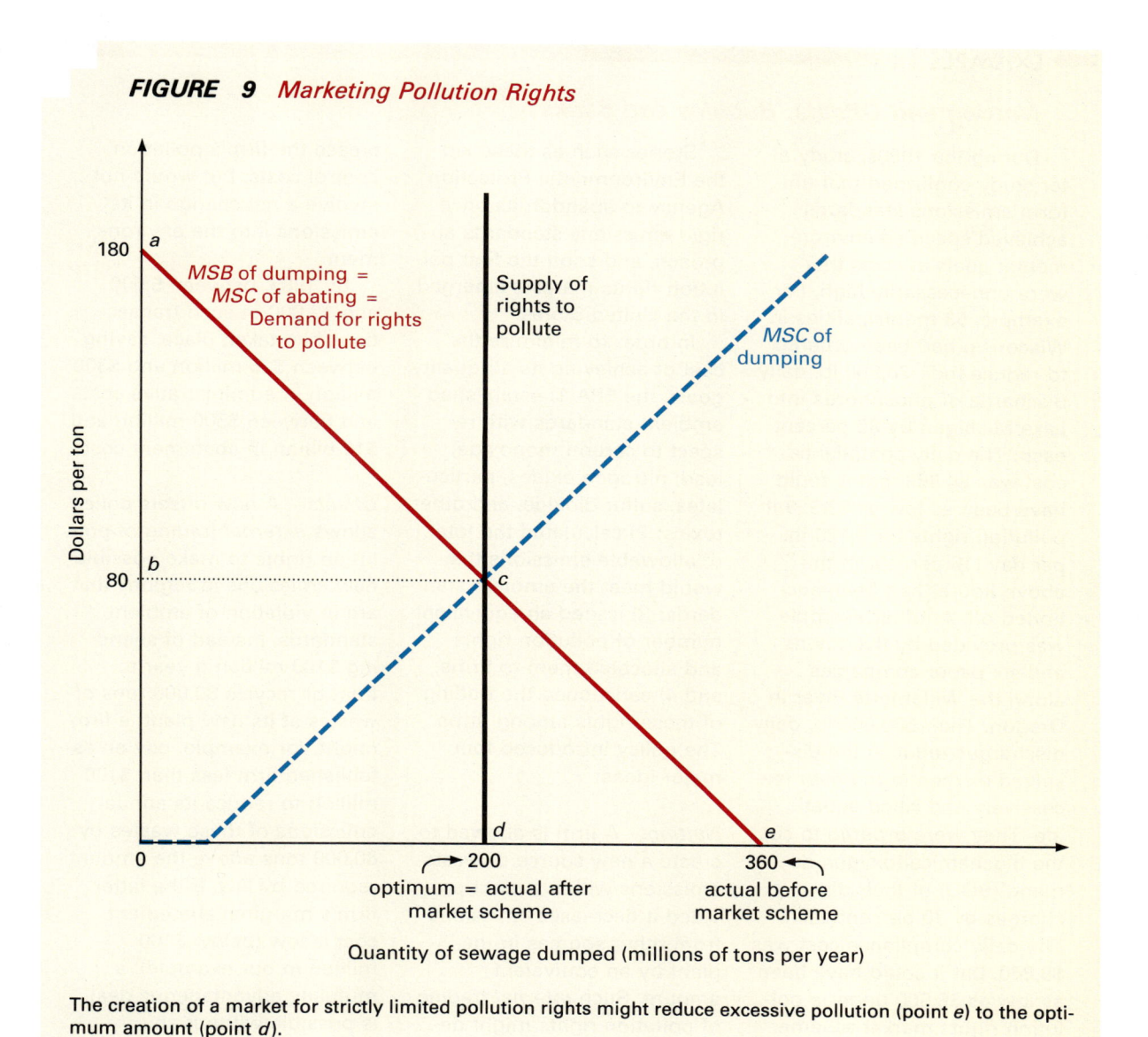

by their customers, making them aware of the social consequences of their actions. If they continue to produce and consume sulfur-dioxide-creating electric power, say, they will be able to have less of other things, such as houses or cars. And the resources released from the production of these other things will be available to carry on the abatement of sulfur-dioxide wastes. Thus, the pollution rights market helps society make a trade-off; fewer houses and cars for cleaner air. Example 4 provides a report on the first pollution rights markets in the United States. Example 5 illustrates another approach to saving nature with the help of market forces.

EXAMPLE 4

Netting and Offsets, Bubbles and Banks

During the 1980s, study after study confirmed that uniform emissions standards achieved specified environmental goals at costs that were unnecessarily high. For example, 53 municipalities in Wisconsin had been ordered to reduce their 20,800 lb. daily discharge of phosphorus into Lake Michigan by 85 percent each. The daily compliance cost was $4,880, but it could have been as low as $3,920 if pollution rights for 3,120 lb. per day (15 percent of the above figure) had been auctioned off. Another example was provided by five towns and six paper companies along the Willamette River in Oregon. Their 560,000 lb. daily discharges reduced the dissolved oxygen in the river excessively and killed aquatic life. They were ordered to cut the biochemical oxygen demand (BOD) of their discharges by 70 percent each. The daily compliance cost was $9,840, but it could have been as low as $8,500 under a pollution rights market scheme.

Stories such as these led the Environmental Protection Agency to abandon its once rigid emissions standards approach, and soon the first pollution rights markets emerged in the United States.

In order to minimize the cost of achieving its air quality goals, the EPA 1) established ambient standards with respect to carbon monoxide, lead, nitrogen oxides, particulates, sulfur dioxide, and other toxics; 2) calculated the total of allowable emissions that would meet the ambient standards; 3) issued an equivalent number of pollution rights and allocated them to firms; and 4) sanctioned the trading of these rights among firms. The policy introduced four major ideas:

Netting. A firm is allowed to create a new source of waste emissions within a plant provided it decreases emissions from other sources in the plant by an equivalent amount. Such *internal* trading of pollution rights might decrease the firm's pollution control costs, but would not involve a net change in its emissions into the environment.

By 1989, between 5,000 and 12,000 of such transactions had taken place, saving between $25 million and $300 million in administrative costs and between $500 million and $12 billion in abatement costs.

Offsets. A new offsets policy allows *external* trading of pollution rights to make possible new emissions in regions that are in violation of ambient standards. Instead of spending $100 million a year to treat or recycle 80,000 tons of wastes at its new plant, a firm might, for example, pay an established firm less than $100 million to reduce its annual emissions of these wastes by 80,000 tons *above* the amount required by law. If the latter firm's marginal abatement cost is low (below $100 million in our example), a mutually advantageous deal is possible without any adverse effect on the environment.

Thus, the state of Pennsylvania created an offset by altering its road-paving practices, which reduced hydrocarbon emissions. It then gave the pollution rights to the Volkswagen Corporation, which agreed to locate its first American production facility in a depressed region of the state. By 1989, some 1,800 of such transactions had taken place, saving hundreds of millions of dollars in pollution control costs.

Bubbles. A new bubbles policy treats all sources of waste emissions that come from a given factory, firm, or geographic area as if they were contained in a "bubble" and constituted a single emissions source. As long as the bubble as a whole meets ambient standards, each source within it is considered to be in compliance with input or emission standards. As a result, all those within the bubble can find the cheapest way of meeting environmental goals. To cut overall emissions by 50 percent, for example, they are free to cut emissions from source A by 100 percent, while not cutting emissions from source B at all. Thus, the Narraganset Electric Company of Rhode Island had been burdened with input standards specifying the use of 1 percent sulfur oil at all plants. Under the new policy, it managed to use 2.2 percent sulfur oil at one plant while another plant was either shut down or was using natural gas that doesn't contain sulfur. The savings came to $3 million per year. By 1989, some 129 such transactions had taken place, saving $135 million in pollution control costs.

Banks. In anticipation of the kinds of trades described in the previous sections, firms can also cut their present emissions by more than the law requires and get credit for this action at a new emissions bank. These credits can then be used later or sold to others. Thus, in Louisville, Kentucky, General Electric acquired several hundred tons of hydrocarbon emission credits for $60,000 from International Harvester. This allowed GE to meet emission standards without having to spend $1.5 million for an incinerator which would have been worthless in two years, when hydrocarbons would no longer be emitted. By 1989, fewer than 100 such deals had taken place. Overall savings were still small.

Sources: Randolph M. Lyon, "Auctions and Alternative Procedures for Allocating Pollution Rights," *Land Economics,* February 1982, pp. 16–32; Philip Shabecoff, "New Policy Widens Pollution 'Sales'" *The New York Times,* April 3, 1982, p. 7; Richard Greene, "Selling Dirt," *Forbes,* May 24, 1982, p. 120; Tom Tietenberg, *Environmental and Natural Resource Economics* (Glenview, IL: Scott, Foresman and Co., 1984), pp. 306–307; and Robert W. Hahn, "Economic Prescriptions for Environmental Problems: How the Patient Followed the Doctor's Orders," *Journal of Economic Perspectives,* Spring 1989, pp. 95–114.

EXAMPLE 5

Green Marketing

In 1990, Jason Clay, a self-styled "environmental entrepreneur," decided to help save the rain forest by making it more valuable in its natural state than in alternative uses, such as clearing it for cattle raising, mining, and the like. In Cambridge, Massachusetts, he founded Cultural Survival Enterprises, a firm devoted to defending people, such as the Indians of the Amazon, whose traditional culture was threatened by modern economic life. The fruits, nuts, oils, and rubber that the rain forest could produce were much more valuable than the timber gained when cutting it down, he argued. What was required was a marketing plan that provided natives with enough cash to resist loggers, miners, and ranchers alike.

Indeed, his company marketed $447,000 of rain forest products in 1990 and $4.5 million (estimated) in 1991. Companies such as Body Shop, Mars, Safeway, and Canada's Loblaw supermarket chain sold Rainforest Crunch—a brittle confection of Brazil nuts and cashews—as well as soaps and furniture polish made from rain forest oils, pigments, and resins. Plans were under way to market honey and killer-bee wax from Zambia, as well as berries, mushrooms, resins, and tars harvested by Indians throughout North America.

Source: T.A.S., "Using Market Forces to Save Nature," *Fortune*, January 14, 1991, pp. 42–43.

Summary

1. If the activities of consumers and producers do not affect third parties, marginal private benefit equals marginal social benefit, and marginal private cost equals marginal social cost. Under such circumstances, any perfectly competitive market produces an actual or equilibrium quantity ($MPB = MPC$) that is also the optimal or efficient quantity ($MSB = MSC$). This chapter, however, deals with situations involving *externalities* in which this happy coincidence is upset because marginal private and social benefits (or costs) diverge.

2. Externalities are direct effects that the actions of some consumers or producers have on the utility of other consumers or on the output of other producers, none of whom have invited these effects. Situations in which the consumption or production activities of some people impose costs in the form of decreased utility or decreased output on other people are termed *negative* externalities. On the other hand, situations in which the consumption or production activities of some people provide benefits in the form of increased utility or increased output for other people are termed *positive* externalities.

3. The British economist Pigou suggested a cure for the broken link, in the presence of externalities, between competitive markets and economic efficiency: 1) Whenever the actual level of production and consumption that the free market achieves by equating demand and supply (and, thus, by equating marginal private benefit and marginal private cost) is larger than the optimal level (that equates marginal social benefit and marginal social cost), the government should reduce the actual level to the optimal level by imposing an appropriately sized excise tax. 2) Whenever the actual level of production and consumption that the free market achieves by equating demand and supply (where $MPB = MPC$) is smaller than the optimal level (where $MSB = MSC$), government

should increase the actual level to the optimal level by granting an appropriately sized excise subsidy.

4. Pigou's analysis was challenged by Coase, who pointed out that high administrative costs might prevent Pigou's tax and subsidy schemes from working. Coase also suggested the possibility, in the presence of low transactions costs, of private efficiency-enhancing deals among parties generating or affected by externalities. In fact, according to the *Coase theorem,* under perfect competition, once government has assigned clearly defined property rights in contested resources and as long as transactions costs are negligible, private parties that generate or are affected by externalities will negotiate voluntary agreements that lead to the socially optimal resource allocation and output mix regardless of how the property rights are assigned.

5. When the conditions for Coasean deals—clearly defined property rights and negligible transactions costs—are not fulfilled, serious problems arise. The tragedy of the commons provides one example: As more and more people use a community-property resource (such as public grazing land or an ocean fishery), its quality progressively declines and it is eventually destroyed.

6. The pollution of nature provides dramatic examples of negative externalities that cannot be cured by private Coasean deals because of high transactions costs. The theory of optimum pollution lays the groundwork for curative governmental action by helping identify a socially desirable level of waste dumping. In the absence of governmental action, the actual level of dumping, however, is likely to be higher. Government intervention dealing with excess dumping can take many forms, including moral suasion, outright bans, setting standards, taxing the dumping of wastes, subsidizing the abatement of wastes, and marketing pollution rights.

Key Concepts

ambient standards
Coase theorem
emission standards
externalities
input standards
marginal external benefit, *MEB*
marginal external cost, *MEC*

marginal private benefit, *MPB*
marginal private cost, *MPC*
marginal social benefit, *MSB*
marginal social cost, *MSC*
negative externalities
neighborhood effects
optimum pollution

pollution licenses
pollution rights
positive externalities
spillover effects
transactions costs

Questions and Problems

1. What would you do about the following externalities imposed on you by your neighbors:

    a. Someone builds a house next door, the shade of which ruins your favorite sunbathing spot.

    b. Someone opens a restaurant, the smells of which drift into your home.

    c. Your neighbor's trees grow and ruin your magnificent 100-mile view.

2. Figure 2 illustrates a negative externality in

production. Invent a similar graph that depicts a negative externality in consumption, such as that caused by noisy motorcycles.

3. Have another look at Figure 2 and identify
   a. the consumer and producer surplus before the tax is imposed.
   b. the consumer and producer surplus after the tax is imposed.
   c. the tax revenue.
   d. the total private benefit, total private cost, and total private net benefit before the tax is imposed (when output equals Q_1).
   e. the total private benefit, total private cost, and total private net benefit after the tax is imposed (when output equals Q_2).
   f. the total social benefit, total social cost, and total social net benefit before the tax is imposed (when output equals Q_1).
   g. the total social benefit, total social cost, and total social net benefit after the tax is imposed (when output equals Q_2).
   h. the total harm done to outsiders when output equals Q_1 and when output equals Q_2.

4. Have another look at Figure 3 and identify
   a. the consumer and producer surplus before the subsidy is granted.
   b. the consumer and producer surplus after the subsidy is granted.
   c. the size of the subsidy.
   d. the total private benefit, total private cost, and total private net benefit before the subsidy is granted (and when output equals Q_1).
   e. the total private benefit, total private cost, and total private net benefit after the subsidy is granted (and when output equals Q_2).
   f. the total social benefit, total social cost, and total social net benefit before the subsidy is granted (and when output equals Q_1).
   g. the total social benefit, total social cost, and total social net benefit after the subsidy is granted (and when output equals Q_2).
   h. the total benefit provided to outsiders when output equals Q_1 and when output equals Q_2.

5. Coase imagined the following situation: A rancher and wheat farmer operate side by side on unfenced land. Depending on how one looks at it, each is imposing negative externalities on the other. When the farmer grows more wheat, more cultivated fields stand in the way of the cattle, and the production of meat must be restricted for lack of grazing land. When the rancher increases the size of the herd, more cattle stray onto wheat fields and trample them; thus more meat implies less wheat. The facts, let us suppose, are as follows:

Size of herd (no. of steers)	Total crop loss (tons/yr.)
0	0
1	1
2	3
3	8
4	15

Assume that each steer brings a profit of $40, that each ton of wheat brings a profit of $10, and that transactions costs are zero. Show that the Coase theorem applies once property rights are clearly assigned either to the farmer (who would have the right not to have the wheat harmed) or to the rancher (who would have the right to let the cattle roam).

6. Figure 2 shows how the imposition of an excise tax on the output of perfectly competitive producers who create negative externalities leads to an increase in total economic welfare (equal to shaded triangle *cde*). Could the same argument be made if the output in question was produced by a monopoly? Explain.

7. Have another look at Figure 3 and identify the size of the bribe that outside parties a) could afford to pay, and b) would have to pay to flower bulb consumers and producers in order to change the free market outcome to the optimal one.

8. "In 1960, Americans produced 2.7 lb. of trash per person per day. By 1990, the figure had climbed to 3.6 lb. and it is still rising. Landfills are filling up at record rates, and new ones cost $400,000 per acre to build. Clearly, we need an immediate campaign to change people's *attitudes* about trash." Evaluate the argument.

9. In 1989, California's South Coast Air Quality Management District issued new and stringent emission standards applicable to 1993 cars and slated to become even more stringent thereafter. Auto industry experts argue that the new standards would put an end to gasoline powered cars by 2007; environmentalists counter that the benefits of switching to cars powered by electricity, methanol, or natural gas far outweigh the costs. Evaluate the arguments.

10. Mr. A: The way to solve the pollution problem is to shoot all pollutants into outer space.

    Mrs. B: You are silly. Technology right here on earth will solve the pollution problem. It is already busily doing so. Consider how sawdust, which used to be a waste, is now pressed into boards. Consider how smelter gases are turned into fertilizer, how cinders become building materials, scrap turns into new steel, ground bottles pave streets and parking lots as "glasphalt," and shredded rubber tires become resilient surfaces for playgrounds. Even plastic can be made photodegradable and consequently self-destructible in direct sunlight.

    Discuss.

11. A 1991 Gallup poll showed 90 percent of Americans being interested in environmentally safe products and packages. Research the issue and determine the extent to which producers have responded.

12. There has been a great deal of concern lately about the "greenhouse effect," in which carbon dioxide released by human activities traps heat in the upper atmosphere, just as glass panes do in a greenhouse. As a result, some have predicted the earth's average temperature by the end of the 21st century will be 5.4° F higher than now, and the oceans will be 30 inches higher. This trend presents an extreme danger to some countries, such as the Netherlands (two thirds of which lies below sea level behind dykes) and the Maldives (the 1,190 low-lying islands of which could literally disappear under the Indian Ocean). What do you think should or could be done?

13. "The whole antipollution effort is an elitist thing, good mainly for the rich. Pollution avoidance costs ultimately show up in higher prices of consumer goods or in more unemployment. Since the poor consume a greater proportion of their incomes than the rich and they will be the ones thrown out of work, the poor will bear these costs disproportionately. Thus well-to-do ecology crusaders are driving the poor people right up the wall."
Evaluate.

14. Some 10–30 miles above the surface of the earth is a layer of ozone, consisting of triple oxygen atoms. The lethal wavelengths of the sun's radiation are absorbed by ozone as they split ozone into paired and single oxygen atoms (which then recombine into ozone). Without this mechanism, searing ultraviolet rays would cause skin cancer and kill all plants exposed to the atmosphere. Unfortunately, methane gas reacts with those single oxygen atoms, thereby depleting the life-preserving ozone layer. Some of this methane comes from natural sources, such as swamp decay. But most comes from human activities, including the flying of supersonic transports (SSTs) at high altitudes, coal mining, growing rice in paddy fields, and fertilizing fields with human and animal wastes. In addition, the ozone layer is being depleted by the release of chlorofluorocarbons, CFCs, that are used in air conditioners and refrigerators as well as in the making of aerosols, cleansers, and urethane foam. What do you think should or could be done?

15. The text discusses New England grazing lands and ocean fisheries as examples of the tragedy of the commons. Can you think of any other examples?

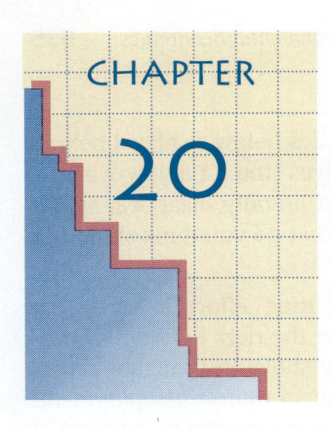

CHAPTER 20
PUBLIC GOODS AND PUBLIC CHOICES

Preview

This chapter focuses on the production and consumption of goods that generate positive externalities to such an extreme degree that literally every member of society can enjoy their benefits at the same time. Moreover, the consumption of such goods by any one person in no way reduces their availability to other people. Such goods are called pure public goods; *national defense or clean air are examples. The crucial role of government in providing such goods is discussed in detail; so is the real possibility that government will fail to provide optimal quantities of such goods.*

Examples

1. Computer Software: A Public Good
2. Breaking Out of the Prison Crisis
3. Privatizing Public School Functions
4. Privatizing Space Projects

As the previous chapter has shown, when households consume or firms produce goods, the effects of these activities may well spill over onto the lives of their neighbors. At some times, these external parties may be able to snatch free benefits; at other times, they may become the reluctant bearers of unwanted costs. A certain degree of publicness is thus attached to many goods. Many goods, clearly, are not **pure private goods** that generate no externalities and, therefore, are characterized by the fact that their buyers and sellers are the only persons affected by the benefits and costs associated with them. The present chapter takes our earlier discussion a step further by focusing on **pure public goods**. Such goods generate *positive* externalities and do so to an extreme degree; they affect not only a few individuals, but literally all members of society at the same time.

The Nature of Public Goods

Picture any society, large or small. It may consist of all the residents of a town, a state, a nation, or any other grouping. A good is considered a pure public good with respect to that society if it provides *nonexcludable* and *nonrival* benefits to all members of that society. We will consider these two characteristics in turn.

Nonexcludability

The concept of **nonexcludability** refers to the property of a pure public good that makes it physically impossible or extremely costly to exclude any individual from the enjoyment of the good once a given amount of it has been produced. Once a given quantity of the good has been made available to even one person, its benefits are also available to all other persons in that society—automatically, simultaneously, and regardless of whether any particular person is making a payment for the privilege. The good's benefits indivisibly accrue to all.

Consider the production of national defense. Once this good has been produced and regardless of the form it takes—whether potential enemies are being deterred by missiles buried in silos, by tanks on the ground, by ships at sea, by planes in the air, or even by laser weapons in outer space—there is no practical way to exclude any individual citizen from the good's benefits. The very act of producing the good makes it instantly and equally available to all.

Consider, in contrast, the production of pure private goods, such as apples or cars, houses or shoes. It is very easy to provide amounts of such goods to some people but not to other people. In our market economy, people who do not pay such a good's price do not get any amount of it; they are effectively excluded from the good's benefits.

Nonrivalness

The concept of **nonrivalness** refers to the property of a pure public good that allows additional persons to consume the good without reducing the good's availability to others. Pure public goods are simply nondepletable. The appearance of additional consumers does not detract from the continued consumption by others. National defense, once again, provides a perfect example. Once a given amount of national defense is being produced, it does not matter whether its beneficiaries number 10 or 1,000, whether there are 50 million citizens or 190 million of them. If one person is protected, all are protected; if the population grows by 7 percent during the year, the level of protection enjoyed by the original group does not diminish on that account.

Consider, in contrast, how different all this is with respect to private goods. Given the annual production of apples, cars, houses, or shoes, the consumption of any one person does reduce the amounts available to other persons; the growth of the population does increase the degree of scarcity prevailing.

Examples

Examples of goods that share the characteristics of nonexcludability and nonrivalness abound. On the national level, consider, in addition to military security, the broadcasting of (unscrambled) radio and television signals, a clean natural environment, a drug-free society, economic justice (to be discussed in the next chapter), the rule of law and order, the preservation of wildlife, sound money, and weather forecasts. Public goods in smaller societies include city beautification projects, crime control, fire protection, fireworks displays, flood control, lighthouses, open air concerts, snow removal on public roads, the town hall clock, townwide mosquito control, and traffic lights. In all these cases and many more it is next to impossible to withhold the benefits from any particular person: My clean air is your clean air; my weather forecast is yours, my snow-free road is yours as well. Nor do additional consumers reduce what others can have. If more people tune in on Channel 3 or glance at the town hall clock, others are not prevented from doing the same thing at the same time. Example 1 has more to say on the subject.

Public Goods and Market Failure

In the previous chapter, we noted that competitive markets, if left to themselves, will underproduce goods with positive externalities. In the absence of government intervention, such goods will be produced in actual amounts that equate marginal private benefit with marginal private cost, but fall short of the optimum quantities at which marginal social benefit and marginal social cost are equal (where the social net benefit is maximized). It was for this reason that Pigou recommended governmental subsidies to encourage a greater production and consumption of such beneficial goods. Because pure public goods involve positive externalities to an extreme degree, it is not surprising that last chapter's problem reappears with a vengeance here: Competitive markets don't merely underproduce pure public goods—they do not produce them at all. As far as the provision of pure public goods is concerned, the competitive market fails altogether. It is easy to see why.

The Free-Rider Problem

Producers of a pure private good can recover the costs incurred in its production for a simple reason. Once it is produced, such a good can be withheld

EXAMPLE 1

Computer Software: A Public Good

Computer software typically meets both of the conditions that characterize public goods. First, there is nonexcludability. Once a program has been created for one person, others can be relied upon quickly to make copies for their own use and can do so at almost no cost. There is no practical way to prevent them from enjoying the full benefits of the program. Second, there is nonrivalness. As is true of scientific knowledge, mathematical formulas, and similar creations of the mind, the use of a computer program by one person does in no way prevents others from using it at the same time. There is no fixed quantity that must somehow be apportioned among rival consumers whose use gradually depletes the available stock.

True enough, creators of software do their best to turn it into a private good. Programs can be copyprotected, but the codes involved can fairly easily be broken and the requisite knowledge spreads quickly among computer users. Why then does any private production of software take place? Here are some possible answers:

1. Some creators apply moral suasion. They appeal to people's consciences: "By breaking this seal you promise not to allow anyone to make copies." Thousands of people are thus deterred from making or accepting illegal copies. Institutional buyers, such as college libraries, in particular, pay hundreds of dollars for items that could be copied for 50 cents.

2. Other creators freely give away their programs. They even urge recipients to make copies and pass them on. Once a user runs the program, however, a message appears, asking for voluntary contributions. Amazingly, thousands of users respond.

3. Computer software is often "bundled" with other items, such as college textbooks. Their price is included in the companion item.

4. Creators of software rely on the fact that at least some users will respect the copyright laws. Again, this is most likely to be true of institutional buyers, such as college libraries.

---

from potential consumers unless an appropriate payment is made. As we have now seen, the nature of a pure public good is such that it is intrinsically impossible, or extremely costly, to confine its use to selected persons. Since the persons producing the good are unable to exclude others from its benefits, such producers have a tough time insisting on compensation payments by the outsiders so favored. "We won't pay," they can say, "and if you don't like it, withhold the benefit from us." Being unable to do so, the benefit-producing persons have to share the benefit with the happy freeloaders. However, benefit-producing persons who do not want to share the benefit with others can simply not engage in the benefit-producing activity at all. They can decide to withhold the benefit from others by also withholding it from themselves. More often than not, this is exactly what people do. That is why the private provision of pure public goods is unlikely to occur.

The unwillingness of individuals to pay for the production of pure public goods and their eagerness to let others produce such goods so that they can enjoy the associated spillover of benefits at zero cost, is called the **free-rider problem**. The name comes to us from the days of cattle rustling in the Old West. At one time, the ranchers of Dodge City got together to form a vigilante group to catch and hang cattle thieves. Initially, everyone contributed to the cost of a security force on horseback and its existence quickly discouraged the cattle thieves. Then individual ranchers realized that they could benefit just as much from the newly produced good—law and order—if they didn't pay their dues. They became "free riders." As more and more ranchers followed the same line of thinking, the security force collapsed and cattle rustling resumed. Thus, the rational behavior of each rancher (reaching for a marginal benefit at a zero marginal cost) led to the irrational behavior of the entire group. This is the kind of situation in which government can help.

Public Finance

Instead of being paralyzed by the free-rider problem, the potential beneficiaries of pure public goods can agree mutually to coerce themselves. They can create a government and endow it with coercive powers for the very purpose of securing the social net benefit that the public good might bring and that would otherwise have to be forgone. A government can procure public goods through **public finance,** or the collection of taxes from all those believed to benefit from the provision of pure public goods and the subsequent channeling of these funds toward the production of such goods, either by government agencies or private firms. (In the latter case, as economists put it, the creation of pure public goods involves government *provision,* but private *production.*)

Consider the case of our Dodge City ranchers. If cattle rustling cost a group of 100 ranchers animal losses worth $10,000 a year (a huge sum in those days) and if such thievery could be stopped by a security force costing $2,000 a year, a social net benefit of $8,000 could be procured. A government could tax every rancher $20 a year, a public or private security force could be hired with the tax revenue, and ranchers as a group could receive a net benefit four times the cost.

CAUTION

> *Governments often arrange for the tax-financed production not only of pure public goods but also of all kinds of other goods that do not possess the characteristics of nonexcludability and nonrivalness. Some of these may be associated with externalities; others may be pure private goods. Consider, at the federal level, commodity stockpiling, postal service, printing, shipbuilding, railroad transportation, social security, and veterans' hospitals. Consider, at the state level, unemployment insurance, liquor retailing, gambling, mental institutions, old-age homes, and universities. Consider, at the local level, public buses, cemeteries, golf courses, housing, libraries, schools, sports facilities, and zoos. In all of these cases, it would be easy to withhold benefits from nonpaying would-be consumers (nonexcludability does not apply); nor are the goods inexhaustible (nonrivalness does not apply). Indeed, some of these goods are produced by government agencies in competition with private firms and sold at market prices. More often than not, however, such goods are financed by government with taxes, produced by government agencies, and then supplied at subsidized prices or even free of charge to selected consumers on the grounds that all citizens merit a minimum share of them, which is why such goods are called* **merit goods.** *In this chapter, however, we focus only on the government's provision of pure public goods.*

The Optimum Quantity of a Pure Public Good

In theory, it is easy to determine the optimum quantity of a pure public good. As in the case of optimum pollution, the process involves little more than a systematic comparison of the marginal social cost *MSC* with the marginal social benefit *MSB* of alternative quantities. Figure 1 illustrates the principle. As long as fewer than 10 units of the goods are being produced, the marginal social benefits (along *ae*) of providing additional units exceed the associated marginal social costs (along *be*). Providing additional units allows people to reap the differences between the two; that is, the marginal social net benefits such as *ab* or *cd*. By the time 10 units are produced, the total social benefit (or the sum of all the marginal benefits) equals 0*aeh*, the total social cost (or the sum of all the marginal costs) equals 0*beh*, and the total social net benefit is maximized as the shaded area *aeb*. This is equivalent, in our earlier example, to Dodge City ranchers reaping a total benefit of $10,000 (a reduction in cattle thefts) at a total cost of $2,000 (the cost of their security force), giving them a total net benefit of $8,000.

By the same token, our graph tells us, it is fool-

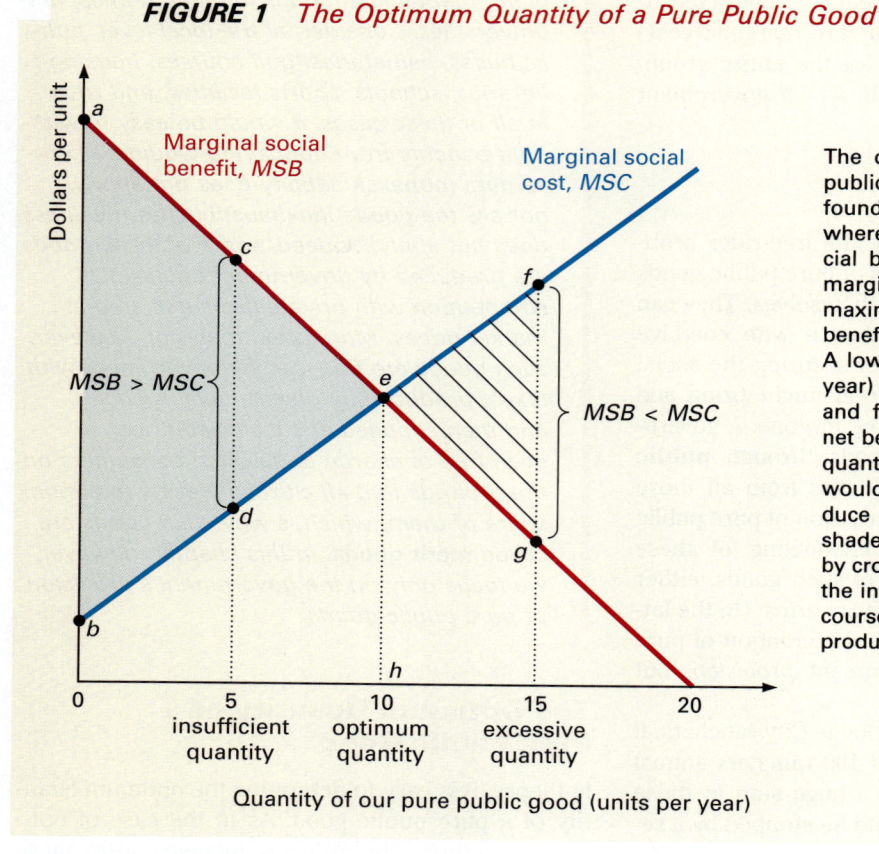

FIGURE 1 The Optimum Quantity of a Pure Public Good

The optimum quantity of a pure public good (here 10 units/year) is found at the point (here at e) where the declining marginal social benefit just equals the rising marginal social cost. This quantity maximizes the total social net benefit (here as shaded area aeb). A lower quantity (such as 5 units/year) would leave $MSB > MSC$ and forgo some of the potential net benefit (such as ced). A higher quantity (such as 15 units/year) would yield $MSB < MSC$ and reduce the net benefit below the shaded maximum (for example, by crosshatched area efg). Without the intervention of government, of course, a zero quantity would be produced.

ish to produce more than 10 units of the public good. Once more than 10 units are produced, the marginal social benefits (along eg) fall short of the associated marginal social costs (along ef). Thus, the total social net benefit (maximized at aeb) begins to decline by the differences. For example, if 15 units of the good are produced, the total social net benefit equals shaded area aeb (a gain reaped from the first 10 units) *minus* crosshatched area efg (a loss associated with the next 5 units).

What is easy enough in theory, however, is often difficult in practice because it is hard to identify the marginal social benefits associated with alternative quantities of pure public goods. After all, consumers do not reveal what alternative units of such goods are worth to them by voluntarily spending money on them as they routinely do in private goods markets. Nor is it easy—in the absence of competition—to bring about the production of any given quantity of pure public goods at the lowest possible cost. Finally, as we will see, there are frequently strong incentives for government officials to push the actual quantity of public goods provided beyond the optimum, even if that optimum can be identified.

The Elusive Marginal Social Benefit

Figure 2 illustrates the nature of the marginal social benefit associated with a pure public good. For simplicity we assume that there are only two individuals in a given society, but what we are about to discuss can easily be extended to any number of people. The marginal private benefits that our two individuals derive from alternative units of a pure public good are illustrated in panels (a) and (b), respectively. Individual 1, for example, receives a marginal private benefit of $a = \$10$ from a first unit of the public good and would, presumably, pay a maximum of $10 for such a unit if it were offered for sale in the same way that private goods are. The same individual, similarly, would receive the additional marginal private benefits indicated by blocks b through e from additional units of the good.

The shaded blocks in panel (b) refer to individual 2 and can be similarly interpreted. Individual 2 has different tastes and that person's marginal private benefits are illustrated by shaded blocks f through j.

Panel (c) combines the two individuals' marginal private benefits and derives the line of marginal social benefit. As the labeling and shading of the various blocks indicate, a *vertical* summation of the marginal private benefits is called for. This is so

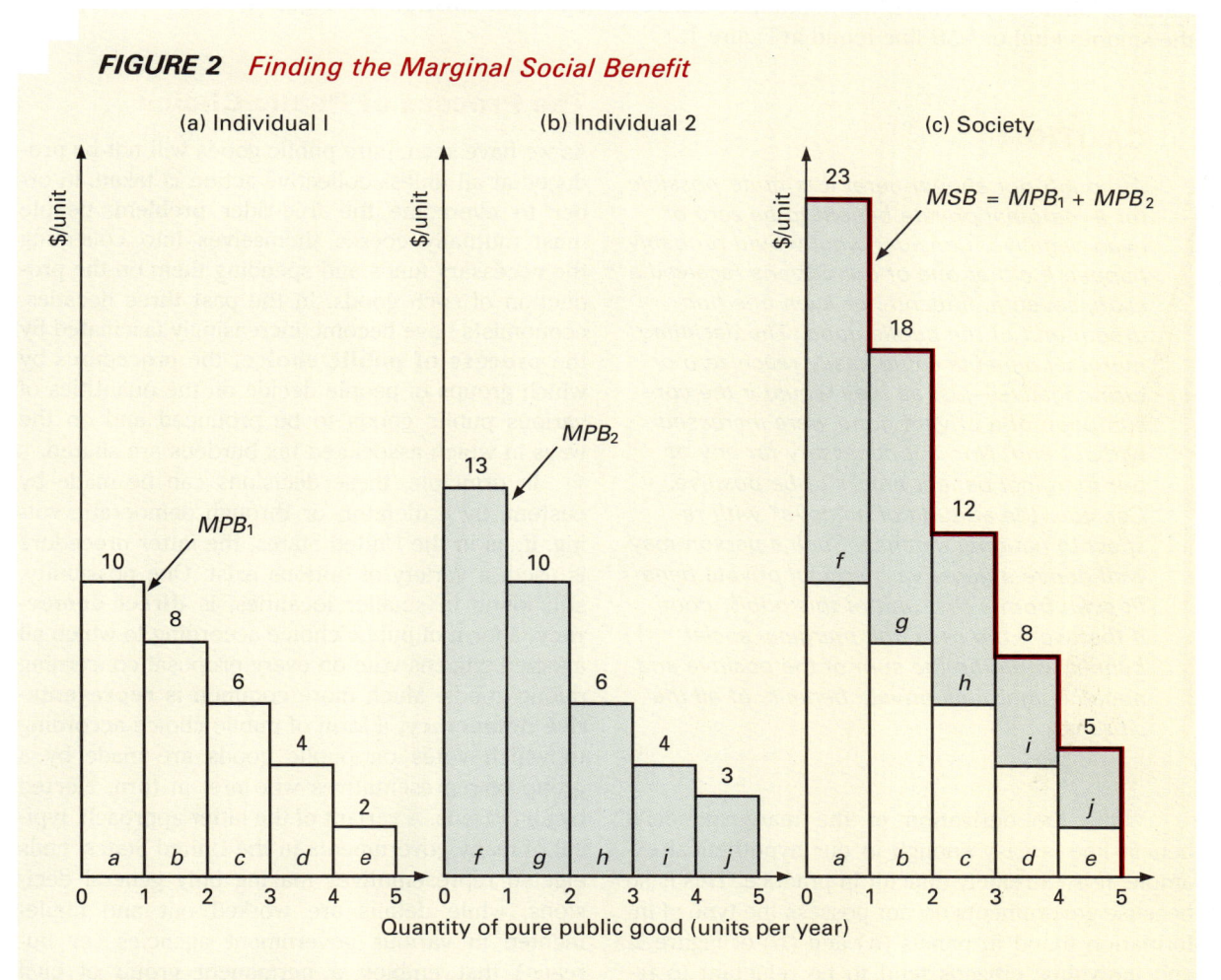

FIGURE 2 Finding the Marginal Social Benefit

The marginal social benefits associated with alternative quantities of a pure public good can be derived by the vertical summation of the marginal private benefits received by all members of the society in question.
Note: What appear to be 10 different units of the good in panels (a) and (b) are really only 5 units, each being consumed by both individuals at the same time. Therefore, the total quantity shown in panel (c) is also 5, and not 10.

because the first unit of the public good consumed by individual 1 is the same unit that is *simultaneously* consumed by individual 2. Thus, the first unit yields a marginal social benefit of $23 (which equals $a + f$). The second unit consumed by individual 1 is, similarly, identical to the second unit consumed by individual 2; hence its marginal social benefit equals $18 (or $b + g$). And so it goes for all the other units. In the end, we derive the *MSB* line in panel (c). Naturally, its stair-step appearance is the result of our simplified example that considers only a two-person society. Had we considered thousands or millions of people, we would have derived the smooth kind of *MSB* line found in Figure 1.

CAUTION

Although not shown here, it is quite possible for a marginal private benefit to be zero or even negative. Consider what would probably happen if either one of our citizens received a sixth, seventh, fifteenth, or even one hundredth unit of the public good. The declining marginal benefits could easily reach zero or turn negative—just as they would if the consumption of a private good were increased without end. Nor is it necessary for any of our marginal benefit blocks to be positive. Consider the attitude of a "dove" with respect to national defense. Such a person may well derive a negative marginal private benefit even from a first unit of this public good. If that were the case, the marginal social benefit would be the sum of the positive and negative marginal private benefits of all the citizens.

While the derivation of the marginal social benefit line is easy enough in our hypothetical example, it is extremely difficult in practice. This is so because governments do not possess the type of information found in panels (a) and (b) of Figure 2, and individual citizens tend to be reluctant to reveal it. If you were individual 1 and the government asked you how much a first, second, third, fourth, or even fifth unit of a certain public good is worth to you, you would be unlikely to answer $10, $8, $6, $4, and $2. You would quite rightly suspect that the next step would be the imposition of corresponding taxes and you would, therefore, have a strong incentive to understate the benefits you expect to get from the public good. Your fellow citizens would do the same thing. Hence the government would be unable to derive the line of marginal social benefit (as in panel (c) of Figure 2) or to equate the marginal social benefit with the associated marginal social cost (as in Figure 1) and then arrange for the production of the optimum quantity. As a result, real-world procedures for selecting the quantities of public goods to be produced are unlikely to find the optimum illustrated in Figure 1.

The Process of Public Choice

As we have seen, pure public goods will not be produced at all unless collective action is taken. In order to overcome the free-rider problem, people must mutually coerce themselves into collecting the necessary funds and spending them on the production of such goods. In the past three decades, economists have become increasingly fascinated by the **process of public choice,** the procedures by which groups of people decide on the quantities of various public goods to be produced and on the ways in which associated tax burdens are shared.

In principle, these decisions can be made by custom, by a dictator, or through democratic voting. If, as in the United States, the latter procedure is used, a variety of options exist. One possibility, still found in smaller localities, is **direct democracy,** a form of public choice according to which all affected citizens vote on every proposal concerning public goods. Much more common is **representative democracy,** a form of public choice according to which votes on public goods are made by a group of representatives who are, in turn, elected by all citizens. A variant of the latter approach, typical of many governments in the United States, finds elected representatives making only general decisions, while details are worked out and implemented in various government agencies (or bureaus) that employ a permanent group of civil servants, called **bureaucrats.** Members of the U.S. Congress, for example, allocate budgets to various executive departments or regulatory agencies, such as the Department of Agriculture, the Department of Defense, the Consumer Product Safety Commission, or the Food and Drug Administration, while the bureaucrats involved decide on the nature and extent of particular projects to be carried out.

No matter which public choice procedure is used, the likelihood of identifying and providing optimal quantities of pure public goods is quite low. The provision of nonoptimal quantities of pure public goods, which is called **government failure,** can be traced directly to problems that are inherent in the process of majority voting, in the delegation of authority, and in the nature of bureaucracy. We will consider each of these in turn.

Majority Voting

Consider a New England town meeting in which all adult citizens meet to decide governmental issues by simple majority vote. Even in such a direct democracy, it is far from certain that optimum amounts of pure public goods will be procured. A series of examples will illustrate the point.

Ignorant Voters

When people spend their hard-earned money on private goods in a variety of markets, they have a strong incentive to be well informed: A wrong decision affects them personally and immediately. Thus, they read labels; they study consumer magazines; they experiment with different products; they even buy advice. Voting at the ballot box, rather than voting with dollars in the market is, however, an altogether different thing. Even in relatively small groups of, say, 100 voters, people realize that their individual ballots will have a negligible effect on the overall outcome of any vote. A single ballot will make a difference only when there is a majority of one—when all other voters are evenly split on an issue—and this will rarely happen. So why should any one voter expend the time and effort to become informed on any given issue of public policy? The marginal benefit, as we have seen, is certainly questionable; the marginal cost is not. Utility-maximizing voters, economists suggest, will remain ignorant—and quite rationally so.

Nevertheless, people may vote in all their ignorance. On the day that the new police station comes up for a vote, certain superficial benefits and costs may loom large. There may be the benefit of having a friendly chat with one's neighbors at the polling place or the joyful feeling that comes with a civic duty performed. There may be a negligible cost of casting that vote if the weather is fine and the polling place is near. Yet more important benefits and costs will be misjudged. Public goods that have easily identifiable benefits, but concealed and large costs (that our ill-informed voters do not see), will be voted in without a second thought. Other such goods that have obvious costs, but harder-to-identify and larger benefits, will be voted down.

Apathetic Voters

Instead of voting ignorantly, many eligible voters do not bother to vote at all. That is likely to happen when the costs of voting are high (the weather is bad, the polling place is far away) and offsetting benefits from the act of voting itself are nowhere to be found. But the absence of many voters is a boon to special-interest groups. Under such circumstances, a well-organized minority can provide itself with great benefits from a government project and do so at the expense of the apathetic voters, each of whom has little to lose. It is far from certain that such an outcome is socially optimal.

The Suppression of Minority Interests

Voting in the presence of general voter apathy allows a minority of citizens to cast a majority of votes and to suppress the interests of the majority. But it is just as possible for a majority of citizens to suppress the interests of the minority. Consider a situation in which all citizens are well informed on an issue and actually vote. Table 1 illustrates how majority voting inevitably suppresses the interest of a minority. Each individual citizen in this 5-person town, we assume, casts a vote based on a comparison of the private benefit and the private cost that the proposed public good is expected to bring to that citizen. In Case I, accordingly, voters A, B, and C vote in favor of the pollution-control project; each voter expects a positive private net benefit. Voters D and E, similarly, vote against the project, expecting negative private net benefits. Yet the project wins approval by a vote of 3:2. Whether they like it or not, those who voted against the project (D and E) will still have to pay their $300 share of taxes each—despite the fact that their personal benefits

TABLE 1 A Town's Vote on Pollution Control

Case I: Social Net Benefit Is Positive

Voters	Expected benefit	Expected cost (tax)	Expected net benefit	Vote
A	$600	$300	$300	for
B	500	300	200	for
C	400	300	100	for
D	200	300	−100	against
E	100	300	−200	against
Total	$1,800	$1,500	$300	for (3:2)

Case II: Social Net Benefit Is Negative

Voters	Expected benefit	Expected cost (tax)	Expected net benefit	Vote
A	$340	$300	$40	for
B	330	300	30	for
C	310	300	10	for
D	200	300	−100	against
E	100	300	−200	against
Total	$1,280	$1,500	−$220	for (3:2)

Under a system of majority voting, a majority (voters A, B, and C here) can easily harm a minority (voters D and E). The net benefit that the majority receives from the public good being voted in may exceed the net cost imposed upon the minority, making the social net benefit positive. (Note the encircled $300 in Case I.) The reverse, however, can also be true: The net benefit that the majority receives can fall short of the net cost that the minority is made to bear, which makes the social net benefit negative. (Note the encircled −$220 in Case II.)

from the project are less. As it happens, the *social net benefit* is positive because the $600 net gain of the majority exceeds the $300 net loss of the minority (note the encircled $300 in the table which indicates the difference between the net gain of one group and the net loss of the other).

Case II illustrates another possibility. Once again, the interests of the minority are suppressed, but this time the social net benefit is actually negative; note the encircled −$220 in the table. The $80 net gain of the majority is more than swallowed up by the $300 net loss of the minority.

The Table 1 example illustrates how different the process of public choice is from the process of private choice that goes on in the marketplace. If 60 percent of shoppers want television sets and 40 percent want bicycles, both groups will be satisfied in due proportion to the *dollar* votes cast. Some will receive television sets, others bicycles. Not so in the public domain. If 60 percent of voters want a new sewage treatment plant and 40 percent would rather do other things, then 100 percent of the people will get the sewage treatment plant and 100 percent of them will be made to pay for it. Indeed, things can be even worse than that.

The Arbitrariness of Results

On many occasions, the outcome of majority voting depends not at all on the preferences of the voters

TABLE 2 *A Winning Combination*

Voters	I. Voting on pollution control			II. Voting on crime control			III. Combined voting on pollution and crime control		
	Benefit	Cost	Vote	Benefit	Cost	Vote	Benefit	Cost	Vote
A	$600	$300	for	$600	$500	for	$1,200	$800	for
B	400	300	for	450	500	against	850	800	for
C	200	300	against	700	500	for	900	800	for
D	100	300	against	200	500	against	300	800	against
E	50	300	against	100	500	against	150	800	against
Total	$1,350	$1,500	against (3:2)	$2,050	$2,500	against (3:2)	$3,400	$4,000	for (3:2)

Under a system of majority voting, it is possible for government projects that would be voted down, if considered separately (cases I and II) to be approved when considered together (case III). The opposite can also happen; projects that would be approved, if considered separately, could easily lose in a combination vote.

but on the way the vote is carried out. When people vote on several issues at once rather than separately, or when they vote in one sequence rather than another, different outcomes can emerge.

Table 2 illustrates how government projects that would be voted down, if considered separately, may, nevertheless, be approved if considered together. If our five hypothetical voters considered their expected benefits and costs and then voted only on pollution control, the project would lose 3:2. The same would happen in a vote on crime control. Yet, in a combined vote (each person's benefits are added together and each person's costs are added together), a majority would *approve* the two projects. Thus, the outcome depends, quite arbitrarily, on the particular voting procedure that is employed.

Table 3 provides an illustration of what is now a well-known fact: When there is a choice among three or more alternatives, and even though all voters have a fixed set of preference rankings, a system of majority voting can lead to absolutely any outcome—depending solely on the *sequence* in which votes are taken. Consider three voters (A, B, and C) who have to choose one of three potential government projects: pollution control, crime con-

trol, or flood control. As the table indicates, voter A ranks the pollution-control project first, the crime-control project second, and the flood-control project last. Voters B and C have different preferences.

Now consider what would happen if a vote were taken pitting pollution control against crime control. Voter A would vote for pollution control; so would C, but not B. The pollution-control project would carry the day by a vote of 2:1. Having eliminated crime control, a second vote could then pit pollution control against flood control. As you can see in our table, voter A would prefer pollution control, but B and C would prefer flood control. Hence *flood control would be the ultimate winner*.

Yet a clever manager of the voting process could achieve quite a different result. Let the first vote pit pollution control against flood control; flood control would win. Let a second vote pit the winner—flood control—against the remaining alternative—crime control. Because A and B would prefer it to flood control, *crime control would be the ultimate winner*.

A third possibility exists as well. Let the first vote consider crime control versus flood control. Crime control would win and flood control would be eliminated. Let a second vote pit the winner—

TABLE 3 Results Depend on Voting Sequence

Voter	Preference ranking		
	1st	2nd	3rd
A	Pollution control	Crime control	Flood control
B	Crime control	Flood control	Pollution control
C	Flood control	Pollution control	Crime control

Under a system of majority voting, the order in which votes are taken can determine the result.

now crime control—against the remaining alternative, now pollution control. Because A and C would prefer it to crime control, *pollution control would be the ultimate winner.*

Which of our three voting sequences correctly reveals the society's preferences? There is no answer. Indeed, this **voting paradox**—that under democratic majority voting the winning choice among three or more alternatives will differ depending on the sequence in which votes are taken—was noted over 200 years ago by the Marquis de Condorcet, a French social philosopher; it was recently highlighted by Kenneth Arrow (born 1921 and recipient of the 1972 Nobel Prize in economics).

Possible Remedies

A number of possible remedies for the problems we have just discussed do exist. The harming of minority interests by majorities that is illustrated in Table 1, for example, could be eliminated by insisting that all votes be unanimous, while also allowing the buying and selling of votes. In Case I of Table 1, the majority of voters (A, B, and C), who stand to reap a net gain of $600 from the pollution-control project, would have to buy the votes of minority voters D and E, who stand to incur a net loss of $300. Their votes, clearly, could be purchased for $300 or more. Thus the Case I project with the positive social net benefit would be carried out, but without harming anyone. In contrast, the Case II project would not be carried out because the majority of potential winners (with a mere net gain of $80) could not possibly bribe the minority of potential losers (with a net loss of $300) to vote for the project.

When the number of voters is large, a systematic vote-buying scheme is unlikely to work because of high transactions costs. In such a case, **logrolling,** or the occasional exchange between voters of support on one issue now in return for similar support on another issue later, might be of help. In Case II of Table 1, for example, Voter E has a lot to lose ($200), while voter C has very little to gain ($10). Voter E might secure a defeat of the pollution-control program by persuading C to vote against it in return for a similar favor.

The voting-sequence problem illustrated in Table 3 might be dealt with by **strategic voting,** a procedure by which voters attempt to achieve their most preferred outcome by selectively misrepresenting their preferences. Consider the voting sequence of pollution control vs. crime control, followed by pollution control vs. flood control, in which flood control is the ultimate winner. Voter A, for whom flood control is least preferred, might change this outcome by first voting for crime control—*contrary* to true preferences. As a result, crime control would win and would then be pitted against flood control. If everyone then voted true preferences, the ultimate outcome would be crime control—preferable to flood control as far as A is concerned.

Unfortunately for A, others can play this game as well; hence the outcome of strategic voting is uncertain. Other procedures can often overcome this uncertainty. They include the replacement of majority voting by **rank-order voting** or **plurality voting,** a procedure in which each voter ranks n projects from 1 (most preferred) to n (least preferred). Then the votes are added together and the lowest number wins. (In the Table 3 example, this procedure is of little help because it yields precisely 6 points for each of the three projects.) Another possibility yet is **point voting,** a procedure in which each voter is given n points that can be allocated at the voter's discretion to potential projects, the votes are added together, and the largest number wins. This procedure takes the *intensity* of voters' feelings into account. Thus, a voter who really wanted the pollution-control project to pass could allocate all of, say, 100 available points to that project, and then not vote on any other issue.

Delegating Authority

Within large groups of people, direct democracy is typically abandoned in favor of representative democracy. As a result, people cease to vote on government projects directly; they vote instead for political candidates who later do the project voting for them. It is easy to see why this delegation of authority is also responsible for a highly imperfect revelation and subsequent satisfaction of people's preferences for pure public goods.

Economists believe that elected representatives, like all people, are engaged in behavior designed to maximize their personal welfare rather than some so-called common good. First and foremost, elected representatives will be keenly interested in preserving their jobs, which means doing whatever it takes to maximize votes in favor of their own future candidacy. As long as the adoption of a proposed government project is believed to bring more votes from people who are pleased (the marginal benefit) than it detracts from people who are annoyed (the marginal cost), a representative is likely to favor the project. Whenever possible, representatives will, of course, reduce the risk of serious vote loss by making vague statements and adopting ambiguous platforms that are nearly indistinguishable from those of their political competitors. As a result, the voters in a representative democracy find themselves voting, on rare occasions, for candidates promising an ill-defined combination of policies. Thus they have all the more reason to remain rationally ignorant on matters of public policy or to abstain from voting. Elected officials, in turn, have all the more leeway in making decisions about public goods that have little to do with the theoretical optimum that we identified in Figure 1.

The Nature of Bureaucracy

There is a third reason for the government's failure to identify and provide optimum quantities of public goods. It has to do with the fact, noted earlier, that elected representatives of the people make general budgetary allocations but then, in turn, delegate much of their power to government bureaucrats. Once again, economists suspect that the behavior of bureaucrats (just like that of elected officials, voters, business executives, or ordinary consumers) is best explained by their desire to maximize their personal welfare. James Buchanan (born 1919 and recipient of the 1986 Nobel Prize in economics), for example, has argued that this view of bureaucrats has a vastly greater explanatory power than an alternative view that describes their actions as driven by a desire to perform "impartial service for the common good." Above all else, says Buchanan, bureaucrats seek to maximize their personal welfare by preserving and advancing their own careers. In a typical government bureaucracy, the achievement of personal goals is closely related to the agency's budget. As a result, the bureaucrats' personal interests translate into a strong desire for large and growing budgets. So far as the agency's budget is concerned, more is always better.

FIGURE 3 *Internalities*

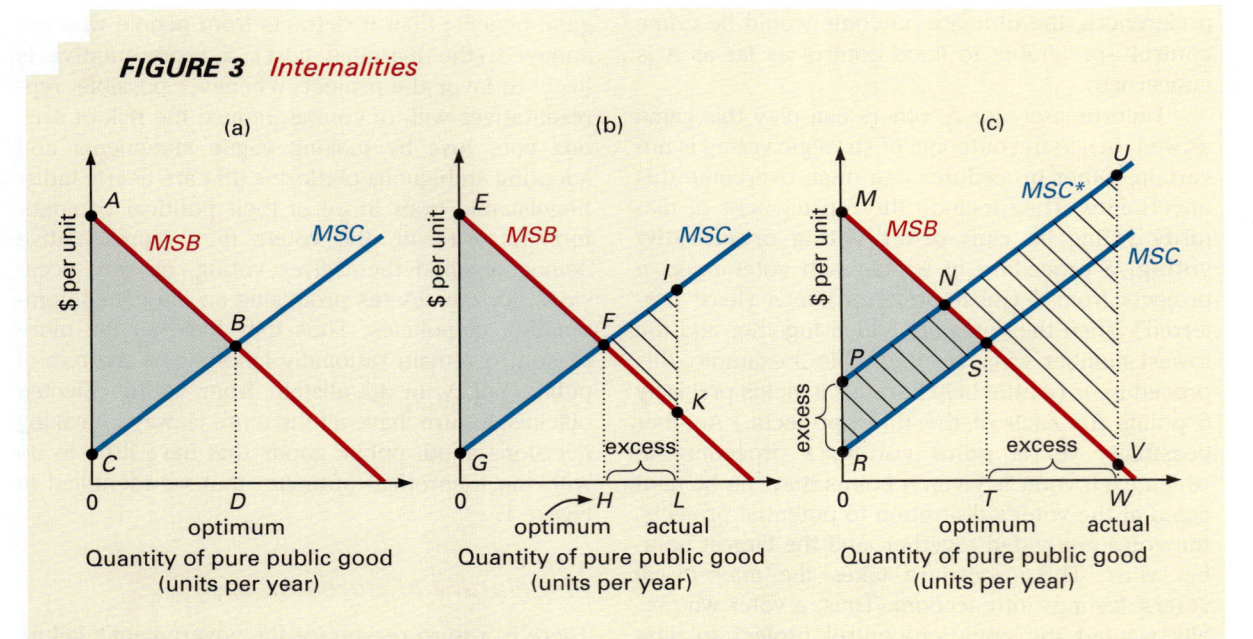

(a) Quantity of pure public good (units per year) — optimum at D. Points labeled A, B, C, MSB, MSC. Shaded triangle ABC.

(b) Quantity of pure public good (units per year) — optimum at H, actual at L. Points E, F, I, K, G. MSB and MSC curves. Crosshatched area FIK indicates excess.

(c) Quantity of pure public good (units per year) — optimum at T, actual at W. Points M, N, P, S, U, R, V. MSB, MSC, and MSC* curves. Shaded triangle and crosshatched excess region.

While pursuing their private internal goals, government officials may well provide an excessive quantity of pure public goods; they may even do so at an excessive cost. As a result, the social net benefit available under ideal conditions, measured by the shaded triangles in panels (a) through (c), may be offset by a crosshatched net social loss, either in part (panel b), fully (not shown), or more than fully (panel c). In the latter case, society would have been better off living with market failure, not producing the public good at all, and simply forgoing the potential net benefit of triangle ABC.

Sooner or later, bureaucrats form an alliance with special interest groups who have much to gain from potential government projects that the bureaucrats might implement. Thus officials in the Department of Agriculture become in-house lobbyists for farmers; officials in the Department of Defense begin to serve defense contractors; officials in the Food and Drug Administration begin to look at pharmaceutical firms as their clients. Jointly, they lobby legislators for higher budgets.

In legislatures, an analogous process occurs. Elected representatives who have strong special-interest constituencies will do their best to sit on committees that deal with matters of concern to the special-interest groups in their home districts. These representatives will logroll with one another until they find themselves on the committee of their choice. Over time, legislative committees will be dominated by representatives who favor the special interests. Thus, an "iron triangle" is formed: bureaucrats, special interests, and legislators—all seeking their *personal* interests—will jointly promote overgenerous budgets for the public goods that are closest to their hearts. This pursuit by elected and appointed government officials of their internal, personal goals instead of publicly announced, official goals has consequences—such as the production of excessive amounts of pure public goods at excessive costs—called **internalities.** Such internalities are linked with government failure just as externalities are linked with market failure.

Figure 3 illustrates what is involved. Panel (a) corresponds to Figure 1 and depicts the ideal situation in which government officials identify and then provide for the production of the optimum quantity of a pure public good, such as 0D. Society's net benefit is maximized as the shaded triangle *ABC*, or the difference between the total benefit 0*ABD* and the total cost 0*CBD*.

Panel (b) illustrates a situation in which government officials, pursuing their personal goals, provide an excessive amount of the public good 0*L* rather than the optimum 0*H*. As a result of the excess provision *HL*, society gets a marginal benefit of *HFKL*; but the marginal cost *HFIL* is larger. Hence, compared to the optimum, society is worse off. The overall social net benefit now equals the shaded triangle *EFG minus* the crosshatched triangle *FIK*. It is still positive, but lower than it might have been. The members of the iron triangle, of course, don't care; they have derived their personal benefits.

Panel (c), finally, illustrates an even worse scenario. Government officials, concerned with their internal goals, provide a vastly excessive amount of the public good, 0*W* instead of 0*T,* and they do so at an excessive cost, measured by *MSC** rather than *MSC*. There is excess staffing, overpricing of equipment, and the like. As a result, the social net benefit is actually negative, equal to the shaded minus the crosshatched area or, more simply, equal to triangle *MNP minus* triangle *NUV*. In this case, society as a whole is worse off than it would have been without any government action at all.

Indeed, it is no accident that the word *bureaucrat,* referring to a person working for a government agency, has derogatory overtones. People have all too often observed the obviously wasteful expenditure of other people's money by government agencies. A few examples will illustrate the point. For years, Senator Proxmire awarded a Golden Fleece to the most wasteful governmental spending program he could find. Once the award went to the National Institutes of Health for a $102,000 study of whether sunfish drinking gin are more belligerent than sunfish drinking tequila. At another time, the Law Enforcement Assistance Administration was honored for its $27,000 study of why prison inmates would like to escape. And the Bureau of Education for the Handicapped (which had persuaded Congress to give it funds to aid an alleged 12 percent of school children who were handicapped) got the fleece after declaring a "handicapped shortage" and launching "Operation Childfind." (The agency had been unable to find 12 percent handicapped children, so it issued a barrage of letters to school officials, made grants to university researchers, and launched a media advertising campaign to help it reverse the handicapped "shortfall.") The whole story, perhaps is best summarized by **Parkinson's law,** pronounced by the British historian in the November 1955 issue of *The Economist*. The "law," of course, is meant to be a humorous exaggeration of the issue. Parkinson's law states that the number of those employed by government agencies will grow at the same rate regardless of whether the volume of work to be done rises, falls, or even disappears.

Remedies for Government Failure

Are there remedies for government failure? A number of suggestions have been made. One possibility is the greater use of **benefit-cost analysis.** This involves the quantification of the expected benefits and costs of potential government projects, the rejection of projects with benefit-cost ratios below unity, and the apportionment of the budget among those remaining projects that have the highest benefit-cost ratios.

Another approach suggests that the excessive costs illustrated in panel (c) of Figure 3 might be avoided by an arrangement that encourages competition among government bureaus that procure public goods. For many years, the air force, army, and navy, for example, separately procured their own planes, which provided legislators with a much-needed yardstick to *compare* the performance of these organizations. The end result was the procurement of higher-quality products at lower governmental cost.

Finally, it is possible to let the government spend tax dollars by exercising demand in the private sector. Such shift of traditional public-sector functions to the private sector is called **privatization.** Examples 2, 3, and 4 illustrate this point.

EXAMPLE 2

Breaking Out of the Prison Crisis

In 1989, some 3.4 million people in the United States were in jail, on parole, or on probation, costing the government $20 billion a year. The United States was incarcerating 426 persons for every 100,000, a number higher than anywhere else in the world. (The corresponding counts were 333 in South Africa, 268 in the Soviet Union, 97 in Great Britain, and 45 in Japan.) Existing prisons were strained beyond capacity; a veritable prison construction boom was unable to keep up with the swelling numbers of offenders. In desperation, governments were making room for prisoners in such unlikely places as homeless shelters, military bases, troop ships, and university dormitories. Following a cautious endorsement of the idea by the nation's governors in 1985, the "corrections system" was converted into a public good produced by a *mixture* of private firms and government bureaus. The measures that reduced costs included:

1. Private firms, including the Corrections Corporation of America, U.S. Corrections, and Wackenhut, were "managing" thousands of inmates in 24 states at 90 percent of government costs.

2. States ranging from Florida and Georgia to New York and Oklahoma set up new types of cheap "boot camps" in which first offenders spent 6 months. Roused daily at 5:15 A.M., the prisoners did pushups, carried rocks, and scrubbed floors with toothbrushes.

3. California set up joint ventures with dozens of private firms to rehabilitate offenders and reduce long-run costs. The prisoners were paid market wages to make clothes and license plates, do farm and road work, restore buses, run airline reservation systems, and build prisons.

4. Some prisoners were released into "intensive supervision," which reduced costs to 18 percent. Under the scheme, prisoners had to meet a probation officer 5 times a week, hold a job, perform community service, submit to random drug tests, and obey a home curfew.

5. Some prisoners were put under electronic house arrest, an even cheaper alternative to the state prison. These prisoners had to be at home to answer random telephone calls and be ever-ready to touch a special wrist band to the phone when called.

As you can well imagine, these changes did not go unopposed. In Torrance County, New Mexico, for example, Bryan Caldwell had just purchased a ranch, in a clean environment, with lots of space. Then the Corrections Corporation of America built one of its prisons next door. Before long, Bryan was reinforcing fences, buying German shepherds, and stocking up on guns. Some neighbors thought the prison would be good for the area by bringing jobs, but the majority had other thoughts. They saw the unzoned desert turning into a prime location for private prisons, making New Mexico into America's "penal colony." They wanted assurances that out-of-state prisoners would never be released in the area and that the county's police and welfare budget wouldn't be burdened by chasing down escapees or taking care of poverty-stricken felons on their release.

Sources: *The New York Times,* March 3, 1985, p. 26; Scott Ticer, "The Search for Ways to Break Out of the Prison Crisis," *Business Week,* May 8, 1989, pp. 80–81; Sandra D. Atchison, "Private Prisons," *Business Week,* June 11, 1990, p. 28; and Chris Black, "Paying the High Price of Being the World's No. 1 Jailer," *The Boston Sunday Globe,* January 13, 1991, p. 67.

CHAPTER 20 Public Goods and Public Choices   551

EXAMPLE 3

Privatizing Public School Functions

In 1990, America's 20,000 school districts spent $4.2 billion to feed some 24 million students. Some school boards, however, have recently concluded that they can save money by hiring private food service companies to do the job. Duval County, Florida, privatized its school lunch program; so did Naperville, Illinois, and Putnam City, Oklahoma. In the latter case, the school district had spent $3.25 million per year to feed its 18,000 students; Marriott did it for $250,000 less.

The trend, furthermore, has been accelerating. In 1987, private companies, such as ARA Services, Canteen, Marriott, and Service America provided 4 percent of school lunches; in 1990, the figure was 10 percent and rising fast.

Some school boards have gone even further. The Miami board turned the entire South Pointe Elementary School over to Education Alternatives, Inc., for a 5-year trial period. The private company, which has had great success in Minneapolis and Phoenix already, will select teachers, design the curriculum, provide all educational materials. The for-profit company plans to operate a "21st century school," making extensive use of computers, telephones in every classroom (so children can involve their parents in their work), and personally-tailored education plans that pair student and teacher for at least six grades.

Sources: Steven A. Holmes, "In Miami, a Private Company Will Operate a Public School," *The New York Times,* December 7, 1990, pp. A1 and D19; and "Privatizing School Lunches," *Fortune,* February 25, 1991, p. 14.

EXAMPLE 4

Privatizing Space Projects

Projects in outer space have long been viewed as the exclusive domain of the federal government. But no more. Since the late 1980s, despite a slower pace than had been anticipated, many private companies have gotten into the act. Consider these examples:

1. In 1989, the McDonnell Douglas Corporation sent into orbit the first privately launched telecommunications satellite. (The government of India paid $50 million for the feat.) Other private companies with similar plans included American Rocket, E. Prime, Martin Marietta, Orbital Sciences, and Space Services.

2. Over 100 private companies, including Amoco, AT&T, Eli Lilly, General Motors, Grumman, Merck, and Space Industries, are pursuing projects involving materials processing. In the weightlessness and vacuum of space, it is possible to develop perfectly formed crystals which are of major importance to drug companies, makers of microelectronics, and users of high-strength metals, such as airplane manufacturers and auto makers.

3. Other private companies, such as the Earth Observation Satellite Company (jointly owned by General Electric, General Motors, and Hughes Aircraft), are engaged in remote-sensing projects. They involve taking pictures of and gathering data about the earth from space. Data about geography, natural resources, pollution, and weather are marketed to the federal government as well as to private firms, including those involved in fishing, lumbering, and oil drilling.

Source: Richard W. Stevenson, "Private Space Projects Lagging," *The New York Times,* June 1, 1989, pp. D1 and D5.

Summary

1. This chapter focuses on the production and consumption of *pure public goods* that generate positive externalities to an extreme degree and provide nonexcludable and nonrival benefits to all members of society.

2. *Nonexcludability* refers to the property of a pure public good that makes it physically impossible, or extremely costly, to exclude any individual from the enjoyment of the good once a given amount of it has been produced. *Nonrivalness* refers to the property of a pure public good that allows additional persons to consume the good without reducing the good's availability to others.

3. In the absence of government intervention, competitive markets produce an inefficiently low quantity of goods that generate positive externalities; in the case of pure public goods, they produce zero quantities. This can be explained by the *free-rider problem,* the unwillingness of individuals to pay for the production of pure public goods and their eagerness to let others produce such goods so that they can enjoy the associated spillover of benefits at a zero cost. The problem can be overcome by *public finance,* the collection of taxes from all those believed to benefit from the provision of pure public goods and the subsequent channeling of these funds toward the production of such goods, either by government agencies or private firms. (In addition, government agencies often collect taxes to produce other goods that are not pure public goods.)

4. In theory, finding the optimum quantity of a pure public good is easy. It is the quantity at which declining marginal social benefit and rising marginal social cost are equal to one another. What is easy in theory, however, is difficult in practice.

5. It is difficult to identify the marginal social benefits associated with alternative quantities of pure public goods because citizens about to be taxed on the basis of benefits they derive have a strong incentive not to reveal how much various units of a public good are really worth to them. As a result, real-world procedures for selecting the quantities of public goods to be produced are unlikely to find the optimum.

6. Other reasons for the production of nonoptimal quantities of public goods, which is called *government failure,* emerge from a study of the process of public choice, the procedures by which groups of people decide on the quantities of various public goods to be produced, and on the ways in which associated tax burdens are shared. A number of alternative arrangements are discussed. It becomes clear that government failure is quite likely because of certain problems that are inherent in the process of majority voting, in the delegation of authority, and in the nature of bureaucracy. Over time, an "iron triangle" may be formed: bureaucrats, special interests, and legislators—all seeking their *personal* interests—may jointly promote overgenerous budgets for the public goods that are closest to their hearts and may produce them at excessive costs.

7. A number of possible remedies for government failure have been suggested. They include benefit-cost analysis, competition among government bureaus, and privatization.

Key Concepts

benefit-cost analysis
bureaucrats
direct democracy
free-rider problem
government failure
internalities
logrolling
merit goods
nonexcludability
nonrivalness
Parkinson's law
plurality voting

point voting
privatization
process of public choice
public finance

pure private goods
pure public goods
rank-order voting

representative democracy
strategic voting
voting paradox

Questions and Problems

1. The text lists all kinds of pure public goods. Make a list of your own.

2. "The characteristic of nonrivalness of some pure public goods applies only to a limited extent; it ceases to hold once the number of consumers grows above a certain point."
Evaluate.

3. Mr. A: "Bus transportation is clearly a pure public good."
Ms. B: "I beg to differ; it's a pure private good."
Mediate the exchange.

4. "The discussion of public goods throws new and interesting light on the long-standing debate of whether labor unions should be allowed to have closed (or union) shops." Evaluate.

5. On occasion, pure public goods can become pure private goods. Can you think of examples?

6. According to the caption of Table 2, projects that would be approved, if considered separately, could, under a system of majority voting, easily lose in a combination vote. Create a numerical example to prove the point.

7. Consider three voters with preferences concerning penalties for speeding listed in the table below.
Prove that, in a system of simple majority voting, whoever controls the voting procedure can also control the results.

8. Reconsider the Question 7 table; prove that "society's" preference ranking is internally inconsistent.

9. Parkinson's law gives the impression that the government bureaucracy is like a giant amoeba, endlessly reproducing itself. Test the claim with respect to the United States.

10. Do some research and find out about the extent of the privatization movement among governments in the United States.

Preference ranking	Voter A	Voter B	Voter C
1st	Issue warning only	$100 fine	Lose license for 90 days
2nd	$100 fine	Lose license for 90 days	Issue warning only
3rd	Lose license for 90 days	Issue warning only	$100 fine

CHAPTER 21
THE REDISTRIBUTION OF INCOME

Preview

In an attempt to create an income distribution that is "fair," governments often tax the income of some people and transfer income to other people, either in cash or in kind. This chapter discusses the nature and effectiveness of major U.S. income redistribution programs, including social insurance (designed to keep people from falling into poverty) and public assistance (designed to help people who are already poor to escape from poverty). An alternative to existing programs, a radically new "negative income tax system," is analyzed as well.

Examples

1. Headstart at Age 25
2. The Welfare Trap

An earlier chapter, "The Personal Distribution of Income: Riches Versus Poverty," analyzed the factors that determine the apportionment of the national income among people. These factors include the sizes and qualities of human, natural, and capital resource stocks owned by individuals, the rates at which these stocks are put to work, and the rental prices that are established in various markets in which the flows of resource services are traded.

Throughout this book, however, we have also noted that governments often try to modify the income distribution that private markets would otherwise generate. Consider price floors for milk or sugar, price ceilings for rental housing, minimum wages for unskilled labor, maximum wages for military draftees. In all these cases and hundreds more, governments seek to redistribute income—from buyers to sellers in the case of minimum prices, and from sellers to buyers in the case of maximum prices. Yet governments can also take a more straightforward approach. They can use their taxing power directly to take income away from some people and then transfer a portion of that revenue to supplement the income of others. (Inevitably, some of the tax revenue is used up in the administration of the income redistribution program.) More often than not, governments, like Robin Hood, take from the rich and give to the poor (although the reverse also occurs), and they do so in order to create a special kind of public good, *distributive justice*. Let us consider some of the ideas underlying this policy.

Notions of Distributive Justice

Although the issue has been discussed for centuries, no general agreement exists about the "proper" slice of the national income pie that any one person should receive. Still, there are many who at least agree that government should promote a state of affairs called **distributive justice,** in

554

which the apportionment of income among people is "fair" because it has been determined not merely by impersonal market forces but also by deliberate actions taken by some human authority. That authority, presumably, establishes and rewards the relative merit of income recipients by reference to personal characteristics that they possess. What should these characteristics be? Here opinions diverge. Some writers, not necessarily American, suggest "hours worked," others point to "human needs," others still to "basic human rights."

Those who favor the *hours-worked* approach would divide the nation's income on the basis of the hours different people have contributed to the process of production, while counting each hour as equally important. For example, if a brain surgeon, a coal miner, a dairy farmer, and a steel worker each worked 35 hours in a week, it would be fair, according to this view, to give each the same monetary income, and thus the same command over goods. Other people, working half as many hours, would be entitled to half as much income. Those working zero hours would get no income at all.

Clearly, this approach is troublesome despite its popularity in some circles. For one thing, as an earlier chapter has shown, wage differentials among different occupations serve important functions, such as channeling the right numbers of people into different fields in accordance with product demand or compensating workers for nonmonetary differences among jobs. In addition, of course, this criteria of "fairness" would condemn many who *cannot* work to having no income at all.

Those who favor the *needs* approach would avoid the zero-income problem just noted but would burden the income-redistributing authority with the impossible task of figuring out everyone's "true needs" and identifying (and rejecting) everyone's "false wants." In addition, this approach, too, would destroy the crucial incentives that allocate workers and other resources in just the right proportions to different occupations. If, for example, everybody's "needs" were taken care of no matter what, why should anybody take on a dangerous or unpleasant job rather than a safe or pleasant one? Why, in fact, should anyone take on any job at all? Redistributing income with a view to giving everyone what is "needed" would require safeguards to make people work and work in the proper places.

The *basic-human-rights* approach typically involves a simple moral judgment: that all individuals are equally important and should, therefore, receive a precisely equal share of the total set of goods produced in any one year. Hence everybody's income should be the same. Once again, the inherent incentive problems are identical to the ones noted in the preceding paragraph. Nevertheless, this absolute-equality standard has had many advocates. The late Abba Lerner, an economist, for example, used to argue that it would be desirable to maximize the total of human welfare, or utility, derivable from the annual output of goods and, given the law of declining marginal utility, that such maximization can occur only if every individual has an equal share of the output total.[1] The philosopher John Rawls has similarly argued for absolute income equality, although on different grounds: Rawls asks us to picture people in a "state of nature" in which all individuals rely only on their own efforts to procure goods. Realizing that great benefits could be reaped by specializing in production and then trading with one another, people in such an "original position," argues Rawls, might draw up a "social contract" that would henceforth govern their relations with one another. What rule of output division would they agree upon for the new society about to be formed? Not knowing what their future position will be—whether they will end up as farmers or janitors, as jet pilots or steel workers, as surgeons or zoology professors—they will consider the matter impartially. For fear of ending up with the lowest-paying job, they will opt for absolute income equality. The same rule, concludes Rawls, should apply to our society where some people, knowing their positions in life, favor inequality only because they have reason to believe that they will end up with the better deal. Rawls favors income inequality, however, if in comparison to an egalitarian division, everyone's income can be raised at the same time.[2]

Actual U.S. programs of income redistribution are not based on any of the preceding arguments,

---

[1] For a detailed presentation of the argument see Heinz Kohler, *Intermediate Microeconomics: Theory and Applications,* 3rd ed. (Glenview, IL: Scott, Foresman and Co., 1990), pp. 506–508.

[2] *Ibid.,* pp. 508 and 512.

nor on any one of various other arguments of this type. Having been enacted at varied points in time and in response to specific problems of the day, they are not based on any master plan. Yet they do share certain features with the theoretical arguments noted here: a longing for a vaguely articulated "fairer" distribution of income and a need to deal with incentive problems that income redistribution inevitably seems to create.

Major Transfer Programs in the United States

Numerous government programs, called **transfer programs,** supply cash or in-kind benefits (commodities and services) to people without requiring them currently to make any payment or render any service in return. These programs are traditionally divided into two categories, social insurance and public assistance. Programs of **social insurance** aim to prevent people from becoming poor due to loss of income that is associated with changes in individual circumstances, such as retirement, death of the family breadwinner, disability, sickness, or unemployment. As a result, eligibility is based on a *status test* and has nothing to do with the overall size of people's income, assets, or liabilities. Nevertheless, these programs clearly seek to prevent people from falling into poverty. Programs of **public assistance,** on the other hand, aim to assist people who are already poor and seek to raise their income above the poverty line. For that reason, eligibility is based on a *means test* and does involve a careful analysis of people's pre-assistance income and net worth. Once a person has passed the status or means test, such a person is entitled to the program benefits specified by law, which is why social insurance and public assistance programs are also referred to as **entitlement programs.**

Since the U.S. government committed itself to a War on Poverty in 1964, entitlement programs have grown significantly in size—whether measured in constant dollars expended overall, on a per capita basis, or as a percentage of the gross national income. Measured in dollars of 1970 purchasing power, for example, overall transfer expenditures rose 6.5 fold from $30.7 billion in 1960 to $199.0 billion in 1987. On a per capita basis, these expenditures rose 4.8 fold from $170 to $816. The percentage of the gross national income thus transferred climbed from 4.5 to 12.9 percent. This growth reflects a variety of factors, including the introduction of new programs, expanded coverage of old programs, growing participation rates in programs, and increases in benefit levels. Let us consider the major types of transfer programs in turn.

Social Insurance Programs

In fiscal year 1987, social insurance programs involved the governmental expenditure of $443.1 billion, which equaled 76 percent of all transfers. Over 81 percent of this amount was paid out in cash, as is illustrated in section A of Table 1.

Social Security

The Social Security Act of 1935 and its amendments, officially known as Old Age, Survivors, Disability, and Health Insurance (OASDHI), provide protection against wage loss resulting from retirement, death, prolonged disability, as well as against the cost of medical care during old age and disability. The OASDI part of the program (line A1 of Table 1) provides monthly cash benefits to retired or disabled insured workers and their dependents and to survivors of insured workers. To be eligible, a worker must have had a specified period of employment in which social security taxes were paid. A worker becomes eligible for full benefits at age 65, although reduced benefits may be obtained up to 3 years earlier; the worker's spouse is under the same limitations. Survivor benefits are payable to dependents of deceased insured workers. Disability benefits are payable to an insured worker under age 65 with a prolonged disability and to the disabled worker's dependents on the same basis as dependents of retired workers. Also, disability benefits are provided at age 50 to the disabled widow or widower of a deceased worker who was fully insured at the time of death (having paid taxes for 40 quarters). A small lump sum benefit is generally payable on the death of an insured worker to a spouse or minor children.

Since 1966, the Medicare program (line A5) has provided two coordinated plans for nearly all people age 65 and over: 1) a hospital insurance plan that covers hospital and related services; and 2) a voluntary supplementary medical insurance plan, financed partially by monthly premiums paid by

TABLE 1 Major Types of Transfer Programs in the United States
(expenditures in billions of dollars, fiscal year 1987)

A. Social Insurance Programs	**$443.1**
Cash	
1. Old age, survivors, and disability insurance (OASDI)	$206.5
2. Railroad and public employee and veterans' pensions	106.9
3. Workers' compensation	29.6
4. Unemployment insurance	18.1
	$361.1
In-Kind	
5. Medicare	$82
B. Public Assistance Programs	**$139.4**
Cash	
1. Aid to families with dependent children (AFDC)	$16.4
2. Supplemental security income	13.6
3. General assistance	6.2
	$36.2
In-Kind	
4. Medicaid	$53.4
5. Food stamps	12.4
6. Public housing	13.2
7. Other[a]	24.2
	$103.2

[a] Includes child care and adoption services, energy assistance, Indian welfare, juvenile delinquency programs, legal aid, migrant worker programs, school lunches, supplementary education for disadvantaged children, vocational rehabilitation, work experience training, and more.

In recent years, about three quarters of transfers in the United States involved social insurance programs; one quarter, public assistance programs. The latter were more heavily weighted toward in-kind assistance than the former.

SOURCE: U.S. Bureau of the Census, *Statistical Abstract of the United States: 1990* (Washington, D.C.: U.S. Government Printing Office, 1990), pp. 351ff.

participants, that partly covers physicians' and related medical services. This insurance also applies to disabled beneficiaries of any age after 24 months of eligibility and to persons with chronic kidney disease.

Social security benefits are funded by a payroll tax on annual earnings of workers (up to a maximum of earnings) and of the self-employed. In 1991, employee and employer each were taxed 7.65 percent of wages up to $53,400; the self-employed were taxed 15.3 percent. In addition, earnings between $53,401 and $125,000 were taxed at 1.45 percent for both employee and employer and at 2.9 percent for the self-employed. The system is referred to as a **pay-as-you-go system** because the social security "contributions" paid by those working in any one year (they are really *taxes*) are typically not saved by the government to finance future benefits, but are immediately paid out to those who are eligible for benefits in that year. The typical private insurance, in contrast, is a **fully funded system** because paid-in premiums are saved to build up a fund the size of which equals the present value of future benefits promised to the insured.

Government Employee Pensions

The Civil Service Retirement System and the Federal Employees' Retirement System are two major programs providing retirement benefits to federal civilian employees and their survivors. Other retirement systems exist for the uniformed services (going back to the Revolutionary War) and for certain special groups of federal employees, such as railroad workers. State and local governments have other programs still. Total 1987 expenditures are shown on line A2 of Table 1.

Workers' Compensation

All states provide protection against work-connected injuries and deaths, although some states exclude certain workers (e.g., domestic help). Federal workmen's compensation laws cover federal government employees, private employees in the District of Columbia, and longshoremen and harbor workers. In addition, the Social Security Administration and the Department of Labor administer a "black lung" benefits program for coal miners disabled by pneumoconiosis and for specified dependents and survivors. Most state workmen's compensation laws exempt such employments as agriculture, domestic service, and casual labor; about half of these laws exempt employers who have fewer than a specified number of employees. Occupational diseases, or at least specified diseases, are compensable under most laws. Total 1987 expenditures are shown on line A3 of Table 1.

Unemployment Insurance

Unemployment compensation programs were introduced in 1935 and are now jointly administered by the U.S. Employment and Training Administration and each state's employment security agency. By agreement with the U.S. Secretary of Labor, state agencies also administer unemployment compensation for eligible ex-service personnel and for federal employees. In addition, they provide unemployment assistance under the Disaster Relief Act and worker's assistance and relocation allowances under the Trade Act. Thus, New England textile workers whose employers go bankrupt as a result of foreign competition may receive funds to move to Texas where jobs in other industries are, perhaps, more abundant. Until 1975, states also administered federal cash allowances to persons being trained under the Manpower Development and Training Act.

Under state unemployment insurance laws, benefits related to workers' past earnings are paid to unemployed eligible workers. State laws vary with respect to the length of time benefits are paid and to their amount. In most states, a waiting period of 1 week must be served before payments begin. Benefits are payable for a maximum number of weeks, ranging from 26 to 39 weeks among the states (most frequently 26 weeks). Under the provisions of the 1970 Employment Security Act and the 1971 Emergency Unemployment Compensation Act, workers can receive an extra 13 weeks of benefits when the national unemployment rate has exceeded 4.5 percent for 3 months and a state's average unemployment plus benefit exhaustion rates add to at least 6.5 percent or when the state rate exceeds 4 percent and is 20 percent higher than the average rate in a corresponding 13-week period during the 2 preceding years. The basic benefit varies greatly among the states; some states supplement it with allowances for dependents.

Unemployment insurance is funded by a federal unemployment tax levied on the taxable payrolls of most employers (defined as the first $7,000 in wages paid each worker during a year). Employers also pay taxes to the states. About 97 percent of wage and salary workers are covered by unemployment insurance. Total 1987 expenditures are shown on line A4 of Table 1.

Public Assistance Programs

In fiscal year 1987, public assistance programs involved the governmental expenditure of $139.4 billion, which equaled 24 percent of all transfers. Unlike in the case of social insurance programs, only a quarter of this amount was paid out in cash, as is illustrated in section B of Table 1. This reflects general attitudes among taxpayers who are unwilling to give aid to the poor without strings attached and, therefore, prefer in-kind assistance.

Aid to Families with Dependent Children

The AFDC program, begun in 1935, is now the largest cash assistance program to the poor, as line

B1 of Table 1 indicates. It is also a joint federal-state program. Originally, it was established for widows and orphans only, but at a later time, separated, divorced, and unmarried mothers were included. Since 1990, all states are required to offer AFDC even to 2-parent families, provided they meet certain income and asset tests and the primary earner is unemployed or unable to work more than 100 hours per month. The number of people aided under the AFDC program has risen very rapidly since World War II, reaching 11 million in 1988. Payments vary considerably from state to state (from a 1988 monthly low of $114 per family in Alabama to a high of $599 in Arkansas).

Supplemental Security Income

The SSI program, noted on line B2 of Table 1, was initiated in 1974 and replaced earlier federal (non-social-security) programs of aid to the aged, blind, and disabled. The program established uniform national eligibility and payment standards; most states supplement the basic SSI payment.

Medicaid

Under Medicaid, all states (except Arizona) offer basic health services to eligible low-income persons. The cost of providing these services is shared by the federal government, but each state determines its own eligibility criteria and may set benefits above the minimum established by federal law. Almost all recipients of cash welfare programs are automatically eligible. In addition, 31 states extend Medicaid to families that satisfy all but the income requirements for welfare and that either have incomes that meet state definitions of "medically needy" or incur medical expenses that lower their remaining incomes to "medically needy" levels. Line B4 of Table 1 lists 1987 program expenditures.

Food Stamps

Under the food stamp program, introduced in 1964 and noted on line B5, single persons and those living in households meeting nationwide standards for income and assets may receive coupons redeemable for food at most retail food stores. The monthly amount of coupons a unit receives is determined by household size and income. Households without income receive the determined monthly cost of a nutritionally adequate diet for their household size. The amount is updated to account for food price increases. Households with income receive the difference between the amount of a nutritionally adequate diet and 30 percent of their income, after certain allowable deductions.

To qualify for the program, a household must have less than $2,000 in disposable assets ($3,000 if one member is aged 60 or older), gross income below 130 percent of the official poverty line, and net income below 100 percent of that line. The 130 percent rule is modified for older and disabled persons receiving social security, veterans' disability, or SSI benefits.

Public Housing

Under various public housing programs, including those initiated by federal housing acts of 1937 and 1949, eligible poor persons can receive free or subsidized housing. In addition, there are programs that subsidize mortgage interest payments and provide governmental mortgage insurance and guarantees. As line B6 of our table indicates, in recent times the local, state, and federal programs have rivaled the food stamp program in size.

Conclusion

As a study of Table 1 indicates, there certainly is no lack of programs designed to improve the economic well-being of needy people. Indeed, the Table 1 data are not even complete. There are other programs, not shown in Table 1, that serve the same goal of weaving a **safety net,** a fabric of social insurance and public assistance programs that prevents people from falling into poverty and possibly helps those already poor to escape from poverty. In 1987, for example, governments in the United States spent $3.9 billion on job training programs, such as the Job Corps and Summer Youth Employment programs, designed to help disadvantaged youths. Governments spent another $10.2 billion on educational aid, including Headstart, college work-study programs, guaranteed student loans, Pell grants, and more. Example 1 elaborates.

Governments in the United States clearly are making a major effort to set up a safety net. Even ignoring the additional programs just noted, Table 1 indicates that governments in 1987 made transfer payments of $582.5 billion—at a time when there

EXAMPLE 1

Headstart at Age 25

One day in 1990, inside a run-down building in New York, a birthday party was in progress. The room was filled with 3- and 4-year-olds, but the party was not for them. It was for Headstart, age 25, a government program designed to help poor children beat the crippling effects of poverty by giving them an early start in school. Looking out of the classroom windows, a visitor could see the scars of poverty everywhere: Vacant lots choked with weeds and trash, smoke-blackened buildings, crack houses, and huge public housing projects where even the balconies had chain-link fences.

Yet, unlike 25 years earlier, almost everyone supported the program. President Bush had just given it a 27.7 percent increase in its budget, the largest in history. The extra $500 million was to be spent in traditional ways: on teachers, nutritionists, social workers, psychologists, health services, and the like—all designed to involve young deprived children and their parents in an early experiment in education.

What has the past taught us? Headstart children have shown greater self-esteem, better attitudes toward school, have had better attendance, and have less often been held back in grades. Compared to children with similar backgrounds and no Headstart, they have been less involved in crime and delinquency. In the long run, academic performance has not been superior and scores on standard tests have remained the same. Perhaps academic proficiency is too much to expect from a one-year outreach program. However, positive social changes affected by Headstart continue to make it a viable program.

Source: Susan Chira, "Preschool Aid for the Poor: How Big a Head Start?" *The New York Times,* February 14, 1990, pp. A1 and B6.

---

were 31.53 million poor persons.[3] Thus, governments made transfers in excess of $18,000 for every poor person in the United States. Why then does poverty persist? The obvious part of the answer is that a portion of transfer payments does not go to people who are poor. Even the relatively rich, for example, are *entitled* to and hence receive social security benefits. A more subtle part of the answer occupies us in the next two sections of this chapter. It has to do with the facts that 1) transfer payments are financed by taxes that burden not only the rich but also the poor and 2) people change their behavior in response to the tax-transfer system.

---

[3] Note Figure 3, The History of U.S. Poverty, 1959–1989, in the chapter "The Personal Distribution of Income: Riches Versus Poverty."

The Effect of Financing Transfers by Taxes

The hundreds of billions of transfer dollars in Table 1 are a gift to their recipients, but rarely are they a pure gift. More often than not, the very persons who receive the transfers also pay some of the taxes that finance them. Involved are personal income taxes, corporate profit taxes, social security taxes, property taxes, and sales taxes, among others.

The Tax Incidence Problem

At this point, we must remember an important fact: Even if governments tried to place taxes on the relatively rich with the aim of later making transfer payments to the relatively poor, the ultimate effect may well be quite different. As we learned in the Chapter 3 section Excise Taxes, the *economic tax incidence,*

TABLE 2 Government Tax and Transfer Rates, United States, 1980 (as a percentage of annual family income)

Family income deciles	Taxes (1)	Government transfers (2)	Taxes minus transfers (3)
1st (poorest 10 percent)	42	158	−116
2nd	23	58	−35
3rd	24	35	−11
4th	25	24	1
5th	26	15	11
6th	26	11	15
7th	26	8	18
8th	27	6	21
9th	28	4	24
10th (richest 10 percent)	29	3	26
All families	27	10	17

This table shows the net effect (column 3) of governmental attempts to transfer income in the United States.
SOURCE: Joseph A. Pechman and Mark J. Mazur, "The Rich, the Poor, and the Taxes They Pay: An Update," *The Public Interest,* Fall 1984, pp. 28–36.

or the way in which the real burden of a tax is ultimately apportioned among people, may well differ from the *statutory tax incidence,* or the way in which the monetary burden of the tax is officially apportioned among people. As illustrated in Chapter 3, Figure 12, Imposing an Excise Tax on Gasoline, even though the government decides who should pay what type of tax at what rate, someone else may nevertheless end up paying it. This is so because the payer of the tax can often shift it onto others. People might shift the tax burden to people from whom they buy something by paying them less than before. They might shift the burden to people to whom they sell something by charging them more than before. Then the true burden of the tax rests with these other people. Thus it is not at all obvious, from looking at the tax laws and the signatures on tax payment checks, who *ultimately* pays how much in taxes. And figuring it out with respect to all the types of taxes that governments levy is an extremely difficult task. It is not the sort of thing one can find out on a regular basis.

Tax Incidence in the United States

The most detailed answer to the question of tax incidence available is given in a somewhat dated study by the Brookings Institution summarized in Table 2. This study defined *family* income as the sum of wages and salaries, fringe benefits, interest, dividends, rents, entrepreneurial income, retained corporate earnings, imputed rent on owner-occupied housing, unrealized capital gains, and pension fund accumulations—but excluded transfers from the definition of income.

Overall, families paid 27 percent of their income in taxes and received 10 percent back in transfers. Thus the net tax burden was 17 percent of total income. Some taxes, such as the federal income tax and estate taxes (not shown), were found to be **progressive taxes;** that is, taxes that take a larger percentage of higher than of lower incomes. Yet the total tax structure (column 1) showed little progressivity. Indeed, at the lower end, the tax structure depicted **regressive taxes,** or taxes that take a smaller percentage of higher than of lower incomes: The proportion of income eaten up by taxes dropped from 42 percent for the 10 percent poorest families to 23 percent for the next 10 percent of families. Families in the remaining income deciles paid almost exactly the same proportion in taxes—between 24 and 29 percent. All this was the result of the regressive impact of corporate profit taxes, of social security taxes, and of all state and local taxes (not shown). The regressivity of these taxes outweighed the progressivity of the federal personal income tax.

Corporate profit taxes (levied on fictitious legal persons, called corporations) are shifted partly to consumers via higher prices and partly to stockholders via lower dividends. Hence all kinds of natural persons ultimately bear them. Social security taxes are regressive because they are levied as a certain fixed percentage of income below a certain ceiling, and not everyone's income is completely below that ceiling. Suppose the tax rate were 8 percent on income up to $50,000 per year. Then a person with a $10,000 income would pay $800, or 8 percent; but a person with a $100,000 income would only pay 8 percent on $50,000, or $4,000, which is 4 percent of income. The employer's portion of social security taxes, furthermore, like property and sales taxes, is likely to be shifted to others via higher prices or lower wages. The poor pay a larger percentage of their low incomes in such taxes because most of their income is wage income and they spend most of it (while the saving by the rich is untouched by such taxes).

Taxes and Transfers Combined

The picture of tax incidence must now be augmented by a look at the impact of transfer payments. The 10 percent poorest families received transfers (column 2) equal to 158 percent of their earned income, and this percentage steadily declined to 3 percent for the richest.

Thus the *net* effect of taxes and transfers was remarkably progressive (column 3): The poorest 10 percent of families augmented their money income by 116 percent when transfers as well as taxes are taken into account. Families in the second decile augmented their income 35 percent; and so on. Net tax rates rose progressively from –116 percent for the poorest to +26 percent for the richest families. More likely than not, this result has been strengthened by the Tax Reform Act of 1986. As a recent study indicates, the act changed federal individual and corporate income taxes by –44 percent for the poorest income decile and for the remaining deciles by –32, –24, –16, –12, –8, –7, –6, –6, and +3 percent. This should reinforce the progressivity exhibited in column 3 of Table 2.[4]

Behavioral Feedback Effects

The imposition of taxes and the making of transfers also has a number of fairly subtle feedback effects on the behavior of both taxpayers and transfer recipients. These involve changes in work effort, saving, family composition, and attitudes that open up the possibility that the entire tax-transfer effort will ultimately turn out to be self-defeating. As two economists recently put it, "While government transfer programs have improved the standard of living for some of the poor through increased benefit levels and relaxed eligibility requirements, they have also stifled the incentives for the poor to improve their own economic status and for the nonpoor to avoid poverty. They have introduced a *perverse incentive structure,* one that penalizes self-improvement and protects individuals against the consequences of their own bad choices."[5]

Taxpayer Disincentives

Taxpayers who are asked to finance transfer payments, it has been argued, will reduce their work effort as well as their saving.

---

[4] Joseph A. Pechman, "The Future of the Income Tax," *The American Economic Review,* March 1990, pp. 1–20.

[5] James Gwartney and Thomas S. McCaleb, "Have Antipoverty Programs Increased Poverty?" *Cato Journal,* Spring/Summer 1985, p. 7. Italics added.

TABLE 3 *A Hypothetical Redistribution of Income*

	Tax rate on R (1)	Weekly hours worked by R (2)	Pre-tax income of R (3) = (2) · $25	Tax revenue and transfer to P (4) = (1) · (3)	After-tax income of R (5) = (3) − (4)
A.	0%	40	$1,000	$0	$1,000
B.	20%	35	875	175	700
C.	40%	30	750	300	450
D.	50%	20	500	250	250
E.	60%	10	250	150	100
F.	80%	2	50	40	10
G.	100%	0	0	0	0

A system of taxes and transfers that changes extreme income inequality (row A) to absolute equality (row D) may well produce disincentive effects so strong that all people are worse off than would be possible under some degree of inequality (row C). Note that for the sake of simplicity, the administrative cost of redistribution is ignored.

Labor Supply

A simple example can illustrate how the government's attempt to redistribute part of a given income from rich person R (who has a well-paying job) to poor person P (who has no job at all) may in fact reduce the overall amount of income available if, as is likely, R decides to work less when taxed.

Consider Table 3. Column (1) shows potential tax rates placed on R to finance transfers to P. Column (2) shows the likely effect of ever-increasing tax rates on R: an ever-decreasing quantity of labor supplied. Column (3) shows alternative levels of income earned by R if R's hourly pay equals $25. In this example, overall income is maximized at $1,000 a week if R is not taxed at all and P receives nothing (row A). If government intervened in the name of distributive justice and insisted on equalizing incomes (row D), society's income total would be cut in half (row D). Quite possibly, taxpayer and transfer recipient might both end up in poverty. A less extreme redistribution policy (row B or C) might avoid this result, at least for R.

Saving

In addition to lower work effort, some types of taxes discourage saving. Consider the social security tax. Because taxpayers are promised future retirement benefits, they are likely to reduce the extent to which they make provisions for old age on their own. Thus private saving falls. As noted earlier, under a pay-as-you-go system, social security taxes collected are not saved by the government either, but are immediately paid out to current beneficiaries who are likely to spend the funds on consumer goods. Thus, social security reduces the nation's saving. (Studies show the reduction to equal at most 20 percent.) As a result, fewer resources are available for the production of capital goods and this cut in investment ultimately reduces the rate of output growth over time.

Recipient Disincentives

The recipients of transfer payments, it is argued, are similarly likely to reduce their work effort and change other types of behavior as well.

EXAMPLE 2

The Welfare Trap

It is often extremely difficult for a poor person to escape from poverty by taking a full-time job because of the way government transfer benefits are reduced as earned income rises. Consider the case of a typical AFDC mother recently highlighted by a congressional investigation. As Table A illustrates, a single woman with two children living in Pennsylvania would receive cash and in-kind transfers of $8,590 a year if she earned no income of her own (row A). This would consist of $4,824 of aid to families with dependent children (AFDC) plus $1,766 of food stamps and $2,000 of free medical care (Medicaid). Now let her earn $2,000 a year at a regular job (row B). Her low earnings would qualify her for an *earned income tax credit* (EITC), a federal in-

TABLE A Earnings, Transfers, and Disposable Income for a Typical AFDC Mother with Two Children, 1989

	Earnings[a]	EITC	AFDC[b]	Food stamps	Medicaid[c]	Social security	Taxes Federal income	State income
A.	$ 0	$ 0	$4,824	$1,766	$2,000	$ 0	$0	$ 0
B.	2,000	280	4,204	1,525	2,000	150	0	0
C.	4,000	560	2,324	1,662	2,000	300	0	0
D.	5,000	700	1,384	1,730	2,000	376	0	0
E.	6,000	840	444	1,799	2,000	451	0	0
F.	7,000	910	0	1,735	2,000	526	0	0
G.	8,000	910	0	1,555	2,000	601	0	168
H.	9,000	910	0	1,375	2,000	676	0	189
I.	10,000	910	0	1,195	0	751	0	210

[a] All calculations assume that, when working, the mother has been on the job for at least four consecutive months. This determines the reduction in transfer benefits shown.
[b] Assumes the standard Pennsylvania allowance and child-care costs equal to 20 percent of earnings up to a maximum of $320 for two children.
[c] The family qualifies for Medicaid for nine additional months after it is removed from the AFDC rolls under 1984 federal law, until earnings exceed $9,000 per year. The 1988 Family Support Act allows Medicaid coverage to continue for twelve months after AFDC is lost, beginning in 1990.

Labor Supply

To the extent that they were earning some income on their own, transfer recipients may decide to earn less; to the extent that they were earning no income (the case of *P* in Table 3), they may be less inclined to look for work. The existence of the social security system, for example, undoubtedly causes many people who would otherwise continue working to retire at ages 62 or 65 (when reduced or full benefits, respectively, become available). The existence of unemployment insurance, similarly, has been linked to a greater likelihood of firms to lay off workers and of workers 1) to quit jobs and 2) not to look for another job until benefits run out.[6] On average, studies show, recipients of transfers reduce

---
[6] Lawrence Katz, "Layoffs, Recall and the Duration of Unemployment," *Working Paper 1825,* National Bureau of Economic Research, Cambridge, MA, January 1986.

come tax refund of $280, even though she has paid no income taxes. On the other hand, once she has been on the job for at least four consecutive months, her annual AFDC and food stamp allowances would be reduced by $620 and $241, respectively. In addition, she would then pay $150 in social security taxes and incur work expenses (such as child care costs) of $600 a year. Overall, her disposable income (cash and in-kind) would rise to $9,259 or by $669. Thus, she would be paying an effective tax of $2,000 − $669, or of $1,331 on her $2,000 earnings, which just about equals 67 cents on every dollar earned.

All this would get worse if her earned income rose further, as rows C through I indicate. In the $4,000 to $6,000 annual earnings range, she would effectively pay taxes in excess of her extra earnings. If her income rose from $9,000 to $10,000 a year, she would lose Medicaid benefits and effectively pay $2.58 for every extra dollar earned. At that point, she would end up with less income ($8,144) than when she didn't work at all ($8,590). Indeed, things could easily be worse than this. Oftentimes, other welfare benefits, such as housing allowances not shown here, are also phased out as earnings rise. Need one say more to explain why the poor—even when they have the opportunity—are sometimes less than eager to work?

Work expenses[d]	Disposable income: cash, food stamps, and value of Medicaid	Effective tax rate on extra earnings
$ 0	$8,590	—
600	9,259	67%
1,200	9,046	111%
1,500	8,938	111%
1,800	8,832	110%
2,100	9,019	81%
2,400	9,296	72%
2,700	9,720	58%
3,000	8,144	258%

[d] Assumed to equal 10 percent of earnings up to a maximum of $100 monthly, plus child-care costs equal to 20 percent of earnings up to the maximum allowed by AFDC, and food stamps ($320 for two children).

SOURCE: Committee on Ways and Means, U.S. House of Representatives, *Background Material and Data on Programs with the Jurisdiction of the Committee on Ways and Means,* 1989.

---

their labor supply and earned income by 23 cents for every $1 of transfers they receive.[7]

To make matters worse, many transfer programs completely discourage recipients from ever looking for a job of their own. This is because benefit levels are rapidly reduced as earned income rises, which can impose extremely high effective tax rates on earned income. Example 2 explains what is involved.

Other Behavioral Changes

Some critics have blamed the present welfare system for more than a discouragement of labor supply, including the destruction of the traditional family and a general lowering of aspirations among a

---

[7] Isabel V. Sawhill, "Poverty in the U.S.: Why Is It so Persistent?" *Journal of Economic Literature,* September 1988, pp. 1073–1119.

significant number of young people. Thus, pre-1990 AFDC eligibility rules specified that benefits could only be paid to a *single* parent with children, which might have encouraged the other parent to move out or never to move in and might have explained the rapid growth of female-headed households that contained mothers with children but no father. Indeed, one study noted that every $100 increase in monthly AFDC benefits had been associated with a 15 percent increase in the number of female-headed households.[8] Yet it is impossible to prove that AFDC has been responsible for growing rates of divorce or separation, for fewer remarriages, or the growing incidence of unmarried mothers living alone rather than with relatives. There certainly is no proof, as sometimes has been claimed, that AFDC has encouraged out-of-wedlock childbearing. What probably is true is this: Vast differences in AFDC allowances among states (varying between $100 and almost $600 per month) do encourage migration of single mothers toward the more generous states.

So far as lowered aspirations are concerned, the evidence is fairly weak as well. Does the welfare system change the attitudes of those who come in contact with it so as to breed a "culture of poverty" including dropping out of school, chronic joblessness, drug use, and crime, and in which children follow their parents naturally into the state of welfare dependency?

An Overall Assessment

What has been the overall effect of the tax and transfer system on the incidence of poverty and the American income distribution in general? One study indicates that in 1985 all types of transfers removed from poverty at least 41.6 percent of all people who would otherwise have been poor.[9] Some 30.3 percent were removed by social insurance cash payments, another 4.2 percent by public assistance cash payments, and another 7.1 percent by in-kind benefits, excluding medical care. This was clearly a considerable achievement; it was particularly impressive among the elderly of whom 71.3 and 14.0 percent, respectively, were kept out of poverty by social insurance or public assistance cash payments alone. (Among the nonelderly, the corresponding percentages were 15.4 and 4.1, respectively.)

A succinct view of what income redistribution has done to the income distribution is provided by Table 4. Clearly, there has been a noticeable, though not dramatic redistribution of income from the richest 40 percent of households to the poorest 60 percent. Can one do better than that? Many observers think so and suggest a dramatic revision of the entire welfare system. We now turn to that issue.

The Call for Welfare Reform

Some critics of existing programs of social insurance and public assistance suggest abolishing the entire patchwork of welfare programs and taking a radically new approach. The federal income tax system is already a progressive one. This feature, these critics say, could be greatly enhanced by making tax rates much bigger at the upper end and much smaller, indeed substantially *negative,* at the lower end. As a result, taxes minus transfers could be much more negative at the lower end (and much more positive at the upper end) of the income distribution that no person would remain below the poverty line. Such a reformed tax system, which would replace all existing transfer programs by a single program paying cash benefits based solely on people's income, is called a **negative income tax system.** Such a system, it is argued, would be simple to administer.

A Negative Income Tax System

The new program might work like this: Every American, every year, would file an income tax return summing up all types of income, which could quite possibly be zero. Each person would then, as the tax law provides, subtract any exemptions and deductions. If the resultant figure were negative or low, as it would be with a zero or low income, the person would get a check *from* the government. The person would "pay" a *negative* income tax. The negative tax could be set at such a rate, argue the proponents of the scheme, as to bring the income of

---

[8] *Ibid.*
[9] *Ibid.,* p. 1100.

TABLE 4 *Two Views of the U.S. Income Distribution in 1989*

Household income quintile	Percent of total income received	
	Before taxes and transfers	After taxes and cash plus in-kind transfers
Lowest	1.5	5.0
2nd	8.2	10.9
3rd	15.9	16.5
4th	25.0	23.4
Highest	49.4	44.2
Total	100.0	100.0

In recent years, the U.S. tax-transfer system has moved the income distribution toward greater equality.

SOURCE: U.S. Bureau of the Census, Current Population Reports, Series P–60, No. 169–RD, *Measuring the Effect of Benefits and Taxes on Income and Poverty: 1989* (Washington, D.C.: U.S. Government Printing Office, 1990), p. 5.

every American above the poverty level. It could abolish low after-tax incomes overnight.

Such a program would automatically reach all the poor, even the working poor, it is argued. It would be irrelevant to inquire into the causes of poverty, whether permanent or temporary. A poor person would automatically get help, whether white or black, farmer or engineer, old or young, employed or unemployed, healthy or disabled. The program would make the present patchwork of welfare programs unnecessary. There would be no necessity for establishing "need." The poor would receive help as a matter of *right*. And that help would be uniform nationwide for people in identical circumstances. Objective rules would be followed rather than the discretionary power of local administrators, which is a feature that has created much abuse in present welfare programs.

The Cost-Incentive Dilemma

In the eyes of those who object to an extremely radical redistribution of income, there is, however, one problem with a negative income tax scheme: In order to preserve work incentives, any scheme guaranteeing a high minimum income to all would require the payment of negative taxes even to many of the nonpoor. Hence, it would be very costly and necessitate extremely high taxes on high incomes. Consider a hypothetical case.

Assume we wanted to give every person an annual income of at least $10,000. A person earning nothing would receive a negative tax of $10,000. Now let the person find a job and *earn* $10,000. Should we reduce the negative tax by $10,000, leaving total income unchanged? Of course not. As Example 2 has shown, this is exactly the sort of thing that many present welfare programs do. Present programs often discourage the poor from seeking income-earning activities by reducing welfare payments by a dollar, almost that, or even more than a dollar for every dollar of earned income received. Hence people lose all incentive to work. Therefore, it is important that the negative tax be reduced by a lot less than any extra income earned. Suppose we taxed earned income and, thus, reduced negative taxes by 25 cents for every dollar earned. Then our friend would find this: Earning $10,000 would impose positive taxes of $2,500, and, thus, offset negative taxes by this amount, but total income would rise from $10,000 to $17,500. It would pay the person to work.

How much would a person have to earn before all of the negative tax revenue was lost? The answer

TABLE 5 How a Negative Income Tax System Might Work

Earned income	25% tax on earned income	Minimum guaranteed income level = negative tax	Total tax collected	After-tax income	Effective tax rate on earned income
(1)	(2)	(3)	(4) = (2) − (3)	(5) = (1) − (4)	(6) = $\frac{(4)}{(1)} \cdot 100$
0	0	10,000	−10,000	10,000	
10,000	2,500	10,000	−7,500	17,500	−75.00%
20,000	5,000	10,000	−5,000	25,000	−25.00%
30,000	7,500	10,000	−2,500	32,500	−8.33%
40,000	10,000	10,000	0	40,000	0%
50,000	12,500	10,000	2,500	47,500	5.00%
60,000	15,000	10,000	5,000	55,000	8.33%
70,000	17,500	10,000	7,500	62,500	10.71%
80,000	20,000	10,000	10,000	70,000	12.50%

(dollars per year)

In a negative income tax system, net positive tax payments begin at an earned income level equal to the guaranteed minimum level (here $10,000) divided by the tax rate on earned income (here .25), or at $40,000 in this example.

is $10,000 divided by the tax rate of 25 cents on the dollar, or .25, which comes to $40,000 a year. At this point, negative taxes would disappear. The formula is simple. Divide the desired minimum income level (our assumed $10,000) by the tax rate on earned income (our 25 cents per dollar), and we find the exact income level at which net taxes paid are zero. People below this income level would get more taxes than they paid. People above it would pay more taxes than they got.

$$\frac{\text{Desired minimum income level}}{\text{Tas rate on earned income}} = \text{Income level at which net positive tax payments begin}$$

Table 5 and Figure 1, which is based on this table, illustrate our example. Note what is implied: In order to give everyone a minimum of $10,000 a year (column 3) and in order to keep the tax rate on earned income at 25 cents on the dollar (column 2), everyone who earned less than $40,000 would receive a net amount of money from the government (column 4). This is not the case at present. Thus the government would either have to be content with losing a great amount of tax revenue or would have to raise taxes significantly on the highest income receivers. After all, the government would have to raise sufficient funds not only to pay all those negative taxes but also to carry on its other activities, such as the provision of public goods. As two rejections (in the 1970s) by the U.S. Senate of a negative income tax bill testify, this is difficult to accomplish at the same time.

FIGURE 1 The Negative Income Tax System

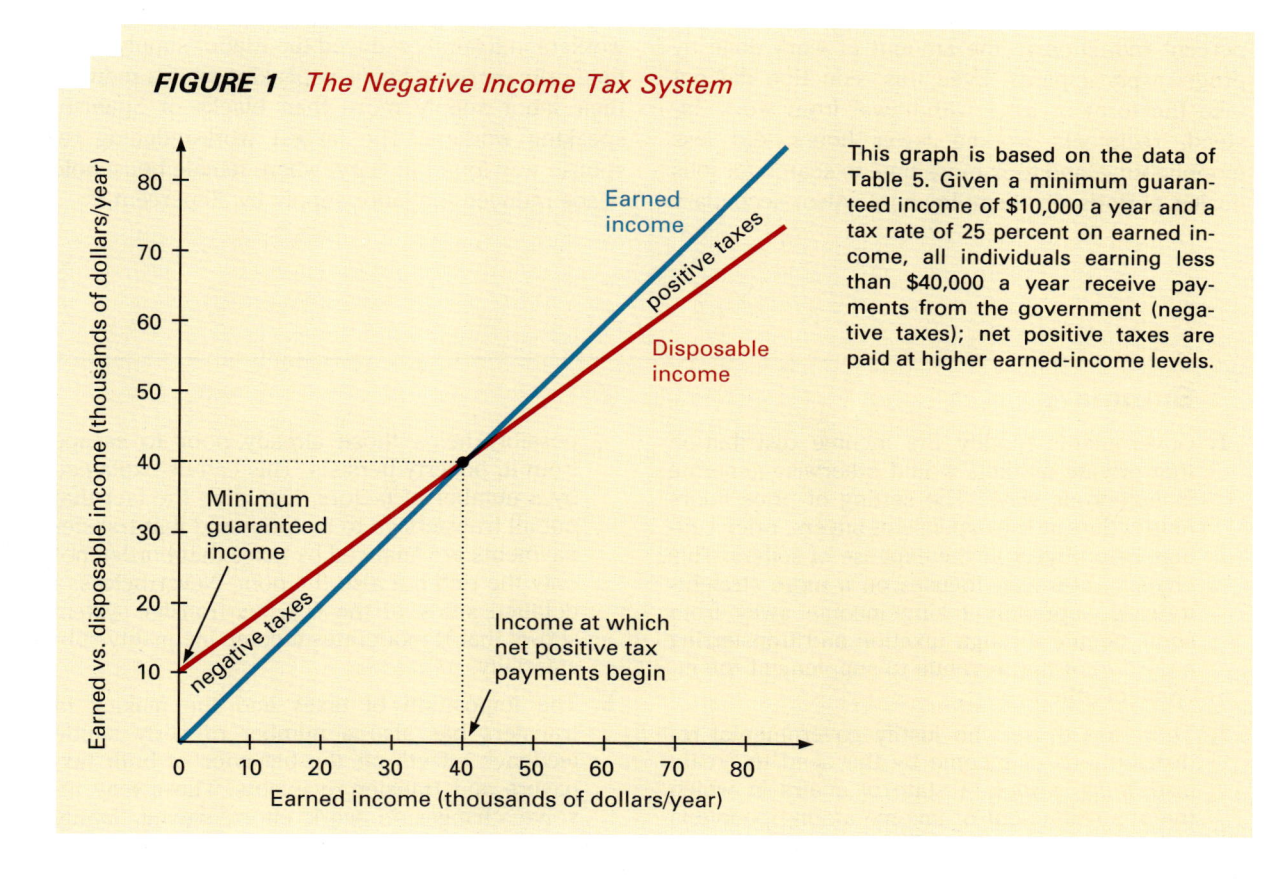

This graph is based on the data of Table 5. Given a minimum guaranteed income of $10,000 a year and a tax rate of 25 percent on earned income, all individuals earning less than $40,000 a year receive payments from the government (negative taxes); net positive taxes are paid at higher earned-income levels.

Indeed, there is no way out of this dilemma. Reducing the income level at which net positive tax payments begin (and thus reducing the overall cost of the program) can be achieved in two ways: First, one can lower the desired minimum income level. (But that may not eliminate poverty). Second, one can raise the tax rate on earned income. (But that may ruin people's incentive to work.)

The Experiments

Nevertheless, beginning in 1968, the U.S. Congress funded a number of large-scale experiments to test the negative-income tax idea. Over a three-year period, some 1,400 male-headed families in New Jersey's six largest cities received cash grants in order to assess the impact on the poor of guaranteed income. Seven different combinations of income guarantee (ranging from zero to $4,325) and tax rates on earned income (ranging from 30 to 70 percent) were tested. Other experiments were conducted with 800 rural families, whites in Iowa and blacks in North Carolina. In the 1970s, further tests were set up with 2,300 families in Seattle and 3,000 families in Denver with particular emphasis on the effects of job training and child day care. Further tests were conducted in Gary, Indiana.

Prior to the experiments, one thought had haunted the program's sponsors: Would the beneficiaries of negative income taxes simply take the money and withdraw from the labor force? Would the rest of society then have to support these people permanently? The results of the experiments showed otherwise. In New Jersey, for example, the labor supply effects were small, involving a 5- to 10-

percent reduction in the amount of work done by program participants. Even this reduction did not take the form of total withdrawal from work. Instead, recipients worked fewer hours, did less moonlighting, and took more time to search for jobs during periods of unemployment. Also, secondary workers in a family reduced their labor supply more than primary ones; English-speaking whites reduced their labor supply more than blacks or Spanish-speaking workers. The largest work-reducing response was found in Gary, where female household heads reduced the labor supply by 30 percent.[10]

Summary

1. Governments modify the income distribution that private markets would otherwise generate in numerous ways. The setting of price floors help sellers at the expense of buyers; price ceilings help buyers at the expense of sellers. This chapter, however, focuses on a more straightforward approach: taking income away from some people through taxation and transferring a portion of that revenue to supplement the income of others.

2. There are those who justify governmental redistributions of income by the need to create *distributive justice,* a state of affairs in which the apportionment of income among people is "fair" because it has been determined not merely by impersonal market forces but also by deliberate actions taken by some human authority, which establishes and rewards the relative merit of income recipients by reference to personal characteristics that they possess. Various characteristics have been suggested, including hours worked, needs, and basic human rights.

3. In the United States, two broad categories of income-redistribution programs exist: social insurance and public assistance. Social insurance programs aim to prevent people from becoming poor due to loss of income that is associated with changes in individual circumstances, such as retirement, death of the family breadwinner, disability, sickness, or unemployment. Public assistance programs aim to assist people who are already poor and seek to raise their income above the poverty line. The major programs in effect in the United States are discussed in detail.

4. Although U.S. governments at all levels are making a major effort to weave a *safety net* that prevents people from falling into poverty and possibly helps those already poor to escape from it, poverty persists. This can be explained by a number of factors, including the fact that not all transfers go to the poor and that transfer payments are financed by taxes that burden not only the rich but also the poor. Nevertheless, a detailed study of the U.S. tax-transfer system shows that it moderates income inequality substantially.

5. The imposition of taxes and the making of transfers has also a number of fairly subtle feedback effects on the behavior of both taxpayers and transfer recipients. These may involve changes in work effort, saving, family composition, and attitudes.

6. The U.S. tax-transfer system in recent years seems to have removed from poverty at least 40 percent of all people who would otherwise have been poor. This effect has been particularly dramatic among the elderly. Overall, as income-distribution data show, there has been a noticeable redistribution of income from the richest 40 percent of households to the poorest 60 percent.

7. Some critics of existing programs of social insurance and public assistance suggest abolishing the entire patchwork of welfare programs and taking a radically new approach. A negative income tax system is one alternative often proposed; it is discussed in detail.

---

[10] Joseph A. Pechman, Michael Timpane, eds., *Work Incentives and Income Guarantees: The New Jersey Negative Income Tax Experiment* (Washington, D.C.: Brookings Institution, 1975); and Robert A. Moffitt, "The Labor Supply Response in the Gary Experiment," *The Journal of Human Resources,* Fall 1979, pp. 477–487.

Key Concepts

distributive justice
entitlement programs
fully funded system
negative income tax system
pay-as-you-go system
progressive taxes
public assistance
regressive taxes
safety net
social insurance
transfer programs

Questions and Problems

1. "Perfect income equality as a basic human right would be a disaster; it would destroy the market economy." Evaluate.

2. Abba Lerner has argued that the total human welfare, or utility, derivable from the annual output of goods can be maximized only if every individual has an equal share of the output total. Using the law of declining marginal utility, try to derive a graphical illustration of Lerner's argument.

3. "Rawls is wrong. What makes him think people are unwilling to gamble? Instead of being fearful lest they end up with the smallest income (which allegedly makes them favor equality), most people are attracted by the chance of getting a higher income than anyone else (which makes them favor inequality)." Evaluate.

4. Ms. A: "Chapter 3, Figure 12, Imposing an Excise Tax on Gasoline, shows how a tax is shifted partially to buyers, partially to sellers. Do you think such a tax could ever be shifted *fully* to one of the two parties only?"
   Mr. B: "Of course. If buyers or sellers were completely *inflexible,* they would end up paying the entire tax."
   Evaluate.

5. Mr. A pays a tax of $500 on a $30,000 income, while Mr. B pays a higher tax of $600 out of $33,000 of income. Is the tax progressive, proportional, or regressive? What would your answer be if the $30,000 and $33,000 figures referred to taxable *property?* (Hint: A proportional tax takes the same percentage from all incomes.)

6. The text claims that U.S. social security taxes are regressive. Given the 1991 tax rates noted in the text, prove the point.

7. Have another look at Table 2. Illustrate the information contained in columns 1 to 3 with three *column charts*. (Hint: You may wish to review Appendix 1A, The Use of Graphs in Economics. You may also consider writing an appropriate title and caption.)

8. A 1971 federal law required all able-bodied beneficiaries under the aid to families with dependent children program to register for work or training by mid-1972 as a condition of continued eligibility. Excluded from this requirement were the ill, the elderly, children under 16, mothers with children under 6, and persons caring for the disabled. Do you think this was a good law? Consider the costs and benefits.

9. "A negative income tax system would be unworkable for this reason: Knowing full well that the government stands ready to make up the difference between people's actual earnings and a decent income, employers would raise their profits by cutting wages. Thus the general taxpayer—by supplementing low-wage incomes—would be supplementing the profits of rich owners of businesses."
   Evaluate.

10. Consider Table 4. Illustrate the information with two Lorenz curves drawn in a single graph.

11. "The way to deal with poverty in particular, and inequality in general, is to do what most Western industrialized nations do: institute a system of generous *children's allowances."* (These are

systematic payments by government to all families with children. Such payments are considered a birthright, independent of family income.) Evaluate.

12. "Income redistribution through government causes more problems than it solves. We should instead rely on *private* charity. Already, many income transfers occur *voluntarily* within families, as between the productive family members, on the one hand, and the children, the elderly, and the sick, on the other. Such intrafamily transfers should be supplemented by voluntary interfamily transfers until poverty is gone." Do some research on the extent of private charity in the United States; then evaluate the statement. (Hint: You may start out by looking at the *Statistical Abstract of the United States.*)

SOLUTIONS TO ODD-NUMBERED QUESTIONS AND PROBLEMS

Chapter 1

1. Given the text and glossary definition of *natural resources,* sand at a beach not yet discovered by people, sunshine, and a school of tuna in the ocean would always be classified in that category. A highway, a college building, and a can of peas would never be so classified (the first two are real capital resources; the can of peas is a consumption good if owned by a household, or real capital if part of a firm's inventory). The 100 cubic feet of coal, cow, and acre of land might be classified as natural resources if the coal was unmined, the cow was a wild animal, and the land was virgin. They might be capital resources if the coal sat in the factory yard, the cow was domesticated and used on a farm, and the land was cultivated. Indeed, they might even be considered consumption goods if a household, say, had purchased the coal and was keeping the cow as a pet and the land for private enjoyment.

3. This statement seems to be true, but is false. An increased quantity of money would in no way increase the flow of real resources (assuming they were fully and efficiently employed originally); thus, neither would it increase the flow of goods available to people. The fallacy might be illustrated with theater tickets and seats. Tickets, like money, could easily be increased a thousandfold; but theater seats, like the annual flow of goods produced, can only be increased with difficulty due to the limited availability of resources.

5. The text and glossary definitions of *free goods* point to the answer. Note the phrase "if the goods could be had for nothing." This condition rarely holds under present U.S. circumstances. Thus governments that acquire highways, schools, and agricultural surplus commodities pay for them (although subsequently, at the time of use, private users of such goods may not have to make any direct payments). Use of the air for communications or waste disposal is often restricted to those who are licensed by the government. Private would-be users of agricultural goods designated as surplus or of coal in the ground can seldom acquire them for nothing.

Even if a good can be had for nothing, the rest of the definition of a free good must be considered. Are the goods "available in larger quantities than all people would want to take in a given period," as the definition puts it? That depends on the way one defines the goods and the time period involved! Consider the use of a zero-toll highway. If the service desired by a user involved travel near New York City, at 55 miles per hour, the good may indeed be free to this user between 3 and 5 A.M. on Mondays. Yet from 8 to 9 A.M. on Mondays, in city-bound lanes, this desired service may not be available because too many people desire it at the same time. Then the free good would become scarce, and unless it was rationed (through physical highway access controls or pricing) the quality of the good would deteriorate. In this case, 55-mph travel from 8 to 9 A.M. on Mondays in city-bound lanes might become totally unavailable and 10-mph travel becomes the closest substitute.

7. See Figure A.1. The threshold situation would be depicted by circles of equal size.

FIGURE A.1 *A Society of Abundance*

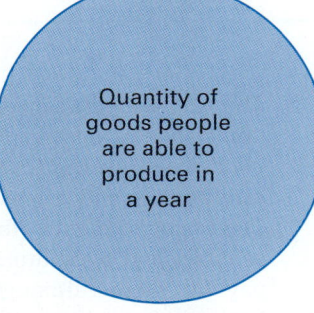

9. See Figure A.2 and compare it with Chapter 1, Figure 2. The frontier would reach farther on the horizontal axis (to *G* rather than *B*) but not farther on the vertical axis.

FIGURE A.2 *Expanding Production Possibilities*

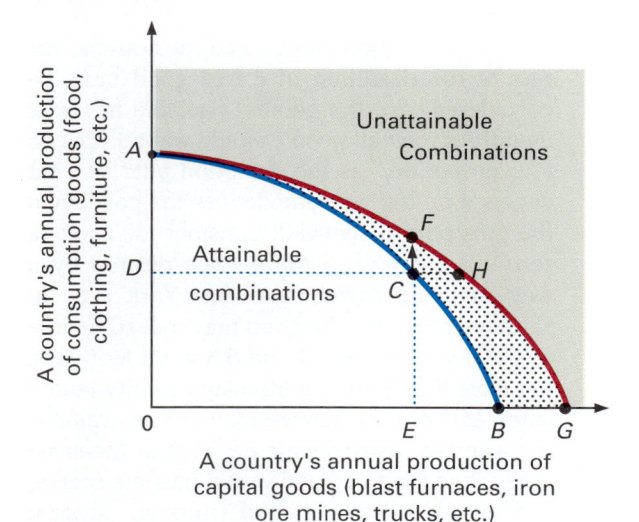

The shaded world of the impossible would shrink by the dotted area. People could still have more consumption goods; for example, by moving from *C* to *F* or to any other point along the color line between *A* and just above *H*.

11. a. Every minute of leisure enjoyed could be used instead working for pay. The income forgone is the opportunity cost.
    b. The saying reflects the very thought noted in (a).
    c. Almost certainly, there would remain a scarcity of time. You may wish to read Staffan B. Linder, *The Harried Leisure Class* (New York: Columbia University Press, 1970). This amusing book notes how the scarcity of time limits people's consumption choices even if the scarcity of goods does not. Also, note the symposium on this book in *Quarterly Journal of Economics,* November 1973, pp. 628–675.

13. All of these statements are *true.*
    a. True. Consider, for example, Chapter 1, Figure 7, but imagine it to refer to a household that must choose between food and clothing. Given a limited money income, more food means less clothing and vice versa. The upper graph may, thus, show food consumption's declining marginal benefits (measured, perhaps, in hypothetical "units of satisfaction"); the lower graph may show food's rising marginal cost (representing forgone marginal benefits of decreased clothing consumption). As in Figure 7, 3 units of food may be optimal. The marginal benefit may, thus, equal $c = 300$ units of satisfaction—a far cry from $z = 0$ units associated with consuming 29 units of food (not shown).
    b. True. Once again, the optimization principle is involved. Even if a government project had positive marginal benefits, it would be foolish to pour resources into a project (say, education) while greater positive benefits could be reaped elsewhere (such as by pouring resources into food production, health care, or foreign aid). These greater positive marginal benefits, should they be sacrificed, would become the greater marginal cost of extra education, and *MC* above *MB* would violate the optimization principle.
    c. True. The optimization principle warns us to forget about totals and to concentrate on *marginal* benefits and costs. Remember the 3-unit optimum level of cancer screening

TABLE A.1 *Alternative Budget Allocations and Their Implications*

Number of $5 million units spent on		Number of lives saved from		
Cancer screening	Heart-attack treatment	Cancer screening	Heart-attack treatment	Total
0	6	0	1,650	1,650
1	5	800	1,600	2,400
2	4	1,300	1,500	2,800
3	3	1,600	1,300	2,900
4	2	1,800	1,000	2,800
5	1	1,900	600	2,500
6	0	1,950	0	1,950

discussed in the text. Then note in Figure 4 how maximizing *total* benefit, TB, would require more than six units of cancer screening—an excessive amount. Or note in Figure 6 how minimizing *total* cost, TC, would require zero units of cancer screening—an insufficient amount.

d. True. We would have more than enough of everything. Thus we could always get more of one thing without incurring the cost of having to give up something else.

15. See Table A.1. The optimal division is the same as that suggested by the optimization principle: Spend three $5 million units (or a total of $15 million) on each program, saving 2,900 lives.

Chapter 2

1. The dumping of wastes on flower gardens rarely happens because real-world governments do establish and protect property rights in scarce real estate. The dumping of wastes in the air happens all the time because real-world governments fail to establish property rights in the scarce waste-absorption capacity of air. Yes, one might avoid the latter in the same way as the former, by seeing to it that government performs the crucial functions required of it in an ideal market economy. One of these functions is to establish property rights in *all* scarce things. See the chapter "Externalities and Environmental Economics" for a more detailed discussion of this issue.

3. There are lots of such instances; here are a few:
    a. Coastal nations have extended their sovereignty from a traditional 3 mile zone beyond their coastlines to 12 and then 200 miles (in order to protect fishing and oil deposits).
    b. A 1982 U.N. treaty (not signed by the U.S.) handed the sea bed (and, thus, two thirds of the earth's surface) to an International Sea Bed Authority that would dole out rights to valuable deep-sea nodules of phosphate, ferromanganese, copper, nickel, and more.
    c. In 1979, the United Nations' Committee on Outer Space approved a treaty that would regulate the expected future exploitation of the moon's resources.
    d. In the 1980s, the Federal Aviation Administration assigned some 3,300 takeoff and landing slots at four major U.S. airports: National Airport in Washington, D.C., O'Hare in Chicago, and Kennedy and La Guardia in New York.
    e. The U.S. Environmental Protection Agency has assigned the limited waste-absorption

capacity of the natural environment to would-be waste dumpers. See the chapter "Externalities and Environmental Economics" for further detail.

5. Government might pump newly created money into the spending and revenue stream flowing through the goods markets to firms (upper loop) and receive goods in return. It might also pump money into the cost and income stream flowing through the resource markets to households (lower loop) and receive resource services in return.

   Government might decrease the money supply by taxing any of the money flows depicted in the graph and then not spending the receipts (taxes on sales, payrolls, incomes, and the like).

7. There is much truth to this. Consider how soldiers fight not only for fear of jail or the firing squad, but also for money, love of country, or their buddies. Or note how citizens soften the impact of bureaucracy by bribing officials or trading in black markets. And note how pure command systems are often overthrown in revolt.

9. Positive: a, b, f, h, i, j
   Normative: c, d, e, g

Chapter 3

1. See Figure A.3.

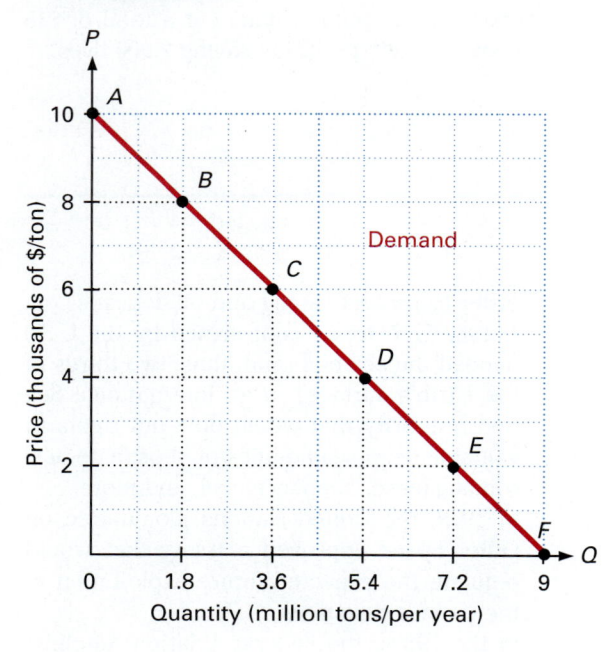

   FIGURE A.3

   [Graph showing Price (thousands of $/ton) on the y-axis from 0 to 10, and Quantity (million tons/per year) on the x-axis from 0 to 9, with points A (0,10), B, C (3.6,6), D, E (7.2,2), F (9,0) on the Demand line]

3. Complementary: $a, b, f, i, j, k, l, n, o, p, t, w$
   Independent: d, g, s, z
   Substitute: $c, e, h, m, q, r, u, v, x, y$

5. Demand is given by $Q_D = 20 - 2P$
   Supply is given by $Q_S = 2P$
   In equilibrium, $Q_D = Q_S$
   Hence $20 - 2P = 2P$
   $20 = 4P$
   $P = 5$

   Given $P = 5$, and substituting, we find $Q_D = 20 - 2(5) = 10$ and $Q_S = 2(5) = 10$

7. a. D shifts right, S shifts right; effect on P uncertain (depends on extent of shifts), Q rises
   b. D shifts right, S shifts left; P rises, effect on Q uncertain
   c. D shifts left, S shifts right; P falls, effect on Q uncertain
   d. D shifts left, S shifts left; effect on P uncertain, Q falls

9. The statement is wrong and mixes up a fall in *demand* (a shift in line D) with a fall in *quantity demanded* (a movement along line D). Consider Figure A.4 and its initial equilibrium at e.

   FIGURE A.4

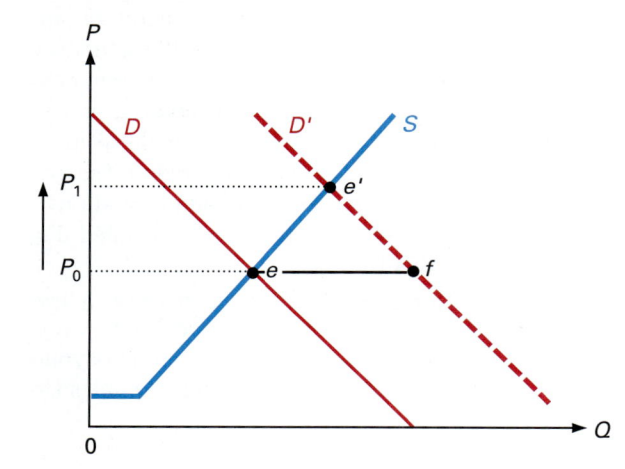

   [Graph showing P on y-axis, Q on x-axis, with curves D, D' (dashed), S; equilibrium points e at P_0, e' at P_1, and f]

FIGURE A.5

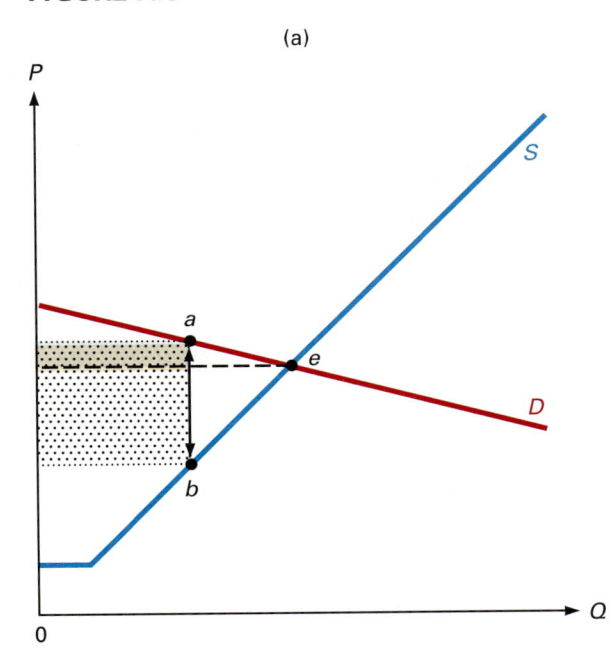

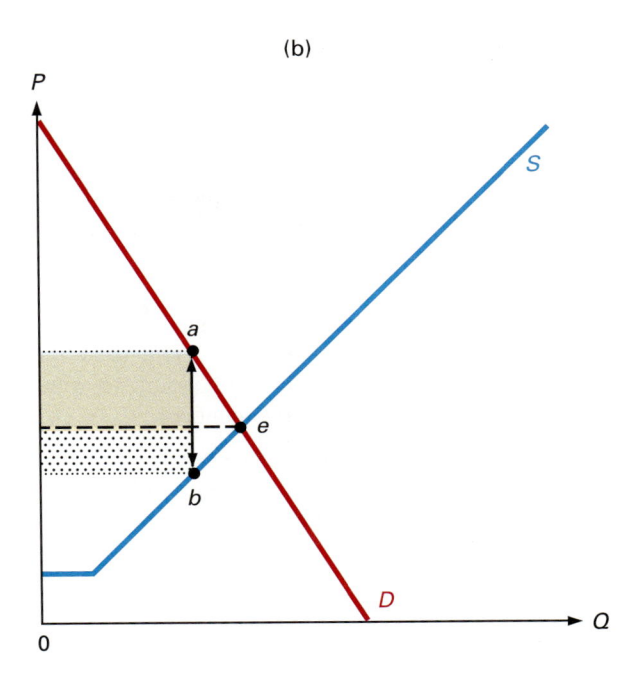

(a)

(b)

Why should price rise in the first place? One possibility, shown here, is a rise in demand from D to D'. (Another possibility, not shown, is a fall in supply.) The temporary shortage (of ef) would raise price from P_0 to P_1, but in the process, *quantity demanded* (not *demand*) would fall (along fe'). Along with a simultaneous rise in quantity supplied (along ee'), the shortage would disappear. We would end up at new equilibrium e', not where we started.

11. Theoretically, as panels (a) and (d) of Chapter 3, Figure 7 indicate, a decrease in demand or an increase in supply would bring about this result. In fact, both of these events did occur: Because of the cholesterol scare, demand fell precipitously. Because of improvements in technology, supply rose. (Hens laying more eggs per week were introduced, so were large-scale production methods; firms with over 100,000 hens became the norm.)

13. As later chapters will show, these graphs are indeed not unrelated. Behind the "law" of downward-sloping demand lies the declining marginal benefit that consumers experience as quantity consumed is increased. Behind the "law" of upward-sloping supply lies the rising marginal cost that firms incur as quantity produced is increased.

15. A superior government could assert property rights in the river and require would-be dumpers to buy dumping permits. By auctioning off permits for only 3.6 million tons (picture a vertical supply line in Figure A.3 at this quantity), an equilibrium price of $6,000 per ton would be established (point C), so quantity demanded would fall along FC.

By auctioning off permits for only 1.8 million tons (picture a vertical supply line at this lower quantity), an equilibrium price of $8,000 per ton would be established (point B), so quantity demanded would fall along FB.

By auctioning off no permits at all (picture a vertical supply line at zero quantity and equal to the graph's vertical axis), an equilibrium price of $10,000 per ton would be established (point A), so quantity demanded would fall to zero as well.

In each case, the city would have to turn to alternatives (such as first-stage, second-stage, or third-stage sewage treatment) in order to cut the quantity it simply dumps down to the allowable amount. (Third-stage sewage treatment produces fertilizer plus drinking water!)

17. If the demand and supply lines' relative slopes were different than in Chapter 3, Figure 12, the burden might be unequally shared. Consider Figure A.5 where an identical per-unit tax (ab) is imposed in two different circumstances. In panel (a), the burden of the tax falls disproportionately on sellers (dotted); in panel (b), on buyers (shaded).

Chapter 4

1. Several answers are possible, such as a) changing the 10 to 25, b) changing the 1 to .4, c) changing the 5 to 2, or d) changing the 1/5 to .5. In all of these cases, the opportunity cost of each good would be identical in both countries. Neither country would have a comparative advantage in either good. (The trick involved: make the *ratio* of cloth hours to wine hours in both countries the same.)

3. All three are possibilities once one realizes that France has a comparative advantage in computers (the marginal rate of transformation being 1 computer for 2 TV sets), while Italy has a comparative advantage in TV sets (the marginal rate of transformation being 1 computer for 3 TV sets or 1/3 computer for 1 TV set).

   Case (a): France +1 computer, −2 TV sets
   Italy −2/3 computer, +2 TV sets } net gain +1/3 computer

   Case (b): France +1 computer, −2 TV sets
   Italy −1 computer, +3 TV sets } net gain +1 TV set

   Case (c): France +2 computers, −4 TV sets
   Italy −1⅔ computers, +5 TV sets } net gain +1/3 computer, + 1 TV set

5. Great Britain in trucks (opportunity cost is 100 cameras per truck, while it is 125 cameras in West Germany); West Germany in cameras (opportunity cost is .008 trucks per camera, while it is .01 truck in Great Britain).

7. The comment is well taken, although it's not really a flaw in the theory. The theory, as presented in this chapter, abstracts from transportation costs. Obviously, international trade is only worthwhile if the gains from it exceed the extra costs that must be incurred for its sake. These costs do include goods forgone as resources are diverted to transportation as well as to negotiating complicated international transactions, setting up foreign-exchange markets, and the like. History shows that it's still worth it.

9. One French computer would trade for at least 2 and at most 3 Italian TV sets. Why? By sacrificing 1 computer, France can always get 2 TVs at home; so it wouldn't take fewer when trading with Italy. By sacrificing 3 TVs, Italy could always get 1 computer at home; so it wouldn't give up more than 3 TVs when trading with France.

11. The calculations can be made from the graph by noting rectangular and triangular areas as follows:

    a. *Change in consumer surplus*

    rectangle *akod* =
    $$6.8¢ \times 18.6 \text{ billion} = \$1.22808 \text{ billion}$$
    triangle *doe* =
    $$\frac{6.8¢ \times 1.12 \text{ billion}}{2} = .03808 \text{ billion}$$
    $$\overline{\$1.26616 \text{ billion}}$$

b. *Change in producer surplus*

rectangle *akmb* =
$$6.8¢ \times 6.14 \text{ billion} = \$.41752 \text{ billion}$$
triangle *mnb* =
$$\frac{6.8¢ \times 5.96 \text{ billion}}{2} = .20264 \text{ billion}$$
$$\overline{\$.62016 \text{ billion}}$$

c. *Tariff revenue*

cross-hatched rectangle *cghd* =
$$2.8¢ \times 5.96 \text{ billion} = \$.16688 \text{ billion}$$

d. *Quota value*

dotted rectangle *gnoh* =
$$4¢ \times 5.96 \text{ billion} = \$.2384 \text{ billion}$$

e. *Deadweight loss*
Two shaded triangles

$$bnc = \frac{6.8¢ \times 5.96 \text{ billion}}{2} = \$.20264 \text{ billion}$$

$$doe = \frac{6.8¢ \times 1.12 \text{ billion}}{2} = \$.03808 \text{ billion}$$
$$\overline{\$.24144 \text{ billion}}$$

13. a. If foreigners truly undersold us in everything, we would demand a great deal of their currency, yet they would not supply any of it, being uninterested in our high-priced goods. The resultant shortage would drive up the exchange rate. Before long, foreigners would cease to undersell us in everything.

   b. Have another look at panel (a) of Figure 6. It is possible that foreigners pay a *portion* of tariff revenue, here exemplified by the difference between P_f and P_t^*, multiplied by hi. On the other hand, as Figure A, Example 1, shows, foreigners may pay no part of a tariff at all. It all depends on whether the imposition of the tariff does or does not reduce the price at which foreigners offer their product to the world market. If the tariff-imposing country buys a significant portion of world output, the world market price is likely to fall; if it doesn't buy much, it won't.

Chapter 5

1. In the absence of cardinal utility measurement (and no one has yet found a way to carry it out), there simply is no way to determine objectively which choice would produce "pleasure that outweighs the pain." Bentham's felicific calculus in unusable in practice.

3. Examples are rare, indeed. Veblen himself mentioned mink coats. Others have suggested that people may buy less at a lower price if they think, perhaps incorrectly, that low price denotes low quality. Rumor has it that slow-selling $1 lipsticks sold like hotcakes once price was raised to $5.

5. If consumer B disappeared, each one of the entries in column 5 would be reduced by the corresponding entry in column 3. This would show graphically by a leftward shift of the entire market demand line. Economists would talk of a "fall in demand."

7. We do not know, unless told what the prices of these goods are. If all prices were the same per pound of product, the answer would be "yes," otherwise it would be "no." See Focus 1, "Jevons' Rule."

9. The question cannot be answered unless we are given the prices of X and Y and the consumer's budget. If the prices were identical and equal to, say, $10/unit of X as well as Y, one could determine the following:

Good X

Quantity consumed	Marginal utility per unit	Marginal utility per dollar
1	50	5
2	40	4
3	30	3
4	20	2
5	10	1

Good Y

Quantity consumed	Marginal utility per unit	Marginal utility per dollar
1	100	10
2	50	5
3	25	2.5
4	10	1
5	5	.5

If now the budget equaled, say, $90, the consumer would optimize by buying $5X$ and $4Y$, equating the marginal utilities at 1 util per dollar and obeying Jevons' Rule:

$$\frac{MU_X}{P_X} = \frac{10 \text{ utils}}{\$10} = \frac{MU_Y}{P_Y} = \frac{10 \text{ utils}}{\$10}$$

Chapter 6

1. Using the Focus 1 formula,

$$AB: \frac{\frac{4-0}{4+0}}{\frac{8-10}{8+10}} = \frac{1}{-.\overline{111}} = |9|$$

$$BC: \frac{\frac{8-4}{8+4}}{\frac{6-8}{6+8}} = \frac{.333}{-.143} = |2.33|$$

$$CD: \frac{\frac{12-8}{12+8}}{\frac{4-6}{4+6}} = \frac{.2}{-.2} = |1|$$

$$DE: \frac{\frac{16-12}{16+12}}{\frac{2-4}{2+4}} = \frac{.143}{-.333} = |.429|$$

FIGURE A.6

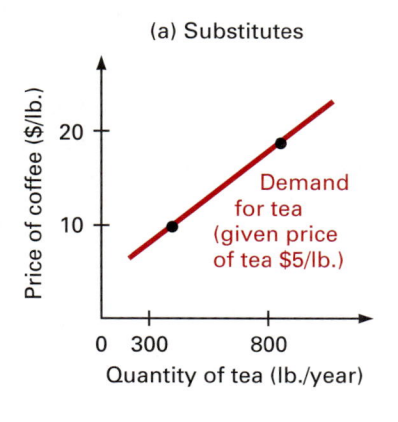

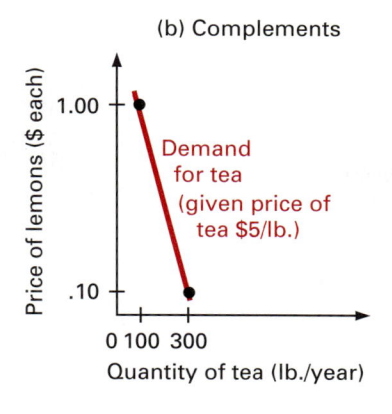

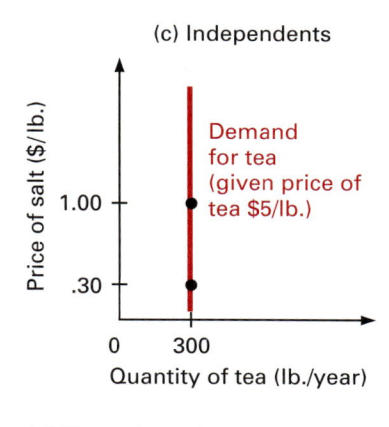

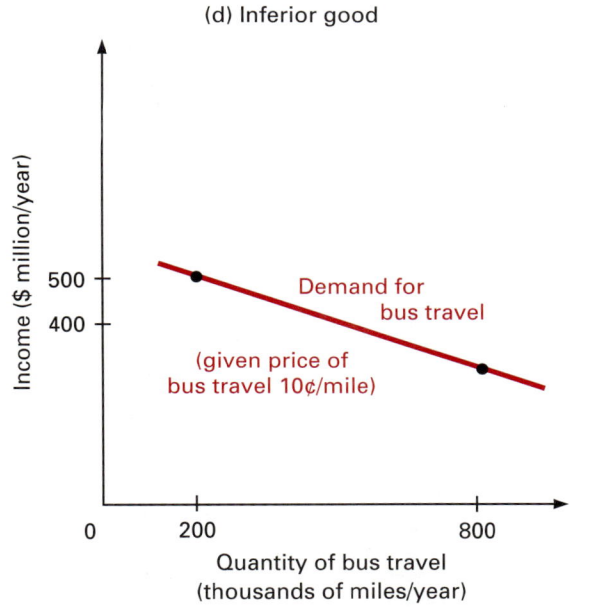

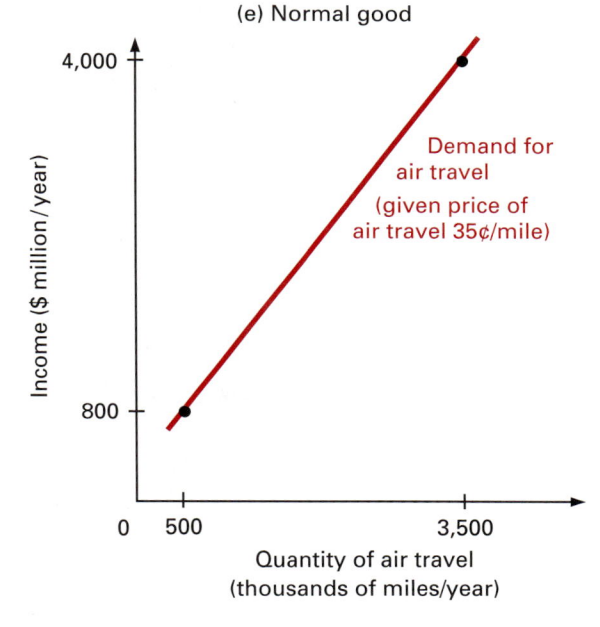

(a) Substitutes — Price of coffee ($/lb.) vs Quantity of tea (lb./year); Demand for tea (given price of tea $5/lb.); points at (300, 10) and (800, 18).

(b) Complements — Price of lemons ($ each) vs Quantity of tea (lb./year); Demand for tea (given price of tea $5/lb.); points at (100, 1.00) and (300, .10).

(c) Independents — Price of salt ($/lb.) vs Quantity of tea (lb./year); Demand for tea (given price of tea $5/lb.); points at (300, 1.00) and (300, .30).

(d) Inferior good — Income ($ million/year) vs Quantity of bus travel (thousands of miles/year); Demand for bus travel (given price of bus travel 10¢/mile); points at (200, 500) and (800, 400).

(e) Normal good — Income ($ million/year) vs Quantity of air travel (thousands of miles/year); Demand for air travel (given price of air travel 35¢/mile); points at (500, 800) and (3,500, 4,000).

$$EF: \quad \frac{\frac{20-16}{20+16}}{\frac{0-2}{0+2}} = \frac{.\overline{111}}{-1} = |.111|$$

3. Using the Focus 1 formula,

$$E_D^{o-p} = \frac{\frac{18-16}{18+16}}{\frac{1-2}{1+2}} = \frac{.059}{-.333} = |.18|$$

5. a. A 1 percent change in price changes the quantity of food (or root beer) demanded by .18 (or 2.22) percent in the opposite direction.

b. A 1 percent change in the price of one good changes the other good's quantity demanded in the same direction by .13, .18, 4.12, and .72 percent, respectively.

7. The company could have raised total revenues by raising its ticket price: Each 1 percent increase in price would have lowered quantity demanded by only .657 percent. In addition, Shakespeare performances were a luxury good, given a positive income elasticity exceeding 1.

9. See Figure A.6. The demand lines of panels (d) and (e) that relate quantity demanded to income are also called *Engel curves*.

11. Of course. When goods are produced jointly (wool and mutton) or when goods are competitive in production (wheat and rye), economists calculate cross-price elasticities of supply, which show the responsiveness of one good's quantity supplied to the price of another good. Similarly, various income elasticities of supply can be calculated—for example, the responsiveness of the supply of a good to incomes earned in the industry could be determined to see how changed incomes change the quantity of inputs supplied to an industry and hence the quantity supplied of the industry's product. In general, though, economists have been less inclined to calculate these other types of elasticities than in the case of demand because such estimates are less useful. Unlike demand elasticities, supply elasticities tell us nothing, for example, about the amount of money spent by buyers or taken in by sellers.

Chapter 7

1. It all depends on whether managerial or market coordination costs are lower. For example, if the needed electricity is acquired more cheaply by buying generators, fuel oil, and labor services and letting a manager supervise its in-house production than by simply buying it from an outside electric power company, the former approach will be taken. The same is true for any other commodity or service, such as those mentioned in the question.

3. Stalin provided bonuses for peasants and workers who fulfilled his planned output targets and he promoted "socialist education campaigns" designed to instill his own values in the minds of his agents. (In addition, of course, he built a terror machine to frighten everyone into following his orders.)

Chapter 7A

1. Consider the following balance sheet:

Consolidated balance sheet of all U.S. corporations
(in billions of dollars, December 31, 1985)

Assets		Liabilities and net worth	
Cash	683	Liabilities	
Accounts receivable	3,318	Accounts payable	892
Government securities	917	Bonds issued	
Inventories	715	short term	1,001
Plant and equipment	3,174	long term	1,699
Land	141	Other liabilities	5,877
			9,469
Other	3,825	Net worth	3,304
Total	12,773	Total	12,773

3. The annual income is a flow concept and irrelevant for a balance sheet; the net worth equals −2,920.

Balance sheet (*as of unspecified date*)

Assets		Liabilities and net worth	
Cash	100	Tuition due	5,000
Clothing	500	IOU	20
Books	400		
Car	1,100	Net worth	−2,920
Total	2,100	Total	2,100

Chapter 8

1. *Marginal physical products*

Range	MPP
A–B	$\frac{+1000}{+100} = +10$ tons/extra hour
B–C	$\frac{+800}{+100} = +8$ tons/extra hour
C–D	$\frac{+600}{+100} = +6$ tons/extra hour
D–E	$\frac{+400}{+100} = +4$ tons/extra hour
E–F	$\frac{+200}{+100} = +2$ tons/extra hour

Average physical products

A: $\frac{0}{0} = 0$ ton/hour

B: $\frac{1000}{100} = 10$ tons/hour

C: $\frac{1800}{200} = 9$ tons/hour

D: $\frac{2400}{300} = 8$ tons/hour

E: $\frac{2800}{400} = 7$ tons/hour

F: $\frac{3000}{500} = 6$ tons/hour

3. The law is, in fact, a special case of the more general law of declining marginal benefits. Compare this chapter's Figure 4, Total, Marginal, and Average Product, with Chapter 1's Figure 4, Cancer Screening: Declining Marginal Benefits, or Figure 5, Heart Attack Treatment: Declining Marginal Benefits. Or look at the chapter "Consumer Preferences and Demand" and review Figure 1, Total Utility Versus Marginal Utility. In all these cases and more, a principle of diminishing returns is at work.

5. a. False. It could increase it by *reducing* the variable input quantity (as from *H* toward *B* in this chapter's Figure 3).
b. False. When marginal physical product *lies above* average physical product, the latter rises. A rising *MPP* that lies below *APP* will still reduce *APP*. And *APP* can rise even with a falling *MPP*, as long as *MPP* lies above *APP* (as to the left of *M* in this chapter's Figure 4).
c. False. When marginal physical product *lies below* average physical product, the latter falls. A falling *MPP* that lies above *APP* (as to the left of *M* in this chapter's Figure 4) will still raise *APP*. And *APP* can fall even with a rising *MPP*, as long as *MPP* lies below *APP*.
d. False. Under the circumstances, *APP* can rise or fall. See this chapter's Figure 4.
e. False. Under the circumstances, *MPP* rises only when total product rises at an increasing rate, before the point of diminishing returns is reached. See this chapter's Figure 3 or 4.

Production function exhibits	Behavior of any input's average physical product under different returns to scale when	
	Scale is expanded	Scale is contracted
Constant returns to scale	APP unchanged	APP unchanged
Increasing returns to scale	APP rises	APP falls
Decreasing returns to scale	APP falls	APP rises

7. In each case, we must figure the ratio of total output quantity to total input quantity (for any input). If both change by the same percentage, the ratio (which is the average physical product) remains unchanged; otherwise it changes, as indicated by the definitions of constant, increasing, and decreasing returns to scale.

   The above table summarizes the consequences.

9. Theater, opera, and symphony showed decreasing returns to scale for all scalar adjustments. (For example, the reduction of all theater inputs to 25 percent reduced theater output to only 28.23 percent; a 4-fold increase of all theater inputs raised theater output only 3.2361-fold.) Ballet, however, was a maverick, showing increasing returns to scale for input decreases and extreme decreasing returns to scale for input increases. (For example, a reduction of all ballet inputs to 25 percent reduced ballet output to 13.15 percent; a 4-fold increase of all ballet inputs raised ballet output only 1.1139-fold.)

Chapter 9

1. The effects are summarized in Tables A.2 and A.3.

TABLE A.2

	Change	Effects on table		
		FC (col. 4)	VC (col. 5)	TC (col. 6)
a.	fixed input price rises	rises	no change	rises
	fixed input price falls	falls	no change	falls
b.	variable input price rises	no change	rises	rises
	variable input price falls	no change	falls	falls
c.	fixed input quantity smaller	falls	output (col. 3) declines and no change	falls
	fixed input quantity larger	rises	output (col. 3) rises and no change	rises
d.	technical knowledge advances	the same inputs (cols. 1 and 2) yield higher output (col. 3), no effects on cost entries *or* given outputs require fewer inputs, all costs fall		
	technical knowledge regresses	the same inputs (cols. 1 and 2) yield lower output (col. 3), no effects on cost entries *or* given outputs require more inputs, all costs rise		

TABLE A.3

	Change	Effects on graph		
		FC line	VC line	TC line
a.	fixed input price rises	shifts up	no change	shifts up
	fixed input price falls	shifts down	no change	shifts down
b.	variable input price rises	no change	origin unchanged, otherwise shifts up	origin unchanged, otherwise shifts up
	variable input price falls	no change	origin unchanged, otherwise shifts down	origin unchanged, otherwise shifts down
c.	technical knowledge advances	e.g., shifts down	e.g., origin unchanged, otherwise shifts down/right	e.g., origin unchanged, otherwise shifts down/right
	technical knowledge regresses	e.g., shifts up	e.g., origin unchanged, otherwise shifts up/left	e.g., origin unchanged, otherwise shifts up/left
d.	fixed input quantity smaller	shifts down	origin unchanged, otherwise shifts left/up	origin unchanged, otherwise shifts left/up
	fixed input quantity larger	shifts up	origin unchanged, otherwise shifts right/down	origin unchanged, otherwise shifts right/down

TABLE A.4

	Change	Effects on graph		
		AFC line	AVC line	ATC line
a.	fixed input price rises	shifts up	no change	shifts up
	fixed input price falls	shifts down	no change	shifts down
b.	variable input price rises	no change	shifts up	shifts up
	variable input price falls	no change	shifts down	shifts down
c.	technical knowledge advances	e.g., shifts down	e.g., shifts down	e.g., shifts down
	technical knowledge regresses	e.g., shifts up	e.g., shifts up	e.g., shifts up
d.	fixed input quantity smaller	shifts down	shifts up	shifts up
	fixed input quantity larger	shifts up	shifts down	shifts down

3. See Table A.4.
5. a. The two forgone potential salary entries would have to be raised to whatever maximum incomes could have been earned if they had previously spent as much time working for pay as they do now. The proper comparison is thus not with the couple's salaries from teaching and editing (referred

to in the opening paragraph of the section Short-Run Costs: Tabular Illustrations), but with these salaries plus additional salaries from, say, extra evening taxi-driving and marital counseling jobs.

b. Considering the forgone salaries of $25,000, the willingness to pay $2,000 for the privilege of being their own bosses might be interpreted to mean that running the new firm brought psychological income of $27,000. One might deduct this $27,000 from the fixed-cost total in order to arrive, ultimately, at a more meaningful profit figure that would indicate the income difference between the old and the new occupation in a more comprehensive sense.

7. Consider the production function given in this chapter's Problem 2. Moving from alternative A toward E, the marginal physical products are +400, +300, +200, +100; hence the law of diminishing returns is operating. At the same time, total cost is rising by +$20,000 at each step (because variable inputs only are changing, they are changing by 1 unit at a time, and they cost $20,000/unit). Since $MC = (\Delta TC / \Delta Q)$, marginal costs are:

Range AB: $\dfrac{+\$20{,}000}{+400} = \$50$

Range BC: $\dfrac{+\$20{,}000}{+300} = \$66.67$

Range CD: $\dfrac{+\$20{,}000}{+200} = \$100$

Range DE: $\dfrac{+\$20{,}000}{+100} = \$200$

All this makes perfect sense. When the law of diminishing returns prevails, successive 1-unit increases in physical variable input yield ever smaller additions to physical output. Hence successive equal increases in variable cost (here $20,000) yield ever smaller additions to physical output. Hence added units of output cost ever more additional dollars.

9. a. See Figure A.7.
b. The average variable cost of any chosen output level VC/Q can easily be calculated as the slope of a ray emanating from origin 0 and aiming at the variable cost curve right above the output level in question.
Example 1: At an output level of 5,000

FIGURE A.7 *Variable Cost Versus Average Variable Cost*

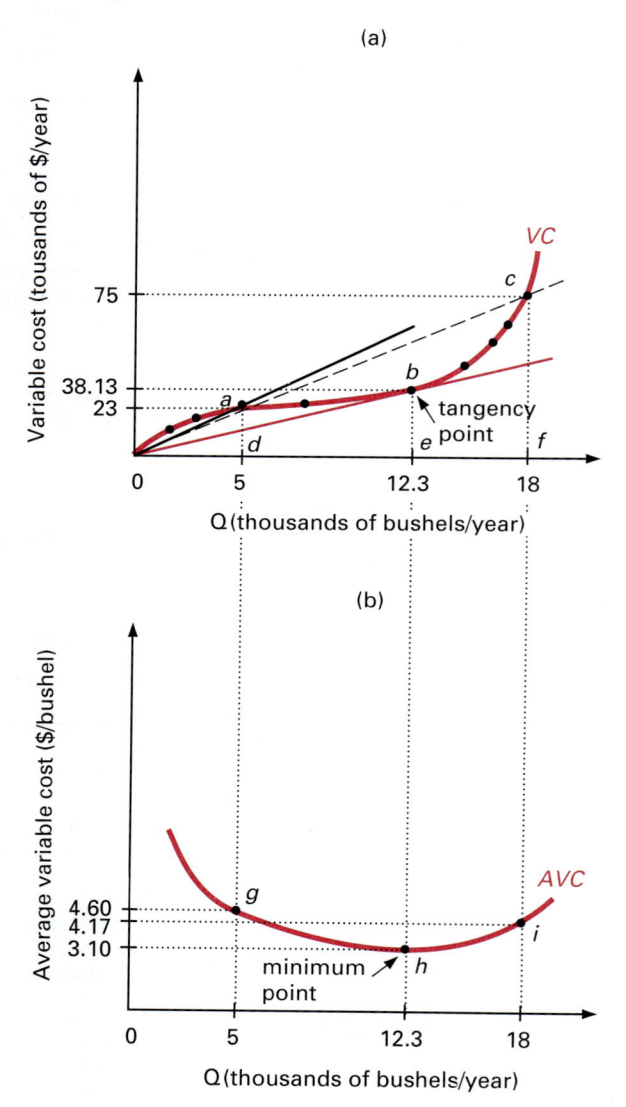

The behavior of average variable cost as output expands—panel (b)—can be gauged from the ever-changing slopes of rays emanating at origin 0 and aiming, successively, at points farther and farther to the right along the variable cost curve—panel (a).

bushels/year (distance $0d$), variable cost equals $23,000/year (distance ad). Hence average variable cost equals $4.60/bushel. This number equals $ad/0d$, the *slope* of a ray from 0 to a and beyond. It is also plotted as the *height* of the AVC curve—point g, panel (b).
Example 2: At an output level of 12,300

bushels/year (distance $0e$), variable cost equals \$38,130/year (distance be). Hence average variable cost equals \$3.10/bushel. This number equals $be/0e$, the slope of a ray from 0 to b and beyond. It is also plotted as the height of the AVC curve—point h, panel (b).

Example 3: At an output level of 18,000 bushels/year (distance $0f$), variable cost equals \$75,000/year (distance cf). Hence average variable cost equals \$4.17/bushel. This number equals $cf/0f$, the slope of a ray from 0 to c and beyond. It is also plotted as the height of the AVC curve—point i, panel (b).

To sum up, picture in your mind a whole series of rays, always originating at 0 in panel (a) and aiming, successively, at points along the variable cost curve farther and farther to the right, such as a, b, and c. The ever-changing slope of these rays, in effect, traces out the behavior of average variable cost as output expands. Note how that slope (and, thus, AVC) continually declines until one ray ($0b$ in our example) just touches the VC line at a single point, such as b. The AVC line in panel (b) declines accordingly as from g toward h. Yet rays aiming at points to the right of tangency point b begin to have ever greater slopes—compare the slope of dashed ray $0c$ with that of the tangency ray $0b$. Accordingly, the AVC line in panel (b) rises, as from h toward i. The point of tangency in panel (a) thus corresponds to the minimum point in panel (b). Points b and h correspond to the identical output quantity (12,300 bushels/year in our example).

11. Since $ATC = (TC/Q)$, it follows that $TC = ATC(Q)$. Therefore, at a, $TC = 10(15) = 150$; at b, $TC = 6(27) = 162$, which is an 8 percent increase in TC and all inputs. Yet output increases from 15 to 27, or by 80 percent.

13. Since $ATC = (TC/Q)$, it follows that $TC = ATC(Q)$. Therefore, as Figure 9 shows, at d, $TC = 2(48) = 96$; at e, $TC = 4(64.5) = 258$. Therefore, in the de range,

$$LRMC = \frac{\Delta TC}{\Delta Q} = \frac{258 - 96}{64.5 - 48} = \frac{+162}{+16.5}$$
$$= \$9.82 \text{ (point } i\text{, Figure 10)}$$

15. See Figure A.8.

FIGURE A.8

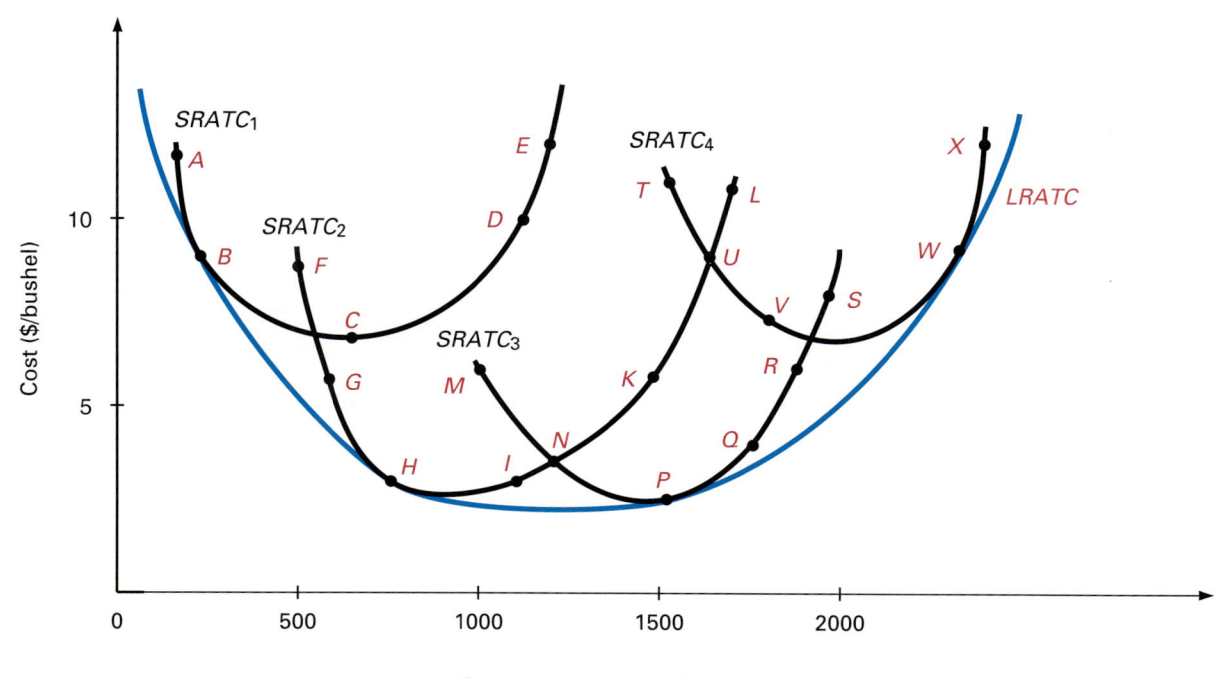

Chapter 10

1. The same principle is applied. The slope of the total revenue line equals $\Delta TR/\Delta Q$, or marginal revenue. The slope of the total cost line equals $\Delta TC/\Delta Q$, or marginal cost. Between point a, on the one hand, and points b and c, on the other hand, the TR slope (or MR) exceeds the TC slope (or MC), so it pays to increase output. At b and c, respectively, the two slopes are equal, hence $MR = MC$ and the output level is optimal. Between b and c, on the one hand, and point d, on the other hand, the TR slope is less than the TC slope (MC); it would pay to reduce output.

3. Yes. Consider points a and d in panel (a) and—vertically below them—points I and B in panel (b).

5. Using the graph or last chapter's Table 3, Short-Run Cost Alternatives—An Expanded View, you can find annual $FC = \$50{,}000$, $VC = \$30{,}000$, and $TC = \$80{,}000$. Total revenue would be $\$2.57$/bushel times $9{,}000$ bushels/year, or $\$23{,}130$. Thus, economic profit would equal $-\$56{,}870$. Shutting down at once could reduce the cost to $-\$50{,}000$.

7. From the given data, you can calculate:

Q	ATC	Q · ATC = TC	MC = $\frac{\Delta TC}{\Delta Q}$
20	14.00	280	
40	11.60	464	9.20
60	9.50	570	5.30
80	8.10	648	3.90
100	7.30	730	4.10
			5.50
120	7.00	840	
140	6.80 (minimum)	952	5.60
160	6.90	1,104	7.60
180	7.00	1,260	7.80
200	7.40	1,480	11.00
			14.00
220	8.00	1,760	
240	9.10	2,184	21.20
260	10.20	2,652	23.40
280	12.00	3,360	35.40
300	14.00	4,200	42.00

The *ATC* data and some of the *MC* data are graphed in Figure A.9. The profit-maximizing output corresponds to point *a* and equals 188 bushels/year. The short-run supply line equals the *MC* line above minimum *AVC* (not known). It certainly includes the *MC* line shown above *b* (minimum *ATC*).

FIGURE A.9

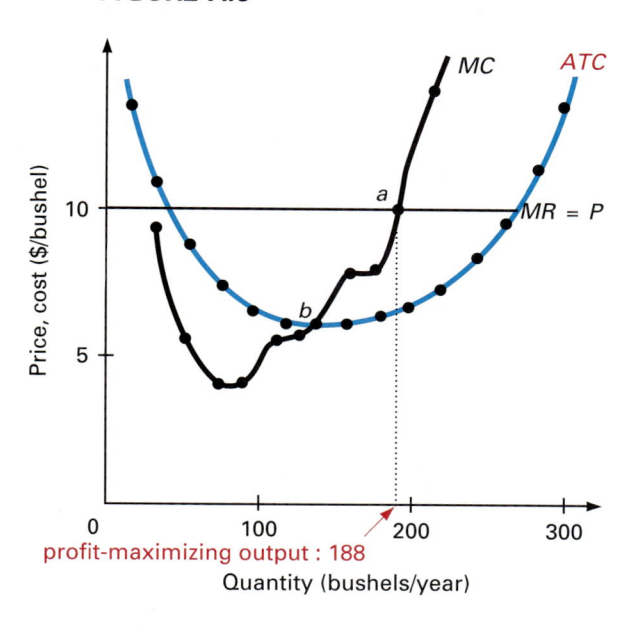

9. See Figure A.10 (on the following page). Given that the firm will choose an output volume of $0a$, the unshaded net benefit in panel (c) equals total revenue ($0abd$) minus the sum of marginal costs = total variable cost ($0abc$), or producer surplus bcd. This excess of total revenue over variable cost inevitably equals the sum of (positive or negative) profit plus fixed cost. Consider this:

$$TR - TC = \Pi$$
$$TR - FC - VC = \Pi$$
$$TR - VC = \Pi + FC$$

11. Input prices would continually rise and cost curves shift up. Supply would shift left, raising product price. Eventually, the product price would be so high that quantity demanded equaled zero. The industry would disappear.

13. It is not a contradiction because the *number* of firms changes, rising in Figure 8 and falling in Figure 9. In each case, the individual firm merely responds to the changing market price (in the fashion suggested by the "law" of supply).

FIGURE A.10

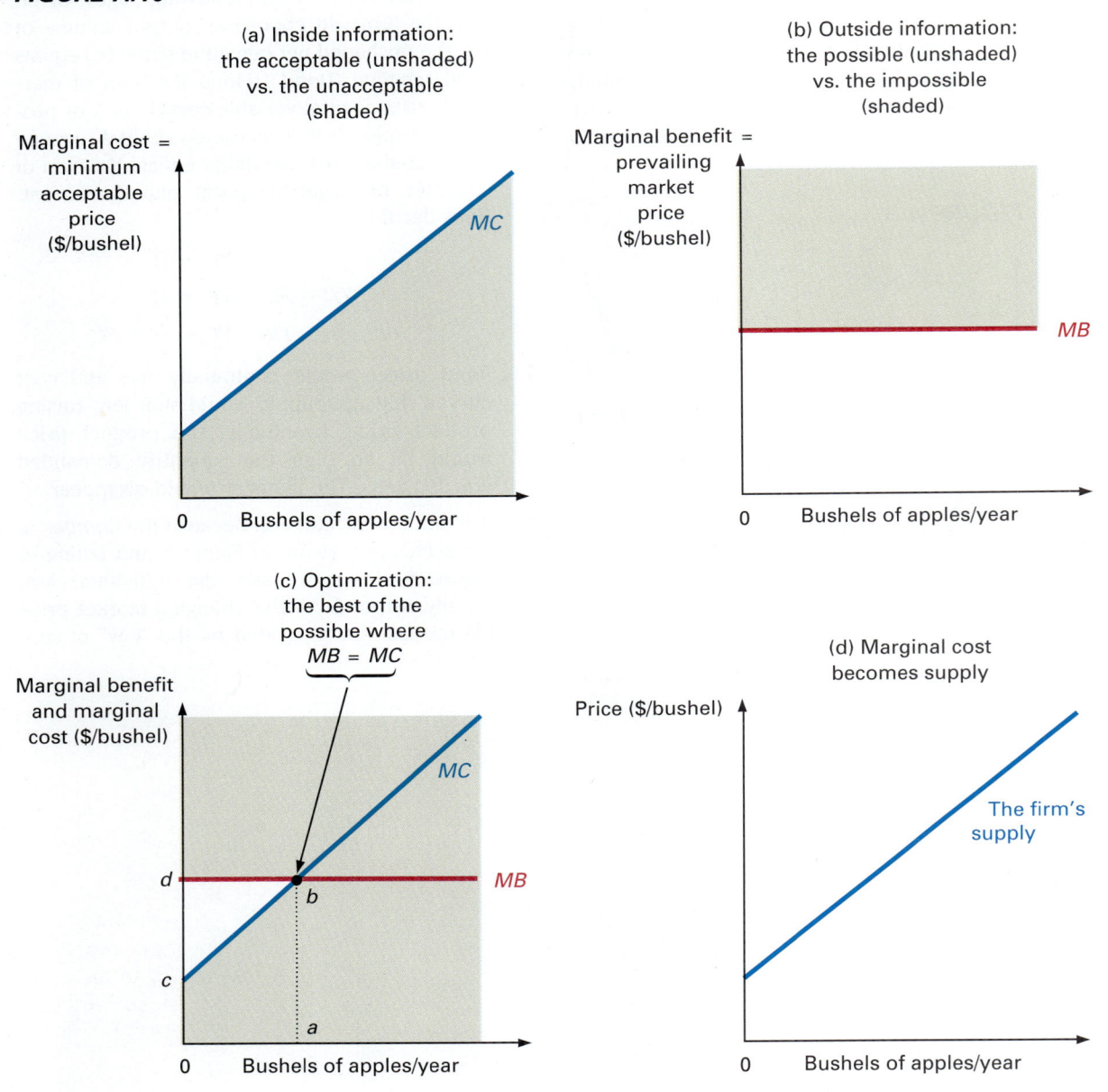

(a) Inside information: the acceptable (unshaded) vs. the unacceptable (shaded)

(b) Outside information: the possible (unshaded) vs. the impossible (shaded)

(c) Optimization: the best of the possible where MB = MC

(d) Marginal cost becomes supply

Chapter 11

1. Aluminum vs. copper or stainless steel; cellophane vs. aluminum foil or wax paper; local newspapers vs. national papers, radio, television; railroad transportation vs. airplanes, buses, trucks; any domestic good vs. imports.

3. See Figure A.11. The move from D to E engenders a $6 million/year revenue loss equal to the dotted rectangle plus a $2 million/year revenue gain equal to the shaded rectangle. The marginal revenue of −$4 million/year divided by

FIGURE A.11

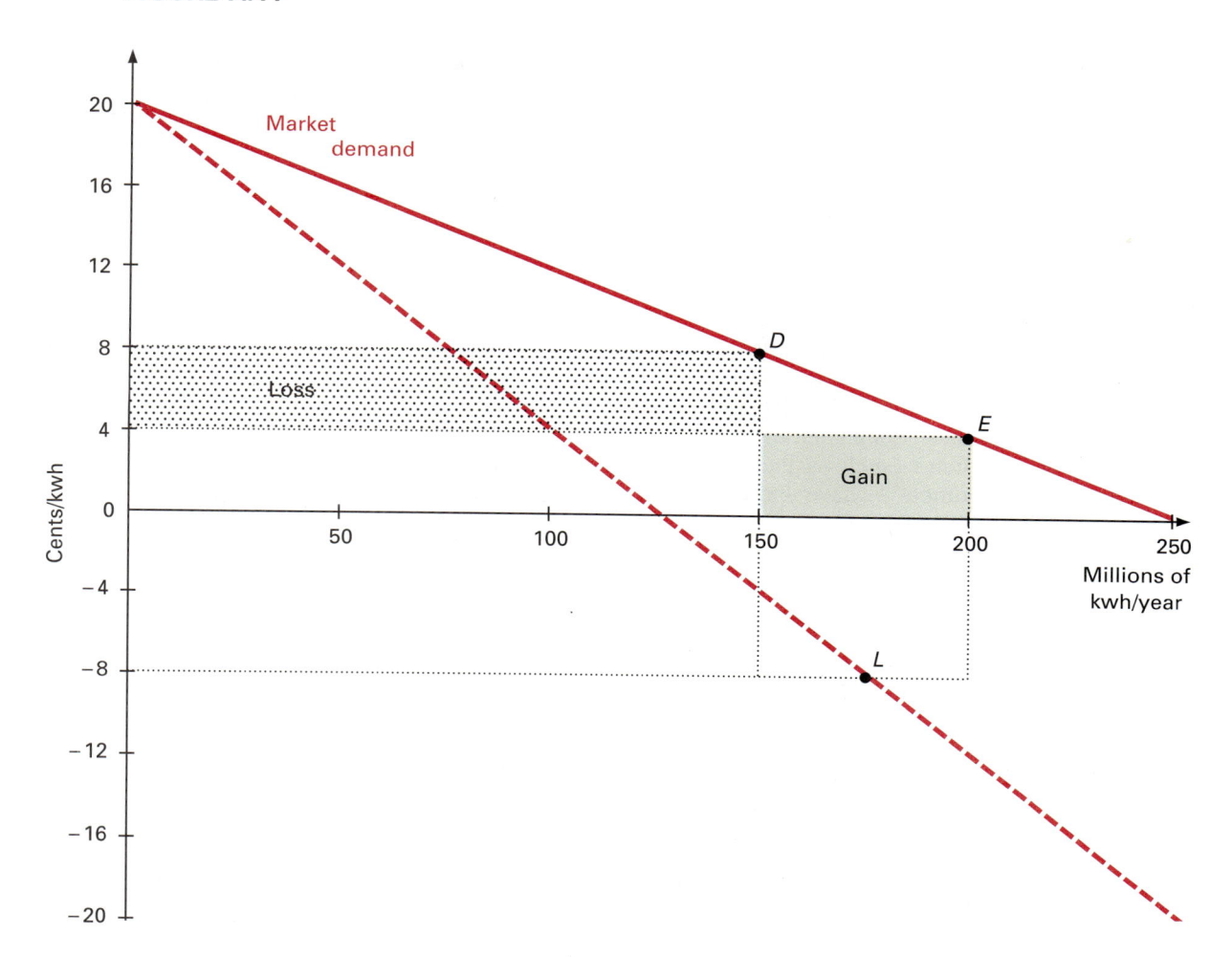

+50 million kwh/year equals −8¢/kwh; it is represented by the average height of the marginal revenue line in the 150 to 200 million kwh/year range (point L).

5. a. Left of B: vertically below a
   Right of B: vertically below d
   At a and d, $TR = TC$, hence $(TR/Q) = (TC/Q)$ which means $AR = ATC$.
   b. It corresponds to the MC minimum. Left of the TC inflection point, TC rises at a decreasing rate, so MC is falling. Right of the TC inflection point, TC rises at an increasing rate, so MC is rising.

7. True. Consider Figure 2. The author would want to maximize total revenue at m and set a price corresponding to demand line midpoint M. The publisher would want to maximize profit and set a (higher) price corresponding to the intersection of declining marginal revenue and (obviously positive) marginal cost (not shown).

9. The government could auction off the licenses. If recipients expected to earn, say, an extra $5 million a year because of their monopoly position and if interest rates were 10 percent, they might pay as much as $50 million for the license. The $5 million per year subsequently earned through the exercise of monopoly power would be the same amount that the $50 million could have earned in a bank. Thus, the recipient of the monopoly right would be neither better nor worse off.

11.

Before (point h):

Total revenue $(P \cdot Q)$	$4,000
– Total cost $(ATC \cdot Q)$	4,000
= Profit	0

After (point d):

Total revenue $(P \cdot Q)$	$4,644
– Total cost $(ATC \cdot Q)$	2,700
= Profit	$1,944

Chapter 12

1. There is no explanation for how the initial price/quantity combination was established in the first place. Also, the model suggests that prices should be more rigid in oligopolistic industries than in those dominated by monopoly. Yet empirical studies (such as those cited in this chapter's footnote 1) have shown exactly the opposite to be true.

3. The total equals $23 in panel (b); $21 in panel (c).

Panel (b):

Buying from A		Buying from B	
#1	$6	#8	$0.50
2	5	9	1.50
3	4		$2
4	3		
5	2		
6	1		
7	0		
	$21		

Panel (c):

Buying from A		Buying from B	
#7	$0	#1	$5.50
8	1	2	4.50
9	2	3	3.50
	$3	4	2.50
		5	1.50
		6	0.50
			$18

5. a. If Firm A introduces product 3, its market share will rise by 4 or fall by 2 or 6 percentage points, depending on whether Firm B introduces product 4, 5, or 6.
   b. If firm B introduces product 6, its market share will fall by 8 or 16 or rise by 6 percentage points, depending on whether Firm A introduces product 1, 2, or 3.

7. See Figure A.12. Assuming that total revenue covers variable cost, the firm would produce

FIGURE A.12

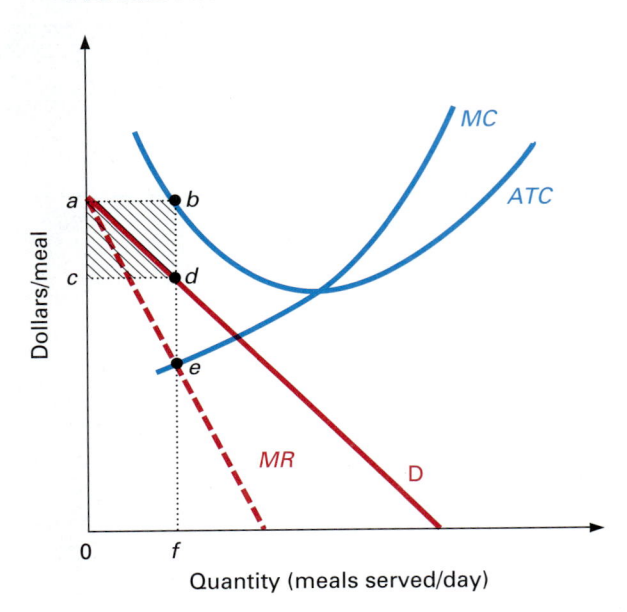

output 0f, equating (at e) marginal revenue and marginal cost. Its total revenue would equal 0cdf; its total cost 0abf; it would be incurring a loss of abdc (the cross-hatched rectangle). If total revenue did not even cover variable cost, the firm would shut down at once and make a smaller loss equal to fixed cost.

If the depicted situation was typical, this firm or similar ones would eventually go bankrupt. As a result, the bankrupt firms' customers would go elsewhere and the demand facing surviving firms would rise. Eventually, losses would disappear and a situation corresponding to panel (b) of Figure 7 could emerge.

9. The same factors noted in the chapter "Monopoly and Cartels" apply here. Economies of scale may provide a technical reason for the exis-

tence of just a *few* firms if the minimum efficient size of a firm is large relative to the market. The exclusive ownership of key resources by a few or government franchises given to only a few can restrict the number of firms in an industry. In addition, high concentration ratios can even be consequence of *pure chance.* Consider the famous experiment conducted by F. M. Scherer. He imagined an industry containing 50 identical firms in year 1, along with a complete absence of entry barriers. Thus, in year 1, each of the 50 firms held a (100/50) = 2 percent market share and the 4-firm concentration ratio equaled 4(2) = 8 percent.

Scherer then programmed a computer to simulate the imaginary industry's history over the course of 140 years, with average sales growing at 6 percent per year, but each firm having a randomly assigned chance of growing somewhat slower or faster than the pack as a whole (which is precisely what one observes among real-world firms). Concentration ratios were then recalculated after every 20 years of simulated history; and this experiment was repeated 16 times. Table A.5 shows his results. Within a few simulated decades, the industry showed the very degree of concentration that is often found in U.S. markets—despite the deliberately assumed absence of the causes of concentration that are traditionally cited. The only explanation is the operation of pure chance.

TABLE A.5

	4-firm concentration ratio at year:							
Simulation	1	20	40	60	80	100	120	140
Run 1	8,0	19.5	29.3	36.3	40.7	44.9	38.8	41.3
Run 2	8.0	20.3	21.4	28.1	37.5	41.6	50.8	55.6
Run 3	8.0	18.8	28.9	44.6	43.1	47.1	56.5	45.0
Run 4	8.0	20.9	26.7	31.8	41.9	41.0	64.5	59.8
Run 5	8.0	23.5	33.2	43.8	60.5	60.5	71.9	63.6
Run 6	8.0	21.3	26.6	29.7	35.8	51.2	59.1	72.9
Run 7	8.0	21.1	31.4	29.0	42.8	52.8	50.3	53.1
Run 8	8.0	21.6	23.5	42.2	47.3	64.4	73.1	76.6
Run 9	8.0	18.4	29.3	38.0	45.3	42.5	43.9	52.4
Run 10	8.0	20.0	29.7	43.7	40.1	43.1	42.9	42.9
Run 11	8.0	23.9	29.1	29.5	43.2	50.1	57.1	71.7
Run 12	8.0	15.7	23.3	24.1	34.5	41.1	42.9	53.1
Run 13	8.0	23.8	31.3	44.8	43.5	42.8	57.3	65.2
Run 14	8.0	17.8	23.3	29.3	54.2	51.4	56.0	64.7
Run 15	8.0	21.8	18.3	23.9	31.9	33.5	43.9	65.7
Run 16	8.0	17.5	27.1	28.3	30.7	39.9	37.7	35.3
Average	8.0	20.4	27.0	33.8	42.1	46.7	52.9	57.4

SOURCE: F. M. Scherer, *Industrial Market Structure and Economic Performance,* 2nd ed., p. 146. Copyright © 1980 Houghton Mifflin Company. Used by permission.

Chapter 13

1. a. The marginal value products are given in Table A.6. The table also shows the demand: column (1) is the quantity demanded for any of the potential wages given in column (2).
   b. At a wage of $60/day, a maximum of 4 detectives would be hired. The 1st, 2nd, and 3rd detective would bring in more than they cost; a 5th or 6th detective would bring in less.

TABLE A.6

Number of detectives (1)	Marginal value product (2)
1	$200
2	100
3	80
4	60
5	40
6	20

3. a. When profit is maximized, $MPP_i \cdot P_o = P_i$. Hence $MPP_i \cdot (50) = 200$, and $MPP_i = 4$ units of output.
   b. $MVP_i = 4(50) = 200$.

5. Consider panel (a) of Figure 3. When MVP_L is above AVP_L (as to the left of m), it pulls the AVP_L up (regardless of what MVP_L itself is doing). When MVP_L is below the AVP_L, it pulls the AVP_L down.

7. Unless the differentials compensated for nonmonetary differences, such as risk to life or disagreeableness of the jobs involved, one would expect a labor surplus in these markets. Such did, indeed, emerge: While 10,000 fire fighters were employed, 12,000 more had to be put on waiting lists. The corresponding numbers were 23,000 and 42,000 for police officers; 10,838 and 36,849 for sanitation workers.

9. Consider why people have to be *forced* to perform jury duty: According to one study,[a] jurors in 1962 received fees of $89.8 million, but their forgone income was $232.9 million, all measured in dollars of 1958 purchasing power.

---

[a] Donald L. Martin, "The Economics of Jury Conscription," *Journal of Political Economy*, July/August 1972, pp. 680–702.

Chapter 14

1. a. See Table A.7.
   b. Equating market-determined W and MVP at $W = \$120$, a maximum of 8 workers. At $W = \$160$, a maximum of 7 workers. (Note the encircled numbers.)
   c. Equating W and MVP at $W = \$120$, a maximum of 5 workers. At $W = \$160$, a maximum of 3 workers. (Note the encircled numbers.)

3. a. See Table A.8.
   b. The firm will employ 3.5 workers (at $250 per week each), equating MLC and MVP at $300.
   c. Equating union-set W and MVP, at $W = \$360$, the firm employs 2 workers; at $W = \$240$, 5 workers.

TABLE A.7

Number of workers	Marginal physical product	Marginal value product	
		Price = $8	Price = $4
1	50	$400	$200
2	45	360	180
3	40	320	(160)
4	35	280	140
5	30	240	(120)
6	25	200	100
7	20	(160)	80
8	15	(120)	60
9	10	80	40

TABLE A.8

Number of workers	Wage per worker per week	Total labor cost	Marginal labor cost	Marginal value product
1	$200	$200	$200	$400
2	220	440	240	360
3	240	720	280	320
4	260	1,040	320	280
5	280	1,400	360	240
6	300	1,800	400	200
7	320	2,240	440	160
8	340	2,720	480	120
9	360	3,240	520	80

5. The monopsony would pay each worker a different wage, equal to the minimum that worker would accept and, presumably, equal to the maximum that worker could get elsewhere. Thus the labor market supply line would become the monopsony's line of marginal labor cost and the firm would employ the number of workers corresponding to point f.

7. See Figure A.13. The firm equates MLC and MRP_L at d, employs N_0 workers and sets the wage at W_0. Thus, the wage lies below the marginal value product by bf. Rectangle abdc denotes monopolistic exploitation; rectangle cdfe, monopsonistic exploitation.

FIGURE A.13

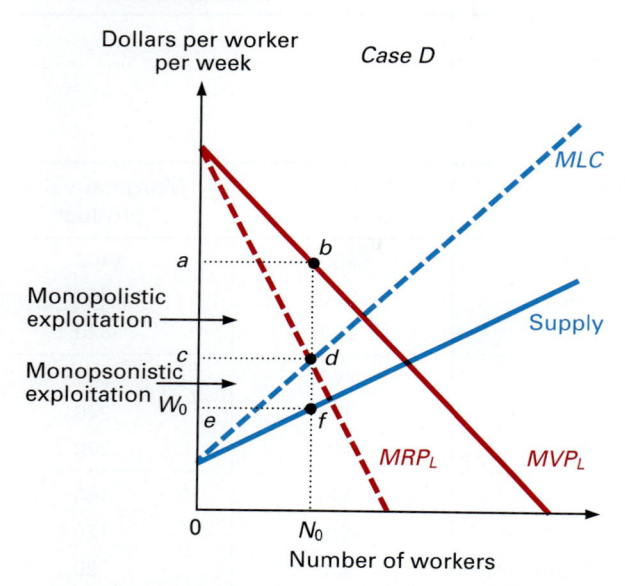

9. Figure 1: Inefficient. Given the chosen wage/employment combination d, potential extra benefits of cdf are being forgone.
Figure 2: Inefficient. Given the chosen wage/employment combination d, potential extra benefits of cdf are being forgone.
Figure 4: Inefficient. Given the chosen wage/employment combination c or f, respectively, potential extra benefits of cmi or fpi, respectively, are being forgone.
Figure 5: Inefficient. Given the chosen wage/employment combination a or d, respectively, potential extra benefits of aec or bdc, respectively, are being forgone.

11. Unfortunately, Mr. A is correct. For one thing, just as observed female/male or white/black wage differentials are not necessarily caused by discrimination, so union/nonunion differentials need not be union-caused. What if unions tend to form in large firms that use lots of skilled labor that would receive higher wages even in the absence of unions? What if unions tend to form in growing, profitable industries in which competitive pressures raise wages rapidly in any case? Even if wage differentials can be traced to unions, measuring their extent is tricky business. We can illustrate this point with the help of Figure A.14. Consider two competitive labor markets with an identical initial wage W_0 corresponding to equilibrium points c and f, respectively. Let a union organize workers in market (a) and impose a wage of W_1. Let the unemployed workers in the union sector (ab) swell the supply of labor in market (b) from S to S^* (with eh = ab). The market (b) wage falls to W_2 according to equilibrium g. Statistics now reveal a union/nonunion wage differential of $W_1 - W_2$, but surely this is misleading. The union has raised the wage of *some* workers from W_0 to W_1; indirectly, it has lowered the wage of other workers from W_0 to W_2. It shouldn't get credit for the $W_1 - W_2$ gap.

An alternative scenario is also possible. Let employers in the nonunion sector pay a *disequilibrium* wage W_3 to keep the union out. (This is called the *union-threat effect.*) Then unemployment appears in both sectors, equal to ab and de, respectively, but the statistics reveal *no* union/nonunion wage differential at all. Everywhere, the wage equals W_3.

But note: Statistical techniques exist that enable economists to determine how effective unions have really been. Recent studies show that about one-third of unions have raised their members' wages from 15 to 20 percent above the level that would have otherwise prevailed (airline pilots and teamsters, for example). Another one-third raised wages from 5 to 10 percent (auto and steel workers). A final third of unions had no effect at all (retail clerks, textile workers).

FIGURE A.14

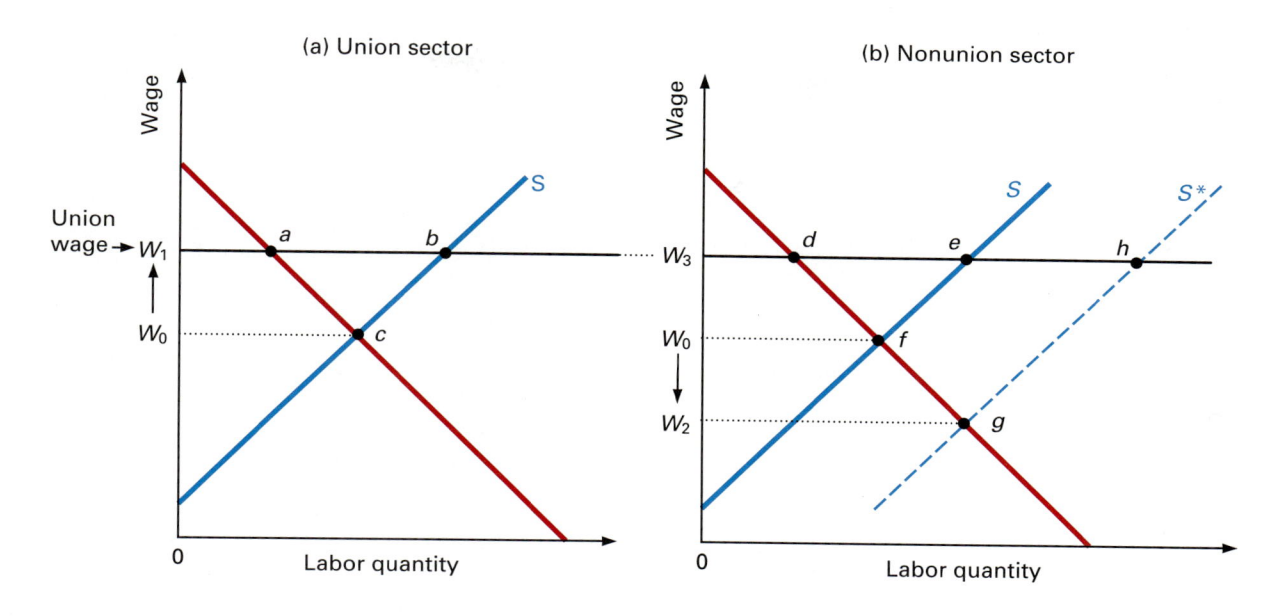

(a) Union sector — Wage axis with Union wage → W_1 (points a, b), W_0 (point c), supply S and demand curves, Labor quantity axis.

(b) Nonunion sector — Wage axis with W_3 (points d, e, h), W_0 (point f), W_2 (point g), supply S, shifted supply S^*, and demand curves, Labor quantity axis.

13. Of course. This chapter's examples of *featherbedding* indicate how productivity might be decreased. For another example, review Example 1, The Amazing Story of Two Ford Plants, in the chapter "The Technology of Production."

    Yet careful studies by economists have shown that unions in U.S. manufacturing industries on the average have *raised* productivity from 20 to 25 percent. This has been attributed to greater worker morale under unionized conditions. In addition, workers who need not fear arbitrary actions of the boss against them are likely to quit less often (saving their firm training costs) and are even interested in cooperating with management on changes that raise productivity. In any case, there is a shock effect on management: It is galvanized into finding productivity-raising changes in order to maintain profit in the face of union wage demands. See, for example, Richard B. Freeman and James L. Medoff, "The Two Faces of Unionism," *The Public Interest,* Fall 1979, pp. 69–93.

15. Middle-age and older women earn less than men of the same age. In 1989, the median annual income of women in the U.S. was $20,466 for ages 45–54 and $18,727 for ages 55–64. The corresponding figures for men were $34,684 and $32,476, respectively. Half of the gap could be explained by differences in education and work experience, some more by part-time employment that is more common among women. The remainder of the gap was associated with confining women to "women's professions," such as cashiers, librarians, nurses, secretaries, waitresses–and *that* is attributable to the kinds of attitudes noted in the question. In 1991, Congress was debating a Nontraditional Employment for Women Act to help solve the problem. (See Tamar Lewin, "Older Women Face Bias in Workplace," *The New York Times,* May 11, 1991, p. 8.)

Chapter 15

1. The formula is $FV_t = PV_o(1 + i)^t$.

    a. *3 percent case*

    $$FV_4 = \$1\left(1 + \frac{3}{100}\right)^4 = \$1(1.03)^4 = \$1.13$$

    $$FV_7 = \$1\left(1 + \frac{3}{100}\right)^7 = \$1(1.03)^7 = \$1.23$$

    $$FV_{19} = \$1\left(1 + \frac{3}{100}\right)^{19} = \$1(1.03)^{19} = \$1.75$$

    b. *7 percent case*

    $$FV_4 = \$1\left(1 + \frac{7}{100}\right)^4 = \$1(1.07)^4 = \$1.31$$

    $$FV_7 = \$1\left(1 + \frac{7}{100}\right)^7 = \$1(1.07)^7 = \$1.61$$

    $$FV_{19} = \$1\left(1 + \frac{7}{100}\right)^{19} = \$1(1.07)^{19} = \$3.62$$

    c. *11 percent case*

    $$FV_4 = \$1\left(1 + \frac{11}{100}\right)^4 = \$1(1.11)^4 = \$1.52$$

    $$FV_7 = \$1\left(1 + \frac{11}{100}\right)^7 = \$1(1.11)^7 = \$2.08$$

    $$FV_{19} = \$1\left(1 + \frac{11}{100}\right)^{19} = \$1(1.11)^{19} = \$7.26$$

3. Consider any dollar amount invested now, $\$D$. In 1 year, the lender has a claim on the principal $\$D$ plus interest (which is $\$D$ multiplied by the annual interest rate i). Thus, after 1 year, $\$D$ becomes $\$D + \$D(i) = \$D(1 + i) = \$D(1 + i)^1$. Since $\$D$ is the present value, we can call the one-year future value

    $$FV_1 = PV(1 + i)^1$$

    which looks very much like the formula in the text.

    What would happen after 2 years? The amount existing at the end of year 1 would be returned, along with interest thereon:

    $PV(1 + i)^1 + [PV(1 + i)^1] i$. Hence

    $FV_2 = [PV(1 + i)^1](1 + i) = PV(1 + i)^2$,

    which, again, looks like our formula.

5. If you had $7 million now, you could invest it in tax-free municipal bonds and earn, say, 6 percent interest per year, or $420,000 per year *forever*, without even touching the principal. But this is what actually happens: You receive, for 20 years, an annual gross amount of $350,000. Deducting 40 percent taxes, the net amount is $210,000. The present value of such a 20-year stream, at 6 percent discount, is as follows:

    $PV_0 = \$210,000$

    $PV_1 = \dfrac{\$210,000}{1.06} = \$198,113.20$

    $PV_2 = \dfrac{\$210,000}{1.06^2} = \dfrac{\$210,000}{1.1236} = \$186,899.25$

    $PV_3 = \dfrac{\$210,000}{1.06^3} = \dfrac{\$210,000}{1.1910} = \$176,322.41$

    $PV_4 = \dfrac{\$210,000}{1.06^4} = \dfrac{\$210,000}{1.2625} = \$166,336.63$

    $PV_5 = \dfrac{\$210,000}{1.06^5} = \dfrac{\$210,000}{1.3382} = \$156,927.21$

    $PV_6 = \dfrac{\$210,000}{1.06^6} = \dfrac{\$210,000}{1.4185} = \$148,043.70$

    $PV_7 = \dfrac{\$210,000}{1.06^7} = \dfrac{\$210,000}{1.5036} = \$139,664.80$

    $PV_8 = \dfrac{\$210,000}{1.06^8} = \dfrac{\$210,000}{1.5938} = \$131,760.57$

    $PV_9 = \dfrac{\$210,000}{1.06^9} = \dfrac{\$210,000}{1.6895} = \$124,297.12$

    $PV_{10} = \dfrac{\$210,000}{1.06^{10}} = \dfrac{\$210,000}{1.7908} = \$117,266.02$

    $PV_{11} = \dfrac{\$210,000}{1.06^{11}} = \dfrac{\$210,000}{1.8983} = \$110,625.29$

    $PV_{12} = \dfrac{\$210,000}{1.06^{12}} = \dfrac{\$210,000}{2.0122} = \$104,363.38$

    $PV_{13} = \dfrac{\$210,000}{1.06^{13}} = \dfrac{\$210,000}{2.1329} = \$98,457.50$

    $PV_{14} = \dfrac{\$210,000}{1.06^{14}} = \dfrac{\$210,000}{2.2609} = \$92,883.37$

$$PV_{15} = \frac{\$210,000}{1.06^{15}} = \frac{\$210,000}{2.3966} = \$87,624.13$$

$$PV_{16} = \frac{\$210,000}{1.06^{16}} = \frac{\$210,000}{2.5404} = \$82,664.15$$

$$PV_{17} = \frac{\$210,000}{1.06^{17}} = \frac{\$210,000}{2.6928} = \$77,985.74$$

$$PV_{18} = \frac{\$210,000}{1.06^{18}} = \frac{\$210,000}{2.8543} = \$73,573.21$$

$$PV_{19} = \frac{\$210,000}{1.06^{19}} = \frac{\$210,000}{3.0256} = \$69,407.72$$

All this sums to a mere $2,553,214.90. (If you only got that amount and invested it at 6 percent per year you could make the 20 withdrawals of $210,000 indicated here and the account would be gone.) Thus, you are a multi-millionaire, but not quite what the lottery officials will make it out to be.

7. Not necessarily. The decreased demand for newly produced paper would decrease the price of paper and, indirectly, the demand for the services of parcels of land full of trees. This would, in turn, lower the rental price of such lots, and, indirectly, their purchase price. If the owners of tree lots had alternative uses that paid more, they might just *cut down* all the trees and do other things with the cleared land!

9. Imagine putting $38,947.31 in a bank account that bears 10 percent interest per year. The following series of transactions prove that such an account is equivalent to the truck described in the question:

Now: original deposit		$38,947.31
1 year later:	interest added	3,894.73
	1st withdrawal	8,000.00
	balance	$34,842.04
2 years later:	interest added	3,484.20
	2nd withdrawal	8,000.00
	balance	$30,326.08
3 years later:	interest added	3,032.61
	3rd withdrawal	8,000.00
	balance	$25,358.69
4 years later:	interest added	2,535.87
	4th withdrawal	8,000.00
	balance	$19,894.56
5 years later:	interest added	1,989.46
	5th withdrawal	8,000.00
	balance	$13,884.02
6 years later:	interest added	1,388.40
	6th withdrawal	8,000.00
	balance	$7,272.42
7 years later:	interest added	727.24
	7th withdrawal	8,000.00
	balance	$ 0 (rounded)

11. The dramatically higher price of crude oil raised the prices of oil derivatives, such as fuel oil and gasoline. Everyone looked for alternatives, such as using coal instead of fossil fuels to produce electricity or using taxis and rental cars temporarily instead of private cars permanently.

    The higher demand for the services of coal mines, taxis, and rental cars raised the income streams derivable therefrom and, thus, raised their asset prices. In coal mining towns, the newfound prosperity among coal miners spilled over to mining supply stores, car dealerships, and residential houses.

13. This is not difficult to explain. Consider a house that provides a net rental income of $8,000 a year. All else being equal, the cut in property taxes raises that annual net income stream. Accordingly, the capitalized value of the house rises as well.

    All this can be seen graphically in Figure 4. If all the blocks rise in height, so does the white area of capitalized value in the graph.

    Incidentally, the $1 to $7 ratio given in the question is quite believable because interest rates were about 14 percent per year at the time. Anyone investing $7 (for example, by spending that much more on a house) could expect an annual return of 14 percent of $7, or roughly $1, in return (for example, by paying that much less in property taxes).

15. It has been said that "God makes models, but He doesn't make many of them." Be that as it may, the gift of nature called *Beauty* is in very limited supply. Modeling agencies are forever battling one another over that supply; in the process, they drive up the price and provide a few women for a few precious years with impressive rents (in a fashion described by this chapter's Figure 5). Recently, for example, Clotilde, a model representing Shiseido's flagship cosmetic line, was earning $190,000 a year. Lauren Hutton, representing Revlon's Ultima II cosmetics, earned $250,000 a year. Cheryl Tiegs was selling her lips, eyes, and face for $300,000 a year to the Noxell Corporation (Cover Girl makeup); she was also marketing her hair and legs to Bristol-Myers Clairesse hair coloring, and the rest of herself to Sears, Roebuck and Co. ("personality jeans").

17. You could calculate the net present value of the dollar stream as

$$NPV = -3{,}000 + \frac{800}{(1+i)^1} + \frac{800}{(1+i)^2} + \frac{800}{(1+i)^3} + \frac{800}{(1+i)^4} + \frac{800}{(1+i)^5}$$

The answer will depend crucially on the relevant interest rate employed in the discounting process. A positive net present value would prove the relocation project to be worthwhile.

19. The jury might figure the capitalized value of the income stream the person might otherwise have enjoyed, such as $60,000 a year for 17 more years. The precise number would depend on the discount rate employed.

Chapter 16

1. Cumulating the tabular data, we get Table A.9.

    TABLE A.9

Income class	Percentage of families in class or lower ones	Percentage of total income received by families in class or lower ones
Under $2,000	77.7	45.4
$2,000–$2,999	90.8	64.9
$3,000–$3,999	95.2	74.1
$4,000–$4,999	96.9	78.6
$5,000–$7,499	98.5	84.4
$7,500–$9,999	99.1	87.6
$10,000 and over	100.0	100.0

    The two Lorenz curves, based on the table here and text Table 1, are given in Figure A.15. The income distribution was somewhat more unequal in 1935–1936.

3. *"Lowest" row*: Among families who were in the lowest income quintile in 1971, only 55.5 percent were still in that quintile in 1978. Some 22, 9.5, 7, and 6 percent, respectively, had moved up to successively higher quintiles.
   "Lowest" column: The families who were in the lowest income quintile in 1978 included 3.5 percent of those who were in the highest quintile in 1971, and, respectively, 6, 13.5, 21.5, and 55.5 percent of those who were in successively lower quintiles in 1971.

5. Answers can vary.

FIGURE A.15

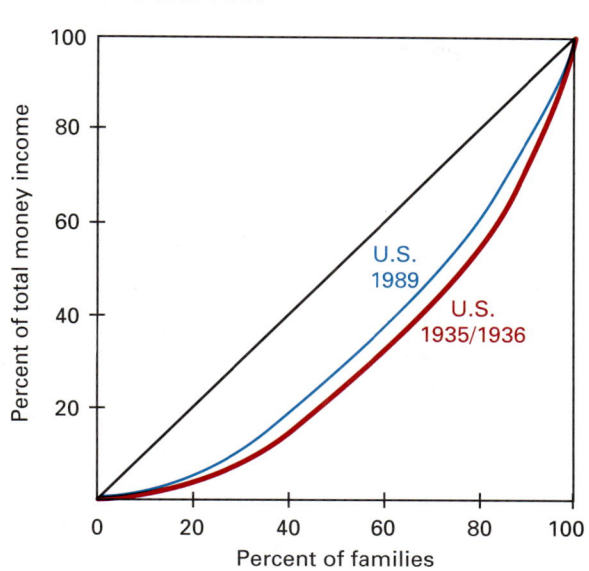

[Lorenz curve graph: Percent of total money income vs Percent of families, showing U.S. 1989 and U.S. 1935/1936 curves]

7. The statement is false. Consider Table 6. It shows that 39.4 + 10.7 = 50.1 percent of all poor persons were very young (under 18 years of age) or elderly (65 years and over) and, thus, unlikely to be helped by jobs. It also shows (indirectly) that many of the remaining poor (aged 18–64) would find it difficult to take jobs: Consider female household heads tied down with small children, the ill and disabled, and those who already work full time. Although precise numbers are not available, clearly a *majority* of the poor cannot be helped by jobs.

9. Here you can let your imaginations roam.... Almost certainly, these countries were not richer in the past in an absolute sense, but, possibly, they were richer *relative* to Italy and Spain. In addition, more likely than not, the world travelers mentioned made comparisons to the richest people in China and India.

Chapter 17

1. At the 8 million unit output level, sold at a price corresponding to point *f*, a profit of *fg* per unit would be made. Thus, total profit would equal *fg* times 8 million, measured by a rectangle clearly smaller than shaded area *abcd*.
   Alternative proof: If output were raised above the profit-maximizing level of 5 million units (and price lowered to sell it), marginal cost along *ef* would continually exceed marginal revenue along *eh*. Extra units sold would, thus, reduce the profit total by the (ever-growing) vertical differences between lines *ef* and *eh*.

3. Courts have in fact decided on all of the cited cases. Their answers: "yes" for a and b; "no" for the rest.

5. The provisions were put in the act in order to make it easier for new firms to enter a market, compete away profit, and push prices down to minimum average total cost. Here, however, are some counter-arguments: Exclusive contracts make it easier for retailers to provide factory-authorized parts and service because they can establish a good working relationship with a single manufacturer. Requirements contracts reduce uncertainty; they enable buyers to count on the receipt of specified quantities at agreed-upon prices. Tying contracts help sellers make sure that their products' reputation is not sullied by breakdowns caused by the use of incompatible raw materials supplied by other firms.

7. Figure 1: $\dfrac{P - MC}{P} = \dfrac{7 - 7}{7} = 0$

   Figure 2: $\dfrac{P - MC}{P} = \dfrac{10 - 5}{10} = .5$

9. a. Each firm would have a .5 percent share; $H = 200 \,(.5)^2 = 50$.
   b. Each firm would have a 1 percent share; $H = 100 \,(1)^2 = 100$.
   c. Each firm would have a 10 percent share; $H = 10 \,(10)^2 = 1{,}000$.
   d. Each of the fringe firms would have a .3 percent share; $H = 70^2 + [100 \,(.3)^2] = 4{,}900 + 9 = 4{,}909$.

11. a. $H = 35.9^2 + 24.6^2 + 6.5^2 + 5.9^2 + 4.3^2 + 12 \,(1.9)^2 = 2{,}032.84$.
    b. According to Table 4 and barring other con-

siderations, the answer is "yes" because the index would only rise by 7.22.
c. Coca-Cola and Dr. Pepper: no; the index would rise by 35.9 (6.5) (2) = 466.7.
Pepsi and Seven-Up: no; the index would rise by 24.6 (5.9) (2) = 290.28.
Note: Both of these mergers were in fact attempted in 1986; both were challenged by the FTC.

Chapter 18

1. This procedure would justify *any* level of profit as precisely "fair." Consider a natural monopoly with an eternal annual profit of $10 million. If the current market rate of interest (which would, presumably, be chosen as a "fair" rate of return) were $i = 10$ percent, the firm's present value PV would be calculated by the special discounting formula as $100 million because

$$PV = \frac{FV}{i} = \frac{10}{.10} = 100$$

Given a rate base of $100 million, the firm's actual profit of $10 million per year would then come to 10 percent of the owners' investment and be judged as "fair."

What if the firm's profit had been $90 million a year? All else being equal, the firm's value would have been computed as $900 million because

$$PV = \frac{FV}{i} = \frac{90}{.10} = 900$$

Given a rate base of $900 million, the firm's actual profit of $90 million per year would still have come to 10 percent of the owners' investment and would still have been considered "fair." The same would be true with any other level of profit; thus the suggested procedure is pure nonsense. Because the "fair" rate of return is used to capitalize the income stream to begin with, any subsequent comparison of profit and capital base will always lead to the same verdict: The return is precisely "fair."

3. Such a procedure would almost certainly encourage cost-reducing innovations over time. The age-old tendency of such firms to permit X-inefficiency (higher-than-necessary cost curves) would disappear because the firms could raise profitability by keeping costs down and wouldn't have to fear that regulators would then punish them by lowering prices. Similarly, firms that pushed cost curves down over time through technical advances would be assured of reaping the rewards of their efforts (as long as they charged a price at or below the long-term cap).

5. Almost certainly, the licensing was undertaken primarily to restrict supply (which tends to raise price) rather than to maintain competence, professional ethics, and the like.

7. The quotation involves a mixture of facts and value judgments. It is certainly true that the elimination of monopoly power hurts those who possessed it. Thus airlines that held CAB-sanctioned route monopolies or trucking companies that held ICC-sanctioned route monopolies may well have to lower prices and give up their once-permanent profit in the face of competition. As a result, the capitalized value of such firms declines. Others tied to the industry are affected similarly. Consider owners of restaurants at air or truck terminals positioned at once-mandated and suddenly-abandoned routes: their profits disappear, their firms become worthless. Or consider the associated labor unions who used to get a share of the loot that regulation extracted from captive consumers. (Examples: Following deregulation, there were 11,000 new competitors in the trucking industry by the mid-1980s. Trucking companies such as the Yellow Freight System, which carried the capitalized value of their monopoly operating rights on their balance sheets, sustained massive declines in their net worth. And the mighty International Brotherhood of Teamsters—whose strikes in the past had crippled the entire economy and whose wages often had run ahead of other unions—

agreed in 1982 to freezing or lowering wages, reducing the frequency of cost-of-living adjustments, and making concessions on work rules.)

Should compensation be made? That is a value judgment, but keep in mind that the original regulation redistributed income from consumers to producers (including workers); deregulation simply reverses the process (although the precise people involved may be different).

9. Answers can vary so far as the value judgment is concerned. As to the factual statement, it is certainly true that people evaluate risks everyday. Consider how they drive 1,000 miles in their private cars because it is cheaper or more interesting, while being fully aware that airline flying would be safer. Consider how they use chain saws and ski, how they smoke and set off fireworks, being fully aware that risks exist. Consider how they eat cheap food at the Greasy Spoon even though food poisoning is less likely at the Fancy Restaurant. Consider how they take dangerous jobs because they like the higher pay.

Under the Federal Coal Mine Health and Safety Act of 1969, for example, miners must be offered periodic free chest X-rays to detect black lung disease. They know that inhalation of coal dust eventually decreases the functional capacity of lungs, which is progressively disabling and can be fatal. They also know that employers must offer alternative jobs to diseased workers, for example, office jobs at reduced pay. Only 10 percent of workers take the medical tests; clearly, they are trading income for health.

Yet there are those who still argue for paternalism because, as they see it, people will never understand the information they get. For example, each year dozens of children die by ingesting balloons, marbles, and small parts of their toys. This happens despite the warning labels required by the Consumer Product Safety Commission. As critics see it, such labels can never be made foolproof. Consider a label "For Ages 3 and Over" that is meant to warn of the fact that small toy parts fit perfectly in a toddler's windpipe. Proud parents who like to think of their 2-year-old as functioning at the level of a 4-year-old may buy the toy nevertheless, looking at the label as a challenge. Even a more explicit label may not help: Consider "Not Recommended for Children Who Still Put Objects in Their Mouths." Even though the intention is the same as before (to warn of a choking hazard), parents may simply believe that the toy in question tastes bad, which is not a big deal. Thus, some observers argue, regulators must do more than spread information; they must be parents to us all and tell us directly which "toys" we may use.

(Barry Meier, "Reading Between Lines of Toy Warning Labels," *The New York Times,* September 30, 1989, p. 48.)

11. In fact, the government has tried, but an economist should ask whether the marginal benefit is worth the marginal cost. In 1970, the Occupational Safety and Health Administration (OSHA) set a 10 ppm allowable limit of benzene in the air and announced its intention to lower that limit further to 1 ppm in the future. At the time, it was estimated that the new regulation would prevent one cancer death every three years (the marginal benefit), but would cost firms $500 million in the first year and $150 million per year thereafter (the marginal cost). Industry executives argued that it was "crazy" to spend hundreds of millions of dollars to save a single life, and they succeeded in having a court set the OSHA regulation aside.

By 1979, the case of AFL-CIO Industrial Union Department vs. American Petroleum Institute reached the U.S. Supreme Court. It was hoped that the Court would decide once and for all whether government regulators had to justify the benefits they sought to achieve by reasonable costs. Yet the Court was unable to reach a majority decision.

It took another decade, until 1989, before a decision of sorts was made. The Environmental Protection Agency issued a benzene standard of its own: Affected industries had to assure that a worker's lifetime chance of contracting leukemia from benzene was no higher than 1 in 10,000. (Robert D. Hershey, Jr., "U.S. Adopts Limits on Use of Benzene," *The New York Times,* September 1, 1989, pp. A1 and A19.)

13. Answers can vary.

Chapter 19

1. Answers can vary, but you might consider a) seeking help from the government or b) making a private deal. For example, the City of Palm Springs forbids the building of houses that cast a shadow on other people's land between 9 A.M. and 3 P.M. And people have paid their neighbors to install fans (to divert smells) or to cut down trees (to preserve a view).

3. a. consumer surplus aeg; producer surplus mge
   b. consumer surplus acb; producer surplus mhi
   c. $bcih$
   d. $TPB = 0aeo$; $TPC = 0meo$, $TPNB = mae$
   e. $TPB = 0acn$; $TPC = 0min$, $TPNB = acb + mhi$
   f. $TSB = 0aeo$; $TSC = 0kdo$; $TSNB = kac - cde$
   g. $TSB = 0acn$; $TSC = 0hcn$; $TSNB = kac$
   h. at Q_1: $mkde$; at Q_2: $mkci$

5. The identical land use will occur in either case; there will be two steers.

    a. *If property rights belong to the farmer*
    The first steer will be retained because the $40 profit that it brings to the rancher is more than sufficient to compensate the farmer for the 1 ton of wheat (worth $10) that the steer would destroy. An appropriate deal will be made.
    The second steer will be retained because the $40 profit that it brings to the rancher is more than sufficient to compensate the farmer for the additional 2 tons of wheat (worth $20) that the second steer would destroy. An appropriate deal will be made.
    The third steer will be removed because the $40 profit that it might bring to the rancher is insufficient to compensate the farmer for the additional 5 tons of wheat (worth $50) that the third steer would destroy. Naturally, there will be no fourth steer because the $40 profit that it might bring to the rancher is insufficient to compensate the farmer for the additional 7 tons of wheat (worth $70) that the fourth steer would destroy.

    b. *If property rights belong to the rancher*
    The first steer will be retained because the associated wheat loss of 1 ton (worth $10) is insufficient for the farmer to compensate the rancher for a potential $40 profit loss.
    The second steer will be retained because the associated wheat loss of another 2 tons (worth $20) is insufficient for the farmer to compensate the rancher for a potential $40 profit loss.
    The third steer will be removed because the associated wheat loss then avoided (5 tons worth $50) is more than sufficient to compensate the rancher for the $40 profit loss.
    The fourth steer will be removed because the associated wheat loss then avoided (7 tons worth $70) is more than sufficient to compensate for the $40 profit loss.

7. a. They could afford $cekg$.
   b. They would have to pay enough to compensate for the loss of consumer surplus (ghk) and producer surplus (geh).

9. Answers can vary, but one should note that the benefits (less smog in the Los Angeles area) may come at costs the nature and magnitude of which are not yet fully understood. Apart from perhaps minor irritations (less acceleration, more frequent or more lengthy fueling), other types of cars produce other problems. To name just one, methanol fumes collect at ground level in pools and present an explosion hazard; when burned, methanol produces the very gases that have been implicated in the so-called *greenhouse effect*. These gases help trap solar energy in the atmosphere and are believed to produce a gradual heating of the entire planet. If this process is unchecked, humanity can look forward to more climate changes in the next century than during the past 10,000 years, leading to melting polar ice-caps, a rise in the mean sea level, the flooding of most cities on earth, as well as changes in weather patterns and land fertility. (See Peter Passell, "Staggering Cost is Foreseen to Curb Warming of Earth," *The New York Times*,

November 19, 1989, pp. 1 and 18 and David Woodruff et. al., "Is America Finally Ready for the Gasless Carriage?" *Business Week,* April 8, 1991, pp. 58–60.)

11. Answers will vary. On April 22, 1991, people celebrated the 20th anniversary of Earth Day—a global epic marked by marches, speeches, and a wave of supposedly "environmentally friendly" consumer products. Marketers everywhere rushed to wrap their products in the glow of environmental good deeds, yet their claims were often little more than merchandising scams, now called "green collar fraud." Consider the following:
    1. recyclability claims: drink boxes for juices and milk still clog our landfills at the rate of 80,000 tons per year because they contain aluminum foil and plastic that can be recycled only in special "hydrapulping" plants available almost nowhere.
    2. degradability claims: First Brand Corporation's Glad Bags and Mobil Oil's Hefty Trash Bags are (partially) degradable in sunlight. In fact, these and other plastic bags end up in landfills and never see the sun.
    3. composting claims: so-called compostable diapers (Pampers and Luvs) require removal of the plastic liners and special treatment facilities available nowhere.

(See Alecia Swasy, "Color Us Green," *The Wall Street Journal,* March 22, 1991, p. B4, and Mark Green, "Recyclable . . . or Just Fraudulent?" *The New York Times,* April 21, 1991, p. F11.)

13. Answers can vary, but one thing should be clear: The antipollution effort absorbs resources and, thus, requires some people to have fewer goods. Who these people should be is another matter.

15. Answers can vary, but consider what happened in the last century on the Great Plains (the Dakotas, Wyoming, Montana, Kansas, Nebraska, Colorado, New Mexico, and Texas), where land, livestock, and water supplies belonged to everybody. When the population on the Great Plains exploded (from 274,000 in 1850 to 7,377,000 in 1900), disaster struck and many of the common resources were destroyed. (The buffalo, for example, became extinct.)

    In this century, consider what is happening on urban freeways (traffic congestion and the decline in transportation quality that it implies is equivalent to too many cows on the commons). Or consider how even national parks are becoming endangered oases. (On one day in 1980, some 25,000 visitors to the *back country* of Grand Teton National Park vainly looked for solitude among cold blue lakes, deep canyons, and snow-capped peaks.)

Chapter 20

1. Answers can vary. How about "national prestige," produced by generous foreign aid, great architecture, national parks, space exploration? How about the results of basic research that might take the form of new mathematical theorems?

3. Both are wrong. Bus transportation is not a pure public good because neither nonexcludability nor nonrivalness applies: It is easy to exclude nonpaying passengers; the space taken by extra people leaves less for others. Nor is the good a pure private one. Consider how people riding buses create positive externalities: Fewer private cars means less road congestion, fewer accidents, probably less air pollution. Thus, one might make a case for Pigouvian subsidies, but hardly for public finance.

5. Answers can vary. Consider indiscriminate broadcasting of television signals—a pure public good. Then consider the invention of scrambling devices or of cable TV, making it possible to exclude people from receiving the signals unless they pay for descrambling devices or cable connections.

7. a. Vote warning vs. fine, winner vs. license suspension.
   Result: license suspension
   b. Vote warning vs. license suspension, winner vs. fine
   Result: fine
   c. Vote fine vs. license suspension, winner vs. warning
   Result: warning

9. Answers can vary, but consider these facts about the federal government: When George Washington was president, 1 in 4,000 Americans worked for the federal government. Some 100 years later, the ratio was 1 in 400. Now it is 1 in 75. Did the work to be done rise in the same proportion?

Chapter 21

1. There is a lot of truth to the statement and it has to do with incentives. Consider, for example, the effects in our market economy of a change in demand from cars to houses that would ordinarily, in the short run, lower prices and incomes in the auto industry and raise them in the home construction industry. These changes would provide the incentives to switch human and other resources from one industry to the other. What if government intervened for reasons of equity? If it taxed suddenly rich construction workers and contractors, and transferred money to suddenly poor auto workers and owners of auto plants in order to equalize their incomes, why should auto workers still move to become carpenters, electricians, plumbers, and the like? Why should owners of auto plants bother to think about not replacing their equipment as it wears out and reinvesting in the construction industry instead? The government's attempt to be "fair" would take the heart out of the price system's message. Instead of telling people that they could recapture their once-higher incomes only by doing what sovereign dollar-voting consumers had decreed (taking resources out of the auto industry and putting them into the home construction industry instead), people would be getting quite a different message: "*No matter whether you produce cars or homes for people, your income will be exactly the same.*" Of course, people would then have little reason to change their behavior; resources would *not* be used for the purposes most wanted by consumers.

   In short, as long as consumers are to be free to decide what products they consume, *differential* payments to resource owners are necessary—based not on effort put in, but on the objective result achieved; that is, based on whether the right kind of output is produced. Without differential payments, there couldn't be rewards and penalties to entice required changes in behavior.

   The incentive problem just noted is even greater if the tie between income received and contribution is broken entirely. Suppose all persons were guaranteed, through an appropriate program of taxes and transfers, an exactly identical income, *independent of* their contribution to production. Such a policy would effectively countermand *all* the orders of the price system with this single message: "*No matter what you do, even if you don't work at all, your income will, ultimately, be the same!*" Under such circumstances, people may wonder about working only two hours a day, if at all. Everyone would be contributing fewer resources for use in the process of production. Society's output and, therefore, society's total money income would collapse. Like children fighting over a pie and spilling half of it on the floor, our egalitarian policies would have destroyed the very thing they were designed to apportion "fairly." The latest message to all, printed above in italics, would turn out to have been a classic Delphic oracle indeed. Everyone's income would ultimately be *the same* all right, but the same *as everyone else's* (and close to zero), not the same *as before*!

FIGURE A.16 *Government Tax and Transfer Rates: United States, 1980*

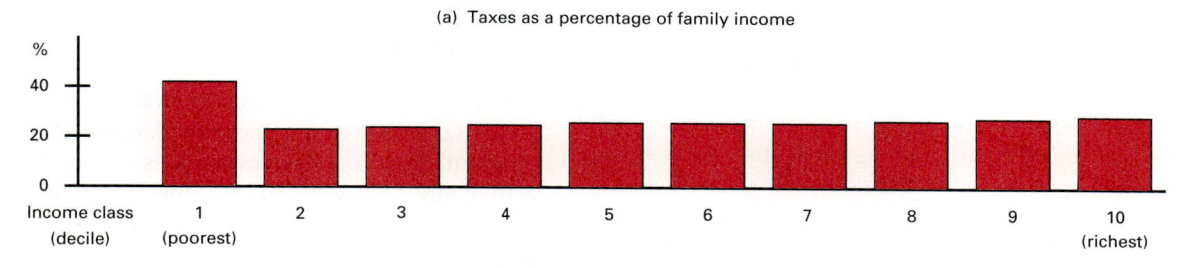

(a) Taxes as a percentage of family income

(b) Government transfers as a percentage of family income

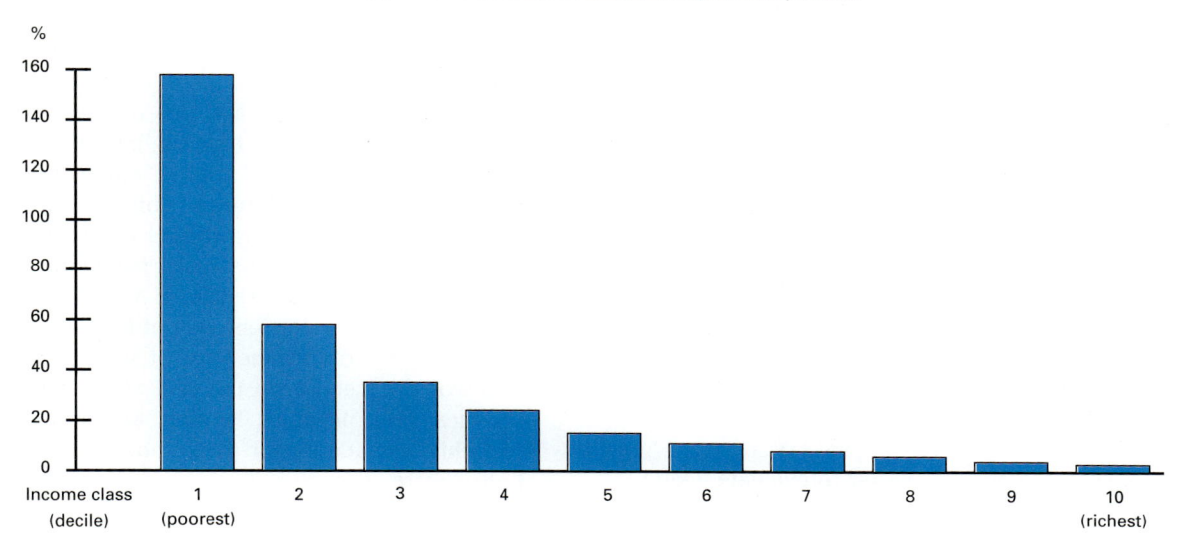

(c) Taxes minus transfers as a percentage of family income

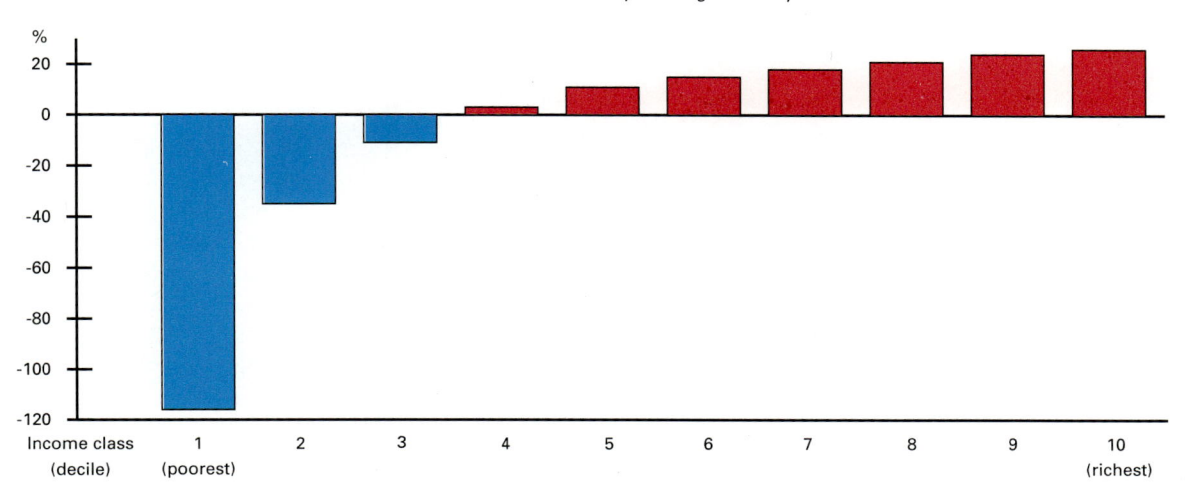

Because families not only receive transfers but also pay taxes, the net gain to them of transfer payments is reduced. Only those in the lowest three income deciles have any net gain at all.

Many thoughtful economists, therefore, are hesitant to recommend creating perfect income equality and breaking the link between income and productive contribution. They recognize that people generally must be given rewards in order to contribute to the process of production at all. Without such rewards, the world's work simply would not get done. They also recognize that people must be given differential rewards if the right things are to be done. Most economists do not rule out, of course, a *limited* redistribution of income of the type discussed in this chapter.

3. Answers can vary.

5. Mr. A pays a 1.67 percent tax on his $30,000 income. Mr. B pays a 1.82 percent tax on his $33,000 income. So the tax is progressive.

   If the tax referred to property, no answer could be given. Progressivity, proportionality, and regressivity are always defined with respect to income. A person with a $30,000 property could have a $1,000 income, and a person with a $33,000 property could have a $100,000 income—or the reverse!

7. See Figure A.16 on the previous page.

9. This is a very difficult matter to evaluate. Quite apart from possible factual inaccuracies (Can employers cut wages at will? Are they rich?), it involves problems similar to figuring out the true incidence of taxes.

11. The proposal rests on the knowledge that a large percentage of the poor are children, many of whom live in fatherless families or families with many children. These allowances might greatly enhance family stability and cut into the vicious circle of poverty breeding poverty. It has been found abroad, furthermore, that such allowances do *not* encourage more births (as some critics fear) and that they *are* spent on the better health and education of children. Unlike the negative income tax, this plan is politically attractive. Public opinion hesitates to support "the lazy poor," but is enthusiastic about "investing in the future of children."

    There are two main drawbacks to this system. It would require substantial payments to families now not poor. Hence, it would be a costly and highly inefficient way of helping the poor. Almost certainly the cost of such a program would exceed even the cost of a reasonably designed negative income tax system. Also, childless adult poor would not be helped at all.

GLOSSARY

abscissa the horizontal axis in a graph (1a)

absolute standard of poverty measurement a standard that defines a person's "needs" as a fixed market basket of bare necessities without which the person cannot survive, and declares the person "poor" if the set of goods available to the person is less than that basket of goods (16)

accounting profit the profit calculated in an income statement, or the difference between sales revenue on the one hand and explicit cost plus depreciation on the other hand (7a)

acreage allotments government restrictions of the total acreage planted with particular crops to or even below that achieved at a given date in the past (18)

ad valorem tariff a tax on imported goods, expressed as a percentage of the good's value (4)

affirmative action plans labor market programs designed not only to end discriminatory practices now but also to make deliberate efforts at overcoming the present effects of past discrimination (14)

agency problem a potential problem that arises whenever people employ others to perform a task on their behalf; the latter (called *agents*) may pursue goals that conflict with the interests of the former (called *principals*) (7)

agent a subordinate who is charged with acting on behalf of a superior, called a *principal* (7)

ambient standards rules that specify the quantity of stated pollutants that a given environment may contain (19)

antidumping rules rules that prevent imports from entering a country if these imports are "unfairly traded" (4)

antipirating agreements agreements among employers to act jointly in the hiring of labor and not to compete with each other for workers (14)

antitakeover laws laws designed to delay or discourage corporate takeovers (11)

antitrust policy systematic governmental efforts designed to limit the market power of monopolies, oligopolies, and other imperfectly competitive firms and to create conditions under which free competition can flourish (17)

antiunion practices employer practices, such as firing workers for joining a labor union, refusing to hire workers sympathetic to unions, threatening to close a firm if workers join a union, interfering with or dominating the administration of a union, and refusing to bargain with a union (14)

appreciation if an exchange rate is expressed as X dollars per unit of foreign money, a fall in the rate denotes an appreciation of the dollar, a rise in the rate denotes an appreciation of foreign money (4)

arc elasticity an elasticity measure that refers to a fairly large section of a demand or supply line (6)

assets things of value owned by a specified party (7a)

autarky a situation of national self-sufficiency in which no economic relations with foreigners exist at all (4)

average fixed cost, *AFC* fixed cost divided by total product (9)

average physical product the ratio of total product to the total quantity of an input used (8)

average revenue, *AR* total revenue TR divided by total product Q; equals product price P (10)

average total cost, *ATC* total cost divided by total product; the sum of average fixed cost plus average variable cost (9)

average value product, *AVP* the total value of output, $Q_o \cdot P_o$, divided by the total associated input quantity Q_i that helped produce the output; also an input's average physical product multiplied by output price, $APP \cdot P_o$ (13)

average variable cost, *AVC* variable cost divided by total product (9)

Averch-Johnson effect whenever the "fair" rate of return that regulators guarantee a natural monopoly exceeds the current rate of interest, its owners will make unnecessary investments in the firm and, thus, fail to produce its output at the lowest possible average total cost (18)

balance sheet a systematic listing, at a particular moment of time, of a specified party's assets, liabilities, and net worth (7a)

balance sheet identity assets always equal or "balance" liabilities plus net worth (7a)

bar chart a graph that portrays data by a series of horizontal bars, the lengths of which are proportional to the values to be depicted (1a)

basing-point system a method of oligopolistic price setting according to which colluding companies, regardless of their location, agree to quote prices equal to those charged by a given firm at a given location (the basing point) plus freight from this basing point to the buyer's location (12)

benefit an advantage derived from an act of choice; an opportunity realized (1)

benefit-cost analysis the quantification of the expected benefits and costs of potential government projects, the rejection of projects with benefit-cost ratios below unity, and the apportionment of the budget among those remaining projects that have the highest benefit-cost ratios (20)

bilateral monopoly a market configuration in which a monopoly seller confronts a monopsony buyer (14)

black markets markets in which goods are traded at illegal prices (or in which illegal goods are traded) (3)

brand loyalty an attitude that causes consumers of a highly advertised product to make automatic repeat purchases of the same brand and to cease sampling other brands (12)

break-even point any output level at which total revenue equals total cost and at which average revenue or price, therefore, equals average total cost (10)

budget line a line in the field of choice showing all the alternative quantity combinations of two goods that a consumer is able to buy at current market prices in a given period by fully using a given budget (5a)

bureaucrats civil servants employed by government agencies (20)

capacity output the output level at which a given plant achieves minimum average total cost (9)

capital budgeting the process of identifying available investment opportunities, selecting investment projects to be carried out, and arranging for their financing (15)

capital resources productive ingredients made by people, including structures, durable equipment, and producer inventories of raw materials, semifinished and finished goods (1)

capitalism an economic system in which the private ownership of natural and capital resources predominates (2)

capitalized value the present value of an asset's future income stream (15)

cartel a conspiracy by all existing sellers in a market to put up a joint front toward buyers, acting as if they were one, and making joint price and output decisions (11)

central economic plan a document specifying the future economic actions of all people in detail (2)

change in demand a change in the quantity of an item that buyers are ready to purchase, if this quantity change is due to a change in some factor *other than* the item's own price, all else being equal; graphically shown by a *shift* of a given demand line (3)

change in quantity demanded a change in the quantity of an item that buyers are ready to purchase, if this quantity change is due to a change in the item's own price, other things being equal; graphically shown by a *movement along* a given demand line (3)

change in quantity supplied a change in the quantity of an item that sellers are ready to provide, if this quantity change is due to a change in the item's own price, other things being equal; graphically shown by a *movement along* a given supply line (3)

change in supply a change in the quantity of an item that sellers are ready to provide, if this quantity change is due to a change in some factor *other than* the item's own price, all else being equal; graphically shown by a *shift* of a given supply line (3)

class-action suits legal suits charging that a given individual has been victimized and the individual's treatment was typical of an entire class of "similarly situated" individuals (14)

closed shop a firm in which only union members are hired (14)

Coase theorem "under perfect competition, once government has assigned clearly defined property rights in contested resources and as long as transactions costs are negligible, private parties that generate or are affected by externalities will negotiate voluntary agreements that lead to the socially optimal resource allocation and output mix regardless of how the property rights are assigned" (19)

cobweb cycle the tendency of the prices and quantities of some goods or resources to rise above and then fall below some intermediate level in successive periods (13)

collective bargaining contracts contracts between labor unions and employers that specify compensation, hours worked, and numerous other conditions of employment for a specified term (14)

column chart a graph that portrays data by a series of vertical columns, the heights of which are proportional to the values to be depicted (1a)

command economy an economic system in which the separate economic activities of people engaged in the division of labor are coordinated on paper by a central planning board, followed by its issuance of detailed verbal commands directed to each person (2)

commercial policy governmental measures affecting international trade (4)

commodities physical objects, like food, clothes, or cars (1)

communism an economic system in which the public ownership of natural and capital resources predominates (2)

comparable worth a standard designed to assure equal pay for equal-quality workers holding jobs of equal intrinsic value (14)

compensating wage differentials see *equalizing wage differentials* (13)

complementary goods two goods such that the consumption of one is typically linked to the simultaneous consumption of the other (3); goods with negative cross-price elasticity of demand (6)

compounding a process that makes dollars of different dates comparable by using the interest rate to compute the future value of present dollars (15)

concentration ratios numbers that show the percentage of domestic sales that is attributable to a stated number of largest domestic firms in an industry, usually the 4, 8, 20, or 50 largest companies (12)

conglomerate merger the combining into one of two or more firms that have neither competitive nor supplier-customer relations and that operate in different industries or geographic markets (17)

consent agreement a deal between a government prosecutor and an accused party, according to which a lawsuit is dropped in exchange for voluntary ameliorative action by the accused (17)

conspiracy doctrine a doctrine according to which courts looked upon unionized workers who "conspired" to raise wages and were, thus, "interfering with freedom of contract" as common criminals (14)

constant returns to scale a situation in which a simultaneous and equal percentage change in the use of all physical inputs leads to an *identical* percentage change in physical output (8)

constant-cost industry an industry with a horizontal long-run supply line (10)

consumer optimum a state of affairs in which it is impossible to raise total utility from a given budget by buying more of one good and less of another (5)

consumer surplus the difference between the maximum sum of money consumers would pay for the quantity traded and the actual sum they do pay for it (4)

consumption possibilities frontier see *budget line* (5a)

copyright an exclusive right to the publishing, sale, or reproduction of a literary, musical, or artistic work (11)

corporate raiders persons who specialize in seeking out corporations for takeover (7)

corporation a legal entity, chartered by government, which is separate and distinct from the persons who own it (7)

cost a disadvantage associated with an act of choice; an opportunity lost (1)

countervailing tariffs tariffs designed to offset the price-lowering effects of export subsidies (4)

craft unions unions of workers who share a common set of skills but do not necessarily work for the same employer (14)

cross-price elasticity of demand the percentage change in a good's quantity demanded divided by the associated percentage change in *another* good's price that causes it, all else being equal (6)

deadweight loss a welfare loss experienced by some people that is not offset by other people's gain (4)

decreasing returns to scale a situation in which a simultaneous and equal percentage change in the use of all physical inputs leads to a *smaller* percentage change in physical output (8)

decreasing-cost industry an industry with a downward-sloping long-run supply line (10)

delay period a typical provision in antitakeover laws, mandating a lengthy waiting period between the time a corporate raider makes a tender offer and the date of its expiration (7)

deliberate coordination see *command economy* (2)

demand line a graphical representation of a demand schedule which lists the relationship between alternative prices of an item and the associated quantities demanded—other things being equal (3)

demand schedule a tabular listing of the relationship between alternative prices of an item and the associated quantities demanded—other things being equal (3)

democratic socialism a capitalist economic system in which a social-democratic or labor party runs the government and introduces programs to modify capitalism, such as limited nationalization of industry, environmental legislation, or a tax system that redistributes income from the rich to the poor (2)

depreciation if an exchange rate is expressed as X dollars per unit of foreign money, a fall in the rate denotes a depreciation of foreign money, a rise in the rate denotes a depreciation of the dollar (4)

derived demand the demand for an input that exists only to the extent that people demand the output that such input helps produce (13)

desire for goods the quantity of goods people would take in a period if goods could be had for nothing (1)

direct democracy a form of public choice according to which all affected citizens vote on every proposal concerning public goods (20)

disclosure statement a typical provision in antitakeover laws, requiring the publication of details about the personal background and finances of corporate raiders (7)

discount rate the interest rate employed in the discounting process (15)

discounting a process that makes dollars of different dates comparable by using the interest rate—then also called discount rate—to compute the present value of future dollars (15)

discrimination in labor markets, a practice according to which employers make irrelevant distinctions among workers and systematically place positive or negative values on personal characteristics of workers that are unrelated to their productivity (14)

distributive justice a state of affairs in which the apportionment of income among people is "fair" because it has been determined not merely by impersonal market forces but also by deliberate actions taken by some human authority that establishes and rewards the relative merit of income recipients by reference to personal characteristics that they possess (21)

dividends corporate after-tax profit divided among stockholders and paid out to them (7)

doctrine of caveat emptor the legal doctrine of "let the buyer beware," according to which buyers alone are responsible for the consequences of their purchases; it is up to them to ascertain the quality of products at the time of purchase and to use these products properly thereafter (18)

doctrine of caveat venditor the legal doctrine of "let the seller beware," according to which sellers are responsible for the effectiveness and safety of their products and are liable for consequences if these products have been negligently produced (18)

double taxation a major disadvantage of the corporate form of business according to which corporate profit is subject to corporate income taxes, while after-tax corporate profit that is paid out to stockholders as dividends is again subject to personal income taxes (7)

dutiable imports imports subject to customs duties or tariffs (4)

economic efficiency a situation in which it is *impossible* to make a person better off without making another person worse off because all *mutually beneficial* transactions have already been carried out (10, 13)

economic equity a situation in which the apportionment of goods among people is considered fair (2)

economic growth a sustained expansion over the long run of a society's ability to produce goods (2)

economic inefficiency a state of affairs in which it is possible to reallocate resources or goods to make some people better off without making others worse off because some potential, mutually beneficial transactions have not yet been carried out (2, 11)

economic power the capacity, based on property rights, to make and enforce decisions on the allocation of scarce resources and, ultimately, the apportionment of scarce goods made with the help of those resources (2)

economic profit, Π accounting profit minus all types of implicit cost not considered in its computation, notably the value of resource services supplied to the firm without pay by its owners (7a); the difference between total revenue and the total cost (explicit and implicit) associated with producing that revenue (10)

economic regulation a type of regulation aimed at particular industries that specifies rules concerning market entry, pricing, output, and the like (18)

economic rent in the labor market, the excess of workers' actual income over the minimum income necessary to bring forth the quantity of labor being supplied (the minimum, presumably, equals the maximum value of the workers' time in alternative uses) (14)

economic stability the maintenance over time of constant or smoothly growing levels of overall output and employment, while preserving a constant general level of prices (2)

economic system the arrangements through which people in a society allocate scarce resources and apportion scarce goods among themselves (2)

economic tax incidence the way in which the real burden of a tax is ultimately apportioned among people (3)

economic theory deliberately simplified and, therefore, unrealistic representations of reality that can be useful in explaining and predicting events that occur in the world's economic systems (2)

economics the study of how people allocate scarce resources that have alternative uses among virtually unlimited competing ends (2)

elasticity an exact measure of responsiveness of quantity demanded or quantity supplied to changes in other variables; the percentage change in quantity divided by the percentage change in whatever variable causes the quantity change—all other things being equal (6)

emission standards rules that specify maximum quantities of stated pollutants that may be released by any one polluter (19)

entitlement programs government transfer program of *social insurance* and *public assistance* (21)

envelope curve a curve to which other curves are invariably tangent, such as the *planning curve*, which is tangent to all the curves of short-run average total cost (9)

equal-product curve see *isoquant* (8a)

equalizing wage differentials wage differentials, as among occupations or regions, that offset nonmonetary differences in the perceived attractiveness of jobs (13)

equilibrium a situation in which there is no innate tendency to change as when quantity demanded and quantity supplied are just equal to one another in a market (3)

escape clause a legal clause making it possible to revoke tariff concessions if a domestic industry is "seriously" hurt by foreign competition (4)

excess capacity the difference between a monopolistically competitive firm's capacity output (corresponding to minimum *ATC*) and its lower, but profit-maximizing level of actual output (12)

exchange rate the price in a foreign-exchange market, expressed (in this book) as so many dollars per unit of foreign money (4)

excise tax a tax imposed on each unit of a good traded in a market (3)

exclusive contracts contracts by which sellers agree to lease or sell a commodity only on the condition that the lessees or purchasers thereof shall not use or deal in the commodity of competitors (17)

exclusive franchise a government grant to a single seller of the exclusive right to produce and sell a good (11)

explicit cost a highly visible cost incurred by a firm that sooner or later involves a payment to an outside party (7a, 9)

export subsidies money paid exporters by their government to promote larger sales abroad (4)

external diseconomies unfavorable changes in the production functions of all firms (that lower output per unit of input), or increases in input prices that are associated with industry growth and that shift cost curves up (10)

external economies favorable changes in the production functions of all firms (that raise output per unit of input), or decreases in input prices that are associated with industry growth and that shift cost curves down (10)

externalities direct effects that the actions of some consumers or producers have on the utility of other consumers or on the output of other producers, none of whom have invited these effects (19)

factors of production see *resources* (1)

fair-price provision a typical provision in antitakeover laws, forcing successful corporate raiders to pay the same price per share to all former stockholders, even to those who refused to surrender their shares before the expiration of a tender offer (7)

fair trade laws laws, now abolished, that allow any manufacturer to fix a minimum price for a product and, if even a single retailer agrees to it, to bind all retailers to it, even those who refuse to sign an appropriate agreement with the manufacturer (3, 18)

featherbedding a labor union practice requiring payment for work not done or not needing to be done (14)

field of choice all the alternative quantity combinations of two goods among which a consumer might conceivably choose (5a)

financial capital a collection of money, bonds, deeds, stocks, and the like; paper claims against real re-sources (1)

firm one of the market economy's major institutions that buys productive ingredients in resource markets, uses them to produce goods, and sells these products in goods markets (7)

first-degree price discrimination a practice according to which the seller charges each buyer for each unit bought the maximum price the buyer is willing to pay for that unit (11)

fixed cost, *FC* the monetary value of fixed inputs used in a period (9)

fixed inputs productive ingredients the quantities of which cannot be varied in the period under consideration (8)

flow a quantity that is related to a given *period* of time (1)

foreign-exchange markets markets in which one country's money is traded for another country's money (4)

free goods goods available in larger quantities than all people would want to take in a given period, if the goods could be had for nothing; thus, everyone's desire for them can be fulfilled at the same time (1)

free-rider problem the unwillingness of individuals to pay for the production of pure public goods and their eagerness to let others produce such goods so that they can enjoy the associated spillover of benefits at zero cost (20)

friendly takeover a takeover undertaken by a "white knight" who is friendly toward the current management (7)

fully funded system an insurance system, typical of private schemes, in which premiums paid in are saved to build up a fund the size of which equals the present value of future benefits promised to the insured (21)

functional distribution of income the apportionment of the national income among large and possibly overlapping groups of people who supply, respectively, the services of human, natural, or capital resources (16)

game any decision-making situation in which people interact with other people and in which these other people actively seek to thwart the attainment of the first people's goals (12)

game theory a method for studying decision making in situations of conflict in which the fates of people seeking different goals are interlocked so that the payoff to people's choices depends not only on them and objective circumstances, but also on other people's choices (12)

gentlemen's agreements informal oral understandings among oligopolists in a given industry on maintaining a specified minimum price (12)

Gini coefficient a numerical summary measure of income or wealth inequality; equal to the ratio of two areas in the Lorenz curve graph: the area between the lines of perfect equality and actual inequality to the area between the lines of perfect equality and perfect inequality (16)

golden parachute an exceedingly generous promise of pay and benefits payable to a top corporate manager in the event of a corporate takeover that eliminates the manager's job (7)

goods commodities and services that people desire (1)

government failure the provision by government of nonoptimal quantities of pure public goods (20)

gross barter terms of trade the ratio of physical import quantity to physical export quantity (4)

greenmail an arrangement that uses company funds for buying up, at extremely high prices, company stock held by corporate raiders (7)

Herfindahl index a sophisticated measure of industrial concentration, equal to the sum of the squared market shares of all firms operating in a market (17)

holding company a corporation established for the sole purpose of acquiring a controlling stock interest in two or more competing corporations and then running their affairs jointly, as if they were a single company (17)

horizontal merger the combining into one of two or more firms that sell closely related products in the same market (17)

hostile takeover a takeover undertaken by a group that is unfriendly toward the current management (7)

Hotelling's paradox oligopolistic competition by means of product differentiation can lead to a situation in which products are hardly differentiated at all (12)

human capital the accumulation of past investments in people's health, general education, and training that raise the productive capacity of people (1)

human resources people able and willing to participate in the process of production, supplying their mental or physical labor (1)

imperfectly competitive markets markets in which one or more of the characteristics of perfect competition are absent (11)

implicit cost a hidden cost that does not involve a payment and that the owners of a firm incur when using their own resources in their firm "free of charge" rather than hiring them out to collect the maximum possible income available elsewhere (7a, 9)

import quota a maximum physical quantity of a specified good that may be imported in a given period (4,18)

income effect the effect of a changed wage that makes an individual supply less labor at a higher wage (and more labor at a lower wage) because being richer incites the desire to consume more leisure (and being poorer, the opposite) (13)

income elasticity of demand the percentage change in a good's quantity demanded divided by the associated percentage change in consumer income that causes it—all else being equal (6)

income statement a systematic listing, for a specified period of time, of a specified party's revenue, cost, and profit (7a)

increasing-cost industry an industry with an upward-sloping long-run supply line (10)

increasing returns to scale a situation in which a simultaneous and equal percentage change in the use of all physical inputs leads to a *larger* percentage change in physical output (8)

independent goods two goods such that the consumption of one is totally unrelated to the consumption of the other (3); goods with zero cross-price elasticity of demand (6)

indifference curve a graph of all the alternative quantity combinations of two goods that in a consumer's view yield the same (unmeasurable) total utility and among which the consumer, therefore, is indifferent (5a)

industrial unions labor unions that collect all workers in a given industry into a single organization without regard to particular skills (14)

industry all the firms operating in a given market and producing an identical or similar product (10)

industry structure see *market structure* (10)

infant-industry argument one of numerous arguments advanced in support of protectionism according to which new industries in a *developed* nation must be protected against more mature foreign competitors while they become established (4)

inferior goods goods of which smaller physical quantities are typically consumed at higher than at lower incomes—other things being equal (3); goods with a negative income elasticity of demand (6)

informative advertising a type of advertising that provides much-needed, truthful information to prospective buyers concerning available sellers, products, prices, and the like (12)

injunction a court decree, enforceable by arrest and jail, forbidding certain actions (14)

input standards rules that specify the type of inputs polluters may use (19)

interlocking directorates arrangements under which two or more competing corporations have at least some members on their boards of directors in common (17)

interlocking stockholdings an arrangement by which one corporation acquires the stock of a competing corporation or purchases (as a holding company does) the stock certificates of two or more corporations that are competitors (17)

internal diseconomies decreasing returns to scale encountered as larger plants are put into operation or increases in costs as a single administrative unit attempts to run ever more plants, which shift a firm's cost curves right and up (10)

internal economies increasing returns to scale encountered as larger plants are put into operation or cost savings reaped through multi-plant operations that shift a firm's cost curves right and down (10)

internalities consequences—such as the production of excessive amounts of pure public goods at excessive costs—that are related to the pursuit by elected and appointed government officials of their internal, personal goals instead of publicly announced, official goals (20)

Invisible Hand see *market economy* (2)

iron law of wages the Malthusian notion according to which population changes assure that wages, ultimately, end up at the level of subsistence (13)

isocost line a line showing all the alternative quantity combinations of two inputs that a producer is able to buy at current market prices in a given period by fully using a given budget and that, therefore, cost the same amount (8a)

isoquant a line that shows all the alternative combinations of two input quantities that yield the same maximum total product and among which a producer would be indifferent from a purely technical point of view (8a)

Jevons' Rule "To maximize utility, a consumer should purchase such quantities of various goods that the marginal utility received per dollar of every good is the same." (5)

jurisdictional strikes strikes wherein workers belonging to one union, in an attempt to force the recognition of a single union, walk off the job to interrupt work being done by fellow workers belonging to another union (14)

keeping-our-money-at-home argument one of numerous arguments advanced in support of protectionism according to which trade restrictions prevent a country's money from ending up in foreign hands (4)

kinked demand line an oligopolist's demand line reflecting the fact that price increases are not expected to be matched by competitors (which will reduce quantity demanded a lot), while price decreases are expected to be matched promptly (which will raise quantity demanded only a bit) (12)

labor boycott an organized attempt by workers to persuade their employers' customers not to buy products of the firms until a labor dispute has been settled (14)

labor union a cartel formed by workers for the joint sale of their labor (14)

"law" of declining marginal benefits "all else being equal, the greater the overall level of any activity during a given period, the smaller will its marginal benefit usually be" (1)

"law" of declining marginal utility "given the quantities of all other goods being consumed, the greater is the quantity consumed of a given good during a period, the smaller will its marginal utility usually be" (5)

"law" of demand other things being equal, as the price of an item falls, the quantity demanded by buyers tends to increase; the opposite is also true (as the price of an item rises, the quantity demanded tends to decrease) (3)

law of diminishing returns "given technical knowledge and fixed quantities of all other inputs, equal successive increases of any one input to any given production process will, after some point (the point of diminishing returns), yield ever smaller increases in output" (8)

"law" of supply other things being equal, as the price of an item falls, the quantity supplied by sellers tends to decrease; the opposite is also true (as the price of an item rises, the quantity supplied tends to increase) (3)

leisure all uses of people's time other than work (13)

Lerner index an index measuring the degree of monopoly power exercised by a firm, equal to the difference between output price and marginal cost, divided by output price (17)

liabilities the debts of a specified party (7a)

limited liability the legal principle that makes each stockholder separately liable for a corporation's debts, but only up to the amount of money already spent when acquiring the stock certificates held (7)

limited partnership a partnership jointly owned by one or more general partners (who carry unlimited liability) and one or more limited partners (whose liability for the firm's debts is limited to their original investment in the firm) (7)

line of actual inequality an actual rather than hypothetical Lorenz curve (16)

line of perfect equality the hypothetical position of the Lorenz curve when income or wealth is apportioned perfectly equally among the members of a group (16)

line of perfect inequality the hypothetical position of the Lorenz curve when income or wealth is apportioned perfectly unequally in the sense that all of it goes to one member of a group and none of it to all the others (16)

lockout a refusal of employers to let workers work until a labor dispute has been settled (14)

logrolling the occasional exchange between voters of support on one issue now in return for similar support on another issue later (20)

long run a time period so long that a firm can vary the quantities of *all* of its inputs (8)

Lorenz curve a graphical device providing a summary of the way in which income or wealth is apportioned among the members of any group and highlighting the extent of equality or inequality among them (16)

luxuries normal goods with an income elasticity of demand greater than 1 (6)

macroeconomics the study of "large" issues that are economy-wide (2)

managed capitalism a different term for *democratic socialism* (2)

managerial coordination costs the resources used to arrange for the coordination of people's specialized activities by a central manager; alternatively, the forgone output these resources might have produced (7)

marginal benefit the change in an activity's total benefit which is attributable to a unit change in the level of that activity (1)

marginal cost, MC the change in total cost divided by the associated change in total product (9); the change in an activity's total cost which is attributable to a unit change in the level of that activity (1)

marginal external benefit, MEB the increased utility or output provided to other people by the extra consumption or production of some people (19)

marginal external cost, MEC the lowered utility or output imposed upon other people by the extra consumption or production of some people (19)

marginal labor cost, MLC the change in a firm's total labor cost divided by the associated change in labor input used (14)

marginal physical product, MPP the physical change in the total product that is attributable to a unit change in one input in the productive process—other things being equal (8)

marginal private benefit, MPB the marginal benefit that the purchaser of a good derives from its consumption (19)

marginal private cost, MPC the marginal cost that the producer of a good incurs in its production (19)

marginal rate of substitution, MRS the rate at which a consumer is able to sacrifice—without any feeling of utility gain or loss—a little bit of one good for a unit increase in another good (5a)

marginal rate of technical substitution, MRTS the rate at which a producer is technically able to exchange—without affecting the quantity of output produced—a little bit of one input (such as capital) for a little bit of another input (such as labor) (8a)

marginal rate of transformation, MRT the rate at which people can exchange, in the process of production, a little bit of one good for a little bit of another (4)

marginal revenue, MR the change in total revenue ΔTR, divided by the associated change in total product ΔQ; under perfect competition only equals product price P (10)

marginal revenue product of labor, MRP_L the change in a firm's total revenue that is associated with a unit change in labor input used; also equal to the marginal physical product of labor multiplied by marginal revenue (14)

marginal social benefit, MSB the change in the total benefit, from the point of view of all members of society, that is associated with a unit change in the consumption of a good (19)

marginal social cost, MSC the change in total cost, from the point of view of all members of society, that is associated with a unit change in the production of a good (19)

marginal utility the change in total utility that is associated with a unit change in a good's quantity consumed—other things being equal (5)

marginal value product, MVP an input's marginal physical product multiplied by output price, $MPP \cdot P_o$ (13)

marginalist thinking the systematic comparison of the marginal benefit and marginal cost associated with any conceivable reallocation of fully used resources (1)

market a framework within which owners of property rights make contact with one another for the purpose of transferring ownership, usually for money (2)

market coordination costs see *transactions costs* (7)

market economy an economic system in which monetary incentives established in markets spontaneously coordinate the independently taken but interdependent economic activities of self-interested people (2)

market failures shortcomings typical of market economies, including inefficiency, inequity, and instability (17)

market share the ratio, in a given year, of a firm's dollar sales in a market to the total dollar sales of all firms in that market, multiplied by 100 (17)

market structure the major characteristics of a market or industry that determine how it is organized, including the number of firms operating in the market, the nature of the product traded, the degree to which market knowledge is available to traders, and the conditions of entry into or exit from the market (10)

marketing quotas government specifications of maximum amounts of various products that particular farmers can legally sell (18)

maximin strategy a game theory strategy according to which a player chooses the best among a list of worst possible outcomes, that is, the maximum among all possible minima (the *maximum minimorum*) (12)

maximum price see *price ceiling* (3)

merit goods certain goods other than pure public goods that are, nevertheless, financed by taxes, produced by government, and supplied at subsidized prices or even free of charge to selected consumers on the grounds that all citizens merit a minimum share of them (20)

microeconomics the study of issues that do not encompass the entire economy and are in this sense "small" (2)

minimax strategy a game theory strategy according to which a player chooses the best among a list of worst possible outcomes, that is, the minimum among all of its opponent's possible maxima (the *minimum maximorum*) (12)

minimum efficient scale the lowest output level associated with the long-run average total cost curve at which minimum long-run ATC can be achieved (9)

minimum price see *price floor* (3)

mixed economies economies in which government occupies an intermediate position that involves more than the minimum role required of it in a laissez-faire, capitalist market economy, but less than the maximum role it would play in a totally planned, communist command economy; thus, there is a mix of private and public decision making (2)

monopolistic competition a market structure in which innumerable firms compete because restrictions to market entry or exit are absent, in which the products traded are differentiated from one seller to the next, and in which traders possess less than perfect market knowledge (12)

monopolistic exploitation of labor a situation in which labor's wage falls short of its marginal value product and this divergence is caused by the fact that the employer possesses monopoly power in the output market (which makes marginal revenue falls short of output price and, therefore, the marginal revenue product of labor falls short of its marginal value product) (14)

monopoly a seller who is the only seller in a market into which the entry of other sellers is severely restricted or even impossible and who is selling an item for which no good substitutes are available (11)

monopsonistic exploitation of labor a situation in which labor's wage falls short of its marginal value product and this divergence is caused by the fact that the employer possesses monopsony power in the labor market (which makes the marginal labor cost exceed any wage that the firm sets) (14)

monopsony a buyer who is the only buyer in a market into which the entry of other buyers is blocked or highly unlikely and for whom sellers have no good substitute (11, 14)

most-favored nation treatment the automatic extension of bilaterally negotiated tariff cuts to other trading partners (4)

national-defense argument one of numerous arguments advanced in support of protectionism, according to which domestic industries "crucial for defense" must be protected against foreign competition (4)

natural monopoly a situation in which a firm's long-run average total cost is declining throughout the range of quantities that might be demanded in the market (11)

natural resources gifts of nature in their natural state; productive ingredients not made by people and as yet untouched by them (1)

necessities normal goods with an income elasticity of demand between 0 and 1 (6)

negative externalities situations in which the consumption or production activities of some people impose costs in the form of decreased utility or decreased output on other people who, to their dismay, are not being compensated for this injury (19)

negative income tax system a reformed tax system that would replace all existing transfer programs by a single program paying cash benefits solely based on people's income (21)

neighborhood effects see *externalities* (19)

net present value the sum of the present values of all the negative and positive components of an investment project (15)

net worth the difference (positive or negative) between assets and liabilities (7a)

nominal rate of interest the percentage by which the dollar amount returned to a lender exceeds the dollar amount lent (15)

non-automatic import authorizations import licenses that are required for specific imports and that can be granted or denied at the discretion of government officials (4)

nonexcludability the property of a pure public good that makes it physically impossible or extremely costly to exclude any individual from the enjoyment of the good once a given amount of it has been produced (20)

nonprofit firms certain firms in the U.S. economy, such as trustee-run corporations, cooperatives, and public enterprises, that are exempt from taxation (7)

nonrivalness the property of a pure public good that allows additional persons to consume the good without reducing the good's availability to others (20)

nontariff barriers nontax measures imposed by governments to protect domestic producers from import competition (4)

nonzero-sum game a game in which the winnings and losses of all players add to a positive or negative number (12)

normal goods goods of which larger physical quantities are typically consumed at higher than at lower incomes—other things being equal (3); goods with a positive income elasticity of demand (6)

normative economics statements about the economy that make value judgments about existing circumstances and prescribe what ought to be (2)

oligopoly a market structure in which a large percentage of sales is made by a mere handful of firms that compete with one another in the sale of homogeneous or differentiated products, in which the entry of new firms is difficult, and in which market knowledge is imperfect (12)

opportunity cost the most fundamental of all concepts of cost; equal to the most highly valued alternative that is forgone in an act of choice (1)

optimal rate of plant operation see *capacity output* (9)

optimization principle "Whenever a subjective evaluation of an activity's marginal benefit MB and marginal cost MC shows (a) $MB > MC$, an expansion of the activity raises welfare; (b) $MB < MC$, a contraction of the activity raises welfare, and (c) $MB = MC$, the activity level is optimal." (1)

optimum plant that plant, among all conceivable ones, with the lowest possible minimum average total cost (9)

optimum pollution a level of waste dumping that equates the marginal social benefit and marginal social cost of such dumping and, thus, maximizes the social net benefit (19)

orderly marketing agreement a multilateral form of voluntary export restraints (4)

ordinate the vertical axis in a graph (1a)

origin the point in a system of coordinates at which the vertical and horizontal axes intersect at right angles (1a)

own-price elasticity of demand the percentage change in a good's quantity demanded divided by the associated percentage change in the good's own price that causes it, all else being equal (6)

own-price elasticity of supply the percentage change in a good's quantity supplied divided by the associated percentage change in the good's own price that causes it, all else being equal (6)

Parkinson's law the number of those employed by government agencies will grow at the same rate regardless of whether the volume of work to be done rises, falls, or even disappears (20)

partnership an unincorporated firm owned and operated by a fixed number of two or more persons (7)

patent an exclusive right to the use of an invention (11)

pay-as-you-go system the U.S. social security system in which social security taxes paid by those working in any one year are typically not saved by the government to finance future benefits, but are immediately paid out to those who are eligible for benefits in that year (21)

perfect competition a market structure characterized by a large number of independently acting buyers as well as sellers; by buyers viewing all units of the traded item as identical, regardless of the source of its supply; by buyers as well as sellers possessing full knowledge relevant to trading in the market; and by the absence of impediments to entry into or exit from this market for either buyers or sellers (10)

perfect price discrimination see *first-degree price discrimination* (11)

peril points legal limits set by Congress below which tariffs may not be lowered by the executive branch of government (4)

personal distribution of income the apportionment of the national income among individuals without regard to the type of income that is being received and, thus, without regard to the type of resource services that are being supplied (16)

persuasive advertising a type of advertising that is designed to divert people's attention from facts to images and to make them buy more as a result of imagined advantages (12)

picket line a line of striking workers parading around the work site, encouraging other workers not to cross the line (14)

pie chart a segmented circle that portrays divisions of some aggregate in such a way that the central angles (and, therefore, the circumference arcs and sector areas) are proportional to the sizes of the divisions being displayed (1a)

planning curve the line of long-run average total cost that is tangent to all the curves of short-run average total cost and indicates the lowest possible average total costs for all conceivable output levels that a firm might produce (9)

plant a firm's physical production facility, as defined by a set of inputs that are fixed in the short run (9)

plurality voting see *rank-order voting* (20)

point elasticity an elasticity measure that refers to a single point on a demand or supply line (6)

point of diminishing returns the inflection point on the total product curve where increasing positive slope gives way to decreasing positive slope and beyond which the variable input's marginal physical products decline (8)

point voting a procedure in which each voter is given *n* points that can be allocated at the voter's discretion to potential projects; the votes are added together, and the largest number wins (20)

poison pills techniques such as selling off the best company assets or taking on dangerously risky ventures that are deliberately designed to make a target company less attractive to corporate raiders (7)

pollution licenses see *pollution rights* (19)

pollution rights transferable certificates allowing the owner to dump one unit of specified wastes into a specified environment (19)

positive externalities situations in which the consumption or production activities of some people provide benefits in the form of increased utility or increased output for other people who, to their delight, are not being charged for this favor (19)

positive economics statements about the economy that are restricted to describing the facts, explaining how they are related, and predicting the consequences of any changes in circumstances (2)

poverty gap the difference between poor people's needed income and their actual income (16)

poverty line an income level that separates the poor below it from the nonpoor above it (16)

poverty rate the percentage of all the people in a given group who are poor (16)

prejudice preconceived irrational opinion that leads to bias against some people and unfair partiality toward others; an attitude of mind that interferes with fair judgment (14)

price ceiling a legal maximum price, typically set below the market equilibrium level, above which transactions are illegal (3)

price discrimination a practice according to which sellers charge a given buyer or different buyers different prices for different units of an identical good, even though such price differences cannot be justified by differences in the cost of serving these buyers (11, 17)

price floor a legal minimum price, typically set above the market equilibrium level, below which transactions are illegal (3)

price leadership a practice common in oligopolistic industries according to which one firm, the price leader, announces and occasionally changes the price of the industry's product, while all other firms immediately follow suit (12)

price setters imperfectly competitive buyers and sellers who have the power to influence the prices at which transactions take place (11)

price system the totality of interdependent prices in numerous markets for goods and resources; the market economy's invisible governor who coordinates people's activities by inducing them to supply less and consume more of surplus things (the prices of which are falling) and to supply more and consume less of shortage things (the prices of which are rising) (2)

price takers traders in a perfectly competitive market who must take or leave the price that the forces of demand and supply have established and who cannot influence that price by any individual actions of their own (10)

price war a situation in which rival firms successively cut their prices below those of competitors and, perhaps, even below their own costs (12)

principal a person who exercises authority over subordinates, called *agents* (7)

prisoners' dilemma game a game in which the best common choice of strategies is unstable, offers great incentives to cheat, and leads to the worst possible choice (12)

privatization the shift of traditional public-sector functions to the private sector (20)

process of production the set of activities by which people, directly or indirectly, make goods available when and where they are wanted (1)

process of public choice the procedures by which groups of people decide on the quantities of various public goods to be produced and on the ways in which associated tax burdens are shared (20)

producer surplus the difference between the actual sum of money producers receive for the quantity traded and the minimum sum they would accept for it (4)

product differentiation deliberate actions taken by producers to make their product, in the eyes of consumers, distinct from the close substitutes that rival firms supply (12)

production function the technical relationship, stated in physical and not in value terms, between alternative combinations of inputs used during a period and the maximum possible output quantities associated with each of these input combinations, given the state of technical knowledge (8)

production indifference curve see *isoquant* (8a)

production possibilities frontier a graph showing all the alternative combinations of two groups of goods the people of a country are capable of producing in a given year by using their flows of resources fully and efficiently, given their present state of technology (1)

productivity the quantity of goods that can be produced *per unit* of any given type of resource (1); also see *average physical product* (8)

profit the difference (positive or negative) between revenue and cost (7a)

progressive taxes taxes that take a larger percentage of higher than of lower incomes (21)

property right the exclusive (but variously qualified) right to the use of something scarce (2)

proprietorship a firm owned and operated by a single person (7)

protectionism the totality of measures governments take to restrict international trade (4)

proxies permissions to vote on behalf of current stockholders at the next stockholders' meeting (7)

public assistance transfer programs that aim to assist people who are already poor and seek to raise their income above the poverty line (21)

public finance the collection of taxes from all those believed to benefit from the provision of pure public goods and the subsequent channeling of these funds toward the production of such goods, either by government agencies or private firms (20)

public-interest theory of regulation a theory according to which government regulates firms in otherwise competitive industries because it wants to achieve certain goals that it considers to be "in the public interest" and that would otherwise not be achieved (18)

pure private goods goods that generate no externalities and therefore are characterized by the fact that their buyers and sellers are the only persons affected by the benefits and costs associated with them (20)

pure public goods goods that generate positive externalities to an extreme degree and provide nonexcludable and nonrival benefits to all members of society (20)

pure rent the economic rent generated by a resource that can neither be produced nor destroyed by people and that is supplied by nature in a fixed amount that remains forever unresponsive to the resource's rental price (15)

quadrant any one of the four quarters in a system of coordinates (1a)

quasi rent the economic rent generated by a resource that can be produced and destroyed by people and that is, therefore, in the long run, supplied in amounts that vary with the resource's rental price (15)

rank-order voting a procedure by which each voter ranks *n* projects from 1 (most preferred) to *n* (least preferred), the votes are added together, and the lowest number wins (20)

rate base the value of the invested capital on which the owners of a natural monopoly are to receive a "fair" rate of return (18)

real capital see *capital resources* (1)

real rate of interest the percentage by which the purchasing power returned to a lender exceeds the purchasing power lent (15)

regressive taxes taxes that take a smaller percentage of higher than of lower incomes (21)

regulation the setting by government of detailed rules of business behavior that specify who may produce what types and quantities of products, the manner in which production takes place, how goods are marketed, what prices may be charged, and more (18)

regulatory lag the length of time, sometimes years, that it takes government regulators of natural monopolies to review a firm's performance and possibly adjust its price (18)

relative standard of poverty measurement a standard that defines a person's "needs" as a market basket of goods that varies over time and space and always equals a designated percentage of the goods that are available to the average person in society; a person is "poor" if the set of goods available to the person is less than that basket of goods (16)

rent seeking a set of activities through which monopolies expend valuable resources not to produce goods but to obtain, strengthen, and defend their monopoly positions (11)

representative democracy a form of public choice according to which votes on public goods are made by a group of representatives who are, in turn, elected by all citizens (20)

requirements contracts contracts according to which buyers agree to purchase all of their requirements of a commodity from a given seller only (17)

reserve clause a clause in a labor contract (often found in professional sports) that gives all rights to the future services of a worker to the worker's original employer (14)

resources ingredients used in the process of production; human, natural, and capital (1)

reverse discrimination deliberate discrimination against some people on the grounds of righting past wrongs against other people (14)

right-to-work laws state laws outlawing the union shop (14)

Rule of Reason a 1911 U.S. Supreme Court ruling according to which only deliberate and unreasonable restraint of trade was illegal under the 1890 Sherman Act, while market dominance as such was not (17)

S-corporations certain small business corporations with 35 or fewer stockholders that can escape double taxation (7)

saddle point the combination of strategies that equates maximin and minimax in a game (12)

safety net a fabric of social insurance and public assistance programs that prevents people from falling into poverty and possibly helps those already poor to escape from poverty (21)

satiation a level of consumption at which total utility has peaked and that is associated with zero marginal utility (5)

saving-our-jobs argument one of numerous arguments advanced in support of protectionism, according to which imports must be prevented from entering the country in order to save jobs in domestic import-competing industries (4)

scarce goods goods available in smaller quantities than all people would want to take in a given period if the goods could be had for nothing; thus, everyone's desire for them cannot be fulfilled at the same time (1)

scarcity problem the fact that it is impossible, in any country and in any period we care to consider, to fulfill the desire for goods by all the people at the same time (1)

screening an activity by which buyers select high-quality sellers and reject low-quality ones (14)

search any activity designed to discover information relevant to proper decision making that is currently possessed by other people (14)

second-degree price discrimination a practice according to which the seller partitions market demand into fairly large (but not necessarily equal-sized) blocks of output units and charges buyers different prices for these blocks but uniform prices for units within blocks (11)

selling costs costs, such as advertising expenditures, designed to increase the demand for a firm's product (12)

services the temporary use of physical objects or people (1)

short run a time period so short that a firm cannot vary the quantity of at least one (and, perhaps, several) of its inputs (8)

shortage a situation such that quantity demanded exceeds quantity supplied at a given price (3)

shutdown point an output level at which total revenue equals variable cost and at which average revenue or price, therefore, equals average variable cost (10)

signaling any activity designed by sellers to convince buyers of the high quality of what is being offered for sale (14)

single tax a tax on pure rent alone, as suggested by Henry George (15)

slope a measure of inclination of a given line or plane from the horizontal; the ratio of rise (or fall) over run (1a)

social cost of monopoly a forgone net benefit, equal to the cumulative excess of marginal benefits over marginal costs between the actual monopoly output and the higher efficient output (11)

social insurance transfer programs that aim to prevent people from becoming poor due to loss of income that is associated with changes in individual circumstances, such as retirement, death of the family breadwinner, disability, sickness, or unemployment (21)

social regulation a type of regulation not targeted at specific industries and concerned with economy-wide issues, such as the health and safety of consumers or workers (18)

socialism see *totalitarian socialism* and *democratic socialism*

special-interest theory of regulation a theory according to which government regulates firms in otherwise competitive industries because self-interested politicians and bureaucrats (who have a lot to gain from this) respond to requests for regulation by those who want to escape the rigors of competition and seek to set up viable cartels (18)

specific tariff a tax on imported goods, expressed as a fixed dollar amount per physical unit (4)

spillover effects see *externalities* (19)

spontaneous coordination see *market economy* (2)

statistical map the portrayal of data about geographic areas by crosshatching, shading, and otherwise differentiating these areas on a regular geographic map (1a)

statutory tax incidence the way in which the monetary burden of a tax is officially apportioned among people (3)

stock a quantity that is related to a given *moment* of time (1)

stock certificates marketable certificates of corporate ownership (7)

stock option the right, often given to top corporate managers, to buy a specified number of corporate shares at a specified price before a specified date (7)

stockholders persons who own a corporation, as evidenced by their holding of marketable certificates of ownership, called stock certificates (7)

strategic behavior a type of behavior that always arises among a small number of actors who have conflicting interests and are mutually conscious of the interdependence of their actions and that tries to anticipate the reactions of others to one's own decisions (12)

strategic voting a procedure by which voters attempt to achieve their most preferred outcome by selectively misrepresenting their preferences (20)

strikes concerted refusals by a body of workers to work (14)

subsistence wage a wage that enables workers to perpetuate their numbers precisely in the long run, because it is just sufficient to supply the needs of any given worker, the worker's spouse, and enough children to replace the parents at their deaths (13)

substitute goods two goods such that the increased consumption of one can, in the view of the consumer, more or less make up for the decreased consumption of the other (3); goods with positive cross-price elasticity of demand (6)

substitution effect the effect of a changed wage that makes an individual supply more labor at a higher wage (and less labor at a lower wage) because total utility can be increased by substituting work and consumption goods for leisure (or the opposites) (13)

supermajority requirement a typical provision in anti-takeover laws, linking the acquisition of corporate control by a raider to unusually difficult conditions, such as the ownership of 85 percent of all shares or an approving two-thirds vote of current stockholders (7)

supply line a graphical representation of a supply schedule (that lists the relationship between alternative prices of an item and the associated quantities supplied—other things being equal) (3)

supply schedule a tabular listing of the relationship between alternative prices of an item and the associated quantities supplied—other things being equal (3)

surplus a situation such that quantity supplied exceeds quantity demanded at a given price (3)

takeover an action in which one corporation or a group of financiers (known as the acquirers) buys a sufficiently large percentage of stock of another corporation (known as the target company) to dominate the stockholders' meeting and take control of the firm (7)

tangent a straight line that just touches a curve at a single point (1a)

tariff a tax on imported goods (4, 18)

technical efficiency a situation in which it is *impossible*, with current technical knowledge, to raise a given firm's output from given inputs or, alternatively, to produce a given output by using less of one input without using more of another input (8, 10)

technical inefficiency a situation in which it is *possible*, with current technical knowledge, to raise a given firm's output from given inputs or, alternatively, to produce a given output by using less of one input without using more of another input (8)

technology the knowledge that people have about how different goods can be produced (1)

tender offer a proposal to buy a controlling interest in a corporation by purchasing stock from current stockholders at a fixed price that exceeds the current market price (7)

terms-of-trade argument one of numerous arguments advanced in support of protectionism, according to which tariffs are needed in order to assure a fair division of the gain from international specialization and trade (4)

theory of absolute advantage an explanation of international trade according to which the citizens of every nation specialize in the production and export of those goods they can produce with fewer units of resources than anyone else, while importing other goods the production of which requires fewer resources elsewhere (4)

theory of comparative advantage an explanation of international trade according to which mutually beneficial trade between two countries arises—regardless of the presence or absence of absolute advantage—whenever one country is *relatively* better at producing a good than the other country, a fact that is indicated by the former country's ability to produce a good at a lower opportunity cost (measured in terms of other goods forgone) (4)

time preference an attitude typical of consumers everywhere that makes them value current goods more highly than future goods of like kind and number (15)

time productivity the ability of producers to cut the production of consumption goods now, use the resources so released to make capital goods, and then employ these capital goods to produce a permanently larger flow of consumption goods in the future (15)

time-series line graph a plot of a variable's magnitude (measured vertically) against time (measured horizontally), with successive dots joined by a continuous line (1a)

total cost, *TC* the sum of fixed and variable costs (9)

total revenue, *TR* market price P multiplied by total product Q (10)

totalitarian socialism see *communism* (2)

transactions costs the costs of negotiating and carrying out voluntary legal agreements, for example, the resources used to bring buyers and sellers together and to facilitate the coordination of people's specialized activities through voluntary market exchanges; alternatively, the forgone output these resources might have produced (7, 19)

transfer programs government programs that supply cash or in-kind benefits (commodities and services) to people without requiring them currently to make any payment or render any service in return (21)

transitivity a characterisic that makes consumer choices noncontradictory and consistent: if A is preferred to B and B to C, then A is also preferred to C (5a)

trust an arrangement placing two or more competing corporations under the "trusteeship" of a single board of directors who are to run the companies' affairs jointly, as if they were a single firm (17)

two-tier wage structure a union-management agreement acording to which a firm may pay lower wages to newly hired employees than to previously hired ones, even if both types of workers do identical work (18)

tying contracts contracts according to which buyers of one good are forced to purchase another good from the same seller as well (17)

undistributed corporate profit corporate after-tax profit retained by a corporation and not paid out to stockholders as dividends (7)

unfair union practices labor union practices, such as refusal to bargain with an employer, featherbedding, striking without 60 days' notice, striking to force the recognition of one union where another has already been certified (14)

union shop a firm in which all employees, within a short time after hiring, have to become union members or at least pay union dues as a condition of continued employment (14)

unlimited liability a legal principle according to which the owners of certain firms are responsible for all business debts without limit—up to the full extent of the owners' personal wealth and regardless of the amount of money the owners have invested in the businesss (7)

util a hypothetical unit of enjoyment that a consumer derives from consumption (5)

utility function the relationship between alternative quantities of a good consumed and the associated total utility reaped by the consumer, other things being equal (5)

utility the enjoyment consumers derive from the choices they make (5)

variable cost, *VC* the monetary value of variable inputs used in a period (9)

variable import levies specific tariffs that are continually adjusted to changing world market prices so as to keep the domestic price constant (4)

variable inputs productive ingredients the quantities of which can easily be varied in the period under consideration (8)

vertical merger the combining into one of two or more firms that are related as suppliers and users of each other's products (17)

Visible Hand see *command economy* (2)

voluntary export restraints, *VERs* agreements between importing and exporting countries according to which the exporting country's government "voluntarily" limits the exports of a specified item to the importing country during a given period (4)

voting paradox under democratic majority voting, the winning choice among three or more alternatives will differ depending on the sequence in which votes are taken (20)

welfare state a capitalist society in which government pledges to protect people not only from the rigors of the marketplace (such as unemployment or inflation associated with business cycles) but also from all other types of misfortunes that might befall them (2)

white knight someone undertaking a takeover who is friendly toward the current management (7)

work the use of people's time in the productive process in return for pay (13)

X-inefficiency a situation, usually attributed to insufficient worker supervision or motivation, in which a given firm is not obtaining the maximum possible output from the inputs it is in fact using (8)

young-economy argument one of numerous arguments advanced in support of protectionism, according to which new industries in a developing nation must be protected against established industries in developed nations (4)

zero-sum game a game in which the sum of winnings and losses inevitably equals zero (12)

INDEX OF SUBJECTS

abscissa 23
absolute advantage, theory of 87
absolute standard of poverty measurement 437, 443–447, 450–455
abundance 21, 72–73
accounting concepts 193–198
accounting profit 194–197, 260
acreage allotments 490
ad valorem tariffs 97
advertising 256, 317, 319–321, 325, 331, 466
affirmative action plans 393
agency problem 180–192, 212, 287
agent 182
aid to families with dependent children 557–559, 564–566
ambient standards 525
antidumping rules 102
antipirating agreements 374
antitakeover laws 187, 464–471, 477
antitrust policy 458–477
antiunion practices 381–382
appreciation (of currency) 92–93, 118
arc elasticity 163, 165, 172
asset markets 410, 412–416, 427
assets 193
autarky 95–97
average fixed cost 229–230, 233, 249–250, 282
average physical product 201–209, 217–218
average revenue 257–259, 282, 288–291
average total cost 229–230, 233–243, 249–251, 262–270, 273–282, 284–285, 292–302, 312–314, 317, 319, 326–327, 415–416, 423, 459–461, 483–485
average value product 348–350, 366
average variable cost 229–230, 233–234, 236, 249–250, 262–272, 281–282, 292–299, 350
average vs. marginal rule 208, 367
Averch-Johnson effect 487

balance sheet 193–194, 198
balance sheet identity 193
ban, of pollution 524–525; of trade 104–105
banks, for pollution rights 531
bar charts 30–31
baseball players' market 378–379, 403
basing-point system 314–315
bees 517
benefit 7; *see also* marginal benefit, marginal external benefit, marginal private benefit, marginal social benefit
benefit-cost analysis 549
bilateral monopoly 386–387, 403
black markets 73–74
bonds 4
bonuses 182, 184
brand loyalty 320–321
break-even point 265–266, 281–282
bubbles 531
budget line 139–145
bureaucracy 547–549, 553
bureaucrats 542
business cycles 462

capacity output 239, 250
capital budgeting 420–422
capital-resource markets 412–416
capital resources 3, 4, 21
capitalism 36–41, 44
capitalized value 410, 412–416, 427
cardinal utility 123

cartels 169, 255, 283–284, 301–302, 304–306, 308, 369, 377–387, 403, 477, 553; *see also* labor unions
central economic plan 40
change in demand 57–58
change in quantity demanded 57
change in quantity supplied 61
change in supply 61, 63–64
charity 572
children's allowances 571–572
choice 6–22
circular-flow (diagram) 41, 343
class-action suits 396
closed shop 381, 386, 553
Coase theorem 515–516, 521
cobweb cycles 355–357, 360
collective bargaining contracts 381
column charts 30–31
command economy 40, 42
commercial policy 110–112
commodities 3
common stock 4, 179, 463
commons, tragedy of 516–520, 535
communism 37, 42, 46–47
comparable worth 394–395
comparative advantage, theory of 87–90, 93–97, 111, 113–115, 117–118
compensating wage differentials 354, 356–359
competition, *see* effective competition, imperfect competition, monopolistic competition, perfect competition
complementary goods 58–59, 83, 157, 173
compounding 407–408, 427
concentration ratios 328–330, 339, 471, 473
conglomerate mergers 467
consent agreements 468–470
conspiracy doctrine 380
constant returns to scale 210–211, 218, 238–239, 242–244
constant-cost industry 275–277
consumer optimum 136–145
consumer preferences 122–145
consumer surplus 93–103, 108, 118, 279, 351–352, 514–516, 534
consumption possibilities frontier 139–145
coordination 40–44, 50–52, 174–175, 189–190, 212
copyrights 285
corporate raiders 185
corporations 176, 179–197
cost 7, 226–251, 286–308; *see also* average total cost, average variable cost, explicit cost, fixed cost, implicit cost, long-run cost, marginal cost, marginal external cost, marginal labor cost, marginal private cost, marginal social cost, opportunity cost, selling cost, short-run cost, total cost, variable cost
cost-incentive dilemma 567–570
cost cutting 245–247
countervailing tariffs 103
craft unions 380
cross-price elasticity of demand 155–159, 172
culture of poverty 566

deadweight loss 99, 118
decreasing returns to scale 212–213, 218, 241–243, 274
decreasing-cost industry 275–277
delay period 187

deliberate coordination 40, 174–175, 189–190
demand 3, 60, 64–81, 83–84, 90–93, 118, 127–138, 149–162, 167–173, 343, 346–349, 351, 353, 355, 360, 363–364, 366, 385, 390, 395, 409, 411, 413, 417, 419, 423–424, 459, 487–491, 508
demand line 55–61, 83, 373
demand schedule 24–26, 55–61, 83
democratic socialism 37, 44
depreciation, of capital 195–196; of currency 92–93, 118
deregulation 493, 499–503, 505–506
derived demand 346
desire for goods 2–3, 6
direct democracy 542
disclosure statements 187
discount rate 408
discounting 407–408, 410, 427
discrimination 387–397; *see also* price discrimination
distributive justice 554–572
dividends 180
division of labor 19, 34–35, 40–44, 50–52, 211; *see also* deliberate coordination, spontaneous coordination
doctrine of caveat emptor 495
doctrine of caveat venditor 495
dominant firms 328, 332
double taxation 180
draft 364
dual labor market 389–390
dutiable imports 110

earned income tax credit 564–565
economic efficiency 278–280, 351–352, 403, 459–460, 476, 507–508
economic equity 44, 433
economic growth 44
economic inefficiency 47, 298, 300, 326, 460–462, 481–485
economic inequity 301, 462, 481–485
economic power 36
economic profit 196–197, 260–270, 273–274, 276–277, 281–282, 292–299, 422–423
economic regulation 479–494, 499–503, 505–506
economic rent 384–385, 403, 409–412, 416–417, 424–425, 427
economic stability 44
economic systems 34–44, 50–52
economic tax incidence 81, 173, 560, 571
economic theory 34, 43–49
economics, defined 43
economies of scale 209–213, 218, 238–244, 247, 274, 284–285
effective competition 330, 332, 334
efficiency *see* economic efficiency, technical efficiency
elasticity 146–173, 290–291
emission standards 525
entitlement programs 556–560, 571
entrepreneurs 177
envelope curve 242–243, 248
environmental economics 507–535
equal-product curves 219–225, 251
equalizing wage differentials 354, 356–359
equilibrium 64–81, 83–84, 94, 349–351
equity, *see* economic equity
escape clause 112
excess capacity 326–327

I-1

exchange rate 91–93, 118
excise subsidy 84
excise tax 74–76, 81, 84, 149, 173, 281, 571
exclusive contracts 465
exclusive franchises 285–287, 308
explicit cost 196, 227–228
exploitation 370, 372–374, 376–379, 386–387, 399, 402–403, 417, 455
export subsidies 103
external diseconomies 274, 276–278, 282
external economies 274, 276–277, 282
externalities 352, 460–461, 507–535

factors of production, see resources
fair-price provisions 187
fair trade laws 71, 489
featherbedding 381, 385
felicific calculus 135, 138
field of choice 139–140, 223–224
FIFO method 195
financial capital 4
firms 41, 174–192, 328, 332
first-degree price discrimination 296–298, 308
fixed cost 227–232, 249–250, 260–270, 281, 292–299, 348
fixed inputs 200–201
flow (vs. stock) 5, 193–194, 405–406
food stamps 557, 559, 564
foreign-exchange markets 90–93, 118
free goods 5, 21
free-rider problem 537–539
friendly takeovers 187
fully funded system 557
functional distribution of income 399, 429–430
future value 407–408, 410, 413–414

game 321
game theory 321–325
gentlemen's agreements 314–315
Gini coefficient 434
golden parachutes 187, 189
goods 3, 5; see also complementary goods, free goods, independent goods, inferior goods, merit goods, normal goods, pure private goods, pure public goods, scarce goods, substitute goods
goods markets 41, 343
government failure 543–551
government role in economy 34–44, 50–52, 54, 70–84, 97–115, 165, 360–365, 392–397, 457–572
graphing 23–33
greenmail 186–187
gross barter terms of trade 109, 118

Headstart 560
health and safety regulation 493–498, 501–504, 506
Herfindahl index 473–474, 477
holding company 462–463
homelessness 448–449
horizontal mergers 462
hostile takeovers 186–187
Hotelling's paradox 315–318, 320, 339
households 41
human capital 4, 359, 435
human resources 3

imperfect competition 283–339, 368–403
implicit cost 196, 227–228
import quotas 99–101, 118, 490
incentives 37–42, 54, 182, 184–185, 562–570

income distribution 399, 429–455
income dynamics 444–445, 453, 455
income effect 345–346
income elasticity of demand 156, 159–162, 167, 173
income inequality, causes of 430–431
income redistribution 554–572
income statement 194–195, 198, 260, 262–269, 292–299, 308, 339
increasing-cost industry 275–277
increasing returns to scale 211–213, 218, 239–241, 243, 247, 284–285
independent goods 58, 83, 157, 173
indifference curve analysis 139–145
industrial unions 381
industry structure 254–255
inefficiency, see economic inefficiency, technical inefficiency
inequity, see economic inequity
infant-industry argument 106
inferior goods 58–59
informative advertising 319–321
injunctions 380
innovation 287–288, 422–423
input standards 525
instability 462
interest rates 406–408, 417–422
interlocking directorates 466
interlocking stockholdings 466
internal diseconomies 274, 276–277
internal economies 274, 276–277
internalities 548–551
international trade 85–118
inventory evaluation 195
Invisible Hand 40
iron law of wages 354–355, 427
isocost line 223–225, 251
isoquants 219–225, 251
ivory trade 104–105

Jevons' Rule 136–137, 145
jurisdictional strikes 380
just price 394

keeping-our-money-at-home argument 109
kinked demand line 313–314, 339

labor boycotts, 377
labor markets 342–403
labor unions 369, 377–387, 403, 477, 553
"law" of declining marginal benefits 13–18
"law" of declining marginal utility 124–127, 571
"law" of demand 55–56
law of diminishing returns 201–209, 214–215, 217–218, 250, 408–409, 412
law of increasing marginal costs 14–18
"law" of supply 61
leisure 344–346
Lerner index 471–472, 477
liabilities 193
licensing 490, 505
LIFO method 195
limited liability 179
limited partnerships 179
line of actual inequality, see Lorenz curve
line of perfect equality 432–433, 455
line of perfect inequality 433–434
loanable funds market 419
lockouts 377
logrolling 546
long run 200, 226
long run costs 236, 238–244, 250–251, 284
Lorenz curve 432–434, 436, 444, 453, 455, 571

loss 265–270, 274–275, 282; and industry contraction 274–275, 282, 422–423
luxuries 158

macroeconomics 45, 48–49
malevolent tastes 388–389
managed capitalism 37, 44
managerial coordination costs 190, 212
marginal benefit 9–18, 22, 260, 343, 347, 351, 371–372, 375–376
marginal cost 9–18, 22, 229–230, 234–236, 242, 249–250, 260–280, 282, 292–302, 306, 308, 312–314, 317, 319, 326–327, 343, 347, 350–351, 371–372, 375–376, 423, 459–461, 483–485
marginal external benefit 510–511
marginal external cost 509–511
marginal labor cost 374–377, 387, 403
marginal physical product 200–202, 206–209, 214–215, 217–218, 221–222, 225, 347, 350, 367, 371–372, 399, 409, 411–412
marginal private benefit 507–515, 540–542
marginal private cost 508–515
marginal rate of substitution 142–143
marginal rate of technical substitution 221–222
marginal rate of transformation 89
marginal revenue 257–259, 261–270, 281–282, 289–301, 306, 308, 311, 313–314, 317, 319, 326–327, 371–372, 387, 423, 459, 461, 483–485
marginal revenue product of labor 370–373, 379, 402, 409, 412
marginal social benefit 507–515, 518, 521–524, 526–529, 540–542, 548–549
marginal social cost 508–515, 521–524, 526–529, 540–542, 548–549
marginal utility 123–138, 344
marginal value product 347–350, 366–367, 370–371, 375–377, 385–387, 403, 409, 412
marginal vs. average rule 208, 367
marginalist thinking 8–10
market 38; see also asset markets, baseball players' market, black markets, capital-resource markets, foreign-exchange markets, goods markets, labor markets, loanable funds markets, natural-resource markets, rental markets, resource markets
market coordination costs 190
market economy 40, 50–52
market failures 458–462, 478–572
market share 473–474
market structure 254–255
marketing quotas 490
marketization 46–47
maximin strategy 323–325
maximum price see price ceiling
maximum wage 364–365, 367
Medicaid/Medicare 556–557, 559, 564
mergers 462, 466–474, 477
merit goods 539
microeconomics 45, 48–49
micromarketing 132–133
minimax strategy 323
minimum efficient scale 243–244
minimum price, see price floor
minimum wage 360–364
mixed economies 42–43
monopolistic competition 255, 309–310, 326–328, 330–332, 334–335, 337
monopolistic exploitation of labor 370, 372–374, 399, 403
monopoly 255, 283–308, 328, 332, 386–387, 403 422, 461, 476, 480–485, 505, 534

monopsonistic exploitation of labor 376–379, 386–387, 399, 402–403
monopsony 284, 369, 374–379, 386–387, 402–403
most-favored nation treatment 112

national-defense argument 103
natural monopoly 284–285, 480–485, 505
natural-resource markets 404–412, 427
natural resources 3, 4, 21
necessities 158
needs 437, 442–443
negative externalities 461, 509–510, 512, 533–534
negative income tax system 566–571
neighborhood effects 509
netting 530
net present value 421–422, 427–428
net worth 193
nominal rate of interest 406
non-automatic import authorizations 101–102
nonexcludability 536–539
nonprofit firms 181–183
nonrivalness 537, 539, 553
nontariff barriers 99–103
nonzero-sum game 323–325
normal goods 58–59, 345
normative economics 45, 54

offsets 530
oligopoly 255, 309–325, 329–339
opportunity cost 7
optimal rate of plant operation 239
optimization principle 10–22, 118, 127–138, 218, 260–270, 281, 291–299, 347–350, 366–367, 371–372, 375–376, 521–524, 526–529, 539–542; *see also* profit maximization, utility maximization
optimum plant 242–243
optimum pollution 521–524, 526–529
orderly marketing agreements 101
ordinal utility 123
ordinate 23
origin 23
own-price elasticity of demand 149–155, 167–168, 172–173, 290–291
own-price elasticity of supply 160–164, 173

PAPO rule 166–171
Parkinson's law 549, 553
partnerships 176, 178–179
patents 285–286
pay-as-you-go system 557
pensions 558
perfect competition 254–282, 342–367, 459–460, 508
perfect price discrimination 296–298, 308
peril points 112
personal distribution of income 429–455
persuasive advertising 319–321
picket lines 377
pie charts 30–31
pinups 397
planning curve 239–241, 250
plant 238–244, 250–251
plurality voting 547
point elasticity 163, 165–166
point of diminishing returns 206
point voting 547
poison pills 186
pollution 520–532, 535
pollution licenses 527–531
pollution rights 527–531
positive economics 45, 54

positive externalities 461, 510, 513, 534
poverty 437, 439, 442–447, 450–455
poverty gap 442
poverty lines 443, 446
poverty rates 447, 450–453
preferred stock 463
prejudice 391
premarket discrimination 392
present value 407–408, 410, 413–414
price ceiling 72–74, 76–79, 364–365, 367, 487–491, 505
price discrimination 296–299, 308, 403, 465–466
price fixing 314–315, 360–365, 367; *see also* price ceiling, price floor
price floor 70–72, 74–75, 84, 360–364, 487–491
price leadership 315
price setters 284
price system 40
price takers 255
price war 312, 324
principal (vs. agent) 182
prisoners' dilemma game 323–325
prisons 550
private goods *see* pure private goods
privatization 549–551, 553
process of production 3
process of public choice 542–547, 553
producer's optimum 224–225
producer surplus 94–103, 118, 279, 351–352, 384, 412–413, 514–516, 534
product differentiation 315–318, 327
production function 200–225, 227, 231–232, 249, 258, 261, 282, 288, 346–347
production indifference curves 219–225, 251
production possibilities frontier 6–9, 21, 90, 118
productivity 4, 19, 201–203; *see also* average physical product
professional licensing 490, 505
profit 193–198, 260–270, 273–274, 276–277, 281–282, 292–299; and industry expansion 273–274, 276–277, 282, 422–423
profit maximization 189, 224–225, 260–270, 281, 291–299, 308, 326–328, 347–350, 366–367, 371–372, 375–376, 387, 402–403
progressive taxes 562, 571
property rights 35–39, 53–54, 514–532
property tax 571
proprietorships 175–178
protectionism 97–118
proxies 186
public assistance programs 556–560, 571
public choice 542–547, 553
public finance 539
public goods, *see* pure public goods
public housing 557, 559
public-interest theory of regulation 487–491
public schools 551
pure private goods 536, 553
pure public goods 460–461, 536–553
pure rent 409–412, 416–417, 424–425, 427

quadrant 23
quasi rent 412–413; *see also* producer surplus
quotas, *see* affirmative action plans, import quotas, marketing quotas

rank-order voting 547
rate base 486
rate-of-return regulation 484–487, 505
real capital, *see* capital resources
real rate of interest 406

real wages 358, 361
redistribution of income 554–572
regressive taxes 562, 571
regulation 478–506; *see also* price ceiling, price floor
regulatory agencies 38–39
regulatory lag 486
relative standard of poverty measurement 439, 442–443
rent, *see* economic rent, pure rent, quasi rent
rental markets 408–413
rent control 77
rent seeking 288, 460, 476
representative democracy 542
requirements concracts 465
research and development (R&D) 207, 287–288
reserve clause 378, 403
resource markets 41, 341–455
resources 3–4; *see also* capital resources, human resources, natural resources
revenue, *see* average revenue, marginal revenue, total revenue
reverse discrimination 396
riches 435–441
right-to-work laws 382
risk bearing 422
robber barons 463–464
Rule of Reason 464

saddle point 322–323
safety net 559
satiation 124, 140
saving-our-jobs argument 107–109
scarce goods 5, 21
scarcity (problem) 2–22, 72–73
scissors diagram 80
S-corporations 180
screening 391
search 389
second-degree price discrimination 298–299, 308
securities 156
selling costs 317
separation of ownership and control 180–181; *see also* agency problem
services 3
sexual harassment 397
short run 200, 226
shortage 39–40, 66–67, 83, 350–351
short-run costs 226–241, 243, 249–251, 284
shutdown point 266–267, 270, 281–282
signaling 391
single taxers 424–425
sleep 346
slope 26–28
social cost of monopoly 300
social insurance programs 556–558, 571–572
social regulation 479–481, 493–498, 501–504, 506
socialism 36–37, 44
space projects 551
special-interest theory of regulation 491–493
specialization, *see* division of labor
specific tariffs 97–99
spillover effects 509
spontaneous coordination 40, 50–52, 174–175, 189–190
standard setting 525, 535
statistical maps 30
statistical prejudgment 389
statutory tax incidence 81, 173, 561, 571
stock (vs. flow) 5, 193–194, 405–406
stock certificates 4, 179, 463

stock markets 180
stock options 184–185
stockholders 179
strategic behavior 310–325
strategic trade model 106–107, 114–115
strategic voting 546
strikes 377, 380
subsidies, and externalities 511–513, 527–528, 534
subsistence wage 354–355
substitute goods 58–59, 83, 154, 157, 173, 308
substitution effect 344–346
supermajority requirements 187
supplemental security income 557, 559
supply 60, 64–81, 83–84, 90–93, 118, 160–164, 173, 260–277, 281–282, 294, 344–345, 351, 353, 355, 360, 363–364, 385, 390, 395, 409, 411, 413, 417, 419, 423–424, 459, 487–491, 508
supply line 61–64
supply schedule 25–26, 61–64
surplus 39–40, 65–66, 83–84, 350–351; *see also* consumer surplus, producer surplus
system of coordinates 23

takeovers 185–187, 189
tangent 27
tariffs 97–99, 103, 110–112, 115, 118
taxation, and externalities 511–512, 525–527, 534
tax incidence 81, 173, 560–562, 571
tax programs 560–570

technical efficiency 203, 278, 459–460
technical inefficiency 204, 222, 286–287, 460; *see also* X-inefficiency
technology 4–5, 199–225, 303
tender offer 185
terms-of-trade argument 109
theory of absolute advantage 87
theory of comparative advantage 87–90, 93–97, 111, 113–115, 117–118
time 406–408, 417–422
time preference 418–419
time productivity 418–419
time-series line graph 29–30
total cost 227–232, 235–238, 249–250, 260–270, 281, 292–299
total product 200–209, 218
total revenue 257–270, 282, 288–299; and price elasticity of demand 168–171
totalitarian socialism 36
transactions costs 190, 192, 514–516
transfer programs 556–572
transitivity 143–144
trusts 463
two-tier wage structure 499–500
tying contracts 465–466

underground economy 52
undistributed corporate profit 180
unemployment 384
unemployment insurance 557–558
unfair union practices 382
union shop 381, 553
unlimited liability 177

utility 122–145
utility function 124
utility maximization 122–145, 344–346
utils 123, 135

variable cost 227–232, 236, 249–250, 260, 262–270, 281–282, 292–299, 348
variable import levies 102
variable inputs 200–201
Veblen effect 129, 138
vertical mergers 467
Visible Hand 40
voluntary export restraints 101–102
voting paradox 544–546, 553
voting procedures, *see* public choice

wage floor 360–364
wage differentials 352–354, 356–359, 394–395
water-diamond paradox 125
wealth 404–405, 434–435
welfare state 44
white knights 187
work 344
workers' compensation 557–558

X-inefficiency 204, 215–216, 218

young-economy argument 103

zero-sum games 322–323

INDEX OF NAMES

Aaron, Henry J. 388
Addison, William 163
Adie, Douglas K. 364
Agnello, Richard J. 520
Alexander, Doyle 379
Aquinas, Thomas 394, 417
Aristotle 394, 417
Armour, Philip 463
Arrow, Kenneth J. 546
Ashenfelter, Orley 362
Averch, Harvey 487

Bakke, Allan 396
Ballengee, Bert 440
Bass, Perry 439
Bastiat, Frédéric 35, 46–47
Battalio, Raymond C. 172
Beattie, Bruce R. 153
Beckenstein, A. 244
Bell, Alexander Graham 470
Bell, Frederick W. 70, 152
Bellante, D. 358
Bentham, Jeremy 123, 135, 139
Bergerec, Michel 189
Biddle, Jeff 346
Black, Shane 245
Blankart, Charles B. 152, 160
Blinder, Alan 314
Böhm-Bawerk, Eugen von 418–419
Boone, Bob 379
Bork, Robert H. 469
Born, Allen 441
Bougeon-Maassen, F. 244
Brandow, G. E. 152
Brien, Michael 395
Brozen, Yale 364
Buchanan, James 547
Buffet, Warren Edward 439
Bush, George, President 39, 133, 492

Caldwell, Bryan 550
Carnegie, Andrew 463
Carter, Gary 378
Chamberlin, Edward H. 337, 399
Chambers, Anne Cox 438
Chapman, W. Fred 159
Cheung, Steven N. S. 517
Christensen, Laurits R. 244
Chung, Connie 418
Clark, John Bates 399
Clarke, Richard A. 441
Clay, Jason 532
Coase, Ronald 175, 189–190, 514–516, 534
Coelho, P. 358
Cohen, Mark A. 471
Condorcet, Marquis de 546
Coughlin, Cletus C. 101–102
Cournot, Antoine Augustin 306, 337
Crandall, Robert W. 496
Cullison, William E. 358
Cunningham, James 395

Daly, Rex F. 152
Davis, Martin S. 418
Dawson, Andre 379
Deng Xiaoping 47
Denison, Edward F. 497
Dewey, John 425
Dickens, Charles 263
Diocletian, Emperor 394
Donnelley, Lawrence P. 520
Dorrance, John T. III 439

Duncan, Greg J. 444–445, 453
Dunlap, R. Terren 475
Dupuit, J. 136

Edgeworth, Francis Y. 123, 139
Edison, Thomas 303
Ehrenberg, Ronald 355, 366
Eisner, Michael D. 418, 446
Ellickson, Robert C. 449
Elzinga, K. G. 153
Engels, Friedrich 400
Evans, Edward P. 187
Evans, Linda 320

Feldstein, M. 152, 160
Fireman, Paul 440
Fischette, Teresa 403
Fisher, Irving 123
Flanagan, Robert J. 355, 366–367, 392, 395
Fletcher, Max E. 315
Flood, Curt 378
Foster, George 378
Foster, Henry S., Jr. 153
Fox, Karl A. 153
Freeman, Richard B. 355
Frey, Bruno S. 48–49
Friedman, Milton 472

Gapinski, James H. 173, 218, 367
Gary, Elbert J., Judge 314
Gates, William Henry III 436–437, 439
Gedman, Rich 379
Gelb, Richard L. 418
George, Henry 424–425
Ghali, M. 358
Gherity, James A. 425
Godwin, Marshall B. 159
Goeken, John D. 287
Goldsmith, James 185
Gompers, Samuel 380, 399
Gorbachev, Mikhail 47
Gossen, Hermann Heinrich 136
Gould, Jay 463
Grabowski, Henry G. 497
Grant, Ulysses, President 460
Green, Leonard 172
Greene, William H. 244
Gretzky, Wayne 403
Guidry, Ron 379
Gutfreund, John H. 440
Gwartney, James 562

Hackenburg, David 517
Hahn, Robert W. 531
Halvorsen, R. 159–160
Hamermesh, Daniel 346
Hand, Learned, Judge 475
Hanley, William T. 159
Hardin, Garrett 520
Hayek, Friedrich A. von 47, 50–52
Heien, Dale 160
Hibbard, Dwight H. 440
Hickok, Susan 108
Hill, Steven 448
Hillegass, Clifton 263
Hilton, George W. 173
Hogan, Dennis, Jr. 519
Hogarty, T. F. 153
Horner, Bob 379
Horrigan E. A., Jr. 187, 418
Hotelling, Harold 315–317, 320, 339

Houthakker, H. S. 153, 160
Hufbaner, Gary C. 108
Hunsucker, Robert D. 441
Hunter, Jim "Catfish" 378

Iacocca, Lee A. 440–441
Ismail, Raghib "Rocket" 403

Jackson, James 429
Jamail, Joe 437
Jansson, Jan Owen 213
Jaynes, Gerald D. 388
Jerome, Robert W. 114–115
Jevons, William S. 123, 136, 139, 306, 425
Johnson, F. Ross 187, 418
Johnson, Leland L. 487
Johnson, Lyndon B., President 437
Johnson, Mike 383
Johnston, William B. 398
Jureen, L. 159, 160

Kagel, John H. 172
Kahn, Alfred E. 499
Karrenbrock, Jeffrey D. 247
Katz, Lawrence 564
Kaufer, E. 244
Kearl, J. R. 48–49
Kennedy, Edward, Senator 499
Kennedy, John F., President 305
Kerr, Baine P. 418
Ketelsen, James L. 441
Khomeini, Ayatollah 417
King, Gregory 165
Kinkead, Gwen 427
Kluge, John Werner 438
Koch, Charles 438
Kohler, Heinz 52, 77, 80, 91, 135, 136, 205, 213, 215, 216, 242, 248, 288, 306, 337, 399, 555
Krugman, Paul 106, 114, 115

Lauder, Estée 436, 438
Leibenstein, Harvey 204, 215–216, 218
Leigh, J. Paul 356
Lerner, Abba P. 471, 555, 571
Lewala, Zacharias 304
Lewis, John L. 381
Liedtke, J. Hugh 184, 418
Lilla, Mark 445
Lipsey, Richard G. 160
Lloyd, W. F. 136
Lyon, Herbert L. 153
Lyon, Randolph M. 531

McCaleb, Thomas S. 562
McCarthy, Walter J., Jr. 441
McCormick, William T., Jr. 440
McCracken, P. W. 473
McNall, Bruce 403
McNally, Dave 378
Mallory, Wilhelm A., Sr. 187
Malthus, Robert Thomas 354–355
Mandel, Morton L. 441
Manning, Willard G. 167
Marin, Alan 356
Markus, Keith E. 108
Mars, Forrest E. 429, 438
Marshall, Alfred 80, 123, 215, 306, 425
Martin, John D. 187
Marx, Karl 113, 399–400, 417–418

I-5

Mazur, Mark J. 561
Menger, Carl 136, 425
Mentzer, Josephine Esther 436
Messersmith, Andy 378
Meyer, Robert H. 364
Milken, Michael R. 418
Mincer, Jacob 364
Moffitt, Robert A. 570
Mohammed 417
Moore, Thomas Gale 364, 473, 491
Morgan, J. P. 463–464
Morgan, James N. 444
Morgenstern, Oskar 321–323
Moses 417
Murphy, R. D. 244
Myrdal, Karl Gunnar 50–52

Nader, Ralph 506
Napoleon 306
Nerlove, Marc 163
Neumann, John von 321–323
Newhouse, Samuel I. 438
Nisbet, Charles T. 153
Nixon, Richard M., President 468

Oaxaca, Ronald 392
Olsen, Kenneth H. 418
O'Neill, June 395
Ong, John D. 441

Packer, Kerry 185
Parkinson 549
Parrish, Lance 379
Paul VI, Pope 70
Pechman, Joseph A. 561–562, 570
Peltzman, Sam 491
Perelman, Ronald Owen 439
Peterson, Jerrold M. 511
Petty, William 399
Phelps, Charles E. 167
Pigou, Arthur C. 215, 510–514, 525, 527
Pinola Joseph J. 441
Posner, Richard A. 491
Prestowitz, Clyde V. 114–115
Price, Robert E. 440
Pritzker, Jay 439
Proxmire, William, Senator 549
Psacharopoulos, George 356

Rachlin, Howard 172
Ragan, James F. 364

Raines, Tim 379
Rangos, John, Sr. 437
Rawls, John 555, 571
Reuther, Walter 381
Rhodes, Cecil 304
Ricardo, David 87, 88, 90, 109, 112, 113, 117, 118, 215, 411
Robinson Crusoe 419–420
Robinson, James D. 418, 440
Robinson, Joan Violet 337, 399, 403
Robinson, Lois 397
Rockefeller, John D., Sr. 463–464, 479
Rojko, A. S. 153
Roosevelt, Franklin D., President 381, 400, 467
Roosevelt, Theodore, President 425, 467, 477
Rose, Pete 378
Rosen, Kenneth T. 427
Rosen, Sherwin 356
Rossi, Peter H. 449
Rothschild, Jacob 185
Rottenberg, Simon 379

Salop, S. C. 468
Salvatore, Dominick 115
Sawhill, Isabel V. 437, 565
Scherer, F. M. 244
Schultz, Henry 153
Schwarzenegger, Arnold 245
Scully, Gerald W. 379
Shaw, George Bernard 48
Sheflin, Neil 382
Shepherd, William G. 328, 333, 475
Sherman, John, Senator 470
Shneerson, Dan 213
Sigoloff, Sanford C. 187
Simon, Julian L. 153
Smith, Adam 19, 34, 40, 46–47, 80, 87, 113, 125, 175, 308, 314, 356, 442
Smith, Philip L. 187
Smith, Robert S. 355, 362, 366
Smith, Shirley 391
Spann, Robert M. 487
Spielberg, Steven 418
Stalin, Joseph 46, 189, 192, 417
Stallone, Sylvester 418
Stauch, August 304
Steiner, Peter O. 160
Stevens, Whitney 187
Stigler, George J. 437, 491
Stiritz, William P. 418
Stone, R. 159
Strawberry, Darryl 378
Suits, Daniel B. 153

Sweezy, Paul M. 313–314, 339
Swidinsky, Robert 364

Tappan, David S., Jr. 441
Taubman, A. Alfred 439
Taylor, A. 152, 160
Taylor, Dan 210
Taylor, Elizabeth 320
Taylor, Lester D. 153, 159, 160
Taylor, R. Lee 440, 441
Taylor, William 188
Terleckyj, Nestor E. 356
Thaler, Richard 356
Thünen, Johann Heinrich von 214–215
Tietenberg, Tom 531
Timpane, Michael 570
Tolstoy, Leo 215–216, 425
Tonelson, Alan 114–115
Torrens, Robert 113
Tregarthen, Timothy 379
Tremblay, Victor 240
Troy, Leo 382
Tsai, Gerald, Jr. 187
Tyson, Mike 417

Vakil, Firouz 153
Vanderbilt, Cornelius 463–464
Van Gogh, Vincent 60
Veblen, Thorstein 129
Vernon, John M. 497
Viner, Jacob 248
Viscusi, Kip W. 356

Walras, Léon 136
Walton, Sam Moore 438
Weber, Brian 396
Weidenbaum, Murray L. 495–496
Welch, Finis 361, 364
Wells, Frank G. 418
Wexner, Leslie 439
White, L. J. 468
Williams, Walter F. 441
Wilson, James A. 520
Winkler, Irwin 245
Wise, David A. 364
Wold, H. 159, 160
Wood, Geoffrey E. 101–102
Working, Elmer 153

Yamamura, Kozo 106
Yarnell, Kenneth A. 187
Yellowitz, Irwin 400

ACKNOWLEDGMENTS

Chapter 2, pp. 48–49, text from "A Confusion of Economists?" The American Economic Review by J. R. Kearl et al., May 1979, pp. 28–37. Reprinted by permission of the American Economic Association and the author.

Chapter 7, Table A, p. 181, from "The Fortune 500: The Largest U.S. Industrial Corporations," Fortune, April 24, 1989, p. 354. Copyright © 1989 The Time Inc. Magazine Company. All rights reserved.

Chapter 7, Table 5, p. 185, from Keith Brasher, "A Far-Flung Corporate Empire" The New York Times, July 12, 1989, pp. D1 and 6. Copyright © 1989 by The New York Times Company. Reprinted by permission.

Chapter 7, Table 6, p. 187, "The 10 Largest Golden Parachutes" May 1, 1989, p. 47. Reprinted from May 1, 1989 issue of Business Week by special permission, copyright © 1989 by McGraw-Hill, Inc.

Chapter 7, p. 177, text adapted from Carrie Dolan "Entrepreneurs Often Fail as Managers". Reprinted by permission of The Wall Street Journal © 1989 Dow Jones & Company, Inc. All Rights Reserved.

Chapter 9, Figure 11, p. 244, from Christionson and Greene, "Economies of Scale in U.S. Electric Power Generation," Journal of Political Economy, August 1976, p. 674. Published by The University of Chicago and reprinted with permission.

Chapter 12, Table 7, pp. 332–333, from William G. Shepherd, "Causes of Increased Competition in the US Economy, 1939–80" The Review of Economics and Statistics, November 1982, pp. 613–626. Reprinted by permission of Elsevier Science Publishers.

Chapter 13, p. 364, text from "Effects of Cohort Size on Earnings: The Baby Boom Babies Financial Bust" by Finis Welch, The Journal of Political Economy, October 1979, pp. 565–598. Published by The University of Chicago and reprinted by permission.

Chapter 16, Tables A and B, pp. 440–441, "Pay For Performance: Who Measures Up ...And Who Doesn't," May 1, 1989, p. 49. Reprinted from May 1, 1989 issue of Business Week by special permission, copyright © 1989 by McGraw-Hill, Inc.

Chapter 16, Table 2, p. 435, data for table The Wall Street Journal, August 22, 1986, p. 6. Reprinted by permission of The Wall Street Journal © 1986 Dow Jones & Company, Inc. All Rights Reserved.

Chapter 16, Table 3, pp. 438–439, table taken from data in FORTUNE SEPTEMBER 9, 1991. Reprinted by permission of Fortune. © 1991 The Time Inc. Magazine Company. All rights reserved.

Chapter 17, Table A, p. 472, data for table "1991 Telephone Rates (5-minute call, peak time)" from Peter Fuhrman, "An Unlikely Trustbuster," Forbes, February 18, 1991, pp. 100–104. Adapted by permission of Forbes magazine, © Forbes Inc., 1991.

Chapter 18, Figure 1, p. 479, graph made from data in FORBES, December 11, 1989, p. 80. Adapted by permission of Forbes magazine, © Forbes Inc., 1989.

Chapter 18, Table 3, p. 503, from Carl H. Lavin, "Battling It Out for Airport Control," New York Times, August 20, 1989, p. F4. Copyright © 1989 by The New York Times Company. Reprinted by permission.

Chapter 19, p. 517, table based on Steven N. S. Cheung, "The Fable of the Bees: An Economic Investigation," The Journal of Law and Economics, April 1973, pp. 11–33. Published by The University of Chicago and reprinted by permission.

Chapter 21, Table 2, p. 516, adapted from Joseph A. Pechman and Mark J. Mazur, "The Rich, the Poor, and the Taxes They Pay: An Update". Reprinted with permission of the authors from: The Public Interest, No. 77 (Fall 1984), pp. 28–36. © 1984 by National Affairs, Inc.